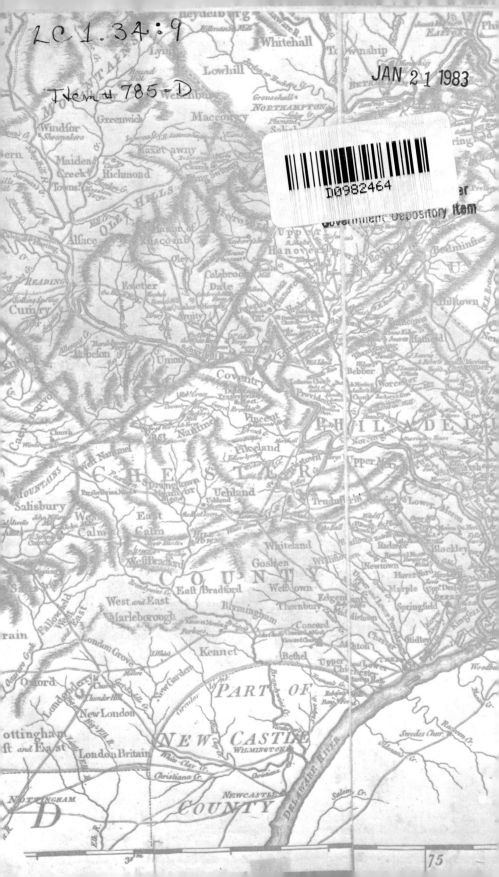

LETTERS OF DELEGATES 1774 ☆ 1789 TO CONGRESS

9

February 1–May 31, 1778

Paul H. Smith, Editor

Gerard W. Gawalt, Rosemary Fry Plakas, Eugene R. Sheridan
Associate Editors

LIBRARY OF CONGRESS   WASHINGTON   1982

This volume is printed on permanent/durable paper.

Library of Congress Cataloging in Publication Data (Revised)

Main entry under title:

Letters of delegates to Congress, 1774–1789.

Includes bibliographical references and indexes.
1. United States. Continental Congress—History—Sources—Collected works. I. Smith, Paul Hubert, 1931–
JK1033.L47   973.3'12   76–2592
ISBN 0–8444–0177–3 (set)   AACR1
ISBN 0–8444–0388–1 (v. 9)

For sale by the Superintendent of Documents, U.S. Government Printing Office
Washington, D.C. 20402

Editorial Method and Apparatus

In its treatment of documents this edition of delegate letters strives to achieve a middle ground between facsimile reproduction and thorough modernization. The original spelling and grammar are allowed to stand except where editorial changes or insertions are required to make the text intelligible. For example, when a badly misspelled word is misleading, the correct spelling is inserted in roman type in brackets after the word. Moreover, words omitted through oversight have been supplied at appropriate places in italic type in brackets. Obvious slips of the pen and inadvertent repetitions are usually silently corrected. Capitalization and punctuation have been standardized according to certain conventions. Each sentence begins with a capital letter, as do all proper and geographic names as well as days of the week and months of the year. Doubtful cases have been resolved in favor of modern usage; otherwise the usage of the original texts has been followed. Generally, abbreviations, contractions, and monetary signs are preserved as they appear in manuscript except when they are ambiguous or misleading. On the other hand, the thorn and the tilde are consistently expanded. "Ye" always appears as "The," for instance, and "rec̃vd" as "received." Likewise, "pr." and tailed *p*'s are always expanded to "per," "pre," or "pro," as the case demands. Finally, superscript letters are always lowered to the line.

Gaps in the text are indicated by ellipses in brackets for missing words and by blank spaces in brackets for missing numbers. Conjectural readings are supplied in roman type in brackets, and editorial insertions in italic type in brackets. Material canceled in manuscript but restored to the printed text is included in italic type in angle brackets ("square parentheses"). Marginalia in letters are treated as postscripts if not obviously keyed to the body of the document, and postscripts which appear without explicit designation are supplied with a *P.S.* in brackets. Documents are arranged chronologically, with more than one document of the same date arranged alphabetically according to writer. Documents dated only by the month or by the year are placed at the end of the respective month or year. Place-and-date lines always appear on the same line with the salutation regardless of their position in the manuscript.

A descriptive note at the foot of each entry provides abbreviations indicating the nature and location of the document when it was copied for this project, except for privately owned manuscripts whose ownership is explained. The descriptive note also contains information on the document's authorship if explanation is necessary, and endorsements or addresses are quoted when they contain more than routine information. Other editorial practices employed in this work are explained in the sections on editorial apparatus which follow.

TEXTUAL DEVICES

The following devices will be used in this work to clarify the text.

[· · ·], [· · · ·]	One or two words missing and not conjecturable.
[· · ·]^1, [· · · ·]^1	More than two words missing; subjoined footnote estimates amount of material missing.
[ ]	Number or part of a number missing or illegible.
[ ]^1	Blank space in manuscript; explanation in subjoined footnote.
[roman]	Conjectural reading for missing or illegible matter; question mark inserted if reading is doubtful.
[*italic*]	Editorial insertion in the text.
⟨*italic*⟩	Matter crossed out in manuscript but restored.

DESCRIPTIVE SYMBOLS

The following symbols are used in this work to describe the kinds of documents drawn upon. When more than one symbol is used in the descriptive note, the first to appear is that from which the main text is taken.

RC	recipient's copy
FC	file copy
LB	letterbook copy
MS	manuscript
Tr	transcript (used to designate not only contemporary and later handwritten copies of manuscripts, but also printed documents)

LOCATION SYMBOLS

The following symbols, denoting institutions holding the manuscripts printed in the present volume, are taken from *Symbols of American Libraries,* 11th ed. (Washington: Library of Congress, 1976).

CSmH	Henry E. Huntington Library, San Marino, Calif.
Ct	Connecticut State Library, Hartford
CtHi	Connecticut Historical Society, Hartford
CtY	Yale University, New Haven, Conn.
DLC	Library of Congress
DLC(ESR)	Library of Congress, Early State Records Collection

DNA	National Archives and Records Service
DNDAR	Daughters of the American Revolution, Washington, D.C.
DeHi	Historical Society of Delaware, Wilmington
ICarbS	Southern Illinois University, Carbondale, Ill.
ICU	University of Chicago, Chicago, Ill.
M–Ar	Massachusetts Archives, Boston
MB	Boston Public Library
MdAA	Maryland Hall of Records, Annapolis
MdHi	Maryland Historical Society, Baltimore
MH–H	Harvard University, Houghton Library
MHi	Massachusetts Historical Society, Boston
MeHi	Maine Historical Society, Portland
MiU–C	William L. Clements Library, University of Michigan, Ann Arbor
MnHi	Minnesota Historical Society, St. Paul, Minn.
N	New York State Library, Albany
NAlI	Albany Institute of History and Art, Albany
NHi	New-York Historical Society, New York
NN	New York Public Library, New York
NNC	Columbia University, New York
NNPM	Pierpont Morgan Library, New York
NOsHi	Oswego County Historical Society, Oswego, N.Y.
NRom	Jervis Library Association, Rome, N.Y.
Nc–Ar	North Carolina State Department of Archives and History, Raleigh
NcU	University of North Carolina, Chapel Hill
Nh–Ar	New Hampshire Division of Archives and Records Management, Concord
NhHi	New Hampshire Historical Society, Concord
NjGbS	Glassboro State College, Glassboro, N.J.
NjHi	New Jersey Historical Society, Newark
NjMoHP	Morristown National Historical Park, Morristown, N.J.
NjP	Princeton University, Princeton, N.J.
NjR	Rutgers University, New Brunswick, N.J.
OClWHi	Western Reserve Historical Society, Cleveland, Ohio
PBL	Lehigh University, Bethlehem, Pa.
PBMCA	Moravian Church Northern Province Archives, Bethlehem, Pa.
PHarH	Pennsylvania Historical and Museum Commission, Harrisburg
PHC	Haverford College, Haverford, Pa.
PHi	Historical Society of Pennsylvania, Philadelphia
PPAmP	American Philosophical Society, Philadelphia

PPL	Library Company of Philadelphia
PPRF	Rosenbach Foundation, Philadelphia
PU	University of Pennsylvania, Philadelphia
PYHi	Historical Society of York County, York, Pa.
R–Ar	Rhode Island State Archives, Providence
RHi	Rhode Island Historical Society, Providence
RNHi	Newport Historical Society, Newport, R.I.
RPJCB	John Carter Brown Library, Providence
ScC	Charleston Library Society, Charleston, S.C.
ScHi	South Carolina Historical Society, Charleston
Vi	Virginia State Library, Richmond
ViHi	Virginia Historical Society, Richmond
ViU	University of Virginia, Charlottesville
ViW	College of William and Mary, Williamsburg, Va.

ABBREVIATIONS AND SHORT TITLES

Adams, *Family Correspondence* (Butterfield)
    Butterfield, Lyman H., et al., eds. *Adams Family Correspondence.*
    Cambridge: Harvard University Press, Belknap Press, 1963–.
Adams, *Writings* (Cushing)
    Adams, Samuel. *The Writings of Samuel Adams.* Edited by Harry
    A. Cushing. 4 vols. Boston: G. P. Putnam's Sons, 1904–8.
AHR
    American Historical Review.
Austin, *Life of Gerry*
    Austin, James T. *The Life of Elbridge Gerry, with Contemporary
    Letters to the Close of the American Revolution.* 2 vols. Boston:
    Wells and Lilly, 1828–29.
Bartlett, *Papers* (Mevers)
    Bartlett, Josiah. *The Papers of Josiah Bartlett.* Edited by Frank C.
    Mevers. Hanover, N.H.: Published for the New Hampshire His-
    torical Society by the University Press of New England, 1979.
Bio. Dir. Cong.
    U.S. Congress. *Biographical Directory of the American Congress,
    1774–1971.* Washington: U.S. Government Printing Office, 1971.
Burnett, *Letters*
    Burnett, Edmund C., ed. *Letters of Members of the Continental
    Congress.* 8 vols. Washington: Carnegie Institution of Washington,
    1921–36.
Clinton, *Papers* (Hastings)
    Clinton, George. *Public Papers of George Clinton, First Governor
    of New York, 1777–1795, 1801–1804.* Edited by Hugh Hastings and
    J. A. Holden. 10 vols. New York and Albany: Wynkoop Hallenbeck
    Crawford Co. et al., 1899–1914.

Delaware Archives
Delaware Public Archives Commission. *Delaware Archives,* 5 vols. Wilmington, 1911–16.

DAB
Dictionary of American Biography. Edited by Allen Johnson and Dumas Malone.

Evans, *Am. Bibliography*
Evans, Charles. *American Bibliography.* 12 vols. Chicago: Privately printed, 1903–34.

Franklin, *Writings* (Smyth)
Franklin, Benjamin. *The Writings of Benjamin Franklin.* Edited by Albert Smyth. 10 vols. New York: Macmillan Co., 1905–7.

Freeman, *Washington*
Freeman, Douglas S. *George Washington, a Biography.* 7 vols. New York: Charles Scribner's Sons, 1948–57.

Heitman, *Historical Register*
Heitman, F. B. *Historical Register of Officers of the Continental Army during the War of the Revolution, April, 1775, to December, 1783.* Washington [Baltimore]: Press of Nichols, Killam & Maffit, 1893.

Henry, *Patrick Henry*
Henry, William Wirt. *Patrick Henry, Life, Correspondence and Speeches.* 3 vols. New York: Charles Scribner's Sons, 1891.

Jay, *Papers* (Morris)
Jay, John. *John Jay; the Making of a Revolutionary: Unpublished Papers, 1745–1780.* Edited by Richard B. Morris et al. New York: Harper & Row, 1975.

Jefferson, *Papers* (Boyd)
Jefferson, Thomas. *The Papers of Thomas Jefferson.* Edited by Julian P. Boyd et al. Princeton: Princeton University Press, 1950–.

JCC
U.S. Continental Congress. *Journals of the Continental Congress, 1774–1789.* 34 vols. Edited by Worthington C. Ford et al. Washington: Library of Congress, 1904–37.

Journals of N.Y. Prov. Cong.
New York. *Journals of the Provincial Congress, Provincial Convention, Committee of Safety and Council of Safety of the State of New York, 1775–1777.* 2 vols. Albany: T. Weed, 1842.

Lafayette, *Papers* (Idzerda)
Idzerda, Stanley J. et al., eds. *Lafayette in the Age of the American Revolution: Selected Letters and Papers, 1776–1790.* Ithaca: Cornell University Press, 1977–.

Lasseray, *Les Français sous les treize étoiles*
Lasseray, André. *Les Français sous les treize étoiles, 1775–1783.* 2 vols. Macon and Paris: Imprimerie Protat Frères, 1935.

Lee, *Letters* (Ballagh)

Lee, Richard Henry. *The Letters of Richard Henry Lee.* Edited by James C. Ballagh. 2 vols. New York: Macmillan Co., 1911–14.

Md. Archives

Archives of Maryland. Edited by William H. Browne et al. Baltimore: Maryland Historical Society, 1883–.

N.C. State Records

North Carolina. *The State Records of North Carolina.* Edited by Walter Clark. Vols. 11–26. Winston and Goldsboro, N.C.: N.I. and J.C. Stewart et al., 1895–1914.

OED

Oxford English Dictionary.

Pa. Archives

Pennsylvania Archives. 9 series, 119 vols. in 120. Philadelphia: J. Severns & Co., 1852–56; Harrisburg: State printer, 1874–1935.

Pa. Assembly Minutes (1778)

Pennsylvania. *Minutes of the Second General Assembly of the Commonwealth of Pennsylvania.* Lancaster: John Dunlap, 1778.

Pa. Council Minutes

Pennsylvania. *Minutes of the Supreme Executive Council of Pennsylvania, from its Organization to the Revolution.* 6 vols. [*Colonial Records of Pennsylvania,* vols. 11–16]. Harrisburg: Theo. Fenn & Co., 1852–53.

Paullin, *Marine Committee Letters*

Paullin, Charles O., ed. *Out-Letters of Continental Marine Committee and Board of Admiralty, 1776–1780.* 2 vols. New York: Printed for the Naval History Society by the De Vinne Press, 1914.

PCC

Papers of the Continental Congress. National Archives and Records Service. Washington, D.C.

PMHB

Pennsylvania Magazine of History and Biography.

Public Records of Connecticut

Hoadly, Charles J. et al., eds. *The Public Records of the State of Connecticut.* 11 vols. Hartford: Case, Lockwood & Brainard Co., 1894–1967.

Rodney, *Letters* (Ryden)

Rodney, Caesar. *Letters to and from Caesar Rodney, 1756–1784.* Edited by George H. Ryden. Philadelphia: University of Pennsylvania Press, 1933.

Rush, *Letters* (Butterfield)

Rush, Benjamin. *Letters of Benjamin Rush,* ed. Lyman H. Butterfield, 2 vols. Princeton: Published for the American Philosophical Society by Princeton University Press, 1951.

Simms, *Laurens Army Correspondence*
Laurens, John. *The Army Correspondence of Colonel John Laurens in the Years 1777–78*. Edited by William Gilmore Simms. New York: n.p., 1867.

Sullivan, *Letters* (Hammond)
Sullivan, John. *Letters and Papers of Major-General John Sullivan*. Edited by Otis G. Hammond. 3 vols. Collections of the New Hampshire Historical Society, vols. 13–15. Concord: New Hampshire Historical Society, 1930–39.

Washington, *Writings* (Fitzpatrick)
Washington, George. *The Writings of George Washington*. Edited by John C. Fitzpatrick. 39 vols. Washington: U.S. Government Printing Office, 1931–44.

Wharton, *Diplomatic Correspondence*
Wharton, Francis, ed. *The Revolutionary Diplomatic Correspondence of the United States*. 6 vols. Washington: Government Printing Office, 1889.

Acknowledgments

To the Library of Congress, the Congress of the United States, and the Ford Foundation this edition owes its existence. It is fitting, therefore, that we take this opportunity to acknowledge the foresight of the Library's administration in planning a timely and comprehensive observance of the American Revolution Bicentennial, of the Congress in funding a Bicentennial Office in the Library, and of the Ford Foundation in making a generous grant in support of this project as a scholarly contribution to the celebration of the Bicentennial era. It is with the most profound gratitude that the editors acknowledge their appreciation to all those who bore responsibility for the decisions that made possible these contributions. Our appreciation is also extended to the innumerable persons who have contributed to enriching the holdings of the Library of Congress to make it the premier institution for conducting research on the American Revolution.

The photocopies of the more than twenty-one thousand documents that have been collected for this project have been assembled through the cooperation of several hundred institutions and private individuals devoted to preserving the documentary record upon which the history and traditions of the American people rest, and it is to their work that a documentary publication of this nature should ultimately be dedicated. Unfortunately, the many individual contributors to this collecting effort cannot be adequately recognized, but for permission to print documents appearing in the present volume we are especially grateful to the following institutions: Albany Institute of History and Art, Algemeen Ryksarchief (The Hague), American Philosophical Society, Archives du ministère des affaires étrangères (Paris), Boston Public Library, John Carter Brown Library, Charleston Library Society, University of Chicago, William L. Clements Library, Columbia University, Connecticut Historical Society, Connecticut State Library, Daughters of the American Revolution (Washington, D.C.), Historical Society of Delaware, Glassboro State College, Harvard University, Haverford College, Henry E. Huntington Library, Jervis Library Association, Lehigh University, Maine Historical Society, Maryland Hall of Records, Maryland Historical Society, Massachusetts Archives, Massachusetts Historical Society, Minnesota Historical Society, Moravian Church Northern Province Archives, Pierpont Morgan Library, Morristown National Historical Park, National Archives and Records Service, New Hampshire Division of Archives and Records Management, New Hampshire Historical Society, New Jersey Historical Society, Newport Historical Society, New-York Historical Society, New York Public Library, New York State Library, North Carolina State Department of Archives and History, University of North Carolina, Oswego County Historical Society, Pennsylvania Historical and Museum Commission, Historical Society of Pennsylvania, University of Pennsylvania, Library Company of Philadelphia, Princeton University, Rhode Island Historical Society, Rhode Island State Archives, Rosenbach Foundation, Rutgers University, South Carolina Historical Society, Southern Illinois University, Virginia Historical Society, Virginia State Library, University of Virginia, Western Reserve Historical Society, College of William and Mary, The Royal Archives (Windsor Castle), Yale University, and Historical Society of York County. And in addition we express our thanks and appreciation to the following persons: Mr. Sol Feinstone, Mr. Creighton C. Hart, Mr. Henry Laurens, Mr. John F. Reed, Mrs. Elsie O. Sang and Mr. Philip D. Sang, Capt. J. G. M. Stone, and Mr. Robert J. Sudderth, Jr.

This work has benefitted not only from Edmund C. Burnett's path-finding 8-volume edition of *Letters of Members of the Continental Congress* but also from the generous cooperation of the editors of several other documentary publications with a common focus on the revolutionary era. From them the Library has borrowed heavily and to them it owes a debt it can never adequately acknowledge. It is a pleasure to give special thanks to the editors of the papers of John Adams, Benjamin Franklin, Thomas Jefferson, Henry Laurens, James Madison, and George Washington. Finally, we owe thanks to the historians who have served on the Advisory Committee on the Library's American Revolution Bicentennial Program, and especially to Mr. Julian P. Boyd, Mr. Lyman H. Butterfield, and Mr. Merrill Jensen, who generously acted as an advisory committee for the *Letters* project.

Paul H. Smith
Historical Publications Office
Manuscript Division

Chronology of Congress

FEBRUARY 1–MAY 31, 1778

February 2   Appoints officers for Canadian expedition.

February 3   Prescribes oath required of all officers of the United States.

February 4   Directs commissioner to the court of Tuscany to seek $1 million loan; receives Committee at Camp recommendation that Jeremiah Wadsworth be appointed commissary general of purchases.

February 6   Reforms medical department; appoints middle department physician general.

February 11   Adopts regulations for commissary general of military stores.

February 13   Requests North Carolina beef and pork embargo.

February 16   Resolves to emit additional $2 million in bills of credit.

February 17   Suspends Board of War's special purchasing agents.

February 19   Relocates Convention Army for security purposes.

February 23   Appoints committee to reexamine feasibility of Canadian expedition.

February 26   Adopts resolves for arranging a prisoner exchange; adopts new Continental Army quotas and recruiting regulations.

February 27   Prescribes death penalty for persons convicted of aiding the enemy.

March 2   Appoints Nathanael Greene quartermaster general and adopts new quartermaster regulations; urges cavalry recruitment; suspends Canadian expedition.

March 3   Authorizes General Burgoyne's return to England.

April 11   Orders Thomas Burke to answer charges of disrupt-
            ing proceedings of Congress; resolves to emit addi-
            tional $5 million in bills of credit.

April 14   Adopts regulations for commissary general of pur-
            chases.

April 15   Responds to Delaware protest that General Small-
            wood's seizure of loyalists infringed the internal
            police of the state; directs General Gates to take
            command of the northern department.

April 16   Rejects motion to refer issue of Continental officers'
            pensions to the states.

April 18   Orders inquiry into the loss of the *Virginia*.

April 22   Orders publication of statement on North Ministry's
            peace proposals.

April 23   Urges states to pardon and forgive penitent loyalists;
            requests Maryland to send troops to suppress Dela-
            ware uprising.

April 25   Resolves that Thomas Burke's withdrawal from
            Congress was "disorderly and contemptuous."

April 26   Holds Sunday debate on half-pay proposal for Con-
            tinental officers.

April 28   Accepts General Conway's resignation.

April 29   Adopts plan to encourage desertion of British mer-
            cenaries seeking land and citizenship in the United
            States.

May 3   Holds Sunday session to consider treaties of com-
            merce and alliance negotiated with France.

May 4   Ratifies the treaties with France.

May 5   Instructs commissioners to secure revocation of two
            treaty of commerce articles.

May 8   Adopts an address to the inhabitants of the United
            States.

May 9   Issues proclamation denouncing seizures of neutral
            shipping by American armed vessels.

May 11   Instructs Massachusetts on safeguarding the rights of the owners of an illegally seized Portuguese vessel.

May 13   Rejects motion to refer proposed officer pension plan to the states.

May 15   Adopts plan to provide half pay for officers for seven years after the conclusion of the war.

May 18   Receives "plan for regulating the army" from the committee at camp.

May 19   Orders emission of $6.3 million in bills of credit to pay interest on loan office certificates.

May 21   Authorizes Massachusetts to assist Nova Scotian revolutionaries at Continental expense; adopts principles for governing prisoner exchanges.

May 22   Resolves to emit additional $5 million in bills of credit.

May 26   Adopts revised "rules" of Congress.

May 27   Adopts new "Establishment of the American Army."

May 28   Revises commissions of the American commissioners to Vienna, Berlin, and Tuscany.

May 30   Resumes twice daily sessions "for the space of one month."

List of Delegates to Congress

This section lists both the dates on which delegates were elected to terms falling within the period covered by this volume and the inclusive dates of their attendance. The former are generally ascertainable from contemporary state records, but the latter are often elusive bits of information derived from the journals of Congress or extrapolated from references contained in the delegates' correspondence, and in such cases the "facts" are inevitably conjectural. It is not possible to determine interruptions in the attendance of many delegates, and no attempt has been made to record interruptions in service caused by illness or brief trips home, especially of delegates from New Jersey, Delaware, Maryland, and Pennsylvania living within easy access of Congress. For occasional references to such periods of intermittent service as survive in the correspondence and notes of various delegates, see the index under individual delegates. Until fuller information is provided in a consolidated summary of delegate attendance in the final volume of this series, the reader is advised to consult Burnett, *Letters*, 3:li–lxii, for additional information on conjectural dates of attendance. Brief biographical sketches of all the delegates are available in the *Biographical Directory of the American Congress, 1774–1971*, and fuller sketches of more than half of the delegates can be found in the *Dictionary of American Biography*.

CONNECTICUT

Andrew Adams
   Elected: October 11, 1777
   Did not attend February to May 1778
Eliphalet Dyer
   Elected: October 11, 1777
   Attended: February 1 to April 3, 1778
Oliver Ellsworth
   Elected: October 11, 1777
   Did not attend February to May 1778
Titus Hosmer
   Elected: October 11, 1777
   Did not attend February to May 1778
Samuel Huntington
   Elected: October 11, 1777
   Attended: February 16 to May 31, 1778

Roger Sherman
  Elected: October 11, 1777
  Attended: April 25 to May 31, 1778
Oliver Wolcott
  Elected: October 11, 1777
  Attended: February 16 to May 31, 1778

DELAWARE

Thomas McKean
  Elected: December 17, 1777
  Attended: February 1 to April 28; May 11–31, 1778 (at Lancaster
      discharging judicial duties, ca. March 9–18, April 7–20)
Caesar Rodney
  Elected: December 17, 1777
  Did not attend in 1778
Nicholas Van Dyke
  Elected: December 17, 1777
  Did not attend February to May 1778

GEORGIA

Nathan Brownson
  Elected: June 7, 1777
  Did not attend in 1778
Joseph Clay
  Elected: February 26, 1778
  Did not attend Congress
Lyman Hall
  Elected: June 7, 1777; February 26, 1778
  Did not attend in 1778
Edward Langworthy
  Elected: June 7, 1777; February 26, 1778
  Attended: February 1 to May 31, 1778
Edward Telfair
  Elected: February 26, 1778
  Did not attend February to May 1778
George Walton
  Elected: June 7, 1777; February 26, 1778
  Did not attend in 1778
John Walton
  Elected: February 26, 1778
  Did not attend February to May 1778
Joseph Wood
  Elected: June 7, 1777; February 26, 1778
  Attended: February 1 to March 17, 1778

MARYLAND

Charles Carroll of Carrollton
  Elected: December 5, 1777
  Attended: April 15 to May 31, 1778
Samuel Chase
  Elected: December 5, 1777
  Attended: March 23 to May 8, 1778
James Forbes
  Elected: December 22, 1777
  Attended: February 1 to April 17, 1778
John Henry
  Elected: December 22, 1777
  Attended: February 1 to May 30, 1778
Joseph Nicholson
  Elected: December 5, 1777
  Declined
William Paca
  Elected: December 5, 1777
  Did not attend February to May 1778
George Plater
  Elected: December 5, 1777
  Attended: April 18 to May 31, 1778
Thomas Stone
  Elected: December 5, 1777
  Did not attend February to May 1778

MASSACHUSETTS

John Adams
  Elected: December 4, 1777
  Did not attend in 1778
Samuel Adams
  Elected: December 4, 1777
  Attended: May 21–31, 1778
Francis Dana
  Elected: December 4, 1777
  Attended: February 1 to May 31, 1778 (on mission with committee
      at camp, ca. January 17 to March 21, 1778)
Elbridge Gerry
  Elected: December 4, 1777
  Attended: February 1 to May 31, 1778
John Hancock
  Elected: December 4, 1777
  Did not attend February to May 1778

Samuel Holten
  Elected: February 20, 1778
  Did not attend February to May 1778
James Lovell
  Elected: December 4, 1777
  Attended: February 1 to May 31, 1778
Robert Treat Paine
  Elected: December 4, 1777
  Did not attend in 1778

NEW HAMPSHIRE

Josiah Bartlett
  Elected: December 25, 1777; March 14, 1778
  Attended: May 21–31, 1778
Nathaniel Folsom
  Elected: April 1, 1777
  Attended: February 1 to April 1, 1778 (on mission with committee
    at camp, ca. January 17 to March 14, 1778)
George Frost
  Elected: April 1, 1777
  Attended: February 1 to April 1, 1778
John Wentworth
  Elected: March 14, 1778
  Attended: May 30–31, 1778
William Whipple
  Elected: December 25, 1777
  Did not attend February to May 1778

NEW JERSEY

Elias Boudinot
  Elected: November 20, 1777
  Did not attend February to May 1778
Abraham Clark
  Elected: November 20, 1777
  Attended: February 1 to April 7, 1778
Jonathan Elmer
  Elected: November 20, 1777
  Attended: May 26–31, 1778
Nathaniel Scudder
  Elected: November 20, 1777
  Attended: February 9 to May 23, 1778
John Witherspoon
  Elected: November 20, 1777
  Attended: February 1–19; May 16–31, 1778

NEW YORK

James Duane
  Elected: October 3, 1777
  Did not attend February to May 1778
William Duer
  Elected: October 3, 1777
  Attended: February 1–3; March 27 to May 31, 1778
Francis Lewis
  Elected: October 3, 1777
  Attended: February 1 to April 4, 1778 (on Marine Committee
      business in Baltimore, ca. January 21 to February 9)
Philip Livingston
  Elected: October 3, 1777
  Attended: May 5–31, 1778
Gouverneur Morris
  Elected: October 3, 1777
  Attended: February 1 to May 31, 1778 (on mission with committee
      at camp, ca. January 24 to April 11, 1778)
Philip Schuyler
  Elected: March 25, 1778
  Did not attend in 1778

NORTH CAROLINA

Thomas Burke
  Elected: May 4, 1777
  Attended: March 10? to April 28, 1778
Cornelius Harnett
  Elected: May 4, 1777; April 25, 1778
  Attended: February 1 to April 25, 1778
Abner Nash
  Elected: April 25, 1778
  Declined
John Penn
  Elected: May 4, 1777; April 25, 1778
  Attended: February 1 to March 19, 1778
John Williams
  Elected: April 28, 1778
  Did not attend February to May 1778

PENNSYLVANIA

William Clingan
  Elected: December 10, 1777
  Attended: February 1 to March 24?; April 25 to May 19? 1778

Benjamin Franklin
  Elected: December 10, 1777
  Did not attend in 1778
Robert Morris
  Elected: December 10, 1777
  Attended: May 13–15, 1778
Joseph Reed
  Elected: December 10, 1777
  Attended: February 1 to April 11, 1778 (on mission with committee
        at camp, ca. January 28 to April 4, 1778)
Daniel Roberdeau
  Elected: December 10, 1777
  Attended: February 1 to April 11; May 26–31, 1778
James Smith
  Elected: December 10, 1777
  Attended: February 1 to April 21; May 5?–23? 1778
Jonathan Bayard Smith
  Elected: December 10, 1777
  Attended: February 1–6?; February 25–March 19?; April 7?–May
        19? 1778

RHODE ISLAND

John Collins
  Elected: May 6, 1778
  Did not attend May 1778
William Ellery
  Elected: May 7, 1777; May 6, 1778
  Attended: February 1 to May 31, 1778
Stephen Hopkins
  Elected: May 7, 1777; May 6, 1778
  Did not attend in 1778
Henry Marchant
  Elected: May 7, 1777; May 6, 1778
  Did not attend February to May 1778

SOUTH CAROLINA

William Henry Drayton
  Elected: January 21, 1778
  Attended: March 30 to May 31 (visited Washington's headquarters,
        ca. May 6–21, 1778)
Christopher Gadsden
  Elected: January 21, 1778
  Declined

Thomas Heyward
    Elected: January 22, 1778
    Did not attend February to May 1778
Richard Hutson
    Elected: January 22, 1778
    Attended: April 13 to May 31, 1778
Henry Laurens
    Elected: January 21, 1778
    Attended: February 1 to May 31, 1778
John Mathews
    Elected: January 22, 1778
    Attended: April 22 to May 31, 1778
Arthur Middleton
    Elected: January 21, 1778
    Declined

VIRGINIA

Thomas Adams
    Elected: December 9, 1777
    Attended: April 16 to May 31, 1778
John Banister
    Elected: November 19, 1777
    Attended: March 16 to May 31, 1778
John Harvie
    Elected: May 22, 1777
    Attended: February 1 to March 18? 1778 (on mission with commit-
        tee at camp, ca. January 24 to February 26, 1778)
Joseph Jones
    Elected: May 22, 1777
    Did not attend in 1778
Francis Lightfoot Lee
    Elected: May 22, 1777
    Attended: February 1 to May 30, 1778
Richard Henry Lee
    Elected: June 24, 1777; January 23, 1778
    Attended: May 1–31, 1778
George Mason
    Elected: May 22, 1777
    Declined
Mann Page
    Elected: November 12, 1777
    Declined

Illustrations

Lancaster and York, Pennsylvania, where Congress convened when the British moved into Philadephia in September 1777 and continued to meet through June 1778, are visible on this southeast quarter of a map of Pennsylvania by Robert Sayer and John Bennett, "exhibiting not only the improved parts of that Province, but also its extensive frontiers: Laid down from actual surveys and chiefly from the late map of W. Scull published in 1770; and humbly inscribed to the Honourable Thomas Penn and Richard Penn, Esquires, true and absolute proprietaries & Governors of the Province of Pennsylvania and the territories thereunto belonging" (London, 1775).

Geography and Map Division, Library of Congress.

On December 26, 1777, Congress appointed a committee consisting of Daniel Roberdeau, Abraham Clark, and William Ellery "to devise effectual means to prevent persons disaffected to the interest of the United States from being employed in any of the important offices thereof." Clark thereupon drew up and submitted to Congress on January 21 a report that prescribed an oath of allegiance for all civil, military, and naval officers in Continental service and made detailed recommendations for preventing fraud in the departments responsible for supplying the army. Congress considered the committee's report on February 3, 1778, and approved their proposed oath while sharply modifying their suggestions for curbing fraud in the military supply system. The passage of this resolution was hailed by several delegates and led James Lovell to express the hope that the states would follow Congress' example, thereby "making it as inconvenient as possible for such vermin to exist among us."

Continental Congress Broadside, no. 38, Rare Book and Special Collections Division, Library of Congress.

The breakdown in the Continental Army's system of supply near the end of 1777 led to fears of the impending dissolution of the army and moved Congress to initiate decisive actions to remedy the situation. The delegates took immediate steps to provide the army with adequate provisions and clothing and began a far-reaching study directed at a major reorganization of the commissary and quarter-master departments. As part of its effort to improve the system of supplying the army, Congress on February 11, 1778, approved a plan for reorganizing the commissary of military stores that had been drafted by the Board of War six days before. Gen. Henry Knox subsequently criticized this plan for making the commissary general of military stores independent of him in his capacity as commander of artillery, but Congress remained committed to a policy that provided a number of checks controlled by the Board of War. The broadside reproduced in this volume is one Knox enclosed with his June 15, 1778, letter to Washington.

Manuscript Division, Library of Congress.

Joseph Reed   142

Reed, whose conspicuous political career in Pennsylvania ended abruptly with his death at the age of 43 barely 18 months after the signing of the Treaty of Paris in 1783, graduated from the college at Princeton in his native New Jersey and studied law at the Middle Temple in London before launching a legal career in Philadelphia in 1770. His months in England were especially significant, for there he not only met his future wife, Esther DeBerdt, daughter of the prominent London merchant and agent for the Massachusetts Assembly Dennys DeBerdt, but made acquaintances and formed interests that stamped him as a moderate devoted to restoring peaceful relations with Britain. Although he took a leading role in the revolutionary movement in Pennsylvania and served both as Washington's military secretary and as adjutant general of the Continental Army in 1775–76, Reed also wrote a dozen advisory letters to Britain's American secretary of state, Lord Dartmouth, in 1773–75, and was one of the persons peace commissioner George Johnstone sedulously sought to cultivate in an effort to open negotiations with the Americans in 1778. As a delegate to Congress he received important assignments that reflected his previous experience with Washington and the army, serving as a member of both the committee sent to headquarters during the Valley Forge crisis and the committee sent to camp the following autumn to complete the reform and "arrangement" of the Continental Army. Although Reed was embarrassed by the public exposure of Johnstone's clumsy efforts to win his support and was accused by Arthur Lee of harboring pro-British sentiments, his popularity was not undermined. Following the British evacuation of Philadelphia in June 1778 he was appointed assistant to the attorney general of Pennsylvania to prosecute the state's loyalists, and he subsequently served three years as president of Pennsylvania.

Painting by Charles Willson Peale. Independence National Historical Park Collection.

William Duer   253

Duer, merchant, financier, and speculator, had a colorful career that few delegates could match. Born in England to a father who was an absentee West Indies plantation owner, Duer was educated at Eton and commissioned an ensign in the British army. After serving in 1764 as aide-de-camp to Robert Clive, the governor-general of India, Duer returned to England and subsequently inherited some of his father's West Indian plantations. He moved to New York in 1773 and soon became a prominent member of the revolutionary movement, serving in that province's provincial congress, committee of public safety, constitutional convention, and militia. Duer's service to the revolutionary cause led to his election to Congress in March 1777, where he served until November 1778. While in Congress Duer was a member of the Board of War and a number of ad hoc committees dealing with problems relating to the Continental Army, particularly those of supply. He distinguished himself as a vigorous defender of New York's interests and as a staunch advocate of congressional authority over the states. Yet Duer's high regard for Congress' institutional prerogatives was not matched by high respect for the delegates with whom he served. "When I was sent here," he wrote to John Jay in May 1777, "I had some Idea that I was entering into The Temple of Public Virtue. I was disappointed and Chagrined." The subsequent course of events merely deepened Duer's disillusionment with Congress, leading him to lament in March 1778: "The parties prevailing in our Army, and the want of Foresight, and Attention to Business in Congress (to say no More) are the principal Sources from whence Various and alarming Evils have arisen." In such a mood Duer left Congress in November 1778, never to return as a delegate, and during the rest of the war he devoted much of his attention to private business affairs.

With the coming of peace in 1783 Duer embarked upon a number of grandiose speculative schemes and served briefly in 1789–90 as assistant secretary of the treasury to Alexander Hamilton. However, Duer's tenure in this position was marked by accusations of official misconduct, and subsequently the collapse of his business ventures led him into debtors' prison in New York in 1792, where he remained, except for a brief interval, until his death seven years later.

From Clarence W. Bowen, *History of the Centennial Celebration of the Inauguration of George Washington* (1892).

Resolve on Pardons, April 23, 1778   463

The arrival in April of news of Lord North's conciliatory proposals initially had a dual effect in America. Patriots were concerned that a war-weary people might prove receptive to British peace overtures, whereas loyalists felt betrayed by what they perceived as Britain's abandonment of their cause. Congress sought to capitalize on the latter sentiment by adopting a resolution on April 23 calling upon the states to pardon loyalists who had served with the British but who agreed to surrender themselves to American authorities by June 10, 1778. Such a resolution, Samuel Chase observed in regard to loyalists two days before it was actually approved, "would thin their Ranks, and detach their friends." Although Congress ordered this resolution to be published in English and German, no German text has been found. The broadside reproduced in this volume bears the following endorsement by Secretary Charles Thomson: "Vote of Congress to receive Returning Sinners."

Rare Book and Special Collections Division, Library of Congress.

Franco-American Treaties of Alliance and Commerce   577

Henry Laurens and William Henry Drayton prepared this account of the diplomatic background and terms of the February 1778 treaties of alliance and commerce with France and had it published as a supplement to the *Pennsylvania Gazette* on May 2, shortly after Simeon Deane arrived in Congress with official texts of these treaties. Some delegates criticized the two South Carolinians for taking this step before Congress ratified the treaties on May 4, but most were so exhilarated by the diplomatic coup in Europe that they took a more indulgent view of the matter. For many months this broadside was the American public's only printed source of information on the precise terms of the treaty of alliance as Congress deemed it impolitic to release an authorized text of the full treaty until November 1778. At the same time Congress also released the full text of the treaty of commerce, parts of which had been published earlier in May. A major reason for the delay in publishing these treaties in their entirety was to allow the American Commissioners at Paris time to secure French consent for deleting two articles from the treaty of commerce that the delegates considered detrimental to American economic interests.

Library of Congress.

Address to the Inhabitants of the United States of America   638

Drafted by a committee appointed on May 6 consisting of Samuel Chase, Richard Henry Lee, and Gouverneur Morris and amended and approved by Congress two days later, this address sought to reinvigorate popular support for continuing the war and thereby blunt the impact of Britain's recently received proposals for Anglo-American reconciliation. Three long, indecisive years of warfare coupled with mounting economic problems made the delegates apprehensive that British peace efforts might find a sympathetic audience even among Americans who had hitherto supported the revolutionary cause. Congress therefore authorized the publication of this address to remind Americans of past British tyranny and present British barbarity and to suggest that the conclusion of an alliance between the United States and France made a final patriot victory inevitable. In order to add force to this address Congress urged that it be read "after divine service" in all "churches and chapels, and other places of religious worship" throughout the country. Although no manuscript copy of the address is now known to exist, Jared Sparks saw a draft of it in Gouverneur Morris' hand over a century and a half ago, and the address as amended and approved by Congress bears the unmistakable imprint of Morris' rhetorical style.

From the Miscellaneous Papers of the Continental Congress, National Archives and Records Service.

Horatio Gates   673

Gates' controversial career as a Continental officer often made him the focus of congressional attention. Born of a humble family in England, Gates entered the British army and served in America during the French and Indian War, but he subsequently left the army, moved to Virginia in 1772, and acquired a plantation. After the outbreak of hostilities between America and Britain his military experience stood him in good stead, as Congress appointed him adjutant general of the Continental Army in 1775. The following year he was promoted to major general and assigned to the northern military department. There Gates became involved in a bitter command dispute with Gen. Philip Schuyler that absorbed much of Congress' attention and was not resolved until Gates finally replaced Schuyler during Burgoyne's invasion from Canada in August 1777. Gates' ensuing victory at Saratoga raised his prestige to its greatest height, which, coinciding as it did with disillusionment over the loss of Philadelphia, led to fears by Washington and his supporters that a conspiracy was afoot to make Gates commander in chief. Although most scholars now believe that the opposition to Washington and the general frustration that was voiced in 1777–78 did not constitute a conspiracy against him, Gates' close relations with several of Washington's opponents tarnished his prestige. After serving as president of the newly reorganized Board of War in 1777–78, Gates returned to the field to take command of the northern and eastern military departments and served at Boston in 1778–79. When the British launched successful attacks on Georgia and South Carolina in 1780 he was named commander of the southern military department, but he suffered a humiliating defeat at Camden in August 1780 which shattered his military reputation and his career.

Painting by Charles Willson Peale. Independence National Historical Park Collection.

Establishment of the American Army, May 27, 1778   762

The sorry state into which the Continental Army had fallen by the end of 1777 led Congress to dispatch a committee to Valley Forge to confer with Washington on ways "for reducing the number of regiments in the continental service, and for reforming the abuses which have too long prevailed in the different departments belonging to the army." The Committee at Camp arrived at Valley Forge near the end of January 1778 and spent a month and a half conferring with Washington and his subordinates on various army problems. Among the most important products of the committee's work was a plan for restructuring the army that the committee first proposed in a February 3 letter to President Henry Laurens and that Congress finally approved on May 27, 1778. Yet consistent with the indecisive manner in which Congress frequently transacted business at this time, the appointment of another committee and many months of additional work were required to implement this plan for reducing the number of regiments and officers in the Continental Army. The broadside reproduced in this volume is the one President Laurens enclosed with his June 4, 1778, letter to Washington.

Manuscript Division, Library of Congress.

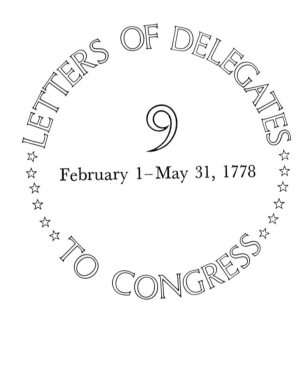

LETTERS OF DELEGATES

9

February 1–May 31, 1778

TO CONGRESS

Francis Lewis to Thomas Johnson

Dear Sir   Baltimore 1st Febry. 1778

Capt. Nicholson of the Frigate Virginia, has applyed to me as a member of the Marine Committee, pointing out the necessity he is under of having a Tender, in order to reconnitre the Bay before he proceeds down with the Frigate.[1]

He informs me that there is now at Annopolis armed boats belonging to this state, under your Excellency's directions, and prays that one of the largest might be lent for that purpose; he intends to embrace the first fair wind to proceed with the Frigate to Sea, and which Congress has very much at Heart.[2] I have the honor to be, Sir, Your most obedt Humbl Servt.   Fra. Lewis

RC (CtY).

[1] See also Marine Committee to James Nicholson, January 28, 1778. Lewis, who had been granted eight days leave of absence from Congress on January 20, was back in Congress by February 9, when he signed a letter from the Committee of Commerce to the Commissioners at Paris. Lewis had taken leave to visit his family in Baltimore and conduct some business for the Marine Committee. See *JCC*, 10:67; and Lewis to Thomas Johnson, January 27, 1778.

[2] Although no response by Governor Johnson to Lewis' request for aid has been found, some efforts by the Maryland Council of Safety to assist Captain Nicholson are described in *Md. Archives,* 16:508, 534–35.

Gouverneur Morris to John Jay

Dr Jay   Camp Valley Forge 1st Feby. 1778.

Congress have sent me here in Conjunction with some other Gentlemen to regulate their Army and in Truth not a little Regulation hath become necessary.[1] Our Quarter Master and Commissary Departments are in the most lamentable Situation. Opportunities have been neglected last Campaign which were truly Golden ones but omnipotent Fatality had it seems determined that the American Capital should fall. Our Sentiments on this Occasion are so perfectly coincident that I will not enlarge. The mighty Senate of America is not what you have known it. The Continental C—— & C——[2] have both depreciated but in the Hands of the almighty Architect of Empires the Stone which the Builders have rejected may easily become Head of the Corner. The free, open and undisturbed Communication with the City of P——[3] debauches the Minds of those in its Vicinage with astonishing Rapidity. O this State is sick even unto the Death and in

3

been able to think of any new Regulations for the Militia which are practicable in our present situation. The System in the main is a good one. Defects in my opinion do not proceed so much from the plan (except the choice of officers) as from the Want of Competent Persons to Execute it. While our state is the Seat of War & I fear it will be so for some Time the Militia will be called for frequently & largely. It improves I think every Day & I am persuaded will in Time be as good as any of its neighbours. You must not judge of it altogether by the Report of Continental Officers. It is fashionable to blame them & it is sometimes carried to a blameable Length.

The State of our Army in respect to the Force & Numbers has kept us much employed. It appeared to me highly reasonable that the Quota of this State fixed before there was any Invasion & with the Capital in Our possession should now be lower'd & I have got it reduced from 12 to 10 in our estimate. I should have got it to 8 if in the Correspondence with the General the Idea of keeping up the whole Number had not been preserved. I intended to have gone farther with this as well as some other Matters if the Gentleman who is to be the Bearer of this Letter did not press me to finish. But I cannot close without suggesting to your consideration the Necessity of forming some plan of executing the Law for supply of Provisions. It appears clearly to me that however well intended the Law will have no Effect if two Persons are to execute it for a whole County. I have thought sometimes a Revival of Committees will have a very good Effect to some purposes. I am sure it will but it may be perverted from its Design.

It is in vain to look for any attempt upon the City under the most favourable Circumstances in other Respects if Provisions are not procured.[1] We are assured that the Army have not now nor ever had more than 4 Days stock before hand for their present Numbers. You will easily Judge the Consequences of bringing a great Body together under present Prospect.

I must conclude or my Paper will not give me Room to say with what Respect & Regard I am, Dr Sir, Your Obed, Hble Servt.

Jos. Reed

Tr (NHi). *Pa. Archives,* 1st ser. 6:218–20.

[1] Reed's comments on the prospects for an "attempt" on Philadelphia were prompted by the Pennsylvania Council's request for such an attack the preceding month. For the background of the proposal and the committee's response to Congress' order directing them to confer with Washington on the proposal's feasibility, see Jonathan Bayard Smith to Timothy Matlack, January 5; and Committee at Camp to Henry Laurens, February 3, 1778.

Committee at Camp Minutes of Proceedings

[February 2–7, 1778]

Feby. 2d. Present as before [Mr. Dana Chairman, Gen'l Fulsom, Gen'l Reid, Colo. Harvie, Mr. Morris].

Recd. a Letter from Qur. Master Lutterlow. (No. 9).[1]

Recd. the returns of the W[agon] M[aster] Genl. Department. (No. 10).[2]

Resolved to recommend to Congress the Draught of a Number of Men to complete the Battalions on the Establishmt. Also fixed the Quotas of the several States.[3] Agreed that the German Battalion belong to Maryland as part of their Quota. James Livingstons & Hazens to be united on the new Establishmt. Under Hazen the Surplus to be added to Warners. Armands to be reduced & thrown into the 9 of the 16 to be kept up.

Took into Consideration Colo. Campbell's application to Congress & denied his request to go in upon parole to solicit his Exchange.[4]

3d. Consider'd Capt. Durkee's & others petition & denied the prayer of it.[5]

Wrote a Letter to Congress on the Expedition agt. Phila. forwarded by Col. Fitzgerald. (No. 11.)[6]

Recd. the Return of Persons employed in the Qr. Mr. Genl. Departmt. (No. 12)[7] & Lutterloh's 2d Letter (No. 13).

Conferr'd with Col. Blaine Dy. Commy. of Issues on the State of Provisions of the Army & recd. his Return of Meat purchased. No. 13.

Recd. from Gen. Green Returns of the Army & an Acct. of Rations drawn during the Month of December.

4t. Conferr'd with Col. Palfrey on the State of the military Chest. Proceeded on the Arrangemt of the Army & the Draughts to fill up the Continental Batalions.

5. Recd. Proposals from Col. Blain in the Provision Department.[8] No. 14.

Recd. a second Lettr. from the Clothier Genl.[9] (No. 15.)

6th. Finished the Resolves on the Drafts. Also Letter to Congress on that Subject—with the Establishment & Arrangement of the new Army.[10]

7. Conferr'd with the Marquis de Fayette on his Return from Congress.[11]

With Col Blain on the State of Provisions[12] forwarded the above Letters of yesterday to Congress.[13]

MS (DLC). A continuation of Committee at Camp Minutes of Proceedings, January 28–31, 1778. The minutes printed in this entry are in the hands of committee members Francis Dana, Gouverneur Morris, and Joseph Reed.

[1] Henry Emanuel Lutterloh was deputy quartermaster general.

[2] For further information on the committee's interest in these returns, see Committee at Camp Minutes of Proceedings, January 28–31, 1778, note 7.

[3] To judge from the correspondence of one of the committee members, some state troop quotas had been discussed and decided previously, although no earlier references to this issue are found in the committee minutes. See Joseph Reed to Thomas Wharton, February 1, 1778.

[4] Lt. Col. Archibald Campbell, who was being held hostage for Gen. Charles Lee's safety, was a prisoner of war at Concord, Mass. His December 18, 1777, petition to Congress was referred to the committee at camp on January 16 and arrangements were made to exchange him for Ethan Allen as part of a general prisoner of war cartel. By April 18 Campbell had been returned to Philadelphia and Allen's exchange was effected on May 6. See JCC, 10:43, 58, 213, 295, 332; John Hancock to George Washington, January 6, 1777; Henry Laurens to Archibald Campbell, January 14, 1778; James Lovell to Samuel Adams, April 18, 1778; and Washington, Writings (Fitzpatrick), 11:70–72, 129, 214, 219, 300, 381.

[5] See Committee at Camp Minutes of Proceedings, January 28–31, 1778, note 3.

[6] See Committee at Camp to Henry Laurens, February 3, 1778.

[7] This list is in PCC, item 192, fols. 159–60.

[8] This is doubtless the list of proposals Blaine copied into his letterbook under the heading "A few Queries for Consideration of His Excellency General Washington and the Honourable the Committee of Congress now sitting at Moore Hall, February 4th 1778." Blaine apparently prepared these proposals after conferring with the committee on February 3. Blaine first proposed to reduce the ration of bread and meat for soldiers until "there is an appearance of a more plentiful supply," and then suggested several measures that might increase the supply of beef and pork: a proclamation urging farmers to fatten more cattle for April and May slaughter; seizure of cattle at Cape May and Egg Harbour, to prevent their falling into British hands; setting the price of pork at £15.10 per barrel; and securing cattle in western North Carolina and Virginia to prevent "forestallers" from buying and holding them off the market. Ephraim Blaine Letterbook, DLC.

[9] That is, James Mease.

[10] See Committee at Camp to Henry Laurens, February 5, 1778.

[11] Since January 30, Lafayette had been in York soliciting additional support for his expedition to Canada and seeking the promotion of several French officers who would accompany him on the venture. Although Congress approved the Canadian expedition, it never gave the "incursion" its wholehearted support. However, most of Lafayette's recommendations for the promotion of French officers were approved on February 2. See JCC, 10:84–85, 87, 107; and Henry Laurens to Lafayette, January 22, 1778.

For the committee's negative response to the proposed Canadian expedition, see Joseph Reed to Jonathan Bayard Smith, February 8; and Committee at Camp to Henry Laurens, February 11, 1778.

[12] For the committee's letter on provisions, see Committee at Camp to Henry Laurens, February 6, 1778.

[13] For the continuation of these minutes, see Committee at Camp Minutes of Proceedings, February 8–14, 1778.

James Lovell to John Adams

My dear Sir   [February 2? 1778][1]

Instead of scribbling any Thing about Inactivity I will endeavour to give you an Idea of our intended progress into Canada.

Janry. 22d. The Board of war brought in a report on the several dispatches received from the northern department, which was taken into consideration whereupon

Resolved that an irruption be made into Canada, and that the board of war be authorized to take every necessary Measure for the execution of the business under such General Officers as Congress shall appoint, and apply for such sums of money as may be thought by them proper & requisite for the expedition.

23d. Congress proceeded to the Election of Gen Officers to conduct the Irruption into Canada and the Ballots being taken Majr. Genl. the Marquis dela Fayette, Majr. Genl. Conway & Brig. Genl. Stark were elected.

Janry. 24th. Resolved That it be earnestly recommended to the Government of the state of New York forthwith to call out four hundred militia of that state under the command of an active & vigilant Officer to serve for the space of four months under the Command of the officer commanding in the northern Department. The said militia when raised to repair to Albany.

28th. Resolved That the Marquis dela Fayette or the General Officer commanding an expedition into Canada be furnished with Bills of Exchange drawn by the President of Congress on the Commissioners of the United States in France to the amount of thirty thousand Livres the said sum to be by him appropriated in such manner as his own prudence may suggest and the exegencies of affairs shall render conducive to the public Interest.

Feb 2d. The Board of War brought in a Report which was taken into Consideration whereupon Resolved That Gen. Washington be informed that in compliance with the request of the Marquis de la Fayette Congress are willing that Major General McDougal should proceed on the intended incursion into Canada if his state of health will admit of it; but if not that the Baron de Kalb be directed to follow the Marquis on the said expedition in case Gen. Washington shall judge it proper. That it is not however the intention of Congress that the Marquis should be detained till Genl. McDougal's intention can be known as the success of the expedition depends upon its being executed without loss of time.

That in compliance with the request of the Marquis dela Fayette commissions be granted to the following French Gentlemen who have produced to the Board of war credentials of their rank & military merit in the French service, and are moreover recommended by the Marquis to be employed under him agreable to their respective ranks, in the intended incursion into Canada, the said officers to be appointed to the command only of such Canadians as may be embodied in Canada. Vizt.

Monsr. Gimat at present aid de camp to the Marquis dela Fayette
to be appointed   Lt Colonel
Monsr de Vrigny   Lt Colonel
Le Chevalier de pont Gibaut   Major
Monsr de Sigonie   Captain
Monsr de Lomagne   Captain
Baron du Frye   Captain

Resolved That Monsr des Epiniers now a Captain in the service of the United States be advanced to the rank of Major in Consideration of the services rendered by his Uncle Monsr. de Beaumarchais and of his having served with reputation in the American Army.

I cannot help giving you a sight of our present Representation.

Quere. To postpone the Consideration of a motion to chuse a Quartr Mastr. Genl. to prepare in concurrence with the Bd. of War a new arrangemt. of that department[2]

N H	Mr. Frost	ay	ay
Mass	Mr. Geary	—	
	Mr. Lovell	no	*
R Is	Mr Ellery	ay	ay
Con	Mr Dyer	ay	ay
N Y	Mr Duer	no	*
N J	Mr Witherspoon	no	divided
	Mr Clark	ay	
Pen	Mr Roberdeau	no	divided
	Mr Clingan	ay	
	Mr Jas Smith	no	
	Mr J B Smith	ay	
D	Mr McKean	no	no
M	Mr Henry	no	*
V	Mr F Lee	no	*
N C	Mr Pen	no	no
S C	Mr Lawrence	ay	ay
G.	Mr Wood	no	no

So it was resolved in the affirmative.

RC (MHi). In Lovell's hand, though not signed.

[1] Lovell probably wrote this letter soon after the last congressional action he discussed in the body of it (the February 2 resolutions concerning officers appointed to serve under Lafayette). It seems likely, therefore, that this is either the February 2 or 7 letter to John that he mentioned in his letter to Abigail Adams printed below under the date March 21, 1778.

[2] This January 31, 1778, vote of Congress is in *JCC*, 10:104.

James Lovell to Benjamin Lincoln

Dear Sir,[1]   York in Pennsylvania Feb. 2d 1778

I am sorry, but not altogether surprised to find from a mutual good Friend that the Resolve of Congress of the 29th of November, which I inclose connected with one of the 12th of that Month supposing a Chance of your not having been furnished with it, has made you uneasy.[2]

I see Circumstances attending your Case which are not common to the Cases of those among the Brigadiers who will be affected by the Arrangement of Woodford and Scott,[3] and also the Cases of St. Clair, Stephen, Mifflin & Stirling.[4]

It had been often possitively declared upon Debates prior to Novr. 29th that the Gentlemen who were created Majors Genl. on the 19th of Febry had signified their entire Willingness that A[5] should have the same Rank as if he had been made a Major General on the same Day with them. Though this Declaration had been made without Effect formerly, yet, it had Influence on the 29th of Novr. when his Name was added in a Resolve which was on the point of passing in regard to two other Officers, whose Case, it was asserted, was similar to his.

This Resemblance was true in a Refference of A. to the 4 other Gentlemen promoted on the Day you was chosen a Continental M.G. but it is not true when referred to your former Situation. And this Nicety was not adverted to at all I believe when the sudden Addition was offered & passed Novr. 29th or if adverted to it did not opperate so powerfully as the Influence of the Declaration before mentioned.

You may be assured that your Name and Character is as highly esteemed in Congress at both Camps, than which I cannot find a more honorable Comparison.

I cannot boast of an Intimacy with you in any measure proportionate to my Regard, but I hope you will let that be no Obstacle to your pointing out to me in a plain Manner how I may in any Measure promote your Happiness which I most sincerely wish to do.

I will depend so much upon finding Credit to my Assertion as to expect to hear from you soon either directly or through Genl. Gates who is the mutual good Friend I have hinted at before.

I am Dear Sir, Your affectionate humble Servant,

James Lovell.

Tr (DLC). Copied for Edmund C. Burnett "from the original, then in the possession of C. F. Libbie & Co."

[1] Benjamin Lincoln (1733–1810), Hingham, Mass., farmer and member of the General Court, 1772–75, had served as a major general of the Massachusetts militia in 1776. He was appointed a major general in the Continental Army in February 1777 and during the Saratoga campaign was seriously wounded. During his ten-

month convalescence Lincoln became concerned about changes in the seniority ranking of Continental generals, but he returned to active duty in August 1778 and the following month was appointed to command the southern department. Although he was in command of the army that surrendered to Gen. Henry Clinton at Charleston, S.C., in May 1780, he was returned to a Continental Army command after his exchange and later served as secretary of war, 1781–83. *DAB.*

[2] For the resolves of November 12 and 29 governing "the relative rank or precedence of officers," see *JCC,* 9:896–97, 981.

[3] For further discussion of the settlement of the ranks of Gens. William Woodford and Charles Scott, see John Penn to William Woodford, November 19, 1777; Committee at Camp Minutes of Proceedings, February 16–20, note 3; and Committee at Camp Statement, March 2, 1778.

[4] Lincoln, Arthur St. Clair, Adam Stephen, Thomas Mifflin, and William Alexander had been promoted to major general on February 19, 1777. *JCC,* 7:133.

[5] The problem of Benedict Arnold's seniority was resolved on January 20, 1778, when General Washington, acting under Congress' November 29 resolve, issued him a new commission as major general dated February 19, 1777. Lincoln mildly objected to the new arrangement in a March 1, 1778, letter to Washington, but he nevertheless returned to active duty August 6, 1778. See Washington, *Writings* (Fitzpatrick), 10:324–26. Lincoln's letter is in the Washington Papers, DLC.

John Witherspoon to Benjamin Rush

Sir   York town Feby. 2, 1778

I was favoured with Your Letter covering two Forms of Resignation. There was nothing exceptionable in any of them. I however gave in that which says you found you could not discharge your Duty as you would &c. which was accepted without a word said by any Person upon the Subject.[1] I am sorry for the Necessity of the Measure & yet I question whether you could have done any thing more proper for Dr. Shippen was fully determined to bring the Matter to a Contest between you refusing positively to serve with you which would have occasioned an Examination & Judgement troublesome to us, hurtful probably to both of you & uncertain in its Issue. I have mentioned to some Members what you proposed to me about the Expedition you know of but they seemed to be at a Loss what Station or Character you could sustain.[2] Some Difficulties are likely to arise on that Expedition. If however it go on & I can find any Opening I shall remember your Proposal. In the meantime as you make use of the Word *Retirement* in your Letter to me I beg you may pay some Regard to my former Opinion upon that subject which you must well remember. I suppose I shall see you at Princeton in a short time as I shall probably go home when Dr Scudder arrives.[3] My Compliments to Mrs Rush & Mr & Mrs Stockton and to the young Folks.

I am Sir your most obedt., humble servant,

Jno Witherspoon

RC (PPL).

[1] Dr. Benjamin Rush's January 30 letter of resignation as physician general of the middle department is in PCC, item 78, 19:205, and Lyman H. Butterfield, ed., *Letters of Benjamin Rush*, 2 vols. (Princeton: Princeton University Press, 1951), 1:193–94. Rush's resignation was an outgrowth of his feud with Dr. William Shippen, Jr., director general of the medical department, on which see James Lovell to Samuel Adams, January 1, 1778, note 1. Witherspoon was chairman of the committee appointed on January 27 to investigate the controversy between Rush and Shippen. *JCC*, 10:93. Rush gave a detailed account of his dealings with this committee in a 1779 letter to Dr. John Morgan in which he claimed that Witherspoon virtually forced him to resign. *Letters of Benjamin Rush*, 1:225–28. See also Committee of Congress to Rush, April 7, 1778.

[2] Although Burnett plausibly conjectured that this "Expedition" was the abortive assault on Canada commanded by Lafayette, it may also refer to a plan Rush had in mind at this time for driving the British out of Philadelphia with a militia force commanded by Gen. Thomas Mifflin. See Burnett, *Letters*, 3:67n.3; and *Letters of Benjamin Rush*, 1:196, 198–200, 2:1200–02.

[3] Nathaniel Scudder took his seat in Congress on February 9. *JCC*, 10:138.

Committee at Camp to Henry Laurens

Sir   No. 11. Camp near the Valley Forge, Feb. 3d. 1778

Your Committee in yesterday's Conference with the General took into Consideration the Memorial of the Council & Assembly of this State, proposing an Attack upon the City of Philadelphia.[1] The happy Consequences resulting from a successful Attempt of this Nature, not only to the inhabitants of this State, but the general Interest, are too many & great, not to excite our warmest Wishes, & most earnest Anxieties. We have therefore weighd every Circumstance with the minutest Attention, & when military Judgment has been requisite, we have endeavoured to supply it with the best Advice & Information. We find it, Sir, universally admitted even by those unacquainted with its Wants & Distresses, that the Continental Army is not equal to the Enterprize in point of Numbers, & it is proposed to supply this Deficiency by a large Collection of Militia from this & the neighbouring States. Such a Collection we presume, as making all due Allowance for the Advantages of Discipline & Experience, will enable us to cope with the Enemy. The Practicability of this Measure seems also to be grounded on a Passage over the River on the Ice, a Supply of Arms, & some Species of Provisions from the Stores of this Army. Any one of which Circumstances failing all Prospects of Success vanish. It is with Sincere Regret Sir, we are obliged to state, that the Continental Army has during the whole Campaign depended upon daily Supplies. No Magazines having been formed, it has not at any Period had 4 days Provisions in Advance. Its late Necessities Congress are acquainted with. When we say they do not now suffer, we say the best the Case will admit. But we need not enter into a Detail of

Difficulties, which have called for the most vigorous Exertions of the States, both collectively & separately to remove. We would only suggest, that if such is the Situation, & such the Prospect when confined to the smaller Scale of the Continental Army, what can be expected, but extreme Famine & Distress, when this Number is doubled & trebled. We cannot from our best Inquiries entertain a rational Hope of subsisting them, during the necessary Preparations. The difficulty of doing it on their March is equally obvious. We may farther add, that coming in from different Distances, & at different Times which the utmost Activity & Circumspection will not prevent, they must suffer every Hardship, & Fatigue which are inseparable from the Want of cover & the Inclemency of the Season.

The State of the Arms is equally unpropitious to our Wishes. The Legislature of this State will alone require for their Militia a greater Number, than can be procured for the Occasion. There would be a Deficiency of many other Articles essential to the Service & equally unattainable. But we need not trespass longer, Sir, on your Time. The course of this Season has furnished the clearest Evidence, how little we can depend upon the Passage of the Schuylkill. Tho twice frozen with every Appearance of continuing so, a sudden Change of Weather has shewn the precarious Footing on which such an Enterprize must stand. This Uncertainty every Day increases—every Person acquainted with this Climate & these Rivers must feel the Weight of this Difficulty.

We need not dwell upon the Consequences of engaging in this Attempt without prosecuting it, or failing in the Execution. They appear to us many & great. The Wisdom & Discernment of Congress will easily perceive them, & make it unnecessary to be more particular.

We shall therefore close the Subject by saying that it has been canvass'd by the military Gentlemen, & has appeared impracticable not only to those who have no immediate Attachment to this State, but those who have, and are influenced by every Motive that is dear to the Heart of Man, to promote & encourage a Spirit of Vigour & Enterprize.

We cannot therefore so far suffer our Wishes to prevail over our judgment, as to recommend the Prosecution of a Measure attended with so many Difficulties, & from which there is so small a Prospect of Success.

We are with the greatest Deference & Respect, Sir, Your most Obedt. & very Hbble. Servs.

Fra Dana	Nathl. Folsom
Jos. Reed	Jno. Harvie
	Gouv. Morris

RC (DNA: PCC, item 33). Written by Joseph Reed and signed by Reed, Dana, Folsom, Harvie, and Morris. Endorsed by Charles Thomson: "Letter from Commee. at Camp, Feby 3. 1778, read 16."
  ¹ For the background of this proposal, which originated in a January 2 letter from the Pennsylvania legislature to Congress, see Jonathan Bayard Smith to Timothy Matlack, January 5, 1778, note. The committee's recommendation against the proposal ended Congress' consideration of an attack on Philadelphia. See also Joseph Reed to Thomas Wharton, February 1, 1778.

William Duer to Gouverneur Morris

Dear sir,   York Town Feby. 3d. 1777 [i.e. 1778]

Mr. George Irwin is so obliging as to forward to you at my Request the Cloth purchas'd by the Delegates of the State of New York for the Use of the New York Troops. You will be kind enough to take the Receipts of the Colonels or Comng. Officers of Regiments to whom the Cloth is deliverd specifying the Quantity by them received. As I am in a hurry to proceed to the Northward¹ having been detaind here much longer than I expected, I beleive I shall not be able to call upon you at Camp on my way homewards.

I am very Affectionately Yours,   Wm. Duer

[P.S.] There has been thirty five Yards taken out of the Quantity Specified in a former Letter from the Delegates to the Cols. Cortlandt and Livingston,² which being deducted will leave the Number of Yards now sent.   W. D.

RC (NNC).
  ¹ Duer was planning to join Lafayette's Canadian expedition as a volunteer, but he soon changed his mind after learning of some uncomplimentary remarks the marquis had made about him. See Duer to Francis Lightfoot Lee, February 14, 1778.
  ² This letter has not been found, but see Francis Lewis's first letter to the New York Convention of January 5, 1778.

Cornelius Harnett to Richard Caswell

                                                      Feb. 3. [1778]

Being disappointed in sending this forward at the time expected, I cannot help mentioning to Your Excellency very Shortly a Matter which hangs heavy at my heart. Whilst all the States are fortifying every Creek & Inlet where Vessels can possibly enter, I fear Our State have Neglected Cape Lookout Bay & Cape Fear River. The Latter is such a harbour, as may at all times be safe for the Enemy to Enter, & ravage the Country at will more especially at this time, when all our Continental Troops are at the distance of 600 Miles from that place.

Cape Look Out is one of the finest Harbours on the American Coast,
& would be a noble Asylum for the Continental and Private Ships of
war to wood & water, as also a Place of Security for Trading Vessels
Chaced by the Enemy. I am distressed beyond Measure to find Our
Sea Coast so much neglected, to please (I fear) a few Individuals who
may be interested in the Matter. I am as befor Your Excellys. Most
Ob &c &c &c   Cornl Harnett

[*P.S.*] I am confined to my room by the Gout, & therefore can not with
that Accuracy I could wish, answer your Queres in regard to Major
Genl. Pay &c. I shall do myself the Honor of writing you in a Short
time on that head. I could wish Your Excellency would fall upon
ways & means to procure all the Salted Pork in your State for the use
of the Continental Army. Congress have every reason to believe the
Army will be greatly distressed for that Article, I hope none will be
Suffered to be Exported. Your Bills will be answered.

RC (PHi). A continuation of Harnett to Caswell, January 31, 1778.

Cornelius Harnett to William Wilkinson

Dr. Sir   York Town Pensylvania Feby. 3d 1778
   I wrote to you a few days ago by Coll Davis. I have not lately been
favoured with any from you. For News I refer you to the Papers Inclosed, indeed we have very little stirring. Our Army remain as mentioned in my last, at Valey Forge.
   I am every day expecting Jackey here, as Mr. Mitchell has promised
to send him as soon as the weather will permit. Be assured I shall be
as Careful of him as I would be of my Own.
   I can not yet meet with a Distiller but have a prospect Of Purchasing a Negro who I am told understands the business very well. I
mentioned to you in several of my Letters that it was absolutely
necessary to send on the Bills recd by you & drawn by Coll Kennon.
I wish you may not delay it too long, you need not be afraid of my
spending the Money, especially when Our Assembly have made such
a Generous Allowance to their Delegates.[1] I have not the least doubt
but this handsome Salary will tempt some Other Gentleman to Covet
my place, & by that means I hope to be relieved from the most disagreeable business I ever undertook in my whole life. I wish I was
fairly out of it. I am, Dr Sir, Your real friend & Obed Servt,
                                            Cornl. Harnett

[*P.S.*] You have never yet told me whether you have paid Mr Black-
more the 100 Dollrs. Continental money I borrowed of him, if it is
not done *I beg you will immediately do it with Interest.*

I desire you will make particular inquiry about my Intimate & worthy friend Mr. Sampson, you have not mentioned his name in one of your letters since I left home. I beg you will present him with my most affectionate regard, tell him I still retain the sincere & disinterested esteem for him I ever had, & which can end only with my life. Your &c,   C. H.

RC (PHi). Endorsed: "recd the 18th March 1778."
[1] On December 24, 1777, the North Carolina Assembly had changed the salary of a North Carolina delegate from $2,000 to £1,600 a year. *N.C. State Records,* 12:66–67, 440–41.

Henry Laurens to James Duane

Dear Sir.   York Town 3d February 1778
   Meeting accidentally with the present good conveyance which may save some days in the dispatch of the inclosed Paper & being so early in the Morning as to prohibit access either to the War Office or Secretary's in order to obtain the proper Address of Indian Commissioners for the Northern department I take the liberty of putting an Act of Congress of yesterday upon Indian affairs under this Cover & of requesting you to deliver it into the proper hands.[1]
   I am with great Respect, Dear Sir, Your most obedient servant,
                              Henry Laurens, President of Congress[2]

RC (NHi).
[1] The enclosed "Act" consisted of instructions for the conduct of the Indian commissioners for the northern department at a forthcoming conference with the Six Nations at Johnstown, N.Y. *JCC,* 10:110–11. This day Laurens also wrote a brief letter to New York governor George Clinton transmitting the section of the instructions requesting him "to appoint a suitable person to be commissioner for Indian affairs in the northern department, and direct him to attend the treaty above mentioned." Bright Collection, NRom; and *JCC,* 10:111. Duane was the man Clinton chose for this task. Clinton, *Papers* (Hastings), 2:791. Duane, who had been deputed by Congress on December 3, 1777, to assist the northern Indian commissioners, was currently in Albany on that mission. See *JCC,* 9:999; and Duane to George Clinton, March 13, 1778.
[2] This day Laurens transmitted copies of December 19, 1777, and January 21, 1778, resolves on the treatment of prisoners of war with brief notes that he wrote to the governors of Connecticut, New York, Maryland, Virginia, and North Carolina. PCC, item 13, fols. 160–62; and *JCC,* 9:1036–37, 10:74–82. He also wrote another brief note this day to Governor Henry of Virginia enclosing "the papers to which you refer in your favour of 24 January." Breckinridge Long Papers, DLC. There is no January 24, 1778, letter from Henry mentioned in the journals or located in PCC. On February 2 Congress did read a January 20 letter from Henry dealing with the problems of supplying the army, but it contained no request for papers. PCC, item 71, 1:131–34; and *JCC,* 10:110.

Henry Laurens to John Laurens

My Dear son,   York Town 3d Febry 1778
   I wrote to you the 28th of the expired Month by Barry.
   I could if time would permit write a Page full of intelligence, but
Monsr le Marquis[1] will relate to you in less time & better.
   You will receive under the protection of the Marquis's retinue two
Camp Shirts, I am promised two more for you very soon. You never
acknowledge the receipt of any article, which exposes us to loss, by
the worst means, fraud.
   In conversation with General Gates without seeking on my side, I
discovered an inclination in him to be upon friendly terms with our
great & good General, it cannot be doubted but that there is the same
disposition on the other side. What would I not give to see a perfect
& happy reconciliation.[2]
   Talking of General Conway's Letter which has been circulating as
formerly intimated, & of which General Gates declared both his ignorance & disapprobation, I took occasion to say, if General Conway
pretends sincerity in his late parallel between the Great F—— & the
great W——[3] he has, taking this Letter into view, been guilty of the
blackest hypocrisy—if not, he is chargeable with the guilt of an unprovoked sarcasm & is unpardonable. The General perfectly acquiesced in that sentiment & added such hints as convinced me he
thought highly of Conway. Shall such a Man seperate freinds or keep
them asunder? It must not be.
   My Dear son, I pray God protect you.   Henry Laurens.

RC (PHi).
   [1] Lafayette.
   [2] For a discussion of Horatio Gates' role in the so-called Conway Cabal against
General Washington, see James Lovell to Gates, November 27, 1777, note 1.
   [3] Gen. Thomas Conway had sarcastically compared Washington to Frederick the
Great in a December 31, 1777, letter to the commander in chief. See Laurens to
John Laurens, January 8, 1778, note 12.

Henry Laurens to John Rutledge

                                                   3d Febry. [1778]
   We cannot tell on what Credit we are at the Court of Versailles,
not having received any intelligence from the Commissioners since
May last. A person lately arrived Express from there delivered me a
large packet which being opened presented a Charte blancke, it contained about 40 folds of clean coarse white Paper—the Packet intended for Congress, supposed to have been stolen & this Counterfeit
put in its place, the person who brought it, informed me that two

packets preceeding that delivered to him had been intercepted by a Merchant at Harve de grace & sent to London, he supposed the one spoken of above, had fallen into the same snare. However we have taken this chap into Custody, several parts of his behaviour having exposed him to suspicion & we are too well convinced of carelessness in Mr. Dean's part with respect to public dispatches.[1] Your Excellency knows that Mr. John Adams is appointed to succeed Mr. Deane, Dr. Franklin is very old & therefore I am persuaded that abilities in addition to his are extremely wanted.

Congress have projected an Irruption into Canada, & had appointed Marquis delafayette 1st, Major Gen Conway 2d, & Brigadier General Stark 3d in Command.[2] The Marquis came from Camp to York, discovered a noble resentment for the affront offered to his Commander General Washington, to whom his appointment had not been intimated by Congress, said he could not go without a General Officer of the Rank of "Major General" in whom he could put confidence, & therefore demanded General McDougal or Baron Kalb & that their appointment should be through his General.

Congress & the Board of War hesitated, the Marquis said if he was disappointed he must immediately go to France to account for his conduct, & that every foreign Officer would accompany him. Had an Irruption of this nature taken place, the World at large must have been informed of the unmeritted insult offered the General & Commander in Chief, & Censure must have followed both on Congress & the Board of War. Ignorance perhaps might have accounted for the conduct of the former, although they were warned against the unjustifiable step. A good deal of struggle was made to elude the Marquis's demands. He was firm & Succeeded & this Morning he took leave of me & proceeded to the Camp in order as he Says, to receive the Commands of his General, to take either General McDougal or General Kalb with him & go rapidly forward to Albany.[3] He speaks of G.C.[4] in the most unfavorable terms, who will be much mortified by this new arrangement.

I count it a misfortune that I do not approve of this Canada expedition because I am almost single in opinion, however there is no Man in our Army so likely to succeed in it as this young Noble Man. He is skilful in the Art of War, is sensible & brave & will have great Influence in Canada with the Noblesse, the Church & the Commonalty. He takes in his suite some eight or ten prime French Officers in order to raise Companies in that Country.

I wish our utmost strength of Men & Money had been collected to the one point for driving the Enemy from this quarter that we would hedge securely in our own proper territory. Canada as well as East & West Florida must in a few years fall into the general Union without loss of Blood or expence of Treasure on our part—& the diversion which we pretend will be made of the Enemy's forces is by no means, according to my judgement, an equivalent for the risque we take by diverting our own forces in the present State of affairs. Hence Your Excellency will perceive how totally So. Carolina & Georgia are effaced from our memory. The Enemy will not be ignorant of our weakness & I am informed by two Men who have made their escape from the Enemy on Delaware that the common talk there was an Expedition against So Carolina in the Spring. These Men are Jeremiah Vane, a Native of Charles Town & Richd. Aislep a Seaman. I supplied them with Sixty Dollars to assist them on their return to our Port, presuming the public of So. Carolina will admit the charge, otherwise it shall be my own expence.

There lies on the Treasury here, 100000 Dollars returned by Mr. G A Hall & upwards of 14000, which had been left in my hands by Mr. Middleton & Mr. Hayward, all the property of South Carolina.

I have the honour to be with great Esteem & Respect &ca.

[*P.S.*] I have heard it avowed in full Congress that we have sustained losses of several hundred thousand Dollars in the Passage from the Board of War to distant departments, not in my time thank God. Is it not very extraordinary we have not taken the trouble even to inquire into this?

LB (ScHi). A continuation of Laurens to Rutledge, January 30, 1778.

[1] For a further account of the theft of the dispatches which the commissioners at Paris had entrusted to Capt. John Folger, see Committe Examination of John Folger, January 12, 1778.

[2] For a discussion of this expedition, see Laurens to Lafayette, January 22, 1778, note 2.

[3] See *JCC*, 10:107. See also Gouverneur Morris to Laurens, January 26, 1778, note 1.

[4] General Conway, whose dispute with Lafayette is also discussed in Laurens to Lafayette, January 22, note 2; Gouverneur Morris and John Harvie to the Pennsylvania Council, January 24, note; and William Duer to Francis Lightfoot Lee, February 14, 1778, note 1.

Henry Laurens to George Washington

Sir,   3d Febry 1778.

My last trouble was under the 27th Ulto. by Messenger Barry.

Your Excellency's favor of the 31st together with General Foremans memorial came to hand last Night, I presented it to Congress & the Subject matter will be taken under consideration this Morning.[1]

Inclosed your Excellency will find an Act of Congress for appointing a Major General under your Excellency's direction to proceed with Marquis delafayette on the intended expedition into Canada.[2]

I have the honour to be &ca.

LB (DNA: PCC, item 13).

¹ Washington's January 31 letter to Laurens, in which he commended to Congress' attention an enclosed letter and memorial from Gen. David Forman of New Jersey, is in PCC, item 152, 5:275–76, and Washington, *Writings* (Fitzpatrick), 10:411–12. In his January 1 letter and memorial to Washington, Forman had proposed that he and his business associates would set up a saltworks in Barnegat, N.J., and sell the salt they produced to the army if Washington agreed to provide a guard of Continental soldiers for the works. PCC, item 152, 5:279–81. Although Congress read Forman's proposal on February 2 and decided to consider it the following day, no further action on it was taken. *JCC*, 10:111–12. Nevertheless, Washington did station Continental soldiers at Forman's saltworks during their construction until he was obliged to withdraw them because of New Jersey's opposition to their use for this purpose. Washington, *Writings* (Fitzpatrick), 11:148–50.

² Congress had resolved on February 2 that either Maj. Gen. Alexander McDougall or Maj. Gen. de Kalb could serve with Lafayette on this expedition. *JCC*, 10:107. As McDougall was too ill to serve, Washington subsequently reported that de Kalb would join Lafayette. Washington, *Writings* (Fitzpatrick), 10:428.

Jonathan Bayard Smith to George Bryan

Dr. Sir   York Town Feb. 3d. 1778
    I wrote you a few days ago by   .¹ Nothing since has occurred worth your notice. The assembly of Virginia has acceded to the Confederation. I do not think however they have treated the matter with form equal to its importance. Does it appear proper to raise so great a fabrick on the slender basis of a simple resolution of the two houses? Will not *legal consequences* follow from this confederation? I apprehend it would be not only proper, but that it would answer many valuable purposes if more form were used, at least if the articles were approved & acceded to by a law of each State solemnly enacted, & in which law perhaps it may be expedient to insert certain matters connected therewith. It is a question in this house, whether suits can be supported for the recovery of p[ublic?] monys in the several states. What think you of this? This may be one object in the act I speak of.
    Please to send the Inclosed² to my good woman.
    I am Dr. Sir, with respect yr. afft. & m h st.   JBS.

[*P.S.*] Have you any acct. yet from Sammy?

RC (PHarH).
¹ Not found.
² Not found.

Robert Morris to Henry Laurens

Sir,   Manheim Feby 4th. 1778
   The Baron de Steuben so Warmly recommended by Doctr Franklin
& Mr Deane, as well as by Monsr Roderique Hortalez & Co. having
done me the honor to call in his way to Congress,[1] delivered me the
enclosed letters, Copies of which I took the liberty to forward to
Your Excellency some time since, but still think it necessary to send
the originals least those Copies might be mislaid. Doctor Franklin
writes in very strong terms of this Gentns. military experience &
Talents to Mr Bache[2] now here & at whose desire I mention it; having
served so long as twenty years under so great a Master as the King of
Prussia one cannot but entertain expectations that the Baron must
be capable of rendering important Services to this country, otherways
the Art Military is not acquirable by opportunity & experience alone.
I have the honor to be Your Excellys Obedt hble servt.
                                                    Robt Morris

RC (DNA: PCC, item 164).
   [1] For an account of Steuben's trip from Boston to York, where he arrived February 5, see John McAuley Palmer, *General von Steuben* (New Haven: Yale University Press, 1937), pp. 117–23.
   [2] Benjamin Franklin's son-in-law, Richard Bache.

John Penn to Robert Morris

My dear Sir   York Feby 4th. 1778
   I intended before this to have seen you at Manheim, Mr. Harnet
being unable to attend Congress having the Gout will make it some
days before I can have that pleasure.
   The design of this letter is to inform you that I wish you would
lay the accounts of the Secret Committee before Congress as soon as
you can possibly, some members at times drop expressions on that
subject that I do not like.[1] There are few men whose ability and
Integrity I have so high an opinion of, as I have of yours. I do not
mean to alarm you by what I have said, but only to induce you to
attend to this matter more than perhaps otherwise you would, when
I see you I shall be more explicit.
   Master Robert is very well, and quite brisk, he visits me at times,
the little Fellow found a 30 dollar bill yesterday in the street, but
gave it to a Girl that was looking for one of that dignity some hours
after. My Compliments to Mrs. Morris & am with great regard &
Esteem, Dear Sir, Your obt. Servt.   J Penn

RC (PHi).

[1] One of the delegates who disapproved of Morris' handling of the Secret Committee's accounts was doubtless President Laurens, who subsequently became embroiled in a controversy with Morris over the issue early in 1779. See Henry Laurens' Memorandum, [ante January 7]; and Robert Morris' letter "to the Public," January 7, 1779. For information on the context in which the subject of the Secret Committee accounts arose in Congress, see also Committee of Commerce to Robert Morris, February 21, 1778.

Committee at Camp to Henry Laurens

Sir   Camp near the Valley Forge, Feby. 5, 1778

In Obedience to the Orders of Congress, we have taken into Consideration the Reduction of the Number of Battalions, the necessary Reinforcements for the Cavalry, Artillery, & Infantry, the Mode of obtaining them, & the necessary Regulations of that Part of the Army.[1] Upon the first of these Heads, we have to observe that the Number of our Army must depend upon the Force which in all Probability will be opposed to it, the Operations which it is intended to effectuate, & the Means of procuring Subsistence. The Force opposed will be very far from inconsiderable, or it will be nothing, for we cannot suppose that Great Brittain will prosecute this War with inferior Numbers to those hitherto employed, when she has such good Reason to believe in the Strength of this Continent.

Considering the Situation of our own Affairs, it will doubtless be expected from our Army that they should cover such Parts of the Country as are exposed to Depredation from the several Posts which the Enemy hold; secure that very important Pass on Hudsons River which Reason & Experience demonstrate to be the Key of America, & at the same Time to act with Efficacy against their main Army now at Philadelphia. The great & increasing Difficulty of procuring Subsistence is perhaps the strongest Reason why our Continental Troops should be numerous. For when it is considered that where they are defective, a much greater Militia must be called into the Field, at an increased Expense of Money, Provisions & military Stores; & that each Success of the Enemy is a fatal Stab to our Resources, by operating thro the Opinions of the People upon our Paper Currency, the Truth of the Position will appear with the strongest Evidence.

Our present Establishment of Infantry, from New Hampshire to North Carolina inclusive, allowing only seven to Maryland is 81 Battalions, which with the 16 additionals is ninety seven; if to this be added the two State Regiments of Virginia & Pennsylvania, the German Battalion, Hazens & James Livingstons Canadian Battalions, Warners Regiment, Armands Corps, & Rawlins's, the whole will amount to 103 complete & incomplete. These we would reduce to

Eighty eight (exclusive of the Regiments of Warner, Hazen, & James Livingston, of whom Mention will be made hereafter) upon the Establishment inclosed & marked No. 1. In Consideration of the Loss of a Part of Rhode Island, we would for the present reduce their Quota to one Regiment, & for the same Reason, would we in like Manner reduce that of Pennsylvania to Ten. The State Regiments of Virginia & Pennsylvania we propose to incorporate into the Continental Regiments to be completed by them respectively, & to consider the German Battalion, & so much of Rawlins's as have been raised in Maryland, as a Part of the Eight Battalions to be completed by that State. Armands Corps & the 16 Additionals we would reduce to nine, & of Hazen's & James Livingstons Canadian Regiments form one upon the new Establishment, & reduce Warners to the same Standard, to be filled up if possible by voluntary Inlistments.

We would continue our Establishment of Artillery, which is four Regiments, in the Manner marked No. 2. And that of our four Regiments of Cavalry, which in the Opinion of your Committee is of the utmost Importance, especially in the open Country of Pennsylvania, we would place on the Footing mark'd No. 3. Our daily Information of the great Pains taken by the Enemy to increase their Cavalry demonstrates the Propriety & even Necessity of putting ourselves in a Situation to meet them with a decisive Superiority.

It will be essentially advantageous for the Care & good Discipline of the Army to add a Provost Corps. The Establishment of which is in the Inclosure No. 4. The Army we would propose to complete would therefore in the whole Infantry, Artillery, & Cavalry amount to 53,822 non commissioned Officers & Privates as will appear by the Inclosure No. 5.

The Reinforcements necessary for this Army will from what we have already said be very considerable, as may easily be determined by a Comparison between the Numbers above stated & the Returns of the Army filed in the War Office. Copies of such Parts of these Returns as relate to each State ought to be sent forward to each respectively with the utmost Expedition together with the Resolutions of Congress for obtaining Recruits. The General has already notified the States of the Deficiencies of such of their Regiments as are now on this Side the Delaware. Upon the Subject of recruiting, we must beg Leave to observe to Congress, that from the great Havock made among the human Species by Sickness & the Sword during the present War, from the Disrepute of our Paper Money, the Disaffection of many Inhabitants of America, & the Arts of the Enemy it hath become utterly impossible to raise any considerable Number of Men by voluntary Inlistment. The Hope of accomplishing this by any Increase of Bounty, Experience hath shewn to be vain & groundless; & to rely upon it will be fatal to the Army & hazard the Safety &

Freedom of these States. No Resource therefore remains, but that of Draughts which in the Opinion of your Committee ought to be adopted as speedily as possible. For if we have any Advantage over our Enemy it arises from that Circumstance of Distance; which as it cannot be removed, so we shall allways be enabled if not wanting to ourselves to make that Use of Contingencies which they seldom can. And this Advantage in the present Instance is of the utmost Importance, because if the Successes of our Arms to the Northward be properly improved by an early Draught so as to have our Army in the Field before the Enemy can obtain any Reinforcements, it is highly probable that something may be done which will go near to terminate the War in our Favour. The Impropriety of giving any Bounty to the Drafts considering the State of our Finances is so apparent, that we need not enlarge upon it. Let us however be permitted to observe, that unless Congress earnestly recommend the contrary, there is great Reason to believe that some of the States may go into that pernicious Measure. By the Resolutions which we do ourselves the Honour to submit to your Consideration,[2] & List of Quotas No. 5, Congress will perceive that including those already inlisted the several States will be called upon according to our Plan for 54,668 Men, which allowing for the Deficiencies that will arise by Death, Desertion & the Train of unavoidable Accidents which take place on such Occasions, will probably give us an Army of effective Men which tho inferiour from these Circumstances to the Establishment of No. 5, may still be capable of acting with Honour & Success.

We have, Sir, as you will perceive by a Perusal of the Resolutions referred to, endeavoured as far as we could to provide against the many Frauds which are practiced to elude the public Service. We cannot hope that these Provisions will be quite effectual but we expect that they will have a considerable Influence in forwarding the full Proportions of continental Troops.

The Regulations we propose for these Troops will partly appear from the several Papers inclosed. Such others as we have conferr'd upon we shall communicate from Time to Time, as they may be completed, but we have placed this great Object of Recruits in the foremost Point of View, as it is the Basis upon which every Thing else depends, & without which all other Regulations would become meer waste Paper.

With the greatest Respect we are Sir, Your most Obed. Hble Servts.

Fra. Dana per Order

P.S. We have thought it best to explain more fully the Nature of the Above Arrangement so far as respects the Difference of Numbers between the old & new Establishment. On the former the Complement of a Battalion was 692 non commissioned Officers & privates—the present 553. Difference 139 with which we propose to fill up the Artillery, Cavalry & complete the 9 additional Battalions having Respect in the Disposition of them to the several States where they have been originally raised. And we shall think it a very happy Consequence if the States so exert themselves that the Surplus should prove an adequate Fund for the above Purpose; as the 9 additionals are officer'd by Gentlemen of approved Character & the Cavalry & Artillery are too important not to require the greatest Attention. In this old Establishment there were 40 commissioned Officers in a Battalion—in the new but 29 tho an Addition is made of one Company of light Infantry.

ENCLOSURES

No. 1. Establishment of the Infantry of the American Armies.

That each Battallion shall consist of nine Companies one of which shall be of light Infantry the light Infantry to be kept complete by Drafts from the Battallion and organized during the Campaign into Corps of light Troops.

Number	Rank	Monthly Pay	Amt.	Daily Rats.	Amt.
1	Colonel	75	75	6	6
8 { 1	Lt. Colonel	60	60	5	5
1	Major	50	50	4	4
6	Captains	40	240	3	18
1	Captain Lt. of Cols. Co.	26⅔	26⅔	2	2
8	Lieutenants	26⅔	213⅓	2	16
9	Ensigns	20	180	2	18
4 {	Paymaster	20	20		
	Adjutant	13	13		
	Quarter Master	13	13		
1	Surgeon	60	60	4	4
1	Surgeons Mate	40	40	2	2
29	Commissioned Officers Pay		991	Rations	75
1	Serjeant Major	@10	10		
1	Qur. Mr. Serjeant	10	10		
27	Serjeants	10	270		
1	Drum Major	9	9		
1	Fife Major	9	9		
18	Drums & Fifes	7⅓	132		
49	Non Com. Officers		440		
27	Corporals	@ 7⅓	198		
477	Privates	@ 6⅔	3180		
504	Rank & File		3378		

504	Rank & File		Rations	504
49	Non Comm.			49
553				553
29	Com. Officers			75
582				628

Total *582*. Pay per Month *4,809* Dollars. Rations per Month *18,840*.

The Field Officers of the light Infantry to be selected from those belonging to the several Battallions, and the PayMaster &c as above. An Addition of 2 Dollars per Month each is made to the Pay of the Serjeants that good Persons may be got for that necessary Office.

The old Arangement non Com. & Privates consisted of 692. Total 732 their Pay per Month 6020 Dollars. Rations per Month 23,790.

The Difference between the Battallions is *150* Dollars per Month and *4,950* Rations.

No. 2. Establishment of the Artillery of the American Armies.

Number	Rank	Pay	Amt.	Rat.	Amt.
1	Colo.	100	100	6	6
1	Lt. Colo.	75	75	5	5
1	Major	$62\frac{1}{2}$	$62\frac{1}{2}$	4	4
12	Captains	50	600	3	36
12	Captain Lieutts	$33\frac{1}{3}$	400	2	24
12	first Lieutenants	$33\frac{1}{3}$	400	2	24
36	second Lieutts	$33\frac{1}{3}$	1200	2	72
5 {	Pay Master	25	25		
	Adjutant	16	16		
	Quarter Master	16	16		
1	Surgeon	75	75	4	4
1	Surgeon's Mate	50	50	2	2
77	Comm. Officers Monthly Pay $3019\frac{1}{2}$			Rations	*177*
1	Serjeant Major	$112\frac{3}{90}$	$112\frac{3}{90}$		
1	Qur. Master Serjeant	$112\frac{3}{90}$	$112\frac{3}{90}$		
1	Fife Major	$103\frac{8}{90}$	$103\frac{8}{90}$		
1	Drum Major	$103\frac{8}{90}$	$103\frac{8}{90}$		
72	Serjeants	10	720		
72	Bombadiers	9	648		
72	Corporals	9	648		
72	Gunners	$8\frac{2}{3}$	624		
24	Drums & Fifes	$8\frac{2}{3}$	208		
336	Matrosses	$8\frac{1}{3}$	2800		Rations
652	Non Com. & Privates at		$5691\frac{3}{90}$ Dolls/Mo.		652

77   Commissioned
    Officers at $3019\frac{1}{2}$ Dolls/Mo.   177
———   ———
729 $8710^{60}\!/_{90}$ 829

Total 729. Pay Per Month $8710^{60}\!/_{90}$ Dollars. Rat. per Mo. 24870.

No. 3. Establishment of the Cavalry of the American Armies.

Number	Rank	Pay	Amt.	Rat.	Amt.
1	Colonel	$93\frac{3}{4}$	$93\frac{3}{4}$	6	6
1	Lt. Colonel	75	75	5	5
1	Major	60	60	4	4
6	Captains	50	300	3	18
12	Lieutenants	$33\frac{1}{3}$	400	2	24
6	Cornets	$26\frac{2}{3}$	160	2	12
1	Rideing Master	$33\frac{1}{3}$	$33\frac{1}{3}$	2	2
6 {	Pay Master	25	25		
	Adjutant	15	15		
	Quarter Master	15	15		
1	Surgeon	60	60	4	4
1	Mate	40	40	2	2
30	Com. Officers. Monthly Pay		$1277\frac{1}{2}$	Rations	77
1	Sadler	@10	10		
1	Trumpet Major	11	11		
6	Farriers	10	60		
6	Qur. Mr. Serjts.	15	90		
6	Trumpeters	10	60		
12	Serjeants	15	180		
32	Non Com. Officers		411	Dollars Per Mo.	
30	Corporals	@10	300		
324	Privates	$8\frac{1}{3}$	2700		
354	Rank & File		3000	Dollars Per Mo.	
32	non Com Officers		411		
386			3411	Rations	386
30	Com. Officers		$1277\frac{1}{2}$		77
416			$4688\frac{1}{2}$		463

Total 416. Pay per Mo. 4688 1/2 Dollars. Rations per Month 13,890.

No. 4. Establishment of a Provost.

		Drs. per Month				
1	Captain of Provosts at	50	50 & 3	Rat. per Day	3
4	Lieutenants	33⅓	133⅓ 2		8
1	Clerk	33⅓	33⅓ 2		2
1	Qur. Master Serjt.	15	15 1		1
2	Trumpeters	10	20 1		2
2	Serjeants	15	30 1		2
5	Corporals	10	50 1		5
43	Provosts or Privates	8⅓	358⅓ 1		43
4	Executioners	10	40 1		4
63			680		70

This Corps is to be drafted from the several Brigades mounted on Horseback and armed and accoutred as light Dragoons. Their Business is to watch over the Regularity and good order of the Army in Camp, Quarters or on a March, Quell Riots, prevent marauding, stragling and Desertion, detect Spies, regulate Sutlers and the like.

No. 5. State of the Infantry, Artillery and Cavalry of the American Army.[7]

Infantry	Batts.		Non Com. & Privates
New Hampshire	3		
Massachusetts	15		
Rhode Island	1		
Connecticut	8		
New York	5		
New Jersey	4		
Pensilvania	10		
Delaware	1		
Maryland	8		
Virginia	15		
N. Carolina	9		
Additionals	9		
Hazens Canadians	1		
Warners	1		Non Com. & Privates
	90	Bats. 553 each	49,770
Artillery	4	652	2,608
Cavalry	4	386	1,544
			53,822

State of the Quotas to be called for viz.

The several States abovementioned to complete their State Battallions according to the original Establishment of non Com. Officers and Privates.

79 Battallions containing each of non com. Officers and Privates 692	54,668
Warner's and Hazens Regts to be completed to the new Establishment of 553 as above by voluntary Enlistments	1,106
Now in the Artillery about	1,000
in the Cavalry about	550
in the Additionals &ca about	1,850
	59,174
Deduct for the Deficiencies in Drafts, Desertion, Death &ca	5,352
	53,822
Make a further Deduction for those sick, naked who may not have joined and the like at least one third	17,942
The army may by the first Day of June equal	35,880

RC (DNA: PCC, item 33). Written by Joseph Reed and signed by Francis Dana. The draft of this letter, written by Gouverneur Morris, is in the Force Collection, DLC. Enclosures: MS (DNA: PCC, item 33). Written by Gouverneur Morris.

[1] This letter with its plan for the new arrangement of the army was read in Congress on February 16. On February 26 Congress agreed to the committee's general recommendations on state quotas and a militia draft to replace voluntary enlistments, but it delayed action on many details of reorganization until the committee returned from camp. The committee's recommendation to discontinue bounty payments was rejected, but Congress did finally take action on the proposals for the engineering department, which the committee discussed in a March 3, 1778, letter to President Laurens. A revised committee plan was eventually laid before Congress on May 18, and after debates lasting several days it was adopted without substantial changes. Putting new measures into effect involved many difficulties, however, and after many delays, Congress on July 9 ordered Joseph Reed and Francis Dana to headquarters to work out details of the new arrangement. A month later Roger Sherman and John Banister were added to this new arrangements committee, but not until November 24 was this chapter in the reorganization of the army finally closed. See JCC, 10:172, 199–203, 11:507, 514–15, 517, 536, 538–43, 550–51, 570, 676, 769, 12:995, 1004, 1154–60; and Committee at Camp to Laurens, March 3, 1778.

[2] A text in the hand of Francis Dana of the committee's eleven proposed resolutions on ways and means of drafting and enlisting men in the Continental Army is in PCC, item 33, fols. 113–16. These resolves are substantially similar to the ones Congress adopted on this issue on February 27. See JCC, 10:199–203.

[3] Morris wrote in the margin at this point: "Each of the Field Officers to command a Company, the Lieut of the Cols. Co. to have the Rank of Cap. Lieutt."

[4] In the margin: "These Officers to be taken from the Line, the PayMaster chosen by the Corps, the others appointed by the Colo from among the Subalterns."

⁵ In the margin: "These Officers to be taken from the Line in the Manner specified for the Infantry, No. 1 [enclosure]."

⁶ In the margin: "These Officers to be taken from the Line in the Manner specified for the Infantry, No. 1."

⁷ For the committee's proposed "Establishment for a Corps of Engineers," which would have been the sixth element in this new "arrangement" of the Continental Army but which was not ready for submission until nearly a month later, see Committee at Camp to Henry Laurens, March 3, 1778.

Committee for Foreign Affairs to Ralph Izard

Sir   York Town in Pensylvania 5 Feby 1778

Your letter from Paris of Octr. 6th last year,¹ being read in Congress, afforded much satisfaction, as it signified acceptance of the Commission which has been sent by Capt. Young; and also held up a prospect of your obtaining a loan of money in Italy. Our apprehensions of danger to our liberties are reduced to one circumstance of the depreciation of our Currency, from the quantity which we have been obliged to issue. The different States are sinking their own emissions, and are going largely into taxation for continental purposes, but it will require more time than we wish before the good policy of taxation can have full effect upon the currency; therefore Congress have given in regard to you, the same instructions as to the Gentlemen at the courts of France and Spain; and we doubt not of your best exertions. We wish you Success in the business of the enclosed resolves,² as well as in every other undertaking for the good of the public, or for your own personal felicity. We must leave you very much from time to time to receive intelligence of our affairs from the other Commissioners to whom we shall have a more ready channel of conveyance than to you.

We are with much regard &c.   Signed   J. Witherspoon

J. Lovell

FC (DNA: PCC, item 79).

¹ Ralph Izard's October 6, 1777, letter to the Committee for Foreign Affairs in which he accepted his appointment as commissioner to Tuscany, is in PCC, item 89, fols. 3–6, and Wharton, *Diplomatic Correspondence*, 2:403–4.

² A reference to Congress' resolves authorizing Izard to borrow one million pounds sterling at 6 percent interest from the court of Tuscany. *JCC*, 10:120.

Henry Laurens to the Marquis de Lafayette

Sir,   5th Febry. 1778.

Virtue & fortitude will subdue "Troops," countermine Cunning Inspectors & bring Presidents¹ embarrassed & entangled between native honour & party plots to subscribe very unprecedented engagements.

The Convention of Susquehana[2] affords me Dear General, the highest satisfaction although I am under some apprehension for the article to be complied with at Lancaster. Be that as it may, you will be at the heels of the contracting party, my fears are therefore confined to the little mischief which an almost exhausted Treasury may Suffer by a demand for an unnecessary & expensive Courier. The Eye of my mind is always fixed on that poor battered Treasury badly filled from a want of judgement & scandalously plundered by the effects of folly & dishonesty.

Proper care shall be taken of Monsr. Valfort's Letter & the disposal duly notified.

There will be an excellent opportunity for writing to France about 10 days hence from Baltimore.

The little Note was destroyed the Morning it was delivered to me. Unless the New Monsr. Lanuville will follow Your Excellency's fortunes as a Volunteer I have no prospect in his favour.

Congress have Resolved to detain the Artillerists &c at Boston on certain terms which Colo. Duplessis is possessed of, advancement of Rank & the pay of the Army.[3] If they have not stratagems in their heads, considering what they have already received, they will accept. If they have, they will be left to prosecute them.

I have the honour to be with every sentiment of respect & attachment &ca.

LB (ScHi).
[1] Laurens is alluding to Col. Robert Troup, Horatio Gates' aide-de-camp; Gen. Thomas Conway, the inspector general of the Continental Army; and Gates himself, the president of the Board of War.
[2] A facetious reference to an encounter between Lafayette and Troup at Anderson's Ferry on the Susquehanna and their agreement to meet at Lancaster. Lafayette, *Papers* (Idzerda), 1:276.
[3] Congress passed this resolve this day, with Laurens casting South Carolina's vote in the affirmative. *JCC*, 10:118–19.

James Lovell to Richard Henry Lee

Dear Sir.   York Janry [*i.e.* February] 5th. 1778.
Your favors of the 15th & 23d of January came yesterday to hand.[1] I am exceedingly pleased with the proceedings of your General Assembly. I hold them out in all my letters to the eastward as a fine example.

I shall send you the oath of Allegiance which passed in Congress yesterday as soon as it comes from the Press.[2] It is our Business to

In CONGRESS,

FEBRUARY 3, 1778.

RESOLVED,

THAT every officer, who holds or shall hereafter hold a commission or office from Congress, shall take and subscribe the following oath or affirmation;

" I   do acknowledge the United States of America, to be Free, Independent and Sovereign States, and declare that the people thereof owe no allegiance or obedience to George the Third, King of Great-Britain; and I renounce, refuse and abjure any allegiance or obedience to him; and I do swear (or affirm) that I will to the utmost of my power, support, maintain and defend the said United States, against the said King George the Third, his heirs and successors and his and their abettors, assistants and adherents and will serve the said United States in the office of which I now hold, with fidelity, according to the best of my skill and understanding." So help me God.

That all officers of the army shall take and subscribe the foregoing oath or affirmation, before the Commander in Chief, or any Major General or Brigadier General.

That all officers of the navy shall take and subscribe the same, before one of the Commissioners of the Navy Boards, or before a Judge or Justice of the Peace of the State, wherein they respectively reside or shall receive their commissions or warrants.

That all persons holding any civil office of trust or profit, under the Congress of these United States, shall take and subscribe the said oath or affirmation before a Judge or Justice of the Peace of the State, wherein they respectively reside.

That every officer having the disposal of public money, or who is or shall be intrusted with the charge or distribution of public stores, shall, at the time of taking and subscribing the foregoing oath or affirmation, also take an oath or affirmation of office in the following words.

" I   do swear (or affirm) that I will faithfully truly and impartially execute the office of   to which I am appointed, and render a true account, when thereunto required, of all public monies by me received or expended, and of all stores or other effects to me intrusted, which belong to the United States, and will, in all respects, discharge the trust reposed in me with justice and integrity, to the best of my skill and understanding."

That every officer, taking the foregoing oaths or affirmations or either of them, shall obtain from the person administering the same, duplicate certificates specifying the time of his taking it or them and also his name and rank or employment.

That every military officer shall deliver or transmit one of the certificates so obtained, to the Commander in Chief or the Commander of a Department, or to such person, as by General Orders shall be appointed to receive the same; and the said commanding officers shall cause the certificates so received to be sent to the Secretary of Congress, and shall keep an exact list of the names of all officers whose certificates shall be received and forwarded, together with their several ranks and the times of their being qualified.

That every officer in the navy shall deliver or send one of the certificates by him obtained to the Navy Board most convenient, who are required to transmit the same, and also a certificate of their own qualifications, to the Marine Committee, as soon as conveniently may be.

That every other person employed in any civil department or office as abovementioned, shall send or deliver one of the certificates by him obtained to the Secretary of the State, to which he belongs, or to such other person or persons, as the Governor or President of such State shall direct. And the Governors or Presidents of the several States, are hereby requested to attend to this matter and to cause the certificates, when received, to be transmitted to the Secretary of Congress.

That each deponant or affirmant shall retain and keep the other certificate, by him obtained, as a voucher of his having complied with what is hereby enjoined him.

Resolved, That every officer civil or military, now in office, shall take and subscribe the qualification above directed, within twenty days after notice hereof; and every person hereafter appointed to any office, by or under the authority of the Congress of the United States of America, shall take and subscribe the same, previous to his acting in such office: And every officer who shall continue or presume to exercise any commission civil or military, under the authority of the Congress of the United States of America, without taking the qualification, in time and manner above directed, shall be cashiered and forfeit two months pay to the use of the United States of America, and be rendered incapable of serving in the army of the said States, and of executing thereafter any office under Congress.

And whereas many persons, employed as Deputy or Assistant Commissaries or Quarter-Masters or in other civil departments are dispersed in various parts of the continent, over whom neither Congress nor the head of their respective departments can have the immediate inspection.

Resolved, That it be recommended to the legislative and executive authority of every State, to take effectual measures for preventing any person, within their State, from exercising any office in the civil department of the army or in any other civil department under Congress, who shall not, when thereunto required by any Magistrate, produce a legal appointment to that office and a certificate of his having taken the foregoing oaths or affirmations, or who shall neglect or refuse to take and subscribe the said oaths or affirmations within the time above limited.

Resolved, That the resolutions passed the 21st day of October 1776, prescribing the form of an oath or affirmation and directing the same to be subscribed by officers holding commissions or offices from Congress, be and they are hereby repealed.

Extract from the minutes,

CHARLES THOMSON, *Secretary.*

Oath of Allegiance, February 3, 1778

take measures with all continental officers whatever. The states will take care of their particular citizens. Maryland besides excluding nonjurors from offices &c makes them liable to a treble tax; which I think falls well in with your idea of making it as inconvenient as possible for such vermin to exist among us.

I ought to have informed you that Mr. *J.A.* has accepted, and that I constantly forward to him letters & papers for F—— & ——— ———.³ Mr. Iz—— also accepts for Tu——, and speaks of the probability of obtaining a Loan in I——y. I have therefore obtained a Resolve (similar to that passed on Decr. 3d) for 1,000,000 stg. upon an interest to accumulate (if it can be obtained) during the war, afterwards to be paid off annually.⁴ You must have heard from your Brother of the great disappointment we met with about our dispatches from France. I have no doubt the robbery was committed on the other side of the water, and by a person near the Commissioners; as besides the main packet, one for you was changed which was under a cover among Gazetts, while a very considerable for the President of Congress, another for me and another for Barnabas Deane and a 4th for R Morris were untouched. But then, all these were upon private concerns, tho their Directions were more tempting than yours could have been. I have the satisfaction of remarking to you that my Letter from Doctr Franklin as well as Genl. Roberdeau's, and all for other Gentlemen from the Doctor or other friends were written with an air of ease & pleasantry which I should not expect to find if the public packet had been quite the reverse.

It is well reported that Howe is paying the Quakers of Chester Co. &c for Horses and other Articles, *upon slight vouchers;* but I cannot find whether this is in consequence of a remonstrance from them or of news from England or whether it is a stroke of good Policy to make them well affected towards his Usurpation.

I am in hopes that we shall get our army both cloathed and fed by the good care of the several states and our own afterwisdom in regard to certain systematic attachments. I think we grow more & more practical daily, I wish we had not waited for the teachings of woeful Experience.

I have not recd. Letters from Boston for a long time. Our good Friends Adams were well the 7th of Janry. I am glad they are in the way to advise Heath in his present difficult task with Burgoyne. I wish you had been present in our debates upon that Subject, I think you must have approved the step of detaining him upon the grounds which appeared for such a procedure.

I am affectionately your humb. Servt.   James Lovell

[*P.S.*] The Committee on the Tyconderoga affair have reported, and the Attorney Genl. of Pensylvania, Sergeant, & he of Jersey, Patterson, are to assist at the Court martial.⁵ Thus Congress have done every thing the enraged People could expect, but from the Papers collected, Minds ought to be prepared to rest satisfied with the ruin of Burgoyne & his Army. This I say in Confidence to you as I was put upon the Committee since you left York.[6]

RC (MH-H).
  [1] Lee's January 15 letter to Lovell is in Lee, *Letters* (Ballagh), 1:378–80.
  [2] On February 3 Congress passed resolutions requiring all civil and military officers to take an oath of allegiance. See *JCC*, 10:114–18.
  [3] Doubtless Franklin and Arthur Lee.
  [4] Ralph Izard, commissioner at the court of Tuscany, had just been authorized to borrow one million pounds sterling. *JCC*, 10:120.
  [5] See also Committee of Congress to Washington, and Henry Laurens to William Paterson, February 7, 1778.
  [6] Lovell had been appointed to this committee on January 20. *JCC*, 10:66. See also John Hancock to Arthur St. Clair and Philip Schuyler, August 5, 1777, note.

Gouverneur Morris to Robert R. Livingston

Dear Livingston.   Camp Valley Forge 5th February 1777 [*i.e.* 1778]
  I received your Letter at York Town. You do me a Species of Injustice by it because you suppose me guilty of Negligences which do not justly lie at my Door.[1] My Heart does not yet charge me with the Guilt of being insensible to the Claims of Friendship. Let us put things on a proper Footing. Take you no note of my Sins of Omission and you shall charge me *justly* with none of Commission. You ask why I am here. I answer that I am sent to regulate our Army. One Word therefore upon the Subject you write on. The Ardency of our Friend's Desire to acquire Honor does him so much Honor that perhaps it would be unfair to let him have more.[2] Seriously. You know me I hope so well as to believe what is most true that Nothing in my Power shall be wanting that will conduce to his Welfare or that of any other Person you may patronize even if unconnected with you. Perseverance, Perseverance that is the great Desideratum. I will promise Nothing but this I tell you, that I hope much More of this hereafter when things are in better train.
  Nothing could have been more agreable to me than to have continued in the Circle of my Friends in our own State But what can be done. I was ordered away and to have staid would have been reprobated by some Persons in our Legislature. I would that I were quit of my congressional capacity which is in every Respect irksome. Stuffed in a Corner of America & brooding over their Situation they have become utter Disagreables. There are no fine Women at York Town. Judge then of my Situation. Worse still I am now in Camp and Lady Kitty & Miss Brown within three Miles of me for several Days past. I cannot go to see them. Politics I can say nothing about for we really

have nothing worth saying. As to news all we have is comprizd in a few inconsequential Anecdotes. The most marked is the Desertion of a young British officer whose Name I do not recollect. Pray remember me to your Lady, Mother & Sisters. I shall write you a long Letter as soon as I have time to think. Oh, I had like to have forgotten that I wished to tell you that Interest should be made with the Legislative of our State to send their Chancellor to the Meeting of those who are to regulate Prices.[3] A measure which we both know to be ruinous. The Genl.[4] sends his Compliments. Your Brother who called on me a few Hours ago desires to be remembered. I again desire it. My Love to Jay.

Adieu, Adieu, remember me, yours sincerely,   Gouv Morris

RC (NHi). Addressed: "The honle. Robert R. Livingston Esqr. Chancellor of the State of New York, Poughkeepsie."

[1] The FC of Livingston's letter to Morris, undated but apparently written at the end of 1777 or the beginning of 1778, is in the Robert R. Livingston Papers, NHi. "But I am in hopes," he had written, "that your rage for pleasure & disapation is by this time gratified & that you may find leasure to attend to your friends."

[2] Livingston had asked Morris to help his brother Col. Henry Beekman Livingston secure command of "a partizan corps with the rank of Coll Commandant if more can not be obtained." Ibid. Colonel Livingston never received such an appointment, and on January 13, 1779, Congress accepted his resignation from the Continental Army. *JCC*, 13:58.

[3] Livingston had vigorously criticized laws regulating prices in the letter cited above.

[4] Washington.

Committee at Camp to Henry Laurens

Sir   Camp near Valley Forge Feb. 6th 1778

In our Letter by Col Fitzgerald on the Expedition against Philada. we slightly touch'd upon the State of this Army in Point of Provisions.[1] But it is a Matter of so much Importance, & the Prospects are so truly alarming that we think it our indispensible Duty to be more particular & submit our Sentiments thereupon to the Consideration of Congress. We have conferred with every Officer in the Provision Department from whom we could expect to receive Information, the Result of which is, that we find this Army has been fed by daily Supplies drawn from the Country at large—seldom or ever having more than four Days Advance; that in some few Instances there has been a total Failure & on one Occasion Necessity compelled the Soldiery to disperse in the Neighbourhood & take indiscriminately the Provisions laid in by the Inhabitants for the Winters Support of themselves & Families. The pernicious Consequences of which we need not enumerate. Of the several Species of which a Ration is composed, we find the Commissary has never been able to furnish any but the capital Articles of Beef & Flour, the Quantity of which has been increased beyond the stated Ration in Lieu of Vegetables which cannot be procured. We are happy to acquaint you Sir that there seems little Doubt of obtaining an ample Supply of Flour. But the great & almost inconceivable Consumption of Flesh in a Country which never raised sufficient for the Subsistence of its own Inhabitants, has so exhausted that Space laying between the Potomack & the North River, that we cannot depend upon a farther Supply than the inclosed Paper intimates. From the Character of Col Blaine the present Deputy Commy. of Purchases & his Success in the Article of Flour we have Reason to believe equal Industry & Attention has been shewn to the procuring Meat & therefore must ascribe the Deficiency to a real Scarcity.

From the very large Issues we had presumed that there must have been some Mistake or Fraud, a Detection of which would have enabled us to make a considerable saving, but upon a Scrutiny & Comparison of the Provision, & Brigade Returns, we do not find any considerable Difference, the large Issues being satisfactorily accounted for, in the Number of continental Troops to be fed (tho' many of them are unfit for Duty thro Sickness & Want of Cloathing) in the Militia, & long Train of Waggon Masters, Drivers, Artificers, Clerks, & other Retainers of the Army.

The Prisoners of War at Boston & in the several Eastn. States, Burgoynes Army, the Guards & Garrison there, & the Forces stationed for the Protection of Rhode Island will we apprehend amount to 12, or 14000 Men. The Troops destined for Canada, & stationed at Albany along the Mohawk & Hudsons Rivers, with those at Fish Kill, Artificers, Retainers &c may be Computed at least at 6000, making in the whole 20,000 Men to be fed with Meat from the East Side of Hudsons River. New Jersey, Pennsylvania & the Delaware State are exhausted. From this collective View of the Subject, & taking it for granted that the Army under General Howe is the first great Object of Attention, we are induced in the first Place to recommend a Perseverance in the Exertion of every Person to procure supplies in every State, not excepting those at a Distance firmly persuaded that after all we have done, or can do, there will be little or no Surplus. And in the second Place, to adopt every Expedient of Œconomy in the Application of them. Among which we beg Leave to suggest the immediate Dispersion of General Burgoyne, & all the other Prisoners, in such a Manner as to require few or no Guards, & to be easily fed from the neighbouring Country. Other Considerations will concur to demonstrate the Propriety of this Measure. We find the Generals Mind impressed strongly with Apprehensions of Danger from keeping such a Body of Officers & Men collected after they suppose the Obligations of personal & national Honour are dissolved.[2]

We think every Nerve should be strained to collect such a Supply of Meat as will feed an Army of 30,000 Men early the next Spring, & are compelled by the inevitable Force of Evidence to say, that the very Existence of this Army depends for its Resources in a great Degree upon the Eastern Country, which failing it must disband, live upon free Quarter in the Country—or perish The Operations of the next Campaign so immediately depend upon some Measures of this Kind, & upon the Wisdom of Congress in forming & executing them that we beg Leave to urge it in the strongest Manner. Should we neglect any prudent Precaution in providing, or divide the Supplies & Resources of our Country into a Number of separate Channels, we very much fear our Efforts will be lanquid & ineffectual in every Quarter, while General Howe with his collected Force will ravage the middle States with Impunity.

We are Sir with the greatest Respect & Regard, Your most Obedt & very Hbble Servs,   Fra Dana per Order

RC (DNA: PCC, item 78). Written by Joseph Reed and signed by Francis Dana. Endorsed by Charles Thomson: "Mr. Dana—Letter from 6 Feby. 1778. Read 16 Feby. respecting comy of provisions & prisoners of Convention at Boston. Referred to a Comee of three. Mr. Gerry, Mr. Wolcott, Mr. Ellery who are to confer with the board of war." An undated draft of this letter, written by Gouverneur Morris, is in PCC, item 33, fols. 141–42.

[1] See Committee at Camp to Laurens, February 3, 1778.

[2] On February 19, Congress requested the government of Massachusetts "to remove, separate and place" the Convention Army "in such manner and in such parts of the said State as may be most convenient for their subsistence and security." JCC, 10:184–85.

Henry Laurens to John Laurens

My Dear son,   York Town 6th. February 1778.

Your favor of the 2d Inst. came to hand late last Night.[1] As you have filled six Pages on the Negro scheme without approaching toward a Plan & Estimate—& as you have totally overlooked every other subject on which I have addressed you in several late Letters— the conclusion that your whole mind is enveloped in the Cloud of that project, is unavoidable. If any good shall arise from a prosecution of it, the merit will be solely yours. For now, I will undertake to say there is not a Man in America of your opinion. Nay you will not be of your own opinion after a little reflection. 'Tis evident you want to raise a Regiment, as evident you have not digested a Plan. Admitting, which I admit only for argument, you have a right to remove a Man from one state of Slavery into another—or if you please into a state of servitude which will be esteemed by him infinitely worse than

Slavery—what right have you to exchange & Barter "Women & Children" in whom you pretend to say you have no property?

The very same observation may be made with respect to the Men—for you have either property in them, or you have not. Admitting the latter which you seem to acknowledge, upon what ground of justice will you insist upon their enlisting for Soldiers, as the condition of their infranchisement? If they are free—tell them so—set them at full liberty—& then address them in the Language of a recruiting Officer to any other free Men—& if four in forty take your inlisting bounty, it will be very extraordinary. This small number will do it through ignorance & three of the four be returned as Deserters in a very short time. All this by no means intimates that I am an Advocate for Slavery—you know I am not, therefore it is unnecessary to attempt a vindication.

The more I think of & the more I have consulted on your scheme, the less I approve of it. Wisdom dictates that I should rather oppose than barely not consent to it. But Indulgence & friendship warranted by Wisdom, bids met let you take your own course & draw self-conviction. Therefore come forward Young Colonel, proceed to So Carolina. You shall have as full authority over all my Negroes as justice to your Brother & Sisters & a very little consideration for my self will permit you to exercise—& so far do what you please & as you please without regard to St. Mary Axe.

You want a Regiment that's certain, go to Carolina & I'll warrant you will soon get one. I will venture to say, sooner than any other Man of my acquaintance—you will have many advantages—in raising a Regiment of White Men.

On the Journey you may think fully & converse with many worthy sensible Men, on your favorite Idea. When you arrive in Charles Town you will have further advantages, if you are disposed to receive them, from the sentiments of your most judicious friends. Your own good sense will direct you to proceed warily in opposing the opinions of whole Nations—lest *without effecting any good,* you become a byeword, & be so transmitted, to Your Children's Children. Give me a day's Notice previous to your appearance here in order that an apartment may be provided for you if possible—for it is barely possible to obtain one.

My Dear Son I pray God protect you & add to your knowledge & learning, if it be necessary, discretion.   Henry Laurens

[*P.S.*] Your friend Fleury this moment takes leave of me & in pouring freely a thousand good wishes, drops a few to you in particular & desires I would tell you so. With some difficulty he obtained leave to pursue the Marquis but failed in his attempt to Climb Rank.[2]

The bearer of this will deliver two more Camp Shirts, I sent two &

a piece of Scarlet Cloth lately by Barry. It gives me some little trouble to collect & send forward these things, why will you not be so kind as to take the very little which is necessary barely to acknowledge the Receipt of them. I have often requested this & have assigned such good reasons for the necessary Check as I should have thought abstracted from the Idea of humoring an old & good friend, would have made a proper impression upon a Man of so much accuracy as I perceive you are when you transact business for or correspond with any body but poor me.

RC (ScHi).
[1] John Laurens' February 2 letter to his father, in which he defended his plan for raising a regiment of slaves, is in Simms, *Laurens Army Correspondence*, pp. 114–18. See also Laurens to John Laurens, January 22, 1778, note 1.
[2] See Laurens to Lafayette, February 7, 1778, notes 2 and 3.

James Lovell to Samuel Adams

Dear Sir   York Town Feb. 6th. 1778
    I write only to tell you that you are exceedingly wanted here, I wish I could add that you will be better accommodated than before, but really I have no grounds upon which to assert that you will be as well off.

    I have at times hoped that we should move nearer Boston, but I now look southward for the next ride if we make one in any other course than to the City of Philadelphia.[1]

    I have been long without a line from you. I hope you go now and then to Faneuil Hall. I am this day told that Doctor Church is gone to Europe and I have also heard that Doctr. Lloyd &c &c have *conformed*. I think I can guess who has acted a Bishop's part upon this occasion.

    You will mediately or immediately get Information from Mr. L [2] about some late Transactions here. I was too much hurried to be more lengthy in Extract.

    Yr Friend & h Servt.   J L

RC (NN).
[1] The following month Gouverneur Morris also expressed hope that Congress might relocate and asserted his intention to move for an adjournment to Hartford, but there is no evidence the subject was seriously considered until April 9, at which time a resolution was adopted to take the subject "into consideration" on the 11th, but the journals indicate that the issue was not taken up until June 24 when Congress voted to adjourn to Philadelphia on June 27. See Gouverneur Morris to Robert R. Livingston, March 10, 1778; and *JCC*, 10:325, 11:641.
[2] That is, President Laurens.

James Lovell to Joseph Whipple

Dear sir   Febry. 6th. 1778

I will not make so little use of your many friendly professions, and your knowledge of the perplexing multiplicity of affairs which naturally lay before Congress, as now to make any other apology for not before answering your very obliging letter of Decr. 29th than by telling you that there have been very few Delegates and very many Foreigners at York Town for some time past. I hope the inclosed Resolve will prove a sifter to many vermin who are eating continental bread.[1] Virginia is acting with her wonted Spirit in filling up her Quota and furnishing 5000 volunteers to open the next Campaign besides providing for the army both Cloathing and Food. They have also a Test. Maryland not only excluded Nonjurors from Office but subjects them to treble Taxation. This last is peculiar to Maryland, but I think it a very good Example for other States. You will have seen what we have done in regard to the affair of Retalliation which you mentioned; and also how far we have exceeded your hints about Burgoyne. It is high time that we should show that we feel Independence as well as profess it. We long ago instructed our Commissioners to show under the authority of our Signature that we had not treated nor would ever treat with Gr Br upon any other footing but our Declaration of July 4th 76.

France is playing a lucrative Game, but it is by no means the highest she has in her power to play; and I think by every account from the West Indies she has already cut the Cards for Dealing. We have been robbed of our Dispatches of Octr. either in France or on the Passage. But I am sure from Doctr. Fr—— Letters to myself that there could be no bad news in the public packet. He writes as gayly as a man of middle Age on general Topics.

Salute, for me, her who most of all Women will welcome you with such a Commission. She does not know from how much honest Love I give it, therefore will place all the Value to your Credit.

I will not now write to the Brigadr.,[2] therefore tell him that J D Sergeant & Mr Patterson are to assist at the Tryals on the Tyconderoga affair, so that Congress have done all that was proper, though the Event may not answer the too warm Expectations of such as were highly chagrined at perhaps inevitable Losses.[3]

I am, Sir, very affectionately, your huml Servt. James Lovell

RC (MHi).
   [1] Probably a reference to the February 3 resolves requiring all civil and military officials to subscribe to an oath of allegiance. *JCC*, 10:115–18.
   [2] That is, William Whipple.
   [3] See Committee of Congress to George Washington, February 7, 1778.

John Penn to Theodorick Bland, Jr.

Dear Sir   York Feby. 6th. 1778
    My having been unwell for some time past is the reason of my not
writing to you as often as I intended. We are informed that the Kings
officers behave with great severity to the Canadians, that by Flogging
those that were taken with Burgoyne on their return, they had compelled all of them to inlist again, tho' expressly contrary to the Convention of Saratoga, and that the Inhabitants in general were much
incensed against their oppressors. Congress have determined to have
an expedition made as far as Mountreal at least, in order to get possession or destroy the enemy's Fleet on the lakes, & in order to induce
the Canadians to exert themselves & Join us, the Marquis De lay
Fayettee will command. Generals McDougle, Conway & Stark attend
him. The men employed will go from Albany and New Hamshire.
The reputation we have acquired in taking Burgoyne, and the dissatisfaction of the people against the English, make me hope for
something Clever, besides it will rouse us a little which we want &
distress the Ministry in their Councils, they will be at a loss where to
send reinforcements if they have any. I informed you that Burgoyne
& his whole Army were to be detained untill the Convention is Confirmed by the Ministry.[1] Burgoyne wrote to Gen. Gates that we had
broke the Convention, on account of his not having so good lodgings
as he wanted, & soon after refused to suffer a discriptive list to be
taken of his Troops wch. was done by Genl. Carlton before he would
suffer our soldiers to come out of Canada. My Complimts. to Mrs.
Bland. I am with great respect, Your obt. Servt.   J Penn

[P.S.] A Committee of Congress is at the Camp with General Washington endeavouring to reform our army. I have not had an opportunity of saying any thing on the subject of Rank since you went
away, nor can it be done before the Committee returns.[2]

RC (DLC). Addressed: "To The. Bland Esqr., Colo. of the 1st Regimt. of Horse,
Prince George Coty., Virginia."
    [1] Penn's letter informing Bland of the suspension of the Saratoga Convention
has not been found, but for a discussion of this matter, see Henry Laurens to
William Heath, December 27, 1777, note 1.
    [2] For further information on the dispute over rank involving Bland and Col.
Elisha Sheldon, commanders respectively of the First and Second Continental
Dragoons, see Henry Laurens to Washington, November 7, note 2; and Penn to
Bland, December 1, 1777.

Committee of Congress to George Washington

Sir   York Town 7th February 1778
   The Committee appointed on the 27th of August 1777 to collect
evidence of the State of the Army in the Northern department & also
the State of the Troops, Military Stores & provisions at the Posts of
Tyconderoga & Mount Independence before & at the times when the
evacuation was determined upon, In obedience to an order of Congress of the 5th Inst., Copy of which will be transmitted by the
President, now forward to Your Excellency in one Packet, an Orderly
Book & two parcels of Papers which together with the Orderly Book,
contain all the evidence the Committee have been hitherto able to
collect.[1]
   Your Excellency will be pleased to give timely Notice to the Gentlemen who are appointed to assist the Judge Advocate in conducting
the Trial.[2]
   We are, Sir, Your Excellency's most Obedt. Servants. By desire of
the Committee,   Henry Laurens, one of the Members.

RC (DLC). Written and signed by Henry Laurens.
   [1] For a discussion of this committee's investigation of the circumstances surrounding the evacuation of Ticonderoga and Mount Independence in July 1777, see John
Hancock to Arthur St. Clair and Philip Schuyler, August 5, 1777, note. Although
Congress expected Washington to proceed with a court-marital of "the general
officers who were in the northern department when Ticonderoga and Mount
Independence were evacuated" on the basis of the evidence collected by the committee, Washington pointed out in a February 27 letter to Laurens that he could not
take this step because of the committee's failure to make "any particular charges
against the Officers who are to be the objects of trial." As a result, Congress appointed a new committee on April 29 to correct this oversight and approved its
report specifying charges against Gens. Arthur St. Clair and Philip Schuyler on
June 20. Armed with this new report, Washington convened separate court-
martials that in September and October 1778 acquitted both officers of all the
charges preferred against them. See, in addition to the Hancock letter cited above,
JCC, 10:125, 238–39, 403, 11:593–603, 628; and Washington, Writings (Fitzpatrick),
10:518–19. See also Laurens to Washington, April 4, 1778.
   [2] See Henry Laurens to William Paterson, this date.

Elbridge Gerry to Samuel Adams

My dear Sir   York in Pennsylvania Feby 7. 1778
   I cannot longer deprive myself of the Pleasure of writing a Letter
to You, altho on other Occasions my Mind sometimes recoils at the
Ideas of Pen & Paper. The Business of Congress in the winter Season
is greatly increased on account of the necessary Reformation Plan &
Preparation for a succeeding Campaign, & at this Time there is half
the number of Members to transact it. Few can stand it as well as our

friend Mr Lovell; he writes Morning, Noon & Night, sickens once a Fortnight, and devotes a Day to Sleep, after which, like the Sun from behind a Cloud he makes his Appearance with his usual Splendor.

The Department of the Commissary General of military Stores is now Under the Consideration of the Board of War, your Letter relative to Major Ayers, shall be communicated to General Gates, who is very attentive to the Business.[1]

The Commissary of Provisions has made frequent Applications to Congress for their Assistance in conducting the Business of his Department;[2] indeed, We have had little Assistance from his Appointment, neither could it be expected from a better Officer whilst the Regulations prevented him from appointing his Deputies, but You well know from whence this Part of the Plan originated, & for what Purpose it has been obstinately supported. It's advocates have finally given it up, after distressing the Army, Congress, & the Continent with it for six or eight Months. I wish We may be successful in Measures to correct the Errors, but it is easier to prevent than remedy an Evil.

The Baron de Steuben is in Town, & is much esteemed as a great Officer & accomplished Gentleman. His proposals will be complied with by Congress, & he expects in a Day or two to repair to the Army. Great Benefit may be derived from his abilities, unless the mistaken Notions of Honor, which mislead our Army, should prevent it. I inclose You some Resolutions of Congress relative to the Tryal of the Officers concerned in the Loss of Ticonderoga: the last Resolve was omitted to be copied at the Secretary's Office, & was not attested, but is correct, & compares with the Journals. I wish that they may be published, to convince the people that Congress are in earnest in probing this Wound, & Officers, that Misconduct of the Army will not pass unnoticed.

By a Vessel arrived at South Quay in Maryland, We are informed that our worthy Friend Doctor Franklin is dangerously ill of a Wound which he received in his Bed from an assassin supposed to be employed by Lord Stormont. The Master informed Mr Samuel Purviance, whose Letter to a Gentleman in this place I have seen, that he left France the 8th Decr., that the News arrived the Day of his sailing, & that advices were received of the Surrender of General Burgoyne's Army, & loss of the Philadelphia, at the same Time. He has brot the King's Speech, which Mr. Lovell will inclose You, it is the Index of a melancholy & desponding Mind.[3] By a vigorous Exertion the ensuing Campaign, & the Smiles of divine providence, I hope We shall be free of the rage of this weak & merciless Tyrant. My best Respects to Mrs & Miss Adams, & believe me to be Sir with much Esteem your Friend & hum Ser,

                                                        E Gerry [4]

RC (NN).

¹ Adams' letter has not been found, but its subject was apparently Maj. Benjamin Eyre, assistant deputy quartermaster general.

² William Buchanan, who replaced Joseph Trumbull as commissary general of purchases in August 1777 and was supplanted by Jeremiah Wadsworth in April 1778. See Committee at Camp to Henry Laurens, January 29, 1778, note.

³ George III's speech on the opening of Parliament in November 1777 became available from several sources at this time and was widely reprinted in American newspapers, including the *Royal Gazette* (New York), January 24: the *Pennsylvania Evening Post* (Philadelphia), January 29; and the *Pennsylvania Packet* (Lancaster), February 11, 1778. It can also be found in *The Parliamentary History of England, from the Earliest Period to the Year 1803*, 36 vols. (London: T. C. Hansard, 1806–20), 19:354–55.

⁴ This day Gerry also wrote a letter to his brother Thomas discussing the disposition of some casks of wine and a vessel carrying a cargo of salt. Of the latter, which was being directed to him from Messrs. J. Gardoqui & Sons, Gerry reported: "if she arrives in the Massachusetts please to Land her Cargo in a good Store & order her to Edenton in North Carolina to the Address of Mess. Hughes & Smith of that Place for a Cargo of produce, giving one of the earliest Notice thereof, & informing the Master that the risque is to be on the Owner's Acct." Gerry Collection, MHi.

Elbridge Gerry to Henry Knox

Dear sir   York in Pennsylvania Feby 7. 1778

I have not yet been able to make any Discoveries that can justify a Suspicion of a Plan's being formed to injure the Reputation of, or remove from office, the Gentleman hinted at in your Favour of Jany the 4th. And the Alarms that have been spread & Jealousies that are excited relative to this Matter appear to be calculated rather to answer mischeivous than useful Purposes; at least, I fear this will be the Consequence.¹ It is essentially necessary to the Authority of an Officer that those who are under him should have a Confidence in his Abilities, & Pride in his Character; & certain it is, that those cannot long exist, where these are frequently called in question. How then can we account for such groundless Rumours, at a Time when the Character of this worthy officer is high in Congress, & when there appears to be an Intention of the Members to support him, but by considering them as the Effect of a party Spirit that is dangerous to the Cause in which we are engaged. I am exceedingly distressed at the Dissentions that begin to prevail in the Army, they augur ill, & whilst uncorrected are of themselves sufficient to reverse our Affairs. I know your firm Attachment to the Cause, & express myself without Reserve, that We may cooperate in preventing an Evil that has frequently involved in Ruin mighty Empires; an Evil that, if not timely prevented, cannot be remedied. How frequently do we find in History, that an artful General has spared no pains or Expence to accomplish such purposes in the Camp of his adversary; & When We consider, that We are at War with a Nation which for Centuries past has been trained to the Business, that our former Connections with her expose us to Dangers from Intrigues, which otherwise could not be carried into Effect, surely too much Caution cannot be used to guard against internal Dissentions. I know not the Source of the Uneasiness which We are speaking of ⟨& being a Friend to both parties shall for the Interest of my Country side with neither⟩ but it would not be any Ways surprizing to me to find the Enemy at the Bottom of the Dispute, & If they did not originate it, they will certainly promote it, unless the officers of the Army should wisely prevent it. The Disputes relative to Rank have probably had some share in exciting this Spirit, but here I must condemn ⟨a great Part⟩ some of the officers in opposing a constitutional Exercise of the Authority of Congress. A Resolution was after the most mature Deliberation entered into in Feby 1777 to appoint General Officers upon three principles, which Respected their former Rank, their Merit, & the proportion of Troops raised by the States to which they severally belonged.[2] This was necessary to give satisfaction to the States, was considered as a wise & politick Measure, & I have reason to believe will be invariably pursued at all Events. But What has been the Consequence of every appointment of General officers made by Congress? If it did not suit the whole Army, Opposition has taken place, & reduced Congress to the necessity of asserting the Rights of themselves & their Constituents, or consenting to give them up in a Manner that would sap the foundation of Liberty. I have ever tho't that such an opposition has been the Effect of Inadvertance, & of not recurring to first principles, but the Injury which the civil Liberties of America derive therefrom is the same as if a premeditated Attack had been made against them. It appears to me that the Army have generally mistaken Notions of Honor, when they suppose that a foreign officer of great Experience cannot be introduced to high rank without disgracing all below him. I have as great prejudices in favour of my Countrymen as any person, perhaps on Earth; And will readily grant, that with the same Degree of Experience & under similar Advantages, no Officers whatever will exceed them in skill & prowess; but can any person suppose that a Year or two in the service of the united States will qualify an officer as well as ten or twenty years service in the armies of Europe? & has not our Cause been almost ruined, does it not at this instant suffer greatly from the want of experienced officers ⟨to introduce Discipline into the Army⟩? Under these Circumstances then is it not evident that the Honor of an Officer who readily consents to promote the service of his Country by giving place to Experience, is established; whilst those who oppose this do it at the Expence of their reputation.

I know of no Promotions of any Consequence that have not been made on the purest Principles, & a full conviction of Merit in the Officer appointed; but such are the prejudices of each Person in

Favour of himself that it rarely happens, when he exercises a Judgment on his own Cause, that he can divest himself of Partiality in every Respect, whence the Necessity of Decisions in all Cases of a legal or publick Nature by disinterested persons.

FC (DLC photostat).

[1] Henry Knox's January 4 letter to Gerry, inquiring about the intrigues against General Washington and defending the general officers' concern with rank, is in Austin, *Life of Gerry,* 1:238–41.

[2] See *JCC,* 7:133.

Henry Laurens to Francis Dana

Sir,   7th Febry 1778

I duly received & presented to Congress both your Letters signed as Chair Man of the Committee at Camp. These being at the Secretarys Office I cannot write the particular dates.[1]

All the Commands I have received for the Committee in consequence of those Letters are contained in two Acts which you will find in company with this.[2]

Vizt—of the 5th Inst adopting a plan for carrying into immediate execution the important business of the Quarter Master General.

of this date—directing the Committee "to consult with General Washington & Report to Congress the proper officers for filling the several departments of the Quarter Master General" which probably means to recommend or nominate proper persons &ca.

The Secretary having sent me only one Copy of the last mentioned Act, I request you will lay this or a Copy of it before His Excellency General Washington.

I am with great Regard &ca

LB (DNA: PCC, item 13). Addressed: "Francis Dana Esquire, Chairman of Committee from Congress, Valley Forge."

[1] See the Committee at Camp's January 28 and 29 letters to Laurens, which dealt with the appointment of a new quartermaster general and a new commissary general of purchases for the Continental Army.

[2] See *JCC,* 10:126–27, 138.

Henry Laurens to the Marquis de Lafayette

Sir,   7th Febry 1778

I had the honour this morning of receiving your Commands by the hands of Lt. Colo. Fleury.[1]

This Gentleman notwithstanding the aid of some able advocates in Congress has failed in his pursuit of a Colonel's Commission, you will wonder less, when you learn that the preceeding day I had strove very arduously as second to a warm recommendation from a favorite General, Gates, on behalf of Monsr. Failly, for the same Rank, without effect. The arguments adduced by Gentlemen who have opposed these measures, are Strong & obvious. We are reforming & reducing the Number of Officers in our Army, let us wait the event, & see how our own Native Officers are to be disposed of—& besides, there is a plan in embrio for abolishing the Class of Colonel in our Army, while the Enemy have none of that Rank in the Field.

Some difficulty attended obtaining leave for Monsr. Fleury to follow your Excellency. Congress were at first of opinion he might be more usefully employed against the Shipping in Delaware & formed a Resolve very flattering & tempting to induce him, but his perseverence in petitioning to be sent to Canada, prevailed.[2]

Monsr. Fleury strongly hopes Your Excellency will encourage him to raise & give him the Command of a distinct Corps of Canadians.[3] I am persuaded you will adopt all such measures as shall promise advantage to the Service & there is no ground to doubt of your doing every reasonable & proper thing for the gratification & honour of Gentlemen of whom your Excellency Speaks & writes so favorably.

The King's Speech of the 21st November which I presume you have seen at Camp, according to my reading & interpretation, is intended as harbinger to propositions. The tone will be reverbrated by Lord North's puppets & the Scene will open.

It is remarkable that on the 21st November the Capture of Philadelphia had not been announced in England—& not less *remarkable,* that except the Speech there is not a Single insertion of European intelligence in the Philadelphia Gazette 31st Jany.

I congratulate with your Excellency on the pleasing accounts received from the spot from whence you are now wandering. If fretting, or wishing, would rand [4] the Roads I would enter heartily upon so cheap a mode of scavaging. Such as they are, may God conduct you, Noble Marquis, happily successfully, through them, that when *you shall think it proper,* you may return & fill those tender breasts with joy which till that time will be the subjects of anxiety.

I have the honour to be with great regard &ca.

LB (ScHi).

[1] See Lafayette to Laurens, ca. February 4, 1778, in Lafayette, *Papers* (Idzerda), 1:279–80.

[2] See *JCC,* 10:127–28, 137–38.

[3] Among the Laurens Papers at DLC is a memorial from Lt. Col. Fleury to Laurens, undated but obviously written about this time, in which Fleury asked the president to have "the Board of the War . . . write to general Lafayete & commend me to him for the first body of Canadians to be Raised."

[4] "Melt"—or, in this context, to clear the roads of snow. *OED.*

Henry Laurens to William Paterson

Sir,   7th Febry 1778

By the inclosed Act of Congress of the 5th Inst. you will be informed that the House have appointed you to assist the Judge Advocate in conducting the intended Trial of General Officers who were in the Northern department when Tyconderoga & Mount Independence were evacuated.

I am ordered to add the request of Congress that you will attend the Court Martial, the appointment & intended sitting of which you will learn from General Washington & give your best assistance to the Judge Advocate & to assure you that Congress will make Suitable provision for your trouble & expences on this occasion.[1]

I am with great Respect

LB (DNA: PCC, item 13). Addressed: "William Patterson Esquire, Attorney General of the State of New Jersey."

[1] Laurens wrote substantially the same letter this day to Jonathan Dickinson Sergeant, the attorney general of Pennsylvania. PCC, item 13, fol. 164. Paterson and Sergeant, citing the press of other official business to which they had to attend, both declined to assist at this court-marital. See *JCC,* 10:238–39, 367; and PCC, item 59, 3:7, item 78, 20:207. For a discussion of the congressional investigation of the evacuation of Ticonderoga and Mount Independence during the summer of 1777 and the courts-martial of some of the army officers involed, see John Hancock to Arthur St. Clair and Philip Schuyler, August 5, 1777, note; and Committee of Congress to Washington, this date.

Henry Laurens to George Washington

Sir,   7th Febry 1778.

I had the honour of presenting in due course Your Excellency's favours of 31st Ulto & 3d Inst. to Congress,[1] the former, which introduced General Foreman's Memorial on Salt Works remains unconsidered & no day appointed. The latter was sent immediately to the Board of Treasury.

I have at present no other Commands from Congress but to transmit—

An Act of the 5th Inst. adopting a plan for filling the Offices of Quarter Master general in the Army.

Another Act of the same date for the trial of the General Officers who were in the Northern department when Tyconderoga & Mount Independence were evacuated. These Your Excellency will find under the present Cover.

The 14th Inst. I transmitted an Act of Congress & divers other papers relative to Baron Stuben.[2] It may not be improper to intimate that the Baron arrived at York two days ago & intends waiting on Your Excellency Some Six or eight days hence.

P.M. Since writing as above Congress have passed a Resolve directing the Committee at Camp to "consult with your Excellency," & "Report to Congress the proper Officers for filling the Several departments of the quarter Master general," [3] by which I presume is to be understood to recommend or to nominate proper persons to be appointed for the Several departments. The Secretary has sent me only one Copy of the Act which I have transmitted to the Committee who will lay it before your Excellency.

Congress have consented that Leiutt. Colo. Fleuri shall follow the Marquis delafayette on his intended expedition into Canada, having been assured that he had first obtained Your Excellency's permission.

I have the honour to be with Sincere Regard & Esteem &ca.

LB (DNA: PCC, item 13).

[1] These letters are in PCC, item 152, 5:275–83, and Washington, *Writings* (Fitzpatrick), 10:411–12, 418.

[2] Laurens is actually referring to his January 14, 1778, letter to Washington.

[3] See *JCC,* 10:138.

Committee at Camp Minutes of Proceedings

[February 8–14, 1778]

8. Sunday.

9. No Committee.

10. Examined Clothr. Genls. Depy.[1] Considered the Establishmt. of Engineers & agreed to recommend it to Congress agreable to the Genls. plan. Monsr. De Portail to give a more particular arrangment of the Companies, & of his Assistants.

Wrote to the Comissary of Hides to attend the Committee.[2]

11th. Wrote Genl. Washington on the proposed exchange of Prisoners by Gen. Howe. (No. 16.)[3]

Wrote to Congress upon the Canada Expedition. (No. 17.)[4]

Pass'd proposals for procuring Horse & Saddles for the Cavalry (No. 18.)

12. Conferred with Genl. Green abt the Qr. Mastr's. Genl. Departmt.

13. Conferred upon the starving condition of the Army.

Wrote to Colo. Cox (No. 19.)[5]

Recd. Lettrs. & Resolutions from Congress respectg. Qr. Mr. Gen. Departmt.[6] Sent Lettrs. to Congress respectg. Canada Expedition & the Qr. Mr. Departmt.[7]

14. Wrote to Gov. Livingston respectg. Waggons to transport Provi-

sions & the mode of obtaining Horses to remount the Cavalry (No. 20).[8] Sent them forward 9 o'Clock. Conferred with Genl. Woodford & others & stated their Case (No. 21).[9]

Wrote to Congress [10] abt. Genl. Varnum.[11]

MS (DLC). A continuation of Committee at Camp Minutes of Proceedings, February 2–7, 1778. The minutes printed in this entry are in the hands of committee members Francis Dana and Joseph Reed.

[1] This is probably a reference to deputy clothier general Daniel Kemper.

[2] The committee's letter to George Ewing has not been found.

[3] See Committee at Camp to George Washington, February 11, 1778.

[4] See Committee at Camp to Henry Laurens, February 11, 1778.

[5] The committee's letter to John Cox, who became deputy quartermaster general, has not been found.

[6] See Henry Laurens to the Committee at Camp, February 7, 1778.

[7] See Committee at Camp to Henry Laurens, February 12, 1778.

[8] This is the committee's letter to Gov. William Livingston dated February 13, 1778.

[9] See the February 17 entry in the committee's minutes of proceedings (February 16–20, 1778) and its March 2 statement.

[10] After a discussion of the army's distresses in their letter to President Laurens, the committee turned to the need of a commanding general in Rhode Island and recommended James Varnum for the post. Varnum did not receive the assignment. See Committee at Camp to Henry Laurens, February 14, 1778; *JCC*, 12:1215, 13:274; and Washington, *Writings* (Fitzpatrick), 11:284.

[11] For the continuation of these minutes, see Committee at Camp Minutes of Proceedings, February 16–20, 1778.

Eliphalet Dyer to Joseph Trumbull

Dear Sir   York-Town Feby. 8th 1778

I received yours of the 13th Ulmo in which you mention the decline of your health, a bad cold and Jaundicy habit. A deccoction of strong soot with the Yolk of an egg repeated a few mornings will relieve you of your Jaundice, as I have found by repeated experience and a long ride not to expose your self to Storms or Night Air is the best relief for a fix'd cold tending to a hectick disorder however you must Consult self on the latter. It gives me much concern that a meer unthought of mistake & accident should give the Governor or you on his Account so much Sollicitude as am Absolutely Certain there was no design in the direction. The letter was Circular, some Assemblys have no upper house. I have often before rectified mistakes of that kind but believe was then Absent or Inattentive but can give the Strongest assurance that it was a meer Accident. But when an Unhappy jealousy prevails there is no wonder of a misconstruction but unhappily at this time many concurrent circumstances tended to Strengthen the suspicion. But the President has since been directed to assure the Governor how it happened [1] and that the supposed Neglect or affront was purely

Accidental and I am Warranted to say there is neither Governor nor President in any of the United States who is held in so much Esteem by Congress as Govr Trumbull, tho there has been a party in Congress and on some occasions I have no doubt some of his family have suffered by it. Yet it is now gone, the same as to you. Tho there has no doubt been some who were Vexed to see the new plan they were so fond of turn out with all the mischievous Consequences of which they were foretold were Vexd, & Chagrind, and ready to Impute the misfortune to any thing & every thing & upon you among the rest rather than their mighty Widome & Judgment should be Impeached, is not this Natural? & Why then such mighty Stress to be laid on such feeble dispairing efforts, of an expiring faction; why again so much alarmed on your not recieving an Answer from a Body to your letter of exculpation, when Congress as such were entirely satisfied & it is rather unusual to direct answers on such Occasions & when the suspicion if any, arose from Individuals; if the body had passed any Censure most certainly they ought to have taken it of when the Occasion was removed, or they better informed but there had been no Censure from the body. Beside the Amazing croud of business has prevented attention to many things, as Answers to letters & the like, which were rather matters of Complaisonice, Congress the Country & Army have suffered sufficiently for this Imprudence of their New regulation, and they are enough sick of it, and if they can possible relieve themselves by New men or measures they are ready to Adopt them: they therefore as well as Genll Gates & board of Warr most ardently wish your attendance, I with them, & nothing but your want of health has excused you in my View, for the security of our Country in no measure ought to be Neglected on Account of any real or supposed affronts or Injuries Whatever, this I must hold, to Vindicate my own conduct, as I never should have seen this place, & sacrificed my Intrest, & the Comforts of my family had not I valued my Country & held my self superior to reproach, Ingratitude or Calumny. I trust it will be no pleasure to you when I tell you that by the New Commissariate plan & the Ignorance, inattention & sloth of many of those employd, our Army has been at times starving, and many advantages over the Enemy lost for want of provisions & at length many of our Army dispersed in the Country & suffered to return home on furlow, & what is worse the most advantageous oppertunities for Attacking the Enemy this Winter & driving them out of Philadelphia could not be taken nor a force called in for that purpose for want of Stores & Magazines of Provisions necessary for that purpose, & fear we may be as destitute in the Spring. The flower most certainly is to be had in this Country yet much doubt where a sufficiency of the meat kind can be provided; they hear much of Capt Wadsworth, the eyes of the publick, the Army, & Congress, are mostly on him, Next to you, as they are told no Inducement will be sufficient to Induce you to Undertake Again in that Department. I dare say Mr Wadsworth might have any terms & moddle the plan as he pleased with your Advice if he would undertake, but I dare not Assure them he will, I wish I knew.[2] Coll Thos has wrote for liberty to resign in the Army on account of his Infirm state of health. I laid in his Memorial to Congress for that purpose but instead of granting his resignation, they have on report of the board of War to which it was referrd lengthened out his furlow to 1st of April & if then not fit for service, he has liberty to resign. Coll Chandler has since applied for a dismission, Complaining of want of health—attended with the Gravel & conclude it will be Granted.[3] A Comtee from Congress has been for sometime attending at Head Quarters for the purpose of regulating the Army &c. It is high time for the several States to be fitting up their quotas in the Army, or the enemy will be Aforehand of us in the spring. My affectionate regards to family & am Yours,

E Dyer

[*P.S.*] I hope you will not forget to settle your old Long Island affairs in these good times.

RC (CtHi).
  [1] See Henry Laurens to the States, December 23, 1777, note 2, and to Jonathan Trumbull, Sr., February 9, 1778.
  [2] See Dyer to Jeremiah Wadsworth, February 10, 1778.
  [3] For the extension of Thomas Dyer's furlough and the acceptance of John Chandler's resignation, see *JCC*, 10:127, 143. President Laurens' February 13 letter to Chandler enclosing Congress' February 11 resolve granting Chandler's request to resign his commission, is in PCC, item 13, fol. 188.

Henry Laurens to George Washington

Sir.   8th Febry 1778
  I beg leave to refer Your Excellency to a Letter which I had the honour of writing to you yesterday & last Night.
  Your Excellency will receive herewith an Act of Congress of the 5th Inst. extending the furlough of Colo. Tho. Dyer, and also an Act of the 3d Inst. & 5 Copies for obliging all Officers Military & Civil holding appointments under Congress to qualify themselves for acting in their respective Offices by taking certain Oaths therein prescribed. Your Excellency will be pleased to take the most effectual means for publishing this Act throughout the Army immediately under your Command. Copies will be sent to other departments of the Army & to each State.
  I remain with very great Regard

LB (DNA: PCC, item 13).

James Lovell to John Adams

Dear Sir   Febry. 8th. 1778.
   Yours of Janry. 9th is before me. Deane had inclosed to Congress
a long minute corresponding history of what you sent me. He doubted
whether Mr. R M had communicated to us what had been sent of the
kind formerly therefore he wrote to him lately with Flying seals under
cover to the President. Mr. R M had been indiscreat in remarking to
T. M. upon the Conduct of the Commissioners as not acting candidly
in their Representations; for which he has made through Congress so
very lengthy Apologies, and totally discarded his infamous brother.
I am not able to write minutely to you but I endeavour to send Papers
which speak for themselves.[1] The long and short of Affairs is that if
we can [gain] assistance to meliorate our currency we may laugh at
Britain.
   Poor Weeks is gone to the Bottom of the Sea with a very valuable
Cargo and every Soul but one who was preserved by a floating Ladder
3 Days before he was taken up.[2]
   Burgoynes affair was known in France and the English ministry
concealed the proceedings about Philadelphia. It does not appear by
the Kings Speech that Auxiliaries are coming. The Detention of
Burgoyne will disconcert the ministry most horribly. An Incursion
into Canada is making by Fayette, Conway & Stark. I think the prospect is good. You will take minutes of any intelligence worth notice
written to Mr. S A or other Friends. I fear to keep Packets open as
Posts & Expresses are altogether uncertain, depending upon information obtained about the River.
   I have directed Mr. Dunlap at Lancaster to put up Sheets of the 2d
Vol of Journals, and forward to you under Cover to the Navy Board.
I hope they will be delivered by the Bearer of this. Your Chest shall go
by the first Carriage of Money unless Bat Horses[3] are made use of.
I suppose you cannot want the Contents except for your Children
though I have not been the less industrious to send them upon that
supposition. But I should risk a total Loss if I sent them to any Stage
short of the east side of Hudson's River. If I can get the Chest on to
Hugh Hughes, I am sure he will push it to Boston.
   I have written to Mr. Dana[4] to contrive at Camp to get yr. other
things forwarded from Mr. Sprouts home wherever it may be. The
Baron Steuben has been most cordially received by Congress. If he
should be so received at Camp it may tend to introduce many advantages into the Quarter Masters Department at least. We had determined upon the following arrangmts. before his arrival. 1. the military duties as laid down in Books. 2. Forage Master. 3. Waggon Mastr.
"to purchase & direct Horses, Carriages &c. 4. Agent for the purchase
of Tents Tools &c.[5] We have also taken the purchasing business from

the Director Genl. of Hospitals and made the Dy. Drs. act as Purveyors. The Dr. Gl. with the Ph[ysicia]n & Surgn. Genl. to order the Invoices, and the two latter to publish in the Hospitals forms of Receipts which are to be the vouchers for all Expenditures, acquainting the Treasury with the forms by immediate duplicates.[6] We hope to save thousands & ten thousands of Dollars by having appointed Auditors for the Camp accounts, but how we shall secure what is due from Paymasters & other Officers who have quitted the Service I cannot tell.[7] Exchequer Courts would allarm the People.

RC (MHi). In Lovell's hand, though not signed.

[1] For further information on Silas Deane's correspondence with Robert Morris about the affairs of Thomas Morris, see Robert Morris to Benjamin Franklin, December 27, 1777.

[2] The *Reprisal,* commanded by Capt. Lambert Wickes, foundered and sank in a storm off the coast of Newfoundland on October 1, 1777, while returning from France. See William Bell Clark, *Lambert Wickes Sea Raider and Diplomat* (New Haven: Yale University Press, 1932), pp. 358–63.

[3] That is, pack horses.

[4] Not found.

[5] For the report of the Board of War proposing these changes within the quartermaster general's department, see *JCC,* 10:102–3.

[6] For the resolves of Congress regulating the hospitals, see *JCC,* 10:128–31.

[7] The resolves of Congress establishing the positions and duties of auditors of accounts are in *JCC,* 10:132–37.

James Lovell to William Whipple

Dear Sir [1]   York Town 8th. Feby 1778.

Your favor of the 12th of January has at length reached me, and gives double pleasure as it assures me of your health and at the same time mentions several things which in your good judgment would essentially benefit the public cause which things had actually received the approbation of Congress. Establishing a fund in Europe for the purpose of sinking our quantity of paper more *expeditiously* than it can be effected by taxes, tho' not more *prudently,* unless we lay great stress upon the gain of time—making due distinction between internal friends and foes many of the latter now actually eating our bread, vile vermin as they are. The public officers being sifted, each State must look to its citizens. Virginia is going on vigorously in this work as well as in recruiting, clothing and feeding the Army. Maryland besides excluding Nonjurors from office is laying a treble tax upon them. Retalliation is another thing you mention. You know where the main clog has been;[2] but he as well as Congress seems *now* determined. You are not the only one of my correspondents who give me information about our commercial matters in France. Mr. J

Adams who succeeds Deane, has sent me an extract of a letter from
that little judicious man McCreary, who gave us a pretty account of
what he had heard and seen in France last year.[3] He sends a striking
picture of the infamy of T.M., but his brother R. had done it before
and had totally discarded him from private as well public affairs.
Congress had in October sent directions to the Commissioners to
suspend Agents. The Baron [4] whom you mention arrived here two
days ago. Congress had sent a very complimentary Resolve to Boston
which did not get to his hand before he set off from thence.[5] If Genl
W—— should be able to make use of his talents as a Qr Mr Genl it
would be of eminent service. We have divided the system into 4 parts.
1st A military genius to perform the scientific parts as laid down in
military books. 2d a Forage Master. 3d Commissary for purchasing
and regulating stores [*i.e. horses*] and waggons. 4th Agents for purchasing tents and other military utensils. We have also taken the purchasing part from the hands of the Director General of Hospitals; the
Deputy D.G. is to act as Purveyor in consequence of the plans of the
D.G. and the Ph. and Surg. Genl conjointly, and the orders of the two
last with such other vouchers as they shall direct and report to the
Treasury from time to time are to be produced in proof of expenditures. Rush has resigned, there being a mortal enmity between him
and Shippen.[6]

As to winter's plan I am egregiously baulked. Howe will rest quiet,
but an incursion is making into Canada, in which many foreigners
are employed with Stark. The Marquis de la Fayette may greatly
influence the Canadian Noblesse.

I rec'd your list of tickets and Mr Thos Smith has undertaken the
check of the books. I wrote to Mr. S. Adams to have the advertisement
altered; I wonder you did not upon seeing the first publication. The
Lottery is *absolutely* to be drawn the 1st of May.

I am truly your friend & humble servant,   J.L.

Tr (DLC).
    [1] Although the recipient of this Tr is identified as John Langdon, the letter was
apparently addressed to William Whipple. Whipple had long maintained a regular correspondence with Lovell and was the owner of the lottery tickets that are
the subject of the last paragraph of this letter.
    [2] This is probably a reference to General Washington.
    [3] William McCreery, a Baltimore merchant who had recently established his
business in Bordeaux, had discussed commercial and political affairs in France and
the activities of Thomas Morris in a September 29, 1777, letter to John Adams,
which is in the Adams Papers, MHi.
    [4] That is, Baron von Steuben.
    [5] See *JCC*, 10:50.
    [6] For further information on the feud between Benjamin Rush and William
Shippen that led to Rush's resignation, see John Witherspoon to Benjamin Rush,
February 2, 1778, note 1.

Joseph Reed to Jonathan Bayard Smith

Dear Sir   Norriton,[1] Feb. 8. 1778

I received your Favour [2] reminding me of Mr. Montgomery & shall not omit any Thing in my Power to serve him, but the Appointment of Chaplains depends so much on the Inclinations & Attachments of the Officers of the Brigades (& very properly in my opinion) that other Interest is of little Consequence; he belongs to Genl. Smallwoods Division, with whom I have some Acquaintance & to whom I will write, tho I have every Reason to believe Mr M. stands exceeding well with them.

I came over from the Committee last Evening. The Reform & Establishment of an Army when so many Circumstances concur to introduce & support Disorder & Confusion is no easy Task. We shall therefore most probably spend more Time here than may be thought necessary by those unacquainted with the Nature of our Business. But from the little Observation I have made during three Years Connection with the Army [3] I have thought more Intercourse between it & Congress & a longer Stay of its Members in Camp when attending military Business would have prevented some Errors & Mistakes which have happened. It is true it is not very agreeable to Gentlemen accustomed to the Conveniencies of domestick Life; but it gives great Satisfaction to the military to think that their Wants, Fatigues & Inconveniencies are known & felt in some Degree by those upon whom they depend for their Honour & Support. A longer Residence in Camp & an Exchange of Sentiments with some Degree of Confidence between Congress & the Army seems at this Time particularly necessary; for believe me we are in a critical Situation & I think are hastening fast towards that Rock upon which opposers of established Government have generally made Shipwreck of their most favourable Prospects. I mean Dissention between the component Parts of our System. Your Acquaintance with History & good Judgment will suggest to you many Instances of the fatal Consequences of a Division in Councils & shew how the jarring Interests of ambitious Men have blasted the fairest Hopes of political Happiness. God forbid that this Country should furnish History with another Instance of the political Suicide. The Danger of trusting to Paper Matters of this Nature prevents my dessending to Particulars; but it is too plain that a general Idea prevails thro the Army & Country of a Want of Harmony between the principal Characters in our political Drama. I should be extremely happy to be perswaded that it was groundless but some Events have happened & they seem to multiply so fast that as a Lover of my Country & feeling an Attachment to its Interests superior to all other Considerations I cannot but perceive & lament it. And the more so as Experience shews how difficult it is to heal such Breaches, tho much Time is lost & irreparable Injury often done the publick Interests in the vain Attempt. A decided Line of Conduct on such Occasions is certainly the best, & when Facts are once established, Wisdom & Policy I think should determine us to give our Confidence & Support to that Character which is the most meritorious, without ballancing between the contending Parties or vainly trying to reconcile them. To you & me & a great Majority of this Country it must be perfectly immaterial by whom its Salvation is wrought out; our only Ambition being to secure its Liberties & rest its peaceful Citizens. Let us therefore early guard against any Designs incompatible with these Veiws from whatever Quarter they may come & whatever their Pretensions, for we cannot suppose our Country should not furnish Characters in this Respect like Caesars Nil actuon reputans, dum aliquid superisset agendum: Who will think no Degree of Honour attained while any remains unattained. Our former Difficulties have been surmounted by Vigour & Firmness. The Power & Strength of the Enemy & common Danger with a Sense of the Justice of our Cause has enabled us to struggle thro' them. The last great Evil, clashing Interests & sinister Ambition only remains; that conquered, Victory is most certainly ours. But I am very clear, it requires more Wisdom & Prudence to combat this than all the others. And that State must be in imminent Danger, when Persons possessing its Confidence in a great Degree have lost Confidence & Harmony with each other. I need not say to whom I refer, when I make these Reflections, nor should I have ventured them on Paper, if I did not see that I should be detained from Congress on this Committee a considerable Time, & that some Measures have been lately adopted calculated in my Opinion to serve other Views than those of Patriotism & which Congress have sanctified without sufficiently attending to their Consequences. I must acknowledge the Unacquaintance of the Committee with some important Facts surprized me, & as I suppose other Gentlemen in Congress are equally uninform'd, I cannot but feel the greatest Anxiety least an unsuspicious Confidence in Men should lead us to the Brink of a Precipice before we perceive our Danger. I am not insensible that some unfavourable Events, & perhaps unimproved Opportunities have made their Impression on some Minds with respect to a very high Character; they have been stronger as those who entertained them have been distant from the Scene of Action; but let these be what they may, that Policy & Wisdom must be very defective which shews its Designs without a reasonable Prospect of accomplishing them. To permit Power to remain in any Hand upon which much depends & at the same Time to adopt Measures to thwart & enfeeble its Exertions I can never agree to—either change the Hands, or support them with your greatest Weight. I observed early last Summer a growing Disgust among Characters

who figure high but trusted to Events to soften or crush it. Those
Events have rather cherished it as they have raised one Scale, & sunk
the other, so as to bring Parties nearer to a Ballance, & unmask'd
Men & Measures much sooner than ordinary Occurrencies would
have done. But however they may cross each other in Ambitions
Road, I apprehend our Path is plain, to take Care the publick Interest does not suffer in the Justle. In the Course of Events, the
Enemy have become possessed of this Intelligence. It is publickly
talk'd both in New York & Philada. that our leading military Characters are hostile to each other, & they draw no small Degree of Consolation from the Circumstance. Congress till lately seemed to stand
neuter, but some late Appointments, & the new Expedition have
countenanced an Opinion that they mean to throw a Weight into
one Scale. Of the Propriety & Justice of the first I shall not say any
Thing. The Characters of Men are too delicate to discuss on Paper,
it is sufficient for my Purpose that such Promotion must wound, &
very sensibly too, the Man with whom while possessed of supreme
military Powers it is our Duty as Members of Congress to be on the
most harmonious Terms. I look upon the Expedition considered
simply, as pregnant with immediate Ruin to this State, & extremely
pernicious to the general Interest. I cannot think it wise to prosecute
a foreign Expedition, when we find it so difficult [to] oppose the
Enemy in the very Heart of our Country. I know in some Instances
it has been found politick to transfer the Seat of War into your
Enemy's Country, but that can only be, when you are able to carry
it on there, which I fear in the present Instance will not be our Case.
A Want of hard Money alone will prove its Bane. I need not tell you,
what indifferent Prospects of Union there are between the Characters
engaged in it. They have entered upon it with such different Veiws,
& with such Sentiments of it, & each other, that I am exceedingly deceived if its very Commencement will not be attended with very
inauspicious Symtoms. If it should prove a Part of a systematical Plan
to lessen a great Character, by drawing off the necessary Supplies of
Arms & Provisons, & render his Exertions feeble & ineffectual, while
every Attention is paid to that Demand, tho' Success should attend
it equal to the Wishes of those who patronize it, we shall have no
Reason to approve it, but if which I really beleive will be the Case,
by attempting to support an Army here, & carry on an Expedition
there, we starve & fail in both we shall never forgive ourselves or be
forgiven by others. I have had the Grounds & Motives of this Expedition fully disclosed to me by a Gentleman who voted for it, but has
since seen his Error: but they prove no more to me, than that an
Object wholly unattainable is very desirable. If it be possible, therefore, my dear Sir, let me beg you to use your utmost Influence to get
this unadvised Measure recalled before it begins to operate on our

Army here, for I am clearly of Opinion that if it is proceeded in, it will enlarge beyond its now professed Limits, & swallow up the Resources of the Army here, the certain Consequences of which will be a disbanding of this Army & a great Recruit to the Enemy's. I know some delicate Feelings will be hurt by a Retraction, & very probably this may be urged against it, but the Interests of our Country & State, the Safety of ourselves, & Families are too dear, & valuable to be sacrificed to Punctilio.[4] Whatever may be thought by some Gentlemen, the Attachments of this Army to its Commander are extremely strong, & very natural. A long Connection, winning Manners, unspotted Morals, & disinterested Views cast a Lustre round him which a Want of Success cannot obscure. They are even strengthned by that Circumstance of Character, which some deem a Blemish: I mean a Diffidence of his own Judgment & Reliance upon that of his Officers. In supporting him, they support their own Opinions & are interested in vindicating the Measures which they have advised. You must be sensible, I have during this Campaign had the best Opportunities of discerning the Springs of many of our Movements, & I do assure you there has been a remarkable, & in some Cases I have thought, an unhappy Unanimity of Councils, but surely so general a Concurrence of Sentiment, in the great Transactions of the Field will go far to justify a General to every considerate Mind. Those who are bold enough to think of a Change, would do well to reflect upon these Circumstances & fix upon a superior Character in all Respects. Untill they do this we are bound by every Principle of Honour, Interest, & Gratitude to discourage every Attempt to lessen his Character, & weaken or counteract his Measures. If there should be any such System formed as I have hinted, & any farther Marks of it appear, let me intreat you, my dear Sir, to oppose it with your best Interests, you can never serve your Country more effectually. In urging this I am not moved by personal Attachment, but a Regard to the publick, & a full Conviction of the pernicious Consequences of Discord, between our deliberative & executive Powers in the military Department. Some perhaps may think it expedient to ballance these Parties, & that it will secure the Scale in the Hands of Congress, but this I fear will be an over reaching Policy, that will defeat its own Purposes. We are yet under no Necessity & from certain Circumstances I think never shall be to seek for this Security. It is fixed in the unchangeable Order & Nature of Things, but if it were not, this is no Time for trying Experiments when a great, & I may say a victorious Enemy is in the very Bowels of our Country. As I have never known the Powers, & Duties of the Board of War. I confess myself very incompetent, to judge of the Nature & Extent of the Evils, which will flow from Division between it and the Commanders of our Armies, but it seems pretty clear that its Influence & Utility must be very limited, if the publick Cause will not be much injured by such a Conflict.

I have troubled you with this long Scrawl tho perfectly ignorant of your private Sentiments, on this important Subject, but if I had been sure they were unfavourable to the Character I mean to support, I should have said as much, depending on your Candour & Discernment to see & pursue the Measures I have suggested upon publick Ground only. My respectful Compliments to our Colleagues; I trust to your Prudence & Discretion to make Use of this free Letter which I should never have wrote if Events did not seem to require it.

I am with much Esteem, Dear Sir, Your very Obed. & Affect., Hbble Serv. Jos. Reed

P.S. I shall be much obliged to you to call at the Post Office in York Town & forward any Letters to me you may find there. Expecting to have attended Congress before this I desired some of my Boston Friends to direct to me there.

Genl. Howe has confirm'd the old Cartel of Exchanges[5]—so that we now hourly expect Gen. Lee out & capable of Service. Nothing else new in Camp.

RC (DLC).

[1] Reed had moved his family to a farm at Norriton, the site of present-day Norristown, Pa., the previous summer when the British threatened Philadelphia. During the period he served with the Committee at Camp, which met generally at either Valley Forge or at Moore Hall about two miles from Washington's headquarters, Reed was therefore within easy reach of home and managed occasional visits to his family. For information on Reed's activities during this period of his public career, see John F. Roche, *Joseph Reed, a Moderate in the American Revolution* (New York: Columbia University Press, 1957), pp. 122–28.

[2] Not found.

[3] Reed had served as Washington's confidential secretary from June to October 1775, as adjutant general of the army from June 1776 to January 1777, and as a volunteer aide with Washington at various intervals during the 1777 campaign.

[4] For Congress' suspension of the expedition to Canada, see *JCC*, 10:253–54. See also Henry Laurens to Lafayette, January 22, 1778, note 2.

[5] As Washington received this information from General Howe on February 9, Reed obviously added this second postscript no earlier than the 9th. See Washington, *Writings* (Fitzpatrick), 10:444.

Committee of Commerce to the Commissioners at Paris

Gentlemen York in Penna. Feby 9th. 1778

The Honorable William Lee Esqr. having been appointed a Commissioner to the Court of Prussia, and Mr. Thomas Morris having been removed from the Commercial Agency, Congress have impowered and directed Us to write to you, desiring you would appoint one or more suitable Persons to be Commercial Agents for Conducting the Commercial business of the united states in France and other parts of Europe. Inclosed is the Resolve of Congress to that purpose.[1]

You will be pleased to make appointments immediately and give us notice by the first opportunity.

We are with great Respect, Your most obed humble servts,

William Ellery

James Forbes

Fra. Lewis

RC (PPAmP). In the hand of John Brown, and signed by Ellery, Forbes, and Lewis.

[1] In their July 20, 1778, letter to President Laurens, the Commissioners at Paris acknowledged the belated receipt of this resolve and the committee's letter and indicated that John Bondfield at Bordeaux and John D. Schweighauser at Nantes, who had been previously appointed by William Lee, were currently the only authorized American commercial agents in France. See *JCC*, 10:139; and Wharton, *Diplomatic Correspondence*, 2:651–52. For William Lee's comments on several merchants seeking commercial appointments at French ports, as well as his indication that he had also appointed Andrew Limozin as agent at Havre de Grâce, see his March 23, 1778, letter to Richard Henry Lee in William Lee, *Letters of William Lee*, ed. Worthington C. Ford, 3 vols. (Brooklyn: Historical Printing Club, 1891), 1:406–11.

Henry Laurens to Nicholas Cooke

Sir,   York Town 9th Febry 1778.

My last was on the 22d January by Messenger Dodd.[1] Your Excellency will receive in Company with this the following Acts of Congress & five Copies of each.

of the 19th December & 21st January past for retaliating upon the Enemy.

of the 3d Inst. for obliging persons holding Commissions & appointments under Congress to qualify themselves for acting in their offices respectively by taking & subscribing certain Oaths therein prescribed. You are requested Sir to cause this to be published in your State in the most effectual manner.[2]

I have the honour to be, Sir, Your Excellency's Most obedient servant,   Henry Laurens, President of Congress

RC (R–Ar).

[1] See Laurens to George Clinton, January 22, 1778, note 2.

[2] For the "Acts" Laurens enclosed, see *JCC*, 9:1036–37, 10:74–81, 114–18. Laurens also transmitted copies of these December 19, January 21, and February 3 resolves with brief letters that he wrote this day to the Massachusetts Council, Gen. Israel Putnam, and President Meshech Weare of New Hampshire. Revolutionary Papers,

FEBRUARY 9, 1778 63

M–Ar; PCC, item 13, fol. 181; and Revolutionary Papers, Nh–Ar. He transmitted copies of the February 3 resolve along with brief letters that he wrote on February 8 to Gov. William Livingston of New Jersey and to President Thomas Wharton of Pennsylvania; and on February 9 to Gov. George Clinton of New York, Pres. George Read of Delaware, and the marquis de Lafayette. PCC, item 13, fols. 163, 165, 179; George Read Papers, DeHi; and Charles Roberts Autograph Collection, PHC. See also Laurens to Patrick Henry, February 10, 1778.

Henry Laurens to William Heath

Sir.   York Town 9th Feby 1778.
   I had the honour of receiving by Mcloski the 5 Inst. your favor of the 10th Ulto. including a late correspondence with Lieutt General Burgoyne,[1] these were immediately reported to Congress & transmitted to the Board of War, from whence a report has not yet ascended, therefore I have no particular Commands relative to your said dispatch. I may however with propriety & pleasure intimate that your conduct towards the British General & his dependants receive the continued approbation of Congress if I may be permitted to make this conclusion from the general sentiments of Members.
   Inclosed with this you will receive an Act of Congress of the 3d Inst. for obliging persons who hold Commissions or appointments under Congress to qualify themselves by taking & subscribing to certain Oaths therein prescribed, which Sir, you will be pleased to publish throughout the department of the Army under Your Command.[2]
   I have the honour to be, With very great Regard, Sir, Your most humble servant,   Henry Laurens, President of Congress

RC (MHi).
[1] The January 13, 1778, letter to Laurens from Gen. William Heath, the Continental commander in Boston, dealt with "some Riotous behaviour" by a few of Gen. John Burgoyne's troops in that city as well as problems related to the maintenance of Burgoyne's captured army. Enclosed with it were letters of January 4 from Burgoyne to Heath and of January 10 from Heath to Burgoyne concerning the unruliness of the British prisoners mentioned above. PCC, item 57, fols. 135–46. Laurens obviously confused Heath's January 13 letter to him with the general's January 10 letter to Burgoyne.
[2] In his presidential letterbook Laurens made the following summary of a letter he wrote this day to Gen. Benedict Arnold: "Acknowledged the Receipt of two Letters from him Committed to Board of War—that I had received no Command from Congress." PCC, item 13, fol. 181. See also *JCC*, 10:74, 139.

Henry Laurens to Jonathan Trumbull, Sr.

Sir,   9th Feby 1778.
   I had the honour of writing to your Excellency on the 14th Ulto. by Major Spencer & on the 3d Inst.[1] by an opportunity Mr. Webber

which offered suddenly & unexpectedly I covered & directed properly to your Excellency Acts of Congress of the 19th December & 21st Jany past for retaliating upon the Enemy.

My Duty is at present to convey the several Acts recited below Vizt.

29th December 1777 for bringing to punishment when practicable such of the Inhabitants of these States as have joined or shall join the Enemy.

26th Jany 78—expressing the approbation of Congress of the measures adopted by Your Excellency & the Council of Connecticut for providing public Stores & provisions &ca.

3d Febry—for compelling persons holding Commissions & appointments under Congress to qualify themselves for acting in their several Offices by taking & subscribing to certain Oaths therein prescribed. Your Excellency is requested to cause this to be made public throughout the State of Connecticut.

Your Excellency will also find inclosed a Warrant on the Loan Office of your State for two hundred Thousand Dollars.[2]

Colo. Dyer has signified to me that the mode of the Address by Congress to the General Assembly of Connecticut, conveyed under a flying Seal in my Letter of the 23d December had been interpretted as a slight & given some offence to Your Excellency.[3] It is at the request of that Gentleman I trouble you with the present explanation. When the paper abovementioned was sent to me I was in extreme pain confined in Bed. I perceived it had escaped Congress in an unusual dress & bespake a new Channel of Correspondence in almost all the States & that there were also some roughnesses in the Composition which required amendment. I therefore requested a sensible Member of Congress whose Sentiments I found to be consonant with my own, to present the piece to the House for a review. This Gentleman, as he informed me, pointed out the objections alluded to, in the House, & proposed a reconsideration, but Congress being deeply engaged in other affairs of great moment declined receiving it, saying in general, the president would send it in a proper manner. Under this intimation I judged it proper to pass the Address through Your Excellency's hands in the manner abovementioned, in order that the Contents might be previously known to your Excellency & the Council. I am persuaded Sir, there was no design in Congress to overlook Your Excellency & I beg Your Excellency will be assured it is impossible for me to attempt the smallest degree of disrespect towards a Character which I have long held in the highest Esteem—under this declaration I have the honour to subscribe with great truth, Sir, Yours &ca.

LB (DNA: PCC, item 13).

[1] See Laurens to James Duane, February 3, 1778, note 2.

[2] Congress had ordered the issuance of this warrant on January 27, 1778. *JCC*, 10:94. Laurens also wrote a brief letter this day to John Lawrence, the Continental

loan office commissioner in Connecticut, informing him of "an Act of Congress of 20th December last cancelling a Warrant on the Loan Office Connecticut for 200,000 Dollars of the 16th September in favour of William Buchanan Esquire which had been returned unpaid." PCC, item 13, fol. 178; and *JCC*, 8:748, 9:1042. Furthermore, he wrote brief notes apprising Joseph Henderson and Eleazar Wales of their February 3 appointment as commissioners of accounts for the northern district and informing Moses Emerson of his February 3 appointment as commissioner of accounts at Hartford. PCC, item 13, fols. 178, 180; and *JCC*, 10:113–14.

³ Laurens had unintentionally offended Governor Trumbull by addressing a copy of his December 23, 1777, circular letter to the states, to the speaker of the Connecticut Assembly rather than to the governor himself. Although Trumbull did not mention his chagrin in his January 16, 1778, reply to Laurens, his son Joseph complained about the putative slight in letters to Eliphalet Dyer and James Lovell, both of whom hastened to reassure the younger Trumbull that Laurens had not meant to give offense to the governor. See PCC, item 66, 1:372–73; James Lovell to Joseph Trumbull, January 27; and Eliphalet Dyer to Joseph Trumbull, February 8, 1778.

Daniel Roberdeau to John Clark

Dr. Sir   York Town Feby. 9th. 1778
    The System of the Auditors department is in the press and has undergone no material alterations, your appointment remains as it did, neither has Congress tho desirous of your services accepted the unconditional Terms of your Letter, as it was unpresidented.[1] I could wish for your own sake as well as on account of the publick wheel [weal] that you would repair to Camp and in your way call here for the System, if you do otherwise I think you will[2] repent, further argument is unnecessary as you are acquainted with my opinion at large. Mr. Clarkson has accepted his appointment in very polite terms and with thanks; "do thou likewise." I shall expect to see you in a few days, but dont neglect giving an answer to Treasury, it is expected, and your acceptance will be universally agreeable. I am, Dr. Sir, Yr. most obt. friend & Servt,   Daniel Roberdeau

P.S. Is not your appointment of 4 dollars per day, and 3 rations for yourself and one for your horse, better than the pay of the Board of War as its members are allowed but 2000 Dollars per Annum?

RC (DNA: PCC, item 41). Addressed: "Major John Clark, at Abbots Town, York County."

    ¹ On January 10, Congress named John Clark and Matthew Clarkson "auditors to audit and settle the public accounts in the main army." Clarkson accepted his appointment on January 28, but Clark, in the "unpresidented" letter of January 24 to which Roberdeau refers, protested the inadequacy of the salary offered and suggested instead that he be employed at a salary to be determined at a future date, after Congress had time to restudy the question of fair compensation. Roberdeau's letter was obviously written in the belief that Clark's stance would redound to his disadvantage if he did not reconsider it, but the latter remained

unmoved until they had a face-to-face encounter, which is explained in the following note. In any event, Clark submitted his letter of acceptance on the 10th and almost immediately set off for Valley Forge. See *JCC*, 10:38, 121, 137, 143; and PCC, item 78, 5:129–40.

² At this point Clark later inserted an asterisk to which he keyed the following statement that he penned at the bottom of the page. "Note. Mr. Roberdeau was of the Board of the Treasury, & when I was going to hand in my resignation he told me with warmth, if I did not accept, I need not be surprised when I should hear myself represented as a *disaffected person*, & my Friends begd. me to accept least I should be injured. J.C."

Eliphalet Dyer to Jeremiah Wadsworth

Dear Sir   York Town Febry 10th 1778

I receivd your kind favour a few days since. Am Extreemly sorry for the unhappy jealousy that has arisen in the mind of the Govr. & Some of his family on Account of the supposed Neglect of Congress in their address to the Speaker of our Assembly Instead of the Governor. Unhappy I say for when jealousies once arise every thing is Construed into Design & Intention of an affront when no such intention is had as was the case in that direction. It was purely a mistake, as the letter was Circular & some States have only a lower house, & it really gives Congress much concern that it happened & that Govr Trumble was so sensibly Affected with it. They have desired the President to excuse the matter to him. I can give the strongest assurance that there is no Govr. or President on the Continent who has the Esteem of Congress equal to Govr Trumbull. He stands with them in the highest point of light as does the late Commissy. Genll. & Pay master Genll in the Northern department. There has Indeed been in time past sometimes & unhappy party or faction in Congress arising from two or three persons. Some of Govr Trumbull family have it is true had their rubbers, but in Genll highly Valued & Esteemed in whatever department they have Acted. They have now & then had a Squib from Individuals but I think they lay too great Stress upon them. There is now no party in Congress. Mr. Trumbull had the Vote of every Individual in Congress in his Appointment to the board of War, they greatly regret his Non attendance. Nothing but his Indisposition excuses him in the opinion of his best Friends, hope he may yet come forward. He seems hurt that he had not receivd an Answer to his letter wrote to Congress exculpating himself from the false & Injurious Aspersions which had been cast upon him that he had obstructed the progress & success in the Commis[saria]te since the New plan was adopted. This might be & doubtless was from some Individuals Vexed, Chagrind and dissapointed that their New plan had succeeded not better that all the ill Consequences which had been foretold & more had come to pass. They would therefore attribute the misfortune to every thing & every person, rather than have their great skill & Wisdome Impeachd. It was the Natural effect of disapointed Malice but is this to be minded or regarded When the safety of our Country comes into question—by no means. Congress being entirely satisfied, & as they had never accused him, it has not been usual to give an Answer. Congress see their error and are sufficiently Mortified therein; they are now willing to resume the old plan or any they can be advised to Effect the great purpose of Supplies to alter & Change men & measures & to do any thing & every thing to that end, they have been Advised to Apply to you in their difficulties as they are assured Mr. Trumbull will never again engage in that department. They have wrote you requesting your Attendance at this place on matters of Importance.[1] I hope you will not fail to attend & that you will bring Mr. Trumbull along with you. A long ride may be most beneficial to his health. If every thing should not be agreable when you come hear I dare say you will be generously paid for your expences & Trouble. Express waiting, excuse inacuraces. My respects to all Friends & am, with sincere Esteem, Yr Hle Servt, Elipht Dyer

RC (PHi).

[1] Wadsworth had been recommended for commissary general of purchases by the Committee at Camp in their January 29 letter to Henry Laurens and on February 9 Laurens had written the following note to Wadsworth: "It is the request of Congress that you will with all possible expedition repair to this place & attend the House on business of Importance & for Public service. All your expences on this occasion will be reimbursed by Congress." PCC, item 13, fol. 180.

On March 30 Dyer was appointed to a committee to confer with Wadsworth and on April 9 Congress appointed Wadsworth the commissary general of purchases. JCC, 10:141, 293, 327–28. See also Dyer to Wadsworth, March 10; and Abraham Clark to Wadsworth, March 29, 1778.

Cornelius Harnett to Richard Caswell

Dear Sir York Town Pensylvania Feby. 10. 1778

I had it not in my power to send you the Pay & Rations of a Major General on the Continental Establishment until yesterday tho' I applied to Our Secry. Mr. Thompson, soon after receiving Your Excellencys favour to Mr. Penn & myself;[1] indeed I have been Confined to my room for these 10 days past by a fit of the Gout, which has prevented my Attendance on Congress much against my Inclination.

Our Grand Army remain in Winter Quarters Hutted at Valey Forge, nothing interesting has lately happen'd in that Qr. Congress are not yet determined to Call for the reinforcement Offerd by No. Carolina, should such an event take place, Your Excellency may be assured of receiving the earliest Notice possible.

I take the Liberty to Inclose the last Paper, which Contains very little except the King's Speech to Parliament. I have nothing particular to mention having written to you a few days ago. I am with the Greatest respect, Your Excellencys Most Obedt & very huml Servt,

Cornl. Harnett

[*P.S.*] I beg leave to present my most respectful Compts. to the Council.

Pay of a Major Genl.—166 Dol. per mo & 15 Rations.

His Aid de Camp 50 Dol. per mo. with rank of Major—no Rations.

His Secry.—50 Dol. per mo.

RC (CSmH). Addressed: "His Excellency Richard Caswell Esquire Governor & Commander in Chief of the State of North Carolina." Endorsed: "Recvd. the 17 March 1778."

[1] Governor Caswell had written a letter to Harnett and John Penn on January 11, 1778, in which he mentioned having also written one to them on December 27, 1777. It is not clear if Harnett is referring to the January letter, which is in *N.C. State Records*, 13:7–8, or the December letter, which has not been found.

Cornelius Harnett to William Wilkinson

Dear Sir	York Town Pensylvania Feb. 10. 1778

I wrote you about a fortnight or perhaps a week ago and have nothing new at present to Communicate. The Army still remain in Winter Quarters at Valey Forge well Hutted, I hear their houses or Hutts are very warm & Comfortable.

I send you the last Paper Containing the Kings Speech &c. Jackey is not yet sent to me. The Weather has been very bad, the Snow now very thick upon the Ground, as soon as this weather Clears up, I expect to have him with me agreeable to Mr. Mitchels promise.

What has been done about Fortifying Cape Fear River? I fear nothing at all. Mr. Hooper & Mr. Maclain are unpardonable in not writing to me. I have been laid up with the Gout for a week Past. I shall write you more at large in my next. I wish you would send on your Bills, not that I shall have Occasion to use them, since Our Assembly have made so generous an allowance to their Delegates. But remember I warn you that Delays are dangerous.

I am, Dr Sir, Your real friend & Ob Servt.	Cornl. Harnett

[*P.S.*] I write Mr Quince by this Post.[1]

RC (NcU).

[1] Not found.

Henry Laurens to Patrick Henry

Sir,   10th Febry 1777 [*i.e.* 1778]
My last to your Excellency was dated the 3d Inst. & conveyed by
the opportunity of Monsr. Lanuville.[1]

My present duty is to forward two Acts of Congress which will
accompany this.

of the 3d Inst. for obliging all persons holding Commissions or
appointments under Congress to qualify themselves by taking & subscribing to certain Oaths therein prescribed, which Your Excellency
will be pleased to lay before the Legislature & also to cause the said
Act to be made public throughout the State of Virginia.

of the 9th Inst. for restraining Malconduct in Continental Officers
Civil & Military & for correcting the abuse of Supernumeraries in the
Civil Line & also recommending to the Legislatures of the several
States to enact Laws for the most speedy & effectual recovery of debts
due to the United States of America.[2]

I likewise send in a seperate Packet by the present Messenger fifty
blank Commissions for private Ships of War with the same number
of Instructions & Bonds at the request of Colo. Fr. Lee the Bonds
when executed to be transmitted to Congress. I have the honour to
be &ca.

LB (DNA: PCC, item 13).
    [1] See Laurens to James Duane, February 3, 1778, note 2.
    [2] Laurens also transmitted copies of these February 3 and 9 resolves on oaths and
Continental officers with brief letters that he wrote this day to the governors of
Maryland, North Carolina, South Carolina, and Georgia. PCC, item 13, fols.
182–85. Furthermore, he transmitted copies of the February 9 resolve on Continen-
tal officers alone with brief letters that he wrote this day to the Massachusetts
Council, the governors of Rhode Island and New Jersey, and the presidents of
New Hampshire and Delaware, and also with a letter he wrote to Washington on
February 13. Ibid., fols. 186–88.

Henry Laurens to Thomas Mifflin

Sir,   York Town 10th February 1778
I beg pardon for having so long detained the Inclosed Act of Congress of 30th January past, *requiring immediately an Account of all
public expenditures by the Quarter Master general.*[1] This delay arose
from my expectation of your speedy return to York.

I am With very great Respect, Sir, Your most obedient servant,
                        Henry Laurens, President of Congress.

RC (NNPM).
    [1] See *JCC*, 10:102–3. For a detailed account of the extraordinarily complicated
business of settling General Mifflin's accounts as quartermaster general, which was

not finished until 1780, see Kenneth R. Rossman, *Thomas Mifflin and the Politics of the American Revolution* (Chapel Hill: University of North Carolina Press, 1952), chap. 12.

Henry Laurens to Josiah Smith, Jr.

Sir,[1]   10th Febry 1778.
    I beg leave to refer you to the Inclosed Act of Congress of the 3d Inst. by which you are approved of to be an Attorney in South Carolina for the United States of America.[2] In obedience to the said Act I have executed a Letter of Attorney which will be transmitted by the Commercial Committee to Mr. Abraham Livingston.[3] I am with great respect &ca.

LB (DNA: PCC, item 13).
    [1] Josiah Smith, Jr. (1731–1826), was a Charleston, S.C., merchant. Henry Laurens, *The Papers of Henry Laurens*, ed. Philip M. Hamer et al. (Columbia: University of South Carolina Press, 1968–), 2:213n.9.
    [2] Acting on a recommendation from the Committee of Commerce, Congress on February 3 appointed Smith and Nathaniel Russell "attornies for recovering all commercial debts due to the United States of America, and for claiming the continental share of all prizes libelled in the admiralty court in the State of South Carolina." *JCC*, 10:114. Laurens notified Russell—who also lived in Charleston—of his appointment in a letter dated the 10th that is nearly identical to this letter to Smith. PCC, item 13, fol. 182.
    [3] No "Letter of Attorney," or letter from the Committee of Commerce to Abraham Livingston, has been found.

Henry Laurens to Thomas Wharton

Sir,   10th Febry 1778.
    I wrote to your Excellency the 8th Inst. by Messenger Barry.[1]
    Under this Cover your Excellency will receive an Act of Congress for restraining & preventing Malconduct in Continental Officers Civil & Military & for correcting the abuse of Supernumeraries in the Civil Line.
    Also an Act of the same date recommending to the Legislatures of the several States to Enact Laws for the most speedy & effectual recovery of debts due to the United States of America.[2]
    I have the honour to be with great Regard &ca.

LB (DNA: PCC, item 13).
    [1] See Laurens to Nicholas Cooke, February 9, 1778, note 2.
    [2] See *JCC*, 10:139–41. Laurens also transmitted copies of these February 9 resolves on Continental officers and debts with brief letters that he wrote on February 13 to Govs. George Clinton of New York and Jonathan Trumbull of Connecticut. PCC, item 13, fol. 189.

James Lovell to John Adams

My dear Sir   Feb 10th [1778]

The week after Mr. C—— was appointed secretary, I saw the P.S. of a letter to Mr. S.A. in which he is said to be a very unworthy person, but he has so good a Character in the estimation of Congress and from Maryland Gentlemen, that I did not think proper to move for a power of Suspension to be given to the Commissioners, as I find it is the opinion of some here that the secretary should be independent.[1]

I hope you will either give me your opinion before you go or write very early upon having conversed with Dr Fr. & Mr. L.[2]

I did not know whether the Commercial Committee had forwarded to you the Resolve of yesterday, therefore I send it on the other page.[3] We are most horridly spunged by Mr Le Balme and others who resigning their Commissions apply in forma pauperis or on pretences of a variety of kinds. I do not think it will do to make the Resolve hinted at by Dr. F to me "that the Commissrs. should be directed not to give even a letter of civil Introduction to any Foreigner," but such letters are pleaded as a sort of implied Convention. Avoid them. Affectionately Yours,   J L

RC (MHi).

[1] Lovell had copied part of Arthur Lee's July 31, 1777, letter to Samuel Adams and had sent it to Arthur's brother Richard Henry. See Lovell to Richard Henry Lee, December 18, 1777. William Carmichael, who had been acting as an assistant to Silas Deane, left France in February 1778 without acting under his official appointment as secretary to the American commissioners in France. He later served in Congress during 1778 and 1779. Arthur Lee included similar warnings in an October 4, 1777, letter to Richard Henry Lee, which is in Richard H. Lee, *Life of Arthur Lee, LL.D.*, 2 vols. (Boston: Wells and Lilly, 1829), 2:116, and also in a December 18, 1777, letter to Samuel Adams, which is in the Adams Papers, NN.

For further information on Carmichael's activities in Europe before his return to America in 1778, see Floyd B. Streeter, "The Diplomatic Career of William Carmichael," *Maryland Historical Magazine* 8 (June 1913): 119–40; and Harry Ammon, ed., "Letters of William Carmichael to John Cadwalader, 1777," ibid. 44 (March 1949): 1–17.

[2] That is, Benjamin Franklin and Arthur Lee.

[3] Lovell enclosed a copy of the resolve authorizing the American commissioners to appoint commercial agents in Europe. *JCC*, 10:139.

Thomas McKean to Sarah McKean

My dear Sally,   York Febry. 10th. 1778.

I received your favor by Sam, and am obliged to you for your attention. There are three shirts & stocks, a cap &c. returned by him. The horses I shall want on Friday night the 27th instant, as I purpose

to make you a visit the next day, & to return on the Tuesday following.[1] You will receive 4 ounces of brown thread and one of white,
price 15/, which is all I can get at present; also some medicines for
worms for Betsey, together with directions.

A Baron Steuben, who was Aid de Camp, Quarter Master General,
& a Lieutent. General to the King of Prussia, is now here, and will
enter into our service. General Burgoyne & his army are to be detained
until his Convention is ratified by the court of Great Britain. Colo.
Coats, Lieutenant of Philadelphia county, & Mr. Gyles, Aid de camp
to General Sinclair, are taken prisoners by the British light horse at
Germantown. Doctor Franklin is said to be assassinated in his bed in
a village called Pacy, abt. four miles from Paris; tho' this account
contains all the particular circumstances attending this horrid deed, I
doubt abt. the truth of it. Our affairs seem prosperous. By the King
of G.Bs. speech, which I have sent you in the last paper, he appears
to be frightened.

Let me hear from you as often as opportunities offer, and believe
that I am, my dear Sally, Your affectionate,   Tho M:Kean

RC (PHi).
[1] McKean had presented his credentials and resumed his seat in Congress on
January 30, 1778. *JCC*, 10:100. This letter to his wife is the only contemporary
evidence that has been found to indicate that McKean may have made a brief trip
to Delaware February 28–March 3, 1778.

Committee at Camp to Henry Laurens

Sir,   Moor Hall 11th Feby. 1778.[1]
We lately did ourselves the Honor to write to you upon the State
of the Commissary's Department; since which the Marquis De la
Fayette hath favored us with a Visit on his Way to the Northern
Army. Altho it may be Presumption in your Committee to give their
Sentiments upon a Subject of so great Magnitude, especially after it
hath been stamped with your Concurrence, yet Sir the deep Concern
which, in common with other Americans we cannot but feel upon
every Occasion of public Importance, forbids us to be silent.[2]

It is not unknown to us how much you wish to prompt our Armies
to a Spirit of Enterprize, nor have we overlooked the Influence of
such a Spirit upon the Complection of all our Affairs. We feel and
acknowlege that Caution may at Times wear the Appearance of
Timidity; especially with the ignorant or the invidious Part of mankind. But Enterprize without the constant Eye of Prudence is at
all Times hazardous, and even the most brilliant Successes frequently
teem with Destruction. Let us then be permitted to examine the

Canada Expedition in two distinct Points of View; first in itself, secondly in its Connection with other Transactions.

As to the first. It cannot be disputed that it is of Importance to give an Alarm to the Enemy in that Quarter, since it may tend to repress the hostile Intentions of the Savages. If an Incursion should be attended with the happy Consequence of destroying those Vessels which it hath cost them so much to build, and of seizing and destroying the Post of St John's, it would cast a Lustre upon our arms in the Eyes of Europe, and perhaps distract the Attention and divide the Force of our Enemies during the Course of the ensuing Campaign. And on the other Hand if a *slight* Incursion should fail of Success, our intestine Enemies would have little Cause of Exultation. But to carry on this Enterprize upon a large Scale demands a very serious Attention; for then it is no longer one of those Minutia wherein a false Step may be easily remedied, it may involve the most serious Consequences. If successful, so far as to gain Montreal and rouse the Canadians, have we Money to prosecute the War in that Country? A Country already drained during three Campaigns, and where the Abundance of Specie hath considerably reduced it's Value. Canada never produced Flesh sufficient to feed an Army at any Time, much less at present; so that of Necessity it would require an increased Number of Men, and a vast Increase of Expence, to send thither that single Article even if we had it in the utmost Abundance. If after our Success the Enemy should send thither a greater Force than they have at present, would it be consistent with the Ties of Honor a second Time to abandon those unhappy People whose zeal may have prompted them to enlist under our Banners or whose Credulity may have tempted them to entrust their Property to our Promises. If we have too much Regard to the Sanctity of public Faith to desert them, where are the Resources by which we are to maintain a large Army for their Protection? And if we could draw those Resources from the very Lap of Abundance, where are the Men to compose such an Army? This Sir would be our Situation should Success attend the Expedition.

Let us then turn our Eyes to the other Side of the Question, and see what would be the Result, if a considerable Expedition should fail. It would produce Desertion among the Troops particularly the Canadians many of which taken at Bennington have since enlisted, perhaps with a remote View of returning to their Families. It would produce Disgrace to our Arms, and all its Consequences upon our Money, upon our People, upon our Friends in Europe, and upon the Enemies we have in our own Bowels. But above all, our Weakness fairly manifested would draw on an Indian War in all its Horrors, dissipating the Force of our frontier Settlements and whelming them in Blood. These are the certain Consequences of a Defeat. And on what do we build our Hopes of Victory? Have not Montgomery and

Burgoyne demonstrated the Imprudence of distant Expeditions across
an inhospitable Wilderness where there is but one Road by which to
advance or retire? Is not the very Season against us? Our Troops are
unprovided against it's Rigors and when it abates which will probably happen by the Time they have crossed the Lake, then they will
be deprived of the Means of accomplishing a Retreat. To these Considerations let us add that those Troops cannot be fed. The Provisions
are (it is said) at Albany, and this may be true, but they cannot be
transported in any great Quantity. The Country from Albany to
Montreal is already drained of Forage, very small Quantities of which
were ever produced in it. To subsist two thousand Men with the
several Retainers and Followers of an Army will require at least four
Tons of Provisions per Day. Forty times this Quantity must be
transported two hundred Miles. That alone will employ about four
hundred Horses during Forty Days and the Forage for them must be
carried above fifty Miles and that across Mountains being only to be
had upon the Grants, if there. We will not pursue this Consideration
but cast one View upon the Business as connected with other Affairs.

And first the want of Arms for our Soldiers next Campaign deserves a serious Notice, for Neglect in those whose Business it was to
take Care of such as have been from Time to Time put in the Hands
of the Militia, or the Impracticability of preventing Abuses even with
the utmost Attention, or both, have so exhausted the continental
Magazines that we shall not have enough by a third at least. So that
every Musket carried into Canada will be in Effect the Loss of a Man
to the main Army; notwithstanding which we are informed that the
arms now at Albany are to be sent thither for the Purpose of arming
the Canadian Militia. Secondly the Article of Provisions is among
those which hath made the most serious Impression upon us. In a
former Letter on that Subject we have assigned the Grounds of our
Conviction, that Recourse must be had to the Eastern States for
Supplies of Flesh, and that even with their Assistance and with all
the Magazines we may now have we shall have the utmost Difficulty
to subsist this Army if it should be of sufficient Strength to operate
successfully against General Howe.

But should the Enemy gain Possession of Hudson's River next
Spring (and if the greatest Exertions are not made to prevent them
they certainly will) these Eastern Supplies would be quite cut off, and
then to subsist an Army in Pensilvania would be impracticable; besides which the Army in Canada tho crowned with Laurels must in
such Case undoubtedly starve. On the other Hand, if these Veterans
instead of being sent against Montreal were stationed at Fish Kill in
addition to the Force now there, they might perhaps keep open that
Communication. Or if their Services should not be necessary at that
Post, they would certainly be an essential Reinforcement to the main

Army, by which it is expected that the capital Efforts of the Enemy will be defeated. And should General Howes Force in Philadelphia be destroyed all their lesser Posts would inevitably fall. But should he be able to ravage the middle States, and drive our army before him (which from the want either of Men, Arms or Provisions may too easily happen) the great Depreciation of our Money (an Evil which first took Rise in a Canadian Expedition) might effectually ruin every Plan either of Offence or Defence during the next Campaign, and so lower our Reputation in the Eyes of Europe that none could be found either to trust or assist us.

We pray Sir that Congress will excuse our Freedom upon this Occasion. Not perhaps so well informed as they are, it is possible that our Opinion may be ill founded; but you will pardon us when we add that it is possible it may not.

We have the Honor to be with the greatest Respect, Sir, Your most obedient and humble Servants,   Fra. Dana by Order

RC (DNA: PCC, item 78). Written by Gouverneur Morris and signed by Francis Dana. Endorsed by Charles Thomson: "Letter from Comee. at Camp Moore Hall 11 Feby 1778 read 16. respecting the irruption into Canada. referred to the board of war, who are directed to report specially thereon & to lay before Congress a copy of the·orders given to the officer."

[1] Morris apparently began composing this letter on February 7, because his draft of it—which is located in PCC, item 33, fols. 121–24—contains references to events of "Yesterday" and "this morning" that occurred on February 6 and 7. "We ⟨Yesterday⟩ lately did ourselves the honor," Morris began, "to write you upon the State of the Commissary's Department, ⟨This Morning⟩ since which the Marquis de la Fayette hath favored us with a Visit." According to the committee's minutes of proceedings, they wrote to President Laurens concerning the commissary department on February 6 and met with Lafayette on the seventh.

[2] The committee's letter was referred to the Board of War on February 16, which returned the problem of the Canadian expedition to Congress on February 23. At that time Congress appointed a committee to "collect the best information they can, relative to the irruption into Canada." The next day Lafayette was cautioned against exposing his troops to hazards due to lack of provisions and supplies, and on March 2 Congress directed Lafayette to "suspend for the present the intended irruption" because it was "not only hazardous" but "imprudent." See JCC, 10:172, 190–91, 193–94, 196, 216–17, 253.

Committee at Camp to George Washington

Sir   Moore Hall Feby. 11th. 1778.

The travelling is so bad that we wish you wou'd not attempt to meet us while it continues. We shall employ ourselves in that part of our business which can be done without your personal attendance.

We have been considering General Howe's letter which you was pleased to lay before us yesterday, and seem agreed and confirmed in the opinion that he hath some latent meaning in those parts of it

In CONGRESS,

FEBRUARY 11, 1778.

RESOLVED,

THAT there shall be one Commissary-General of military stores; whose business it shall be to receive and deliver all arms, ammunition and accoutrements of every species and denomination——to provide and contract for all such articles as may be wanted in this department, according to the directions he shall receive from the Board of War and Ordnance——to receive and collect returns from all the different States, where there are any Continental arms and stores; draw them into one general return, and on the first day of every month, deliver one to the Board of War and Ordnance:

In case of vacancy occasioned by death, resignation or otherwise, of any of the Commissaries, Commissary's, Deputies or Conductors, which may happen in any department near to where the Commissary-General may be, he shall have permission to fill such vacancy pro tempore, until it shall be confirmed or disapproved by Congress:

All monies to be drawn on account of military stores, to be by application of the Commissary-General, or his Deputies, to the Board of War and Ordnance; and all monies so drawn, to be accounted for by him, once in every six months, to the Board of Treasury, or to such Auditors or Commissioners, as the said Board shall direct.

All Commissaries, Deputy-Commissaries or Conductors, who may have money advanced them by the Commissary-General, for the use of their several departments, to keep regular accounts, and produce vouchers and receipts for the sums paid, and account for the same to the Commissary-General once every month, or as often as called for:

All Continental Armourers, shall be under the direction of the Board of War and Ordnance, and of the Commissary-General of military stores; the Armourers to receive from the said Commissary all arms to be repaired, make returns of the state of repairs when demanded, and deliver the arms when repaired, into his store: The principal Armourer or Armourers, at each and every Armoury to be accountable for all such arms, as he or they shall receive, until they are repaired and delivered to the Commissary-General, his Deputies or Assistants; and the said Commissary-General shall see that every method is taken by the Armourers, to hasten the repairs of the arms: the principal Armourers to receive money from the Commissary-General for the contingent expences of their departments, and the Commissary-General shall produce their accounts and vouchers at the adjustment of his accounts:

That there be as many Deputies, Assistants, Commissaries, Deputy-Commissaries, Conductors and Clerks, as the exigency of the service shall require, to be appointed by the Board of War and Ordnance; and the said Board are from time to time to report all such appointments to Congress:

That the pay of officers in the department of the Commissary-General of military stores be as follows;

Commissary-General	100 Dollars per month and 6 rations a day.	
Deputy-Commissary-General, of which there shall be one in each military division of the States	75 ditto	5 ditto
Commissaries each	60 ditto	4 ditto
Deputy-Commissary each	50 ditto	3 ditto
Conductors each	40 ditto	2 ditto
Clerks each	40 ditto	2 ditto

The Commissary-General shall be allowed forage for two horses; his Deputies, Assistants, Commissaries and Conductors, to be allowed forage for one horse each, and the Captains of the Artillery Artificers respectively, when duty requires their travelling to collect materials &c. forage for an horse.

... for the future, ... be annexed to ... Office ... in this department, except they belong to the regiment Artillery Artificers, are to take place as Officers of that corps; the pay also, which they receive as Officers in that regiment, to be included in the pay herein settled for the Officers of the Commissary-General department:

That a return be made to the Board of War and Ordnance, once every month, of all Officers employed in the civil branch of ordnance and military stores:

All Commissaries, Deputy-Commissaries, Conductors and Clerks; who shall have the separate charge of any stores, are on the first day of every month to make out an exact return of all cannon and military stores, of every species and denomination, one copy whereof they shall transmit to the Commissary-General, who is to put then into one general return as heretofore directed, and one other copy thereof, the said Commissaries, Deputy-Commissaries, Conductors or Clerks are to send to the Board of War and Ordnance:

All the Artillery Artificers that are or may be employed at any Armories, Laboratories, Founderies or Military Magazines (those employed with the army in the field excepted) shall be under the immediate direction, and subject the orders and command of the Commissary-General, or the Officer directed by him to take the charge of the same:

The Quarter-Master-General, his Deputies and Assistants, shall give the Commissary-General, every assistance & teams for the removal of public stores, and in case there be no Quarter-Master in the department or place, from whence the stores are to be removed, the Commissary-General shall have power to procure teams in the way and manner that will best promote the public service:

All Officers, Artificers and others, in the ordnance and military department shall be governed by the rules and articles of war in the same manner, as other Officers in the Artillery of the United States:

The Commissary-General shall give such forms or returns, and instructions to his Deputies, Assistant-Commissaries, Conductors, &c. as the service and situation of their department shall require. And all Officers in this department are to attend to such orders and instructions as they shall receive from time to time from the Board of War and Ordnance, or the Commissary-General:

All regulations incidental to the department, and not enlarging the powers and authorities here given, shall be settled and made by the Board of War and Ordnance:

The Board of War and Ordnance shall transmit from time to time, as the service shall render necessary, transcripts of all returns received from the Commissary-General of military stores, and also accounts of all ordnance and stores under their care, or belonging to the United States, and of the places where the same are deposited, to the Commander in Chief of the armies of the United States, in order that he may make such requisitions of supplies for the army under his immediate command, or for the separate departments, as he shall think proper, and give such advice and directions as to the disposition of them, as circumstances may from time to time require:

The Commanding Officer of Artillery for the time being in the grand army, with the chief Engineer, Commissary of Artillery, and eldest Colonel of Artillery in camp, or such of them as are at present with the army, shall be a subordinate Board of Ordnance, under the direction of the Commander in Chief or the Board of War and Ordnance, for transacting all business of the ordnance department necessary to be done in the field, and to have the care of all ordnance and stores at camp, and in case of sudden exigency, the Commissary-General of military stores shall be obliged to obey their directions, as to any supplies wanted by the army out of the stores not in camp; and the said Board shall correspond with, and report their proceedings to the Board of War and Ordnance, from whom they are to receive any necessary assistance.

Resolved, That the pay of Col. Benjamin Flower's corps of Artillery Artificers shall be for all those, who engage to serve the United States as such for three years or during the war, Twenty Dollars a month, besides the same bounty, cloathing, and every other benefit allowed by Congress to the Continental Artillery; the Officers the same pay as others of equal rank in the Continental Artillery; and that Colonel Flower augment the four companies ordered to be raised in January last, add other companies to the said regiment, and if necessary, encrease the pay of Officers and men in the same, agreeable to such orders as have been given for that purpose, by General Washington, and that he be required forthwith to transmit a copy of such orders to Congress:

That if the exigency of the service makes it necessary to employ, at any time or place more Artificers, than the Commissary may have inlisted or can enlist, then he, his Deputies, or Assistants, may engage them for the time of such necessity, on the most reasonable terms possible, with the approbation of the Board of War and Ordnance.

Extract from the Minutes,

CHARLES THOMSON, *Secretary.*

Commissary Reforms Broadside, February 11, 1778

which were then pointed out. We flatter ourselves you will not take it amiss that we express to you our sentiments upon the proposition of a general exchange made at this time, by General Howe.[1] We think he wou'd not do this, but for very cogent reasons, and altho we are not able to conjecture what they are with any very strong probability: yet this is clear that he confines his proposed exchange to Officers and Soldiers, and is totally silent as to Citizens. As the latter were expressly comprehended in the original Cartel proposed by himself, and agreed upon between you; and as he has been called upon by Congress, if not by yourself, to explain certain passages in his former letter which you laid before Congress, and explictly to declare in what light he held the faithful Citizens of these States, who by the fortune of war, or other accidents had fallen, or shou'd fall under his power, yet he has never deemed proper as we can learn, to make any reply at all, much less a full and satisfactory answer on that subject. We cannot but think that he affects to consider every such Citizen as a rebel unexchangeable; and answerable to the Laws of England, and therefore treats them, if possible, with more rigour and cruelty than those whom he is pleased to say, properly fall under the denomination of prisoners of war. Impressed with the manifest injustice of such apprehensions which if well grounded, we deem a breach of his faith plighted in the Cartel, we cannot but think the present a happy opportunity of drawing forth from General Howe the most explicit declarations on a subject of so great importance to every mere Citizen of these States, and making a renewal of the Cartel, the sine qua non of an exchange.

We are Sir, with much esteem & respect, your obedient humble Servants, Fra Dana by Order

RC (DLC). Written and signed by Francis Dana.

[1] General Washington had undoubtedly given the committee a copy of William Howe's February 5, 1778, letter, which is in the Washington Papers, DLC. Although consideration of a general exchange of prisoners continued for several months, the tentative plan of Generals Washington and Howe finally collapsed under the weight of congressional opposition and British unwillingness to conclude an official agreement with the Americans. See Henry Laurens to Washington, March 15, 1778, note 1.

According to Elias Boudinot, who resigned as commissary general of prisoners on April 17, 1778, after the cartel negotiations collapsed, the committee decided after meeting with Washington and his staff to oppose the proposed cartel. Many years later Boudinot made the following observation on the committee's opposition to the cartel: "The Committee of Congress soon discovered their Sentiments, agt an Exchange, and urged it as the Opinion of Congress—That the settling this Cartel should be merely ostensible for the purpose of satisfying the Army and throwing the blame on the British, but true policy required us to avoid an Exchange of Prisoners just at the opening of the Campaign. We absolutely refused to undertake the Business on these principles—if we went, we were determind to make the best Cartel we could for the liberation of our Prisoners—That we would not be made Instruments in so dishonorable a measure. Genl. Washington also resented it, and said his Troops looked up to him as their protector, and that he would not suffer an opportunity to be lost of liberating every Soldier who was then in Captivity let the Consequence be what it might. The Committee were much disgusted and soon left the Army, (where they gave much dissatisfaction) and returned to Congress." J. J. Boudinot, ed., *The Life, Public Services, Addresses and Letters of Elias Boudinot, LL.D., President of the Continental Congress,* 2 vols. (Boston: Houghton, Mifflin and Co., 1896), 1:75. See also *JCC,* 10:197–98, 266–68, 294–95, 367, 369–71.

Henry Laurens to Baron de Kalb

Dear General,   11th Febry 1778.

I have before me the several favours which you have honoured me with under the 1st & 7th Inst. The former importing your sentiments upon the propriety of suspending the embarkation of Lieutt. General Burgoyne & his Troops affords me singular satisfaction.[1] Convention's & suspension's are new articles in the American War & perhaps there is not an Instance in History of a General's having so completely betrayed himself the Dupe of his own policy. Mr. Burgoyne's duplicity will be quoted as a precedent by future Writers, while the resentment of Congress will be recorded as an example of Sound policy. In these Ideas & under a consciousness of having passed my own Vote from conviction of the rectitude of the measure, I rest content within & assured that Congress will be vindicated in every disinterested Court in Europe.

I shall have the pleasure to deliver to morrow Morning a Commission of Lieutt. Colonel to the Chevalier Dubuysson,[2] whose impetuosity had nearly rendered his journey fruitless, a hint from you on this head without intimating the notice I have taken, may be of particular service to a Young Gentleman by leading him to reflect that hurry & urgency, which may be extremely necessary in a quick March, are exceedingly disgusting to a deliberative body of Representatives particularly so, when the application is for Grace & favor. Congress had not promised Monsr. Dubuyson the present Rank until he should be returning to France. Had I been as rapid in presenting your Letter as the young Gentleman was vehement in his desires, he would have returned a Major owing to his Minor judgment.

I wish you Dear General a good Campaign, that you may Succeed in the intended enterprize, & return with Glory.[3] Believe me to with very great Esteem & Regard.

LB (ScHi).

[1] For a discussion of the suspension of the Saratoga Convention by Congress, see Laurens to William Heath, December 27, 1777, note 1.

[2] This day Congress granted this rank to the chevalier Dubuysson, subject to the stipulation that he only command Canadian troops raised in Canada. *JCC,* 10:142.

³ Kalb was second in command of the soon to be aborted Canadian expedition that had been placed under Lafayette's command. See Laurens to Lafayette, January 22, note 2; and Gouverneur Morris to Laurens, January 26, 1778.

Committee at Camp to Henry Laurens

Sir   Camp near the Valley Forge Feb 12. 1778

We had flattered ourselves that before this Time the Pleasure of Congress would be made known to us respecting the Qr. Masters Department.[1] We fear our Letter upon this Subject has miscarried, or the Consideration of it yielded to the Pressure of other Business. You will therefore pardon us, Sir, when we again sollicit your Attention to it as an Object of the last Importance, on which not only the future Success of your Arms but the present Existence of your Army immediately depends. The Influence of this Office is so diffusive thro every Part of your military System, that neither the Wisdom of Arrangement, the Spirit of Enterprize, or favourable Opportunity will be of any Avail, if this great Wheel in the Machine stops or moves heavily. We find ourselves embarassed in entering upon this Subject, least a bare Recital of Facts should carry an Imputation (which we do not intend) on those Gentlemen who have lately conducted it. We are sensible great & just Allowances are to be made for the Peculiarity of their Situation, & we are perhaps not fully acquainted with all their Difficulties. It is our Duty Sir to inform you, it is not our Intention to censure, & be assured nothing but a Sense of the Obligations we are under to postpone all other Considerations to the publick Safety could induce us to perform this unpleasing Task. We find Sir, the Property of the Continent dispersed over the whole Country. Not an Encampment, Route of the Army, or considerable Road but abounds with Waggons left to the Mercy of the Weather, & the Will of the Inhabitants. Large Quantities of entrenching Tools have in like Manner been left in various Hands under no other Security that we can learn, than the Honesty of those who have them in Possession. Not less than 3000 Spades, & Shovels, & the like Number of Tomahawks have been lately discovered & collected in the Vicinity of the Camp, by an Order from one of the General Officers. In the same Way a Quantity of Tents, & Tent Cloth after having lain the whole Summer unnoticed in a Farmers Barn, & unknown to the Officers of the Department, was lately discovered & brought to Camp by a special Order from the General. From these Instances we presume there may be many other Stores yet unknown, & uncollected, which require immediate Care & Attention.

When in Compliance with the Expectations of Congress, & the Wishes of the Country, the Army was thrown into Huts instead of retiring to more distant & convenient Quarters, the Troops justly expected every Comfort which the surrounding Country could afford; among these a provident Care in the Article of Straw would probably have saved the Lives of many of your brave Soldiers, who have now paid the great Debt of Nature. Unprovided with this, or Materials to raise them from the cold & wet Earth, Sickness and Mortality have spread thro' their Quarters, in an astonishing Degree. Notwithstanding the Diligence of the Physicians & Surgeons of whom we hear no Complaint, the sick & dead List has increased one third on the last weekly Return, which was one third greater than the Week preceding, & from the present inclement Weather will probably increase in a much greater Proportion. Nothing Sir can equal their Sufferings except the Patience & Fortitude with which the faithful Part of your Army endure them. Those of a different Character desert in considerable Numbers. We must also observe that a Number of the Troops have now been some Time prepared for Inoculation, but the Operation must be delayed for Want of this & other Necessaries, within the Providence of this Department. We need not point out the fatal Consequences of this delay in forming a new Army, or the Preservation of this. Almost every Day furnishes Instances of the Small Pox in the natural Way. Hitherto such Vigilance & Care has been used, that the Contagion has not spread, but surely it is highly incumbent upon us, if possible, to annihilate the Danger. We need not point out the Effect this Circumstance will have upon the new & draughted Troops if not carefully guarded, they are too obvious to need Enumeration. In Conference with the Forage Master on this Subject (which tho in Appearance trivial is really important) he acquaints us that tho out of his Line, he would have procured it if Waggons could have been furnished him for that Purpose.

The Want of Horses & Waggons for the ordinary, as well as extraordinary Occasions of the Army presses upon us if possible with equal Force. Almost every Species of Camp Transportation is now performed by the Men, who without a Murmur patiently yoke themselves to little Carriages of their own making, or load their Wood & Provisions on their Backs. Should the Enemy encouraged by the growing Weakness of your Troops, be led to make a successful Impression on your Camp, your Artillery would now undoubtedly fall into their Hands for Want of Horses to remove it. But these are smaller and tolerable Evils, when compared with the imminent Danger of your Troops perishing with Famine, or dispersing in Search of food. The Commissaries in Addition to their Supplies of live Cattle, which are precarious, have procured a Quantity of Pork in New Jersey, of which by a Failure of Waggons not one Barrel has reach'd the Camp, tho Orders were given for that Purpose as early as the 4th Jany. In yesterdays Conference with the General he informed us, that some

Brigades had been four Days without Meat & that even the common Soldiers had been at his Quarters to make known their Wants. At present Sir there is not one Gentleman of any Rank in this Department tho the Duties of the office require a constant & unremitted Attention.

In whatever View therefore this Object presents itself, we trust you will discover that the most essential Interests are connected with it. The Season of Preparation for next Campaign is passing swiftly away—be assured, Sir, that its Operation will be ineffectual either for Offence or Protection, if an Arrangement is not immediately made, & the most vigorous Exertions used to procure the necessary Supplies. Permit us to say, that a Moments Time should not be lost in placing a Man of approved Abilities & extensive Capacity at the Head of the Department who will restore it to some degree of Regularity & Order, whose provident Care will immediately relieve the present Wants of the Army & extend itself to those who must be satisfied before we can expect Vigorus Enterprize or Success.

When your Committee reflect upon the increased Difficulties of procuring Waggons, Horses, Tents, & the numerous Train of Articles dependent on this Office, without which your Army cannot even move, They feel the greatest Anxiety least the utmost Skill, Diligence, & Address will prove insufficient to satisfy the growing Demands. All other Considerations vanish before this Object and we most earnestly wish Congress may be impress'd in a proper Degree with its Necessity & Importance.

A Report has reach'd us that Col Lutterlogh is a Candidate for the Office of Quarter Master General. We have therefore been led to make some Inquiry into his Character & Conduct. We would be far from doing Injustice to his Abilities & Experience in a subordinate Line but exclusive of the Danger of intrusting so confidential an Office to a Stranger whose Attachment to this Country must be light & transient, & whose Interest may be so easily distinguished from ours we cannot find that he possesses Talents or Activity equal to the Discharge of this important Office. We find that in the Course of the Campaign necessary Tools & Stores have often been wanting—important & seasonable Movements of the Army delayed, in some Instances wholly frustrated & favourable Opportunities lost thro the Deficiencies of this Department. The rapid Marches of our Army & unforeseen Disasters which attended it during the Summer justly claim some Allowance, but that Disorder & Confusion prevail thro the Department which require some able Hand to reform & reduce, is a certain but melancholy Truth.

Unacquainted with the Resolution of Congress with Respect to Genl. Schuyler we have hesitated what farther to propose. Time is so extremely precious, that we are unwilling to lose a single unnecessary Moment, & have therefore been induced to extend our Views to the Disapprobation of this Gentleman & make some Provision for that Event. A Character has presented itself,[2] which in a great Degree meets our Judgment & Wishes; we have opened the Subject to him, & it is now under his Consideration. When we are at Liberty we shall introduce him to your Notice, but Delicacy forbids our doing it, until he has made up his Mind on the Subject, & given his Consent to the Nomination. Another Gentleman of extensive Connections, great Activity, & comprehensive Genius, but intirely in civil Life, has also been proposed.[3] As he is at a Distance we have not been able to consult him, & are restrained by similar Motives of Delicacy from making his Character & Name a Subject of Discussion without his Consent.

By the Time we are favoured with the Determination respecting Genl Schuyler & he should not be approved we hope to be able to announce both these Gentlemen for your Consideration.

We are with the greatest Respect and Regard Sir, Your most obedt. & very Hbble Servts.

RC (DNA: PCC, item 33). In the hand of Joseph Reed.

[1] Apparently the committee had not yet received the plan Congress had adopted on February 5 to reorganize the quartermaster general's department, which was communicated in a February 7 letter directing the committee to consult with General Washington on nominees for the posts to be filled in that department. See *JCC*, 10:126–27, 138; and Henry Laurens to the Committee at Camp, February 7, 1778.

[2] This is undoubtedly a reference to Gen. Nathanael Greene, with whom the committee consulted this day. See Committee at Camp Minutes of Proceedings, February 8–14, 1778. See also Committee at Camp to Henry Laurens, January 28, 1778.

[3] It has not been determined to whom the committee was referring.

Committee at Camp to Henry Laurens

Sir,   [February 12–25? 1778][1]

Maturely reflecting upon our Situation & Circumstances relative to the great Article of Provisions the lamentable Defect of which presses so sorely upon us and comparing our probable wants with the natural Resources of this great Country we are convinced that if the proper Measures had been used the present Evil would not have been felt.

Permit us then Sir a little to investigate the Causes by which we feel ourselves reduced to the present Situation. We place the Depreciation of our Money in the foremost Point of View and add that it hath in a great Measure arisen from the Giving of Commissions upon the Price of Commodities to those employed in Purchases. The second

Cause certainly arises from a Want of Genius & Activity in the Head of the Commissary's Department, added to a total Ignorance of our Resources or the Means of drawing them forth with Ease and Expedition. A third Cause flows from a Want of the Means of Transporting the several necessary Articles to Camp. A fourth is the total Neglect of every Thing but the immediate and pressing Emergencies which arise without looking forward to provide for or rather [prevent?] such Emergencies for altho it may be impracticable to point out the precise Theatre of the War Yet if Magazines were laid up in the several probable Places the worst which could happen would be a little additional Expence in Transportation. The last Cause is a plentiful source of this and numerous other Evils, the Want of Money which presses so hard that we are told on good Authority that private Persons buy Wheat in the Vicinage of this Camp two shillings per Bushel cheaper than the public Agents.

To consider these Things in their Order we observe first that the Allowing Commissions which Congress have altered long ago we cannot suppose will be revived for Reasons the most obvious and as to the general Depreciation complained of the wise Measure of Taxation will probably prevent it from increasing Notwithstanding the proposed Regulation of Prices on which we shall say Nothing submitting the Propriety of it to those great Tests of political Wisdom, Time & Experience. Our Sentiments upon the Head of the Department we have already communicated and suppose that the Attention of Congress will be called to it in a Manner becoming its Importance.[2] And as to the want of Waggons & the like We cannot but believe that the Assistance of the Legislature of this and the Neighbouring States, if properly applied to afford to a prudent and provident Quarter Master Genl. (and such a Man we expect soon to recommend), will remove this Evil.

The fourth Cause demands a little more Consideration. And first let us consider the now immediate want for the next Season and then what is of more Importance perhaps the Means of obtaining Supplies for the Campaign of the Year 1779 and the Winter preceeding it. On the first Head Nothing seems to be left but to urge the Husbandmen of Virginia, Pennsylvania & New Jersey immediately to prepare as many Cattle as they can for the next Summer forthwith, to procure all the Pork which can be had in the Eastern and Southern States, to have large Supplies of Fish laid up from the Rivers of Virginia particularly the Potowmack in the ensuing Spring and to get all the Cattle which can be bought in the Eastern States. Flour is out of the Question as there can be no want of that Article if the smallest Attention be paid to it.

As to the Magazines for the Winter and Campaign succeeding the next the first Measure will be to contract immediately for as many fat Cattle as can be had in Virginia and North Carolina to be delivered at convenient Places in September next and forwarded on to the Banks of the Delaware or Hudsons River there to be killed and salted up. A considerable Quantity of Pork may be had in like Manner in those States and the State of Maryland, the Hogs to be driven to the Places where they are to be salted up and of the Fish put up as aforesaid a large Quantity should be kept as a Reserve for the Winter. Dried Fish also should be purchased in the Eastern States during the Course of the next Summer as also all the salted Provisions which may be brought in by the Cruizers and which being laid up in the best Manner can be depended upon. Pork may be had also to the Eastward perhaps in the mutilated State of New York in considerable Quantities especially as the Article of Salt now begins to grow cheaper and tho that which is made by boiling will not preserve Pork yet if the Hogs be driven alive to Places where Stores of blown Salt and Nitre are laid up the public Agents may preserve that which is bought for the Army in the greatest Perfection. The large Beeves in the Eastern States salted next Fall should be stall fed and not killed untill the Spring 1779 and then Salted up for the Use of the Summer as great Waste happens from the killing of Cattle in the hot weather besides which the Troops are not so healthy on fresh as on Salt Provisions. Contracts should be immediately made from Massachusetts to Pennsylvania inclusive for very great Quantities of Vinegar An Article the most necessary of all others to the Health of the Troops. Pease for the Winter Season should be contracted for in Maryland and Virginia for the Summer following in the northeastern Parts of the State of New York. Onions should be contracted for on Connecticut River, other Vegetables in the different Parts of the several States which may probably be near the Seat of Action. Old Corn should be bought up & Kiln dried in the Southern Parts of New Jersey which will there answer well for Indian or Mush Meal so as to prevent it from souring. We recommend Salt Provisions particularly because greater Waste and greater Villainy will prevail in the Distribution of fresh besides which the Beeves being killed at particular Places their Skins and some Hogs Skins can better be preserved for the public Use than at the various Encampments & at a much smaller Expence.

It will add much to our Resources to reduce the cumbersome and unweildy Staff of the Army. This hath been partly attempted already. We shall pay such farther attention to it as we can and also to the Detection of Frauds many of which we are too sensible must prevail tho it is we fear very difficult to point out the particular Villains.

The Want of Money is perhaps as inexcusable as any other Want. The Means of obtaining it on Loan are certainly inadequate to the End. Pardon us our Freedom but judge of our Feelings when we hear that very great Sums might be had in the Neighbourhood even of this

Camp were there any Persons duly authorized to receive it. This probably is the Case in many other Places. It is true Congress have now the cheapest Mode of procuring what they do borrow but certainly with a little more Expence they might borrow much more and the Difference between Purchases for Money and Credit is such as will greatly overbalance the Expence of procuring Money. We shall not debate further but beg Leave to recommend this Matter to the serious Attention of Congress. We are Sir &c.

FC (DNA: PCC, item 33). In the hand of Gouverneur Morris. Endorsed: "Letter on Supplies."

[1] When Morris wrote this undated letter has not been determined, but its contents suggest that it was written between February 12 and 25. The committee's statement that they "expect soon to recommend" a quartermaster general indicates a date sometime after February 12, when apparently they first learned from Jonathan Bayard Smith that Gen. Philip Schuyler would not be an acceptable candidate for this post, but before February 25, when they nominated Gen. Nathanael Greene. It may be significant for the dating of this letter that the committee first officially consulted with Greene about the quartermaster general's post on February 12, for it contains a reference to a nominee "we expect soon to recommend."

The committee's focus on "the next Season" and "obtaining Supplies for the Campaign of the Year 1779," on the other hand, would indicate that the committee had completed much of its work attempting to solve the current supply problems of the army that were the subject of a series of committee letters to state and commissary officials on February 16, 17, and 20.

The committee's opposition to the commission system also points to a date before the committee had conceded commissions should be allowed to quartermaster and commissary officials as indicated in their February 25 letter nominating Greene quartermaster general.

See Joseph Reed to Jonathan Bayard Smith, February 13; and the committee's letters to Thomas Johnson, February 16, to George Clinton, February 17, to Ephraim Blaine, February 20, and to Henry Laurens, February 25, 1778.

[2] See the Committee at Camp to Laurens, January 29, 1778.

Thomas McKean to George Read

Sir,   York, February 12th, 1778.

Your favor of the 29th of December did not reach me until the 24th of January, when, duly reflecting upon every circumstance, I thought it my duty to come here, though, I confess, I am almost tired of serving my country so much at my own expense. I left home on [the] 29th of last month, and went into Congress next morning, where I found only nine States represented, and, including myself, but eighteen members, though five, now at the camp, and some others are expected in a few days. I hope General Rodney and Major Van Dyke will come as soon as possible;[1] but don't tell them that I lived in a little Dutch tavern, at an enormous expense, for ten days, before I could get other lodgings, and that I still am on sufferance.

The situation of Delaware gives me constant anxiety. The choice of representatives in October, 1776, and *their* choice of officers, have occasioned all its misfortunes. Nothing but effectual laws, vigorously executed, can possibly save it, and there seems to me not the least prospect of the former, and when I learn that not a single step is taken towards collecting the fines under the present inadequate militia law, or to punish the most imprudent traitors, or even the harboring of deserters, I despair of any law, tending to support the freedom, independence, and sovereignty of the State, being executed, especially in Kent and Sussex. The conduct of the General Assembly, having neither imposed a tax for reducing the paper bills of credit, nor passed the laws necessary even in times of profound peace, much less for competing their quota of troops, putting their militia on a respectable footing, etc. etc., is too conspicuous not to cause the disagreeable animadversions I am obliged continually to hear.

I shall endeavor to procure the account against the State, from the Auditor-General, as soon as possible. The votes of Congress, since January, 1776, printed by Aitken, are not yet come to hand, though they have been sent out of Philadelphia. I shall send you all that can be got, not knowing to what time they are printed up.

Who can I propose in exchange for the President? Do inform me, if you can think of any one. None occurs to me but Governor Franklin, and hearing a gentleman say that he could do more mischief than the President could do good, and for other reasons, which will readily suggest themselves to you, I have little hope of success from that proposition.[2] I was told the other day that he lodged at widow Jenkins's, along with his *old friends* Robinson and Manlove, and seemed very *happy*; these observations, and many others, from different gentlemen, whenever I name him in private to any member, almost discourage me; however, after I hear from you, I shall attempt to have him released (though I could wish my colleagues to be present and assisting), lest it should be thought that I was indifferent about the event.

Notwithstanding all the diffidence you so modestly express of yourself, the State of Delaware think themselves happier, and I am sure they are in wiser hands than those of your predecessor.

In answer to your favor by your brother you will receive ten thousand dollars to be expended in recruiting only,[3] as Congress have lately purchased clothing, to a very great amount, at Boston, etc., and the battalion will be furnished by the Clothier-General. If more should be wanted you will be pleased to write to em again, but I should advise that the recruiting officers should first render you an account of the expenditure of this sum. No letter from General Smallwood has yet appeared in Congress; when it does, I shall attend to it. The whole affair, in my opinion, respecting the schooner, rests with the Judge of Admiralty in the first place, and must be decided upon the resolves of Congress (there being none but what you have relating to this subject) and the laws of England. An appeal lies to Congress. The case is undoubtedly in favor of the State, and not the first possessor, whether a wreck or dereliction.

I have no news but what Major Read can tell you, and, therefore, shall conclude with my best compliments to Mrs. Read.

Sir, your most obedient, humble servant,   Thomas McKean

MS not found; reprinted from William T. Read, *Life and Correspondence of George Read, a Signer of the Declaration of Independence* . . . (Philadelphia: J. B. Lippincott & Co., 1870), pp. 298–300.

¹ Read returned this discouraging reply to McKean's inquiry about the attendance of Delaware's other delegates: "As to the presence of your colleagues on this or any other occasion, shortly, you are not to expect it. Mr. Rodney is very necessary here, and as to Mr. Van Dyke, the situation of his family will keep him for awhile." Ibid., p. 306.

² Despite episodic discussions in Congress of the question of President John McKinly's exchange, Congress did not agree to exchange McKinly for William Franklin until September 14, 1778. Ibid., p. 306; and *JCC*, 11:769, 816, 818, 12:898, 908–12.

³ See *JCC*, 10:128.

Committee at Camp to William Livingston

Sir   Camp at Valley Forge Feb. 13. 1778

We have had the Honour of composing a Committee of Congress appointed to confer with his Excellency General Washington on the Affairs of the Army & concert with him such Measures as might enable him to open the Campaign with Spirit & Vigour. We were proceeding on this important Business when the critical Situation of the Army in the Article of Provisions was disclosed to us. We are extremely concerned to find Sir, that after subsisting our Army a long Time by casual & almost daily Supplies, they are now in Danger of experiencing a total Stagnation. Some Brigades have not tasted Flesh for four days & the Commissaries give us little Hopes of Relief beyond what we are about to suffer. We need not enlarge Sir upon the alarming Consequences of such a Situation. To break up the Camp at this Season of the Year when every Officer & Soldier supposed himself settled for the Winter, the Baggage Waggons dispersed & every Conveniency of March removed would be extremely distressing. But such Circumstances are comparatively trivial with the Effect it would have upon the General State of our Affairs. Should the Army from their present Distresses mutiny, refuse Obedience to their Officers, spread thro the Country on free Quarters or disperse with an Intention to return to their several States your Excellency can be at no Loss to judge what Matter of Triumph & Exultation it would afford our Enemies of every kind & proportionably distress Liberty & their Country. Be assured Sir we are not drawing an imaginary Picture. Very alarming Prospects open upon us & oblige us to sollicit your Attention & that of the Gentlemen in Authority about you to our situation. They inform us that they have purchased considerable Quantities of Pork in your State which they cannot forward to the Army for Want of Waggons. They excuse themselves by charging the Quarter Masters with Neglect—who transfer the Blame to the Constables & other Civil Officers. In the mean Time the Army suffers. Permit us Sir, to ask another vigorous Exertion of that Zeal of which you have so often manifested on other Occasions. On An early Transportation of Provisions to Camp the Continuance of the Army depends & there has never perhaps been a Period when it stood in greater need of the faithful Assistance of the civil Powers. The Provisions to which we refer have been collected in the Western Part of your State. They appear to us to be considerable when compared with Exportation of former Times. If any Plan could be adopted to turn the Surplus beyond the Necessities of the Inhabitants to the Supply of the Army it would prove a most seasonable Relief.

We would also beg Leave to ask your Excellency's Aid in another Matter of great Importance tho not of such pressing necessity. We consider the remounting our Cavalry as a Matter of the greatest Moment. Its Utility to the Army & the Protection it affords to the Inhabitants not only by checking the plundering Spirit of our Enemies, but preserving our faithful Citizens from their mean kidnapping Designs are too obvious to need a further Illustration. But unhappily the Duty of the last Campaign has left us few Horses fit for service. If there is any one State more able to satisfy than another this capital demand it is New Jersey where for many Years the Inhabitants have bestowed peculiar Care in the Raising of a Breed of valuable Horses. We find ourselves much embarrassed with this Branch of our Duty. And shall think ourselves extremely happy so far to intrust you in it to call your Attention to this Subject. We have thought long that if some Gentlemen of Character & of Knowledge in this Business would thro you favour us with their Opinion what Number of Horses might be procured in New Jersey for the Cavalry[1]—at what Prices & in the best Mode still having respect to the Conveniences of the People & the demand of the service it would have a very happy Effect & perhaps guard us against some Measures which our deficient Knowledge might lead us to pursue. General Heard, Mr Wilson Hunt of Hopewell, Gershom Lee of Arnswell, are Persons upon whom we are informed dependance may be placed. We could wish their sentiments in writing & pointed as much as possible to the above Inquiries. Should we be so happy as to obtain your Assistance you will be pleased to forward the Result to the General to be further communicated.

We remain with the greatest Respect & Regard, Sir, Your most Obed & very Hbble servts

FC (DNA: PCC, item 192). Written by Joseph Reed and endorsed by him: "Letter to Gov. Livingston respectg. procuring Waggons & remountng Cavalry."
[1] Reed wrote in the margin beside this paragraph: "Horses at least ¼ blooded 15 Hands high & not less than 4 years old will be required."

William Ellery to William Churchill Houston

Dr. Sir,   York town Febry. 13th 1778.

I received your letter seasonably, and have sent its enclosure to Mr. Marchant. I have been under much concern for my good old landlord and his family; but my solicitude is relieved by his appointment to the office of a hospital chaplain in the middle department; an appointment for which he is greatly indebted to our worthy friend President Witherspoon.

When I left Philadelphia I fully expected to have returned to it— to have spent many useful and pleasant evenings with Mr. Sprout and you, in untying some metaphysical Knot, in attending to your solution of some mathematical problem or physical question, and catching by snatches some knowledge of the French Language—but alass!— instead of this pleasure I am condemned to drag through the winter amidst a people who have but one idea, and whose manners are as different from the English as their language.

You, it seems, have leaped out of the frying-pan into the fire of business. What think you of leaping back again? Mr. Rush hath resigned, and the office of Dep. Sec. is now vacant.[1] But you are become a parliament man and are immersed in politicks; and perhaps, mounted in the chariot of glory, look down upon so low an office with disregard. Come then a delegate.[2] I should be exceedingly glad to see you here in any shape. I received a letter from Mr. Channing a few days ago. He and his family and mine were well when he wrote. Your kind Inquiry after their health, and your wishes to see my Spectacles are very obliging. I should rejoice to speak to you and your good lady face to face as a man speaketh to his friend.

We have not taken Rhode-Island yet. Inglorious Expedition. We have lost Philadelphia! But this would be nothing if avarice and peculation did not rage irresistibly. The Love of country & public virtue are annihilated. If Diogenes were alive, and were to search America with candles, would he find an honest man? I knew an honest man once in office. Believe me to be his Friend.

William Ellery

P.S. **Dr.** Witherspoon will acquaint you with a Resolve of Congress lately passed, which may give some check to the Shoals of Officers who are rioting on the Spoils of the Publick.[3]

RC (PHi). Addressed: "William C. Houston Esqr., Princeton, New Jersey."

[1] On January 28 Congress had accepted the resignation of its deputy secretary Jacob Rush, who had been Houston's successor in that post. See *JCC*, 8:874–75, 10:95–96.

[2] Houston, who had recently become a member of the New Jersey Assembly, later served in Congress in 1779–81 and 1784–85. *Bio. Dir. Cong.*

[3] On February 3 Congress had approved the administration of an oath designed to prevent the misuse of public money or stores by Continental officials. *JCC* 10:115–16.

James Forbes to Thomas Johnson

Sir   York Town Feby. 13th 1778

I shoud have don my self the honour to have wrote you before now, had I any thing worth communicating. This is to informe you that the appointment of Commershall agents in France has been moved for in Congress, in consequince of Mr Wm Lee's being appointed a Commissiner to the Courts of Vienna & Barlen, and of a Letter from Mr Robt Morris, recommending Mr Jno Ross to suchseed his Broter.[1] I put Mr Jushua Johnson in the nomination, and I believe, had Congress made the appointment, he woud have been chosen, but they resolved that the Commissiners in France shoud appoint them, and they are wrote to on the 9th Instt. for that purpose,[2] had I known how to have directed to your Brother, I woud have wrote him on the Subject.

The Committee that went to Camp for reforming the army is not yet returned, nor have we heard from their, for som time, the communication being stopt by the River being impassible. The Demands on Congress for money is immence, it cant be emitted fast enuff, and I apprehend the demand will encrease in proportion to the Emission.

Commissiners appointed in this State, & the Board of War are empowerd to purchase 50,000 Bbls Flour,[3] & all the Pork & Beef they can get, and lay it up in Magazeens, for a supply, in case the Commissary falls short in his purchas, which there is grate reason to fear, their is very grate complaints of his department from every quarter. Congress have had noe accounts from Europe since I have been here. Ten States only are represented in Congress, & one half of them, by one member only. Masechusits, New York & Virginia have noe representation. I shall doe my self the honour of writing you when any thing offers worth communicating and am very respectfully, Sir, Your most Obedt Hble serv.   James Forbes

RC (MdAA).

[1] Forbes' assertion that Morris had recently written a letter recommending Ross to succeed his brother Thomas Morris should be compared with Morris' own testimony on the subject written a few days later. In response to a report that the Committee of Commerce desired him to "recommend Mr. Ross for one of the Commercial agents in Europe," Morris replied "I am too sick of recommending agents ever to do it again." See Robert Morris to the Committee of Commerce, February 17, 1778.

[2] See Committee of Commerce to the Commissioners at Paris, February 9, 1778.

[3] For Congress' January 15 and February 12 resolutions on the purchase of flour, which were amended on February 14, see *JCC*, 10:54, 152–53, 166–69. Congress had in fact specified the purchase of only 30,000 barrels of flour, but the Board of War had directed the purchase of 20,000 more. For the consequences of the appointment of these commissioners, see Daniel Roberdeau to Thomas Wharton, January 16, 1778, note 2.

Elbridge Gerry to Nathaniel Appleton

Dear Sir   York in Pennsylvania Feby 13. 1778

Congress having ordered 20,000 Loan Office Certificates amounting to 10,000,000 Dollars to be forthwith struck under the Direction of the Board of Treasury,[1] I have to request your Assistance in procuring Colours for the Borders if the Treasurer should find it necessary to send to Boston for this Purpose.

Being with much Esteem your very hum serv,   E. Gerry

RC (PHi). Addressed: "To Nathaniel Appleton Esqr Commissioner of the Loan Office Boston."

[1] See *JCC*, 10:59.

Henry Laurens to Richard Caswell

Sir,   York Town 13th Febry 1778.

I beg leave to refer to a Letter which I had the honor of writing to your Excellency under the 10th Inst.[1] and which will accompany this. Yesterday your Excellency's favor of the 11th Ulto. reached me. I immediately presented it to Congress and from thence it was transmitted to the Board of Treasury.

Enclosed herein your Excellency will receive an Act of Congress of this date earnestly requesting an immediate restraint to be laid on the exportation of Beef & Pork from the State of North Carolina to which I refer,[2] and remain with very great Respect, Sir, your Excellency's mo. huml Servt.   Henry Laurens, Prest. Congress

Tr (Nc–Ar).

[1] See Laurens to Patrick Henry, February 10, 1778, note.

[2] Congress wished to have exports of beef and pork from North Carolina embargoed in order to ensure adequate supplies of both for the Continental Army. *JCC,* 10:156.

Francis Lightfoot Lee to John Hancock

Dear Sir   York Town Febry. 13. 1778
    The State of Virginia having occasion to advance some French Gentlemen in Boston a sum of Money, & not being able to procure a bill of exchange in this place, I as a delegate for that State am obliged again to have recourse to your friendship.
    I hope therefore you will be kind enough to advance to Lt. Colo. Marrie, on application, two hundred pounds lawfull for which your draft upon the Delegates here will be honourd at sight.[1]
    Your order on us for 600 Dollars advanced to Captains Pierre & Cayotte has come to hand, and is paid, but we have heard nothing of the Gentlemen.[2] All my bror. delegates are at present away, therefore I alone have the honor of subscribing myself, with much esteem, Yr. mo. hble. St.   F. L. Lee

FC (Vi). In a clerical hand, except the last sentence and signature which are in Lee's hand.
    [1] At the foot of this copy of Lee's letter to Hancock, Lee also copied his note of this date to "Leiut Colo. Marree at Boston": "Monsr. Loyeaute, who has enter'd into the service of the State of Virga. has desired me to lodge in your hands two hundred pounds money of Boston for purposes expressed in his Letr. to you. Finding it difficult to procure at this place a bill of Excha. upon Boston I have desired the honble. Mr. Hancock to advance that sum to you. If therefore you will please to present the inclosed Letter, I make no doubt you will receive the money." For a plan being considered in Virginia for importing military stores from France, see Richard Henry Lee's February 23 letter to Arthur Lee in Lee, *Letters* (Ballagh), 1:388–89.
    [2] On the Virginia delegates' earlier efforts to secure the services of several French artillerists, see Richard Henry Lee to Patrick Henry, October 8, 1777, note 3.

Joseph Reed to Jonathan Bayard Smith

Dear Sir   Camp Valley Forge, Feb. 13. 1778
    I wrote you by Mr. Young (Mr. Mease's Clerk) a long & confidential Letter which I hope will reach you safely. I have since that Time received your Favour & find we are not to expect Schuyler for our Qr. Master. I feared it & am really sorry for it as it is a Matter of great Importance & we are now much at a Loss whom to propose. After much Hesitation we have at last turn'd our Eyes upon General Green as a Character in the Line, a Man of good Judgment apprized of the Wants & Difficulties of the Army & much intrested to releive them.

We have proposed to him but he hesitates & I fear will refuse. After casting round I can think no one else preferable to Col. Cox!—you know his Activity, Address & great Knowledge of the Resources of the Country.[1] It will never answer to divide the Department with the Hope that inferiour Characters may do the Duty separate which they cannot perform united. Be not misled my dear Sir, to countenance any Plan of this kind; it will be better far better to put an inferiour Character into the whole Department & let all Hazards be run. We have been much puzzled to determine on this Subject & suppose what we have done will occasion much Speculation. However we declare ourselves or at least I may for my own Part that I am influenced by no other motives than such as interest every Friend to his Country. Least we should be supposed to conceal or keep back from Congress any Information or in short to have less Candor than we ought to have I thought it best with the Approbation of the other Gentlemen to let you know whom we have in View. You will make such Use of it as your Prudence & Skill may direct.

We have nothing new. In the Haste of despatching an Express an Inclosure was omitted. I forwarded it to Mr Thompson immediately but least that should miscarry or be delayed I now inclose you a Duplicate which you will please to deliver him to be annexed to our Letter on the Subject of Provisions—If the other has not got to Hand.

Our Troops sicken, die & desert fast. I very much fear we shall have an ineffective Army in the Spring.

My Complts. to our Colleagues & beleive me Dear Sir, Your Affect. & Obed., Hbble serv.   Jos. Reed

RC (DLC).
[1] For the Committee at Camp's consideration on February 12 and 13 of Nathanael Greene and John Cox for appointment as quartermaster general and assistant quartermaster, see Committee at Camp Minutes of Proceedings, February 8–14, 1778.

Rhode Island Expedition Commissioners to Henry Laurens

Sir,   Providence February 13th. 1778.

Agreeable to the Resolve of Congress of December 12th appointing a Committee to inquire into the Causes of the Failure of the Expedition against Rhode Island,[1] we met at Providence on the Sixth Day of February, and having been previously notified by General Whipple that he should not attend the Service, and not hearing from Mr. Benson[2] we concluded to proceed with a bare Quorum rather than the Business should be disadvantageously delayed, tho' we wished much for the Assistance of those Gentlemen in so important an affair. Mr. Paine being hindered on the Convention of Committees at New Haven Occasioned his not arriving at Providence, till the 6th current, at which time we immediately sent Summonses to the Examinants; exceeding bad travelling delayed our Expresses, and we suppose has hindered several General Officers who live at a Distance from arriving at this Time, it also happens that public Concerns of great Importance require each of us to be absent next Week, and for some Time, and therefore finding that we cannot at this Time finish the Examinations to Satisfaction, tho' we have made considerable Progress in them, we have concluded to adjourn to the fourth Monday in March at this Place, and have notified all Examinants to be present,[3] and hoping that Mr. Benson will be able to assist us with his Presence, we have wrote him on the Subject.[4]

We take Liberty through you to inform the Honble Congress of our Proceedings, and hope this unavoidable adjournment of our business will not be disagreeable to them.[5]

We are with Esteem, your humble Servants,

RT Paine

Oliver Ellsworth

Hy Marchant

RC (DNA: PCC, item 78). In a clerical hand and signed by Ellsworth, Marchant, and Paine. Endorsed by Charles Thomson: "Letter from R. T. Paine, O. Ellsworth, H. Marchant. Providence Feby 13. 1778. Read March 12."

[1] For a discussion of the background and work of this committee, which was investigating the failure in October 1777 of a joint expedition by Massachusetts, Rhode Island, and Connecticut against the British occupying force in Rhode Island, see Laurens to the Rhode Island Expedition Commissioners, December 15, 1777, note 1. Congress had actually appointed the commissioners on December 11, 1777. JCC, 9:1022.

[2] Gen. William Whipple of New Hampshire and Egbert Benson, the attorney general of New York, had also been appointed to this commission. JCC, 9:1022.

[3] See also Rhode Island Expedition Commissioners to Laurens, March 27, 1778.

[4] The commissioners' letter to Egbert Benson has not been found.

[5] Robert Treat Paine also made some pertinent remarks about his work on the commission in a private letter he wrote this day to Elbridge Gerry. Having been detained at a convention of states in New Haven, he noted, "I did not arrive here till the Friday after the Monday appointed for our meeting. We went immediately upon business, tho' with great reluctance with a bare quorum but we thought if we excused our selves one after another, it would throw the requisitions of Congress into a faint point of light, & so I undertook this fatiguing business meerly from Patriotic principles, & to put a good face on our Affairs; otherwise, a large Sum would not have tempted me to have been Absent from Genl. Court, forming Constitution, regulating money &c to say nothing of private affairs. We are obliged to Adjourn to 4th Monday in March, when we hope to finish to Satisfaction; you will oblige me if you will inform me how the Expences of this business are to be born, & whether any allowance is to be made to us by Congress for the Service." Emmet Collection, NN.

Committee at Camp to Henry Laurens

Sir,   Moor Hall 14th Feby. 1778.
The Distresses of our Army we cannot paint if we would. We would not if we could, since it would answer no Purpose to give you the Pain of reflecting upon this which you cannot perhaps alleviate, tho indeed a careful Appointment of certain officers may prevent them in future. Without entering into that Detail at present, we have to observe that Distress in an Army always furnishes Materials for factious and de-signing Men to work upon. Those who know Mankind know that such Men exist, and according to the common Chances of Humanity, it may well be supposed that our army is not without them. But be this as it may, there are a Kind of Men in the World, who from the Pride of Opinion do great and lasting Mischeif. If for Instance, a Person of this Cast should (possibly from an Unwillingness to be situated in the Enemy's Neighbourhood) have assigned, among other Reasons against the Post we now occupy, that the Army would be distressed for Want of Provisions & Forage; he would now, to vaunt his own Judgment, dwell upon the present Sufferings in the per-nicious Stile of Exageration. Whether soothing Language would not lend more to inspire the Soldiery with patient Fortitude, no one can be at a Loss to determine.

Without troubling Congress with any Application of these Ideas, We take Leave to observe, that as there is a Want of General Officers in the continental Line at Rhode Island it might not be improper *immediately* to send one thither. We do ourselves the Honor to recommend to this Post a Gentleman from that State, Brigadier Gen-eral Varnum whose Character and Abilities are so well known to Congress that we shall not presume to dilate upon that Subject.[1]

We are Sir with the deepest Respect, your most obedient & humble Servants,   Fra Dana, by Order

RC (DNA: PCC, item 78). Written by Gouverneur Morris and signed by Dana.
[1] On Congress' decision to disregard the committee's recommendation, see Com-mittee at Camp Minutes of Proceedings, February 8–14, 1778, note 10.

William Duer to Francis Lightfoot Lee

My dear sir,   Reading Feby. 14th. 1777 [*i.e.* 1778]
You will be much surprised to hear of me from Reading, where I have been detain'd three or four Days in Expectation of receiving a Letter from York Town, the Substance of which is (I am told) a very Extraordinary Conversation betwixt the Marquis de la Fayette, and Genl. Conway, of which I had the Honor of being the Topic.[1] In the

Course of a Discussion betwixt these Officers of the Expedition against Canada,[2] the Marquis Exprest his Astonishment, that *I* should be trusted to go on it, as he had been inform'd that my political Character was that of *a Tory*.[3] *Risum teneatis, Amici*,? if you can, your risible Muscles are not so flexible, as I take them to be. I think it is no difficult Matter to guess at the Quarter, whence this Insinuation comes, or the Purpose for which it is design'd. I am happy, however, to learn it in Time, for however I despise the Insinuation it will furnish me with this Useful Lesson not to risque my own Reputation, and Ease of Mind by troubling the Young *Telemachus* with the Presence of a Person, whom he cannot consider as a *Mentor*. Before I was informd of this Matter my Imagination suggested to me that the Pleasure, which the Marquis Exprest of my going with him as a Volunteer appeard more the Result of French *Politisse* than of Inclination; yet, as I was of Opinion my Presence might be useful to the Public, I was willing to sacrifice my own feelings to a more important Consideration. To persist in this Resolution at present would be a Breach of Self Duty, as I must in such Case sacrifice my own Ease, and (possibly) my Reputation, without the Hope of possessing with the Marquis that Influence, which might be necessary for Effecting Purposes beneficial to the public Weal. I have thought it my Duty to communicate this Matter to you in order that you may mention it to the Board of War[4] and to Congress, who probably depend on my going into Canada, and may thereby be prevented from taking such Measures with respect to that Expedition, as Policy may suggest. I think a Committee of Congress ought without Delay to be sent into Canada should our Troops oblige the Enemy to retire to Quebec; and though I owe too much to my own Feelings to Volunteer it, where I am lookd upon in a Suspicious Point of View, I will if Congress think proper, act as one of such a Committee, provided Mr. Law of Connecticut whose Probity and good Sense be well known in Congress be appointed to act with me. Should Congress think proper to take any Measures on this Subject, they will be pleasd to communicate it to me as early as possible, directing their Letter to the Care of Genl. Schuyler. I shall now proceed from myself to the Public.

In my last Letter[5] I inform'd you that I should endeavor to prevail on Genl. Mifflin to join the Board of War without delay. I accordingly explain'd to him the Manner in which the Resolution respecting his Settlement of the public Accts. had past,[6] and gave my Opinion, that it ought not to be consider'd in the rigorous Sense which at first View it appears to Convey. All my Endeavors, I am sorry to say, have proved fruitless, his Feelings appear to me greatly wounded, and what has tended to aggravate them is the Return of Mr. Butler from York Town without a Farthing of Cash; although the Department is in a most Miserable Condition for Want of that Article. I have taken much Pain to make myself acquainted with the State of the Department, and am fully convinced, that unless active and Experienc'd Officers are immediately appointed to conduct the different Branches of it, and be properly Supplied with Cash, in order to enter into the immediate Execution of the Business, that We shall not be able to take the Feild 'till very late next Year, for Want of Waggons, Camp-Equipage &ca. Nay, I doubt whether this will be the Worse. The Supply of the Army depending upon an Active and judicious Discharge of this Office, a Defect in this Point, added to other Causes, will I fear occasion the Dissolution of the Fragments of a once Powerful Army.

Your Zeal, my dear sir, for the Cause we are engaged in, will I trust engage you to rouse Congress from their Languour, and not to cease urging them on this Point, 'till Matters are put in a proper Train. So much Time has elapsed without any thing being done with respect to this Matter, that I doubt whether the Exertions of any Person whom Congress can at present appoint will atone for what has past. But should they appoint Persons of Ordinary Talents, or even Persons of Ability, but living at a Distance (whence great Delays must necessarily accrue in their Entering into the Execution of their Office) the most fatal Consequences must Ensue. Some of the Principal Misfortunes in the Commissary's Department were derived last year from this Source. Considering the present critical Situation of Affairs the Persons to conduct this Business ought in my Opinion to be Appointed either out of the Army, or amongst Persons in this State and that of Jersey, who have had some Experience in the Department. There are two Persons in Pena. who in my Opinion are well calculated to conduct two of the Branches respecting the furnishing Waggons and Forage. I mean Mr. Mark Bird and Colo. R.L. Hooper. The former is a Man of great Influence, and Property, and brought up from his Youth in a Business, which from its Nature, is capable of furnishing good Quartermasters, namely the Iron Factory; the second, you know from the Accounts and repeated Testimonies we have received is undoubtedly a Man of Business. To this it may be added that they have already been Employ'd in that Business, which must necessarily give them an Advantage over Persons, whatever their Talent may be, who have not yet applied them in this Channel.

From Principles of public Duty, I am induced to mention these Persons; but I must observe that in my Opinion nothing can Effect a radical Cure to the Mischiefs which prevail in that System, and introduce Vigor, and Œconomy, not only in that, but in the other military Departments, but the ordering Genl. Schuyler to the Army, and prevailing on him to accept of the Qu. Ma. Department; and in Conjunction with the Comrs. of the War Office to model it, as they shall deem Expedient. I trust you know me too well to think I have so often urged this from any Considerations of personal Friendship. Were I to consult his Peace of Mind, I should be against his Accepting it; because I know the Opposition he would meet with from many who make their Harvest, by destroying all Order in the Administration of public Affairs. My Mind is imprest with the Strongest Conviction of the Necessity of calling forth his Talents for the public Service; and Congress will I am afraid be obliged to acknowledge it when it may be too late to remedy the Evils which accrue from the Cruel and unjust State of Suspense he is at present kept in.[7]

Shall I beg your Attention whilst I enter into some Minutiae with Respect to this Department, which have come to my Knowledge.

1st. There is not at present at Camp Sufficient Strength of Teams and Horses to move the Artillery and Baggage of the Army, should the Movements of the Enemy render a Retreat necessary.

2. Were more Horses and Teams supplied at this Time for Want of a proper Supply of Forage, a judicious Mode of Feeding, and a proper Discipline in the Arrangement and Care of the Teams, they would before the month of April is past be in as miserable a Condition as they are at present.

3d. Upwards of two thousand horses have been Expended in the course of the last Campaign in the Q.M. Department; and from what I can learn few (if any) of the Harness belonging to these Horses have been preserved.

4. Through Want of proper Management and Care of the Tents, few if any of them can be made Serviceable for the next Campaign.

5. No Magazines of Forage from what I can learn is as yet laid up for the Spring Service.

This is a faint Sketch of the State of this Department. I leave it to yourself to draw the Inferences. I shall only observe that it is lamentable to consider that we, whose Resources in this and the Comys. Department are in many Respects much preferable to those of the Enemy, should be in danger of having our Army disbanded from a Want of these Branches being conducted with Spirit and Skill, at a Time when the Enemy are making every Preparation for opening the Campaign early, and profiting by our Want of Attention, and the Exercise of a false humanity (it deserves the Name of Treason!) which induces us to leave in their Power as much Forage, and as many horses, as are necessary for enabling them to act with Vigor in carrying on this wicked, and Cruel War.

Another Object, which demands your immediate Attention and in which a Delay must be fatal, is the Supplying the Comrs.[8] with Cash for forming the Magazines. I have conferred with Colo. Hooper, and the other Gentn. in this Quarter on the Subject, and am convinced, that if they are immediately supplied, nothwithstanding the

Time which has been lost they will answer the Expectation of Congress; if not, all Prospect of forming Magazines in Time on this Side the Susquehanna must be given up. I trust therefore that they will be Supplied immediately with Money. I believe the Treasury Board are alarmed at the large Sums daily demanded for the public Service, but, when they consider that almost all the Articles in the Comys., Quarter Masters, and Cloathing Department, exceed on an Average four Times the Price at which they were purchased not twelve months Since, and that this is Season, in all Wars, where the largest Expenditures are necessary, their Wonder on this Point must cease. However painful the Reflection, more Money (and that a very large Sum must be immediately emitted) but this is like giving Water to a dropsical Man: a ruinous Expedient. It will give Ease for a short Time—but unless our Finances are better managed, than they have been, (or indeed ever can be by a Committee of Congress) the Sinews of War must fail and Congress lose Entirely the Opinion the public once formed of their Wisdom. Less than a Year must, I am confident, exhaust our narrow System of temporary Expedients, and Contracted Measures. The State of the public Debt, and the critical Situation of Affairs call loudly for the Care of Men of Superior Abilities, of Capacity, to form some great comprehensive Plans for our Relief— Men, who will not be biassed by a Consideration to particular States, much less Individuals; or content themselves with a languid Official Execution of their Duty; but apply to the important Business of our Finances with a Steadiness arising from a Conviction of their own Talents, and Integrity, and with the Zeal of Men, who are passionate for their Purpose. Such Men it is the Duty of Congress in my Opinion to find out as quick as possible, to entrust the Super Intendence of the Treasury to them, and to Support them in the Execution of their Office, and in the Plans they may Suggest for introducing public Œconomy, and supplying our Funds. I know it has been a Doctrine pretty generally received as Orthodox in Congress that the Treasury should only be entrusted to the Management of the Members of Congress, and my Colleague Mr. Duane (who to do him justice attended faithfully to it, and managed it with Reputation) is a Sanguine Partizan for this Opinion; yet, whoever considers how few Members of Congress could ever pretend to the Character of Financiers, the Evils, which flow from a constant Fluctuation of Members of the Treasury, and the Partiality in public Advances too often shewn to particular States, and individuals, from a political Complaisance which the Members are inclined to shew to each other, and the Impossibility there is of Members of Congress giving up Sufficient Time to the Board, to make themselves Masters of the Business, and to enable them to conduct it with Advantage to the Public, and with Satisfaction to Individuals, whoever, I say, considers these Points, must be of Opinion that the Evils arising from the present mode of Conducting the Treasury infinitely overballance any Advantage, which can result from its being under the Management of Members of Congress.[9] The only Advantage, which I ever heard mention'd as attending the present Mode, was its being a powerful check against Frauds, and improper Application for public Money. But, Surely, there is no magical Influence in the Name of a Committee of Congress, which can of itself produce these valuable Ends. These must be effected by Strict Integrity, Knowledge of Business, and close Attention in the Committee who Super Intend the Treasury—and the same Qualities may be found in Commissioners to be appointed by Congress for this Purpose, at least in equal, and so far as it respects Attention, and Skill, in a Superior Degree. I wish therefore that the Treasury Department, as well as every other Executive Department of Congress was thrown under Commissioners. Every possible Precaution ought certainly to be taken that these Persons should not only be well qualified by their abilities, but, by an unsuspected Integrity of Character, for the Exercise of a Trust, of such high Moment—but if no one was to be appointed to it, but after being a certain Space of Time in Nomination, and by the Voice of nine States, the public would have every Security for a faithful Discharge of this trust which could be expected. An additional one (if deem'd necessary) might still be added; and that is a Committee of Congress to be appointed by the Ballot of nine States, whose Business it should be to inspect monthly the Proceedings of the Commrs. and to report to Congress their Opinion of the Mode in which the Treasury Business has been conducted. Should you agree with me in this Opinion (which I trust you will in a great Measure) you will ask perhaps where are the Men to be procur'd who are fit for this Business, and who are willing to execute it. I must confess that I do not think there are many Men in America, who can be considered as Financiers, our contracted dependant System of Government not affording Scope for Abilities of this Species. Yet some undoubtedly might be found whose Genius fits them in a peculiar Manner for such a Line of Business. Two occur to me at present Mr. R. Morris of this State, and my Colleague Govr. Morris. With respect to the former, you know him so well, that it is unnecessary to enlarge upon his Character—the latter, tho' Young, has turned his thoughts and Course of Reading much to the Subject of Money as a Science, and from his Genius would I am convinced make an Useful, and Shining Member in such a Department. Some others in the different States might be fix'd on, with whom I am not acquainted. Whether or no if Congress thought proper to make such an Establishment these Persons would accept, I cannot tell; but this I am certain of—that they ought to do it, as the Situation of public Affairs calls for the Talents of every Person in that Line, where he can be most Useful to his Country. My Mind is so strongly oppressed with these and Several other Matters relating to our public Matters, that I cannot find ease till I unbosom myself, and I know no one to whom I can do it with greater Frankness than yourself. A long Experience of you in the Course of last Year had convinced me of your Abilities to judge, and of your Determination to persue what is Right. I am interrupted from proceeding further by a Messenger who brings an account from the Army, which I have Daily expected. I have obtained a Copy of the Letter concerning the Situation of our Army, which I transmit to you.[10] If Congress has not received the Acct. make such Use of it as your Prudence may Suggest. For my own Part, when I consider the Character of our present Councils, and that of the principal Leaders in our Army, I am induced to prepare My Mind for an Event (which unless a Miracle interposes) will certainly happen, the Dissolution of the Army. Whether or no this may prove Eventually for the Worse, I am at a Loss to determine. Some great public Calamity may call forth the Spirit of Enquiry into the Causes of our misfortunes, rouse all our public Bodies from their Languour, compell the Prejudices of States and Individuals to bend to the public Good, and call forth those Spirited and determined Whigs both in our Councils, and in our Armies, by whose means only this Revolution (like all others which have ever happend) will be brought to an Issue.

You may perhaps think me too Sanguine in harbouring such an Idea, but when you Consider the Justice of this War, and take a retrospective View of the Extraordinary Events which have happen'd in it, and the Instruments with which we have labour'd you will be induced to cry out as a good Catholic, Non nobis Domine.

Dr. Potts is kind enough to take charge of this Letter, I flatter myself from the necessary Changes which will be made in our Medical System, and from the Harmony which (I trust) will subsist betwixt himself and Dr. Shippen the most beneficial Consequences will be derived in the Management of our Hospitals.[11]

I beg you to tender my Respects to Mrs. Lee, and to remember me to the Members of the Board, particularly our Fellow Labourer in the Vinyard Dick Peters. Tell him I meditate writing him in Folio, the next Attack I have of the Cacoethes Scrib.

You will oblige me in making my Compliments to Mr. Arnet,[12] and Mr. Penn, and Mr. Langworthy, and Mr. Wood, my old Mess mates.

As I have some Matters which I propose communicating to you from this Place I shall stay here till I have finished another Letter to you. Since I have been out of the Vortex of Confusion in York Town, Two Matters have suggested themselves to me, the one an Expeditious, and Cheap Mode, of procuring a Body of Horse for the next

Campaign, the other, in my Opinion as certain Mode of recovering the Navigation of the Delaware, and thereby obliging the Enemy either to Surrender, or to hazard a Retreat through the Jerseys with the Loss of their Shipping. Twenty five thousand Men with good Generals to conduct the different Divisions of the Army, will I think be Sufficient.

However you and the Board of War will judge of both when I communicate the matter fully.

God bless you, and Yours!   Wm. Duer

P.S. I have particular Reasons for wishing that Congress was immediately furn[ishe]d with an Exact Muster of the Conl. Army, particularly the Main Army. It is high Time we should know the Worst of Matters and prepare against it as Wise, as Brave men ought.

RC (ViU). For a more elaborate discussion of this letter, see Louis Gottschalk and Josephine Fennell, eds., "Duer and the 'Conway Cabal,'" *American Historical Review* 52 (October 1946): 87–96.

[1] Gottschalk and Fennell doubted that such a "Conversation" took place, pointing out that Gen. Thomas Conway had left York the day before Lafayette arrived there on January 30, 1778, to receive instructions from the Board of War for the forthcoming Canadian expedition. Ibid., p. 90n.9. Unfortunately, they were unaware of the fact that Lafayette and Conway met at Lancaster on January 29 and conversed alone together "for a considerable time," a meeting discussed in "Extract of a Report from Mr. Thomas Sandford" [January 1778], Washington Papers, DLC. It was undoubtedly during this meeting that Lafayette made the unflattering remarks about Duer described in the present letter.

[2] For a discussion of this abortive expedition, see Henry Laurens to the marquis de Lafayette, January 22, 1778, note 2.

[3] Lafayette detested Duer because of Duer's critical attitude toward the marquis' cherished friend Washington. In a January 27, 1778, letter to President Laurens, Lafayette had called Duer and Gen. Thomas Conway "the two greatest ennemys and most insolent calumniators of my friends" and had singled out Duer in particular as one who "has the reputation in the country, to be a tory, and you'll know by several instances that he is a rascall." Lafayette, *Papers* (Idzerda), 1:260. See also ibid., pp. 285–87.

[4] Of which both Duer and Lee were members.

[5] Not found.

[6] See Henry Laurens to Thomas Mifflin, February 10, 1778.

[7] General Schuyler was under investigation by Congress for his role in the evacuation of Ticonderoga and Mount Independence in July 1777. For a discussion of this investigation, see John Hancock to Arthur St. Clair and Philip Schuyler, August 5, 1777, note.

[8] Commissioners.

[9] Although Duer was not the only delegate who was in favor of entrusting the administration of the treasury department to nonmembers of Congress, it was not until April 15 that the Board of Treasury submitted such a plan to Congress. See *JCC*, 10:349–51.

[10] Possibly Washington's comprehensive January 29 report to the Committee at Camp. Because Duer later mentioned "the former letter I sent you from Genl. Washington," it seems likely that the enclosure was a letter from the general, but it is not perfectly clear from Washington's surviving correspondence which letter

Duer actually sent to Lee. See Washington, *Writings* (Fitzpatrick), 10:362–403; and Duer to Francis Lightfoot Lee, February 19, 1778.

[11] Dr. Jonathan Potts had been appointed "deputy director general" of the medical department "in the middle district" on February 6 and was therefore subordinate to Dr. William Shippen, Jr., director general of the entire medical department. *JCC,* 10:131.

[12] Cornelius Harnett.

John Henry to Thomas Johnson

Sir   York Town Feby. 14th 1778.

Congress a day or two ago took up the appointment of commercial agents, and concluded to refer the same to the commissioners in France. Mr. Ross and your Brother were in nomination. If you have an opportunity it would be well to write to Mr. Johnson.[1] I do not at present know in what part of France he resides, possibly upon inquiry, I may be informed. At this time I do not know of an opportunity, but as soon as there is one I shall write to him myself.

Besides our accounts lately from the W Indies, we are informed by a Letter from Richd. H. Lee to his Brother, that there is a large Snow arrived at York Town 42 Days from Bourdeaux loaded with salt and dry Goods. The Capt. and Supercargo say the Number of Troops sent to the W. Indies, is certainly very considerable. Among them are a very powerful body of Artillery and too thousand dismounted Cavalry. What the latter can be for puzzles me. These Gentlemen say that altho the utmost care is taken to quiet the Minds and Suspicions of G.B. that a war will most certainly take place in the Spring. They further say the Spanish Ambassador, the Duke de Choiseul and Dr. Franklin have had frequent and long conferences.

The State of our Army is critical. Four month pay, if not more are due them, and no Money in the Treasury to satisfy their just and reasonable Demands. The press is at work, and attended with all vigilance and care, and has been for some time past; near a Million a week is now made, and yet our Demands are greater than we can answer. They come in from all parts of the Continent. The avarice of our people and the extravagant prices of all commodities, joined with the imperfect management of our Affairs, would expend the monies of Chile and Peru.

For the want of pay, of cloths, and provisions our army is decreasing every hour, not by one or two at a time, but from seven to twelve. By a Letter from Col. Smith[2] he tells me some of the troops have been eight Days at different Times without meat and only a bare allowance of flour. The State of Pennsylvania has passed a Law appointing certain commissioners in every County of the State, with full power to purchase or to seize at stated prices all provisions necessary for the army. These Men are subject to the orders of Congress as to the quantity of each article of provisions to be purchased or seized.[3] Besides this the Board of War have authority from Congress to purchase twenty thousand Barrels of flour and other provisions necessary for the army. From these resources I expect fifty thousand Barrels of flour and quantities of other provisions, but to what amount is uncertain. Our commissary Genl. does not at this time I am informed, know that he has five thousand Barrels of pork or Beef—upon such foundations the existance of our army depends. At whose door this prospect of ruin lies, time will discover.

What think you of Dr. Franklins assassination; with some Gentlemen here, the tale has the appearance of probability, with others it is esteemed a fact. I hope both opinions are groundless. His death will stagnate our system in France and probably shatter some of the Doctors flattering hopes of serving his country through the sides of France.

Will the Test go down?[4] Will the Law for recruiting our quota of Troops succeed. The Committee at camp I understand will recommend measures for filling the Army, which I expect will not be very agreeable to our people.

N. Carolina has agreed only to part of the Confederation, the other States I believe have done nothing with it as yet.

Virginia, New York and Massachusetts Bay is unrepresented.

I am Sir your obedient and very hble Servt,   J. Henry Junr.

RC (MdAA).
[1] See James Forbes to Thomas Johnson, February 13, 1778.
[2] Lt. Col. Samuel Smith of the Fourth Maryland Regiment.
[3] Pennsylvania passed "An Act for the better supply of the armies of the United States of America" on January 2, 1778. *Minutes of the Second General Assembly of . . . Pennsylvania,* October 1777 session, p. 40. DLC(ESR).
[4] Perhaps a reference to the Maryland "Act for the better security of the government" adopted on December 23, 1777, which imposed a test on Maryland citizens. *Votes and Proceedings of the House of Delegates of the State of Maryland,* October 1777 session, pp. 13–14, 48–51, 56–57, 68. DLC(ESR). However, Henry may have merely had in mind Congress' February 3 resolutions requiring a test oath of all officers holding commissions, which only Maryland delegates James Forbes and John Henry opposed on a roll call vote. *JCC,* 10:114–18.

Henry Laurens to David Mason

Sir,   14th Febry 1778.
     Your favour of the 29th Ulto. came to hand the 7st Inst. by Ephraim Harris, who is to be bearer of this. I presented it immed-

iately to Congress, where it was Committed to the Board of Treasury from whence you will receive the necessary returns.[1]

Harris Complained of being without Money. I sent him to Colo. Buchannan for whose dispatches he has been detained several days & that Gentleman has Supplied him as he informs me with forty Dollars.

I am with great Respect

LB (DNA: PCC, item 13). Addressed: "David Mason Esquire, Colo. of the 15th Regiment of Virginia, Williamsburg."

[1] Although the journals contain no mention of Congress' response to Mason's letter, John Banister subsequently mentioned "a considerable sum lately sent him for the troops" in a letter to Patrick Henry of April 10, 1778.

Committee at Camp Minutes of Proceedings

[February 16–20, 1778]

16. Wrote to Govr. Johnson on the article of Provisions a similar Letter to that sent to Govr. Livingston.[1]

Conferred with Colo. Bayard.[2]

17. Submitted State of the Case of Genls. Muhlenburgh, Weedon, Woodford & Scott relating to Rank to a Board of Genl. Officers.[3]

Wrote to Govr. Clinton for aid in procurg or transportg Provision.[4]

Recd. from the Genl. Copies of the Instruct. to certain Superintendants for the purchasing Flour, and other papers relative to that business. Referred for Consideration.

18. Took into consideration the above papers & reported against the Contract as unnecessary & unreasonable & exorbitant.[5] Genl. not present.

19. Mr. Harvey left the Committee.[6] Settled the order of promotion as follows.[7] Promotion shall be *regimental* to the rank of Captain inclusively. From that rank to that of Brigadiers inclusively to be in the line of the *State*. Promotion from that rank, in the line of the army, *at large*. The Genl. laid before the Committee, Duportail recommendation of Capt. de Murman for an Engineer with the Rank of Major. Referr'd.[8] Colonels power of granting Furloes. The Article of War, touching Capital Offences, weak (*nothing—Corporal Punishment must be introduced such as whipping*) 100 Lashes only insufficient.

Mr. Lawrence judge Advocate's Letter laid by the Genl. before the Committee, on the subject of the articles of war.[9]

Consid of Marquis Fayette's Proposition respectg the Marquis de la Tour de pin[10] & agreed to write a cavil declining his Offers of Service.

20. Recd. Letters from Col. Mifflin & Young Waggon Master Genl to Col. Lutterlogh on Waggons. Also from Capt. Selin Commandg. Officer of Armands Corps requesting Directions respectg it. Referr'd to the General.

Wrote Blane Dy. Comy. Genl. of Purchs. respecting the purchase of Fish in Maryland[11] & Lettr. to Govr. Johnson introducg him.[12] (N. 22.)[13]

MS (DLC). A continuation of Committee at Camp Minutes of Proceedings, February 8–14, 1778. The minutes printed in this entry are in the hands of committee members Francis Dana, Gouverneur Morris, and Joseph Reed.

[1] See Committee at Camp to William Livingston, February 13, and to Thomas Johnson, February 16, 1778.

[2] See Joseph Reed to John Bayard, March 8? 1778, note 1.

[3] The dispute among the brigadier generals of the Virginia Continental regiments over their seniority had been before Congress for more than a year, and after several attempts to resolve the problem, Congress referred it to the Committee at Camp. For further information on the disposition of this dispute, see John Penn to William Woodford, November 19, 1777, note 3; and Committee at Camp Statement, March 2, 1778.

[4] See Committee at Camp to George Clinton, February 17; and Gouverneur Morris to George Clinton, February 17, 1778.

[5] Three agents of the Board of War had been directed to purchase flour and to establish supply magazines in Pennsylvania under a January 15 resolve of Congress. Robert L. Hooper, Nathaniel Falconer, and Jonathan Mifflin, Jr., apparently exceeded the limits of their authority and certainly angered Pennsylvania officials by purchasing flour and "several other articles wanted in the army" at prices that exceeded those set by the state government. On the same day that the committee began its deliberations on the activities of these purchasers, Congress, acting on information provided by the Board of War, denounced their conduct and directed the board to "recal and suspend" them. See JCC, 10:54–56, 166–70, 172–74, 176–77; Pa. Archives, 1st ser. 6:303–14; PCC, item 78, 11:259–83; Daniel Roberdeau to Thomas Wharton, February 17, note 2; William Duer to Francis Lightfoot Lee, February 19, note 1; and Gouverneur Morris to John Harvie, February 19, 1778.

[6] John Harvie returned to York in an apparent effort to explain the committee's findings and recommendations to Congress. See Gouverneur Morris to John Harvie, February 19, 1778.

[7] This was part of the general arrangement of the army that the committee had been sent to camp to undertake.

[8] After preparing its plan to rearrange the engineer corps, the committee agreed to recommend Jean Bernard de Murnan to Congress for the rank of major in the corps. Congress took no action until January 13, 1779, when it appointed Murnan a major in the corps of engineers "to take rank as such from the 1st day of March last, and to receive pay and subsistence from the 1st day of February last, the latter being the time he was employed by Brigadier du Portail, and the former the time he was directed by the Commander in Chief to act as major." See JCC, 13:57–58; Committee at Camp Minutes of Proceedings, March 1–7; and Committee at Camp to Henry Laurens, March 3, 1778.

[9] John Laurance's February 5 letter to General Washington is in the Washington Papers, DLC. Laurance reported that the articles of war needed no alteration except to allow commanding officers authority to call courts-martial and to increase the permissible number of lashes so that whipping could be used as an intermediate punishment for desertion instead of the death penalty. For further infor-

mation on Laurance's career as judge advocate and for a discussion of these two points raised by Laurance, see Robert H. Berlin, "Administration of Military Justice in the Continental Army during the American Revolution, 1775–1783" (Ph.D. diss., University of California at Santa Barbara, 1976), pp. 96–111, 141–45, 161–65.

[10] That is the marquis de la Tour du Pin de Montauban. See Lafayette, *Papers* (Idzerda), 1:227–28, 232, 233n.

[11] See Committee at Camp to Ephraim Blaine, February 20, 1778. A letter Blaine wrote to the committee this day from "Camp, Pawlings Ford," containing complaints against the Board of War's purchasing agent Robert L. Hooper for buying up wheat for forage that should have been used for flour, is in the Ephraim Blaine Letterbook, DLC.

[12] Not found.

[13] For the continuation of these minutes, see Committee at Camp Minutes of Proceedings, February 22–28, 1778.

Committee at Camp to Thomas Johnson

Sir.   Camp at the Valley Forge 16th Feby. 1778

We have the Honor to compose a Committee of Congress appointed to confer with the General upon the Affairs of the Army & with him to concert Measures for opening the Campaign with Vigor and Activity. During the Progress of this important Business the critical Situation of the Army on the Score of Provisions hath filled our Minds with Apprehension and Alarm. Fed by daily Supplies and even those uncertain we have to fear a total Want. Some Brigades have not tasted Flesh in four Days and the Evil great as it is seems rather to increase than diminish. The Commissaries inform us that they have not only met with Great Difficulties in Purchasing Provisions in your State but that they cannot even transport what they have purchased for the Want of Waggons & the like. Whether these Apologies are justly founded we will not presume to say but this is certain that upon an early transportation of large Quantities of Provisions to this camp from the State you preside over the very Existence of our Army depends. Let us then intreat you Sir to exert the full Influence of your Abilities to forward such Supplies as may have been already bought up and also to obtain by such Measures as you may think most adequate to that Purpose as much as can be spared by the Inhabitants from their own particular Consumption.

We have the Honor to be, respectfully, Sir, your most obedt. & humble Servants,

Francis Dana   Jno. Harvie

Nathel. Folsom   Gouv. Morris

RC (MdAA). Written by Gouverneur Morris and signed by Morris, Dana, Folsom, and Harvie.

Francis Dana to Elbridge Gerry

Moore Hall, Camp Valley Forge
My Worthy Friend   Feb. 16, 1778.

Your favour of the 8th instant[1] I had the pleasure of receiving on the 13th, and am much obliged to you for the variety of matter it contains. Before I pay a particular attention to it, I will give some account of the state of our army, which demands a most serious consideration. A great proportion of the soldiers are in a very suffering condition for want of necessary clothing, and totally unfit for duty: but even this evil would have been patiently endured had not another, irresistible in its nature, taken place, the want of provisions. Congress will wonder, when we acquaint them, that the army, or any part of it, have wanted bread, since but a short time before we assured them that there was no probability of a deficiency in that article, and that there was a sufficiency already purchased and engaged. We founded this opinion upon the information of colonel Blane.[2] Several brigades complained they had been destitute of flour two, three and four days. We reexamined colonel Blane, who assured us that if such a want took place, it must be owing to neglect in the issuing commissaries or quarter-masters, as flour was deposited in the magazines. An enquiry was instituted at head quarters, the result of which was a general blame; but such is the dependence of the army, even upon some scoundrels, that they dare not proceed to punish the most negligent at present, lest the sufferings of the army, instead of being relieved, should be increased. I yesterday mounted my horse and rode into camp and passed through several brigades, some of which were said to have been destitute of flour several days, enquiring separately of all the officers I knew, of different ranks, and am satisfied that by comparing their accounts I learnt the real state of these brigades: indeed the accounts were not very different. For flour they had not suffered; but upon an average every regiment had been destitute of fish or flesh four days. On Saturday evening they received, some three-fourths and others one half pound of salted pork a man—not one day's allowance: nor have they assurance of regular supplies in future. We do not see from whence the supplies of meat are to come. The want of it will infallibly bring on a mutiny in the army. Sunday morning colonel Brewer's regiment rose in a body and proceeded to general Patterson's quarters, in whose brigade they are, laid before him their complaints, and threatened to quit the army. By a prudent conduct he quieted them, but was under a necessity of permitting them to go out of camp to purchase meat as far as their money would answer, and to give their certificates for the other, and he would pay for it. The same spirit was rising in other regiments, but has been happily suppressed for the present by the prudence of some of their officers. But no prudence or management, without meat, can satisfy the hungry man. In plain terms, 'tis probable this army will disperse if the commissary department is so damnably managed. Good God! how absurd to attempt an expedition into Canada, when you cannot feed this reduced army! All the meat you have in magazines or can purchase in any part and transport here, will not be more than sufficient to satisfy the daily wants of this army for months to come. This consideration induces me to set my face against that expedition, which I think I foresee will be extending from time to time, till it becomes a great object. I lament it was not confined to its original limits. Is it yet too late to reduce it? The passes on the North river must be secured, or without question this and the neighbouring states of Jersey, Delaware and Maryland must be evacuated by our army. They cannot be fed with meat but from beyond that river. But more on this subject when I have the pleasure of meeting you.

Your's,   F. Dana.[3]

But to return to your letter. I am sorry Congress have divided the Quarter Master General's department; for upon a critical examination into the causes of the failure of supplies seasonably arriving in Camp, we find they arise principally from the scandalous neglect that has taken place in that department. That this neglect cou'd have been in a good measure remedied by the Quartr. Mast. Genl. being of the Line and *constantly* attendant upon the army, and thoroughly acquainted with its wants. His orders must be obeyed thro every branch of the department upon the peril of life, and untill some villains are hanged or quartered great will be the obstructions in it. Baron Steuben has not yet arrived in camp.[4] I hope he will answer your expectations. Remember what Chatham said, "confidence is a plant of slow growth in an aged bosom." I joined in recommending Genl. Schyler with diffidence; it was therefore I stated the objections for the particular consideration of Congress. Press on the appointment of Wadsworth vigorously. As to the Field Deputies, I am fully convinced of the expediency of their appointment. Guard against intrigues & cabals as effectually as possible. The utmost caution shoud be used in pitching upon characters. Speaking of intrigues and cabals I am *naturally* reminded of a certain Brigadier General. We have presumed to point out a station for him.[5] Don't let this movement be delayed. I shall give you a surprising ancedote or two, of another General Officer, who, among you, has the reputation of a man of courage. I was much releived by your information respecting the treasury. Go on vigourously by all means, much yet remains to be done in that line. I had heard of the infamous attempt upon the venerable Doctr. Franklyn's life, before the arrival of your letter. I hope he will survive it. I did not receive the letter from our friend J Adams, which you say was inclosed. You must have long since seen our proposals for reinforcing our army by drafts from the militia, and arrangement of the new Battalions. I think it is an œconomical plan & hope it will be acceptable. The appointment of Gentn. of the law to assist & cooperate with the Judge Advocate in a certain tryal is not a very pleasing thing in camp.[6] It is I believe a novelty. I hope the committee have been industrious in collecting evidence. Genl. St. Clair is gone to Boston, *perhaps to Cambridge.* As to my going to France I shou'd have no objection to go as Secretary; in any other character, I am sure I shall never have an opportunity. If I had, I shou'd think it my indispensable duty to decline it. I have a passionate desire to visit Europe once more, and am firmly determined to do it when this Storm is over.[7]

Please to present my regards to Messrs. Ellery & Lovell. I will write them both as soon as possible. Inclosed I shall send a letter from our friend J. Jackson to me and another to Mr. Rose. You will please to execute his desire in my stead.

I am, with much esteem, your friend &c.   Fra Dana

Austin, *Gerry,* 1:245–48. RC (MHi). Endorsed by Gerry: "Moore Hall Lettr, **F.** Dana Esq. Feby 16, 1778, ans[were]d 26th." Only the last two pages of the RC have been found; these apparently became separated from the opening pages of the letter before they were printed by James T. Austin in his life of Gerry in 1828. Although Austin included a complimentary close and Dana's signature with the portion of the letter he printed, the content and physical appearance of the surviving portion of the manuscript suggest that Dana actually wrote it as part of the original letter rather than as a postscript.

[1] Not found.

[2] The Committee at Camp had met with Ephraim Blaine on February 3 and 7. See Committee at Camp Minutes of Proceedings, February 2–7, 1778.

[3] Remainder of letter taken from the RC.

[4] Baron von Steuben arrived at camp on February 23 and conferred with the committee on February 27. See John M. Palmer, *General Von Steuben* (New Haven: Yale University Press, 1937), p. 129; and Committee at Camp Minutes of Proceedings, February 22–28, 1778.

[5] In their February 14 letter to Henry Laurens, the committee had recommended Brig. Gen. James Varnum to command the American forces in Rhode Island.

[6] For further information on Congress' efforts to appoint additional lawyers to assist in the trial of Generals Schuyler and St. Clair, see Henry Laurens to William Paterson, February 7, 1778.

[7] Dana's name had apparently come forward in Congress when William Carmichael was named secretary to the commissioners at Paris on November 28, 1777. Although Carmichael's character had recently been aspersed by Arthur Lee, no immediate change was made in the appointment. Only after Carmichael returned from France in June 1778 and the American diplomatic mission was reorganized in 1779 was Dana appointed secretary to the minister plenipotentiary to negotiate peace, John Adams. See *JCC,* 9:975; 15:1128; and James Lovell to Richard Henry Lee, December 18, 1777.

William Duer to George Washington

Sir,   Reading Feby. 16th. 1777 [*i.e.* 1778]
I esteem it my Duty to inform you that a certain Mr. John Biddle
has lately gone into the Enemy, who has an Exact Draft of your
Camp; before he went in he told a Person confidentially that he
could put the Enemy in a Way of investing it in such a Manner as
to cut off your Communication with the Country, and thereby prevent the Supply of Provisions &ca. How far this can be Effected your
Excellency best knows;[1] but what has occasioned it [to] make a
Strong Impression on my Mind is a Declaration of Major Genl
Sinclair[2] to a Freind (who some Time ago communicated it to me)
that in his Opinion such an Event might happen unless two Bridges
were thrown across the Schuylkill in order to facilitate the Retreat of
the Army, if the Enemy were to make this Attempt.
As I am a Stranger to the Geography of the Country, it would be
impertinent in me to add any Reflections of my own: I have therefore contented myself with communicating this Matter and doubt not
your Excellency will pay that Attention to it which you shall think
it deserves.
I am with great Respect, Your Excellency's most Obed. Hble. servt.
                                                    Wm. Duer

P.S. This Mr. Biddle has been for a considerable Time Emplyd as a
Depy. Surveyor in the Proprietor's Service, and is an Excellent Drafts-
man.

RC (DLC). Endorsed by Duer: "Mr. Duer desires Mr. Morris will open this Letter,
and if he thinks proper communicate the Contents in such Way as he shall think
best."
[1] Washington explained the utter impracticability of John Biddle's scheme in
his February 21 response to Duer. Washington, *Writings* (Fitzpatrick), 10:497–98.
[2] Arthur St. Clair.

Pennsylvania Delegates to Thomas Wharton

Hond Sir,   York 16th Feby 1778
The Delegates take the liberty to send enclosed, the last resolve of
Congress, relative to the purchase of Provisions &c for the Army.[1]
They have not lost a Moment since the Voting of the money, which
was on Friday last,[2] to procure a Warrant & have it passed the Treasury, But upon applying to the Treasurer it was impossible to procure more than 16 quire Amountg to £52,000 at this time, as he
was pressed by Prior Orders. The same hour it was received one quire
of the Draught was put into Majr. Scotts hands, one Do. into Majr.

Dills, who had waited two days (after advancing £150 of his private money in purchases) 2 Do. were sent by Majr. Dill to the Cumberland Comy. which he engaged to deliver on Saturday, And the remaining 12 quire we send by the bearer which is the whole of the 52,000 Dollars. We hope your honr. & the Council will approve of the advances to the York & Cumberland Comissrs. which we should not have done without a special Order, if it had been practicable to send an Express, but the River forbad it. We hope the unhappy, & we fear fatal delay, in this business in the distressed State of our Army will not be attributed by our State to any Neglect or want of Zeal in their Delegates, And we heartily pray that a Moment longer, may not be lost in a business so pressing & necessary, we shall if agreable to your honour & Council, Urge the Treasurer to Compleat the residue of the War[ran]t for 300,000 Dollars in favour of our state with all possible dispatch.

We have the Honour to be, with all due respect, your hble Servts (by order of the delegates)   Jas. Smith

17th. Mr. Dickson takes the Charge of this but without the money. The Delegates hope to be able to draw the whole tomorrow & will send it in safe Custody to the River by Thursday Noon, where they will deliver it to your Excellencies Order & hope some proper Person may be Ordered from Lancaster to receive the same at the River.

Your Excell most obedt,   Jas Smith
By order of the [. . . .]

RC (RPJCB). Written and signed by James Smith.

[1] For this February 14 resolve, see *JCC,* 10:166–70.

[2] According to the journals, this resolve was adopted on Thursday, February 12. See *JCC,* 10:155. For the efforts of the delegates to get this money delivered, see also Daniel Roberdeau to Wharton, February 17; and Pennsylvania Delegates to Wharton, February 18, 1778.

Committee at Camp to George Clinton

                                                    Camp near the Valley Forge
Sir   Chester County Pennsylvania Feb. 17. 1778.
We have the Honour of composing a Committee of Congress to confer with his Excelly. General Washington on the Affairs of the American Army. We find ourselves interrupted in our Progress to form an Arrangement & make the necessary dispositions for the ensuing Campaign by a most alarming Scarcity in the Article of Meat. The Course of the Enemy thro this State & the continued Draughts of our own Army have exhausted a Country which never raised sufficient Flesh for its own Consumption. Your Excellys. Discernment

will easily point out to you the variety of melancholy Events which such an Evil must produce & how affecting they must be to the Interests of the United States. Mutiny, Desertion, a Spirit of Depredation, & Plunders ending at last in a total Dissolution perhaps of the Army, a Subject of great Exultation to our Enemies & Depression to our Friends will be the immediate Consequences of this deplorable Failure, unless some Remedy can be provided. Some of the Troops have been 4 days without Meat & the Prospects of the Commissaries are so light & precarious that Necessity obliges us to disclose our Situation & call most earnestly for your Assistance. Our limited Knowledge of the Resources of your State & its present Condition forbids our pointing out any precise Mode in which this important Business of Supply can be effected & it is the less necessary as the Zeal & Judgment manifested so frequently by your Excellency & the Gentleman in Authority with you will so amply supply our Deficiency. We could only hint that if from the peculiar Circumstances of the State of New York it can afford us little [or] no Relief in furnishing this necessary Article of Subsistence it may possibly do much in the Transportation of it from other States. Our Situation obliges us to call for Help of every kind & from every Quarter & we flatter ourselves it will have its due Effect in animating the faithful Inhabitants of your State to the most vigorous Exertions.

We are with the greatest Respect & Regard, Your Excells. most Obed & very Hbble Servts.

FC (DNA: PCC, item 33). In the hand of Joseph Reed and endorsed by him: "Copy of a Letter to Govr Clinton dated Feb. 17. 1778 on Provision. Forwarded the same Day."

Committee of Commerce to Robert and Samuel Purviance, Jr.

Gentlm.   York Town 17 Febry. 1778.

The day before I left Baltimore, it was reported there, that a large French ship was on shore on the Coast near Chingoteague, and that they were taking part of the Cargo out in order to lighten her. The Agent from France arrived here yesterday and informs us that a 50 Gun ship laden for the Congress may be abt this time expected at the Capes from St Domingo,[1] and is anxious to know if that ship reported to be on shore may not be the same, of which please to get the best information you can and inform me—also whether the Virginia has embraced the opportunities of these fair winds to put to Sea, which I am very anxious to know.[2] I am, Gentlm., Your very Humble Servt,

         Fras Lewis, Chairman of Commercial Committee

RC (MdHi). Written and signed by Francis Lewis.

[1] According to Silas Deane's September 10, 1777, letter to the Committee for Foreign Affairs, which introduced Caron de Beaumarchais' agent Jean Théveneau de Francy, the French vessel expected from Santo Domingo was the *Therese,* sent by Hortalez & Co., the firm set up to funnel French supplies to America. Wharton, *Diplomatic Correspondence,* 2:392–93.

[2] For the loss of the *Virginia,* see Marine Committee to the Middle Department Navy Board, April 8, 1778, note 1.

Eliphalet Dyer to William Williams

Dear Sir   York Town 17th Febry 1778

I most sincerely thank you for Your two last clever long letters & not too long. I feel my self in some measure relievd in being joined by two Colleagues[1] but the distresses of our diminished Army the little prospects of Magazines being laid up sufficient for an Increase equal to our demands fill me with much Anxiety. The southern States say you must not depend upon us, when we turn our eyes eastward they say we must not depend upon them. It is in the meat kind we principally fear a failure; as to bread we trust we are in a way to be Supplied. Indeed there is considerable quantityes of pork laying up to the southward as far as North Carolina but it seems almost impossible to get it transported here in season. The Navigation is Obstructed by the Enemy, Waggons almost worn out & the cost amazing. There is no Stop to the Continual Cries for money from every quarter & every department, it is made & Issued as fast as possible but that with every other resource falls much short of the Increasing demands. But why do I dwell on the dark side? We have put our hands to the plow & must not look back but persevere & Trust in the Almighty for deliverance. I hope the Governor before this time is somewhat pacified & his jealousies removed, as all was meer Accident without design or the least Intention of so much as Neglect.[2] Am very anxious for Mr. Trumbull on Account of his ill State of health tho am glad to find his resentments in some measure abated & that if his health permits he will attend the board.[3] His presence there is much desired but it seems Providence denies us his help when to Appearance it is most wanted. The Commissary & Qtr. Master Department is in a most ruinous State but on report of board of Warr the qtr master Department is divided up into 3 or 4 branches which is agreed to.[4] Their is now the military part which requires a person of skill & abilities in that way, a forrage Master part to procure forrage, Another for Waggons, & Another to Collect Tent, warlike Stores & the like & we are now looking out for persons proper to head each. Congress are quite sick & discouraged on their late plan in the Commissary Department & of the persons employd in the Execution, &

we have lately received a letter from the Genll & other Genll Officers recommending Coll Wadsworth as the only Gentn they can think of whose abilities & exertions can under Providence relieve us & Tho Congress have not yet dismissed Buc——n yet they have Unanimously sent of an express to Coll Wadsworth to come forward immediately to Congress;⁵ And dare say if he comes he may have almost his own plan & Terms if he will only undertake as they entertain the highest Opinion of his Abilities & think him the only person Next to Mr Trumbull who can effect their purpose. I hope he will not fail to come forward soon. He will be well rewarded I trust for his trouble even if he should not undertake but hope he will as I know he loves his Country & is Zealous in her cause. Why in the name of common sense could you the most averse to Frenchmen after we had been plagued beyond measure to send one the most Insignificant of all upon us and recommend him to me who could not speake a word of French nor he of English. I received the letter & that was all & sent him to Mr. Lovell but he can have no birth and seems to have no Claim or any thing or quality to recommend him. You doubtless before this will have Various rumours of a Canada Expedition & may wonder among our many wants we should undertake this wild plan. The Truth is Genll Gates had laid the plan & made every preparation for Genll Starks with a party under him at the proper season to make an irruption into Canada as his Accounts were the Garrison at St. Johns & Chamblee were Very Weak, the Canadians highly dissaffected to the Britons, large Stores for the Indians in Montreal, & that by a sudden push they might soon fall into our hands & if not we might burn or destroy their Navigation on the lake which would Intirely prevent the Enemy from Anoying us from that quarter for a year or two. Beside the report of our forming a discent on Canada again would reach the Court in Great Britain and must perplex their Counsells in carrying on the Warr for the Ensuing year & would divide their forces as they would doubtless send a considerable post to Canada. We imagine it will have that effect even if we do not succeed & we expect our forces to return again before the lake breaks up & will be ready to give their assistance on the North River. There is, it is true a Considerable Number of French Officers gone that way viz Marq. Fiatte, Genll Conway, I believe Baron Kalb, Cols Young, Fleury & several others of spirit to Convince the French in Canada that France is really engaged on the side of America which may prevent their joining or giving any assistance to the few British Troops now in Canada. I have many letters to write & no room or place to write in being dislodged of my old lodgings by the sickness of Mr. Spongler with whom I lived of a Violent pleurisy of which he died about 2 days agoe. My sincere regards to all Friends & am with sincere Esteem, yr Hle Servt,   Elipht Dyer

[*P.S.*] Our friend Esqr Wales has forgot me. I have wrote him once or twice[6] since I had any from him one of which I know he has received, therefor wait for an Answer or line from him which should be glad to receive as I make a point not to fail of an Answer especially to one whom I Esteem & am glad to Correspond with. Remember me kindly to him.   E D

P.S. Since the above we have just receivd a letter from Genll Washington that a Cartel is settled between him & Genll How for a full exchange of Prisoners which will redeem all our privates and a great part of our officers. This I believe was effected by some late spirited resolves of Congress, a Copy of which will Indeavour to send you.[7]

E D

RC (CtY: Pequot Library deposit).
   [1] Samuel Huntington and Oliver Wolcott, who presented their credentials to Congress on February 16. *JCC*, 10:170.
   [2] See Henry Laurens to the States, December 23, 1777, note 2.
   [3] Governor Trumbull's January 24 letter to President Laurens, indicating that his son Joseph would attend the Board of War when his health improved, was read in Congress on February 16. See PCC, item 66, 1:378; and *JCC*, 10:171.
   [4] The Board of War's report was read on January 30 and approved on February 5, but it was replaced by another plan on March 2. See *JCC*, 10:102–3, 126–27, 209–10; and Committee at Camp to Henry Laurens, February 25, 1778, note 2.
   [5] For Congress' request to meet with Jeremiah Wadsworth to discuss his availability as a replacement for Commissary General of Purchases William Buchanan, see Dyer to Wadsworth, February 10, 1778, note. No specific recommendation of Wadsworth by Washington has been found, but Dyer may have had in mind the Committee at Camp's January 29 recommendation to President Laurens, which was made after conferring with Washington.
   [6] Not found.
   [7] For the January 21 resolves on treatment of prisoners, see *JCC*, 10:74–82. Washington's February 8–14 letter to President Laurens, which reported agreement between Washington and Howe to negotiate a general prisoner exchange, is in PCC, item 152, 5:287–89, and Washington, *Writings* (Fitzpatrick), 10:428–30. On congressional opposition to the prisoner cartel that contributed to the ultimate collapse of negotiations, see Committee at Camp to Washington, February 11, note; and Henry Laurens to Washington, March 15, note 1, and April 8, 1778, note 4.

John Henry to Thomas Johnson

Sir   York Town Febry. 17th 1778.
   I wrote to you yesterday.[1] Since that Time, we have had an Express from Camp, by which we are acquainted that Genl. Washington and Genl. Howe have agreed upon an exchange of prisoners. This is an agreeable piece of news. The former Dispute is waved for the present. The Law of retaliation has had this good effect.
   Enclosed you have a piece of the Earl of Abingdon.[2] It is just put into my hands. I have not read it. It is said to have reputation.
   I am Sir with great respect, Yrs.   J Henry Junr.

RC (PHi).

¹ Not found.

² *Thoughts on the Letter of Edmund Burke, Esq. to the Sheriffs of Bristol, on the Affairs of America*, a vigorous attack on Edmund Burke's defense of unlimited parliamentary supremacy. For the Americans' use of Abingdon's tract to revive sagging American morale during this bleak period, see Paul H. Smith, comp., *English Defenders of American Freedoms, 1774–1778* (Washington: Library of Congress, 1972), pp. 193–230. It is clear from the correspondence of Thomas Wharton, president of the Pennsylvania Council, that he and Robert Morris had a hand in subsidizing the publication of an American edition of the pamphlet by John Dunlap at Lancaster at this time. Ibid., pp. 194, 196n.3.

Gouverneur Morris to George Clinton

Sir.   Camp Valley Forge 17th Feby. 1778.

This half private half public Letter arrives to tell you that an American Army in the Bosom of America is about to disband for the Want of somewhat to eat. We write to you as Governor from the Committee a *general* Letter.¹ To your private Ear and for your particular Information let me say that our Troops have been upon the Point of disbanding three times. One dangerous Mutiny quelled with Difficulty. The neighbouring Country twice laid under military Contribution to little or no Purpose. The sly broad Brims² who do not take Arms against us in great Numbers are assiduous in the Task of undermining our Resources and when we are starved from a Piece of Ground Howe need but appear and it smiles with Abundance. I know our State can furnish little or no Provisions but Something or other may perhaps be done and if so let it be done.³ Not a Word of Politicks. I know none and from the State of New York I can hear none. Yes one Piece of News. Howe is so fearful that the World should know his situation or his Army know what passes in the World that he examines every Letter of every Body going to or coming from any Place and all this under very severe Penalties on those who shall presume to smuggle. Desertion prevails in his Army, Resignation among the Officers of it. Ours is not without both of these Diseases. But when you consider that the Poor Dogs are in an Enemy's Country without Cloaths to wear, Victuals to eat, Wood to burn or straw to lie on the wonder is that they stay not that they go.

Let me intreat that I may immediately have a Return of the Officers in Gansevoorts, Van Schaicks & Dubois's Regiments containing their merit that is to say let the best Captain be put on the Top of the List, the next best next and so on for each Regt. Those Officers who are worse than indifferent marked with an asterisk * those very good with a Star ★. Let me at the same time have a Copy of a Rank Roll made out for the late Convention by their Committee of Appointment and on it the Vacancies which have since happened. Secrecy in this

Business as far as conveniently practicable without too great an Affectation of it will be of Advantage. The Returns I have mentioned are necessary for the new arrangement of the Army and with Expedition. I have no time to sport with my Pen nor even to write to my other Friends as the Express who is to carry this Waits. For Gods Sake let me hear that you are raising at the very least Farthing a Tax of half a million Dollars. Pounds would be still better. Taxation will raise, feed and Clothe an Army better than any thing human or all Things human beside it. I have said let me repeat it when our Confederation is fixed, the several Governments organized, heavy Taxes laid and levied and civil and *more especially* criminal Proceedings regularly *rigidly* had then and not till then the American War will end.[4]

My Respects to all who deserve them; to Jay & Livingston my Love. I say nothing of my Colleagues because I suppose by this time two are gone Northward tother South.[5] Adieu. Believe me sincerely, yours,

Gouv Morris

RC (NN).
    [1] See Committee at Camp to Clinton, this date.
    [2] Quakers.
    [3] Morris also evinced his concern about the Continental Army's current supply problems by drafting a proclamation for General Washington on February 18 that called upon the people of New Jersey, Pennsylvania, Maryland, and Virginia to supply cattle to the army. See Washington, *Writings* (Fitzpatrick), 10:480–81.
    [4] Governor Clinton's March 5 reply to Morris' letter is in Clinton, *Papers* (Hastings), 2:791–92.
    [5] Morris is referring to James Duane, who was assisting the northern Indian commissioners in Albany; William Duer, whom he supposed to be on his way to join Lafayette's Canadian expedition; and Francis Lewis, who, unbeknownst to Morris, had recently returned to Congress after a leave of absence in Baltimore.

Robert Morris to the Committee of Commerce

Gentlemen,   Manheim Febry. 17th. 1778
    Agreable to my promise you will find inclosed herein a Manifest of all the Tobacco that has been bought by the Secret Committee shewing what has been exported, what quantity arrived, how much taken & lost and what remains except that it is not in my power to ascertain the exact quantities in the hands of Mr. J. H. Norton of Williamsburg, Mr. Benjn. Harrison junr., Carter Braxton Esquire, Messrs. James & Adam Hunter and Thos. Pitt Esquire. The latter I think did send me an Account of his purchase but if he did it is mislaid. This Gentleman had not the money sent him, time enough to lay the whole out before prices rose above his limits, he therefore must account for the Balance in Money unless you choose to order him to

Invest it now in Tobacco, the other Gentlemen have Tobacco to nearly the Amount of their balances as the deficiency only arises by the breach of bargains they made for it, several not delivering the full quantities they agreed for. I have employed myself a few days in entering up & adjusting a very long accot. between the Committee & my House W[illing] Morris & Co. which was employed to Conduct their purchases & find a balance in their favour of about £5000 Curry. Several articles of account however are not included therein as I cannot at present ascertain them exactly but when the whole are included I believe the Committee will be still more indebted to them, besides £6000 they are to be paid for the ship Lord Camden taken on her Return from France & Insured by the Committee.

Enclosed herein you will receive a letter I have written to Mr. John Ross which I have signed agreable to your desire[1] by which you will see I have directed 142 hogsheads Tobacco on board the Snow Speedwell, Capt. Kent (indeed this was ordered to him last spring) 120 hhds per the Brigt. Braxton, 476 hogsheads per the Brigt. Governor Johnston, & 269 hogsheads by the Brigt. Morris, Capt Gunnison, to be Consigned to him or his order on accot. of the United States Amounting to 1007 hogsheads in all & if it arrives safe will over pay his advances, but we cannot Count upon the whole to arrive, I have desired each Vessel to [set] out the first opportunity. There Remains

492 hogsheads	on Board the Chase	} under care of Steph.
117 hogsheads	on Board the Snow George	} Purviance
ditto	on Board the Ship Virginia, under care of Mr. Braxton	
ditto	on Board the Brigt. under care of Steph. Steward	
ditto	in the hands of the Gentlemen mentioned in the general Manifest all unappropriated and of course I suppose will be applyed towards satisfying the demands or Claims of Monsr. Francy.	

You will also find herein a paper of Entries proper to be made in the Books of the Commercial Committee for the purpose of transferring the balances therein ascertained from the Books of the Secret Committee wherein I have made Correspondent Entries and did intend to have continued this practice as fast as I settled any Accounts therein, had I been left to pursue this business agreable to the offer made in Congress. I thought it essentially necessary to settle these as the foundation of your present operations & would now send you the Books but the Crossing of Susquehannah is yet too dangerous before they shall wait your orders which you may depend shall be instantly complyed with.

The Charter Party for the Brigt. Governor Johnson is amongst the Committees papers but as her Voyage is transferred to your care had best be deposited with yours. The Brigt. Morris belongs to the Continent, she was bought by Jno Langdon Esquire in New Hampshire & her Cost & charges must be transferred to your Debit. The Snow Speedwell, Capt. Kent, was valued at £2000 Virginia Curry by persons appointed for the purpose, she is my property & no Charter party has ever been made but the Committee must in this as in all other Cases Insure the value of said Vessell, in proportion as their part of the Cargo is to the whole, and the same with the Brigt. Boston in which I am interested with Mr. Braxton & Mr. Ross, this Brigt. might have been sold both before & since she loaded for £3000, which I deem her salvation and should be glad you would either order Charter parties to be made out for these Vessells or Enter on your Minutes that you are Insurers thereon against all Risques untill the Cargoes are landed, at the Valuations I have mentioned in the proportions that your part of the Cargoes bears to the whole on board. The letting these Vessells take in Goods for the public has been of great prejudice to the Owners as they could long Since have sold them if disengaged to good profits but instead of that they have been long detained on heavy expenses, part whereof they think you should pay & respecting which I shall speak to you when I come to York.

I am now at the 19th Febry & find myself disapointed by Messrs. Hunters of Fredericksburgh who promised our Accot. Currt. with them by the last post but it is not come, therefore I will leave the Sum a blank for the present. That they are accountable to you for, it is however above £9000 this Currency & soon as I receive their account the proper Entries shall be made in the Secret Committee Books for transferring that balance also to you. I must observe however, that a part of this balance has come into their hands from the Sales of Goods saved from Ship Esther & Brigt. General Mercer since that price of Tobacco was above the purchasing limits, consequently these Gentlemen will have some Money & some Tobacco to accot. for, they are Men of honor & good Merchants and will deliver every hogshead of the Tobacco they bought. I have ten Hogshead of Tobacco on Board the ship Chase & ten Hogshead on board the Snow George for which I was to pay Eighteen Guineas per Ton freight, but as it is probable the destination of these Vessells must be altered and that the Cargoes will be assigned to Monsr. Francy, you may have these twenty hogsheads also at the first Cost & charges if you choose it. If not they may go forward on my account as first intended and you'l please to give me an answer to this offer. I have just received a letter from Mr. J Brown dated the 15th Inst. desiring me to return Messrs. Hewes & Smiths letter to the Committee, this I did by Monsr. Francy. He also says you wish for an extract of their letter to me on the subject of the Pattys Cargo of Salt & it shall be enclosed herein. I cannot help remarking that Colo Aylett seems fond of raising his own reputation at the expense of other people, he made last Summer several attacks on Colo. Braxton by insinuation as he does now on Mr. Hewes & I believe both these Gentlemen to be Men of as much honor & honesty as Colo. Aylett or any others upon Earth.[2] I believe at the same time that Colo. Aylett is an active Commissary but he seems too full of Suspicions & too free in writing them and Congress should guard against giving in too readily to the belief of such things, or they will not get any Men who value their Characters to serve them. On the 13th November last I wrote Messrs. Hewes & Smith[3] if any Salt arrived there belonging to the Public not to Sell, but Store it untill they should receive the Committees order as it would all be wanted for the use of the Army &ca. They acknowledge the receipt of this letter in theirs to me of the 11th December from which the enclosed extract is taken by which you'l find they had sold the Pattys Salt previous to the Receipt of my orders & that Colo. Aylett himself was in some measure the cause of it.

Soon after the Patty arrived in North Carolina with her Salt on Public Account, a Snow Nancy, Capt. Forster, belonging to Mr. Ross & myself arrived there also with a Cargo of Salt on our Account & Messrs. Hewes & Smith with equal precipitation & without orders proceeded to make Sale of it for which they justify themselves in the Same manner as they do for the Sale of the public Salt, however this Cargo arriving latter then the Pattys they had not sold the whole of it when my orders respecting it reached them. Soon as I heard of this Snows arrival in No. Carolina I offered the Cargo of Salt to Mr. Buchanan (not respecting Messrs. Hewes & Co. would make any sale untill they heard from me) and he told me Mr. Aylett being Deputy Commissary of purchases in that Department he would buy it, but Mr. Aylett being distant from me & the price of salt low in No. Carolina Compared to what it was here I determined not to lay mine & my Friends property at his mercy.

Therefore I wrote to Messrs. Hewes & Smith[4] proposing that they should measure the Snow Nancys Cargo of Salt, value it at the then Current price & then make a large purchase of Green Pork on the best terms in their power, Cure & Barrell it, ready for Sale to those that should want, and the concern in this Pork to be in thirds, one of which their Accot., ⅓d Mr. Ross & ⅓d mine. By this mode Mr. Ross & myself gave up one third of our Salt at a low price for the Sake of being ⅔ as interested in the Pork, this proposal reaching Mr. Hewes & Smith before all the Nancys Cargo of Salt was sold but long after the Pattys was gone, they adopted the plan & executed it as far as the remains of the Nancys Cargo enabled. I have mentioned this matter in order to clear Mr. Hewes of any unworthy Suspicion being confident he does not deserve them and I hope Congress will never countenance them by gratifying Colo. Aylett with orders to make the enquiry he offers. What I have mentioned about the Nancys Cargo of Salt & the Pork scheme may probably be remembred by Mr. Brown, by Mr. Gerry, Mr. Peters & some others in York as I told them last Winter the orders I had given and added that I expected the Pork to be put up in consequence would some day or other prove a seasonable supply to the Public. The Price of £18. per Barrell is very high but I should have made more of the Salt if it had not been so applyed for I Sold another Cargo that arrived since for £7 this Curry per bushl. and the purchaser is gone down from Pennsylvania to receive it there & bring it up at his own risque & expense, whereas the Nancys Cargo Sold at 60/ to 70/ that Curry per bushel & the Green Pork Cost 100/ to 120/ per 100 lb besides Barrells, Salt, Cooperage &ca &ca and you well know that all kinds of charges are raised to a most enormous pitch, Mr. Hewes also writes me that if Mr. Aylett had not wanted that Pork for the Public Service he could & would have had above £20 Virga. Curry for every Barrel of it.

Mr. Brown says you have wished I would recommend Mr. Ross for one of the Commercial agents in Europe.[5] I have told you Gentlemen his deserving Character but I am too sick of recommending agents ever to do it again, he says also that Colo. Harrisons plan is approved except the Commissions of one per Cent on return Cargoes in which I agree with you & think if instead of one per Cent he were allowed one quarter per Cent on a certain sum on every Cargo that returns to him for his care & trouble herewith it might do very well.

I think there is no points mentioned in any of your or Mr. Browns Letters that this and my preceeding Letters has not answered.

Last Night I recd. a letter from Mr. Willm. Wilkinson of Wilmington of which I take the Liberty to inclose you a Copy and if you were not previously informed the arrival of those Stores you will now give the necessary order respecting them or rather let the Marine Committee do it as these articles are more properly in their department. With much Respect & Esteem, I remain, Gentlemen, Your obedt. humble Servant.   Robt. Morris

P.S. I am this moment informed by a Gentleman that saw a person lately from the City of Philadelphia that the report of a Riot in London is well founded as he heard Bill the Bookseller read an Account of it in an English paper. He says General Howe offers (in hand Bills) free passages in the Transports to any persons or Families that desire to remove to England.

Tr (ScHi).
    [1] See Committee of Commerce to Robert Morris, January 30, and to John Ross, February 21, 1778.

² For additional information on charges made by deputy commissary general of purchases William Aylett against Joseph Hewes and Robert Smith, see Henry Laurens to William Aylett, April 22, 1778.

³ Not found.

⁴ Not found.

⁵ For James Forbes' understanding of what was being done to appoint commercial agents in Europe, see Forbes' letter to Thomas Johnson of February 13, 1778.

Daniel Roberdeau to Thomas Wharton

Sir,   York Town Feby. 17th. 1778

My Colleague Mr. James Smith obtained a warrant for 300,000 Dollars to be remitted to you for the purchase of Provisions, reserving as he informs me 52,000 which he has put into the hands of the Commissioners for this County and Cumberland. The low state of the Treasury has occasioned since a devision of the 300,000 Drs., one half to the Board of War & Ordinance, and the other half for this State, both being for the same purposes, the Bal[anc]e of your moiety vizt. 98,000 will I expect be ready this day, to go under the care of someone of the members of Assembly who may be passing through. As Mr. Smith undertook this business in my absence, being at the Treasury, when the Grant obtained, I shall leave the whole to his management.[1] I shall urge forward the supplies of Cash as you shall from time to time advise to be necessary, and I beseach Council not to put too much confidence in any Servant under them, lest some wheel in the machine should rust or clog to the injury of the cause which now labours in the Article of Provisions. The exuberant care of the late board of war in providing Superintendants over the Commissioners in the respective Counties, and the delegacy of their choice, has occasioned a good deal of perplexity. Last evening a modest request came before Congress to indemnify the Superintendants in violation of the provision act, in having given more than the stipulated prices, this is refered with the depositions concerning Mr. Hooper to a Committee.[2] You will see by the resolve of last Saturday that a new System has been contrived to accommodate the appointment of Superintendants to the late law of the State and to prevent any interference.[3] Mr Smith informs me he will transmit the System which prevents me. I beg Council will urge the respective Commissioners to the purchase of live Stock; as to flour, I have no fear of a plentiful supply, but through the lack of meat provisions our army is even now greatly distressed, and without the most vigorous exertions I fear the consiquence. If any thing prevents our Capital being speedily regained it will be the want of provisions. Virginia is ready to supply 5000 Volunteers and No. Carolina as many with their Governor to march at their head besides their Quota of Continental Troops, but they cannot be called for without provisions, therefore let me beseech Council to strain every nerve of exertion and make timely applycation to Congress for Cash from time to Time. Next to the want of provisions there is no one thing so distressing to our publick affairs as the want of the aid of Mr. Rittenhouse, on whom the Treasury has depended for a little work in his way, to help forward a speedy emission which is always most necessary at this season, but especially so on account of the enormous prices of every article of supply to the army. I have urged his comming forward again & again hitherto in vain, therefore I beg the interposition of Council and that that Gentleman will be entreated not to delay his coming here, a moment longer. With respectful Salutations to Council I am, Sir, Yr. most obt. huml. Serv.   Daniel Roberdeau

RC (PHarH).
[1] See the Pennsylvania Delegates' letters to Thomas Wharton of February 16 and 18, 1778.
[2] Deputy Quartermaster Robert L. Hooper had been under attack from Pennsylvania officials since early November 1777, and although recently exonerated of the original charges brought against him, his more recent activities as one of the Board of War's special purchasing agents led to renewed opposition. At the state's insistence, Congress this day directed the Board "to recal and suspend" Hooper, Nathaniel Falconer, and Jonathan Mifflin from their recently created posts, but Hooper continued to remain under attack for months. See JCC, 10:172–74, 176–77, 194; Charles Henry Hart, "Colonel Robert Lettis Hooper," PMHB 36 (January 1912): 60–91; Roberdeau to Wharton, January 16, note 2; William Duer to Francis Lightfoot Lee, February 19, note 1; and Thomas McKean to Nathanael Greene, June 9, 1778.
The orginal charges brought against Hooper by Pennsylvania were the subject of the Board of War's proceedings on January 21, 1778, of which there is no record in PCC, but a copy of the board's minutes for that date survives in the Peter Force Miscellany, DLC. In the hand of the board's deputy secretary Joseph Nourse, the document reads:
"Colonel Hooper voluntarily attending the Board, on a Charge against him, by the Executive Council of Pennsylvania, for favoring the Enemies of America, and oppressing it's Friends in the Execution of his Office, as Deputy Quarter Master General in the Service of the United States; And the Council of the said State altho' repeatedly applied to for that purpose, not having transmitted any Evidence in support of their allegation, the Board are of Opinion, that the Complaints be dismissed, and Colonel Hooper discharged from any farther attendance on Account of the said unsupported information.
"The Board taking into Consideration the Charge made by Mr R Wilson against Colonel Hooper concerning his obstructing the Commissary's Department, in the purchase of wheat, & having maturely considered the Circumstances on which Colonel Hooper's Conduct was founded, & the testimonies of several respectable public Officers, in the Service of these States, in his favor, are of Opinion, that Colonel Hooper's Conduct is not reprehensible.
"Resolved, that the Order of this Board of the 22d of December last restraining Colonel Hooper in the purchase of Wheat for the Quarter-Master's Department be rescinded and that it be recommended to Colonel Hooper and the Assistants under him to cultivate harmony with the persons employed in the Commissary

Department in Order that no Competition may arise in the purchase of any Articles, necessary for the Use of the respective Departments."

This document is also interesting for the light it casts upon the operation of the board at this date, because this session was perhaps the last time it convened in its traditional role as essentially a congressional committee. Although reorganized in November 1777, it did not actually function in its reconstituted form until late January 1778. The members of the board attending on January 21 to consider Hooper's case were Charles Carroll of Carrollton, William Duer, John Harvie, Edward Langworthy, Francis Lightfoot Lee, and Jonathan Bayard Smith. See also Committee on Emergency Provisions to Thomas Wharton, December 30, 1777, note 1.

³ For Congress' resolves concerning the collection of provisions for the army in Pennsylvania adopted on February 14 replacing those passed on February 12, see *JCC,* 10:152–53, 166–70.

Committee at Camp to John Laurance

Sir   Moore Hall Feb. 18. 1778.

The Committee of Congress setting at Moore Hall request your Attendance when the Business of your Office will admit & desire you will at the same Time bring up with you the Resolves of Congress & Laws or other Regulations of this State empowering Court Martials to try Persons (other than of the Army).

We are induced to call upon you from a Report which has reach'd us that the Court Martial hesitates to try the Person lately concerned in the Attempt to seize Justice Knox.¹

I am by Desire of the Committee, Sir, Your most Obed. & very Hbble Serv,   Jos. Reed

RC (NOsHi). Written and signed by Joseph Reed. Addressed: "To Col. Lawrence Judge Advocate."

¹ Reed later reported to a friend that one man had been hanged for the kidnapping of Justice Knox. See Reed to John Bayard, March 8? 1778.

The Committee at Camp responded to the rash of recent "partisan" raids by urging Congress to authorize enlisting Indians to serve as a protective screen for eastern Pennsylvania and to prescribe specific punishments for persons convicted of engaging in such raids. Congress not only approved the recommendation to employ Indians but on February 27 authorized courts-martial to impose the death penalty for partisan offenses occurring within 70 miles of an American post where a general officer was stationed. See Committee of Congress to Henry Laurens, February 20; Henry Laurens to Francis Dana, March 1, 1778; and *JCC,* 10:204–5, 12:1282.

The British-controlled *Pennsylvania Evening Post* (Philadelphia) enthusiastically reported many successful loyalist raids in eastern Pennsylvania during this period, and in the February 17 issue published a list of captured "militia officers, justices of the peace, and collectors of fines under the new state, and some other disaffected persons."

Henry Laurens to Robert H. Harrison

Sir,   18th Febry 1778.
Your favor of the 5th Inst. by the Southern post reached me but this Morning whence I conclude it has been lying some days at Lancaster.[1]

No Man who has transacted half the quantity of promiscuous business which has passed through your hands but must have been startled at one time or another in his progress by a mistake Similar to that for which you so politely apologize, nothing but ignorance or illiberality would even insinuate against you a charge of improper desire.

I am perfectly satisfied Sir, & should have been extremely sorry you had given your Self a moments disquiet upon the present occasion, if the accident had not fortunately afforded me a good opportunity of assuring you of my Respect & Esteem for your Character & that under this profession I am very truly, Sir, your obedt. Servant

LB (ScHi).
[1] Robert H. Harrison (1745–90), a Maryland lawyer, served as Washington's military secretary with the rank of lieutenant colonel from 1776 to 1781. *National Cyclopædea of American Biography*. His February 5 letter to Laurens has not been found.

Henry Laurens to John Laurens

My Dear son,   York Town 18th Feby 1778.
Your Letter of the 15th[1] which I received yesterday affords me particular satisfaction, I am persuaded you will fret no less, when you receive what I shall have to offer in reply, when time will permit. At present I am obliged to defer minute answers to that & several, perhaps not less than half a dozen, of your late favours, which have come dropping in like Militia Men upon a Retreat.

My present address will be confined to one subject. The Baron Stuben has done me the honour to request a Letter to you. The Baron has learned that you speak French & that you are not une Mauvais Garçon (I have no dictionary, tell me if my French is mauvais) & is desirous of taking you into his acquaintance. I intreat you to pay to this reputable stranger your devoirs, & to render him every degree of attention consistent with your prior engagements. This is saying every thing that is needful to a Gentleman of your politeness & sensibilities & leaves me scarcely room to add that your Respects to the Baron Stuben will be particularly grateful to me.

My Dear son, I pray God, protect you.   Henry Laurens

[*P.S.*] Through various indirect Courses I am informed that about the Middle of January a Fire broke out on Elliot Street Charles Town & spread till it had destroyed about 350 Houses—that the loss, besides the buildings, is in Merchandize immense—it happened in the night.

RC (MHi: William Gilmore Simms Collection deposit, 1973).
  [1] John Laurens' February 15 letter to his father is in Simms, *Laurens Army Correspondence*, pp. 124–25.

Henry Laurens to George Washington

Sir,   18th Febry 1778.

Since I had the honour of transmitting to your Excellency, papers collected as Evidence by the Committee appointed to enquire into the Causes of the Loss of Tyconderoga & Mount Independence,[1] those Members of the Committee who had the papers in hand for Inspection & arrangement & from whom I received them, have informed me there were several which they had not intended to have troubled Your Excellency with—particularly a long anonymous Letter.

Inclosed herein Your Excellency will be pleased to receive & to add to the former a Narrative of transactions &c. at the Said Posts, confirmed by the affidavit of Capt. Jesse Leavenworth.

I have the honour to be With great R[espect]

LB (DNA: PCC, item 13).
  [1] Laurens had transmitted these papers with his February 7 letter to Washington.

North Carolina Delegates to Richard Caswell

Sir   York Town Pensylivania Feby 18th. 1776 [*i.e.* 1778]

We have had the Pleasure of receiving your Excellencys favours of the 27th Decr & 12 Ultimo,[1] for which we return you our thanks. Congress have a high sense of the intended exertion of Our State, and should the Militia be called for we shall be careful to represent the Necessity of a supply of Money, Arms &c &c & that they may have a Supply of Provisions on their March. The pay of a Major General as received from our Secretary is 166 Dollars per month and 18 Rations, his Aid De Camp 50 Doll. per month with rank of Major and no Rations; a Secretary 50 Doll. per Month. The extracts from the journals of the General Assembly will meet with Our particular Attention, You may depend we shall make use of our best endeavours to find out Capt Hampsteads retreat.[2]

We are sorry it is not in Our Power to give your Excellency any Interesting Intelligence, Our Army still remain in Winter Quarters hutted at Valey Forge, the Enemy have not as yet thought proper to molest them. A Committee of Congress is now at Head quarters with Intention to make such Reformation in the Army as may be judged necessary. Congress are exceedingly anxious that the Several States should exert themselves in Completing their Battalions. We have heard nothing lately of Colo Shephard.

The prices of Leather skins &c are excessive high, but they are articles which must at any rate be procured; we shall in our next Inform you whether Congress will choose to give still a greater price for those articles. We wish your Excellency would be pleased to inform us whether there is not a Quantity of Salt Pork in the hands of Private persons, this is an Article which will be very much wanted for the Army the next Campaign as the Supplies from the Eastward have fallen very short of the Expectations of Congress. We shall write you more fully in our next, and have the Honor to be with respect, Your Excellency's, Most obt. & very huml. srvts.   J Penn

Cornl. Harnett

[*P.S.*] Inclosed are the two last papers.

Since writing the above we have received letters from General Washington in which we are informed that Genl. Howe has agreed to an exchange of Prisoners; Officers for officers, Soldiers for Soldiers & Citizen for Citizen, so that our poor Country-men will soon be released from their cruel confinement. Congress a few days ago Resolved that as Genl Howe had refused to suffer anything to be purchased for the releif of our prisoners in his hands that he should be obliged to send all the necessaries his prisoner's with us might want & that the same Severity should be practised towards British Prisoner's as was inflicted on ours,[3] this Resolution has produced a change in Mr Howes conduct. He paid some high compliments to Genl Washington and at the same time censured Congress, but was answered by our General that he would always resent any afront offered the Representatives of a free People under whose authority he acted, and that he had ever avoided saying anything of the Conduct of those Genl. Howe served.   J Penn

C Harnett

Tr (Nc–Ar).
    [1] Governor Caswell's January 12, 1778, letter to the North Carolina delegates is in *N.C. State Records*, 13:7–8.
    [2] See North Carolina Delegates to Thomas Johnson, February 20, 1778.
    [3] See Congress' January 21, 1778, resolves on prisoners of war in *JCC*, 10:74–82.

Pennsylvania Delegates to Thomas Wharton

May it please your Excellency   [February 18, 1778]
Yesterday evening the Resolve of Congress of Saturday was sent enclosed by Mr Dickson[1] with an Account of the Recet of 52,000 Dollars received by the Delegates, out of which 13,000 Dollars was paid to the York & Cumberland County Comissrs. The Remainder being 39,000 Dollars & 100,000 Dollars received this day is forwarded by the Sherif of York County, as there is not a Moment to be lost he is sent to day, which will we hope prevent the trouble of sending to the River as mentioned in the Postscript of yesterdays Letter. As the Superintendts are dismounted on the East side the River, it might not have been so proper to apply to the usual place for a Guard & Convoy & makes it more necessary for the Comrs. on the East side to exert themselves, lest the Army should suffer.
We have the honour to be, may it please your Excellency, your most obedt Servts (by order of the Deleg),   Jas. Smith

RC (NN). Written and signed by James Smith.
   [1] See the postscript to Pennsylvania Delegates to Wharton, February 16; and Daniel Roberdeau to Wharton, February 17, 1778.

Oliver Wolcott to Laura Wolcott

My Dear,   York Town 18 Febry. 1778
I arrived here the 15 Well after having been detained about Two Days by the Susqhennah. I performed the Journey with much less faticuge than I expected and my Horse held out bravely, and has suffered Nothing. I am Now with Mr. Huntington at a publick House well and in comfortable Circumstances. We hope soon to get into private Lodgings, but We do not know where and find that they are Not to be had but with the greatest Dificulty and Expense. The latter is so great that I understand that a single Man exclusive of Hors keeping cannot probably live under at least ten pounds per Week. Every thing here bears an enormous price. The Town is much more pleasant than Baltimore but publick and private Virtue I suppose is much the same here as there.
We have no European News. An Exchange of Prisoners between Washington & Howe is agreed upon. Govr. Clinton is impowerd to secure the North River which has been totally neglected.[1] Genl. Putnam will douptless be soon ordered to join the Main Army and Genl. McDougall will probably Command on that Station.[2] An Order has gone to the States requesting them to fill up their Battalions—Measures taken to support a large Force in the spring, but

to get Provisions of the Meat kind is difficult. I fear that the Operations this Way will not be so early as Might be Wished. The State of
Pensylvania is Languid and divided—but I hope that their Vigor
such as it is, is increasing. But I have not been here long enough so
to understand the State of Affairs as to give much of a detail of any
Thing. The Post I understand is this Moment going off, to Me unexpected, so that I can add Nothing[3]—except my Earnest Wish that
the Almighty Being who has hitherto taken care of Us would still
extend his protecting Care over us and our Children and grant us
such Direction and Support as may be necessary for us. I am by the
Blessing of God well and injoy a Freedom of Spirits. God I trust
will take Care of this Land—and will bring us together again in
Peace. Trust in your Maker, and he will do you good. I am yours,
affectionately,   Oliver Wolcott

RC (CtHi).
   [1] See Henry Laurens to George Clinton, February 19, 1778, note 3.
   [2] In his February 8–14 letter to President Laurens, General Washington had
expressed the hope that Alexander McDougall's health would permit him to preside over an investigation of the October 1777 loss of the Hudson River forts
Montgomery and Clinton in the New York Highlands, which were under the
command of Israel Putnam. But it was not until March 16 that Washington requested McDougall to assume command of the Highlands and undertake this
investigative assignment. To the aging Putnam, whose inattention to the demands
of his command had generated criticism from many sources, Washington explained
that this change was necessitated by the "prejudices" of New Yorkers against him
and that, after meeting with the board of inquiry, he was to return to Connecticut
to superintend Continental recruiting. See Washington, *Writings* (Fitzpatrick),
10:429, 451–52; 11:94–97. On Putnam's eventual acquittal, see Gouverneur Morris
to John Jay, April 29, 1778, note 7.
   [3] Wolcott also wrote a letter to his wife on February 21, which contained little
more than an assurance that he was in good health and the following brief report
on issues pertaining to Congress. "Burgoynes Army are by Order of Congress to be
distributed in such Parts of the Massachusetts as the Executive Councill of that
State think Most for their Security and safety, till the Convention shall be ratified.
No News from Europe—likely some of our Mails must be lost. Congress are intent
upon Reinforcing and supplying the Army. A general Cartel for the Exchange of
Prisoners I believe I told you in my last, is agreed upon." Wolcott Papers, CtHi.

William Duer to Francis Lightfoot Lee

Feby 19. 1778

   I have this day seen a letter from Genl. Gates as president of the
board of war directing general Mifflin to inform the commissioners
appointed by the board to superintend the purchasing provisions &c
that Congress had determined that the measures pursued by the State
of Pensylvania were adequate to the supply of the army on the east side
of Susquehannah and had therefore directed that they no longer pro-

ceed on that business, but lay all their accounts &c before Congress.[1] Just when the resolution came to hand a considerable supply of provisions & forage was forwarding to head quarters by the persons appointed by the board of war & a great number of teams impressed for this purpose. The order of Congress has put a stop to the whole, so that all prospect of keeping the army together is now at an end and you may expect every moment to hear of its dissolution. The former letter I sent you from Genl. Washington painted to you their critical situation.[2] Since that time about 1000 barrels of flour have been sent down by water from this place by Col Bird. But the river is now fallen & there is no probability of procuring an adequate number of teams in time agreeable to the laws of this state.

This you may declare to Congress as a fact that warrants have been out agreeable to the laws of Pensylvania for a month past for procuring teams for the use of the army & that none have as yet been procured in that way. The consequence of which is that all the horses in the army are now famished for forage and a mutiny has already arisen for want of a timely supply of provisions. It will be more than we have a right to expect, when the army disbands, which I think in a few days it must, if a great part dont join the enemy. A few nights ago thirteen of the Artillery (the best corps in the service) twelve of whom were sergeants deserted in a body to the enemy. This you may rely on as fact.

Tr (PHarH). In the hand of Charles Thomson and endorsed by him: "Extract of a letter from Mr Duer to col F. L. Lee in Congress Feby 19. 1778." This is undoubtedly the copy of Duer's letter that on February 21 Congress ordered to "be sent by express to the executive Council of Pensylvania" and which Daniel Roberdeau sent to the Pennsylvania Assembly. See *JCC*, 10:189; and Daniel Roberdeau to the Pennsylvania Assembly, February 21, 1778.

[1] On February 17 Congress had ordered the suspension of three superintendents who had been appointed by the Board of War to purchase flour in Pennsylvania for the Continental Army. Congress took this action not only because Pennsylvania had appointed its own commissioners to make this purchase, but also because the board's appointees "without any authority, in direct violation of the laws of Pensylvania, and contrary to the instructions given by the Board of War, have presumed to fix and ascertain the prices of several articles wanted in the army, much higher than fixed by law in the State." On February 21 Congress, having read this extract of Duer's letter to Lee, decided to send a copy of it to the Pennsylvania Council, together with a resolve requesting the council to forward to the army "by every possible means, supplies of provisions, (especially of the meat kind,) and forage, with the utmost dispatch." See *JCC*, 10:54–56, 166–70, 176–77, 189. The council complied with Congress' request on February 24 by issuing a circular letter to this effect to its purchasing commissioners. See *Pa. Archives*, 1st ser. 6:294; Daniel Roberdeau to Thomas Wharton, January 16, note 2; and Committee at Camp Minutes of Proceedings, February 16–20, 1778, note 5. In order to avoid exclusive reliance on state authorities in this matter, Congress also ordered the Board of War on the 21st to make immediate purchases of "meat and forage for the army . . . having respect to the prices fixed by the laws of the State of Pennsylvania." *JCC*, 10:189. It is pertinent to note in this context that Duer

and Lee were both members of the old Board of War, which had only recently
relinquished its authority to a new board made up of nonmembers of Congress.

[2] Duer may be referring to Washington's comprehensive January 29, 1778, report
to the Committee at Camp. See Duer to Lee, February 14, 1778, note 10.

Henry Laurens to George Clinton

Sir,   19th Febry 1778.
I had the honour of writing to your Excellency the 13th Inst.[1] by
Jones & since, of reporting to Congress your Excellency's favor of the
16th Ulto. which had been just thirty one days on its tour by way of
Baltimore.[2] This may lead your Excellency to account for the delay
of former Letters, probably none have miscarried, I acknowledged
the Receipt of those of 20th & 31st December in mine of the 22d
January by Dodd, but I have observed that the conveyance by Post
is precarious, the Channels from the principal Office require much
attention to keep them in tolerable order for public benefit.

Inclosed herein Your Excellency will be pleased to receive an Act
of Congress of Yesterday authorizing & requesting you to superintend
the business of obstructing, fortifying &c the passes of North River
agreeable to the Resolution of Congress of the 5th November last, a
Copy of which will accompany the other, together with a Warrant on
the Loan Office of New York for 50,000 Dollars for defraying expences
of the intended works as far as that Amount will extend.[3]

In a seperate packet Your Excellency will receive by the bearer
hereof Brown, six Copies of Acts of Congress of the 5th & 6th Inst.
establishing divers regulations in the Civil & military Lines of the
Army & appointing Auditors of accounts in the Army under General
Washington.[4]

I have the Honour to be &ca.

LB (DNA: PCC, item 13).
[1] See Laurens to Thomas Wharton, February 10, 1778, note.
[2] Governor Clinton's January 16, 1778, letter to Laurens is in PCC, item 67,
2:102–3.
[3] See JCC, 9:865–68, 10:180–81. Ironically, Clinton urged passage of such a
resolution in a February 3 letter to Laurens that was read in Congress on February
23 and referred to the Board of War. In this letter, however, Clinton pointed out
that to fortify the Highlands properly, engineers and heavy artillery were needed
as much as money. See PCC, item 167, 2:106–7; and JCC, 10:192.
[4] See JCC, 10:124, 132–37. According to a notation in his presidential letterbook,
Laurens this day sent copies of these resolves to the governors of Rhode Island,
Connecticut, and New Jersey, the presidents of New Hampshire and Pennsylvania,
the council of Massachusetts, and the commanding officer in Boston; and on
February 21 to the governors of Virginia and North Carolina. PCC, item 13, fol.
193. Laurens also indicated that the resolves destined for the executives of Pennsylvania and New Jersey would be delivered by New Jersey delegate John Witherspoon.

Henry Laurens to Joseph Trumbull

Sir,   York Town 19th February 1778

I am directed by Congress to inform you that in expectation of your recovering health & Strength & being enabled thereby to attend the Duties of your appointment at the Board of War in a short time, no other appointment will be made on account of the delay which shall be unavoidable on your part.[1]

I have the honour to be with great Regard, Sir, Your Obedient & most humble servant,   Henry Laurens, President of Congress.

RC (Ct).

[1] Although Congress had decided on February 16 to reserve Joseph Trumbull's seat on the Board of War after learning of his willingness to serve "as soon as his health will permit," continued illness finally compelled Trumbull to resign from the board in April. He died in July 1778. See *JCC*, 10:171, 363; and Laurens to Joseph Trumbull, November 27, 1777.

Henry Laurens to George Washington

Sir,   19th Febry 1778.

Since writing the 13th Inst. to your Excellency by Sharp,[1] I have received the Honour of your Excellency's several favours of the 3d & 8th continued to 14th Inst. together with the divers Letters & papers referred to in the latter.[2] These were all presented to Congress & remain under consideration.

Inclosed herewith your Excellency will receive Acts of Congress under the 5th, 6th & 9th for establishing divers regulations & restraining abuses in the Army & for appointing Mathew Clarkson & Major John Clarke Esquires Auditors of Army Accounts.

Also an Act of the 17th deciding who are to be excluded from the benefit of the Months extra pay ordered by a Resolve of the 29th December.

This will be delivered to your Excellency by the Baron Stüben who proceeds to the Army with the Rank of Captain, granted by a Brevet Commission at the Barrons special Instance in order to guard against inconveniences which might attend him, if he should without any Commission in his pocket be made a prisoner.

Upon the arrival of this illustrious Stranger at York Town,[3] Congress ordered a Committee consisting of Mr. Witherspoon, Mr. McKean, Mr. F.L. Lee & Mr. Henry to wait upon & confer with him to pay the necessary Compliments on his appearance in America & to learn explicitly his expectations from Congress & the Committee were directed to deliver me the Substance of their conference in writing, to be transmitted for your Excellency's information. All that I have received or know on this head will be seen on an Inclosed paper marked Committees conference with Baron Stüben to which I beg leave to refer your Excellency.

I have the honour to be with great Respt.

[*P.S.*] The Baron declines the Commission abovementioned or any other for the present.

ENCLOSURE

Committee Report on Baron von Steuben

The Baron Stuben who was a Leiutenant General and Aide de Camp to the King of Prussia—desires no rank—is willing to attend General Washington, and be subject to his orders—does not require or desire any command of a particular Corps or Division, but will serve occasionally as directed by the General—expects to be of use in planning Encampments &c. and promoting the discipline of the Army—he heard before he left France, of the dissatisfaction of the Americans with the promotion of foreign officers, therefore makes no terms, nor will accept of any thing but with the general approbation and particularly that of General Washington.

Signed by Mr. Witherspoon   Mr. F.L. Lee

Mr. McKean   Mr. Henry

LB (DNA: PCC, item 13). Tr (DNA: PCC, item 19). In a clerical hand and endorsed by George Washington: "Copy—Examined. Go. Washington. Mount Vernon Novr. 10th. 1787." The text of the enclosure printed above is taken from a transcript of the original committee report made for Washington in 1787 and forwarded by him to Congress to help the delegates determine the justice of Baron von Steuben's claims for compensation for his revolutionary war services. See Washington to Charles Thomson, November 10, 1787, PCC, item 19, 5:581–82. The original MS report has not been found.

¹ See Laurens to Patrick Henry, February 10, 1778, note.

² Washington's letters are in PCC, item 152, 5:283–89, and Washington, *Writings* (Fitzpatrick), 10:418, 428–30. Along with the second letter Washington sent copies of eight letters pertaining to an exchange of prisoners that he and Gen. William Howe had written to each other between January 8 and February 10. Washington Papers, DLC.

³ Although Congress believed that this "illustrious Stranger" had been a lieutenant general in the Prussian army, Steuben was in fact a former aide-de-camp to Frederick the Great who had attained only the rank of captain and had not been in the king's employ since 1763. See John M. Palmer, *General von Steuben* (New Haven: Yale University Press, 1937), pp. 1–5, 29–52, 97–98, who argues that Benjamin Franklin was responsible for exaggerating the baron's military attainments in order to facilitate congressional acceptance of his services as a volunteer officer.

Although the fact is not recorded in the journals, it is clear from Laurens' letter and from other sources that on February 6, the day after Steuben's arrival in York, Congress appointed a committee consisting of John Henry, Francis Lightfoot Lee, Thomas McKean, and John Witherspoon to meet with the baron and ascertain his terms for serving in the Continental Army. Palmer, *General von Steuben*, pp. 122–23. Steuben himself described his meeting with the committee, which apparently wrote its report on February 6 or 7, in a memorial he submitted to the U.S. Congress in August 1789 to justify his claims for further compensation for his military service:

"At the arrival of the Baron de Steuben, in the year 1777 [i.e., 1778], he was received by Congress with marks of distinction, and, the day after his arrival, was waited on by a committee of Congress, composed of Dr. Witherspoon, Mr. Henry, of Maryland, and a third, whom at this time he cannot recollect. This committee demanded of the baron the conditions on which he was inclined to serve the United States, and if he had made any stipulations with the commissioners in France. He replied that he had made no agreement with them, nor was it his intention to accept of any rank or pay; that he wished to join the army as a volunteer, and to render such services as the commander-in-chief should think him capable of, adding that he had no other fortune than a revenue of about six hundred guineas per annum, arising from places and posts of honor in Germany, which he had relinquished to come to this country; that, in consideration of this, he expected the United States would defray his necessary expenses while in their service; that if, unhappily, this country should not succeed in establishing their independence, or if he should not succeed in his endeavors for their service, in either of those cases he should consider the United States as free from any obligations towards him; but if, on the other hand, the United States should be happy enough to establish their freedom, and that he should be successful in his endeavors, in that case he should expect a full indemnification for the sacrifice he had made in coming over, and such marks of their generosity as the justice of the United States should dictate; that, if these terms were agreeable to Congress, he waited only their orders to join the army without delay. The committee were pleased to applaud the generosity of his propositions, in thus risking his fortune on that of the United States. The committee then left him in order to make their report. The next day, Congress gave him an entertainment; after which the President, Mr. Laurens, told him it was the desire of Congress that he should join the army immediately, which he did." Walter Lowrie and Walter S. Franklin, eds., *American State Papers Class IX Claims* (Washington: Gales and Seaton, 1834), pp. 11–12.

The same memorial includes affidavits drawn up and signed by Lee, McKean, and Witherspoon in 1785 and 1788, attesting to the accuracy of Steuben's account of his meeting with them, as well as 1785 letters from Horatio Gates and Richard Peters, the president and secretary of the Board of War in February 1778, on the baron's dealings with the committee. Ibid., pp. 12–13. For a detailed treatment of Steuben's long and not entirely successful quest for remuneration from the Continental and Federal Congresses, see Palmer, *General von Steuben*, pp. 297–306, 323–27, 330–31, 352–54, 362, 374–77.

James Lovell to Samuel Adams

My dear Sir,   Yk 19th Feb. [1778]

I have only time to give you the Anatomy of French Politics as they stood Sepr. 10th 77.[1] America undertook war of her own motion upon great provocations given by England and without consulting France, though doubtless depending in a degree upon the political *Interests* of that Nation. Complaints therefore against her while she pursues what *she judges* to be that Interest are unjust. She did not foment your Divisions nor was she consulted upon their probable consequences. Will you *force* her to take an *open* part? Is it not her wisest line to aid you *secretly*. In which case Britain must either see & *not* see or else must *begin hostilities* against France. In the former Case you will have every necessary article to enable you to support your rising Independence. In the latter France will be justified by all her Neighbours in vigorously repelling all attacks of the English. At present, should his Christian Majesty declare War, he must endure the Charges of boundless Ambition in taking an unprovoked Opportunity to assault Britain during the Moment of her greatest Embarrassments. The Threat of your Reunion with Britain unless France *openly* unites herself with America is impolitic as the bare possibility of such a Reunion should make France cautious of any hazardous step. Shall it be said "join us, & we will never reunite?" Will it not be answered "prove that you will never reunite & I will openly assist you". Convince the World that no Extremity is capable of making you renounce that Independence which you have not seditiously & tumultuously declared but calmly & methodically adopted.

And now Dr Sir you and I will not quarrel with such Politics as these, if, instead of leaving us to depend only on the natural Greediness for gain which is the commercial Punctum Vita Monsieur Louis will *lend* us the sine qua non to provide Bait for carrying on that Shark Fishery.

Shall you be able to defend yourselves against Burgoyne and at the same time *draught* without giving bounty to fill up the continental Quota with 12 months or 9 months men very early this Spring? No other remedy is left I think for all our Evils.

It is said as the Term of the German Auxilaries is expired they refuse any Obedience to Howe. Perhaps this has brought on the general Exchange, as England must pay for all that are lost.

Adieu, be happy.   JL

RC (NN).
 [1] The following account of the French diplomatic position vis-a-vis the United States probably stems from a conversation Lovell had with Jean Théveneau de Francy, the agent of Caron de Beaumarchais. Francy had left Paris on September 10 and arrived in Portsmouth, N.H., on December 1, 1777. His papers were laid before Congress on February 20. Although Francy carried a letter of introduction from Silas Deane, dated September 10, 1777, he did not bring official letters from the commissioners at Paris. See *JCC,* 10:185; Pierre Augustin Caron de Beaumarchais, *Beaumarchais Correspondance,* ed. Brian N. Morton (Paris: A. G. Nizet, 1962–), 3:235n.2; Wharton, *Diplomatic Correspondence,* 2:392–93; and Committee for Foreign Affairs to the Commissioners at Paris, March 24, 1778.

Gouverneur Morris to John Harvie

Dear Harvie,   Moore Hall 19th Feby. 1778.

I write to you at the Request of my Brethren. You have forgotten two or three material things which you ought to have taken with you.[1] In the first Place the Memorandums extracted from the Papers sent to Genl. Washington from Reading.[2] They are as follows. 1. Congress have directed 30,000 Blls. and the Board of War 20000 more. 2ly. 2½ Per Cent is allowed to the Superintendants of Purchases & 2½ to the Purchasers. 3ly. 7 Clerks & 7 Storekeepers at 7 different Magazines; on this Note that only 5 are charged in our Estimate owing to Negligence in making the Calculations. 4thly. Each Superintendent to have an Office and a Clerk with as many Assistants as he chuses to employ, the wages of which are discretionary. 5thly. The Purchasers of Grain & Flesh to be seperate. 6thly. a House and Clerk to be kept at Allen Town. 7thly. The Price of Wheat to be limited at 12/ and eight Bushels to be processed for one Bushel of Flour. 8thly. Waggons to be employed at Discretion. 9thly. Millers to be allowed £4 per 100 Bushels for grinding &ca. and 4d per Barrill for putting on a Lining Hoop. 10thly. 2 Millers, 3 Coopers & 2 Woodsmen to be inlisted for a Year for each Mill & exempt from Military Service. 11thly. Millers to Employ Teams to haul Timber for Staves & Hoop Poles at Discretion & Sheds or Stores to be built at their Mills if *necessary*. 12thly. Coopers to be allowed 18d. per Barril for making, It owed to Coopers, Wages of Woodsmen not settled & Millers allowed for boarding them 15/ per Week. 13thly. It is observed that the Prices fixed by the Assembly for Oats, Spelts, & Corn are not sufficient (Remark that these People complained not long ago & the Truth is that the Assembly fixed the Prices higher than they were before) the Deputies of the Superintendants, Millers &ca are desired to purchase grain for *Forage* and draw on the *Superintendants* (not Quarter Master whose salary is fixed) and to allow for Rye 12/ Spelts & Oats 7/6 & Corn 9/. 14thly. The Millers are to be allowed 8d per Bushel for the Oats they may purchase and are to grind the other Grain as before. Lastly it is to be observed that they acknowlege Meat is not to be purchased.

You neglected also some Articles which we computed to be purchased in different Parts. I run them over to you as follows: first 18,000 Barrils of Fish which will require 20,000 Bushels of Lisbon or Bay Salt to be laid up in the State of Virginia as many of them as possible Shad and the Quantity to be governed by the Quantity of this Salt which can be procured. 2d. 20,000 Barrils of Pork in the Southern States requiring 10,000 Bushels of common Salt & 5 Tons of Salt Peter the Salt to be merely Dissolved in Water and the Salt Peter mixed with it and poured cold on the Pork packed close. The

Pork should be cut into Pieces of 4 lb each and 60 such Pieces put into each Barrill. This will save greatly in dealing it out and prevent Roguery. The like should be observed with respect to all Provisions put up and that will prevent the Necessity & Expence of Inspectors &ca. 3dly. 7,000 B of Pork should also if possible be bought in the Eastern States. 4thly. All the Prize Cargoes of Salted Provisions should be carefully purchased for the public Use, also a great Quantity of Cod Fish. 5thly. 40,000 Bushels of Pease should be immediately contracted for in the middle or southern states for the Consumption of the ensuing fall and Winter, also 30000 Bushels of Pease in the County of Tryon in the State of New York for the Use of the Summer 1779 and Onions on the Banks of Connecticut River in the Township of Wethersfield particularly. 6thly. 10,000 Beef Cattle to be bought up in Maryland, Virginia and North Carolina and forwarded from Time to Time untill the first of September & 7000 in like Manner in the Eastern States.

I enclose you also a Calculation I made this Morning on what the Flour ought to cost and compared it with what it will cost if these Gentlemen go on. Adieu. I wish you Health and Pleasure. I am yours,

Gouvr Morris

RC (DNA: PCC, item 78).
[1] John Harvie left camp this day to return to Congress. Committee at Camp Minutes of Proceedings, February 16–20, 1778.
[2] A copy of these memoranda relating to the activities of the Board of War's special purchasing agents, in the hand of Pennsylvania delegate Jonathan Bayard Smith, is in the collection of Smith's papers at DLC.
For further information on the controversy surrounding the activities of these agents, which led to a request that all memoranda and instructions pertaining to their work be supplied to the Pennsylvania Council, see Committee at Camp Minutes of Proceedings, February 16–20, 1778, note 5.

Robert Morris to John Brown

Dear Sir   Manheim Feby 19th. 1778
I have duely received your letters of the 3d, 13th & 15th Inst. & have made the necessary Entries from the Acct Currt you sent me charging you with £522.18.7 Curry in a New Account and when you pay the balance due the Virginia Delegates you will transmit me those Vouchers. Colo Lewis cannot get a Waggon to bring the Medicines, I believe Doctr Shippen will send one for them. I intended sending the money to pay Mr Helligass for Mr Rowes bill, but have just received a letter from Messrs. Purvianaces of Balto. who are the proprietors of that draft, telling me they are to receive the money for it from my Friends there. Pray mention this to Mr Helligass for I can only pay it in one place. I do not incline to sell the Pipe of Wine I

have in York but rather think of storing some more there soon as I can get them Carted over. Pray what price wou'd my Salt stored at Mr Irwins fetch in York at this time?

I thank you for forwarding my letters & for the mention of Mr Whites absence. Bob must remain until I hear from him, poor fellow he has escaped the Measles by being from home. Tom & Bill are just got well out of them & Mr Nesbitt is got downstairs again. Youl see by my letter to the Commercial Committee[1] that I have taken due notice of every thing you mentioned of or from them. You will find herein the Govr. of New Orlean's letter which you may forward to Colo Richd Henry Lee with my Compliments, I also enclose a letter for Messrs. Robt & Saml Purviance at Baltimore which respects the Twenty hogsheads of Tobo I have offered to the Committee; if they agree to accept that offer then I beg you to return me this letter, but if they decline the offer then forward the letters to Messrs Purviances.

Under Cover is also a letter for Mrs. Duncan.[2] I have desired her to draw on me payable at Messrs. Mease & Caldwells for £2500 to £2600 Curry. If you can assist her to get money for such a draft it will save me the trouble of sending it to her, unless she chooses to receive it in Baltimore, agreable to another proposal I have made her.

I am Dr Sir, Your Sincere Friend & Obed hble servt,

Robt Morris

P.S. I told Mr. Fitzsimmons if he wanted any business done at York, Goods sold &c you wou'd do it for a Coms. & perhaps he may interest you in something or other when he goes to Virginia.

RC (NjP). Addressed by John Swanwick: "To Mr. John Brown, Secy. to the Marine Committee at Mr. Stakes's Tavern in York Town." At the foot of Morris' letter Swanwick also added the following instruction to Brown. "Mr. Morris desires you will forwd. the other letter for Mr. Harrison too."

[1] See Robert Morris to the Committee of Commerce, February 17, 1778.
[2] Not found.

John Penn to Robert R. Livingston

Dear Sir   York Town Feby 19th. 1778

I never recd. your favr. of the 10th of Jany untill three days ago. I am much obliged to my Friend James Duane esqr. for procuring me the Correspondence of a Gentn. of your merit, As I know no Person so well qualified to serve America at the Court of France, in the Important office you mention, I own I was anxious that you should be appointed, but you know Sir local attachments and prejudices are to be found even in Congress, this was the reason that you stay at home.[1]

I applied to the Treasury Board, who declare that since the date of your letter 600,000 Dollars have been sent to your State. Your Govr. is invested with all the powers that General Gates had, for securing the passes on the No. River, and is requested by Congress, to take effectual means to have that Important service done as soon as possible.[2] General Putnam will be removed from the Command he now holds. Will not General Parsons do under General Clinton for some time. I fear General Washington cannot spare McDougle, a Major Genl. must be sent to Rhode Island, Heath having resigned,[3] you know the officers of that Rank in our Army at present. I wish I could praise them. Our Committee is still at the Camp. How long they intend to remain I know not, but all the resolutions they make will be of no consequence unless an attempt is made to put them in execution soon.

Congress some time ago Resolved that as Genl Howe had refused to permit any necessaries to be purchased in Philada. for our prisoners, he should be obliged to send provisions for his soldiers in our hands, and that every act of severity committed on our prisoners should be retaliated on his. This I believe has induced Genl Howe to agree to a general exchange, officers for officers, soldiers for soldiers & citizen for citizen, so that our poor fellows will soon be released from their Captivity.[4] We are endeavouring to relieve the wants of our Soldiers. I am persuaded nothing will be omitted that can be done by Congress.

Do prevail on Mr. Duane to return to Congress as soon as he can, indeed his presence is absolutely necessary. I am obliged to attend the House, & have only time to add that I shall be glad to know your sentiments on any subject you may favr. me with. I am with great respect, in haste, Dear Sir, Your obt. Servt.   J. Penn

RC (NHi).

[1] Livingston had obviously commented on Congress' selection of John Adams on November 28, 1777, to replace Silas Deane as an American commissioner to France and evidently regretted that he had not been chosen instead. See *JCC*, 9:975.

[2] See *JCC*, 10:180–81.

[3] Penn must be referring to the resignation of Gen. Joseph Spencer, the former Continental commander in Rhode Island, which Congress had accepted on January 13, 1778. *JCC*, 10:47. Gen. William Heath was the commanding officer in Boston.

[4] See Committee at Camp to Washington, February 11, 1778, note.

Joseph Reed to Jonathan Bayard Smith

Dear Sir   Camp near Valley Forge Feb. 19. 1778

Mr Harvey one of the Committee returning I just give you a few Lines. Almost every Day produces some Instances of the pernicious Effects of an Influence which I described in a former Letter & the one I am now going to mention is perhaps as extraordinary as ever happened. Under the Idea of purchasing 50,000 Bbbls of Flour a System of Power & Extravagance is formed which will surprize you. It at one Stroke demolishes the Militia Law, Waggon Law, regulating Law & Provision Law, erects an arbitrary Power over the Property of the People to be exercised by a Sett of Gentlemen in avowed Opposition to the Authority of the State. The enormous Profits or if I may so express myself the Jobbing Part of it Col Harvey will explain to you. We have made a Calculation on the System here which that Gentleman will shew you. It is founded on their own Plan of Instructions ramified into a Number of Particulars & appears to be formed as a Provision for Dependents, establish an Influence subversive of the Government & fix a Precedent for future Peculation.

Col. Cox has been sent for but is not yet come to Camp. Perhaps my long Acquaintance & Connection with him may mislead my Judgment but I profess I do not know a Man whose Versatility of Genius, Activity, Readiness at Expedients & Acquaintance with the Country better qualifies him to fill the Qr. Master's Department. Green will not accept but on Condition Cox is joined with him & agrees to give up what is called the lucrative Part, this perhaps may have some Effect upon our Friend who has some profitable Schemes on the Anvil. Green only goes in it from public Motives; he is not an interested Character. He thinks he might be of some Use in the military Part of this Office but disclaims what may be called the civil Part.

I was very sensible that the Service on which you have appointed us is very difficult, but my dear sir, I have no Idea of declining or evading any Duty which this great Cause requires tho Life itself should be hazarded. This Principle strange as it may seem has I believe hurt my Preferment & injured my private Interests, but as I am not ambitious, nor interested beyond a certain Degree & that I hope limited to moderate Bounds I feel perhaps less Mortification than most Men & have the Happiness of believing that Time will discover my Enemies & those of the publick to be the same.

The Papers that will give you a perfect Insight into the Contract I have mentioned you will find at the Board of War & consist of Instructions from the Board of War, to the Superintendants—their Plan of conducting the Business as framed by Falconer, Mifflin & Hooper—their Instructions to the Millers, their Letter to the Board of War.[1] A Letter wrote by R.L. Hooper as Dy Quartr. Mastr. Genl.

Joseph Reed

to the Purchasers encreasing the Prices of Spelts, Oats & Corn beyond the Act of Assembly.

We are going into the Huts this Week to execute the most disagreeable Commission, to wit, the Selection of proper Officers.

Col. Harvey waits so that I can only add my best Respects to our Colleagues & am, Dear Sir, your Affect. & Obed., Hbble Servt.

Jos. Reed

RC (DLC).
[1] For these papers, which Smith obtained a few days later as the result of a request from the Pennsylvania Council, see Smith to Thomas Wharton, February 26, 1778.

Committee at Camp to Ephraim Blaine

Sir,   [February 20, 1778][1]

We inclose you a Letter of Introduction to Govr. Johnson.[2] Upon the Subject of Fish we have to observe that from our Accounts of that Business your Informant must have deceived you as a Barrell will hold more than eighty probably more than one hundred Shad. The Quantity of Salt he hath not exagerated as it requires a great Deal and of imported Salt too for that which is made in this Country will not answer. The Fish ought to cost very little per hundred say three or four Dollars; for this they may probably be purchased especially in the River Potomack tho' that is out of your present rout. The Cost on the whole will be great but [the army] must not starve. We are Sir &ca.

FC (DNA: PCC, item 33). Written by Gouverneur Morris and endorsed by Francis Dana: "Copy of Lettr. to Mr. Blane from Committee."
[1] Although this FC is undated, it is undoubtedly the letter described in the committee's minutes this day as written to "Blane Dy. Comy. Genl. of Purchs. respecting the purchase of Fish in Maryland." See Committee at Camp Minutes of Proceedings, February 16–20, 1778.
[2] The committee's February 20 letter to Thomas Johnson has not been found but a brief abstract of it was printed in *Stan V. Henkels Catalog*, no. 683 (April 5, 1892), item 312.

Committee at Camp to Henry Laurens

Sir,   Camp near the Valley Forge, Feb. 20th 1778.

We are to acknowledge your Favour of the 7th Inst., received the 13th inclosing the Resolves of Congress on the Qr. Master Gens. Department. The Subject is very important, & we only wait for some farther Information when we shall do ourselves the Honour of laying our Sentiments before Congress on the material Alteration proposed in this Office.

We now, Sir, beg Leave to submit to your Consideration, a Proposition of employing a Number of Indians in the American Army.[1] We have fully discussed it with the General, & upon the maturest Deliberation are induced to recommend it to Congress. We are of Opinion no Measure can be adopted so effectual to break off the pernicious Intercourse which the disaffected Inhabitants of this Country still hold with the Enemy, from which they derive the greatest Advantages. Exclusive of the wholesome Supplies of Provisions by which they refresh their numerous Sick, & check the Advances of the Scurvy, it is the most sure & certain Source of Intelligence. Thro' this Channel they are constantly apprized not only of every material Transaction of our Army, but of the Quarters of our Troops & Situation of such active Whigs as are either occasionally passing, or yet reside within the Reach of their Excursions. Hence almost every Day furnishes an Instance of some Surprize & Capture. From repeated Successes they grow confident & venture in small Parties a considerable Distance, carrying off with them such straggling Officers, Soldiers, & incautious Whigs as they find in their Route. Their Progress in this Business is the more alarming as they are now joined by a Number of Tories perfectly acquainted with the Country, well mounted & equipp'd, who not only serve as Guides to the British Horse, but venture upon separate Expeditions. The Terror of these Excursions is so great, that it will, unless seasonably check'd, endanger the Communication of the Army with its Supplies & absolutely deprive us of all Assistance from our Friends in the lower Parts of the three Counties of Bucks, Chester, & Philada.[2] We can foresee but two Objections to employing the Indians on the Flanks & Advance of the Army. The Danger of indiscriminate Injury to the well & ill affected, & Prevention of Desertion from the Enemy. But his Excelly. is of Opinion both may be obviated by proper Precautions, or at least so far guarded as to justify the Expediency of the Measure, & render the Experiment less hazardous than it may appear at first View.

But we do not, Sir, confine our Ideas to the present Moment, we think the restless Spirits of the Savages will not allow them to remain inactive. If we do not find Subjects to employ them on, we fear our Enemies will, & we have only to chuse whether these shall be British Troops or the Inhabitants of our defenceless Frontiers. As it is in Contemplation to form a Flying Army composed of light Infantry & rifle Men under the Direction of Officers distinguished for their Activity & Spirit of Enterprize, it is proposed to mix about 400 Indians with them; being thus incorporated with our own Troops, who are designed to skirmish, act in Detachments & light Parties, as well as lead the Attack, we hope their Irregularities will be restrained & any

Excesses prevented. We fear a greater Number would rather injure than promote the Service, as they claim Access at all Times & on all Occasions to the Commander in Chief & expect Cloathing & Douceurs which we fear our scanty Supplies will not afford but in very moderate Quantities. The Number therefore we propose we flatter ourselves may be easily procured, their good Humour preserved & sufficiently answer the Purposes we have in View.

Nor do we think ourselves less warranted to say that there is great Reason to believe the Novelty of their Appearance in the Field, the Circumstances of Horror & Affright which attend their Attack, will have a great Effect upon the Minds of Men wholly unacquainted with such an Enemy. Upon the foreign Troops we doubt not it would operate in a high Degree, & when we consider upon what trivial Circumstances the Fate of Battles often turns, & the constant Attention shewn by the nice Observers of the human Heart in the military Line to every Thing which can discompose & terrify it, we trust we shall not be thought visionary or chimerical.

Upon the whole, Sir, by the Request & Desire of the General we beg Leave to recommend it as a Measure of Policy & Utility worthy the Attention of Congress. If it should meet your Approbation, Col. Gist a Gentleman of much Acquaintance & Experience with the Southern Indians will most chearfully receive your Commands & is recommended to us by General Washington as a Man of approved Spirit & Conduct, in whom the greatest Confidence may be safely reposed.

The Situation of the Oneidas to the Northward is such, that perhaps it will be found our truest Interest to take them into Service, even if little is expected from them. They are threatned by the surrounding Tribes & declare that unless we can protect them, they must however reluctantly take up the Hatchet against us or be intirely cut off. We cannot protect them unless we take the Nation into our Country, which may be done by setling their Wives & Children for the present in the State of New York, as the Commissioners may think proper, and bringing their Warriours to the Army, for whose Fidelity & Perseverance we shall then have the best Pledges, without the Odium of demanding them.

We are, with the greatest Respect & Regard, Sir, Your most Obedt. & very Hbble servts.   F. Dana by order

P.S. Having communicated this Letter to his Excelly. he wishes to add that no Time is to be lost in coming to a Resolution & dispatching Col. Gist, as the Distance is very great & the previous Ceremonies & Preparations will take up some Time—And that Col. Gist being now detached with a Party of ficticious Indians upon the Lines cannot

attend Camp so soon as was intended, but will set out in a very few
Days if the Plan is approved.

RC (DNA: PCC, item 33). Written by Joseph Reed, and signed by Dana.
¹ This letter was read in Congress on February 26 and referred to the Board of
War, which reluctantly endorsed the employment of "400 Indians with the grand
army." On March 4, Congress consequently authorized Washington to employ
Indians "in such a way as will annoy the enemy without suffering them to injure
those who are friends to the cause of America." *JCC*, 10:203, 220–21. See also Committee of Congress to Laurens, March 2, 1778, note.
² For Congress' adoption of the death penalty to deter loyalist raiding and kidnapping, see *JCC*, 10:204–5; and Committee at Camp to John Laurance, February
18, 1778.

Henry Laurens to John Avery

Sir,¹   20th Febry 1778.
You will receive by the bearer of this a seperate Packet containing
twenty five Signed Commissions & Instructions for private Ships of
War from these States, together with the same Number of Bonds to
be duly executed by the commander & one Sufficient Surety, I meant
to say the Commanders respectively to whom the Commissions shall
be granted & when so Executed to be transmitted to Congress.

These Commissions &ca are sent to you at the request of the
Honble. Mr. Dana now of a Committee from Congress in General
Washington's Camp.² I am with great Respect.

LB (DNA: PCC, item 13).
¹ John Avery was the deputy secretary of the Massachusetts Council.
² Francis Dana had made this request in a February 14 letter to Laurens that has
not been found. See Laurens to Dana, this date.

Henry Laurens to the Committee at Camp

Sir,   York Town 20th February 1778
I had the honour of addressing you on a subject of high importance
the 7th Inst. by Messenger Barry who returned without a Line from
you, nor have you touched on the Quarter Master's department in
your favor of the 14th, hence several Members of Congress entertained suspicions of the miscarriage of my Letter & therefore moved
the House to the Act of this date which you will receive inclosed in
this, desiring you will by the return of the present Messenger nominate proper persons to fill the Quarter Master's Department, conformable to the plan adopted.¹

In order to supply the place of the original, admitting what is barely possible, that it has not reached you, I will subjoin a Copy of my said Letter of the 7th by which you will perceive the intention of Congress was that you should consult with General Washington; I presume the same is now meant although not expressed in the present Resolve which was concluded rather in haste this Evening.

I am with very great Regard, Sir, Your obedient & humble Servant,
Henry Laurens, President of Congress

RC (DNA: PCC, item 192). Addressed: "The Honorable Francis Dana Esquire for the Committee from Congress—at Valley forge Camp."

[1] For the Committee at Camp's response to this resolve, see its February 24 and 25, 1778, letters to Laurens.

Henry Laurens to Francis Dana

Sir   20th Febry 1778.

I was last Night honoured with your favor of the 14th.[1] My memory is too modest to attempt to prove a negative, but it pleads ignorance of your having applied to me for Cruizing Commissions & their companions, although you may, as you intimate have Spoken to me cursorily on the Subject, be that as it may, you shall be no longer charged with remissness on that score, I will send a set of 25 tomorrow morning by a Messenger whom I shall dispatch with orders from Congress, for "seperating & placing General Burgoyne's Troops in such manner & such parts of Massachusets as may be most convenient for their subsistence" &ca.[2]

I thank you Sir, for your concern for my health, I have not only not been tormented by the Gout for near a Month past, but by obstinately persisting in the severe discipline of Cold Water have gained more strength in my ankles than I should otherwise have had till the warm weather had come in to my relief.

Your description of the miseries of the Army affected me beyond common feeling, altho' I thought myself prepared by having perused it at home, I could not go through the reading your Letter in Congress. Deep sympathy for the poor Suffering Soldiers blended with as deep indignation against the infamous delinquents who have been the authors of their distress, forbid utterance.

You say you will learn Characters, I think Sir, from the slight acquaintance I have had the honour of making with you, You have too much fortitude & integrity, either to be flattered or frighted by any Character & that when you have fully investigated, you will tell your Country in the presence of their Representatives where originated the Evils complained of. I wish you had been here *yesterday*

& *today*. I wish for you *every day* & I wish you not to come away *too soon* from your present Charge.

I am with very great respect.

LB (ScHi).
¹ This particular February 14 letter from Dana has not been found.
² See Congress' February 19 resolves on this issue in *JCC*, 10:184–85.

Henry Laurens to William Heath

Sir,   York Town 20th February 1778

Yesterday I wrote you a very few Lines by Messenger Browne whom I dispatched on very special business to Governor Clinton.¹ By him I also sent you a Packet containing several Copies of Acts of Congress of the 5th, 6th & 9th Inst. for establishing divers regulations in the Civil & Military departments of the Army &ca.

Soon after that Messenger departed, Congress confirmed the Inclosed Act of the 19th for seperating & placing the Troops included in the Convention of Saratoga in such manner within the State of Massachuset as shall be most convenient for their subsistence & security.²

The Inclosed piece of Paper which I writ in Congress this Evening & slipped into the hand of a Member of the Treasury Board will shew you Sir that I have not been unmindful of your Calls for Money. The subjoined answer is all I am authorized to say on that head. I shall persevere in applications & I hope you will find means for subsistence until you receive the promised supply.

I have the honour to be, with great Respect, Sir, Your obedient & most humble servant,   Henry Laurens, President of Congress.

ENCLOSURE

I earnestly intreat the Gentlemen of the Treasury to inform me what I shall advise General Heath respecting a transmission of Money, for which he has *seriously* & *repeatedly* called. The General will feel himself extremely unhappy, should Congress lay new Commands on him which will produce new expenses, without affording him assistance to discharge Arrears. Ansd. that the Money will be sent next Week or the Week after, unless some unforeseen Accident should prevent it.

RC (MHi). Enclosure: MS (MHi). In the hand of Laurens except for the last sentence, which was written by Elbridge Gerry, the member of the Board of Treasury to whom Laurens wrote the note.
¹ See Laurens to George Clinton, February 19, 1778, note 4.
² See *JCC*, 10:184–85.

Henry Laurens to the Massachusetts Council

Honorable Gentlemen,   York Town 20th February 1778

Yesterday by Messenger Browne I directed a Packet to Your Honorable House containing six Printed Copies of Acts of Congress of the 5th. & 6th. Inst. for establishing divers regulations in the Military & Civil Lines of the Army &ca.[1] At the same time was conveyed to you another Packet which had not been properly noted in my Copy Book & my memory does not help me to the Contents. Permit me therefore to request you Gentlemen to inform me what is contained in the said Packet, in order that I may cause the necessary amendment to be made if it shall appear there has been an omission.[2]

Be pleased to receive under this Cover an Act of Congress of yesterday's date authorizing & requesting you to make the proper & necessary seperation & disposition of the Troops comprehended in the Convention of Saratoga & for other purposes thereinmentioned, to which I beg leave to refer you.

I am with very great Respect, Honorable Gentlemen, Your obedient & very humble servant,

Henry Laurens, President of Congress.

RC (M–Ar).
[1] See Laurens to George Clinton, February 19, 1778, note 4.
[2] No reply to Laurens' request by the Massachusetts Council has been found.

Henry Laurens to James Wilson

Sir,   20th Febry 1778

The Case I alluded to yesterday, in which I desired to retain you, on behalf of the Respondent is An Appeal by Capt Francis Arthur from a Decree in the Court of Admiralty in South Carolina founded upon the Verdict of a Jury against the Brigt. Success & Cargo— Weyman the Libellent now Respondent.[1] I expect from Charles Town every hour authenticated Copies of Acts & proceedings of the Court, when these come to hand I may again trouble you. In the mean time I am with great Respect, Sir, Your obedient humble Servt.

LB (ScHi). Addressed: "James Wilson Esquire, York Town."
[1] For further information on this case, see Laurens to John Lewis Gervais, October 18, 1777, note 4. The journals give Captain Arthur's forename as George. JCC, 8:738. See also Laurens to Wilson, March 26, 1778.

North Carolina Delegates to Thomas Johnson

Sir   York Feby. 20th. 1778

Having heard that Joshua Hampstead is now in Maryland, we take the liberty to inclose to your Excellency, a Copy of a Resolution of the General Assembly of the State of North Carolina, relative to his Conduct, requesting that you would be pleased, to give such directions as you may think proper for securing the said Hampstead in order that Justice may be done that State, and transmit an account of what is done to Governor Caswell.[1] We have the Honor to be with great respect, Your Excellency's most obt. humble Servts.

J. Penn

Cors. Harnet

P.S. If not too Troublesome we shall be much obliged to your excely. to let us know if this man is in Maryland & what is done in regard to him.   J P

C.H.

RC (NjHi). Written and signed by Penn, who also signed for Harnett.

[1] On December 21, 1777, the North Carolina Assembly had approved a resolve instructing the North Carolina delegates to secure the apprehension of "Joshua Hampstead late Commander of the armed Brigantine Pennsylvania Farmer" who "has grossly abused the trust reposed in him by this State on a voyage which he lately performed to the West Indies by order of this State, by refusing to deliver the articles which he brought in for public purposes to the persons authorized to receive them and that he has in some instances made sales thereof and applied the monies to a very considerable amount to his own use and has retired to some other State beyond the operation of this State." *N.C. State Records*, 12:419. No reply by Governor Johnson of Maryland to the North Carolina delegates' plea for assistance in this case has been found.

Committee of Commerce to Robert Morris

Sir   Commercial Committee York Feby 21. 1778.

We acknowledge the Receipt of your favours of the 7th, 8th, 12th and 17th instant.[1]

In answer to that of the 7th respecting our misterious Commerce we laid it before Congress together with Monsr. Hortalezs Letters (one of which was a highly finished Political performance) who have added two members to the Commercial Committee to take the same into consideration.[2] They will enter upon the business this afternoon, and when Congress Shall have determined upon this important matter, we will give you the Result.

In answer to that of the 7th respecting the New Brigantine at Baltimore &c we have some Time Since ordered her to be loaded with

Tobacco for France. She is to go as a Packet to be armed and Commanded by Captain Read.[3] We have ordered the Two Vessels which last arrived at North Carolina from Hispaniola to be loaded with Tobacco and Consigned to Mr. Carrabasse. The Brigantine Success, Captain Harris, now at Edenton, was ordered before her Sailing from Boston to proceed from Carolina to Bilbao to the address of Messr. Gardoqui & Sons. Congress have ordered General Hand to send Provisions to the Arkansaws.[4]

In Answer to the 8th would observe that we think Mr Duer would have been very illy employed in telling you any thing that might have passed in Congress in which you were concerned; especially we think him highly culpable in representing to you that the Commercial Committee had complained to Congress that their not having the Books in their possession was a grievance to them; because it was a gross misrepresentation. Messrs. Forbes & Ellery who were the only members of the Commercial Committee then present, laid before Congress General Hands Letter &c respecting the Rattle Trap. Some of the Members were dissatisfied with that undertaking and asked a Multitude of questions about it. The Instructions given to Captain Willing were read; but still they wanted more light, when accidentally it was mentioned that the Books and Papers of the Secret Committee were in your hands. This occasioned a Conversation about them, which, if we could, we should think it not worth our while to relate. Let it suffice that so far from complaining against you on account of the Books, the Members of the Committee were for your retaining them 'till they should be settled.[5]

We laid this Letter before Congress who desired us to inform you that they would have you still keep the Books in your possession and settle them as soon as you could.

We have asked your advice frequently and freely, and have as often and as freely received it and shall continue to trouble you while we remain of the Commercial Committee (which we hope for reasons we have already mentioned to you will not be long)[6] whenever we find ourselves embarrassed.

In answer to yours of the 12th we leave the disposition of the Indies intirely to you.

Yours of the 17th is now before Congress and will be answered in due Time.

We have the Honor to be Sir, Your Obed Hble servants,

Fra Lewis

William Ellery

RC (NjGbS). In the hand of John Brown and signed by Ellery and Lewis.

[1] Except for the fragment of his February 7 letter quoted in the next note, only Morris' February 17 letter has been found.

[2] Elbridge Gerry and Henry Laurens were added to the committee on February 20 for the purpose of considering the papers presented by Jean Théveneau de Francy, an agent of Caron de Beaumarchais' firm Roderique Hortalez & Co.. *JCC,* 10:185. In his February 7 letter to the committee, a fragment of which is in Lee Papers, MH–H, Morris explained that "Mr. Francy says Mr. Beaumarchais' engagements are with Individuals who expect & wish for some returns to inspire them with fresh confidence & that the business of his mission to America is to receive whatever he can & settle the Accounts . . . that done to establish a permanent system for future supplies of money & goods."

There are two long 19th-century reports by the United States Congress on Beaumarchais' claims in U.S. Congress, House Select Committee, *Reports of the Select Committee . . . on the claim of the Representative of the late Caron de Beaumarchais,* 15th Cong., 1st sess., 1818, H. Rept. 111; and Committee of Foreign Affairs, *Committee of Foreign Affairs Report on the Claims of Beaumarchais' Heirs,* 20th Cong., 1st sess., 1828, H. Rept. 220. Both reports contain detailed descriptions of Beaumarchais' dealings with the Continental Congress as well as many contemporary letters and papers relating to them. Among these is a September 10, 1777, grant of powers by Beaumarchais to Francy to go to America "to solicit and recover all debts, relative to all the cargoes past, present, and future, sent by [Roderique Hortalez & Co.] to America," which is also printed in *JCC,* 10:320–21.

For the committee's negotiations with Francy, see Committee on the Claims of Roderique Hortalez & Co. Report, March 5; Robert Morris' Proposed Report on the Claims of Roderique Hortalez & Co., March 12; and Committee of Commerce to the Commissioners at Paris, May 16, 1778.

[3] See Marine Committee to Thomas Read, January 13, 1778.

[4] On January 30 Congress read and postponed consideration of Edward Hand's January 17 letter to the committee requesting instructions on James Willing's request that provisions for his expedition be sent to "the Arkansaws, a Spanish port on the Mississippi." But on February 19 Congress authorized Hand to send provisions to Willing, after considering Hand's February 12 explanation to the Board of War that provision boats could be sent part of the way under the protection of George Rogers Clark, who was embarking on an expedition against the British at Kaskaskia. See *JCC,* 10:101, 184; PCC, item 159, fols. 402–4, 431, 435–36; and Committee of Commerce to Oliver Pollock, November 21, 1777, note 1. For further details about Willing's raiding expedition through the Natchez district of West Florida, see Robert V. Haynes, *The Natchez District and the American Revolution* (Jackson: University Press of Mississippi, 1976), chap. 3.

[5] On the accounts of the Secret Committee, see Committee of Commerce to Robert Morris, January 30; John Penn to Robert Morris, February 4; and Robert Morris to the Committee of Commerce, February 17, 1778.

[6] For the committee's earlier comments about the need for reorganizing responsibility for commercial affairs, see its January 30, 1778, letter to Morris. The ever increasing work load of the committee coupled with its constantly fluctuating membership certainly affected the efficiency of the committee's operation and made continuity of policy most difficult. Although reform was mentioned during the spring of 1778, nothing concrete developed and the committee as reconstituted in December 1778 continued to be composed of members of Congress. See Committee for Foreign Affairs to William Bingham, April 16, and to Arthur Lee, May 14, 1778; and *JCC,* 12:1216–17.

Committee of Commerce to John Ross

Sir,   Commercial Committee York Feby. 21st. 1778
    Your Friend Mr Robt Morris having laid before us a Copy of your
Letter to him dated at Passy 7 October last whereby we observe the
American Commissioners at the Court of France had granted you a
Draft on their Banker for four hundred & fifty thousand Livres to
make good your Engagements and relieve you of Advances made in
the Execution of certain Contracts and Orders of the Secret Committee of Congress which Sum you had promised to replace when you
should be enabled by Remittances on the Public Account. In order to
enable you to comply with this Promise we have directed the following Parcells of Tobacco to be addressed to you or your Order
    142 Hhds per the Snow Speedwell, Capt Kent, from Virginia
    120 Hhds by the Brig Braxton, Capt James, Do
    476 Hhds by the Brig Governor Johnson, Capt Auchenleck, Do
    269 Hhds by the Brig Morris, Capt Gunnison, Do
1007 in all, which if they arrive safe will be more than sufficient
for your Reimbursement.[1] These Cargoes are directed to Messrs. Sam
& J.H. Delap at Bourdeaux, Mr John Danl Schweighauser at Nantes,
Messrs. Berard Brothers at Port L'Orient, Mr Andw Limozin at Havre
de Grace, Mr Mark Gregory at Dunkirk, Mr A Grieg at Marstrandt.
The Captains will make the first safe Port they can, & the Consignies
will consult you as to the Sales and account with you for the Net
Proceeds of these Cargoes, the sooner therefore you lodge proper
Directions respecting them the better. You must have these Cargoes
sold to the best Advantage, receive the Net Proceeds and credit the
United States therewith, retain in your hands any Balance justly due
to you on your former Transactions for the Public, pay the Commissioners the Amount of what they have advanced to you or such part
thereof as you are enabled by these Cargoes to pay and if after these
Arrangements a Balance becomes due to the United States We authorize & direct you to invest the same in an Assortment of Articles suitable for Clothing our Army which you will please to ship by such
good Opportunities as you can meet for any of our Ports consigning
the same to our Order, and divide the Quantities to be shipped on
different Vessels so as not to risque too much on any one. We depend
on your Care & accustomed Zeal to have this Business done to the
best Advantage. The Vessels that carry the Tobo. are all chartered
except the Brig Morris, Capt Gunneson, which belongs to the United
States; you must therefore supply the Captain what may be necessary
for the Ships Disbursements and also with a Cargo of Salt with which
you will order him back to any safe Port he can make in these States
consigning the same to our Order & transmitting us a Bill of lading

for the Salt and his Receipt for Amot. of Supplies to the Vessel. The others you have only to pay the Freight of the Tobacco to the Captains & you have done with them. These Vessels are all loaden & ready to sail & have been so a considerable Time. They are watching for our Enemies ships to be a little off their guard so that an Oppertunity may present for slipping out, therefore if they do not arrive soon as you could wish still we hope they will get safe at length. With much Regard, We remain, Sir, Your Obdt Hble Servts. Robt Morris

P.S. If you can procure Insurance on these several Parcells of Toba. valuing each Hhd at £30 Sterlg. and Premm. not to exceed 25 per Cent we authorize you to make such Insurance, in order to secure the Remittance either by safe arrival or by the Recovery of such Insurances.

Tr (PPL). A copy of the letter enclosed by Robert Morris with his February 17 letter to the committee.

[1] For the committee's explanation of how this letter came to be written and the August 1 resolve consigning the described cargoes to the commissioners at Paris, see *JCC*, 11:738–40. See also Committee of Commerce to Robert Morris, January 30; and Robert Morris to the Committee of Commerce, February 17, 1778.

Henry Laurens to the Committee at Camp

Gentlemen   In Congress at York Town. 21st February 1778.

I beg leave to refer you to my Letter sent this Morning by Messenger Barry & to the Inclosed Act of Congress this moment confirmed by which you are authorized in conjunction with General Washington to make the proper appointments for the Quarter Master's department, without further delay.[1]

I have the honour to be with great Regard, Gentlemen, Your most obedient servt,   Henry Laurens, President of Congress.

RC (DNA: PCC, item 192).

[1] See *JCC*, 10:185; and Laurens to the Committee at Camp, February 20, 1778.

Henry Laurens to Thomas Johnson

Sir,   York Town 21st February 1778.

I wrote to Your Excellency the 10th Inst by Eph. Harris.[1] Please to receive under this Cover an Act of Congress of the 18th for embodying a sufficient Number of Militia for guarding Prisoners to be stationed at Fort Frederick &c—& in a seperate Packet six Copies of Acts of the 5th & 6th Inst. for establishing divers regulations in the Civil

& Military departments of the Army & for other purposes therein mentioned.[2] These dispatches General Weedon is so obliging as to take charge of.

I have the honour to be, With great Regard, Sir, Your Excellency's Obedient & humble servt,

Henry Laurens, President of Congress.

RC (MdAA).
[1] See Laurens to Patrick Henry, February 10, 1778, note.
[2] See JCC, 10:124, 132–37, 180.

Henry Laurens to George Washington

Sir   21st Febry 1778

I had the honour of writing to your Excellency the 19th by Barry. Under the present Cover Your Excellency will be pleased to receive— An Act of Congress of the 19th for seperating the Troops included in the Convention of Saratoga & for other purposes.

Of the present date for appointing by Your Excellency's Order a Major General to releive Major General Spencer in the Command of the Troops at Rhode Island.[1]

And for hastening supplies of Meat & Forage to the Camp.

Another Act of the present date for appointing proper persons without delay to fill the several Offices of the Quarter Master's department.

In consequence of the Act of the 19th Your Excellency is requested to suspend the transmission to Sir William Howe of the requisition for passports for Vessels to transport Fuel &c to Boston for the subsistence of General Burgoyne's Troops until Congress shall have further deliberated on that matter.

I have the honour to be with very great Esteem.

LB (DNA: PCC, item 13).
[1] On March 10 Washington ordered Gen. John Sullivan to take Gen. Joseph Spencer's place as Continental commander in Rhode Island. Washington, *Writings* (Fitzpatrick), 11:57–58.

Henry Laurens to Thomas Wharton

Sir.   York Town 21st February 1778.

I troubled your Excellency with a Letter on the 10th Inst. by the hand of Monsr Dubuysson—& on the 19th[1] by the Reverend Doctr Witherspoon I conveyed a packet containing six Copies of Acts of Congress of the 5th & 6th Inst. for establishing divers regulations in the Civil & Military Lines of the Army & for appointing Auditors of Army Accounts &ca. These may be added to several preceeding dispatches which I have had the honour of transmitting to Your Excellency & which remain unacknowledged.

Your Excellency will be pleased to receive in company with this, an Act of Congress of the present date earnestly recommending to the Executive Council of this State to exert the whole power of the State to releive the Army under General Washington now reduced almost to the very last extremity from a want of provision of Flesh & Forage, & referring to a Letter from the General of the 15th Inst. to Robt. L. Hooper & others, & to an extract of a Letter from Mr. Duer to Colo. Lee of the 19th. Copy of the said Letter together with the extract Your Excellency will find with the other Paper.[2]

I dare not Insult Your Excellency & the Honorable Council by urging that not a moment should be lost, or that on Your exertions rest the safety of our Union & Independency. All attempts to such incitement, I am persuaded are equally unseasonable & unnecessary. I have therefore only to conclude wishing success to Your Excellency's Orders & endeavors & repeating that I am, With very great Respect, Sir, Your obedient & Most humble servant,

Henry Laurens, President of Congress

RC (NN).

[1] See Laurens to George Clinton, February 19, 1778, note 4.

[2] Washington's February 15 letter to Robert L. Hooper, Nathaniel Falconer, and Jonathan Mifflin, who had been appointed by the Board of War to purchase supplies in Pennsylvania for the Continental Army, is in Washington, *Writings* (Fitzpatrick), 10:463–64. The enclosed extract of William Duer's February 19 letter to Francis Lightfoot Lee is printed in this volume under that date. See also note 1 to that letter.

Daniel Roberdeau to the Pennsylvania Assembly

Sir,   York Town Feby. 21st. 1778

I have the honor to address my Constituents the Representatives of this State now assembled, on subjects the most distressing and alarming, the deficiencies in the Commissaries and Quarter masters departments which threaten the dispersion of our army and all the horrid train of Evils consiquent to this State more immediately, and to the common cause more general in its baneful influence. The Letters and resolves of Congress ordered to be forwarded[1] makes a particular discant on the distresses of our army unnecessary from me. I have only to assure the Honble. House that under God the Salvation of our Cause now depends on you as from your Situation timely supplies of provisions especially meat, of forage and Waggons and *immediate* conveyance can only be expected, and without the most vigorous exertions you may depend the army will disperse, nothing but indispensable duty would extort a secret which might by being divulged prove ruinous, therefore what is my duty, is equally the duty of your Honble. House now the fact is disclosed to impose the most inviolable restraint on yourselves that our Enemies may not triumph in our Disgrace. Congress will begrudge no expence attending the exicution of your order in dependance on which is now the whole trust of Congress, for an immediate supply, or in other words for preventing the most direful distress. It would be impertinent in me to attempt to inforce a Subject so important on your Honble. House. Congress have displaced Officers who infringed the Law of the State respecting the prices of Articles.[2] To this Enemies will attribute the Evils we should deprecate, but our cause does not depend on the weak efforts of a few individuals, much less on any restless spirits among us who probably in the struggle mean to overset the freedom of this State. Your endeavours I trust will be succeeded. I am most respectfully, Sir, Yr. most obt. & very huml servt,   Danl. Roberdeau

P.S. A moments delay may be our ruin, which must apologize for my hasty scrawl which I have not time to copy or correct.

RC (PHarH). Addressed: "The Honble. James McLene Speaker of the House of Representatives of the Province of Pennsilvania, Lancaster." Endorsed: "Recd. & read in Assy. Feb. 24, 1778, p.m."
  [1] See JCC, 10:189.
  [2] For the issue of these "displaced Officers," see William Duer to Francis Lightfoot Lee, February 19, 1778, which was one of the documents Roberdeau enclosed with this letter.

Jonathan Bayard Smith to Joseph Reed

Dr Sir,   Lancaster Feb. 21st. 1778.
    Yours of 8th met me at this place where I have been very much indisposed with a severe cold. In conformity to your request, I wrote to York town concerning any letters for you, & directed them to be sent down. Tomorrow, I expect, I shall go over myself.
    It gave me real pleasure to find your sentiments on some important subjects so perfectly coincide with my own. In many instances I have dreaded the effects of measures, tho' at the same time a principle of charity, & a confidence in the zealous attachment of those who favored them, almost forbid any suspicions of undue motives. The Generals conduct on occasions truely affecting to a man honor, evinces how much more infintely he prefers the good of his country to any personal considerations. If in any instance Congress has seemed to favor an

adverse party, it ought not to be resolved into a design of injuring him; a concurrence of untoward circumstances have impelled to these steps which appear most exceptionable, & the tendency of which I foresaw & dreaded. If an individual or two are unhappily under the influence of an undue impression, the effects, it is to be hoped, will be very circumscribed, & the evil will carry in itself its own remedy. At the same time, something should be done to prevent the body of the people, especially of this state, losing their confidence in the Commander in Cheif. Rectifying the conduct of the different departments & putting an end to the impositions, & irregularties of some of the agents, would do much towards accomplishing this important end. If it were possible to avoid *seizures* & acts of force except in particular cases many disaffected persons, more of the indetermined, & all real whigs would be with us. By the present system of conduct, we suffer a fearful encrease of disaffection.

You have much to do, & however anxiously I wish to have your aid & counsil in Congress, yet I cannot wish you from your present post 'till the important business shall be *well* done. This will require time & patience; nor is it improbable that new business will present itself every day.

As I rise from my bed to embrace an opportunity by Colo. Bayards boy; & now feel myself worse, I must refer myself to another opportunity of being more full on several subjects. In general you may depend on my conduct being such in Congress as, considering my abilities, such sentiments as yours ought to produce. Inclosed you have a copy of Abingdons pamphlet which perhaps you have not seen.[1]

I am Dr. Sir, with great respect, Yr v h st.   J B Smith

RC (NHi).
[1] See John Henry to Thomas Johnson, February 17, 1778, note 2.

Committee at Camp Minutes of Proceedings

[February 22–28, 1778]

22. Recd. Presidts letter dated 20th.
23. Recd. Do. dated 21st.
    Conferred with Colo Cox[1] & Genl. Green.
24. Conferred with the same Gentn.
25. Closed the business of the Quarter Master Genl. Department.[2]
26. General not present.
27. General called away. Conferred with Baron Steuben. Sent dispatches to Congress respecting the Qr. Mr. G. Department.

28. Agreed to apply to the States of New-Jersey, Pennsylvania & Maryland[3] to procure Horses for the Cavalry & Sadles.[4]

MS (DLC). A continuation of Committee at Camp Minutes of Proceedings, February 16–20, 1778. In the hand of Francis Dana.

[1] For additional comments on the committee's meeting with Col. John Cox on the subject of his availability for appointment as deputy quartermaster general, see Joseph Reed to Jonathan Bayard Smith, February 24, 1778.

[2] See Committee at Camp to Henry Laurens, February 25, 1778. For other committee recommendations on the quartermaster general's department, see also the committee's letters to Laurens of January 28, February 12 and 24, 1778.

[3] See Committee at Camp to Thomas Wharton, February 28, 1778.

[4] For the continuation of these minutes, see Committee at Camp Minutes of Proceedings, March 1–7, 1778.

Gouverneur Morris to Robert R. Livingston

My dear Friend.   Moor Hall Camp Valley Forge 22d Feby 1778

Whether you receive all the Letters I write I know not but this I know that I get none from you which is not pleasing to me. Indeed I ought to write two or three for one because in the first Place one of your Letters is intrisically worth more than mine and would be so valued even by a Bookseller. In the next Place I can only satisfy the idle Curiosity which may arise in the Breast of a Man of *Leizure* about what is going forward in a foolish World which he *says* he wishes to retire from. You can inform me of what I love and value most in the World for you can satisfy those Yearnings about the *natale Solum* which forbid us to be immemorous of it, you can give me a Map of that political Spot which hapless Wanderer as I am I must travel through, above all (excuse a Republican for laying so great a Stress here) you can send me Tidings of the Friends I love and value more than the world. Pray remember me to them all of every Sex, Age and Complection.

While I write a Dispute is going on at my Elbow about Taxation which like every other political Subject Every one is as you know a perfect Master of. The Contest is whether Bonds should be taxed. A Gentleman from Massachusetts contends that they should, One from Jersey that they should not. Both *may* be right. I, as you know, hate disputes but I love the State I was born in and as I am confident this Measure will be followed among our neighbours from a mistaken Policy of the landed Men and possibly from some Propriety in it under our present Circumstances which indeed I cannot see It is my wish to Advantage alienâ insaniâ. Let me intreat that nothing of this kind may take Place among us. Thank God our Government is such that the *true* Interests of the State can be pursued. I have no Money, all the little Property I have is in Land, I therefore speak freely, perhaps my Sentiments may from that Circumstance have Weight with those who suppose me interested (with what Propriety or on what Grounds I know not) and who will acknowledge that I have not always judged wrong. If the several States N York excepted tax Money N York will be inhabited by all the monied Men on the Continent & consequently raise a Revenue from all the Rest which indeed greater political Abilities as well as greater Sufferings in the common Cause intitle them to. Besides this such immense personal Property in the Country will add vastly to the Value of Lands and of the Produce of Lands. At the same Time it will give such a Spring to Commerce as will necessarily render our Merchants Carriers to the other States (and our Farmer's Sons may be Merchants if they will) thereby adding a further Increase to the Property of the State. By these Means shall we become the Bankers of America and consequently regulate Exchange in our own Favor. To all which I add that of Necessity immense Stores of Merchandize will flow in to make the great Ballance of Trade which as you know cannot be all in Money and indeed ought not. These carried up Hudsons River will form vast Magazines in the Heart of America: the true source of Victory. Hence shall we derive a splendor to our arms (which our Neighbours will oblige us to brighten or I am much mistaken) and a controuling Influence in the Councils of America. Great Things depend on small more than small Men think for. And however little Wits may laugh let us not forget that this is the Seed time of Glory as of Freedom. Adieu again I say remember me to my Friends particularly Jay. Remember me very particularly to Mrs Livingston. When you see your Mother and Sisters assure them of my faithful Remembrance.

I am Dear Robert, yours sincerely,   Gouvr Morris

RC (NHi). Addressed: "honle. Robert R. Livingston Esqr. Chancellor of the State of New York, Manor of Livingston or Poughkeepsie." Endorsed by Morris: "To be put in the Post Office at Lancaster."

Committee of Commerce to John Langdon

Sir   Commercial Committee, York 23d Febry. 1778
We have agreed with Mr. Francey that the Flamand shall go to South Carolina and there take in A Load of Rice for France. She will be upon our risque to Carolina and the Captain of her being unacquainted with the Coast, and there being a possibillity of her taking a Prize on her Passage, We have agreed with Mr Francey to send in her a Continental Navy Captain and two or three Officers and Eight or Ten Seamen if to be had.

We write to the Navy Board in the Eastern Department for that purpose.[1] If they should not be able to furnish them in Season you must put on board a proper Person who is acquainted with that Coast. You will give the Flamand all the dispatch in your power.[2] We are Sir, Yr. Obedt servts,   Fra. Lewis

William Ellery

James Forbes

P.S. You will make out Triplicates of the Ship Flamands Disbursments which you have paid, get the Captain to Sign them, and send them forward to us as soon as you can. We acknowledge the receipt of yours of the 8th Ultimo and return thanks for your attention in giving us a discription of the Flamand.   F L

W E

J F

Since writing the above Mr Francey informs that he had left orders with a Freind at Portsmouth to pay the Ships Debts, therefore there is no Occasion for what we have said above.

RC (Capt. J. G. M. Stone, Annapolis, Md., 1973). In the hand of John Brown and signed by Ellery, Forbes, and Lewis.

[1] See Marine Committee to the Eastern Navy Board, this date.

[2] In a March 3 revision of his February 21 letter to John Langdon, Jean Théveneau de Francy requested Langdon to assist Capt. Fassy in preparing the *Flamand's* papers and dispatching the vessel promptly. He also requested Langdon's cooperation in settling the accounts of Hortalez & Co.: "I am Very much pleased with all the members of the Congress, & I do not expect to meet with the least difficulty; however I cannot Settle nothing, as the different invoices Concerning what is arrived of our goods upon the Continent, have not been Sent yet to the Commercial Committee; it seems to me you had told me that you Sent last year the amount of what you did received by the *Mercury* & *Amphytritte*, it was never received; I beg of you to have a copy of it made & to Send it directly along, with the amount of what is come in the packet *Niere Bobie* & upon *le Flammand.*" Capt. J. G. M. Stone Collection.

Although the Committee of Commerce was advanced $20,000 on February 26 to purchase a cargo of rice for the *Flamand,* her captain subsequently refused to go to South Carolina. See *JCC,* 10:199; and Committee of Commerce to Langdon, May 7, 1778.

A January 11, 1778, letter from Francy to Caron de Beaumarchais, discussing his activities in Portsmouth and Boston since his arrival in America in December, is in Pierre Augustin Caron de Beaumarchais, *Beaumarchais Correspondence,* ed. Brian N. Morton and Donald C. Spinelli (Paris: A. G. Nizet, 1962–), 4:28–30.

Henry Laurens to Matthew Smith

Sir,   23d Febry 1778

This Morning I received & presented to Congress your favour of the 16th & agreeable to your request Congress have consented to your resignation.[1] I am sorry that a want of health has obliged you to this measure, I wish you a perfect recovery & am with much Respect, Sir, your obedt. humble Servt.

LB (DNA: PCC, item 13). Addressed: "Lieutt. Colo. Math. Smith of the 9th P[ennsylvania] Regiment, Paxtang, Lancaster County. By James Wilson."
[1] See *JCC,* 10:190. Lt. Colonel Matthew Smith's February 16 letter to Laurens, in which he announced that he wished to resign his Continental commission because he was afflicted with "Several Bodyly Complaints," is in PCC, item 78, 20:191.

Marine Committee to the Eastern Navy Board

Gentlemen   Feby 23d. 1778

The French Ship Flamand now in Portsmouth New Hampshire is directed by the Committee of Commerce to proceed forthwith to Charles Town in South Carolina there to be laden'd with Rice &c for France. This Ship mounts 18 Six pounders and is navigated with 70 Seamen and fast sailes. The Committees intention is to give this Ship a Commission in expectation of picking some Prizes on the passage to Charles Town, and for that purpose you are requested to send out of your department a Captain and two Lieutenants in the Continental Service who have not at present an Actual command together with Eight or ten Seamen in order to conduct any prizes that may be taken into Port. In navigating the Ship as a Merchant Ship the French Captain is to have the command, but in giving chase or in an engagement the Continental Captain and his officers are to have the sole direction. The Captain & Officers apptd. to this service should be persons who have some knowledge of the Carolina Coast. They are upon their Arrival at Charles Town to return as soon as may be to their former station in your department. Should they be so fortunate as to take Prizes on the Passage, One half will be set apart for the Continent. The Continental Captain and his Officers will draw one eight and the French Captain and his Officers and Crew will be intitled to the other ⅜ths. If you should or should not be able to procure a suitable Captain, officers and seamen, you will give seasonable notice thereof to the Continental Agent at Portsmouth that the ship may not be unnecessarily delayed.[1]

We have given Orders to our Agent in Maryland to purchase 2000 Barrels flour and 30 Tons bar Iron and to have the same transported to the Inlet of Senepuxent on the Sea Coast in Maryland about 50 Miles to the southward of the Capes of Delaware.[2]

You will immediately on receipt hereof dispatch the Continental Schooner at Bedford, and charter as many small fast sailing Vessels and dispatch them for that Port as you shall think will be sufficient to carry the above quantity of Flour to such Ports or places in the

Eastern States as you shall think proper to direct. Our Agent William Smith Esqr. will give the necessary orders for having the Vessels loaded immediately on their arrival. You will endeavour to get Masters for those Vessels who are acquainted with the Coast and Inlet above mentioned and if you cannot Charter Vessels without Insureing them we empower you so to do having them properly valued. We are, Gentn, Yr hble Servants

LB (DNA: PCC Miscellaneous Papers, Marine Committee Letter Book).
    [1] "The Continental Agent at Portsmouth," John Langdon, had also been the subject of a brief February 12 letter from the Marine Committee to the Eastern Navy Board, which requested it to direct Langdon to make future applications for money directly to the board. PCC Miscellaneous Papers, Marine Committee Letter Book, fol. 126; and Paullin, *Marine Committee Letters*, 1:201.
    [2] See the committee's February 24 letter to William Smith.

Daniel Roberdeau to Thomas Wharton

Sir   York Town Feby. 23d. 1778
    The papers by you transmitted to the board of War were refered to Congress, read and committed to be returned,[1] accordingly I do myself the honor of handing them to you, and hope the violators of the Laws of the State will be brought to condign punishment. I am with respectful Salutations to the Honble. Council, Sir, Yr. most obt. & very huml. Serv.   Daniel Roberdeau

RC (PHarH).
    [1] These were probably documents read in Congress on February 18 relating to the Board of War's investigation of the conduct of a British prisoner of war relief party that lodged in Lancaster January 21, 1778. See *JCC*, 10:180; *Pa. Archives*, 1st ser. 6:216, 268–69; and John Harvie and Gouverneur Morris to the Pennsylvania Council, January 24, 1778, note.

Committee at Camp to Henry Laurens

Sir   Moor Hall 24th Feby. 1778
    We have been honored with your several Favors of the twentieth and twenty first Instant with the Enclosures. We now beg Leave to acknowledge the Receipt of them and to assure Congress thro you that their Committee will pay the utmost Attention to their Commands by placing the Quarter Master's Department (as far as lies in their Power) upon such a Footing and in such Hands as will provide for the various Wants which now distress the Army and shakle the General and at the same Time to obviate that iniquitous System of Peculation which History informs us hath prevailed in former Ages

and in other Countries which our Scale of Observation leads us to
believe are not entirely unknown in this. These Sir are Objects of the
utmost Importance. Add to these that the Department is at present
involved in inextricable Confusion. Genius, Industry, Integrity and
the Manner of doing Business are absolutely nay indespensibly
necessary.

Notwithstanding the Powers which Congress have thought proper
to entrust us with we shall not presume absolutely to fix the Appointments but are at this Instant engaged in making all the necessary
Arrangements after which we will submit the whole to them Not
doubting but that we shall be able to put Matters in such a Train as
will produce desirable Consequences. The principal Gentlemen are
now with us and hope so far to complete the Business this Day.[1]

We are Sir, your most obedient & humble Servants,

Fra Dana
by Order

RC (DNA: PCC, item 33). Written by Gouverneur Morris and signed by Dana.
[1] The committee completed its work on the quartermaster general's department
on the next day. See Committee at Camp Minutes of Proceedings, February 22–28;
and Committee at Camp to Henry Laurens, February 25, 1778.

Samuel Huntington to Jabez Huntington

Sir   York Town 24th February 1778
You will See King Gorge's Speach at the opening of his parliament
before this comes to hand which is as late as any Intelligence we have
from there. The Assembly of Virginia have fully approved & acceded
to the Articles of Confederation; have not heard the determination
of any other State on the Subject.

A general Cartel for exchange of prisoners hath taken place between Generals Washington & Howe,[1] which is all the Intelligence I
am able to communicate more than you will find in the public papers.
I am Sir with much Esteem, your humble Servant,

Saml Huntington

RC (CtHi).
[1] See Eliphalet Dyer to William Williams, February 17, 1778, note 7.

Henry Laurens to George Clinton

Sir,   24th Febry 1778.
My last to your Excellency was dated the 19th Inst. & went by
Messenger Brown.

Yesterday I had the honour of presenting your Excellency's favour of the 3d Inst. to Congress.[1] The importance of the necessary works for obstructing the passes of North River & the near approach of the time when it may be in the power of the Enemy to oppose all our attempts awaken reflections truly alarming.

In the Letter above referred to, was inclosed an Act of Congress of the 18th Inst. authorizing & requesting Your Excellency to superintend & quicken the dispatch of that business & Congress still flatter themselves with an assurance that through Your Excellency's influence & exertions the whole intended work will be completed. I will take the liberty of reminding the House this very day of those essential articles Engineers & proper Artillery.[2] In the meantime, in order to guard against accidents I judge it necessary to forward duplicates of the said Act & of the Warrant for fifty Thousand Dollars which your Excellency will find within.

I have the honour to be with very great Regard &ca.

LB (DNA: PCC, item 13).
[1] Governor Clinton's February 3 letter is in PCC, item 67, 2:106–7. See also Laurens to Clinton, February 19, 1778, note 2.
[2] On March 4 Congress resolved to place additional cannon at Governor Clinton's disposal to defend the Highlands. *JCC*, 10:221.

Henry Laurens to Samuel A. Otis

Sir,   24th Febry 1778

Very late this Evening your favor of the 24th Ulto. came to hand,[1] I will present it to Congress to morrow, but as the Messenger by which this is intended will proceed earlier than our Meeting, I will barely acknowledge the receipt of your Letter which has travelled much more deliberately than you could have expected.

And I mean to afford you the further satisfaction of assuring you the Resolves of Congress which you intimate have affected an individual, Mr. Jackson, were certainly not intended to apply to him or personally to any other Gentleman & that they were grounded upon general information of the exhorbitant demands which had been made for such Merchandize as you had attempted to purchase for the use of the Army.[2]

The Letters which you wrote on that occasion to Congress are at present in the Secretary's Office & at this time of Night not accessible, therefore I cannot possitively say, the name of Jackson is not mentioned in them, but my memory which in such Cases is not deficient, assures me it is not, & you may, if it be needful, Safely aver to that Gentleman that neither his name nor conduct were animadverted in

Congress, this would probably have happened, had your Letter exhibited either or both in an unfavourable light.

Be all this as it may, when I say you merit thanks for your attention to the public welfare in your department, I believe I speak the sentiments of every Member of Congress.

Notwithstanding the great discouragement given by the present sluggishness of public Spirit, let us proceed Sir, set our faces against the phalanx of Avarice & peculation, however countenanced by splendid Characters, however powerful & triumphant, & through good Report & Evil Report strive, & we shall at length stem the power of those Engines calculated for our destruction & played by the hands of Enemies in disguise. These will otherwise soon shew to the World, our pretended work of Independency a second Babel in perspective.

I am with great Respect &ca.

P.S. 25th A.M. the Messenger having been unavoidably detained affords me an opportunity of adding, that I have presented your Letter to Congress & that it was well received & your conduct applauded.

LB (DNA: PCC, item 13).

[1] In this letter Samuel A. Otis, the deputy clothier general in Massachusetts, described his efforts to carry out the resolves Congress had passed on December 31, 1777, to enable him to purchase clothing for the Continental Army at fair prices. See PCC, item 78, 17:285–87; and JCC, 9:1071–73.

[2] Jonathan Jackson was a Massachusetts merchant who had tried to charge Otis "2000 per Cent" for clothing and who therefore may very well have thought that Congress' December 31, 1777, resolves against extortionate sellers were personally directed at him. See PCC, item 78, 17:285–87.

Henry Laurens to Thomas Wharton

Sir.   York Town 24th Feby 1778

I had the honour of writing to Your Excellency the 21st.

Yesterday Mr. Joseph Simons of Lancaster addressed Congress with a Letter which Your Excellency will find inclosed—meaning as he has explained, to obtain permission for going within the Enemy's Lines in order to account with Mr Franks. Congress judged it best to refer this application, for determination, to the Supreme Council of the State; thence Your Excellency receives the present trouble.[1]

I am with great Regard & Respect, Sir, Your Excellency's Most humble servant,   Henry Laurens, President of Congress

RC (CtY).

[1] Although Congress noted receipt of a February 18 letter from Joseph Simons, he is not mentioned in the *Pa. Council Minutes* or the correspondence in *Pa. Archives*, 1st ser., and it is not known how the Pennsylvania Council disposed of his request to enter the British lines. *JCC*, 10:190.

Marine Committee to William Smith

Sir   February 24th 1778
We request you will immediately on receipt hereof purchase 2000 Barrels of Common Flour with 30 Tons of bar Iron and forward the same as soon as may to Senepuxent with directions to a proper person there to receive and deliver the same to such Masters of Vessels as shall arrive there for that purpose. We have by Express this day directed the Navy Board for the Eastern Department to send from thence round to Senepuxent small fast sailing Vessels that may be sufficient to take off the above quantity.

We shall apply to Congress for money to enable you in the execution which we shall send you by the first safe conveyance.[1] We shall rely upon your care and expedition in this affair & are Sir, Your humble servants

LB (DNA: PCC Miscellaneous Papers, Marine Committee Letter Book).
[1] On April 11 Congress authorized the committee to send their Baltimore agent Smith $10,000 to purchase the flour and iron. *JCC,* 10:338. The committee's April 14 letter informing Smith that this money would be delivered by Capt. David Porter is in PCC Miscellaneous Papers, Marine Committee Letter Book, fol. 141, and Paullin, *Marine Committee Letters,* 1:228. See also Marine Committee to William Smith, January 10 and June 19; and Committee of Commerce to Francis Lewis, Jr., March 6, 1778, note 2.

Joseph Reed to Jonathan Bayard Smith

Dear Sir   Moore Hall Feb. 24. 1778
It gives me much Concern that our Business proceeds slower than Congress seem to expect. I trusted that our private Communications would at least have softned the Violence of Expectation. We attribute most of the Peculation, Waste, & Derangement of our Affairs to an injudicious Choice of Officers. With these Sentiments you must not be surprized to find us cautious & slow, especially in a Department of so much Confidence & Power as that of a Qr. Master General. When we see Confusion & Disorder reigning thro the whole Army by the Defects of this Office & unaccounted Millions, we think we cannot be too cautious & esteem it Time well spent to look out the most worthy Characters, & draw them into the publick Service. I hinted to you that we had a Design on Col. Cox. We sent for him & he is now with us. But you know he is a Man of too much Sagacity to engage without due Consideration of all Circumstances. He is employed in very extensive Concerns both of Iron & Salt for which he has made great Preparations the Benefit of which he must lose & alter his whole Arrangements. You will not wonder therefore if he takes Time & I

believe you will agree that if he can be brought in we shall have a Prospect of bringing Order out of this Confusion. I presume you understand from what I mentioned before than Gen. Green is to be at the Head of the Department, Col. Cox to stand second, & they are to have the Appointment of their Subs. Be not misled, my good Friend, with Utopian Ideas of dividing Departments & Offices which the Practice & Experience of all Nations shew us ought to be united. Wander as far as we will from established Rules & Systems we shall find sooner or later we must return. A Dislike & even Rage against every Thing English has precipitated us into a Labyrinth of Error & Expence from which the wisest Heads will find it difficult to extricate us. We are resolved not to be Parties in plunging you deeper; if we cannot raise the publick above Water we shall at least let you feel your own Way. Characters fit for the Department are not to be found in the Army; if they were your Affairs would not be in the wretched Condition they now are. If we have the World to chuse out of; Congress can select better than we can; their Knowledge is more extensive & should they err they will not have the same kind of Responsibility. I know you cry out precious Time is wasting, it is so but great Haste is not often the best Speed. Experience must tell you how easy it is to put a Man in Office & how difficult to get him out. There has been to use an odd Expression a Cullibility[1] in Congress that has surprized me. How many rash Appointments have been made which we all lament & the Consequences of which we feel thro the whole System.

You will therefore my good Sir, oblige us if you will in a Way of which you are very capable vindicate us from the Imputation of causeless Delay.

I am anxious to hear whether you have received a long Letter I wrote you about 10 Days ago. The Messenger waits so that I have only Time to desire my best Regards to our Associates & add that I am with sincere Regard, Dr Sir, Your most obed. & very Hbble Serv.

Jos. Reed

[*P.S.*] One James Woolard a Post or Express from Congress has been taken by a Party of the Enemy's Tory light Horse.

RC (DLC).
[1] Although the usage of cullibility was in decline by the late 18th century, gullibility was apparently seldom used before the 19th century. *OED*.

Committee at Camp to Henry Laurens

Sir   Camp near Valley Forge, Feby. 25. 1778
Agreeable to the Promise made in our Letter of yesterday, we

have in Concert with the General, compleated the Arrangement of the Quarter Master Generals Department; which now only waits for the Fiat of Congress. By your Resolutions of the 5th Inst.[1] we find, that it is the Intention of Congress, to divide the Quarter Master's Department into four capital Branches. The Quarter Master properly so called: The Commissary of Forage; the Commissary of Horses &c, and the Agent of Purchases. Permit us, Sir, to represent that so many independent Officers without a controuling Chief, must necessarily involve Interference with each other, infinite Confusion, & a Variety of Controversies, which must be terminated by the Commander in Chief, or in other Words, that the General must be, what he has been during the last Campaign, the Quarter Master General of the Army. Besides this, we have to observe farther, that each of these Officers must necessarily be empowered to draw publick Money, & of Consequence, that the Chance of Frauds, & Amount of Expenditures will be greatly increased by so many separate Departments. Add to this, that when any Abuses, & more particularly when any Deficiencies shall be felt, it will be easy for these Gentlemen to shift the Blame from one to the other, rendering it impracticable to detect either Ignorance, Indolence, or Inequity. Many additional Reasons might be adduced to shew[2] how dangerous such an Experiment may prove; but the Wisdom of Congress will doubtless supply them, & upon reconsidering this Business in all its Connections, & Dependencies see a Propriety in placing this very executive Department, under one controuling superintending Power, whose Activity, & Influence may regulate, pervade & animate the whole System.

Let us now, Sir, cast our Glance upon the Administration of Affairs heretofore. We mean not to censure or commend, but it is our Duty to inform. We hesitate not to say, that the Abuses which have crept in are such, that no Finances can support a System like the present. Men without Morals, without Character, & without Property have been, & are intrusted with the Disposal of publick Money, & private Property. The Number of little, piddling, pilfering Plunderers in the Character of Deputies, & Deputies Assistants is sufficient almost to form an Army, & does form a kind of Army, not indeed to act against the Enemies, but against the Friends of America; to sour the Minds of the People, & exhaust the Resources of the Country. And not only is the Expence almost infinite; the Neglect is as great perhaps as fatal. This may appear to be the Language of Exaggeration, but whatever Ideas arise from a View of the general Complexion, they fall much short when we examine some particular Features. We are told, Sir, that in some capital Purchases, the enormous Commission of 5 per Cent hath been allowed: We know that the publick pay 2½ per Cent upon every Ounce of Forage consumed by this Army. We fear that publick Teams have been employed at the publick

Expense, to transport private Property from distant States, while publick Property has there lain neglected, & our Troops been left to suffer for Want of the usual Camp Transportation. We are also obliged to add that at this Moment, not a Horse, Waggon, Tent, or intrenching Tool, as we are informed, is purchased for the next Campaign, & every Gentleman who rides thro' the Country will see it strewed with publick Stores perishing from Neglect. Such being the melancholy Situation to which we have been reduced, it hath become indispensably necessary to call forth Characters, of known & approved Abilities, to introduce a thorough Reform, & make the necessary Provision for the ensuing Campaign. Genl. Schuyler appeared to your Committee best adapted to these Purposes, but[3] least he should not be approved, we have cast our Eyes upon other Persons. It might well have been supposed that on this Occasion, we were not inattentive to the Merit, which it is said Baron Steuben possesses. If it were practicable to divide this Department without great Injury to the publick Cause, & if that Gentleman really possesses the necessary Qualifications; we cannot but think, there would be a manifest Impropriety in trusting a Foreigner for whose Attachment we have at best but a very slender Security, with a Power to accelerate, impede, or obstruct at his Pleasure every Movement of the Army, & to dispose of large Sums of Money, in such Manner & for such Purposes as he may think proper, (for large Sums he must have the Disposal of, tho' it be only to defray what is called petty Expences of an Army) such Expences amounting annually to a very considerable Expenditure under the Name of *Contingencies*. Young Men, Sir, fired with a Love of Glory, may indeed seek Honour at the Hazard of Life, in our American Wildernesses; but Men who make a Trade of War, are seldom animated by or act upon such enthusiastick Principles; neither can their Education, their Profession, or the Form of Government they have lived under, inspire such Veneration for the Rights of Mankind, as will lead to a Conduct purely disinterested. With Respect to these Gentlemen therefore, it must be evident, they are either sent hither for the particular Purposes of those by whom they are sent; or they come hither for particular Purposes of their own. If the former of them be the real Motive, it is unwise to trust them too far, because it is not possible allways to discover the sender; or even then what are his Intentions. If on the contrary, they come from the latter Motive, they come to make a Fortune, & they will make a Fortune at the Expence of their Employers; & having made it they will at an enormous Exchange send their Money to Europe, or at an enormous Price make Purchases of Land here, & in either Case go home, & wait with Indifference the Close of the Contest. Some Circumstances countenance an Opinion that Instances of this kind may be found.

We proceed now to state the Arrangement which we propose to make, premising that it is upon the Characters of Men principally, & not upon Paper Systems that our Success must depend. We propose Sir to have a Quarter Master General, & two Assistant Qr. Masters General appointed by Congress, & that these three be allowed for their Trouble & Expence one per Cent upon the Monies issued in the Department, to be divided as they shall agree & including an Addition to the Pay of the Waggon Master Gen. & his Deputy which is absolutely necessary. The Gentlemen we have in View are Genl. Green, Col. Cox, & Charles Pettit Esqr. the two former of whom have consented to take the Department on these Terms, & upon these only. The latter has not been consulted, but we have Reason to believe he may be prevailed upon to serve. The Arrangment among them is as follows: That General Greene as Qr Master General shall perform the military Duty, attend to all the Issues, & direct the Purchases. That Col. Cox (who we will venture to say is perhaps the best qualified for that Purpose of any other Man) shall make all Purchases, examine all Stores, & the like, which his Knowledge of the Country & of Business will enable him to do with Advantage to the publick. And that Mr. Pettit shall attend to the keeping of Accounts, & of Cash; which is not as heretofore to be instrusted to any Deputy. A perfect Harmony & good Understanding among these Gentlemen, will we apprehend render it unnecessary by any Resolutions to mark out the Bounds of their several Departments, which at best would be attended with no good effects, & in all human Probability would leave something to be done which it would be no Body's Business to do. Forage Masters, Waggon Masters &c must of Necessity be in the Appointment of the Qr. Mastr Genl. who is, or ought at least to be responsible for their Conduct as forming a Part of the general System. Great Abuses have already prevailed from the multiplying such Offices, of which we shall say no more at present, it being a Task at once tedious and disagreeable.[4]

We have had great Difficulty in prevailing with these Gentlemen to undertake the Business. They object the advanced Season, the Confusions of the Department, the Depreciation of our Money, & exhausted State of our Resources, as rendering it almost impracticable to do that essential Service which they conceive their Duty to require of them. Besides which, each has private Reasons of his own. Genl. Greene was very unwilling to enter into this large Field of Business, which tho it will not, & indeed ought not to exclude him from his Rank in the Line, will of Necessity prevent his doing the active Duty of a General Officer. Col. Cox whose private Business[5] is known to be very lucrative, was unwilling to quit it, & break off Engagements which he hath largely entered into for the manufactory of Salt & Iron, and to accept a Compensation much short of it, for doing publick

Business to a much larger Amount, & with increased Labour. Mr. Pettit now Secretary to the State of New Jersey an Office which will make a genteel as well as permanent Provision for his Family, cannot be expected to quit it without an adequate Compensation. In short, Sir, we are confident that nothing but a thorough Conviction of the absolute Necessity of straining every Nerve in the Service, could have brought these Gentlemen into Office upon any Terms. To give a Commission upon publick Money is doubtless a Temptation to the Officers to peculate, & should in general be avoided. In the present Instance however the general Position we believe admits of Exception. Every Man has his Price in a good Sense, that is to say no Man will undertake great Labour without the Prospect of some proportionate Gain, & whatever fair Promises People may make every one will have the Price at which he estimates his Labours, by Right, or by Wrong. To pay such a Price as a Salary to the Officer, would in one Point of Veiw, be preferable, but would produce most dangerous Effects in the Army. Upon raising the Salary of one Officer, every other would expect a similar Increase, & when once the Mode is begun, no one can tell where it will end, unless indeed in publick Bankruptcy. It is true that a Commission is a Temptation to enhance the Price of Articles purchased; & it is possible enough that this Temptation will have its Effect. Let us then suppose a Quartr. Master Genl. inclined to defraud the Publick of 1000 Dollars, would he do it by giving 200,000 for that which ought to be purchased for 100,000, thereby giving an Alarm: or would he charge the publick with the Loss of Articles in his Department to that Amount, or the like; for which a thousand opportunities would daily present themselves, without the Possiblity of Detection. The Fact is that in this particular Department, if those at the Head of it are not vigilant & honest, the publick may, nay, must be defrauded of immense Sums by an Infinity of Ways, in Spite of every Check which the Ingenuity of Man can devise. And of all the Means of defrauding, the swelling of Commissions by greater Expenditures, is the most liable to Detection & produces the worst Consequences to the offending Party himself. There is therefore no Possiblity of obviating Peculation, but by drawing forth Men of Property, Morals, & Character—these are the only solid Basis of Security, & if such Men watch each other, which would be the Case according to our Proposed System; we have all the Precautions which the Nature of the Case will admit. The Commission of 2½ per Cent now paid on Forage alone, will we believe exceed the Allowance of the new Establishment. There will be a Saving then even here, but that from which we hope most, is the Sagacity, & Knowledge of Business which these Gentlemen possess, & which will provide that we are not destroyed by the Insects of the Office.

Upon the whole we must submit this Business to Congress, who are alone competent to a final Determination. If they conceive our Plan, & the Persons we have named to be proper they will confirm it; & if not we have to intreat that they will lose no Time in adopting such Men & Measures as shall appear more adequate to the Objects we have in View. The Delays of the Committee have arisen from the Necessity of consulting the Gentlemen, prevailing on them to accept, & knowing their terms. To trouble you with the whole of this Detail would be tedious & useless, but we beg Leave to assure you that not a Moment hath been spent unnecessarily, as we were under a Necessity to look thro' the widest Circle of Acquaintance & Character, to find some of those very few Men who are capable of filling such important Offices, and it is with Pleasure we add, that in the Opinion of your Committee their Researches have not been in vain.

Nothing now remains but to express to Congress our anxious Wishes that their Resolution may be speedy. Every other Preparation for a vigorous & decisive Campaign will be ineffectual & vain if this great Department remains much longer unfilled by suitable Characters & we hope to be favoured with your Determination by an immediate Express.

We are with the greatest Respect & Regard, Sir, Your most Obedt. & very Hbble Servt.   Fra Dana, by Order

P.S. We had almost forgot to add the great Necessity there is of immediately calling for a State of the Preparations for the next Campaign in the Qr. Master Gens. Department specifying what Articles are in Readiness, where deposited, where engaged & in what Quantities. Let the Arrangement be what it may, such a Return is indispensably necessary to enable the Gentlemen mentioned above or any others who may be appointed to proceed without farther Loss of Time, or unnecessary Expence.

While the above Dispatch was preparing the Enemy with their whole Horse & a large Body of Foot came out; the latter halted about 10 Miles from the City on the other Side the Schuylkill, while their Horse proceeded 15 miles farther up passing several Waggons with Pork on their Way to Camp of whom they took no Notice but pressed on to a Drove of 130 Cattle on their Way from Connecticut which they have carried into Town with them together with about 30 Militia whose Times were out & were returning home without Arms. The nakedness of the Troops & Difficulty of subsisting them on the East Side of the Schuylkill, together with the reduced Condition of our Cavalry prevents the Army from covering that Country as could be wished, & is a Subject of serious Concern to every one who duly reflects upon the advantageous Consequences of it to the Enemy in almost every Point of View.

We understand Dr. Parke & a Son in Law of James Pemberton (named Morton) have without any Permission from Head Quarters passed thro' on their Way to Winchester, we beg Leave to submit to Congress how far such Freedoms ought to pass unnoticed & whether it will not be adviseable to prevent their returning.[6]

We have been much surprized lately to find that the Resolution of Congress passed last October empowering a Court Martial to try Persons other than of the Army who shall be found carrying on an Intercourse with the Enemy, will not reach those Villains who come out to kidnap & deliver to the Enemy the active Friends of their Country.[7] There are a Number of these Offenders now in Custody who must either escape with Impunity (the Court martial having declined passing upon them) or they must be executed by the special Authority of the General. An Authority which he will not exercise but in Cases of the last Necessity. We submit to Congress whether it is not necessary to revise the above Resolution & also to give some Direction about these Criminals whose Discharge will greatly dishearten our Friends & give just Cause of Alarm & Discontent to the faithful Adherents of these States. Besides the great Encouragement given to these Practices if no Punishment can be devised for those now in our Hands, we fear it will bring any farther Resolution of Congress on this Subject into Contempt & in a great Degree countenance the dangerous Intercourse carried on between the City & the dissafected of the Country.[8]

RC (DNA: PCC, item 33). Written by Joseph Reed and signed by Francis Dana. FC (DNA: PCC, item 22). In the hand of Joseph Reed.

[1] See *JCC*, 10:126.

[2] In the FC the following passage was deleted at this point: "that Congress have been deceived into the Resolutions above mentioned from Misinformation or some other Cause but we cannot go so far as we could wish into this Business at present."

[3] In the FC the following passage was deleted: "supposing (what from the Silence of Congress on that Head we suppose it to be the Fact) that he would not be appointed."

[4] Responding quickly to the committee's new proposed "Arrangement"—"instead of that agreed on the 5 day of February"—Congress appointed Nathanael Greene quartermaster general and named John Cox and Charles Pettit his assistants the same day this letter was read in Congress, March 2, 1778. Congress also resolved to allow them commissions of 1 percent and granted the quartermaster general the appointment of "forage masters, waggon masters, and other officers in the department." See *JCC*, 10:210. See also Committee at Camp to Henry Laurens, January 28 and February 12; and Committee at Camp Minutes of Proceedings, February 22–28, 1778.

[5] In the FC the following passage was deleted: "is worth to him at least ten thousand Pounds annually."

[6] On March 2, Congress directed the Board of War to order the apprehension and confinement of "said Parke and Morton." *JCC*, 10:211. See also Laurens to Dana, March 3, 1778, note 3.

[7] *JCC*, 9:783–84.

[8] For Congress' response to the threat posed by such partisan activity, see Committee at Camp to John Laurance, February 18; and Committee at Camp to Henry Laurens, February 20, 1778.

Henry Laurens to James Duane

Dear sir   York Town 25 Febry 1778

I had reserved my self for paying proper respects to your several favors of the 8 & 18th Inst.,[1] the latter received but half an hour ago, in a leisure moment at Night—but the Cry, "Susquehanna will be impassable to morrow" hurried me at the usual hour homeward with a determination to attempt the needful, before the Evening service & to send off this Messenger in time to pass that dreadful Styx—but all in vain. Visitor upon visitor, application upon application has rendred my purposes to write by light of the Sun, I mean as I wished to have written, fruitless. I must either detain the bearer till tomorrow & Hazard a detention at the River three or four days longer when the most important concerns are depending upon his dispatch or reluctantly submit to tell you I will write fully by an opportunity which I must make in four or five days from this. I am persuaded you will commend me for preferring the latter & beleive me to be with very sincere Regard, Dear sir, Your obedient & most humble servant.   Henry Laurens

RC (NHi).
[1] Not found.

Henry Laurens to Baron de Kalb

Dear General.   25th Febry 1778.

Although I missed the opportunity of paying my respects to you this Morning by Major Rogers because I had intended to have taken a leisure minute in the Evening, yet I am reduced to the Same dilemma which his Speed would have placed me in. The Cry is, Susquehanna will be impassable to morrow & therefore the present Messenger must be hurried away at a moments warning. You will from this Consideration excuse brevity.

Your favour of the 14th[1] I had the honour of receiving last Night & have delivered the largest packet for Versailles which it had inclosed to Baron Holzendorff—the other shall go by some other good conveyance. I was rejoiced at the perusal of your Certificate in favor of the Baron. I had always reserved a design in case of need to have made a tender of Acts of kindess to that unfortunate Gentleman, but if he can by claims of right obtain the necessary relief, the great purpose will be answered & himself not unnecessarily subjected to obligation. The latter I mention, only in reference to the feelings of every Gentleman, not from my own estimation of such Acts which are indispensably our duty when such occasions call.

I beg you will Dear General, do me the honour to present me in the most respectful terms to the Marquis,[2] I have nothing worthy his notice at this moment otherwise it should be employed in paying my devoirs to His Excellency. 'Tis not impossible but that something may accompany or speedily follow this, which may veil the gay prospects of the Duplessis, the Fluery's &ca &ca.[3] If any such thing shall happen I shall sympathize with those ardent Sons of Mars, just so long as Wisdom & sound policy will countenance their Mourning. I bear a grateful remembrance of their merits & they are always included in my good wishes.

I had almost forgot to inclose under this Cover the Letter you sent for Monsr. delaBalme, he left York a few days ago & probably will be with you before this Address. Dear General, excuse the unavoidable effects of being hurried by Rivers, & be assured I am with the most perfect Esteem & Respect.

LB (ScHi).
[1] A transcript of Kalb's February 14 letter to Laurens is in the Laurens Papers, ScHi.
[2] Lafayette.
[3] Congress was already having serious doubts about the wisdom and practicability of Lafayette's projected assault on Canada, and on March 2 it decided to suspend the enterprise. *JCC*, 10:217. Kalb was Lafayette's second in command.

Jonathan Bayard Smith to Joseph Reed

Dr. Sir   York Town Feb. 25th. 1778
On arriving at this place I find myself indebted to you for two letters.

I wish the idea of employing Genl. Schuyler in the department referred to could have met the approbation of Congress.[1] Besides the objections arising from his present situation which founded the *declared* impediment, I found on conversing with gentlemen privately that they feared the ill effects of an intrigueing mind; a temper unfriendly to the dispositions of officers in the army & its peace; & that out of the sphere of his particular influence & knowlege of the country he would not be able to conduct the great business. This last objection I own was counter to every idea I had formed of the man. Colo. Cox will be an happy acquisition to the public in any line. But in the line intended I beleive he may be peculiarly useful. His veiws & schemes of his own are many & extensive; however I hope he will find himself able to reconcile his private with his public duties, especially as your interposition with him cannot fail to have great weight. Whether Genl. Green will not be too great a loss to the Line, I am not competent to determine. He is certainly one of a very few who made the art of war a study, & are become acquainted with its principles. As to dividing the department you must long ago have recd. the opinion of Congress on the subject. Tho' it carries an idea of a distribution, yet does it not exclude that of one Genl. head. Your veiws of this are just. Unity of action in no one department can be maintained on any other principle than that you mention.

The several transactions respecting the laying up provisions of flour &c. in this state are truely unaccountable, unless one should give way to some very disagreeable reflections. The State feel themselves truly uneasy. Last Monday Council received a Letter from the board of war informg. that the purchase of flour on the East side of Susquehanna was now unnecessary & that the Commissioners were directed to stop their hands in purchasing that article & to confine themselves to the purchase of meat. Council have directed a copy of the several papers on this subject to be sent to them & yesterday I procured an order of Congress for this purpose.[2] I wish the order of Congress, & the application of *the delegates of a State* had been met with rather more attention at the board than they were. However the copics are making. I beleive the assembly & Council will very seriously address Congress on the subject. Not many days ago Congress stopt any purchases by the superintendents on the East side of the River, & the money was sent to the Council. An additional 20,000 bbls are ordered to be procured, & the State Commrs. are now directed to discontinue their purchases of flour on the East. The tendency & effect cannot be doubted, even if we unwillingly admit the seeming principle of this proceeding. But is not the whole plan? Why collect flour? Can it not at any time be found in the mills? Will not these magazines be tempting objects to the enemy, both for distressing us, & helping themselves? Or should adverse circumstances take place, as last year, is All this flour collected, to be again & again transported, & finally dispersed again thro' the Country nobody will know where, till suffering the violence of all weathers, the injuries of moving & want of care, & the poison of unseasoned casks, it will be lost & perish. At this very time our flour may be found in farm houses & feilds havg. lain there 8 or 9 months, 30,000 & 20,000 bbl. purchased under the directions of the board of war & 50,000 by Mr. Blaine; the whole in the middle department cannot be necessary. I do not think it proper. This article can never be wanted in this Country if the Quarter Masters department gives due assistance.

Congress yesterday passed thro' the plan for reinforcing the army with drafts from the militia.[3] I fear it will have a tendency to draw us back again to 3 months men. Nor does it appear to be practicable in this State, Delaware, perhaps Jersey & I am told not in Maryland. As the body of the people are so circumstanced that the loss of one year must be the ruin of their families or at least their very great distress, those who return in the winter will find unprovided families, & with them become a burden on the public, instead of being a source of its strength & riches. A few repetitions will render the evil general & perhaps decisive if the experiment should succeed. But the trial made with the flying camp forebodes the event, especially as that was for 5 months only, & this for 9 months. The disadvantages arising from having to redeem persons from captivity who are to yeild no future services by an exchange of others who are to serve during the war are manifestly against us; & the danger of meeting an enemy disciplined & hardy with new troops every campaign is alarming. Perhaps the Committee had good reason to think this mode was the last resource. I am truly sorry for it. Sure I am these things & many more could not have escaped them. Their propositions have suffered no alteration that I remember except that in the first proposition recommending to reinforce *the army by drafts,* these words are admitted immediately following *or in such other manner as shall be effectual.*[4]

I observe an exchange on the old cartel is likely to take place. Can Nothing be done for our freinds who are cruelly confined in the goals of Britain & who are sent to the East Indies? Of the last circumstance Congress has undoubted testimonies.

Genl. Burgoyne has had the resolutions to detain him communicated to him. Genl. Heath writes that the officers are affected with concern & dissapointment rather than with sulleness or resentment. He has required the officers arms to be deposited with him till they imbark. B. says he will collect them but that they must remain in his own hands on honor not to distribute them again. An aid from B. is now in York Town on the subject of his detention.[5]

Feb. 26.

Not having an opportunity of forwarding the above, I have to thank you for yours of 24 Inst. which came to hand this Evenning. I have heard no complaints concerning the slowness of your proceeding. Indeed such is the importance, multiplicity & delicacy of the matters you have to do, that time, much time, must be necessary to do it well. Of this I have reason to beleive Gentlemen here are fully convinced. However taking it for granted that you have had hints on this head, I shall omit no opportunity of giving my sentiments freely. Much dependence is had on your proceedings. The consequences of doing Your business thoroughly may be great. If the army, or if the Congress should be disappointed the effects may be fatal. Indeed it may be a matter of some doubts whether the continuance of a Committee in camp would not be productive of great advantages. The several letters I have the pleasure of from you are

of Feb. 8 from Norriton, which I suppose the long one, as you call it, & which I consider as confidential.

Feb. 13 Camp Valley forge

Feb. 19 do.

Feb. 24 Moore Hall⁶

RC (NHi). In the hand of Jonathan Bayard Smith.

¹ For the Committee at Camp's recommendation of Philip Schuyler as Thomas Mifflin's replacement as quartermaster general, see Committee at Camp to Henry Laurens, January 28, 1778.

² This "order of Congress" is recorded in the journals under the date February 25. JCC, 10:194. See also the following entry.

³ Congress doubtless "yesterday passed thro" this plan in committee of the whole; it was not actually adopted until February 26. JCC, 10:199–203.

⁴ For President Laurens' addition of these words to the committee report as originally submitted, see JCC, 10:200.

⁵ See Henry Laurens to Richard Wilford, March 1, 1778.

⁶ Remainder of RC missing.

Jonathan Bayard Smith to Thomas Wharton

Sir,   York Town, Feby 26th, 1778.

I have the honor to inclose copies of sundry papers as directed by your excellency, together with some extracts from the minutes of Congress.¹

It would have given me pleasure to have despatched these papers sooner, but, though no time was unnecessarily lost in obtaining the order of Congress, or in applying to the board of war, yet finding the board not able to make out the copies immediately, for want of Clerks, we were some time before we could find a person to do it.²

There are other proceedings on the same subject; but from the nature of them presume you have received copies; particularly some resolutions of Congress of 14th Feby Instant.

I have the honor to be, with very great respect, your Excellency's and the Council's very humble servant,   Jona B. Smith

MS not found; reprinted from Pa. Archives, 1st ser. 6:303.

¹ Smith obtained these documents relating to the procurement of flour in Pennsylvania by the Board of War in consequence of a Pennsylvania Council request of February 23. See JCC, 10:194; and Pa. Archives, 1st ser. 6:293–94, 303–14.

² Smith had sent the following message to Wharton the preceding day. "In obedience to your orders we this morning early obtained an order of Congress to the board of war for the copies of several papers you referred to. The board have not yet been able to give us the papers, but we hope to have them ready to send forward tomorrow." Gratz Collection, PHi.

The difficulties Smith encountered in obtaining these papers is recorded in the drafts of two letters he wrote to President Gates of the Board of War at this time. The first reads: "You will oblige the delegates of this State by ordering a copy of the papers to [be] made aggreably to the inclosed Resolution, as soon as possible, as I have a person now waiting to carry them to Council. I will wait on the Honble. board for the copies in about two hours." The second: "Major Young waits on you for the copies of papers directed to be made for the State of Penns. Or if they are not done he will receive from you the originals at my request, & make out the copies. After which is done I will be careful that the originals shall be returned to yr. office." The former is undated; the latter reads "Feb. 26." Jonathan Bayard Smith Papers, DLC.

Committee at Camp to Thomas Wharton

                                           In Committee of Congress.
Sir   Moore Hall, Camp. Feby. 28th. 1778
    The Cavalry of our army requires the most vigorous exertions to be put on so respectable a footing as to enable us to meet the Enemy the ensuing Campaign on equal terms.[1] Experience hath so fully demonstrated the value and importance of this Corps, not only to the ease and security of the Troops in the Field, but to the protection of the faithfull inhabitants of the Country, whose persons and property are exposed to the depredations of the enemy, that we are of opinion there is no part of our establishment which so strongly applies to the feelings of the People and calls for greater attention. Under every disadvantage which a new raised Corps always labours, and especially in a service intirely new, this Body hath performed the most essential services during the last campaign. What may we not therefore now expect from them when experience and acquaintance with their duty has qualified them to discharge it? When we are become better acquainted with the character of Officers, and the Men are more familiarized to Danger and Discipline?

    We promise ourselves Sir the greatest advantage from a decisive superiority in Horse in the open Country where the Scene of Action will probably lie, and are the most anxious on this subject as the Enemy are evidently increasing their number by every means they can devise, purchasing and stealing Horses for the purpose whenever they can be found. They have already two Troops of Tory Light Horse who are cheifly employed in kidnapping those civil Officers who are distinguished for their activity in executing the trust reposed in them by Government. The consequence of this to our infant States are too obvious to need enumeration. We are sorry to say they have lately had such successes as will probably encourage their progress in this mischievous business, and extend it very far unless they meet with some seasonable check. We apprehend therefore your Excellency and the Gentlemen in Authority with you will fully concur with us in the propriety and necessity of recruiting this Corps with all possible dispatch, and favor us with your best assistance in so doing. The Regiments are nearly completed with Men Natives of the Country whose time of Service in the Infantry having expired, readily enlisted in the Horse. These Men inured to fatigue, danger and discipline have only to learn the special duties of that Service, and will form excellent Dragoons. The great difficulty under which the Service labours is the want of Horses and Saddles to mount them. On the one hand to wait the Tedious process of collecting Horses in the common mode by purchase either by Officers or Agents uncontroled by any immediate Authority will occasion great fraud and delay. On the other hand to use force in any degree appears oppressive and leaves such lasting discontent in the minds of the sufferers as not only sours and disaffects to the general Interests of the Country but to the particular State where the exertion is made. We have been therefore extreemly solicitous to find some expedient to reconcile these clashing Duties, an expedient which may provide for the present exigence of the service without wounding too deeply those feelings and attachments which all Men have for their property in a greater or lesser degree. At length Sir, as the safer and more effectual mode we have concluded to rely on the wisdom and public spirit of the Gentlemen in Authority in this and the neighbouring States, and to request their exertions in the following mode. We have made calculations of the number of Horses and common country Saddles and Bridles proper for the Cavalry which may be had from Virginia, Maryland, Delaware, Pensilvania & New-Jersey respectively. The State we suppose will then calculate what number the several Counties can furnish by a reasonable assessment, and then appoint proper persons in the Country to purchase them on the best terms they can, allways attending to the following description. That the Horse be sound and clean limbed not less than Five years old this Spring, nor exceeding Twelve years—Geldings at least $14\frac{1}{2}$ hands high and not less than one quarter blooded. We do not limit any price either as a purchase money, or a compensation to those employed in the business, because we presume they will be men of integrity and property who besides the Interest they have in common with us that the public expences be not causelessly enhanced will have a due regard to their own characters. In order to provide for payment it is proposed that a number of Loan Office Certificates be lodged with the Executive Authority of the State to be paid on the First Day of May under such Limitations and Checks as will most effectually guard against Fraud or Mistake, The whole amount to be finally settled between Congress and the State when the business is completed. We must request that the persons who may be appointed to make the purchases, be directed from time to time to make returns of their doings in this business to yourself, and that you wou'd please to order a general return to be made to the Quarter-Master-General, and also to the Board of War. The number of Horses, Sadles and Bridles estimated for this State is Two hundred and fifty which we beleive will not appear by any means too large for its resources. We doubt not but on this occasion your Excellency and the Gentlemen of the Legislature will favor us with a continuance of those exertions, the beneficial effects of which we have already experienced. We greatly regret that this business has been so long delayed, and fear the service will suffer in consequence of it as some time is necessary to train the Horses before they can be brought into the field. We hope therefore it will receive all possible forwardness from the Gentlemen who are to take it up as the utillity of the measure will depend greatly on dispatch.

 We are Sir, Your most obedient, humble Servants,

Fra Dana, by Order

RC (PHi). Written and signed by Francis Dana.
 [1] The committee wrote nearly identical letters this day to Thomas Johnson, governor of Maryland, and William Livingston, governor of New Jersey, assigning them quotas of 350 and 300 horses respectively. See *Md. Archives,* 16:522–24; and PCC item 192, fols. 143–46.

Committee of Commerce to Edward Hand

Dear Sir   Commercial Committee, York Town 28 Febry. 1778
 Application having been made to this Committee, by Col. Anthony Steel, D P Q Mr. General, in your Department, for the payment of a Bill drawn by Capt James Willing on said Col. Steel in favor of John Gibson or order, for Three hundred pounds, as also for payment of an account for sundry Articles he furnished Capt James Willing for the use of the armed Boat Rattle Trap's Crew, amounting to Two hundred and fifteen pounds, 12/6.

 It appearing on the Minuts of this Committee, that by a letter dated 21st Novemr. last, directed to you Sir, you were requested to supply Capt James Willing with a Boat, and all other necessaries, for his intended Expedition.[1]—In order that the same may be conducted through 'its proper channel, we must now request you Sir, to Issue your order to the said Depy. Qr. Masr. General for the payment of both the above sums, pursuant to our endorssments thereon. We are Sir, Your very Humble Servants,   Fras Lewis

William Ellery

James Forbes

RC (NN). Addressed: "The Honble Brigadr General Hand att Fort Pitt. Favored by Col. Steel." Written by Lewis and signed by Lewis, Ellery, and Forbes.

[1] See Committee of Commerce to Oliver Pollock, November 21, 1777, note 1, and to Robert Morris, February 21, 1778, note 4.

Marine Committee to Nathaniel Shaw, Jr.

Sir   February 28th 1778

We have received your Letter of the 2d instant & in consequence of your demand for money you have advanced for the Marine Service we have paid Mr. John Hertell whom you sent for that purpose Five thousand Dollars and have delivered to him a Warrant on the Loan Office of your State for thirty five thousand Dollars making 40,000 Dollars to your debit. Since the appointment of the Navy Board at Boston it has been our determination that all applications for Money and other Matters relative to Marine affairs should be made to them, for which reason we have charged that Board with the above sum and you must Credit them for the same. As it is high Time your Accounts with the Marine Department were settled, we request that you will with All expedition produce them to the Navy Board who will settle and pay the balance that may be due to you and in future you are to be governed intirely by their directions in Marine Affairs.[1]

We are sir, Your hble servants

LB (DNA: PCC Miscellaneous Papers, Marine Committee Letter Book).

[1] The committee's letter this day to the Eastern Navy Board, advising them of payment to Shaw, the Continental prize agent at New London, Conn., and requesting that "when he furnishes his Account Current you will please to transmit to us a Copy thereof for our Inspection before we order payment of the balance," is in PCC Miscellaneous Papers, Marine Committee Letter Book, fol. 129, and Paullin, *Marine Committee Letters,* 1:205–6.

Jonathan Bayard Smith to Thomas Wharton

Sir   York Town Feb. 28. 1778

On other side you have copy of a letter yesterday Evenning read in Congress.[1] It was referred to a Committee whose report you shall be made acquainted with. As I was that day confined to my bed cannot say what strictures were made on the subject by Congress.

The packet of copies[2] was returned to me from the ferry as the river was impassable. I this morning had the honor of forwarding it by Genl. Wilkinson.

I am, Sir, with very great respect, your Excellencys & Councils very humble Servant,   Jona. B Smith

RC (PHarH).

[1] Horatio Gates' February 26 letter to Henry Laurens is in PCC, item 147, 1:529–32, and *Pa. Archives,* 1st ser. 6:315. In it Gates voiced the Board of War's "regret that much confusion & contradiction has attended the management of" the board's plan for laying up 50,000 barrels of flour at several magazines in Pennsylvania, which had been the source of a controversy with state officials for more than a month. For the inception of this plan, see Daniel Roberdeau to Thomas Wharton, January 16, 1778, note 2.

[2] See Jonathan Bayard Smith to Thomas Wharton, February 26, 1778.

Committee at Camp Minutes of Proceedings

[March 1–7, 1778]

March 1. Forwarded Letter to Gov. Livingston by Col. Cox.[1]

2. Wrote to Congress by Colo. Guest.[2] Agreed to recommend M. de Murnan to Congress for a Major in the engineering department.[3]

3. Conferred with the Majrs. Generals at Head Quarters.

4. General not present. Wrote to Congress upon the Engineering Departmt.[4]

5. Wrote to Congress abt Colo. Baylers procurg Horses in Virginia.[5]

6. Genl. not present.[6]

7. Genl. not present. Arranged the New-Hampshire Battalions, and conferred with the Jersey Colonels.[7]

MS (DLC). A continuation of the Committee at Camp Minutes of Proceedings, February 22–28, 1778. In the hands of Francis Dana and Joseph Reed.

[1] That is, the committee's February 28 letter to William Livingston, for which see Committee at Camp to Thomas Wharton, February 28, 1778, note.

[2] See Committee at Camp to Henry Laurens, March 2, 1778.

[3] For further information on the appointment of Jean Bernard de Murnan, see Committee at Camp Minutes of Proceedings, February 16–20, note 8; and Committee at Camp to Henry Laurens, March 3, 1778.

[4] See Committee at Camp to Henry Laurens, March 3, 1778.

[5] See Committee at Camp to Henry Laurens, March 5, 1778.

[6] For one of the issues that came before the committee this day, see Committee at Camp to Washington, March 6, 1778.

[7] For the continuation of these minutes, see Committee at Camp Minutes of Proceedings, March 8–12, 1778.

Committee at Camp to Henry Laurens

Sir   Moor Hall 1st March 1778.

It is the peculiar Misfortune of America beyond almost every other State in the World to remain ignorant of the Situation of its Affairs untill the critical Moment when the Knowledge of them can be of little or no Avail. Congress doubtless expect that all Arms which

wanted Repair last Winter should by this Time have been made fit
for Service. We just now received a Note from the General by the
Bearer of this Letter informing us that the Armoury Department is
in the most deplorable Situation.[1] Mr. Dupree came this Day from
Lebanon to give him Information upon the Subject and in the Course
of our Inquiries gives us but too much Reason to beleive that a fatal
Neglect prevails at every of the public works in the State. There are
at present 6,000 Stand of Arms wanting Repair perhaps more. Let us
intreat Sir that Congress will cause instant Inquiry to be made into
the Representations Mr. Dupree will make and provide Means to
have all the Arms put into Repair without Delay. It being out of the
line of your Committee they are obliged to trouble you on this Occasion which they hope Congress will excuse.[2] We have the Honor to be,
Sir, your most obedient & humble Servants,

Fra Dana, by Order

RC (DNA: PCC, item 33). Written by Gouverneur Morris and signed by Francis
Dana.
   [1] Washington's misdated February 29 letter to the committee is in Washington,
Writings (Fitzpatrick), 10:530.
   [2] Congress read this letter on March 6 and referred it to the Board of War.
JCC, 10:227. The committee's and General Washington's complaints about the
public armorer apparently led to Congress' April 18 order to the Board of War
for an investigation of his performance. As a result of this inquiry, the board
replaced public armorer Thomas Butler with William Henry, whose appointment
was confirmed by Congress on April 23. See *JCC*, 10:366, 380–81; and Charles
Thomson to Horatio Gates, April 18? 1778.

William Ellery to Nicholas Cooke

Sir   York Town March 1st. 1778
   The reason why I have not wrote to you for some time past is,
because nothing particular respecting either our State or the army
hath taken place; and the general resolves of congress are printed in
news-papers or transmitted by the President.
   France still persues her old equivocal line of conduct. Sometimes,
with a peremptory tone, she orders our Trade from her ports; at another she connives at, and even countenances our armed and commercial Vessels. She is intirely governed by the principles of policy
and interest. She says that she ought not to declare herself, until she
is led to it by an open rupture of the English, of which we shall soon
be the pretext or the subjects; that we shall obtain her alliance by
continuing to solicit her secret friendship and succours; until we convince her that no extremity is capable of making us renounce that
Independency we have adopted, and by contenting ourselves with an
assistance as underhanded as it is efficacious, and thereby leaving the

English to retard the alliance of France with us by their pretending not to see what they endure or to hasten the period by hostilities which France is determined to repel vigorously.

This is the language of France; from which it seems that we must fight our own battles; unless Britain should come to an open rupture with France, which, I think, is not much to be expected. To enable us to fight them successfully it is indispensably necessary, that our continental battalions should be filled as soon as possible.

By a resolution of Congress on this subject, which you will receive by the express who carries this, you will see that we are to complete only *one* of our battalions, the *two,* considering our circumstances, having been reduced to *one.*[1] The number of recruits that we shall have to raise, as by the return, is eight Sargeants, nineteen corporals and one hundred and thirty nine privates; which I hope will be collected at the place of rendezvouz early in the spring. I am informed that Col. Green is gone to our state to raise a regiment of blacks. I wish that ⟨*they*⟩ He may not be encouraged to recruit, until our continental battalion and State battalions shall be completed, and the Enemy be removed from the State. It appears to me very inconsistent that we should be required to fill up only *one* battalion, on account of our exposed, perilous situation, and that recruiting, for another purpose than for our defence, should go on.[2]

The late Resolution of Congress authorizing and requesting the Executive council of Massachusetts to remove and separate Genl. Burgoynes troops, and place them in such parts of the State as might be thought proper,[3] and the information I have received, that a number of the militia from thence and Connecticut have arrived in our State, have in some measure relieved me from the anxiety I have long endured; but still so long as the enemy's troops continue on Rhode-Island, and their fleet in the Bay, nothing but a force sufficient to awe them can secure our long-extended shores from ravage and devastation. In my humble opinion we have not a man of any colour to spare, Our Towns, our Shores, our fields require every hand to defend and cultivate them.

We are about obstructing and fortifying Hudsons River, in order to secure the communication between the southern and northern states; altering the System of the commissariats and quarter-master, which departments with the Clothiers have been most miserably executed the last campaign; calling public officers to account, and taking every method we can devise to fill up and supply our Army, and correct Abuses. I hope they will prove efficacious; but so great, alass! is the corruption and avarice of the people, that it is extremely difficult to find persons, to fill the public offices, who will, by their honest exertions, give efficacy to public measures.

Congress have directed Genl. Washington to send a proper Major Genl. to fill the place of Genl. Spencer.[4] It is not yet determined who is to pay the expence of the R. I. Expedition.[5] I have not urged a determination; because Massachusetts hath been a long time and is still unrepresented, one of her members[6] being of a committee now at Head Quarters. There are so many and such large demands on the treasury for supplying the great departments of the army, that an application for a considerable Sum would be ineffectual. I opposed the last Warrant being issued on our Loan-Office, but in vain. So soon as those departments shall be supplied, our State may have a chance. If the Assembly should think proper they can send forward an Abstract of their Accounts against the United States with directions to their Delegates to apply when a good time shall present. If Loan Office certificates would answer it would mightily facilitate a Grant.

Some of the citizens of this state having been lately kidnapped and carried into Philadelphia, Congress have resolved that all offenders taken within 70 miles of the main army or any detachment or post, under the command of a General, shall be tried by a court martial, and suffer the pains of Death.[7]

A certain northern expedition is for good reasons laid aside.[8] Several Vessels have lately arrived at the Southward from the W. Indias with Cloths, Blankets, Tents &c. Those from Martinico were convoyed clear off the Island by a French Frigate. Some Loads of Salt have also arrived, but still that article is scarce. Could not this Article be made in Charlestown and Westerly in great abundance? And may it not be adviseable to encourage this necessary manufacture?

By the fifth Article of confederation no state shall be represented by less than two members. I submit it, whether it will not be adviseable to chuse four or five at the next election, and keep three upon the spot that the State may be always represented. If only two should be present, One may fall sick and the State for a considerable time be unrepresented to its great Detriment.[9]

I expect soon to see a colleague with orders for a ratification of the confederation.[10] Most sincerely praying for the perpetual establishment of the Sovereignty, Freedom and Independence of the United States of America, and particularly for the deliverance of the distressed State of Rhode Island and Providence Plantations from her Enemies, I have the honor to be with the highest respect, yr Excellency's most obedt hble Servant,   William Ellery

P.S. Two hundred and eighty six dwelling houses & a number of Stores in Charlestown So. Carolina have lately been destroyed by Fire.
The Resolution last hinted at, and another desiring the several

States to send forward their accounts of supplies to prisoners &c I see are in the Paper which I now inclose.[11]

I find that I have made a mistake in the number of Sargeants & Corporals wanted to complete our Battalion. The number I have mentioned is the number wanting to complete two battalions.

RC (R–Ar).

[1] See *JCC,* 10:200.

[2] There was no truth to the report that Col. Christopher Greene was planning to raise a black regiment in Rhode Island, as Ellery later admitted in an April 5 letter to Governor Cooke.

[3] For this February 19 resolve, see *JCC,* 10:184–85.

[4] See Henry Laurens to Washington, February 21, 1778, note.

[5] Congress finally decided on August 7, 1778, to assume the cost of the unsuccessful October 1777 expedition against the British in Rhode Island. *JCC,* 11:761. See also Henry Laurens to the Rhode Island Expedition Commissioners, December 15, 1777, note.

[6] Francis Dana.

[7] Congress passed this resolution on February 27, with Ellery voting in the affirmative. See *JCC,* 10:204–5.

[8] According to the journals Congress suspended Lafayette's Canadian expedition on Monday, March 2. See *JCC,* 10:216–17.

[9] The Rhode Island Assembly enlarged the state's congressional delegation to four members in May 1778. William R. Staples, *Rhode Island in the Continental Congress, 1765–1790* (Providence: Providence Press Co., 1870), pp. 177–78.

[10] Ellery received the Rhode Island Assembly's instructions regarding the Articles of Confederation on April 18. See ibid., pp. 133–35; and Ellery to Cooke, April 25, 1778.

[11] See *JCC,* 10:197–98.

Henry Laurens to Richard Caswell

Sir,   1st March 1778.

On the 21st Ulto. I conveyed under the care of General Weedon a packet directed to Your Excellency which contained Six Copies of Acts of Congress of the 5th & 6th Febry for establishing divers regulations in the Army—since which I have had the honour of receiving & reporting to Congress Your Excellency's favor of the 7th Ulto. which was referred to a special Committee in whose hands I believe it remains, as I have received no Commands.[1]

Under the present Cover Your Excellency will find two Acts of the 26th Febry to which I beg leave particularly to refer.

1. for filling up the Continental Battalions, accompanied by a return from the Board of War shewing the Numbers wanted to complete.

2. for ascertaining the Amount of necessaries supplied British Prisoners from the commencement of the present War.[2]

I have the honour to be with the highest Esteem.

P.S. General Burgoyne has remonstrated with Congress on the suspension of the embarkation of his Troops, which has made no impression except, if I may speak my own feelings, to confirm my sentiments on the propriety of the Act of Congress of the 8th Jany.[3] By a subsequent application, which shews he had not entertained very sanguine expectations of success in the first, he applies for leave to embark himself & family for Great Britain upon certain conditions—this will be granted.[4] His several addresses are decent & unexceptionable. I trust great good will arise from the politeness & Civility of Congress, contrasted with the treatment of American Officers, prisoners of the Britons, & we have remaining time & Subjects enough for retaliation admitting we shall be driven to necessity.

LB (DNA: PCC, item 13).

[1] Governor Caswell's February 7 letter to Laurens is in PCC, item 59, 1:81, and *N.C. State Records*, 13:22–23. Enclosed with it were various papers relating to the case of Capt. John Folger, who was under confinement in Lancaster because of his suspected complicity in the theft of some dispatches from the American commissioners in France to Congress. See PCC, item 59, 1:83–108. Congress finally decided on May 8 that there was no evidence to prove Folger had been involved in the purloining of these documents and ordered his release. See *JCC*, 11:482. For further information about this case, see Committee Examination of John Folger, January 12, 1778.

[2] This day Laurens also sent copies of these two February 26 resolves to Govs. Thomas Johnson of Maryland and Patrick Henry of Virginia and President Thomas Wharton of Pennsylvania. PCC, item 13, fols. 203–5. In addition, he transmitted copies of the February 26 resolve on supplies for British prisoners of war to Commissary of Prisoners Elias Boudinot, Clothier General James Mease, and Director General of Hospitals William Shippen, Jr. Ibid., fols. 202–3. Finally, this day he sent copies of the February 26 resolve on British prisoners and a February 21 resolve "on the propriety of keeping a dep. Pay Master at Baltimore" to Paymaster General William Palfrey. MH–H.

[3] That is, the resolve suspending the Saratoga Convention, which would have allowed Gen. John Burgoyne's captured army to return to England. See *JCC*, 10:34–35.

[4] Congress decided on March 3 to allow General Burgoyne, "the officers of his family and his servants" to return to England. *JCC*, 10:218. See also Laurens to Richard Wilford, March 1, and to John Burgoyne, March 6, 1778.

Henry Laurens to Francis Dana

Dear Sir,   1st March 1778.

'Tis now late Sunday Evening & your favor of the 25th Ulto.[1] has but this Instant made its appearance, had it been less deliberate in its progress & not made so long a halt at the Waggon Tavern I might yesterday have received authority for confirming your Acts in the arrangement of the Quarter Mr. General's department. As the case now Stands, to morrow is mortgaged & it will be difficult to bring the business upon the tapis before Tuesday, however I will make an attempt & if not baulked by some Six-deep Orator will get it in edge-way in the afternoon.[2]

Upwards of 750,000 Dollars have been lately Issued for the department in the present hands, these I should therefore hope have Supplied you very amply or have provided large Legacies for their successors.

In obedience to your Commands Sir I will transmit another quarter of an hundred Commissions & their proper Companions to Mr. Avery. You may Smile when I tell you that I yesterday granted two Commissions for Cruizing on the Ohio & Mississipi.

A Resolve will go to General Washington by the present Messenger which will probably reach those partizans whom you were afraid would escape justice,[3] & there is one upon the Anvil which I parted with yesterday every Stitch Crimson, it will return tomorrow probably with small white facings.[4] We are vex'd I assure you sir, & we shall roar when we come to hear the story of the Connecticut deserters. This I am determined to keep a secret to the very proper moment for disclosing the melancholy subject.

An Act upon your Resolves for filling up the Continental Battalions will also now go to the General.[5]

I will not rashly assert that we perform a great many good things, but truth will witness that we work hard. I can seldom begin to sit at this Table before 9 oClock at Night & as Seldom rise from it before 12 & at it again before day light.

There was a time some 12 or 13 Years since when I abandoned the means of pocketing Thousands per Annum under the Idea of retiring from the hurry of business. If this be retirement, I most devoutly wish to go to work again.

The loss of the Cattle is horrible, I begin to dread the Enemy's driving the Army into the City & Sending a detachment for your humble Servant & Company, I have in the mean time been calculating how to repair the lack of so much Beef. This may be done by a Recommendation from the Committee to the Army to observe Lent which will begin on Wednesday by three Pan Cake days in each of the Six Weeks, but upon my seriousness Sir, if we are not more watchful, if we cannot or will not recover that affected or real virtue which ground our first Steps into this dispute our Lent will be extended far beyond 40 days, but if I am to fast & choose my Spot, let it be at Mount Tacitus[6] where I am certain of a constant supply of excellent Trout & Bream. I am weary of the [levities?] of York Town.

You intimate good sir, that most of the Evils which have attended our Camp flow from gross neglect & abuse in the department of Qur. Mr. general, if it be so, & I am inclined to beleive it, why are we so Courtly & mincing? Is there a name under Heaven that shall sanctify the peculator or Screen the man whose neglect of Duty has brought thousands to misery & Death? Forbid it torpid patriotism of 1775. No! let the Offender be dragged forth, & the people told, this is the Man! God awaken us. I am with very great Respect.

LB (ScHi).
¹ See Committee at Camp to Laurens, February 25, 1778.
² Congress approved the committee at camp's proposed "arrangement" of the quartermaster's department on March 2. *JCC*, 10:210–11.
³ On February 27 Congress had passed a resolve designed to deter loyalist Americans from turning over to the British "such of the loyal citizens, officers, and soldiers of these states, as may fall into their power." See *JCC*, 10:204; and Committee at Camp to Laurens, February 20, 1778.
⁴ Perhaps Laurens is alluding to the resolve Congress passed on March 2, reaffirming its January 8 suspension of the Saratoga Convention. *JCC*, 10:216. The resolves on this issue that Congress deleted from the journals are much sharper in tone than the one it allowed to stand. Ibid.
⁵ See *JCC*, 10:199–203.
⁶ One of Laurens' South Carolina plantations.

Henry Laurens to John Laurens

My Dear son,   York Town 1st March 1778
I beleive I have not writ you a line since that by Baron Stuben, to which I have received your answer under the 24th.¹ I am anxious to know whether he will find amusement & employment in your Camp & whether he is likely to be a valuable addition to the Main Army. It is remarkable that your General has kept a profound silence on that Officer's name although I have had occasion to announce it to His Excellency in three several Letters.

Beleive me my Dear Son the present times present us with a variety of modes which contribute to, & effectuate, the equalizing Estates which though very wicked are still infinitely preferable to burning a whole Town. I received last Night a further account of that accident from a Travelling Officer who happened to be an Eye Witness, but even this person cannot relate to me such particulars as ought from authority to have reached us fifteen days ago, either authority has been very dilatory or its Messenger is so. However according to this Gentleman's report the destruction is as great as the most apprehensive mind could have figured upon a first impression. 11 Houses on the Bay of Charles Town, & no more South of Queen Street were left standing—& there are strong grounds for suspecting the Fire was kindled by Emissaries of our Enemies. Four Men of War were close in with the Bar all the day of the Fire & the Night following continued false fires as if to conduct persons expected from on Shore. The Randolph, another Ship & three Brigantines were equipped, well

Manned & lay ready to Sail on the 28 January intended to attack the little Squadron of the Enemy which consisted of a Frigate of 28, one of 20 Guns & two Armed Brigantines. We shall soon hear the Issue of this enterprize; if good, it will be more than I expect. We out reckon the Enemy in Guns & Men, but their experience & discipline made an overmatch of two to one against us. If we are beat the loss will be felt severely in the 1st & 2d Regiments which have contributed large Officers & Men for the expedition. I hope their bravery will be rewarded with success.

What shall I do for my Dear son reduced to Breeches, there is not an Inch of such Cloth as you want in York. James made one search & a Taylor upon whom I can depend, a second, & both returned empty, our hopes of a supply from Charles Town are cut off. I must write to Baltimore & to Boston, why had not my Dear Son laid in a larger stock. He will find the Doctrine of equalizing altogether inconsistent with Military uniformity. Here's a fragment of Blue Cloth just enough the Taylor says to make you a Coat.

I would give the value of ten pair of Breeches rather than learn or think & I shall now be continually thinking so—that you are confined to one pair dirty or tattered. You will learn in time to make better provision for your self.

I suspect that some in your Army supply themselves with necessary articles from the City[2] & hold it no more criminal to do so in the present state of affairs than it was of old for a Religious hungry David to eat the hallowed Bread of Ahimelec when there happened to be none other. Indeed in all the States the Resolve against purchasing British Manufactures in cases of extremity hath been dispensed with—& it is a moot point in my mind whether we ought any longer to adhere to the Rule.[3] There is much to be said in favor of a Repeal.

The article of Powder was promised by my Hair Dresser but he has not brought it in. James will go & enquire for it, if he succeeds you will receive it by the bearer of this.

We hear repeated Accounts of advantages gained by the Enemy in small parties making Prisoners daily of Officers & Men from your Army—that the Major of a Colonel Stuart, together with a Company of Taylors & all the Clothing intended for the Colonel's Regiment were taken at New Town by a party of twenty Light Horse & the Major at the head of the Taylors beyond doubt, paraded into the City—that desertions are numerous & continued every day—& in a word that Your Camp is in the power of General Howe & that he may compel you to fly from it when he pleases & leave your Baggage & Artillery, or give you the Choice of being Prisoners of War or cut to peices.

I was just going to ask, are these things so? when a L[etter] from the Committee came to hand,[4] which informs me of an irreparable loss which you had suffered of 130 head of Cattle turned by the Enemy's light Horse into the City. I am apprehensive these give a true description of your helpless state nor shall I be very much surprized however much I may be affected by it, to hear that you are routed by the Enemy's Army & feel that Congress are seized upon by a detachment. The prospect is gloomy indeed. There are a few villains who have brought us to this precipice who deserve to be hanged but they have powerful Advocates. Give me your sentiments fully on our deplorable situation.[5]

An Officer who came in here a few minutes ago gives me hopes of procuring buff Cloth for your present necessity. You see how I patch a Letter together, exposed to continual interruptions & diverted from the most important & serious subjects to Buff Cloth & Breeches.

I had intended to have spoken to you again on the subject of your black Regiment but I have not time at present, however let me tell you you mistook my meaning in some parts of the last Letter on that affair.[6] I did not even intend to insinuate that you were possessed by illaudable ambition. It is evident you wished for a Command; speaking of you honestly as a fellow Citizen, & you know partiality is not to be found in the Catalogue of my vices, I think you would not, young as you are, disgrace a Regiment. I intended to have recommended you to a practicable Road & to draw you off from a pursuit which in the opinion of every body would prove fruitless & which I exceedingly feared might soil your excellent character with a charge of singularity, whimsicality & Caprice. This however I have ever taught you to despise when set in competition with Duty & with honourable Acts.

Your scheme, with respect to your own progress in it would have ended in essay, but you would not have heard the last jeer till the end of your life, meaning if you had gone precipitately into the prosecution. An attempt of that magnitude may originate with an Individual but must be extended after very mature deliberation by the Collective wisdom of States. I wish for an hours serious conversation with you on these points.

I suppose you to be strongly attached to General Washington & I do not wonder you are so—every Gentleman loves & Esteems that great & good Man but when the proper time shall come that you feel an inclination to retire from that Army & turn your attention to your own Country I hold it probable that you may obtain a Commission & soon raise a respectable Regiment. From such Ideas & reflections I was led to write in the terms which I perceive you misapprehended, but we will postpone the subject for discussion on some future day.

I know not what my Country Men are about nor why they have so shamefully neglected to fill their Representation in Congress. I have been long striving to shame them into the performance of their duty. As the Assembly met at Charles Town on the 5 January I hold it probable that Delegates were chosen among their earliest Acts & that the Men, whoever they are, will soon be at York & bring me permission to return, which I am determined to do immediately after I can meet & take leave of you. You will make such use of this intimation as you shall judge necessary.

I feel a strong inclination to send into Philadelphia & New York about an hundred Guineas to be applied to the relief of some of the most necessitous of our Soldiers who are Prisoners there. Tell me your thoughts. If Rich Men would open their hearts & their Purses freely what infinite advantages would be gained to our Army & to our cause in general.

My best Respects to Monsr. le Baron Stüben.

My Dear son, Adieu.   Henry Laurens

RC (MHi: William Gilmore Simms Collection deposit, 1973).

   [1] John Laurens' February 24 reply to his father's February 18 letter is in Simms, *Laurens Army Correspondence*, pp. 130–31.

   [2] Philadelphia. See also ibid., pp. 134–35.

   [3] A reference to the nonimportation agreement embodied in the Association approved by Congress on October 18, 1774. *JCC*, 1:75–77.

   [4] See Committee at Camp to Henry Laurens, February 25, 1778.

   [5] John Laurens sought to allay his father's apprehensions in his March 9 response to this letter. Simms, *Laurens Army Correspondence*, pp. 134–41.

   [6] See Laurens to John Laurens, February 6, 1778.

Henry Laurens to William Livingston

Sir.   1 March 1778

On the 19th Ulto.[1] by the hand of Doctr. Witherspoon I had the honour of transmitting to Your Excellency a packet containing several Copies of Acts of Congress of the 5th & 6th Febry for establishing divers regulations in the Army &c & on the 27th & no sooner of receiving your Excellency's favor dated the 4th & 13th. This I presented immediately to Congress & obtained the Inclosed Resolve of the 28th February relative to the Warrant on the Loan Office New Jersey of the 24th January. Congress at the same time Resolved that 5000 Dollars should be paid into the hands of the Delegates of that State to be transmitted by them for the purposes of recruiting the Battalions & apprehending Deserters.[2]

Your Excellency will also find under Cover with this two Acts of Congress of the 26th February one for fitting up the Continental Battalions accompanied by a Return from the War Office shewing numbers wanted to complete.

The other for ascertaining the Amount of necessaries supplied British Prisoners from the commencement of the present War. To

these several Papers I beg leave to refer & remain, Sir, Your Excy's
&c &c.

LB (DNA: PCC, item 13).
   ¹ See Laurens to George Clinton, February 19, 1778, note 4.
   ² On January 24, 1778, Congress had issued a warrant for $10,000 to Joseph
Borden, the Continental loan officer in New Jersey, to assist Governor Livingston
in carrying out some July 31, 1777, resolves on the recruitment of Continental
soldiers and the apprehension of deserters. But, as Livingston pointed out in a
February 4–13 letter to Laurens, because the warrant only mentioned recruitment
he did not know if he could also use the money to apprehend deserters. Accordingly, Congress on February 28 authorized applying the warrant to both purposes
and issued $5,000 to the New Jersey delegates for the governor's use, Livingston
having also informed Laurens that loan officer Borden was out of cash. See JCC,
10:89, 208; PCC, item 68, fols. 329–31; and Laurens to Livingston, December 29,
1777, note 1.

Henry Laurens to George Washington

Sir   1st March 1778.
   My last was on the 21st Ulto. by Messenger Millet since which I
have not been honoured with any of Your Excellency's favors.

   Under Cover with this Your Excellency will receive the following
Acts of Congress.

   1. of the 26th February, for filling up the Battalions of Continental
Troops.

   2. An Act also of the 26th Febry, for ascertaining the Amount of
demands for supplies of necessaries by the several States &ca for the
use of British prisoners.

   3. of the 27th for the Speedy punishment of any of the Inhabitants
of these States who shall be detected in acting as Marauders & parti-
sans on the part of the Enemy.

   In a separate packet I likewise forward six half quire of blank
Oaths of Office & of Allegiance for the use of the Army.

   I have the honour of being specially charged to signify to your
Excellency that Congress highly approve of your Excellency's conduct
in support of the Civil authority of the United States as expressed in
your Excellency's Letters in answer to General Howes Letter of the
19th January & 25th February.¹

   I am also directed to intimate to your Excellency as a recommendation from Congress that every proper precaution be taken against
putting it in the power of the Enemy to take any unfair advantages
in the Exchange of prisoners & that Congress take for granted General
Lee is included in the late Stipulation between Your Excellency & the
British Commander & have therefore refrained from repeating a

Special demand for the restitution of that Officer.

I have the honour to be with the highest Regard &ca

LB (DNA: PCC, item 13).

[1] See *JCC*, 10:179, 194, 197–98. In his January 30 and February 10 letters to General Howe, Washington had defended Congress against the British general's criticism of its handling of prisoners of war and its suspension of the Saratoga Convention. Washington, *Writings* (Fitzpatrick), 10:408–9, 444–46. Howe had offered these criticisms in letters to Washington of January 19 and February 5, not February 25. Washington Papers, DLC.

Henry Laurens to Richard Wilford

Sir,   1st March 1778.

I duly received your Notes of yesterday's & the present date, the latter accompanied by the No. 2—intimated when you did me the honour of a visit the other day. These shall be, meaning the Packet & the paper contained in it presented to Congress to morrow Morning, thence according to the ordinary course of business the papers will be referred to a Committee, & the necessary or usual forms will cost two or three days which might have been saved had the packet been earlier delivered, for I learn the Committee on No. 1. are prepared to Report at the next Meeting of Congress. Be that as it may, rest assured Sir, of my endeavors to bring the whole under consideration without the formality of a second reference, from the tenor of Lieutt. General Burgoyne's application in No. 2 which I think may be comprized in one question, there is some prospect of succeeding.[1]

I am with great Respect &ca.

LB (DNA: PCC, item 13).

[1] Lt. Richard Wilford, an aide-de-camp to Gen. John Burgoyne, had brought to York two letters from Burgoyne to President Laurens dated February 11. In the first, which was read in Congress on February 26 and referred to a committee of five, Burgoyne rejected congressional charges that he had violated the Saratoga Convention and asked the delegates to repeal their January 8 suspension of this agreement so that he and his captured army could proceed to England. While this letter was still under consideration Wilford presented Burgoyne's second letter, in which the general asked permission for "myself, the officers of my family . . . and my servants" to return to England in the event Congress persisted in its refusal to implement the convention. Congress referred this letter to the same committee and on the basis of its reports decided on March 2 to confirm the suspension of the convention, although on the following day it did grant permission to Burgoyne and his dependents to return to England. At the same time, however, the delegates turned down requests by Burgoyne to allow three other officers not of his family to accompany him to England, and by Wilford to transmit to Gen. William Howe via Washington copies of other papers from Burgoyne he had brought with Burgoyne's letter. Instead Congress ordered Wilford to give copies of the papers for Howe to the Board of War for eventual transmittal. On the other hand

Congress did agree to a request by Burgoyne to permit a Canadian officer captured at Saratoga to return to Canada, as such officers were eligible for this favor under the terms of the convention. See *JCC*, 10:196, 207, 210, 216, 218–19; PCC, item 57, fols. 177–79, 183–84, 191, 199, 207–14; and K. G. Davies, ed., *Documents of the American Revolution, 1770–1783* (Dublin: Irish University Press, 1972–), 15:38–44. For a discussion of Congress' reasons for originally suspending the Saratoga Convention, see Laurens to William Heath, December 27, 1777, note 1.

Committee at Camp Statement

Moor Hall 2d March 1778.

State of the Case of Brigr. Genls. Mulenbergh, Weedon, Woodford and Scott with their Claim of Rank.[1]

	July 1775.	Woodford was appd. Colo. of the 2d Virginia State Regt.
19	Sepr.	Woodford reecived his Commission & Scott was appointed his Lt. Colonel.
13	Feby. 1776.	Woodford was appd. Colo. of the 2d Virginia Cont. Regt., Mercer of the 3d, Stephens of the 4th & Mulenbergh of the 8th. Scott Lt. Colo. of the 2d and Weedon of the 3d.
5th	April.	The 5th Virginia Regt. become Vacant.
3d	June.	The 3d. Regt. became vacant and Mercer was made a Brigr. Genl. over Woodford in which he chearfully acquiesced.
9th	June.	Scott was appointed Colo. of the 5th & Weedon of the 3d Regt. Scott by this appointment claimed Rank of Weedon which was allowed by Weedon.
	Sept 1776.	Stephens was appointed a Brigr. Genl. over Woodford wheron he resigned.
21st	Febry. 1777.	Mulenbergh, Weedon and Woodford were appointed Brigr. Genls. Congress declaring at the same time their Rank should be afterwards settled (vid Resolve).[2]
22d	Feby	Congress placed Woodford last by a Resolution (vid Resolve).[3]
1st	April 1777.	Scott was appointed a Brigr.
19th	Aug.	Upon a Dispute of Rank in the Pensilvania Line a Board of General Officers determined on the Principle that Rank & Precedence should be settled among Officers according to the Standing they held in the Army immediately before their present Coms. excepting Promo-

	tions for Merit (vid Proceedings of the Board).

12th Novr   Congress by their Resolution confirm this Principle (vid Resolve).[4]

29th   Congress direct the Genl. to regulate the Rank of Genls. Arnold, Woodford and Scott agreable to their Resolution of the 12th Novr. (vid Resolve of 29th).[5]

Genl. Arnolds Rank hath been regulated accordingly and he placed in the Position he would have held if originally promoted according to the Rank he then held.

Claim

Woodford claims to Rank as the eldest Brigr. because before his Resignation he was the eldest Colo. to which Resignation he was compelled by the Injustise done him.

To this Claim Scott assents but Mulenbergh & Weedon oppose it upon the Principle that Woodford having resigned held no Rank at the time of his Promotion.

Scott claims to Rank before Weedon because he did so when they were Colonels.

To this Claim Weedon objects.

The within Case and the Claims thereon having been referred to the Committee of Congress they request the Opinion of a Board of General Officers on the foregoing State of Facts which is submitted to them as more properly cognizable by Gentlemen of the Army than those in a civil Line.   Fra Dana, by Order

MS (DNA: PCC, item 33). Written by Gouverneur Morris and signed by Francis Dana.

[1] The committee prepared this "State of the Case" of the seniority among four Virginia brigadier generals as an aid to a board of officers which had been convened by General Washington at the committee's request.

The committee had originally conferred with Gens. William Woodford, George Weedon, and Charles Scott on February 14 and prepared a "State of Facts relative to the claims of Brigadier General Mulenburgh, Weedon, Woodford & Scott," to which they obtained the signatures of each officer except Peter Muhlenberg, who was absent in Virginia. They then sent the signed statement to Washington and recommended that he convene a board of general officers to obtain their opinion on the claims summarized. That document remains in the Washington Papers, DLC.

Before the board of officers convened on March 4, however, the committee prepared the statement which is printed here and which contains more detailed information on the case, especially the substance of several resolutions of Congress relating to seniority. Subsequently the board unanimously reported that, "in the original promotion of Those Gentlemen . . . They ought to have been Arranged in The following Manner, viz. Woodford, Mulenburgh, Scott, Weeden." On March 19 Congress accepted this "opinion" and directed Washington to issue the four generals new commissions.

Although Woodford, Muhlenberg, and Weedon had threatened to resign if the dispute was not settled to their satisfaction, only Weedon finally did when Congress denied his August 14 request to reconsider their March 19 decision. See *JCC,* 7:142, 9:981, 10:269, 11:807; Washington, *Writings* (Fitzpatrick), 10:183–88, 246, 449, 490–91, 11:1, 21–22, 87–88; PCC, item 152, 5:369; letters from Woodford, Muhlenberg, and Weedon to Washington of February 19, April 10, and April 13, 1778, respectively, in Washington Papers, DLC; and Committee at Camp Minutes of Proceedings, February 8–14, and February 16–20, 1778, note 3.

² See *JCC,* 7:141.
³ See *JCC,* 7:141–42.
⁴ See *JCC,* 9:896–97.
⁵ See *JCC,* 9:981.

Committee at Camp to Henry Laurens

Sir   Moor Hall 2d March 1778.

We did ourselves the Honor to write to you some Days since upon the Propriety of taking Savages into the public Service, to act as light Troops upon out Posts, advanced Parties and the like.¹ In Conversation with Baron Steuben upon the Subject, He observes that the Austrians always use the Croats (a Kind of white Indians) for such Purposes and to so good Effect that the King of Prussia imitated them by enrolling a Body of Irregulars to Cover in like Manner his Army but without answering the End, as new Soldiers too frequently desert which is fatal when very great Dependence is placed upon them.² Colo. Gist who is made the Bearer of this Letter will do himself the Honor to satisfy Congress in such further Enquiries as to the Utility of this Corps as they may think it expedient to make.

Colo. Gist will be happy in rendering every Service to the Continent which is in his Power consistent with that Attention which Justice requires to his private Affairs. In a former Embassage of this Kind he involved himself in a very considerable Expense so much beyond the Extent of his Funds that he was obliged to mortgage his Plantation for Money which has been applied to the Public Service. Public Honor requires that the Account he will deliver for this Expenditure should be speedily and satisfactorily adjusted. And Prudence will lead him to provide that Monies be advanced him for his personal Charge, and the Maintenance of the Indians with him. This Gentleman hath also a farther Demand upon the public for Goods which he promised to seventeen Savages who were employed usefully last Summer upon the Eastern Shore of Maryland and altho these Goods were not specificated in any Bargain with them, yet what he says to them in future will have little Influence unless they see some Kind of Performance to follow on such general Promises.

In Order that no Mistakes may arise in future upon this Subject and also inasmuch as it may flatter the Vanity of these People (which is *not* taking them by the *strongest* Side) he suggests the Propriety of making out the Terms upon which they are to be taken in Service and this in Writing from Congress but how far this may be proper we will not pretend to say, submitting it entirely to your superior Discretion.

Colo. Gist also expects the Liberty to take with him a faithful Assistant, who is to provide for the Indians upon their Route, a Business which it is impracticable for the Principal to attend to, his time being taken up in the Management of those whom he conducts, preventing or adjusting little Differences which arise between them and the Inhabitants and the like.

When the Savages shall have arrived it will be necessary to have with them Interpreters, as there would be Danger in permitting them to go out in detached Parties without the Power of making themselves understood. Indeed there would be great use in having a few Men from their Neighbourhood to serve as Irregulars with them which would prevent perhaps Mistakes which might be fatal. For these Reasons the Colo. thinks it would be proper to employ some few Interpreters and also to enlist for the special Service about fifty Men, of which as many as possible are to understand the Indian Language.

Upon the whole sir we cannot but think that much Good would arise from employing these turbulent Borderers as they would certainly keep the Enemy Compact, prevent Desertion in our Troops, make us Masters of Intelligence and give us Pledges of their Fidelity.

We are, sir, respectfully, your most obedient & humble servants.

Fra. Dana, by Order

RC (DNA: PCC, item 33). Written by Gouverneur Morris and signed by Francis Dana. Endorsed: "Letter from the Comee. of Congress at Camp March 2, 1778. read 6. referred to the board of war. (Acted Upon)."

[1] For the committee's previous letter recommending the employment of Indians with the army, see Committee at Camp to Henry Laurens, February 20, 1778.

[2] For a discussion of irregular warfare in 18th-century Europe, see Peter E. Russell, "Redcoats in the Wilderness: British Officers and Irregular Warfare in Europe and America, 1740 to 1760," *William and Mary Quarterly*, 3d ser. 35 (October 1978): 629–52.

Committee for Foreign Affairs to William Bingham

Sir   York Town 2d March 1778

The Committee of Secret correspondence, which almost a year ago was denominated the "Committee for foreign Affairs" stands indebted to you for many letters both of interesting advice and ingenious political speculation. Happening to be the only member of that Committee at present in York Town, I now take up my pen, not to form apoligies for their long past silence so much as to make a beginning of the act of justice due to you. I really fear that the collected ingenuity of the members will be put to it to offer, for a main excuse, any thing better, than that they relied upon your getting frequent intelligence of the state of our affairs from the commercial Committee. In short, Sir, I am so deeply concerned with the gentlemen in this affair that I know what they ought to do; and I am so well acquainted with their just manner of thinking that I will venture to confess in their name, that their past omission of corresponding with you is, in a considerable measure unaccountable. It is certainly better to step forward, towards a man of candor, in the straight line of honest confession than in the Zigzag tract of awkward apology.

Your letters, exclusive of their intrinsic Merit, have been more particularly acceptable to Congress from the Circumstance of our having [been] deprived of the satisfaction of receiving intelligence from the hands of our commissioners in Paris, since May last year. Besides those of their dispatches which have been lost at Sea, We know One has been examined and culled by some perfidious villain who substituted plain sheets of paper for the real letters of our friends. This was probably done in Europe before the bearer of it, a Capt. John Folgier, embarked with it for America.[1]

Your Ideas of the policy of the Court of Versailles appear quite just from the corroborating testimony of whatever information we can collect in any way.

The Course of gazettes which accompany this will so well communicate our home affairs that I shall not enlarge upon them. I will only say in brief that you may rest assured Independence is so absolutely adopted by America as to leave no hope for Britain, that we shall ever relinquish our claim. It must therefore be only to delude her own Islanders and her neighbors that She pretends to expect the contrary.

In addition to the misfortune which you mention respecting the Lexington we are told of a greater and one which will more intimately affect you respecting the Reprisal which is said to have foundered on the 1st October. Your acquaintance with Capt. Wickes will lead you to lament greatly the loss of so valuable an officer, and so worthy a man. I enclose you a list of your letters as they came to hand,[2] both for your own satisfaction, and to command your belief of my regard for You as a faithful corresponding Agent and of my consequential professions of being &ca.   (Signed) J Lovell
                                                        for the committee
                                                        for foreign affairs

FC (DNA: PCC, item 79).
    [1] For further information on the theft of the public dispatches, see Committee Examination of John Folger, January 12, 1778.
    [2] The list has not been found, but most of Bingham's surviving letters to Congress are in PCC, item 90; and Continental Congress Miscellany, DLC.

Committee for Foreign Affairs to
the Eastern Navy Board

Gentlemen   York Town 2 March 1778

The Committee of Congress for foreign Affairs, directing letters from time to time to your care, doubt not of your attention to forward them to our Commissioners and agents abroad, or to others as they may happen to be directed. You will be pleased to attend to the character of the person who may take charge of Packetts or letters, to any public Officer beyond seas, and to give direction for sinking the papers, when in imminent danger of falling into the hands of the Enemy. You are desired also to take the trouble of sending to the printers in Boston for the Gazettes in course, as you happen to have opportunities of enclosing them to our Commissioners in France either directly or thro' Mr. Bingham, our Agent at St. Pierres, Martinique. By ordering each printer to keep one course of papers, you can never be in want of a number proper for a packet; if you send for them to the Offices alternately, as Vessels offer, the printers may make a charge to the Committee of Congress for foreign Affairs or to your board on our account.[1]

We are &c,   (Signed) James Lovell, for the Committee

FC (DNA: PCC, item 79).

[1] On April 6 the Eastern Navy Board acknowledged the receipt of both this letter and a March 12 letter from the committee that has not been found. The board assured the committee of its attention to the dispatch packets, but on June 12 it reported that a brigantine carrying dispatches to Bilbao, Spain, had been captured. On July 6 the board reported that it was still awaiting opportunities to forward dispatches to France and Martinique. The board's April 6, June 12, and July 6 letters, which are addressed to James Lovell, are in PCC, item 37, fols. 109, 113, 117.

William Ellery to William Whipple

Dear Sir   York town March 2, 1778

Mr Francy is here. He hath offered the Flamand to Congress; but we have not purchased her. We were informed by Mr Langdon to whom we had written on the subject that she was unfit for our service.[1] She is ordered to South Carolina for a load of rice.

I take notice of what you say respecting the 74 gun ship. I was against building such huge ships, because I thought it would be very difficult if not impossible to man them. But would not the timber now prepared be too large even for such a frigate as you mention? And would not there be a loss in hewing it down to a proper size? I shall lay this matter before the Committee[2] when they can be got together which is as difficult to accomplish now, as it was formerly. I wish we could collect a number of our frigates together and give the British ships a drubbing, which now block up Chesapeake and the entrance into Charlestown South Carolina. Nicholson hath made two attempts to get out, but was so narrowly watched as rendered it impracticable. A gentleman who lately arrived here from thence, tells us, that Biddle and three State vessels were to go over the bar that day after he left Charlestown with a determination to attack the British ships who were of about equal force. I am anxious for the event.

France preserves her old equivocal line of conduct. We are constantly receiving supplies of one kind and another from Hortalez & Co. Several vessels have lately arrived from the West Indies with necessary articles and more are expected; but not withstanding this, and the unremitted exertions of Congress, so miserable is the conduct of every department that the army is not supplied with any one necessary article. We are altering the commissariate plan and are looking out for a new Commissary General. We have chosen General Green Quarter Master General in the room of General Mifflin resigned, and a Col Cox and a Mr Petit two very good characters assistant Q.M. G's so that I hope things will go on better in that department than they have done.[3] That of the Clothier General wants rectifying. Avarice and corruption run through, disorder and confound the execution of all our measures.

What effect the regulation of prices will have I cant say. I wish it had been universal, that a full experiment might have been made of its efficacy; although I was never fond of the measure. Unnatural restraints eventually do no good.

I delivered the account you enclosed to Mr Penn who promised me that he would send it to their government, such characters ought to be carefully watched, for they are capable of doing and disposed to do much mischief.

General Howe is upon the kidnapping plan at present and hath been not unsuccessful. To prevent this evil Congress have subjected all marauders and kidnappers to suffer death by a Court Martial, that are taken within 70 miles of the main army or any detachment under the command of a General.[4]

Before this reaches you, you will have heard that the executive Council of Massachusetts are authorized and requested to remove Genl. Burgoynes troops, separate and place them in such parts of that State as they may think proper. Malititular General hath wrote a letter to Congress, endeavoring to exculpate himself from the charges on which the suspension of the Convention is founded and desiring Congress to recede from their resolution. Upon which it is resolved that nothing therein contained is sufficient to induce Congress to recede from their resolution. Imagining that he might fail in this application he hath by one of his Aids laid before Congress another that he might with his suite be permitted to go to Britain on their parole. This is committed. What a strange reverse of fortune this vain glorious man hath experienced!

The Reverend Prelate's letter was an old story when I got here.[5] The virtuous gentleman you inquire after was allowed by his State, six month's absence from Congress, that he might settle his private affairs about which and the adjustment of the accounts of the Secret Committee I suppose he is employed at his place about twenty miles from this place.[6] It is true that S.D. is recalled and J.A.[7] appointed in his room and it is true that I am with much respect, Yrs,

Wm Ellery

[P.S.] Folsom is well at Camp as a Committee Man. Frost is hearty.

Tr (DLC).
    [1] See Committee of Commerce to John Langdon, February 23, 1778.
    [2] This probably refers to the Marine Committee, of which Ellery was a member.
    [3] See JCC, 10:210–11.
    [4] See JCC, 10:204–5.
    [5] This is a reference to the Rev. Jacob Duché's October 8, 1777, letter to Washington in which the Anglican cleric had urged the commander in chief to open peace negotiations with the British. See Henry Laurens to Robert Howe, October 20, 1777, note 2. Ellery had returned to Congress on November 17, 1777. JCC, 9:931.
    [6] The "virtuous gentleman" in question was Robert Morris. See Morris to the Committee of Commerce, December 17, 1777, note 1.
    [7] Congress had recalled Silas Deane as one of the commissioners to France the preceding November and replaced him with John Adams. JCC, 9:946–47, 975.

John Henry to Nicholas Thomas

Sir.   York Town March 2d 1778.
    The inactivity of both Armies, arising from the Season of the year, affords little intelligence worth communicating.

The wants and distresses of our army no doubt has reached your ears, to recapitulate them would give you unnecessary pain as it is out of your power to afford any relief. They have rec'd a short temporary supply. How long it will continue I do not certainly know, but I have great reason to believe but a few Weeks. The causes which have produced these Evils, I trust will be a subject of serious inquiry. It is highly necessary they should, if no other views were to be answered by it, than the prevention of such mischiefs in future. Where men are virtuous and active, and properly supplied with money it appears to me, unaccountably strange, in a country like this the very lap of plenty, that an army like ours should be on the very brink of distruction for the want of common necessaries. And what is beyond measure astonishing, many of the soldiers for the want of a little straw to ly upon are daily droping into the grave. I wish for better times, and I am sure we have a right to expect better Men and management. Many of the officers in the great civil Departments I am firmly persuaded are highly criminal and I expect will be found so.

One of the principal subjects for which our Assembly stood adjourned to this Day,[1] has not yet been taken up in Congress. The Confederation will be generally approved by the states. Virginia has acceded to it and some other states. No Carolina has agreed to part only. In the principal point on which your Delegates are instructed, I despair of succeeding in.[2]

The Success under our late recruiting Law I am unacquainted with. The necessity of filling up our Batallions agreeable to our quota, will appear by some late resolves of Congress which have been transmitted to our Governor to be laid before the General Assembly.[3] The mode principally recommended is the last effort that should be made. Whither it is to be embraced at this Time, is left to the wisdom of the Legislature.

I shall continue to give you such Intelligence as we have and am Sir with great respect your obedt. and very hble. servt.

J. Henry Junr.

RC (MdAA). Addressed: "The Honble. Nicholas Thomas Esqr., Speaker of the House of Delegates, Maryland." Although Thomas had presided during the October–December 1777 session of the Maryland House of Delegates, he resigned the speakership before the assembly reconvened in March 1778. Henry's letter was therefore doubtless opened by the new speaker, William Fitzhugh.

[1] Although the preceding assembly had adjourned to the first Monday in March—i.e., March 2—it did not actually reconvene until the 17th.

[2] For the assembly's instructions on the subject of the Articles of Confederation, see *Votes and Proceedings of the House of Delegates of the State of Maryland,* October 1777 session, pp. 48, 55, DLC(ESR). The "principal point" to which Henry alluded concerned Maryland's claim to western lands. As expressed in the assmbly's instructions, Maryland was "justly entitled to a right in common with the other members of the union, to that extensive tract of country which lies to the westward of the frontiers of the United States." Ibid., p. 48.

[3] See Henry Laurens to Richard Caswell, March 1, 1778, note 2.

Committee at Camp to Henry Laurens

Sir,   Moor Hall 3d March 1778.

When we did ourselves the Honor of transmitting to Congress the Plan of an Arrangement for the American Army we omitted that of a Corps of Engineers,[1] the Utility of which was and is equally evident with that of others though our Ideas upon the Subject were not at that Time entirely fixed and since that Period a Variety of other Researches have prevented so far our Attention that we have not yet submitted it to your Consideration. Enclosed is the Arrangement we determined on for that Corps together with their particular Duty on which we have only to add that the Officers should be Men of warranted Integrity and if possible great Mathematical Genius to the End that we may not in future be necessitated as at present to employ Officers of foreign Birth and Connections in this very confidential Part of our military Operations.[2]

On the Subject of Engineering we are further to observe to you that there is a Want of Assistants in this Line since every considerable Detachment ought not to be unprovided with a Person tolerably skilled in it. To supply this want, a Monsieur Murnan warmly recommended to us by General Portail offers himself to us and wishes to serve the Continent with the Rank and Appointment of a Major. Comparing his Pretensions with those of the Herd of his Countrymen and estimating them in the Scale of Abilities his Request appears to your Committee moderate and ought in their Opinion to be accepted since in this Department we must employ them on their own Terms.

A very alarming Circumstance draws our Attention at this Time and renders an immediate Application to Congress absolutely necessary. Want of Discipline in our Army from Causes which it is needless now to travel through occasions in most Instances a Relaxation of the Attention due to the Orders of the General. In Nothing is this more evident or more dangerous than in the Furloughs given by Colonels to their Men By Reason whereof our Numbers suffer a daily Diminution leaving only the Skeleton of an Army. True it is by the Articles of War only two Men are to be furloughed from any Company but this Article if strictly complied with would reduce us greatly the Companies being very numerous and but few men in each. How much greater then the Evil when by *Pretence* of the Article and in Defiance of general Orders this Privilege is extended according to the Disposition of the Colonel and the Importunities of his Men. We have therefore to request the immediate Repeal of this Article and that in future the Commanders of the respective Departments be invested with the sole Power of granting Furloughs.[3]

We have the Honor to be with great Respect, Sir, your most obedient humble servants,   Fra Dana, by Order

ENCLOSURE

An Establishment for a Corps of Engineers, Artificers &ca. to consist of 2 Battalions of 8 Companies each, 100 Men to a Company including Officers.

Feild & Staff Officers in each Battalion	Pay per Month in Dollars	Their extra Allowances per Month in Dollars
1 Colo. or Chief Engineer	60	15 for a Clerk
1 Lieut. Colo. or Chief director	50	15 for a do.
1 Major or Sub director	40	15 for a do.
1 Surveyor	33⅓	30 for 2 do.
1 Adjutant		
1 Chaplain		
1 Surgeon		
1 Mate	} Pay the same as in Battalion Service	
1 Quarter Master		
1 Pay Master		

Each Company to consist of the following Officers, Artificers &ca. their monthly pay the same as in the Battalion Service.

		Extra Allowance per day when employ'd in the Works
1 Captain or Engineer in Ordinary		½ Dollar
1 Capt. Lieut. or Engineer extraordinary		⅜
1 Lieutenant or Sub Engineer		⅓
1 Ensign or practitioner Enginer		¼
4 Serjeants or Foremen of Band	each	⅙
4 Corporals or Seconds do	do	⅐
2 drums & Fifes	do	do
30 Carpenters or Wheel Wrights	do	⅛
5 Smiths	do	⅛
6 Masons	do	⅛
25 Miners & Sappers	do	⅛, in time of Seige ¼ dollar
20 Laborours	do	1/12

100.

Arrangement of the Engineering Department

No.	Rank	Pay	Amt.	Rat.	Amt.
1	Captain	50	50	3	3
3	Lieutenants	33⅓	100	2	6
4	Serjeants	10	40	1	4
4	Corporals	9	36	1	4
60	Privates	8⅓	500	1	60
72	Monthly pay		726	Daily Rat.	77
				Monthly Rat.	2,310

Three Companies upon the above Establishment to be instructed in the Fabrication of Field Works as far as relates to the manual & mechanical Part. Their Business is to instruct the fatigue Parties to do their Duty with Celerity and Exactness. The commissioned Officers to be skilled in the necessary Branches of the Mathematics. The noncomd. Officers to write a good Hand. Duty of the Corps to repair Injuries done to Works by the Enemy's Fire & to prosecute Works in the Face of it. ⟨*The Corps to be under the Direction of the Chief Engineer and to have the Care of the intrenching Tools.*⟩

RC (DNA: PCC, item 33). Written by Gouverneur Morris and signed by Francis Dana. Enclosure: MS (DLC). In the hand of Morris and Dana.

[1] See Committee at Camp to Henry Laurens, February 5, 1778.

[2] Another copy of the enclosure's second page, entitled "Arrangement of the Engineering Department" and in Dana's hand, is in PCC, item 33, fol. 109, where it was later placed among the enclosures with the committee's February 5 letter to Laurens on the arrangement of the army.

[3] For congressional response to this request, see Henry Laurens to William Heath, March 7, 1778, note.

Cornelius Harnett to William Wilkinson

Dear Sir   York Town March 3. 1778

Your several favours of the 7, 14 & 26 January & 4 Ultimo are now before me. I have lately had one of the Severest fitts of the Gout, I ever had in my life, I have been confined to my room these 5 Weeks unable to help myself, having it in both feet, one knee & my right hand & arm, it is with great pain that I am able to hold a pen in my hand this day. I am sorry to hear Meridith is taken, I wish the fact could be Assertained in regard to his being put in Irons &c. Jackey is not yet with me; Mr. Mitchel promises to send him as soon as the weather will permit. I think I shall bring him home with me, as we are likely to have Warm work the Next Campaign, you may for the present send him to Mecklingburg School. In yours of the 26 Jany. I received Coll Kennons Bills on the Continental Treasury, Viz No. 25, Bill for 1000, No 26 for 1000, No 33 for 500, No 34 for 500, No 35 for 500 ammounting in the whole to 3,500 Dollars. I shall present them for payment as soon as I am Able to Attend the Treasury bord, which I hope will be in a very few days.[1] I am sorry indeed for the great Loss sustained by the Inhabitants of Charles Town, it was a dreadful fire.

I write Mr. Maclain a few lines by this Post & shall write my friend Hooper very fully by the Next.[2] Our Army remains as before at Valey Forge. Unless the several States exert themselves to compleat their Batalions Our Continental Army will Cut a poor figure in the Spring, we have not even heard of a Schyrmish lately. I hope to see you in April & am, Dr Sir, Your affect & Obed Servt,   Cornl. Harnett

[P.S.] In the midst of my Distress, my Man Sawney ran away from me. I have with much ado hired a little Dutch Boy to make a fire for me. A Servant is not to be had here. I beg you will hire Herons Josh to come to me or some other free man. I don't know whether I shall ever get Sawney again, it is said he intended to go to Philadelphia. He turned Out to be one of the greatest Villains Living, if I was to tell you some parts of his behaviour it would amaze you. You may purchase a horse for Josh if he'll Come, & I can perhaps sell the horse here for as much as he Costs.

Yours &c   C. H.

RC (Nc–U).

[1] On March 7 President Laurens laid before Congress the bills of the late Col. William Kennon, acting paymaster and commissary to Virginia and North Carolina troops serving in Georgia. A week later the board of treasury reported in favor of paying Kennon's bills, but Congress rejected this report and ordered it to be recommitted. Not until October 30, 1778, when Congress next considered the issue, did it order payment of Kennon's bills. See JCC, 10:232, 255–57, 12:1071, 1079.

[2] Neither of these letters has been found.

John Henry to Thomas Johnson

Sir.   York Town March 3th. 1778.

I was informed some Time ago by Col. Smith, that the recruiting Service was much injured for the want of the continental Bounty. If that is the case I should be glad to be informed of it. The Treasury here will now supply it.[1] Genl. Green is made quarter Master General, this I hope will be attended with the most happy effects. The Expedition into Canada is suspended for the present and the Troops ordered to the North River for the fortification and defence of it.

I am Sir with great respect, your obedt. and hble Servt.

J Henry Junr.

RC (MdAA).

[1] See Henry to Johnson, March 6, 1778.

Henry Laurens to Francis Dana

Sir,   3d March 1778

Yesterday I had the honour of sending forward a Letter written the preceeding Evening as a private to yourself to which I beg leave to refer.

Congress upon my presenting the Committees Letter from Camp dated the 25th Febry, entered upon the subject without hesitation & confirmed divers Resolves which you will find in the Inclosed Act of yesterday's date by which you will be pleased to govern your future proceedings relative to the department of Quarter Master General.

A duplicate of this Act I shall transmit by the bearer of this to Major General Mifflin. All the present Members of Congress entertain the most Sanguine hopes that the department will now be conducted with the greatest propriety & benefit by Major General Green & the Gentlemen his Coadjutors. It occurs to me that in your long Letter you omitted one capital article, Money; from an assurance that the important business cannot be conducted without the aid of that necessary, I will take the liberty at our meeting to day to introduce the Subject[1] & I make no doubt but a proper grant will be immediately Resolved. The late Qur. Mr. general was Supplied with upwards of 300,000 Dollars a very few days ago, from whence some benefits will no doubt arise in the new arrangement.[2]

Congress have directed the Board of War to give orders for apprehending those Excursors from Philadelphia towards Winchester & if taken to imprison them.[3]

I have the honour to be &ca.

LB (DNA: PCC, item 13).

[1] It is not apparent from the journals what Laurens actually did "to introduce the Subject," but he may have simply assumed it would receive adequate attention from the committee appointed to take into consideration "an extract of a letter from one of the committee at camp, relative to the purchase of provisions from the army," which was laid before Congress this day by John Harvie. It is also not clear what use Congress made of this committee's report, which was introduced on March 11, but apparently it was rendered superfluous by the resolves pertaining to the commissary's department that Congress adopted on March 13. See *JCC,* 10:219, 244–45, 248–52.

[2] In fact Congress had entrusted $400,000 to then Quartermaster General Thomas Mifflin on February 19. Nathanael Greene had replaced Mifflin in this office on March 2. See *JCC,* 10:182, 210.

[3] On March 2 the Board of War had been ordered to apprehend Dr. Thomas Parke and Robert Morton for having "presumed to undertake a journey from Philadelphia to Winchester, without calling at head quarters, or obtaining permission from any lawful authority." See *JCC,* 10:211; and Committee at Camp to Laurens, February 25, 1778. Parke and Morton were relatives of James Pemberton, one of several Philadelphia Quakers who had been exiled to Winchester, Va., in September 1777 on account of their allegedly seditious activities against the patriot cause. See John Hancock to William Livingston, August 30, 1777.

Henry Laurens to John Laurens

My Dear son,   York Town 3d March 1778

Permit me to refer you to what I had the pleasure of writing by the Light Horse Man, Sharp, yesterday.[1]

The bearer hereof is another Light Horse Messenger. He will deliver a bundle containing 1½ Yards of yellowish Cloth enough the Taylor reports for 2 pair Breeches or a Wastcoat & Breeches. This I obtained as a very great favor & at the very moderate Sum of 48

Dollars. You wrote only for Cloths but where are materials for making up. Mr Hair Dresser recommends to you to substitute flour until he can by his art procure a better article for your hair.

In my last dispatches I forwarded a miniature of the General to Mrs Washington from Majr. Rodgers which he packeted in my presence & requested my care of. I think I have seen a performance of yours which discovered superior skill; maybe I am mistaken, but be that as it may, if you have materials, time & inclination you will do me a singular pleasure by sending me a half length of your draught.[2] The Major says the General has a remarkable dead Eye. This did not strike me in either of the three or four times when I saw him. Once I had as good a veiw as Candle light could afford & I am seldom deficient in such strictures.

General Burgoyne has transmitted to Congress a long remonstrative Epistle on the Suspension, to which we shall return a very laconic & decisive answer. This event must have been preconceived by the unfortunate General, who had therefore put into the hands of his Aid de Camp a Messenger Capt Wilford a No. 2 to be delivered after the receipt of our answer, but without waiting, he enabled me to report it yesterday. This contains a request, that himself & certain Officers chiefly of his family may under proper restrictions embark for England. I have communicated to several Members my sentiments and I believe a vote will pass in his favor Nemine Contradicente. I think good may be produced from this Political condescension. However let me say the representation he has made of the state of his health & private affairs including his Character is an appeal to humanity—or in the General's own term to our Generosity. I shall be exceedingly mortified if we neglect the opportunity of contrasting American liberality to British Cruelty. Should the favor be abused we have subjects enough remaining for full retaliation. The General may adopt any Motto, he has now learn'd that derivative is not higher than original honour & power, his Addresses to Congress in the name of their President are decent & unexceptionable. This is paving the way to a right understanding.

I mean to trust a plain Letter or two by Capt Wilford who will probably pass through your Camp & apply to you.

I write now as I am generally driven to do in my Addresses to you, in haste. God Bless & protect you.   Henry Laurens

RC (MHi: William Gilmore Simms Collection deposit, 1973).

[1] Laurens' last extant letter to his son John, which is dated March 1 in his private letter book in the Laurens' Papers, ScHi, was apparently dispatched on the second. It is also pertinent to note that John Laurens mentioned receiving two March 3 letters from his father, though only one has been found. Simms, *Laurens Army Correspondence,* p. 134.

[2] John replied on March 9 that his talents were not equal to the task of painting or sketching a portrait of Washington or anyone else. Ibid., pp. 138–39.

Henry Laurens to the Marquis de Lafayette

Sir,   the 4th March 1778.

I am much honoured by the receipt of your Excellency's Letter of the 19th Febry.[1] which was delivered to me by Colo Kosciuszko in person, but not early enough by 24 hours to prevent my troubling Baron de Kalb to say "I had nothing to offer the Marquis delafayette on the 25th except respectful Compliments & good wishes." [2] This would not have been true, had Your Excellency's favor been delivered to me soon after the delivery of a Letter dated the 20th Febry & signed by your Excellency which was sent to me by the Board of War uncovered for the information of Congress.[3]

I had read this last mentioned Letter to Mr. Lovel before the meeting of Congress & remarked to him that from the Stile & tenor, it must have been intended for the president of Congress. This sentiment which scarcely required further aid, was confirmed beyond all doubt, by the preface of your Excellency's private Letter. "I intend to write to you as president of Congress," but unluckily this was not presented to me till the afternoon of the 20th. It was then the Colo. introduced by General Gates, did me the honour to call at my little apartment. I can account in no way for the miscarriage of the Letter intended for Congress, but by concluding an error in the superscriptory, & the omission within, of the customary direction, for it cannot be beleived the Board of War would otherwise have made so unbecoming an appropriation; & their hurry of business apologizes for the want of that nice attention which was necessary to discover from the contents of the Letter that it was manifestly designed for Congress. From this mistake, if it be really one, it follows that I have no Commands on me from Congress directed to your Excellency, who will hear from the Board with whom Your Excellency apparently corresponded.

Nevertheless, as it is neither out of the Line of the presidents Duty nor inconsistent with his Right as a Delegate, I shall do myself the honour of conveying a Copy of the Act of Congress of the 2d Inst. passed upon Resolving to suspend the intended Irruption,[4] meaning from thence to prove that Congress maintain an high opinion of your Excellency as a Soldier & a Gentleman & you may depend upon it Sir, the approbation contained in that Act, is genuine, not merely complimentary. Admitting the phraseology to be not quite unexceptionable, I should be criminally silent were I not to declare, the intentions of Congress respecting Your Excellency's honour & merits, are altogether so. I will in this case presume to answer for each Individual Member. I love to walk in the Light & to dwell on these bright scenes. Your Excellency, I flatter myself, will indulge my silence on some particulars alluded to in your Excellency's Letter of the 19th.

I might be led to disclose sentiments which might seem unfavorable to a Gentleman,[5] whom I esteem a Man of good & upright intentions, whose mistakes are more the effect of credulity than of turpitude of mind or principles. Those who mislead him will be dragged forth at length to public veiw. Methinks they are in such hands at present as will not Spare them. You Sir, who are a Bystander are best qualified to judge, & most likely to judge impartially.

My wish is, that we may detect & punish all peculators, projecting, insidious, mischievous Knaves, & that no Name under Heaven may screen the villain. But I would deal gently with those whose errors are of the head, whose general tone speaks the public good. And at all hazards & expences I will to the utmost of my abilities Support & defend the disinterested patriot—at the same time most sedulously avoid every whisper which may tend to fan the flame of party. Hence your Excellency will perceive my motives for touching certain Subjects with caution. When I am clear, no Man will Speak with more chearful boldness, but by casting at an object in a Mist, I may wound an Innocent, or a friend.

If ever Man stood on a firm Base, you do My Dear General, you are possessed of what Bacon calls the "vantage ground of Truth"—from whence you may look down upon the Crooked vales & paths below.

My hopes are sanguine that from the American patriotism of Marquis delafayette & from his native virtue a power will be raised which will effectually repress the Monster, party, now ravaging the fairest Characters in this Country. God forbid Sir, you should entertain a thought of leaving our United States at this juncture.

"My opinion Dear General of *your situation,*" is, that you are at Albany & often in very good Company, & very far from the inglorious precipice which you seem to suggest. The notoriety of your whole conduct & the Resolves of Congress shield you against every possible unfavorable insinuation. Your Excellency will find that Body, Congress, however it may, by artful Men, be sometimes a little Bamboozled, to consist of honest well disposed minds and if "Wisdom is justified of her Children" I appeal to their Acts in general. Fall the blame of the late abortion where it ought, or where it may, or by good maneuvring on one side & tameness & acquiesence on the other, let a thick veil be drawn over it, not the smallest spark or speck of Censure can possibly light on Marquis delafayette; that General has performed every thing which had been prescribed to him. He has overshot the expectation of some who presumed to beleive & assert that he would be deficient in "activity," & the intended expedition "some days advanced before his appearance at Albany"—in a word 'tis but just that I should repeat, your Excellency is spoken of by Members in Congress with Respect & Admiration. The Air around the Marquis is serene & his own Breast tranquil; a Blunder, not his own, has afforded an opportunity for a display of Wisdom which has gained him the confidence of the people, hence my Dear Sir, you will perceive that you may with very great propriety & decency, return to your late Miltary Post.

I shall add to the Act of Congress above mentioned one of the 24th Ulto. which by three last words added at my particular request injoins you to report the reasons of your Conduct "to Congress." [6] Your Excellency may possibly think this anticipated by the Letter of the 20th Febry—& if the Board of War shall have transmitted Copies of these Resolves the present Inclosed will appear to be superfluous, I have however confined my self within the sphere of my Duty, relying upon Your Excellency's indulgence to excuse me for making an Address which is altogether private, the Vehicle for two public Acts.

I know not what to say relative to General Putnam's Command, it appears to me that Gentlemen wish him away, & at the same time are loth to offend the good Man—if it be from his unfitness their wishes arise, the sacrifice is very politic & unwarrantable.

I remarked in a late Act by General Gates he retained the stile of Commander of the Troops in the Northern department, I know of no Resolve by which he has been divested of that Command & I have heard it said lately that there would be a necessity for his taking the Field again in the Spring.

Your Excellency having now a proper opening to correspond with Congress may if you shall judge it proper suggest a plan for employment of such troops as are at present under your Command & such as may be collected. I feel the utmost confidence that Congress will pay becoming attention to every thing your Excellency shall be pleased to offer.

I have the honour to be with the Highest Esteem & Respect.

P.S. I should not like our correspondence to be talked of by everyone who calls himself or who may seem to be friend. I am afraid of nothing but lies & misrepresentation.

A Note in the Margin of your Letter "I beg you will engage Congress to read over all the papers I send to them," is a clear proof the Letter of 20th Febry was intended for Congress altho' it might have been by mistake directed to the Board of War. I had not perceived this Note till the present Moment.

LB (ScHi).

    [1] This was a private letter to Laurens in which Lafayette deplored the fact that it was impossible for him to carry out the expedition against Canada that Congress had appointed him to command. Lafayette, *Papers* (Idzerda), 1:295–97.

    [2] See Laurens to Baron de Kalb, February 25, 1778.

    [3] This letter, in which Lafayette described at length the obstacles in the way of a Canadian expedition, is in Lafayette, *Papers* (Idzerda,), 1:305–8.

⁴ On March 2 Congress had ordered the Board of War to instruct Lafayette to suspend his expedition against Canada and to assure him that the delegates did not hold him responsible for its failure. *JCC*, 10:216–17.

⁵ This is probably an allusion to Gen. Horatio Gates, the president of the Board of War and the main planner for the assault on Canada, to whose ignorance of the "immense number of debts, the want of cloathing, want of men, want of every thing indeed to be wanted" in the northern department Lafayette attributed much of the blame for the failure of the Canadian expedition. Lafayette, *Papers* (Idzerda), 1:295–96.

⁶ On February 24 Congress had ordered the Board of War to instruct Lafayette to "regulate his conduct" as commander of the Canadian expedition "according to the probability of success" and to "report the reasons of his conduct." But to whom the marquis was supposed to report is something of a problem. According to the rough journals, which consist of Secretary Thomson's daily entries of proceedings in Congress, Lafayette was supposed to report "to the board ⟨& to⟩ Congress," whereas the "Transcript" journals, which contain the proceedings of Congress as revised for publication, state that his reports were to go "to the board of war and to Congress." See PCC, item 1, 14:29, item 2, 7:2031. Worthington C. Ford, whose text of this order in *JCC* is taken from the rough journals, decided that the deletion of "& to" before "Congress" meant that Lafayette only had to report to the Board of War and thus rendered his text accordingly. *JCC*, 10:193. Yet although it seems clear from Laurens' testimony and the evidence of the "Transcript" journals that Congress also expected to receive reports on the Canadian expedition from Lafayette, General Gates, the president of the Board of War, transmitted a text of the February 24 resolve to Lafayette that only mentioned the board as a recipient. Lafayette, *Papers* (Idzerda), 1:349. It is impossible to say if this was merely an innocent error by Gates or an effort on his part to control the flow of vital military intelligence to Congress. As the chief author of the Canadian expedition, Gates may well have desired to screen reports of its failure before passing them on to Congress, though admittedly this is merely conjecture.

Marine Committee to Thomas Johnson

Sir   York Town 4th March 1778

We have been honored with your letter of the 11th Ultimo addressed to Mr F Lewis A Member of this committee.¹

The offer you therein make us of furnishing the Brigantine Baltimore Packet, with Six Pieces Canon, four pounders with their Carriages, Rammer Rods, Spunges &c, or as many thereof as may be compleat, we accept, and will order payment for the same as soon as the value is ascertained agreeable to the mode you propose.

We beg leave to request Your Excellency to order those Canon &c to be sent up to the Point at Baltimore in the manner most convenient.

We have hitherto been unfortunate in our attempts to get the Frigate Virginia to Sea. The Committee have this day resolved that Capt. Nicholson be ordered to make one other attempt; we are informed that it will be necessary that he be furnished with a tender for giving him intelligence in the Bay, also a proper Pilot to carry the

Ship out, as the want of a Pilot rendered his last Attempt Abortive. For these reasons we must intreat your Excellency to permit Captain Nicholson to A further use of the Tender he was lately furnished with, as well as to impower him to procure a good Pilot in Such manner as you shall think fit, for we are informed he cannot procure one without your Sanction.

We have the Honor to be, Your Excellencys most humble Servts,

Fra Lewis   Abra. Clark

Geo. Frost   Saml Huntington

Willm Ellery

RC (MB). In the hand of John Brown and signed by Clark, Ellery, Frost, Huntington, and Lewis.

[1] See Francis Lewis to Thomas Johnson, January 27, 1778.

Marine Committee to James Nicholson

Sir   March 4th 1778

Your letters of the 25th & 26th ultimo per Lieutenant Barney are now before us. We are concerned to find your last attempt in getting the frigate Virginia to Sea had been fruitless; but as your letters inform us such is the fondness your Officers and Seamen retain for the Ship that you think they will chearfully make another trial, This has induced the Committee to resolve that another trial be made as soon as possible and to expedite the same they have this day requested Governor Johnston to continue to you the use of the Tender, as well as to furnish you with, or empower you to procure an able and Skillful Pilot.[1]

By information from Lieutenant Barney we have reason to apprehend our late Agents will not supply the Ship unless more Money is put into their hands, this we are restrained from doing until the large sums already placed there is accounted for, and least this should throw embarrassments in your way the Committee have this day appointed Stephen Steward Esqr. of West River their Agent for supplying the Virginia and have put money into his hands for that purpose,[2] we shall rely upon your giving him all the Assistance in yr. power. We assure you that we retain a tender regard for your Character, and hope you will by this succeeding attempt be enabled to wipe off any malicious reflections (if any there be for we know of none) on your character.

Enclosed you have Lieutenants Plunket and Barneys Commissions. Wishing you success We are sir, Yr. hble servants

LB (DNA: PCC Miscellaneous Papers, Marine Committee Letter Book).

¹ For the subsequent surrender of the *Virginia*, see Marine Committee to the Middle Department Navy Board, April 8, 1778, note 1.

² The committee's letter appointing Steward their agent for supplying the *Virginia* and directing him "to call on Mr. Francis Lewis jr. at Baltimore for four thousand Dollars" is in PCC Miscellaneous Papers, Marine Committee Letter Book, fol. 129, and Paullin, *Marine Committee Letters,* 1:206–7.

Gouverneur Morris to George Clinton

Sir,   Moor Hall, 4th March 1778.

I take the liberty of writing to you upon a subject of the utmost importance to our State. By following so much of St. Paul's advice as to become all things to all men I find clearly from the very best authority that without nice management we shall certainly loose the State of Vermont. The Eastern States are determined that they shall not be oppressed to use their phrase. The prejudices of the people are against us so are their interests. Designing men take advantage of these circumstances to forward their own private views. Tis absurd to *reason* against the *feelings* of mankind. Neither is it much to the purpose whether our claim is *right* for if it be, the most which can be said for us is that we have *right* without *remedy*. What are their claims? Occupancy, settlement, cultivation and the Book of Genesis. What their plea? Their mountains their arms their courage their alliances. Against all this what can we produce? Why forsooth a decision of the King in council and a clause in the confederacy. How ridiculous for wise men to rear any edifice of hope upon so slender a foundation. But how are we to act? to give them up? No! We must go to the mountain if the mountain won't come to us. They complain that the capital is too far off: carry it nearer not merely for their sakes but for our own. They complain of our impeachment of their title. Give them good title; we want *subjects* not *land*. They complain of the quit rents: abolish them. We cant have more of a cat than the skin. A *good* government, a *free one* I mean, will always command the wealth of its people. Hudson's river ensures us that of Vermont and Vermont ensures us Hudson's river. For Vermont must be fortified all over and vast magazines of military stores must be laid up in Vermont and when any body presumes to attack us from the eastward we shall know what to do. All this is not yet enough: you must apply to their feelings. Suppose for instance the legislature should take up the case of Vandyke, Ethan Allen and other our subjects and make very pointed resolutions for the liberating of them. Suppose for his services and sufferings a part of Kemp's land should be given to him and that part if any such there be which eastern gentlemen claim. Apply yourself to Warner's weak side. Baily is still a considerable man among them. Let splended acts of justice and generosity induce these people to submit early to our dominion for prejudices grow stubborn as they grow old. This business my dear sir hath long pressed upon my mind with a weight and impression which I cannot describe. It is under heaven the great thing needful to us and though I laugh whenever Vermont is named yet I cannot almost use the poetical language intended for another occasion and say "tis laughter swelled with bursting sighs."[1]

MS not found; reprinted from E. P. Walton, ed., *Records of the Governor and Council of the State of Vermont,* 8 vols. (Montpelier: J. & J. M. Poland, 1873–80), 3:291–92, where it is identified as an extract of a letter from Morris to Governor Clinton, "furnished to the *New York Herald,* in 1842, by Col. Beekman of Flatbush, N.Y."

[1] Ironically, Morris' conciliatory approach to the problem of establishing New York's authority over the area that later became the state of Vermont proved to be unpopular among New Yorkers and was an important factor in the state legislature's refusal to reelect him to another term in Congress in August 1779. See Max M. Mintz, *Gouverneur Morris and the American Revolution* (Norman: University of Oklahoma Press, 1970), pp. 134–37.

Robert Morris to John Brown

Dear Sir   Manheim March 4th. 1778

I have your several favours of the 19th, 23d & 28th Ulto & thank you for the letters enclosed therewith, I Credit you for the money paid Colo. Lee agreable to his receipt.

I am glad the price of Salt is so much reduced & wish it may never rise again, however mine Cost me £16 per bushl. in Balto beside Cartage &c therefore it must remain untill I can see further about it. I dont wonder at Mad[eir]a Wine rising so fast, it grows scarce & in a little time none will be left. I must not sell any of mine, yet awhile, I hope the Salt does not incommode Mr. Irwin. Be pleased to present my Compts to him & Mrs Irwin. I shall see them again by & by. I pr[opose] soon as the Roads grow better if I can get Waggons to send some Wine & Spirits over to York, pray you to ask Mr. Irwin & Mr Donaldson if they can store them for me. I have not heard lately from Mr Fitzsimmons so do not know whether he is gone to Virginia or not. You may depend it will be a pleasure when I can put you in the way of making Money and I hope opportunities may offer this Spring.

My Compts to Mr. Francy. He may depend on my sending forward immediately any letters that come to my hands for him; none have appeared yet.

If the Committee take the twenty hogsheads of Tobo. they must order them to be included in their bills of Loading and I will charge them for the Cost, therefore no harm can be done by the letter going to

Messrs Purviance as you had informed them how the matter stood. Mr Slough has undertaken to get the Steel for me. Will you enquire of Mr. Hahn from who I bought some Hemp when in York whether he has any more or can get any more & what price he will take for it. Also mention the quantity, or perhaps you may hear of some with some other person. I thank you for mentioning Bob & am Dear Sir, Your obedt hble servant,   Robt Morris

Mr. Brown.[1] If Genl. Roche de Fermoy is in York deliver him the enclosed with my Compts. if not send it after him wherever he is gone too.   RM.
  Please give the enclosed to Mr. McCalmond.

RC (NjP).
[1] This postscript is in the hand of Morris' clerk John Swanwick.

Committee at Camp to Henry Laurens

Sir   Camp near Valley Forge, March 5. 1778.
  Col. Baylor who commands one of our Regiments of Cavalry being on his Way to Virginia, we avail ourselves of the Oppy. to lay before you what we have done, & what we propose to do, with Respect to that Corps. Our own Judgment so perfectly coincides with that of the military Gentlemen, on the Necessity of placing it on the most respectable Footing, that we have made it one of the principal Objects of our Concern & Attention. We have been happy to find, that three of the Regiments are nearly completed with Men recruited from those Troops whose Terms of Service expired this Fall, & readily inlisted in the Horse, tho totally averse to continuing in the Foot. But a large Supply of Horses, Arms & Accoutrements will be essentially necessary to enable them to take the Field with Effect. After forming a Variety of Plans to make this necessary Provision, we were obliged to reject them as too burthensome & oppresive, upon the People, or subjecting us to the most dangerous Frauds. At length Sir we adopted the following as most reconciliable to the Demand of the Service, & the Feelings, or Prejudices of the Country. We estimated the Number of Horses necessary for the Purpose, over & above those which have been & may be taken from the Vicinity of the Enemy; of which we quota'd a part on the States of New Jersey, Pennsylvania, Maryland & Delaware, the Remainder to be procured in Virginia & North Carolina. We wrote to the respective Governors of the three first States in the most pressing Terms stating the Importance & Urgency of the Service,[1] & requesting them by the most early & vigorous Exertions to procure the Number assigned, together with com-

mon Bridles & Saddles, in such Mode as would be most easy to the People, & effectually guarded against Fraud, Mistake, & Extortion. We did not limit any Price, because we were fully convinced the publick Service was last Year materially injured by this false Oeconomy. In the Rate of Purchases being fixed below the current Price of a good Horse, the Officers to whom this Business was intrusted were obliged either to leave their Men dismounted, or purchase those of an inferiour Quality, In many Instances totally unfit for the Service, & the Money thereby intirely lost. And we have no Doubt from the concurrent Testimony of all the Gentlemen with whom we have conferr'd on the Subject, that had a generous Price been then given which an Addition of a few Pounds would have made, we should now have had a very respectable Number of good Horses, instead of those little, wretched, useless Animals which disgrace our Service, & consume our Forage. It is expected that the Gentlemen appointed by the States will not only conform strictly to the Description we have sent, but be Men of such Character & Knowledge, as to give the best Security against Fraud & Imposition; & acting under immediate Controul & Authority they will perform their Duty without adding to those discontents which the unnecessary, arbitrary Seizure of Property justly creates. These Letters we have Reason to believe, will find the Legislatures of Jersey, Pennsylvania & Maryland sitting who will we trust take effectual Measures to execute this Business with Dispatch, as the only probable Means to ward off the Necessity of using Compulsion. As to the Delaware State, the Debility of its Government, & indeed the Dereliction of Power by the executive Officers, had induced us with the Concurrence of the General to put the Business so far as relates to them, under the Direction of General Smallwood who commands at Wilmington, untill some proper Authority shall intervene. Wtih Regard to Virginia & North Carolina, from which we expect very great Assistance the Assemblies having lately adjourned, & their vast Extent of Dominion rendering it extreamly difficult to diffuse the necessary Information & Powers we have concluded to recommend to Congress to make Use of Col. Baylors Services. His Judgment in Horses, Knowledge of the Country, Fortune, & Character are such as induce the fullest Confidence, & more especially as his own military Character & Interest are so intimately connected with a faithful & honourable Discharge of the Trust. It is proposed to furnish him from the Treasury with 50,000 Dollars or more if it can be spared, & to enable him for the Remainder to receive from the Loan Officer of Virginia from Time to Time Certificates the Appropriation to be accounted with him when the Business is completed. With due Attention & Accuracy we think the Mode may be so guarded that the Publick will be exposed to no other Danger than that of the Loss of the Interest Money on the Certificates while on Hand, & even against this if it should be thought of sufficient Consequence, we conceive a Provision may be made. Upon the whole we beg Leave to assure you, Sir, that our Determinations have been the Result of much Deliberation & there has been no Subject on which we have had greater Embarasments. We flatter ourselves that when we have an Oppy. of laying our Reasons more largely before Congress we shall be able to remove any Doubts which may arise of the Propriety of the Mode we have adopted, & be favoured with your full Approbation.[2]

We must refer you to Col. Baylor for a particular State of the Cavalry at present who will answer such Inquiries as may be thought necessary.

We are with the greatest Respect & Regard. Sir, Your most Obedt. & very Hble Servt.   Fra Dana, by Order

RC (DNA: PCC, item 33). Written by Joseph Reed and signed by Francis Dana.

[1] See Committee at Camp to Thomas Wharton, February 28, 1778.

[2] For the arrangement of cavalry as finally adopted by Congress on May 27, see *JCC*, 11:540–41.

Committee of Commerce to Robert Morris

Sir,   York March 5th 1778

The affairs of Messrs Hortalez & Co. have been laid before Congress, and referred to a Committee who reported this day. The Consideration of this intricate and important Business is postponed to Monday next. As you are better acquainted with this mysterious commerce than we are, and are capable of giving us great Assistance in making any future Contracts that may be entered into with Mr. Francy in behalf of that house, We should be exceedingly glad to see you here by that time,[1] and are with great Respect, Your very hble Servants.   Fra. Lewis

William Ellery

RC (NhHi). Written by Ellery and signed by Ellery and Lewis.

[1] Evidence that Morris did indeed make a brief appearance in York during the following week is contained in the March 10 postscript to his January 12 letter to William Bingham stating that he was "just setting out for York," and in a March 13 letter to Jonathan Hudson from the committee's secretary, John Brown, reporting that "Mr. Morris is now here." Brown's letter to Hudson is in the American Revolution Manuscripts at PYHi. For Morris' contributions to the contract negotiations, see Robert Morris' Proposed Report on the Claims of Roderique Hortalez & Co., March 12, 1778.

Committee on the Claims of Roderique Hortalez & Co. Report

[ante March 5 1778][1]

The Committee to whom were referred Sundry Letters received by the Commercial Committee relative to the Claims of Messrs. Rodrique Hortalez & C. of Paris Report—That Considerable quantities of Cannon, Arms, Amunition, Cloathing & other Stores, shipped by the House of Roderique Hortalez & Co. in different ships & Vessells from France & the West Indies, for the use & account of these United States, That the greatest part of these articles have been delivered to the agents of these States, and it is the opinion of this Committee that the Said States are justly charged for the whole Amount thereof.[2]

Resolved, That the Commercial Committee be authorized & empowered to receive from the Agent or Attorney of Said Roderique Hortalez & Co. the Invoices & other Documents Relative to these transactions, in order to ascertain the Amount of their debt, & make report to Congress from time to time of their proceedings for Confirmation.

Resolved, That the Commercial Committee be authorised & empowered to pay to the said Agent or Attorney, Such Sums of Continental Money as he may from time to time require, fixing the rate of Exchange on every such payment, at the Current or Equitable course of Exchange at the date thereof.

Resolved, That the Said Committee be authorized & empowered to ship such Cargoes of American produce as they may find convenient & proper, from time to time, for France, for the purpose of discharging this debt, consigning such Cargoes to the House of the said Roderique Hortalez & Co. and Whereas it appears to your Committee from the several Letters laid before them, that the Said Roderique Hortalez & Co. are inclined to enter into a Contract with the United States of America for a future Supply of all such Cannon, Arms, Ammunition, Cloathing, & other Stores, together with Specie which they may from time to time order, the Conditions on which such Contract is proposed to be entered into, is herewith presented for the consideration of this Honorable House, and if approved,

Resolved, That the Commercial Committee be authorized & empowered to Contract with Mr. Francy, Agent or Attorney to the said Roderique Hortalez & Co. for the payment of all such supplies as have been already shipped or shall be hereafter shipped agreeable to the orders of said Committee & to the terms of the Contract.

MS (ScHi). In the hand of Henry Laurens.

[1] This date has been assigned because it seems likely that this was the report on the claims of Roderique Hortalez & Co., the appellation adopted to cloak the

commercial operations of Caron de Beaumarchais, that was read in Congress on
March 5. See *JCC*, 10: 185, 192, 225.

[2] The attending delegates' unfamiliarity with the history of "this mysterious commerce" with Beaumarchais explains their reluctance to approve such an unqualified
acknowledgment that the United States "are justly charged for the whole Amount"
claimed before they had had an opportunity to hear from their more knowledge-
able colleague Robert Morris, who was at this time at his home at Manheim.
Consequently Congress postponed consideration of this report and Morris was
urged to come to York to assist in evaluating the claims. See Committee of Commerce to Robert Morris, March 5; John Penn to Robert Morris, March 6; and
Robert Morris' Proposed Report on the Claims of Roderique Hortalez & Co.,
March 12, 1778.

For background on Beaumarchais' commercial transactions and his claims against
the United States, see Wharton, *Diplomatic Correspondence*, 1:369–86. See also
Committee of Secret Correspondence to Silas Deane, October 1, 1776, note 3.

William Duer to Robert Morris

My dear Friend   Reading March 5th 1778
. . . .[1] I should imagine my dear Friend, you can be no Stranger to
the present critical Situation of our Army, and the late Embarassment
which the Ignorance and Faction of a thin C——ss have thrown in
the Way of forming Magazines for the Army. The Consequences will
in my Opinion, occasion its Dissolution very Shortly unless both they,
and the State of Penna. cease to interfere with the Military Departments. This Circumstance, the Necessity of attending to our Finances,
in order to supply the Exegencies of the next Campaign, and the
means for bringing a force into the Field, and introducing in it,
Discipline, and a Spirit of Enterprise call for the immediate Attention
of every Lover of his Country, and particular[l]y of you who (without
Flattery which I abhor) possess Talents to serve it at this Juncture,
and whose Connection, with a State which is likely to be made a
sacrifice of, demand in a peculiar degree all your Exertions. Let me
my dear Sir conjure you to attend Congress on the Return of the
Committee from Camp. I am sensible private Convenience cannot
operate upon your mind at this Crisis, provided you have a Prospect
of being useful. Mr. Lee writes me from Congress that several members are daily Expected.[2] Mr. Hancock will be there in a few days,[3]
and if my Presence can induce you, I will after I have secured my
Baggage at Coryell's Ferry (for w'h I set out this day) return and stay
one month. Perhaps my dear Friend, the Joint Exertions of some [of]
us may save our Country, and revive the Expiring Reputation of
Congress, at least it is our Duty to try it.

I write in a great hurry, and in much anxiety of mind: which must
plead my excuse for Incorrectness. Let me know by a letter to Reading
whether you will attend Congress; if you do I will immediately pro-

ceed to Manheim on my Return from Coryell's[4] and go with you. Write to Colo. Jos Reid to attend I am sure that his and your Presence will give a Right Turn to the Votes of Pensilvania and Delawar without which the endeavors of the other States will be useless. God bless you and your Family to whom I beg to be particularly remembered.   Wm. Duer

[*P.S.*] This Letter will be delivered to you by Dr. Stringer of Albany an Acquaintance of mine whom I take the Liberty of recommending to your attention.   W.D.

Tr (DLC). Copied for Edmund C. Burnett from the original manuscript then in the hands of Stan V. Henkels.

[1] Ellipsis in Tr. According to a notation by the copyist on the Tr, the omitted section of the letter dealt with Duer's "excuse for delaying at Reading."

[2] Francis Lightfoot Lee's letter to Duer has not been found.

[3] John Hancock did not return to Congress until June 19. See *JCC*, 11:621.

[4] "Congress" in Tr. This is obviously a scribal error because, as Burnett cogently argued, "it seems quite clear that Duer is proposing to return from Coryell's Ferry by way of Manheim and go to Congress with Morris." Burnett, *Letters*, 3:108n.3. A 19th-century extract of this letter, taken from the original manuscript, also reads "Coryell's" instead of "Congress." See William B. Reed, *Life and Correspondence of Joseph Reed*, 2 vols. Philadelphia: Lindsay & Blackiston, 1847), 1:365n. It should be noted that in this work Reed gives March 6, 1778, as the date of Duer's letter.

Henry Laurens to Francis Dana

Sir,   5th March 1778

I beg leave to refer to a Letter of the 3d Inst. by the present & Messenger who was that day repulsed by Susquehana & is now going to make a second attempt.

Shall I request the favor of you to present the Inclosed Act of Congress to the Quarter Master General & the two Assistant Quarter Masters general respectively & to excuse me to those Gentlemen for this mode of Address—which the present moment has obliged me to adopt. The Act was done on the 2d but these duplicates have been detained from me until this Instant.[1]

Yesterday Congress received a piteous narrative of the article of Tents in a Letter from Colo. Butler to the Board of War dated 26th Febry. I wished to have sent you a full Copy but time will not permit, therefore shall extract & inclose one or two Paragraphs & Copy of a Calculation of the Number of Tents expected to be ready the 20th April.[2] This being laid before General Green will give him a proper momentum & that Gentleman may expect in a day or two extended Resolves on this Subject.

Congress have Resolved to authorize General Washington to raise a Body of 400 Indians & by this hand I transmit their Act for that purpose.[3]

I have the honour to be &ca.

LB (DNA: PCC, item 13).
  [1] See *JCC*, 10:210.
  [2] These enclosures have not been found.
  [3] See *JCC*, 10:220–21; and Committee at Camp to Laurens, February 20 and March 2, 1778.

Henry Laurens to George Washington

Sir,   5th March 1778.

The present Messenger will deliver to your Excellency with this, a Letter which I had the honour of writing the 1st Inst. & which has been detained by Susquehana.

Inclosed herewith Your Excellency will be pleased to receive the following Acts of Congress.

1. 2d March for appointing a Quarter Master General & two Assistant Quarter Masters general & for other purposes in that department.

2d. 2d & 3d March Containing divers Resolves relative to Lieutt. General Burgoyne & the embarkation for Europe of himself, family & Servants.

3d. 4th March Empowering your Excellency to employ in the Service of the United States a Body of not exceeding 400 Indians.

I have the honour to be with the highest Esteem.

LB (DNA: PCC, item 13).

Committee at Camp to George Washington

Sir   Moor Hall 6th March 1778.

Upon considering the Matter referred to the Committee by your Letter of this Morning, We are of Opinion that a very able Officer should have the Command on Hudson's River. And if Either Putnam or Heath must be sent to Rhode Island we should prefer the former.[1] A new arrangement may be made by Congress before the opening of the Campaign especially if Genl. Gates should (as we suppose he will) incline to take the Field. The Committee Sir sensible that you are best acquainted both with the Characters of Men and the Exigencies of the Service beg you will make such Disposition as on the whole shall appear most eligible.

We are Sir, your most obedient & humble Servants,

                                        Fra Dana by Order

RC (DLC). Written by Gouverneur Morris and signed by Francis Dana.

[1] Washington had asked the committee's opinion on whether Israel Putnam, who was currently under investigation for his performance as commander of the American forces in the New York highlands, or William Heath, the commander in Boston, would be acceptable to Congress as the new army commander in Rhode Island to replace the recently resigned Joseph Spencer. The committee's reluctance to endorse either Heath or Putnam probably contributed to Washington's March 10 appointment of John Sullivan to the Rhode Island command. Washington, *Writings* (Fitzpatrick), 11:31, 57–58.

Committee of Commerce to Francis Lewis, Jr.

Dear Frank[1]   York Town. 6 March 1778

The Commercial Committee having directed Wm. Smith Esquire of Baltimore, to purchase Flour &c for the public service,[2] he will call upon you for six Thousand Dollars which you will pay him taking duplicate receipts for the same, specifying his being accountable to the Commercial Committee of Congress. For the same I am, Dear Frank, Your's Affectionately,   Fra. Lewis

RC (PU). Written and signed by Francis Lewis.

[1] Lewis' elder son Francis was conducting his mercantile business from Baltimore at this time. In August 1778 he was appointed a signer of Continental bills of credit. *JCC*, 11:790. For another instance of the use Congress was making of the younger Lewis in Maryland see Marine Committee to James Nicholson, March 4, 1778, note 2.

[2] Although it can be readily documented that the Marine Committee made a request to William Smith to purchase flour and iron for the use of the navy, this letter is the only surviving indication that the Committee of Commerce had made a similar request. Smith may have been purchasing flour for both committees, but it is also possible that Lewis, who was a member of both committees, inadvertently substituted "Commercial Committee" for "Marine Committee" in this note to his son. See Marine Committee to William Smith, February 24, 1778.

John Henry to Thomas Johnson

Sir   York Town March 6th. 1778.

Col. Samuel Smith arrived here yesterday and acquainted me with the difficulty he met with in the recruiting Service, for the want of the continental Bounty. Upon his solicitation and the prospect of advancing the public Service, I have procured from Congress ten thousand Dollars to be transmitted to you, to be distributed in such proportion among the recruiting officers as you may judge most proper.[1] Col Smith has undertaken the carriage of this money, which I hope you will receive in a few Days. It is the earnest request of Congress that the Battalions from each state, should be filled up as early this spring as possible. Maryland I hope will not be backward. The draught of the Militia recommended by Congress I fear will meet with many obsticles in the Legislature. Should that measure fail, I am at a loss to discover what expedient can be fallen upon. The Expedition into Canada is suspended. Genl. Burgoyne and two of his officers upon his earnest request to Congress is permitted to embark for England. Enclosed you have a copy of the resolve upon which the ten Thousand dollars mentioned above was granted, by which you will see part of the money is to be applied towards paying the premium for taking up deserters.

I am Sir your very hble. Servt.   J Henry Junr.

RC (MdAA).
[1] See *JCC*, 10:225.

Henry Laurens to John Burgoyne

Sir.   York Town in Pennsylvania 6th March 1778

By the hand of Lieutenant Wilford on the 26th February I received the honor of Your Excellency's Letter of the 11th of that Month, No. 1 & upon the 2d Inst. of another Letter from Your Excellency of the former date No. 2. These in due course I presented to Congress & I have received in charge to transmit to Your Excellency the three Acts undermentioned, which will be found within the present Cover.[1]

1. An Act of the 2d March confirming the Act of January 8th for suspending the embarkation of the Troops in the Convention of Saratoga.

2. An Act of the 3d March enabling Lieutt. Wilford to transmit certain papers to General Howe.

3. An Act of the same date for granting Passports for Your Excellency with the Officers of Your Excellency's family & Servants to embark to Great Britain & for other purposes therein Resolved.

To these several Acts Sir, I beg leave particularly to refer, as containing all that Congress have judged necessary for me to return to Your Excellency's Letters above recited.

I have the honour to be, with all proper Consideration, Sir, Your Excellency's Obedient & Most humble servant,   H. Laurens

Tr (MHi). Written and signed by Laurens. This is the duplicate letter that Laurens enclosed in his letter of this date to Gen. William Heath, the commanding officer in Boston who was responsible for the supervision of Burgoyne and his army.

[1] For further information about these "three Acts," see Laurens to Richard Wilford, March 1, 1778, note.

Henry Laurens to Nicholas Cooke

Sir.   York Town, 6th March 1778.

On the 19th Ulto. I had the honor of directing a Packet to Your Excellency which contained several Copies of Acts of Congress of the 5th & 6th of that Month for establishing divers regulations in Military & Civil Lines in the Army.[1]

You will receive Sir under the present Cover two Acts dated the 26th.

1. for filling the Continental Battalions, to which is added a Report from the Board of War shewing the numbers wanted to complete.

2. for establishing the Amount due for necessaries supplied British Prisoners from the commencement of the present War.[2]

I am with very great Respect, Sir, Your Excellency's Most humble servant,   Henry Laurens, President of Congress

P.S. 7 March. Your Excellency will also find inclosed an Act of this date recommending that Wednesday 22d April be observed as a day of General fasting &ca.[3]

RC (R–Ar).

[1] See Laurens to George Clinton, February 19, 1778, note 4.

[2] This day Laurens also enclosed copies of this resolve with brief letters that he wrote to the directors general of hospitals in the eastern and northern military departments. PCC, item 13, fol. 213.

[3] Laurens wrote substantially the same letter on March 6 to the Massachusetts Council, Gov. Jonathan Trumbull of Connecticut, and President Meshech Weare of New Hampshire; on March 7 to Gov. George Clinton of New York; and on March 9 to Govs. John Rutledge of South Carolina and John Houstoun of Georgia. See ibid., fols. 210, 212, 215, 218; Revolutionary Letters, M–Ar; and Meshech Weare Papers, Nh–Ar. On March 7 and 9 he also transmitted copies of the March 7 resolve on a general fast to President Thomas Wharton of Pennsylvania and Govs. Thomas Johnson of Maryland, Patrick Henry of Virginia, and Richard Caswell of North Carolina. See PCC, item 13, fols. 212, 216–17.

Henry Laurens to William Heath

Sir,   York Town Pennsylvania. 6th March 1778.

The last I had the honour of writing to you was dated the 20th Ulto. & forwarded by the hand of Messenger Ross, since which I have been favoured with yours of the 7th & 14th of that Month[1] which were duly presented to Congress, but I have received nothing in Command for you, except what appears in the Inclosed Acts of the 2d & 3d Inst. containing divers Resolves respecting Lieutt. General Burgoyne, his Officers & Troops—to which I beg leave particularly to refer, as I also do to a duplicate of a Letter which I have written of this date to that Gentleman which will likewise be found inclosed herein.[2]

I have this Instant jogged the Treasury again & received for answer—"Money for General Heath will be sent on Monday or Tuesday next."

Nothing is said by Congress in their present Acts respecting General Burgoyne's Accounts, my private sentiment is, that the former Orders exist & are not superseded by anything Inclosed, however I shall have a further opportunity of speaking to this point to Morrow if Congress will enable me.[3]

I have the honour to be, With great regard & esteem, Sir, Your obedient & most humble servant,

Henry Laurens, President of Congress.

RC (MHi).
   [1] General Heath's February 7 and 11 letters to Laurens, which were read in Congress on February 25, are in PCC, item 70, fols. 145–48, 215; Laurens erred in giving February 14 as the date of the latter.
   [2] See Laurens to John Burgoyne, this date.
   [3] See also Laurens to Heath, March 14, 1778.

Henry Laurens to the Marquis de Lafayette

Sir   York Town. 6th March 1778.

I feel myself very happy Dear General upon reflecting that the Letter which I had the honour of writing yesterday has nearly anticipated the necessary answers to your Excellency's favor of the 23d Febry which I am honoured with this afternoon[1]—had not Major Brice been detained by the Board of War my said Letter would have been one day's Journey advanced.

Were I to attempt an intimation of the public opinion of Your Excellency, the whole would end in repetition of what is contained in my last.[2] I may nevertheless add by way of anecdote the remark of a Sensible candid Man, when he had heard your Letter of the 20th Febry read. "I," said he, "was averse to this Irruption into Canada not because I thought badly of the scheme but because I feared the Marquis being a Young Man full of Fire would have impetuously rushed our Soldiers into too much danger—but his present conduct convinces me he is wise & discreet as well as brave, I now esteem him a worthy valuable Officer." Once more, be assured you have gained great reputation in this Country & that there is not the Smallest ground for your apprehensions of the contrary.

I know not how to account for the Ideas of those who planned & announced the intended Expedition, it is probable if they are ever called upon they will be at as great a loss in that respect as I am, a

Subject this, which I wish not to dwell upon. With regard to you Sir, it is clearly evident, that the part which Your Excellency has acted will be known throughout America & spoken of with applause. I dare not predict the Sentiments of Congress respecting a seperate Command, however, I am persuaded every Individual holds you equal to the trust. If you are pleased to propose an eligible plan I may say with confidence it will receive a respectful consideration & tis my private sentiment there will be little hesitation upon availing the public of your Excellency's offers of service.

I submit to you Sir, in such Case, the propriety of corresponding directly with General Washington & procuring his opinion to be transmitted to Congress & also with General Gates as an Officer & a patriot not as part of the Board of War.

I am sensible of the distress the Northern department has been in from a want of Money, of late there have been large remittances & such further sum will immediately follow as the Treasury Board assure me will afford complete relief. If we all followed your Excellency's example & attended business at all hours until it was finished our affairs would be in much better plight than they are.

I do not know who promised Monsr. Failly a Colonel's Commission, I know Congress refused him one, altho' he applied under the strongest recommendation from General Gates. I cannot, even with Mr. Brice's aid, decipher the name coupled with that of Monsr. "Failly."[3]

If it shall be determined that your Excellency shall remain in the Northern department it will become necessary in a proper part of some one of Your Letters to Congress to require Blank Commissions.

When a proper opening invites, I shall with great pleasure intimate Your Excellency's attention to the Interests of these States demonstrated in pledging your own in Support of the public Credit,[4] which I am persuaded will be gratefully received & acknowledged.

I have ordered 6000 Dollars of my own funds to be packeted & delivered to Major Brice for which I have taken his Rect. to deliver the same to your Excellency.

I shall put that Gentleman in the way to enquire the course of Exchange in Lancaster. If he finds it at 400 per Cent or upwards Bills for about the value of One Hundred Louis d'or each set may be transmitted & made payable to me. I will endorse them to the purchasers—there ought to be at least five Bills to a set.

Major Brice will inform Your Excellency how closely I am confined to this Table at all intervals from personal attendance in Congress & plead an excuse for all my errors & omissions.

I am just closing dispatches for Leiut General Burgoyne who having found a pen capable of writing Congress properly has obtained leave to embark himself & family for Great Britain. I will in a few days transmit to your Excellency the particulars of this negotiation. At present I am obliged to conclude, which permit me to do by repeating that I am with the most Sincere & respectful regard & attachment, Sir, Your Excy's obliged & Obt. Servt.

P.S. I have this moment a hint given me that the Board of War mean to recommend the recall of your Excellency & General deKalb to join General Washington & that General Conway will remain where he is—do not Dear Marquis suffer this to discompose you.[5]

I shall expect—I was going to say—that Congress will well weigh this point—but that Inst. General Gates came in, I put the question to him, he says it is intended to make it agreeable to your Excellency because there is no Command yonder worthy of you.

LB (ScHi).
[1] This letter is in Lafayette, *Papers* (Idzerda), 1:318–20.
[2] See Laurens to Lafayette, March 4, 1778.
[3] Gen. Horatio Gates, the president of the Board of War, had advised Congress to grant a colonel's commission to Philippe-Louis, chevalier de Failly, and a captain's commission to René-Jean Guillaume Luce—the officer whose name Laurens could not read—but Congress had refused to do so on February 5. Despite this setback, however, Failly and Luce had gone on to join Lafayette's Canadian expedition and to insist that they had indeed "been promised" these commissions. See *JCC*, 10:123; and Lafayette, *Papers* (Idzerda), 1:317. Gates' letter of recommendation to Congress, which is undated but was clearly written in February 1778, is in the Laurens Papers, ScHi.
[4] See Lafayette, *Papers* (Idzerda), 1:319.
[5] On March 13 Congress authorized Washington to recall Lafayette and Baron de Kalb to his army, and ten days later it ordered Gen. Thomas Conway to report to Peekskill, N.Y., to serve under Gen. Alexander McDougall. *JCC*, 10:253–54, 280. Lafayette feared that if he and Kalb rejoined Washington while Conway remained in Albany, Conway would assume command at Albany under the immediate authority of Gen. Horatio Gates, who was still commander of the northern department. As a firm supporter of Washington, Lafayette naturally viewed this prospect with alarm because Conway and Gates were reputed to be bitter rivals of the commander in chief. See Lafayette, *Papers* (Idzerda), 1:318–19; and Laurens' second March 24, 1778, letter to Lafayette, note 2.

Marine Committee to Unknown

Gentn   Marine Committee, York March 6th 1778
The Honorable the Board of War having Occasion for the under mentioned Stores, You are hereby directed to deliver to their order the whole, or such part of Said Stores as you may have under your care belonging to the Public. We are Gentn. Your humble servts,

Fra. Lewis	Abra. Clark
William Ellery	James Forbes

10 Barrels Pitch	1000 wt. of Oakum
10 Barrels Tar	1 Barrel of Rozin
5 Barrels Turpentine	20 lb of Thrums for mops

RC (MeHi). In the hand of John Brown and signed by Clark, Ellery, Forbes, and Lewis.

John Penn to Robert Morris

Dear Sir   York Friday morning [March 6, 1778]
   Doctor Richman[1] & myself never got to this place untill yesterday about two oclock, we crossed at the Falls, you may easily guess how disagreeable our situation was, when we reflected that we had left Manheim & were breathing in a little cold Tavern, however fasting after feasting may be necessary, tho' we should have had enough of the former at this place.
   Mr. Francy's business was taken up last evening.[2] The Committee reported that all the Consignments should be made to Hortales & Co. and a Contract made with their House for large supplies in future. As I thought we were not very good merchants, I proposed that the affair should be postponed untill Monday, in order that you might be requested to attend that day by the Commercial Committee and that all who wished to have you would make it a point to agree to the postponing, it was accordingly agreed to unanimously. It was proposed afterwards that by particular direction you should be sent for, this was refused as not parliamentary, tho' almost every man would be glad to have you here. I hope my dear Sir you will excuse my being the means of giving you the trouble of coming to York as I really think it of great Importance to America to have a Gentn. of your abilities present when a Subject of such Magnitude is on the Carpet. If you come get here on Sunday evening as Mr. Francy is uneasy at being detained. We will not keep you more than two days. Master Robt. is well, Mr. Richman's boy will come to day, & shall immediately carry him his Mama's present. With great respect I remain, Dear Sir, Your obt. Servt.   J Penn

RC (PHi). Endorsed by Morris: "York Friday 6 March 1777 [i.e. 1778] Jno. Penn Esqr."
   [1] On March 7 Congress acquitted Dr. William Rickman of charges of negligence in connection with the inoculation of some Virginia and North Carolina troops and restored him to the office of director of the hospital at Alexandria, Va., from which he had been suspended by Congress on December 20, 1777. See JCC, 9:1039, 10:230–31.
   [2] See Committee on the Claims of Roderique Hortalez & Co. Report, March 5; and Robert Morris' Proposed Report on the Claims of Roderique Hortalez & Co., March 12, 1778.

Cornelius Harnett to William Wilkinson

Dear Sir   York Town March 7 1778

I wrote you the 3d by Post, since which I have not been able to attend Congress, Owing to the very bad weather, I hope the next week I shall be able to do Duty as usual.

My Man Sawney has been run away ever since the 5 Feby. & I have not heard a word of him, I suppose he will if Possible get to Philadelphia. I wish Heron's Josh could come to me in Time but I fear he cannot, I can't meet with a Servant at any rate, I dont know but I shall be Obliged to endeavour to return home on horse back & leave Carriage and all behind me. It is impossible to describe to you the Vilany of my fellow—he has robbd Our Qr. Master of more than £100 worth of Goods &c. Capt. Doherty is just setting off. I shall write you more fully by next Post & am with true esteem, Dr Sir, Your affec & Obedient Servt,   Cornl. Harnett

[*P.S.*] Compts to all friends.

RC (PHC).

Henry Laurens to Samuel Adams

Dear Sir   York Town 7th March 1778.

You may remember the anxiety which I expressed upon hearing of the Portuguese Vessel being carried into Boston as prize, neither you nor I knew then who were Owners of the Captor, I am sure I did not.

Congress two days ago received a Memorial on that affair from the Honorable Robt. Morris Esqr. which exhibits after much candid narration, a Prayer, "that Congress will cause a fair & public Sale to be made of the Vessel & her Cargo, that the charge & expense arising on the Sale be paid & the remainder or Net Proceed be invested in Loan Office Certificates bearing Interest for the Benefit of the true & Lawful proprietors of said Vessel & Cargo."[1]

The Ideas of the Memorialist are, that from this very partial restitution of original property—"The original Owners will obtain JUSTICE & REPARATION," in which from the prejudice of my Education I have the misfortune to differ extremely.

That "the Owners of the Phœnix will be relieved of all their difficulties." This sentiment precisely accords with my own, but unfortunately I cannot from any consideration unite with any set of Men in an attempt to dupe Congress into a participation of the Crimes or follies of those good Owners. Then closes the pious peroration— "thus, the National Fate & Credit of these Infant States will remain

Inviolate." Had this been intimated by any Man of less understanding & Virtue than the Memorialist I should have been prompted to pronounce it—"Matchless impudence & Ignorance." Now I suspend a sentence.

This Phœnix Memorial is however Committed to five & had preengaged strong Advocates.

The Memorialist altogether pleads ignorance of the orders given to seize Portugueze Vessels[2] & adds his renunciation of the Act sometime after the Vessel arrived at Boston. These might have made a different impression upon my mind, had it not been hardened by a retrospection to three or four antecedent circumstances & by the present definition of Private "Justice & Reparation" And of public "National Faith & Credit." I now perceive these calling aloud for a thorough Investigation of the Crime committed, & that it is necessary if the Laws are defective for punishing Pirates & the prompters of Pirates that we ought by doing complete Justice to the Injured Original Owners, & by affixing a Public Stigma upon the Offenders, display to the World that we entertain a just sense of, & that we are determined to keep Inviolate "the National Faith & Credit of these Infant States."

I have spoken these things freely Sir, in the confidence which you have heretofore been pleased to vest in me. This is a public matter & will be followed with great consequences, it is in the Power of the People & tis their Duty by wise determinations to draw them to contribute to, I should say to establish the Honour of the American Union, without regard to private considerations.

I am to request of you Sir if the Proceedings in Admiralty are not very prolix to obtain a Copy of & transmit them by the bearer hereof who is furnished with Money to pay the Office Fees & I shall flatter my self with hopes of your sentiments in addition.

Will you further oblige me Sir by directing the bearer where he can upon the best terms purchase for me a piece of Cambrick & a piece of Silk Hankerchiefs, I have given him a particular description of the articles wanted & Money to pay the Cost. Pardon me for this freedom & beleive me to remain with the most sincere Esteem & Regard, Dear sir, Your obliged & obedient servant,

Henry Laurens

[*P.S.*] I presume our friend Mr. J Adams is now far advanced towards Versailles.

RC (NN).
  [1] For further information about the case of the illegal seizure of the Portuguese snow *Our Lady of Mount Carmel and St. Anthony* by the American privateer *Phoenix*, see Robert Morris to John Rowe, October 27, 1777, note 2. Morris' undated memorial to Congress "on behalf of the owners of the Pheonix Privateer" was read in Congress on March 6 and referred to a special committee of which

Laurens was not a member. See PCC, item 44, fols. 49–50; and *JCC*, 10:227. Morris himself was one of the owners of the *Phoenix*.

[2] In his memorial to Congress Morris claimed that the captain of the *Phoenix* had been under orders to seize only such Portuguese vessels as he found preying upon American shipping. PCC, item 44, fol. 49.

Henry Laurens to Thomas Conway

Sir, 7th March 1778.

In due course I had the honour of receiving your favour of the 2d Ulto. For some days I suspended an answer because it was then doubtful whether you were on this side the Lakes. Now you are to be found, permit me to inform you Sir your Letters for France are still in this Room. Baron Holzendorff by whom I intend to forward them is unhappily detained here. To morrow or next Day he will commence his journey & will take the charge upon him. I have the honour to be &c.

LB (ScHi).

Henry Laurens to Benjamin Farrar

Sir,[1] 7th March 1778

Three days ago I was honoured with your favor of 11th Febry. by the hand of our worthy friend the Reverend Mr. Turquand whom I immediately warned of danger to which your families & effects might otherwise have been exposed on the Water & even at any landing place after having once embarked & proceeded down the Mississippi, directed him to the best means for guarding against such danger, & in a word I have according to your request given him the best advice & assistance in my power in all respects, which renders it unnecessary to add that I wish your whole party, beleiving them to be in Strict friendship with these United States of America, happiness & prosperity.

I am, Sir, Your obedient & most humble Servant.

LB (ScHi).

[1] Benjamin Farrar, a South Carolina physician and planter, had served either in the South Carolina Assembly or Provincial Congress from 1765 to 1776 and been a leading supporter of the South Carolinian Regulators. Farrar's father-in-law Tacitus Gaillard, also a former South Carolina assemblyman and provincial congressman, was thought to be a lukewarm patriot and therefore felt obliged at this time to leave South Carolina with his family and settle in West Florida. Although Farrar and his family also left South Carolina with the Gaillards, they did not remain with them for more than a few years because after the war Farrar is known

to have practiced medicine in South Carolina. See Walter B. Edgar and Louise Bailey, *Biographical Directory of the South Carolina House of Representatives* (Columbia: University of South Carolina Press, 1977), 2:240–41, 265–67.

Henry Laurens to William Heath

Sir.   York Town 7th March 1778.

I beg leave to refer you to the inclosed duplicate of what I had the honour of writing to you yesterday by Mr. Peck to which I add a Copy of General Burgoyne's.

You will receive inclosed an Act of Congress of this date for restricting the granting furloughs in the Army.[1]

I have pressed the Treasury to embrace the present opportunity by Frederick Weare an honest careful Man & of good responsibility to transmit for your department 50 or 100 Thousand Dollars in part of the whole Sum intended & I hope the recommendation will meet success. A like Sum to be forwarded by Mr. Dodd who is to follow some day in next Week will assist you for the present moment, & more ample supplies will be sent by other conveyances.

I have the honour to be, With great Regard & Esteem, Sir, Your obedient & most humble servant,

Henry Laurens, President of Congress.

[*P.S.*] I just now learn that twenty Thousand Dollars will be delivered indeed are delivered to the bearer Fred Weare.

RC (MHi).

[1] Congress gave greater authority over the issuance of furloughs to "the Commander in Chief, or commander of a department" in response to a recent Committee at Camp report on abuses by regimental colonels, whose authority to issue furloughs was thereby restricted. See Committee at Camp to Laurens, March 3, 1778, which was read in Congress on the sixth; and *JCC*, 10:227, 230.

Henry Laurens to the Marquis de Lafayette

Sir,   7th March 1778.

Major Brice left me yesterday & carried with him Six Thousand Dollars on Account of your Excellency & two Letters which in obedience to your Excellency's command I had the honor of writing under the 4th & 6th Inst.

I spoke again this morning to General Gates on the subject of recalling Your Excellency to General Washington's Army & although we differed in opinion I really beleive he means well. However when the recommendation came before Congress, I could not consistently with honour & Love to my Country, forbear intreating Congress to hear my Sentiments. I marked out the good your Excellency was performing in the Northern department & the effect which an Order of recall *from the Board of War,* might have. The House agreed to postpone the Consideration of that Report & nothing will be done until we hear from Your Excellency.[1]

When Your Excellency writes to Congress You will certainly take no notice of the above. You may ask us how you are to be disposed of & so forth, in which Your Excellency needs no hint or information from me. Permit me to intreat you Sir, if you speak of or refer to the Letter of the 20th Febry, avoid disclosing that kind of resentment which may bring on disagreeable altercation.[2] I dread the consequences of keeping up the flame of party by disputes among ourselves & so far as I feel myself affected or affronted I am willing to make a sacrifice to peace by passing quietly over the bagatelle. If there was any design in the forestalling that Letter, Major Brice has said enough to inflict ample punishment upon the offender. The dread of being detected & brought to light will be no small degree of punishment.

The stream of Tallow Candle which just now fell on the paper will show your Excellency that I am writing when many other people are fast a sleep or otherwise amusing themselves in Bed & upon my honor I have not time to Copy again. I know Your Excellency's goodness will accept of a sincere inclination to wait on you, in atonement for these imperfections.

Your Excellency desired to have News Papers. I may have some to send by the next Messenger, some five or six days hence, at present I am without any. I do not account the inclosed York Print to be a news paper.

By this conveyance I transmit to Govr. Clinton an Act of Congress for the Commanding Officer in the Northern department, relative to obstructing the passes in Hudson's River &c.[3] I know not to whom it will be delivered, the direction is general & tis late Saturday Night when no explanation from Congress can be had.

Adieu, Dear General, permit me the honour again of subscribing, yours &ca.

[*P.S.*] The Gentleman[4] who was to have met or gone volunteer with your Excellency I am informed is yet within 40 miles of York & I am afraid his Spirit is transfused by every opportunity & that it is always more or less at work here.

LB (ScHi).

[1] See Laurens to Lafayette, March 6, 1778, note 5.

[2] In his February 20 letter to President Laurens, Lafayette had sharply criticized the Board of War's planning of the abortive Canadian expedition. Lafayette, *Papers* (Idzerda), 1:305–8.

[3] See *JCC*, 10:221–22. This day Laurens also transmitted copies of the March 4 resolves on the defense of the Hudson and a March 7 resolve on restricting furloughs with a brief covering letter addressed to the "Commanding Officer of the Army in the Northern department," which was received by Lafayette in that capacity before he left Albany to rejoin Washington's army. See PCC, item 13, fol. 213; and Lafayette, *Papers* (Idzerda), 1:362.

[4] William Duer.

Henry Laurens to Israel Putnam

Sir,   7th March 1778.
I had the honour of receiving & Reporting to Congress on the 26th, your favour of the 10th of that Month,[1] this was immediately committed to the Board of War & I have received no other Commands from Congress save the Inclosed Act of the present date for restricting the granting furloghs in the Army.

The Treasury have already Sent pretty large Sums for supplying the Military Chests in the Northern Armies. These I am assured will soon be followed by farther Sums & that such measures are now in motion as will discharge arrears in every quarter. I trust there will be no failure on the part of that Board. Next Week Congress mean to take under their Consideration the State of our public funds when probably the establishing a Loan Office near your Army agreeable to your proposition will be taken into view. I have the honour to be &ca.

LB (DNA: PCC, item 13). Addressed: "Major General Putnam, Hudsons River."
[1] General Putnam's February 10 letter to Laurens, in which he described his efforts to fortify the Hudson and suggested the establishment of a Continental loan office at Poughkeepsie for him to draw upon whenever he needed money, is in PCC, item 159, fols. 121–28. Putnam's letter, according to the journals, was read in Congress on February 27. *JCC*, 10:204. Putnam also noted the need for such a loan office in a February 13 letter to Washington, an extract of which the general forwarded to Congress where it was read on March 5. See *JCC*, 10:225.

Francis Lewis to the New York Convention

Sir,   York Town 7th March 1778
I had the honor to write you the 25th Ultimo to wch. beg leave to refer you.[1]

As my worthy Collegue Mr Duer, is long ere this arrived with you, he will minutely inform you with every material circumstance relative to the publick transactions here, to the time of his departure, since which nothing of considerable notority has happened.

Your letter of the 11th Janry. with accounts & Vouchers for the expenditure of monies &c in supporting the Prisoners of War, I immediately laid before Congress, who ordered them to the Auditors Office, but such is the present low State of the Treasury, and the large demands thereon, from the Quar. Masr. General's & the Commissary of provisions departments that the payment of those Accounts must be for sometime postponed;[2] It may be necessary to inform you that Congress has lately passed a Resolve, that all the States from New Hampshire to Virginia exhibit their accounts relative to prisoners of War on or before the 15th day of April next, on failure, to be excluded, from payment,[3] this Resolution has been sent out to the several Governors by Express; The two last articles charged in your Account, has the appearance of Abitary enties and may require an explanation, this I hint at for your government, when you furnish an account of such articles as were omitted in the former.

The Northern Expedition under the Marquis de Fiette, is by Congress deemed impracticable, therefore set aside.

By a private letter received yesterday from Mr. Clement Biddle a Commissary, we are informed, that Genl. [Wayne] who went over to the Jerseys with a party in order to distroy the forage engaged a party of the British light Infantry whom he totaly routed, and the major part of them were killed or taken prisoners.

I herewith send you a pamphlet,[4] reprinted at Lancaster, together with this days Pensylvania Gazette for your perusal having nothing more material to add but that I am still the only member here representing our State.

I have the honor to be with great respect, Your most Obedient & Humble Servant, Fra Lewis

RC (NN). Addressed: "Honble. Pierre Van Cortlandt Esquire."

[1] Not found.

[2] In his January 11 letter to the New York delegates, Pierre Van Cortlandt, the president of the New York Convention, reported that pursuant to an August 15, 1777, resolve of Congress which did not reach the convention until November, he was enclosing accounts of the money New York had expended on prisoners of war. *Journals of N.Y. Prov. Cong.*, 1:1114. The accounts themselves have not been found. Lewis presented them to Congress on February 18 and they were then referred to the Board of Treasury, but this is the last mention of them in the journals for 1778. *JCC*, 10:179.

[3] This resolve was passed on February 26. *JCC*, 10:198.

[4] See John Henry to Thomas Johnson, February 17, 1778, note 2.

Jonathan Bayard Smith to Thomas Wharton

Sir York Town March 7 1778

The delegates had the favor of your Secretary's letter with copy from James Young Esq.[1] It is extremely painfull to hear & to make complaints on one side or other. We did not communicate the contents to Congress, 'till yesterday, when we felt ourselves called upon, by the conversation of Gentlemen on the floor among themselves. I find this morning that they have the Counterpart, & that proper & full information was said to have been given to the waggon masters. I hope your Excellency received the papers I had in charge to transmit to you, & which went by Genl. Wilkinson.

Our army is now arriving at an important period. The Campaign will probably open soon. Much depends on its being well reinforced. I hope this state will not fail to exert its utmost influence.

I am, Sir, with very great respect, your Excellencys most humble servant,

Jona. B. Smith

RC (PHi).

[1] Pennsylvania officials were embarrassed in their efforts to relieve the distress of Continental troops at Valley Forge when two brigades of Northampton County wagoners refused to obey orders and attempted to return home. The episode was dramatized by the fact that four men were drowned and several wagons and horses were lost in their attempt to recross the Schuylkill River, and Deputy Quartermaster Henry Lutterloh dispatched the brigades' leader, Michael Snyder, to Wagon Master General James Young for trial "to make an example of him to Deter others from the like attempt." For Young's correspondence with Pennsylvania Council Secretary Timothy Matlack on this subject, and several other documents related to the state's efforts to provide transportation for the Continental quartermaster and commissary services during this difficult period, see *Pa. Archives*, 1st ser. 6:276, 282–83, 289–90, 298–99, 319–21, 330, 337–39, 343, 348–49, 352–54. See also Jonathan Bayard Smith to James Young, March 11, 1778.

Committee at Camp Minutes of Proceedings

[March 8–12, 1778]

8. Sunday Conferred with the General & Major Generals & the Commissioners on the subject of the Cartel.[1]

Conferred with Colos. Levingston & Cortland of New-York & the Mass Colonels upon arrangemts.

9. General not present.

10. General not present.

11. At Head Quarters. Conferred upon the Cartel.

12. Wrote to Major Chase[2] about the Tents.[3]

MS (DLC). Conclusion of Committee at Camp Minutes of Proceedings, January 28–March 12, 1778. In the hand of Francis Dana.

[1] For further information on the problems surrounding the proposed prisoner cartel with the British, see Committee at Camp to Washington, February 11, note 1, and March 9? 1778; and Henry Laurens to Washington, March 15, 1778, note 1.

[2] See the committee's March 14 letter to Thomas Chase, deputy quartermaster general at Boston.

[3] For information on the return of the committee members to Congress following the conclusion of their work at camp, see Committee at Camp Minutes of Proceedings, January 28–31, 1778, note 1.

Joseph Reed to John Bayard

Dear Sir[1]   [March 8? 1778][2]

A close Attention to our Business & some Engagements abroad have hitherto prevented my answering your Favour of the 25 February. Nothing could give me more Pleasure (because I am sure it would redound to the Honour of the State & the common Interest) to have its Powers vigorously & effectually exerted in every Thing that respects the Supply & Accomodation of the Army. My Opinion was against its taking this Position, because I feared the Difficulties which have ensued. But the great Apprehensions & Anxieties of the People to which so great a Regard was shewn as to detain the Army on this Spot seem to me to have been improperly expressed, if the utmost Attention is not shewn to render their Situation supportable; comfortable it can never be. The Troops certainly have a Claim upon the Authority of this State & I know no Circumstances more likely to prove fatal to this Government than to press so earnestly for the Cantonment of the Army here & then to fail in its Attempts to furnish the necessary Supplies. The General & many others are very sensible that the Operations of the State have been enfeebled & frustrated by the Interference of Officers in various Departments who have made their military Power an Instrument of Offence against the State. They are therefore not only convinced of the Propriety but wish the Powers of the State to [be] fairly tried & if they shall be found in all ordinary Cases equal to the Demands I believe the most effectual Measures will ever be taken to repress either the malevolent or ambitious Procedures of any of its Enemies so far as they are attempted under the Colour of military Authority. The Presidt. very properly transmitted to the General a Copy of Mr. Young's letter on the Transaction mentioned in your Letter. We do not at present hear of any Scarcity of Provisions in Camp, but we only live as the vulgar say from Hand to Mouth. The Affair of the Waggons mentioned in my last was much exaggerated. The Desire some Persons have to avail themselves of every Circumstance unfavourable to the State led them to speak much larger than the Truth would admit. There were but a few Horses & only one or two Men drowned by their Rashness & Folly. We now have a Body of Continental Troops posted from Barron Hill as far as your Place which keeps that Country in some State of Security & has very much broke the Intercourse which notwithstanding the Risque of Horses & corporal Punishment the vile & disafected still persisted in. The Fellow apprehended on Justice Knox's Account was executed at Bartholemew's Tavern & left hanging as an Example to other Offenders of the same kind—he acknowledged the Justice of his Sentence & hoped his Fate would be a Warning to others. I was very apprehensive he would have escaped from the Lenity of our Officers but the Committee remonstrated to [*them*] so strongly upon the Subject that I believe he was executed by the General's special Authority. Two men of the same Gang will soon share the same Fate as also a Person apprehended for purchasing Horses for the British Army.

The Success of the Party at Newtown in Bucks was very Alarming & occasioned a very general Inquiry where Lacy was; as we do not know precisely his Strength & Situation in other Respects we ought not to censure what perhaps on a Knowledge of all Circumstances we should approve. But I think one Thing is clear that the publick desire no Benefit from his Command & therefore I hope it is not attended with any Expence. Pray what do you design to do with the Galley Men. They are very burthensome where they are, & from all Accounts there is very little Prospect of getting any Service from them. And at all Events they ought not to be a State Charge any more than the Defence of Hudsons River, our Circumstances now rendering them of little other Value than to preserve the Communication of the Delaware; in every other Point of View they are now of more Consequence to New Jersey than Pennsylvania. From Gen. Howes State of the Defence of the River they did very little Damage to the British Shipping.

The Congress have now passed a Resolve comprehending fully the Case of these Kidnappers.[3]

The Commissioners for Exchange were to have met the 10th Instt. but some Circumstances have happened which I believe will postpone it. I saw the Generals Letter making handsome Mention of your Son,[4] but no Notice was taken of him in the Answer or in any Letter since.

We have engaged Col. Cox in the publick Service upon Terms that we think liberal to both but from the long Delay of the Answer from Congress I very much fear it does not go on smoothly there. We shall I believe return to York Town next Week at least some of the Gentlemen, it being necessary that one should stay to receive the return Expresses & forward the Dispatches. This I suppose will fall to my Share. However I mean to go up to Congress as soon as possible tho the Circumstances of my Family will not admit of my staying long. I have been lucky in getting a very good House at Fleming Town New Jersey about 40 Miles from this, & 27 from Trenton 12 Miles from the Delaware in a pleasant healthy Country. Mr. Cox & Mr. Pettit will be in the Neighbourhood & I have Reason to think you might also be accomodated if you are not fully resolved upon Bohemia. If you relish it let me know & I will write up to my Friend in that Country.

Pray make my Complimts. to the Gentlemen of my Acquaintance with you & believe Me with real Regard, D Sir, Your Affect. Friend & Hbble Servt.

Jos. Reed

March 9th. 1778

Since writing the above we have had a new Arrangement of the Qr. Masters Departmt. Genl. Green is appointed Qr. Mr. Genl., Col. Cox first Assistt. & Charles Pettit second.[5] The latter has been brought in contrary to my Inclination, but there was no getting Cox without him. He would not engage his Character & Fortune without some suitable Character in whom he could confide to manage the Books & Accounts. I hope & believe this Choice will be acceptable to New Jersey & this State where the Operations are most likely to be.

RC (DNA: PCC, item 31).

[1] John Bayard, who had been elected speaker of the Pennsylvania Assembly on February 20, 1778. An old friend of Reed's and a fellow militia officer, Bayard had made a visit to Valley Forge in December as a member of the Pennsylvania Council and met with the Committee at Camp on February 16. *DAB*; and Committee at Camp Minutes of Proceedings, February 16–20, 1778. Although the letter's recipient is not identified on the manuscript, the reference in paragraph four to "your Son" is to Bayard's son James, who had been taken prisoner by the British.

[2] In addition to the fact that Reed added a postscript to the letter on March 9, this date has been selected because the "Circumstances" that Reed believed would entail postponement of the prisoner exchange conference mentioned in paragraph four below had come to General Washington's attention on March 7. See Washington, *Writings* (Fitzpatrick), 11:38.

[3] This resolve was adopted on February 27. *JCC*, 10:204–5.

[4] For Washington's January 20 letter to William Howe, see Washington, *Writings* (Fitzpatrick), 10:323–24. That Reed's relationship with Washington was an intimate one during this period is also suggested by the fact that the draft of the general's March 7, 1778, letter to Thomas Warton is in Reed's hand. Washington Papers, DLC; and ibid., 11:45–48.

[5] Reed's personal relationship with many of the persons consulted on army "arrangements" during the period that he was with the committee at camp is of more than incidental interest. Reed, John Cox, and John Bayard had been the second, third, and fourth ranking officers respectively of Daniel Roberdeau's Second Battalion of Philadelphia militia, and Charles Pettit was Reed's brother-in-law. John Roche, *Joseph Reed, A Moderate in the American Revolution* (New York: Columbia University Press, 1957), pp. 5, 32, 60.

Committee at Camp to George Washington

Sir   [March 9? 1778][1]

The Committee at Moor Hall have employed such Time as they could spare from many Interruptions this Morning in a Conference upon the very important Subject of the Cartel now about to be established. And altho they may not be (and probably are not) so well acquainted with some Facts as other Gentlemen, and having perhaps different Feelings upon the Subject may view the same object in a different Point of Light, yet they conceive that the Ideas of Citizens may not be quite useless to Gentlemen of the Army now about to determine on the dearest Rights of Citizens at least of unfortunate ones. Neither will it be improper that as Members of Congress they should endeavor to explain and to vindicate some Resolutions of Congress which must in the Course of this Business become Matter of Debate and which (in the Opinion of some Gentlemen not improperly) have been already stigmatized as cruel and unjust.[2] Your Excellency's Request superadded to these Considerations leads the Committee to go into the Matter a little at large, a Measure which on so important a Transaction their Duty seems to require.

Without entering into the Deduction of an historical Train of Facts we shall simply refer to those which apply to particular Propositions but it appears to us absolutely necessary to investigate if possible the precise Situation which the contracting Parties stand in as well absolutely as relatively to each other. For since no Fact can be clearer than this that Interest alone (and not Principles of Justice or Humanity) governs Men on such Occasions it becomes necessary to know our Interest and theirs which can alone be collected from such Situations.

And here because it frequently happens that Soldiers particularly young Soldiers are dazzled with Misconceived or ill applied Notions of Honor it may be well to step a little on one Side and explain our Sentiments. Honor mutually pledged appears to the Committee to be the *ostensible* Security of Compacts prompted and complied with for mutual Ease, Security or Advantage. The Current of History will shew us that this Security is for the most Part only *ostensible* and were History silent our own melancholy Experience in the present War after the first Cartel settled will evince the Truth of the Observation at least as far as the Business before us requires. But allowing that it were more than *ostensible,* allow it to be *real,* we cannot conceive that it hath any Thing to do with adjusting the Terms of the Compact. It is in publick what Honesty is in private Transactions and tho Honesty obliges a Man to pay what he owes, it hardly obliges a Man to run in Debt.

The Enemy possessing Quebec, Halifax, Rhode Island, New York, Philadelphia & Florida are distressed for Men to make a proper Defence at these several Places in the Begining of the ensuing Campaign, they being at present ignorant where the Storm which they suppose to be collecting will fall, and fully convinced that the Loss of any capital Post will do them more essential Injury than the Failure of an Expedition or a considerable Defeat. Besides this it is with Difficulty they can procure Subsistence for their present Force in America and their Supplies of Money begin to run low. They are therefore much affected by the Resolutions of Congress compelling them to send Provision in Specie or pay for it in hard Money at a par Exchange.

Having mentioned these Resolutions it is not amiss to attempt to clear them from the Imputation of Inequity. And first it must be observed that in every Compact between beligerent Powers to ascertain Money Matters Recourse must be had to a tertium interveniens or middle Rate, neither Party being willing to trust the Honesty of the other seeing that if he did, that other by exercising the allowed Sovereignty of a State might raise or lower the current Coin so as to suit his own Convenience according to the Circumstances and Exigencies which might arise. A fortiori on the present Occasion is such Precaution necessary to us the Value of whose Money is from the Nature of the Case more fluctuating than that of other Nations. Besides which the Enemy deny that it is Money and have not only the Will but in a great Measure the Power too of governing its Value and further have exerted themselves to depreciate it by Methods totally unprecedented among honest Men. If then it were agreed that both Sides should pay for the Subsistence of Prisoners in the Money of the respective Countries, what would be the Consequence but that our Resources must be entirely exhausted in maintaining our Enemies and this by Reason of their Knavery and our Folly. Besides this it would be declaring upon the very Face of the Transaction that our Money is not worth a Quarter of what it is uttered for by Congress, which is the next Step to making it worth nothing at all. With a View to these Inconveniences Congress fix the Medium to be in Spanish Milled Dollars worth each one paper Dollar of the Currency of these States & 4/6 Sterling. Nor does the Objection of Inequity lie so strongly as Gentlemen suppose even in their own favorite Point of View, for it is permitted to them to pay in Specie; & if they can do it cheaper and more conveniently than in Gold they certainly will, but the Fact is their Provision costs them more than ours even on this *inequitable* Exchange as it is called and we shall have to pay for so much as is furnished to our Prisoners according to what it costs them and not as we might have bought it in the Country. Nor shall we be permitted to replace our Deficiency in Provisions unless they happen to want Subsistence. For this we find was the Case at first, and tho the Liberty of sending in Flour and Wheat as they grew short in these Articles was (on that Principle and for their Advantage) extended to an Amount for purchasing other Necessaries Yet even then they by Proclamation obliged us to sell our Wheat at their Price or in other Words to pay for their Commodities just what they pleased. And tho it may be said that this Proclamation applied chiefly or only to their own Territory, yet when it is known (and the Fact is) that the Inhabitants of that Territory never did raise Wheat beyond their own Consumption the slight thin Pretence only exposes their Conduct.

But to return, it is evident that the Interest of the Enemy now calls upon them loudly for an Exchange of *Men* And therefore it is by no Means a Matter of Surprize that Genl. Howe after having delayed it so long is from these Circumstances brought to urge an Exchange with such Rapidity.

On the other Hand the Capture of Burgoyne & the Leizure allowed the United States to breathe from the late Exertions will enable them to bring no despicable Force into the Field earlier than the Enemy can be well supported by additional Numbers; besides this, the Maintaining so large a Number of their Prisoners will bring in considerable Supplies of solid Coin while the Liberty which a Principle of Retaliation now fully adopted compels them to allow our Prisoners will enable us to maintain them with comfort among the Enemy whereas if exchanged they would scatter abroad thro the Country and make little or no Addition of Strength to our Army. At the same Time the Want we feel of good Officers and the Sufferings of our Sailors and Citizens call upon us to establish a Cartel. Our Interest therefore is to push the Exchange of Officers, Mariners and Citizens. The Mariners indeed will not be exchanged on the ensuing Conference but must take their Chance upon the great and useful Retaliation which Genl. Howe with great Propriety condemns because it affects his Interest, which was greatly forwarded by rendering American Prisoners so miserable as to disincline them to the Service of their Country if not absolutely forced to abjure it.

The Exchange of Officers will We believe be admitted by the Enemy tho from the Delays affected there and the parole System adopted there is very good Reason to suppose that they will expect great Sacrifices on our Part in the Exchange of Privates and also some Relaxation in the *inequitable* Demand of Subsistence. But the Exchange of Citizens they will if possible avoid because it is their Interest to render the Acceptance of civil Offices extreemly dangerous since without civil Officers there can be no civil Government and the Enemy have Discernment enough to discover that civil Governments will be a more effectual Bar to their Claim than any Army upon Earth and this for Reasons your Excellency is so fully possessed of that it is needless to run thro the Detail.

Hence it follows that the Exchange of Citizens should be a sine qua non of the Treaty; it should be made the great Corner Stone, Unless the Enemy will (which they will not) agree to carry on the War upon those benevolent Principles which we set them a fair Example of by Releasing all such of their Citizens as fell into our Hands. The next Part of the Treaty should we conceive be the Exchange of Officers, and here as well as in the Exchange of Citizens we ought to insist that former Agreements be complied with on their Part before we take a single Step further in the Business, The great Security of public Faith being a regular & rigid Exaction of the Performance of every Promise on the Part of our Enemies while we have the Power of compelling Performance which will be the Case so long as we prudently retain their Soldiers in our Hands.

Another Resolution of Congress presents a very considerable Obstacle in the Way of this Exchange and that is a Resolution directing that the Subjects of the several States found in Arms shall be delivered to the States respectively.[3] The Enemy will doubtless expect either a direct or at least an implicative Repeal of this Resolution but as neither the one or the other can be in the Power of the Commissioners would it not be proper either to obtain a Confirmation of their Authority from Congress or else to instruct the Commissioners to insert a general Clause to the following effect viz. "Provided always that Nothing herein contained shall be construed in any wise to affect any Acts of the British Parliament or Resolutions of the American Congress." But if it shall be thought most adviseable to obtain from Congress a Confirmation of the absolute Power of the Commissioners we then submit to your Excellency the Propriety of directing them to provide that the Troops raised by the Enemy in America shall be last exchanged and also a special Provisoe that nothing in the Articles contained shall be construed to prevent either Party from proceeding judicially against those who by the Event of this Contest shall appear to have been Rebels. The Reason of which Observation is this, that so long as the Troops raised among us are entitled to the Privilege of equal Exchange the Enemy will be enabled to carry on the American War in a great Measure by the Strength of America; besides this it is no small Inducement to interested Men to join them, that at the worst Great Britain will make it an Article to save the Property of her Adherents in America, and altho Prudence may as it probably will lead us to go a great Way in our Compliances to get Rid of a very burthensome War, yet certainly Prudence will now dictate to hold out a Beacon to the wavering in Terrorem.

Should a Cartel take Place then in setling the Terms, great Attention should be paid to the *Valuation* which both with Regard to civil and military Characters should be made on Republican Principles, that is the Officers should be estimated very low when compared with the Privates whether Citizens or Soldiers, and besides this they should be exchangeable for each other only, that is to say civil Officers for civil Officers, military for military, Citizen for Citizen and Soldier for Soldier. The Reasons of which considering the disproportionate Number of Officers and those too of high Rank among us are too evident to dwell upon.

In adjusting Accounts we cannot but be of Opinion that the full Value of our Money should rigidly be insisted on and before the Ballance is struck it should be agreed how such Ballance is to be paid, for which a Variety of Modes presents itself. If Neither Gold or Paper will answer (for if they will not acknowledge the legality and Value of our Money they certainly should not be permitted to pay their Debts with it) then it may be proper for the Americans to pay in Wheat and the English in Cloth at limited Prices which would be for the mutual Advantage of both Parties or to establish some other Mode alike in the Power of both to comply with.

The Enemy will probably make a very considerable Demand of Prisoners taken at Fort Washington, but before a Tittle of this is complied with, for the Sake of the Influence it may have on future Transactions the Question must be settled whether Prisoners on Parole are or are not at the Risque of those who grant the Parole and this must be made an Article of the Treaty; for if they are not then when old Prescott dies Lee should be considered as released because upon calling for Prescott he could not come in and therefore the other would not be bound. But if they are then we are not to account for one more of these Men than are now alive. However supposing the former to be the Rule established which we beleive ought to be the Case, then a manifest Distinction is to be taken between the common Accidents of Nature and other Circumstances. For clearly should the Enemy after dismissing Prisoners on Parole waylay them and put them to the Sword We should not be held to redeem them. Again if their Death was rendered equally certain by previously administering Arsenick the Determination ought to be the same. And surely no good Distinction can be taken between Death brought on by a Detention of the Necessaries of Life and an Exhibition of the Principles of Death. If therefore it should appear that these unhappy Men were by hard Treatment so reduced that great Numbers necessarily died we ought not to be held to account for them and a very favorable Opportunity now offers to stickle for these unhappy People to the uttermost, and in order that the Enemy may find it to their Interest to treat Prisoners better in future they should not be suffered to take the least Advantage of their own Wrong. The Commissioners therefore should be directed to estimate the Number of these Prisoners very low and further to start an Objection whether even any of them are to be exchanged. In as much as the Capitulation of Fort Washington was clearly broken and altho it may not be proper to insist on this Matter yet it will be of Use to raise it because in Treaty the Claim of an Adversary should be opposed on every just and honorable Ground since by that Means it may be much lessened if not totally avoided, besides which the only Security for their future good Faith consists in making them pay for their former Iniquities.

Another Claim they may perhaps set up is that of Restitution for the Men taken at the Cedars but on this Occasion the Case of Fort

William Henry last War is so fully in Point that they cannot say much on the Subject.

On the whole Sir We have to intreat that the Commissioners will not suffer a Headlong Desire of releiving the Miseries of our unhappy fellow Countrymen or a blind Attachment to Principles which the Enemy disregard (they having in Fact nothing to do in the making of Treaties) to lead them into a hasty Acquiescence in the Enemy's insidious Proposals for such their Proposals will and indeed ought to be if they would maintain the Character of able Negotiators. But that on the other Hand they will industriously Consider that on a proper Management & Use of the present Opportunity the Rights and Interests of this Country do most materially depend. And we cannot but wish for many Reasons that they may be careful not to interfere with the Resolutions of Congress which may involve in it very disagreeable Altercations.

It is true that by insisting on these various Points the Treaty may become intricate and after all the whole Matter fall to the Ground. But if it should, who will suffer most by the Accident. This is a Question which should be maturely weighed because upon a proper answer to it must depend the Steps to be taken on our Part. And at any Rate should the Exchange be ever so desirable the best Way to bring it about will be by an apparent Indifference whether it ever takes Place.

FC (DNA: PCC, item 33). In the hand of Gouverneur Morris and endorsed by him: "Draft of Part of a Letter to Genl. Washington upon the Subject of Exchange. superceded by a Conference."
[1] This undated letter was written after March 6 but before the committee's March 11 conference with General Washington on the prisoner cartel. It could not have been written before March 6, because the last page of it was drafted on a sheet containing the lined-out beginning of another letter datelined "Camp near Valley Forge, March 6, 1778," and it was probably written after the committee's conference with Washington on the cartel which is noted in the committee minutes of proceedings for March 8. As Washington did not attend the committee's meetings of March 9 and 10, the committee discussions described in this letter could have been held on either day. See also Committee at Camp to Washington, February 11, note 1; and Laurens to Washington, March 15, 1778, note 1.
[2] References to Congress' resolutions of December 19, 1777, and February 26, 1778, establishing restrictions on exchanges of prisoners. *JCC*, 9:1036–37, 10:197–98.
[3] See *JCC*, 9:1069.

Edward Langworthy to William Palfrey

Dear Colonel,   York Town 9th March 1778.

Your esteemed favor came to hand the 6th instant & am extremely sorry there should be the least uncertainty of your returning to your

Post.[1] I have no doubt but the Committee will pay the greatest attention to your Business & I am certain the Members of Congress in general have a proper Sense of your Services, so that I have the most sanguine Expectations that things will be settled to your Satisfaction. Tis strange the Auditors are not yet arrived at Camp, the Congress expected the business to be entered upon before this time, as Messrs Clarkson & Clark were appointed as long since as Feby the sixth.[2]

I cannot express to you my feelings for the Comfort & support of our little Army, our prospects are gloomy & distressing, but I hope that that virtue which has been tried by suffering will still persevere & that the Congress will be induced to make proper Exertions against our Enemies early this Spring. General Howe must certainly be greatly reduced in Numbers, otherwise you would have heard more of him during the Winter; by some News Papers procured from New York it appears that their reinforcements will be very inconsiderable the next Campaign & there appears to be very great discontents in London & other parts of England.

Lieutenant Wilford Aid de Camp to Genl Burgoyne has been here with a Letter from the General addressed to the President of Congress.[3] It was referred to a Committee who were of Opinion that nothing contained therein was sufficient to induce Congress to recede from their Resolves of the 8th day of January last, respecting the Convention of Saratoga. The General on account of his ill state of health has leave to embark for England, by Rhode Island, or any more expeditious Route, with the Officers of his Family & his Servants. A Parole is to be taken from the General, Colonel Kingston & Doctor Wood.

Lieutt. Wilford requested permission to go into Philadelphia in order to deliver to Genl Howe duplicates of the Papers by him presented to Congress; but this could not be granted, however he was directed to deliver them to the board of War that they might be transmitted to Genl Washington who may send them by a Flag to Philadelphia.

Our distresses in every department for the want of Money have been very great & alarming; the Treasury board heretofore have acted on principles that do not suit the present Exigencies of Affairs. We are now determined to adopt a different Conduct & I think there will be a better supply of Cash in future;[4] I shall be glad if other requisites for the next Campaign can be so easily procured. Like you I have fears for the disaffection & inactivity of this State.

The Treasury board are now employed in drawing up a Report for the Loan Offices for the Year 1778, Ten Millions of Dollars are to be borrowed on this plan—by a Letter just received from Genl Putnam it appears that he thinks it would be proper to have a Loan Office near that Army.[5] If I remember, you was wishing for something of this kind at your Camp. I should be glad to hear from you on this head soon.

I have lately seen Doctor Shippen, who has desired me to procure for the use of the American Hospitals two Tons of Bowen's Sago Powder.[6] He greatly approves of it & says it should be used in every Part of the Continent. The greatest difficulty will be to get it here, as there is no sending it by Sea. Mr Harnet for upwards a Month past has been very ill in the Gout, he was glad to hear of you. The Compliments & good Wishes of the Ladies await you—& that you may have an happy Interview with your family is the sincere wish of, yours affectionately,   Edwd Langworthy

RC (MH–H).

[1] Palfrey had been thinking of resigning as paymaster general for several months. In a January 5 letter to Washington written at Lancaster, he had reported his intention to go to York the following day to settle the affairs of his department and indicated that once this was accomplished he intended to resign, citing his expenses at camp and the press of personal affairs in Massachusetts. Washington Papers, DLC. The origin of Langworthy and Palfrey's friendship is not known, but they probably had become acquainted while Palfrey was in York at that time. In January 1778 Langworthy had been appointed to both the old Board of War and the Board of Treasury—committees Palfrey had consulted directly in his attempts to improve the operation of his department and obtain funds. *JCC*, 10:45–47, 51–53, 60. Although Palfrey did return to New England in April 1778 for a lengthy stay with his family, and thereafter periodically reaffirmed his desire to resign, he was repeatedly dissuaded and continued as paymaster general until Congress appointed him consul to France in November 1780. Unfortunately, he was lost at sea en route to that post. See *JCC*, 18:1018; and John Gorham Palfrey, *Life of William Palfrey* (Boston: Charles C. Little and James Brown, 1845), pp. 427–41.

[2] The auditors for the army had been appointed on January 10, and it was the resolves outlining their duties that had passed on February 6. See *JCC*, 10:38, 131–37; and Daniel Roberdeau to John Clark, February 9, 1778.

[3] See Henry Laurens to Richard Wilford, March 1, 1778, note.

[4] In addition to the $2 million emission Congress had authorized on March 5 upon the recommendation of the Board of Treasury, emissions of $1 million, $5 million, and $500,000 were authorized on April 4, 11, and 18. See *JCC*, 10:223, 309, 337–38, 365.

[5] See Henry Laurens to Israel Putnam, March 7, 1778, note.

[6] On Langworthy's earlier efforts to introduce Bowen's sago powder to the medical department, see Langworthy to Benjamin Rush, December 26, 1777.

Henry Laurens to William Cooke

Sir,   9th March 1778

Your Letter of the 10th Jany. reached me no earlier than the 6th Inst. I presented it the next Morning to Congress, when the Contents were taken under consideration and it was Resolved to accept your

resignation, as you will see by an Act of the 7th Inst. here inclosed.[1]
I am with great respect.

LB (DNA: PCC, item 13). Addressed: "Colo. Willm. Cooke, 12th Pennsylvania Regimt."

[1] See *JCC*, 10:228. Cooke's letter of resignation is not in PCC. Five days after Laurens wrote this letter Cooke was court-martialed "for disobedience of orders in sundry instances," convicted, and publicly reprimanded. Washington, *Writings* (Fitzpatrick), 11:52, 81–82. It is pertinent to note that when Cooke wrote his letter of resignation he was absent without leave from his regiment.

William Duer to Robert R. Livingston

My dear Freind   Baskenridge March 10th. 1778
I received your Letter of the 30th Jany.[1] at Reading where I had stopt for some days in my Way homewards in Expectation of meeting with my Colleague Mr. Philip Livingston who I had reason to expect would have been at that Place about the 8 or 10 Feby. On the Receipt of your Letter, in which you mention that you had wrote to Morris on a Matter of the utmost Importance to our State,[2] desiring me to open it in Case he should be loitering on the Road, I determined notwithstanding a very Weak State both of Body and Mind to return to Congress at York Town (where the Letter for Morris was stopt) in order to attend to its Contents, in Case I should not find Mr. P. Livingston at this Place, for which I immediately set out. Being disappointed in my Expectation I am just going to set out for Congress (and in Case Mr. Morris should not have returned thither from Camp (where he has been for five weeks on a Come. for reforming the Army) I shall open the Letter and attend to the Matters you recommend. At the Same Time, my dear Freind, It is a Duty which I owe myself to inform you, and by your Means, my Freinds in the Governt. of our State, that I cannot possibly stay there more than three Weeks. It is now near two Years since I quitted home, during which Time I have not paid the least Attention to my private Affairs, which are in the Utmost Confusion—and if not speedily attended to may involve me in Difficulties injurious in the highest degree both to my Fortune and Reputation, especially in matters which I transacted for the Public.
Independant of this Consideration my Health is much shattered by an Intermitting Fever which has been hanging upon me during the Course of last Summer and Fall, and my Mind much Impair'd by a Close Attention to Business, and by an inexpressible anxiety which I cannot help feeling for the State of our Public Affairs which I am sorry to tell you in my Opinion (and I think I am not of a desponding [cast?]) wear a most unpromising Aspect. It would take

William Duer

a Volume to point out the Various Causes to which in my Judgment this is to be imputed, did I think it prudent to enter into a Detail. Suffice it to say, that the Parties prevailing in our Army, and the want of Foresight, and Attention to Business in Congress (to say no More) are the principal Sources from whence Various and Alarming Evils have Arisen. Notwithstanding Common Sense must have convinced any but Fools that betwixt the Close of One Campaign, and the Opening of another, would be *the* great Period of public Business, a Number of Gentlemen acquainted with the Business of Congress returnd to their homes, and left a few (and very few) Men of Business and real Patriotism to struggle against Men actuated by contracted State Politicks, and render'd impenetrable to all the Efforts of Reason by the Superlative Dint of stupidity. This my dear Freind is no Exaggerated Picture; judge then what have been my Feelings from what your own would be in such a Case.

Mr. Morris was only two or three Days at York before he went to Camp on the Business I mentioned. I wish he had been there longer that he might have a greater Oppertunity than I am sure he has had of judging of the Character of Parties in the Army, and the Views of Individuals in Congress. I am afraid (nay I am certain) he does not sufficiently know this which will involve the Public in my Opinion in a greater Labyrinth of Evils than we are in at present. You know he is like the Elephant in War often times more destructive to his Freinds than his Antagonists.

I am confident from a close Attention which I have paid to the Conduct of Individuals both in the Army and Congress for more than 10 Months past that I am pretty well Master, of their public Character and Intentions, and I may venture to say that notwithstanding Parties run pretty high in the Army, from which have flowed an Inactive Campaign, a Relaxation of Discipline, and all its Concomitant Evils, that a Wise and Virtuous Body could turn even these Parties to Advantage during the Course of the present Year, but this I am afraid will not [be] the Case. I shall esteem it my Duty however to make one last Effort on my Return to Congress, where I am in hopes Mr. Robert Morris and some other Men of Business and Integrity will be on my Return. With this Reinforcement something may perhaps be done to alter the present sickly state of public Affairs.

I enclose a Letter to Genl. Schuyler which you will oblige me in forwarding; likewise one for my Clerk Mr. Archibald Stewart,[3] whom I beleive you will find at Poughkepsie; if he is not there, be kind enough to make Enquiry after him, and to convey this Letter to him; which materially concerns my private affairs. God bless you my dear Freind, and all your Connections, and beleive me though a remiss Correspondent, Your very Sincere and affectionate Freind. Ask yourself whether they are incompatible Characters.   Wm Duer

[*P.S.*] The Hurry I am in has made me write in Hieroglyphics; I hope you will be able to expound them.

RC (NHi).
    [1] The FC of Livingston's letter to Duer, dated January 29, 1778, is in the Robert R. Livingston Papers, NHi.
    [2] For the FC of Livingston's January 29 letter to Gouverneur Morris, see ibid. Livingston's main concern in this letter was securing the defense of the Hudson. For the steps Congress had already taken to achieve this goal on February 18 and March 4, see *JCC,* 10:180–81, 221–22.
    [3] Neither of these letters has been found.

Eliphalet Dyer to Jeremiah Wadsworth

Dear Sir   York-Town March 10th 1778
    A day or two after the President wrote you Inclosing a resolution of Congress requesting your speedy Attendance at this place I wrote you to the same purpose.[1] By your last & one from Coll Williams am Informed you had not recievd that from the President. Congress have long been sick of the late Commis[saria]te System. They find it sufficiently ineffectual, they were determined to Alter, they have from Various quarters been Advised to you to head that Department, they thot it prudent to have you present, to advise to a plan which you dare Venture yourself upon but by your delay they are oblidged to Indeavor to settle a plan in the best manner they can, but dare say when you come they will readily Admit of such alterations as you think Necessary. They are willing to make it worth any Gentn. Accepting. They Wish to have the Army Supplied. At any rate, I hope you will make no delay in coming forward, the season is advancing, our preparations ought to be seasonable for the insuing Campaine. We ought to make an early Effort to dislodge the Enemy before any reinforcements may come from Great Britain, tho Planet Struck at the fate of Burgoyne yet are determined to make one Vigorous Effort more which God Grant may End in the destruction of all their future Schemes against America. Hope no one this year will stand upon Terms but join heart & hand for his Country. Am with Sincere Esteem Yr Hle Servt,   Elipht Dyer

RC (CtHi).
    [1] See Dyer to Wadsworth, February 10, 1778.

Eliphalet Dyer to William Williams

Dear Sir,   York Town March 10th 1778
    I receivd your kind favour per Mr Torry, and am really much Oblidged to you for the repeated favour of your Correspondence

since you left this place. Mr Trumbull being sick have been deprived of that repeated Intelligence I Used to have from him of my family, & sincerely rejoice that a kind Providence has so far restored him to health but yet much fear for his full recovery, as the Symptoms of his disorder appear to me of a dangerous kind, but hope for the best. Our Diminished Army have lay Very quiet this winter, the detachments from the enemy have ravaged the Country round about them & lately came out upwards of twenty miles and carried off unmolested 130 head of fine Cattle sent by Coll Champion Between Delaware & Schuylkill[1] & it has been with the greatest difficulty that our Army have been supplied from day to day. Indeed we have no fear for Flower in the Country, but the army has been much distressed for the want of forrage. Their Waggon horses many dying for want of food & the difficulty to procure Waggons has much distressed the Army & we are still in great Anxiety how to supply them with meat till the summer fed cattle may relieve them, especially as we wish for a large reinforcement as early in the spring as possible to take the first advantage to break up Hows Army, before he can be reinforced, which requires every Exertion of every State. The Scarcity of Provisions, of forrage, of carriage, the excessive prices, our exhausted finances & every Circumstance attending our affairs instead of discouraging ought to Animate us to a more earnest, early, spirited, & most Vigorous Exertion. Congress are doing all they can, they are diligent & attentive & we seem very Quiet since D——r[2] went away. We have called upon & requested the Govrs & Councils of the several States to give all their aid & assistance in procuring necessaries, much in the same form as we had Govr Trumbull & his Council, & hope it may have a good Effect. We have regulated the Qr Master Department, appointed by Recommendation of Genll Washington & our Comtee at head Quarters, Genll Green, Major Cox & one Mr Pettit of the Jerseys to head the Various branches of that Department but I fear we have not persued the best plan for the purpose. We have been waiting for the Arrival of Coll Wadsworth to make a new plan & regulation in the Commissy Department to form it so as to be Agreable to him, but at present are disappointed, the principal and main business of Jones the Express was to carry letter to him, tho we had some letters for Boston. Am surprised at his failure in delivering the letters by which means are Obliged to proceed in our plan without his advice, but believe if Gain will Tempt him we shall put it on as favorable a footing as he could desire, beside he will have the Appointment of all to Act under him. I hope you will forward him here with all speed, all the purchases will be on Commissions as also his pay. Am rather sorry our Assembly when they passed the Regulating Act did not postpone the time for its taking effect till, at least till they were Informed the other States came into it. The operation must be suspended till abt middle June at least as to price of fat beef. I conclude the president has sent the resolution for building barracks in Connecticut which passd some time agoe, as also a resolution Authorising the Executive of every State to suspend all Continental officers behaving unworthily &c.[3] The news of Burgoynes defeat & surrendry gave a Shock to the Parliament house but resumd Courage after a few days & are determind to attack us with redoubled Vigor the coming season, hope we may be too soon for them & that the Almighty may deliver us, have now 6 or 8 letters to write & must conclude by assuring you that I am with sincere Esteem & regard Yr Hb Servt,

Elipht Dyer

[P.S.] The Disturber, I mean B——ke[4] has just come after Inducing Nth C——na to dissent from Confederation [or?] a great part of it, is now in Congress to the Universal sorrow & of every member.

Soon after I finishd my letter Brown Arrivd with yours of the 4th Instant. Congress wish our Assembly had lengthned out the time of the regulating Act taking Effect at least with respect to Beef till the middle of June & have by their resolve recommended it to the Consideration of our Assembly.[5] Champion must be supplied or our Army will fail. It is Impossible to supply them wholly from the Southard. We have not received Accounts from the other States whether they have adopted the report of the Comtee regulating prices. Yrs,

E D

Be assured there is not the most distant thought of removing Genll Washington, nor ever an expression in Congress looking that way, is a Tory lye from the beginning.

RC (MB). Endorsed by Williams: "Col. Dyer, at York Town, Mar. 1778—soon after I left him & Congress there. A note on the Cover, that the Cattle taken were Jersey, not Champions Cattle."

[1] It was obviously this passage that led Dyer to explain on the cover of this letter, as Williams noted in his endorsement, "the Cattle taken were Jersey, not Champions Cattle."

[2] William Duer.

[3] See the resolves of December 20, 1777, and February 9, 1778. JCC, 9:1047–48, 10:139–40.

[4] Thomas Burke. See Burke's Notes on the Articles of Confederation, December 18, 1777, note.

[5] On March 9 Dyer's Connecticut colleague Oliver Wolcott had been appointed to a committee to consider commissary Henry Champion's complaint that the Connecticut act regulating the price of live beef was impeding his procurement efforts for the army. The committee report, in Wolcott's hand, suggested that Congress advise the Connecticut Assembly to suspend or repeal its Regulating Act, but the resolve finally approved by Congress on March 11 merely referred Champion's letter to the assembly and recommended that it "devise a remedy for the evil complained of or feared." See JCC, 10:233, 235, 244; and Dyer to Jonathan Trumbull, Sr., March 12, 1778.

John Henry to Thomas Johnson

Dear Sir   York Town March 10th. 1778.
Upon the representation of Col. Samuel Smith who was here last Week, I obtained from Congress ten thousand Dollars for the recruiting Service. I sent it by him to you, and I expect you have received it before this Time. If that Sum will not do, I beg you will be kind enough to acquaint me.

I am informed the Committee of Congress at Camp have among other States, applied to the State of Maryland for the purchase of a Number Horses for the purpose of forming a Body of light Cavalry.[1] If you should approve of the plan or should you lay it before the Assembly, and it is adopted by them; I trust some estimate of the expence will be made that the money may be forwarded from this place. Should the recruiting service require a greater number of Dollars I believe they may be had.

I believe you need not intertain any fears of the expedition against Canada going forword. The advanced Season of the year, and the feeble preparations in that department have effectually put an end to it. I most cordially join with you in opinion, that it is the interest as well as the true policy of this country to collect their force to a single point by strengthening the hands of Genl. Washington. But this I fear will not be the case. It is the opinion of some, and they have weight with a certain class of Men, that the whole force of the Enemy will be turned towards the East the next campain. A military Gentleman in high office supports this opinion. Should it prevail in Congress I think it will injure the Middle States in a high degree, as well as the common cause at large. The Virginia Frigate is ordered to make another attempt; if she fails the measure you propose I expect will be adopted.[2]

Virginia will this afternoon offer to ratify the confederation. No other state is prepared. I shall take this opportunity of stating the objections to it, from Maryland, tho I have little hopes of this matter being soon determined. I fear it never will in our favour.

We had intelligence last night of one of our armed vessels in the Delaware, near Cristeen having taken two Ships and a small sloop of war. We have not heard the Cargoes. I beleive this news may be relied on.

Enclosed you have some of the Debates of the House of Lords and Commons. They will amuse you. Twenty thousand additional Troops for the Service of 1778 is voted without a division.

With great regard I am sir your most obedt. and very hble. Servt.
                                                        J Henry Junr.

RC (MdAA).

¹ See Committee at Camp to Thomas Wharton, February 28, 1778, note.
² See Marine Committee to Thomas Johnson and to James Nicholson, March 4, 1778.

Henry Laurens to William Livingston

Sir,   10th March 1778
    The last I had the honor of writing to your Excellency was dated the 1st Inst.
    Yesterday your Excellency's favour of the 5th Inst. with an Inclosed Report of the suspension of supernumerary & profligate Officers reached me & was immediately presented to Congress. The House expressed great satisfaction with your Excellency's proceedings respecting those Officers & committed the papers to a Select Committee of three who have not yet Reported.¹
    Inclosed herein Your Excellency will receive an Act of Congress of the 7th Inst. for holding on Wednesday 22d April a General Fast throughout the United States.²
    I remain with great Regard

LB (DNA: PCC, item 13).
  ¹ In his March 5 letter to Laurens and accompanying report to Congress, Governor Livingston described how, in the course of carrying out a February 9 resolve authorizing the states to remove supernumerary Continental civil or military officers "not immediately appointed by Congress," he had dismissed five members of the "Quarter masters & Commissaries department" in Princeton. See PCC, item 68, fols. 333–37; and *JCC*, 10:139–40. On March 11 Congress instructed Laurens to thank Livingston for his action and resolved to reimburse state officials for expenses they might incur in carrying out the February 9 resolve. *JCC*, 10:242.
  ² Laurens also wrote a brief letter this day to Washington transmitting copies of March 7 resolves on holding a general fast and regulating the grant of military furloughs. See PCC, item 13, fol. 218; and *JCC*, 10:229–30.

Henry Laurens to Thomas Wharton

Sir,   York Town 10th March 1778.
    I had the honour of writing to Your Excellency the 7th Inst. by Messenger Millet & yesterday of receiving & presenting to Congress your favour of the 3d Inst. which was thence Committed to the Board of War & I have received no commands respecting the Contents,¹ but in the course of duty, aggreeable to Your Excellency's request I now transmit Six Commissions for Cruizers with Instructions & Bonds.
    I remain with very great Esteem & Regard, Sir, Your Excellency's Obedient & Most huml servant,
Henry Laurens, President of Congress

RC (MH–H).

[1] President Wharton's March 3 letter to Laurens, which was primarily concerned with urging other states to share more of the burden of supplying wagons, is in PCC, item 69, 1:477–79, and *Pa. Archives*, 1st ser. 6:327–29. It does not appear that Congress took any action on this letter other than referring it to the Board of War.

Henry Laurens to Christopher Zahn

Dear Sir,[1]   10th March 1778.

I am sorry you have not enabled me to acknowledge the Receipt of a single Line from my Neighbor Zahn since we parted in June last. Although I am not under the dominion of a very anxious mind & that I repose the utmost confidence in your judgement as a Planter & attention as an Attorney & Friend, yet from various considerations it would have given me pleasure to have received an account from yourself, reflective & prospective, of affairs at Mount Tacitus. Persuaded as I am that every thing is going forward under your usual good management, you will nevertheless admit, that a desire of knowing whether we can afford to expend & to give fifty or Five hundred, is not a criminal passion—especially in a Man who while his usual income is greatly straightned is exposed to such exorbitant charges for common, I should say, very mean subsistence as are Sufficient to impoverish a very large Estate. Only think of paying £11.7.6. Carolina Money for a pair of shoes, Negro shoes, for George, & articles in proportion.

Our Neighbor the Revd. Mr. Turquand is now in York Town transacting business for the Society at Red Stone with whom he is connected,[2] he informs me the families are all pretty well except the old Gentleman who has lost the little patience he carried from Santé. Poor old man he discards his business with me in this part of the World to be quite of a different nature from that he used to talk of in the piaza, he has found it necessary to accept of Services from me, when I might not only have witheld them, but have put him to great inconvenience. To do him acts of kindness when the opportunity was fair, gave me the most pleasure & satisfaction.

Mr. Turquand desires his Compliments.

This will probably be delivered to you by Mr. John Christian Senf an ingenious, sensible, Young Gentleman, who in the last summers Campaign was taken prisoner by General Gates's Troops. He had been a Lieutenant Engineer under General   . Sometime after he had been Captured, he determined to abandon the infamous Cause into which his Prince had plunged him without his own consent, & to become an Inhabitant & Citizen among a free people. General Gates was so well pleased with his whole behavior as to give him the

Rank of Captain of Engineers & to recommend him strongly to me. I have for several reasons which this Gentleman will explain to you if you converse together, advised him to seek his fortune in the Southern Climates.[3] If he has health & a few friends I am of opinion he will find it there. He is an excellent draughtsman & equal to every kind of surveying business. These with other qualifications which he is possessed of, will enable him to go through the first efforts in a new Country with tolerable ease; & after a little experience he will be competent to helping himself, in the meantime I request all my freinds to shew him countenance. Perhaps we may soon employ Capt. Senf if he does not obtain better business to resurvey Mount Tacitus. Your Civilities to him will not be thrown away.

I say nothing of my private affairs under your direction being confident of your friendly attention in every respect & flattering my self with an assurance of hearing from you very soon.

General Burgoyne having learned to address Congress in a becoming Stile & having earnestly requested leave to go to England for his health & for the vindication of his conduct Congress have consented.

Our public affairs in general are not in so good a train as I could wish, but every defect is owing to a Langour in the States. Consider Sir, what is the Cause & what may be the consequence, of Congress's being reduced to the number of 13 to 17 Members. The States are off their Guard & fallen a Sleep—was not our Enemies as weak as our selves we should be ruined, but they may make a grand effort & destroy us. It is our duty to make a great Stroke & drive them out. This might easily be done were we half so animated as we pretended to be in 1775.

You will smile when I inform you I have granted Many Commissions for Cruizing on the Delaware, Cheesapeck Bay & even on the Ohio & Mississipy. On the Delaware many valuable prizes have been made, I have just now an Account that four of our Armed Boats had taken two ships & an Armed Schooner & were in pursuit of several more who were coming up the River. The Men of War had retired for the Winter to Rhode Island. The Enemy lately lost near New York in a Snow Storm two Frigates & several Armed Vessels. From the King of Englands speech to His Parliament & their Answer & debates I think it would not be very hazardous to prophesy that terms of accomodation will soon be offered. I am for preparing every means in readiness for an early blow as the best posture we can be found in for receiving propositions for peace.

I am with very great regard.

LB (ScHi).

[1] Previously identified in volume seven of these *Letters*.

[2] During his stay in York, Rev. Paul Turquand also sought in vain to secure payment by Congress of some bills of exchange he had brought with him from South Carolina. *JCC*, 10:233, 257.

[3] Evidently Laurens had more in mind than advancing the fortunes of a young man when he directed Captain Senf to South Carolina. Writing from Charleston, S.C., on August 11, 1778, Senf informed Laurens that he had just returned from a trip to Georgia and East Florida and would soon send him "the Plan of Fort Howe & Fort Tonyn" in the British province. Laurens Papers, DLC. It is clear from Senf's letter that Laurens was expecting this "Plan." Later in the war Senf became colonel of engineers in the South Carolina militia. See Edward McCrady, *The History of South Carolina in the Revolution, 1775–1780* (New York: Macmillan Co., 1901), pp. 367, 679.

James Lovell to Samuel Adams

My dear Sir   March 10th. 1778.

It was mortifying to hear the Delegates from several states this day assert that they were instructed respecting the Confederation, while the two Cyphers from Massachusetts could produce nothing. Our State is expected to be found in the Fore-front upon such Occasions. I think the determination of the States upon this point must have a great effect upon the ensuing Campaign and I therefore wish to hear from our Assembly.[1]

I think it not amiss to say that whenever Congress sends a Recommendation to the States its but right & fit that regular public Returns should be made whether the Recommendations are fully or partially complied with or rejected. How otherwise can future plans be properly laid, or the general continental works carried on? Connecticutt, modest Connecticutt is exemplary in her attention to the Propriety which I have hinted at. I fear the States are insensible of the Hazard which our Cause runs this Spring for want of an Army early ready for action. The Enemy have been nursing their Horses, preparing Carriages and refreshing the Soldiers, While everyone of these things has been neglected on our part. You had cause to expect a degree of ruin in the Commissary's line, but you hoped the Quartermaster's would be properly attended to. Alas, it is worse conducted than the former. I am suspicious that regulating acts have been attempted for the *last* time. The States which feeling strong in their own Virtue shall attempt it will be sacrificed by others, which are less virtuous, and can produce easily from history anecdotes against the measures. I think I shall never again consent to such a Remedy even in a desperate Disease.

I have received a long letter from Mr. John Amory upon the subject of his Exile. Mr. Payne forwarded it to me from Providence. I would have you converse with Brother Appleton upon the Subject and tell *him* to write to me. He was a great Friend to Mr. Amory and knows how things were conducted at the late visit. I am willing the Gentleman should have the fairest chance. But when he addressed

his Letter to me he addressed it to one who has resigned Father &
Mother, Brothers and Sisters with many Friends male & female. He
desires me to put a Memorial into Congress for him, as he was
surprized into an Ooath of Allegiance which *binds* his conscience.[2]

RC (NN). In Lovell's hand, though not signed.

[1] When Congress had transmitted the Articles of Confederation to the states
for their consideration in November 1777 it had called upon legislatures to invest
their delegates "with competent powers . . . to subscribe articles of confederation
and perpetual union" by the "tenth March next." *JCC*, 9:932–35. Notwithstanding
the sense of urgency that prevailed in Congress at that time (a motion to give the
states until May 1 to return instructions to their delegates had been defeated
on a roll call vote), several states had not responded to this call by March 10.
Thus Lovell was mortified that he had not yet heard from the Massachusetts
General Court and was somewhat embarrassed that Virginia rather than Massachusetts was "found in the Fore-front" on this occasion. As a noted authority has
explained: "On March 10, 1778, Virginia was the only state prepared to ratify
without qualification or criticism." Merrill Jensen, *The Articles of Confederation:
an Interpretation of the Social-Constitutional History of the American Revolution,
1774–1781* (Madison: University of Wisconsin Press, 1940), p. 190.

Actually six states had been heard from by March 10 (Virginia, North Carolina,
Maryland, New York, Connecticut, and Pennsylvania), and four others (Georgia,
South Carolina, Rhode Island, and New Hampshire) had adopted instructions
although they had not yet reached York. By coincidence, Massachusetts adopted
instructions authorizing her delegates to sign the Articles the very day Lovell
penned this letter to Adams. Adams enclosed the General Court's March 10
instructions to its delegates in a March 27 letter to Lovell, but there is evidence
that word of their adoption reached York as early as March 20. See Adams,
Writings (Cushing) 4:18; and Cornelius Harnett to Richard Caswell, March 20,
1778, note 1.

For a discussion of the states' responses to Congress' call for ratifying the Articles and the various revisions suggested or insisted upon by several of them, see
Jensen, *Articles of Confederation*, pp. 185–94. See also Thomas Burke to Richard
Caswell, March 12; John Henry to Nicholas Thomas, March 17; Cornelius Harnett
to Richard Caswell, March 20; and James Forbes to Thomas Johnson, March 24,
1778.

Several developments conspired to keep Congress from returning to the subject
of the Articles for many weeks, however, and not until June 20 did the final debate
on revision of the Articles begin. Almost simultaneously Congress learned that the
British were evacuating Philadelphia, and the delegates were unable to complete
the document and prepare an engrossed copy for signing and ratification until
after Congress returned to the Pennsylvania capital in July. See *JCC*, 11:485, 556,
625, 628, 631–32, 636–40, 647–58, 662–71, 677–78, 681, 712; and Jensen, *Articles of
Confederation*, pp. 194–97.

[2] In his March 31 response to Lovell, Adams made the following observations on
John Amory's relations with Massachusetts. "You mention your having receivd a
Letter from Mr John Amory, with his Request that you would put a Memorial
into Congress for him. He tells you 'he was surprized into an Oath of Allegiance.'
He informd the Committee of both Houses that he was not compelld to take the
Oath. He could not recollect the Form or Tenor of the Oath he had taken. He
wished to live peaceably in his Native Place and he declared he would not take
up Arms against the British King. In what Manner could Congress interpose for
him? if you should comply with his Request? His Residence in this State was
deemd by the General Assembly to be dangerous to the State. Will Congress order

or recommend that he should reside in it notwithstanding? I will desire Mr Appleton to write to you on the Subject." Sol Feinstone Collection, DLC microfilm. No
evidence has been found to indicate that Lovell took any action in Amory's behalf,
and Amory did not return from exile in Great Britain until 1784.

Gouverneur Morris to Robert R. Livingston

Dr Livingston.   Camp Valley Forge 10th March 1778.
At the Rate our Letters usually travel I think it very far from
improbable that I may see you as soon as you see my Letter for immediately upon my Arrival at Congress which I hope will be in a
few Days I intend to endeavor to procure {an adjournment to Hart-
ford}.[1] This Measure will I trust be attended with very beneficial
Effects. It is very advantageous to be in a good Neighbourhood. Mankind are less apt to neglect Things immediately under their Eye. Tis
true it may tend to throw Obstructions {into Hudsons River}—but I
know many in the World who do not consider this as an Object quite
undesirable. Should this my Intention take Place we may immediately
and in future have a much freer and readier Communication of
Councils which I trust will produce neither public nor private *Dis*
Advantages. You may probably ask why I dislike my present Situation.
I answer that I think it in every Respect too remote. I would wish to
be within Ken of every Scene of Action from whence you may gather
something in Favor of my Curiosity. The greater Part of the People of
this Country to their Honor be it spoken are {wicked tories}. They
are not of a very active Disposition. Indeed the Propn. of Germans
and Quakers cannot well be supposed to be so. The Irish are *true*
Irishmen. When I consider all Things together the State of Things
here appears {gloomy} so that there is Room to beleive the State will
be cleared of it's Tories. A Set of Scoundrels at the Head of whom
are {Gates and Mifflin} are very busy in an Attempt to ruin the
{General} of America.[2] I will not promise them Success, but what
will surprize you is that they have made a {*tool* of Duer}. This hath
been effected by making use of a strong Affection for {foreigners}
which has not escaped your Observation. {Profusion} prevails to a
very surprizing Degree in all the {public offices}. I do not find that
the Legislature of this State laid a Tax and therefore our paper
Money is {worth nothing}. Patience, Attention and that great *Desideratum* political Knowlege must be exerted. Duer hath been
waitting at Reading a long Time for old Phil[3] and is thence going to
Jersey on Business as he calls it. Adieu my Friends. My Love & Respect to your Fire Side. Remember me to all who desire it. Yours,
                                                              Gouv Morris

RC (NHi).

[1] Words printed in braces in this text were written by Morris in cipher.

[2] For a discussion of the opposition to Washington in and out of Congress during the winter of 1777–78, see James Lovell to Horatio Gates, November 27, 1777, note 1. Former Virginia delegate Benjamin Harrison made some pertinent comments about rumored anti-Washington machinations in a letter he wrote from "Berkely James River" on March 3 to former North Carolina delegate Joseph Hewes: "I have been greatly alarmed by some letters I have received from my worthy friend, and accounts through other channels, that there was a party formed against our general, both in and out of Congress in favor of the Saratoga Hero. I give the greater credit to this, when I consider who they are that compose our Board of War, men who are most of them avowedly his enemies, and some of them too who are using every endeavor to rise by his fall. In the name of wonders how came it thus constituted? Are the good and virtuous of you, and I know there is a great majority of such, taken in? Indeed I fear it and venture to foretell, that if you have not your eyes and ears about you, America or at least, this part of it will soon be in very great confusion." *N.C. State Records*, 13:61–62.

[3] Philip Livingston.

Jonathan Bayard Smith to Thomas Wharton

Sir   York Town March 10. 1778

On other leaf is copy of parts of a letter from Colo. Hartley to the board of war on the subject of recruiting his battalion; & the boards letter to Congress on the subject; both which were referred to the delegates of this State.[1] As not to comply with the proposition made might appear an unnecessary obstruction to reinforcing the army on one hand; or on the other a compliance might involve consequences not expected, the delegates advised with the Committee from the state now here, & finally take the liberty of referring to your directions, as they did not conceive themselves authorized to interfere.

The states are severally called upon to raise their old quota of troops. The number of this state regiments is diminished to 10.[2] The supernumerary men are to be transferred to the horse, artillery, & other unconnected corps. Of the 16 Regiments (so called) 9 only are to be kept up; &, I suppose, will be alloted to particular states, & filled up as above. Colo. Hartleys will probably belong to us as its natural connexion. To concur with his proposition, will give him the men more immediately; & allowing him to employ his officers may expedite the recruiting service; perhaps be the means of procuring recruits, either from connection or attachment, which others would not pick up. He has expectations from the borders of Maryland; filled his regiment formerly with quick success, & appears to be sanguine now. With respect to the money he appears to be prudent & cautious. But as we may perhaps not foresee all the effects, or its full connection with the state of Pennsylvania, we beg leave to sollicit your earliest advice & direction, as no time ought to be lost. We beg leave only to add that the complement of each battalion is also to be reduced; & that though some states have discountenanced these unconnected regiments, yet some others have given them the benefit of their state bounties. I am, Sir, with very great respect in behalf of the Delegates, Your Excellency's & Councils most ob. h. servt.

Jona. B Smith

RC (MeHi).

[1] See *JCC*, 10:235. For the extracts of the two letters pertaining to Col. Thomas Hartley's regiment that Smith enclosed to the Pennsylvania Council, see *Pa. Archives*, 1st ser. 6:351–52. See also Henry Laurens to Thomas Wharton, March 31, 1778; and John B. B. Trussell, Jr., *The Pennsylvania Line: Regimental Organization and Operations, 1776–1783* (Harrisburg: Pennsylvania Historical and Museum Commission, 1977), pp. 139–46.

[2] For the new state quotas that Congress adopted on February 25, and which the states were "required forthwith to fill up by drafts from their militia," see *JCC*, 10:200. For an indication of how the Committee at Camp arrived at the quota established for Pennsylvania, which the committee originally recommended to Congress in its February 5 letter to President Laurens, see Joseph Reed to Thomas Wharton, February 1, 1778.

Henry Laurens to John Lewis Gervais

My Dear Sir,   11th March 1778.

Sympathize with me when I complain that near four Months have elapsed since the date of the last public or social Letter to me from Charles Town—consider how I must appear & what I must feel when publications have been made in all the American papers of a wasting Fire in the Capital City of the State from whence I ascended & I am left as unable to answer enquiries into that Calamity as I am ignorant, when *our State* will be represented? when *our State* intends to Ratify Confederation? when I expect Instructions to defend against Arthurs Appeal? questions which distress me every time they are asked.

Concerning the Fire I have learned enough to make me feel deeply for my fellow Citizens. Let me entreat my worthy friend Mr. Manigault & Yourself to charge my Brother's Estate & my own with ample Sums in contribution to the relief of the necessitous. On such an occasion be not so cowardly as to fear even the reproach of ostentation. You will see what other people give & go rather beyond proportion in subscribing for me—when I learn particulars I may say more on the subject.

Baron Holzendorff is now returning to France by way of Chs. Town, he will have a lamentable & pitious tale to relate. I think he has too much ground for complaint, but it is not proper for me to expatiate on the subject at this time.[1]

I have lent him 400 Dollars to help him onward after I had learned that he had been reduced to make sale of his Silver Mounted Sword & the Epaulets from his Coat. Do not conclude from hence that he is disliked, on the contrary except one or two, he enjoys the esteem & respect of every Body, but there is a Spirit in this World which will tyrannize and refuse to do justice—when it is in power—& at the same time submit to be bullied out of Millions.

The Baron had proposed to publish in Philadelphia & had receiv'd great encouragement to do so, an Essay on the Prussian Tactics but our being obliged to abandon that City, defeated his design. I wish he may receive encouragement for the work in Charles Town. He will inform you pretty fully & clearly of all our intelligence from the Army.

I presume my House has received some of my distressed neighbors lately burnt out otherwise I would chearfully consent to his request of lodging there until he can obtain a passage. I do not say a word about him to the President[2] because I reserve many things as more proper for private conversation but be assured he is respected by General Washington, General Gates, General deKalb & I may add what is abovementioned on this head, & I wish the courtesy of some of *us Americans,* may soften his resentment against others—which if added to that of many other disappointed & complaining French Men, may represent us in very unfavorable coulours in Europe a circumstance which Seems to be treated by certain persons with a contempt which discloses a want of knowledge of the World.

This will be delivered to you by Captn. John Christian Senf, lately a Lieut. & Engineer in General Reidesel's Hessian Troops. This Gentleman was made prisoner in the action of the 19th October near Saratoga. General Gates countenanced him & from reflection upon the Cruelty of his late Master in compelling him to engage in the present War he determined to change Countries & breathe in the Air of Liberty. General Gates Commissioned him to be a Captain of Engineers but here are so many foreigners, the pay allowed by the public so small & every article of subsistence so extravagantly Dear I have after receiving a very warm recommendation of him from the General advised him to try his fortune in a more Southern Latitude. He is an ingenious Sensible Man, & may be made very useful in public life as an Engineer or in the Service of Individuals as a Surveyor. You will soon discover his abilities & so far patronize him as to direct him how to apply them to the best purposes; I am sure he will be found of great benefit in directing & superintending any of our public Works. I have lent him 150 Dollars for expenses on his journey & should he remain any days unemployed I request you to advance him a farther necessary Sum on my account. Capt Senf is a Saxon & speaks a tongue which you have no aversion to. I shall therefore refer you to himself adding only, that considering him a modest & ingenious

Man I shall rejoice to learn that I have pointed a Road which may lead him to honour & Independence.

I have taken up so much time on behalf of these Strangers scarcely a moment remains for my own affairs but what can I say respecting them. I confide in your Self & my other friends that you will do all you can in my absence to save me from ruin & exert your endeavors to obtain leave for me to return & take the burthen from your hands.

I beg you will introduce Capt Senf to General Howe & excuse me to the General for not writing by this opportunity, tis impossible. Colo. Holzendorff & Capt Senf will relate to you how I am excercised except half an hour which I sometimes hammer out to Sixty minutes drinking Tea & chatting with the very pretty Ladies in this House. I am perpetually 19 or 20 Hours in the day going round like a Mill Horse. Congress have had so much business before them & I believe were never more in want of proper powers for transaction.

The Chief Justice[3] will expect a Line from me, I will do myself the honour of writing next opportunity & several other friends I hope will give me a little further Credit.

I thank Mr. Loveday for his Letter & intend very soon to write to him. I know he will proceed without being offended by my silence. I had almost forgot to say I am willing to give Mr. McCullough every reasonable Indulgence for his debt—let him have an opportunity of attempting to improve for his own benefit the Talents put into his hands. I believe him very honest & am desirous of befriending him.

Adieu My Dear Sir. Present me with respect & affection within your own Walls & in proper terms to all of our friends.[4]

LB (ScHi).

[1] For further information about Congress' alleged failure to appreciate the merits of Baron de Holtzendorf, see Laurens to Baron de Kalb, January 1, 1778, note 2. Among the Laurens Papers at DLC is a series of four letters that Holtzendorf wrote to Laurens at various times in 1778.

[2] President John Rutledge of South Carolina.

[3] William Henry Drayton.

[4] At the end of this letter Laurens noted in his letter book: "Inclosed the first interview with Capt. Wilford." Laurens Papers, ScHi. This enclosure has not been found. Richard Wilford was the aide sent to Congress by General Burgoyne to secure permission for his return to England.

Henry Laurens to Robert Howe

Sir   11th March 1778

Under Cover with this I have the honour of transmitting the following Papers.

1. An Act of Congress of the 7th. Inst. restricting the granting Furloughs in the Army.

2. A Commission appointing Nicholas Eveleigh Esquire Dep. Adjutant General for the States of So. Carolina & Georgia with the Rank of Colonel in the Army from 8th June 1777.

3. A Commission appointing Henry Purcell Esquire Dep. Judge Advocate for So. Carolina & Georgia with Rank from 8th June 1777 of Lieut. Colonel.

4. A Commission appointing Ferdind. deBrahm Esqr. Engineer with the Rank of Major in the Army 11th Febry 1778.[1]

I have the honour to be with Respect

LB (DNA: PCC, item 13).

[1] Laurens also notified De Brahm, Eveleigh, and Purcell of their appointment to these offices in brief letters that he wrote to them this day. PCC, item 13, fols. 220–21. For further information on the appointments of Eveleigh and Purcell, see Laurens to Howe, August 9, 1777, note 1. Gen. Robert Howe was commander of the southern military department.

Henry Laurens to John Rutledge

Dear Sir,   11th March 1778

I had the honour of writing to Your Excellency 30th Jany. continued to 3d Febry. by the hands of a Mr. Gray who received from me a large consideration for promised care & dispatch.

I am sorry to say our public affairs are not a whit mended since the gloomy account in my last.

Repeated daily clamors from every quarter for want of money & provision—the Quarter Master General's, the Commissary General & Clothier General's several departments in the most wretched situation particularly the former two.

The necessary works on North River extremely backward & strong fears expressed that we shall be in no State, when the River is navigable, to defend the Passes, in that Case Albany & all our Stores will be demolished.

The Army under General Washington mouldering away & still in danger of disbanding for want of provision.

The New Board of War has hitherto wrought nothing beneficial, have been bickering with the Executive Council of the State[1] & not run very smoothly with Congress.

The intended Irruption into Canada ended before it commenced. In this business the Marquis de Lafayette has acted with wisdom which has gained him much reputation—but he is seriously chargrined with the planners of that amusement & if I have the honour of any Influence it shall be, I may say it has been exercised to dissuade him from resentment at this critical juncture.[2] Your Excellency may recollect I regretted being almost alone in opposition to that indigested romantic Scheme. You Sir, who know the world so well, will not be surprized when I add, I can scarcely find a Man in Congress, now, who favoured it. Except my own I do not remember three dissenting voices—now—well "I never liked that Canada Expedition" is unanimous. I am extremely glad we have not sacrificed our Men. The want of Members in Congress is still to be deplored, were my Countrymen sensible of the daily waste of time, when affairs of the utmost importance demand attention & are neglected or slovened over, partly from a want of Numbers & partly of abilities, I am persuaded some of them would fly to remove the reproach which lais particularly severe upon our State.

I have been strongly tempted to resign the Chair in order to gain an opportunity for offering my sentiments upon subjects, which, tho' of great moment, came within the narrow Circle of my understanding. I am apprehensive of being under the necessity of transmitting a proof of this in three of Colo. Kennon's Bills sanctified by Your Excellencys testimonial which I fear will nevertheless, after certain illiberal remarks upon Your Excellency's Certificate, be returned protested to Charles Town. Had I been upon the floor I am persuaded this would not have happened—if the House is so unwise as to refuse payment tomorrow I shall think it my Duty to accompany them by a Special detail of the causes.[3]

I had lately the honour of a correspondence with the Renowned General Burgoyne, which Your Excellency will be well informed of by perusing Copies of our Letters & of the Acts of Congress upon that occasion which will be covered with this. If I had wanted confirmation of my sentiments on the Acts of Congress of the 8th January I should have received it from the General's Letters.

Our Commissary is now extremely busy in exchanging prisoners, 'tis said General Lee is actually on his way to Valley Forge but I suspend belief until I receive an account of his arrival. Tis very evident from Sir William Howe abating of his former demands which had put a stop to exchange, that he is in great want of Men & entertains no sanguine hopes of a speedy reinforcement from Great Britain. The Exchange will augment his Ranks about 1200 hearty fellows. We shall have a large remainder not less than 7000 including the Troops of Saratoga—but the Enemy outnumbers us in Officers. From accounts I have received we have not enough to meet theirs by 200—it seems we have had sad Rubbish under the guise of Officers.

I had little apprehension in June last that I was coming to this part of the World in order to grant Commissions for Cruizing Ships on the Delaware, Cheaspeak Bay, & even on the Ohio & Mississippi. Upon Delaware from whence the British Ships of War had retired to Rhode Island we have been amazingly successful, many Vessels have been captured & some very valuable. I have just received an Accot. of

Captn. Barry's taking two Ships chiefly laden with forage, an affecting stroke to the Enemy—a schooner Armed with 8 4-poundr. & 12 4-pound howitzers, having 1 Lt. Engineer, 15 Artificers & several Officers Wives & some Cargo on board; the Schooner a remarkable fine Vessel, all this effected by Armed Barges.

In Company with the bearer of this will go a young Gentleman[4] who had been a Lieut. in the Hessian Troops under General Burgoyne, was taken prisoner & after mature deliberation detested & abandoned the Cause in which he had been involuntarily plunged by his Prince. General Gates was so well pleased with him as to give him a Commission of Captn. Engineer, & recommended him very warmly to me. The public have no employment for him here, I have therefore encouraged him to seek his fortune in South Carolina where a Man of his abilities cannot be long out of business. He is said to be a good Engineer & is certainly an excellent draughtsman. If Your Excellency should have room for him in public Service he will prefer it, otherwise he means to offer himself as a Surveyor of Lands, a profession in which after a little experience he will become eminent, admitting his integrity equal to his ability, which both General Gates & myself think there is room to believe.

We have this very Evening received an intimation of a most horrid & dangerous conspiracy. If the secret information shall prove grounded, it will appear that Sr. William reduced to play a desparate Game would aim to be better acquainted with Congress. However, with all the air of probability, the tale is yet mysterious, we are pursuing measures to unfold it.[5] Great Britain would chearfully return to the Year 1763, but with difficulty will be brought to address America in the stile lately observed by her Northern Generals.

I condole with my friends & fellow Citizens Sufferers by the late Fire in Charles Town. The particulars I cannot learn, but enough is come to my knowledge to convince me of the great distress of the Inhabitants & that all these States will feel the Stroke in some degree.

I lately paid from the fund of So. Carolina in the public Treasury 20,246 Dollars for your Excellency's draughts in favor of Benja. Farrar Esquire for 14092 & 6154 Dollars. That Gentleman with Mr. Gaillard &ca. are still on the Monongahela & not a little apprehensive of being seized by some American Cruizer when they have reached the British Line on the Mississippi. I have done everything in my power to guard them against such danger, but I am not clear whether the Board of Wars pass will destroy the effect & validity of the presidents Commission by order of Congress.[6]

I request Your Excellency will allow Colonel Gervais to peruse Mr. Burgoyne's Letters & other papers on his affair & that Your Excellency will not permit any Copy or extract to be taken.

I have the honour to be with very great Regard & Esteem.

P.S. I intreat your Excellency to order the packets for Georgia to be sent immediately forward at Continental Expense.

LB (ScHi).
   [1] See, for example, Daniel Roberdeau to Thomas Wharton, January 30; and William Duer to Francis Lightfoot Lee, February 19, 1778, note.
   [2] See Laurens to Lafayette, March 4 and 6, 1778.
   [3] See Cornelius Harnett to William Wilkinson, March 3, 1778, note 1.
   [4] John Christopher Senf.
   [5] This is the only mention of this "mysterious" tale in the surviving correspondence of the delegates.
   [6] See Laurens to Benjamin Farrar, March 7, 1778.

Marine Committee to John Barry

Sir
                                                          March 11th 1778
   We have received your letter of the 8th instant and congratulate you on the successful commencement of your expedition and hope it will be attended with Similar advantages to the Public and Glory to the gallant Commander, brave officers & men concerned in it, throughout the whole course. The good opinion you have of your Prize Schooner[1] has determined us to purchase her for a Cruizer, you will therefore obtain the consent of the Partys who took her, have her fairly valued, and take her at that valuation for the public. She is to be called the Wasp, and as you have represented her to be properly equiped in every particular for an Armed Vessel, you will see that she is officered & manned as soon as possible, take the command of her yourself or bestow it on some brave, Active, prudent officer. You will employ her there so long as you shall think prudent, but should you apprehend there will be danger of her falling into the hands of the enemy you will send her out of the Bay into Senepuxent, Chincoteague or any of the Inlets on the Coast, where you will be able to collect a full Complement of Men if not well manned before. That done let her take such Station off Cape Henlopen as to be able to descry the enemies Vessels coming in & going out of the Capes and to secure a retreat should she fall in with any Vessels of Superior force. We observe that you have advised General Washington of your Success, and expect you have furnished him with Inventories of what was on board your Prizes. Any Articles which he may direct to be kept for the use of the Army you will retain having them properly valued and deliver them as he may direct. With regard to the general distribution of the Prize Money it is our opinion it should be distributed according to the number of Men & Guns in each Boat concerned in the Capture. As to the distribution among the officers and Men in the Continental Boats (If no previous agreement had been entered into)

it must be made agreeable to the Continental Regulations, but if those Regulations should appear not to be adapted to the peculiar circumstances of your expedition, we consent that you should enter into such agreement with your officers and Men as shall be most satisfactory to you & them. We approve of your consulting the Honorable Nicholas Vandyke Esqr when necessary and would have you agreeable to your Instructions, put your Prize goods under his care or any other person you may think proper,[2] and continue to pursue the main object of your expedition with all your usual vigour and activity. The Prisoners you have taken or shall take you will deliver to the commander of that Department of the main Army which may be most Convenient to you. We thank you for the early inteligence of your Success—your well known bravery and good conduct gives us Strong hopes of hearing from you often on Similar Occasions.

With the best wishes for your Success, We are sir, Your very hble servts

P.S. Please to transmit to us an Inventory of the effects you have Captured. Enclosed is Lieutenant Cokelys receipt for 50 Dollars which he will account with you for.

LB (DNA: PCC Miscellaneous Papers, Marine Committee Letter Book).

[1] For details on Barry's capture of the British schooner *Alert,* and its subsequent recapture, see William Bell Clark, *Gallant John Barry* (New York: Macmillan Co., 1938), pp. 148–53.

[2] On April 24 the Marine Committee wrote the following note to Nicholas Van Dyke, a Delaware delegate who did not return to Congress until September 1778. "Captain Barry hath informed us that he hath appointed a Mr. Hall Agent in behalf of the Continent for the Prizes he took in his Cruize on the Delaware and that when distribution should be made that Mr. Hall would deposit the Continental share in your hands. If that should be the case, and you should come to Congress soon, we wish you would bring the Money with you, or otherwise transmit the same by a Safe hand to the Navy Board at Baltimore." PCC Miscellaneous Papers, Marine Committee Letter Book, fol. 143; and Paullin, *Marine Committee Letters,* 1: 231. See also Marine Committee to Barry, March 26, 1778.

Jonathan Bayard Smith to James Young

Sir   York Town 11th March 1778

The frequent complaints made concerning the Waggon service induced me to trouble you with this letter. I shall mention two instances & will be much obliged to you for a state of the case in general, & for your sentiments on the particular instances I now refer to.

Your letter to Council was transmitted to the Delegates of this State, & we had occasion to communicate it to Congress.[1] It was said in reply that the Supperintendents had regularly turned over the whole transactions & given the proper orders for delivery to the Commissioners, and upon application from the Waggon Masters inform'd them that they had done so & referred to them.

The other Instance is that upon application for Waggons to move 2 tons of Iron you had refused to saying that no Waggons were to go out of the State.

As I imagine those things only need to be explained I wish for information, & shall be glad to receive it or on any other occasion from you.[2]

I am Sir with respect, your very Obt Sert,

Jona. B. Smith

Tr (PHarH).

[1] It is not clear from Smith's letter which of Wagon Master Young's letters to the Pennsylvania Council had been forwarded to the state's delegates, but for several references to documents bearing upon Young's activities at this time, see Jonathan Bayard Smith to Thomas Wharton, March 7, 1778, note.

[2] Young's response to Smith has not been found, but for his transmittal of it through the Pennsylvania Council, see his March 17 letter to council secretary Timothy Matlack, *Pa. Archives,* 1st ser. 6:366.

Thomas Burke to Richard Caswell

Dr Sir   York Pennsylvania March 12th. 1778

I had the honor of addressing you some short time before my departure from home, which was not so early as I expected when I took leave of you in Newbern, owing to unavoidable delays which I assure you Sir I surmounted as soon as it was in my Power. The intollerably bad roads kept me three weeks nearly on my Journey and I find on my arrival here things by no means in such forwardness as I wish. The army is at present much in the same Situation that it has been all the Winter, a Committee of Congress is at Camp in order to Enquire into and regulate the abuses and Insufficiencies therein. The Congress are much alarmed on account of the scarcity of Flesh provisions and many splendid projects are Contemplated but I fancy nothing will do unless the possessors of that Commodity can see prospects of gratifying their avarice. This vile principle if any thing can, will mar our Cause, for though America abounds with provisions we cannot get sufficient for a few Thousand men without spending millions in the purchase of it. The Congress have yet Resolved on Nothing relative to our Militia, indeed I cannot find that they have any Idea of a plan of Operations or System of Warfare for the next Campaign, and are not able to determin whether they will want them or not. I am myself of Opinion that our army will neither take the field early enough or be of Competent Strength when it is Collected, and I fear we shall be able to undertake Nothing against the Enemy, but must act still on the Defensive and prolong the War. This is far from being agreeable to my Ideas of good policy—but without force Sufficient for an Offensive War, it is all that can be done.

Virginia is the only state who has yet wholly agreed to ratify the Confederation. The 24th of this month is assigned for passing upon it again, by that time I suppose all the States will be Instructed. Maryland and Connecticut have produced theirs. The former desires the western boundaries of the States claiming to the Mississippi or South Seas to be Ascertained by Congress, and that all the Country west of the frontiers not granted to Individuals should be Common Stock. The latter desires that no Standing Army be kept up in time of peace by the United States, or Pensioners supported by them, except persons disabled in war, that the quota of the public Expence be in proportion to the Number of People in each State. I shall Endeavour to procure Copies of the Several Instructions, and transmit them to you, but I suppose the next Assembly will not take it up. They will deem it prudent to know the Sense of every other State before they finally determin. I refer you to Mr Penn for Intelligence. I believe I was mistaken in supposing the tenth of May the time of our Election. Mr Penn informs me it was the 28th of April, if this be so I shall return sooner than I expected, for having no powers beyond the day, and hoping the assembly will not require me to serve here any longer my stay would be useless. I hope the Assembly will take this into early consideration. If I shall observe any thing of Importance before Mr Penn's Departure (who only waits for good weather, and the roads being a little settled) I will add it.

I have the honor to be, with the greatest Esteem and respect, your Excellency's Obed Servt,   Thos Burke

RC (Nc–Ar).

Eliphalet Dyer to Jonathan Trumbull, Sr.

Sir   York Town 12th. Mar. 1778.

I had the Honor of yours by Torrey & since by M Brown, with the Inclosures. On Colo Champions Letter to M Buchanan being read in Congress, it produced all that Sollicitude & Concern the Subject required.[1] On the one Hand to recommend to the Assembly & State of Connecticut, who, they acknowlege, have ever distinguished themselves, not only in their ready Compliance with the Resolutions of Congress, but in their great Attention to every Thing which tended to the Good of the Common Cause & Interests of the United states— to revoke what they had so lately recommended them to adopt, would discover a Want of Consideration & too great a Fickleness in the

Representative Body of the United States, & might much lessen the Influence of their future Resolutions. When they first recommended to the several States to appoint Committees to meet at N Haven for the Purpose of Regulating Prices &ca,[2] they found themselves, at that Time, on the Brink of a Precipice—such a rapid Progress of the Increase of Prices on every Article necessary to raise as well as support the Army, the amazing Demands on the Treasury, arising from such an Increase, become beyond all possible Provision for Supplies, or would very soon be the Case—besides sinking the States in such an immense Debt, from which they never could emerge. Congress being sensible that this Rise did not wholly spring from the large Emissions of Bills or a Scarsity of Articles necessary for Consumption, but from a corrupt, avaricious, unnatural, infectious Disease which was spreading through every State, & which Nothing but extraordinary Remidies could check & Controul. That this was truly the Case appeared from the Prices being as extravagant in the States South of this, where the Bills were very scarce, as where there was the greatest Plenty. Therefore as the last Resort, with the other Remidies proposed, a Recommendation for a Regulating Act, in which the several States should unite, was what would effect some valuable Purpose—but at present we have received no Confirmation but from the State of Connecticut, the other States are generally much slower in their motions, & more feeble in their Efforts, but I could have wished, from the critical Scituation of our Affairs with Respect to Provisions, & the absolute Necessity of Supplies of Beef coming from the Eastward, that the Effect of the regulating Act, so far as respects Stallfed Beef, had been suspended 'till about the middle of June. Congress have immediately referred back Colo Champions Letter & their Resolution thereon to our Assembly, which is expressed in general Terms, as they would not appear to give any possitive Directions, which should interfere with the Rights of the Legislature of any particular State, but they really Wish, hope & expect, that the Act, so far as it respects Stall fed Beef, be suspended for a Time, for Ruin will ensue, unless every Obstruction be removed to every possible Supply of Beef 'till Summer fed Cattle can be procured.

I am &c.   Eliphalet Dyer

Tr (M–Ar).

[1] See Dyer to William Williams, March 10, 1778, note 5.

[2] Congress had recommended on November 22, 1777, that the New England states send commissioners to New Haven in January 1778 to establish price regulations and that they enact laws to enforce these regulations. *JCC*, 9:956–57.

Henry Laurens to George Clinton

Sir,   York Town 12 March 1778.

I beg leave to refer Your Excellency to my last Letter under the 7th Inst.[1] by Messenger Millet & also to two Acts of Congress which I have the honour of forwarding within the present Inclosure. Vizt.

1. of the 11th Inst. for defraying the Expences incurred in the several States by carrying into Execution an Act of the 9th February for suspending and removing supernumerary & delinquent Officers.

2. of the present date Recommending that each of the United States, keep at least three Members constantly in Congress during the War.[2]

I remain with perfect Regard & Respect, sir, Your Excellency's Most Obedient & Most humble servant,

Henry Laurens, President of Congress

RC (Privately owned original, 1974).

[1] See Laurens to Nicholas Cooke, March 6, 1778, note 3.

[2] Laurens also transmitted copies of these two resolves with brief letters that he wrote this day to Pres. Meshech Weare of New Hampshire, the Massachusetts Council, and Gov. Nicholas Cooke of Rhode Island; on March 14 to Govs. Thomas Johnson of Maryland and Richard Caswell of North Carolina; on March 15 to Pres. Thomas Wharton of Pennsylvania; and on March 16 to Gov. John Houstoun of Georgia. See PCC, item 13, fols. 223, 230; Red Series, R Ar; Signers of the Articles of Confederation Collection, NNPM; Red Books, MdAA; and Norton Collection, OClWHi.

Henry Laurens to Jonathan Trumbull, Sr.

Sir,   12th March 1778.

I beg leave to refer Your Excellency to my last Letter under the 6th Inst.[1] by Messenger Millet & also to sundry papers which I have the honour of forwarding in company with this. Vizt.

1. An Act of Congress of the 11th March submitting a Letter of the 28th Febry from the Commissary General of purchases to the Consideration of the Legislature of Connecticut.[2]

2. The Letter referred to.

3. An Act of the 11th for defraying the Expences incurred in the several States by carrying into Execution an Act of the 9th Febry. for suspending & removing supernumerary & delinquent Officers.

4. An Act of the present date recommending that each State hold constantly in Congress at least three Members during the War.

I remain with perfect Esteem & Respect assuring Your Excellency of my fervent wishes for the recovery of your health. &ca.

LB (DNA: PCC, item 13).

[1] See Laurens to Nicholas Cooke, March 6, 1778, note 3.
[2] See also Eliphalet Dyer to William Williams, March 10, 1778, note 5.

Henry Laurens to Jonathan Trumbull, Jr.

Sir,   York Town, 12th February [*i.e.* March] 1778.
I thank you for the justice you have done me in your favour of the
5th February which reached me no earlier than the 8th Inst. The
abatement which my past direction of Addresses made to your proper
stile, was not only inadvertent on my part, but the effect of misrepresentation from the Secretary of Congress from whom I had enquired
in order to avoid error, or giving Offence.[1]

Upon reading the Journal after the Rect. of Your Letter of* . . .,[2]
your name & the erroneous Title, of course occurred. I judged this a
proper juncture for correcting the mistake. For this purpose I intimated to the Secretary the claim which you had made in a Letter to
me, & received a reply so very rugged, as had nearly carried me beyond
the limits within which every Gentleman will confine himself in a
Public Assembly.[3] I treated the asperity of Mr. Secretary with silent
contempt, & appealed by reading Your Letter, to Congress. The Secretary turned to the Journals & produced Resolves from whence he had
derived *his* Resolutions. Other Gentlemen were at the trouble to
prove from the same Journal of a subsequent date Vizt. on the 28th
July 1775[4] that you had been appointed Pay Master of the   *[5]
department. I was asked if I had seen Your Commission? That I was
satisfied with your assurance of the fact & would not affront you, or
any Gentleman, by such a demand, appeared to me the best reply to
so giddy a question. The House happened to be extremely anxious
to proceed upon business of the highest importance, & as most of the
Members acquiesced in this opinion "that Colo. Trumbull should be
properly addressed" & I beleive took it for granted the Journal would
be altered, I judged it unnecessary to press the subject any further.
I have delivered my sentiments in Public, & also to Colo. Dyer in
private conversation, who promises me he will embrace a favorable
opportunity for obtaining an amendment of the improper Entries.

General Gates has assured me that he knows you are Commissioned
Pay Master General, this happened not from my seeking confirmation, but accidentally in the course of conversation, & I can perceive
no impropriety but directly the contrary, in Mr. President Hancock's
addition to the Resolve, which was intended to designate Jonathan
Trumbull Esqr. to be chief or principal Pay Master within a certain
district—and from the Character I have received of that Gentleman,
considered with the depreciated value of *general* in the Civil Line, I

cannot be persuaded to beleive that sheer thirst of Title, prompted his present Claim.

I flatter my self Sir, that enough is said to assure you, I am not chargeable either with a want of respect for you, or of attention to my duty, in any of my former addresses; & that I am with great Esteem & Regard, Sir, Your obedient & humble servant,

Henry Laurens. Private

RC (CtHi). Addressed: "Jonathan Trumbull Junr. Esquire, Pay Master General in the Northern department." LB (ScHi). The LB is correctly dated "12th March 1778."

[1] Jonathan Trumbull, Jr., had been elected "Pay master of the forces for the New York department" on July 28, 1775, and thereafter was variously referred to in the journals as "deputy pay master in the Northern Department" or "pay master general of the northern department." Laurens had addressed him as "Dep. Pay Master General Northern department" in a letter of January 22, 1778, prompting Trumbull to write a February 5 letter of complaint that is in neither PCC nor the Laurens Papers. Henceforth Secretary Thomson usually referred to Trumbull in the journals as "pay master in the northern department." Trumbull resigned this office in July 1778 to devote himself to settling the accounts of his recently deceased brother Joseph, the former commissary general of the Continental Army. See JCC, 2:212, 11:709–10; PCC, item 13, fol. 148; Burnett, Letters, 3:127n.5; and DAB. For another recent example of the Trumbull family's sensitivity to imagined congressional slights, see Laurens to Jonathan Trumbull, Sr., February 9, 1778.

[2] Asterisk and cllipsis in RC. To this asterisk Laurens keyed the following sentence at the foot of the letter: "the Letter which inclosed one from Mr Appleton —this being at the Treasury Board I cannot quote the precise date." The journals record that Congress read this particular letter from Trumbull on March 12 but give no date for it. See JCC, 10:245.

[3] For another example of Laurens' dissatisfaction with Secretary Thomson in this period, see Laurens' Notes on Half-Pay, April 17–21, 1778.

[4] At the end of the LB copy of this letter Laurens noted: "N.B. 14th sent him a distinct Cover a Copy of the Resolve 28 July 1775."

[5] Blank and ellipsis in RC. To this asterisk Laurens keyed the following sentence at the foot of the letter: "I have not the Journal before me & neither Colo. Dyer nor I can recollect precisely."

Robert Morris' Proposed Report on the Claims of Roderique Hortalez & Co.

[ca. March 12, 1778][1]

The Committee to whom Were referred Sundry letters received by the Commercial Committee relative to the Claims of Messr. Roderique Hortalez & Co. of Paris, report that Considerable quantities of arms, ammunition, Cloathing & other Stores have been received in different Ships & Vessels from France, & the West Indies, at Several ports in these united States, that the Same Were Shipped by the Sd.

Rod. Hor. & Co. or by their order & delivered to agents of these States for the use & Service thereof.

That the united States are indebted to the Said Rod. Hortalez & Co. for what may be justly due for the Cost, charges in France of the Said goods or Stores as well as for the freight to America, & that this debt ought to be paid With interest to be estimated according to the mercantile Custom or usage of that Country.

That the Commercial Committee Should be authorised & impowered to receive from the agent or attorney of Sd. R. H. & Co. the invoices & other documens relative to these transactions whereby to ascertain the amount of this debt, & make report to Congress from time to time of their proceedings for Confirmation.

That the Commercial Committee be authorized & impowered to pay to the Sd. agent Such Sums of Continental Currency as he may from time to time require fixing the rate of exchange on every Such payment at the Current or Equitable Course of exchange at Date thereof.

That the Commercial Committee be authorized & impowered to Ship Such cargoes of American produce as they may find Convenient & proper from time to time for France for the purpose of discharging this debt, Consigning Such cargoes to the order of the American Commissioners at the Court of France, giving them regular advice of every cargo they Ship.

That the Said Commissioners be instructed to appoint proper agents to receive Such cargoes as arrive, inspect their Condition, ascertain the quantities, qualities & Current prices of every article & tender the Sd. Cargoes at those prices to the Sd. R. H. & Co. or their agents, but if refused on their parts, then the Sd. agents to make the most advantageous Sale of the Cargoes, & remit the amount of the net proceeds as the Commissioners may order.[2]

Second plan proposed by Mr. M——

Whereas Rod. H. & Co. of Paris have Shipped or Caused to be Shipped or loaded on board Sundry Ships or Vessels Considerable quantities of Cannon, arms, ammunition, cloathing & other Stores most of which have been Safely landed in America & delivered to the agents of the united States for the use & Service thereof,

& whereas the Sd. R. Hortalez & Co. are willing & desirous to Continue Supplying these States with Cannon, Mortars, bombs, arms, ammunition, Cloathing & every Sort of Stores & Specie that may be wanted or required, provided Satisfactory assumption be made & assurance given for the payment in France of the just Cost, charges & freight of the Cargoes already Shipped as well as those to be hereafter Shipp'd & for Specie to be advanced,

& whereas Some Cargoes of American produce have already been

Shipped to the address of Sd. R. Hortalez & Co. or their assigns for Sale on acct. of the united States, net proceeds Whereof to be applyed in part discharge of their Claims,

Now Know ye that J.L. Defrancy agent for the Sd. R. Hortalez & Co. by them especially appointed & impowered to act fully & effectually in all things on their behalf as appears by a Certain letter of attorney or instrument of writing dated the   day of year   , Copy Whereof is hereunto annexed, doth for & on behalf of the Sd. R. Hortalez & Co. in Virtue of the Sd. power in him Vested, Contract, agree & engage to & with F. Lewis &ca a Committee of Commerce properly appointed & authorised by the Hble delegates of the united States of N. America in Congress assembled to enter into, execute, ratify & Confirm this Contract for & on behalf of the Sd. united States as follows.

1st. that the Cost & charges of the Several Cargoes already Shipped by R. Hortalez & Co. Shall be fairly Stated at the Current prices & usual mercantile charges of the date at which they were Shipped to the Satisfaction of the Said Committee.

2d. that the freight of the Sd. Cargoes Shall be charged agreable to the Contract made by & between Mr. Beaumarchais, Mr. Deane & Mr Montieu.[3]

3d. that all orders for Cannon, Mortars, bombs, arms, ammunition, Cloathing or other Stores which may hereafter be transmitted to Messrs. Rod. Hort. & Co. or delivered to their agent in America by the Sd. Committee or any other persons properly authorised by Congress to transmit or Deliver Such lists or orders Shall be executed & Shipped With all possible dispatch.

4th. that all articles to be hereafter Shipped for America in Virtue of this Contract Shall be provided as nearly to the orders as possible, at not higher than the Current prices & attended with the most moderate charges not higher than the usual mercantile charges of the place from whence they are Exported.

5th. that good Ships Shall be chartered on the most moderate terms for transporting the Stores to America & Carrying back Such cargoes as the Committee Shall choose to Ship in them.

6th. that agents appointed under authority of Congress Shall have free liberty to inspect the quality & require the prices of all articles to be Shipped for the acct. of the united States, With power to reject Such as they judge unfit or too high charged. They Shall also be parties in the charters of Ships to be Employed in this Service.

7th. that whatever bills of exchange the Hble. Congress Shall have occasion to draw on the Sd. R. Hortalez & Co. not Exceeding livers per ann. Shall be punctually honoured.[4]

In Consideration Whereof the Sd. F. Lewis &ca. Commercial Committee of congress by Virtue of the powers & authority to them delegated by the Hble. Congress, do for & in behalf of the Sd. united States Covenant, agree & Engage to & With the Sd. Rod. Hor. & Co. by their Sd. agent as follows.

1st. that remittances Shall be made by exports of American produces & otherways to the American Commissioners at the Court of France or Such agent as Shall be appointed under authority of Congress,[5] for the express purpose of discharging the debt already justly due or hereafter to become justly due in Consequence of this agreement.

2d. that   per Cent interest Shall be allowed on the debt already due, as well as on what is hereafter to become due to the Sd. R. H. & Co. in Virtue of this agreement computing the Same from the usual periods of Commercial credit on goods Exported & discounting these from interest on all payments from the dates of which they are made.[6]

3d. that Any payment of Continental Currency in America required by Sd. R. H. & Co. or their agent and agreed to by congress, Shall be Computed at the Current or equitable course of exchange at the date of the payment & interest be discounted on the amount from that date.

4th. that the remittances to be made for the purpose of extinguishing the debt now due, or to become due to the Said R. H. & Co. Shall be made at Such times & Seasons, as Shall be most Safe & Convenient for the American interest; but are to Continue untill the entire debt—principal & interest—Shall be fully & fairly discharged.

5th. that   per Cent Commission Shall be allowed to the Sd. R. Hortalez & Co. in the amount of the invoices, freights & monies paid & disbursed by them for acct. of the united States.[7]

6th. that   per Cent Commission Shall be allowed the Sd. R. Hortalez & Co. on the amount of all payments made to them on acct. of the united States.

Tr (ScHi). In the hand of Jean Baptiste Lazarus Théveneau de Francy.

[1] Robert Morris wrote this proposed report sometime after March 10, the day he left Manheim for York, and before March 16, the day the committee's revised report was submitted to Congress. It was on March 12 that Congress recommitted the committee's March 5 report. Francy made this copy soon after Morris drafted it and apparently sent it to Henry Laurens, a member of the committee Francy considered sympathetic to his situation and in whose collection of papers it is now located. See JCC, 10:245, 261; and Committee of Commerce to Robert Morris, March 5, 1778, note 2.

Morris' proposed report, although revised by the committee as explained in note 4 below, formed the heart of the committee report that was submitted to Congress on March 16, and many of the articles in Morris' proposed contract survive verbatim in the final document. The revised report was considered in the committee of the whole on the 17th and 20th and debated and postponed by Congress on the 23d. After further consideration on April 6, Congress adopted contract terms on the 7th and empowered the Committee of Commerce to execute the instrument as approved. The wording as published in the journals under the proceedings of April 7 is identical to the contract executed with Francy on April 16 by William Henry Drayton, William Duer, William Ellery, and James Forbes that is in the Correspondance politique, États-Unis, Archives du ministère des affaires etrangères, and which was reproduced as document no. 1913 in Benjamin Franklin Stevens, comp., *B.F. Stevens's Facsimiles of Manuscripts in European Archives Relating to America, 1773–1783,* 2107 facsim. in 24 portfolios (London: Photographed and printed by Malby & Sons, 1889–95). See *JCC,* 10:261–63, 274, 281, 313, 315–21, 356. See also Committee of Commerce to Morris, February 21, note 2; Committee on the Claims of Roderique Hortalez & Co. Report, March 5; and Committee of Commerce to the Commissioners at Paris, May 16, 1778.

[2] At this point in the manuscript Francy penned the following note, which Edmund C. Burnett erroneously attributed to Laurens in Burnett, *Letters,* 3:157. "N.B. this was the plan proposed by Mr. M—— to Settle what has been done, I do not make any observation upon it, because you comprehd much better than I can do the whole meaning of it. Upon remarks of Some other Gentlemen of the Commercial Committee, Mr. M—— has altered that first plan of Settlement, & has blended what has been done & what is to be done, So that what is done Should be almost the rule of what is to do, & I am Certainly Very far from agreeing to it." Immediately following this note, Francy copied Morris' proposed contract with Hortalez & Co. under the heading "Second plan proposed by Mr. M——," a somewhat misleading label since the proposed contract complements the report.

Francy's copy of Morris' proposed report is the manuscript that Burnett described as the "first plan of Robert Morris," which he had seen when he originally searched the Laurens Papers but could not locate when he was preparing his notes on the subject for publication. Although he carefully compared Morris' proposed contract with the final version as printed in *JCC,* 10:316–18, Burnett was unable to identify the handwriting and mistakenly identified it as "the instrument apparently in the form in which it was brought before Congress." See Burnett, *Letters,* 3:157n, 243n.

[3] This contract is in Wharton, *Diplomatic Correspondence,* 2:171–72.

[4] In the final version of the contract, which authorized committing up to 24 million livres annually, a concluding proviso was added stating that this seventh article would become binding only after it was jointly ratified by Hortalez & Co. and the American commissioners at Paris. *JCC,* 10:317–18.

[5] Although there are numerous minor variations between Morris' proposed contract and the document finally approved by Congress, the most significant difference concerns the consignment of American remittances. Morris' proposed report and contract attempted to establish congressional control over these remittances by consigning them to the American commissioners at Paris or a congressional agent. But before submitting its March 16 report to Congress the committee revised this first article and added a new second article that permitted consignment of American remittances directly to Hortalez & Co. although subject to the inspection and control of a congressional agent. This attempt to compromise objections raised by Francy apparently succeeded but did not entirely please the French agent. In an undated letter to Laurens, which was probably written about March 16, Francy further explained his concerns. "Receive my best thanks for your attention & care in what Concerns my affairs & tho' I am Convinced it is not my personal interest you have regard for, I am extremely grateful of what you do for me & much Sensible to it. I hope I will convince you I am worthy of the good opinion you have conceived of me.

"The report you have been So good as to Send to me is the Same which we did agree upon in the Commercial Committee after a long debate Concerning the remittances to be made; as that point was the most essential of all, I only did opposed to it without examining very close all the others which after reading them again Seem to me to be right enough, tho I do not like at all, that it is entirely left in the power of the Commercial Committee to send Some remittance, whenever it will be agreable to them; it is effectually agreed between us, that all the vessels fitted on public account for the express purpose of discharging a part of the debt Shall be directed to the house, but the Commercial Committee may notwithstanding Send fifty, without directing a Single one to us, they can always Say 'this is not to discharge a part of your debt,' & I have nothing to answer. I objected to it, & it was answered to me that if I did not truste the public faith, it Should be better not to enter into any Contract; what I Should have Complied with willingly, if I was not Convinced that it is of the greatest importance for the relief of the brave & honest men at the head of the machine to See one of the chief points established upon a proper train. However I shall be glad to have your opinion upon that article as well as upon the great authority which is given to an agent & which can be the Source of many & many difficulties, if he is not a very honest man & a better patriot than many others; at least I request your utmost attention upon the choice of Such an agent, you must be very Sensible how much it is important not to leve it in the power of the Commercial Committee to appoint one.

"I will do myself the honour of calling upon you in ten minutes to ask your advice about my objections which I cannot make publickly to oppose the report as I have agreed to it." Laurens Papers, ScHi.

⁶ This and all subsequent articles in the proposed contract correspond to the article bearing the next higher number in the final version.

⁷ Congress on April 13 authorized the commissioners at Paris "to determine and settle with the house of Roderique Hortales & Co., the compensation, if any, which should be allowed them on all merchandise and warlike stores, shipped by them for the use of the United States, previous to the 14 day of April, 1778, over and above the commission allowed them in the 6th article of the proposed contract." *JCC*, 10:342.

Pennsylvania Delegates to Thomas Wharton

Sir,   York Town March 12th. 1778

Peter Ozeas this day from Lancaster informed one of us that it was the desire of the Speaker and Coll. Morgan that he Ozeas should apply to a Magistrate here to apprehend Mr. Wm. Todd Coachmaker of Philad, who Mr. Ozeas says on his own knowledge issued Counterfeit Continental money in Reading. Mr. Todd having left this Town this morning we applied to the board of war for two light horse men and a proper Officer to follow Todd to Baltimore and bring him back, who are to set off this Evening.¹ In tracing this affair we are informed that Todd has ordered his Servant with a portmantua back to Pottsgrove, while he goes another way, this adds to the suspicion raised by Ozeas's information, therefore we have thought it of sufficient importance to furnish this information that you may have an Opportunity to send a prudent person to pursue the Servant, and to watch a happy nick of time when the Servant may be charged with counterfeit money, Letters, or other information for the fuller conviction of Mr. Todd, and to discover any accomplicies in the black design that may be against the general cause. We must exercise an Oliverian[2] deligence, secrecy and jealousy and search to the bottom of any Conspiracy, for an early conviction and example may have the happiest tendency to suppress so diabolical a Spirit, which otherwise may prevail to our ruin, therefore Council we doubt not will take every prudent and vigorous step to detect such vile Machinations. We should not on a verbal information have proceeded to any measure, but that Ozeas's testimony concerning the issuing the money may be sufficient, failing of further information which we earnestly desire as a matter of very high importance. We have further information on the same authority that Todd has been lately near the Enemys lines and has dry good to sell. We are respectfully, Sir, Yr. most obt. huml Servts.   Danl. Roberdeau

                                                            Jona. B. Smith

P.S. The Servant is a white man.[3]

RC (PHarH). Written by Roberdeau and signed by Roberdeau and Smith.
  [1] For a letter of this date from the Board of War to President Wharton concerning William Todd's apprehension, see *Pa. Archives,* 1st ser. 6:360–61.
  [2] A synonym for Cromwellian. *OED.*
  [3] Roberdeau and Smith also wrote the following brief letter to the Pennsylvania Council this day. "The Committee of Council and Assembly, who left us this day intimated the desire of the State to offer to Congress our Gallies and Zebechs, on reflection the Delegates think it of such importance that they request particular instructions on the head, lest they should act contrary to your, and the intention of the State. We shall expect Instructions and are, Sir, yr most obt huml Servt, Daniel Roberdeau. Jon'a. B. Smith." *Pa. Archives,* 1st ser. 6:359. The "Committee of Council and Assembly" referred to had laid a "representation" before Congress on the issue of the Continental Army's dependence upon the state for "establishing the necessary magazines" of wheat and flour. Ibid., pp. 333–36; PCC item 69, fols. 485–98; *Pa. Council Minutes,* 11:434–35; and *JCC,* 10:239. See also Henry Laurens to George Clinton, March 24, 1778, note 2.

Joseph Reed to George Washington

Dear Sir   [March 12, 1778]
    I fear the Arrangement of the Pennsylv. Battalions will be very inconveniently delayed if Gen. Wayne should stay out of Camp much longer, as he is the only General Officer of this State whose Assistance we can expect.
    If his Stay in Jersey is not very important I submit to your Excelly. whether it would not be best to call him into Camp as the whole Business of the Arrangement &c. now waits for him.[1]

RC (PHi). In Reed's hand, signature clipped. Endorsed: "12th March 1778 from Genl. Reed."

[1] As this letter is located in the Anthony Wayne Papers, PHi, Washington doubtless forwarded it to Wayne and probably enclosed it with his March 15 letter to Wayne ordering him to Valley Forge immediately. See Washington, *Writings* (Fitzpatrick), 11:86–87.

Oliver Wolcott to Laura Wolcott

My Dear,   York Town 12th March 1778

I have recd. a Letter from Oliver of the 4t inst. by which I had the Pleasure to learn that you and the Family were well. I think you will gratify my Wishes in letting me hear from you every Oppertunity. I have Wrote to you Three Letters, the last of which you may have recd. by this Time which was inclosed in a Letter to Dr. Smith.[1] Nothing Material has occurred since my last. Whatever Information I am able to give of publick Affairs is mentioned in my Letter to Mr Adams,[2] which he will let you See. And from thence be induced to beleive that the Regulating Act will be of no long Duration.[3] I intended to have Wrote to Mr. Reeve. You will present my best Compliments to him. How our Project goes on I have not heard. Oliver will continue to Write to me and let me know his Veiws. I am comfortably Lodged in a private House with a good Family with Mr. Huntington, but We are Obliged to Dine Abroad, but our Dutch Landlady gives us Incouragment that she will before long provide Dinners for us.

I still injoy my Health. May I not forget from whom the Blessing is derived. I shall Write to you by every Oppertunity. Take Care of your Health and may the Almighty Bless you. Let our Children know my tender Regard for them. As None of us have a Waiter from Connecticut Who might be more usefull to us than one here as he Might help any of us on our Return if Necessary, I had thot, therefore of sending for Whiting Stanly. You may if you please let me know wheither he would probably come if Sent for—or any other who may be as much depended upon. I told you that Mr. Huntingtons Servant had returned. I hope you have got the Flower of Mr Read. Goods it is said are much fallen at Boston. You will not depend upon Things being Cheaper than they are at present. Every Thing here bears an enormous Price except flower. Wheat may be had for 10 or 12/ per Bushell this Currency. My best Regards to my Friends and be assured of my inviolable Affection for you.   Oliver Wolcott

RC (CtHi).

[1] Wolcott's letter to Litchfield physician Reuben Smith has not been found, but his brief March 6 letter to Laura is in Wolcott Papers, CtHi. "At present," he had explained to Laura, "I am with Mr. Huntington at private Lodgings, which are good and the Dutch Family with whom We live are Very Neat, simple and kind.

We hope that We shall before long make such an Interest with the Family as to perswade them to get Dinners for us. But at present We go abroad for them. Congress adjourn to Dine at one o.Clock and so Meet in the afternoon. This Practice is much more agreable than to sit till 5 or 6 o.Clock and I think it expedites Business.

"I Wish to hear from you every Opportunity. I have not heard any Thing from Home since I left it. I Wish that you would suffer no unnecessary Anxiety. I trust that God will take Care of us and our Children. For myself I injoy more Health and Freedom of spirits than I expected. Indeed they are good. As to What News I could give I have Wrote in a Letter to Dr. Smith. I shall Write to you every Oppertunity. Your Happiness is the Object of my most fervent Wishes. May the Almighty Protect and Bless you and our Children. I am yours, with the tenderest Affection, Oliver Wolcott."

² Not found.

³ See Eliphalet Dyer to William Williams, March 10, 1778, note 5. For Wolcott's further comments on this subject, see his April 25 letter to Andrew Adams.

James Duane to George Clinton

Sir   Manour Livingston 13th March 1778

Your Excellency's Dispatches of the 25th of February did not reach me 'till I was proceding to attend the Treaty with the Six Nations.¹ The Scene in which we have been employed as well as the Want of a direct Conveyance, have deprived me of an earlier Opportunity of returning an Answer.

I think I informd your Excellency that I set out with the Marquis de la fayette from this place the 15th of February for Albany: his Instructions referring him to me for Information.² I had sufficient Reason to believe that the Enterprize which he was to conduct cou'd not go forward: Unwilling however that the most remote discouragement shoud be ascribed to our State, I resolved to leave him to Judge from his own observations and totally unprejudic'd & uninfluenc'd. He soon discovered the Want of almost every Necessary of which he had been led to expect an abundant Supply.

The Number of men was greatly deficient. They were destitute of warm Cloathing; their pay in Arrear, and both the Officers and Privates visibly averse to the Expedition. If the Army had been in the best Condition, and highest Spirits, a sufficient number of Teams (1300 being thought necessary) coud not have been collected in Season; and to encrease the difficulties, Forage it was *impracticable* to procure. The *Irruption* of the Enemy last Summer having prevented the Harvest in the Northern and North Eastern Parts of this State. Excepting Provisions, Ammunition and the Corps of Militia to be raisd in this State, nothing was ready; and the Opinion of the General Officers, as well as the publick at large, was strongly opposed to the Probability of Success had every one of these Impediments been removed. The Marquis who attentively examined every Circumstance saw with inexpressible Chagreen the Obstacles which clouded his prospects of Glory, and, after having flattered himself with sanguine Hopes of performing a distinguished Service to this Country, was oblig'd to relinquish the Enterprize without an Attempt to accomplish it. He has, it must be confessed, some Reason to be vexed and disgusted, advised, as he was, to announce to his Court, the Confidence reposd in him by being elevated to the Command of such an Expedition; and not in the least suspecting that General Gates cou'd be deceiv'd in the Circumstances of a Department which he had Just left, and which coud have undergone no material Alteration.

The Plan of Congress, when I was last upon the Floor, was by a sudden Irruption with 3 or 400 Volunteers, to attempt to burn the Enemy's shipping at St John's, and to offer a very considerable Bounty in Case of Success; The Command to be given to General Starke who was suppos'd to be very popular in New Hampshire the western frontiers of the Massachusetts, & the Grants; and in every other Respect qualified for the undertaking.[3] The adventurous Spirit of the Inhabitants in these parts, the Dangers to which they must now be exposd while the British Vessels command the Lakes, and the prospect of a great Reward, if they shoud succeed in the Attempt, were thought sufficient Considerations to Justify the Proposition. To me it was given in Charge by Congress, to confer with General Starke & deliver him his Instructions and explain their Views This occasiond my repairing to Albany as soon as I coud give him notice to meet me. At first he seemd sanguine that the scheme woud be acceptable and vigorously supported by those over whom he had an immediate Influence: but on examination it was found that a Reward which depended only on a prosperous Issue, was too slender a Motive for the Undertaking. A proposal was therefore made to Congress to allow the Volunteers pay at all Events, & the Bounty in Case of Success: But on General Gates's Arrival at Congress the Plan was enlargd into its' present Form, and the Command conferred on the Marquis.[4] Imagining it woud be agreeable to you to have a full View of this Transaction I have been thus circumstantial. I shoud have mentiond to your Excellency when I had the pleasure of seeing you, the original Plan; but as it Depended on Secrecy I was enjoind to communicate it only to General Starke.

Altho' we proposd to hold the Treaty with the Six Nations between the 15th & 20th of February it was not till the 27th that we had notice of their Assembling. We repair'd to John's Town the 28th, but they were so tedious in their movements that the Business was not opend untill Monday the 9th Instant. The Number of Indians was something above 700, consisting of Oneidas, Tuscarores, Onondagoes, a few Mohawks, and three or four Cayugoes: but not a single Senaca attended. The latter had the Insolence even to affect their Surprize that while our Tomahawks Stuck in their Heads, their Wounds were bleeding, and their Eyes streaming with Tears for the Loss of their Friends at the German flatts, we shoud think of inviting them to a Treaty!

The Speech from Congress[5] was in a Tone becoming the Dignity of Congress and the Spirit and Power of the United States. The generous and upright Conduct of these States towards the Six Nations, and their Ingratitude, Cruelty and Treachery were pointed out, and Satisfaction peremptorily Demanded. The faithful Oneidas & Tuscarores were excepted and distinguished. They were applauded for their Integrity and Firmness, and assurd of our Friendship and Protection.

An Onondagoe Chief spoke for the guilty Tribes. He exculpated himself & the Sachems, threw the Blame on the Headstrong warriors who no longer woud listen to advice, laid a proper Stress on the example of our own internal Divisions and Oppositions, and painted in strong Terms the Influence of the *Bribery* and Artifices employd by Butler and the other *Creatures* of the Crown.

An Oneida Chief answered for that Nation and the Tuscarores with a Spirit and Dignity which woud not have disgracd a Roman Senator. He pathetically lamented the *Degeneracy* of the unfriendly Tribes; predicted their final Destruction; and declard the *unalterable* Resolution of the Oneidas & Tuscarores, at every Hazard, to hold fast the Covenant Chain with the united States, and with them to be buried in the same Grave; or to enjoy the *Fruites* of Victory and Peace. He fully evinced the Sincerity of these Professions by desiring that we woud erect a Fortress in their Country and furnish a small Garrison to assist in their Defence. This being promisd on our part; He concluded with a solemn assurance that these two nations woud at all Times be ready to cooperate with Us against all our Enemies.

In a private manner they warnd us against the Onondagoes who they lookd upon as our Enemies notwithstanding their seeming Contrition for their passed Conduct: and affirmed that there was not the least doubt but that they, the Senecas, & Cayugoes, woud renew their Hostilities early in the Spring; & that Butler woud take possession of Oswego and get it fortified: For which Events they entreated us to be prepard.

In our Reply we applauded again the Courage & Fidelity of the Oneidas & Tuscarores. The other Nations we observed were not sufficiently represented to Justify our Treating with them. We directed therefore that a Council of their Confederacy shoud be assembled at Onondagoe as soon as possible; that our demand of satisfaction shoud be there publickly made, and from the hostile nations, an explicit Answer returnd: that they shoud be reminded of our upright and their *own treacherous* Behaviour: that our Cause was Just; that the Hand of the united States coud reach the remotest Corner of the Country of the Senacas; and that we trusted the good Spirit whom we servd woud enable us to punish all our Enemies & put it out of their power to do us further Injury.

The Inhabitants of the County who attended in great numbers were highly satisfied with the manner in which the Treaty was conducted. I think it will probably have a considerable Influence on the Onondagoes, upwards of an hundred of whom were present. They are much intermaried with the Oniedas & will be apt to follow their example. At Least that Tribe will be divided: But from the Senecas and Cayugoes, & the greatest part of the Mohawks, nothing but Revenge for their lost Friends, and tarnished Glory, is to be expected: especially while our Enemies are so plentifully supplied with the means of Corruption: and we cannot furnish our best Friends with the necessaries of Life even in the Course of Trade.

I hope the Facts I have suggested, which passed under my own Observation, will be sufficient to give your Excellency a competent Knowledge of the Temper and Disposition of the six Nations; and to enable you to take seasonable Measures for the Defence of our Frontier Inhabitants: at least so far as may depend on the Exertion of our internal Strength. I have conversed with the Marquis who was at the Treaty on this Subject. He has already orderd Troops to Schoharie and Cherry Valley, and directed an Engineer to lay out a fort in the Oneida Country. Sure I am that nothing in his power will be wanting for the Security of every part of this State.

As I was on my Journey to John's Town when I was honourd with the Receipt of your Dispatches: it was too late for your Excellency to execute your Trust respecting the Appointment of an Additional Commisr. for Indian Affairs. Before I left Congress it was pressed upon me to accept the office. I declind it, And on my promise to assist the Commisr. at the propos'd Treaty if necessary, the matter rested for that Time. When I met the Commisrs at Albany the beginning of January to fix the Treaty, it Appeard that there was no prospect of General Wolcot's, and no certainty of General Schuyler's Attendance. We concluded therefore to recommend it to Congress to appoint additional Commissioners, which occasioned the power committed to you.[6]

The Reason which inducd me to decline the Office of Commisr when my Acceptance was requested by Congress, is this. The Jurisdiction of this State over the Country of the Six Nations is unquestionable as well as ancient, on it depends the legality of all our Setler's in the Mohawk Country. Apprehensive that the Interference of Congress might one time or other cross the Rights or the Interests of the State, & that as a Trustee for Congress I might be embarrassed and restraind in supporting our separate & exclusive Jurisdiction, I did not see my way clear to engage in it: As far as I can Judge there is some Weight in the Objection. I am however not the less obliged to your Excellency for the Testimonial of your good Opinion in offering me the Appointment: When I pay you my Respects I shall take an Opportunity of conversing further upon it.

Having now, Sir, finished the Duties enjoined me by Congress on my Recess, in which to this Time I have been employd, I from this day consider myself as entring on that Respite from publick Business with which, thro' your Interposition, the Legislature have been pleasd to indulge me.[7]

I have the Honour to be, with the greatest Respect, Sir, your Excellencys most obedient huml Servant,   Jas Duane

P.S. Col. Livingston desires me to inform your Excellency that he will give the Person who is to direct the Construction of the Slitting Mill all the Encouragemt he can reasonably ask. Not knowing how he values his services it is difficult to mention a price: but rather than be disappointed he would allow him 20/ a day; a Sum he mentions at Random.

Tr (DLC).

[1] No February 25 "Dispatches" from Governor Clinton to Duane have been found, but on February 22 Clinton did write to Duane to notify him that he had appointed him a special commissioner for Indian affairs in the northern department. Clinton, *Papers* (Hastings), 2:791–92. Congress had instructed Duane on December 3, 1777, to assist the regular northern Indian commissioners in their dealings with the Six Nations, and he had been periodically engaged in this task since January. See *JCC*, 9:999; and Duane to Henry Laurens, January 12, 1778. There are minutes of the meetings between the commissioners and the Iroquois that Duane attended in January and April 1778 in the Philip Schuyler Papers, NN.

[2] See the instructions for the Canadian expedition in Gen. Horatio Gates' January 24, 1778, letter to Lafayette. Lafayette, *Papers* (Idzerda), 1:249–50. Duane provided an earlier description of his encounter with Lafayette in a letter he wrote to Clinton on February 19:

"The day I dispatched my last Letter to your Excellency I was honourd with a visit from the Marquiss defayette in his Route to this City. It was his Request and the wish of the honourable Congress that I shoud attend him & give him any Information in my power. I had about the same time receivd a pressing Letter from the Commissioners of Indian Affairs to assist them at the approaching Treaty with the Six nations which will be attended with difficulty & be probably followd by an open Rupture with the Senecas and Cayugaes if they are as implacable and determind as our Advices lead us to expect. From these Considerations tho' highly inconvenient after so long an absence from my Family I repaird to this City. The Marquiss is very assiduous and active and examines and will judge for himself. It is plain that he finds neither the Troops nor preparations in the Condition he expected; nor has he met I believe with any Person civil or military in this Quarter who approves of the Enterprize: tho' from this part of the State he will receive every thing he asks & they can grant. His Zeal for this Country for which he has given marks even of Enthusiasm, & his ardent desire for Glory lead him to wish the

Expedition practicable: but he is too considerate to pursue it rashly or without probable Grounds for a successful Issue. I must mention To your Excellency a Circumstance which shews the Liberality of his disposition. He determind on his entering Canada to supply his army thro his own private Bills on France to the amount of 5 or 6000 Guineas and to present that sum to Congress as a Proof of his Love to America & the Rights of human Nature!" Duane Papers, NHi.

[3] For further information about this "sudden Irruption," see Duane to John Stark, December 16, 1777.

[4] For a fuller account of the genesis of Lafayette's abortive Canadian expedition, see Henry Laurens to Lafayette, January 22, 1778, note 2.

[5] For the text of this speech to the Six Nations, which Congress had approved on December 3, 1777, see *JCC*, 9:994–98.

[6] See Henry Laurens to Duane, February 3, 1778, note 1.

[7] According to an account he submitted to the state of New York, Duane claimed payment for his "Services as a Delegate in Congress and on Committees of Congress from the 3d day of April 1777 to [March 17, 1778], at 7 dollars per day, being 348 days." Miscellaneous Manuscripts, NN.

Samuel Huntington to Jabez Huntington

Sir   York Town 13th March 1778
I am favoured with yours of the 5th Instant per Brown, am not a little concernd what may be the Effect of the Regulating Act in Connecticutt, with regard to the Article of beef at least; it being to take place So Soon. Congress have passed a Resolution on that Subject in very general terms which will be forwarded by Brown.[1]

Several of the States I am pretty Certain will not adopt the Act Supposing it Impossible however desirable to be put in practice. Is it not prudent to Suspend it at Least in Connecticutt until you find the Sentiments of other States on the Subject?

We have late Intelligence that three of the Enemies vessels are taken in the Delaware by our Capt. Barry with others, also a Report that General Waine has killed & taken nineteen of the Enemy on Jersey Side but know not the particulars, have no European Intelligence later than you will find in the public prints.

Remain Sir, your Humble Servant,   Saml Huntington

RC (MH–H).
[1] See Eliphalet Dyer to William Williams, March 10, 1778, note 5.

Henry Laurens to the Marquis de Lafayette

Dear General,   13th March 1778
It is now late in the Evening. I am just returned from Congress & have much business to prepare for a Messenger who is to make his excursion at the dawn of tomorrow & therefore only a Moment to

intimate that Congress by a side wind this afternoons meeting were induced, but not without debate, to Resolve that General Washington be authorized to recall Marquis delafayette & Baron deKalb to the Main Army.[1]

This may reach you before a Mandate from the General & will afford so much more time to make necessary arrangements for the retrograde journey.

I have the honour to be Noble Sir, with the highest Respect &ca.

LB (ScHi).
[1] See also Laurens to Lafayette, March 6, 1778, note 5.

Committee at Camp to Thomas Chase

In Committee of Congress   Camp Valley Forge March 14th 1778

Congress having upon the application of the Commander in Chief ordered a number of Bell Tents to be prepared for the use of the army, We were this day informed by him that it appeared by a return made by Mr. Butler (agent of General Miflin) that you had, in pursuance of the resolution of Congress, purchased a considerable quantity of Duck, and ordered the same to be made up into Bell Tents, and that upon further enquiry he found that such Kind of Tents, tho wanted, were by no means so necessary at present as tents for the Men, and requested us to give you directions immediately to make up all the Duck not already made into Bell Tents in your possession into Tents for the Men which we accordingly do.[1] You will therefore immediately upon the receipt of this give your necessary orders for the making of the last sort of Tents, notwithstanding the resolution of Congress or any directions you may have received to the contrary from the late Quarter Master General or any other person.

We are &c.   F D, by Order

FC (DNA: PCC, item 192). Written and signed by Francis Dana.
[1] Chase was deputy quartermaster general at Boston. Congress had ordered the purchase of 1,000 bell tents on January 6, 1778. JCC, 10:24.

Committee for Foreign Affairs to John Dunlap

Sir   York Town 14 March 1778

Please to send an *advertiser*,[1] regularly as you publish it, to the Committee for foreign Affairs. If you can send a continuation from the beginning of this year till now, you will commence your charge at that period.

In the name of the committee,   (Signed)   J. Lovell

RC (DNA: PCC, item 79).

[1] The *Pennsylvania Packet, or the General Advertiser,* which Dunlap had published in Philadelphia before the British occupation of the city, was published in Lancaster, Pa., from November 29, 1777, to June 18, 1778.

Henry Laurens to William Heath

Sir,   York Town 14th March 1778

Permit me to refer to my last of the 7th Inst. by Messenger Millet.

Congress came to no determination relative to adjustment of Accounts by General Burgoyne, therefore that matter remains open to your own determination.[1]

I this Moment applied again to the Treasury, rather to the Board of War & Ordnance, enquiring if a further Aid of Money had been forwarded—the Answer—"the whole Sum intended will be sent off to day"—confirmed by a Gentleman of the Treasury who is sitting by me.

I remain with perfect Esteem & Regard, Sir, Your obedient & Most humble servant,   Henry Laurens, President of Congress.

RC (MHi).

[1] See Laurens to Heath, March 6, 1778, a duplicate of which he had enclosed with his March 7 letter to the general.

Henry Laurens to Patrick Henry

Sir   14th March 1778.

Colo. Baylor was so obliging as to take under his protection my last Letter to your Excellency dated the 9th Inst.[1]

This will be accompanied by two Acts of Congress to which I beg leave to refer Vizt.

1. of the 11th Inst. for defraying expenses incurred by carrying into execution an Act of the 9th Febry for suspending or removing supernumerary & delinquent Officers.

2. of the 12th Recommending to the several States to keep constantly in Congress at least three Members during the War.

I shall by this opportunity transmit to Colo. Charles Harrison a Resolve of Congress ordering the Regiment of Artillery under his Command immediately to join General Washington.[2]

I have the honour to be with great regard &ca.

LB (DNA: PCC, item 13).

[1] See Laurens to Nicholas Cooke, March 6, 1778, note 3.

[2] See *JCC,* 10:226, 253. Laurens notified Colonel Harrison of this resolve in a brief letter he wrote to him this day. PCC, item 13, fol. 228. Washington had

requested the transfer of Harrison's artillery regiment to his army in a February 27 letter to Laurens. Washington, *Writings* (Fitzpatrick), 10:520.

Henry Laurens to George Washington

Sir,   14th March 1778.

My last to Your Excellency was dated the 10th Inst. per Messenger Barry.[1]

Inclosed with this your Excellency will receive an Act of Congress of the 13th,

Ordering Colonel Harrison's Regiment of Artillery from Virginia to join the grand Army without delay—And authorizing Your Excellency to order Major General Marquis delafayette & Major General Baron deKalb to rejoin the Army, & also to recall Colo. Hazen's or order any other Regiment from the Northward.

I have the honour to be with perfect Regard & Esteem &ca.

LB (DNA: PCC, item 13).
[1] See Laurens to William Livingston, March 10, 1778, note 2.

Henry Laurens to William Aylett

Sir,   15th March 1778

Inclosed within the present cover you will receive An Act of Congress dated yesterday for purchasing for the Army Neat Cattle & live Hogs in your department by means of the aid of John More Esquire together with a Copy of the said Act which you will be pleased to transmit to Mr. More & proceed on the intended business with all possible dispatch. Congress repose the highest confidence in your Zeal & abilities & you may rely upon being properly supported by supplies of Money.

I am with great regard & Respect.

LB (DNA: PCC, item 13). Addressed: "Colonel William Aylett Esquire, D[eputy] C[ommissary] of Purchases, Virginia."

Henry Laurens to John Laurens

My Dear son,   York Town, 15 March 1778

While James Custer is Copying a very short Address to Your General, I will employ my self in acknowledging the receipt of your favours of the 28th February & 9th Inst.[1] At another opportunity I may reply specially to parts which at present must lie dormant.

I will certainly this day, make some provision for those distressed fellow Citizens of whom you speak & address Mr Franklin through your means.[2] There are obvious objections against a proposal by me for more general contribution. I have once or twice hinted such a thing, & made very little impression; tis my Duty Charitably to conclude that every Man does in private as he pleases & that every one does somewhat toward the relief of sufferers in our great Cause. Nevertheless my only sentiments in this peculiar case are, that our Light should shine before Men. Were we possessed of the Spirit of Patriotism which flashed in 1775, there would be Contributions at this critical moment not only for the comforting of sick & Naked Prisoners but for the relief of all suffering Soldiers—for the support, conservation & augmentation of the Army & we should enable Your General that great & good Man to drive out our Invaders—but alas! that virtue now appears to have been a mere *flash*. Every Man has bought his Yoke of Oxen, has married a Wife & stays to prove them. Often have you heard me ludicrously express my fears that my Countrymen in general would prove only good for the Quarter— not for the Course. The present time too well confirms the remark. From the best accounts, from all Accounts, & I have opportunities of receiving the best, you lie at the Mercy of our Enemies, who may disposses & drive you, & in that Act animate our bosom-Enemies, throw the States into consternation & shake our Independency. Yet alas! although all see & acknowledge the danger is not in fancy only, yet time is toyed away—a Senate of 13 Members, seldom above 17—against whose honesty & good meaning I make no exception—Wisdom is justified of her Children. I have in my own name called & called again upon the States to fill up their several Representations—the Governors & President see & acknowledge the necessity—& there it ends. Men are engaged in private veiws—some are afraid of Expence & coarse fare & others of being exposed in high Characters & dangerous situations— & too too many are labouring at all hazards to add field to field. The Villains of exalted Rank who have been plundering our Treasury & starving our Cause contribute all their force to keep us down & my jealousies that some of these are in contact with Sir William grow strong.

If there are Patriots, Men who love Country more than pelf, let them step forth & cast their gifts or loans into the Treasury, some by Money & some by services without Reward. Others may, because they have ability, give both. I would wish to be in the first Class & subscribe to morrow five or ten thousand Pounds Sterling & if these were found insufficient, *all my Estate* shall be given for saving the Public— & perhaps there will be found in this proposition much of prudent calculation—give part to save the remainder. Be that as it may, or put me into either Class I am chearfully disposed to proceed provided

I have any prospect of success, but at present I have none. Proper subscriptions by, sure we may find on this continent from New Hamshire to Georgia, 500 wealthy Men, would raise near three Millions Sterling, return your Paper into the Treasury & animate the Middle & lower Ranks of people to adventure Life & fortune in proportion. I have sounded some breasts on this important subject—but all were cold, applaud the scheme—"if Men would do so it would certainly relieve us"—& there was all. Can I then believe that Men are in earnest? Yes I see they are in Earnest to plunder the Common Stock. The very manner of our proceeding in the Issuing our Money leads rapidly on to ruin. What complaints has your General been making for many Months past—without the least good effect—how have delinquents not only been skreened—but held up in triumph & can you prevail on me to remain longer among such People? No. I will rather insist upon your abandoning them. But indeed, *there,* are sometimes my hopes, *where you are*—A species of Patriotism may at length spring forth from the Army & so far save this Country as to drive out the Enemy & punish sluggish torpid friends. These Ideas have been long in my mind. I may have expressed them in some late uncopied Letter. If they are worth your reflexion, retain my meaning & destroy the Paper record.

I dont understand your meaning where you mention DuPlessis books, neither can James assist me, that Gentleman left no Books here.

Baron Holzendorff is gone to So Carolina exceedingly chagrined by the treatment he met with here. Poor Man, I almost wept when I learned by a mere accident, that he had been obliged to sell his Silver hilted Sword & Epaulets &c. to pay for his Lodging. I instantly put him a step above such necessity—& have given him Letters to Charles Town which will secure him tolerable quarters there & a Passage to his own Country.

My Dear son, I pray God protect you,   Henry Laurens

RC (ScHi).
    [1] These letters are in Simms, *Laurens Army Correspondence*, pp. 131–41.
    [2] John Laurens had suggested that his father send a sum of money to Thomas Franklin, Washington's agent in charge of relief for American prisoners of war held captive by the British in Philadelphia. Ibid., p. 137. Franklin's efforts in behalf of these captives are described in his February 16 "Declaration" and William Howe's February 17 letter to Washington in PCC, item 152, 5:327–41. No letters from President Laurens to Franklin have been found.
    [3] In order to combat the problem of poor attendance among the delegates, Congress had resolved on March 12 that henceforth every state should constantly maintain at least three delegates in Congress. *JCC*, 10:245–46.

Henry Laurens to William Livingston

Sir   15th March 1778.
I had the honour of writing to Your Excellency the 10th Inst. by Barry.

Inclosed within the present Cover Your Excellency will be pleased to receive two Acts of Congress under the 11th Inst. & one of the 12th to which I beg leave to refer.

1. for presenting the thanks of Congress to Your Excellency for your Excellency's attention to the public Interest by carrying into effect in New Jersey the Act of the 9th Febry. for suspending or removing supernumerary & delinquent Officers.[1]

2. for defraying expenses which may be incurred by carrying by the said Act of the 9th Febry into execution.

3. Requesting the States respecting to keep constantly attending Congress at least three Members during the War.

I have the honour to be &ca.

LB (DNA: PCC, item 13).
[1] See also Laurens to Livingston, March 10, 1778, note 1.

Henry Laurens to George Washington

Sir,   15th March 1778.
Last Night Sharp arrived with your Excellency's several Letters under the 7th, 8th & 12th Inst. containing the sundry papers referred to, which shall all be presented to Congress to Morrow.[1]

I return Sharp immediately with the inclosed Letter[2] which had been lying a day for want of a proper Messenger, & as there appears to be a degree of solicitude that the Marquis delafayette & Baron de Kalb should rejoin your Excellency without loss of time, I will not detain the Resolve of Congress which is within that Letter a moment unnecessarily. I remain with the highest Esteem & Regard &ca.

LB (DNA: PCC, item 13).
[1] Washington's March 7–8 and 12 letters to Laurens are in PCC, item 152, 5:317–24, 349–52, and Washington, *Writings* (Fitzpatrick), 11:37–45, 72–74. In them Washington complained of congressional interference with a prisoner exchange he was attempting to negotiate with General Howe, citing in particular resolves of December 19, 1777, and February 26, 1778, that made the conclusion of such an agreement contingent upon British repayment of the expenses incurred by the states in caring for enemy prisoners of war. Congress decided on March 18 that Washington could ignore these resolutions in treating with Howe, but on the 30th it approved a set of instructions for the commissioners appointed by Washington to negotiate the prisoner cartel, requiring them among other things to make Gen. Charles Lee's exchange a precondition to a general prisoner exchange and to

adhere to a December 30, 1777, resolve making loyalists serving in the British army liable to trial for treason in their respective states. Washington vigorously objected to these instructions in an April 4 letter to Laurens, arguing that they were ill-considered and would very likely "destroy the Idea of a Cartel." Washington's letter gave great offense to a number of delegates and touched off a heated debate in Congress, culminating in the dispatch of a presidential letter signed by Laurens on April 14 that generally defended the controversial instructions while advising Washington to use his discretion in applying them. By the time Washington received this letter, however, negotiations with Howe had collapsed, having foundered on the British commander's refusal to offer anything stronger than his personal word of honor as a guarantee for the proposed cartel. See *JCC*, 10:258, 266–67, 294–95, 314, 329–41; Washington, *Writings* (Fitzpatrick), 11:216–20, 276–77; Alexander Hamilton, *The Papers of Alexander Hamilton*, ed. Harold C. Syrett et al. (New York: Columbia University Press, 1961–), 1:445–78; Thomas Burke's Proposed Statement to Congress, April 13; Laurens to Washington, April 14; and Thomas Burke to Richard Caswell and to the North Carolina Assembly, April 29, 1778. For a discussion of British and American policies on prisoner exchanges, see Larry G. Bowman, *Captive Americans: Prisoners during the American Revolution* (Athens: Ohio University Press, 1976), pp. 103–15.

² See Laurens to Washington, March 14, 1778.

Committee at Camp to George Clinton

Sir,   In Committee of Congress.   Camp 16th March 1778

We do ourselves the Honor to enclose you the Arrangement of a continental Regiment upon the new Plan agreed to by the Committee according to which the old Battallions are to be modelled.¹ It is at the same Time intended to dismiss from the Service such Officers as had better not be in it and should there be some worthy Men who cannot be employed consistently with our Plan to recommend them to Congress to make Provision for them. You will therefore be pleased to form the Regiments raised within your State (excepting such as are in this Camp upon this Establishment) with as much Speed as the Nature of the Business will permit and transmit to this Committee a List of the Officers by you appointed and also such as are deserving and cannot be provided for. The Commissions will then be made out. The Method we followed was to obtain from the Field Officers of the Regiments who were to be confided in the Characters of the inferior Officers. Whatever Means shall appear to you best calculated for the Purpose your Good Sense will undoubtedly lead you to pursue. You will much oblige us Sir and contribute greatly to the public Service by taking the Trouble of this Business upon you.

We are respectfully, Your Excellency's most obedient & humble Servant,   Fra Dana, by Order

RC (NN). Written by Gouverneur Morris and signed by Francis Dana.

¹ The committee's enclosure in this letter has not been found, but it was almost certainly identical to the arrangement of an infantry regiment enclosed with

Committee at Camp to Henry Laurens, February 5, 1778, and printed with that
letter as enclosure no. 1. See also Gouverneur Morris to Clinton, this date.

William Ellery to William Vernon

Dear Sir,   York Town. Mh. 16th. 1778.
   On the 11th instant I received yours of the 5th and Mr. Jno.
Adams's of the 6th of February. Two paragraphs of the latter I will
transcribe; because I know it must give you pleasure. "Dear Sir I had
yesterday the pleasure of receiving your letter of the 22d of January
and beg leave to assure you I shall pay all proper attention to its
contents, by rendering to the Gentleman you recommend every service in my power.[1]

   "I had been before introduced to that young gentleman by his
father; for whom I have concieved a great deal of esteem, and from
what I have seen and heard of the son I think him ingenious and
promising; but as I shall have an ample opportunity to become more
acquainted with him, I shall be better able hereafter to speak of him
from my own knowledge, and you may depend upon it, that nothing
shall be wanting on my part, towards recommending him in proportion to his merit." I most heartily congratulate with you on your
Sons being under the patronage of so worthy a gentleman, and hope
he will be a blessing and an honour to his father and his country.
He early treads the great stage of the world, may his steps be directed
by unerring wisdom, and boundless goodness!

   I read that part of your letter, respecting the 74 at Portsmouth,
and a Paragraph of one I recd., about the same time and upon the
same Subject, from Mr. Whipple, to the marine committee, and it
was agreed to stop the building of her for the present. These huge
ships are too costly and unwieldy; and it will require as many men
to man one of them, as to man three or four frigates; besides we
cannot with all the naval force we can collect be able to cope with the
British navy. Our great Aim should be to destroy the trade of Britain;
for which purpose Frigates are infinitely better calculated than such
large Ships. Mr. Whipple proposes to the marine committee to put
the timber prepared for the 74 into a frigate to mount 30 18 pounders
on one deck and this proposal I believe would be complied with if
our finances were not at present very low and the demands of the
great departments of war very high. I wish we may be able to finish,
man, and get to sea, in the course of the next summer, the frigates
that are now in hand; but I very much doubt it. It gave the marine
committee great Satisfaction to find that the Warren had got out.
We have since heard that She had arrived at Boston, which we hope
will prove true. I hope you will get out the Providence and Columbus.

The Virginia hath made two fruitless attempts to pass out Chesapeak. She is order'd to make another. There ar four or five Men of war in that bay; but I cannot think it so difficult to pass by them, as it is to pass those in our Bay. Our last accounts from Charlestown So. Carolina were, that Capt. Biddle with three State armed Vessels were determined to go over the Bar, and attack several British Vessels of about an equal force with them. I cannot forbear being anxious for the Event.

The marine Committee lately ordered Capt. Barry of the Effingham to take the four Boats, belonging to the Frigates, which are Sunk in the Delaware, and proceed on a Cruise upon that River.[2] On the 7th instant Two of them, the other two had not then got below the city, joined by five boats, half manned, attacked (near Bombay hook) and took two of the Enemy's transport ships, one mounting six four pounders, the other two swivels; and also a Schooner with eight 4-pounders, twelve 4-pound howitzers and 32 men, properly equipped for an armed vessel. They first boarded the Ships, and, learning from them the Strength of the Schooner, Capt. Barry prudently sent a flag to the Schooner, ordering the Capt. of her to submit, and promising that he & his officers, on compliance, should be allowed their private baggage; whereupon they thought proper to strike. As the Ships were loaded only with forage, Capt. Barry, after stripping, burn't them. The Schooner, being a suitable Vessel for a Cruiser, he is order'd to purchase and employ on the Delaware so long as he thinks it may be safe. She had in a variety of useful and valuable Articles. This gallant Action reflects great Honour on Capt. Barry, his officers and the Crews of those Boats. The other two boats have since got down, and in their way took a small Sloop, with fresh Provisions, bound to the City. I expect every day to hear of their further Success. These boats will annoy and injure the enemy more, in my opinion, than both the Seventy fours would if they were built, equipped and manned, at least upon the Delaware.

With regard to the Fish, Mr. Whipple writes. "I have never been able to procure any fish that I think worth sending to you or your friends. They ask 20 dollars per Quintal for such as I would not, by any means, make use of. I do not suppose it possible to get any of the first Quality at present; when I can you may depend I shall not be unmindful of your order."

I thank you for the Stick of Sealing wax. I had been obliged some times to secure my Letters with the Wax taken from Letters I had received.

Please to write to me frequently, and send me all the news you can collect. The two armies are in statu quo. Nothing material hath lately turned up. You will have hear'd, before this reaches you, that the intended Irruption into Canada is laid aside. We are obstructing and fortifying Hudson's River, collecting men and provisions &c &c for the next campaign. The last will be the most difficult to accomplish. To have subdued both the British Armies in one Campaign was not more than I expected the last; but it would have left us nothing to do the ensueing Campaign.

With the Aid of Heaven we will crush the Serpents head next Summer, and force our Enemies to be at peace with Us! I have room only to add that I am, Yrs,   Wm Ellery

RC (RNHi).

[1] The "Gentleman" in question was Vernon's son William, who was seeking a position in "a good, reputable, mercantile house" in France. See Daniel Roberdeau to John Adams, January 22, 1778. The elder Vernon was a member of the Eastern Navy Board.

[2] See Marine Committee to John Barry, March 11, 1778.

Henry Laurens to Andrew Williamson and William Thomson

Dear Colonel[1]   16th March 1778.

The bearer hereof Rudolph Maxmillian Vanderpen has in his pocket a Commission by which he was appointed an Ensign or Coulor bearer somewhat, as I apprehend, below the Rank of Ensign in our establishment & above the degree of Serjeant. He says when he Entered into the British service he was promised an Ensigns Commission, which he often applied for in vain. The Commanding Officer neglected or refused to grant what he knew to be justly due to him, & therefore he held himself released from all engagement on his part, & embraced the first opportunity of coming within our Lines. He was sent from General Washington's Camp to York Town—here the Board of War have supported him & General Gates has requested from me a Letter to a friend in South Carolina where the poor fellow says he will be willing to Serve in any capacity he may be thought equal to & he intends to take the moderate walk of 700 Miles to the Banks of Sante & Savanna Rivers to put fortune to the test.

It is contrary to a Resolve of Congress to inlist into Continental Service any prisoner of War or Deserter[2] & under the latter denomination this person whatever may be his apologies, must be held. But he may be usefully employed in Garrisons or Rangers within the appointment of the State—and as active young Men if they have any merit may always find beneficial employment in So. Carolina, I venture to shew him the way to the hospitable Doors of my friends Colo. Thomson & Colo. Williamson whose benevolence will cast an eye of attention upon a Stranger who pretends to a sense of honor. I think appearances are in his favor that he will become an additional useful Inhabitant.

I am with great regard &ca.

LB (ScHi). Addressed: "Colo. Williamson, Ninety Six, & Colo. Thomson, Amelia."
  [1] Both Williamson and Thomson were colonels in the South Carolina militia.
  [2] Congress had passed this resolve on February 26. *JCC,* 10:203.

Gouverneur Morris to George Clinton

Sir.   Camp 16th March 1778.

By a Letter from the Committee which the Bearer will deliver to you We have requested your Excellency to assist in arranging or rather paying our Regiments.[1] Let me intreat that the utmost Attention be paid to removing every Officer who is unfit for the Post he fills since upon this will in a great Measure depend the Success of our Arms and not only that but also our Funds which can never be made equal to the horrible Expenditures which become necessary as much from the Want of good Discipline as any other Cause. The Want of Money in the several Departments is a Complaint reverberated to us from all Quarters and arises as much as any Thing from Neglect in those who should have thought a little more of paying while very liberal in contracting Debts. But surely it would be wise in the State immediately to tax very heavily even if it should answer no other Purpose than to pay their own Subjects for what is it after all but this that in the one Case the Continent pay an Interest for the Debt and in the other they do not. The bad Policy of delaying Taxation is so evident that the People ought to take exemplary Vengeance upon those whoever they may be who are Causes of such Delay. For God's Sake is it intended that our Neighbours shall make such Advances during the War as to leave us groaning under an immense Burthen of Debt at the Close of it? Are Gentlemen ignorant that Money is like Water which always seeking a Level runs to the Place from whence it is dipt out? Woeful Experience will demonstrate to them that the State which lays heavy Taxes for ten years will at the End of that Period have as much Money and as many Commodities as the State which has not taxed, but a truce to these Observations. In the Letter from the Committee we neglected (unless I mistake) to send you the Arrangement which shall therefore be done in this Letter. Let me observe apropos that by the broad Terms of our Letter Warner's Regiment is subjected to you.[2] On this Occasion you will not slip the Opportunity of paying him the proper Compliment and at the same Time exercise an Act of Authority which will speak very intelligibly. My Respects to all our Friends.

I am sincerely yours,   Gouvr Morris

RC (DLC).
[1] See Committee at Camp to Clinton, this date.
[2] Col. Seth Warner commanded a Continental regiment of Green Mountain Boys who were determined to make Vermont a separate state independent of New York. *DAB.*

Jonathan Bayard Smith to Thomas Wharton

Sir   York Town March 16. 1778
Above you have copy of a resolution this day passed by Congress.[1] The second resolution was moved but referred to a Committee who are directed to confer with Council thereon. The Committee are Mr. Clark, Mr. James Smith & Mr. Henry.[2]

This affair appears to be of a delicate nature & may possibly tend to embarrass if not to injure. The veiw of Congress is I apprehend to be informed if possible of the intended precautions to be taken by the state preventive of any ill effects from liberating Messrs. Penn & Chew.

I have the honor to be, with great respect, your excellencys most ob. h. st.   Jona. B. Smith

RC (NjP).
[1] For Congress' resolve directing the Board of War "to deliver over to the order of the president and council of Pensylvania, the prisoners sent from that State to Virginia," see *JCC,* 10:260.
[2] See Committee of Congress to Thomas Wharton, March 18, 1778.

John Henry to Nicholas Thomas

Sir.   York Town 17th March 1778
I should have done myself the pleasure of writing to you by the last post, but as the Confederation was to be taken up on the Day he left this place, I deferred writing untill I could have it in my power to acquaint you what was said upon that Subject, but before Congress rose the post had left Town.

Virginia ever desirous of taking the lead in this great Contest, was prepared and offered to ratify the Confederation. She stood, single, and enjoyed a secret pride in having laid the corner stone of a confederated world. Massachusetts Bay, Connecticut, New York, New Jersey, Pensylvania, and South Carolina will confederate. The Delegates of some of these States have not yet received their Instructions, but are in daily expectation of them. New Hampshire, Rhode Island, Deleware, and Georgia could give Congress no satisfactory information of what had been done in their several States, as they had received no authentic Intelligence upon this subject. There can be no doubt but these States will confederate. The Instructions which the Delegates of Maryland received from the Genl. Assembly were stated upon this occasion to Congress. Several of the States being unrepresented [and] few members prepared to combat our objections, produced [but a] short Debate. The matter now stands posponed till the twenty fifth of this month.[1] As to the two first objections, from the present Temper of the House I believe they will meet with very little opposition. But as to the last, which requires Congress to be invested with full power to ascertain and fix the western Limits of those States which claim to the Mississippi or South Sea all attempts will be vain and fruitless; Equally unsuccessful will prove the Efforts made to obtain a right in common to that extensive Country which lies to the Westward of the frontiers of the United States, the property of which was not vested in Individuals at the commencement of the present war. Much has been already said in Congress upon this subject, and the opinions of those who will have the determination of it, has been long made up. The Argument may be renewed but the Decision will be the same. The bare mentioning of the Subject rouses Virginia, and conscious of her own importance, she views her vast Dominion with the surest expectations of holding it unimpaired.

North Carolina has agreed only to the first, second, third, eighth and 12th, the second and third Sections of the fourth, and the last section of 9th Articles which she has instructed her Delegates immediately to ratify. But the remaining Clauses and Articles, which, she believes, contains matters of the highest importance and involving what may materially affect the internal Interest and sovereign Independency of the state and which is not immediately necessary and essential to the success of the present War, ought not to be ratified till there is full time for mature and deliberate consideration.

Connecticut has instructed her Delegates to obtain an alteration in the mode of supplying the common treasury with money by changing it from the value of Landed property to the Number of Inhabitants; if this cannot be done the Delegates are still impowered to ratify.

Congress have with great earnestness, and with a Desire of impressing on the Minds of the several States the necessity of filling up their Battalions, recommended a Draft of the Militias, or other measures that may be effectual. This I know will be a serious piece of Business in our State and dangerous to persue. How it can be effected and at the same time preserve the Temper of the people, I know not. It is possible the Legislature may fall upon ways and means without adopting the odious plan of Drafting.[2]

The enclosed paper of 7th March you will see a recommendation for the forming a Body of Horse.[3] The advantages are many and great, to be derived from a strong Body of Light Cavalry, in the opinion of your Commander in chief. If the plan alluded to should be so fortunate as to bring forth into the field a considerable Number of young Gentlemen of property and spirit, it cannot fail of producing the most salutary effect. The Legislature will give it every encouragement I hope in their power.

In the enclosed papers you see the reasonings and grounds upon which the Embarcation of Genl. Burgoyne and his troops is suspended. Since this resolution passed, Genl. Burgoyne upon his particular application is permitted to go to England.

We have little News worth communicating. The Success of Capt Barry in the Deleware you have heard. He has lost his schooner after a very obstinate engagement. A large Spanish Ship was lately taken off our Capes. A French Ship said to be worth, as things are now rated, five hundred thousand pounds is arrived in Carolina.

Congress is ex[t]remely thin, which you will discover by a resolve which has or will be soon sent you.[4]

I am sir with great respect your most obedt. and hble. Servt.

J. Henry Junr.

RC (MdAA).

[1] There is no mention of this postponement in the journals, but Thomas Burke's March 12 letter to Richard Caswell states that the debate on confederation was postponed to March 24.

[2] See JCC, 10:199–203; and Henry Laurens to Richard Caswell, March 1, 1778, note 2.

[3] For Congress' March 2 resolutions on raising troops of cavalry, see JCC, 10:214–15.

[4] See Henry Laurens to George Clinton, March 12, 1778, note.

Committee of Congress to Thomas Wharton

Hond. Sir,　　　　　　　　　　　　　　　　York 18th March 1778

Your Excellencies Letter in Council of the 7th Instant,[1] relative to the Prisoners sent from the State of Pennsylvania to Viriginia, was read in Congress and a resolution thereupon entered into directing the Board of War to deliver them to the Order of your State, which Resolution we presume has been transmitted, in the usual channel.[2]

The latter part of the Letter which mentions the case of the Honble John Penn and Benja. Chew Esqrs. occasions the Subscribers to trouble Your Excellency herewith, they having been appointed by Congress a Committee to Correspond with your State, & bring in a report to Congress on that Subject; Those Gentlemen as Crown Officers & holding Comissions under the Authority of the King of Great Britain, prior to the declaration of Independency, & yet taking no active parts (that we know of against us) since that Period, renders their situation very peculiar, in the first point of view, they seem, under their present restraint, Prisoners of the United States; what is to be done with them consistent with Justice & the publick safety, is a question of much importance. If enlarged & permitted to go into Philadelphia, what mischief may our Enemies doe, under a Colour of their Authority, even without their consent. If permitted to go at large in those parts of Pensylvania in possession of the Whigs, as they are so intermixed with Tories, very mischievous consequences may arise. If confined in Pensylvania for refusing a Test it may occasion discontent & caballing.

Congress have no objection (we are inclined to think) to their being returned, under the Authority of the State, provided it can be done without danger to the State of Pensylva. in particular, or the United States in general.

The Comittee request such Information on the Subject, as your State may think proper to Comunicate, to enable them to form their opinion, and report to Congress, for their determination.[3]

We have the honour to be, with great respect, your Excellencies most obedt. Servants,　　　　　　　　　Abra. Clark

John Henry Junr.

Jas. Smith

RC (PHi). Written by Smith and signed by Smith, Clark, and Henry.

[1] Wharton's March 7 letter to President Laurens is in PCC, item 69, fols. 481–82.

[2] See Jonathan Bayard Smith to Thomas Wharton, March 16; and Charles Thomson to Israel Pemberton, April 8, 1778. For information on the circumstances surrounding the arrest and exile of these Pennsylvanians to Virginia, see John Hancock to William Livingston, August 30, 1777.

[3] For the Pennsylvania Council's response to this letter, see *Pa. Archives,* 1st ser. 6:380, 389–90. For the disposition of the case of Penn and Chew, who were ordered returned to Pennsylvania and discharged from their parole pursuant to Congress' resolution of May 15, 1778, see *JCC*, 11:497, 503; and Henry Laurens to Benjamin Chew and John Penn, May 15, 1778. Their arrest and confinement the previous summer is discussed in Henry Laurens to John Rutledge, August 12 and 15, 1777.

Cornelius Harnett to William Wilkinson

Dear Sir　　　　　　　　　　York Town March 18th 1778

Since my last we have received no interesting Intelligence from the Army, they remain still in quiet possession of Valey-forge Camp.

I am apprehensive my Servant has attempted to go to Philadelphia & perhaps is got there. I can however hear nothing of him, altho' I have distributed advertisements all over the Country, & have imployed some of our light Horse to go in pursuit of him, but to no purpose. I expect to set off the middle of April, & I fear, without a Servant to attend me, as not one is to be had here as yet on any Terms.

Jackey is not yet come to me. Mr. Mitchell promised by letter to send him as soon as the weather would permit; indeed we have had no weather fit for any person to travel for two months past. I have again written very pressingly to Mr. Mitchell[1] for the Child & expect every day his answer. He lives now at a place called Potsgrove some where down towards Philadelphia.

It is hoped General Washington will be able to Open the Campaign with some vigorous exertions.

Burgoyns Army is Stopped, You will see the particulars in the inclosed News papers; I was not at Liberty to Communicate this Intelligence sooner.

I shall bring Your Nephew home with me; as I do not think it prudent to leave him at present in this Country; indeed the Schools in general are broke up, perhaps he may be sent to Mecklingburg, to be of advantage to him. If Mrs. Harnett will Consent I will send Neally with him, but this we can conclude upon after my return.

Your Bills I fear will not be paid. I wish you had not been Concerned with them. I ever Cautioned you against having any Connexion with that man Kennon but to no purpose; but it was unpardonable to have no Other Indorser than his Clerk. The business of Congress was taken up the whole day on Kennons Bills on Saturday last, and from the Complexion of the House, I am well satisfied they will not be paid. I shall bring it on again, & if they are not paid, I shall have them regularly Protested, which is I fear, all that can be done at present; & will send them on by Post, to give you an Oppertunity of endeavouring to procure payment from his Executors or Administrators, upon my word you have Acted exceedingly imprudent, to say no worse of it. You will be obliged to Commence a Suit, & throw good money after bad. I think I foresee what will happen on this Wild goose transaction. It is surprising to me that you could not take the Currency of your own Country for what you sold rather than take Bills drawn by a Man whose estate was universally believed insolvent, and only Indorsed by his Clerk. You will give me leave to tell you, that such a transaction Can not be reconciled to Common Sense. You have only lost 3500 Dollars by this *prudent* Step. *Shew this paragraph to Mrs. Harnett if you dare.*[2]

I am Dr Sir Your sincr friend & Ob Servt,   Cornl. Harnett

P.S. Since writing the foregoing, I have been favoured with yours of the 12 Feb. which I shall answer by Next Post.

RC (NcU).
¹ Not found.
² See also Harnett to Wilkinson, March 3, 1778, note 1.

James Duane to Robert Morris

My dear Friend   Manour Livingston 19th March 1778
    When I left Congress I was charged with Business which has kept me abroad and unsettled ever since I came to this State. This has been the Chief Reason of my not doing myself the pleasure of enquiring after your Health & of assuring you that however remote, you possess a Share in my Remembrance and Affections.
    I have written a long Letter to Congress[1] by this Conveyance to which I refer you for a full View of the Condition of this Department, the Temper of the six nations, and the Dangers to which we shall in all probability be exposed the approaching Campaign. I flatter myself that you will continue to be a warm advocate for the Protection which is necessary to preserve the shatterd Remains of a State which is equally the Object of *British,* and *savage* Malice. From the want of every necessary Preparation in the Northern Department, I am apprehensive that it is concluded that the Victories last Campaign, have placd us in a State of safety. Nothing however is more remote from Truth. The Sencas & Cayugaes the most powerful nations of the Confederacy instead of being humbled by their Defeat are enragd at their Disgrace; have refusd to attend the late Treaty from which I am Just returnd; and openly threaten Revenge. Butler intends to take possessn. of Oswego which will give the British Troops & their savages the greatest advantages in distressing our Frontiers; & I see no sufficient obstruction to discourage the Enemy's Troops & Fleet in the City & Harbour of New York from revisiting Hudson's River and compleating the Desert which they began last summer. They have unquestionably ample Means and to suppose they will not be exerted, if it is only to create an alarming Diversion in favour of General Howe, woud be Folly in the extreme.
    While I have Room to feel with Sympathetic Concern the Dangers and distresses of Pensylvania I shoud do my Friend Injustice to doubt his Anxiety for our Safety. I therefore please myself with a full Assurance that he will give all the weight to my Representations to Congress which they shall appear to him to deserve.
    There is one subject I have touched upon—the Illiberality of leaving General Schuyler eight months suspended in the Light of a Criminal without Examination or Trial.[2] The justice of such a procedure [*is*] out of the Question. Do you think, my dear Sir, that the Reputation of Congress must not be injurd, & the publick Service

prejudiced by so unexampelled a Delay? Will the impartial world be satisfied with the plea that such a Length of time was necessary to find out a Charge of maleconduct, or Evidence to maintain it? Will not Gent. who value their Honour be terrified from hazarding, what is so dear to every good Man, with such austere or such lukewarm masters, who seem prone to suspect a Crime, and indifferent whether the accusd shall ever have an opportunity to vindicate his Innocence? I do not know what passes in other States but here this unreasonable Treatment of officers of high Rank & Confidence is a Topic of general Conversation. Genl Schuyler wants no Office from Congress; He wishes to resign. He can in that Case be highly servicable to his own State; & yet he dare not resign least it shoud be ascribd to his unwillingness to undergo, what he most wants, a publick & impartial Enquiry and Trial. In the mean time the winter has passed away & the Campaign opening when it will be perhaps impracticable for the witnesses & a Court martial to be convend. Is not this sporting with Peoples Reputations and Peace of Mind? You my dear Sir who have an abundant portion of Sensibility, who know how precious a Jewel is a good name, who woud advocate Innocence, as much as you abhor Guilt, will I trust with manly freedom press forward the Trial of General Schuyler without further Delay both upon principles of private Justice & publick good. If Evidence cannot be discoverd in eight months the presumption is violent that none exists—especially after the publick Call which has been given, as well as the personal Applications which have made for this purpose. If it is to be taken up as a principle that there can be no Trial 'till Evidence shall be found; there may never be a Trial or Enquiry, & this after an Accusation and Suspension woud be a palpable Denial of Justice. But I will not enlarge.

I had the unhappiness, my dear Sir, on my Return home to find Mrs. Duane's Health greatly Impaird. The Dangers and Alarms to which she was exposd during the whole Summer joind to the fateagues & distress of a precipitate Flight, and my unexpected long absence, were too violent for her Fortitude and in a manner destroyd her whole nervous System. She recovers very Slowly and it requires all my Care and Attention to keep her in that Flow of spirits which is absolutely necessary to give her any Chance for Health.

Consider my dear Friend what a drawback this is from the Happiness I proposed to myself in rejoining my Family after so long an Absence. May Heaven preserve you & yours that first of all earthly Blessings Health. Your Fortitude will give you Contentment and Patience under all the Calamities we suffer in our persons or feel for our Friends. Present my affectionate Compliments to my dear Mrs. Morris, tell her that we often speak of you & her with unfeignd Regard, & that I am incapable of forgetting the Kindness and Hospitality with which I have been always entertaind at every place which called Mr. Morris its owner.

Do, my dear sir, write me the news. If you have none, write only that you & your family are well; & that you still remember, your truly affect Friend & most Obedt Servant, Jas. Duane

[P.S.] I have expected Mr Duer every day for three months which is the Reason I do not write. I fear the Return of his Indisposition. If he is still with you present him my respectful Complimts as well as to my other colleages & all in whose Remembrance I have a place.

RC (NAII).
 ¹ No doubt Duane is referring to his March 16 letter, which was read in Congress on the 28th but is not now in PCC. *JCC*, 10:291.
 ² For discussion of the congressional investigation of the role of Gen. Philip Schuyler and other officers in the July 1777 evacuation of Ticonderoga and Mount Independence, see John Hancock to Arthur St. Clair and Philip Schuyler, August 5, 1777; and Committee of Congress to Washington, February 7, 1778, note 1.

Edward Langworthy to William Palfrey

Dear Colonel, York Town, March 19th. 1778
 I am extremely sorry to observe that you give the least hint of leaving the Army, tho' I'm conscious you could do more for your family in a Private Station & that your Abilities & knowledge of mercantile Affairs could not fail of procuring you great Success; but my Dear Sir, it may be dangerous to the great & glorious Cause to suffer private motives to influence us at this Time.

True it is, you have made a great Sacrifice already & therefore should think you justifiable to conduct your future Life in whatever mode might be agreeable; but I cannot but express my Wishes that you would continue to move in that Sphere, in which it is my real Opinion, no Man in America will do better than yourself.

Life is a probationary State & a disinterested Conduct for the Liberties & good of Mankind will not fail of the Smiles & blessing of that great Being, who governs all & turns our hearts according to his pleasure.

I believe it is happy for the Continent that the Committee were sent to Camp, General Fulsom arrived here yesterday, when will the other Gentlemen return? We decrease in Members every Day; Mr Penn & Mr Harvey return to their respective States this week, so that the Congress will want assistance; Do give Mr Morris a hint of this. New York has agreed to the Confederation & directed her Delegates to ratify the same.

Mr Wood my Colleague sate out for Georgia yesterday.¹ I shall not leave Congress till the beginning of June & shall do my endeavor to get the Powder of Sago &c here as soon as possible & will send some likewise to Boston. [Of] this shall particularly inform you herea[fter.]

As I apprehend you will get into Tra[de] as soon as you leave the Army, I hope [you] will not fail to correspond with me. If the present Cloud should blow over, I am certain it would be for our mutual advantage.

We have had several Debates this week relative to the Exchange of Prisoners & the Liquidation of Accounts &c; as for my part, I am for relieving at all Events our distressed Friends from Captivity & have given my vote accordingly.[2] Col. Harnet desires his respectful Compliments to you. The Nymphs of the Stove Room smiled at your Ingenuity & remember you with pleasure.

I am, Dear Colonel, Your well wisher & very humble servt,

Edw Langworthy

RC (MH–H).

[1] Although Joseph Wood had been in Congress since mid-November 1777, no letter written by him during his period of service has been discovered, nor has evidence been found to indicate precisely when he last attended Congress. Wood was last recorded as voting on February 27; he did not participate in the roll call votes of March 13, 14, and 18. See *JCC,* 9:931, 10:205, 250–51, 256, 267–68.

[2] For the March 18 resolution authorizing Washington to exchange prisoners of war without awaiting final settlement of British prisoner accounts, while retaining the settlement of accounts as a prerequisite to negotiating a general cartel for future prisoner exchange, see *JCC,* 10:266–68.

Henry Laurens to William Aylett

Sir   19th March 1778.

I beg leave to refer you to my late Letter of 15th Currt.[1] which General Scott was so polite as to take under his protection & to promise he would deliver on his way to Williamsburg.[2] Within the present Inclosure you will receive two Copies of an Act of Congress of the 13th Inst. for appointing a Commissary general of purchases, & for ascertaining the allowance for purchasing provisions &c.—to which I beg leave to refer, requesting you to transmit one Copy to John Moore Esquire who I hope is now acting vigorously & Successfully in the line of the late appointment.

I am with much regard &ca.

LB (DNA: PCC, item 13). Addressed: "Colo. William Aylett Esquire, Williamsburg, by John Penn Esqr."

[1] See Laurens to Aylett, March 15, 1778.

[2] Laurens also wrote a brief letter this day to John Carter of Williamsburg, informing him of his March 16 appointment as Continental prize agent in Virginia.

Carter took the place of John Tazewell, who had recently resigned as prize agent and to whom Laurens addressed a brief letter this day containing word of congressional acceptance of his resignation. See PCC, item 13, fol. 232; and *JCC*, 10:259.

Henry Laurens to the Massachusetts Council

Honorable Gentlemen   19th March 1778

My last by Messenger Brown on the 12th Inst.[1] Within the present Inclosure you will receive an Act of Congress of the 16th for obtaining information from the several States of their determinations respecting the Recommendations of Congress &ca.[2] to which I beg leave to refer the Honorable Council & remain with very great Respect, Honorable Gentlemen, Your obedt. humble Servant.

24th. The Honorable Mr. President's favor of 23d Febry. reached me no earlier than yesterday. I have presented it to Congress—the Answer is anticipated by an Act of Congress of 15th Febry transmitted in mine of the 20th by Ross.[3]

LB (DNA: PCC, item 13).
[1] See Laurens to George Clinton, March 12, 1778, note 2.
[2] The enclosed "Act" of March 16 requested "the governors and presidents of the states . . . to transmit to Congress . . . attested copies of the acts passed by their respective legislatures, in pursuance of recommendations of Congress, which they may have received since the 1st of November last; and of all acts which they may hereafter pass, in consequence of future recommendations." *JCC*, 10:260–61. November 1, 1777, was the date of Laurens' election as president of Congress. Laurens also enclosed copies of this "Act" with brief covering letters that he wrote this day to the governors or presidents of New Hampshire, Rhode Island, Maryland, Virginia, North Carolina, and Georgia. See PCC, item 13, fols. 231–33; Meshech Weare Papers, Nh–Ar; Emmet Collection, NN; and Red Books, MdAA.
[3] The Massachusetts Council's February 23 letter is not in PCC. With his February 20 letter Laurens had enclosed a February 19 resolve requesting the council to disperse Gen. John Burgoyne's captured troops throughout Massachusetts. *JCC*, 10:184–85. Congress did not meet on February 15, a Sunday.

Daniel Roberdeau to Thomas Wharton

Sir,   York Town March 19th. 1778

The enclosed resolution was this Evening proposed to Congress, and after some debate committed to the Delegates of this State; we therefore request Instructions from The Honble. the Council on the head, with their result on the other matters refered to them by us as soon as possible.[1] A resolution has passed Congress recommending to this State to call out five hundred Militia which will be forwarded

to you by the President to which please to be refered.[2] I am in behalf
of my Collegues very respectfully, Sir, Yr. most obt. huml. Servt.

Daniel Roberdeau

RC (PHarH).
[1] For the Board of War's proposal that "to check any Insurrections" the government of Pennsylvania be requested to deposit with its county lieutenants "sufficient Quantities of Ammunition to be used in an Emergency," see *JCC*, 10:270.
For the Pennsylvania Council's March 21 reply reporting that they had instructed
the Lancaster town major "to add 20,000 cartridges to the stock on hand, as a
provision against emergencies," see *Pa. Archives*, 1st ser. 6:380.
[2] No such letter of transmittal from President Laurens has been found, but for
Congress' resolution requesting Pennsylvania to deploy 500 militiamen to protect
magazines at Bethlehem, Easton, and Reading, see *JCC*, 10:269–70.

Jonathan Bayard Smith to Thomas Wharton

Sir,   York Town March 19th. 1778

Upon an application from the settlers at Wioming or as they call
it "The Town of Westmoreland" congress agreed to establish one
Company of troops there for its immediate defence for one year.
Congress has expressed this in the same terms in which a similar
resolution passed two years ago & which I beleive was adopted on the
consent of the Delegates from Connecticut & this state.[1] At the same
time establishments were formed for the defence of the other frontiers
by establishing other corps both with regard to Pennsylv. & Virginia.
The house is prepared for the same measures now on application (I
believe) for that purpose. But the affair I imagined had been left to
the Commissioners now at Pittsburgh at least as far as it respects the
Vicinity of that place.[2]

In a letter received from Genl. Washington yesterday he speaks of
the Enemys representation concerning the treatment of the flag
bearers & seems to labor under considerable difficulties on that head.
An order passed Congress some time ago for obtaining from the
Honble Council a state of that transaction as far as Council or persons under their authority were concerned. I wish it were done.[3]

The Committee ordered to report on the memorial of the Assembly
& Council have not yet had an opportunity of laying before Congress
their report.[4] I have seen what they propose. Among other matters,
they recommend that the prices fixed by the state be adhered to; &
that the waggon hire be settled agreeable to the act of our state.

I have the honor to be, with great respect, your Excellencys obedt.
& very humble Servant,   Jona. B. Smith

RC (PHi).
[1] For Congress' August 23, 1776, resolution on this subject, see *JCC*, 5:698–99.

² For the Westmoreland petition which was read in Congress on March 13, the Board of War's March 14 report on it, and Congress' order that "one full company of foot be raised in the Town of Westmoreland," see *JCC*, 10:247, 257, 261–62, 263.

³ For Washington's March 7–8 letter on "the treatment of the flag bearers," which Congress resumed consideration of (rather than "received," as Smith states) on March 18, see Washington, *Writings* (Fitzpatrick), 11:37–45. The episode that gave the general "considerable difficulties on that head" is discussed in John Harvie and Gouverneur Morris to the Pennsylvania Council, January 24, 1778. For the council's February 16 report on the subject and their March 21 response to this letter, see *Pa. Archives*, 1st ser. 6:268–69, 380.

⁴ See Henry Laurens to George Clinton, March 24, 1778, note 2.

John Banister to Frances Bland Randolph

York. Pensylvania. 20th March. 1778

The hurry of Business in this Place and the constant attention required for the discharge of the important duties of Congress, admit of little time for paying that Regard I owe to my Friends so frequently as I wish.¹ Besides these Reasons an incommodious Lodging without Fire in the Morning or Evening renders it almost impossible to write the letters which Inclination and the strongest attachment to my little Circle of Friends at Matoax would impel me to, but in a few days I hope some of these obstacles will be removed & then I shall be regular in corresponding with you & the Girls.² In the Mean time I beg you not to forget your share in this agreeable Intercourse. There is not the least News of an interesting Nature, but thus much you may rely on the Campaign now approaching will be great in its Events. The Pertinacity of the English still continues, & their steady persuit of the Conquest of America is their favorite object, for which Purpose they voted a Reinforcement of twenty thousand Soldiers, & in all instances at the opening of their Session the Parliament have submitted to dictatorial Majesty by echoing back his Speech, & without even a Question voting the required Supplies.

Tell the Girls I shall write them by the next opportunity & to beleive that nothing would be more pleasing to me than to hear of their Improvement, in the attainment of every valuable accomplishment, it is by these means they will either be happy or deserve it.

How is my Friend Miss Hall? This is the highest Stile of Regard I am at Liberty to entertain for any of your charming Sex.

But is it not hard that I am to loose this precious Season of my Life, cut off as I am from the Society of my female Friends, & perhaps forever from a Connection I most ardently wish and deem essential to Happiness? Mr. Penn has just called for the letter & I must conclude by wishing you every felicity & assuring you that I am most affectionately, your Friend,   J Banister.

[*P.S.*] I wrote so hastily with Mr. Penn hurrying me that I fear you'll not be able to read the letter. Respects to Mr. Buchanan & his Lady & Mr. Leigh.

RC (ViW).
   ¹ Banister had taken his seat in Congress on March 16. *JCC,* 10:258.
   ² This letter was doubtless written to Frances Bland Randolph (1752–88), a sister of Banister's late wife Elizabeth. Frances, the young widow of John Randolph of Matoax, became the wife of St. George Tucker in September 1778, among whose papers Banister's letter is now located. Jonathan Daniels, *The Randolphs of Virginia* (Garden City, N.Y.: Doubleday & Co., 1972), pp. xx, 97, 111.

Cornelius Harnett to Richard Caswell

Dear Sir   York Town 20 March 1778
   I have been laid up with the Gout which has prevented my writing to Your Excellency for some time past having had it in my right hand. Nothing has as yet been determined on in Congress relative to Calling out the Militia of No Carolina. The Army remains still at Valey Forge, & we have been for some time alarmed with the great Scarcity of flesh to feed them. My friend Burke thinks this an Artificial Scarcity; in this we differ much in Opinion, as I am Convinced the want is real, as we have not been Able as yet to lay up any Magazines of Provisions, & have had only sufficient to Supply the immediate wants of the Army; I am firmly of Opinion if we fail at all in the Vigour of our Opperations, it will be owing to this Circumstance; & by that means, I fear the war may be prolonged, and our Army reduced to the Necessity of carrying on a defensive war only. I hope I may be mistaken, many Gentlemen think I am; The Provision not coming on as fast as we wish, may perhaps be owing to the badness of the weather, which has rendered the roads almost impassable; how my Collegue (Penn) will get on, I know not, he is the bearer of this & I beg leave to refer you to him for further information in regard to Congress Matters. General Washington has it much at heart to Open the Campaign with Vigour before the Enemy can possibly receive reinforcements.
   Our Committee are not yet arrived from Camp, but are daily expected. It is expected they will, on their arrival, Open a new field for Congress.
   I intend to set off on my return home some time towards the middle of April, I shall then have been ten Months from my family, and as Our Assembly pay their Delegates so very Liberally, I have neither expectation or wish to return again, as I am convinced there will be many Candidates for the Honorable imployment, I am not one; 'tho

I shall think it my Duty to serve my Country to the best of my poor abilities, in any Capacity, either with or without pay.

I suppose the Genl. Assembly will be adjourned before my return, I am sorry they had not Continued thier Present Delegates until they were relieved by Others, this might have prevented Our State from being unrepresented in Congress for two or three Months at least, which must be the case as matters now Stand.

Virginia has impowered her Delegates to ratify the Confederation. The Members from Massachusets have also private Letters informing them that their State has also done it.[1] I do not hear of any Other States doing it as yet; Connecticut wish the Quota to be fixed by the Number of people in each State; every Other Objection of theirs has little weight.

Every member of Congress seems to wish for a Confederacy except my good friend Burke who laughs at it as a Chymerical Project, it does not strike me in that point of view. I think that unless the States Confederate a door will be left open for Continual Contention & Bloodshed, and *that,* very soon after we are at peace with Europe. I heartily wish I may be Mistaken. I have the honor to be with the greatest respect, Your Excellencys Most Obed & very hul Servt,

Cornl. Harnett

P.S. Upon enquiry I find the Delegates from the several States have power to ratify the Confederation, but are to endeavor to get some Alterations made if possible. Mr. Penn will give Your Excellency further information on this subject. The Gen. Assembly of N. York have agreed unanimously and have by Commission empowered their Delegates.[2] As I have been informed some aspersions have been thrown out to the Prejudice of Mr. Penn, I must in justice to that Gentleman's Character assure your Excellency that his Conduct as a Delegate and a Gentleman has been worthy and disinterested.

RC (NcU).
  [1] See James Lovell to Samuel Adams, March 10, 1778, note 1.
  [2] The New York legislature's instrument of ratification, signed by Governor Clinton on February 16, is in *JCC,* 11:665–68.

Henry Laurens to Egbert Benson

Sir,   20th March 1778.

Your Letter of the 31st December which I had the honour of receiving the 27th Jany. was immediately presented to Congress.[1] The Members then present expressed generally their regret that you had declined acting in the Commission for the intended "Enquiry" at Providence & ordered the Letter to be filed by the Secretary.

From the method in which I found Congress habituated & against which I have sometimes remonstrated, it is not the president's province to acknowledge the Receipt of Letters without the authority of a Resolve or special order, nor indeed can he in many Instances even recite the date but by the aid of a good memory, hence I flatter myself Sir, you will be persuaded to beleive, the seeming neglect of your former address is not imputable to me. At the same time tis my duty to declare the opinion of Congress, from the sentiments delivered by Individuals, appeared to be, that an appointment in your Stead would have arrived posterior to the period first assigned for that Enquiry, & that the four other Gentlemen named in the Commission would all have given their attendance to the business.

This Morning the Honble Mr. Lewis put into my hand & I presented to Congress your Letter of the 7th Inst. directed to the Delegates from New York. The House made no order, but the unanimous Voice indicated an earnest desire that you will if your affairs can possibly admit of your absence from home join the other Commissioners, if they shall have judged it necessary to adjourn to a further day from the intended meeting on the 4 Monday in the present Month & give me leave from the best assurance to add Sir that in such Case your Services will be highly acceptable.

I have the honour to be with very great Regard & Esteem &ca.

LB (DNA: PCC, item 13).

[1] Egbert Benson (1746–1833), a New York lawyer, served on the New York Council of Safety, 1777–78, as attorney general of the state, 1777–87, and as a delegate to Congress, 1784, 1787–88. *Bio. Dir. Cong.;* and *DAB.* On December 11, 1777, Congress had appointed Benson one of five commissioners to investigate the failure in October of an expedition against the British in Rhode Island. The December 31 letter in which he declined this appointment is not in PCC. See *JCC,* 9:1020, 10:93, 271; and Laurens to the Rhode Island Expedition Commissioners, December 15, 1777.

James Lovell to Samuel Adams

Dear Sir,   [March 20? 1778] [1]

Mr Dana is likely to be at Camp a Fortnight longer. I will make no Comments upon this. I have mentioned something like it as often to you as if *you* was the procuring cause of a regulation which has not *yet* proved beneficial to our state, for which end it was doubtless calculated. I must insist upon it that more than are necessary for a vote ought always to be attending, as a necessary provision against accident.

A small Letter from Bingham with some English news papers having cost us nearly £180 has turned my mind towards travailing charges and the long Etcætera of washing, botching and patching. The two last multiply upon me, and being the subjects of draughts upon the privy purse, rather than dittos against the public Treasury, I find them as much as can possibly be spared from the appropriations for my Family. How shall I contrive to obtain from the Assembly of our State an Allowance of the 260 dollars which I now totally despair of recovering by advertisement. You know the disposition of the People who alone can grant it. If they are not disposed to do it I must contrive to leave this place upon your return and Jew-like buy & sell Salt till I have thus piously recovered from the poor & needy what was alike piously taken from me by some *industrious* money getting man in THAT GREAT CITY.

I have wrote to Doctr. Cooper[2] all that was scratching over for our Martinique Correspondent's letter. As to Affairs in this quarter they are just as *you* would naturally imagine from your former knowledge of the discipline of our Camp. You may tell your acquaintance how that is. I am sure I need not tell you. Pray endeavour that the eastern Recruits should not come forward 5 Weeks too late. Our Dilatoriness will give Howe opportunity to reestablish his Reputation early this Campaign I fear. At present it is much sunk among the Quakers and their Likenesses. New York has sent her Confirmation of the Confœderation in a most elegant and formal manner engrossed and fortified with the Great Seal of the State to be lodged among the Papers of the Continent the most precious. Our State is little attentive to such things and yet they are far from improper. I am Sir, affectionately yr humble Servant,   J L

RC (NN).
   [1] This undated letter was apparently written shortly after March 19 when the news of New York's ratification of the Articles of Confederation arrived at York but before Francis Dana's return from army headquarters on March 23, 1778.
   [2] Not found.

Henry Laurens to George Washington

Sir,   21st March 1778
   My last to your Excellency was under the 15th by Sharp in which I had acknowledged the receipt of your Excellency's favours of the 7th, 8th & 12th & which I now repeat because I have heard nothing since of that Man who in common course should have been at Camp on the 16th. Within three days past I have had the honour of presenting to Congress Your Excellency's several dispatches of the 14th, 16th & 17th.[1] Those of the 7th, 8th & 12th are still in the hands of a Committee from whom may be expected a special Report respecting the many opprobrious terms & epithets scattered throughout the Papers

from Sir Willm. Howe, applied to the good people of these United States & to their Representatives in Congress, which were heard by the House with great Indignation. From expressions of sentiment by Members on all sides, it appears to be the general opinion, that such papers should have been marked with the contempt of an immediate return.

Your Excellency will be pleased to receive within the present Inclosure three Acts of Congress.

1. 18th March—Authorizing Your Excellency to settle a general Cartel & to proceed to an Exchange of Prisoners.[2]

2. 19th—for adjusting the Rank of Brig. Generals Woodford, Muhlenberg, Scott, Weedon respectively.[3]

3. 21st for confirming the powers vested in Majr. General McDougal by Your Excellency & for other purposes.[4]

I have the honour to be with the highest Esteem & Regard &ca.

LB (DNA: PCC, item 13).
[1] These letters are in PCC, item 152, 5:373–75, 379–80, 385–87, 393–94, and Washington, *Writings* (Fitzpatrick), 11:81–82, 90–94, 103–4.
[2] See also Laurens to Washington, March 15, 1778, note 1.
[3] See also Committee at Camp Minutes of Proceedings, February 16–20, 1778, note 3.
[4] In the first of his two March 16 letters to Laurens, Washington pointed out that although he had recently appointed Gen. Alexander McDougall to take command in the Highlands, it was uncertain whether McDougall would have any authority over the forts in the area as under the terms of a February 18 resolution on the defense of the Hudson these seemed to fall into the domain of New York governor Clinton. See *JCC*, 10:180; and Washington, *Writings* (Fitzpatrick), 11:91. In effect, Congress decided on March 21 that McDougall's authority should take precedence over Clinton's. *JCC*, 10:275.

Henry Laurens to Thomas Wharton

Sir,   York Town, 21st March 1778

The last I had the honor of writing to you was dated the 15th Inst. by Messenger Sharp.[1] On the 10th I transmitted to Your Excellency by the hand of the Reverend Mr. Duffill a Packet containing six Commissions for Cruizing Vessels together with Bonds & Instructions. This intimation proceeds from an application which was made to me yesterday by the Honble Mr J.B. Smith, for Commissions for the use of the State. If a further supply is wanted or that the Packet above alluded to hath not reached Your Excellency please to inform me & Your Excellency's Command shall be immediately obeyed.

This will be accompanied by four Acts of Congress to which I beg leave to refer.

1. 16th March for obtaining necessary information of the deter-

mination of each of these States respecting Acts of Congress transmitted to each from & after the 1st November 1777.

2. The same date—for delivering over to the order of the President & Council of Pennsylvania certain Prisoners confined in Virginia & for appointing a Committee to correspond with the State of Pennsylvania on the Case of the Honble John Penn & Benja. Chew.[2]

3. 19th Requesting the Government of this State to Station certain numbers of Militia for the defence of Magazines of Military & other Stores, at Easton, Bethlehem & Reading.

4. 20th for filling Magazines of Provisions, Payment of Waggon hire due to the Inhabitants of these States &c.[3]

I have the honour to be, With great Regard, Sir, Your Excellency's Most obedient humble servt,

Henry Laurens, President of Congress.

RC (PHi).

[1] See Laurens to George Clinton, March 12, 1778, note 2.

[2] See also Committee of Congress to Wharton, March 18, 1778.

[3] For further information about the provenance of these resolves, see Laurens to George Clinton, March 24, 1778, note 2. On March 23 Laurens transmitted to former Quartermaster General Thomas Mifflin the portion of these resolves instructing him "to cause an immediate payment to be made of all wages justly due from him to the inhabitants of the State of Pennsylvania, whose waggons have been employed by him in the continental service." PCC, item 13, fol. 239; and JCC, 10:273–74.

James Lovell to Abigail Adams

Dear Ma'am   York Town, 21st. of March 1777 [*i.e.* 1778]

I am to thank you, in my own name, and on the public account, for that exercise of laudable patriotic prudence, which you have modestly termed the "Freedom" of inclosing to me Mr. McCreary's letter to your worthy Husband. I read it in Congress, and I think it will be useful to the commercial Committee.[1] The same Gentleman wrote to Mr. Adams in Sepr. some interesting history,[2] of which he gave me a copy, just before he undertook his late vast Sacrifice to his Country's Wellfare. I fear I shall have wounded you by carrying your mind back to a day which you ought to strive to forget, by confining your imagination strictly to that of your future reunion: but, your billet under my eye, by developing your character, made my pen mark the expression "*vast* Sacrifice," while my heart acknowledged its individual portion of the debt of gratitude, which *our* Mr. Adams may charge against the Public.

All the intelligence which we received from France, about the period of Mr. McCreary's letter, was of the same tenor; our friends in

Martinique wrote in like style on Decr. 3d; but, on the 28th of that month and the 26th of January we have an ecclaircisement of the gallic finesse.[3] The most open protection is afforded to our trade, privateers are fitted out, and their prizes not only sold, but a duty of 1 pr. Ct. regularly paid upon their cargoes towards the governmental revenue. The Governor of Antigua has no resource left but impotent threats to the General at St. Pierres of the Resentment that may arise in the breast of his Britannic Majesty, when the affair is properly represented. I suspect that England will more easily draw France in to open War by talking about Reconciliation than by boasting of subduing us by force. Louis thinks the latter impossible: his only fears are about the former.

I cannot give you any thing agreable from this neighbourhood. I cannot promise you that we shall owe our prosperity to our own spirit and preperations, in any degree comparable to what we shall owe to the Enemy's embarrassments and the unmerited favour of Providence, but, our hope of the latter is hardly supported in a ballance by the Justice of our Cause, counteracted by the *selfish* spirit of the Times: Justly may I be turned to the Parable of the Beam and Mote while I beg YOU to count me among yr. affectionate humb Servant[s].

RC (MHi). In Lovell's hand, though not signed. Adams, *Family Correspondence* (Butterfield), 2:403–4.

[1] Abigail had probably sent a copy of William McCreery's October 10 and 25, 1777, letters to John Adams, in which McCreery presented a generally gloomy portrait of Europe's attitude toward the United States and recommended the appointment of a commercial agent at Bordeaux. There is no evidence in the journals that the letters were read in Congress, but for further information on Lovell's use of another McCreery letter in Congress, see Lovell to William Whipple, February 8, 1778.

The originals of McCreery's October 10 and 25 letters are not in the Adams Papers, MHi, but a copy of them in Abigail's handwriting is.

[2] This is probably a reference to McCreery's September 29, 1777, letter to Adams, which is also in the Adams Papers, MHi.

[3] For further information on the receipt of William Bingham's letters, see Committee for Foreign Affairs to William Bingham, April 16, 1778, note 1.

James Lovell to Abigail Adams

[March 21? 1778][1]

I have written to Mr. Adams 8 Times since the 21st of January which was the last of 4 that he acknowledged on the 6th of February.[2] If I directed them all to the Care of the navy Board he will get them. Should any of my slovenly scrawls of Friendship fall under your eye, not containing matters connected with Mr. A's *foreign* employmt. you will be pleased to purify them by fire. Of this kind perhaps were those written the 30th of Janry., 2d & 7th of Febry. All later, I guess, went under Cover to the navy Board. I am not certain but that the 3 mentioned might have gone thither also. I directed the Express to call on Mr. Thaxter who will doubtless send you a proof of his dutiful affection which he is never backward to express when speaking of you to, Your most humble Servant,   James Lovell

RC (MHi).
    [1] Although this document contains few clues for ascertaining the date Lovell wrote it, a June 24 letter from Abigail to Lovell suggests that it may have been a postscript to Lovell's March 21 letter printed separately in the preceding entry. The evidence on this point is not clear, but Abigail's reply contains the following pertinent passage: "The Letters which you mention in yours of March 21 as having wrote to my partner arrived since his absence and were delivered to me, and agreable to his direction I opened them all, and perused them with a pleasure which the communicative manner of your writing must always give to your correspondence." As the brief, undated document printed here explicitly mentions eight letters from Lovell to Adams, and nothing in the preceding March 21 entry fits this reference, it is a plausible conjecture that the two were originally parts of a single letter. The editors of the *Adams Family Correspondence* stated that Abigail's June 24 reference to "yours of March 21" was erroneous and pertained instead to Lovell's April 1 letter to her, but that interpretation seems less convincing than the alternative assumptions discussed here. See Adams, *Family Correspondence* (Butterfield), 2:404–5, 3:7, 48–50.
    [2] Of the eight letters Lovell had written to John Adams since January 21, only three—printed under the dates February 2?, 8, and 10 above—have been found.

Henry Laurens to John Laurens

My Dear son,   York Town 22d March 1778
    As my last was, so will the present Address to you be—a hurried over performance. Indeed I should not have troubled you if the five Letters which will accompany this had not called upon me. Impart all that is proper for me to know of the intelligence from St Mary Axe.[1] I send you also a bundle of Carolina News Papers which you may return for my reading at some leisure hour—lend them to General McIntosh & assure the General I have endeavoured at several times to pay my respects to him, but the repeated term "acquaintance" at each attempt rendered stagnant Pen & Ink. I will struggle to get the better of this disorder & hope soon to express myself in the Stile of a Friend, not worn out, nor even tired by service.
    Chief Justice Drayton & another I believe Mr. late Speaker Mathews are on the Road with the Mantles of Delegates to Congress.[2] We certainly want numbers. The addition of abilities can never come amiss. My Country men have Voted me permission to return when I please, but have rechosen & put me at the head of the list. Is not this somewhat embarrassing? Has not some mischievos fellow applied the remark, Moultrie to Grant "You know the Man"? but I must go—

either southward or Eastward. Your attachments give me little room to hope for the happiness of seeing you before I go, for my departure will be without Ceremony. If I could travel as I once could, it would be impossible for me to move an hairs breadth more distant without first embracing you, but to the times, except in Cases of honour & Conscience, when we *must,* we *may* submit.

God Almighty protect you, My Dear son.   Henry Laurens

RC (MHi: William Gilmore Simms Collection deposit, 1973).

[1] The street in London where a number of Laurens' relatives lived.

[2] William Henry Drayton took his seat in Congress on March 30 and John Mathews on April 22. *JCC,* 10:294, 374. Laurens apparently learned about the election of Drayton and Mathews from a February 16 letter of Pres. John Rutledge, which also informed Laurens of his own reelection as delegate and enclosed the South Carolina Assembly's February 5 instructions on the Articles of Confederation. See Frank Moore, ed., *Materials for History Printed from Original Manuscripts* (New York: Printed for the Zenger Club, 1861), pp. 93–95.

James Lovell to Samuel Adams

23d [March 1778][1]

I miss-dated my inclosed Scrawl. Brother Dana is this day in Congress but he will immediately return to Camp. He is bent to be at home in May; he has been very industrious in serving the public, but it seems his own countrymen are totally laying open his Farm to destruction; I must also intreat for other reasons than his or Mr. Geary's releif that you & your Brethren would come forward. I think another Delegate, at least, should be chosen as Mr. J A is taken from the Corps which was to relieve those who have stood a sad winters Campaign in York Town. I do not grudge my Labour; but, verily without I get relief in the point of my Loss on the 19th of Sepr. I cannot afford to tarry where the same needle work, which an industrious wife would perform gratis in an hour, is charged 5 Dollars and every species of wear & tear is in proportion to that of Linnen. But I will not go on with this Topic further than to say that raggedness afflicts me, *in such times as these,* only when I view myself as a Delegate. As a Citizen of America strugling for Liberty I dispise Hunger, Thirst, Tatters, Cold and all the mud & mire of Baltimore & York Town which are as little terrific to me as Imprisonment & Chains.

RC (NN).

[1] Although Lovell did not note the month and year of this document, it was apparently written—as a postscript to a letter that has not been found—on March 23, 1778, the day Francis Dana probably returned from headquarters. Dana's presence is noted in the yeas and nays recorded on March 24, and two Massachusetts delegate letters written at about this time contain references consistent with other observations Lovell made below. Elbridge Gerry noted in a March 28 letter

to Jeremiah Powell, for example, that Dana planned to return to camp, and in a March 29 letter to Powell, Dana indicated his intention to return home at the end of April. See *JCC*, 10:283; and letters from Gerry and Dana to Powell of March 28 and 29, 1778, respectively.

Virginia Delegates to Patrick Henry

York Town, Pennsylvania 23 March 78.

Nothing of moment having occurred since Col. Lee's last letter,[1] we have only to communicate the earnest desire of congress that our new levies of troops may be sent forward to camp with the utmost expedition. The necessity of pushing this business with vigour arises from the present weakness of our army, and the great probability of the enemy's taking the field early with augmented force, and over running the country, or attempting something decisive against our army before it is reinforced. The next grand object is to secure all the provision that can be engaged for the troops, as many disappointments and difficulties have intervened to lessen the prospect of the abundant supplies that were expected.

Colonel Harrison's regiment of artillery is much wanted at camp, and congress wishes them to march immediately.[2] It is reported, and we fear not without foundation, that the troops at Rhode Island have embarked with an intention of joining General Howe. If this is the case, without the greatest exertions it is much to be apprehended the enemy will open the campaign with great advantage over us. We are with the highest respect.

Your Excellency's mo. obed. Servants.

Francis Lightfoot Lee.

J. Banister.

P.S. Since writing the above General Smallwood mentions in a letter to General Washington,[3] that a fleet of Vessels, ships &c, amounting to near an hundred, had passed by Wilmington and anchored at Reedy Island, he supposes they are going to forage either up the bay or Potomack.

MS not found; reprinted from Henry, *Patrick Henry*, 3:152–53.

[1] Not found.

[2] See Henry Laurens to Patrick Henry, March 14, 1778, note 2.

[3] William Smallwood's March 17 letter to Washington, which was read in Congress this day, is in PCC, item 152, 5:409. For Washington's March 18 letter to Congress transmitting Smallwood's "intelligence of the Enemy's motions on the Delaware," see *JCC*, 10:279; and Washington, *Writings* (Fitzpatrick), 11:106.

Committee for Foreign Affairs to the Commissioners at Paris

Honorable Gentlemen   York Town 24 March 1778[1]

I cannot consent to omit this oportunity of addressing a few lines to you, though the state of our military operations affords nothing material.

The manners of the Continent are to much affected by the depreciation of our Currency. Scarce an Officer civil or military but feels something of a desire to be concerned in mercantile speculation, from finding that his salary is inadequate to the harpy demands which are made upon him for the necessaries of life, and from observing that but little skill is necessary to constitute one of the merchants of these days. We are almost a continental tribe of Jews, but I hope Heaven has not yet discovered such a settled profligacy in us as to cast us off even for a year. Backward as we may be at this moment in our preparations, the Enemy is not a condition to expect more success in the coming, than in former campaigns. We have the debates of the British Parliament to Decr 5 and perceive that the old game is playing called RECONCILIATION, but, depend upon it, they are duping themselves only.

Yesterday a private letter from Doctor Franklin, dated Octr 7th was presented containing the only political intelligence which Folgier brought safe with him Viz: "Our affairs, so far as relates to this Country are every day more promising." [2] This with a letter from Mr Barnabas Deane, who tells us his brother apologizes for his brevity by saying "he was sending an important packet to Congress" is all the explanation we have of the nature of your dispatches, of which we were robbed. I enclose a list by which you will see the breaks in our correspondence. I send a pamphlet which contains, I hope, the general ideas of America in regard to what Great Britain may be tempted foolishly to call her successes.

We think it strange that the Commissioners did not jointly write to Mr de Francey, considering the very important designs of his coming over, to settle the mode of payment for the past cargoes sent by Roderique, Hortalez & Co and to make contracts for future.[3] It is certain that much eclaircessement is, at this late moment, wanting.

But I dare not enlarge, for fear of losing this sudden good oportunity. I therefore close with assurances of the most affectionate respect.

Your very humble servant (Signed)   James Lovell, for the
                                       Committee for foreign
                                       Affairs.

FC (DNA: PCC, item 79).

¹ This day, "at noon," Lovell also wrote another brief letter on behalf of the committee to the commissioners: "An express going immediately for Boston I can only send a copy of the hasty lines which I have dispatched within this hour to go in a cutter from Chesapeake bay. The Gazettes which will be regularly sent by the Eastern navy Board; and private letters from your friends in New England, by whatever opportunity may convey this, will make my abrupt manner a less disappointment to you than it would otherwise be." PCC, item 79, fol. 185.

² An October 7, 1777, letter from Franklin to Lovell discussing his experiences in France with importunate foreign officers is in the Adams Papers, MHi, and Franklin, *Writings* (Smyth), 7:65–67. But since that document does not contain the passage quoted here by Lovell, Franklin obviously wrote another letter of that date which apparently has not survived.

³ See Robert Morris' Proposed Report on the Claims of Roderique Hortalez & Co., March 12, 1778, note 1.

James Forbes to Thomas Johnson

Dear Sir   York Town March 24 1778

Yours of the 21st Inst by Mr Howard came to hand yesterday,¹ by him you will receive the 100,000 Dollars, the State of Maryd to be accountable for the same, as Mr Howard coud not carry the money, I have got from the Board of War a Dragoon to goe with him to Baltimore & from thence he says he can contrive it. A Letter came to hand a day or two agoe from Genl Smallwood to Genl Washington informing of a large Fleet being gone down the Delawair of upwards of one hundred saile, many of which are small Vessells, said to have Troops on board.² By information from deserters from Philaa they have only eighteen days provisions on hand, therefore concluded only to be sent on a Forredging party to the State of Delewair, or perhaps to the Chesepeak Bay.

Mr Chase is just arrived, but seems to be determind to make but a short stay, on Account of the very bad accommodations this place affords.

Your Lettr to Genl Gates on the Subject of an Embargoe & the Virga Frigate was committed and a report ready but it has not yet been taken up in Congress. I apprehend an Embargoe on provissions will take place, but am affraid a general one will not be agreed to.³ When any thing material occurs shall do my self the honour of writing you & am very respectfully, Sir, your most Obedt Servt,

James Forbes

N.B. Virga & N York only have agreed in form to the ratification of the Confederation. Most of the other States have proposed amendments but the Members say they are instructed to ratify, if the amendments cant be obtaind. Noe time fixt for taking up this matter in Congress.

RC (MdAA).

[1] For the Maryland Council's March 21 letter to the Maryland delegates, see *Md. Archives,* 16:546.

[2] See Virginia Delegates to Patrick Henry, March 23, 1778, note 3.

[3] Johnson's February 27 letter to the Board of War was read in Congress on March 5 and referred to a committee of which Forbes was a member. For the action Congress finally took in June on the subject of an embargo, see *JCC,* 11:569, 578–79.

Henry Laurens to George Clinton

Sir,   24th March 1778.

Since the date of my last trouble to Your Excellency of the 12th Inst. by Brown I have had the honour of presenting to Congress Your Excellency's favours of the 5th & 7th.[1] The latter came through General Washingtons hands. The first was committed to a Special Committee who have not yet Reported.[2] I have no other Commands on me relative to the very important subjects of your Excellency's Letters but an Act of Congress of the 21st requesting Your Excellency & Govr. Trumbull to afford General McDougall every assistance in your power for perfecting the defence of the North River which will be found within the present Inclosure, together with another Act of the 16th for obtaining information from the Several States of their determinations respectively on the recommendations of Congress.[3]

Mr. Morris being still on Duty in a Committee at General Washingtons Camp, the State of New York remains unrepresented, I need not intimate to your Excellency that our Union is suffering in its most essential Interests from a want of full & competent Representation. Every state must have felt the Ill Effects of our general delinquency, I hope we shall awaken by degrees & in time to ward off a lash which may otherwise prove intolerable.

I have the honour to be &ca.

LB (DNA: PCC, item 13).

[1] Governor Clinton's March 5 letter to Laurens is in PCC, item 67, 2:122–23, and Clinton, *Papers* (Hastings), 2:868–71. His March 7 letter has not been found.

[2] On March 10 Congress appointed a committee to consider a March 5 representation from the Pennsylvania Assembly and Council, which charged that the state's efforts to supply food to Washington's army were being hindered by the Board of War's interference with the state's commissaries, by the Continental quartermaster general's offer of higher prices for wheat and flour than those allowed by state law, and by the failure of Continental officers to pay Pennsylvania wagoners for hauling supplies to the army. The following day Congress also referred to this committee a March 6 letter to the Board of War from Gov. Thomas Johnson of Maryland, which criticized the actions of Pennsylvania food purchasing agents in Maryland and asked for their removal from the state. At length the committee submitted its report, and on March 20 Congress passed resolves designed both to remove Pennsylvania's causes of complaint against Continental officials and

to confine the activities of her purchasing agents within the bounds of their state. See *JCC*, 10:239, 241–42, 258–59, 272–74; and PCC, item 69, 1:485–90, item 70, 1:245.

On March 16 Clinton's March 5 letter was referred to the committee considering the representation from Pennsylvania and the letter from Governor Johnson. Although Clinton's letter dealt primarily with the problems of defending the Hudson River, it also mentioned the existence of an illicit trade between the hinterland and British-occupied New York City. No report on this illicit trade by the "Special Committee" has been found, but on March 21 Congress did take steps to secure the defense of the Hudson in response to a report on the subject from the Board of War. See *JCC*, 10:258–59, 275–76; and PCC, item 67, 2:122–23.

[3] Laurens also enclosed copies of these March 16 and 21 acts with a brief covering letter that he wrote this day to Gov. Jonathan Trumbull of Connecticut. PCC, item 13, fol. 241.

Henry Laurens to Baron de Kalb

My Dear General duKalb   24th March 1778

Your Packets for France which accompanied the Letter of 10th Inst.[1] which you honoured me with by the hand of ———— shall be carefully disposed of. One will go by a Swift Sailing vessel from Baltimore to morrow or next day—the other probably will be put into the hand of Monsr. Francy.

British Administration were shocked to the Center by the account of the Surrender at Saratoga, but in their palest moments, nothing like concession dropped from their quivering lips, & I am persuaded that while France continues vibrating from side to side according to appearances, they will not submit to anything less, than their Ideas of Constitutional terms to restore America to the State the Colonies were in at the period of 1763—so far they would chearfully stoop.

Baron Holzendorff is gone & as well satisfied as an unfortunate Gentleman could be who had found that fellow feeling still existed among Men liable to common misfortunes.

I have no less than three Letters of Major Du Bois not yet presented to Congress. I beg that Gentleman will be assured the delay is not imputable to me. I shall embrace an inviting opportunity to represent his Case & then he may depend upon receiving immediately the necessary information.[2]

Inclosed I convey a packet lately received from Colonel Kershaw, if there is any thing in which I can be serviceable you know Dear General you may with the utmost freedom Command your obedient humble Servant

LB (ScHi).
[1] Kalb's March 10 letter to Laurens is in the William Gilmore Simms Collection deposit, MHi; a transcript of it is in the Laurens Papers, ScHi.
[2] On April 1 Congress read a March 10–11 letter from Maj. Pierre-François de Bois, requesting $1,000 to pay for his travel expenses back to France. On May 19

the Board of War recommended that Congress accept Bois' resignation from the Continental Army and pay him "a sum of money" to cover his journey home. Congress then referred this recommendation to the Board of Treasury, which is the last mention of the matter in the journals. See *JCC,* 10:299, 404, 11:491, 508; and PCC, item 78, 2:403–10.

Henry Laurens to the Marquis de Lafayette

Sir,   24th March 1778.
   I am honoured with Your Excellency's favor of the 12th Inst. by the hands of Colo. Armand.
   Whatever had been the design, or if it might have been, as Your Excellency charges, intended "deception" of the Board of War I dare again aver, that Congress were not in the project for leaving General Conway in a seperate Command in consequence of recalling Your Excellency & Baron de Kalb from Albany. I have been more than a little astonished by the freedom of Speech in treating upon that Gentleman's Character—severe & harsh sentiments have not only been whispered but loudly sounded in my hearing, & even one Gentleman in whom I know he had reposed the greatest confidence gave him up by a *mild* declaration that he was *afraid* General Conway was too *indiscreet* a Man to be *trusted* with a Command. Thus are Men deceived in this Rascally World. Poor Conway beleives quite a different Creed. I have not the least doubt but that he has wrapped himself secure in the friendship of some, who by fair & soft personal addresses have tempted him to a confidence, while he is shy of others from whom he has experienced only Candor & plain dealing. God knows what he is, I have not yet fully heard all sides, nor have I very deeply considered what I have heard. But this I will venture to say to you Dear Marquis, according to the Maxim of an ancient Lawyer "whatsoever a Man sowith that shall he reap," if he is *deceitful,* he is paid in his own Coin. I protest humanity shrinks at hearing Men traduce the Character whom they have taught to place a confidence in them—to hear ferocity, sheer Courage, eminent qualities in the Brute Creation, acknowledged to be the *only* virtues in the mind of a favorite. Is it possible for Men to speak of a friend as they do of a Mastiff? Then steps in *another Set,* who attempt to strip him even of that specious Virtue. In a word the General once honoured me by asking for my advice, I gave it honestly, he literally pursued, but indirectly, most effectually contravened it. I have therefore no great encouragement to become a *volunteer* Councellor, but should my sentiments be again demanded, I would find room for inserting, "be advised by me General & return to France where there is a greater Croud."

Congress have ordered a Letter to be written to Your Excellency which I shall Sign by direction & transmit herewith together with a Resolve of yesterday,[2] Ordering General Conway to Peeks Kill under the Command of Major General McDougall, there had been more than a few opinions for ordering him to York Town.

I trust your Excellency will do Congress the Justice to beleive they had never entertained the most remote intention to give you offence. I add & repeat with great pleasure that Your Excellency is held by each Individual in the highest Esteem & the House very much relies upon the greatness of your Mind for security against groundless exceptions to any part of their conduct respecting yourself. These indeed are Sentiments not dictated by Congress, but I know they are warranted. However your Excellency may retort that my declaration in this case will require a little skill to reconcile it with the total Silence on the Subject of the piracy committed upon the packet of 20th Febry.[3] Even this most extraordinary conduct cannot be fairly urged as an exception to the professed Esteem & Regard for Marquis delafayette, although it may be inconsistent with that Veneration which the Representatives of the 13 United States should ever preserve for their own Character if they expect to escape Contempt throughout the Universe. I should have been happy if your Excellency had passed that affair over for reasons which I had assigned but since it has been talked of & since the parties accused are acquainted with the circumstance, I am made very unhappy by a conduct which will endanger us to be exposed to future & greater Insults.

It is impossible to do anything for the officers mentioned by Colo. Armand until the arrangement at Camp is completed & tis probable Your Excellency will meet the Committee there. I shall then transmit a Duplicate of Mr. Duplessis Commission & of the Resolve upon which it is founded.[4]

It appears to be more & more the wish & purpose of Gentlemen here to return General Gates to his late Command in the Northern department & there was lately the appearance of a pretty little attempt to render that Command Independent of all Orders but those of Congress.[5] This will account to you at once for the silence on that head. How Major General McDougall may approve of being superceded after he shall have gone through the drudgery of Mechanical operations in & about the River is a matter of uncertainty.

With respect to Great Britain, believe me Sir, Administration was greatly shocked by the Account of Mr. Burgoynes surrender but it does not appear from any hints dropped on their part that they were disposed to terminate the dispute with America by any thing like a Concession to Independence. There may & there possibly will be attempts to treat for peace & accomodation some time before the ordinary course of opening the Campaign, but I do not expect any thing substantial to follow, but blows. In the mean time the Monied people of England are really alarmed & begin to subscribe for the support of the War. This is a maneuvre which I always dreaded, if the infection spreads our American troubles will not soon be removed. On this side the Water there is too much ground to fear some grand exertion, or some injurious sly stroke, will appear against Valley Forge, Wilmington or perhaps York Town before General Washington is sufficiently reinforced to admit of detachments or even of facing the Enemy with his whole present Army.

I most sincerely wished your Excellency a seperate Command, but since that has not happened, with equal earnestness I wish to hear of your Excellency's safe arrival at Valley forge, where possibly this may kiss your hand & upon that presumption Colo Armand means to take the Camp in his Route.

I dare not detain that Gentleman a moment longer, he is as impatient to be gone as he would be if he was going to be Married, he will admit of no delay. He has experienced none from me as an Individual. I have the honour to be with the most sincere *Esteem & Regard* &ca.

[*P.S.*] Inclosed are two Letters left here for your Excellency.

LB (ScHi).
    [1] This private letter to Laurens is in Lafayette, *Papers* (Idzerda), 1:350–52.
    [2] See the next entry.
    [3] That is, the Board of War's opening of Lafayette's February 20 letter to Laurens. See Laurens to Lafayette, March 4, 1778.
    [4] Lafayette had lost the chevalier de Mauduit Du Plessis' commission as brevet lieutenant colonel and the January 19, 1778, resolve of Congress that granted it. See *JCC,* 10:64; Lafayette, *Papers* (Idzerda), 1:351; and Laurens to Du Plessis, April 28, 1778.
    [5] On April 15 Congress directed Gen. Horatio Gates to repair to Fishkill, N.Y., and resume active command of the northern department. *JCC,* 10:354–55.

Henry Laurens to the Marquis de Lafayette

Sir,   24th March 1778
    Your Letters of the 11th & 12th of this Month[1] have been laid before Congress. They have considered the apprehensions you express, that you & General Kalb are to leave the command of the Troops in that part of the continent where you now are, to General Conway, and your request, of permission to go to France, founded thereon. They wish you to be assured, that they have a very high sense of your merit and attachment to America. They judge it of advantage to the public Service that you and General Kalb be present with the grand army, but when they came to this determination, had not yet resolved

on a disposition for General Conway, and had no intention to make any injurious to your honour. They expect this declaration, and the disposition since made for General Conway,[2] will make it unecessary to grant the permission you request.

By order of Congress.

LB (DNA: PCC, item 13).

[1] These official letters to Laurens are in Lafayette, *Papers* (Idzerda), 1:344–50. Lafayette's letters had been referred to a committee of three on March 19, which reported on the 21st that another committee should be appointed "to prepare the draught of a letter, to be signed and sent by the President, to the marquis, in answer to the said letters." Thomas Burke, Francis Lightfoot Lee, and Thomas McKean, the delegates named to this committee, then produced the present letter. See *JCC,* 10:269, 278.

[2] On March 23 Congress decided to order Gen. Thomas Conway to serve at Peekskill, N.Y., under the command of Gen. Alexander McDougall, thus relieving Lafayette's fear that Conway would remain in command at Albany upon the departure of himself and Kalb. See *JCC,* 10:280; and Laurens to Lafayette, March 6, 1778, note 5. Laurens notified Conway and McDougall of this resolve in brief letters that he wrote to them this day. PCC, item 13, fol. 240. On the same day he wrote to Jonathan Trumbull, Jr., paymaster general in the northern department, and informed him of a March 23 resolve ordering him to supply McDougall with money for as long as the general remained in command in Peekskill. See ibid.; and *JCC,* 10:280.

James Lovell to George Washington

Sir   March 24th 1778.

You will form a Judgement upon the following Extract of a Letter from the Honble Thos. Cushing by weighing it with the various Intelligence which you receive from other Quarters. It has been long on the Road from the Difficulty of passing Hudson's River where the Express lost his Horse on the 11th of this Month.

"Sir   Extract   Boston Feb. 28th. 1778

"Mr. Hancock having just informed me that he shall send off an Express tomorrow morning for Congress, I embrace the opportunity to convey to you a peice of Intelligence I have just received from Mr. Wm. Davis, a Member of our House, who left Dartmouth last Thursday. He says he was credibly informed there that some persons (having by some means or other got the Countersign) went from Tiverton to Newport to gain Intelligence of the Enemy's Designs, they returned from there on Monday Evening the 23d Instant. They inform that all the Women & Children belonging to the British Troops were gone to New York and the Invalids gone to England. That the Troops were making preparation for Embarking, and the Officers had been heard to say that General Howe had given orders for them to be in Readiness to sail for Philadelphia by the 20th of

March. It is conjectured Genl. Howe has sent for these Troops, to be in force to make some Capital Movement with regard to General Washington.

"A prize of considerable Value taken by a continental Vessel of War is arrived at Dartmouth. Some of the Prisoners are arrived in Town. We hear Lord Howe has wrote Govr. Cook that he will send all the marine Prisoners he has on hand to Providence, in Case we will return as many in Lieu of them when we have them in our Possession."

I beg to be allowed by your Excellency to add a few words about a private concern of one John Gray who has this morning surprized me by appearing in the Land of the Living, as I had thought it impossible he could have survived the hardships I left him exposed to on the 10th of Octr 1776 at Halifax. He is a very honest Fellow who has never received any Pay for the Period of his Imprisonment from the 25th of Sepr. 1775 to the 15 of July 1777. He bore all the Hardships of his Imprisonment with Resolution, and fulfilled his Promise of enlisting the day after his Liberation. He tells me he has once appeared before you. If he should be again under the Necessity of doing it upon the Subject of his Wages, I hope you will consider him as a brave faithful Soldier upon the proof of my knowing his Behavior some months in Prison and hearing Col Allens Testimony of his former Conduct. Perhaps the Colonel will shortly be at Liberty to patronise the Lads who long suffered with him. In the mean time I shall write to the major of the Regiment in which Gray is serving at Lancaster, that your Excellency may not be interrupted by this Subject further unless it should be found unavoidable.[1]

By a Letter from Martinique of the 26th of Janry.[2] it appears that the General there gives the fullest encouragement to the American Cruisers, that the Duty of 1 per Ct. on prize Goods was regularly received at the Custom House, and that the Governor of Antigua is outrageous with the French General and impatiently threatens him with "the Resentment which may arise in the Breast of his Britannic Majesty" when the Affair shall be represented to him.

I am, with much Regard, Your Excellency's obliged humble Servant,   James Lovell

RC (DLC).
[1] Washington replied to Lovell on March 29: "You may depend upon my paying Gray his wages upon application. If he ever applied before, I refused to settle with him then, because he wanted the proper testimonials." Washington, *Writings* (Fitzpatrick), 11:172.
[2] Almost certainly a reference to William Bingham's January 26 letter to Congress. For further information on the receipt of Bingham's letters, see Lovell to Bingham, April 16, 1778, note 1.

Henry Laurens to William Heath

Sir,   York Town 25th March 1778

The last I had the honour of addressing you with, was under the 14th Inst. by the hand of a Messenger Brown.

Yesterday I presented to Congress Your favors of the 10th & 12th together with the Papers referred to.[1] It affords me pleasure to repeat that your correspondence with the British General at Cambridge from every sentiment expressed by Individuals continues to receive approbation, if my own was worth your acceptance it should with great warmth be added.

Your Letters are Committed to the Treasury from whence I am in hopes you will receive supplies of Money hereafter in such seasonable times as to guard against those or such distresses as you have lately been reduced to.

Congress are not at all inclined to indulge Lt. Colo. Sutherland, indeed he could scarcely have expected it from his cautious & indirect application, as an old acquaintance I feel for that Gentleman's distresses, Would to God, there had been, or that there was even now, any sympathy on the other side.[2]

About ten days ago a part of the Enemy's Shipping proceeded down the Delaware about 150 Sail half of them small Vessels, made no shew of Soldiery on Deck as they passed Wilmington, the last account of them was at Reedy Island, they are gone foraging in the lower parts of Jersey or Delaware or to destroy our Salt Works if conjecture is to be trusted.

I have the honour to be, With great Regard, Sir, Your obedient & humble servant,   Henry Laurens, President of Congress[3]

RC (MHi).

[1] General Heath's March 10 letter is in PCC, item 157, fols. 97–99, and his March 12 letter is in PCC, item 57, fol. 239. See also PCC, item 57, fols. 219–38, for the papers Heath sent to Congress. These are also conveniently listed in *JCC*, 10:282.

[2] Lt. Col. Nicholas Sutherland's March 4 application to Heath for leave to return to England because of his affliction "by a Disorder which has hitherto baffled every Effort of Medicine" is in PCC, item 78, 1:153–55. There is no record in the journals of any action by Congress on this application by Sutherland, a British officer in the Forty-seventh Regiment of Foot, or on another one he made directly to Congress on April 11. See ibid., fols. 157–62.

[3] Laurens also sent the following message to Heath later this day. "The Bearer William Dodd who has hitherto in the business of a Messenger to & from Boston merited the Character of a diligent discret Young Man, in the Moment of his departure demands from me two hundred Dollars without which he cannot proceed. His present chief errand is, to conduct a large Sum of Money from the Treasury & Board of War for the use of the Commissary of Purchases in the Northern department & therefore he ought, if he is intitled to receive any supplies here, to have obtained the necessary Sum from one of those Offices, but at this time of

day both are shut up. Should I refuse to enable him immediately, another day will be passed before he can proceed. I have therefore judged it best to grant him the Sum he required. I take the liberty of requesting you to enquire & inform me if Mr. Dodd is not particularly in the service of the State of Massachusetts & if he is, to give an intimation of this advance to the proper Board or Office in order that his Account may be properly charged & a loss avoided which may otherwise attend this irregular payment either to the public or more properly to myself whose Wages will not bear it." Heath Papers, MHi.

Henry Laurens to George Washington

Sir,   25th March [1778]
   I had the honour of writing to Your Excellency on the 21st Inst. by Fred. Weir.
   This will inclose Duplicates of Acts of Congress of the 19th January & 18th March[1]—also an Act of the 23d for accepting the Resignation of Colonel Webb.[2]
   Colo. Armand who promises to deliver this with great expedition will not afford me time to send to the Secretary's Office for the dates of two of Your Excellency's favors which I think came to hand since my last,[3] these shall be properly noted when I have the honour of next addressing Your Excellency, meantime I remain with the utmost respect & Esteem &ca.

LB (DNA: PCC, item 13).
   [1] See Congress' January 19 resolves on pay for captured American officers and its March 18 resolves on the prisoner exchange Washington was negotiating with General Howe. JCC, 10:61–62, 266–68.
   [2] Col. Charles Webb had requested leave to resign from the Second Connecticut Regiment because the "Sickness and Hardships that I have undergone for near two years past, have so far enfeebled my Constitution as to render me incapable of enduring the Fatigues of a Campaign." For Webb's case, see his letter to Jedediah Huntington of March 13, 1778, in PCC, item 152, 5:391.
   [3] Since Laurens' last letter to Washington on March 21 Congress had read two letters from the general written on March 16 and 18. See JCC, 10:278–79; PCC, item 152, 5:385–87, 405–6; and Washington, Writings (Fitzpatrick), 11:92–94, 106.

Henry Laurens to William Smallwood

Sir   26th March 1778
   Within the present Inclosure you will be pleased to receive an Act of Congress of this date by which you are directed to secure the persons of Thomas White, Charles Gordon, & such other inhabitants within the State of Delaware as you shall upon good grounds suspect to be dangerous to the Independence of the United States of America, to which I beg leave to refer.[1]

Congress esteem this measure to be of the highest importance and repose equal confidence in you for executing the Charge with dispatch & efficacy. I have the honour to be with great Respect.

LB (DNA: PCC, item 13). Addressed: "Willm. Smallwood Esqr. Brigadier General Commanding a detachment from the Army at Wilmington in Delaware."

[1] Earlier in March the Maryland Council had intercepted and forwarded to its delegates in Congress a letter of Thomas White, a Kent County, Del., judge, allegedly indicating his involvement in "an iniquitous conspiracy" against America. Upon a motion by the Maryland delegates, Congress therefore ordered General Smallwood to arrest White and Charles Gordon, a disaffected New Castle County, Del., lawyer, as well as all other inhabitants of Delaware suspected of disloyalty and "send them under guard to such safe place or places as he shall think proper." Col. David Hall, one of Smallwood's subordinates, carried out the actual arrest of White and Gordon with the aid of Caesar Rodney and then began to experience serious difficulties. The Delaware Council instructed Rodney—who had meanwhile become president of the state—to detain the prisoners "untill the general Assembly Should Consider the propriety of seizing the persons of those men other than under the authority of the State," and White and Gordon obtained a writ of habeas corpus from the chief justice of the state, who demanded that Smallwood explain "what the Offense is with which they are charged, and the cause of their Imprisonment by the Military." Smallwood thereupon affirmed his determination to keep White and Gordon under arrest, telling Rodney that he could not disobey "an express Order derived from the supreme Authority of the United States of America" and advising the state to apply to Congress for redress of grievances if its authority was infringed. The Delaware Assembly blocked implementation of Smallwood's arrest order, however, and the general reported the matter to Congress. In response Congress dispatched a letter to Rodney on April 15 justifying its order to arrest White and Gordon by citing the imperative need to halt the growth of loyalism in Delaware. Although Rodney did not dispute the desirability of arresting the two men, he insisted that Congress should have entrusted this task to Delaware. As for Gordon and White, the former escaped and made his way to England while the latter remained on parole to General Smallwood at least until 1779. See *JCC*, 10:285, 328, 351–52, 11:519; PCC, item 161, 1:147–60; Rodney, *Letters* (Ryden), pp. 257–59, 262–63, 267, 298, 300–301; Harold B. Hancock, *The Loyalists of Revolutionary Delaware* (Newark: University of Delaware Press, 1977), pp. 84–85, 107; Laurens to Caesar Rodney, April 15; Thomas McKean to Caesar Rodney, April 28, 1778; and John Dickinson to Caesar Rodney, May 10, 1779.

Henry Laurens to James Wilson

Sir,   26th March 1778

I beg leave to refer to what I had the honor of communicating when you were last in York respecting Capt. Arthur's Appeal from a Decree in the Court of Admiralty at Charles Town in South Carolina, Weyman vs. Brig. Success &c,[1] & now to request your attention to the proceedings of the Court, which the bearer hereof is charged with & will deliver, in a Roll properly directed.

You will likewise receive under the present Inclosure Mr. Attorney General Moultries sentiments disclosed in a Letter to me together with the Act of Assembly for establishing the Court of Admiralty in that State.

The proceedings in Court & Attorney General's opinion extend to a great length, but if my Ideas are just, it will be more laborious to read the papers than to discuss with efficacy the true points upon which a final determination will depend.

The Committee of Congress for hearing Appeals will meet on Tuesday & Wednesday the 5th & 6th May & it is expected this business will then be a Subject for their consideration & I shall be glad to have it so.

I know the necessary attendance on your part will be both expensive & troublesome, therefore you will pardon me Sir for adding that a liberal acknowledgement will be made on mine.

I am with great regard, Sir, Your obedt. Servant.

P.S. Since writing as above I have learned of your excursion to Maryland. I therefore send only this by a transient hand & not by an express Messenger as I had intended & I will detain the papers until I have the pleasure of hearing of your return to Carlisle.

LB (ScHi).
[1] See Laurens to Wilson, February 20, 1778.

James Lovell to George Washington

Sir   York Town March 26th 1778

A Gentleman belonging to Boston, Capt. Fritz, having arrived from France had intended himself the honor of waiting upon your Excellency in person to deliver the enclosed letter and several articles therein referred to. But having had a disagreable, hard journey from North Carolina, and finding that he is to expect worse in his approach to your Camp with his heavy loaded carriage & two or three horses, he has left under my Care the articles referred to in the letter; which I will forward to your Excellency by any person whom you shall order to call upon me, or, by any very good Opportunity which I may happen to have, before you shall signify your will by a Line.[1]

Since I began, I hear your Lady is with you; therefore I drop an expectation that you would desire me to send a part of my charge to Virginia. I shall be industrious to find a safe conveyance to your Quarters. As the things have been very carefully preserved hitherto, I am anxious that they should not be injured under my aim to show you my forwardness to prove myself, your Excellency's most humble Servant,   James Lovell

P.S. Mr. De Francy the Bearer of this having been already introduced to your Excellency, I think he cannot now stand in need of any testimony that I should, otherwise, have taken pleasure in giving to his merit. Mr. De Francy kindly takes charge of the articles in question.

RC (DLC).
[1] Washington reported to Lovell on March 29 that the "letter and several articles therein referred to" had been delivered by Jean Théveneau de Francy. See Washington, *Writings* (Fitzpatrick), 11:172, 325–26.

Marine Committee to John Barry

Sir   March 26th 1778

We have received your Letter of the 20th instant covering an Inventory of the goods lately Captured, and are sorry that your Prize schooner had unfortunately been retaken;[1] and that the Militia instead of affording you Assistance had pilfered so much of the goods you had saved. We think with you that the Bay will be the best place for your meeting with success & hope you will use your utmost diligence in getting your small Squadron speedily down there.

With regard to the Prize goods you have Captured one half in our opinion belongs to the Continent. If it had fully appeared that the Schooner Alert was a Vessel of war and belonged to the Crown of Great Britain, or was duely commisionated a privateer by his Britannick Majesty and you had held she would have been solely the property of the Captors. We inclose herein A Resolve of Congress of the 30th of October 1776.

As to the bounty offered by Congress for burning the Ships of War and Transports of the enemy it was confined intirely to the fire Ships fitted at Philadelphia last fall.

We have advanced your officer Mr. Clarkson Eight hundred Dollars for which sum we have inclosed his receipt and you are to be accountable for the same.

We are sir, Your hble servants

LB (DNA: PCC Miscellaneous Papers, Marine Committee Letter Book).
[1] See Marine Committee to John Barry, March 11, 1778, note 1.

John Banister to Patrick Henry

York 27th March 1778

My letter of yesterday[1] mentioned the embarkation of some Troops from Rhode Island, and I now find that the Conjectures respecting their Destination were well founded. General Washington in a letter of the 24th tells Congress that some People of Rhode Island having got the Enemy's countersign mixed among them & became fully acquainted with their intended junction with Howe which in a very few daies will be effected.[2] The General in his letter is earnest in his address to Congress & more than usually so, that they would send forward the intended Recruits for the Army & seems in no doubt of the Enemy's Intention of being in the Field early in full Force to act with vigor. If they get Possession of this State they may easily keep up their Army. The General says few of the drafts "Said to have been made in Virginia & Carolina" are arrived at Camp. He desires that none may halt on their march under Pretence of getting equipt. The Carolina Troops who marched last fall are not up as far even as this Place.

The Virginia Volunteers would do well to come into Service if a formidable Body can be induced to venture out on this most critical occasion. It is not improbable that Genl. Howe expecting Troops from England either late in the Season or *not at all* is determined, as he knows the weak State of our Army, to make an Effort against it before Recruits shall arrive to reinforce it.

I thought it my duty to give you this Intelligence before they can reach you 'thro the slow Movements of Congress, that so *happily* Virginia may be active in rescuing a Sister State *perhaps an Army* from Ruin. The Signal Service of being instrumental in such *good* needs not a Comment. I am with every Respect Sir your Excellencys Mo. Obed. Servant,   J Banister

[*P.S.*] Another embarkation is made at New York & I am clear they are drawing all to a Point in which we should imitate them.

RC (PHi).
    [1] Not found.
    [2] For Washington's March 24 letter to President Laurens, which was read in Congress this day, see Washington, *Writings* (Fitzpatrick), 11:137–40.

Elbridge Gerry to Robert Treat Paine

My dear sir   York in Pennsylvania 27th March 1778
    I am much obliged to You for a particular Relation of the principles upon wch. the Convention at N Haven proceeded, in forming their Resolutions relative to the fixing Prices; Congress have been so much engaged since the Receipt of the Acts of the Convention, as not to have been able to express their opinion upon them, but I have not heard from any Gentleman the least Hint of Disapprobation & for my own part think You have conducted upon true principles of policy.[1] I fully agree with You upon the Salutary Effects wch would

result from lessening the Quantity of Money in Circulation, & wish
to have your Opinion upon the Expediency of attempting to take
from the Continental Currency 15 or 20 Millions of Dollars, by stopping the Circulation & obliging the Holders to invest their Money
in Loan office Certificates; this is in agitation & inter nos, I shall
endeavour to push it thro. I need not assure You, that nothing shall
be wanting on my part, to urge the States to a Compliance with the
Resolution of Congress for taking their Money out of Circulation,
since I have ever entertained the most sanguine Hopes from such a
Measure.

I am glad to find that the Commissioners are in Earnest upon the
business of investigating the Causes of the shameful Failure of the
Expedition against Newport, & hope that they will be able to give a
good account of the Matter. Congress have passed a Resolution relative to the Time & Expence of the Commissioners, Copy of wch is
inclosed.[2] It is certainly right that the former should be considered
as well as the latter, & the Commissioners must be judges of a Reasonable allowance.

Congress have not received returns from the southern Conventions
of their proceedings upon the regulating Business. There is a Delay
in the Matter & I am not yet informed of the Cause of it.

With respect to General Burgoyne & the other prisoners of the
Convention, the Council of M Bay are desired to make a proper Disposition of them & have full powers for this purpose.

I want to say much more on many subjects but am obliged to attend
the House on a Business of Importance & conclude with my best
respects to all Friends, yours very sincerely,   E Gerry

RC (MHi).
  [1] Although a congressional committee, of which Gerry was a member, prepared
a report on the recommendations of the New Haven Convention, Congress took no
direct action on the "Acts of the Convention." See *JCC,* 10:47, 55, 172, 260, 322–24,
11:472, 843. For further information on Congress' response to the New Haven
Convention, see Oliver Wolcott to Andrew Adams, April 25, 1778, note 3.
  [2] For this March 27 resolve, see *JCC,* 10:290.

Henry Laurens to George Clymer

Sir   27 March 1778

I duly received & presented to Congress the Letter you honoured
me with under date the 7th Inst. together with several papers referred
to.[1]

Congress appeared to be impressed by a sense of your Zeal & attention to the duties & importance of the Commission in which you are
engaged but laid no Commands on me by Act or Resolve, therefore

I have at present only to add my own good wishes & assurances that I am, With great regard & Esteem

P.S. The French Letter which came inclosed in yours contains nothing of moment; that written in Spanish remains a dead Letter; if Colo. Morgan will be so obliging as to acknowledge the Receipt & at the same time intimate that we have no persons capable of translating Spanish it may induce the Governor of Orleans to address hereafter in French.

LB (ScHi).

¹ George Clymer was one of three commissioners who had been sent by Congress to investigate conditions at Fort Pitt, including the suspected disloyalty of George Morgan, the agent for Indian affairs in the middle department. See *JCC*, 9:942–45, 1018, 1026, 10:191–92; and Committee of Congress to Edward Hand, October 24, 1777, note 1. Writing from Fort Pitt on March 7, Clymer reported to President Laurens that fellow commissioners Samuel McDowell and Sampson Matthews of Virginia had not yet joined him, that he had decided to invite the Delaware Indians to a conference at the fort, and that he had carried out a resolve of Congress authorizing the people of Bedford County to raise three volunteer companies for defense against the Indians. See PCC, item 56, fols. 93–95. Enclosed with this were letters of August 8, 1777, from Bernardo de Galvez, the governor of New Orleans; of November 19, 1777, from Francisco Cruzat ("Francis Crurati" in the journals), the lieutenant governor of Illinois; and of March 2, 1778, from George Morgan. Cruzat's and Morgan's letters are in PCC, item 78, 5:119–21, 15:317–18; the one from Galvez has not been found. See also Laurens to George Morgan, April 9, 1778.

Henry Laurens to the Marquis de Lafayette

27th March 1778.

I was honoured this Morning Dear & much Respected Marquis by the receipt of your favor of the 20th.¹

What branch of any of my Letters, the inadvertent disclosure of which could have occasioned you pain—It is most certain I never intended to communicate & I am persuaded I have not promulged sentiments inconsistent with the Interests of the public nor derogatory to the honor of my Station; & perfectly sure I am from the integrity of my heart that I have written nothing which can be construed into slander. It would be indecent to whisper across a Street & impertinent to read my private correspondences to every Man who calls to see me, but while I am peculiarly careful not to expose what is intrusted to me in the Letters of my friends, I am equally anxious for the fate of my own. I may safely be so since I cautiously avoid every thing inflammatory, every thing like party whisper & every thing that can spread the present deplorable discord.

If I judge truly, the "little article," which Your Excellency alludes to, is the Postscript of my Letter the 6th Inst.[2] I read that to General Gates & the fact was public, therefore the intimation can give no offence. In a word permit me to assure Your Excellency that neither the manner nor the matter of the late disclosure affects me with the Slightest degree of Chagrin, except my feelings for the vexation which that circumstance had given you.

Your Excellency's Letter to Congress is Reported & Committed to a Select Committee. Our business of this nature proceeds slowly, therefore I will not detain the Messenger but return him to morrow Morning with this. Such determinations as Congress may make in consequence of the expected Report from Committee will in all probability meet you at Valley forge.[3] I presume you will commence your retrograde journey soon after the return of the present bearer.

An authentic account from Holland of 25th October assures us the States have demanded restitution for a Dutch Ship taken in the Channel by an English Man of War under pretences of her being American built—that all the capital Houses in Trade (Hope & Comp. excepted) have united in application for Convoys to their West India Trade & that the number of friends to American Independence increased daily in that Country.[4]

Yesterday a Gentleman from Virginia imported a peice of intelligence of extraordinary magnitude—which had just arrived from the French West Indies. France, Spain, Portugal, Prussia & Poland have concurred in sentiments to recognize the Independence of these United States. I will not say this is impossible but have advised the printer to preface the Account by such an apology as will save him hereafter from the charge of forgery.

Your determination Dear Marquis to do nothing which may in any degree injure the American Cause is the fruit of a Noble Heart— indeed were you to retire at this Instant unhappy consequences.[5]

LB (ScHi).

[1] Lafayette's private March 20 letter to Laurens is in Lafayette *Papers* (Idzerda), 1:366–69.

[2] In the letter cited above, Lafayette insinuated that he had shown Gen. Thomas Conway the postscript of a March 6 letter from Laurens stating that the marquis and Baron de Kalb were to rejoin Washington's army while Conway was to remain behind in Albany, which would have made Conway acting commander of the army there.

[3] Lafayette's official March 20 letter to President Laurens was referred to a committee this day, but no report on it has been found. See *JCC*, 10:287; and Lafayette, *Papers* (Idzerda), 1:362–65.

[4] Congress had received this "authentic account" in the form of an October 14, 1777, letter to the committee of foreign affairs from Charles W. F. Dumas, Congress' agent at The Hague. Wharton, *Diplomatic Correspondence*, 2:407–8. Laurens erred in giving the date of this letter as October 25.

[5] For the continuation of this letter, see Laurens to Lafayette, April 8, 1778.

Henry Laurens to George Read

Sir.   York Town 27th March 1778.

Within the present Inclosure you will receive two Packets under date of the 9th & 10th Ulto. which I had pressed upon the Honorable Mr. McKean to take into his care & forward but he declined. I intreat you to be assured that notwithstanding any seeming delinquency on the part of the President of Congress in his correspondence with Deleware he is by no means chargeable with the smallest neglect, although I will not detain you at present with proofs or apologies. The bearer of this to Wilmington is on the wing & I must embrace the opportunity to transmit by him the Letters above mentioned together with the several Acts of Congress enumerated below.

1. 26th February for filling the Continental Battalions to which is annexed a Return from the Board of War shewing the Numbers wanted to compleat.

2. Same date for ascertaining the Amount of Accounts for necessaries supplied British Prisoners from the commencement of the present War.

3. 7th March for setting apart Wednesday 22d April for a General Fast.

4. 11th March for defraying the expences incurred by carrying into execution a Resolve of Congress of the 9th February last.

5. 12th March Recommending that each State send at least three Members to Congress during the War.

6. 16th March for obtaining from the several States information of their proceedings on the Recommendations of Congress &c.

If you will be pleased to inform me the best or to point out a particular mode for conveying dispatches hereafter I shall pay that regard, which I hold to be due to your advice, & depend upon me Sir, for as strict an attention to Delaware as I regularly observe to every State in the Union within the circle of my Duty.

I have the honour to be, With very great regard, Sir, Your obedient & Most humble servant,

Henry Laurens, President of Congress

P.S. This Instant the Secretary has sent in & you will receive with other papers an Act of the 19 March Recommending to the several States to take the most effectual measures for raising their quota of Men &c.

RC (Henry Laurens, Flat Rock, N.C., 1973).

Gouverneur Morris to Robert R. Livingston

Dear Livingston   Camp 27th March 1778.

I hear by Accident of an Opportunity directly to you. Whether I shall meet with it I know not but I will not on that Account omit writing. The little Billet I received from you the other Day accuses me of Neglect which I can by no Means charge myself with. To obviate such Accusation I seize this Moment in which I have Nothing to say to you because I hear *Nothing* from you, *Nothing* from the State and I fear you are doing *Nothing*. A letter from the G—— tells me you are busy passing Bills of very little Importance and that the greater Business is neglected. Is it possible my Friend that the State of New York can think of passing a *regulating Act*. How hath this Madness got hold upon them. Can a Requisition of Congress sanctify Absurdity. Will any people under the Sun knowingly swallow Poison because recommended by a Phisician? When the Way is so open by Taxation can any Persons be so absurd as to think of putting a Stop to the Evil by any other Mode. Alas we like all other People must profit I find by our *own Experience*. Adieu. My Love to all our Friends. Remember me to Jay very particularly the more so because I fear he wants such a Remembrancer. This I conclude from not having received a single scrip of a Pen from him in Answer to many letters I have written. Again Adieu. Yours sincerely,

                                                   Gouvr Morris

RC (NHi).
[1] Gov. George Clinton.

Rhode Island Expedition Commissioners to Henry Laurens

Sir   Providence. March 27th 1778.

We did ourselves the honor of addressing you on the 13th Feby. last upon the subject of our proceedings in pursuance of the Resolve of Congress of Decemr 12th for enquiring into the causes of the failure of the Expedition against Rhode Island.[1] We then inform'd your Honor that after spending a Week on the business & not being able to finish it we adjourned to the 23d of March at which time we met & have finished the Enquiry in the best manner we found ourselves Capable; & we hope the manner in which we have executed it will give Satisfaction to the Honble. Congress.

We are very sorry the Execution of this Commission has been so long delayed, & we wish to satisfy the Honble. Congress that it has not arisen from a want of due attention in us who were honored with the appointment; the severity of the season at which the Enquiry was appointed, the exceeding badness of the travelling, our previous Engagements in public business of great importance, were the real causes.

The business of our Commission is a matter of such great expectation & Concern, that it was with great reluctance we enter'd upon it with a bare quorum of the Commissrs. & nothing but the Idea of embarrassing the Administration of Congress by neglecting their requisition, & the danger of having this matter too far postponed or totally neglected, induced us to undertake it. We hoped for the assistance of Mr Benson on the Adjournment, but have not been happy enough even to hear from him on the subject.

In pursuance of this business we have attended to the Questions pointed out in our Commissn. & have proposed them to every person whom we could judge capable of answering them & we have proposed some other questions which we thought tended to throw light on the subject; we have also collected all the proceedings & determinations of all Councils of War, & the opinions of each member of Council & all other papers respecting the matter which have come within our knowledge; we have also procured a Copy of the Enquiry made by Committees from the New England States, into the causes of the failure of this Expedition, all which we herewith transmit.

In the execution of this business certain expences have arisen, some of which, viz. Waiter, Expresses procured by our order by the Sheriff, Wood & Candles, The Honble. the Council of the State of Rhode-Island proposed advancing on Acct. of the United States, but it was thot more convenient the Accounts should be paid by Mr. Tillinghast Continental Agent after they had been examined & allowed by the Honble. Council of War; & accordingly we drew an Order on Mr. Tillinghast for that purpose, as also for 28 Dollars for the Clerks & also for 200 Dollars for the actual expences of the three Commissioners on their first meeting, & we have proceeded in the same manner for the expence of this meeting being 32 Dollars for the Clerks, & 78 Dollars for the actual expences of the Comissnrs. and stated the same in Acct. to Mr. Tillinghast. As the Honble. Congress had given no direction for the payment of these expenses, we thought the method we have taken would be most satisfactory, & hope it will prove so.

We are with great Respect, your honor's most humble servts.

> Rob Treat Paine
>
> Oliver Ellsworth
>
> Hy. Marchant

RC (DNA: PCC, item 78). In a clerical hand and signed by Ellery, Marchant, and Paine.

[1] For an account of the work of these commissioners, see Laurens to the Rhode Island Expedition Commissioners, December 15, 1777, note.

Elbridge Gerry to the Massachusetts Council

Sir,   York in Pennsylvania 28th March 1778
I must beg Leave to request that You will communicate to the Honorable Assembly my Intentions of returning Home in the Month of April or Beginning of May next,[1] that the Place which I have the Honor to hold may not be vacant from their Want of seasonable Information.

The State of Massachusetts since January last has been unrepresented in Congress, in Consequence of a Resolution appointing Mr Dana on a Committee for reforming the Army. He has lately returned from Camp for the Advice of Congress on a Subject of Importance, & having obtained it, is again to meet the Committee. Many States require but one, others two, & Massachusetts alone three Members present to have a Vote, & should the same Rule continue with respect to the latter, It may hereafter be found necessary to have at least four Members present for preventing the Inconveniences which necessarily result from the Want of a Voice in Congress.[2]

FC (MH–H). Endorsed by Gerry: "Copy of a Letter to the Presidt of the Council of M Bay March 28, 1778."
[1] Gerry did not return home in 1778.
[2] Massachusetts continued to require the presence of three delegates for representation in Congress. *JCC*, 13:17–18. But on April 23, 1778, after considering Gerry's letter and one from Francis Dana of March 29, the General Court directed the absent members of its state delegation to proceed to York "as soon as possible." Journal of the House of Representatives, January 7–May 1, 1778, DLC(ESR).

Cornelius Harnett to William Wilkinson

Dear Sir   York Town March 28. 1778
I wrote you some time ago perhaps about a fortnight. I send you the Last papers. As for News nothing has happened, but what you'll meet with in the papers. Your Bills will not be paid, I hope you'll endeavour to get it out of Coll Kennons Estate. As soon as Congress determines the matter, I shall have them protested, & bring them home with me. I will not upbraid you again with your great knowlege of business in transacting this matter, I only wish you had got the Indorser to have been a person of property.

My Servant, I can hear nothing of, some think he is gone to visit Genl. Howe; God knows how I shall get home, unless you received my Letter about sending me a Servant. I must endeavour to get on by hiring One, from Stage to Stage.

I dare not tell you how ill I have been, how ill I am now; or how soon I expect to be better. But Mrs Harnett must not know it. I ride out on horse-back every day & think I mend.

Make my respectful Compliments to all my friends & believe me, Dr Sir, Your sincere friend &c,   Cornl Harnett

[*P.S.*] I beg you will Shew Civility to Major Lucas, for my sake & his own.

RC (PHi).

Henry Laurens to John Laurance

Sir,   York Town 28th March 1778
Your Letter to Mr. Duane of the 18th November was presented to Congress the 9th Inst. and was yesterday taken under consideration, when it was Resolved to augment your Salary as will appear by an Act of Congress for that purpose which I have the honour of transmitting within the present Inclosure.[1]

I am with great Respect, sir, Your obedient & most humble servant,
                    Henry Laurens, President of Congress.

RC (NHi). Addressed: "John Laurance Esquire, Judge Advocate general in the Army of the United States of America, Valley forge Camp."
[1] In his November 18, 1777, letter to James Duane, who was then a member of the Board of Treasury, Judge Advocate General Laurance had complained that he was being underpaid and had asked Congress to give him "Pay and Rations equal to those of a Colonel" as well as "Provender for two Horses." PCC, item 78, 14:251–52. On March 27 Congress decided to allow Laurance "seventy-five dollars per month [*the regular monthly pay for a colonel*], his former rations, and forage for two horses." See *JCC,* 5:853, 10:290.

Henry Laurens to Ebenezer Learned

Sir,   28th March 1778.
Your favour of the 12th which reached me the 23d Inst. having been taken under consideration in Congress, the House Resolved to accept the Resignation of your Commission & within this Inclosure you will receive the Act for that purpose.[1]

Permit me to add as an Individual that from the high opinion I have entertained for your excellent Character as a Soldier & a Citizen I regret the loss which the public will Suffer in one part on this occasion. I wish you perfect recovery of health & have the honour to be, With great Esteem & Respect &ca.

LB (DNA: PCC, item 13). Addressed: "Brigadier General Ebenezer Learned Esquire, Boston."

[1] In his March 12 letter to Laurens, Ebenezer Learned, who had been appointed a Continental brigadier general on April 2, 1777, had asked for permission to resign from the army for reasons of health and Congress had granted it on the 24th. See *JCC*, 10:281; and PCC, item 78, 14:203–4.

Henry Laurens to Casimir Pulaski

Sir[1]   28th March 1778.

I have the honour of presenting within this Inclosure an Act of Congress of this date for confirming your Rank of Brigadier General in the Army of the United States & for enabling you to raise & Command an Independent Corps &ca to which I beg leave to refer.

Permit me to assure you of my warmest wishes for your Success, and that I am with very great Respect &ca.[2]

LB (DNA: PCC, item 13). Addressed: "Count Paulaski, York Town."

[1] The young Polish patriot Casimir Pulaski (1748–79) had arrived in America in July 1777 with a letter of introduction from Benjamin Franklin, and he had quickly won the favor of Washington, who advised Congress to appoint him commander of the Continental cavalry. Congress obliged the commander in chief on September 15 by creating the post of "commander of the horse . . . with the rank of brigadier" and appointing Pulaski to it. But Pulaski's appointment offended a number of American cavalry officers, and after repeated clashes with them he resigned his command early in March. With Washington's support, however, Pulaski next sought authority from Congress to raise and command "an independent Corps composed of 68 Horse and 200 foot," which Congress granted this day. See *JCC*, 8:745, 10:291; Washington, *Writings* (Fitzpatrick), 11:80–82; and *DAB*. See also Laurens to Washington, March 30, 1778.

[2] This day Laurens also wrote a brief letter to Jonathan Trumbull, Jr., the paymaster general in the northern department, transmitting "A Warrant on Derick Ten Brock Esquire Commissioner of the Loan Office New York dated yesterday for Twenty Seven Thousand three hundred & thirteen Dollars." See PCC, item 13, fol. 246; and *JCC*, 10:290.

Abraham Clark to Jeremiah Wadsworth

March 29. 1778.

Mr. Wadsworth is desired to peruse the enclosed regulations,[1] and Signifie his Pleasure whether he is willing to Accept the appointment of Comsy. genl.—and whether he find any defect in the System of Consequence Sufficient to require a reconsideration—the information may be given to Mr Dyer or his Humble Servt,   Abra Clark

RC (John F. Reed, King of Prussia, Pa., 1972). Addressed: "Jeremiah Wadsworth in York Town." Endorsed by Wadsworth: "Letter from Mr A Clark 29 March recd same day."

[1] The "enclosed regulations" were undoubtedly those approved by Congress on March 13 and drawn up by "the committee to revise the commissary's department." Clark was a member of this committee, which had been appointed on January 14, 1778, while Eliphalet Dyer had long been urging Wadsworth to accept the office of commissary general of purchases. Congress approved three alterations Wadsworth requested in the commissary system and "unanimously elected" him commissary general on April 9. See *JCC,* 10:51, 192–93, 207, 235, 241, 247–52, 327–28; and Dyer to Wadsworth, February 10 and March 10, 1778.

Although Clark's letter is clearly dated March 29 and is so endorsed by Wadsworth, it may have been written one day later. March 29 was a Sunday, and according to the journals Clark, Dyer, Elbridge Gerry, and Francis Lightfoot Lee were appointed on the 30th to meet with Wadsworth "and enquire whether he will undertake the office of commissary general of purchases." *JCC,* 10:293. But since Clark may have been writing in his capacity as a member of the previously appointed committee on the commissariat and referred Wadsworth to Dyer simply because Dyer was a fellow Connecticut resident who had been promoting Wadsworth's appointment, the letter has been placed as Clark dated it.

Francis Dana to the Massachusetts Council

Sir   York Town March 29th. 1778

As the time I proposed, when I left home, to tarry at Congress, is nearly expired, and I am unwilling our State shou'd be unrepresented in that Assembly;[1] I take the liberty to trouble you with my intention of leaving Congress in the latter end of April, or the beginning of May next. Mr. Gerry will I believe, return at the same time. And as our General Assembly have thought fit to require *Three* to make up their representation in Congress (which by the way is attended frequently with much inconvenience, and I think ought to be reduced to *Two*) it will be necessary Two of the other Delegates shou'd come forward by the time Mr. Gerry and myself intend to set off for home.

I am Sir, with much esteem & respect, your most obedt. & obliged humble Servant,   Fra Dana

P.S. Please to present my respectful Compts. to the Members of the Board.

RC (M–Ar). Addressed: "Honble. Jeremiah Powell Esqr., President." Endorsed: "In the House of Representatives April 23d. 1778, Read & committed to the Committee on the Letter from Elbridge Gerry Esq. Sent up for Concurrence. J. Pitts Spkr pro Tem. In Council April 23d. 1778, Read & Concurred. John Avery DyScy."

[1] For Elbridge Gerry's testimony that Massachusetts had in reality been unrepresented in Congress for some time, because of Dana's attendance at the Committee at Camp, see Gerry to the Massachusetts Council, March 28, 1778.

Henry Laurens to John Laurens

My Dear Son,   29th March 1778.
    In a very few words let me acknowledge the Receipt of your favors of the 22d & 25th Inst.[1]

General Duportail is a sensible Man & I beleive merits the highest respect—had it been necessary he might have commanded my services. Count Poulaski is gratified by a Resolve of Congress for raising an Independent Corps.

Neither Mr Duplisses nor Mr De Balme have deposited any Books with me, unless there should be some in the Coffers of the latter which he has lodged in this House under my protection.

I listen attentively to your reasonings & flatterings for inducing me to continue in the present appointment. No Man has so much influence over me as my worthy friend my Virtuous Son John Laurens. If after half an hours conversation he will confirm his present advice, I will be governed by it, but I think he will then veiw things in a different light. However I am not determined—you know I never do determine until it becomes necessary. When Mr. Drayton & Mr. Mathews arrive I shall make an arrangement for an interview with you provided I determine on a Journey Southward.

Present me respectfully to Baron Stuben, he has always my warmest wishes & I will express them in a Letter in a very few days. The Brevets to his Aids de Camp were intended to intitle those Gentlemen to Rank, pay & Rations.[2] I think if those Commissions were not, they ought to have been intimated to the General. I will look into that matter to morrow or as soon as I can, but I am weary of troubling Congress with my opinions & sentiments on Army Etiquet. Your General has not the Talent of our Colo. O Roberts. Otherwise whenever Congress overleaped him, he would, & perhaps in a quite different Stile, give the necessary hint.

It grieved me the other day, as it has done upon many similar occasions, to be made the Instrument of transmitting positive orders to the Commanding Officer of a detachment from General Washingtons Army without passing through the Medium of the General. I spoke of it & intreated to pursue a regular course, the answer was by a Gentleman who entertains high notions of the sublimity of his own judgement. What Sir have not Congress a right to give what Orders they please to their Officers? Is it possible I can err in being of a contrary opinion with necessary references to that respect which is due to a Commander in Chief & to the well ordering & safety of the Army. Consider I intreat you & answer me. I refer in this Instance to a late Order to General Smallwood[3] a Copy of which you will find inclosed & my inquiry is for information. If I am right in my present Idea, I have been so in a numberless past Instances & I will speak to the Members out of Congress & put them upon their guard against improper Acts which I am persuaded have not been pursued from any design to affront the General. Some Men hold power & omniscience to be Synonymous, I do not. Inclosed with this I transmit you a Letter which I have just received of the 8th March from my good friend the late President Rutledge together with his Speech to the Council & Assembly of So Carolina in the Act of his Resignation,[4] an Act which involves very momentous considerations & upon which I formed my Judgement, upon the first veiw, I am not ignorant that this may be called a moot point the question admitting much debate & of very refined argumentation, to be determined, or perhaps more properly, undecided by nice Casuistry. An honest plain answer will contain your Sentiments & I will candidly inform you mine & compare Notes. That Restless Spirit continues like the troubled element in which he has been so long dabling I mean an old Neighbor of ours.[5] I see he has been at the bottom of this untoward event. As there subsists a friendship between your General & Mr. Rutledge I think it will not be improper to offer the General a perusal of these papers. If he will take that trouble & shall think proper to disclose his opinion I am persuaded it will afford Mr. Rutledge pleasure & will be very complimentary to me. General Duportail hurried me into an opinion that I should not have had time to fill half the 1st page, otherwise I would have addressed my Son on a more decent piece of paper. You will excuse me & be assured of my continued Ardent Love & increasing Esteem & Respect.

[*P.S.*] Carefully return Mr. Rutledge's Letter &ca & soon.

LB (ScHi).
    [1] These letters are in Simms, *Laurens Army Correspondence,* pp. 143–49.
    [2] See *JCC,* 10:280. Washington did not know if he was supposed to pay the salaries of Steuben's aides and consequently they had had to draw their pay "on account." Simms, *Laurens Army Correspondence,* p. 148.
    [3] See Laurens to William Smallwood, March 26, 1778.
    [4] In his March 8 letter to Laurens, John Rutledge explained that he had recently resigned as president of South Carolina because he opposed an effort by the state legislature to make both its upper and lower houses popularly elected. See Frank Moore, ed., *Materials for History Printed from Original Manuscripts* (New York: Printed for the Zenger Club, 1861), pp. 103–6.
    [5] Christopher Gadsden may have been the "Restless Spirit" Laurens had in mind. Ibid.

Henry Laurens to George Washington

Sir   29th March 1778
    Since my last of the 25th by Colonel Armand I have had the honour of presenting to Congress your Excellency's favours of the 24th &

24th Inst.[1] The former Committed to the Board of War & not reported—the latter came under Cover from Colo. Lewis of Virginia accompanied by his Commission which Congress have received & accepted that Gentleman's resignation.[2] Congress by an Act of the 24th Inst. accepted also the Resignation of Brigadier General Learned.

Inclosed herein Your Excellency will receive two Acts of Congress, Vizt.

1. 19th March Recommending to the several States to take the most speedy & effectual measures for raising their respective quota of Men for procuring complete sets of Accoutrements &ca.

2. 28th March for authorizing Count Poulaski to raise an Independent Corps &ca retaining his Rank of Brigadier General in the Army.

Colonel Armand is now or will probably be in Camp in a few days, I therefore judge it proper to return the Inclosed Letter directed by your Excellency to that Gentleman.[3] I have the honour to be with the utmost Esteem & Respect.

LB (DNA: PCC, item 13).
[1] Washington's two March 24 letters to Laurens are in PCC, item 152, 5:415–19, and Washington, *Writings* (Fitzpatrick), 11:137–40.
[2] See *JCC*, 10:292.
[3] See Washington, *Writings* (Fitzpatrick), 11:147–48.

Henry Laurens to George Washington

Sir,   30th March 1778

I had the honor of writing to Your Excellency Yesterday by General duportail.

At reading the Journal this Morning Congress reconsidered the Act of the 28th for authorizing Count Pulaski to raise a Seperate Corps & expunged the words "Prisoners &" which Stood in the last Sentence & your Excellency will receive within the present Inclosure a Copy of the Act as now amended.[1]

I likewise inclose an Act of Congress of this date for securing the Exchange & inlargement of Major General Lee & for other purposes relative to the intended Cartel for the Exchange of Prisoners to which I beg leave to refer.[2]

I have the honour to be with great Regard & Esteem &ca.

LB (DNA: PCC, item 13).
[1] The printed journals do not record the deletion of the phrase "Prisoners &" from the March 28 resolve authorizing Casimir Pulaski to raise an independent corps, and the rough journals for this part of March 1778 are missing from PCC. However, the phrase is crossed out in the manuscript report of the Board of War

proposing the creation of this corps. PCC, item 147, 1:557. Congress had forbidden the enlistment of prisoners of war or deserters into the Continental Army in a February 26 resolve, but Washington raised the issue of exempting Pulaski's corps from this ban in his March 14 letter to Laurens. Perhaps Congress rescinded permission to Pulaski to recruit prisoners because of Washington's March 12 warning to Laurens that this practice would undercut efforts to end General Howe's policy of "obliging or permitting the prisoners in his hands to inlist." See *JCC*, 10:203, 291; and Washington, *Writings* (Fitzpatrick), 11:73, 81. Despite Congress' resolves and Washington's orders forbidding this practice, however, Pulaski, with the encouragement of the Board of War, proceeded to enlist prisoners of war anyway, thereby offending both the delegates and the commander in chief. See Washington, *Writings* (Fitzpatrick), 11:337; and letters to William Atlee from Laurens, May 29, and from Thomas McKean, June 5, 1778.

[2] See *JCC*, 10:295; and Laurens to Washington, March 15, note 1, and April 8, 1778, note 4.

Francis Lewis to the New York Convention

Dear Sir,   York Town, 30 March 1778.[1]

I had the honor to write you the 25th Ultimo & 7th Inst. acknowledging your favor of the 11th January,[2] and pursuance to your request, & my duty, I shall proceed to give you every information in my power relative to the Public Weal.

About two Months ago Congress sent a Committee of their Body to Camp in order to consult with the General upon a mode for regulating the Army. Mr Danna, one of that Committee is returned with a Report for the new arrangement of the Army in which it is proposed to reduce the present establishment to 88 Battalions, each to consist of one Colonel, one Lieut Colonel, one Major, six Captains, one Capt. Lieut., Eight Lieuts, nine Ensigns, The Staff to be appointed out of the Line. The Qr. Mrs. General for the Grand Army are already appointed, vizt Major Genl. Green, with a Col. Cox & Mr. Pettit (both of this state) as assistant Qr. Masrs. General. There has been great complaints of neglect & peculation in this department, into which a strict inquiry will be made.

The Report proposes half pay to all Commissioned Officers on the new Establishment, who shall remain in the service at the end of the War. Congress has already employed a Week, de diem in diem, debating warmly upon this point, & nothing yet determined. The half pay scheme meets with great opposition, the House divided in a Committee of the Whole, the Question not yet put, but will I believe tomorrow, if carried in the affirmative (wch is still with me a doubt) it will be for a limmited term of years, & not for life.[3]

By a letter from General Washington receivd last night, we are informed the Enemy are preparing for an Expedition.[4] They have ordered Troops from Rhode Island & Nw. York round to Philadelphia, from which Manoeuvre the General conjectures, that they do not expect any considerable reinforcemts from Europe this Campaign, or they would not take the Field so early. Should their designs be against Genl. Washingtons Army, it is at present in a weak State. Should they be routed, or obliged to retreat, from the negligence of Quarter & Forrage Masr, they have not Horses to bring off their Artillary & Military Stores &c.

Governor Casswell from N. Carolina is on his march with 5000 Volunteers for the Grand Army, and Virginia has 5000 more, but we know not as yet what has been collected in the other states by Inlistments or drafts. If the public reports we have from abroad be true, we have nothing more to do than to exert ourselves this Campaign, & our Independence will have a permenant Establishment.

Our Magazeens of Provisions are filling daily, especialy of the bread kind and we have lately advice of the arrival of large Supplys of Arms, Amunition, & Cloathing, in the out Ports, both to the Eastward & Southward, but from the badness of the roads & scarcety of Waggons, few as yet have been conveyed to the Army.

I forgot to inform you that it has been also moved in a Committee of the Whole, that a bounty should be given to the Soldiers at the end of the War, of fifty dollars each & a suit of Cloths, over and above the bounty of Land formerly voted.

The Marquis de la Fyette is in high esteem with the Congress. He appears to be a nobleman, with a high sence of honor, & I hope nothing will be done to give him the least disgust.

The Polish General Polasskey is appointed to raise an Independent Corps of sixty Draggoon, with 200 light Infantry, to Rank a Brigdr General; I believe he will prove a valuable Officer.

Congress is anxious to know if the Forts on Hudson River are carrying on with Vigour as they have the security of that River very much at Heart; such has been the large demands for money that the Treasury was nearly exhausted, but hope it is now in such a train, as to be soon and amply replenished.

General Wayne with a party made lately an excursion into the Jerseys where he was followed by a party of the Enemy. They skirmished & were driven back with the loss of Eight or nine taken & some wounded, Genl. Wayne distroyed large quantities of forrage & returned. The Enemy took from us a drove of 120 black Cattle near Corrells ferry on the West side the Delaware comming for our Camp. If General Washington is not soon reinforced, I fear he will be obliged to quit his ground & cross the Sassquehanna. Should that happen, the Enemy will have the States of Pennsylvania, Delaware & Maryland in their possession, & Virginia must be our Asylum.

My worthy Collegue Colo. Duer returned to Congress last week, so that now our State is represented. Mr. G. Morris is still at Camp, we expect he will join us in a fortnight.

The following is exctract from a letter I this day received a Baltimore. "In a Vessell that arrived here last Monday from Martinque, a gentleman came Passinger who reports that Mr. Bingham shewed him a letter, which he received from Parris, the day before this Gentlm left the Island, the purport of which was that Doctor Franklin was received by the French Court as Ambassador from the United States of America, & that a packet for Congress came in this Vessell which was landed on the Eastern Shore." The packet here mentiond, is not as yet received by Congress.

We have also this day received a letter from a Capt of French Ship of 32 Guns 170 Men just arrived at Nuburn N. Carolina, with a Valuable Cargo consisting of Articles suitable for our American Army, of which he makes an Offer to Congress. I have a list of the several Articles, but time will not permit me to send you a Copy. Let it suffice, when I say, that in my opinion we have lately arrived on this Continent a sufficiency of Supplys for our present wants, nay more, if they were properly collected to their respective magazeens.

Be assured Sir I shall give the Honble Council every material information that comes to my knowledge. I have the honor to be, Sir, Your Most Obedt Humbl Servt,   Fra. Lewis

RC (MeHi).

[1] Burnett, who did not use the RC of this letter, printed a Tr of it under the date April 10, 1778. Burnett, *Letters*, 3:163–64.

[2] Lewis' February 25 letter has not been found. The convention's January 11 letter to the New York delegates is in *Journals of N.Y. Prov. Cong.*, 1:1114.

[3] Congress was considering a half-pay plan that had been worked out between Washington and the Committee at Camp and submitted to Congress on March 26 by two committee members—in all likelihood Francis Dana and Nathaniel Folsom. It was, as Lewis indicates, a highly controversial proposal, and after much debate and intricate parliamentary maneuvering Congress finally approved an amended version of it on May 15. See *JCC*, 10:285–86, 289–93, 298–302, 357–60, 362–63, 372–74, 391–98, 11:482–83, 485, 491, 495–96, 502–3. For a discussion of earlier plans for half pay, see Committee at Headquarters to George Washington, December 10, 1777, note. See also Henry Laurens to George Washington, May 15, 1778, note 2.

[4] Washington mentioned British troop movements in New York and Rhode Island in letters he wrote on March 29 to Henry Laurens and James Lovell. Washington, *Writings* (Fitzpatrick), 11:171–72. Congress did not read the letter to Laurens until April 1. *JCC*, 10:300.

Joseph Reed to Robert H. Harrison

Dear Sir   Moore Hall, March 30. 1778

In Consideration of Capt Lees Merit & Services as well as those of the Officers of his Troop the Committee had it in Contemplation to

promote him to the Rank of Major to give him the Command of a
separate Corps consisting of two Troops upon the new Establishment,
one Captain, one Capt. Lieutenant, 3 Lieutenants, 2 Cornets, Mr.
Lindsey to be Captain of the 2d Troop & Mr Peyton Captn. Lieutenant of the 1st.—the new Officers nominated by the General. This
was our Idea which we designed to have suggested to his Excelly &
which if he approves we shall recommend to Congress, but as yet, it is
only thought of.[1]

Our respectful Compliments wait on the General. I am, Dr Sir,
Your most Obed, Hbble Servt.   Jos. Reed

RC (DLC).
[1] For General Washington's April 3 letter to Congress recommending that Capt.
Henry Lee be given "command of two troops of Horse on the proposed establishment with the Rank of Major, to act as an independent partisan Corps," see Washington, *Writings* (Fitzpatrick), 11:205–6. Congress approved the recommendation
on April 7. *JCC,* 10:314–15.

Henry Laurens to Richard Caswell

Sir   31 March 1778
I had the honor of writing to your Excellency by the Honorable
Mr. Penn on the 19th Inst.—if I then transmitted an Act of Congress
of the 16th, the inclosed which I found on my Table will prove to be
a supernumerary sent in by mistake from the Secretary's Office.[1]

Your Excellency will likewise receive within this Inclosure an Act
of the 19th Recommending to the several States to fill up their respective quota of Men for the Army, to March them to the place of
Rendezvous & to provide complete sets of accoutrements &ca to
which I beg leave to refer.[2] I have the honor to be with much Esteem
& regard.[3]

LB (DNA: PCC, item 13).
[1] The enclosed resolve of March 16 called upon the states to inform Congress of
the acts they had passed in pursuance of recommendations they had received from
Congress since November 1, 1777. See Laurens to the Massachusetts Council, March
19, 1778, note 2.
[2] Laurens also enclosed copies of this March 19 resolve with brief letters that he
wrote this day to the Massachusetts Council, the president of New Hampshire, and
the governors of Rhode Island, Connecticut, New York, Maryland, and Virginia.
See PCC, item 13, fols. 235, 249; Meshech Weare Papers, Nh–Ar; Revolutionary
Papers, M–Ar; Red Series, R–Ar; John F. Reed Collection, King of Prussia, Pa.;
and Red Books, MdAA.
[3] Laurens also wrote brief letters this day to Peter Boyer of Boston, notifying
him of his appointment as "an Auditor of Accounts in the Northern District;"
and to William Denning of New Windsor, Conn., informing him of his appointment to "the Commission upon Accounts at the Board of Treasury." See PCC,
item 13, fol. 248; and *JCC,* 10:293.

Henry Laurens to Matthew Locke

Dear Sir,   31 March 1778.

Monsieur Capitaine lately brought me your favor of the 25th Febry. & yesterday Thomas Bell arrived & delivered the Marquis delafayette Baggage. I thank you for all your kindness upon this account & will chearfully pay your advance for Monsr. Capitaine when Mr. Brandon or any other person brings a draught.[1] That Gentleman lost on the Road the Horse which you supplied him with but he cannot clearly discribe the place from whence the Beast Strayed. If you can recover him I am persuaded you will & hold him in readiness for the Marquis's order or account for so much as he may sell for.

If Marquis delafayette had been upon the Spot he might have added to the Sum which I have paid Mr. Bell for his Waggon here, but I think I have gone as far as appear to be equitable & have exceeded the Sum you agreed for. I have paid him 470 Dollars equal to £188—upwards of three pounds per day for a light load out, & empty return is certainly a very enormous price with which Mr. Bell seems satisfied.

LB (ScHi).

[1] For further information about Laurens' efforts to enlist the assistance of Locke and others for Michel Capitaine du Chesnoy, a French officer who had come to America with Lafayette in the summer of 1777 and afterward been incapacitated by illness, see Laurens to Locke, January 25, 1778. Congress granted Capitaine a commission as captain of engineers on April 16. *JCC*, 10:356.

Henry Laurens to Thomas Wharton

Sir   31st March 1778

My last to Your Excellency was the 24th Inst. by Messenger Wier.

Within the present Inclosure your Excellency will receive two Acts of Congress,[1] of the 19th & 1 of the 27th Inst.

1. Recommending to the several States to raise their respective quota of Men & March them forward with all possible expedition, to provide complete sets of accoutrements &ca.

2. For recruiting Colo. Thomas Hartley's Regiment,[1] to which I beg leave to refer and remain, with great respect &ca.

LB (DNA: PCC, item 13).

[1] This resolve stated that if Pennsylvania granted the state bounty to those who enlisted in Colonel Hartley's Eleventh Pennsylvania Regiment they would be credited to Pennsylvania's quota of Continental troops. *JCC*, 10:288. See also *Pa. Archives*, 1st ser. 6:351–52; and Jonathan Bayard Smith to Wharton, March 10, 1778.

Henry Laurens to James Wilkinson

Sir[1]   31st March 1778.

I received & presented this Morning your favor of the 25th Inst. of Congress.

The House has directed me to intimate their acceptance of your resignation of Secretaryship at the Board of War & to return your Letter, which contains other matter improper for the cognizance of Congress & inadmissible as a deposite. In obedience to this order I shall transmit the Letter within the present inclosure.[2]

I have the honour to be with much Respect &ca.

LB (DNA: PCC, item 13). Addressed: "Brigadier General James Wilkinson, Manheim. By General Fulsom."

[1] James Wilkinson (1757–1825), the son of a Maryland planter, had obtained a captain's commission in the Continental Army in 1776 and risen to the rank of lieutenant colonel the following year. He served as Gen. Horatio Gates' adjutant general during the Saratoga campaign and was the messenger who delivered official news of Gates' victory to Congress, thereby gaining the recognition that led Congress to appoint him brigadier general in November 1777 and secretary to the Board of War in January 1778. Wilkinson's promotion to such high rank for so slight a cause was highly resented in the army and led him to resign his commission early in March 1778. Later in the month he also resigned as secretary of the Board of War owing to his inability to get along with board president Horatio Gates, who never forgave Wilkinson for inadvertently revealing the contents of the celebrated letter to Gates from Gen. Thomas Conway that exposed the so-called Conway Cabal. See *JCC*, 9:851, 856, 870, 10:21, 26, 226, 297; and *DAB*. See also *DAB* for a short sketch of Wilkinson's highly controversial post-revolutionary career, which included, among other things, treasonable dealings with the Spanish and involvement in the Aaron Burr Conspiracy.

[2] Before returning Wilkinson's letter of resignation, which is dated "Manheim March 25, 1778," Laurens made the following copy of it:

"I beg leave to inform you, that I find myself obliged to decline the seat which the most Honorable Congress voted me in the Board of War, as the sedentary life which attends that duty would be ruinous to my Health. Permit me to add that I could not consistently do business under Major General Gates after the uncandid, artful, unjust & ungenerous practices he has employed to dishonour me." Laurens Papers, ScHi.

In his memoirs, however, Wilkinson printed a different text of his letter of resignation, which he dated "Reading, March 29, 1778." "While I make my acknowledgments to Congress for the appointment of secretary to the board of war and ordnance, I am sorry I should be constrained to resign that office; but after the acts of *treachery* and *falsehood*, in which I have detected Major-general Gates, the president of that board, it is impossible for me to reconcile it to my honour to serve with him." James Wilkinson, *Memoirs of My Own Times*, 3 vols. (Philadelphia: Abraham Small, 1816), 1:409–10. Laurens' copy of Wilkinson's letter of resignation obviously demonstrates that the March 29 letter is a fabrication and, as some historians have long held, that Wilkinson's memoirs must be used with caution.

Francis Lightfoot Lee to George Weedon

Dear Sir,   York Town March 31. 1778

I am sorry to inform you that the report of the board of Genl. Officers was sent by the Comtee, to Congress, & is agreed to. I laid the whole matter before them, but they were of opinion, that the surest way of not injuring the feelings of Military Gentlemen, was to conform to the ideas of the Gentlemen of the Army. This, I assure you, was the principle, which directed their determination & not any preference given the other Gentleman.[1] I did not know who was Your Post master, but being inform'd he was not well affected, I thot it my Duty to mention it to some Gentn in the Neighbourhood. I am glad my information was not well founded.

I wrote some time agoe to Mr Dick about his Son, prisoner in England; shd. be glad to know if he recd. the Letr. You will do an essential service by hastening on the men. It is the opinion of the board of War, not to wait for inocculation, as there is little danger of infection while in the feild. I am Dear Sir, Your very humble Sevt.

                                        Francis Lightfoot Lee

RC (PHC). Addressed: "To General George Weedon Fredericksburg Virginia."

[1] On April 12 Weedon sent a copy of Congress' March 19 resolution placing him last in the seniority arrangement of the brigadiers in the Virginia line to Richard Henry Lee, whom he asked to inform Congress that he would not serve "in the present Arrangement." Lee Family Papers, ViU. Responding to Weedon the same day, from "Belleview" in Virginia, Richard Henry urged him to remain in the army. "I am much concerned at the resolution of Congress that you have sent me a copy of," Lee explained, "because I am perfectly satisfied from the knowledge I have of this matter that it is unjust with respect to you. No affected knowledge of military rule is necessary here, common sense is sufficient without other aid to determine the question. When you were appointed Brigadier, Mr. Woodford was no more an Officer in the Continental Army than I am. He was out by his own choice, and with respect to him, your appointment was unoppugnable. When therefore Mr. Woodford was made a Brigadier from a Citizen, what pretext could there be for complaint that you were above him? I regard Gen. Woodford as a good Officer, but without flattery, I do not think his Talents superior to yours, and this alone, could in my opinion, justify the resolve. I must confess to you, that altho I thought well of Gen. Woodford, I found my feelings much hurt, both as a public man, and a friend to our righteous cause, when he resigned his commission. I thought it could not be justified upon any principles that I was able to try it by, and so I think still. Having thus given you my thoughts on this point, I will with your leave put down how I should, if in your situation, think and act on this occasion. And perhaps I am in some degree qualified to judge because I too have as a Citizen been not only injured in this way but in a much worse. I did then, and would now reflect, that the Sacred cause of Liberty and my Country supercedes all other obligations and every other consideration; and therefore when I find that Country mistaken and acting upon wrong principles with respect to me, altho my feelings might be greatly hurt I should be more affected for the operation that the example might have upon the minds of others than for my particular injury, but I would continue to exert every faculty in the service of my

Country. I should certainly not resign, and by continuing to Act, convince Mankind of my superiority to what you call 'the evil spirit of intrigue,' and indeed to every other consideration but the love of my Country. Military Men, in these days, are apt to carry their ideas of honor too far, for I cannot help thinking with St. Paul that Temperance, even in virtue, is proper. As I wish you to continue in the Army, so I could wish you would not insist on my doing the disagreable business of Bearing your resignation." Allyn K. Ford Collection, MnHi.

For information on the dispute respecting the seniority claims of the Virginia brigadiers and Weedon's subsequent resignation despite the pleas of friends, see Committee at Camp Minutes of Proceedings, February 16–20, note 3; Committee at Camp Statement, March 2, 1778, note 1; and Harry M. Ward, *Duty, Honor or Country, General George Weedon and the American Revolution,* Memoirs of the American Philosophical Society 133 (1979), chaps. 7 and 8.

Cornelius Harnett to Jethro Sumner

Dear Sir   York Town 1st April 1778

I received your favours of the 19th & 27 & do not recollect to have done myself the Pleasure to answer either of them. My great Indisposition must plead my excuse; I received from Coll Clark the dates of the Colls. Commissions now in Camp belonging to the N Carolina Brigade, you or he is mistaken in a day—you say the 15th, he the 16 Apl. 1776, this will be easily rectified by having recourse to the Commissn.

Mr. Pen & myself while he was here Moved Congress several times to have the Brigadiers recommended by Our Genl. Assembly immediately Commissioned; but as there are several Other Colonels, in Other Brigades, who are also to be appointed, Congress have postponed the matter until the Gentn. are fixed upon. In order that they may rank agreeable to the dates of their Commissions as Colonels.[1]

This measure must very soon take place, & hope to have it in my power to Congratulate you & Coll Clark, on yr. Appointment, Mr Burke says he will not Stir in it.[2]

I would advise you on receiving the Commission, to get leave of Absence for a few Months to return to the Southward which will I hope effectually restore your health, & enable you to return to the Army in the most Vigorous part of the Campain. I shall set Out from hence about the 15, or betwixt that, & the 20 Instant, at furthest;[3] & shall be very happy to travel with you if Convenient. I am with great esteem, Dr Sir, Your most Obed Servt.   Cornl. Harnett

RC (NcU). Addressed: "Coll. Jethro Sumner of the No. Carolina Brigade, Lancaster."

[1] On December 15, 1777, the North Carolina Assembly passed a resolve calling for the promotion of Cols. Jethro Sumner and Thomas Clark to the rank of brigadier general, and on February 10 the North Carolina delegates presented it to Congress. Congress did not act on the assembly's request until January 9, 1779,

when it promoted Sumner and Col. James Hogun, another North Carolina officer, to brigadier general. See *JCC,* 10:142, 12:1260, 13:46; *N.C. State Records,* 12:209; and Harnett to Thomas Burke, November 13, 1777, note 2. Burnett, *Letters,* 3:148n.2, errs in stating that Sumner and Clark became brigadier generals on December 29, 1778—on that day the North Carolina delegates merely repeated their recommendation of them to Congress.

[2] Burke may have professed indifference to the proposed promotions because in the previous year he had been sharply criticized by a number of North Carolina officers for reportedly favoring the appointment of Edward Hand of Pennsylvania as brigadier general of North Carolina troops. See Burke to Francis Nash, August 16, 1777. Eventually, however, Burke did oppose Clark's promotion and was instrumental in inducing Congress to pass over Clark in favor of Col. James Hogun. See Burke to Richard Caswell, January 10, 1779.

[3] Harnett received leave of absence from Congress on April 23 and left York on the 26th. See *JCC,* 10:384; and Henry Laurens to Richard Caswell, April 27, 1778.

James Lovell to Abigail Adams

Dear Ma'am   York Town Apr. 1st. 1778

When I tell you that no Credit is to be given to the late Report of an attempted Assassination of Doctor Franklin, you are not to attribute my Assertion to an Endeavour to give Relief, *at all Adventures,* to the anxious Mind of an amiable Sufferer. Had your Letters of the 1st. and 8th of March[1] reached me before this Morning, I could not have given you so much Satisfaction as at present. I could only have told you that no Letter of mine had "confirmed" the Report. I did, it is true *convey* it to Boston, in hopes that I should procure a Contradiction of it, by Intelligence received at the eastern Ports later in Date than what Capt. More brought to Maryland. He left Bordeaux the *12th.* of December and had pickt up his Story at Blaye before that period. But we have a fresh Packet from Mr. Bingham our Agent at Martinique in which he gives us the Substance of Letters from Paris dated Decr. *22d,* ten Days after More left his Outport.[2] Mr. Bingham's Correspondents are certainly a Class of Men who could not be ignorant of a capital Event respecting our Commissioners near a Fortnight after it is said to have happened, and who also would not have omitted to mention the Attempt upon Doctr. Franklin's Life, if it had really been made. The Connecticutt Gazettes tell us the Doctor was well about the *31st* of December.

Call me not a Savage, when I inform you that your "Allarms and Distress" have afforded me *Delight.*

I assure you, Ma'am, that my Intimates think me not devoid of the most tender Sensibilities: But, if you expect that your Griefs should draw from me only sheer Pity, you must not send them to call upon me in the most elegant Dresses of Sentiment and Language; for, if you persist in your present course, be it known to you before hand, that I shall be far more prompt to admire than to compassionate Them.

I do not at all recollect the subject of those letters which you mention to have fallen under your eye after the sailing of the Boston, I rely altogether on your discretion to burn or foward them.[3] I have a degree of curiosity to know what was the purport of that from which you scratched the name, and delivered it to the Judgement of Genl. W[arren].[4]

I have honestly confessed to you my delight springing from your afflictions, you must not therefore attribute it to Mr. G[erry]'s Celibacy, only in part, that he takes *singular* pleasure in finding your "Heart was not at Ease."

You must take this last as *my* opinion, for Mr. G—— instantly disavows the truth of it. Let us set this down as a great symptom in his favour that he knows and means speedily to turn into the truest road of earthly felicity. May you, Dear Ma'am, only leave that road to enter the eternal Paradise.

RC (MHi). Adams, *Family Correspondence* (Butterfield), 3:1–2.

[1] Only the first of these has been found, for which see ibid., 2:396–97.

[2] For the receipt of William Bingham's letters, see Committee for Foreign Affairs to William Bingham, April 16, note 1.

[3] Lovell is referring to his February 8 and 10 letters to John Adams.

[4] Abigail had passed on to James Warren a letter from Lovell that has not been identified, but which in her response she described as "that in which you gave ample scope to your immagination with regard to the Robbery of the publick packets." Adams, *Family Correspondence* (Butterfield), 3:49.

Thomas McKean to George Read

Sir,   Yorktown, April 3d, 1778.

When I attended the general assembly of this state in December last, they obtained a promise that I would give a little assistance in draughting some bills at their adjournment in March, at which time I, accordingly, in pursuance of a letter from the speaker, went to Lancaster, and, having stayed there ten days, returned to York on the 19th. During this interval, your favour of the 4th of March,[1] by lieutenant Frazer, arrived at York, and by the advice of the express, was opened by the president and read in congress. It was well there was nothing private in it, and I must confess you gave me more agreeable prospects of our little state, and more sincere pleasure, than any thing relating to it had done for three years past. I congratulate you on the whig election in Sussex. With such a general assembly as the present, which could I have done, or rather, could I not have done? Sure I am, you will make a proper use of this most fortunate occurrence, in which there appears visibly the hand of Providence, which can alone save this deluded state. Though the resolve for completing the quota of troops, by draughting in the several states, passed against my consent, yet as Virginia, Maryland, Pennsylvania, the four New England governments, &c. have agreed to it, I should have been glad if the general assembly had even proceeded no farther in that business; this would have showed a respect for the recommendation of congress, encouraged the recruiting service by making it the interest of every individual in the state, and prevented an opinion that I had wrote to the general assembly against the measure, which I never did; nor, indeed, did I ever hint the matter to any person whatever. As to the proviso in the second section of article 9th of the confederation, quoted by you, to wit; "provided also that no state shall be deprived of *territory* for the benefit of the United States," my opinion is, that it must be referred to the subject matter of the preceding paragraph, and may, by a fair construction, mean, that in a contest between two states respecting boundaries, the territory taken from the one shall be added to the other, and not adjudged for the benefit of the United States; and yet I confess I have apprehensions, that it may, hereafter, be insisted to mean what you seem to fear. Some gentlemen with whom I have conversed on this affair say, if the intention of congress was, that Virginia, &c. should be deemed at present to extend to the south sea, yet no injury could arise from thence to any of the United States; for that Delaware, for instance, has a right to apply for one or more townships for their troops, to be laid out equally with Virginia in that state, without paying any purchase money or any other expense, more than that of surveying, &c. which Virginians themselves must pay; and that, if that state increases in inhabitants, it will have to pay more towards the support of the government of the United States, and in the same proportion lessen the burden of the other states; but if Virginia, &c. grow too large, the people themselves will insist upon a new state or states to be erected, even if the congress should be passive; and no good reason can be assigned for refusing such a requisition, whenever it may be proper to grant it. The Stockbridge Indians in New Hampshire and Connecticut, the Oneidas in New York, &c. were I suppose the objects of the 4th section of the same article: The 3d section of article 9th, seems to have been calculated for the disputed lands between purchasers under Maryland and Delaware, and Maryland and Pennsylvania; but upon the whole, it may not be an improper method of adjusting such controversies. If Delaware had been represented in congress, at the time the finishing was given to the confederation, it would, I am persuaded, have been a public benefit, as well as a particular one to that state; but matters are too far gone, I fear, to procure any alterations, so many states have already empowered their delegates to ratify it; however, I will exert every nerve to accomplish any measure which shall be recommended by my constituents, who may think it advisable to direct their deputies to endeavour to procure any explanation of certain doubtful expressions in different articles, if they should not think it proper to do more.

Nothing has been effected with regard to president M'Kinley;[2] but as the cartel for a general exchange is now debating, and settling between three commissioners on the part of general Washington, and the like number on the part of general Howe, in Germantown, where they met on the last day of March, I hope in a few weeks, something favorable for him may be done.

If you can procure any clothing for the Delaware battalion, it may be useful, but I am confident there is sufficient for the whole army, already purchased by congress, for above a year; and yet I am told the most of the troops are naked—peculation, neglect of duty, avarice, and insolence, in most departments abound; but, with the favor of God, I shall contribute my part to drag forth and punish the culprits, though some of them are high in rank, and characters I did not suspect.

You will also receive a little pamphlet of the earl of Abington's, which is worth your perusal.[3] General Rodney is not yet arrived, nor could I procure a lodging for him in town when he comes; indeed, when I return, I shall be at an equal loss for myself; this is discouraging, but we must not expect much comfort during this great and glorious struggle. It is reported Howe is recalled, and is to be succeeded by lord Townshend: this will be an active, and I fear a bloody, campaign.

April 12th, at Lancaster. I find you give up the command in chief to general Rodney, so that perhaps it may suit you to come to congress.[4]

I am, Sir, Your most obedt. friend,   Thos. M'Kean

MS not found; reprinted from John Sanderson, *Biography of the Signers to the Declaration of Independence,* 9 vols. (Philadelphia: R. W. Pomeroy, 1820–27), 4:65–69.

[1] George Read's March 4 letter to McKean is in William T. Read, *Life and Correspondence of George Read, a Signer of the Declaration of Independence . . .* (Philadelphia: J. B. Lippincott & Co., 1870), pp. 303–7. It was read in Congress on March 12. *JCC,* 10:246.

[2] See McKean to Read, February 12, 1778, note 2.

[3] McKean doubtless enclosed a copy of the Earl of Abingdon's *Thoughts on the Letter of Edmund Burke, Esq. to the Sheriffs of Bristol, on the Affairs of America* (Oxford, 1777), which had just been reprinted in Lancaster by John Dunlap. For further information on Abingdon's pamphlet, see John Henry to Thomas Johnson, February 17, 1778, note 2.

[4] On March 31 the Delaware Assembly elected Caesar Rodney, a brigadier general

in the state militia, to replace Read as president of Delaware, Read having served as acting president since John McKinly's capture by the British in September 1777. Rodney, *Papers* (Ryden), pp. 256–57. McKean wrote a letter of congratulations to Rodney on April 8 that has not been found, but see Rodney's April 18 reply in *Delaware Archives*, 3:1449–50.

Marine Committee to John Langdon

Sir   April 3d. 1778

We have received your Letter of the 3d of March, and must confess that it gives us great concern that you should have been thrown into so disagreeable a Situation for want of a proper supply of Money. So great and so frequent have been the demands on the Treasury for that necessary article that it hath been out of our power to furnish the Navy Board agreeable to our wishes. It is on this account principally that we have wrote to them directing them to stop the building of the seventy four gun ship at Portsmouth.[1] You will drop the building of her for the present & take proper measures for securing and seasoning the Timber provided for her. We shall procure an order on the Treasury or a warrant on the Loan Offices eastward if possible to enable them to supply you with some money; hereafter when the great departments of the Army shall have been supplied therewith, we will endeavour at the payment of all our debts, and don't doubt but that we shall be able to accomplish it, in the mean time you must make your self and your Creditors as easy as possible. We are satisfied with your conduct and believe that the Building of the Ships at Portsmouth hath been conducted with as much œconomy and advantage to the Continent as in any of the United States.

The Navy Board at Boston are empowered to settle all Marine Accounts in their Department—the Commercial Accounts must be transmitted for settlement to the Committee of Commerce. We are with respect, Sir, Your very humble servts

LB (DNA: PCC Miscellaneous Papers, Marine Committee Letter Book).
[1] See Marine Committee to the Eastern Navy Board, April 6, 1778.

Henry Laurens to Pierre Etienne Du Ponceau

Sir,[1]   York Town 4th April 1778

I am much indebted for your favor of the 2d Inst. The common Civilities which I had the honor of shewing you in York Town were as far short of my wishes as they were of that attention which is due to every polite stranger, let the times & circumstances by which my inclinations were cramped be my apology.

Your sentiments Sir, respecting the Contest in which we poor Americans are engaged are truly liberal, they are Noble. If I were not perfectly assured of their consistency with the eternal Laws of truth & justice I would abandon the Cause & persuade you to follow the example before I subscribed to this Letter, but conscious as I am of the righteousness of our Claims, it is with pleasure I hear your determination to persevere in the line of Duty which was the object of your free Choice.

I wish you frequent trials & upon every occasion success & honor & I beg you will rank among your friends, Sir, Your most obedient & humble servant,   Henry Laurens

RC (NNC). Endorsed: "I arrived in America at Portsmouth N.H. 1 Decr 1777. This letter dated 4 months afterwards proves that at that period my mind was fixed to remain in and devote myself to this Country. This is a precious paper for me. P.S.D. 25 May 1831."

[1] Pierre Etienne Du Ponceau (1760–1844), French-born author and lawyer, arrived in America in December 1777 as Baron von Steuben's secretary and was appointed captain in the Continental Army on February 18, 1778. He acted as Steuben's aide-de-camp until illness forced him to retire from military life in 1779, and then served as Robert R. Livingston's under secretary of foreign affairs from 1781 to 1783. After the war Du Ponceau settled in Philadelphia where he enjoyed a long and distinguished career as a lawyer, legal scholar, and philologist. *DAB*.

There is no basis for the suggestion in Burnett, *Letters*, 3:227n.6, that Laurens probably wrote this letter "in response to a communication from Du Ponceau of a date subsequent to May 11." Both the RC of the letter and the LB, which is in the Laurens Papers, ScHi, are clearly dated April 4, and there is nothing in the letter itself to indicate a later date.

It is interesting to note that in an autobiographical reminiscence written in 1836 Du Ponceau observed of his relationship with Laurens: "Henry Laurens . . . was to me as a father, by the excellent advice he gave to me, as well verbally, as by letters, after we separated." "Autobiographical Letters of Stephen S. Duponceau," *PMHB* 40 (1916): 176.

Henry Laurens to William Heath

Sir,   York Town 4th April 1778

Yesterday I had the honor of presenting to Congress your favors of the 21st & 24th March & although I have received no particular commands relative to their several Contents I am warranted by the general Voice of Members to intimate that you have received the applause of the House for your determinations respecting the adjustment of Accounts with General Burgoyne.[1]

I hope you have received the late large remittance of Money from the Treasury as well as the smaller Sum sent by Messenger

Millet & that you are releived from the trouble which, I am sensible, the want of it must have occasioned you. I remain with very great Esteem & Regard, Sir, Your most obedient servant,

Henry Laurens, President of Congress.

RC (MHi).
[1] General Heath's March 21 and 24 letters to Laurens are in PCC, item 157, fols. 97–102. In the first he described how he had required Gen. John Burgoyne to abide by a December 19, 1777, resolve forbidding the release of British prisoners of war until they had paid for the supplies they had received from their captors in "provisions or other necessaries, equal in quality and kind to what have been supplied, or the amount thereof in gold and silver, at the rate of four shillings and six pence for every dollar of the currency of these states." See *JCC*, 9:1037. In the second he reported a rumor that Great Britain was sending 30,000 reinforcements to America under the command of Sir Jeffery Amherst.

Henry Laurens to Baron Steuben

Dear sir,   York Town 4 April 1778.

I can no longer submit to remain a subject of my own reproaches nor refrain from asking your forgiveness for my delinquency respecting the very polite Letters which you have honoured me with under the 12th Ult. & 2d Inst.[1]

Beleive me Sir, I am made very happy by repeated Accounts of the great utility of your presence & aid in our principal Camp joined with Your Excellency's intimations of Contentment in the very humble station which for the benefit & improvement of the American Army you are pleased to submit to. I entertain the most confident expectations that good discipline will be established in Front & Ranks by Your Excellency's Inspection & superintendence & I am as fully persuaded that suitable acknowledgements will be made on the part of the People in their Representative body & by thousands individually as occasions shall offer.

Accept I intreat you Sir of my particular thanks, of my sincere wishes for Your Excellency's health & continued success. When shall I become an official correspondent? the opening may possibly depend upon the return of the Committee from Camp, when our worthy Commander in Chief may announce to Congress your conditionary appointment & meritorious services. I wish it may be soon, that your mind may be more composed. Permit me to assure you Dear Baron, in every case where I can consistently with that of these Infant States, I shall be devoted to your Interest & honor.[2]

A Gentleman late from Charles Town brings no advice of Mr. Leterjettes arrival nor have I from any quarter received Letters for Your Excellency. York Town affords no interesting intelligence. I

have therefore only to repeat that with the highest Esteem & Respect,
I have the honor to be, Sir, Your Excellency's Most obedient & Most
humble servant,   Henry Laurens

RC (PHi).
    [1] Steuben's letters to Laurens of March 12 (in which he expressed a wish for a
major general's commission but stated that in deference to a request by Washington he would not yet ask Congress for one) and April 2 are in the William Gilmore Simms Collection deposit, MHi.
    [2] See also Laurens to Steuben, May 5, 1778.

Henry Laurens to George Washington

Sir,   York Town 4th April 1778
    Since my last of the 30th Ulto. per Barry I had the honor of receiv-
ing & presenting to Congress Your Excellency's favor of the 29th of
that Month which having been taken under consideration the Inclosed Act was this day Resolved—for impowering Your Excellency
when you shall judge it necessary to call on the States of Maryland,
Pennsylvania & New Jersey for Five Thousand Militia Men, Armed
& accoutred.[1] I have the honour to be, With great Esteem & Respect,
Sir, Your Excellency's Most obedient & Most humble servant,
                               Henry Laurens, President of Congress

P.S. Evening 9 oClock. Monsieur de Francy this moment delivered
me Your Excellency's favour of the 1st Inst. which shall be presented
to Congress on Monday. Mean time permit me Sir to intimate that
I had backed the Report of your Excellency's Letter of the 27th Febry
with an information to Congress that one Gentleman of the late
Committee on the Ticonderoga Enquiry had retired & that it was
impracticable for me to give that attention which was due to an
affair of such importance. A new Committee was immediately appointed, these Gentlemen some 8 or 10 days ago offered a Report,
when Mr. Duer interposed arguments which induced the House to
postpone the Consideration for two days. I have taken the liberty
to name that Gentleman because his declared motives for delay were
coupled with assurances of particular considerations respecting General Schuyler. This very Morning I called on Mr. Duer & reminded
him of his engagements, urging the painful situation in which his
freind & the other General Officers remained. He replied, "I will soon
bring on that business." Your Excellency's present Letter will prove a
further incitement.[2] I have very long felt for the Gentlemen who are
subjects of the Enquiry & although it was with extreme reluctance
I obeyed the order of Congress, to be of the original Committee, after
having urged such reasons for exemption as appeared to me very

forcible, yet I cannot charge myself with delinquincy at any stage in the course of our proceedings. To account for the uncouth & entangled state of this Enquiry, would not be half so difficult as it might be impertinent to the proper line of my correspondence. From this consideration I shall only add, that I trust Your Excellency's present application will have that weight which is justly due.

H L

RC (DLC).

[1] Washington's March 29 letter to Laurens, in which he relayed reports from various sources that British reinforcements were on their way to Philadelphia, is in PCC, item 152, 5:421, and Washington, *Writings* (Fitzpatrick), 11:171–72.

[2] Washington's April 1 letter to Laurens, which was read in Congress on the sixth, is in PCC, item 152, 5:423–24, and Washington, *Writings* (Fitzpatrick), 11:195–96. Washington had reiterated in it the point originally made in his February 27 letter to the president that he could not proceed with courts-martial of officers involved in the evacuation of Ticonderoga and Mount Independence unless Congress first specified charges against them. Although Congress had referred the February 27 letter to a special committee which suggested on March 28 that the committee at camp should apprise Washington of the charges, Congress finally assigned the task of enumerating charges to another committee appointed on April 29 whose bill of particulars it approved on June 20 and sent to Washington. See *JCC*, 10:226, 292, 310, 403, 11:593–603, 628; John Hancock to Arthur St. Clair and Philip Schuyler, August 5, 1777, note; and Committee of Congress to Washington, February 7, 1778, note 1.

The report of the "new Committee" presented to Congress "some 8 or 10 days ago," which Burnett was unable to find a record of in the journals, is undoubtedly the report offered to Congress on March 28 by the committee appointed on the sixth to consider Washington's letter of February 27. Congress postponed consideration of this report until March 30 but did not then take it up again. See *JCC*, 10:292; and Burnett, *Letters*, 3:151n.4. It is noteworthy that Laurens was often so preoccupied with his presidential duties and extensive correspondence that he is not always a reliable witness on the chronology of events in Congress.

William Ellery to Nicholas Cooke

Sir,   York-Town April 5th 1778

Since my last nothing new hath occurred at home, and by the unfortunate shipwreck of Capt. Weeks and the robbery of the Dispatches committed to the care of Capt. Folger we have been disappointed of the Intelligence expected from France.[1] We have received no advices from our Commissioners since last May; so that I have nothing to communicate, from that quarter, which can be depended upon. The indirect news, published in the inclosed News-Paper, from Martinico came from a good hand, and deserves as much credit as any account that does not procede immediately from the fountain.[2]

A Number of ships lately arrived at Philadelphia, it is said, with

Soldiers from New-York, and we have a report from the eastward that the Troops at Rhode-Island were embarking to reinforce Genl. Howe, with a view to enable him to make an efficacious attack upon our encampment before the recruits from the several States shall have joined the main army. It is of the utmost importance that the states should fill up their battalions and send them forward immediately. I find that my information, respecting the negroe Regiment, was not good.[3] Since I had the honour of writing to you, one of the committee from camp hath informed me that it was not the intention that we should have two battalions in the field, that the surplusage of our recruits, above the number necessary to complete our one battalion, was to remain in the state so long as it should continue to be invaded. Inoculation is carried on in camp with such great success that recruits may come forward without any reluctance. Out of three thousand six hundred, which were lately inoculated at Valley forge, eleven only died of the small pox.

An Important questions are on the carpet, whether an establishment of half pay for life or term of years shall be allowed to *military* commissioned officers who shall continue in service to the end of the war? Whether any provision shall be made for the widows of those Officers who have fallen or shall fall in battle, and whether some allowance shall be made to such soldiers as inlist during the war and shall continue in the service to the end of the war? The first is the great question. A Question of such magnitude, in my opinion, that I am one of those who think that it ought to be referred to the consideration of the States. At present it is postponed at large.[4] When it shall be resumed it will be moved that it should be so referred; but whether the motion will meet with success or not is uncertain. I could wish to be instructed by my constituents how to give my voice especially on the capital question; will beg leave to expect it. If I should be called upon, before I receive the Instructions I wish, and shall expect, to give my vote, I shall do it as shall appear to me to be right, and if I should not jump in Judgment with my constituents I hope I shall not be censured.

Congress have recommended it to the States to transmit as early as possible such Acts as they have passed in pursuance of Resolutions of Congress, since the first, I think it is, of November last. I wish that our state may attend to the recommendation. I have not received any authentic Information of what hath passed our Assembly for a long time, and what I have heretofore received were such abridgments of Acts as were of but little use.

The circumstances of my family are such as to necessitate my return home immediately after the election, I hope therefore that the Assembly will order on to Congress, the Delegate which may be chosen directly. By a private Letter I am informed that your Excellency means to resign.[5] I am sorry for It behoves at this time, especially, that sound patriots should fill the several offices in Government. Whether you continue in or go out of office, I shall always entertain a high regard for your excellency on account of that sound steady patriotism which you have discovered and preserved during your administration, and am with the greatest Respect, your Excellency's most obedient, humble,   William Ellery

[P.S.] Please to excuse interlineations & incorrectness. I have not time to copy.

RC (R–Ar).
[1] See Committee Examination of John Folger, January 12, 1778.
[2] See Committee for Foreign Affairs to William Bingham, April 16, 1778, note 1.
[3] See Ellery to Cooke, March 1, 1778.
[4] Congress had postponed consideration of the half-pay issue on April 2. *JCC*, 10:302.
[5] Cooke declined to stand for reelection as governor of Rhode Island and was succeeded by William Greene in May 1778. William R. Staples, *Rhode Island in the Continental Congress 1765–1790* (Providence: Providence Press Co., 1870), pp. 178–79.

John Henry to Thomas Johnson

Dear Sir.   York Town Apl. 5th. 1778. In Congress
     The enclosed[1] is the Invoice of the Goods which you desired to obtain from Mr. Morris. The price and the quality you will perceive by the Invoice, if you incline to take one half of them, it will be necessary to send down proper persons to receive them.
     I am Sir with great respect, yrs.   J Henry Junr.

RC (MdAA).
[1] Not found.

Henry Laurens to Horatio Gates

Sir,   6th April 1778
     Within the present Inclosure you will receive a paper containing Information against Mr. Swanwic a young Gentleman at present in the service of the Honorable Robert Morris Esquire to which for particulars I beg leave to refer.[1]
     By order of Congress I shall transmit one Copy of the Paper to Mr. Morris & request him to make an immediate & full enquiry into the conduct of the Young Man respecting the charges alleged against him. Congress desire the Board of War will pursue such measures

as shall appear proper & necessary for discovering facts if there has been a criminal or unjustifiable correspondence between the said Mr. Swanwic & any person under protection of the Enemy. The Board may judge it necessary to dispatch proper persons to inspect without alarm the papers of the Mother of the Culprit. The Name of the Informant is known but reserved for the present at her particular desire.

I have the honour to be with very great Regard & ca.[2]

LB (DNA: PCC, item 13). Addressed: "Horatio Gates Esquire, President of the Board of War, Lancaster."

[1] See also Laurens to Robert Morris, April 6; and Robert Morris to Laurens, April 7 and 13, 1778.

[2] Laurens also wrote a letter this day to Col. David Mason, informing him that Congress had referred his March 21 letter to the Board of Treasury. PCC, item 13, fol. 253. Mason's letter is not in PCC, and there is no record of any further action on it in the journals.

Henry Laurens to Robert Morris

Sir,   York Town 6th April 1778

In obediance to an order of Congress passed this Morning I transmit a Paper within the present Inclosure containing an information against Mr. Swanswick a young Gentleman in your service, to which for particulars I beg leave to refer you.

Congress request & confide in you, to make immediately the most diligent & effectual enquiry into the conduct of Mr. Swanswick respecting his correspondence with Philadelphia & other charges intimated in the Paper referred to. The Name of the person who gave the Information is known but at present reserved by her particular desire.

I have the honour to be, Sir, Your obedient & Most humble servant,
                              Henry Laurens, President of Congress.

RC (Creighton C. Hart, Kansas City, Mo., 1974).

Marine Committee to the Eastern Navy Board

Gentlemen   March [*i.e.* April] 6th 1778[1]

We acknowledge the receipt of yours of the 20th Feby., of the 2d & 17th of March last, and are exceedingly pleased to hear that the Warren, after having been so long cooped up in the Bay had got out to sea. We have since heard that she is arrived at Boston and carried in two or three Prizes.[2] We should be glad to get the Providence and other armed Vessels out of the River, and at a less expence than we find will attend it, but they must be got out let the expence be what it may, if it should be practicable and from the success that hath attended such attempts we infer its practicability. We highly approve of the Conduct of the Board in getting out the Warren and don't doubt but that they will exert themselves in getting out the Providence & Columbus, especially as the season for brisk, steady north winds will in a Short time be over, and we are sure that you will exercise frugallity wherever it may be beneficial.

The Demands upon the Treasury from the great departments of the Army are so large and frequent that they cannot be supplied. We have however procured Three Warrants—One on the Loan Office of New Hampshire for 30,000 Dollars—One on Massachusets Bay for 40,000, and One on Connecticut for 30,000 making 100,000 Dollars transmitted herewith for the use of your Board.[3] We chose to have them on those different States, because Money will be wanted in each. If the Money cannot be had at the offices, the Certificates may be disposed of—you will take care that Mr. Langdon hath his share. We have already advised you that we have paid Mr. Shaw 40,000 Dollars and charged the same to your Account, part of which money we presume will be applied towards fitting out the Trumbull &c. The Warrants we returned to you corrected we are glad to find have reached you.

We have determined to stop the building of the Seventy four at Portsmouth for the present, and desire you will give orders accordingly, and for seasoning of the Timbers prepared for her. You will man and equip the Warren with all possible dispatch and order her out on a Cruize to the West Indias with directions to Captain Hopkins to apply to Mr. Bingham at St. Pierre Martinico or Mr. Ceronio at Cape François, Hispaniola, for such supplies as he may Chance to want, and send the Prizes he may take to their address or to the Continent as he may judge proper. You will further direct him towards the Close of his Cruize to go to Cape François, call upon Messrs. Ceronio & Carrabasse for such goods as they may have to ship and take in what he can conveniently bring to the Continent without hurting the Ships sailing. You will furnish us with a Copy of the Instructions you shall give him.

By the Notes in the Margin and endorssment on the Account which you sent to us for inspection, and which we now remit you will see what part thereof is allowed and what rejected.

Before discharging the wages of those and any other Continental officers, you will procure from the Continental Agents in your district accounts of the Monies they have paid them on that score. We have ordered the Paymaster of the Navy in this district James Read Esqr to transmit to you a State of Captain Olneys Account, and the Accounts of such other officers now in the Eastern Department as may have received any Monies of him.[4] Enclosed is a Resolve of Congress respecting the pay, Rations and allowances of Officers not in Actual service and during their Captivity and under Parole.[5] We wish Vessels for the flour and Iron speedily. We congratulate Captain Rathbourne upon his success, but cannot think he is entitled to the whole of the ship Mary and her Cargo. The question was put in Committee & they came to the following Resolution—"It is the opinion of this Committee from the representation of the said Board, that by the Resolves of Congress the Captors are only intitled to One half of said Vessel & Cargo." Enclosed is a Copy of the Resolves referred to.[6] You will see that a Claim is put in on behalf of the Continent. We shall write to Mr. Landais by this opportunity—it is out of our power to comply with his wishes.[7] We have a number of Captains out of employ, and it would be imprudent to pass by them. We shall immediately write Samuel Tuder and Captain Lawrence at Poughkeepsie on Hudsons River to send forward to you at Boston the sails of the two frigates, which were saved at the time said frigates were burned and which is in their possession, If they should receive directions from you therefore.[8] One of those frigates was 28 and the other 24 Guns. The sails of the 28 may suit one of the Ships building at the Eastward as they are large, and the sails of the 24 may suit for some of the sails of the other. You may direct both or either of the suits of Sails of these burned frigates to Boston or Norwich or part to one place or part to the other as you shall judge proper—they had two suits each. We are satisfied with your report respecting Mr. Roche. How he came to be suspended by a Resolve of Congress from his command of the continental ship of war the [Ranger] when he never was appointed to the command of her we cannot tell.[9] Captain Roche laid a plan before Congress, which they referred to the Marine Committee to carry into execution, whereupon they empowered Mr. Langdon to build a Vessel of war, and employed Captain Roche to advise and assist about the building &c. He wrote the Committee a Letter dated the 29th of December last at the close of which he mentions that he had waited with that patience that became a Gentleman in his situation living on his own Money for Six Months, wages &c being stopped ever since his suspension and that he waited impatiently for our further orders. He hath a right, as you have reported in his favour, to his wages, and therefore would have you enquire into what time he hath been paid, and what per month, and pay him off.

We have no vessel to give him the command of without passing by several good Commanders who now hold Commissions and are out of service. If he will accept of a Lieutenancy on board of one of the Frigates and you think him a proper person we shall have no objections, otherwise we shall not consider him any longer as being in the service of the Continent.

We approve of your altering the name of the Industrious Bee to that of the General Gates altho we think it would have been a higher compliment to have given his name to a frigate. We cannot determine upon a proper person to command the frigate at Salisbury, We would have the berth left open for Captain Manley as he may be exchanged, and for the present the Charge of her be given to the person who you may judge suitable for a first Lieutenant of her. We leave to you to determine respecting the Lieutenants who are desirous to make a Cruize of a few Months. Inclosed are the Rules & Regulations of the Navy. Congress has ordered us to Revise them.[10] If you can suggest any New Rules or alterations that will be necessary, we would be glad you would propose them, and if you can by any means procure a British Privateers Commission, send it forward to us. Coppies of Captain Judds and the Captain of the Jamaica Packets may answer—they were taken by Captain Harding of the Connecticut State ship and their Commissions are in the Maritime Court of the Middle District Massachusets. We have ordered Mr. Barnabas Deane of Connecticut to lay his Accounts against the frigate Trumbull before you,[11] which you will please to examine and transmit to us a Copy of his account Current when we shall give Orders for the paymt. of the balance that may be due to him.

We are Gentlemen, Yr humble Servants[12]

LB (DNA: PCC Miscellaneous Papers, Marine Committee Letter Book).

[1] Internal evidence clearly indicates that this letter was actually written in April.

[2] After running through the British blockade off Newport, R.I., the *Warren* took two prizes before arriving in Boston on March 23. "Papers of William Vernon and the Navy Board," *Publications of the Rhode Island Historical Society* 8 (January 1901): 214, 229–30.

[3] These warrants were ordered by Congress on April 4. *JCC*, 10:308–9.

[4] No letter from the Marine Committee to James Read has been found.

[5] See the resolve of March 20 in *JCC*, 10:272.

[6] According to these October 30, 1776, resolves on prize distribution, Continental naval officers and crew were entitled to one half of the value of captured merchantmen, transports, and store ships and the entire value of British war ships and privateers. John Peck Rathbun unconvincingly contended that the armed merchant brig *Mary*, which he had taken during his recent occupation of Fort Nassau, Bahamas, belonged in the latter category. See *JCC*, 6:913; and "Papers of William Vernon and the Navy Board," *Publications of the Rhode Island Historical Society* 8 (January 1901): 217.

[7] On April 7 the Marine Committee wrote the following note to Capt. Pierre Landais, a French naval officer who had been commissioned by Silas Deane to command the *Flamand* on her recent voyage to America: "It would give us much pleasure could we at this time comply with your wishes by giving you a command in the Continental Navy, but it is entirely out of our power, without neglecting Several good Commanders who are already in Commission but unemployed, and whose merit and former services we cannot over look." PCC Miscellaneous Papers,

Marine Committee Letter Book, fol. 138, and Paullin, *Marine Committee Letters,* 1:222. In June Landais was appointed commander of the frigate *Alliance.* See *JCC,* 11:484–85, 625. For further information on the checkered naval career of Landais, see Charles O. Paullin, "Admiral Pierre Landais," *Catholic Historical Review* 17 (October 1931): 296–307.

[8] The Marine Committee's brief April 7 letter to Augustin Lawrence and Samuel Tuder, requesting them to forward the sails according to the directions of the Eastern Navy Board, is in PCC Miscellaneous Papers, Marine Committee Letter Book, fol. 137, and Paullin, *Marine Committee Letters,* 1:222.

[9] For further information about John Roche, see Marine Committee to John Langdon, October 17, 1776; and Executive Committee to John Hancock, January 25, 1777, note.

[10] The journals of Congress do not record a resolve specifically ordering the revision of "the Rules & Regulations of the Navy," but on March 5 Congress had directed the Marine Committee "to revise the commission and instructions heretofore ordered to be given to the commanders of privateers and letters of marque and reprisal, and the resolutions heretofore passed, relative to captures by sea, and report such a form of a commission, and such instructions, as they judge proper and suitable to our present circumstances." No comprehensively revised naval regulations were ever submitted by the Marine Committee, however, and in July 1780 the Board of Admiralty—the committee's successor—proposed that Congress appoint a special committee to assist in completing the work. See *JCC,* 10:225, 17:661–62.

[11] The Marine Committee's letter to Barnabas Deane, requesting that he submit his accounts to the Eastern Navy Board, dated April 11, 1778, and signed by Henry Laurens, is in the Deane Papers, CtHi, and *Collections of the Connecticut Historical Society* 23 (1930): 126.

[12] The Marine Committee also wrote the following note to the Eastern Navy Board on April 6: "You have inclosed with the other papers herein the Sailing Instructions and Signals by Day & night for the enemys Transports & Ships under convoy. They were lately taken onboard a Transport in the River Delaware and we wish Copies of them may be given to the Commanders which you send out of your Department as they be serviceable. You will take care to dispatch the ship Providence as soon as possible. We leave it to you to order her Cruize as you may think proper sending us a Copy of the Instructions you give the Captain." PCC Miscellaneous Papers, Marine Committee Letter Book, fol. 136, and Paullin, *Marine Committee Letters,* 1:219.

Marine Committee to Thomas Read

Sir   April 6th 1778

We have been favoured with your letter of the 21st of March and hope you have by this time got the Brigantine Baltimore nearly fitted. We observe you are under some dificulty in procuring Seamen; but as we have this day been informed that Captain Nicholson of the Frigate Virginia left behind him fifteen of his men, with two of his officers, we would have you immediately endeavour to secure these men for your Vessel as they are in the Continental Service.[1] Upon your applying to Mr. Stephen Steward he will furnish you with what tobacco you may further want to compleat your lading, and ship the remainder of your Crew on the best terms you can.

As Mr. Fanning is one of the officers Captain Nicholson left behind, should you want an officer of his Rank we would advise you to engage him for your Vessel if agreeable. We are sir, Your hble servants

LB (DNA: PCC Miscellaneous Papers, Marine Committee Letter Book).

[1] This day the Marine Committee requested Capt. Thomas Plunkett, an officer of the Marine Corps, to "deliver over the Men belonging to the Virginia to Captain Read and we will order the payment of such wages as is due to them." The committee also informed Plunkett that "there is no employment for you at the Northward, therefore you are at liberty to engage in any business that you think proper and when vacancy happens we shall inform you." PCC Miscellaneous Papers, Marine Committee Letter Book, fol. 137; and Paullin, *Marine Committee Letters*, 1:220.

Robert Morris to Benjamin Chew

Manheim in Pa. April 6th. 1778. "Your Letter of the 31st Ulto.[1] was delivered to me yesterday morning & as I then expected Mr. President Wharton and some other Gentn. to come here from Lancaster I detained your Messanger in hopes of sending you such information this Morning as might be relyed upon but the Lancaster Gentn did not appear & I am entirely disappointed therefore it is only in my power at this time to assure you of my inclination to procure you that relief you wish for & further that I will try to effect it by every probable means I can think of.[2] What may be the event of my endeavours I will not promise but you shall be informed soon as it is in my power to tell you any thing with certainty. You are considered as a Prisoner of this State & as such all applications on your behalf must first be made to the Council. I shall therefore go to Lancaster on this errand & if afterward it should be necessary to apply to the Continental Board of War or Congress I will repair to York Town." Laments the hardships Americans have been exposed to by the war and explains Pennsylvania's recent test act requiring former crown officers who had not renounced their commissions to take an oath of allegiance by July 1.[3]

FC (DLC). In the hand of John Swanwick. Addressed: "Benjn. Chew Esqr., Union Iron Works, New Jersey."

[1] A lengthy extract from Chew's letter is in *Stan V. Henkels Catalog*, no. 1183 (January 16, 1917), pp. 184–85.

[2] For the disposition of Chew's case, see Committee of Congress to Thomas Wharton, March 18, 1778, note 3.

[3] For Chew's reaction to the passage of this law, which actually required compliance by June 1 rather than July 1 as Morris stated, see Henry Laurens to Benjamin Chew and John Penn, May 15, 1778, note 1.

Committee of Congress to Benjamin Rush

Sir.   York Town, April 7. 1778.

Your letters of the 25th of February, to General Washington, & of the 9th of March, to Mr. Roberdeau, of which we presume you have draughts, having been laid before Congress, produced an Order, of which the inclosed is an authenticated copy.[1]

We wish to proceed in this business, so as to obtain the most perfect information of the mal-practices, if there are any, of the Director General; & to this end, we desire that you will be pleased to ascertain with precision, & transmit to us, the charges, & upon oath the evidence you have, or can procure, against him; also, the names of the Witnesses, & places of their residence.

If there are any difficulties in the way of your collecting the evidence upon this important subject, you will be pleased to point them out; with, if in your power to do so, the means of removing them.[2]

We are, Sir, Your most humble servts.

Wm. Hy. Drayton

Saml Huntington

W. H. D. for Mr. Banister

RC (PPL). Written by Drayton and signed by Drayton and Huntington.

[1] On April 3 Congress had directed this committee to investigate renewed charges by Benjamin Rush that Director General William Shippen was mismanaging the medical department and embezzling hospital supplies. *JCC*, 10:303. For Rush's February 25 and March 9 letters containing these allegations, see PCC, item 78, 19:211–26, or Lyman H. Butterfield, ed., *Letters of Benjamin Rush*, 2 vols. (Princeton: Princeton University Press, 1951), 1:200–208. For information on the feud between Shippen and Rush which had recently led to Rush's resignation as physician general of the middle department, see James Lovell to Samuel Adams, January 1, 1778, note 1.

[2] In his April 20 response to the committee's request, which was read and tabled on June 4, Rush warned of the difficulties inherent in requiring witnesses to travel to York and recommended a court-martial as a more appropriate method of dealing with Shippen. See PCC, item 78, 19:233; *Letters of Benjamin Rush*, 1:210–11; and *JCC*, 11:568.

Henry Laurens to James Duane

Dear Sir,   York Town, 7th April 1778.

I have been in possession of your favour of the 16th March about 8 days. After you are informed that Congress have in the mean time been sitting every day from 9 A M to the same hour at night & some times an hour longer you will not wonder that I have not so fully executed every one of your commands as otherwise I should have done, but be assured Sir none of them shall be unnoticed.

Your Letter enclosed nothing relative to Mr Holt the name excepted, I remain therefore utterly ignorant of your & his purpose respecting an application of the Money intended for him. You will be so good as to supply this deficiency.[1]

Our Accounts from Great Britain are as you will read in the inclosed Paper—from this City below—no appearance of excursive steps until reinforcements shall be received. Deserters assert positively that General Howe's Baggage is embarked & that he will follow it immediately upon the arrival of Lord Townsend who is expected daily, to assume the Command. Admitting the embarkation, a change of Command is implied.

An Exchange of Prisoners was intended & Commissioners had met at German Town the 31st March. Last Evening I received dispatches from our General, from whence I infer, the business is interrupted by a late Act of Congress which I transmitted the very day on which the Commissioners had convened.[2] The Letter has not yet been presented to Congress, but has undergone severe strictures from a knot of our friends who called here late at night & conned it over. I will give no opinion at present, yet I have the vanity to think if you were in York we should not differ; had you been present, certain ambiguities, I do not say contradictions, would not have taken place in our Acts—but this is tender ground. I will wait the event of that debate which in three or four hours I shall *hear* in the multitude of Counsellors. General Lee in the mean time has reached Valley forge on his Parol only—an actual Exchange it is said would have taken place but for the circumstance just now alluded to.

Intelligence from Fort Pitt, very dark—the Officer McKee who had been at large on Parol, gone off to Detroit & carried with him an Interpreter & four other Men, the Savages engaged in daily butcheries on the guardless Country people. Our Commissioners had at length assembled, they write sensibly & seem resolved to proceed with vigour. Colo. Morgan had passed a stout enquiry & was acquitted with honor & the Court have subjoined to the acquital an handsome recommendation.[3] Since the flight of McKee the minds of the People have been again agitated by suspicions of General Hand who has renewed his intreaties for a successor in order that he may come within.

Baron Stüben has condescended to Act the Drill Master as well as the Inspector in Camp, he has hit the taste of the Officers, gives universal satisfaction & I am assured has made an amazing improvement in discipline. A Young correspondent of mine who is a very honest Man & not very ignorant & who had always regretted the deficiency of discipline, tells me if I were present I should be enchanted by the change suddenly made in the grand Camp.[4]

I am confident if the States are in earnest & will send *in* reinforcements in time to partake the benefit of the Current reform we shall not be driven much further from the Ocean. The present newly adopted encampment, General duportail assures me, is tenable against the Enemy's utmost efforts by their present powers.

We are menaced & not slightly, with the loss of all our good Officers unless a Peace establishment is made. This has appeared to me, unjust, unseasonable & a compliance under *threats,* dangerous & the reasonings in favor of the measures "a total loss of virtue in the Army," the worst adopted in the whole circle of ratiocination for converting me. In the first place I cannot beleive it—if I could, I would say, every Man to his Tent—tis a matter of indifference to me whether the Tyrants name be George or Dick—not an argument adduced in favor of the measure but will apply generally to every Person zealously engaged in the present dispute & to thousands more forcibly than to our Officers in general. The Remedy proposed is also inadequate to releif, upon the grounds on which the Claim is set up. Half pay to commence seven Years hence will not add a Shirt nor a bottle of Wine to a complainant General Officer in the mean time. I will not be further troublesome at this Instant, I may hereafter submit my sentiments at large to your better judgement with permission. The object is stupendous; veiw it in either light—the danger of losing *"All" "All"* your *"good"* Officers—or that of getting *"no more"* Men & "losing those you have"—one of these Evils may be remedied—but from my own feelings I trust, who have already lost a great Estate & am in a fair way to part with the present small remainder, there are many Thousands whose hearts are warm with the reasonings which induced the original Compact & who have not bowed the Knee to Luxury nor to Mammon.

'Tis time to turn to your Letter, from whence I have thus digressed, from casting my eye on your Complaint of the dearth of News. You will forgive all that is said too much, I have not time to retrospect, nor genius nor inclination for refining phrases into no meaning, besides, I dare trust you Sir with my first thoughts, those upon the half pay establishment are rooted in my mind. Hitherto the strongest arguments in favour of the measure have been the *necessity,* & for avoiding the consecutive threatned evils. The Justice & propriety of the Act would have made some impression upon such a heart as mine, but "portents & prodigies are lost on me." The project we are clearly informed originated in a sphere above Regimental Command; it was a work extremely practicable to roll it down Hill, the application comes in not directly, but through a medium & Clothed with terror, but whither am I again wandering.

P.M. 3 oClock. I just returned from the Chair, & while the morsel is removing from the Cabouse to the Table, before I take up your

Letter let me add a word. If you delight in contracting an enormous debt to a Crafty powerful foreign State, your absence from this Mornings service has lost you much pleasure.[5] I have executed your several Commands & while I think of it let me add, your public Letter was in due time, presented to Congress & referred to the Board of War from whence I have learned nothing concerning it—unless the Board have included the subject of yours in their Report on General Schuylers Letter, not yet considered in the House.[6]

The arrival of Majr. General McDougall at FishKill has anticipated an answer to your enquiry, who is to command in the Highlands? but, whatever might have been General Washington's intention when he ordered that Gentleman to repair to that Post, tis probable his Command will be but temporary—it has been said & repeated that General Gates must soon take the Field & in your quarter & although this is mere out of door talk, I would wish you to understand it, as said to a Member of Congress.[7] Under the same stipulation if you & I were tete a tete, might attempt to account for the amazing neglect of North River. I might add at least twenty other neglects, & possibly as many Acts which ought to have been neglected, make an aggregate of these & transfer the whole to the debit of the general Account of the thirteen UNITED FREE AND INDEPENDENT States of America. What Representation had ye for upwards of three precious Months, when those things were done which ought not to have been done, & those left undone which ought to have been done. Why—9 States—9 or 11 Members when we could collect them— seldom 15—17 made a very full House. You well know Sir, the unavoidable drudgery of Committees requires more *hands*. I am not competent to Lecture upon *heads,* nor need I attempt description to a Gentleman so well acquainted with the sagacity of the Stock which he left upon hand. Be this as it may, I do aver & will maintain the United-States & not their few Pack Horses are blameable. The United States have acted & 'tis far from impossible may be whipped, like Children. Often have I lamented the neglected state of North River as well as of many other essential works. Whatever may be the event, I shall feel some consolation from a reflection, which it would be unbecoming to boast of. I still trust we are not quite too late; tis true danger appears. That *Lion* which I have beheld for three Years past Couchant, always well apprized of his unexerted powers, is now roused, his Eyes flash & he growls; if he has strength to Roar & expand, we shall retrospect with pain. Be it so; let us not be stricken by fear, let us be animated & Wise. There is Wisdom in America, let it be collected, strength & success will be the Issue, but no time is to be lost. I do not hold it impossible, we shall hear of some attempts to accomodation as a prelude to the ensuing Campaign; admit the belief of a change in the Command at Philadelphia & the suggestion will not appear extravagant, but we need not distress our minds by apprehensions that the very first article will be a confirmation of American Independency, & who can dry eyed contemplate submission?

Your hint respecting a Committee for North River & that department is valuable, but in our meagre state respecting numbers & qualities, can we spare a respectable detachment? When could we have spared such a one? Why, My Dear Sir, may we not appoint Men of abilities including diligence, of the vicinage to act as Commissioners & to receive compensation from the Public for devoting their whole time & attention to the Public service? This consideration if we pursue it will head us into a large field from whence we shall not be able to return before night, therefore let us go back.

The Marquis has indeed as you observe been in an awkward situation. I have sometimes felt pain on his account, but most from an inspective view of consequences which might follow a vindictive assertion of his honour. I trust however that his greatness of mind & his attachment to our Cause will dictate the propriety of seeming a little blind & a little unfeeling upon a late determination.[8]

I entertain an high opinion of that Noble personage. As a General & a Commanding Officer I am persuaded he would have given great satisfaction in the Northern department. When I reflect upon the alacrity with which he obeyed the order of Congress to penetrate Canada, his Zeal for the public Interest & upon the propriety of his whole conduct during that short lived Command & at the same time take into view certain concomitants to the Act of remanding him to Valley forge,[9] I admire his magnanimity & grieve for the mistakes of some of our good friends.

If you said any thing in your public Letter relative to your Freind General Schuyler, as I think you did tis not at present in my power to reply particularly; I surrendered the Letter the Morning it came to hand to the Board of War where it now sleeps. We have indulged the New Board in an exceeding bad practice, making Reports & detaining the subject referred, you perceive in an Instant how many inconveniences this produces, one which I feel is, an inability in many Cases to answer Letters with perspicuity & dispatch. ☞ I am speaking to a Member. I write to the General Officially.

Such Money as may remain in your hands of the trifle intended for St. Lawrence give if you judge it proper to the Child or Children you sometime ago mentioned or to any of my poor fellow Citizens who may have suffered by the hand of violence or the misfortune of War on North River & whom you may think a more necessitous object.

God protect you & yours, free from the assaults of our Enemies, you being safe, your neighbors will be so, I include you all in my prayers & I beg you will beleive I always hold you in a very respect-

able light & am with great Regard, Dear sir, Your obedient & Most
humble servant.   Henry Laurens

Dear sir,   8 April 1778
After your Packet had been sealed up, I discovered a mistake which
this is slipped in to inform you of & to save you some trouble. I am
in possession of Mr. Holt's Letter & will by the very first opportunity
pay into the hand of Mr. Morris or of his Agent here if he does not
come within the course of this Week to York, the intended Money
300 Dollars. You may tell that Gentleman *now*, that 200 comes from
a Brother Printer John Wells Junior who lately had his own House
in Charles Town burnt over his head in the dreadful conflagration in
that Town, but had the good fortune by accumulated assistance to
save his vast collection of Books, his household furniture, Paper,
Types & almost everything & within a Week of the accident proceeded
in his Publications.   H. Laurens

RC (NHi).
¹ For further information about Laurens' efforts to assist John Holt, a New York
printer whose equipment had been destroyed by the British, see Laurens to Duane,
December 24, 1777.
² For a discussion of the controversy caused by Washington's objections to
Congress' March 30 instructions for the commissioners appointed by him to
negotiate a prisoner cartel with the British, see Laurens to Washington, March
15, note 1, and April 8, 1778, note 2.
³ This day Congress read a "letter of 31 March . . . with sundry papers enclosed"
from the commissioners it had sent to investigate conditions at Fort Pitt. See
JCC, 10:313; and Laurens' letters to George Clymer, March 27, and to the
Commissioners at Fort Pitt, April 9, 1778.
⁴ See John Laurens' March 28 letter to his father in Simms, *Laurens Army
Correspondence*, pp. 146–49.
⁵ Laurens was apparently skeptical about the contract that Congress this day
authorized the Committee of Commerce to conclude with Beaumarchais' agent
Théveneau de Francy. *JCC*, 10:315–21.
⁶ Duane's "public Letter" was dated March 16 but has not been found. *JCC*,
10:291. Regarding the "Report on General Schuyler's Letter," see Laurens to
Philip Schuyler, April 8, 1778.
⁷ Congress resolved on April 15 to order General Gates to return to active command of the northern department. *JCC*, 10:354.
⁸ No doubt Laurens is referring to the March 2 suspension of the Canadian
expedition commanded by Lafayette. *JCC*, 10:216–17.
⁹ On this point, see Laurens to Lafayette, March 6, 1778, note 5.

Robert Morris to Henry Laurens

Sir   Manheim April 7th. 1778
I am honoured with your letter of yesterday & not a little surprized
at the Contents of the paper enclosed therein; but I believe & hope
the information it contains is founded on Suspicion more than fact.

Be that as it may, I am determined to make a strict examination into the Young Gentlemans Conduct[1] and at all events to remove him from my employ whether innocent or guilty, because I am sensible his connections will constantly expose him to suspicion, indeed I shou'd have done this long since but his knowledge of the French & German Languages has been very usefull to me, the insinuation that he makes false translations is groundless for I know sufficient of the French myself to detect an imposition of that kind. I do not recollect any public matters that can have come to his knowledge, the communication of which cou'd be any ways usefull to the Enemy or detrimental to us. I do not say this in paliation of his crime, for if he has given any kind of information or attempted it, I will never forgive him but on the contrary most readily Consent to such punishment as he may deserve. I have the honour to be Your Excellencys Most Obedt hble servt. Robt Morris.

RC (DNA: PCC, item 137).
[1] For the "examination" of John Swanwick, which was the subject of Laurens' April 6 letter to Morris, see Morris to Laurens, April 13, 1778.

Oliver Wolcott to Laura Wolcott

My Dear, York Town 7 April 1778

I Wrote to you (I beleive it was) the 18 Ultimo which I hope you have recd. This is my fifth Letter to you since I came to this Place[1]— and which will be sent by Mr Frost a Deligate from N Hamshire or Col Dyer who will probably Return to Morrow.[2] I have heard nothing from you or any of my Freinds since Oliver's Letter of the 4t Ultimo, But as I expect that Brown will Return in about a Forthnight I hope by him to receive a Letter from you. I find that the Conveyance by the Post is so Very uncertain that I shall Venture by him but few Letters whose miscarriage could give me any concern. By the Blessing of God I still injoy my Health and am free from those sundry Disorders which some Time ago so much Afflicted Me. You will therefore suffer no Anxiety on my Account as I hope any Solicitude in that respect will be as unnecessary as it will be unavailable. The same protecting Providence which has hitherto preserved me will I trust Return me to my Family in safety. Your Cares I know must be many besides any Concern for Me. Alleviate them as farr as you can, and put your Trust in the Protection of that Being on whom alone Confidence is to be placed.

Nothing material has Occurred in these Parts since my last. It is reported with some Degree of Credibility that about 1500, or 2000 Troops have lately joined Genl. Howe from N York. Whether merely for the Purpose of Stregnthening his Army in Case of an Attack, which I am sorry to say that I see no probability of soon, or to be employed to Act offensively against our Army, is uncertain.

A Scandalous Languor still exists amongst the People of this State. I suspect that they have not yet suffered that Chastisment which is Necessary for them. There Wants nothing (according to human Probability) but a proper Spirit in this People to put an end to the War— But which thro' their infamous Baseness, may be drawn out to a considerable Length, unless the Power of G. Britain should be diverted, by a War with her Neighbours, of which there is no certainty. Material Intligence may be dayly expected, but as you have foraign News earlier at the eastward than We have here, you will probably receive it sooner than any Information I shall be able to give you. The Regulating Acts have no Effect in this State. Nothing of the kind has any Existence at the Southward, and you may depend upon it that the Operation of Acts of this Nature, will soon be suspended or Abrogated every where, And perhaps Congress will Advise to Repeal this Act. You will present my kindest Love to my Children, Family and Freinds, and be assured of My tenderest Affection for you.   Oliver Wolcott

P.S. My half years Service will expire next June when I shall expect to be releived by Mr. Adams or some other of the Gentlemen Appointed to Attend Congress.

RC (CtHi).
    [1] Wolcott's fourth letter to his wife from York is dated March 12, 1778.
    [2] Although the exact date of Eliphalet Dyer's departure from York is not known, he was granted a leave of absence by Congress on April 3 and was not recorded as voting after that date. *JCC,* 10:305.

Henry Laurens to the Marquis de Lafayette

8th April [1778]
    Notwithstanding what is said above I have detained this Messenger 13 days from day to day hoping the next wou'd produce Commands from Congress but the Committee to whom your Letter was referred have not yet Reported. Excuse us good Sir. We are indeed deeply engaged in very important & complicated businesses, but in order to remove an anxiety which this long delay must have occasioned I will not keep this back an hour longer. I think you will soon be at Valley forge, where Baron Stüben is making great improvements & giving much satisfaction to every Body. Will you Sir be so obliging as to inform Major DuBois that I have duly presented his addresses to Congress, that these are referred to the B. of W.[1] & that the moment

I am furnished with Subject I will do myself the honour of writing to him.[2]

LB (ScHi). A continuation of Laurens to Lafayette, March 27, 1778.
  [1] Board of War.
  [2] See also Laurens to Baron de Kalb, March 24, 1778.

Henry Laurens to Henry Lee

Sir   8th April 1778.
  I have the honour of transmitting under the present Inclosure an Act of Congress of the 7th Inst. for promoting you to the Rank of Major of Horse & to the Command of a seperate Corps of two Troop as an acknowledgment of your distinguished Merit.[1]
  Permit me Sir, to congratulate with your friends upon this occasion to wish you continued successes and accession of Glory, & beleive me to be with great Esteem, Sir, your most Obedient humble Set.

LB (DNA: PCC, item 13).
  [1] Congress took this action at the behest of Washington and the Committee at Camp. See JCC, 10:315; and Washington, Writings (Fitzpatrick), 11:205–6. Henry "Light Horse Harry" Lee (1756–1818), after distinquishing himself as a cavalry officer during the southern campaign of 1780–81, held a succession of responsible public offices, serving as a delegate to Congress, 1785–88, member of the Virginia ratifying convention, 1788, governor of Virginia, 1791–95, and U.S. congressman, 1799–1801. DAB; and Bio. Dir. Cong.

Henry Laurens to Philip Schuyler

Sir   8th April 1778.
  On the 28th Ulto. I had the honor of receiving & presenting to Congress your favor of the 15th which was immediately referred to the Board of War from whence a Report came up the 3d Inst. but this has not yet although frequently offered, been taken under consideration, consequently I have received no Commands.[1] I have on this & a similar Case detained the bearer hereof from day to day hoping upon each the next would have produced the desired effect at length, persuaded it will save some expense to the public & even afford you Sir, some satisfaction. I have submitted to the importunities of Mr. Green by consenting to his return—but I cannot let him go without adding a word on the Subject which must, most nearly, affect your mind.
  Some time in February the Committee appointed to Enquire into the Causes of the loss of Tyconderoga &ca presented such Evidence as

had been collected to Congress & by order, transmitted the whole to General Washington, & then the Committee were discharged. The General in a Letter of the 27th Febry. intimated a necessity for Stating Charges. A new Committee was thereupon appointed, who soon after offered a Report which was about to be determined upon the 28th Ulto. when the Honorable Mr. Duer interposed arguments which induced the House to postpone the intended consideration for two days. I take the liberty to name that Gentleman because his declared motives for delay were coupled with assurances of particular considerations respecting General Schuyler & because there can be no ground for doubting the goodness of his intentions. On the 4th Inst. I called on Mr. Duer, reminded him of his engagement & urged the painful situation in which his friend was suspended—yesterday I directed the Secretary to repeat the call. General Washington has again written upon the Subject, I was in hopes this would have proved an incitement, but all remains still dormant. I hope to give no offence, but I will this very Morning remind Congress of the business again.[2]

Be assured Sir, I have long Sympathized with Gentlemen who are Subjects of that Enquiry, abstracted from all Ideas of Censure or applause, & although it was with extreme reluctance I obeyed the order of Congress to be of the Original Committee after having offered such reasons for exemption as appeared to me to be forcible, yet I cannot charge my Self with delinquency at any stage in the course of our proceedings. To account for the uncouth entangled State of this enquiry would not be half so difficult as it might be improper in the line of official correspondence, therefore I shall only add that my endeavors shall be continued for putting it in motion.

I have the honour to be with very great respect.

LB (DNA: PCC, item 13).

[1] General Schuyler's March 15 letter to Laurens is in PCC, item 153, 3:286–91. In it Schuyler reported on a recent conference with the Six Nations at Johnstown, N.Y., and urged adoption of certain measures to secure New York's northern frontier, including a preventive strike against the Mohawk's, Cayugas, Onondagas, and Senecas; seizure of British posts at Niagara and Oswego; and increased trade with the Oneidas and Tuscaroras. Not until June 11, however, did Congress approve a report by the Board of War on "the cruelties lately exercised by the savages on the frontiers of New York, Pensylvania and Virginia," which was based upon Schuyler's letter as well as others from the commissioners for Indian affairs in the northern department and the commissioners at Fort Pitt. See *JCC*, 11:587–91; and Barbara Graymont, *The Iroquois in the American Revolution* (Syracuse: Syracuse University Press, 1972), ch. 7.

[2] See also Laurens to Washington, April 4, 1778, note 2.

Henry Laurens to George Washington

Sir,   York Town 8th April 1778

I had the honor of writing to your Excellency the 4th by Jones, since which I have presented to Congress Your Excellency's favors of the 1st, 3d & 4th.[1]

Upon reading the first I took occasion to intimate to Mr. Duer the distressed situation of his friend General Scuyler as described by the General himself in a late Letter of 15th March & this Morning suggested again to the House the demands of all the General Officers subjects of the suspended Enquiry. I shall repeat the same to Morrow & having just now obtained the concurrence of Gentlemen in private conversation that Congress are Guardians of the Honor of their Officers I flatter my self there will be no further delay of this business.[2]

Your Excellency will receive under the present Inclosure an Act of Congress of the 7th for promoting Captain Lee to the Rank of Major of Horse & to the Command of a seperate Corps. I perceive it is not expressed in the Act but I am warranted to assure Your Excellency it is the particular desire of Congress that suitable declarations of that Gentleman's Merit should be expressed either within the intended Commission or by annexing to it the abovementioned Act, a Certified Copy of which Major Lee will receive by the present dispatch.

Consideration of Colonel Lee & Major Swasey's applications is postponed a few days for particular reasons.[3]

I shall direct the Secretary of Congress to collect the dates of late Resignations of Colonels in the Virginia line & transmit an Account to Your Excellency when obtained.

Your Excellency's last Letter of the 4th is at present the subject of a special Committee, 'tis probable a Report will be offered to Morrow Morning.[4]

Previous to the receipt of your Excellency's advices Congress had determined to make a purchase of divers articles set forth in Captn. Cottineau's schedule of his Cargo & for this purpose a Gentleman will proceed to morrow on his journey to Cape Lookout by whom Your Excellency's Letters will go forward.[5]

I have the honor to be, With the highest Esteem & Regard, Sir, Your Excellency's Obedient & humble Servant,

Henry Laurens, President of Congress

[P.S.] I detain'd the Bearer to this hour 3 oClock the 9th hoping to have transmitted an answer to Your Excellency's Letter of the 4th.

RC (DLC).
[1] These letters are in PCC, item 152, 5:423–34, and Washington, *Writings* (Fitzpatrick), 11:195–96, 205–6, 216–19.

[2] See also Laurens to Washington, April 4, 1778, note 2.

[3] Congress did not accept the resignations of Col. William Lee and Maj. Joseph Swasey of Massachusetts until June 24. *JCC*, 11:640. Lee's letter of resignation, dated January 24, and Swasey's, dated March 17, are in PCC, item 78, 14:189, 20:197.

[4] Washington displeased many delegates by criticizing in his April 4 letter the instructions Congress approved on March 30 for the commissioners he had appointed to negotiate a prisoner cartel with the British. On April 7 Congress referred Washington's letter to a committee consisting of Samuel Chase, Francis Dana, and William Duer, which three days later submitted to Congress a draft reply to Washington drawn up by Duer. In its original form Duer's letter was so critical of Washington that it provoked heated debate among the delegates and led Thomas Burke to absent himself from Congress, depriving the delegates of a quorum. At length the delegates deleted some of the harsher passages in Duer's draft and approved a letter on the 13th that defended the March 30 instructions but gave Washington discretion to modify them as he saw fit. Laurens signed this letter on April 14 and sent it to Washington in the form of a presidential letter. See *JCC*, 10:314, 329–34, 335–37, 339–41, 343–44; Laurens to Washington, April 14; and Thomas Burke to Richard Caswell and to the North Carolina Assembly, April 29, 1778. See also Laurens to Washington, March 15, 1778, note 1.

[5] See Laurens to Denis Nicolas Cottineau, April 9, 1778.

Marine Committee to the
Middle Department Navy Board

Gentlemen   April 8th 1778

Agreeable to your application in your letter of the 21st of February last, we inclose a Warrant on the Loan office of the State of New Jersey for Eleven thousand Dollars to enable you to pay Mr. Taylor for the shot he furnished for the use of the navy. We shall now answer the queries you presented for our consideration in that Letter.

first. We have already ordered the Paymaster to remove his office to Baltimore when your Board removes to that place.

2d. We would by all means have the Commissarys store at Bordenton immediately broke up. Congress has resolved that no Rations or Subsistance Money shall be allowed to any officers but such as are in Actual Service—inclosed is the Resolve dated the 20 March last.

3rd. We would have you examine the Accounts of your clerk and Treasurer yourselves, and appoint or nominate a new one just as you please.

4th. The Agents at Baltimore will be notified that they are responsible to your Board for the settlement for their Accounts.

As the New Signals for the Navy have been sent to the Navy Board of the Eastern Department and have been given to several Commanders we think it would be improper to alter them at this time, however as it may be necessary hereafter to change the Signals, we would be glad if you would compose a sett.

The want of officers at present makes it impracticable to hold a Court Martial for the trial of the officers who commanded onboard the Continental Vessels that were destroyed in the Delaware. Congress having ordered us to revise the Rules and Regulations of the Navy, we would be obliged to you to propose any alterations or amendments which you may think necessary to be adopted.

We acknowledge the receipt of yours of the 12th of March and are pleased to hear that you had lodged the Stores in places of greater safety. We are glad to inform you that the Virginia frigate has got to sea.[1] Mr. Read the Paymaster having represented that the duties of his office did not require his constant attendance he had our permission to transact some business for the Board of war. Congress has not appointed him to any new office—you will please to write to him and advise him to return to his office if he hath not already returned. You have enclosed an account of Maxwell & Loyals which we refer to you for examination. We suppose you will require them to exhibit the particulars of the Charges in the said Account with the vouchers we have marked the drafts paid by this Committee since our removal from Philadelphia, and you have in your Books an account of what had been paid before. You have also inclosed a Receipt of Lieut. Robert Harris's late of the Ship Reprisal for 150 dollars paid him by the Navy Board at Boston which please to order to his debit in the Paymasters Books. We have your favour of the 25th of March and approve of the offer you have made the General of Rice, Codfish and Oil for the use of the Army. You will take the Commissarys Receipt for those articles and charge him in your Books. The Board of war have had [under] consideration that part of your letter which relates to Captain Robinson and we suppose will communicate their sentiments thereon to General Washington who doubtless will take proper measures for his releasement.[2] We are Gentlemen, Your hble servants

LB (DNA: PCC Miscellaneous Papers, Marine Committee Letter Book).

[1] At this point is keyed the following note: "An account since received that she unfortunately go on a Bank in the night and was next morning taken by the enemy. Captain Nicholson and nine of his Crew who were all that chose to venture in the Barge escaped to shore." On the loss of the *Virginia*, see William M. Fowler, Jr., "James Nicholson and the Continental Frigate *Virginia*," *American Neptune* 34 (April 1974): 135–41.

[2] Isaiah Robinson was detained in Philadelphia while under a flag of truce when it was discovered that he had permitted Capt. Nathaniel Galt to accompany him under the guise of a private seaman. Washington demanded Robinson's immediate release in his March 22 letter to General Howe and reiterated his request in May. See Washington, *Writings* (Fitzpatrick), 11:129–30, 395-96, 458.

Jonathan Bayard Smith to Thomas Wharton

Sir   York Town April 8th 1778.

Understanding from Colo. Cox that the purchase of horses for the army in your state was impeded for want of money, I was led to enquire into the circumstances, as warrants had issued in your favor for 80,000 dollars so long ago as 30th of March. Accordingly I found in the Treasury office one warrant on your Loan Office for 50,000 dollars which is inclosed,[1] & one other on Mr. Hillegas for 30,000 ds. Respecting the latter it will not answer any purpose to rely on it *'till we can get Mr. Rittenhouse to finish what he has in hand.* Perhaps a greater service cannot be rendered the public than that of urging his assiduity.

With very great respect, I have the honor to be, Your Excellencys most ob. hl servt.   Jona. B. Smith

[*P.S.*] If the 30,000 ds. should be indispensably necessary any directions from your Excellency shall be attended to.[2]

RC (PHi).
   [1] For this warrant, which is entered on the minutes of the Pennsylvania Council for April 8, see *Pa. Council Minutes,* 11:461.
   [2] Wharton's April 9 response, in which he asked Smith to forward the $30,000 authorized "and as much more as can be conveniently spared," is in the Jonathan Bayard Smith Papers, DLC.

Charles Thomson to Israel Pemberton

Sir,   York town April 8. 1778
   I was out of town when the resolution respecting you passed Congress.[1] Upon receiving your brothers letter yesterday I called on the board of war to know what they had done in the matter & was informed that they expected an application from the Council of Pensylvania; but no application being made they had not taken any steps in pursuance of the act of Congress. However they proposed to take your case into consideration this morning & I hope will give orders for your coming down. I communicated your letter to Jos. Uptegraf, who I expect will find a conveyance for this. I am sorry for the death & sickness of your friends. Inclination as well as humanity easily lead me to do you any service in my power.
   I have sent to the board of war & received a copy of their proceedings respecting you. The act of Congress is inclosed in the letter to your brother James.
   I am, sr, Your humble servt.   Chas Thomson

RC (PHi).
   [1] See *JCC,* 10:260; and Committee of Congress to Thomas Wharton, March 18, 1778. For the exile of Pemberton and several other Pennsylvania Quakers in Virginia and circumstances leading to their release in the spring of 1778, see Theodore Thayer, *Israel Pemberton, King of the Quakers* (Philadelphia: Historical Society of Pennsylvania, 1943), pp. 225–31; and Robert F. Oaks, "Philadelphians in Exile: The Problem of Loyalty during the American Revolution," *PMHB* 96 (July 1972): 322–24.

Thomas Burke to Richard Caswell

York Pensylvania April 9th. 1778.

No State has yet absolutely instructed its Delegates to ratify the Confederation except Virginia and New York, and none except those and Connecticut, Maryland and our State have transmitted any instructions at all.[1] The Congress have at present no leisure for entering upon it being much engaged in what relates to the Army. A Committee which has been a long time at Camp, has proposed some alterations in our Military System, tho I think they have not reformed any of its capital abuses which are want of discipline in the men and want of industry in the Officers. They have proposed to reduce the number of battallions from 116 to 88 and the number of Officers in each battallion from 40 to 29.[2]

Two subjects very much engage our attention at present, and we all wish on one of them to be particularly informed of the sentiments of our constituents. These subjects are, a general exchange of prisoners, and an establishment for the Officers of the army after the War. The former meets with many difficulties from the opposite views and interests of the contending powers, and also from the secret wishes of some Officers in the Army. This last is conjecture, but many of us are convinced of the reality of its foundation. The enemy want their men and officers, but are very unwilling to let us avail ourselves of the experience and abilities of General Lee, we want the General and have determined that his releasement shall take place, or no exchange at all be permitted. We insist that the enemy shall pay for the provisions we give their troops, when prisoners, in hard money, or replace them in Quantity and Quality. They are unwilling to agree to this. We are desirous that all traitors should be delivered over to the Civil Magistrate to be punished agreeable to the Laws of the States to which they respectively belonged. The Enemy are unwilling to admit this distinction, but desire all to be considered as prisoners of war. Finally Sir we are many of us persuaded that some Officers in the Army wish not for the release of General Lee because his enterprising disposition and martial genius will be a strong contrast to their want of both, and we find by undoubted testimony, that it is a prevailing opinion in the Army that no regard ought to be paid to the Penal Laws of the States in settling the exchange of Prisoners but that all ought to be deemed prisoners of War. A letter from General Washington relative to this affair is now before Congress wherein he recommends that the Laws be suffered to sleep in his expression, and that a rule of practice be adopted directly contrary to them; but this proposal met with very great and almost general opposition and indignation in Congress.[3] It appears to most of us that giving up a matter of this kind is betraying our independence and in effect giving a licence to the enemy to recruit in our country. If we suffer our citizens who adhere to our enemies, and actually take arms against us to be considered as prisoners of war, and subject to no municipal laws, I see not where our independence remains, and we cannot conceive that even Congress can dispense with such Laws much less a Cabinet Council of Military Officers. These are the sentiments, I believe of a great majority in Congress as well as mine, and I venture to say the matter will be peremptorily insisted on.

The other matter, that is, the establishment for Officers has cost us much time and debate, but the favourers of it have not yet ventured a Question on it, the proposal is from the Committee who were at Camp, strongly supported by the Commander in Chief. It is to make a provision of half pay for life after the end of the War for all Officers who shall continue in service until that period, and to extend this provision to the Widows of Officers who may be Slain, also to make such half pay transferable under the Controul of Congress and to subject the Officers to be again called by Congress into the service occasionally. In support of this it was alledged that at present the Officers having no permanent interest in their Commissions, it is not possible to reduce them to discipline, because whenever the necessary strictness and severity is observed they threaten to resign a Commission which affords them no prospects but of pain, danger, fatigue, and ruin to their private fortunes. That it is unjust to sacrifice the time and property of the men whose lives are every day exposed for us without any prospect of compensation, while so many who are protected by their valor and exertions are amassing princely fortunes, that unless something of this kind is done we cannot long expect to have an Army, because the Officers being unable even to subsist on their pay have already expended much of their private property and would be entirely ruined were they to continue; in a word Sir that without it we can have no discipline, and almost no army. On the other hand it is alledged that the Officers in the Army are and ought to be actuated by the principles of patriotism and public spirit, and ought to disdain motives of private interest, that enough will always be found to command our Troops who will deem the service of their Country and its gratitude a very ample compensation. That making such an establishment will involve the idea of a standing Army in time of peace to be at the disposal of Congress and that the rights of the States of appointing the regimental Officers will be reduced to nothing, that its effect will be to keep a great number of People idle Pensioners on the public who ought to be restored to useful industry, that it will be burthening the country with an expence for Officers at the same time that the Soldiery must be supplied from the Militia. That since it cannot certainly produce an army exclusive of the Militia no good can be derived from it, for which we ought to hazard such inconveniences. But the most formidable argument is that the Congress being instituted only for the purposes of War have no power without particular instructions, to make any peace establishment. For my own part Sir, I cannot help admitting the force of the arguments for this measure so far as they prove the necessity of holding up the prospect of some adequate Compensation for the Officers and Soldiers likewise, but I do not approve of the mode proposed. The arguments drawn from Patriotism and public spirit may be fine and specious, but I choose to trust to some principles of more certain, lasting and powerful influence for the defense of our country. There will be room enough for their full operation after every thing else in our power is done. The fear of a standing Army arising from this establishment, has no great weight with me. This War will make too many of our people Soldiers to leave us any thing to apprehend from a standing Army in one generation. The few in each State whom the fatigues and consequent infirmities of a long and painful War will induce to indulge an indolent ease are not in my opinion an object of any consequence, the argument of want of power is no more conclusive against this than against borrowing money which must be paid and its interest in the mean time kept up by revenues which must continue long beyond the War, but it is not conclusive against either if the necessity for raising and keeping together an army be admitted. The argument with respect to the power of the States, in appointing the regimental Officers cannot be denied, but I hope after the present war we shall not have occasion to exercise that Power again in the age of any man now living, In short Sir I could get over all the objections if the number of Battallions were so reduced that no State should be obliged to keep up more than they can man exclusive of draughts from the Militia, but so long as it tends only to keep Officers in pay without regular troops under them, so long as our State are required to keep up a number so much beyond their proportion and ability, I cannot agree to it. It will not have the effect of producing a good army which may prevent the necessity of calling on the Militia, and so long as a country must employ its Militia, the expence and injury arising from it is sufficient burthen without an established list of Pensioners. I shall use my endeavour to have the number of Battallions from our State reduced because I am convinced they cannot be filled by recruiting and to fill them with draughted militia is much too heavy and unequal a burthen for us. And if the establishment can be so moddled as to make provision only for Officers who shall have regular troops to command I shall consent to it, if it shall be determined during my stay.

Tr (MH–H). Endorsed: "Mr. Burke to Govr. Caswell—Extract."

[1] Burke seems to be in error on this point as there is evidence indicating that states other than those he mentions here had already transmitted instructions on

the Articles of Confederation to Congress. President John Rutledge enclosed South Carolina's February 5 instructions with a February 16 letter to Henry Laurens that apparently arrived in York around March 22. See Laurens to John Laurens, March 22, 1778, note 2. The Pennsylvania Assembly, which adopted instructions on March 3, appointed a committee to bring them to York and consult with the Pennsylvania delegates about them. It is not known when the committee was actually in York, but on March 14 it reported to the assembly that it had completed its work. *Minutes of the Second General Assembly of . . . Pennsylvania*, February 1778 session, pp. 51, 61, DLC (ESR). A copy of the Pennsylvania instructions is in the Jonathan Bayard Smith Papers, DLC. Furthermore as early as March 20 the Massachusetts delegates learned unofficially of the Massachusetts General Court's March 10 instructions on the confederation, though not until March 27 did Samuel Adams transmit a certified copy of them to James Lovell. See Lovell to Samuel Adams, March 10, note 1, and April 18, 1778, note 7. Although the Massachusetts instructions evidently did not reach York until April 18, it is difficult to believe that the Pennsylvania and South Carolina instructions were not presented to Congress before the ninth. And finally, President Josiah Bartlett transmitted the New Hampshire Assembly's March 5 instructions on the articles with a March 14 letter to the New Hampshire delegates, but it is not known when these documents reached York. No New Hampshire delegates attended Congress between April 7 and May 21, and the last known New Hampshire delegate letter written before April was George Frost's January 31, 1778, letter to Bartlett. See Bartlett, *Papers* (Mevers), pp. 176–77.

For texts of the instructions from the states that had sent them to their delegates by the time Congress resumed debate on the Articles of Confederation in late June, see *JCC,* 11:662–71. It should be noted, however, that their placement in the journals at this point is the result of an editorial decision by Worthington C. Ford, the editor of this volume of the modern printed edition of this source, for they were never entered in the journals by Secretary Thomson, and the order requiring the delegates to "lodge with the secretary, their powers for ratifying" was added to the manuscript journals under the date June 27 sometime after July 9, 1778. See PCC, item 1, 16:144, 17:6. The texts of these instruments of ratification, the originals of which do not survive, are taken from PCC, item 9.

[2] See Committee at Camp to Henry Laurens, February 5, 1778.

[3] See Henry Laurens to Washington, March 15, note 2, and April 8, 1778, note 4.

Henry Laurens to the Commissioners at Fort Pitt

Gentlemen.   9th April 1778

Two days ago I was honoured with yours of the 31st Ulto. which was immediately presented to Congress & now remains the Subject of a Select Committee.[1] Until that Committee shall Report I shall receive no Commands. In the mean time I may inform you that Congress approve of your opinion the result of an enquiry into the conduct of Colonel George Morgan, have ordered it to be entered upon the Journal & published.[2]

The bearer James McLeland is charged with four thousand Dollars to be delivered to Colonel Morgan for defraying the expence of building & Arming Boats on the Ohio.[3]

I immediately upon being authorized by an Act of Congress I shall dispatch a Special messenger to wait on you.

I am with very great Esteem.

LB (DNA: PCC, item 13). Addressed: "Sampson Mathews, Geo Clymer & Sam. McDowell Esquires, Commissioners on the Western frontier, Fort Pitt."

[1] The commissioners' March 31 letter to Laurens, which recommended a number of measures for defending the frontiers of Pennsylvania and Virginia and was signed by George Clymer and Sampson Matthews, is in PCC, item 78, 2: 445–46. The committee to which it was referred submitted a report on "the protection of, and operations on the western frontiers" that Congress approved on May 2. JCC, 10:313–14, 11:416–17. Committee member Jonathan Bayard Smith—not William Ellery, as Worthington C. Ford asserts in JCC, 11:416n.3—summarized the commissioners' letter and made preliminary suggestions for the committee's report in the following undated notes written sometime before May 2:

"Two Regiments to be raised for 2 years.

"12 Comps. in Virginia & 4 in Pennsylvania.

"Order of Congress for sending down McKee, Gitty [Girty] & Elliot.

"Request from Hand to be recalled & a successor to be recalled [i.e. appointed].

"A Commissary of provisions to be appointed & to act as P[ay] M[aster] & Q[uarter] M[aster] in Rockingham Co. &c. N.B. Capt Pat. Lockhart of Botetourt recomd.

"Colo. Morgans letter to Colo. Buchannan with copy of Contract to be referred to the board of war.

"A Commy. to be appointed for the Counties of Rockingham, Augusta, Rockbridge, Botetourt, Montgomery & Washington & Green Briar.

("That 2 Regiments be ordered immediately to Pittsburg Viz. Colo. Russels of Virginia and Colo. McCoys of Pennsylvania for the immediate defense of the frontiers.)

"That Genl. Washington be directed to order to Pittsburg one of the most reduced Virginia & one of the most reduced Pennsylvania Regiments & That their officers take effectual means for recruiting them in the Western Country to their full Compliment, & be authorized to take recruits to serve for 1 year unless sooner dismissed by Congress which said recruits shall receive 20 ds. bounty & the same cloathing as other Continental soldiers. And every noncommd. officer & private who shall furnish himself with a blanket, musket or Rifle & accoutrements shall receive the same allowance therefor as is given by Congress to the drafts from the militia for filling up the Continental Regiments." PCC, item 78, 2:445–46.

Most of the points raised by Smith were dealt with in the committee report. For further information about the background and work of the commissioners, see Committee of Congress to Edward Hand, October 24, 1777, note 1; and Laurens to George Clymer, March 27, 1778, note.

[2] See Laurens to George Morgan, this date.

[3] See JCC, 10:325.

Henry Laurens to Denis Nicolas Cottineau

Sir,[1] 9th April 1778

Inclosed with this you will receive two Letters from His Excellency General Washington which came yesterday to my hands.[2]

The Honble. Mr. Lewis will address you on behalf of Congress in order to treat with you for the purchase of divers articles of your Cargo.

I have requested that Gentleman to attempt the purchase of a few trifles on my private account if to be done without prejudice to the public—the particulars set forth in a paper under this Cover.[3] I shall make payment in a Bill of Exchange on London or Nantz or in Gold which will have due consideration with you in ascertaining the prices.

If I can be useful to you in this Country or South Carolina proper intimations will find me very much Sir Your most humble Servt.

LB (ScHi). Addressed: "Captn. Cottineau, New Bern, by Mr. Lewis."

[1] Denis Nicolas Cottineau de Kerloguin (d. 1808), commander of the French privateer *Pallas*, subsequently received an American naval commission from Benjamin Franklin in 1779 and served under the command of John Paul Jones. Lasseray, *Les Français sous les treize étoiles*, 1:167–68. Cottineau had arrived at Cape Lookout in February with a varied cargo of goods—including clothing, coffee, linen, medicine, silk, spices, and wine—which he promptly offered for sale to Washington. He also sent word of his cargo to Congress, which agreed to purchase such parts of it "as are necessary for the Army" and dispatched Francis Lewis, a member of the Marine Committee, to North Carolina to complete this transaction. See *JCC*, 10:298, 333; *N.C. State Records*, 13:85, 93, 111, 119–20, 126; and Laurens to Washington, April 14, 1778. See also Cottineau's letter to Washington and the invoice of his cargo, both dated February 26, 1778, in the Washington Papers, DLC.

[2] The only extant letter Washington wrote to Cottineau around this time is dated April 4. Washington, *Writings* (Fitzpatrick), 11:215–16.

[3] A list of the "few trifles" that were the subject of this enclosure was also copied into Laurens' private letterbook with this letter.

Henry Laurens to the Chevalier de La Neuville

Sir
                                                              9th April 1778

Having so good an opportunity as this by the Honble. Mr. Lewis I cannot forbear to pay my respects to you although I have not the pleasure of saying all that I wish & what I know would be agreeable to you.

The Camp Committee are not yet returned nor have they Reported the intended arrangement of Officers, consequently everything in that branch remains just in the State they were in when you left York Town.[1]

Mr. Lewis can further inform you to whom I beg leave to refer & I have only to add assurances of being, With great respect & regard &ca.

LB (ScHi). Addressed: "Monsr. Lanuville, New Bern."

[1] See Laurens to Chevalier de La Neuville, January 27, 1778.

Henry Laurens to John Laurens

My Dear Son   9th April 1778.
My last I beleive was by Jones since which I know I have received
a Letter from you but 'tis not at hand, yes here 'tis of the 6th.[1]
We are very nearly of one opinion on our late Presidents resigna-
tion.[2] I want the papers.
You will receive by Ross the bearer of this all your Blue Cloth &
Buttons per Accot. inclosed, if superfluous you have a right to return
them.
I am greatly distressed by circumstances now in agitation respecting
your friend, I think I once said "I hope he will never afford him or
them his own consent to hurt him." [3]
My Dear Son Adieu.

LB (ScHi).
    [1] The letter in question seems to be the one dated April 5 in Simms, *Laurens
Army Correspondence,* pp. 153–54.
    [2] See ibid. for John's comments on the recent resignation of South Carolina
president John Rutledge.
    [3] Laurens had made a remark to this effect about Washington in his January 8,
1778, letter to John.

Henry Laurens to George Morgan

Dear Sir,   9th April 1778
The day before yesterday I had the honor of presenting to Congress
your favour of the 7th Inst. which was referred to a Select Committee
& remains unreported,[1] consequently I have received no Commands
on that subject, nevertheless I cannot suffer Mr. McLeland to return
without intimating that the Enquiry into your conduct by the Commissioners at Fort Pitt is approved of by Congress, that the House have
ordered it to be entered upon the Journal & to be published to the
World, a circumstance which with the utmost pleasure I communicate
by the earliest opportunity.[2]
Mr. McLeland is charged with the four Thousand Dollars applied
for by General Hand for building Armed Boats, for which Sum you
are to be accountable.[3]
I am with great regard.

LB (DNA: PCC, item 13). Addressed: "Colonel George Morgan Esquire, Fort Pitt."
    [1] In reality Morgan's letter was dated March 31 and read in Congress on April 7.
JCC, 10:313. This letter dealt with Indian affairs in western Pennsylvania—
particularly the recent escape from Fort Pitt of former British deputy Indian
superintendent Alexander McKee—and was referred to the same committee that

was considering a March 31 letter from the commissioners at Fort Pitt. See Laurens to the Commissioners at Fort Pitt, this date, note 1. Morgan's letter is not in PCC, but a text of it is available in Reuben Gold Thwaites and Louise Phelps Kellogg, eds., *Frontier Defense on the Upper Ohio, 1777–1778* (Madison: Wisconsin Historical Society, 1912), pp. 254–56. In the previous year Morgan had been cleared of allegations that he had conspired with McKee and others against the American cause. See ibid., pp. 184–87; and Committee of Congress letters to Edward Hand and to Unknown, October 24, 1777.

² The March 27 certificate of the commissioners at Fort Pitt, exonerating Indian agent Morgan "of the charges against him, of infidelity to his public trust, and disaffection to the American cause," is in *JCC*, 10:314–15. See also Committee of Congress to Edward Hand, October 24, 1777, note 1; and Laurens to George Clymer, March 27, 1778, note.

³ See *JCC*, 10:325. Morgan had requested this money in the March 31 letter to Laurens cited above.

Thomas McKean to Sarah McKean

Lancaster April 9th 1778. McKean had gone to Lancaster for a meeting of the Pennsylvania supreme court. "I arrived here on Tuesday morning and was escorted into Town by a number of Gentlemen of the Law, Justices of the peace &c. besides the Officers, who met me near to Mrs. Scott's. Matters have been conducted equal to my most sanguine hopes, indeed every thing is as I would wish it." Concerning Charles Lee's parole and public affairs in Delaware: "General Rodney is appointed President of the Delaware State. General Lee will be here today; tho' I believe, he is not yet finally exchanged. . . . The Inhabitants of Delaware are said to be on the verge of a total Revolution to Whiggism, and that the most spirited measures are adopted there."

RC (PHi).

Marine Committee to William Phillips, Isaac Smith, and Ebenezer Storer

Gentlemen¹   April 9th 1778
    Enclosed is a Copy of A Letter from Colo. Benjamin Tuper to the President of Congress with A Resolve of Congress thereon.² You will please to enquire of Mr. Watson whether the Vessels & Cargoes have been sold—if not you will dispose of them and pay to the Captors the several proportions justly due to them. We are Gentlemen, Your humble servants

LB (DNA: PCC Miscellaneous Papers, Marine Committee Letter Book).
    ¹ The recipients were "commissioners appointed by the Marine Committee, to

settle and adjust the accounts of prizes with the agents appointed by General Washington." *JCC*, 10:326.

² In his March 19 letter, which is in PCC, item 78, 22:557–59, Benjamin Tupper had requested assistance in obtaining his share of two British vessels captured by him in October 1775 at Washington's order. Tupper's letter was referred to the Marine Committee on March 31 and the committee's report, recommending that the commissioners be required to pay the captors their due shares, was approved on April 9. *JCC*, 10:297–98, 326.

John Banister to Patrick Henry

Sir.   York. 10th, April. 1778

Nothing having occurred since I had the honor of adressing you last,¹ a very few days since, I have only to inform you that a warrant is made against the treasurer to the amount of the advance you mention,² and that it may be sometime postponed, to make way for some immense supplies of money wanted now for the quarter master and commissary departments, previous to a possibility of the armies being able to act with effect. So soon as it can be obtained with propriety it surely *shall* be, and forwarded. The thousand pounds Col Mason received he must pay on demand out of a considerable sum lately sent him for the troops. It is, I cannot help again repeating, a misfortune to our affairs, that the men were not sent forward uninoculated, since innumerable experiments justify a communication of that disorder in camp, besides saving a train of ills consequent upon the method hitherto practised of doing it at a distance.

I have the honor to be with the highest respect your excellency's mo. obd. and Mo. hble. Servt.   J. Banister.

[*P.S.*] General Lee is here on parole.

MS not found; reprinted from Henry, *Patrick Henry*, 3:154–55.
¹ See Banister to Henry, March 27, 1778.
² This day Congress ordered a warrant for "33,333 ⅓ dollars" to reimburse Henry for provisions advanced to the Continental army. *JCC*, 10:329.

Marine Committee to James Maxwell and Paul Loyall

Gentlemen   April 11th 1778

We have determined for the present to stop the building of the Frigates in Virginia. We find on examining your Account that you have neglected giving us Credit for the following Sums which will make a considerable balance in our favour.

Your draft of the 9th July last in favour of Wm. Holt for	£ 390. 0.0 Va Curry.
A Warrant on the Loan Office in Virginia for 10,000 Dollars transmitted you the 24th of November last @ 6s per Dollr.	3000. 0.0
Your draft of the 5th March last in favour Wm. Holt for	243.11.0

Virga Currency   £3633. 0.0

Mr. Stodder tells us that you have not received any Money on the Warrant on the Loan Office transmitted you the 24th of November. If there should be no money in the Office you must negotiate the Loan Office Certificates. We inclose you a Resolve of Congress empowering you & Mr. David Stodder Master builder of the Frigates to consider and Report what allowance if any you think ought to be made to Thomas Hoggard for the frames of the Frigates over and above the prices originally stipulated.[1] When we shall resume the building of those Frigates we shall be glad to have your superintendancy of them. In the mean time we are with great respect Gentlemen, Yr humble servants

LB (DNA: PCC Miscellaneous Papers, Marine Committee Letter Book).

[1] This resolve, approved on April 9, was passed in response to Thurmer Hoggard's March 20 letter to the Marine Committee, which is in PCC, item 78, 11:293. See *JCC*, 10:313, 326.

Marine Committee to David Stodder

Sir   April 11th 1778

We have determined for the present to stop the building of the Frigates in Virginia of which you are the Master builder and are willing that you should enter into the employ of the State of Virginia,[1] and continue therein until we shall thank proper to resume the building of them or you shall be ordered to build other vessels for us. In the mean time we would have you take particular care of the Ships Frames and Materials for building so as to prevent any rot or embezzlement, and shall make you a reasonable allowance for your trouble therein. When we shall have an opportunity to converse with the Honorable Richd. Henry Lee Esqr. who was the Gentleman that agreed with you respecting the terms of your employment we shall be able to determine upon an allowance to be made you. So soon as we shall have decided on this matter we will give you notice thereof, and at the same time will inform you whether the terms you have proposed for your future service is agreeable. In the mean time we are Sir, Your humble Servants.

LB (DNA: PCC Miscellaneous Papers, Marine Committee Letter Book).
[1] This day the Marine Committee also sent a brief note to Governor Henry, acknowledging their agreement "that Mr. Stodder should be employed by your State in building small Vessels upon condition that he shall resume the building of the Frigates or build any other vessels for the Continent when we judge proper." PCC Miscellaneous Papers, Marine Committee Letter Book, fol. 141; and Paullin, *Marine Committee Letters,* 1:228.

Delegates' Pledge of Order

April 12. 1778.[1]

We the subscribers members of Congress pledge our honor to each other that we will meet punctually at the hour of adjournment, that on any subject in debate (except in Committee of the whole house) we will not speak more than ⟨fifteen⟩ Ten[2] minutes, seldom more than once, never more than twice, and that we will unite in supporting order & preserving decency and politeness in debate.[3]

Francis Lightfoot Lee, Va.	James Lovell
⟨Samuel Chase, Md.⟩[4]	Fra. Dana
Wm. Duer, N Yk.	Edward Langworthy
J. Banister	Saml Huntington
Wm. Hy. Drayton, Nay[5]	John Henry, Md.
Jas. Smith	Nath. Scudder
William Ellery	Cornls. Harnett
James Forbes, Md.	E Gerry

MS (DLC). In the hand of Charles Thomson and signed by all the delegates whose names are appended. Endorsed by Thomson: "Engagement of the members to meet punctually at the hour of adjournment, to support Order & preserve decency & politeness"; and by an unidentified hand: "Signed in the handwriting of the Members April 12th 1778."
[1] According to the journals Congress did not convene on Sunday, April 12, 1778.
[2] Francis Dana deleted "fifteen" and wrote "Ten" above the line.
[3] The delegates' decision to enter into this agreement was undoubtedly prompted by a wish to avoid a recurrence of the sort of obstructionist behavior in which Thomas Burke was currently engaged. See Burke's Proposed Statement to Congress, April 13, 1778. Years later William Ellery discussed Congress' decision to limit the duration of speeches by delegates in a letter he wrote to Benjamin Huntington.
"I recollect that while I was a member of Congress it was more the practice to speechify in that assembly, than I believe in any other on the Continent; but the most frequent and the most lengthy were not the most graceful or the most pertinent speakers. Long speeches were found to be so disadvantageous, that, when Congress sat at York Town, the principal speakers agreed not to speak longer than 15 minutes. A man must have a great deal to say, or be very verbose indeed who cannot deliver his sentiments on almost any subject in that time. If an oration

is to be pronounced or papers to be read and commented upon half an hour might not be too much; but orations are not a sort of speeches proper for Legislative bodies; nor is it common to vouch or support what is advanced in Congress by papers, authorities, and comments." See Ellery to Huntington, July 4, 1789, Thomas C. Bright Autograph Collection, NRom.

[4] In the margin next to his deleted signature, Chase wrote the following explanation: "struck out because violated by several of the contracting parties."

[5] The "Nay" after Drayton's signature, in another hand, suggests that he too may have subsequently repudiated this agreement, but in the absence of other evidence this must remain a conjecture.

William Duer to Robert Morris

My Dear Sir   York Town 12th April [1778]
. . . .[1] It is said that my Friend Gouverneur Morris is at your *Chateau.* For the sake of our Country, my dear Morris, entreat him to push on and come with him yourself. From a want of Representation in the State of New York, and several other Embarrassments we cannot bring as many members absolutely essential to our Safety, without you, especially the Establishment for the Army. I am desired by all your Friends in Congress to press you on this matter; and I flatter myself we shall not plead in Vain. If G. Morris should be at Lancaster, pray write to him in the most pressing Terms, to come forward. . . .[2]

My dear Friend do not fail to accompany Mr Morris; ten or twelve days of your Joint attendance will do more good than six months of your Presence one month hence.[3]

Tr (DLC). Copied for Edmund C. Burnett "from the original, then in possession of Mr. Stan V. Henkels of Philadelphia."

[1] Ellipsis in Tr. According to a marginal note by Burnett, the omitted opening of Duer's letter "merely states why he had not gone to Manheim."

[2] Ellipsis in Tr. A marginal note by Burnett states that the omitted section concerned "a parcel for Mrs. Morris and her health."

[3] Gouverneur Morris was back in Congress by April 15 when he voted and received a committee assignment. *JCC,* 10:352–53. Although Robert Morris made a brief trip to York the following week to see Charles Lee, he did not return to Congress until about May 13, just in time to help secure congressional approval of the controversial half-pay plan for Continental military officers. *JCC,* 10:495.

Thomas Burke's Proposed Statement to Congress

Mr President   York April 13th 1778[1]
I receive the proceedings of the house with respect, and (Protesting that until the Laws of the State I represent shall expressly declare the

Contrary, I shall hold myself accountable for my Conduct in Congress to that State, and no other power on Earth) I shall use the freedom which according to my Idea belongs to a republican, and a representative of a Sovereign People in the answers I shall make.

I consider the minutes of the tenth of April as a charge of a breach of order in the thing, and a Contempt in the manner.

I admit that withdrawing without the permission of Congress is a breach of order, and I hold that no member can deny his personal attendance at reasonable hours or even his Sentiments on any question debated before him, except by special leave of the house, without incurring the Penalties on misbehavior in office and I have only to allege *in excuse* that I had uniformly observed the members of Congress withdraw themselves at pleasure from attendance on Congress, and without reprehension that I thought it not improper to use a liberty which had been denied, as I conceive, to no other member, when I deemed the subject of too much Importance to be debated and determined, at a time when the faculties of the members were tired by the attendance of a whole day and when my own particular Indisposition rendered me incapable of giving that attention which I thought my duty to my Constituents required.

As to the manner, I am not conscious of having Intended a Contempt. I did not, nor do I now admit that less than Nine States can make a Congress. I understood not that the Message came from the President, but deemed that it came from Colonel Duer[2] whose name the messenger particularly mentioned, from whom he delivered a private message to the Delegate from Georgia[3] requesting his company as a favor, and to whom I intended my words should be conveyed. Before my departure, I heard Mr Lovell from Massachusetts say to the House "there is no farther occasion to call the states, this declaration is decisive" in which I thought the House acquiessced, and that the adjournment was compleat. The Delegate from Georgia, who always answer the last in order, accompanied me under the same persuasion. With respect to the minutes of the eleventh, protesting that as a Delegate representing a free and Sovereign People, I am entitled to entire freedom of Debate, I say that the Expressions minuted were accompanied with and explained by other Expressions not minuted which declared my sense to be, that Congress have a power so far as to enforce the attendance of the members, that if the hours of attendance were ascertained by Congress I would punctually attend, but if not I must use my own Judgment, at the risque of any consequent punishment, as to the time being reasonable when my presence is required, that I am at all times ready and willing to Submit my Conduct and opinions to my Constituents, in whose Justice I have the firmest Confidence, and to whom I owe, as a duty, to prevent, if I can, the decision of important matters, when members cannot duly attend to them, that Conviction of Error always did, and always shall precede Concession with me.

That (abstracted from the breach of order under Consideration which I meant not to Justify, but excuse) my general political opinions were that undue, or unreasonable exercise of any power, tho' lawful power, is Tyrannical, and that no freeman is bound to submit to it. That every freeman must use his own Judgment on it before he determines to disobey, for until he does disobey there can be no subject for any other Judgment and it remains for his Country to decide whether he is mistaken or not, and if he is, he incurs the penalties provided by Law. That it is Criminal in members of Congress to withold their attendance when the public safety required it, but that they are to be Judged and punished by the Laws of the States they represent, and no other power.

These Sentiments however expressed, I avow, and as to the Language, I know no obligation I am under to use a Courtly Stile. My expressions are usually what first occur and in this Instance were not intended to offend.

I shall only add that I mean not by any thing I have here said to submit myself to any Jurisdiction, but that of the state I represent, such submission being in my Idea injurious to the majesty thereof, nor do I mean to forego any of my own rights as a Citizen entitled to the benefit of the Laws, and Constitution of the free State of North Carolina.   Thos. Burke

The Above writing I compared with Mr. Burkes Defence & it contains the express words spoken or read by him in Congress.
Witness my hand.   Cornl Harnett

MS (NcU). Written and signed by Thomas Burke, with attestation and signature by Cornelius Harnett. Endorsed by Harnett: "Mr. Burkes Defense April 13th, 1778."

[1] This manuscript consists of the justifications Burke was prepared to offer Congress this day for his action in withdrawing from Congress without permission, on the evening of April 10, during debate on a reply to Washington's April 4 letter to President Laurens that he regarded as excessively critical of the commander in chief. Burke's unauthorized withdrawal, which temporarily deprived Congress of a quorum, and his peremptory refusal to obey a request that he return immediately to Congress affronted many delegates and led them to consider various disciplinary measures. In the end, however, Burke's unflagging insistence that he was amenable only to the jurisdiction of North Carolina led Congress to confine itself to passing a resolve on April 25 that sharply criticized Burke's behavior but referred further action on it to the North Carolina Assembly, which in August 1778 pronounced itself satisfied with Burke's conduct and his defense of the state's authority over its delegates. For further information about this controversy, see *JCC*, 10:334, 336–37, 339, 386–91; *N. C. State Records*, 12: 769, 792, 825, 843–45; Henry Laurens to Richard Caswell, April 27; and Burke to Richard Caswell and to the North Carolina Assembly, April 29, 1778. Finally, it is necessary to point out that Burke

had already submitted a written defense of his conduct to Congress on April 11, which has not been found, and that Congress refused to read the present document. See *JCC*, 10:339, 386; and Burke to the North Carolina Assembly, April 29, 1778. See also Henry Laurens to Washington, April 8, 1778, for a discussion of Congress' response to Washington's April 4 letter.

[2] William Duer was a member of the committee that drafted the reply to Washington's April 4 letter Burke found so objectionable. *JCC*, 10:314.

[3] Edward Langworthy, who had withdrawn from Congress with Burke, but who returned to Congress on the evening of April 10 as soon as he was requested, a fact Burke neglected to mention in this document. *JCC*, 10:334.

James Lovell to Joseph Trumbull

Dear Sir   13th Apr. 1778

Your favor of the 2d gave me vast satisfaction as it goes near to insure to me the restoration of your Health & Limbs. I think you had best determine to lay aside all thought of coming to this Place.[1] The Employment you were invited to would be inevitable Destruction after the Shock you have had. You will ever hereafter require Exercise and good Accommodations where your own or your Physician's Will could decide in points of Regimen. Here you can command no course of Diet. I am not Galen enough to say whether the Lime water which tears your Countryman's Bowels out would not serve you. It has driven several Delegates home to their native springs. I have not been affected with it disagreably in that respect which I hinted as to Mr. Wolcot & Mr. Huntington: and I do not think I ought to charge the Cramp in my Breast to any thing but Quilldriving perpetually.

Mr Wadsworth will conduct the Commissary's Department,[2] and I think your *Constitution* requires that you should *assist* him. I will not enlarge on that point as you discover a Disposition in your letter both well suited to your present State of Health and your Character as a *true* Patriot.

If the Army is not *immediately* filled up to the full compliment called for, what we have yet felt is a trifle to what we may expect. I say the same in Regard to Congress. The Sickness or *Will* of one man out of 7 now here destroys its Existence. I will tell you hereafter why this ought not to be if you stand in need of being told. My respectful & affectionate Compliments to your Father's & yr. own family.

J L

RC (CtHi).

[1] Lovell had been urging Trumbull to assume his seat on the new Board of War. See Lovell to Trumbull, January 27, 1778.

[2] For further information on Jeremiah Wadsworth's acceptance of the office of commissary general, see Abraham Clark to Wadsworth, March 29, 1778.

Robert Morris to Henry Laurens

Sir   Manheim April 13th. 1778

I embrace the opportunity of the Honble Governeur Morris Esqr. to inform Congress that Colo. Conner & myself entered into an examination of young Mr Swanwick on the Morning after the date of the former letter I had the Honour to write you Concerning him.[1] He produced to us the sundry letters he had received from his Father & Copies of those written to him since the loss of Philadelphia, but so far from treating of Political subjects, they appear to have laid it down as a fixed point between them, not to meddle with any thing of the kind, least it might produce an interruption to their Correspondance, which the Father in one of his first letters says, he is desirous of continuing for the Sole purpose of knowing what passes with respect to his own Family & affairs and that he desires no other kind of information from the Son, in short the letters he produced & the propriety of his behaviour on hearing the charge against him Convinced both Colo Conner & myself of his perfect innocence, it has made me very happy to find him so, because if he had been guilty, the greatest ingratitude & perfidy wou'd have been involved in the Crime. Colo. Conner will communicate his Sentiments to the Board of War & I have the Honor to Remain Your Excys Obed hble servt.

Robt Morris

RC (DNA: PCC, item 137).

[1] See Morris to Laurens, April 7, 1778. Lt. Col. Morgan Connor's April 11 letter to Laurens reporting the results of his investigation of John Swanwick, "In Obedience to orders from the . . . Board of War," is in PCC, item 78, 5:151. Swanwick himself had offered an impassioned rebuttal of the charge that he had engaged in a treasonous correspondence with his father in an April 8 letter to Laurens that was read in Congress on the 15th. See PCC, item 78, 20:203-4.

Henry Laurens to George Washington

Sir,   York Town, 14th April 1778

In obedience to the directions of Congress, I am to acknowledge the receipt of your letter of the 4th instant.[1]

Congress with great concern perceive that your sensibility is wounded by their resolutions. Placing the firmest confidence in your prudence, abilities and integrity, they wish to preserve that harmony with you, which is essential to the general Weal. You may rest assured that far from any intention to give you pain, their resolutions have no other motives or end but the public good. They therefore hope that you will not in future be distrest by apprehensions as injurious to their honor as they are to your own feelings.

However different the views of Congress may seem to you now from what you supposed them to be when you entered into your late engagements with general Howe, Congress certainly had nothing in view, but a proper respect to the dignity, safety & independence of these States.

The duplicity of general Howe and authentic information that the gentlemen appointed by you to negotiate the cartel held opinions repugnant to the sense of Congress, constrained them in a matter of such high moment, as forming a general cartel, to express their sentiments in an explicit manner; lest they might have only to lament, when it was out of their power to remedy a misapprehension on points deeply affecting in their judgment, the safety & honor of these States.

Congress expected that you would consider their resolutions of the 30th Ult. in the light of private instructions calculated to shew their sense with respect to the general outlines of the proposed cartel: a practice usual with the supreme power of every state in similar cases.[2]

You observe that a strict adherence to all the resolutions of Congress must of necessity destroy all idea of a cartel, but as a distinction can easily be made betwixt such of the resolutions of Congress as flow from general principles of policy, and those which arise from circumstances which have rendered a variation from time to time necessary, it is conceived that an attention to this discrimination will rid you of those embarassments, which you may, at first view, think yourself entangled with.

The resolution of Congress of the 19th December respecting the mode of settlement for supplies to the Enemy's prisoners seems not to have been sufficiently attended to.[3] It is left at the option of the enemy to pay either in coin dollar for dollar or in provisions &c equal in quantity and kind to what is furnished. Whatever objections may be made against the first mode, there surely cannot be a more just and equal ratio than the latter. Genl. Burgoyne lately made the same objections on this point, which occured to you, but on being reminded of the alternative offered by the resolution, he acquiesced, and the victuallying ships are now actually delivering provisions in payment for what they received. The commissaries of prisoners on each side may pass receipts for the rations received expressing the quantum of each article received for the subsistence of the prisoners in the power of the contracting parties and the balance may be paid in provisions or in coin, at the option of either party. The mode suggested by you is liable to this strong objection, that it would lay us under the necessity of furnishing the enemy's prisoners with us as well as ours with them with provisions; which certainly would be a capital advantage to them, if we consider the distance whence they must derive their supplies.[4]

The resolution of the 30th December was a measure naturally flowing from the treason acts, which the respective states have passed in consequence of the express recommendation of Congress.[5] On a mature deliberation, they are convinced that a deviation from it would be subversive of our character as an independent people & inconsistent with sound policy. No act of Congress can suspend the operation of the laws of the different states, and therefore they cannot consent that any measures should be adopted in the proposed cartel which may contravene this resolution. It does not however appear to Congress that any embarrassment will arise in this matter unless the enemy should insist upon an article in the cartel that Americans taken in arms shall be intitled to the benefit of an exchange. Under the terms of "Officer for Officer, soldier for soldier" &c which are generally used in cartels traitors would no more be included by the laws of nations than deserters. The carrying this resolution into practice can depend only on the will of the several states who in this respect must be presumed to be governed by principles of policy, of which they must necessarily be competent judges.

With respect to the resolution concerning genl. Lee, at his request, Congress are willing that you should wave his exchange for major genl. Prescot as a preliminary article; it is however their intention that no cartel be acceded to unless it be expressly admitted therein, that general Lee be exchanged for general Prescot.[6]

Congress have taken measures for purchasing such articles of captn. Cotteneaus Cargo as are necessary for the Army.[7]

By order of Congress,   Henry Laurens, President

RC (DLC). In the hand of Charles Thomson and signed by Laurens. The text of this letter in Laurens' presidential letterbook bears the following endorsement: "The following is Copy of a Letter, produced by amendments in Congress on a draught prepared by a Committee in Answer to General Washington's Letter of the 4th April—the draught presented the 9th, debated at divers meetings & Resolved the 13 April ½ h. 9 OClock PM." The committee draft upon which this letter is based was written by William Duer and is in *JCC*, 10:329–33. See also note 1 below.

[1] For discussion of why Washington's April 4 letter provoked this unusually formal reply from Congress, see Laurens to Washington, March 15, note 1, and April 8, 1778, note 4.

[2] Anyone who reads Congress' March 30 instructions to Washington on the subject of negotiating a prisoner exchange with General Howe will readily understand why the commander in chief concluded that they were designed to be carried out to the letter. *JCC*, 10:295.

[3] This resolution forbade the release of British prisoners of war until the British first repaid their captors for maintenance costs in "provisions or other necessaries, equal in quality and kind to what have been supplied, or the amount thereof in gold and silver, at the rate of four shillings and six pence sterling for every dollar of the currency of these states." *JCC*, 9:1037. The British objected to this resolve because of the depreciation in the value of Continental currency, and Washington's suggested modification of it in his April 4 letter to Laurens did not commend itself to the delegates. Washington, *Writings* (Fitzpatrick), 11:216–17.

⁴ At this point in the debate on the committee draft Congress voted five states to three, with one divided and two abstaining, to delete a sentence that would have authorized Washington to disregard the December 19 resolve "provided a Mode is adopted for subsisting Prisoners upon a Principle of Equality to the contracting Parties." *JCC* 10:331.

⁵ This resolve declared that all inhabitants of "these United States" who voluntarily entered British service and were captured in battle would be "delivered up to the respective states to which they belong, to be dealt with agreeable to the laws thereof." *JCC*, 9:1069. Naturally, the British insisted that loyalists who fell into this category should be treated as ordinary prisoners of war who were subject to exchange, and Washington advised Congress that it would be prudent if this resolve were "suffered to sleep." Washington, *Writings* (Fitzpatrick), 11:217.

⁶ The foregoing paragraph was inserted in the committee draft in place of three other sharply worded paragraphs reminding Washington of Congress' insistence that Gen. Charles Lee had to be exchanged for Gen. Richard Prescott before a general exchange of prisoners could take place. *JCC*, 10:332–33.

⁷ In the committee draft this paragraph was originally preceded by another paragraph severely chastising Washington for "permitting the Enemy's Officers, Prisoners with us, to go in on Parole, before ours are sent out." Congress deleted this paragraph by a vote of five states to three, with one divided and two abstaining. *JCC*, 10:333.

Henry Laurens to George Washington

Sir,   14th April 1778.

Since my last of the 8th by Ross I have had the honor of presenting Your Excellency's dispatch of the 10th to Congress, this together with the several Extracts of Letters which accompanied it are referred to a Committee & remain subjects for consideration.¹

Under Cover with this Your Excellency will receive a Letter of the present date signed by special order, to which I beg leave to refer.

I remain, With the highest Regard & Esteem, Sir, Your Excellency's Most obedient & Most humble servant,

Henry Laurens, President of Congress.

RC (DLC).

¹ Washington's April 10 letter to Laurens, which dealt mainly with the need for Congress to approve the new arrangements for the army proposed by the Committee at Camp, is in PCC, item 152, 5:439–46, and Washington, *Writings* (Fitzpatrick), 11:235–41. Unlike most of his official letters to Laurens, Washington wrote this one in his own hand. With it he also enclosed letters from Gen. Israel Putnam on prospects for recruiting in Connecticut, from Gen. Alexander Mc-Dougall on the state of his new command in the Highlands, and from Col. Israel Shreve on "the destruction of the Salt, and Salt Works at Squan" in New Jersey. McDougall's letter, dated March 29, and Shreve's, dated April 7, are in the Washington Papers, DLC; Putnam's letter has not been found. On April 15 Congress approved a report from the committee to whom all these letters had been referred ordering Gen. Horatio Gates to repair to Fishkill, N.Y., and resume active command of the northern department, hoping thereby to resolve some of the problems in this area noted by McDougall. *JCC*, 10:341, 348, 354–55. It is also pertinent to

note that on the following day Congress rejected a motion to record in its
journals portions of Washington's March 24 and April 10 letters to Laurens urging
approval of the half-pay plan. See *JCC*, 10:357–58; and Washington, *Writings*
(Fitzpatrick), 11:138–39, 237–39.

Oliver Wolcott to Laura Wolcott

My Dear,   York Town 14t April 1778
   I was Very happy to receive your Letter of the 6t instant, tho' at
the same Time that part of it which gave Me an Account of your
Want of Health touched Me with a Very sensible Greif. I was in
hopes that the Disorders which have so frequently afflicted you would
not have returned, tho' I believe from my own experience that they
are difficult to eradicate. My Seperation from you was always a most
disagreable Circumstance to my being Sent on publick Business, and
every Repetition of an Appointment of this Nature becomes less
agreable. As no one I beleive has a greater Relish than I have for
domestick Injoyment, so I beleive I may flatter myself that after my
present Tour of Duty which will conclude in Two months from this
Time not only my own Wishes But that of my Country, will be gratified by my returning to enjoy in future domestick Peace. I shall Write
to Mr. Adams that either he or some Other Gentleman appointed to
attend would releive me as early in June as can be done. My half
year's Service counting to next Novr. will fully expire by that Time,
and I shall not have a single Wish to prolong the Period, And if my
Health shall continue in any tolerable Degree till that Time it is the
utmost that I can hope for. The Service in Attending Congress is
more Arduous than I had before known it. We sit sometimes till
between 10 and 11 o'Clock at night, but in those Cases We have an
adjourment at Noon. I have been so confined as not to have been on
Horsback since I came here, which I find has been some Injury to my
Health. At present I am not so well as to attend Congress. Yesterday
I did not attend nor shall do so to Day. I am not confined to my
Chamber nor in any Danger of a Fever, I suppose my Disorders are
rather Billious and which will pass off by a Diarrhea which exercises
me pritty freely, so that I expect to be as well as usual in a Day or
Two. A Turn of this kind both Col Dyer and Mr. Huntington have
had since I came here. I beleive it is a kind of seasoning for the Climate and mode of living. I feel myself much better than I did yesterday. I shall have my Horse Bro't in a Day or Two to a Stable near to
where I live and intend to Ride Very frequently. You take Notice
that I mention in one of my Letters that I was well and injoyed a
flow of Spirits. A Flow of Spirits you seem to consider as hardly
proper to be felt at the present Day. I hope you did not suppose I

meant by it any Gayety of Temper. Your own Experience I beleive will convince you that a Flow of Spirits in me is to be a little above Dejection. As to the Gloominess of the Times which you mention, Times I admit are bad, but I do not beleive that God will Consign this Country to Destruction, Light in due Time will arise and the happy Days of Peace, Fair, equitable and just Peace will Return. Suffer not your Mind to be under any overwhelming Solicitude on this Acco. God will take Care of this People, and I trust that both you and I shall live to see the most convincing Prooffs of it in the establishment of their Independency and safety.

Your Cares on Acco. of the Family are great. I hope I shall soon be in a Condition to bear a part of them. What you mention concerning Mr. Peirces[1] Kindness I can only say that the Affairs in the Northern Department are intirely unsettled. It is I think most probable that the Peekskill and Albany or Northern Department will be united. If so Mr. Trumbull will hold them both unless Mr. Palfrey P[ay] M[aster] Genl. should Resign, if so which I think is rathar improbable, Mr. Trumbull who has been for a long Time uneasy at not being at the Head may suceed him. If an Oppertunity presents I do not know that I shall object against Oliver's accepting Mr Peirces Kindness. The Army is a good schoole for a yong Man to learn Men and Manners in—None perhaps better if he is brought into an acquaintance with the higher and most improved Characters in an Army as well as that infinite Variety which Makes up the Mass of it. Mankind are unreservedly exemplified in an Army. An easiness of Manners and Address may there be obtained by proper Attention and Care. An Army is likewise unhappily the school of what are called fashonable Vices, tho there is No Vice but what dishonours him who possesses it, and the Deformity of it in some Instances is only concealed by the concommitant splendor of Noble Virtues. But you will perceive by what I say that I do not on the whole object agt his Accepting the offer when proposed. Altho I think that will be Very uncertain. Not but that I think Mr. Peirce ought to fill any Vacancy which might happen, but that perhaps will not be the Case. Mr. Trumbull who has Wrote some pretty offensive Letters to Congress because he has not been treated with more particular Marks of Respect one would imagine did not much care about holding the office.[2] But as it yeilds him a Salary of 125 Dollars per month without his personally attending to it scarcly any at all, I presume he will condescend to hold it, tho' I am Very sure that such sinecure pay must be too much by farr below the Merit of any one of that Family. Their Claims on the Head of Merit I believe have rendered them a little ridiculous. But this to you only. I am as still as a Mouse and I hope you will not doubt my Prudence. While I am here I shall mark the events and if any Thing happens I shall give my opinion upon it farther. I hope Oliver will not set his Heart upon this Business. It is a precarious Event, and if realised the advantage will be doubtfull. As to the Conducting of the little Farming Business, I can give you no advice.

As to the Regulating Act the Achan[3] not only of all good Policy but of common Sence, Congress will I suppose in a few Days Recommend that it be suspended, at least I hope they will.[4] No Regard is paid to any Act of this Kind in this State. No such Act to the Southward of it Exists nor ever will. If Connecticut Maintains a Regulation of this kind, they will be the only State in the Union that will do so. Tho I know that our State will not do it, for this plain Reason because it is impossible, absolutely impossible in the Nature of Things, for such an Act to exist. So I find I am got upon a New Sheet. I shall now be fully able to answer every part of your Letter which I may Very well do considering how few I have to acknowledge. As to the Business which Mr. Reeve was to transact for me it seems to have been done in part for which I am oblidged to him. I have long tho't that I should never be Rich, indeed I am almost sure of it. Perhaps a pritty narrow Fortune will be best for us. The trading Business is carryed on at great Risque, tho I am glad he has purchased but I will not depend upon much success. How farr to engage in the Naval Way I shall be intirely Satisfied with your Determination. This you may be assured of. You mention the Vast Number of Militia Cases bro't to Court—which I am sorry there should be any occasion for. I hope some better Regulation will be devised for calling out the Militia, indeed I hear that six Battalions are to be under some nay to go on service upon an Emergency. Pecuniary Punishment will I fear be but of little Service to any but the Prosecutors—tho' I think at the same time it will be a matter of much dificulty to Adopt a mode effectual to call forth the Strength of the Country. Dr B's Case which you mention is undoubtly a Very singular one, such I beleive as is not to be found in any Law Book. But as I always considered him a Man of an extraordinary Turn, a correspondent Conduct might therefore be expected from him.

As to News I shall put that if I have any (which at present I do not know that I have) in Mr. Reeve's Letter.[5]

And now I do not know what I can add farther, But to advice you to take the best care of your Health in your Power, and attend to the use of those Prescriptions which Dr. Wolcott gave—free yourself as farr as you can from Anxious Care. Remember that he who does not suffer a sparrow to fall to the ground but under his providential appointment and who knows the Wants and Desires of all his Creatures will do that which upon the whole will be best for every one who humbly confides in his providential Goodness. Your own Experience has taught you that you have suffered many unnecessary Inquietudes. I am sure that mine has done so in Numberless Instances. Let us then commit all our Concerns to the Disposal of our Maker who I beleive will order that concerning us, which shall be for our greatest advantage.

This is my Sixth Letter, my last was by Col Dyer which you will receive in a Day or Two. I have Wrote Dr. Smith and Mr. Adams each a Letter, which I do not know whether either of them have recd.[6] I need not tell you how acceptable your Letters will be to me. Those by Brown will come safe. My tenderest Love for my Children and Family. My Ardent Wishes for your Happiness.[7]

Oliver Wolcott

RC (CtHi).
[1] John Pierce of Litchfield, Conn., who was appointed assistant paymaster general of the Continental Army in February 1776 and was promoted to deputy paymaster general in June 1779. Heitman, *Historical Register,* p. 328.
[2] For Jonathan Trumbull, Jr's "pretty offensive Letters" complaining about how he was addressed by Congress, see Henry Laurens to Jonathan Trumbull, Jr., March 12, 1778, note 1.
[3] "The troubler of Israel." 1 Chron. 2:7 and Joshua, chapter 7.
[4] See Wolcott to Andrew Adams, April 25, 1778, note 3.
[5] Wolcott's letter to Tapping Reeve has not been found.
[6] Wolcott's letters to Dr. Reuben Smith and Andrew Adams have not been found.
[7] For the continuation of this letter, see Wolcott to Laura Wolcott, April 19, 1778.

John Banister to St. George Tucker

My dear Sir,[1]   York Pensylvania 15th April 1778
'Tis true the Phaeton to whom you allude in yours of the 29th part, has like the first of that Name fallen never to rise again, but was not so effectually cooled by falling into an Element of an opposite kind.[2] The Mild Planet, whose Course the modern adventurer of that Name had wished to have guided, receded from him with so gentle a Radiance that the Impression remains, perhaps too strongly to be obliterated.

Cruel Necessity if it should be so! since no other Remedy is probable. But you who are much versed in the military and can maneuvre equal to Stueben himself, can you not as heretofore, by marching and counter marching find out the Causes of Movements in Friend as well as Foe? There are more things in Heaven and earth than even Phylosophy will teach.

But where a Planet looks with amicable benignity on a Saint, may he not invoke her to explain the Causes of certain *Influences,* why attraction ceases in some and goes on in other Instances? and then as a Phylosopher why the finest feelings and some of the tenderest Emotions of the Soul do not always awaken the same in others, by Sympathetic Power. Perhaps inimical Interpositions have been thrown in the way to spoil the Concord.

Perhaps poisoned falsehood propagated Good Name in Man or Woman, dear my Friend, is *the immediate Jewel of* their Souls &c &c.

This planetary object was great indeed! weighing down in substantial good even an Empire. Could not an obscure letter be *erected* upon a Consultation of the Stars, and the Result of certain Maneuvres? Such as, How the Responses of the Oracle might be; take Care 'tho of too much ambiguity. If you can go deeper into the obscure than this, being understood, magnus eris mihi Apollo; Apollo, you know, did deal in obscurity when he patronized Physic. To there? I come off decently with my Deity, I thought *otherwise* when I had got him obscured, do allow him to be fairly brought off now & I promise never to risque him again in so dangerous a Post. But no matter so I am hid from vulgar Eyes in these confidential Communications.

How delightful a change in Systems and prospects of alliances, in four or five daies! On it I congratulate my Friend; but in the System of politics how comes it that another Power is introduced on the Stage? Such Jarring interests cannot consist together. It is therefore time for the Power first engaged in the Campaign to come to an explanation upon so delicate a Subject, lest the Balance of Power should not be rightly adjusted, in settling definitive Treaties. France & Spain seem to be at a Stand as to an interfereance with America's Quarrel for her just Rights, indeed I never expected any assistance from them but What was immediately conducive to their Interest. Nor is it to be expected from any Nation, but if these Powers are equal with the advantages America may throw into the Scale, to G. Britain's navy, they would consult that darling Passion of Men & Nations immediately to begin hostilities. An argument was very well concluded upon the advantage attending such an accession of Force to America, by General Lee. A Gentleman in Company a few Minutes ago insisted that Hostilities carried on by France against G. Britain would not aid America. The Gen. replied that the Argument required no other Refutation than to suppose we stood a better chance against that Nation with 20 thousand than four thousand Men.

However at all Events the Americans are doomed to stand another Campaign unaided by any Force but that which should be derived from their own heroism & virtue. Wonder not at the use of the Words *Heroism & Virtue,* without them no Nation ever persevered in the defence of its Liberties. Did we certainly possess these republican virtues the Strength of the Continent might be called out, to the instant destruction of the Invaders of our Country.

Ill judging ambition & the Lust of Gain has induced our Fellow

Subjects beyond the Atlantic to rob us of Possessions which had they but been wise & contented we cultivated for their use.

I wish the same cursed Love of Wealth and Selfish attachment may not equally act upon us, & render our resistance too feeble to admit of Speedy decision. It is said the King of Prussia, considering the German Mercenaries as so many Beasts for Slaughter, has laid a duty upon every individual, a duty which amounts to a Prohibition of their passing 'thro his Territories. Inform Mr. Osborne if you take one sixth of my Share in the commercial Scheme formed when I last saw you. If so pay him £250 for Col. B Harrison of Brandon, & he will give you a Receipt for £100 as Stock and the £150 as you can tell him. I am in daily expectation of letters from you & should hope you will not fail to let me know everything interesting as well to the Saint & his connections as to his & your affect. Friend,   J. Banister

[*P.S.*] Mr. Adams arrived this day & our state is represented[3] which gives me great satisfaction 'tho I shall be obliged to give closer attendance on Congress. That is from morning untill Evening. The last Crisis is sent you of which I can say little except for the Zeal of the author.[4]

RC (ViW).
[1] St. George Tucker (1752–1827), Williamsburg jurist, had come to Virginia in 1772 from his native Bermuda to study law at the College of William and Mary. In 1775 Tucker was admitted to the Virginia bar, but during the war he turned temporarily to mercantile pursuits and was involved in several trading ventures to supply salt and military stores to the army. After serving with the Virginia militia from 1779 until the end of the war, Tucker returned to the practice of law and eventually received appointments to several judicial posts and a law professorship at William and Mary. See Mary H. Coleman, *St. George Tucker* (Richmond, Va.: Dietz Press, 1938), chaps. 2–6; and Charles T. Cullen, "St. George Tucker and Law in Virginia, 1772–1804" (Ph. D. diss., University of Virginia, 1971), passim.
[2] In Greek mythology the sun god Helios granted his mortal son Phaethon's wish to guide the sun chariot for a day, but Phaethon was unable to control the immortal horses and would have set the earth ablaze if Zeus had not killed him with a thunderbolt, causing his body to fall into the Eridanus River. *Oxford Classical Dictionary*. Banister's cryptic classical allusions in the first five paragraphs of this letter were probably stimulated by a letter from Tucker on the subject of his courtship of Frances Bland Randolph, the sister of Banister's late wife. The young widow Randolph was apparently more reserved than the impassioned Tucker wished, but his persistence was eventually rewarded and the couple were married in September 1778. See Coleman, *St. George Tucker*, pp. 38–42.
[3] Virginia had been unrepresented since March 24, when the Virginia General Assembly's December 1777 resolution temporarily authorizing two delegates to represent the state in Congress expired. When Thomas Adams joined Francis Lightfoot Lee and Banister on April 16, the state's quorum requirement of three delegates was satisfied. Banister's comments in his April 16 letter to Washington that Virginia was not represented, as well as the journal's entry on Adams' arrival in the middle of Congress' session on the 16th, indicates that this postscript was

added after Adams arrived. See *JCC*, 9:1064, 10:358; and Banister to Washington, April 16, 1778.

⁴ Thomas Paine's *Crisis. Number V. Addressed to General Sir William Howe* was published in Lancaster in March 1778 by John Dunlap. Evans, *Am. Bibliography*, no. 15951.

Henry Laurens to Caesar Rodney

Sir,   York Town 15th April 1778
    Congress are acquainted by general Smallwood that their late order to him to secure the persons of Thos White and Charles Gordon & others of your state, whose going at large he might deem dangerous & to send them to a place of security has given some disgust to your government and that an habeas corpus is granted to procure their discharge. I am directed to inform you of the grounds of the above order, the objects of which were the security of your state and the safety of the other states.¹

    Congress had received information, on which they rely, that a very great majority of the inhabitants of Kent & Sussex and a part of New Castle are disaffected & many of them avowed & bitter enemies to our independance, Congress esteem themselves bound in duty to watch over & to endeavour to preserve the genl welfare,² and have heretofore exercised similar powers in the other states without giving any offence.

    Resolved in Congress & sign'd by order, By, Sir, Your obedient & Most humble servant,   Henry Laurens, President

RC (NN). In the hand of Charles Thomson and signed by Laurens. This letter is based upon a committee draft that Congress amended and approved this day. See note 1 below.

¹ On April 10 Congress read a letter of the eighth from Gen. William Smallwood, in which he described the difficulties he had encountered in carrying out Congress' March 26 order to arrest certain "disaffected" persons in Delaware, and referred it to a committee consisting of Samuel Chase, William Henry Drayton, and Joseph Reed. Five days later the committee submitted to Congress a draft letter to President Rodney, in the hand of Chase, which vigorously defended the right of Congress to interfere in the internal affairs of states whose governments appeared to be too weak to cope with disaffection. The delegates eliminated Chase's forthright statement on Congress' right to intervene in state affairs but made only minor verbal changes in the rest of the draft. *JCC*, 10:328, 351–52. General Smallwood's April 8 letter to Laurens and enclosures are in PCC, item 161, 1:147–60. See also Laurens to Smallwood, March 26, 1778.

² At this point in the committee draft the delegates deleted a passage affirming Congress' right to intervene in the internal affairs of any state that became "disaffected" or was "unable to execute its own government." *JCC*, 10:352.

Henry Laurens to William Smallwood

Sir,   15th April 1778

Your dispatches of the 8th Inst. were presented to Congress early the 10th.

The Inclosed Act of the present date assures you that your conduct under the Order of the 26th March is highly approved & implies the subsisting force of that Order until it shall be carried into full effect.[1]

I take the liberty to conveying within this Inclosure a Letter formed by Congress & addressed to the President of Delaware which I request you to forward, & for your farther information I will add a Copy of that Letter.

I am with great regard & Esteem.

LB (DNA: PCC, item 13).
[1] See *JCC*, 10:352–53; and Laurens to Smallwood, March 26, 1778.

John Banister to George Washington

Sir   York 16th April 1778

In conscquence of a letter from Govenour Henry to the Virginia Delegates, directing the Payment of thirty thousand Dollars, as an additional Bounty granted the Soldiers who have reinlisted into the Virginia Regiments, I am to inform you that the money shall be paid in any manner you may please to direct.[1]

It was with the most painful Sensibility that I perused your last letter on the Subject of the present State of the Army,[2] and am equally concerned in reflecting that I do not see effectual Measures taken to ward off the impending Blow.

As to the Establishment, I am under no doubt of its being adopted & put upon a ground of Stability.[3] Its not having taken effect as yet has been owing to a thin Representation. Virginia the Leader in this great Business, for want of the constituent Number to form a Representation, remains a Cypher without Suffrage, at this Momentous Period.[4] Did I not fear to intrude upon your Hours of essential business I should sometimes write to you for my own information on military subjects; here being the greatest Ignorance in every occurence of that kind mixt with an inactivity that permits affairs of the greatest magnitude to lie dormant & give place to local Trifles. I have said with freedom in a few words what has often occured when I have been here. I wish I had the Capability to apply an instant Remedy for nothing procrastinated will do. However the military establishment will come out soon. God knows what other Regulations may take place. Virginia's drafted Men will come on soon & I beleive may amount to 1700 instead of 2000 voted, as it is highly probable more men desert of those compelled into Service than if they had entered voluntarily. Col. Harrison's artillery Regimt are on their march. Would volunteers, provided they can be had, be of Service to your operations? Certain it is they will not come out in such Numbers as some have conjectured, but I beleive a considerable Body, perhaps two Battalions may be induced to venture their Persons in this time of danger.

I am with the highest Regard & attachment, your Excellency's mo. obedt. & mo. hble Servant,   John Banister

[*P.S.*] The Order on the Paymaster if it is to go 'thro his hands will [*be*] 30 thousand & 80 dollars, the 80 being for a Soldier which I have desired Col. Meade to pay him.

RC (DLC)

¹ Banister also joined Francis Lightfoot Lee in a brief note to Washington this day informing him that the "Bounty Money of twenty Dollars to each Soldier . . . shall be paid on demand to your Order, in whatever manner you shall appoint, either by order on the Paymaster Genl. or in any other way more eligible." Written by Lee and signed by Lee and Banister, this letter is in the Foreman Lebold Collection, ICHi. Washington's April 23 reply is in Washington, *Writings* (Fitzpatrick), 11:302–3. See also Virginia Delegates to Washington, April 29, 1778.

² See Washington's April 10 letter to President Laurens, which was read in Congress on the 13th, in Washington, *Writings* (Fitzpatrick), 11:235–41.

³ For Washington's lengthy April 21 reply, in which he stressed the urgency of establishng half pay for officers after the war in order to curtail the alarming resignation rate among them, see ibid., 11:284–93.

⁴ This letter must have been written before Thomas Adams took his seat in Congress later this day. See *JCC,* 10:358.

Committee for Foreign Affairs
to William Bingham

Sir,   York Town 16th of Apr. 1778

Herewith you have a copy of what I did myself the pleasure of writing to you on the 2d of last month; since which we have received your favors of Janry. 14 & 26, Feb. 8 & 21st.¹

Your draught of 23554.9.9 in favor of the secret (now commercial) committee has been duely paid. The four first charges in your account current like many other sums on similar occasions here have been expended to no sort of profit to the continent; but I hope we have seen the last of such expences.

Your situation must have been very disagreable indeed in consequence of the failure of remittances from hence. Large quantities of Tobacco have been long stored; but our bayes & coasts are so infested by the enemies ships of war that it is impossible for us to conduct agreable to our earnest wishes of maintaining the best credit in our commercial concerns abroad. It is probable that a commercial board, not members of Congress, will very soon be established so that the whole time of the conductors may be spent in exertions for the public benefit in that branch of continental business.[2]

The want of intelligence from our Commissioners at Paris makes it improper for us to draw largely on them at present; therefore you must content yourself with the œconomical bounds of the power which is given to you by the within resolve of Congress of this day.[3] Be assured that all possible attempts will be made for your relief by remittances of our produce.

I find it impossible to convey to you any thing of a plan of opperations for this campaign. The enemy having the sea open to them must have the Lead in military matters; we must oppose or follow them just as they think fit to attempt an advance or to retire. It is hardly probable they will again attack New England without large reinforcements.

Our Correspondent at the Hague is very regular, but his intelligence is never in season to form the ground of any of our proceedings. We have packets from him regularly to the letter Y Decr. 16th[4] though our Commissioners have not been able to convey one safely since May last. Tis strange that they cannot succeed thro you. But, indeed you appear also to know but little of them.

Mr. Deane being wanted here, Mr. John Adams sailed the 17th of February to take his place at the Court of Versailles. It is probable you will hear of his arrival before this reaches you. It seems needless to desire you to give us early notice of that and other foreign intelligence. Your usual punctuality needed not the spur of the information which I have given you of our present great ignorance of the situation & transactions of the Gentlemen at Paris.

I am with much regard, sir, your Friend and humble Servant,

James Lovell, for the Comme for for. affrs.

RC (PHi). Written and signed by James Lovell.

[1] Extracts from Bingham's letters of December 28, 1777, January 26, February 8 and February 21, 1778, were printed in the *Pennsylvania Packet or the General Advertiser* (Lancaster), April 1 and 8, 1778. Bingham's January 14, letter has not been found, but his February 8 letter is in PCC, item 90, fols. 29–32, and his January 26 and February 21 letters are in the Continental Congress Miscellany, DLC.

[2] This reorganization plan was not executed. See Committee of Commerce to Robert Morris, February 21, 1778, note 6.

[3] Congress authorized Bingham to draw on the commissioners at Paris for "100,000 livres tournois." See *JCC*, 10:356.

[4] For Charles W. F. Dumas' correspondence with the committee, see Committee for Foreign Affairs to Dumas, May 14, 1778, note.

Committee for Foreign Affairs to the Commissioners at Paris

Gentlemen   York Town April 16th. 1778.

This, with my affectionate wishes for your prosperity, may serve to acquaint you that Congress has this day resolved "That William Bingham Esqr agent of the united states of America, now resident in Martinico, be authorized to draw bills of exchange at double usance on the Commissioners of the united states at Paris for any sums not exceeding in the whole one hundred thousand livres tournois, to enable him to discharge debts by him contracted on account of the said states, for which draughts he is to be accountable."[1]

Mr. Bingham will forward the American Gazettes with this billet of advice, and tell you why we have enabled him to draw upon you when we have stores of produce laid up in magazines for exportation. He will also inform you of our anxiety to know something of your proceedings & prospects, an uncommon fatality having attended your dispatches ever since the month of May last.

I am, with much esteem, Gentlemen, Your very humb. Servt.

James Lovell, for the Commttee for for. affairs

RC (PPAmP). Written and signed by James Lovell.
[1] See *JCC*, 10:356.

James Lovell to Abigail Adams

[April 16? 1778][1]

Having mentioned to you a packet from Mr. Bingham I will give you a sketch of the contents.[2] *Great* Britain is meanly covering her commerce in Dutch bottoms for by obtaining Burgher's Briefs at St Eustatius the British merchants become *Dutch subjects* and sail under the *protection* of the Flag of a people whom they affect to think their *inferiours.* The Grand Seignior is said to have given orders to seize all the Russian vessels, in the ports of his dominions, so that war was expected to be declared betwixt these two powers. It was expected also that the port of Lisbon would be shut after the 1st of January against all armed vessels belonging to his Britannic majesty. A powerful confederacy was forming against England, it had taken a consistence, and the basis of its political views was the Independency of America. In consequence of several conferences between the Commissioners of these United States and the French ministry couriers had been dispatched to Vienna, Lisbon & Madrid and as soon as they returned France would acknowledge the Independency of America.

"These accounts arrive thro' such a variety of Channels that the most incredulous can hardly doubt their authenticity. The letters that convey them are dated at Paris the 22d of Decr."

American vessels sailing from St. Pierre's are regularly conveyed by French frigates, and many French merchantmen take the benefit of that Protection, as they remember the conduct of Britain before she last declared war. Custom-house formalities and fees of Office were not demanded of Capt. Chew who was allowed to wear his pendant, altho a French Commodore was then in port. Our Flag is thus put on a respectable footing, *and the rising Constellation* which is now in place of the British Union is a Device greatly admired in our Colours.

When any more authentic particulars arrive "respecting the Doctor" *or a nearer friend,*[3] I shall aim to "mitigate your Anxiety" being your affectionate humble Servant   J L

RC (MHi).

[1] This is the last sheet of a letter of undetermined length that Lovell wrote to Abigail Adams in April 1778. This date has been assigned because the letter contains information Lovell received in a letter from William Bingham that he acknowledged in his April 16 reply to Bingham.

[2] Lovell obtained the following information from William Bingham's February 8 letter to the Committee for Foreign Affairs. See also Committee for Foreign Affairs to Bingham, this date, note 1.

[3] That is, Benjamin Franklin and John Adams.

Gouverneur Morris to Robert Morris

Dear Morris.[1]   York Town 16th April 1778.

I received two or three Letters from you while I was at Camp which I did not answer because I had nothing to do not as you conjecture because I was busy. This is no Paradox to a Man who is alternately immersed in Business and Pleasure or if you will Indolence. The distressed Appearance of your State I pity and have the Pleasure to inform you that we yesterday in Committee prepared a short Report to releive you of the Burthen of one of your Battallions.[2] As to the sixteen they will be reduced to nine and incorporated for that Purpose into each other. That the Enemy are taking Post at Billings Port is a lamentable Circumstance in one sense but it shews their Intention of acting on the defensive in the main which to the Inhabitants of this State is not an unpleasant Idea. We Rebels should always remember the Saying of Macbeth "Come what come may Time and the Hour run thro the roughest Day." In the Evening we shall rejoice. Adieu, Adieu, yours sincerely,   Gouvr Morris

RC (NjR). Addressed: "The honle Robert Morris Esqr. Chief Justice of the State of New Jersey, Trenton."

[1] Robert Morris (ca. 1745–1815), the illegitimate son of Gouverneur's uncle Robert Hunter Morris, was chief justice of New Jersey from 1777 to 1779. *DAB*.

[2] On April 15 Morris was added to a committee that had been appointed on the eighth to consider a representation from the New Jersey Council and Assembly that carefully explained why New Jersey was unable to raise its full quota of Continental troops and asked for reinforcements to help defend the state. At that time Congress had also referred to this committee a petition to Gov. William Livingston from a number of civil and military officers in Cumberland County, N.J., requesting assistance in their efforts to repel British raiders. Two days after Morris' appointment Congress approved a committee report drafted by him that recommended reducing New Jersey's Continental quota from four infantry regiments to three and referring to Washington her requests for reinforcements. See *JCC*, 10:322, 355–56, 361. The representation of the council and assembly, dated April 3, is in PCC, item 68, fols. 347–49; the Cumberland County petition, dated March 28, is in the Washington Papers, DLC. It is pertinent to note that Congress had originally set New Jersey's quota at four regiments on February 26 in response to a proposal by the Committee at Camp of which Morris was also a member. See *JCC*, 10:200; and Committee at Camp to Henry Laurens, February 5, 1778, enclosure no. 5.

Gouverneur Morris to Sarah Morris

Dear Madam,[1]   York Town in Pennsylvania 16th April 1778

I sit down to let you know I am in this World tho in a very remote Part of it. I have heard of you but not from you since I left Morrisania. Neither have I had the satisfaction to learn that of the many Letters I have written you have ever received one.[2] It would give me infinite Pleasure to hear of my Friends yourself in particular but since it is my Lott to know no more than the Burthen of General Report I must be contented. I receive great Pain from being informed that you are distressed on my Account. Be of good Chear I pray you. I have all that Happiness which flows from conscious Rectitude. I am blest with as great a Portion of Health as usually belongs to the share of Mankind. Content with what I have and what I am I look forward serenely to the Course of Events confident that supreme Wisdom & Justice will provide for the Happiness of his Creatures. It gives me Pain that I am seperated from those I love but comparing this with what thousands suffer I dare not repine. Let me earnestly recommend to you so much of either Religion or Philosophy as to bear inevitable Evils with Resignation. I would that it were in my Power to solace and comfort your declining Age. The Duty I owe to a tender Parent demands this of me but a higher Duty hath bound me to the Service of my Fellow Creatures. The natural Indolence of my Disposition hath unfitted me for the Paths of Ambition and the early Possession of Power taught me how little it deserves to be prized. Whenever the present Storm subsides I shall rush with Eagerness into the Bosom of private Life but while it continues and while my Country calls for the Exertion of that little Share of Abilities which it hath pleased God to bestow on me I hold it my indispensible Duty to give myself to her. I know that for such Sentiments I am called a Rebel and that such Sentiments are not fashionable among the Folks you see. It is possible (tho I hope not) that your maternal Tenderness may lead you to wish that I would resign these Sentiments. But that is impossible and therefore for the present I cannot see you. Let me however intreat that you be not concerned on my Account. I shall again see you. Perhaps the Time is not far off. I am much distressed for Wilkins.[3] I sincerely love and respect him and I fear that we are seperated for a very long Season. Pray remember me to him most affectionately and to my sister. She too has been much wounded. The Loss of her Infant must have distressed her greatly but perhaps her own Experience may have led her to prize Life at its just Value and if so it is a Blessing she may not think so estimable as to wish it for her Child. Remember me most tenderly to all her little Infants to Isaac particularly who I am told hath not forgotten me poor Child. I hope it may be in my Power to return his Attention by the Protection of a Parent. God forbid he should need it or any of them. Remember me to Mrs. Ashfield[4] and her Children for I think she hath more than one. I wish her Husband had acted more consistently, but enough of this. And now my Dear Madam let me again intreat you to make yourself happy. Discard the gloomy Ideas which are too apt to croud into the Mind in your Situation and Time of Life. There is enough of Sorrow in this World without looking into Futurity for it. Hope the best. If it happens, well; if not, it is then Time enough to be afflicted and at any Rate the intermediate Space is well filled.

Adieu. Yours most affectionately,   Gouvr Morris

RC (NNC).
[1] Sarah Morris (d. 1786), Gouverneur's mother, was a loyalist whose pro-British sympathies made Morris himself an object of suspicion in the eyes of some of his contemporaries. Max M. Mintz, *Gouverneur Morris and the American Revolution* (Norman: University of Oklahoma Press, 1970), pp. 126–29, 172.
[2] This is the only letter Morris wrote to his mother during his term of service in Congress that has been found.
[3] Isaac Wilkins, the husband of Morris' sister Isabella, was an Anglican minister who remained loyal to Britain and was living in exile in England. Ibid., pp. 37, 47.
[4] Morris' sister Catherine was also a loyalist living in England with her husband Vincent Pearse Ashfield. Ibid., pp. 39, 47.

Jonathan Bayard Smith to Thomas Wharton

Sir,   York Town April 16 1778.
    I had the honor of receiving yours of   .[1] In consequence of your desire expressed, that a warrant for the remaining 30,000 dollars

should be passed in your favor on the Loan Office of this state, I have procured a warrant for 20,000 dollars, which is inclosed.[2] That for 30,000 on the Treasurer yet lies here, & may perhaps be paid in 10 days or a fortnight; but it depends on circumstances which cannot be ascertained. These three warrants make 100,000 dollars *for the purchase of horses,* as the warrant specifies.

Your Excellency will excuse my hinting the necessity of forwarding the accounts of the prisoners taken from the enemy. By a resolution of Congress of February   last those accounts were to be rendered before 15 April, or the State omitting were to suffer any losses consequent on the event.[3]

I beleive orders will issue to suspend any further purchases of flour. Large quantities are procured we are told in Maryland. If so a return of the proceedings of our Commissioners & their accounts will be called for.

With very great Respect, I have the honor to be, Your Excellencys most ob. hle St.   Jona. B Smith

[*P.S.*] Having written the above abroad I have it not in my power to fill up one or two blanks.

RC (PHC).
    [1] President Wharton's April 9 letter to Smith is in the Jonathan Bayard Smith Papers, DLC.
    [2] For this enclosure, see *Pa. Council Minutes,* 11:466.
    [3] For this February 26 resolution, see *JCC,* 10:198. Wharton's April 17 response to Smith is in *Pa. Archives,* 1st ser. 6:427.

Henry Laurens' Notes on Half Pay

[April 17–21, 1778]

Congress, Friday 17th April 1778.

Journal—"Congress resumed the consideration of the Report from the Committee of the whole & the first paragraph being read, it was moved to Resolve &c."[1] (called for as Order of day).

At reading the Journal the 18th remarked on this Entry & repeated what he had said when the Entry was made.

That it was incomplete. This Report from the Committee of the whole having been read for information, the first Paragraph read for debate had become a subject of debate, an amendment reduced to writing by Mr. Duer seconded delivered at the Table, Read by the President applied & explained & the question so far put as "You Gentlemen who agree to this amendment will signify it by saying Aye."

Then & not before, "It was moved to Resolve" &c & Mr Duer withdrew the proposed amendment.[2]

Tuesday the 21st the above Entry on the Journal being called for
by a Member & Read—

The President again intimated to the House the imperfection of
the Entry—

"Gentlemen, I must again observe to you this Entry on the Journal
will not convey to the Reader Ideas competent to the fact—the first
Paragraph had been read for debate, an amendment had been offered,
read & a question upon it half put."

☞ The Secretary persists in keeping the Journal thus unfairly
misrepresenting the proceedings of the House.

After the Yeas & Nays—Tuesday 21st April.

Copy Journal
Motion was made to strike out "an establishment" & insert, "It is
expedient a Provision." Resolved in the affirmative.[3]

Then the Resolve on Friday 17th well Read as follows.

First It is expedient a Provision, [instead of—"that an establishment"][4] of half Pay be made for the Military officers commissioned by
Congress who now are or hereafter may be in the service of these
States & shall continue therein during the War & who shall not be
annexed to any Corps of established Troops or hold any office of
Profit under the United States or any of them & that such [establish-
ment] Provision take place after the conclusion of the present War."

This Motion, which in itself had undergone a Question upon
Order being thus taken under Consideration & in part amended, a
Motion was made for dividing the Question which caused some debate but the manner in which the division was desired declared in
writing as follows.

"The House was Moved that the Question be divided & that the
sense of the House be taken, whether any provision shall be made for
Officers &c."

The President rose & said his Duty Constrained him to speak to
the House—"that this Motion contained no division of the Question
in debate but was a complete new motion which he could not put
without express Command."

Mr. Huntington & other members objected in like manner—debates
& some disorder ensued—the President admonished the House against
disorder & intemperate reflections.

A majority of probably two to one insisted upon having the Question put as it had been reduced to writing. The President replied he
could not apply the words so reduced to writing to any part of the
motion & give it the appearance of a division, except by taking up

some & suppressing or skipping over other words in the Motion. The Member who had reduced the said division or new motion to writing, expressed great surprize & added it is the easiest thing in the World. The President requested his assistance, & delivered the Motion to that Member Mr. Chase who read it as it is reduced to writing & averred it to be a division of the Question. The President resumed the Papers & again requested the Order of the House. Some of those Members who had complained of the division & were against admitting the motion to be a division, exclaimed they were borne down & all said, any how, any how, we see the Gentlemen will have it in their own way—put the Question.

The President then read the Motion again & put the Question.

"You Gentlemen who agree that a Provision shall be made for the [Military] Officers Commissioned by Congress &c. [☞ The words of half pay suppressed & the word Military introduced, by order] when you are called upon will signify it by saying Aye—Contra, when called upon will say No. The Yeas & Nays were called & appear on the Journal.[5]

Instantly after calling the Members, Mr. Chase presented the following motion read by himself & by the President.

"The Question moved & put that such Provision for the Officers be one half of their present Pay."

But the House adjourned without debate or putting the Question.[6]

It is asserted by Gentlemen that Officers & some of high Rank in the Army have declared ("I have heard one & of high Rank too") that they were not for Peace.

They desired War for a support, as they had no fortunes to live upon.

Query. Is it necessary to make further Provision for Men who declare that what they already enjoy is a desirable subsistence, or for Men who at the expence of the Blood & Treasure of their Country wish to enjoy their present subsistence?

Query. Is there no danger that Men of this disposition will, when once an half Pay establishment is fixed do everything, & submit to any terms for compassing Peace even submitting to accept another half Pay for this purpose from the Enemy? Thus Gentlemen in their reasonings upon different subjects in which the Officers of this Army are introduced, destroy their own arguments used in support of a Peace establishment.

It is unjust—
the Motives & considerations not applicable
the demand unseasonable & a compliance dangerous.
the Remedy proposed grievous to the People & inadequate to[7]

Unjust, because it is inconsistent with the original compact— Officers were not compelled but eagerly solicited Commissions knowing the terms of service—because every argument, of loss of Estate, neglect of family—forfieture of domestic happiness—the exorbitancy of prices for every specie of goods for the necessary support or Comfort of Life is applicable to thousands of our fellow Citizens with greater force & in some degree to every Inhabitant of the United States engaged in the Compact with this great difference in favor of Officers that they are Provided with Rations or daily food, with Servants, with Horses at the Public expence & with Clothing from[8]

MS (ScHi). In the hand of Henry Laurens. This text has been produced by conflating two physically discrete but organically related manuscripts among Laurens' papers. The first is seven pages in length and consists of three distinct sections: a brief account of congressional action on half pay between April 17 and 21 (pp. 1–2); a more extended description of Congress' treatment of this issue on April 21 (pp. 3–6); and Laurens' own reflections on the subject of half pay (p. 7). The second manuscript is two pages long and contains further observations by Laurens on half pay that are somewhat similar to those in his letter to William Livingston of April 19, 1778. These four sections of the composite MS have been set off from each other in the printed text by the use of extra space.

[1] For the subject of this "Report," which proposed half pay for commissioned officers who remained in service at the end of the war, see Francis Lewis to the New York Convention, March 30, 1778, note 3.

[2] William Duer's amendment was undoubtedly the motion for "an establishment of half pay" that is entered in the journals under the date April 17. *JCC*, 10:362–63. Since the original manuscript journals for the period March 19–May 1, 1778, have disappeared, the printed journals do not reflect the alterations Laurens describes in this section of his notes.

[3] By this action Congress amended the motion on half pay first offered by William Duer on April 17. *JCC*, 10:362–63, 372–73.

[4] All square brackets in this printed text appear in the MS; they are not editorial insertions.

[5] See *JCC*, 10:373–74.

[6] Chase offered his motion again on April 25 and its substance was incorporated into the half-pay plan Congress finally approved on May 15. *JCC*, 10:392, 11:502. See also *JCC*, 10:393n.1.

[7] Sentence incomplete. During a discussion of half pay in his April 19 letter to William Livingston, Laurens noted that "the Remedy proposed is not adequate to Relief."

[8] Remainder of MS missing.

Henry Laurens to James Duane

Dear sir,　　　　　　　　　　　　　　York Town 17th April 1778

I troubled you with a Letter the 7th Inst. by Messenger Green to which I beg leave to refer.

Mr. Morris continuing to be absent from York Town I yesterday paid into the hands of his Agent Mr John Browne Three hundred Dollars on Account of Mr. John Holt for whose information I now transmit through you a Copy of the Receipt which I directed to be taken for that Sum, in which I was governed by the Contents of Mr Holt's Letter, & having no further use for the Letter I return it to you within the present Inclosure.[1]

We are now in the Wane of April, you know what is undone, done & doing for securing the important passes of Hudson's, on the possession of which our connexion with the Eastern States so intimately depends. Congress have ordered General Gates to repair immediately to Fish Kill & there to Command the Troops at that Post & the whole Northern department, & have empowered him to call out Militia from N.H., M.B., C. & N.Y., as well as from Rhode Island if the Enemy should evacuate that State.[2]

Here, we are still encamped at Valley forge, reinforcements arrive very gradually. General Lee's opinion is the Enemy may March when they please to Lancaster. I am strongly inclined to add "& be cut off." That Gentleman is at present on parol; Congress had restricted the Commander in Chief to an article, as a Preliminary upon which the progress toward establishment of a general Cartel should depend, that Majr. General Lee should be exchanged for Majr General Prescot, but at the General's special request this article is varied & now appears an Instruction.[3] General Lee is exceedingly anxious to be exchanged, intimates that General Howe had assured him he should be, & was equally apprehensive of ill effects following a dogmatic preliminary. General Howe, he was persuaded, would instantly withdraw his Commissioners. I am ignorant of the present state of the business of Exchange, the Commissioners had met at Newton, but there has happened some untoward explanations between the Commander in Chief & York Town & I have had no return to a late Letter signed by Order.[4]

General Lee assures me the British Officers of his acquaintance generally wish for accomodation & that not a few of them approve of our opposition. My pleasure was heightned by another assurance that our suspension of the Convention of Saratoga is censured by none & applauded by many, excepting the Prolixity of our reasonings upon that occasion. He explodes the Idea of a Change in the Command at Philadelphia.

We are now busily engaged on the Report for an half pay establishment. Long & warm debates for many a day had led us to the threshold of the Report from the Committee of the Whole. We had Entered fairly the Door, by reading the whole for information—the first Clause for debate & had received an amendment which was read by the Chair & the question half put, when we were turned out by a New Motion—debates arose upon the point of order, referring to that Motion,[5] an agreement entered upon the journal, which I shall inclose for your information,[6] was also called for & insisted upon in aid of the general reasonings for order, against receiving the new motion—after long & fervorous arguments the Question was put. You Gentlemen who admit this Motion to be in order will signifie it by saying Aye &c. How say you Sir? I intreat your answer.

That you may fully understand this circumstance I should not omit, that the proceedings of the House in debating the Confederation & other Questions were cited as precedents, & replied to, by referring to the special agreement in the present Case & likewise by alledging that the variations which were quoted had been made by "general Consent." I speak again to a Member of Congress. I have stated the Case with brevity & candor.[7]

RC (NHi).
[1] See also Laurens to Duane, April 7, 1778, note 1.
[2] Congress resolved on April 15 to order Gen. Horatio Gates to return to active command of the northern department and gave Francis Dana, William Duer, and Gouverneur Morris the task of drawing up instructions for him. Morris drew up the instructions, and in order to prevent further ill will between Washington and Gates, he placed special emphasis in the document on the need for close cooperation between Gates and the commander in chief. The instructions themselves were written in the form of a presidential letter, which Congress approved and Laurens signed on April 20. The RC of Laurens' April 20 letter to Gates, which is in the Gates Papers, NHi, is identical to the text of Morris' draft instructions in JCC, 10:368–69. See also JCC, 10:354–55; and Gouverneur Morris to Washington, April 18, 1778.
[3] See JCC, 10:295; and Laurens' first April 14, 1778, letter to Washington.
[4] See Laurens' letter cited in the preceding note.
[5] See also Laurens' Notes on Half Pay, April 17–21, 1778.
[6] Laurens sent Duane the following manuscript, consisting of the text of an April 1 agreement by Congress on the issue of half pay followed by two sentences of commentary by Laurens:
"In Congress 1st April 1778
"Congress took into consideration the Report of the Commee of the whole respecting an establishment or allowance to Officers after the War. After debates it was agreed that amendments be moved & made in the Report but after the amendments are made & the Report is gone through, the whole Report shall be open to debate whether it shall be adopted by Congress or be sent to the States and their opinion taken previous to the final determination of Congress."
"If the New Motion was out of order a reference to the above agreement will make the violence of out voting appear to have been more violent.
"This to a Member of Congress." Duane Papers, NHi. See also JCC, 10: 300–301.
[7] For the continuation of this letter, see Laurens to Duane, April 20, 1778.

Henry Laurens to the Marquis de Lafayette

Dear Sir,   17th April 1778.

I beg leave to refer Your Excellency to my last dated 27th March & 8th Inst. dispatched by your Albany Messenger & which will probably have come round to Your Excellency's hands by the time this will have the honor of reaching them. The Committee on Your Excellency's public Letter of the 20th Ulto. have not yet Reported, hence it appears to have been right that I detained the Messenger no longer.[1]

Two days ago I had the honor of receiving by favor of Doctor Treat Your Excellency's Letter of the 28th March[2] together with the 6 sets of Bills of Exchange intended for the Canada Irruption, these I laid before Congress & then called them.

Congress have Ordered General Gates to proceed to Fish Kill & take upon him the Command of the whole Northern department.

Monsr. Capitaine's Commission will be made out & properly expressed respecting Rank,[3] this Morning he talks of going to Camp to Morrow & is afterward to be employed on a Survey of Susquehanna.

I have the honour to be with the highest Esteem & Regard

[P.S.] Monsr. Segon is of the Count Pulaski's Corps a Captain,[4] he is now on the Recruiting service, when I know where to reach him I will forward your Excellency's Letter to him.

LB (ScHi).
[1] See Laurens to Lafayette, March 27, 1778, note 3.
[2] This letter is in Lafayette, *Papers* (Idzerda), 1:384.
[3] See *JCC*, 10:356.
[4] Louis-Gaëtan de Sigounié, who had been recommended for employment in Pulaski's corps by Lafayette in an April 10 letter to Laurens. Lafayette, *Papers* (Idzerda), 2:23–24.

Henry Laurens to George Washington

Sir,   York Town, 17th April 1778

I had the honor of addressing Your Excellency the 14th by Barry.

I am now to present & refer Your Excellency to two Acts of Congress which will accompany this.

1. of the 14th for empowering the Commissary of Purchases to appoint & remove subordinate Officers & for divers establishments & regulations in that department.[1]

2. of the 15th for appointing the Honorable Major General Gates to the Command of the whole Northern department of the Army & for maintaining the Possession of Hudson's River.[2]

I have the honor to be, With the highest Esteem & Respect, Sir, Your Excellency's Most obedient & Most humble servant,

Henry Laurens, President of Congress.

RC (DLC).
[1] See *JCC*, 10:344–48.
[2] See *JCC*, 10:354–55.

Samuel Chase to Unknown

Dear Sir.   York Town. 18th April, 1778.

I have Nothing to communicate worthy of your Notice. We have no Letters from our Commissioners at Paris since the 26 of last May— two Packets were taken, that we know of, one was gutted. Two Captains, one named Fritz, the other named Compstock who give the account inclosed.[1] Treachery & Villainy are not confined to any Country, but I am concerned that Maryland should produce so black a Traitor.

The enclosed Paper contains the Subject of my last Letter[2] in a more clear and distinct Manner. I would have it communicated to the assembly, if sitting. Adieu. Yours faithfully,   Saml. Chase

RC (PHi).

[1] A copy, in Chase's hand, of the depositions of Henry Fritz and William Comstock concerning the treason of Capt. Joseph Hynson of Maryland, which is in the Red Books, 10:55, MdAA. Fritz and Comstock had learned from Jonathan Williams at Nantes, who had received the information from Silas Deane, that Hynson "had turned Traytor & gone to England with Dispatches." For the theft of these dispatches, see Committee Examination of John Folger, January 12, 1778.

[2] Not found.

Henry Laurens to Thomas Dyer

Sir   18th April 1778

Your favour of the 30th March reached me the 11th Inst. & was immediately presented to Congress. The House have in compliance with your request accepted your resignation.[1] I sincerely wish the respite from fatigues which you may now enjoy, may be a means of reinstating you in sound health & enable you again, if it shall be necessary, to appear among the defenders of the Liberties of your Country. I am yours &ca.

LB (DNA: PCC, item 13). Addressed: "Colonel Ths. Dyer, Lebanon."

[1] On April 11 Congress had approved Col. Thomas Dyer's request to resign his commission in the Continental Army "on account of his indisposition." JCC, 10:337. The March 30 letter of Colonel Dyer, the son of Connecticut delegate Eliphalet Dyer, is in PCC, item 78, 7:175.

Henry Laurens to William Livingston

Sir,   18th April 1778

Within the present Inclosure Your Excellency will receive three Acts of Congress.

1. of the 16th March for obtaining from the several States information of their proceedings on the Recommendations of Congress.

2. of the 19th March recommending to the several States to raise their respective quota of Men & March them forward with all possible expedition & to provide complete Sets of accoutrements &ca.

If the delay of these had been the effect of neglect in my Sphere I should trouble your Excellency with a request to pardon me.

3d. of the 17th Inst. founded on a Report from a Committee to whose consideration a Representation from the State of New Jersey had been referred.

A Copy of this last mentioned Act together with Copies of the Representation & of a Petition from several Officers to your Excellency I shall transmit by this bearer to His Excellency General Washington.[1]

Your Excellency's several favors of the 17th March & 9th Inst. came duly to hand & have been presented to Congress, I have received no particular commands respecting them.[2]

I have the honour to be &ca.

LB (DNA: PCC, item 13).

[1] For further information on the April 17 committee report and the accompanying paper referred to here by Laurens, see Gouverneur Morris to Robert Morris, April 16, 1778, note 2.

[2] In his March 17 letter to Laurens, which was read in Congress on the 26th and referred to the Board of Treasury, Livingston stated that he had appointed Thomas Stockton "issuing commissary" at Princeton and no longer needed a warrant for $5,000 from Congress to help him raise recruits for and apprehend deserters from the Continental Army because money was now available from Joseph Borden, New Jersey's loan office commissioner. See PCC, item 68, fols. 343–46. For further information on the warrant in question, see Laurens to Livingston, March 1, 1778, note 2. Laurens neglected to inform Livingston that Congress had approved Stockton's appointment on March 26. *JCC*, 10:284–85. In his April 9 letter, on the other hand, Livingston simply thanked Congress for a March 11 resolve commending him for having removed certain supernumerary Continental officers in New Jersey. See PCC, item 68, fol. 351; and Laurens to Livingston, March 10, 1778, note 1.

Henry Laurens to John Stark

Sir   18th April [1778]

Within this Inclosure you will receive an Act of Congress of yesterday's date Resolving that you be imployed to act under the Command of General Gates who is ordered to take upon him the Command of the whole Northern department.

This casual opportunity affords me the particular pleasure of assuring you Sir, of my great respect for your Character, a Character deservedly famed for equal Zeal & intrepid bravery in defence of the

Rights & Liberties of our Country, this I might upon the best foundation assure you is the sense of all your fellow Citizens but at present I mean only to signify, & to request you will be pleased to accept, the sentiments of Sir yours &ca

LB (DNA: PCC, item 13). Addressed: "Brigadier General Stark, Bennington."

Henry Laurens to George Washington

Sir,   York Town 18th April 1778.
I beg leave to refer Your Excellency to my Letter of yesterday by McKlosky.
This will cover Copy of a Petition by several Officers Civil & Military of New Jersey to His Excellency the Governor of that State. Also Copy of a Representation by the Legislative Council & General Assembly of the same State to Congress; together with an Act of Congress of the 17th Inst. Resolved upon the Report of a Committee to whose consideration the papers abovementioned had been referred.[1]
I have the honor to be, With the highest Esteem & Respect, Sir, Your Excellency's Most Obedient & most humble servant,
              Henry Laurens, President of Congress.

P.S. Your Excellency will also find inclosed an Act of Congress of this day for forming a Plan for the general operations of the Campaign.

RC (DLC).
[1] For further information on this issue, see Gouverneur Morris to Robert Morris, April 16, 1778, note 2.

James Lovell to Samuel Adams

My dear sir   Apr. 18th. 1778.
Your favors of Feb. 29 & Mar 31st came to hand this afternoon.[1] Col. Campbel is actually gone into Philadelphia, and I suppose my old fellow sufferer is before this time among his friends.[2] There has been a variety of managemts. in the affair that may tend to your amusement at some future leisure moment. Howe most evidently had rather have to do with any body rather than Congress; there being this difference that he cannot induce us to believe him any thing better than a deceitful rogue, while some others confide altogether in his *honor* and often put themselves into situations to have their "feelings hurt" by our decisive Resolves which are therefore wished

to "sleep."[3] I may venture to tell you, at so great a distance as Boston is from *this* place, that Genl. Heath has acquitted himself greatly to his own honor as an executive officer upon the Resolves of Congress. Surely there is no odious comparison in what I assert.

Since the date of your last, you must have seen my letter to Mr. Appleton respecting Mr. Amory[4] and I think you must have judged the Spirit of it not to be against the proceedings of the Genl. Assembly.

We are now come to the Season when certain birds of passage return who seldom appear in our flock during winter. I will not enlarge upon the *advantages* of the regulation of this year for our vote in Congress. Esqr. C——[5] the patron of yeas & nays will give you after opportunity of examining that matter. 4 & 4 and 1 divided lost a question against the voice of D & myself, Brother G being very ill[6]—a question of the highest importance, so that you may expect soon an half pay System upon which the existence of the army this campaign is said, "religiously" at one time, & "devoutly" at another to depend.[7] It is said to be Œconomy, Justice & Necessity. The last really is not altogether fictitious, the second does not exist, and the first is quite problematical. Distinctions ought however to be made between an half pay establishment and a *military* establishment, the latter being a curse, the former a nuisance. Can less than 9 states *appropriate money* in the manner hinted above? Can it be called a contingent expence of this war? I am Clearly of opinion, not. I wish all the *old Geese* were here, as Mr Childs called our worthy select men on a certain time.

Genl. Gates is to go immediately to the north river having the command of the posts there & the superintendance of the whole northern department. I tell *you* he is to assist at a council of War in his way, to determine upon the plan of operations for the campaign.[8]

Genl. W—— tells us Massachusetts is most allarmingly deficient in her quota; pray exert yourselves. Our cause is greatly at hazard.

I have mentioned to Docr. Cooper all the scraps of foreign news which have lately reached.[9]

I hope Lot *Gray* (Hall) has paid you cash. My poor wife needs no addition to her present trouble.

The public letter and instructions came to hand with your favors,[10] and will be duely respected.

Apr. 19th. Sunday M[ornin]g. Mr. Geary is something recovered this morning; he will take a ride this delightful day, and he must certainly be relieved from Congress shortly; but I warn you of great difficulties as to Lodging, and I advise you to be composed upon the thought of not being accommodated here. Mrs. C—— will move to Philada. or to some other part. I am sorry to find the regulating law passed, you will be desired to suspend the execution till Congress know what the Southern states will do. We owe this to the eastern states who have sacrificed their Judgements to our Recommendations when others have not. I think such laws may not be without some good effect so suspended.[11]

We have got Col. Wadsworth at the Head of the commisariate *unfettered* strictly so;[12] Had the same Steps as now been taken with Trumbull a year ago amazing sums would have been saved and Howe have been reduced to the greatest Extremity last fall if we may depend upon the causes assigned for past inactivity. Let us look forward with hope.

Mr. John Purveyance has told me within two days that he has got my Almanac from a Soldier at Mount Holly who found my stripped pocket Book on a wharf below Bondford's Coffee House the morning after I ⟨was robbed⟩ lost it.[13] I now give up all thought of finding my money, as the manner in which the book was found proves I had been robbed. I can take my oath as to the 260 Dollars lost in it; and wish for your advice about applying for it as an inevitable expence. I do not see how I can possibly make it up to my family. It costs me as much here to patch my old Cloaths as would have given me and two of my Children a Suit of new not long ago. I wish you could find a number of men willing to come on with you to this political scene of drudgery, so that I may try some other for awhile. I do not see how I can quit unless 4 come up for I should not be easy to have our vote at the risque it has been for near 4 months. N Hampshire & Delaware are not represented R Is 1, Mas 3, Con 2, N Y 2, N J 1, Pen 2, Mary [3], Virg 3, N C 2, S C 3, G 1. Col. R.H.L.[14] is on his way but stopped by a dying brother. Col. F[15] is going home Ld. Lt. of a County. I hope we shall go on very briskly with the Journals as Mr. Dunlap has put up a press here. He is a very active man. I think the States have been very patient so far; There will be a dreadful mix & medly of Resolves & Treasury minutiæ. I find the supervisal of the press a poor interlude to the business in Congress. It is too much like leaving *work* to saw wood, but by no means so salutary.

I cannot refrain from telling you a little Camp Doctrine in the face of our Resolve vizt. that *citizens* of Philada. and any others who *take up arms* with the Enemy in their progress thro the Continent, *are changeable* as prisoners of war. I hope no State will give up its treason acts even to Congress much less to one of its officers.[16] Affectionately your humble Servant.   J L

RC (NN).
    [1] Although Adams' February 29 letter to Lovell has not been found, a draft of what was probably his March 31 letter is in the Adams Papers, NN, and Adams, *Writings* (Cushing), 4:16–19. This draft is dated March 27, but since it discusses some of the points Lovell addressed himself to in this letter and since Adams noted

on it that he sent the RC to Lovell by "Express April 2 1778," it is likely that the RC bore a later date than the draft.

[2] Lt. Col. Archibald Campbell was finally exchanged on May 6 for Ethan Allen, who had been a "fellow sufferer" when Lovell was a prisoner at Halifax in 1775–76. See Committee at Camp Minutes of Proceedings, February 2–7, 1778, note 4.

[3] Lovell is referring to Washington's April 4 letter to President Laurens, in which he criticized Congress' efforts to regulate his negotiations with General Howe for an exchange of prisoners and suggested that one of Congress' resolves be "suffered to sleep." See Washington, *Writings* (Fitzpatrick), 11:216–19.

[4] Not found, but see Lovell to Adams, March 10, 1778, note 2.

[5] Undoubtedly a reference to Samuel Chase, the first delegate formally to propose that Congress record roll call votes in the journals. See Thomas Burke's Notes of Debate, February 27, 1777.

As recently as April 16, a dispute had arisen in Congress over the question of whether a member could decline to answer during a call for yeas and nays, at which time Congress resolved "that when a member is called upon to answer ay or no, he may not of right withhold his voice." *JCC*, 10:359.

[6] Lovell was referring to fellow Massachusetts delegates Francis Dana and Elbridge Gerry.

[7] Lovell must be referring to Congress' April 17 vote on a point of order relating to half pay. *JCC*, 10:362–63. Although this point of order was carried by a vote of five states to four with one divided, it is the only vote on half pay before April 18 in which Lovell and Dana were the only Massachusetts delegates voting in the negative.

[8] Congress this day gave "leave" to Generals Gates and Mifflin to attend a council of war at Washington's headquarters to form a "plan for the general operations of the campaign." *JCC*, 10:364, 368–69.

[9] Lovell's letter to Samuel Cooper has not been found.

[10] Undoubtedly a reference to the General Court's instructions to the delegates to ratify the Articles of Confederation. See Lovell to Adams, March 10, 1778, note 1.

[11] On April 8 the committee on the New England convention recommended that certain proceedings of the convention be recommended to the southern states for consideration and that in the meantime the northern states suspend their plans for regulating prices. The report was considered on May 7, but it was not until June 4 that Congress, in a separate action, recommended that state laws regulating prices be suspended or repealed. *JCC*, 10:322–24, 11:472, 569–70.

[12] For Jeremiah Wadsworth's appointment as commissary general of purchases on April 9, see *JCC*, 10:327–28.

[13] For information on Lovell's lost pocketbook, see Lovell to Robert Treat Paine, September 24, 1777.

[14] Richard Henry Lee.

[15] Apparently Francis Lightfoot Lee, who did not, however, leave Congress to return home until the end of May.

[16] Lovell is referring to General Washington's continuing efforts in the face of congressional opposition to gain recognition of the principle that Americans who enlisted in the British armed forces should be considered prisoners of war if captured rather than turned over to the states to be tried for treason. See Henry Laurens to Washington, April 8 and 14, 1778.

Thomas McKean to Thomas Rodney

Lancaster, April the 18th 1778. Asks Rodney to postpone a Delaware admiralty court hearing on prize goods from the schooner *Alert* seized by the privateer *Christiana,* whose owners McKean was representing, because his duties as Pennsylvania Supreme Court justice would prevent his attendance. "With pleasure would I attend on that day, but that I am obliged to hold a court of Oyer and Terminer &c for York court at York on the 21st where I shall be detained the whole week, and the week following I must hold the like court at Carlisle for the county of Cumberland . . . . I should have it in my power to attend, and (God willing) will attend the trial of this cause at any time after the twelfth of May, that will be most convenient and most agreeable to the Gentlemen on the other side."

RC (PHi).
  [1] On April 20, while still at Lancaster, McKean also wrote a personal letter to his wife, Sarah, reporting his imminent return to York. "I am just setting out for York-Town, and am well, tho' I sat up all Saturday night on a trial." McKean Papers, PHi.

Gouverneur Morris to George Washington

Dear Sir,   York Town 18th April 1778[1]
   I expected before this to have written to you "Provision is made for the American Officers" but that Thief of Time Procrastination hath kept it off from Time to Time. The Question is now an Order of the Day and as such takes Place of every other Business. When it will be determined I know not but this I know that it shall be finished one way or the other before any Thing else Let what will happen.[2] I am confident it will go right if something very extraordinary does not happen. In the Interim nothing is done. I feel as severely on this Occasion as you can do but it is impossible to make Men of Business out of ———. All will yet go well. We have determined to send Gates to Hudson's River where he is to command very largely. But he is to receive Instructions which shall be proper.[3] You are directed to call a Council of *Major* Generals in which the Chief Engineer is *officially* to be a Member and to which by a Subsequent Resolution Genls. Gates & Mifflin were *ordered* to repair.[4] As these Gentlemen ought not to receive Orders *immediately* from Congress they are as you will see permitted to leave the Board of War upon *your* Order. This *Amendment* was for that Reason acquiesced in *nem con.* Colo. Harrison will I believe be again appointed a Member of the Board

of War.[5] This I mention by the bye. I add my Wish that your Business and his Inclinations may be so ordered as to accept of it. For this I have many Reasons. Every Man of Business knows that Words are of great Weight and we receive Reports from the Board of War every Day. I need say no more except that it is not always possible to weigh Sentences with that Accuracy in a public Assembly which is practicable in the Closet. It is astonishing that Congress who certainly are not without sufficient *Apprehensions* should at so critical a Moment as the present be so supine but this is human Nature and we must bear it. I have a Remedy in Contemplation but that as to present Exigencies will be after *Meat* Mustard. If you were an unconcerned Spectator it would divert you to see that altho a Majority of our House have been agreed in a certain Point ever since Mr. Dana arrived here yet Nothing is done.[6] A propos of your Council of War. Should you determine on any Thing which considering the Course of human Affairs is I confess rather improbable Let Congress know Nothing about it. A Secret should never be trusted to many Bosoms. I will forfeit any Thing except Reputation that it will not be *well* kept even by those necessarily confided in. I know your many Avocations and therefore I insist that you do *not answer* any Letter from me. Should you have Reason to *write* a Letter it is another Affair.[7] Remember me to Mrs. Washington.

I am respectfully, Sir, your humble servant   Gouvr Morris
Sunday Evening.

RC (DLC).

[1] Although Morris clearly dated this letter 18th April 1778, he may actually have written it on Sunday, April 19, for he wrote "Sunday Evening" opposite his signature at the close of the document, and the letter appears to have been written at a single sitting.

[2] This exaggerated statement cannot be reconciled with what is known about the proceedings of Congress during this period. Even a casual glance at the journals reveals that the delegates transacted a large volume of other official business while the subject of half pay was under consideration.

[3] Morris himself drafted General Gates' instructions as commander of the northern department and Congress approved them on April 20. See *JCC*, 10:368–69.

[4] See *JCC*, 10:364. Washington informed Morris on April 25 that the only objectionable feature of these resolves was their failure to include artillery commander Henry Knox as a participant in the council, an oversight Congress corrected two days later. See *JCC*, 10:397; and Washington, *Writings* (Fitzpatrick), 11:305–7. On April 20 Henry Laurens transmitted "Under blank Cover" to General Mifflin a copy of the April 18 resolve directing him to meet with Washington. PCC, item 13, fol. 265.

[5] Not until October 29, 1778, did Congress appoint Washington's military secretary Robert H. Harrison to the Board of War. Harrison, who had already declined a similar appointment in November 1777, also turned down this one. See *JCC*, 9:874, 945, 971, 12:1077, 1086, 1147.

[6] Morris means that a majority in Congress favored the half-pay plan for Continental military officers that Committee at Camp members Francis Dana and Nathaniel Folsom had laid before the delegates on March 26. See *JCC*, 10:285–86;

and Edmund C. Burnett, *The Continental Congress* (New York: Macmillan Co., 1941), p. 311.

⁷ Washington's April 25 reply to Morris is in Washington, *Writings* (Fitzpatrick), 11:305–7.

Charles Thomson to Horatio Gates

Sir   [April 18? 1778][1]

I am ordered to inform you it is the pleasure of Congress that the board will confer with Col Butler & report the measures which you judge proper for correcting the abuses & inconveniences attend[ing] the management of affairs in that department.

The board is empowered to defray the expences of Col Butler while detained in town on this business.   Chas Thomson secy

FC (DNA: PCC, item 147).

[1] Thomson wrote this letter in response to Congress' April 18 resolve directing the Board of War "to make strict enquiry into the mode in which the armourer's department has been hitherto conducted . . . and if they judge necessary, to dismiss the persons who have been hitherto employed in that business, and to engage others in their stead." In response to recommendations made in the board's April 21 letter to President Laurens, Congress on April 23 confirmed the board's dismissal of public armorer Thomas Butler and the appointment of William Henry of Lancaster, Pa., in his stead. See *JCC*, 10:366, 380–81; and PCC, item 147, 2:13–16. See also Committee at Camp to Henry Laurens, March 1, 1778, note 2.

Samuel Huntington to Jabez Huntington

Sir   York Town 19th April 1778.

I am honourd. with your favour of the first Instant by Brown and happy to receive the Intelligence you communicate.

We are Anxious to have further European Intelligence, have nothing from there later than the 9th Decemr in the London papers which you have probably obtaind as the Navigation is less obstructed to the Eastward than this way. Capt. Wattles is arrivd in this Town on his way from South Carolina. The Troops from Virginia begin to come forward, one Regiment has arrivd to Join the grant Army, could wish all the Continental Troops might be hastened with all possible Expedition, as I am pretty Sanguine Should the United States make a vigorous exertion equal to their abilities in due Season this Campaign would prove decisive. I am Sir, your humble Servt.

Saml Huntington

RC (Sol Feinstone, Washington Crossing, Pa., 1976).

Henry Laurens to William Livingston

Dear Sir,   19th April 1778

Nothing is more common than petit excuses for delinquency in epistolary correspondence. "I have been so harried with business—have not been very well—Your Letter was unluckily mislaid," or something or other clumsily introduced to Cloak sheer Idleness; when these occur in my own line I smile at my friends shortsightedness. Never had any poor Culprit better ground for building to the utmost extent of his inabilities an elaborate apologetic preface than is at this instant in possession of your Excellency's Debtor. He might without impeachment of his veracity aver he has discovered the Art of uniting Liberty & Slavery, that for two Months past his Masters have confined him Morning & afternoon often till 9 & even past 10 oClock at Night, fixing him immoveable for Six hours together to be bated & Stared at, giving short intervals for refreshment & that as were allowed to him were necessarily devoted to public business including much Trash of incessant applications by French Men & other as light headed Men who watch his Entrance into his Room as keenly as a well [fee'd] Bailiff attends the nocturnal excursion of some poor fellow who has been too liberal with his Taylor & Vintner. I might urge that I seldom write but when other people are amusing themselves in Bed—what becomes of Sunday? that's my day of Rest—I write all day & discharge half a week's arrears. Will you say you have not more than once toyed away an hour talking nonsense with the pretty Girl above stairs & sometimes below stairs since the 26th Febry. when you received the Governor's Letter of the 5th. No I wont tell a Story, but this is my only relief, I am lame & can neither walk far nor ride for exercise. 'Tis a much surer & pleasanter means for reanimation than lounging the hour in an Elbow Chair if I had had one, cogitating & grumbling upon the cares & Labours of the drudge of a political manufactory—but waving further interrogation calculated to ensnare me, let me answer in a word, I have writ oftner by once within six Months past to Governor Livingston than I have upon any Subject in my private Estate, & perhaps the *seeming* indifference has arisen from the same reflection, I know neither of them will suffer from my silence. Be that as it certainly is, when I am called upon, I ought to answer & I promise in return for the very honorable dunns which I have lately received, to write whenever I can lay hold of matter however concise which I shall think not unworthy the Governor's notice. I will do myself the honor of attending his Levee as constantly as possible, should there be an appearance of a little obtrusion now & then in subject or manner I shall know who will not be to blame.

What will you say to yonder long Letter under the two short ones!

maybe not a word more at present, 'tis Sunday & although very early
I am fatigued & from the labors of the past Week I feel a Sterility
upon my natural barrenness. I must get off as well as I can, I'll tell
the Governor a Cock & a Bull Story about an important subsisting
debate in our Club, amuse him with my friend Chief Justice Drayton's speech upon Articles of confederation[1] which as a Special favor
I have obtained for the purpose, add Copies of a very honorable
correspondence lately held with the fallen Hero of River Bouquet,[2]
endeavor to draw His Excellency into a decision of Questions upon
parliamentary Order & then conclude by repeating what is as true as
any thing ever said by any Chief Justice Hero or Parliament.

Sir, We have within a Month past, improved many whole days &
some tedious Nights by hammering upon a plan for an half pay
establishment for Officers who shall continue in the Army to the end
of the present War—a most momentous engagement, in which all our
labour has not yet matured one single Clause nor even determined
the great leading questions to be, or not to be. The Combatants have
agreed to meet to morrow vis a vis & by the point of Reason & by
somethings proxies for Reason put an end to the Contest.[3] I'll be
hanged they do.

Had I heard of the Loss of half my Estate, the account would not
have involved my mind in such fixed concern as I feel from the introducing of this untoward project. A Refusal to gratify the demand of
the Officers will, as we are menaced, be followed by resignations from
all those who are valuable—an acquiescence without an adequate
provision or doceur for officers of the Militia as well as for all the
Soldiery will be attended by a Loss of Men & prove a Bar to future
energy in those Classes. We shall have no Army.

If we provide pensions for one part of the people from the labour
of the other part who have been equally engaged in the struggle
against the common Enemy & who to say the least have suffered equal
losses, the enormous debt which will thereby be entailed on posterity
will be the least evil, constitution will be tanted, and the Basis of
Independency will tremble.

Advocates for the Measure say, "the present pay of Officers is not
sufficient to support them in Character, their Estates are exposed to
waste & loss from their personal absence, they might by various ways
& means from which they are now cut off, improve their fortunes as
their friends & acquaintance are daily doing. You must not confide in
that virtue which you talk of as the Cement of the original compact,
there is none or very little of such principle remaining, upon your
decision of this great question depends the existence of your Army &
of your Cause. If you say No—All, All, your good Officers will leave
you." This is the substance & amount of pro.   Con starts—"the de-

mand is unjust, unconstitutional, unseasonable, a compliance under menaces, dangerous—the reasoning from loss of virtue & insufficiency of the present pay not convincing.

Unjust because inconsistent with the original Compact, Officers were not compelled but eagerly solicited Commissions knowing the terms of service, loss of Estate, neglect of family, sacrifice of domestic happiness, exorbitancy of prices of every specie of goods for the necessities or comforts of Life, applicable to every Citizen in the Union & to thousands who are not officers with greater force & propriety.

Unjust because without superior merit, Officers demand a seperate maintenance from the honest earnings of their fellow Citizens many of whom will have been impoverished by the effects of the War & rendered scarcely able to pay their quota of the unavoidable burthen of equal Taxes—unjust in the extreme, to compel thousands of poor industrious Inhabitants by contributions to pamper the Luxury of their fellow Citizens many of whom will step out of the Army in to the repossession of large acquired or inherited Estates, of some who have accumulated immense fortunes by purloin & peculation under the Mask of patriotism.

Tis held possible by these naughty Cons to produce more than one case in point.

Compliance with a demand unjust as it is extraordinary with a penalty affixed & delayed till the people are reduced to the awful alternative of losing the Army & their Liberties would be dangerous, because it would be establishing a precedent to the Soldiery—because it would be to Tax the people without their own Consent—because the people would have no security against future arbitrary demands— because the attempt is to deprive the Representative of free Agency & to reduce that Body to a State of subserviency—because it would lay the foundation of a standing Army, of an Aristocracy, the demand militates against Articles of Confederation—because it would have a tendency to waste the Army by discouraging the Militia & yeomanry in general to take the field, abate the fervor of the warmest friends & invigorate the hopes & endeavors of every Class of our Enemies" &c &c &c.

The assertion of loss of virtue is not admitted as a fact because the plan originated in a sphere above Regimental Command from whence it was easy to Roll down the glaring temptation.

Insufficiency of the present pay cannot be admitted because the Remedy proposed is not adequate to relief—half Pay to commence at a distant period will not supply present wants—"succeed in the first attempt & by the same means we will compel Congress to augment pay."

If Officers withdraw & the loss of the Army & Liberty are to be

conselective events, by what "various ways & means" may officers
improve their fortunes, where will be those lucrative employments
which it is pretended they now envy—but officers may retire when
they please—so may senators & what then?

A whole quire of Paper would be too narrow to range in, upon
this topic. It is fortunate for you Sir that General Gates, an English
News paper & two or three members of Congress steped in & knocked
out of my head more than would have filled another sheet. If I can
beg that News paper which contains some good things it shall accompany the other papers. Let me conclude this head by observing the
Cons move to postpone the consideration of the plan until the several
States shall be fully informed & consulted.[4] Here a strenuous advocate
let out the Cat—no I am afraid the people will not consent. What!
dare we bind the people in any Case without or against their Consent,
tis very near akin to burding them in all Cases. I must confess the
affair for an affair of such magnitude has been poorly conducted by
the managers.

A Report of the whole, called for in a certain Assembly being the
order of the day—read once for information the first paragraph read
for debate an amendment offered & received a question on the
amendment half put—a new proposition was started irrelative to the
paragraph & amendment, contrary to general consent & having a
tendency to set aside both—Question is it in order to receive & put
to Vote the proposition?

A question was moved upon the order; Question is the latter
motion or the first subject for a previous Question?[5]

From what has been said Your Excellency will collect enough to
determine on the article of confusion. That Mass of paper lying there
which I lug every day to & fro would give a more explicit answer to
this point than, as I think, becomes me. My own Spirits such as they
are keep in pretty equal tone. Men may bear pain with great equa-
nimity in general, yet be impelled by sudden twitches to bawl out &
sigh for a moment.

Things in public life were in extreme disorder when I had last the
honour of writing to your Excellency & besides I beleive other things
in private were as crooked. I fancy I was a Bed with Gout. Some
departments, which as I dont mean to be invidious I will not part-
ticularize, are shifted into more promising hands & I intertain hopes,
if we have an Army, it will be better supplied than it has been with
entertainment for Men & Horse but take a general view & the prospect
is still extremely mortifying. However, we have lately received
acquisition of some abilities though not half enough & tis pretended
the Spirit of reformation is at our threshold. My Colleague Drayton
has given earnest of his determination to set his face against fraud in
every shape & to call upon those men who detain unaccounted Mil-

lions.[6] Thank God we have other virtuous sensible Men to aid him. I believe things were at the time allude[d] to at the worst—nothing but complete ruin could have proved the contrary.

General Burgoyne had reached Rhode Island & probably embarked about the 5th Inst. His arrival in England will produce an excellent fund for polemics.

Congress have directed General Washington to convene a Council of Major Generals including the two Gentlemen of the Board of War & the General Officer of the Corps of Engineers in order "to form such a plan for the general operations of the Campaign as the Commander in Chief shall deem consistent with the general welfare of these States." General Gates from the Council will proceed to Fish Kill & take upon him the Command of all the Northern department.

I learned yesterday that the works upon North River were going forward under great exertions of Industry. Officers assist in manual labour. Apprehensions of losing the important passes & their apendages on that River through a strange delay & perplexity of orders wearing the appearance of infatuation have often exercised my patience.

The knowing ones here will bet that terms of accomodation will be a prelude to the Campaign, I dont pretend to be related to that family, but I expressed the sentiment upon Reading the Speech of the 20th November.[7]

No public good can be derived from Spreading such opinions, a plausible pretence to treat in earnest will bring the Union into a critical situation & will demand all the Wisdom of the thirteen States to counteract a finesse.

But for the visit above mentioned I should have dispatched the bearer at 9 oClock this Morning, my Chain was broke, I went to Church & have finished in the Evening—& ought to be charged one day's expence of the Messenger.

I sincerely wish your Excellency health & Safety being with the highest Esteem & Respect &ca.

LB (ScHi).

[1] See William Henry Drayton, *The Speech of the Hon. William Henry Drayton Esquire, Chief Justice of South Carolina. Delivered on the Twentieth January, 1778* (Charleston: David Bruce, 1778). Evans, *Am. Bibliography*, no. 15785.

[2] An allusion to Gen. John Burgoyne and his grandiloquent proclamation of June 20, 1777, which was issued from his "Camp at the River Bouquett" and long annoyed Laurens. See Laurens to John Lewis Gervais, August 17, 1777, note 5. No doubt Laurens sent Livingston copies of the correspondence relating to Congress' decision to permit Burgoyne and a number of other British officers to return to England. See Laurens to Richard Wilford, March 1, and to Burgoyne, March 6, 1778.

[3] Congress did not resume consideration of the issue of half pay until Tuesday April 21. *JCC*, 10:372–74.

[4] See *JCC*, 10:358–60.

[5] See *JCC*, 10:362–63; and Laurens' Notes on Half Pay, April 17–21, 1778.

⁶ After taking his seat in Congress on March 30, William Henry Drayton had wasted little time in getting down to business. On Saturday April 4 he offered a motion—on which Congress voted to postpone consideration—"that on Monday next Congress be resolved into a committee of the whole to consider the situation of affairs of the United States." *JCC*, 10:306. Although the journals fail to identify the author of this motion, there is a text of it in Drayton's hand in the Laurens Papers, ScHi. It is not known what specific purpose Drayton had in view when he proposed his motion.

The Laurens Papers also contain a March 29 letter from Drayton to Laurens, written at "Suttons Tavern Sunday Noon," in which Drayton asked Laurens to arrange accommodations for him "as I am informed lodging is very difficult to be procured at York."

⁷ An apparent reference to George III's November 18, 1777, speech to parliament, in which the king expressed hope that the conflict with America would soon be settled. See Elbridge Gerry to Samuel Adams, February 7, 1778, note 3.

Oliver Wolcott to Laura Wolcott

[April] 19t [1778]

Brown has been detained longer than I expected. I have now the Pleasure to acquaint you that I am entirely well. I beleive my Disorder was owing to the use of the Waters here which are bad—and which I find has produced the same ill effects in all upon the first using of them. I shall drink this Water but Seldom.

Genl. Gates is appointed to Command on Hudsons River and the Northern Department which are now united. So that I suppose Mr. Peirce's Expectations will not be gratified. So that the matter which you mentioned in Regard to Oliver is about at an end. Mr. Wadsworth of Hartford is appointed Commissry Genl.¹

I have ordered 460 dollars to be left with you to be sent to Mr. Edwards of Stockbridge for his Services as Commissioner of Indian Affairs.² As I have got this Allowance for him, I have delivered an account of a like Nature for myself to the Officers of the Treasury and hope it will be admitted, if so Shall inform you of it.

RC (CtHi). A continuation of Wolcott to Wolcott, April 14, 1778.
¹ See *JCC*, 10:327–28.
² This payment to Timothy Edwards, who like Wolcott served as a commissioner for Indian affairs in the northern department, had been authorized by Congress on March 23. *JCC*, 10:264, 279.

Charles Carroll of Carrollton to Charles Carroll, Sr.

Dear Papa,   York 20th April 1778

I begin to be settled. I now lodge at one Dowdell's in the same house with Mr. Henry. Our lodgings, all things considered, are well enough. We breakfast at home but must dine abroad. The principal business now before Congress is the report of the Committee, which went to camp for putting the army on a new establishment: when the report is gone thro' & confirmed by the House, I will give you the heads of it. Recruits come slowly on to join Gen. Washington, whose army I fear is much weaker than the Enemy's. Gen. Gates will soon go to the high lands on Hudson's river & command a distinct corps to be stationed there for the security of that post. This corps will I fancy be augmented to 8000 men. I have had some conversation with Gen. Lee, who was in this place a few days ago on his way to his Farm in Virga.[1] He says Howe has 14000 men in Pha. I fancy he is imposed on & that the Enemy is not so strong. I judge of their strength by their inactivity. When we have done with the arrangement of the army, we shall proceed to the regulation of finances, which demands the immediate & serious attention of Congress.

The Cartel is in suspence. I do not imagine an Exchange will take place; an insuperable bar to it will be a resolve of Congress, which considers Americans inlisting with the Enemy as Traytors, & subject to the treason laws of the Several States to which they may respectively belong. This Resolve Congress can not depart from; nor can Howe submit to it.

We have had no letters from our Agents in France since last May. One Mr. Francy, an Agent of Beaumarchais, is now here & has entered into a contract with Congress. He had agreed to advance us 24 millions of Livres, but it is specified in the agreement that we shall not draw for more than £100,000 Ster, till he receives the approbation of his Employer. I have not the least doubt but that Beaumarchais is the go between, or the Agent employed by the French court; for of himself he has no estate; this information I had from Mr. de Coudray. I have no doubt but that France & Spain will aid us with money & the necessaries of war, but I am equally persuaded in my own mind they will not yet a while engage in a war with G B, unless they should be drawn into it by some unforeseen accident, & contrary to their present System of politicks.

I hear our Assembly has raised the Tax to 25/ in the hundred. I think they have done well. You must keep a considerable sum of money by you to answer the demands on our estates, for the public assess[men]ts & county levies. We must not have less than £4000 by us to answer these demands & current expences.

The Enemy will, I am persuaded, make a vigorous effort this Campaign; at present we are very ill prepared to receive them. However as our lives, our property, & Liberty depend on the event of this Contest, I hope the People will rouse from their lethargy, & act with a vigor & spirit suitable to the important & glorious cause in which they are engaged.

I write this to Molly as much as to you. I hope she is assured of my affectionate love, & that she will take great care & use much industry to recover her health. I hope she will send me the thread stockings when finished; by this time I dare say Miss Betsy has finished the pair she was about when I left home. My love to little Poll & Charles, & Mrs. Darnall. I hope you are well. Use gentle exercise, keep up your Spirits, mine are good notwithstanding the prospect is a little cloudy at present; but we have surmounted greater difficulties, than what we have now to contend against, and I trust we shall surmont these. The American motto should be "tu contra audentior ito." My complts to Capt Ireland, Jemmy Howard & the Doctor. I am, Yr. affectionate Son,   Ch Carroll of Carrollton

P.S. 4 o'clock.

We recd. this morning letters from the General of the 18th instant.[2] The Treaty for an exchange of prisoners is broken off, and upon the very point we could wish vizt. the Commissioners of Gen. Howe acknowleging that it was only a personal treaty on his part by which his own personal honor would be bound, & not the faith of his Nation. The General has sent us a printed copy of the draughts of two bills;[3] we do not know whether these bills have been brought into Parliat. or passed into laws; but considering their insidious tendency, I imagine they are by this time Acts of Parliat. The first is

A draught of a Bill for declaring the intentions of Parliat. concerning the exercise of the right of taxation over the Colonies.

This Bill, after reciting that the views of Parliat. have been misrepresented, enacts that Parliat will not impose any duty, tax, or assessment payable within the Colonies, except only such duties as it may be expedient to impose for the regulation of commerce, the net produce of such duties to be always paid & applied to & for the use of the Colony in which they shall be respectively levied, in the manner as duties &c collected by the authority of the respective Assemblies are ordinarily paid & applied.

In short this bill only enacts into a law the proposal made by Lord North in 1774.[4]

The second draught is of a Bill

To enable the King to appoint Commissioners with sufficient powers to treat, consult, & agree upon the means of quieting the disorders in America.

The principal provisions are as follow—to appoint commissioners

1. to treat of grievances which may exist in the Colonies with any body or bodies political & corporate.

2. to treat with said Bodies of & concerning any aid or contribution to be furnished by all or any of the Colonies or of any other regulations or matters as the Commissioners may consider necessary or convenient for the honor of his Majesty.

NB—nothing agreed upon to be conclusive till confirmed by Parliat.

3. to order a cessation of hostilities; to suspend the act of the 16th of the present King for cutting off all intercourse with the Colonies; to suspend all the Acts passed since the 10th of February 1763, all this to be done at the discretion of the Commissioners in all *such places* as they shall think proper.

4. to grant pardons to all such persons as they shall think proper & deserving of them.

5. to appoint Governors with the usual powers of Governing in all such places as they shall think fit.

I have given you the substance of these two famous or rather infamous bills; for the obvious intention of them is to mislead & divide our People. The Ministry begin to see they can not conquer us but by dividing. You must excuse inacuracies & blunders. I write in a great haste having my hands full.

Ch. Carroll of Carrollton[5]

RC (MdHi).

[1] Gen. Charles Lee's visit to Congress had also prompted Robert Morris to undertake a hurried trip to York from his home at Manheim to converse with the general, but Lee had already set out for Virginia before Morris arrived. "I am a good deal hurt at missing the opportunity of taking you by the hand," Morris explained in an April 24 letter to Lee. "That pleasure I expected at this place [Manheim] for I did not believe you wou'd have passed us by without a Call. Finding however that You intended from York for Virginia I went over on Saturday [*April 18*] but you had set out. I sent after you to the first Stage, You had left that also and I came back here on Sunday." Allyn K. Ford Collection, MnHi.

[2] Washington's April 18 letter to Congress is in PCC, item 152, 5:447–48, and Washington, *Writings* (Fitzpatrick), 11:276–78.

[3] See Evans, *Am. Bibliography*, nos. 15827, 15828. For Congress' response to the receipt of Lord North's conciliatory bills, see Henry Laurens to James Duane, April 20, 1778, note 1.

[4] Carroll undoubtedly had in mind Lord North's conciliatory plan of February 1775. See *JCC*, 2:62–63.

[5] Carroll also apparently wrote the following postscript to his father at about this time.

"P.S. I recd. this day a letter from General Smallwood from Willmington dated the 17th instant in which he informs me that during the winter 8 valuable vessels have been taken by our People in the Delaware, 4 whereof fell to the Share of his detachment: that in the course of the winter he has taken 200 British soldiers & sailors; that the spirits of the Tories in Pha. are greatly depressed by the late advices from England; that Howe has 10,000 effectives in Pha. & has lately recd. a reinforcement from N York of 2000 as it is given out; that he passed Deards into Pha. who was by that time under way for England, as he (Smallwood) had good reason to beleive."

The precise date of the document cannot be determined, but both its physical appearance and content suggest that it was written on April 20 or 21. On April 20 Congress read an April 17 letter written from Wilmington by Smallwood to President Laurens (which was also the subject of Carroll's April 21 letter to Thomas Johnson); and "the late advices from England" depressing Tory spirits in Philadelphia were undoubtedly Lord North's conciliatory proposals, which were printed in the *Pennsylvania Evening Post* and *Pennsylvania Ledger* on April 15. Moreover, the postscript was written on a separate sheet of paper that cannot be matched with any of the surviving letters Carroll wrote during this period, and it clearly does not belong with Carroll's April 22–24 letter, which was begun just two days after the April 20 letter printed above. Because it is even more apparent that it does not belong with the May 3 letter to his father with which it was placed in the Carroll Family Papers, MdHi, it has been quoted here to call attention to it in the context in which the editors believe it was written.

Samuel Chase to Thomas Johnson

Dear Sir,   York Town. 20 April 1778
  General Howe has sent out of Philadelphia a Cart loaded with Hand-Bills, expressing to be A *Draught* of a *Bill* to declare the Intentions of Parliament, concerning the Exercise of the *Right* of imposing Taxes, within the Colonies.

  And be it Enacted & declared, That the King and Parliament, after the Passing the Act, will not impose any *Duty, Tax* or *assessment whatsoever, payable within any of the Colonies, except only such Duties,* as it may be expedient to impose *for the Regulation of Commerce:* the Net-produce of such Duties to be paid and applied to the Use of the Colony, in which levied, in such Manner, as other Duties collected by the Authority of the general Courts or assemblys of such Colony, are ordinarily paid & applied.

  A *Draught* of a *Bill* to enable his Majesty to appoint Commissioners to treat, consult and agree upon Means of quieting Disorders in the Colonies.

  And be it enacted etc. That—Persons to be appointed by his Majesty, shall have Power to treat, consult and agree, with such Body or Bodies political & corporate, or with such assembly, or assemblies of Men, or with such Person or Persons, as they shall think meet, of & concerning *any Grievances or Complaints,* existing or supposed to exist, in the *Government* of any of the Colonies, or in the *Laws and Statutes* of this Realm, respecting the *same,* and of or concerning *any aid or Contribution* to be furnished, by all or any of the Colonies respectively, *for the common Defence* of the Realm, and the Dominions thereunto belonging, and of & concerning such *other Regulations, provisions, Matters & things,* as, upon mature Deliberation of the Commissioners or any ——— of them, shall be thought *necessary or convenient for the Honor of his Majesty and the common Good of all his Subjects:* Provided that no Regulation, provision, Matter or thing, so proposed, treated, consulted or agreed shall have *any other* force or Effect, or be carried *further* into Execution, than is mentioned in this Act until approved by Parliament.

Provided also that the Commissioners or any ———— of them may order & proclaim a Cessation of Hostilities, on the part of his Majestys Troops, in any of the Colonies, for any Time, & under any Conditions or Restrictions, they shall think convenient, and such order & proclamation may revoke & annul, according to their Discretion.

And be it Enacted That the Commissioners or any ———— of them, may by proclamation suspend the operation & Effects of the Act of Parliament, of the 16th year of his Majesty, "for prohibiting all Trade & Intercourse," or of any of the provisons or Restrictions therein contained, for such convenient Time as they think proper.

And be it Enacted That the Commissioners etc. shall have Power to suspend, in such places, & for such Times, as they may think fit, *during the Continuance of this act,* the operation & effect of all or any of the Act or Acts of Parliament, which have passed, since 10th of February 1763, & which relate to any of the Colonies, so far as the same does relate to them.

And be it Enacted That the Commissioners etc. shall have Power to grant a Pardon or Pardons to any Number or Description of Persons, within any of the Colonies, & to appoint a Governor in any Colony, with such power, as heretofore granted by his Majesty.

The act to continue in force till 1st June 1779.

Published by order of the Commander in chief, Robert Mackenzie Secretary, Philada. 14 April 1778

Two opinions prevail here. Some think this insidious Scheme originated in Philadelphia, others the far greater Number beleive it came from the Ministry. The manifest Intention is to amuse Us with a Prospect of Peace & to relax our Preparations. I hope my Countrymen will have too much good Sense to be deceived. I think it would be adviseable immediately to publish this Attempt, but I hope it will be attended with some Remarks to expose its Design, & remove the baneful Effects it may have on the credulous & weak among the People. Mr Paca has Leisure—it ought not to be attempted to be suppressed.

Captain Nicholson informs, that a Number of Recruits are enlisted for the Enemy in Worcester and Somst. Counties, 90 came to the fleet, when he was on board. It is reported the disaffected in Queen Ann's County have rose, & Congress were yesterday acquainted with an Insurrection in Sussex County. The Malignants are assembling in Arms at Jordans Island. You will be applied to by Congress to order 300 of your Militia, with two field Pieces, & 28 Artillerists, to march there.[1]

The Randolph Frigate is said to be lost. She engaged a 50 Gun Ship for an Hour, and both Sides drawing off to repair their Damage, she by accident blew up, and every Soul on board perished. The proposed Cartel is broke off. Our Commissioners had full Powers, & their Act would have bound the *public* faith, Howes Commissioners had not full Powers, & could only engage his *private* Faith, and that too only during his Command. The Exchange on Parole will continue.

No other Part of my last[2] was to have been private, but Genl. Lee's Name. I am inclined to think Baltimore fort remains in the same defenceless State as I mentioned to the assembly a year ago. There is a great Mistake in my Letter about the Quantity of Continental Arms. I meant to say Congress had fifteen thousand Arms, & above two hundred field pieces. I suppose I folded the Letter before it was dry, & that Circumstance added to the Naughts. I will scize the first favourable Opportunity to apply to Congress for some Mony, but our Demands to pay & buy provisions are very pressing.

My Compliments to the Council, Your Affectionate and Obedient Servant,   Saml Chase

RC (MdAA).
[1] See Charles Carroll of Carrollton to Thomas Johnson, April 21, 1778, note 1.
[2] Chase's last letter to Johnson has not been found, but since a portion of this paragraph is addressed to the subject of "the Quantity of Continental Arms" available to Maryland, it is obvious that Chase is responding to the Maryland Council's April 7 letter requesting the delegates "to apply to Congress for Arms and Field Pieces and Accoutrements," pursuant to an April 4 resolution of the Maryland Assembly. See *Md. Archives,* 21:15.

Samuel Chase to George Washington

Dear Sir,   York Town April 20 1778
I wish some Mode would be adopted to pursue the Release of our Subjects, who are taken by the Enemy, not in Arms. The Situation is truely distressing. Humanity and Policy combine to urge Us to take some speedy and effectual Measures to obtain their Discharge but one of two Modes occurs to Me, either to declare them not objects of Capture, or to seise the Friends of Great-Britain, and detain them to redeem ours with the Enemy.

The Case of Mr. Gunning Bedford is attended with some particular Circumstances. He was taken by a Party of our Enemy abt 13th of February, and has been confined in the New Jail ever since, and even threatened with Punishment as a *Robber* for stopping some People carrying provisions into the City. I am informed General Howe will exchange him for one ———— Cooke, in Northumberland County.[1]

I beg Leave to Solicit your favor for Mr. Bedford, he formerly held the Commission of Muster Master General, and by his Conduct can expect no favor from the Enemy.

I beg your acceptance of my best Wishes for your Health & Happiness and You may be assured that I am, Your Affectionate and Obedient Servant,   Saml. Chase.

RC (DLC).

¹ For Washington's April 27 response to Chase, reporting that he could not act on Chase's request because Mr. Cook was apparently held by the state of Pennsylvania and was not a military prisoner subject to his jurisdiction, see Washington, *Writings* (Fitzpatrick), 11:316–17.

John Henry to Thomas Johnson

Dear Sir.   York Town Apl. 20th. 1778.

I have procured the inclosed paper with some difficulty. When you have read it, if the Assembly should be setting, I wish you would send it to the Speaker. Different opinions prevail here with regard to the Authenticity of it. For my own part I have no doubt, from what I have lately seen in the English papers, but these two Bills before this time, are enacted into Laws. I dread the impressions it will make upon the minds of many of our people. If it should, and I have no doubt of it, make its appearance in the form of a Law, it will prove more dangerous to our cause than ten thousand of their best troops. It will in a Day or two be under the consideration of Congress.

The Cartell for the General Exchange of prisoners is at an End. Upon our commissioners examining the powers of the Commissioners on the part of Genl Howe, they discovered he meant the treaty to be of a personal Nature, founded on the mutual Confidence and Honor of the contracting Generals, and had no Intention of binding the Nation, or of extending the Cartel beyond the limits and Duration of his own Command. They declared themselves ready to treat with us on this footing, with their present powers which they deemed adequate to the purposes of their Meeting. Upon this point the treaty broke off. I lament the Situation of our prisoners, and must approve of the Conduct of our Commissioners. A Cartel upon so narrow a foundation as the personal Honor of Genl Howe would be of little use to us and of short duration, liable at any time to be set aside by a subsequent Commander or by the British King without a breech of Honor. This Conduct will teach us a lesson respecting Genl Burgoyne and his Army.

I make no doubt you have heard of the insurrection in the Delaware State. By a Letter from a Mr Patterson we are informed that a considerable Number of the disaffected have assembled at a place near the head of Chester River. They are exerting themselves to add to their Numbers and those who will not join them, they deprive of their Arms and Amunition. It is said here they have British officers among them and expect to be reinforced from Philadelphia. This Matter is viewed here as very serious by some. Mr. Carrol gives his Compliments to you and desires me to acquaint you that there is a considerable quantity of provision at Charles Town at the Head of our Bay which appears to be in a dangerous Situation. There is also as I am informed by Mr. S. Stewart quantities of provisions at Princes Ann in Somerset, and other places in that neighbourhood, which it would be fortunate for us if we could remove them without Delay.

When I wrote to you, some Weeks ago, I informed you, that I had procured ten thousand Dollars for the recruiting service which I sent down by Col S. Smith, I have never heard whether you have recd. it.[1] If you should write to any of the Delegates, by the next post, I should be obliged to you to acquaint us with the receipt of the Money if it has reached your hands.

I am Sir with great respect, yrs.   J. Henry Junr.

RC (MdAA).
[1] See John Henry to Thomas Johnson, March 6, 1778.

Henry Laurens to George Clinton

Sir,   York Town 20 April 1778.

My last was dated 31st March by Green.[1] This morning I had the honour of presenting to Congress Your Excellency's favor of the 7th Inst. together with the Proclamation which came inclosed—these are referred to a special Committee.[2]

Under this Cover Your Excellency will be pleased to receive an Act of Congress of the 15th Inst. for appointing General Gates to the Command of the whole Northern department & authorizing him to call for Militia from New York & the Eastern States &c.[3] In the General's Instructions he is directed when convenient to confer with & take Your Excellency's advice & assistance.

General Howe is now circulating as far as his own & the power of his Emissaries extend a Paper said to have been received by the February Packet, but printed in Philadelphia, 'titled
                    "Draught of a Bill (Private)
for declaring the intentions of the Parliament of Great Britain concerning the exercise of the Right of imposing Taxes within His Majesties Colonies Provinces & Plantations in North America."
"Draught of a Bill to enable his Majesty to appoint Commissioners

with sufficient Powers to treat consult & agree upon the means of quieting the disorders now subsisting in certain of the Colonies Plantations & Provinces in North America."

"Whereas the exercise of the Right of Taxation by the Parliament for the purpose of raising a Revenue has occasioned disorder, &c.— It is expedient to Declare that the K & P. will not impose any Duty &c. for the purpose of Revenue, except for the Regulation of Commerce &c. the N't produce to be applied for the use of the Colony in which the same shall be respectively levied—Commissioners to be appointed by His Majesty & authorized to treat with Body & Bodies political & Corporate with Assembly or Assemblies of men—Person or Persons—to proclaim a Cessation of Hostilities—to suspend the operation of the Act of 16th Geo 3d prohibiting Trade & Intercourse—to suspend for time all the Acts relative to the Colonies passed since 10th febry. 1763—to grant pardons to any number or description of persons to fill up Vacancies in the Offices of Governors & Commanders in Chief in the Colonies" &c. &c.[4]

The last article is nugatory & must have arisen from their ignorance that every place is full.

I need not trouble Your Excellency with my sentiments on this attempt nor on the proper means for exposing it to complete contempt & ridicule.

I differ with Gentlemen who suppose the performance originated under authority in England; it appears to me to be destitute of the most essential marks; if the MS., crossed the Atlantic it must have been the production of a Jacob Henriques or a Moses Lindo. I believe it to be of Philadelphia manufacture probably under hints from the other side of the Water & sent abroad like a Sibyl's Letter—'tis not improbable I may be obtruding a subject, which before this can reach Your Excellency will be known at large; be that as it may, if I can possibly obtain a Copy of the whole draught it shall accompany this for although I think it should be treated with contempt—yet not silent contempt—it is at present in the hands of some Gentlemen who will exert their Talents in stricturizing.

Your Excellency will have heard of the seperation of the Commissioners for establishing a Cartel, the conduct & determinations of the Gentlemen who appeared on our part is highly applauded by Congress—will do themselves honour & our Cause, service. I have the honour to be with the greatest Esteem & regard Sir Your Excellency's obedient & most hum. Serv't,

Henry Laurens, President of Congress.

Reprinted from Clinton, *Papers* (Hastings), 3:197–99. The text of this letter in Laurens' presidential letterbook contains only the first two paragraphs of the letter printed here. PCC, item 13, fol. 267.
[1] See Laurens to Richard Caswell, March 31, 1778, note 2.

² This day Congress appointed a committee consisting of Samuel Huntington, Francis Lightfoot Lee, and Jonathan Bayard Smith to consider Governor Clinton's April 7 letter and his enclosed proclamation inviting settlers in Vermont to recognize New York's authority over them. Huntington drafted a report that rebuked efforts to create an independent state of Vermont and declared that "no number or body of people" had the right to set up a new state "without the Consent of the State or States in which they are or were Included at the time the Congress were at first Elected & Convened for the Safety & defence of these United States; & the approbation of Congress." This report was submitted to Congress (it is not known when), but Congress never read it—in part because the delegates felt they had more pressing business to attend to but also, one supposes, because they were disinclined to tackle such a sensitive issue involving so many conflicting interests and no clearcut way to reconcile them. See *JCC*, 10:367; Clinton, *Papers* (Hastings), 3:144–46; and New York Delegates to Clinton, July 21, 1778.

³ Laurens also transmitted copies of these resolves with brief covering letters that he wrote this day to Gov. Jonathan Trumbull of Connecticut and to the Massachusetts Council. PCC, item 13, fol. 266; and Revolutionary Letters, M–Ar. In addition he sent "under Blank Cover" to President Thomas Wharton of Pennsylvania "an Act of Congress of the 17th April for preventing further purchases by Pennsylvania Commissioners." PCC, item 13, fol. 265; and *JCC*, 10:361.

⁴ On April 21 Laurens also dispatched copies of this "Draught of a Bill to . . . appoint Commissioners" to absent delegates Samuel Adams and Henry Marchant. Laurens Papers, ScHi.

Henry Laurens to James Duane

20th April [1778].

I wish time permitted, I would attempt some amendment of the hurried sketch above, I know you will excuse its imperfection. I write all my private Letters by scraps as I can catch half an hour & half an hours disposition, the intervals between Public business nature claims as her own for lounging or amusement & we have often little family quarrels upon this score.

General Howe has as far as his own & the Power of his Emissaries have extended sent abroad a spurious draught of a Bill insinuated to be Parliamentary, importing an intended proposition for reconciling differences & quieting disturbances in the Colonies. Governor Clinton shall be furnished with a Copy—which you will of course see—probably you will have seen one sooner—your Morris & our Drayton have it in hand. I make no doubt but that we shall return it decently tarred & feathered.¹

The Commissioners at New Town for establishing a Cartel for Exchange of Prisoners have done as did Balaam & Balak, 24 Numbers 25 V.² Those on our part have gained great Credit, their conduct & proceedings were spirited, perspicuous, honorable to themselves & their Constituents & must do our Cause service in the Eye of the Enemy. General Howe's dictates to his Agents & their servility are all shabby, & will expose them *all* to ridicule & contempt.³ By the bye, remember to whom I speak, a certain Club of which you are a Member have very fortunately got out of a scrape. You shall see the whole, except the latter stroke, in Print very speedily.⁴ I whispered to a friend, *this* may be passed to the Credit of Providence.

Adieu Good Sir. I wish you all happiness & remain, with great Respect, Your obedient & most humble servant,

Henry Laurens.

RC (NHi). A continuation of Laurens to Duane, April 17, 1778.

¹ On April 22 Congress approved and ordered publication of the address drawn up by the committee appointed on the 20th to formulate a response to the news of Lord North's conciliatory bills. *JCC,* 10:374–80. This address first appeared in the April 24 issue of the *Pennsylvania Gazette.* In addition to Gouverneur Morris and William Henry Drayton, Francis Dana was also a member of the committee that drew up this document. *JCC,* 10:367. According to his own testimony, Morris was the author of this address. See Gouverneur Morris to John Jay, May 3, 1778.

² "And Balaam rose up, and went and returned to his place: and Balak also went his way."

³ Washington informed Congress of the failure of his negotiations with the British for a prisoner cartel in an April 18 letter to Laurens that was read in Congress on the 20th. See *JCC,* 10:367; and Washington, *Writings* (Fitzpatrick), 11:276–78. The progress of these negotiations can best be followed in the reports of the commissioners representing the American side in Alexander Hamilton, *The Papers of Alexander Hamilton,* Harold C. Syrett et al., eds. (New York: Columbia University Press, 1961–), 1:445–78.

⁴ It is unclear whether Laurens is predicting or describing the decision Congress made on April 21 to publish its resolves of that date commending the conduct of Washington's commissioners during their recent negotiations for a prisoner cartel with the British. *JCC,* 10:370–71. The delegates had made a serious allegation about the commissioners in the April 14 letter to Washington they had prepared for Laurens' signature.

Henry Laurens to Jonathan Trumbull, Sr.

Sir

20th April [1778]

I shall inclose within the present Cover, Copy of "Draught of a Bill &ca"—a most insidious paper said to have arrived from England in the February Packet & now circulating as far as the power of General Howe & that of his Emissaries extend. The paper is evidently calculated to ensnare weak minds, & to disunite the Citizens of these States. Its wicked designs ought to be compelled¹ everywhere, with the utmost energy. A Report has already reached people of all Ranks that terms of accomodation are offered by Great Britain. Every Man of common discernment will at first reading discover the poison contained in these terms but there are Weak Men who must be supported & Wicked Men who must be confronted in order to prevent the intended Evil from taking effect. Whether this paper really came from England or was manufactured in Philadelphia is uncertain. I am very well satisfied in my own mind it is not circulated under the direction of parliament because it is deficient in one essential mark—it is however an Engine of Administration or the Slaves of Administration.

If no other Copy shall have reached the Eastern States I request Your Excellency will cause one Copy to be made & transmit it to a friend in Boston[2] who will apply to it such remarks as will prove an effectual antidote against the intended venom &ca.

LB (ScHi).
[1] Laurens obviously meant "repelled."
[2] Presumably Samuel Adams.

Henry Laurens to Joseph Trumbull

Sir,   20th April [1778]
In consequence of a Representation lately made to Congress by the Honble. Mr. Huntington, of your infirm State of health & continued desire from that consideration to be excused from taking a Seat at the Board of War, an Act was Resolved the 18th Inst. for accepting your resignation, Copy of which you will receive within this Inclosure.

I sincerely wish you perfect recovery of Strength & have the honour to be, with great Respect &ca.

LB (DNA: PCC, item 13).

Henry Laurens to Meshech Weare

Sir,   York Town 20th April 1778.
Since my last under the 31st March[1] I have not been honoured with any of your favors.

Within this inclosure your Honor will receive an Act of Congress of the 15th Inst. for appointing Major General Gates to the Command of all the Troops in the whole Northern department & empowering him to call for Militia from New York & the four Eastern States &c.

As I have never been honoured by a Line from you in acknowledgement of the many Letters which in obedience to the orders of Congress I have transmitted to you within the last six Months, I request Sir, you will be pleased to direct your Secretary to return me the dates of such as have reached your hands, which will enable me to compare with my Copies & to make the necessary supply, if any of my Letters shall appear to have been miscarried.

I have the honour to be, With great Respect, Honorable Sir, Your obedient & Most humble servant,

Henry Laurens, President of Congress.

RC (Nh–Ar).

[1] See Laurens to Richard Caswell, March 31, 1778, note 2.

Marine Committee to Jonathan Trumbull, Sr.

Sir

April 20th 1778

We have the honor of acknowledging your Letter of the 2d inst. and very unhappy in not being able to comply with the request of your Excellency and your Council of safety.[1] The gallant conduct of Captain Harding intitles him to notice; but when you Sir, and your Council of safety consider that by the destruction and Capture of several of our frigates their Captains are thrown out of actual service, you will easily perceive that it would be doing not only injustice to those officers some of whom at least are very valuable, but to the Continent to pass by them, and appoint to the command of the frigate at Norwich any Gentleman who hath not had A Command in the Continental Navy let his merit be ever so great. It would particularly disapoint the expectations of Captain Hinman who hath wrote to us on the subject should we honor Captain Harding with the Command of that frigate. Indeed it is not with us to appoint it is our duty only to nominate and recommend. We beg leave in answer [to] the last paragraph in your Excellencys letter to observe, that it is not the practice of States to recommend Navy Officers, and that Captain Saltonstal was nominated to Congress by the Marine Committee in consequence of recommendations from the Delegates of your States. We are with great respect yr. Excellencys Most Obedt servants

LB (DNA: PCC Miscellaneous Papers, Marine Committee Letter Book).

[1] In his April 2 letter to the Marine Committee, Governor Trumbull had recommended that Seth Harding, an outstanding captain in the Connecticut Navy, be appointed to command the Continental frigate being built at Norwich and had noted "that of the many appointments in the Navy hitherto, this State has never nominated one." James L. Howard, *Seth Harding, Mariner* (New Haven: Yale University Press, 1930), pp. 61–62. In spite of the Marine Committee's negative response, Trumbull persisted in his efforts to secure this appointment for Harding, whom Congress finally commissioned on September 25, 1778, to command the Connecticut frigate, which they named *Confederacy*. See *JCC*, 12:951; and Marine Committee to Trumbull, September 25, 1778. For Harding's exploits as commander of the *Confederacy*, see Howard, *Seth Harding*, chaps. 5–6.

Charles Carroll of Carrollton to
Thomas Johnson

Dear Sir,   York 21 April 1778.

By a letter from Gen. Smallwood of the 17th instant from Willmington we are informed of an insurrection of the Tories at a place
called Jordans Island 10 miles from Dover. Smallwood apprehends
this insurrection may become very serious unless speedily suppressed.
His letter is referred to a committee of which I am one. We shall
report that you be requested to call out 300 of the militia from the
adjacent counties of Maryd. & put them under a spirited & active
officer, who will receive his instructions from a committee of Congress.[1] I beg your attention to this business. Smallwood writes that
we have considerable stores at Charles Town, which he fears may be
taken or destroyed by these Insurgents. If we have any considerable
Stores at Charles Town, or at any other place near the bay they run
an equal or greater danger of being destroyed by parties from the
Enemy's Shipping. You can not take too much precaution to secure
these or any other stores that may be near the water.

Mr. Henry has sent you a copy of draughts of two Bills, which
as they are of a most insidious tendency, I make no doubt have long
since been passed into Acts of Parliat. I wish you would employ
some ingenious writer to combat & expose the perfidiousness of our
Enemies. They stop at nothing. The whole british Nation seems
rising against us; they will unite art & force to conquer us. I am
persuaded they will send over during the course of the summer &
fall at least 14000 men, principally british.

Is it not strange that the lust of domination should force the
British nation to greater exertions, than the desire of liberty can
produce among us?

By the Mercury Packet in 7 weeks & 3 days from Falmouth we
hear that all hopes of an amicable settlemt. between the Turks &
Russians were at an end. By a courier which arrived at Warsaw the
middle of Decr. there was reason to believe hostilities had then, or
were on the point of being commenced.

The Elector of Bavaria is dead. His death may possibly involve
Germany in a war. If our People would but exert themselves this
campaign we might Secure our liberties for ever. Gen. Washington
is weak; reinforcements come in slow. Try, for God Sake & the Sake
of human nature, to rouse our countrymen from their lethargy. Gates
will command a body of men in the Highlands on Hudson's river
for the Security of its navigation. The Congress do worse than ever.
We murder time, & chat it away on idle impertinent talk. However
I hope the urgency of affairs will teach even that Body a little dis-

cretion. I wish you health & happiness and am with great regard,
Dr. Sir, Yr. most hum. Servt.   Ch. Carroll of Carrollton

RC (MdAA).
¹ Gen. William Smallwood's April 17 letter to President Laurens was read in
Congress on April 20 and referred to a committee consisting of Carroll, Samuel
Chase, and William Duer. Although the general surmised that the insurrection
consisted of "more smoke than Fire," the insurgents did pose a threat to military
stores collected at Charles Town and he thought it prudent to call for outside
assistance because "my influence with the Legislature here is very Slender." The
latter reference is to difficulties he had recently had with Delaware officials over
the arrest of Charles Gordon and Thomas White, for which see Henry Laurens
to Smallwood, March 26, 1778. On April 23 Congress adopted resolves pursuant to
the committee's report calling on Maryland to march 300 militiamen and artillerists with two field pieces into Delaware, and authorizing the committee to apply
to the states of Delaware and Virginia as well if they should deem this necessary
to defeat "all disaffections, conspiracies and insurrections" threatening the Del-
marva peninsula. The committee apparently did not find it necessary to call for
further action at this time, however, for no such committee letters have been
found. Congress' resolves on the committee's report were transmitted to Maryland
by President Laurens. See JCC, 10:368, 383–84; PCC, item 161, fols. 179–82; and
Henry Laurens' April 24 letters to Thomas Johnson and to William Smallwood.

Samuel Chase to Thomas Johnson

Dear Sir,   York Town April 21. [17]78, Tuesday Night 11 o'Clock
   Congress this Evening recd a Letter from Gen. W. enclosing a
Philada. Paper of the 17 Ulto. The Draft of the two Bills (mentd.
in mine of this Day) are published in it. Dispatches arrived there last
Tuesday, in 28 days. Under the London Head of 19 February ———,
on the Tuesday preceding Leave was given to bring in the two Bills.
   Lord Norths Speech is in it, on making the proposition.
   Short late acts for your Satisfaction. "Our Army is great, our
Navy is great, our Men in Health, in Spirits, & well supplied, but
the Resistance of America is greater; & the War has lasted longer,
than was at first apprehended, much longer than any friend to this
Country could wish, & I do not think it will end in this Campaigne.
In the present Situation of affairs only three propositions can be
made—1st. to strengthen our forces & continue the War upon the
present plan. 2. to recal it from America, and 3. to offer Terms of
Conciliation to her. The first is attended with too great an Expence
of Men & Mony, *an Expence which Conquest itself wod. not balance.*
The second is to subscribe to the Independy of America. The third
is that which appears to Me to be the best and the wisest. I wish for
an open Conference with America—he then explained his plan as
expressed in the Bills.
   "I will say hold out to the Colonies a Cessation of the Exercise

In CONGRESS,

APRIL 23, 1778.

WHEREAS Perfuafion and Influence, the Example of the Deluded or Wicked, the Fear of Danger, or the Calamities of War, may have induced fome of the Subjects of thefe States to join, aid or abet the *Britifh* Forces in *America*, and who, tho' now defirous of returning to their Duty, and anxioufly wifhing to be received and reunited to their Country, may be deterred by the Fear of Punifhment: And whereas the People of thefe States are ever more ready to reclaim than to abandon, to mitigate than to increafe the Horrors of War, to pardon than to punifh Offenders:

RESOLVED, That it be recommended to the Legiflatures of the feveral States to pafs Laws, or to the Executive Authority of each State, if invefted with fufficient Power, to iffue Proclamations, offering Pardon, with fuch Exceptions, and under fuch Limitations and Reftrictions as they fhall think expedient, to fuch of their Inhabitants or Subjects, as have levied War againft any of thefe States, or adhered to, aided or abetted the Enemy, and fhall furrender themfelves to any Civil or Military Officer of any of thefe States, and fhall return to the State to which they may belong before the 10th Day of *June* next. And it is recommended to the good and faithful Citizens of thefe States to receive fuch returning Penitents with Compaffion and Mercy, and to forgive and bury in Oblivion their paft Failings and Tranfgreffions.

Extract from the Minutes,

Charles Thomfon, *Secretary.*

York-Town: Printed by HALL and SELLERS.

Resolve on Pardons, April 23, 1778

of Taxation, & I will not subject it to any Conds. or to the Demand of any specific Contribution. I do not see that any other Concession can be made without admitting the Complete Indy. of America—but wod. be the Effect of that Independy? I cannot see into futurity, but it is big with every possible Evils. *Independy with a cordial Love between Us is one thing; with an Union with our Enemies, fatal.* From their Indy a Danger arises from a great Naval Power; a Danger also to our other Possessions. I do not think that we should yield to it, till our Resources are much lowered. Indy. is not beneficial to America, she cannot be so happy, so easy, cannot have such personal Liberty, as if she remains dependant on Us." Moved for the Bills.

This Minute received the enclosed from our President.

I forgot—Ld North—"it is necessary to hold out some Inducemt to the Colonies, *collectively* & *seperately.* Some may not & some may renounce *their* Independency."

Two things are in my opinion essentially necessary—a respectable Army, a full Congress. Every Nerve shod. be exerted to fill our Ranks. I am of opinion that it would be prudent for every assembly or executive immediately to publish a Pardon to all their Subjects who have taken arms etc, who shall return to their Country & take the Oath of allegiance before a limitted Time.[1] Think well of this. I beleive it would thin their Ranks, and detach their friends. We *know* our people, many of them, are desirous of quitting them. If possible keep our assembly together—if broke up convene them early in June. I wish Mr Stone wod. come up. I wish Paca wod. quit his Judges Seat, & that our assembly wod. appoint him. I did intend Home, but I beleive I shall stay & see it out. The Hour to try the Firmness & prudence of Men is near at Hand. I am really diffident of Myself, I shall endeavor to act my Part well. My Soul has been chagrined at certain Conduct, but I love my Country, & shall with pleasure retire after Peace is established.

I am tired—tis 12 oClock. Adieu, Your Friend, Saml Chase

RC (MdAA).

[1] This proposal was probably already under consideration, for Congress on April 23 adopted a resolve recommending that the states offer pardons "to such of their inhabitants or subjects, who have levied war against any of these states . . . and who shall surrender themselves . . . before the 10th day of June," and urging the "faithful citizens of these states to receive such returning penitents with compassion and mercy, and to forgive and bury in oblivion their past failings and transgressions." See *JCC*, 10:381–82.

Henry Laurens to Samuel A. Otis

Dear Sir,
                                                            21st April 1778.
I beg you will accept my best thanks for your favour of 27th March & for the trouble you gave yourself in purchasing the articles by

Brown to add also a tender of my services, which you will be so good as to Command whenever you may have occasion.

By the return of Mr. Brown I now transmit you two Hundred fifty seven Dollars & a scrap which if I am not wrong will balance the account Excepting the remembrance of being with great respect &ca.[1]

LB (ScHi).
[1] This day Laurens also sent Henry Marchant a copy of a March 27 "Act of Congress for paying the Expence of Commissioners to enquire into the causes of the miscarriage of the expedition against Rhode Island." See PCC, item 13, fol. 267; and *JCC*, 10:290.

Virginia Delegates to Patrick Henry

Sir   York 21 April 1778.

General Howe having industriously circulated the Draught of a Bill, said to be the ground of an Act of Parliament intended to be passed, with a view no doubt of diverting the People of America from their grand object of Preparation and defence, and General Washington having transmitted a few Copies of it to Congress expressly to put it in their Power to guard against the baneful Effects with which this political stroke of G. Britain, if not counteracted, may be attended, we think it indispensably necessary to give you *thus early* the Substance of this intelligence & the Draught of the Bill: "A Draught of a Bill to declare the Intentions of Parliament, concerning the exercise of the Right of imposing Taxation within the Colonies."

"And be it hereafter declared that the King and Parliament, after the passing this Act, will not impose any duty, Tax, or assessment whatsoever, payable within any of the Colonies, except only such duties, as it may be expedient to impose, for the Regulation of Commerce: the Net produce of such duties to be paid and applied to the use of the Colony, in which levied, in such manner, as other duties collected by the authority of the Genl. Courts or assemblys of such Colonys are ordinarily paid & applied."

A *Draught* of a *Bill* to enable his Majesty to appoint Commissrs. to treat, consult, and agree upon Means of quieting the disorders in the Colonies.

"And be it enacted that Persons to be appointed by his Majesty shall have Power to treat, consult and agree, with such Body or Bodies political, and corporate or with such assembly, or assemblies of Men, or with such Person or Persons, as they shall think meet, of and concerning *any Grievances or Complaints* existing or supposed to exist, in the Government of any of the Colonies, or in the Laws and *Statutes* of this Realm respecting the *same* and of or concerning any *aid* or *Contribution* to be furnished, by all or any of the Colonies respectively, for the common defence of the Realm, & the Dominions thereunto belonging, and of and concerning such *other Regulations,* provisions, *Matters & things,* as, upon mature deliberation of the Commissrs., or any ——— of them, shall be thought necessary or convenient for the Honour of his Majesty, and the common Good of all his Subjects; *Provided,* that no Regulation, Provision, matter or thing, so proposed, treated, consulted, or agreed, shall have *any* other force or Effect, or be carried farther into execution, than is mentioned in this Act, untill approved by Parliament.

"*Provided also,* that the Commissioners, or any ——— of them, may order and proclaim a Cessation of Hostilities on the part of his Majesty's Troops, in any of the Colonies, for any time, and under any Conditions or Restrictions they should think convenient, and such order & Proclamation may revoke & annul according to their discretion. *And be it enacted,* that the Commissrs, or any ——— of them, may, by Proclamation, Suspend the Operation & Effects of the Act of Parliament, of the 16th Year of his Majestys Reign, for prohibiting all Trade & Intercourse, or of any of the Provisions or Restrictions therein contained, for such convenient time as they may think proper. *And be it in acted,* that the Commissrs. shall have Power to suspend, in such places, & for such times, as they may think fit, during the Continuance of this Act, the operation and Effects of all, or any of the Act or Acts of Parliament, which have passed since the 10th of Feb 1763, and which relate to any of the Colonies, so far as the same does relate to them. *And be it enacted,* that Commrs. shall have Power to grant a Pardon, or Pardons to any Number or description of Persons within any of the Colonies, and to appoint a Govenour in any Colony, with Such Powers as heretofore granted by his Majesty.

"The Act to continue in Force 'till 1st 1779."

Philda, April 14, 1778.   Published by order of the Commander in Chief.   mander in Chief.   Robt. Mackenzie, Secty.

Respecting this proposal & Scheme of the Enemy whither it be genuine from Parliament, or a Production of General Howes, we have only to observe that it may mislead the ignorant, & alienate the Minds of the wavering unless it is made public, & with its Publication such Strictures are made upon the probable Effects of it as may contribute to place the Subject in its true Light before the People. We are with the highest Respect Your Excellency's most Obed. Servant,

Francis Lightfoot Lee

John Banister

T. Adams

RC (Vi). Written by Banister and signed by Banister, Adams, and Lee.

Charles Carroll of Carrollton to
Charles Carroll, Sr.

Dear Papa   22d April 1778

Yesterday evening we heard from the General, who transmitted us a Pha. newspaper containing Lord Norths introductory speech to the two bills which I mentioned in my last. His Speech I will send you by the first opportunity; it shews that the British Ministry are seriously alarmed at the expence & consequence of this war. I am firmly of opinion; that if we can keep the Enemy at bay this campaign, & prevent their making any considerable impression, That G B will acknowledge the Independency of these 13 united States next winter or spring. The war between the Turks & Russians, the death of the Elector of Bavaria, & the foreseen consequences of that event or at least the dreaded consequences, perhaps, the suspicions of a treaty between our Agents & the Courts of France & Spain and the heavy expence of this war may have determined the Administration to this measure. I believe also they mean to lull us into security, & that they will send this Summer & fall very powerful reinforcements to Gen. Howe. North's speech discovers great despondency; perhaps there may be some policy in this, the better to deceive us & make us remiss in our preparation.

The Raleigh continental Frigate is arrived at Porsmouth in New Hampshire in 32 days from France; the Alfred, which sailed with her, is taken by the Enemy. We have not as yet received any dispatches from our Agents in France by the Raleigh; perhaps the express may be on the road. It will be astonishing if we receive no letters from them by this opportunity. My love to Molly, Mrs. Darnall & the little ones. God grant you all health. I am, yr. affectionate Son,

Ch. Carroll of Carrollton

P.S. As the speech will be printed this evening I shall send it to you, that you may judge for yourself. The President has informed some gentlemen (as he says from good authority) that Sir Wm. Howe is recalled & Sir Henry Clinton succeeds him in the command. This piece of information, I believe, comes from his son, who is one of General Washington's aids.

2d P.S. 24th. I thought to have sent you the Speech before this but the Express has been delayed by other business. I hear nothing more of Howes being superseded. Imagine it is not true; tho' by Ld. North's Speech it is pretty plain the Ministry do not approve of his conduct. I am afraid this severe weather will destroy all the forward fruit. Let me know in yr. next whether yours has suffered from it.

RC (MdHi).

Samuel Huntington's Proposed Resolution

[April 22–23? 1778][1]

Resolved, That notwithstanding the Unmeritted, Injurious & Cruel Treatment the United States of America have receivd from the hands of Great Brittain, they are ever willing & desirous to put an end to the Calamities of War; & ⟨disposed to⟩ not averse from[2] entering into a ⟨Friendly & Commercial perpetual alliance with Great Brittain⟩ Treaty for Peace and Commerce between the two Countries[3] for the mutual Interest & Benefit of both ⟨Nations⟩, Upon Terms not Inconsistant with the Freedom, Sovereignty & Independance of these States; or with any Treaties that are, or shall be made with any other Sovereign power before Such ⟨Alliance⟩ Treaty be formed.

MS (ScHi). In the hand of Samuel Huntington with amendments by Henry Laurens. Endorsed by Laurens: "Proposal for Treaty with Great Britain."

[1] It seems likely that this resolution was introduced either on April 22 while Congress was considering how to respond publicly to Lord North's conciliatory proposals or on the 23rd in the wake of the defeat of a motion for deleting a paragraph from the April 22 resolutions that required Britain's withdrawal of military forces or explicit recognition of American independence as a prerequisite to peace negotiations. See JCC, 10:379, 382–83. Henry Laurens' subsequent comments about this proposed resolve in his April 28 letter to John Laurens and in his May 1 letter to Rawlins Lowndes suggest that it was drafted prior to April 30, the date assigned by Edmund C. Burnett in his edition of delegate Letters. It also seems unlikely that such a resolve would have been introduced after April 27, the date Congress read a letter from George Johnstone to Robert Morris, which indicated that the British peace offer was intended to counter successful American negotiations in Paris. It is probable, nevertheless, that Congress did not take it up formally until April 30, when the journals indicate that "Congress proceeded to take into consideration the state of America with respect to foreign nations," and May 1, when a motion on the subject was postponed. On this point see Wm. Henry Drayton's Proposed Resolution, May 1, 1778, note. See also Burnett, Letters, 3:207; and Henry Laurens to Robert Morris, April 27, note 1, to John Laurens, April 28, and to Rawlins Lowndes, May 1, 1778.

[2] Preceding three words added by Laurens.

[3] Preceding nine words added by Laurens.

Henry Laurens to William Aylett

Sir,

22d April 1778

I have been honoured by the receipt of your favors of the 28th March & 3d Inst. These together with Govr. Henry Letter which attended them were presented to Congress the 13th Inst. & Committed.[1]

I have received no other direction but to transmit the Inclosed Act of the 14th for authorizing Mr. Hawkins to proceed in the purchase of Beef &ca & desiring you to continue in your Office until Colo. Wadsworth Commissary general of purchases shall give farther orders.[2] I had detained this Act a few days expecting to have sent it by the Bearer of Money for the Commissary's department in your district.

The Committee have not yet reported on the information given by you respecting the disposal of Salt by Messrs. Hughes & Smith, but as your attention to the public Interest in general & particularly in that Instance is highly applauded & as the reputations of those Gentlemen are also in question, I persuade myself the Committee will not suffer the subject to sleep under their hands, & that a full investigation of facts will soon be made for the satisfaction of all parties.[3]

At a time when extortion, purloining, peculation & unjust appropriation of public Money together with a Thousand other Acts equally unbecoming Men professing to be supporters of the Virtuous Cause of these Infant States appear within the observation of every discerning Citizen every day I cannot resist an inclination to thank a fellow Labourer who discovers some attention, some disinterested attachment to public Interest. Your conduct is generally approved as I judge from the Voice of Delegates in Congress; if my particular thanks are worth your acceptance, I beg you will receive them. It is not my intention to insinuate censure nor to pass an hasty judgement against the Gentlemen at Edinton who have not been heard in their defence although from your State of the Case, they have had time & opportunity for that purpose, but admitting you have in some particulars mistaken facts, Your Zeal & Candor merit thanks & you have mine most heartily.

Let us attack the Vices above mentioned & the whole Catalogue concomitant, & consecutive Attack vigorously when we discover them to be the practice of Men who for safety & support confide in established Character.

Bring to punishment one Capital transgressor & an hundred petit Knaves will fall by the same blow.

If we attend honestly to the expenditure of public Money, Issues from the Treasury will be restrained & the Comparative value of our Currency preserved. The greatest Enemies to these distressed States are those faithless false friends who under a pretence of serving the public have with sinister views plundered the Treasury, forced Emission upon Emission, depreciating the Exchange exactly in proportion to the increase in quantity.

Thank God there are some who have acted with a single Eye to public welfare, in this confidence it is with pleasure I assure you I am with great Regard &ca.

LB (DNA: PCC, item 13).
[1] The two letters from William Aylett, deputy commissary of purchases in Virginia, and the one from Governor Henry are not in PCC.
[2] This day Laurens also wrote a brief covering note to John Hawkins of Williams-

burg, Va., transmitting "an Act of Congress of the 14th Inst. Resolving that you proceed to purchase Beef, Cattle & Bacon agreeable to your contract with Governor Henry." See PCC, item 13, fol. 269; and *JCC*, 10:348. Unfortunately Hawkins died soon after the passage of this act. See Patrick Henry to the Virginia Delegates, May 26, 1778, PCC, item 78, 1:189–90.

[3] The precise nature of Aylett's charges against former North Carolina delegate Joseph Hewes and his business partner Robert Smith is unclear, but in a May 11 letter to Laurens Aylett alleged that he had bought 1,400 barrels of pork from Hewes that had been insufficiently salted owing to the high price of salt. PCC, item 78, 1:165–71. There is no evidence in the journals that Congress ever took any action against Hewes or Smith on this charge. See also Robert Morris to Committee of Commerce, February 17, 1778.

Henry Laurens to Baron de Kalb

Dear General   22d April [1778]

Although I have been four days in possession of your favor of the 16th[1] yet from a perpetual close engagement with variety of other businesses I am reduced to the necessity of writing in the last minute of Major Roger's stay at York Town. You will kindly make the proper inference.

I am extremely mortified by the account you give of the State of the Packages from Camden. Suspicions that such rascally tricks might be played as you have now experienced, had induced me to give Mr. Henry of Lancaster to whom I had directed the charge of the Trunks to be particularly attentive to the condition in which they should be delivered. I shall write to Colo. Kershaw on this subject & he will make the narrowest scrutiny in order to fix if possible the Roguery to some point.

Your Letter for France shall be taken proper care of.

With respect to the melancholy circumstance of Doctr. Phile, depend upon me Sir, every thing in my power shall be done to releive him, but I cannot flatter him with hopes of success from the application of any person himself excepted & the subject deserves the utmost exertions of a Parent.[2] If his health will permit he ought to fly in pursuit of his Child. If this cannot be done let him at least transmit me proper directions signed by himself.[3] These I will transfer to my friends & there will then be some ground for proceeding which will enable my friends in case of need to call in the aid of Government. Let me repeat everything in my power shall be done to serve Baron Kalb & any of his friends; in this particular instance, a stronger tie than common friendship bends me to listen—humanity commands my interposition. I would wish to make it with propriety.

I have not a moment for politics but I intreat you do not think of returning to France hastily.

Adieu, Dear Sir, I am perfectly & very Sincerely

LB (ScHi).

[1] A transcript of Kalb's April 16 letter to Laurens is in the Laurens Papers, ScHi.

[2] This is the first mention of one of the more bizarre problems that came to Laurens' attention during his career in Congress. Dr. Frederick Phile was a Philadelphia physician who had known Kalb since the latter's first visit to America in 1768. Before the British occupation of the city, according to Kalb's account in the letter cited above, Phile and his wife had befriended a certain "Colonel White of Georgia" and a woman White claimed was his wife but who was in fact his paramour, and had agreed to allow the childless couple to bring up as their own the Philes' twelve-year-old daughter Elizabeth. Soon after White and his mistress had returned to Georgia with Elizabeth, however, Phile learned that the colonel's real wife was living in New York and was shocked to realize that his daughter was being raised by an adulterous couple. But when he sought to arrange the return of his daughter, Phile was rebuffed not only by his two false friends but also by Elizabeth herself, who had the effrontery to claim that White and his lover were in fact her real parents! As Phile was unwilling to travel to Georgia himself because he was serving as a physician at a Continental hospital in Pennsylvania, he turned for help to his old friend Kalb, who for his part asked Laurens to urge the Georgia delegates to intervene and secure the return of Elizabeth to her parents. Laurens did not ask the Georgia delegates for their assistance, but he did promise Kalb that he would enlist the aid of some of his South Carolina friends to bring the girl home. Unfortunately, the final outcome of this curious episode is not recorded in the surviving correspondence between Laurens and Kalb. See also Adolf E. Zucker, *General de Kalb, Lafayette's Mentor* (Chapel Hill: University of North Carolina Press, 1966), pp. 70–71.

[3] See Laurens to Kalb, April 28, 1778.

Marine Committee to Thomas Read

Sir   April 22d. 1778

We have received your Letter of the 13th instant and are now to observe that the Captains of the Chase & Snow George were not considered as Continental Officers in the agreement the Committee of Commerce made with them, therefore no arguments can be drawn from that agreement to support the unreasonable demands of your Lieutenants, who if they will not go with you at the Continental pay must quit the service. We have directed Mr Steward to pay the wages due to the Seamen belonging to the Virginia and trust that Captain Nicholson will co-operate with you in getting such a Number of those Seamen to enter on board the Baltimore as you may want.[1] We shall send down the Hemp wanting for your Brig very soon & are sir, Yr. very hble Servants[2]

LB (DNA: PCC Miscellaneous Papers, Marine Committee Letter Book).

[1] For information on the Committee of Commerce's subsequent use of the *Baltimore*, see the committee's May 28 letter to the Commissioners at Paris.

[2] This day the Marine Committee also wrote the following letter to Richard Ellis, the Continental agent at New Bern, N.C. "We have received your Letter of the 2d of March last advising us of your having received from the Marshal of the

Court of Admiralty at your place Two hundred & Sixty Nine pounds 12s for the two thirds of the Net Sales of the Prize Sloop Tryall taken by the Continental sloop Providence and sent into your port. We are now to inform you that by the Rules and Regulations of Congress the Captors are intitled to One half of the Prize, and that you had ommitted to enclose in your letters the Account Sales, nor have we received your letter of the 9th Feby. Considering the high prices at which Vessels are sold, we cannot help being surprized at the small sum which the Sloop sold for, therefore we must request you will inform us on that head and whether she had any Cargo on board or not." PCC Miscellaneous Papers, Marine Committee Letter Book, fol. 143; and Paullin, *Marine Committee Letters,* 1:230–31.

Robert Morris to Thomas Mumford

Sir   Manheim in Pensylvania, April 22d. 1778

I am employed at present in Settling the Accounts of the Secret Committee of Congress, you stand Charged in their Books with the Sums advanced but have no Credits. It is therefore necessary that you send me Invoices & bills of Loading for the Cargoes Shipped, charter Parties for the Vessells hired, Protests & proper Documents to support any charges for Capture, losses, freights &c, you will also send me acct sales of the Cargoes that arrived, Invoices & bills Loading for the returns, the Accts Currt formed thereby, an Acct of the delivery of the returns or receipts from those they were delivered to or Copies of such rects.[1]

If these papers come in time I will have them examined & Entd. If they do not your Acct must stand open untill some other person is appointed to settle what I am obliged to leave unfinished.

I am Sir, Your Obedt hble servt.   Robt. Morris

RC (NNPM).
[1] Morris wrote a similar letter this day to John Langdon, which is in the Capt. J. G. M. Stone Collection, Annapolis, Md. A transcript of it is in the Lee Family Papers, MH–H.

John Banister to St. George Tucker

My dear Sir   York 23d April 1778

Time previous to the departure of my Acquaintance Col. Harnet being very short, only admits of my acknowledging your kind attention from Wmsburg and begging you'd omit no opportunity of giving me repeatedly the Pleasure of hearing from you and [. . . .] *Sub Sigillo Silentii it shall be rest you assured,* as much as if eternal Night & its attendant Silence had spread its dominion over all things. I wish my attachments were not so immutably fixed. You know to what this alludes.[1] Hard very hard indeed, but no more of this. The enclosed will inform you fully of a very important Measure the British Parliament have no doubt adopted through the Recommendation of Lord North, as the Bill was ushered into the house of commons by a long explanatory Speech of his which you will see opens the design & Se[cret] of the intended Law. On this the Congress have made their Strictures shewing the Terms inadmissible, as [being] incompatible with American Independance.[2]

It appears the British Court begin to think seriously of the bloody business they are engaged in, & I am not without hopes their next Proposal will be a Treaty with the admission of Independence, for as L——d North justly observes Independence with the Friendship of America is one thing, but her Independence and alliance with the Enemies of Britain is another, and how different in their Effects. Now is the time for Britain to form an advantageous Connection with America, or yield her as an Ally to the superiour policy of France. I cordially wish the former both from interest & opinion of the People. I look forward to August with Impatience. This is a life of real *hard*ship, unintermitting Employment. Adieu. May all that's etherial in you be pure & serene, & your Mercury be reduced to a moderate State of Sublimation.

Yr. affec. Friend   J Banister

[*P.S.*] Mr. Banister presents to his F——d St. Geo. a Brother Delegate Mr. Harnet, a Gentleman of Sense & Merit, & he insists that Mr. Tucker pay his Respects at Battersea to Mr. Harnett.

RC (ViW).
  [1] Banister is probably referring to Anne Blair, of Williamsburg, Va., whom he married in 1779. She was a sister of the jurist John Blair, Jr., and a confidante of both Tucker and Frances Randolph. See Mary H. Coleman, *St. George Tucker* (Richmond, Va.: Dietz Press, 1938), pp. 38, 41–42; and Frederick Horner, *History of the Blair, Banister, and Braxton Familes before and after the Revolution* (Philadelphia: J.B. Lippincott Company, 1898), p. 97.
  [2] For this congressional response to the North ministry's conciliatory bills, see *JCC,* 10:374–80; and Henry Laurens to James Duane, April 20, 1778, note 1.

Charles Carroll of Carrollton to Thomas Johnson

Dear Sir,   23d April 1778
By this opportunity you will receive draughts of two bills and Ld North's speech ushering them into the house of Commons. I have little doubt myself but that these Bills have long since been cloathed with all the formalities of law. If Lord North's speech is genuine (and I think we have no reason to suspect it to be otherwise) we may fairly conclude that the Administration begin to see the impracticability of

reducing these States, or of retaining them, when reduced, in such a state of subordination as to be useful to G B. The heavy & encreasing expence of the war, a Jealousy of France & Spain, perhaps the appearances of an approaching rupture in Germany about to be occasioned by the death of the Elector of Bavaria, the actual commencement of hostilities between Russia & the Porte have forced the British Ministry on this measure. However I am satisfied they will try the arts of negotiation first, in order to divide us, if possible, and will hazard another campaign, before they acknowledge the Indepence of these States: to withstand their hostile efforts this campaign, which I am convinced will be vigorous, and to counteract their insidious profers of reconciliation, it will be absolutely necessary to have a very respectable force in the field this year; and if a right & dexterous use is made of the Minister's speech, it will probably much promote the recruiting service among us. In a word, if we guard agt. their insidious offers on the one hand, and can resist their warlike efforts on the other during the ensuing campaign, I have not the least doubt but that they will acknowlege our Independency next winter, or Spring, particularly if no alliance between these States or any other European power be concluded in the interim.

The Raleigh continental Frigate is arrived at Porsmouth in 32 days from France; the Alfred which sailed with her is taken; we have not yet recd by this opportunity any dispatches from our Commissioners at Paris, tho I do not yet despair of receiving them, as the Express may be on the road.

The Congress has passed some observations on the two draughted Bills, to counteract their obvious design, or at least the possible bad effects they might produce in the minds of the People, if published without such strictures. These Observations will be printed to day; they will be immediately distributed throughout the United States.[1] I fear they are not so perfect as they ought to be, but the hurry of business & the want of time must & will, no doubt, sufficiently apologize with an impartial Public for all their imperfections. I am with real regard, Dear Sir, Yr. most hum. Servt

Ch. Carroll of Carrollton

RC (MdAA).
[1] See Henry Laurens to James Duane, April 20, 1778, note 1.

James Duane to Henry Laurens

Dear Sir,   on publick Service Albany 24th April 1778
I have passed some days in this City in Conference with the Commissioners of Indian Affairs on General Washington's Application

for a party of the Oneidas and Tuscaroroes to join the grand Army.[1] Every Measure in our power has been taken to accelerate a Requisition which his Excellency has so much at Heart. These Nations have sent an Answer to a Speech from the Commissioners on the Subject, which will be transmitted by the Board. In the mean time as I this moment heard of an Opportunity by Express, I shall mention the Substance. They say that the Number of 200 is more than can be obtaind; but if the Troops and Fortress which they solicited are furnished agreeable to the Commisrs promise they will send forward a party of their Warriors; the number they do not ascertain. I presume the Result of the Council of the Six Nations now assembled at Onondago to deliberate on the Talk from the honourable Congress will enable us to form a true Judgement of the Dependance which may be placed on the Cooperation of those Nations. If they see a prospect of Tranquility on their own Borders some of them will turn out & Join our Arms with alacrity, otherwise it is hardly to be expected.

Since I wrote you a State of Affairs in this Department in my Letter of the 16th of March[2] one of my Predictions is verified. The Enemy with a Number of Vessells and Troops have appeard at Ticonderoga. A Party of 600 have landed and defeated the Militia of that neighbourhood. The whole Northern frontier is in Confusion. They apply earnestly for Assistance, and declare that without it they must again abandon their Farms of which many of them have so lately regaind the possession. But what Succour can be afforded? The Inhabitants of Tryon County are still apprehensive of an attack from the Westward; and from Albany Northward, which has been the principal Scene of the last Campaign the people may be said to be at work *for their Lives*; for if they do not at this Season get in their *Summer* Crops—(*fall* they have none)—they must starve. In the mean time all the Continental Troops except three small Regiments barely sufficient to guard the Publick Stores and Magazines and Laboratory at this place are drawn away. These Regiments are Graton's of about 210, Alden's 300, and Warners 124 Including N. C. Os. Van Schaacks of this State which was 500 strong I saw go away with great Reluctance on my part. Of our five Battallions none are now left us but Gansevoorts which garrisons Fort Schuyler, and the remains of Du Bois's employed in the defences of Hudson's River. If this State was in any tolerable Security it woud be my first Ambition to see the Forces which it has raised fighting the Battles of their Country in the most conspicious Field of Glory; but while We are exposed in every Quarter I cannot but entertain disagreable Apprehensions from the feeble Condition in which it is left. I have done the little in my power to prevent the Distresses which threaten us by my endeavours to possess Congress of the true Circumstances of our Affairs in my Letter before alluded to. That it has not had some weight I pray God may not prove a publick misfortune.

We expect daily the Resolution of the Indian Council at Onondago. Much depends upon it, and I wait here to receive it and assist the Commissioners in the Measures which may be further necessary in their Department.

I have received particular Pleasure in taking a view of the Laby. & Park of Artillery & military Stores at this place. Everything is in the most excellent order, and great Honour is due to Major Stevens of the Massachs. who commands the Corpse of Artillery in this Department. The Conduct of this young Gentleman in the Field & in conducting the publick Works is so distinguished as to entitle him to Favour & Applause. The Committee of Congress who visited Ticonda. in November 1776[3] appointed him Major of a Corpse of Artillery to be raised & to consist of three Companies of Artillery & one of Artificers to serve in the Northern Department. The 9th of the same month he recd a Commission from Congress appointing him Major *Commadant* of that Corpse. He is much dissatisfied on finding that Col. Crane considers him as Major of his Regiment of Artillery; which Mr. Stephens thinks a Degradation; & seems determind to Join the Grand Army as a Volunteer if it is insisted on. The officers of his corpse are equally averse to such an Arrangement. These are the Facts which I promised to State to Congress, & for the Truth of which he refers to Major General Gates. I wish as Major Stevens has undergone severe Service, with great Reputation, & without any promotion, that a suitable attention may be paid to his Merit. He declares that he is contented to retain his present Rank in a separate Command. If He can be gratified consistent with the good of the Publick, it seems to be a very small Reward for a series of services so distingushed; & in the last Campaign so eminently successful.[4]

I have the Honour to be, with the greatest Respect, Dear Sir, Your most Obedient humble Servant,   Jas. Duane

[*P.S.*] There are still great Complaints of the want of money in this Department. The Commissy. of Purchases is disabled from complying with his Contracts, & the fat Cattle intended for the Army fall into private Hands for fear of the Operation of the regulating Law which has taken place in this & other states. The Paymasters of Van Schaack's & Gansevort's Regiments have taken up large Sums to silence the clamours of the Soldiers. It was well that they were Gent. of credit & connections, or this Seasonable Remedy woud have been out of their power. There are 200,000 Dollars in the Military Chest; but it is said Mr Trumbull has directed this money to be removd to the Fish Kills; And that if it remaind here there are no means to issue it; as a General Officer's warrant is necessary. If the operations of the Enemy to the Northward become more serious; and already they are very distressing to the frontier Inhabitants; what is to be done? Is not Gen. Carleton at the head of 3000 men with the entire command of the Lakes which conduct him to our very Doors still formidable; If not for the purposes of Conquest at least for those of Ruin and Desolation?

RC (DNA: PCC, item 78). Endorsed by Charles Thomson: "Letter from Jams. Duane Esq 24 April 1778. read May 4. copy thereof to be sent to Genl Washington & one for gen Gates."

[1] Washington had made this "Application" in a March 13 letter to the commissioners for Indian affairs in the northern department, whom Duane had been assisting in their dealings with the Six Nations. Washington, *Writings* (Fitzpatrick), 11:76–77.

[2] Not found.

[3] For a discussion of the work of this committee, see John Hancock to Philip Schuyler, September 27, 1776, note 4.

[4] Even before Duane's letter arrived in York, Congress resolved on April 30 that in recognition of his distinguished service as commander of artillery in the northern department Maj. Ebenezer Stevens "take rank by brevet as a lieutenant colonel of foot." *JCC,* 10:410.

John Henry to Thomas Johnson

Sir   York Town Apl 24th. 1778

I am desired by the Delegates to acquaint your Excellency that we have this Day procured from Congress thirty thousand Dollars for the recruiting service.[1] Col. Williams applied to us for Money for that purpose, and we have thought it proper to allow him out of that Sum eight thousand Dollars; the remaining twenty two Thousand will go from this place by Mr. Hamilton an Express sent up by Col S. Smith. I have desired him as soon as the express reaches him, to send him forward to you.

As to Arms and Blankets, I can promise you nothing certain at this time. A few have lately arrived in the Eastern States. The Board of war have promised me our troops shall have their proportion of them. Every step is taken to procure Arms, and I hope as the troops come forward the Board of war will be able to supply them. The Arms of the state I would keep. Not one of them should, if I could prevent it, come out of the state, but upon the most urgent Necessity. I have just left the Board of war, and they are desirous and willing that you should have the goods now at Cambridge made up in Baltimore. And if you will be kind enough to write particularly what you want, they will immediately authorise you to take such Articles and to distribute them among the Maryland Troops.

You will receive by an Express which left this place to Day Lord North Speech, the two Bills which occasioned it and the Strictures of

Congress upon them. They were drawn up in haste, but I trust they will be sufficient to shew the wickedness of the Ministry.

I am Sir with great respect, yrs.   J Henry junr.

RC (MdAA).
[1] See *JCC,* 10:385.

Henry Laurens to Richard Caswell

Sir,   24th April [1778]
Since my last of the 31st March by Lieut. Thomson I have had the honour of receiving & presenting to Congress Your Excellency's favour of the 26th of the same Month.[1]

Within the present packet Your Excellency will receive twelve printed Copies of a Speech said to have been made in the British House of Commons by Lord North, Draughts of Bills referred to by His Lordship & an Act of Congress of the 22d pointing to those supposed performances in the Councils of old England & earnestly calling upon the States for their contribution to put the Army in the most respectable State for meeting the Enemy with the Sword or the Olive branch.

Last Night intelligence was received of great commotions in the City of Philadelphia, the Officers of the Enemy's Army expressing loud dissatisfaction at the appearance of an unfavorable change of affairs, & the Citizens clamoring their apprehensions of what may happen to them. Admitting all this to be true, it may be mere shew, & we ought not to trust for safety from crafty manœvres. Let us endeavor to be prepared for meeting either Generals or Ambassadors with a formidable force as the only means of procuring terms for an honorable peace. General Lee had assured me some days since that many Officers in the British Army are good Whigs & speak their sentiments freely & none of the whole group satisfied with their late & present employment. I have good authority for saying that General Howe is recalled & 'tis said Sir H Clinton is to be at the head of the Army.

A dangerous attempt to Insurrection is discovered in the State of Delaware & parts adjacent in Maryland, Congress have adopted such measures as appear necessary for suppressing the parties concerned in it & for bringing them to punishment. I have the honour to be &ca.

LB (DNA: PCC, item 13).
[1] Governor Caswell's March 26 letter to Laurens is in PCC, item 72, fols. 35–36, and *N.C. State Records,* 13:72–73. In it he acknowledged receipt of the resolves enclosed with Laurens' March 1 letter to him.

Henry Laurens to Nathanael Greene

Sir   24th April 1778

Your favour of the 20th reached me the 22d.[1] I presented it to Congress whence it was committed to the Treasury & has produced the Inclosed Warrant on the loan Office in New Jersey for 50000 Dollars. Congress had very lately made such draughts on that Office as neither Mr. Borden nor your self had been apprized of, the amount of which, the Delegate from Jersey supposes will have nearly emptied the Office of Money, for this reason & no other your application is not fully answered.

I have the honour to be &ca.

LB (DNA: PCC, item 13).

[1] Quartermaster General Greene's April 20 letter to Laurens, in which he requested "an Order on the Loan Officer of New-Jersey for One hundred and fifty thousand Dollars . . . to give Vigour to the Purchasing of Horses and other necessary Supplies," is in PCC, item 155, 1:63. Congress read Greene's letter on the 24th and approved a warrant on the New Jersey loan officer for only a third of the amount requested. *JCC,* 10:384.

Henry Laurens to Thomas Johnson

Sir.   York Town 24 April 1778[1]

My last went by Lieutt. Thomson under the 31st March.[2] Much time has elapsed since I have been honoured with any of Your Excellency's favors.

If Your Excellency will be pleased to intimate the Receipt of my Letters, Congress will have the satisfaction of knowing when their several Acts transmitted to Maryland are in a state of safety, I shall be enabled to detect miscarriages if any should happen, & in the course of my duty to supply deficiencies.

Within the present Inclosure Your Excellency will receive an Act of Congress of the 23d Inst. for detecting disaffection & defeating conspiracies & Insurrections in the district therein mentioned, together with Copy of a Letter from General Smallwood of the 17th & Copies of two Letters which the General refers to.

Your Excellency will likewise receive in the same Packet 12 Copies of a Speech said to be Lord North's in Parliament, draughts of Bills which he refers to & an Act of Congress of the 22d April pointing to the supposed Speech &c.[3]

I have the honour to be, With great regard, sir, Your Excellency's Obedient & humble servt,

                                        Henry Laurens, President of Congress.

RC (MdAA).

¹ Laurens also wrote substantially the same letter this day to Governor Henry of Virginia. PCC, item 13, fol. 270.

² See Laurens to Richard Caswell, March 31, 1778, note 2.

³ Laurens noted in his presidential letter book that this day he also transmitted to Gov. William Livingston of New Jersey and President Caesar Rodney of Delaware twelve copies of Congress' April 22 reply to Lord North's conciliatory bills. PCC, item 13, fol. 274; and JCC, 10:374–80. At the same time he sent copies of this reply and an April 24 resolve "for transporting Provisions & Stores from the Southern States across Cheasepeake" to President Thomas Wharton of Pennsylvania. PCC, item 13, fol. 273; and JCC, 10:385.

Henry Laurens to John Penn

Dear Sir,   24th April [1778]

By the Seals affixed to the inclosed Letter you will see that I had opened it, that is to say, had in my usual way cut the paper round the first Seal, which was no sooner done than I discovered the error without seeing the Contents the whole of which I am as ignorant as you at the present moment are. It had come in a number of public Letters when Mr. Drayton was sitting with us & anxious to communicate intelligence to that Gentleman, I had begun to open this, supposing it to have been directed to me, he was Witness to the accident & to my instantly mending the breach.

Inclosed with this you will receive three Copies of an Act of Congress of the 22d Inst. founded on the appearance of preceeding Acts said to be Lord Norths Speech & draughts of Bills referred to. Supposing these to be Sibyl's Letters, our Act I trust, will do no harm. The States will learn the temper of their Delegates & I hope be animated to the utmost exertions for reinforcing the Army. The general opinion is in favor of the genuineness of the Speech &ca. & last Night intelligence from the City imported marks of confirmation. Tis said the Army & their Landlords were in commotion the former exceedingly dissatisfied with the politics at St. James's, the latter with "Conscience trembling for their Sins." I may laugh at all this & admit it to be so, but as nothing looks so much like an honest Man as a Rogue, I would act & earnestly wish all these States to Act as if the whole was manœvre. Admitting this suspicion to be grounded in experience, we ought to be ready & early with a formidable Army in the Field.

A formidable appearance will oblige our Enemies to dulcify their propositions if they mean to hold out any, for peace. Never trust appearances on the part of an Enemy.

General Gates will begin his Journey to Morrow for Fish Kill where he is to take Command of the Northern Army. In the way he is to call at Valley forge & assist in a Council of Major Generals for establishing a plan of operations for the Campaign. General Mifflin will attend him.

I could write you a sheet full of affairs but yonder Bill will fright me presently, & I have been sitting in this spot from 1/4 past four, tis now near Nine.

Adieu Dear Sir, I wish you health & every degree of happiness which is worth twenty humble servants.

LB (ScHi). Addressed: "John Penn Esquire, New Bern, by Wm. Stuart."

Henry Laurens to William Smallwood

Sir   24th April [1778]

Your favor of the 17th with the papers referred to I had the honor of receiving & presenting in due course to Congress. A special Committee of Mr. Duer, Mr. Chase & Mr. Carrol are appointed by Congress in order to confer with the Goverments of Maryland, Virginia & if needful Delaware on proper measures for supressing the threatned Evils intimated in your late dispatches. From these Gentlemen you will receive the necessary information.[1] I have only at present to Inclose an Act of Congress of the 23d Inst. reviving late powers vested in General Washington & extending the term to the 10th August next.

I am with very great Esteem &ca.

LB (DNA: PCC, item 13).
[1] No committee letter to Smallwood has been found, but for a discussion of this issue, see Charles Carroll of Carrollton to Thomas Johnson, April 21, 1778, note.

Henry Laurens to George Washington

Sir,   York Town 24th Ap. 1778

Since my last of the 18th Inst. by a Messenger returning to Govr. Livingston, I have had the honor of presenting to Congress Your Excellency's Letter of the 20th.[1]

Your Excellency will be pleased to receive under the present Cover.

1. An Act of Congress of the 21st Ap. approving the conduct of the Commissioners appointed by Your Excellency to treat with British Commissioners for Exchange of Prisoners &ca.[2]

2. for granting Pardons & recommending to the several States to enact Laws for that purpose (dated 23d).

3. of the 23d renewing the Powers formerly vested in Your Excellency & extending the term to 10th August next.[3]

4. Copy of Instructions to Major General Gates appointed to Command the Forces in the Northern department.[4]

5. of the 22d contained in a Pennsylvania Gazette confirming the Report of a Committee on your Excellency's Letter of the 18th.[5]

In a separate Packet will be found about fifty Copies of the last mentioned Act which Your Excellency will be pleased to disperse in such a manner as shall appear best for accomplishing the good purposes intended.

A Packet containing about 200 Copies of the Act for Pardons, these if I understand Congress for I have received no special direction, are to be dispersed at proper opportunities in the City of Philadelphia & whereever else good effects may be expected—Congress taking for granted that each State will enact a proper Law under the present recommendation. There will probably be a further quantity in the German Tongue sent from Lancaster.[6]

I have the honor to be, With the highest Esteem & Regard, Sir, Your Excellency's Most obedient & humble servant,

Henry Laurens, President of Congress

25th. Late last Night Your Excellency's favor of the 23d together with the sundry papers referred to reached me & shall be presented to Congress this Morning.[7] Your Excellency's Letter to General Lee shall be immediately dispatched to the General in Virginia.[8] General Gates intimates to me his determination to wait General Lee's return to York & with him to proceed to Valley Forge.

RC (DLC).

[1] Washington's April 20 letter to Laurens is in PCC, item 152, 5:511, and Washington, *Writings* (Fitzpatrick), 11:281–82.

[2] For the events leading up to the adoption of this resolve, see Laurens' letters to Washington of March 15, note 1, April 8, note 4, and April 14, 1778.

[3] Congress' last grant of authority to Washington to requisition property and imprison persons within the vicinity of his headquarters had expired on April 10. See *JCC*, 9:1014–15, 10:384.

[4] See Laurens to James Duane, April 17, 1778, note 2.

[5] A reference to Congress' April 22 response to Lord North's conciliatory proposals, a text of which Washington had enclosed with his April 18 letter to Laurens. See *JCC*, 10:374–80; and Washington, *Writings* (Fitzpatrick), 11:276–78.

[6] See Laurens to Francis Bailey, April 28, 1778.

[7] Washington's April 23 letter to Laurens is in PCC, item 152, 5:515–17, and Washington, *Writings* (Fitzpatrick), 11:300–302. With it he enclosed an April 17 letter from William Tryon, the last royal governor of New York, requesting Washington to acquaint his men with Lord North's conciliatory bills, as well as a copy of the April 3 *Pennsylvania Evening Post* containing a bogus February 19 resolve of Congress, which stated that all Continental soldiers, both those now in the army and those who later enlisted, had to serve for the duration of the war. A number of delegates were offended by this British propaganda ploy, which moved Secretary Thomson to write the following indignant letter of denial to an unidentified correspondent on April 27:

"I am much obliged by your favor. If it was possible to be surprised by any chicanery of the enemy, this might perhaps have that effect. The only circumstance that excites any kind of wonder is their folly and stupidity in attempting a forgery which is so easily detected by every inhabitant of the States who reads the public papers. However, to remove every doubt, I assure you, that no such regulation ever passed, nor was any such ever moved in Congress." *Pennsylvania Packet,* May 6, 1778.

[8] See Washington, *Writings* (Fitzpatrick), 11:295.

Thomas Burke to Richard Caswell

Dr Sir.   York April 25th 1778

Mr Harnett will inform you of every thing which I can write about at present. I shall therefore refer you to him, and spare you the trouble of reading.

The enclosed paper[1] will shew you the present temper of our Enemies, and the disposition of Congress. I will make on it no other comment than to observe that nothing is necessary to ensure our success but vigorous efforts. This opinion which I have so often declared, is every day more and more justified, and I hope will be finally sanctified by the happy event of our struggles.

I hope before this the assembly have made a new choice of Delegates, and supplied my place with a more able citizen. I shall set off on the fourth of May and leave what public papers are in my hands directed for the succeeding Delegates. Altho' I shall remain here until that day, yet I do not find myself entirely clear on the propriety of voting in Congress after the 28th Inst. I am told by Mr Harnett that on that day, in last year the election of Delegates was made, and on the preceding day in this year, trust in that case the term of my service ends. The commission under your hand being dated the 4th of May and having in some former letters promised to remain here until then to execute any command of the state, I will keep my promise tho' I assure you Sir, every hour is and will be a very heavy one to me, until I can return to the station of a private Citizen, secure under the protection of the Laws and constitution of my Country. Every day Sir, convinces me more and more, that such a station is the only happy one, and nothing but my deference to the opinion of my Country and my wishes to serve the cause of Freedom should ever have drawn me from it, or will withhold me now from it. Happy is it, for those Countries who are at a distance from the war. They are secured from the depradations of the Enemy, and their civil rights from most violent infractions. The Rights of private citizens, and even of our sovereign Communities are at present so little regarded in Congress that any rumor will determine a majority to violate both, and it is hardly safe to oppose it. Every argument against the unlimited power of Congress to judge of necessity, and under that

Idea to interpose with military force is heard with great reluctance, hardly with patience, and the internal police and sovereignty of states, are treated as chimerical phantoms. One instance I will give you. Genl. Smallwood was ordered by Congress to apprehend two men, in the Delaware State, under a suggestion that they were inimical, and that the state was unable to exercise any act of government, tho the assembly was then sitting. He did apprehend them. They applied for a Habeas Corpus. The Chief-Justice granted it, the officer refused to obey and applied to Congress for advice. The Congress approved the officers conduct, and was with difficulty prevented from ordering him in express terms to proceed in direct opposition to the habeas Corpus—and they forbore this only under an Idea that approbation of his former conduct would determine him to proceed.[2] I need not tell you I opposed these things. You know my pertinacious attachment to civil Rights, and my immovable determination to oppose every thing that may give color to an arbitrary exercise of Power under an Idea of right. I shall probably give you another instance before long wherein our state and I myself am concerned. I have upon a late occasion insisted so far on the sovereignty of the state, and my being amenable to no other jurisdiction, that I have given very great offence to Congress.[3] An accident involved me in the dispute, and so far as it regarded me personally I should have waved all opposition, but I delivered occasionally in debate my political Opinions of the power of Congress and the sovereign and exclusive Authority of the states, over these Delegates. These Opinions were not relished and I was required to make some apology. I very frequently apoligised for the Terms and manner in which they were conveyed, tho' I could not perceive any thing offensive in them, but I persisted in the Opinions, and declared I could not give them up without an Outrage to my honor in telling a falsehood and what I deemed a treason to the state I represented in giving up her sovereignty. Nothing however would do, but retracting the opinions, and it was in vain to require this of a man who would die in support of them. I shall trouble you no more at present on this subject, but at some future time will give it to you, with all its circumstances. My Country will I suppose one day judge of it, but I shall not desire it during the present struggle. I should be very sorry that any thing would interrupt the public harmony which is so necessary to our success, a time of peace and tranquility will better suit the investigation of Civil Rights and relations. I wish you sir, all imaginable happiness, and am with the greatest sincerity your Mo. Ob. servt.[4]   Thos. Burke

Tr (Nc–Ar).

[1] Probably the April 24 issue of the *Pennsylvania Gazette,* which contained Lord North's proposals for reconciliation and Congress' April 22 response to them.

[2] For further information on this subject, see Henry Laurens to William Small-wood, March 26, and to Caesar Rodney, April 15, 1778.

[3] See Burke's Proposed Statement to Congress, April 13, and his letters to Caswell and to the North Carolina Assembly of April 29, 1778.

[4] Burke informed Cornelius Harnett, who left York on April 26, that he wished Governor Caswell to regard this letter as confidential. "The Letter from Mr. Burke," Harnett wrote to Caswell from Wilmington, N.C., on May 25, "he desired me to mention to you was only for your own private Information. I hope before he left Congress the whole was erased from the Journal." NjMoHP.

William Ellery to Nicholas Cooke

Sir   York Town April 25th 1778

Mr. Collins arrived here last Saturday with emaciated horses after having passed through a very deep and difficult road. Your Letter to the President of Congress and the state accounts are referred to the treasury board who will soon report thereon to Congress. We should urge this matter on; but it would be impossible for Mr Collins to procede with his horses without being recruited, and the longer he stays here the more money he will probably recieve. I could wish that the Assembly in their Letters had mentioned what part of the ballance it would have suited them to receive, in Loan-Office certificates. However I shall do what I think will be agreeable to my constituents.[1]

The confederation is not yet taken up; if it should be before I return I will pay a religious regard to your instructions.

I observe that the State have fitted out a Vessel to purchase a load of provisions at Maryland, Virginia, or North Carolina. If she had been dispatched in the winter it would have been better. The navigation then was less hazardous, and provisions much cheaper than at present. I wish her a prosperous voyage, and will honour the bills that the Capt. of her may draw upon me on account of the state. In a letter I wrote to the Assembly[2] sometime past I informed them that I had paid out off the ten thousand dollars, which Mr. Marchant had retained of the 200,000, a bill of exchange drawn by Timothy Coffin late master of the Diamond on Mr. Marchant and myself in favour of Richard Ellis and endorsed to Ruben Hussey or order, of which as no notice hath been taken in any letter I have received from Governt., I am afraid my Letter miscarried.

Mr. Collins informs me that the Delegates which will be chosen at the ensuing election will not set out until some time in June. I should be loth to leave congress, the state unrepresented, but my health, and the unhappy situation of my family require that I should be at home as soon as possible, wherefore let me intreat you to send forward two of the delegates at least immediately after the choice.

This will be accompanied by a late Speech of Lord North, the Draught of two bills and the remarks of Congress on the latter. The design of this ministerial manœuvre is obvious.

We have nothing new. I continue to be with great respect, your excellency's most obedient and most humble Servant, W Ellery

[*P.S.*] Since I wrote the foregoing I have seen a printed hand bill of the two Drafts contained in the news paper with a certificate of Govr. Genl. Tryon.[3] A copy of said Certificate I now inclose.

W E

RC (R–Ar).

[1] On May 1 Congress ordered payment of an advance of $150,000 to John Collins for delivery to Rhode Island in response to Governor Cooke's April 4 letter to Congress. *JCC,* 10:367, 414, 11:415. Collins was a member of the Rhode Island Council who had been sent to York to obtain reimbursement for the state's expenditures on Continental account. See Ellery to Cooke, January 4, 1778, note.

[2] Not found, but see Ellery to Cooke, December 14, 1777.

[3] The handbill containing texts of Lord North's conciliatory bills and William Tryon's April 15 statement attesting to their authenticity is listed in Evans, *Am. Bibliography,* no. 15827.

William Ellery to William Vernon

Dear Sir   York Town April 25th. 1778

I am now to acknowledge the receipt of yours of the 4th of March and the fourth of this month.

The Boston hath on board a pretious cargoe.[1] May she carry it safe to France! The Enemies ships do indeed swarm in the Seas of America and Europe; but hitherto only one of our Frigates hath been captured on the Ocean. Two have been burned in North River, two sunk in Delaware, one captured there, and one in Chesapeak. The Alfred we are just informed was taken on her passage home by two frigates in sight of the Rawleigh. The particulars of this capture and why she was not supported by the Rawleigh we are ignorant of. I hope Capt. Thompson is not culpable. I entertain a high opinion of him. The Columbus is a trifling Loss, and I should not much lament the Loss of the Alfred if her brave Captain, officers and men were not in the hands of a cruel enemy.[2] Our little fleet is very much thinned. We must contrive some plan for catching some of the Enemy's Frigates to supply our Losses; but we must take care not to catch tartars. It is reported that Capt. Biddle of the Randolph, in an engagement with a sixty gun ship, was blown up. We have been so unfortunate that I am apt to believe almost any bad news; but this report I cannot believe. I fear for the Providence, I know but little respecting her captain, and only one of her other officers.

General Burgoyne and his family are allowed by Congress to go to Britain on their parole and Col. Anstruther to Rhode Island to solicit an exchange between himself and Col. Ethan Allen, if an exchange of the latter for Lt. Col. Campbell should not be agreed, which is the case; so that Anstruther must return on his parole. I know nothing about the Hessian officers you speak of, but presume they had permission to go to Newport from proper Authority.

I am sorry to hear that we are so much neglected by our Sister States, and hope that the arrival of the new General[3] will be attended with favorable circumstances. He is an officer of Spirit and I trust will take due care of the State and the tories. When Thomas Cranston Esq. came off the Island, he played the hypocrite so artfully as to induce some people to believe that he had changed his principles.[4] I wrote to one whose credulity was imposed upon by him my Sentiments on the occasion.[5] Sooner will an Æthiopian change his Skin or a Leopard his spots, than Tories will become Whigs. I am told that he came from Newport to make a conveyance of his Estate to his son, it may be so, but such a fraudulent conveyance will not I trust protect it from confiscation. The ten other infamous scoundrels you have given me a list of, I never had the dishonour to be acquainted with. I am of your opinion that some persons of consequence in the Towns of S. & N. Kingstown are busy in procuring men for Whitmore's regiment, and by proper management it may be, if true, fully known. The way might be this. Let Genl. Sullivan bribe some artful persons who are connected or will connect themselves with those who are supposed to be disaffected in said or any other towns to converse with them on the subject of our political disputes, and fall in with their sentiments, in this way they may become acquainted with the principals among the Tories, and after having obtained sufficient proof to convict them they may be dragged forth to public view and receive the punishment which such perfidious miscreants deserve. A plan of this kind was successfully executed in the State of New York, and cannot fail of success in any state provided proper persons are employed. It is of great importance that the Tories should be known, not only to prevent the mischief they may do, but that the States where they lurk may have their Estates to enable them to discharge the debt contracted by a war which they have encouraged, and are still supporting by every means in their power, against their country. If you approve of the measure I have hinted for detecting our internal secret enemies I hope you will mention it to General Sullivan.

If it should be thought proper to have an addition of one to your Board, it would have more weight coming from the board than from a member in his private capacity, and I don't know any Gentleman who would be more agreeable to Congress than Mr Whipple.

We have nothing new, but a melancholy account of the Randolphs blowing up in an engagement with a fifty gun ship. It is supposed that every Soul perished.

Inclosed is the last York paper which contains mighty manœuvres. It ought to be immediately reprinted in Providence. You will therefore deliver it to the Printer so soon as you shall have read it. I am with great Respect, Yrs,   William Ellery

RC (RHi).

[1] The *Boston* was the vessel that carried John Adams to France to serve as an American commissioner at Paris.

[2] See Marine Committee to John Bradford, April 28, 1778, note 2.

[3] John Sullivan, who had been appointed Continental commander in Rhode Island by Washington on March 10. Washington, *Writings* (Fitzpatrick), 11:57–58.

[4] In December 1777 the Rhode Island Assembly had ordered Thomas Cranston, a loyalist and former speaker of the assembly "lately come off from the island of Rhode Island," to be examined by the Rhode Island Council of War. After having been subsequently confined to the home of John Smith in Johnston, R.I., Cranston was allowed in May 1778 to live on his son's farm in North Kingstown and in the following year was permitted to travel freely in the American-held parts of the state. See John R. Bartlett, ed., *Records of the State of Rhode Island and Providence Plantations in New England,* vols. 8–10 (Providence: Cooke, Jackson & Co., 1863–65), 8:344, 397–98, 557.

[5] The letter in question has not been found.

William Ellery to William Whipple

Dear Sir,   York Town April 25th 1778.
I am to acknowledge the receipt of your's of the 6th instant.

Very happily for us the Flamand is not at our expense while she lies in Portsmouth; however that hath not prevented the Committee of Commerce from doing every thing in his power to dispatch her.[1] The demand of money for the great departments of the Army have been so large and frequent as to prevent our supplying the Navy Board agreeably to our wishes. We have lately procured warrants upon the Loan Offices in New Hampshire, Massachusetts and Connecticut and have desired the Navy Board to give Mr Langdon his share of them.[2] The want of money and the impossibility of getting hands for the 74 if she were built hath occasioned us to order the building of her to be stopped;[3] these reasons and the blockade of Chesapeake hath caused to cease building the ships in Virginia.[4] Could you have thought it? The keel stem and stern post of one of those frigates are but fixed, and the other is not half finished, notwithstanding the carpenters have been employed about them upwards of a twelve month. If we were disposed to build a Navy and were to proceed at this slow rate and the enemy were to continue to capture and force us to destroy our frigates as they have done for a twelve month past, it seems to me we should never have so many frigates afloat as there are States in the Union.

You have heard of the loss of the Virginia and how it was occasioned; it would give me pain to repeat it. The destruction of the Columbus is a trifling affair, nor should I much regret the loss of the Alfred, if her officers and men were not in the possession of the enemy. Capt Thomson was in sight when the Alfred was taken by two frigates. I shall suspend my judgment on this matter until I know the particulars.

I rec'd a letter lately from Mr Vernon in which he mentions that an addition of one should be made to the Navy Board and you as a suitable person. I have wrote to him that such a proposal would come with greater weight and propriety from the Navy Board than from him in his private capacity, and desired him, if the Board thought it proper, to mention to them to propose it to the Marine Committee.

Your State have shamefully neglected sending forward a representation. I imagined when you knew what happened last June by Rhode Island's not being represented you would have pointed out a measure to prevent such an evil happening by your State.[5] One of the most important affairs is now on the carpet, that of a military establishment of half pay for life, for such military commissioned officers as shall be in the service at the end of the war and New Hampshire unrepresented. When it was known that the old members could not continue to act until the new ones arrived the latter ought to have been ordered on in season.

Mr Burgoyne and his suite had leave from Congress to go to Britain on parole. General Lee is parolled for General Prescot and was here a few days since. The Cartel hath broke off on Genl Howe's refusing to pledge the public faith for the performance of what should be stipulated. The Epilogue would have pleased me better if the praise had been more judiciously bestowed. The name of the Marquis de la *Fayette* is printed wrong. It will be reprinted here and the name printed right.

This will be accompanied by Lord North's new conciliatory speech, two drafts of Bills with remarks thereon by Congress and a certificate from Wm Tryon. Our enemies are endeavoring to accomplish that by their insidious arts which they have not been able to effect by their arms. We are counteracting them.

Last evening we rec'd the melancholy news of the Randolph, Capt Biddle, blowing up in an engagement with a fifty gun ship. Our little fleet diminishes fast. We must contrive somehow or other to catch some of the enemy's frigates. Can you tell us how to do it? Our small vessels I think are the most successful. Instead of looking up to 74 gun ships we should look down to swift sailing 10 or 12 gun sloops.

I have only time to add that I am with great esteem, your most humble servant,   Wm. Ellery.

[*P.S.*] Give my regards to Mr Stevens, Gen Folsom & Dr Stiles if he should be at Portsmouth.

Tr (DLC).
[1] See Committee of Commerce to John Langdon, February 23, 1778.
[2] See Marine Committee to the Eastern Navy Board, April 6, 1778.
[3] See ibid.
[4] See the Marine Committee's April 11 letters to David Stodder and to James Maxwell and Paul Loyall.
[5] Ellery is probably referring to Congress' May 22, 1777, decision to confirm Gen. Philip Schuyler's appointment to command the northern military department. According to James Lovell, five states voted for confirmation, four against, and two were divided, so that if Rhode Island, which was hostile to Schuyler, had been represented in Congress and had cast a negative vote Schuyler's command would not have been confirmed. See *JCC*, 8:375; and James Lovell to Horatio Gates, May 22, 1777.

Oliver Wolcott to Andrew Adams

Sir,   York Town 25 April 1778

I Wrote to you a few Days ago mentioning that I Wished that either you or some other Gentleman Appointed to attend Congress would releive me by the latter End of May or the beginning of June at farthest which I hope will be attended to. Mr. Huntington who will Return with me, has wrote to Mr. Hosmere upon the Subject.[1] It is unnecessary for me to Write to Mr. Elsworth, tho' perhaps I may do it by this Express, but you will settle this matter amongst yourselves. I have inclosed some Publick Papers to you upon which I shall make no comment. You will see what the unanimous Opinion of Congress is upon this Event. The Authenticity of the Bills and speech I beleive are not to be doupted of. We have no news from Philadelphia that can be depended on, but what are contained in these Papers. Nothing Material has occurred since my last. Mr. Sherman came here yesterday.[2]

I am Sir, Your most Obedient Servt.   Oliver Wolcott

P.S. Since I Wrote my last I have recd. your favour of the 2d March, I hope I may Acknowledge more such. As to the regulating Act Mr. Sherman speaks favourable of its operation in our State and thinks if it might be generally adopted it would answer the End intended. How farr he may be Right (which I much doubt of) it is unnecessary to say. But it is certain that the Measure will not be adopted, and nothing but the multiplicity of Business prevents its being recommended (so farr as I can form [an] Opinion) to the States who have passed [Laws of] this Kind to suspend them.[3] It is in Contemplation to sink 20,000,000 Dollars of the first Emissions in a Loan and pay the Annual Interest in Bills in France till the principal shall be paid.[4] This or a Measure similar to it may be adopted. It is proposed that the Bills called in shall be destroyed. If We can sink the sum it will give a Credit to the money.

The Randolph frigate is lost, Blown up in an Engagement.

RC (PPRF).
[1] Samuel Huntington's letter to Titus Hosmer has not been found, but in his May 6 letter to Thomas Mumford, Hosmer reported: "At my return I met two Letters from Judge Huntington urging me to attend and take his place in Congress by the first of June. It will be out of my Power to be there so soon, but think I may be able to set out from home by that Time." Robert J. Sudderth, Jr., Collection, Lookout Mountain, Tenn., 1973. Hosmer took his seat in Congress on June 23 and Andrew Adams followed on July 9, 1778. JCC, 11:632, 677.
[2] Roger Sherman attended Congress on April 25. See JCC, 10:389.
[3] See James Lovell to Samuel Adams, April 18, 1778, note 11.
[4] For the April 8 committee report on reducing the quantity of Continental bills of credit and paying interest on loan office certificates with bills of exchange drawn on the commissioners at Paris, see JCC, 10: 322–24. After debating these proposals on May 7, Congress postponed consideration of the subject and subsequently referred them to the Committee of Finance established in August 1778. Similar proposals were included in that committee's October 28 recommendations and on December 16 Congress resolved to take certain emissions out of circulation. JCC, 11:472, 843, 12:1073–75, 1223–24.

Oliver Wolcott to Laura Wolcott

My Dear,   York Town 25t April 1778
I wrote to you a few Days ago by Brown,[1] wherein I informed you that I was well, by the Blessing of God I continue so. Nothing Material has Occurred since my last except what you will find in the inclosed Paper. The British Administration seem to be shifting their Ground. I mean so farr as to depend more upon dividing than conquering the Country. But as No other Intelligence has been recd. than what is contained in Ld. North's Speech and the Drafts of the Bills No certain Opinion can be formed of the real Veiws of the British Administration. Thus much they Confess their Disappointment and Embarrassment on account of the American War. But it is our Business not to Relax our Exertions but on the contrary put them forth more Vigorously, as I really beleive upon a proper Exertion on our Part the Independency of America will be established within one year.

As I mentioned to you that I had Wrote to Mr. Adams that either he or some one other of the Gentlemen Appointed to attend Congress would releive me by the latter End of May or the beginning of June at farthest. I hope my Request will be complyed with so that by that Time I may Return Home. For altho I do now injoy Health and have done so since I came here more than what I had Reason to expect, and my Situation here is quite comfortable in a kind & Virtuous Family, yet my own Inclination as well as an Attention to my Family, induce me most strongly to Return and live with them. This will go by an unknown Express but I hope it will come safe to Hand.

Mr. Sherman came to Congress yesterday. Mr. Huntington will Return with me.

My kindest Love to my Children and Friends. Take Care of your Health and may the Almighty Bless you.

I am yours, with the Tenderest Affection,   Oliver Wolcott

P.S. It is in Contemplation to sink 20,000,000 Dollars in a Loan and pay the annual Interest in Bills on France. This measure may be adopted—and if so I think that it will by calling in and burning so large a Quantity give Credit to the Whole—and perhaps particularly raise the first Emissions which are proposed to be sunk in this manner. As the Payment of the Interest in Bills will while the Interest shall continue have the same Effect to the Lender as tho the Principal was in specie, This may therefore induce such People as have the first Emissions not to part with them or rather induce such as Wish to be Lenders to procure such Bills. As every one well knows that a Certificate whenever it may be necessary to turn it into money may easily be done.

The Randolph Frigate is lost, Blown up in an Engagement.

RC (CtHi).
[1] See Wolcott to Laura Wolcott, April 14, 1778.

Committee for Foreign Affairs
to William Bingham

Sir,   York Town April 26th. 1778

Herewith you have a triplicate and copy of my former letters. I now send you the proceedings of Congress upon an appearance of two draughts of Bills said to have been read in the British Parliament. Since Congress took notice of them Govr. Tryon has sent out copies with greater marks of authenticity than those bore which first came to hand. He certifies that he has "his majesty's command to cause them to be printed and dispersed, that the people at large may be acquainted with their contents, and of the favourable disposition of the people of Great Britain towards the American Colonies."

I will not attempt to lead your judgement upon these proceedings of our Enemies. I will only add an anecdote of their late conduct nearly related to that of counterfeiting the continental currency.

They have published, in all our forms, a forged resolve of Congress, purporting a consignment of power to Genl. Washington to *detain* in his army *during the war* all militia men who have enlisted or been draughted for nine months or a year, and to treat as deserters such as attempt to leave him at the expiration of their present agreements.[1] Perhaps you will see this properly stigmatized in some of our eastern papers conveyed in the vessel which may carry this assurance of my being with much Regard, sir, your Friend & humble Servant,   James Lovell, for the Committee for foreign affairs

RC (PHi). Written and signed by James Lovell.
[1] See Henry Laurens to Washington, April 24, 1778, note 7.

Henry Laurens to Samuel Adams

Dear Sir,   26 April [1778]
I have barely a moment for acknowledging the Receipt of your favor of the 9th Inst.

I have put under Cover with this 7 Copies of an Act of Congress of the 22d to which is prefixed a Speech said to be Lord North's & draughts of the Bills mentioned in my last of the 21t by Brown. The late Govr. of New York Mr. Tryon has wasted a good deal of paper & some time in transmitting Copies of the draughts to General Washington, Govr. Livingston &ca—which he modestly enjoins them to publish. No doubt your State has been or will be insulted in the same manner.

His directors & himself will now learn that Congress are not unwilling to expose their weakness in the most effectual manner throughout the World.

Able Men are exceedingly necessary in Congress at this time. I anxiously wish to see Mr. S. Adams.[1]

I am &ca.

LB (ScHi).
[1] This letter may not have reached Adams before he left Boston early in May to return to Congress. See Adams, *Writings* (Cushing), 4:24–25.

Henry Laurens to George Clinton

Sir,   26th April [1778]
When I did myself the honor of writing to Your Excellency the 20th Inst. by messenger Brown I had taken some pains to procure

the Copy of "Draught of Bills" &ca which accompanied my Letter, supposing I was then transmitting a thing which would be new at Poughkeepsie, but from the measures which, I now know, have been pursued by the late Governor of New York[1] it is highly probable he had before that date attempted to Insult Your Excellency with a packet of Printed Copies of that paper Certified by himself & ushered by a modest Injunction upon your Excellency to disperse them. Such has been Mr. Tryon's conduct towards Governor Livingston, General Washington, &c &c, an expence & trouble which might have been spared, since Congress from the first appearance of the Stratagem had determined to expose it in the most effectual manner to public view. In pursuance of such Resolution I have now the honour of transmitting within the present Inclosure twelve Copies of an Act of Congress of the 22d Inst. confirming the Report of a Committee on General Washingtons Letter of the 18th containing the said Draughts, to which is prefixed Lord North's speech at the introduction of the Bills into parliament.

Your Excellency will also find inclosed an Act of Congress of the 23d for granting pardons to certain characters therein described & Recommending to the several States to enact Laws or issue Proclamations for that purpose.[2] In a seperate packet are 50 Copies of this last mentioned Act which Your Excellency may judge necessary to disperse immediately. Congress were induced to this measure from well founded suggestions that great advantages would follow.

I have the honour to be with the highest Esteem & Regard &ca.

LB (DNA: PCC, item 13).
[1] William Tryon.
[2] Laurens noted in his presidential letter book that this day he sent copies of the same "Act of Congress" to President Meshech Weare of New Hampshire and Gov. Richard Caswell of North Carolina. PCC, item 13, fol. 278. He also enclosed copies of this act with brief covering letters that he wrote on April 28 to Presidents Thomas Wharton of Pennsylvania and Caesar Rodney of Delaware. Ibid., fol. 285.

Henry Laurens to Nicholas Cooke

Sir,   York Town 26 April 1778

Since my last of 31st March[1] by Green I have been honored by Your Excellency's favor by the Honorable Mr. Collins whose Accounts are in the proper course & he appears to be satisfied that all possible attention is paid to him. Times & circumstances restrain us in public & private capacities from doing all we would wish with respect to a Gentleman of Mr. Collins's distinction as a Patriot & a Man of honor.[2]

Inclosed with the present Cover Your Excellency will receive—

12 Copies of an Act of Congress of the 22d, confirming the Report of a Committee to whom General Washington's Letter of the 18th was Committed.

2 Copies of an Act of the 23d for granting Pardons & Recommending to the several States to enact proper Laws or Public Proclamations for promoting the good purpose in view.

'Tis not improbable Your Excellency has been insulted by Mr Tryon or some other weak Instrument of Tyranny with Copies of the Draughts for Bills exhibited in Parliament by Lord North which are prefixed to the above-mentioned Act of the 22d & modestly injoined to disperse them. This measure has been taken by Mr Tryon towards General Washington, Governor Livingston &c &c. He will now learn that Congress are by no means desirous of keeping them secret.

I have the honor to be, With very great regard, Sir, Your Excellency's Obedient & Most humble servt,

Henry Laurens, President of Congress

RC (R–Ar).
[1] See Laurens to Richard Caswell, March 31, 1778, note 2.
[2] See William Ellery to Cooke, April 25, 1778, note 1.

Henry Laurens to William Heath

Sir,   York Town, 26 April 1778

By my Copy Book it appears that my last Letter was dated the 4th Inst by one Green but I feel something like remembrance of having written to you about the 20th by Messenger Brown.[1]

Two days ago I had the honor of presenting to Congress your favors of the 6th & 9th by Millet together with Copy of General Burgoyne's Parol & of the agreement referred to.[2] As nothing was said respecting the original Parol 'tis to be presumed Congress are well satisfied that you retain it, in your hands.

Yesterday I signed a Warrant for 250000 Dollars to be immediately transmitted to Mr Hancock Paymaster Eastern department whence I trust you will soon be guarded against such troubles as you have lately experienced from a want of Money for Public use.[3]

Inclosed with this I transmit 7 Copies of Acts of Congress of the 22d Inst., to which is prefixed a Speech said to be Lord North's & two Draughts of Bills introduced by His Lordship into the British Parliament. Tis not improbable you have been insulted by the late Govr of New York or some other such Agent of Tyranny with Copies of the Speech & Bills & a modest injunction to disperse them. He has been silly enough to address General Washington, Governor

Livingston &c in such terms. He will learn from our present proceeding that his diligence was waste of time.

I have the honour to be, With great regard, Sir, your very obedient servant,   Henry Laurens, President of Congress

RC (MHi).
  [1] April 4 is the date of Laurens' last extant letter to Heath.
  [2] Heath's April 6 and 9 letters to Laurens are in PCC, item 157, fols. 105–10. For a discussion of Congress' decision to allow General Burgoyne and other British officers to return to England, see Laurens to Richard Wilford, March 1, 1778, note. According to the journals, Congress considered Heath's letters on April 25. *JCC*, 10:390.
  [3] Heath had described his financial difficulties at length in his April 6 letter to Laurens.

Henry Laurens to the Massachusetts Council

Sir,   York Town, 26th April 1778
  Since my last to the Honorable the Council of Massachuset under the 20th Inst by Messenger Brown,[1] I have been honoured with your favor of the 2d inclosing a Representation from Mr. Allen. This is Committed & rests a subject for consideration. The event shall be communicated immediately after I shall have received Commands.[2]

Within the present Inclosure be pleased to receive.

12 Copies of an Act of Congress of the 22d confirming the Report of a Committee on General Washington's Letter of the 18th &c.

2 Copies of an Act of the 23d for granting pardons & Recommending to the several States to pass Laws or Issue Proclamations for that purpose.

I have the honor to be, Honorable Sir, Your most obedt. & most humble servt.   Henry Laurens, President of Congress

RC (M–Ar). Addressed: "The Honorable Jeremiah Powell Esquire, President of Council, Massachuset, Boston."
  [1] See Laurens to George Clinton, April 20, 1778, note 3.
  [2] The Massachusetts Council's April 2 letter to Laurens and the enclosed March 10–11 "Representation" to the council from John Allan are in PCC, item 65, 1:296–303. In this "Representation" Allan, a Nova Scotian supporter of the American Revolution, advanced various proposals for securing the support of the "Eastern Indians" of Nova Scotia for the American cause. Both documents were referred to the Board of War on April 25, but no report on them has been found. *JCC*, 10:390. For further information on Allan, see George A. Rawlyk, *Nova Scotia's Massachusetts: A Study of Massachusetts-Nova Scotia Relations 1630–1784* (Montreal: McGill-Queen's University Press, 1973), pp. 241–46.

Henry Laurens to Jonathan Trumbull, Sr.

Sir   26th April [1778]

When I writ to your Excellency by Messenger Brown the 20th Inst.[1] I had been at some trouble to procure the Copy of "Draughts of Bills" &ca which went inclosed with my Letter, from an opinion that I should have offered somewhat quite new, but If I may be allowed to judge, from the measures which have been adopted by the late Governor of New York for affronting Govr. Livingston, General Washington &c &c, Your Excellency had before that date been insulted by Mr. Tryon with several printed Copies of the Draughts Certified by his own important signature & Ushered by an immodest injunction to disperse them.[2]

That active Agent might have saved his directors & himself some expence & trouble. Congress had from the first appearance of the paper Resolved to transmit it into every Corner of these United states. Far from apprehensive of any evil consequences it is the desire of the House that it should be presented to the consideration of every Man of common understanding throughout the Land. In pursuance of this sentiment, I have the honor of transmitting within the present Inclosure 12 Copies of an Act of Congress of the 22d Inst. confirming the Report of a Committee on General Washingtons Letter of the 18th containing the said Draughts to which is prefixed a speech said to be Lord North's when he introduced the Draughts into Parliament.

Your Excellency will also receive an Act of Congress of the 23d for granting pardons to certain Characters therein described, & Recommending to the several States to enact Laws or Issue proclamations for that purpose. Congress ever induced to this measure from well founded suggestions that great advantages would follow. I have the honor to be with very great Regard.

LB (DNA: PCC, item 13).

[1] See Laurens to George Clinton, April 20, 1778, note 3.

[2] Laurens' surmise was correct. See Connecticut Delegates to Jonathan Trumbull, Sr., May 18, 1778, note 2.

John Mathews to Thomas Bee

Dear Sir,[1]   York Town April 26th. 1778

I Arrived here the 21st Inst. after a most disagreeable Journey indeed.

I inclose you a paper[2] (which if you have not seen) will amuse you, & I imagine some parts will not a little surprise you. Compare

the Speech of the Minister, with the last Speech from the Throne.
Lee is exchanged. Tryon was imprudent enough, a few days agoe to
write to Washington inclosing several of the Acts, desired him to
disperce them thro' his Camp. When the Acts were posted up in
Philadelphia The Officers tore them down in a most riotous manner
swearing they were all cheated, for they were promissed the Rebels
should be conqured, & their Estates divided amongst them. The
Physic begins to work you see, All we have farther to do, is, to give
them one good dose more this Campaign, & the business is done. The
speech, the Acts, the exchange of Lee (which did not happen 'till
after these acts came out, he had been out on Parole some time before), the sollicitude to disperse these Acts amongst our people all
serve to shew those dam'd Villains are heartily sick of the business.
However Congress takes it up in a different point of View, as all
meant to throw dust in our eyes, & are preparing for a Vigorous
Campaign. I think these manuvres of the Enemy will have this Good
Effect. The house of Bourbone has all along been Jealous of our still
hankering after an accommodation, & alliance with Great Britain,
which has kept them very cautious in their conduct towards us. These
Acts tend immediately to that purpose, & being so suddenly, & I may
say, unexpectedly pass'd upon them, will oblige them instantly to
declare themselves what part they mean to take with us, for they have
been playing fast & loose with us too long. However before these acts
made their appearance, we have had greater reason to think they
would do something this summer, than we have yet had, but this
beleif arises merely from hear say, for we have not had one line from
our Embassadors since last May yet the information comes through
such a Channel, that we have some reason to give Credit to it. I do
not think Lord North altogether insincere, nor do I think he would
be incorrigibly obstinate against admitting our Independency. You
will observe these remarkable expressions in his speech. "The first
proposition is attended with too great an expence of Men & money,
an expence which Conquest itself would not balance." Again. "Independency, with Cordial love between us, is one thing, with an
union with our Enemies, Fatal." I think this last sentiment means a
great deal. I could make many other observations on it but time
nor my paper (for I assure you its a scarce article here) will not allow.
Another inducement I have to believe Ld. North earnestly wishes
peace, & would not be totally averse to Independency, is the formidable appearance France particularly now wears, & which will prevent
his sending a man to America this year, tho' we have had a most
pompous account of 32,000 to be raised in the different parts of the
Kingdom, for that purpose. So far, France certainly renders us some
service. You will observe the report of the Committee, speaks doubt-
fully of the validity of the two Acts[3] but that was before, we received

them from Tryon, which are certified by him, to have actually pass'd. The report fully shews you the Ideas of Congress on this important subject. As this is a matter of as great & momentous concern as any that can come before Congress (except that of real treaty) I would therefore wish my conduct on every such occasion to be known to my Country, & leave to their Judgment whether I am right, or wrong. I do therefore declare the whole report met with my most hearty concurrance. I could then wish, If Commissioners should come out this summer, (as I really believe they will) & they have such powers as Congress can consistently treat with them upon, That a special meeting of the Legislature should be call'd, on this most Important subject, that their delegates may know their sentiments, & receive instructions accordingly. I just drop the hint to you, that you might be prepared for such an Event. I have not consulted any of my Collegues on this Subject, but I think the necessity of such a measure is so self evident that they must concur with me in this opinion, I am sure I should not think myself Justifyed in stirring one step in this business without. I have not time to add more than that I am Dr. Bee, with sincere Esteem Yr. most Obdt. Servt.

Jno. Mathews

P.S. 27th. We received an express late last night (for tho' Sunday, we are obliged to do business, three nights out of five that I have been in Congress, we have sat 'till nine & ten oClock, so that you may imagine our business not trifling) from the General, Informing us that he had just received an account that he could depend on, That the Commissioners from England were daily expected in Philadelphia. They are Lord Amherst, Admiral Keppel, & Genl. Murray.[4] From such Men I am sure we can expect Nothing decisive, neither of whom have one single Qualification Requisite for such a business. They come out with their full *Military* Commissions also. On such Conduct, & such Men, I could say much, but time will not permit. Genl. Howe is certainly recalled & Clinton to take the Command.

RC (ScC). Tr (ScC). RC damaged; missing words supplied from Tr.

[1] For Bee's identification, see these *Letters*, 1:255.

[2] Undoubtedly the April 24 issue of the *Pennsylvania Gazette,* which contained texts of Lord North's proposals for Anglo-American reconciliation and Congress' April 22 response to them.

[3] See *JCC,* 10:374–80.

[4] Washington's April 25 report to Congress on the identity of the British peace commissioners was in error. Washington, *Writings* (Fitzpatrick), 11:307–8. The Earl of Carlisle, William Eden, George Johnstone, Admiral Richard Howe, and Gen. William Howe were the peace commissioners actually appointed by the king, though only the first three served. See Weldon A. Brown, *Empire or Independence: A Study in the Failure of Reconciliation, 1774–1778* (Baton Rouge: Louisiana State University Press, 1941), pp. 244–48.

Charles Carroll of Carrollton
to Charles Carroll, Sr.

Dear Papa,   27th April 1778

I have yours of the 23d instant. I return you Skerrett's letter, act
upon it as you see best. Brown is an orderly industrious fellow, & I
would wish to keep him, but I think his demands are exorbitant. I
wish Molly could recover faster, but her perfect recovery must be
the work of time & proper regimen. I am sorry for the death of bold
Robin; his death is a real loss. General Amherst, General Murray
& Admiral Keppel are the Commissioners coming to treat with
America. General Howe is certainly recalled; Sir Henry Clinton is to
succeed him in the command, but I apprehend, only until the arrival
of General Amherst, who I imagine will have the supreme Command.
From the inclosed letter, & the articles of News in the printed handbill, which you sent me, I have no doubt but that preliminaries of a
treaty have been entered into by our Agents at Paris. I suspect Carmichael is taken by the Enemy, as he sailed from France, or left
Paris, the 27th of last Decr. Govr. Johnston's letter gives us the first
authentic information of such a treaty being on foot, & accounts for
Ld North's Speech & the two acts which it ushered in to the House
of Commons. We have recd no advice from our Agents since last May;
surely several dispatches have been intercepted by the Enemy. I am,
Yr. affectionate Son,   Ch. Carroll of Carrollton

P.S. General Lee is Exchanged for Gen. Prescot and several other
officers have been lately exchanged for officers of like rank.

RC (MdHi).

Charles Carroll of Carrollton to Thomas Johnson

Dear Sir,   Monday 27 April 1778

We have yr. letter,[1] & have written this day to Mr Morris for the
articles therein mentioned; our letter is gone by an Express, which
the President had occasion to send in order to return the original of
the inclosed copy of a letter from Govr. Johnstone to Mr. Morris.[2]
Your application to Congress for 100,000 Dollars shall be laid before
Congress tomorrow. We will write you the result by the first opportunity.[3] Gen. Amherst, General Murray, & Admiral Keppel are the
Commissioners coming out under the Act of Parliat. for offering
terms of peace & reconciliation. General Howe is recalled, & Sir
Henry Clinton is to succeed him, but I apprehend only till General
Amherst's arrival; I think, as he is one of the Commissioners, he will
have the supreme command of the army.

I think we may fairly conclude from Govr. Johnstone's letter, & from the articles in the newspapers, which you have seen, that some treaty or the Preliminaries of a treaty have been entered into between France & our Commissioners. We have had no letters from them since last May; several no doubt have been intercepted. The Administration getting wind of this treaty have been induced thereby to offer terms to this Country: but no terms short of Independence are in my opinion admissible without the utmost danger & disadvantage to these States. I am with great esteem, Dr. Sir yours &c,

Ch. Carroll of Carrollton

N.B. Do not print Governor Johnstone's letter, as [it is] a private letter. General Lee is exchanged for General Prescot.

RC (MdAA). Addressed: "To His Excellency Governor Johnson Esquire of Maryland, Annapolis, to be opened in his absence by the Council."

[1] The Maryland Council's April 23 letter to their delegates is in PCC, item 70, fol. 249, and *Md. Archives,* 21:54.

[2] For information on the subject of the enclosed copy of George Johnstone's February 5 letter to Robert Morris—which is in the Red Books, 10:78, MdAA—see Henry Laurens to Robert Morris, April 27, 1778, note 1.

[3] The next day John Henry wrote the following brief letter to Governor Johnson: "I have just time to drop you a line and to inform you Congress have granted to the State of Maryland, one hundred thousand Dollars. It will be sent forward tomorrow or next Day.

"Mr. Carrol will give you the News of the Day which is very important." Red Books, MdAA.

For Congress' order directing that $100,000 be paid to the Maryland delegates, see *JCC,* 10:402.

Henry Laurens to Richard Caswell

Sir,   27th April 1778

I had the honor of writing to Your Excellency the 24th by Messenger Stuart. Yesterday by the hands of the Honorable Mr. Harnet under a blank Cover I conveyed Copies of an Act of Congress of the 23d for granting pardons & recommending to the several States to enact Laws or issue Proclamations adopted to obtain the great end in view. As this may possibly reach your Excellency before Colonel Harnet's arrival at New Bern I judge it necessary to forward another Copy of that Act under its Cover.

No part Sir, of the various transactions of business in my Office nor all the hard labour of the last Six Months has occasioned me so much pain as I feel at this Instant from the Duty of transmitting a paper which Your Excellency will find inclosed containing minutes of Congress respecting the Honble. Mr. Burke one of the Delegates from North Carolina, from the 10th to the 25th April, which Your Excellency is requested to lay in due time, before the Assembly of that State.[1] The Honorable Gentleman who is most nearly concerned in this Novel untoward circumstance intends to return to Carolina in a very few days. The course of my Duty constrains me to the present transmission, but I am persuaded it is not the desire of Congress to take advantage of Mr. Burke nor to hurt his Character by impressions made in his absence on the minds of his fellow Citizens, or without affording a reasonable time for his appearance at the tribunal of his Country, where only the Honorable Gentleman holds himself amenable.

I have the honour to be with the most perfect Esteem

P.S. As Govr. Tryon has been sending Lord North's draughts of Bills to the several Governors & General Officers in this Quarter 'tis not to be doubted your Excellency has been or will be insulted [in] the same way by some other Tool of the British Ministry.

LB (DNA: PCC, item 13).
  [1] See *JCC,* 10:334, 336–37, 339, 385–91. See also Thomas Burke's Proposed Statement to Congress, April 13, 1778, and his April 29 letters to Caswell and to the North Carolina Assembly.

Henry Laurens to Thomas Johnson

Sir,   York Town 27th Ap. 1778.[1]
  I beg leave to refer Your Excellency to my last under the 24th Inst. by Messenger Stuart.
  The present will be accompanied by two Acts of Congress Vizt.
  1. of 24th April for transporting the Public Provisions & Stores across the Chesapeak Bay or otherwise.
  2. of 23d for granting Pardons & Recommending to the several States to pass Laws or Issue Proclamations for that purpose.
  I remain With great Regard, Sir, Your Excellency's Obedient & humble servt,   Henry Laurens, President of Congress

RC (MdAA).
  [1] Laurens wrote virtually the same letter this day to Governor Henry of Virginia. Hamilton-McLane Family Papers, DLC.

Henry Laurens to the Marquis de Lafayette

Dear Sir,   27th April [1778]
  Should I remain totally silent Your Excellency may possibly pause & make some enquiry into the reason.

I will therefore go so far by the present Messenger as to assure your Excellency that by the next I will do my self the honor to reply to your late favors which now lie before me. The constant attention of Congress to business of late & the multiplicity cut out for my employment in the intervals between adjournment & meetings have kept me extremely hard at work. But I never forget, & I beg your Excellency will give me leave to repeat, that I am always, I am &ca.

[*P.S.*] Mr. Duplaisis shall have the papers required by the next conveyance.[1]

LB (ScHi).
[1] See Laurens to Lafayette, March 24, note 4, and to Du Plessis, April 28, 1778.

Henry Laurens to William Livingston

Dear Sir   27th April [1778]

You will have heard long before this can have the honor of kissing your hands, that Commissioners are daily expected from Whitehall to offer, or to treat on, terms for peace. You will also have heard the Names of the illustrious Characters marked on the other side for the Momentous work, & the Contents of an Interesting Letter dated House of Commons 5th Febry., Governor Johnson to Robert Morris Esquire, speaking in too plain language the Governor's opinion in favour of a dependent connexion,[1] which I suppose to be the sentiment of many Men in Britain, and if Administration despair of beating they will make use of our friends to chouse us,[2] but that is not the end of my troubling your Excellency in such haste as I am at present obliged to write.

We are verging Sir towards an important Crisis, it may become necessary to appoint Citizens for meeting & conferring with yonder Commissioners, all the Wisdom of America will be required, shall we confine our selves in the election of persons on our part to a particular State or Circle, or shall we call proper Men from any or every part or place in the Union?[3]

Permit me Sir under this Cover to transmit Copies of an Act of Congress of the 23d Inst. for granting pardons & Recommending to the States to enact proper Laws or Issue proclamations for that purpose.

I remain with the most sincere attachment &c.

LB (ScHi).
[1] See Laurens to Robert Morris, this date.
[2] "To dupe, cheat, trick." *OED*.
[3] It is interesting to note that Congress had deleted from the draft of its April

22 reply to Lord North's conciliatory bills a proposal by Gouverneur Morris to call upon the states "to send a full and adequate Representation to Congress" to consider the question of entering into negotiations with British peace commissioners. See Morris to John Jay, May 3, 1778. Laurens' own suggestion to invite leaders from outside Congress to consult with the delegates on this issue became irrelevant as soon as official news of the signing of treaties of alliance and commerce with France arrived on May 2.

Henry Laurens to the
Middle Department Navy Board

Gentlemen,   27th April 1778
Under this Cover you will receive an Act of Congress of the 18th Resolving that an Enquiry be made into the Causes of the loss of the Frigate Virginia which Congress expect you will enter upon as early as possible.[1]

I have conversed with Mr. Smith[2] & received his promise of giving you every assistance in his power & have written to Mr. Stewart whose aid I believe you may likewise depend upon.

I have the honor to be with great regard.

LB (DNA: PCC, item 13). Addressed: "John Nixon, Fra. Hopkinson, & John Wharton Esquires, Commissioners of the Navy Board at Borden Town, New Jersey."

[1] See JCC, 10:363–64. The Continental frigate Virginia, Capt. James Nicholson, had run aground and was captured by the British off Cape Charles, Md., on April 1. There is no evidence that the Navy Board ever submitted a report on this matter to Congress or the Marine Committee, but see William Ellery to William Whipple, May 31, 1778. See also William M. Fowler, Jr., "James Nicholson and the Continental Frigate Virginia," American Neptune 34 (April 1974): 135–41.

[2] William Smith, the Marine Committee's agent in Baltimore.

Henry Laurens to Robert Morris

Sir,   27th April 1778
Late last Night I was honoured with your favor of yesterday which with the papers inclosed were immediately communicated to several Members & this Morning presented to Congress.[1] The House ordered a Copy of Govr. Johnsons Letter to be taken by the Secretary, and I now return within the present inclosure that Letter & the draught of the Bills. You will also find in company with these a Letter put into my hands by the Delegates from Maryland[2] & Six Copies of an Act of Congress of the 22d Inst. to which is prefixed the above mentioned Bills & a speech said to be Lord North's when he introduced the Bills into Parliament.

I have the honour to be &ca.

LB (DNA: PCC, item 13).
¹ Morris' April 26 letter to Laurens, which was written from his home in Manheim, reads:

"I have this moment received the Packet which I send here enclosed as it came to my hands from Lancaster, the paper published in Philadelphia has already been before Congress, the letter from my old Friend Govr. Johnston, has unfolded to me what I suspected from the first State, the Government of Great Britain are alarmed at the prospect of our forming Foreign alliances & from that apprehension has sprung Ld Norths Conciliatory Measures.

"I thought it my Duty to communicate such authentic intelligence to Congress immediately least they might not be apprized of any preliminarys being in their way from France. When Congress have done with the letter I shall thank you to Return it to Sir Your Obed & hble servt., Robt Morris." PCC, item 137, fol. 233.

The enclosed letter was one of February 5 from George Johnstone (1730–87), a member of Parliament and former governor of West Florida who also served as one of the British peace commissioners who arrived in America in June 1778. *DNB*. In this letter, which was written before his appointment as a commissioner, Johnstone urged Morris to give serious consideration to the proposals for reconciliation that Lord North was about to lay before parliament but inadvertently lessened the force of his plea by revealing that he had just "learned some preliminarys of a treaty have lately gone from France," thereby confirming delegate suspicions that British peace offers were designed to offset American diplomatic successes in Paris. In PCC, item 78, 13:65–66, there is a copy of Johnstone's letter by Charles Thomson containing this note: "Copy from the Original which was read in Congress April 27. 1778—returned to Mr. Morris." But there is no mention of Johnstone's letter in the journals.

² The Maryland delegates' letter has not been found, but in his April 28 reply to them Morris wrote:

"I am honoured with your favour of Yesterday and as no person has a stronger desire to serve the State of Maryland or oblige the worthy Patriots that bear the burthen of Government in it, than I have, you may depend on my taking immediate measures to secure for you the preferrance of those Articles you write for, if such are in the Cargo of the Brigt unfortunately Stranded at Matompkin. Mr. Nesbitt is interested in this Vessell & has the management of the Concern. He is now at Lancaster & probably taking his measures in respect to these Goods but I will immediately send your letter to him and urge a Complyance with the Contents and I think the Goods you want are there." Red Books, MdAA.

Henry Laurens to Stephen Steward

Sir,¹   27th April [1778]

Within the present Inclosure you will receive an Act of Congress of the 19th² Resolving that an enquiry be made into the causes of the loss of the Frigate Virginia & you are therein appointed one of the Commissioners for that purpose. Congress from your Zeal for public Interest, confide in you to engage in this enquiry when it shall become necessary. Mr. Smith of Baltimore has been properly notified of his appointment & will probably confer with you on the Subject.

I am with great respect.

LB (DNA: PCC, item 13). Addressed: "Stephn. Stewart Esquire, West River, Maryland."

[1] Steward was the Marine Committee's agent in charge of supplying the *Virginia*. See Marine Committee to James Nicholson, March 4, 1778, note 2.

[2] That is, April 18. See *JCC*, 10:363–64.

Henry Laurens to George Washington

Sir,   York Town 27th April 1778

I had the honour of writing to your Excellency the 24th Inst by McClosky.

Yesterday about ½ p. 5 oClock P M Your Excellency's favor of the 25th was brought to me in Congress & was immediately presented.[1] The Person who had been the bearer of it was anxious to obtain a receipt for the Letter to express the time of delivery & he complained of unnecessary detention half the day at Susquehanna Ferry—this intimation will answer his purpose.

I am directed by Congress[2] to request Your Excellency will immediately require all Officers Civil as well as Military in the Army, who are at present delinquent, to comply with the terms of an Act of Congress of the 3d February last by taking the Oath of Allegiance & Abjuration & that Your Excellency will be pleased to cause the necessary Certificates as speedily as possible to be returned & if occasion shall be given which is supposed to be scarcely possible the Name or Names of such persons as shall refuse.

The Bearer hereof will deliver three Packets containing about 600 Blanks which will hasten the business of Admistring Oaths—more shall be sent by the next Messenger.

In considering the article of provision to be made for Officers who shall continue in the Army to the end of the War Congress had proceeded so far last Night as Resolving that one half the present Pay be continued during Life without exceptions of Country, to all such Officers as shall also take the Oath of Allegiance & actually reside within the United States.[3] This Resolution & the whole plan for Military Establishment is subject to further discussion respecting the propriety of transmitting it to the several States for concurrence.

I have the honour to be, With the highest Respect & Esteem, Sir, Your Excellency's Most obedient & Most humble servant,

Henry Laurens, President of Congress.

RC (DLC).

[1] Washington's April 25 letter to Laurens, which discussed further reports about British plans for reconciliation, is in PCC, item 152, 5:525, and Washington, *Writings* (Fitzpatrick), 11:307–8.

[2] There is no mention of this order in the journals, but Congress' dissatisfaction

with the army's failure to comply with its February 3, 1778, resolves requiring Continental officers to subscribe to oaths of allegiance is evident in the following draft resolve demanding compliance with its previous directive.

"It having been represented to Congress that officers in the Army of these States, and other *(holding Appointments)* officers under their authority, have neglected to make the Declaration & take the Oath prescribed by the Resolve of Congress of the   Day of   177 , Resolved that a Number of Copies of the said Declaration & Oath, omitting the Words 'and Honour and' in the latter part thereof, be immediately printed & sent to General Washington, and the Commanding officers in the different Departments: That the General & such Commanding officers, on the Receipt thereof, take & subscribe the said Decla. & Oath, in the presence of some one or more of the Major Generals or Brigadiers of the Army, That all the General officers under the immediate Command of The General, take & subscribe the said Oath & Decla. in his presence: That the General officers in any of the Departmts. qualify before the Genl officer commanding in such Department: That the field officers qualify before the Brigadier or General of their Brigade or Division: That the other Commd. officers qualify before some one of the field officers of their Battalion: That the Quarter Master, Commissary Genl. of Purchases & Issues, Muster Master Genl. & all officers of the Staff qualify before some one of the Genl. officers of the Army: That all Qualifications be returned to the Secretary of Congress, and every person neglecting to qualify within One Month after such Copies of the sd. Decla. & Oath shall arrive in Camp or any of the Departments, & notice thereof given in General orders, shall be [dis]abled to serve in the army or to execute any office under Congress."

This undated document, in the hand of Samuel Chase but located in the papers of Henry Laurens, may have been the immediate cause of the present order to Washington. See Laurens Papers, item 22, ScHi; and *JCC*, 10:114–18.

In his May 1 response to this directive, Washington explained his previous failure to secure the required oaths. "In compliance with the request of Congress, I shall immediately call upon the Officers in the Army to take the Oath of Allegiance and Abjuration. This I should have done, as soon as the Resolution passed, had it not been for the state of the Army at that time, and that there were some strong reasons which made it expedient to defer the matter." See Washington, *Writings* (Fitzpatrick), 11:331–32; and *JCC*, 10:114–18.

[3] Congress approved this resolve during a special Sunday session on April 26. *JCC*, 10:394–96.

Henry Laurens to George Washington

Sir,   York Town 27th April 1778.
The News Papers which I received from Your Excellency in company with the honour of Your Excellency's Letter of the 18th afford me sometimes amusement in intervals from the necessary duties of my present station & I am particularly indebted to Your Excellency for the notice which is included in the kindness of this favor.

Your Excellency is too well acquainted with the Integrity of your own heart & too well assured of the good opinion of your Country Men to admit any anxious impressions from the forgeries of an Enemy. I am disposed to vote for every exertion in our power in order to defeat their designs against us, except following such of their examples as will when related in history greatly abate from that

Character for Generosity which England & upon good grounds once boasted.

The late attempt by publishing forged Resolves of Congress within a Garrison'd Town immediately under the Eye of a Commander in Chief appears to me to be mean & scandalous, & must be considered in the same light by every good Englishman Military, or in Public or private Life.[1]

We are now verging towards a most important Crisis when all the Wisdom of these States will be required. Permit me Sir, to lay before you my private sentiments; If the time shall come for appointing a Deputation for treating with British Commissioners on terms for establishing Peace I hold it necessary that able Men be called forth for that purpose from any place within the Union without confining our election within any one State or Body.[2] I intreat Your Excellency's pardon for this freedom & that you will believe me to be with the most sincere Esteem & attachment, Sir, Your obliged & Most obedient servant,   Henry Laurens

RC (DLC).
[1] See Laurens to Washington, April 24, 1778, note 7.
[2] Washington informed Laurens on April 30 that he favored peace negotiations with the British only on condition that they recognize American independence. See Washington, *Writings* (Fitzpatrick), 11:326–27.

Thomas Burke to Henry Laurens

Sir   York April 28th 1778
The Instrument authenticating my last Election as a Delegate from North Carolina is dated May the 4th 1777. Both my Colleagues have informed me that they believed the Election was made on the 28th of April preceeding. The Constitution of the State requires the Election of Delegates to be annual, and it is a fundamental principle that the Constitution is a fixed rule of Conduct for all the powers of the State, which cannot be dispensed with, or deviated from, unless the Collective Body of the People give special authority for that purpose. All these circumstances induce me to believe that my power of Representing the State is at an End. The Instrument refer'd to is on the Journals of Congress and they can determin whether my attendance can be longer commanded. I request you Sir to lay the matter before them for their Opinion that my absenting myself may not be deemed a Contempt or breach of Order.[1] I should have Submitted my difficulty at a more early day in my place, but that I was unwilling to Interrupt the attention of Congress which was employed on objects far more Important. The same Cause kept me silent on another Matter which I shall now beg leave to mention in this which

I suppose the only way remaining, for I hope my Country has yielded to my earnest request, and excused me from the Delegation.

I feel myself under a sense of very respectful Obligation to you and most of the Gentlemen of Congress for the solicitude which appeared for me on a late Occasion, and am persuaded that nothing but my being so unhappy in my Expressions as not clearly to convey my Ideas could have occasioned a mistake which is on your Journals. I am there represented as attempting to Justify withdrawing from Congress without permission, in an Instance which Interrupted very important business.[2] Such Justification is, sir, what I never did attempt, nor do I think that or any other breach of order Justifiable. My attempt was intended only to excuse my departure under particular Circumstances, by alleging that the same thing had been usually done by the other members without reprehension and that the time and Occasion were not improper for using a Liberty which had been denied to no other member. I am also represented as sending an Indecent Message to the House which I protest was never my Intention. The matter respecting the member from New York,[3] I never conceived myself called upon to answer, but it is not of Consequence enough to trouble you with. I do not mean now Sir to withdraw this matter from the Jurisdiction of my Constituents, it is in the train I wish it to be. To them I hope I can shew that the House intirely mistook my Meaning and when it can be done without injury to the Common Cause, I shall solicit their attention to the Subject, but not before if I can avoid it. My sole purpose at present is to prevent Gentlemen whom I greatly esteem and respect from retaining Impressions of me which I am unconscious of deserving. This I hope to Effect by declaring that I hold no Citizen in any rank or station Justifiable in doing any act, on any pretence, which may tend to the public prejudice, or in forbearing to do any act which is requisite for public Service. That I hold no man Justifiable for using Language or Manners Not sufficiently respectful to the assembly or Society of which he is a member. That attendance in Congress at all times when requested by the President either in or out of the House is in my Opinion what every member is absolutely bound to; and the House itself is Judge of the respect with which the whole or any of the members is to be treated in debate, and I only meant to Insist on the right each freeman must Necessarily have of Judging for himself on the reasonableness or unreasonableness of every Exercise of Power, and on the peculiar Right of the States to apply any punishment which should go beyond Censures. These I advanced occasionally in debate, as general political Opinions not in Justification of any thing that had happened but in answer to some things thrown out by other Gentlemen which seemed to me to hold up Opinions very different from them for the adoption of the House. I hope they are not dangerous, and that persisting in them is not disrespectful to the honorable Members. If the Language and manner in which I delivered my Sentiments was not sufficiently respectful in the Opinion of the House, I beg they will attribute it to Inadvertance, or Imperfection of Temper, not to design. I beg they will believe that no man is more unwilling to give offence, no man more sincerely laments it when it happens through warmth or earnestness of Natural disposition.

I have the honour to be, with great Respect and Esteem, Sir, your very obedient Servt,   Tho Burke

RC (DNA: PCC, item 78).
¹ This day Congress refused to determine whether or not Burke could continue to represent North Carolina. See *JCC*, 10:399–400. Burke remained in York until May 5, but since he did not participate in any of the roll call votes recorded in the journals between April 28 and May 4 it is apparent that he stopped attending Congress after the 28th. See *JCC*, 10:400–401, 409; and Burke to Richard Caswell, May 5, 1778. Burke's May 5 letter to Governor Caswell should not be construed as evidence that he attended Congress after April 28, for it contains no information that could only have been known by an attending delegate and as early as April 25 Burke had promised the governor that he would stay on in York until May 4 regardless of whether or not he attended Congress after the 28th.
² See *JCC*, 10:390–91.
³ William Duer. See *JCC*, 10:386–89.

Henry Laurens to Francis Bailey

Sir   28th April 1778
The bearer hereof Joseph Sharp, is ordered to call on you. I confide in you to dispatch by his hand without much detention, the 200 Act of Congress of the 23d Inst. for granting pardons which you engaged to print in the German Tongue. Direct them in a packet to His Excellency General Washington and one hundred German publications of Lord North's Speech on the draught of Bills & Act of Congress of the 22d, if you have so many in print. Otherwise I request you to send that number to the General as soon as they are ready & the remainder to me.

If you have or can procure for me a Rheam of good writing Paper please to send it by the earliest safe opportunity & oblige, Sir, Your most obedt Servt.

[*P.S.*] Transmit your account & payment shall be immediately made to whom you direct.

LB (DNA: PCC, item 13). Addressed: "Francis Bailey, Lancaster."

Henry Laurens to the Chevalier de Mauduit Du Plessis

Dear Duplessis[1]   28th April [1778]

If I had time & abilities equal to my affection for you & my inclination to let you know it, I would write you a Letter as long as from here to Valley forge, at least I would return word for word to all the Letters I am indebted for, these would reach nearly to Lancaster. Circumstanced as I am you will excuse me for saying no more than the needful, by which you must not misunderstand as if I meant to reproach you for having said more, tho' certainly one dunn for your Commission was enough. You are careless of your papers, lose them & then harrass the poor President to double his labour without increasing *his* pay or his Rank—none, or none but a few of you Messieures Francois, who will work upon such terms. However taking for granted that Your Brevet Commission & the Resolve of Congress in your favor are really lost I now transmit you another of each which you will receive under this Cover. I wish you all manner of happiness & beg you will beleive me to be with great Regard, Dear Sir, Yours &ca.

LB (ScHi).

[1] Thomas-Antoine, chevalier de Mauduit Du Plessis (1753–91), a French artillery officer, entered Continental service in April 1777 as brevet captain of artillery and was made brevet lieutenant colonel by Congress on January 19, 1778, because of his "gallant conduct . . . at Brandywine, Germantown, and his distinguished services at Fort Mercer." *JCC*, 10:64. Du Plessis returned to France with Lafayette in 1779 and came back to America in 1780 as an officer in Rochambeau's army. Lasseray, *Les Français sous les treize étoiles*, 1:304–6. See also Laurens to Lafayette, March 24, 1778, note 4.

Henry Laurens to François-Louis Teissèdre de Fleury

Sir,[1]   28th April [1778]

I find my self indebted for your several favors of the 10th, 10th, 14th & 25th February, & this day I have been further honoured by the receipt of your 25th Inst.[2]

Congress will not attend to applications relative to Rank in the Army until an arrangement which is still under consideration shall be completed.

I have however conversed with friends on the particular subjects of your Letters & learned their sentiments.

It is admitted, that through the importunate & incessant pressing of different French Gentlemen for grade there may be instances of Commissions granted to some which seem to others injurious to themselves respecting relative Rank, but on the other hand it is insisted, as an undoubted fact, the Commissions in almost every case granted to Foreigners are comparatively disgraceful to the American Officers, & that there is no just ground for complaint by the former, that in order to avoid such mistakes for the future, as through a hurry of business, a business altogether new in this quarter of the World, have heretofore happened, it is necessary to wait until Congress shall be possessed of a Complete list of the Army & to grant no more Commissions except in very extraordinary Cases; Your case is not allowed to be one, unless it shall be said you have received extraordinary promotion in acknowledgement of extraordinary services & that an extraordinary degree of attention has been paid to you as a Foreign Ally, extraordinary in comparison with the ordinary course of proceeding towards many very meritorious Sons of America.

These I say are private sentiments drawn from friends among my Coadjutors in Congress, & a direct application to the House after I have been so well informed of the minds of Members would not only produce no good effect but in my opinion would be offensive. Nevertheless if you judge it proper to risque & will direct a Memorial immediately to Congress it will become my Duty to present it & you may rely upon the fidelity as you may upon the friendship of, Sir, your most obedt servt.

P.S. I have within a few days past seen repulses given to written requests made by General Gates for Commissions to officers of whose merits he spoke very warmly in two Instances, upon the principles above mentioned.[3]

You remark that you have made a journey of 6000 Miles—that length will reach much further than the remotest part of France, but my Dear Sir, reflect a Moment how many thousands are wishing to travel all that distance for moderate promotion & the assurance of an Asylum.

LB (ScHi).

[1] François-Louis Teissèdre de Fleury (1749–?), a French infantry officer, entered Continental service in May 1777 as a captain of engineers and was promoted to lieutenant colonel on November 26 "in consideration of the disinterested gallantry which he has manifested in the service of the United States." He was involved in the preparations for Lafayette's aborted Canadian expedition and upon his return to Valley Forge was named "Sub Inspector" of the army by Washington the day before Laurens wrote the present letter. Fleury returned to France in 1779 on leave from the Continental Army and returned to America in 1780 for another two years of service with Rochambeau. See Lasseray, Les Français sous les treize étoiles, 2:425–33; JCC, 9:967; and Washington, Writings (Fitzpatrick), 11:313.

[2] A February 25 letter to Laurens from Fleury and the chevalier de Mauduit Du

Plessis, in which the two lieutenant colonels argued that they were deserving of higher rank, is in Frank Moore, ed., *Materials for History from Original Manuscripts* (New York: Printed for the Zenger Club, 1861), pp. 95–98. A heavily mutilated April 24 letter from Fleury to Laurens, in which Fleury urged Laurens to find employment for a lieutenant colonel whose name has been torn from the manuscript, is in the Laurens Papers, DLC.

³ There is no record of these "repulses" in the journals or in Horatio Gates' letters as president of the Board of War in PCC, item 147.

Henry Laurens to Nathanael Greene

Sir,   York Town 28th April 1778

I had the honor of writing to you the 24th by Messenger McKlosky.

This Morning I presented a Letter to Congress of the 25th Inst. which I had received from Majr. General Mcdougall, an extract of which you will find within the present Cover, transmitted in obedience to the order of Congress.¹

I am with great Regard, Sir, Your obedient & humble servant,

Henry Laurens, President of Congress²

RC (MH–H).

¹ This day Congress read an April 23, not April 25, letter from Gen. Alexander McDougall describing some of the problems he had encountered upon assuming command in the Highlands. Although the journals record only Congress' decision to refer this letter to the Board of War as well as part of it to the Board of Treasury, a marginal note on the RC by Secretary Thomson indicates that a copy of the section dealing with McDougall's need for forage was also sent to Quartermaster General Greene. See *JCC*, 10:398; and PCC, item 161, fols. 87–94.

² Laurens also wrote a letter to Greene on April 30, describing the steps he had taken to succor an unnamed messenger of Greene's who had contracted smallpox and "now lies dangerously Ill at the House of Mr. Clebins on the Lancaster Road about 7 Miles hence." Laurens Papers, ScHi.

Henry Laurens to Baron de Kalb

Dear General   28th April [1778]

I have received the favor of yours of the 24th.¹ The Packet which came inclosed in it for Paris I have sent to my friend William Smith Esquire at Baltimore with necessary directions for conveyance.

My freinds at South Carolina shall be intreated to interpose in the case of Doctor Phile & I am persuaded every proper Act in their power will be attempted to rescue his Child.²

I remain with great regard

LB (ScHi).

¹ A transcript of Kalb's April 24 letter to Laurens is in the Laurens Papers, ScHi.

² See Laurens to Kalb, April 22, 1778, note 2.

Henry Laurens to John Laurens

My Dear son,   York Town 28th April 1778[1]
    This Evening Your kind favor of yesterday[2] inclosing a Letter directed to my Daughter came to hand, this shall be forwarded by an Express Messenger to morrow who will be a Month ahead of Monsr Francy.

I am glad our Act of the 22d pleases you—it appears to me to be sufficiently energetic for the present purpose—the last paragraph one excepted will point out to the illustrious Commissioners from White Hall, from whence to take their departure & save much time which might otherwise have been spent in Ceremonious preliminary.[3] My sentiment is that this little Clause of 7 Lines nullifies many Pages of their Instructions, it certainly contains a complete answer to the Laborious performances of Lord North & the Labours of the blood thirsty Tryon. The Tit for Tat, which your General lately gave to the Quondam Governor must exceedingly mortify a Man of his arrogance.

Some of our people here have been exceedingly desirous of throwing abroad in addition to the Resolutions an intimation of the willingness of Americans to treat with G Britain upon terms not inconsistent with the Independence of these States or with Treaties with foreign powers.[4] I am averse. We have made an excellent move on the Table—rest until we see or learn the motions on the other side—the whole World must know we are disposed to treat of Peace & to conclude one upon honorable terms. To Publish therefore is unnecessary—it would be a dangerous Act, encourage our Enemies & alarm our friends.

Your Ideas respecting New York square precisely with my own.[5] I wish the States & the People of the States could be roused to fill a reputable Army. You have thousands of Men scatter'd over the Country in the Character of Servants to Officers &c &c. Why are not they collected. There is amazing laxness of discipline somewhere or perhaps too generally in your Army. What does Hartley's Regiment in this Town? Congress ordered it to Camp a fortnight ago.[6] Their Idle Drums & Fifes twice a day by my window jarr upon my soul. Thus are we & thus we suffer our selves to be treated.

I have in hand the article you desire for Summer wear, sent for it from Boston, you shall have it by the present or the very next Messenger.

Try to say somewhat to the several heads of my Letters in order to rep[air] my Memory, for I have not time to Copy generally in the very wane of time I take up a piece of Paper to tell you in the best manner so short a moment how very truly & affectionately & respectly I am your faithful friend,   Henry Laurens

RC (MHi: William Gilmore Simms Collection deposit, 1973).

[1] Laurens apparently wrote a letter to John on April 27 that has not been found. In his private letter book for that date Laurens tersely noted "sent without Copy" in reference to an April 27 letter to his son. It is doubtful that the letter referred to is the same as the one printed here because Laurens used different messengers on the 27th and the 28th to transmit letters to Valley Forge. According to his letter book Samuel Wilkinson, the messenger he employed on the former date, carried the letter of the 27th to John, while Joseph Sharp bore Laurens' letters of the 28th. Laurens Papers, ScHi.

[2] See Simms, *Laurens Army Correspondence,* pp. 162–65.

[3] The next to last paragraph of Congress' April 22 response to Lord North's conciliatory bills stated that the United States would not negotiate with British peace commissioners unless Great Britain "as a preliminary thereto, either withdraw their fleets and armies, or else, in positive and express terms, acknowledge the independence of the said states." *JCC,* 10:379.

[4] See Samuel Huntington's Proposed Resolution, April 22–23? 1778.

[5] John had deprecated some unnamed proponents of a plan for taking New York City "by storm." Simms, *Laurens Army Correspondence,* p. 164.

[6] There is no mention of this order in the journals.

Henry Laurens to Henry Lee

Sir   28th April [1778]

I had yesterday the honor of presenting your Letter of the 24th to Congress & this Evening by order of the House I issued a Warrant on the Treasury for 50,000 Dollars for the use of your Corps of Horse payable to Lieutt. Rudulph to whom the warrant is delivered.[1] Some difficulties arose in Congress respecting the propriety of seizing Horses within the State of Maryland which occasioned a Report from the Board of War on that head to be laid aside for future consideration, in the mean time I have referred Mr. Rudulph to a Gentleman one of the Delegates from that State who had promised to point out places to him where he may purchase good Horses at about £125 per Horse, & avoid the violence & danger of seizing private property. Mr. Rudulph will undoubtedly communicate such information as he may receive.

I remain with great regard.

LB (DNA: PCC, item 13).

[1] Major Lee's April 24 letter to Laurens is in PCC, item 78, 14:225–26. In it he announced that the bearer, Lt. John Rudolph of Lee's recently formed battalion of light dragoons, would wait upon Laurens "to receive instructions concerning procuring horses, and obtaining a sufficient sum of money for the purposes of recruiting and purchasing accoutrements," and argued that in view of the high price of horses it was "absolutely necessary, that some powers be given to certain persons to impress for the service and pay according to valuation on oath." Although the Board of War prepared a report proposing to grant Lee authority to impress horses on "the Peninsula formed by the Delaware and Chesapeake Bays," Congress, as Laurens delicately informed the major, decided that this report should be "laid aside for future consideration." See *JCC,* 10:401–2.

Henry Laurens to George Washington

Sir,   York Town 28th April 1778.
I wrote to Your Excellency yesterday by Wilkinson. This Evening Your Excellency's favor of the same date containing Copy of a Letter to M. General Tryon & Extracts from Govr. Livingston & General Heath came to hand.[1] These shall be presented to Congress to morrow.

Within the present Cover Your Excellency will receive an Act of Congress of 27th. for enabling the General commanding the Artillery to be of the intended Council if your Excellency shall judge it proper.[2]

The bearer hereof is charged with a packet containing 500 Copies of the Oath of Allegiance & Abjuration, & he is directed to call on Mr. Bailey Printer at Lancaster for 200 Copies of the Act for granting pardons printed in the German tongue.

This Morning I reported to Congress a Letter from Major General Conway requesting leave to resign his Commission, which the House immediately Resolved to accept; I shall transmit to General Conway the proper notification by the next Express Messenger to Albany.[3]

I have the honour to be, With the highest Esteem & Regard, Sir, Your Excellency's Obedient & humble servant,
                              Henry Laurens, President of Congress.

RC (DLC).
[1] Washington's April 27 letter to Laurens is in PCC, item 152, 5:529–31, and Washington, *Writings* (Fitzpatrick), 11:313–14. His April 26 letter to Maj. Gen. William Tryon is in Washington, *Writings* (Fitzpatrick), 11:309. The April 13 letter from Gen. William Heath and the April 15 letter from Gov. William Livingston, extracts of which Washington sent to Congress, are in the Washington Papers, DLC. The extract from Heath's letter dealt with a perennial problem in his Boston command—"the great and almost insuperable embarrassments under which we labour here on account of the insufficient Supplies of money"—and was as usual referred to the Board of Treasury. It should be noted, however, that on April 27 Congress had already taken steps to relieve Heath's financial distress. *JCC*, 10:397–98. The extract from Livingston's letter described the New Jersey governor's loss of a February 28 letter from the Committee at Camp dealing with the procurement of horses for the Continental cavalry and requested Washington to apprise him of "the mode therein prescribed for the Payment" of the mounts he purchased. Congress did not resolve Livingston's perplexity until May 16, after he had actually purchased some horses for the cavalry and had written a letter of inquiry to Congress about the method of payment. See *JCC*, 11:501, 505; and Committee at Camp to Thomas Wharton, February 28, 1778, note.
[2] See *JCC*, 10:397; and Gouverneur Morris to Washington, April 18, 1778, note 4.
[3] General Conway's April 22 letter to Laurens is in PCC, item 159, fols. 473–75. In it he vehemently criticized his commanding officer Gen. Alexander McDougall for having removed him from the scene of action by assigning him to Albany, lamented the waste of his military talents, and asked Laurens to "Make my resignation acceptable to Congress." Congress, no doubt eager to rid the army of an

inveterate malcontent, promptly voted eight states to one to accept Conway's resignation, with only Virginia casting her vote in the negative. Despite Conway's subsequent claim that his April 22 letter was not intended to be a letter of resignation—a claim few readers of it would accept—Congress took no action to reinstate him. See *JCC*, 10:398–99; PCC, item 159, fols. 477–79; and Laurens' letters to Rawlins Lowndes, May 1, to Conway, May 7, to John Rutledge, June 3, to Lafayette, June 5, and to John Laurens, June 5, 1778.

Henry Laurens to Jacob Christopher Zahn

Dear Sir, 28th April 1778

Before this day you have received my last Letter under the 10th March by the hand of Captn. Senf.

Six days after that had been dispatched I had the pleasure of being confirmed in my opinion that my affairs under your direction were not neglected, because you had not written to me by every opportunity. Such assurance I received in your Several favors of the 6th December, 22d January & 16 Febry. which demand, & I beg you will be pleased to accept, my hearty thanks. I will not trouble you with even a Single direction respecting my Plantations. Order, direct & advise in every case relative to them as if they were your own, I shall be content with events & gratefully express my acknowledgements of your friendship.

I have long since adopted the advice of the Man recorded in history "Wise"—"whatever the hand findest to do, do it with all thy might," & I pursue this precept with most ardor, when applicable to the service of my Country or my friends. Hence you may account for the very little attention which I have given for some time past to my private concerns, these I submit to providence & to my friends under Providence, trusting that my labors for the public will not work detriment to my self.

You must not expect to see me very soon, although I had about two Months ago determined to return to my native Clime immediately after I should obtain permission.

When the House of Assembly were pleased to grant me leave to return, they were also pleased to re-elect me for this Station, this I received as an Intimation of their desire that I should remain, & as it reached me at a juncture when our public Cause had assumed a very gloomy aspect, I immediately declared to my Son & to my Colleague the Chief Justice, that I would not turn my Back upon the appearance of danger & difficulty. I am determined to continue in the service of my Country maugre all particular considerations, until we have a full Congress or some favorable changes in the affairs of our Union, or until my Colleagues are well initiated in the weighty businesses which they are sent to engage in. These are weighty indeed, & the due proper discharge of them require always very great diligence, and more wisdom than I am possessed of. All the States have been exceedingly remiss in their respective Representations in Congress, a remissness which will cost them Millions of Dollars & which had one time exposed our Cause to the most imminent danger. Had General Howe been a Soldier of enterprize he might have made prisoners of the *little* Congress, dispersed our *little* Army, destroyed all our public Stores & returned with very triffling loss to Philadelphia or have taken post at Lancaster & kept a competent Garrison in the City.

We begin now to be in better order & if the Enemy is disposed to pursue the War we shall still be able to make at least a respectable defensive Campaign.

North River which has been too shamefully neglected & whose defenceless condition had endangered the loss of our communication with the Eastern States is now nearly secured by proper works within the Water & upon the Commanding Banks. General Gates will proceed to morrow to take the Command of that department, called the Northern. In his way he is to join a grand Council at General Washintons Head Quarters where a plan for the operations of the ensuing Campaign is to be formed.

General Lee who is now exchanged for General Prescot will be present.

A General Cartel for the Exchange of prisoners was lately on the tapis & Commissioners from each party had met for establishing Rules, but were seperated in the preliminary steps. General Howe refused to engage on behalf of the King His Master, our Commissioners would not accept of engagements which would not extend to bind his successors in Command. Upon this point, our Commissioners retired, & have gained great applause. There was great propriety in their support of the dignity of these free & Independent States. From certain mean & scandalous proceedings immediately under the Eye of General Howe & undoubtedly consistent with his knowledge such as forging & publishing Letters in the name of General Washington & Acts of Congress in my name it can hardly be questioned that he had sinister views in refusing to bind his successor & we now find he is recalled & is to be succeeded in command by Sir Henry Clinton or some other which he must have known at the time the Cartel was in agitation. Last year he gave us *dead* & *sick* Men in return for well fed hearty fellows, this year he had Studied some new artifice perhaps to give us *no Men.*

General Lee assures me the British Officers approbate our conduct in detaining the Troops comprehended in the Convention of Saratoga. This affords much satisfaction to a person who had so large a share in that business as I had. He adds there are numbers among those officers who often express their wishes for our success & beleive that even the Commander in Chief thinks our Cause just.

This seems wondrous strange!

The papers which will accompany this will shew you Great Britain desire of Peace & the mean Stratagem which she is substituting for honest intentions in order to deceive us. Possibly the Act of Congress of the 22d April may teach her Ministry to know we are not quite blind, nor quite Idiots.

We have been long battleing in Congress on a half pay establishment to take place after the present War for our Officers which I hold to be inconsistent with our original Compact, unjust in a comparative view with the Militia & with the Soldiery in general unconstitutional & dangerous. Upon these Several branches I have endeavored to reason against the measure & may by & by shew you my sentiments. If the Question is carried it will be by a bare Majority of one State.

Mr. Tryon the late Governor of New York, has had the imodesty to insult General Washington & all our Generals commanding at Posts in the Northern & Eastern departments as well Governors of States with Copies of the Draughts of Bills offered by Lord North to parliament with an injunction to make them public among the Officers & Soldiers of the Army & the people in general. In return to such effrontry, General Washington has sent him the Act of Congress of the 22d April, shewing the Quondam Governor that 'tis the wish of Congress his Curious draughts should enjoy an unrestrained circulation. At the same time he also transmitted him an Act of Congress of the 23d April for granting pardons, a Copy of which you will find here inclosed, desiring the said Governor to exert his powers to communicate the contents to the persons who are the objects of its operation, & concludes with a sneer upon Mr. Tryon—"The benevolent purpose it is intended to answer will I persuade myself recommend it to your Candor."

Thus I think the Governor's account is Balanced by a retort which he would not have expected & which will therefore be the more mortifying to a Man of his arrogance.

It is said that Lord Amherst, Admiral Keppel & General Murray are named as Commissioners for treating with Congress & that they are daily expected. When they arrive at Philadelphia they will meet half their business done by the Act of the 22d. The paragraph, next to the last, will point out to them where to begin their negotiation & save much trouble of preliminary which otherwise they might have judged necessary.

My circumstances are such as afford me only scraps of time for writing private Letters & none to Copy & amend. You will therefore account for the imperfections of this & be so good as to accept it rough as it is & believe me very sincerely, Dear Sir with affection & Esteem

LB (ScHi).

Thomas McKean to Sarah McKean

My dear Sally,   York Town. April 28th. 1778.
    I have only time to tell you I am well, and am just setting out for Carlisle. Last week Jacob Bone was condemned to die for Burglary, and Elisabeth Wilderness burned in the left hand with the letter M for manslaughter in killing her own husband with a knife. She has by him eight children all alive. Mr. Montgomery will give you a News-paper with intelligence of great importance. Lord Amherst, Admiral Keppel and General Murray are appointed Commissioners to treat about peace or rather reconciliation. I hope to see you on Friday, and in the meantime remain, My dear Sally, Your most affectionate,
                                                              Tho M:Kean

RC (PHi).

Thomas McKean to Caesar Rodney

Dear Sir,   York-Town April 28th. 1778.
    Your favor of the 18th instant came safe to hand.[1] If the General Assembly continue to sit a few weeks and I can be informed of that intention, and that it would be agreeable to them, I shall do myself the honor to wait upon them upon notice, being anxious to render any and every service in my power to that virtuous Body. The affair of the hundred men I have not yet had opportunity to move,[2] but am told three hundred are ordered to be raised on the Eastern shore for the purpose you mention, which it is thought will be sufficient. I congratulate you on the success of Lieutt. Colo. Pope and should be glad to know whether any prisoners were taken and what has been done with them.[3] The Congress sometime ago passed an Act for the apprehending Charles Gordon & Thomas White Esquires & such oth-ers as were notoriously disaffected and active agt. their country in the Delaware State.[4] This took its rise from a motion of the Delegates of Maryland, founded on an Information given to, and an intercepted letter of Thomas White's laid before, the Governor and Council of Maryland, and some kind of claim they had to the persons named, they being lately subjects of that State, living upon their borders & carrying on an iniquitous conspiracy within that State. The intention

was to have them imprisoned in Maryland, and to prevent any revenge on the part of these men or their adherents agt. the Executive Power of the Delaware State, and also to prevent their being rescued out of our Goals by the Enemy or the Tories, or their being liberated by habeas corpus, as the General Assembly had not suspended the habeas corpus Act. I have heard that they have since been taken, and discharged by ha. cor. and that Gordon has again joined the Enemy. Tho' it was perfectly right to enlarge them on this commitment, yet the charge made agt. them by Congress would have been sufficient ground for my brother Chief Justice to have bound them to the Good Behaviour. I should have mentioned this affair to you or Mr. Read before but that it was ordered to be kept secret, lest the execution of it should be frustrated. I was called upon to name some of the most dangerous men in the State to be added to the others, but I refused, alledging the people there were now becoming good Whigs, and I hoped there would be no occasion.

Now for most important intelligence. You will receive ten papers herewith, published by Congress, which will give you part of it, and which I must beg you will distribute among the Members of the General Assembly. The Bills have been passed into laws, and Lord Amherst, Admiral Keppel and General Murray are the Commissioners. This whole affair will (I know) surprize you, but it has been owing to preliminaries for a treaty with Congress from France being intercepted, tho' the duplicates have not yet been received here. I have not a fear of an Acknowledgmt. of our Independance, and an honorable peace, if British Honors, Offices & Gold do not tempt and corrupt your Members of Congress & the Generals & principal officers in the Army. Do Sir, as I have not time to write to any body else, press the General Assembly to send two more Delegates here, and inform them that you know with certainty I am determined never to give up the Independance of the United States, after so much expence of blood & treasure, whilst I have a breath to draw; that I shall neither be allured nor intimidated into it; and that, if this resolution should not meet with their fullest approbation, they would be pleased to remove me immediately.

God grant us virtue & fortitude in this hour of trial. I have worked double tides (as the Sailors say) all the last week, being every day in Court, and also in Congress, which latter sat on the Fast Day and also yesterday. Our Officers will be allowed half pay for life, under sundry limitations & restrictions, the thing not finished but near it. The Bell tolls for Congress. Adieu. I am, dear Sir, Your most obedient humble Servant, Tho M:Kean

RC (Sol Feinstone, Washington Crossing, Pa., 1979).

[1] Rodney's April 18 letter to McKean is in Rodney, *Letters* (Ryden), pp. 260–62.

[2] Rodney had requested Congress to authorize the raising of these men to "be

stationed in Kent." See ibid., p. 261; and Charles Carroll of Carrollton to Thomas
Johnson, April 21, 1778, note.

[3] For information on Delaware's efforts to suppress the loyalist uprising which
occasioned this exchange between McKean and Rodney, see Harold B. Hancock,
The Loyalists of Revolutionary Delaware (Newark: University of Delaware Press,
1977), pp. 80–82.

[4] For further information on the attempted arrest of Charles Gordon and
Thomas White, see Henry Laurens to William Smallwood, March 26, 1778, note.

Marine Committee to John Bradford

Sir   April 28th. 1778
   We are now to acknowledge the receipt of yours of the 8th Current,
inclosing an Inventory of the Continental part of the goods Captured
by Captain Hopkins, we wish to hear of the arrival of his Prizes, but
are afraid they are retaken. You will deliver to the order of the Board
of war the 26 Pieces of coarse sheeting
         24 Bolts Oznabrigs
          9 doz felt hats
         17 Sadelles & their furniture
         81 Pieces napped Cottons
         200 ready made bags enumerated in that Inventory.
   Such of the other articles as the Navy Board may want for the use
of the Navy, you will deliver to them and sell what remains to the
best advantage. We are sorry to hear of the death of Captain Chew,
but are glad at the same time to find that he died bravely fighting a
Ship of Superior force.[1] The loss of the Alfred gives us much concern
and we are not a little surprized to hear that the Raleigh should be
in sight at the time of the Capture and not give her assistance especially when it is said that the force of the enemy was inferior to that
of our Ships, however we shall suspend our judgment until this matter shall be fully inquired into.[2] By advice from our Continental
Agent in Charles Town we have the melancholy intelligence that the
Randolph which sailed from Charles Town in February last in Company with four Armed Vessels fitted out by that state during the
Cruize in Longitude 53, latitude 13.30 the fleet fell in with a British
man of war of 50 Guns. A severe engagement between her and the
Randolph ensued and after it had continued 12 minutes the latter
unfortunately blew up and in all probability every soul perished.[3]
The British ship immediately on the explosion gave chase to the
other Vessels, who were enabled to make their escape by Captain
Biddles having shot away the ships bowsprit and Mizen top Mast. If
this most unfortunate accident had not taken place in all probability
the Randolph and the Armed Vessels had given A good Account of

the 50 Gun ship. Our little fleet is much diminished.[4] Hopeing that we may be more fortunate in future, We are Sir, Yr. most obed servants

P.S. Inclosed is a Resolve of Congress of this date[5] Appointing William Burke a Captain in the Navy, and directing that he should receive from the time he was Appointed to the Command of the schooner Warren to this day according to the Rate of Pay settled when he was so Appointed. We now desire that you will settle his account and pay him Agreeable to the said Resolve. You will please to inform us who was the Captain next in Commission to Captain Manly of the five Vessels fitted out by order of General Washington.

LB (DNA: PCC Miscellaneous Papers, Marine Committee Letter Book).

[1] Samuel Chew was killed on March 4 while engaging a British privateer mounting twice as many guns as his brigantine *Resistance*. Morgan, *Captains to the Northward*, pp. 118–19.

[2] At his June court-martial Capt. Thomas Thompson was found guilty of failing to bring the *Raleigh* to the assistance of the *Alfred* during its capture on March 9, whereas the conduct of the *Alfred's* captain Elisha Hinman was vindicated by a court-martial in February 1779. For further discussion of the *Alfred's* capture and the subsequent courts-martial, see ibid., pp. 122–25, 148, 154–55. See also Marine Committee to the Eastern Navy Board, May 8, 1778.

[3] Capt. Nicholas Biddle and all but 4 of his 315 crewman perished on March 7 when the *Randolph* exploded while engaging the 64-gun ship *Yarmouth* off Barbados. For Biddle's naval career and last cruise, see William Bell Clark, *Captain Dauntless, the Story of Nicholas Biddle of the Continental Navy* (Baton Rouge: Louisiana State University Press, 1949).

[4] The Continental Navy had suffered significant losses during recent months. The *Randolph* tragedy, followed by the surrender of the *Virginia*, left only seven of the original thirteen Continental frigates, and five of the seven were not in service. The *Warren*, after taking two prizes on her maiden cruise in March, was idle at Boston awaiting crew and the *Trumbull*, unable to clear the bar, remained trapped in the Connecticut River. The unfinished frigates *Effingham* and *Washington* would be burned in the enemy's May raid up the Delaware and the *Raleigh*, after acquiring a new captain, would be captured in September. The sixteen vessels purchased in 1775 and converted to form the nucleus of the Continental fleet had fared even worse than the frigates. With the loss of the *Alfred* and the *Columbus* in March, and several smaller craft during the May raid, only the sloop *Providence* remained active and she was being rebuilt at New Bedford between February and July. Although the purchased frigate *Queen of France* and sloop *General Gates* would soon be active in American waters, at this moment American hopes for naval success turned to European waters, as the frigate *Providence*, reaching open sea on April 30, sailed for France to join the sloop *Ranger* and the frigate *Boston*, which had recently carried John Adams to Bordeaux. See Howard I. Chapelle, *The History of the American Sailing Navy* (New York: W. W. Norton & Company, Inc., 1949), pp. 53–55; and Morgan, *Captains to the Northward*, chap. 5.

[5] For this May 1 resolve, see *JCC*, 10:412. For a discussion of Burke's brief career with the Continental Navy as captain of the *Resistance*, see Morgan, *Captains to the Northward*, pp. 119–21.

Gouverneur Morris to John Jay

Dear Jay.   York Town 28th April 1778.

This Letter is to be handed to you by Genl. Gates. Let me recommend him to your particular Attention. Vermont you will say prevents this.[1] Policy may have induced him to flatter those People when he wanted their Assistance. Let us take it up on that Ground. In his present Command he will want the Assistance of our State, the cordial Assistance of its Rulers. I have promised this. I write to you, to Livingston[2] & jointly with Duer to the Governor.[3] This is sufficient and you will all three I am confident exert yourselves whenever Necessity shall [require it?].

I am, yours &ca.   Gouvr Morris

RC (NNC). Addressed: "Honle John Jay Esqr. Chief Justice of the State of New York, Fish Kill or elsewhere."

[1] Some New Yorkers were wary of Gates because of his cooperation during the campaign of 1776 with some local Vermont committees whose authority was not recognized by New York. Walter H. Crockett, *Vermont, the Green Mountain State,* 5 vols. (New York: Century History Co., 1921), 1:532–33.

[2] Morris did not write to Robert R. Livingston until May 3.

[3] See New York Delegates to George Clinton, April 30, 1778.

Robert Morris to John Brown

Sir   Manheim April 28th 1778

Amongst the letters Christian brought me last night were the several you will find enclosed herewith, which being intended for the Marine Committee & Commercial Committee You will deliver them with my Compliments and I think the Commercial Committee wou'd do a very just & proper thing if they were to give Mr Livingston orders to Continue sending Cargoes of Rice both to Mr Ceronio & Mr Bingham as fast as he can, they have suffered exceedingly by making advances for the Public but *particularly the former* and they ought to be relieved. If Mr. Ceronio does not receive remittances it is probable he may be Imprisoned; he has been threatned with that Fate by his Creditors & he has served us with a Zeal and Fidelity that merits much better things. I wou'd order Mr Livingston however not to ship Indigo for the loss on that will be great, but then he shou'd ship the more Rice which will produce a proffit.

The Schooner Lewis, Capt Rowan, was employed it seems to carry Cap Pickles to New Orleans, but I am informed by a Gentn now here, that the Crew Rose & after landing Pickles & Rowan near the Havannah they carried the Schooner into Providence which breaks up that plan.

I thank You for the Contents of your letter of yesterday & remain, Dr sir, Your Obedt hble servt.   Robt Morris

P.S. I hope you have got Capt Osmans bills accepted and ready for payment as he is the bearer of this.

RC (NjP).

Thomas Burke to Richard Caswell

Dr. Sir.   York April 29th 1778.

You will receive from the President of Congress some Extracts from the Journals relative to me which will appear very odd to you if uninformed of several attending circumstances.[1] The history of the matter is as follows: A letter was received from General Washington relative to some resolutions of Congress which stood in the way of an Exchange of Prisoners;[2] the House in general determined not to recede from the resolutions he complained of, which I believe I mentioned to you in a former letter. A Committee was appointed to draught a letter in answer. The draught was reported, and it appeared to several of us exceptionable in many parts, particularly in some Eulogisms on the whole Tenor of the resolutions of Congress relative to the Exchange of prisoners which we thought neither consistent with Truth or Modesty, and also in several charges against the General of suffering the Dignity and Honor of the United States to be Injured, charges which were I am persuaded void of all foundation. The whole indeed appeared to several Gentlemen as well as to me to indicate in the framers a disposition not friendly to the General, nor such as so good, so Important, so public spirited and Disinterested a Character deserves.[3] One Paragraph had taken up the whole afternoon[4] in debate. The members of the Committee had let themselves very largely into many foreign matters, declaimed very vehemently but to no other purpose than confirming us in our former opinions, and fatiguing every faculty. At length the exceptionable parts of the Paragraph were expunged and it received a very different dress. The members of the Committee strenuously urged that we should proceed and finish the letter that night, tho' it was then after ten o'clock. The principal opposition they met with through the day was from General Reid, of Pennsylvania, Mr. Drayton, of South Carolina and myself. I labored under a very Distressing fit of an intermitting fever, which heightened by the part I was obliged to take in the Debate, and the noise of loud, incessant Declamation, occasioned so violent pain in my head that I was totally unable to attend any longer. Mr. Harnett has been several days confined and there were only Nine States represented. In vain was all this and much more which was equally forcible, urged against Sitting any longer. The Question for adjournment was put, and before it came to me I was very apprehensive it would pass in the Negative and I determined to withdraw if no other way was left, to prevent our proceeding so improperly on business of such Importance. Those who know the Opinions that had long prevailed relative to a party against a certain great officer,[5] will not deem this resolution an absurd one, tho' perhaps it was not the most prudent that could have been formed on the Occasion. The event took place nearly as stated in the Journal and I withdrew;[6] the Messenger attended me soon after with a message which from his manner of Delivering it and from my knowing there could be no Congress without me I did not conceive to have come from the President, but from Mr. Duer, of New York, with whom I was on Terms of particular intimacy, and who I imagined, presuming on that Intimacy, had sent for me in order to his facilitating his carrying through the Letter, which seemed to be a favourite object with him. I returned an answer which I intended for him and in which I was not choice of expressions. Next morning[7] the matter was opened by a member from Massachusetts,[8] in a very illiberal manner, but with general observations, and general Inferences of Danger and Inconvenience if such practice was to be permitted. I rose immediately, observed that the application was doubtless intended for the Event of the preceding Evening, (I did not at this time know that my answer had been reported) and therefore said nothing relative to it to the particular Event. I said little more than I was indisposed, and my faculties had been so much fatigued by the whole day's attention that I found myself unable to discharge my duty, and I conceived very few other members were. To the general Observations and Inferences I answered that an unreasonable exercise of any Power was Tyrany, and that to keep a member at such unreasonable Hours and under such circumstances was in my opinion Tyrannical, and that I would not submit to it but by force on my person; that I considered every freeman as having a right to judge for himself when the Exercise of any Power was unreasonable, and if I erred in my judgment the power of punishing lay with the State I represented. If Congress should determine to what hour the members should attend in the afternoon as it had in the forenoon I would punctually attend, but while it was undetermined I must use my own judgment, at the risk of Incurring whatever Penalties my Country should adjudge. The members of the Committee who had framed the letter, now united, and labored strenuously to make a Mountain of this Mole-hill, talked vehemently of the insolence of appealing to the States, declared their disposition to proceed to Commitment or to Expulsion and lamented that the circumstances of Congress made my presence Necessary and prevented them from moving to such purposes. They talked very much of the Contempt in calling any act of a Majority of Congress a Tyrany. I now perceived that I was on ground which it became my Duty to maintain with consequences to myself never so fatal. I addressed the President and declared I would sit patiently until every Gentleman in the House who chose to speak should exhaust the whole of his eloquence. I would only request them that if they chose to use any abusive language (for much had been used) they would reserve it for some other place, and when every one should have done I would reply. I accordingly sat very patient for Hours, and at length when every one who chose it had entirely done I delivered the following Sentiments: That my opinion of the power of Congress over its members had been often given in that Assembly and was well known to be that no member could refuse his attendance or even his Vote when called on, that the States furnish quotas of Council as well as Troops, that either would be furnished in vain if the Individuals assigned could refuse to perform the requisite Duty, that my name stood to this opinion on the Journals, but the Individual must of necessity Judge whether the particular Instance in which his performance is required be reasonable or not. If he judges wrong or disobeys without just reason he incurs the penalties provided for misbehavior in office, but the power of judging and punishing Delegates was never Committed to Congress by any Express act of the State I represented, that the opinion that each freeman had a right to judge of the reasonableness or unreasonableness of any act of power, and even to resist it if unreasonable at the risk only of the Judgment of his Country, I held to be the grand Principle of Whiggism and the best Security for public Liberty, a principle which I would never forego but with my Life, that the other opinion relative to the jurisdiction of the State over its delegates seemed to me to Involve the Sovereignty of the State and its Security in a representation since it would be impossible for its representatives to assert and maintain its rights with firmness and freedom if subject to arbitrary Imprisonments, and punishments by Congress & that I would never retract it but by the Express order of the State, who alone had power to give it up. That I would not justify the particular breach of order under Consideration, but hoped it might be excused because it was not unusual nor under its particular circumstances even improper.[9] That as I discovered great favour in all the members except a few towards me on this occasion I was exceedingly sorry my Conduct or Language had given offense; that nothing was further from my intentions, that the words I used were the only names I knew for the things I wanted to express, that I held it an unworthy Business for a republican and a representative of a free and sovereign People to be looking out for courtly Expressions. That had the matter been opened with any regard to Liberality, a few words which I would have said would have Satisfied the House, and put an end to it, but as the matter was managed it became Inconsistent with my Duty and my honor to make any Concession without expressly insisting on my opinions. That with this reservation I would make any apology the House should require, but without it I could make none which would not involve a breach of Trust to my Country, and no punishment could be devised which I would not meet sooner than be guilty of such an offence. The members of the Committee still persisted; nothing would do but an Explicit acknowledgement of what they pleased to call my Error. I rejoined only that I knew no power who could make a man change his opinion before he was Convinced of his Error, that I was not and therefore would not acknowledge it. They proceeded now to enter on the Journals such a state of facts as they pleased. I desired only that they would enter a fair and full statement, that such as they offered were far from being so. After some time it was said by the Gentlemen that I should have an opportunity of answering and could set forth any that were omitted. In my answer I acquiesced, and so did the House. They then proceeded to take down some of my Expressions in debate. I required them to take down all that would speak my full Sense, and not detached Expressions; that I would give it to them as fully as they could wish, being firmly resolved not to retract one Iota of it. But I was answered, as before, that I could supply the deficiencies in my answer, and I acquiesced. The Entries were made and the president announced them in form. I thanked him for his politeness of manner, told him I hoped I could satisfy the House that no disrespect was Intended to them, but that I avowed my opinions as I delivered them in debate; that I persisted in them, and insisted on entire freedom of Debate. I was required to return an answer to the next adjournment, which was to be in the afternoon, and I desired no longer time; but afterwards the House changed it to Monday, which was the next day of Business.[10]

Reprinted from *N.C. State Records,* 13:403–7. FC (Nc–Ar). The FC is a twelve-page manuscript in Burke's hand; eight pages are a draft of Burke's letter to Caswell, and four contain additional passages apparently not used.

[1] See Henry Laurens to Caswell, April 27, 1778. For further accounts of Burke's dispute with Congress, which is the main subject of Laurens' letter, see Burke's Proposed Statement to Congress, April 13, and his letter to the North Carolina Assembly, April 29, 1778.

[2] After this sentence in the FC Burke wrote a brief summary of Washington's April 4 letter to President Laurens on the subject of negotiating a prisoner exchange that he omitted in the letter he sent to Governor Caswell. For a discussion of the significance of Washington's letter, see Henry Laurens to Washington, April 8, 1778, note 4.

[3] Following this sentence in the FC Burke wrote: "We deemed it unjust and impolitic to give an unnecessary affront to an Officer who had so well deserved of his Country, and was still so important to our affairs."

[4] In the FC Burke originally wrote "forenoon, and the afternoon until ten oclock."

[5] Washington.

[6] At this point in the FC Burke first wrote and then deleted: "and Congress could not proceed."

[7] April 11.

[8] Probably Francis Dana. See the following note.

[9] After this sentence in the FC Burke intended to insert the following passage: "That a Gentleman from Maryland and an other from Massachusetts, both very warm on the present Occasion, had on the forenoon of the same day by withdrawing put a stop to business, the first for no better reason as he himself declared than an Engagement to dine, and the latter because he was not attended to when speaking withdrew in a passion and Congress was under the Necessity of adjourning." Samuel Chase and Francis Dana were the two delegates in question. Burke states in his memorial to the North Carolina Assembly, which is the next document in this volume, that the two delegates who withdrew from Congress were members of the committee considering Washington's April 4 letter to Laurens, which consisted of Chase, Dana, and William Duer.

[10] The FC contains two lengthy passages that do not appear in the Tr of Burke's letter to Caswell. The first relates to Burke's examination before Congress on April 24, when the delegates refused him permission to present a written rebuttal of the charges against him, and reads as follows:

"But I was determined to Seize so favorable an Opportunity whatever might be the Consequence to myself for Establishing a precedent of the Exclusive Jurisdiction of the State over its own Delegates a power which I deemed so Essential for preserving her sovereign Rights, and which I found some Gentlemen so much disposed to usurp. I desired to return my answer, and insisted on it before Mr Harnett should depart. I desired to do it in writing, but that you see was denied. I urged some reasons for doing it in that way, but did not press it much. My main Object was preserving the rights of the state, what regarded myself personally I did not think of Consequence sufficient to take up time with, but chose rather to rely on the Candor and Justice of my Country. I offered the president a paper which contained my answer and was signed with my hand requesting him as a Gentleman to look it over, while I should read my answer, that he might be able to Certify that it Contained it but the Gentlemen of the Committee and one other Gentleman clamored against it and he declined taking it." See also *JCC*, 10:386–89.

The second passage consists of a long defense of Burke's views on the accountability of North Carolina delegates to state authority, which was probably intended to serve as a peroration to his letter to Caswell, and reads:

"When my Country Constituted Delegates with Powers to bind in all matters not inconsistent with her Instructions, when she impowered them to declare Independance and expressly reserved to herself the Controll and Instructions of her own Members in the Common Council, when she declared in her Constitution that they should be subject to Impeachments, I am persuaded she did not intend to submit them to the arbitrary discretion of that Council, or of partial combinations in that Council where they are to Obey her Instructions to submit to her Control and in Opposition to whose will she must expect them to observe her Instructions, and assert her rights, and in Conjunction with whom alone she can do acts to Injure her, and by such acts deserve Impeachment, and punishment. In short I cannot think she meant to subject them to a power whose Interests it may be to prevent them from serving her with fidelity in the manner she Intends. New York once Instructed her Delegates to withdraw from Congress if Delegates from some of her revolted Counties should be received. I think she did [not] imagin the Congress had power to imprison them for obeying her Instructions. Some Gentlemen are now very fond of an Idea of Converting Back Lands into a fund to borrow money upon as Common Stock, and arguments of State Necessity are become as fashionable here as they were in the Court of Charles the first. I am inclined to think if such a Vote were to pass Congress, some of the States would Instruct their Delegates to withdraw, ours I am persuaded would not chuse that they should be imprisoned for obeying. In short Sir, I think the good Sense of my Country will determin that such a Power is not to be given over their Delegates, and that Judging and punishing them must be reserved to the State alone. They will readily Conceive that few men have firmness Sufficient to assert her ⟨their Rights in defiance of the resentment of Arbitrary unlimited power, who can imprison their Persons or proceed to any other punishments their violence may suggest, and they will not I presume leave Citizens in whom they choose to Confide exposed to partial Combinations which may have in View the subversion of their most Important Interests—but if I am mistaken Sir, I hope they will Condemn my motives for bringing before them a Matter which I could have very easily suppressed, could I have Consented to waive what I deemed Essential to their Sovereign Majesty."

At the end of this passage Burke noted in the margin: "Having written the above I sent it to the president, requesting him to peruse it and mark in the margin wherever he might think me mistaken, assuring him I was desirous of saying nothing to Extenuate or Exaggerate and he wrote me a letter which you will find enclosed." The letter Burke mentions is undoubtedly the one President Laurens wrote to him on April 30. Although there is nothing in the physical appearance of the FC to suggest where Burke planned to insert the first of these two long passages in his letter to Governor Caswell, there can be little doubt that he meant the second to serve as the conclusion. It is not clear why Burke left this passage out of the Tr and instead ended his letter to Caswell so abruptly. Consequently, it is possible that the Tr itself may be incomplete.

The conjecture that the Tr is incomplete is supported by the existence among the Secretary of State Papers, Nc–Ar, of a four-page manuscript in Burke's hand that is almost certainly a continuation of the present letter. This document, a partial draft of a letter which appears to begin precisely where the Tr ends but which still seems to lack a conclusion, is heavily corrected and reads as follows:

"I brought in my answer in the afternoon and delivered it to the President, but when he was going to read it the same Gentlemen of the Committee Opposed it and insisted it should not be in writing, and that it should not be at all that Evening. This Occasioned the words to the member from New York [William Duer], and upon this the whole afternoon was spent in altercation of so trivial and Illiberal a nature that I will not trouble you with it. The Expressions were Indiscreet, but they Escaped me while I was under the first Emotions arising from Such want of candor as was Evident in the Conduct of certain men. I perceived that proceeding to Shew the grounds of my belief of a Combination would lead me into discovering Certain Suspicions which you can easily discover from what has gone before, but which it would have been the highth of Imprudence to have declared Openly. I fixed the Expressions personally to One, and there let it rest. I told the House I would appolgize to them if they required it, but nothing more. I still believed the Fact, and could not Descend to the falshood of saying I did not. On Monday I declared myself ready to return an Answer. The Journals were altered, at the Instance of the Gentlemen of the Committee, the word return was Struck out, & it was made to read 'answer thereto.' I objected against it but in vain, altho I had the authenticated Copies in my pocket which I shall carefully preserve. The matter Slept for many days, and would have Slept forever had I permitted it, ⟨but I would not give up the opportunity of a precedent which Should clearly bring So important a right of the State to a Decision, and therefore

I insisted on bringing it on before Mr. Harnett should depart. I urged as a reason for returning my answer in writing Besides the particular Circumstances, that Since every Delegate was subject to proceedings in his own State, the Defence Should appear at the same time, and with the same Degree of authenticity with the charge, that Congress in this Differed from parliament that the members of Parliament are Questionable in no Court or place out of Parliament, the members of Congress must necessarily be amenable to their States or the Control of the States over them is entirely lost. The House however was entangled with parliamentary Doctrine, and I took little pains about it. My grand object was preserving the right of the State, what regarded myself personally I did not think of Consequence Sufficient to take up time with,⟩ but chose rather to rely on the Candor and Justice of my Country, ⟨*or if I could not Satisfy them to Submit patiently to their decision be it what it would than to lose so favorable an Opportunity of furnishing matterials for Establishing their Essential rights. I read the answer of which a Copy is inclosed, and previously requested the President to read a Copy of it which I laid on the table Signed with my Hand, the Gentlemen of the Committee, and One other Gentleman, clamored against it. I told the president I only asked him the favor as a Gentleman, the first in rank amongst us but if he refused it I could not insist on his taking it. He answered that while he was in the chair he could do nothing but by order of the House.⟩* Mr. Harnet who was at the table took it up and perused it while I read that of which it was a Copy. He has it Still in possession, and I hope will deliver it to you, I never Saw it more—what followed you will see from the papers transmitted, and it will also appear whether the Censure of the House is well or ill founded—on this Sir I shall Say nothing. The House Shewed great regard for me During this whole proceeding and were often upbraided with mean Condescension to an Individual by the members of the Committee. I assure you Sir I found it exceedingly difficult to persevere against the public and private entreaties of so many worthy characters, who being persuaded that some kind of Concession was Necessary and yet anxious for my personal welfare labored Strenuously to induce me to make even the Color of a Concession and there is no doubt such would procure a vote for obliterating the whole proceeding. But they entirely mistook the principle by which I was actuated, it was not pride but [a] Sense of Sacred Duty to my Country, and had I made any Concession it should have been as ample as an Individual ought to have made to the most respectable assembly on Earth but I hope my Countrymen believe that as no Power could force So no Influence could persuade me to make a Concession Injurious to their Majesty. Such a One Seemed to me to be required, and it was impossible—to me Sir as an Individual the Issue of this Business cannot be very Important. I wish only to lead hereafter the Life of a private Citizen, and I have been long anxious to return to that Station, but as it involves very Important Rights of my Country I wish it to be examined with great attention, tho' not until it can be done without endangering the harmony which ought to Subsist between the States during the present important Crisis. ⟨*I am happy to think it is in Such a Train that tho' my Country may Condemn my Conduct, yet they may assist her own rights. Nevertheless She can resolve to reserve to herself the power of Judging and punishing officers who She entrust with her most Important Interests, and protect them from the danger of violent and arbitrary Combinations which might be employed to the excluding them from their Duty at times the most Critical to her Interests and for the most wicked purposes. She can enable them to perform her Instructions, without apprehending arbitrary punishments from any other Power. She can make it Necessary, that every Charge against them Shall be full and Impartial.⟩"*

Thomas Burke to the North Carolina Assembly

[April 29, 1778][1]

I beg leave to submit to the assembly the following State of Facts and the proofs relating to them, also of my motives and Sentiments which gave occasion to the transmissions from Congress.[2]

General Washington had written complaining of some Embarassments in forming a Cartel occasioned by several resolutions of Congress which he deemed inconsistent and requesting something to be done to remove them.[3]

A Committee was appointed to draught an answer. A draught was reported and it was the subject of Debate on the 10th of April. It was in many parts in my opinion exceptionable and I together with some other members opposed those parts. The members of the Committee were very strenuous in their Endeavours to carry it through. The Exceptionable Parts seemed calculated to wound the General's Sensibility, and I could perceive no Necessity for it. After the Day until ten O'clock at Night had been Spent in debate on One paragraph which was at length amended, an adjournment was moved for, and the Committee Strenuously pressed to go through the remainder of the Letter that night tho at so late an Hour. I who had Sustained a principle part in the Debate was totally unable to continue any longer by reason of the violence of a fit of an Intermitting fever under which I labored.[4]

I admit that I withdrew &ca.

My reasons were the following

The subject under Debate was a Draught of a Letter to General Washington reported by a Committee in answer to one relative to the Exchange of Prisoners in which he complained of being wounded in his feelings and embarrassed by Some resolutions of Congress which appeared to him inconsistent.

The Draught seemed exceptionable in many parts which tended to give pain to the General without answering any good purpose, and they were opposed by some other members and myself. The whole day until 10 at night was taken up with debate on One paragraph which was at length amended. At that late hour the members of the Committee pressed very Strongly to proceed and finish the letter before adjournment.[5] They Seemed very strenuous for carrying through the draught as reported. I was of Opinion that it ought to undergo many amendments which from that day's debate I perceived could not be Effected without[6] very Strenuous Opposition. I deemed it therefore very improper to proceed when our faculties were exhausted. Besides this General reason I had one peculiar to myself. I had been obliged to take a principle part in the Debate altho during the whole afternoon I labored under a severe fit of an Intermitting fever, and at the time when the Question for adjournment was debated was so oppressed with the head ach attending it as to be[7] unable to give due attention to any Subject. ⟨*I found that my Endeavours were necessary for procuring the Amendments to the report and could not reconcile it to my Duty, or to my Sense of Justice, honor, or Utility to let it pass without using every Endeavour in my power to have it amended in the exceptionable parts.*⟩

I have penetrated the personal character of General Washington. In my Judgement he is a good officer and most excellent Citizen, moved only by the most amiable and disinterested Patriotism, he perseveres in encountering extreme difficulties, dangers and fatigues under which he seems Sensible of no uneasiness but from the misfortunes of his Country, and of no pleasure but from her success. His few Defects are only the Excess of his amiable Qualities, and tho I am not of opinion that any Individual is absolutely Essential to the success of our Cause, yet I am persuaded his loss would be very severely felt, and would not be easily supplied. With this Idea of him, I could not but deem it very impolitic to hazard giving him disgust when no good cause required it. Nor could I avoid deeming it unjust, and ungenerous to give unnecessary offence and Insult to so worthy a man who had so well deserved of his Country. Had a Majority of Congress been for it, I would nevertheless have used my most strenuous endeavours against it, for neither as the Citizen or Magistrate will I ever forgoe the Sentiments of the Independent republican, but as I had great reason to believe that very few in Congress would agree to such a Measure if rightly understood and even the few would err rather through excess of misplaced Zeal than ill disposition, there were still Stronger reasons for my wishing to prevent its passing when it could not receive due examination, and when I was *totally* incapable of performing my Duty. The Debate of the preceding day had Convinced me that even my Endeavours were not altogether unnecessary—the Sequel of the Business sufficiently Evinced that I Judged not amiss. The report underwent long and strenuous debates and was finally amended nearly agreeable to my Idea. Tis true that departing without leave is in strictness a breach of order, but it had been usually done without reprehension, and I only used the same liberty which every other member had frequently done and in some recent Instances by two members of the Committee on Occasions far from being so proper or excusable as that under Consideration.[8]

The answer which the Congress were pleased to call Indecent I hope will appear to the assembly in a very different light when they hear the Testimony which was given on the Occasion, an Authenticated Copy is annexed, to which I pray the assembly to refer.[9] I hope it will from thence appear that the Congress were not then in a Capacity as a Body to send any Message or receive an Answer, and that the message appeared not to have Come from the President, but from a private member,[10] and that the answer was intended for that private member alone.

To avoid taking up the time of the assembly I shall only refer to the answer which I delivered to Congress for an Explanation of the Minutes of the eleventh and tho' I might very well insist upon the dangerous Infraction of the freedom of Debate which must result from Censuring A member of that assembly upon Expressions picked from what falls from him in Argument and so Arranged as not to Convey the whole of his meaning, yet knowing that this will not escape the present Assembly who are watchfully attentive to all the Rights of freedom, I shall for my own part waive it and plainly declare that the Sentiments expressed and avowed in the answer were by me delivered in Debate and in Language Such as I usually Speak which tho' perhaps not refined enough for the Courts of Princes, might escape Censure in a republican assembly. Those Sentiments are mine, and I did refuse to retract them, they are Convictions fixed in my Mind and the result of much thinking, and long Investigation of the Rights of free men. I have not changed my Opinions nor can I without Conviction of their being erroneous, to say I had would be false, and a Meanness which no power could force me to.

The Opinion respecting the exclusive power of the States to Judge and punish their Delegates appears to me Necessary for their future Independance and Essential to their Sovereignty, and I think that when this state invested me with the power of representing them in the united Council of the free, Independent, Sovereign States of America the Supporting and defending that freedom, Independance and Sovereignty which was always my Duty as a Citizen, becomes so in a much greater Degree as a Delegate and to have yielded any thing Injurious to them was in my Idea a henious Treason.

The Congress refused to receive this answer in writing and altered the Journal which Contained the first order at the making of which every One expected my answer was to be returned in writing and I yielded to the partial insertion of my words and the mistate of the facts under an express declaration they should be able to correct them by my answer, but the members afterwards thought it unparliamentary, tho' in truth there is no Similitude in this respect between the Congress and Parliament, Members of Parliament being Subject to no Jurisdiction out of Parliament. The Thing Insisted upon by Several Members in Congress was Concession, they Endeavoured to Extort it by Illiberal Declamation, and by threats of the most Summary Violence, Such as even Imprisonment of my person, and expulsion. Others endeavoured to obtain it by argument, and friendly Liberal persuasion. To the first I confess I could not yield even the Semblance of an appology, and doubt not my words conveyed some part of the resentment which I could not help feeling for such Treatment. To the Second, I declared my sincere Concern if any thing in my Language or manner appeared not sufficiently respectful to Congress, that my Terms were the only names I knew for the things I wanted to express, that tho' my manner was perhaps expressive of resentment and Indignation it was plainly directed against Individuals who had given great provocation, but that no man was more deeply impressed with a Sense of respect for Congress and I was far from intending to give Offence. But the Sentiments I delivered being still unchanged and being in my opinion Essential to the rights of the States, and of the Citizens Individually, any Concession relative to them would be a Sacrafice of those rights, and a Meanness which I hoped the Congress would not expect, and which it was impossible to bring me to.

It is sufficient to hear them in their places because the charge and defence is before the ultimate Judge, but Members of Congress are or at least in my Opinion, ought to be amenable to their Constituents and the Charge and defence ought to come before them with equal authority. The Copy before the assembly is one that was laid on the table while I [awaited?] the answer, and was taken up and perused by Mr Harnet while I was reading. He kept it afterwards in possession. At any time upon Such an Occasion I should have deemed it my Duty to have behaved as I did in the present Instance, but I was particularly Sollicitous to pursue this matter to its utmost length for the following reason.

Since the first of my attendance in Congress I perceived some Individuals to have an Extraordinary propensity to acts of power, and to have often urged Congress to exercise them where there was no apparent Necessity, in such a manner as must be Contrary to the Established Laws and Constitutions of the States. In very many Cases the prudence and Circumspection of Congress rendered such attempts abortive, in some a Majority have been induced to Concur, and Individuals have been Seized, banished or Imprisoned by Resolutions of Congress against whom Rumors were the only Testimony, and who if insnared by this powerful and uncontrollable Body must be [. . . .] Frequent attempts have been made to prevail on Congress to take into their own Hands the Political Administration of one State,[11] and on pretence that their Institutions were defective, Power was given to a Military Officer in an other to Seize, Imprison and remove whomsoever he might Suspect,[12] under a Suspicion that their magistrates were not well affected, and over the Same State and part of two others a Power was given to a Committee of Congress to exercise the most unlimitted dictatorial Powers,[13] on a groundless Supposition of an Insurrection.[14] In short some Individauls from too much Zeal not tempered Sufficiently with wisdom and foresight, from apprehensions too lively and Judgements a little defective, from a busy Enterprising Disposition not quite enough Controll'd by caution and Circumspection or from some other defect of Capacity very frequently gave too much importance to trifling objects[15] and generally Suggested and urged the Exercise of acts of mere arbitrary power as remedies on every Occasion. Of late this Disposition was become more extensive, and appeared more frequently, and whoever spoke of the Internal Police or rights of the States as restraining the power of Congress was generally exposed to Sarcasm or ridicule. State Necessity was urged on all Such Occasions as Sufficient to Justify every act of power. I who am firmly persuaded that arbitrary Power has a Natural tendency to abuse, and am therefore Jealous of it in any Hands, who have marked the force and progress of precedents and have observed that those which have happened under the direction of Virtuous men have given Authority to Corrupt men to Violate the rights of mankind have always Considered this propensity as dangerous so far as it tended to Establish Precedents of such acts of Power exercised by Congress as are repugnant to or Inconsistent with the purposes of its Institution and the rights of the States.

When on the present Occasion I perceived Several of the Same Individuals assuming a power to Judge and punish at discretion the representatives of the Sovereign Independent States it appeared to me very dangerous even to permit the mention of such power undisputed. If not disputed it might pass into a general Opinion that Such power existed in Congress, if carried into Effect and submitted to it would be established by precedent. I therefore determined Instantly to dispute the power and to persist so as to bring the matter to a clear decision. I insisted on the right of the States to Judge and punish their own delegates, and that Congress could do nothing but represent their Conduct. I was certain whichever way Congress decided it would be important. If they Exercised the power, the States would perceive that it deprived them of all security in their members by their being Subjected to the arbitrary power of an assembly which is without Controll, and can be punished for no wrong, and in which they must often assert the rights of the State at every hazard, and of Course would remonstrate against it. If on the other hand, Congress should only make a representation to the State a precedent would be Established in favor of the Exclusive Jurisdiction of the State over its representatives. The Confederation being then under Consideration I hoped this matter might be Considered by the assembly before they finally Concluded their deliberations thereon, and I hoped it would clearly point out to them the propriety of Instructing particularly on that clause which declares that "freedom of speech and debate shall not be impeached or Questioned in any Court or place out of Congress."

A clause which in my humble Opinion is not only Contrary to our Constitution, but takes away the Controll of the States in a very great measure over its Delegates.[16] The Congress is the only power which can usurp or encroach on the rights of the States. The freedom of Speech is Necessary for Opposing the Congress in such attempts. To them only or to Combinations of them can that freedom give Offence, and it will always give Offence when it opposes favorite pursuits. They only can be interested to restrain the freedom of Speech, they therefore ought never to have the power of punishing it or calling it in question. On the other hand the States can have no interest to restrain the freedom of speech of their Delegates. That freedom must be always used for their advantage or in support of their rights, and should a Delegate vote or speak in a manner inconsistent with his Instructions or his Duty, he ought to be Subject to the punishments provided by the Laws of the Country, and with us being subject to legal Impeachment and Trial give him the same Security with every other Citizen. This clause precludes every State from even making Laws for the punishment of offending Delegates for to what End should laws be made to punish men who cannot be impeached or called in question in any Court or place out of Congress. To Congress only must we Complain of our Delegates, for sacrificing to them our rights, Congress is to Judge the offence and inflict the punishment, and it can hardly be expected that it will be deemed an Offence to be Complaisant to the prevailing Combination.

The assembly having concluded on this matter has prevented much of the good I intended but I hope however my wishes will not be entirely disappointed.

One other matter had Considerable weight in determining me to persist in this affair.

While every Citizen of this State is happily Secured by the Constitution and Laws against every arbitrary Exercise of power, is Secure of an Impartial trial by his Country on every accusation, the Case of a Delegate would be extremely hard was he to be Subjected to the arbitrary will of a Combination in an assembly which may be enraged against him for an Opposition which his Conscience may tell him it is his Duty to make. Nothing is more easy than for Such a Combination Secure of a Majority and therefore Secure of Impunity to give repeated provocations until the object of their vengeance is Constrained to use some Expressions which taken by themselves and unconnected with the rest of his discourse may be made the foundation of a persecution against him, and then he is to be tried, Condemned and punished by an Assembly who have no Law to Judge by but mere arbitrary will and who are at once Judge, party, witness and Executioner—who are without Controll and may do any wrong with impunity. I confess as this is a situation I should be very unwilling to be in myself, I should deny that any freeman ought to be in, and had I had no other motive than merely this I should not have submitted to the power claimed by some Gentlemen in Congress. I hope I never shall betray the smallest right of any of my fellow Citizens to avoid any thing which power can impose on me. Lest any thing which I have here said should seem to derogate from the Virtue of the present Congress I beg leave to declare that nothing can be further from my Intention, nor do I believe any Set of men Existed who had Views more disinterestedly directed to public good, even the Individuals I mention as too much disposed to acts of power, are men of the greatest public Spirit and Integrity, and eminent for abilities. If in the particulars I mentioned they erred as in my opinion they did, I am certain they were moved by nothing but a zeal for the public Service which perhaps hurried them too fast to attend to distant Consequences, or prevented their perceiving objects in the proper point of Light.

I do not pretend that I myself have never been in this predicament. I confess I am warm in my Temper, ⟨and apt to decide in favor of bold and vigorous Measures⟩ and feel a Zeal too which I doubt not often transports me too far. Conscious of this, ⟨and being very attentive to motives, and from that attention Convinced of their rectitude,⟩ I heard every gentlemans Sentiments I believe, with Candor, and tho differing from my own doubted not their being Suggested by the same Desire of doing public Service—but I conceived it my Duty to use my own Judgement on all Occasions and I always used it because such as it was my Country Confided in it, and when it differed from other men, Integrity required that I should follow it. Thence Debate necessarily ensued but Enmity I hope never. Nothing therefore should be Imputed to Such Motives. I do not pretend that I never Consented to, nor recommended the exercise of acts of power, every man knows that such will be always unavoidable in times of public Struggles. But my professed Maxims are that Such should never be exercised but so far as plain and Evident Necessity requires and on very important Occasions that whoever exercises an act of power Should not be the ultimate Judge of the Necessity but should rely on it as an excuse but not a Justification. That it should always be Exercised in such a manner as not for a precedent for future Occasions—because such should depend entirely on its own circumstances.

Whenever I have recommended or agreed to acts of power I hope I have kept in view these maxims. I always opposed them on every other ground. I have thought some not quite so attentive to them, I suppose because they were not equally persuaded of their Truth.

In the matter before the assembly some things appear to me not altogether reconcileable to the Idea I have given of Congress. They have Insisted on a man's retracting his Opinions, and Censured him for not Complying, they have given partial abstracts from his words, they refused to insert his answer along with the charge against him, and they have asserted a thing directly Contrary to that answer and to the Testimony taken before themselves.

These and many other Inconsistencies arise from a vain endeavour to adapt to Congress the rules of the British parliament. Many Individuals who form the Congress have been accustomed to observe Such rules in the provincial assemblies during the late monarchical Government, and have not yet clearly perceived the difference between an Elective assembly which knows no monarchical power to restrain, Corrupt or disturb it, and One which has Occasion for great and extraordinary powers to protect itself from the fraud or Violence of an hereditary controlling Magistrate, in a word between a power which if it assumes to act arbitrarily cannot be checked and between a Power which may be dissolved and divested of all authority and Capacity, Injured by a superintending Magistrate.

Concession was required from me because Concessions were usually required in parliament.

My answer was refused in writing because such was not usual in parliament, ⟨*Tho there be this plain difference, A member of parliament Answers no where out of parliament, and the same persons hear and Judge the Offence & Deffence.*⟩

To enlarge on this matter would take up too much time: it [*is*] an evil which I hope experience will cure and in the mean time can do no great mischief if the States are firm in supporting their own rights and protecting their Citizens.

I hope I have not transgressed in being so full on this Subject, less would not have sufficiently laid the matter before the Assembly in that light which in my opinion it's importance deserves.

MS (Nc–Ar). In the hand of Thomas Burke.

[1] Although Burke apparently prepared this memorial for submission to the North Carolina Assembly in August 1778, it is printed here because it complements the account of his dispute with Congress given in his letter of this date to Governor Caswell. See also *N.C. State Records*, 12:769, 792, 825, 843–45.

[2] See Burke's Proposed Statement to Congress, April 13, and his letter to Richard Caswell, April 29, 1778.

[3] See Henry Laurens to Washington, April 8, 1778, note 4.

[4] Burke wrote the preceding two sentences at the bottom of the eighth page of the MS and left no indication of where he intended to insert them in the text. They are printed here because there is a slight break in the MS at this point and their substance seems to fit this paragraph.

[5] Burke originally wrote "the letter that night."

[6] After "without" Burke first wrote and then crossed out "much debate and."

[7] Burke originally wrote "totally unable."

[8] See Burke to Richard Caswell, this date, note 8.

[9] See Burke's Proposed Statement to Congress, April 13, 1778.

[10] William Duer.

[11] Burke probably had in mind Congress' interference with the government of Pennsylvania in 1777, on which see William Duer to the New York Convention, April 17, 1777, note 2.

[12] See Henry Laurens to William Smallwood, March 26, 1778, note.

[13] After "Powers" Burke first wrote and then deleted: "under an Idea that their Civil Magistracy was not well affected, or had not power sufficient to prevent Offender."

[14] Burke is referring to the appointment on April 23 of a committee "for enquiring into, detecting and defeating all disaffections, conspiracies and insurrections on that neck of land comprehended betwixt the Delaware and Chesapeake Bays." *JCC,* 10:383.

[15] After "objects" Burke first wrote and then deleted: "and yet were entirely unimpressed by the Importance of great objects."

[16] Burke wrote "Dele" in the margin next to the first and last sentences in this paragraph so that it is difficult to determine whether he meant to delete the whole paragraph or just these two sentences.

Charles Carroll of Carrollton to Charles Carroll, Sr.

Dear Papa,   29th April 1778
I was glad to hear by Mr Digges that you were all well, and that Molly was recovering fast.

I wrote to you by last Post, & inclosed you a copy of Governor Johnstone's letter to Mr. Robert Morris. By that you will see, some treaty is in agitation between our Agents & France, & that the fears of an alliance between these States & France were the principal occasion of inducing the British ministry to propose terms, & of Ld. North's contradictory, false, & humiliating Speech. I wish we could hear from France, we are in daily expectation of hearing from thence: our dispatches, when we receive them, will probably let us more fully into the reasons of this sudden change of British politicks.

Have you got as yet returns of our different assessments? It is necessary to have them, in order to ascertain what we shall have to pay on this year's assessment. The 25/ in the hundred is a heavy tax: however I think the measure right. If the rest of the States tax in proportion, they will soon retrieve the credit of the money, & convince the English nation that we are in earnest & determined to maintain our Independance. We heared the day before yesterday from Camp; nothing new. It is said our army is increasing. A respectable army, & good management will secure our Independance without running any great hazard. My opinion always was, & now more than ever, to avoid a general action. Delay must ruin the Enemy. I wish you a long continuance of health & am yr. affectionate Son,

                                        Ch. Carroll of Carrollton

P.S. My complts. to yr. neighbours, the Capt. & Jemmy Howard.

RC (MdHi).

Connecticut Delegates to Jonathan Trumbull, Sr.

Sir.   York Town 29th April 1778

We are honor'd with your Excellencys favour of the 3d Inst. by Brown. Note the Contents. With regard to the Regulating Act the State of Pensylvania have Suspended it & the other States to the Southward, of this have done nothing on the Subject, not so much as appointed Committees to meet & take the matter under Consideration as we can learn. A Committee of Congress, appointed to take into Consideration, the doings of the Committee at New Haven, have made their Report that the proceedings of the Committee at N. Haven be Sent to all the Southern States, & recommended to their Serious Consideration & that the Northern States Suspend the Act, in the mean time until they have further advise on the Subject from Congress, but no Resolution of Congress, is as yet passed on their Report but we Expect it will soon be brought upon the Carpet.[1]

Congress have in Contemplation a plan for making a large reduction of the Circulating quantity of Bills as the most natural, & easy method of Supporting their Credit, hope this plan may soon be perfected.

It appears to us from the best Sentiments we are able to Collect, that the Southern States never will adopt the regulating Act.

The marine board Seem'd Sensible of Capt. Harding's Merit & on your Excellencies recommendation would have made his appointment accordingly had it been possible[2] but their had been a predetermination that Capt. Hinman Should take the Command of that Frigate if he arrives in Season; Indeed their are a number of Capts in the Continental Navy which they think may not be pass'd over, as several of them have now no Vessels & Consequently are out of Employ tho' on Wages. We wish to be favour'd with an Acct of Mr. Bushnell Expences; as we are fully of Opinion, that his genious ought to be encouraged & Rewarded at a Continental Expence, & shall take the Earliest Opportunity to urge it.[3]

The States of Virginia & N York have fully Acceded to the Articles of Confederation. South Carolina, Pensylvania, Rhode Island, & Massachusetts have Instructed their Delegates to move for some alterations with power to rattify Some what Similar to Connecticut. Some of the States have not yet furnished their Delegates with their proceedings upon the Subject. Col Wadsworth is appointed Comy. Genl. on his own plan, we hope his Activity & abilities will remove

the Embarrassments which have been too sensibly felt ever Since
Commissary Trumbull left that Dept. Genl. Gates is Ordered to take
the Command of the posts on Hudsons River & the Northern Department.

It is said that Feby. Packet, from England, is arriv'd at Philadelphia, but no Intelligence Transpires.

We are with much Esteem, your Excellencies most Obedient,
Humble Servants,   Saml. Huntington

                                          Oliver Wolcott

Tr (Ct).

¹ See Oliver Wolcott to Andrew Adams, April 25, 1778, note 3.

² See Marine Committee to Jonathan Trumbull, Sr., April 20, 1778.

³ For references on David Bushnell's exploits with his submarine *Turtle,* see
Benjamin Franklin to George Washington, July 22, 1776, note.

James Lovell to John Adams

Dear Sir   Apr 29th. 1778. York Town
I promise myself much from the eight or nine scrawls which I have
sent to you since your departure from America,¹ in the spirit, I own
to you, with [which] Indians make their presents of feathers or bark.

I must depend upon your imagination to comprehend what I will
not undertake to describe—our chagrin and perplexity at our total
ignorance of the situation & transactions of the Commissioners at
Paris and other parts of Europe. I ask you a plain question, or two.
How often have the Gentlemen at Paris wrote to Congress since June
last? Have copies and triplicates of their Dispatches been sent? Do
you know who robbed Folgier? ² Is there more reason to think it
was done by the English court than the French, if it was done at all
by court influence? Do not our mercantile concerns and the interest
of individuals therein furnish the best clue of the robbery?

I must refer you to the printed papers for the conduct of our
enemies. Tryons certified Bills did not come out 'till after our committee had reported. He sent packets to Genl. W——,³ Gates & others
requesting that they would not prevent the dispersion of the Bills
among the Officers & people at large, I have not Tryon's letter by me
just now but it will be printed shortly with Genl. W——s answer as
follows.

Sir   Head Quarters Valley forge, Apr. 26. 1778
Your letter of the 17th and a triplicate of the same were duly
received. I had had the pleasure of seeing the draughts of the two
Bills, before those which were sent by you came to hand and I can

assure you they were suffered to have a free currency among the Officers & men under my command, in whose fidelity to the United States I have the most perfect confidence; and the inclosed Gazette, published the 24th at York Town, will show you that it is the wish of Congress they should have an unrestrained circulation.

I take the liberty to transmit you a few printed copies of a resolution of Congress of the 23d instant, and to request you will be instrumental in communicating its contents; so far as it may be in your power, to the persons who are the objects of its operation. The benevolent purpose it is intended to answer will, I persuade myself sufficiently recommend it to your candor. I am, Sir, Your most Obedt. Servt.   Go Washington

Majr. Genl. Tryon at New York

The enemy just at the time when they are affecting to treat with us are sending forth in the Gazettes of Philada. & New York a forged Resolve of Congress, purporting our grant of a power to Genl. W——to regard all militia men, enlisted or draughted for 9 months or a year, as soldiers *during the war* and to treat them as *deserters* if they shall attempt to leave the camp on the expiration of their present *Agreement*.

We have this day offered 800 acres of Land with certain Stock named to any capt. in the British Service, not a Subject of the King of Gr. Br., who shall bring off with him self 40 Men, and proportional rewards to Officers of inferior rank & to the Soldiers.[4]

This is taking up the enemy's practice. I do not like it because the offers are much too great. The same Generals who have managed the war are not to negotiate reconcilliation. Ld. Amherst is said to have arrived at New York and to have freed all our many prisoners there, upon parole. This is not certain; but He, Admiral Kepple & Genl. Murray are said to be nominated Commissioners. Is it not droll that I should send such news to France; but not expecting to hear from the Gentlemen there this season, I propose to let them know that we do get a little European intelligence other ways. Mr. D——at the Hague writes very punctually tho we treat him as we are treated by others.[5] I hope that we shall some time or other be told what is the proper recompence for that Gentleman's Services. I wrote to him last year that it was needless, for him, to be at the trouble of any thing more than to correspond with the Commissioners.[6] He is punctual however; and his letters down to Y. have reached us and tho little interesting have cost us great Sums indeed; one above from Boston £50 sterling nearly.

RC (MHi). In Lovell's hand, though not signed.

[1] In his July 9, 1778, reply to this letter, Adams stated that he had received none of these "scrawls." Wharton, *Diplomatic Correspondence,* 2:642.

[2] See Committee Examination of John Folger, January 12, 1778.
[3] That is, General Washington.
[4] See *JCC*, 10:405–9.
[5] For C. W. F. Dumas' correspondence with Congress, see Committee for Foreign Affairs to Dumas, May 14, 1778, note.
[6] See Committee for Foreign Affairs to Dumas, August 8, 1777.

Gouverneur Morris to John Jay

Dear Jay.   York Town 29th April 1778[1]

I won't dispute who has written most. I have written more than twice what you acknowledge to have received but this is of no Consequence.

I am sorry for your Session but I wish you had marked out what Taxes have been laid, what Salaries given & a few more striking outlines of Legislation. These with what I know of your Men would have enabled me to imagine proper Lights & Shades.

My *arithmetical* Friend[2] will not find much from the Sum you mention worth casting up. Remember my Love to him.

I chuse that my Friends should write freely and those who know me must know that such Freedoms need no Apology. I never thought the Person you allude to so steady as could be wished.[3] We have all of us our weak Sides. Would to God that were the worst.

What you mention relative to our Plan of Rights shall be attended to.[4] I am a busy Man tho as heretofore a pleasurable one.

Let your Governor cleanse the Augean Stable in his State which no public Body would do tho it stink under their Noses. I am laboring at Arrangements of various Kinds. God prosper me and give me Patience & Industry. It was a good Wish from one who knew my Wants.

We have ordered Troops from the Highlands but we will send thither a Genl.[5] who shall be impowered to call forth the Swarms of the Eastern Hive. Men were necessary at the Valley Forge. I have a good Knack at Guessing. I guess the Enemy won't Attempt Hudson's River.

I do think of Vermont and unless I mistake Matters shall be managed to Effect without bellowing in the Forum which I beleive hath been a little too much the Case.[6] But why should I blame impetuous Vivacity. Hath it never led me into an Error?

Putnam will soon be tried.[7] The Affair of Schuyler & St Clair laboured under aukward Circumstances. Their Friends & their Enemies appear to me to have been equally blind. I enclose Extracts from the Minutes made the other Night to possess myself of the real State of Facts. There are some other Entries from Time to Time. It was erroneous to order a Committee simply to collect Facts; they should have been directed to state Charges. This Morning my Colleague being absent I got a Committee appointed for the latter Purpose. Sherman, Dana (Massachusetts) & Drayton (South Carolina).[8] This was unanimous and yet I would have undertaken to argue for it in a Stile which would absolutely have ruined the Measure. You know it would have been easy to say *Justice to these injured Gentlemen* instead of *Justice to an injured Country* requires &ca.

Great Britain seriously means to treat. Our Affairs are most critical tho not dangerously so. If the Minister from France were present as well as him from England I am a blind Politician if the thirteen States (with their extended Territory) would not be in peaceable Possession of their Independency three Months from this Day. As it is, expect a long War. I beleive it will not require such astonishing Efforts after this Campaign to keep the Enemy at Bay. Probably a Treaty is signed with the House of Bourbon ere this, if so a spark hath fallen upon the Train which is to fire the World. Ye Gods what Havock does Ambition make among your Works.

My dear Friend Adieu. My Love to your Wife. Remember me to all my Friends of every Rank & Sex.

I am yours,   Gouv Morris

P.S. I meant to have said the present is within the spirit of our Constitution *a special Occasion*. The foregoing is in Answer to yours of the 14th.

RC (NNC). Addressed: "Honle John Jay Esqr. Chief Justice of the State of New York at Poughkeepsie or elsewhere."

[1] Although the dateline is smudged and Jay himself thought it read "April 28th," it seems clear that Morris actually wrote the letter on the 29th, the day Congress appointed the committee "to state Charges" discussed herein. *JCC,* 10:403.

[2] Robert R. Livingston, who, as Jay had explained to Morris on April 14, "was to have told me the Amount of certain *Sums* you set him." See Jay, *Papers* (Morris), 1:469. This may well have been a playful reference by Livingston to a February 22 letter from Morris that forecast a bright economic future for New York if only the state government adopted a wise policy of taxation.

[3] Although Morris had apparently discussed "the Person you allude to" in a March 16 letter to Jay that has not been found, it seems clear from other evidence that the man they both had in mind was Chancellor Robert R. Livingston, who was pessimistic about the internal changes being wrought by the Revolution in New York. See ibid., pp. 468–69, 484; and George Dangerfield, *Chancellor Robert R. Livingston of New York, 1746–1813* (New York: Harcourt, Brace and Co., 1960), pp. 106–10.

[4] "I wish," Jay had requested Morris on the 14th, "you would write and publish a few civil Things on our Constitution, censuring however an omission in not restraining the Council of Appointment from granting Offices to themselves, with Remarks on the Danger of that Practice." Jay, *Papers* (Morris), 1:469. Evidently Morris never complied with this request.

[5] Horatio Gates. See *JCC,* 10:354–55, 368–69.

⁶ See also Henry Laurens to George Clinton, April 20, 1778, note 2.

⁷ Morris' prophecy did not come to pass as soon as he expected. Not until July did a military court of enquiry acquit Gen. Israel Putnam of culpability in the October 1777 loss of Forts Clinton and Montgomery in the New York Highlands, and not until August 17, 1778, did Congress accept the court's verdict. See *JCC*, 11:743, 803–4; and Washington, *Writings* (Fitzpatrick), 12:244–45, 352–53.

⁸ Congress appointed this committee on April 29 "to examine the evidence collected, and state charges against the general officers who were in the northern department when Ticonderoga and Mount Independence were evacuated." See *JCC*, 10:403; John Hancock to Arthur St. Clair and Philip Schuyler, August 5, 1777, note; and Committee of Congress to Washington, February 7, 1778.

Virginia Delegates to George Washington

Sir   York 29th April 1778

In compliance with your letter in answer to ours respecting the Paymt of the Bounty to the reinlisted Virginia Soldiers,[1] we now send you thirty Thousand Dollars, by particular direction of the executive of our State ordered into your Hands; it should however have been negotiated in a less troublesome way to you, but the warrant was thro mistake made out in our Names. Eighty Dollars are sent by Mr. Banister, for the use of a Soldier one Abner Howell from his County, where he has written to Col. Meade to find out.[2]

I am for myself & Colleagues with the highest Respect & Esteem yr Excellency's mo. obed. & mo hble Servant,   J Banister

RC (DLC). Written and signed by John Banister.

[1] See Banister to Washington, April 16, 1778.

[2] Banister's letter to Richard Kidder Meade has not been found.

Committee for Foreign Affairs to the Commissioners at Paris

Gentlemen   No. 6 (Copy)   York Town Apr. 30th. 1778

By the Gazettes which accompany this letter you will see that the Enemy are entering upon a plan which must shortly perplex us much, unless we receive dispatches from you to enlighten us as to your Situation & Transactions of which we have had no information since the latter end of May. As we have heard of the loss of Capt. Johnston and Capt. Wickes and know that John Folgier was robbed, we cannot charge our present want of letters to negligence in you; but we think you should not rest satisfied without sending triplicates of your dispatches.

The commercial Committee will transmit to you the contract which they have enterd into with the agent of the House of Roderigue Hortales & Co. The heads of wch. contract happening to be at hand are inclosed.[1]

We have read a letter written by a friend (Govr. Johnston) dated House of Commons Feb. 13th. in which we are told that "you had concluded a Treaty wth. France and Spain which was on the Water towards us." [2] Imagine how solicitous we are to know the truth of this before we receive any proposals from Britain in consequence of the scheme in Ld. Norths speech and the two Draughts of Bills now sent to you.

The state of our foreign connections is a subject now before Congress; and, dubious as we are about your transactions, some resolutions will probably be formed to be transmitted to you by a special conveyance shortly,[3] when a general account of our Affairs will also be sent. We have little uneasiness about the Strength of our enemy. Our currency must be supported in due credit; after which we may bid defiance to Britain and all her German hirelings. We wish every advice and Assistance from You for the support of such Credit.

I am with great Regard, Gentlemen, your humble Servant,

James Lovell

RC (PPAmP). Written and signed by James Lovell.

[1] Congress had approved the terms of this contract on April 7 and the Committee of Commerce had executed it with Théveneau de Francy on April 16. *JCC*, 10:315–21, 356. For further information on the subject, see Robert Morris' Proposed Report on the Claims of Roderique Hortalez & Co., March 12, 1778, note 1.

[2] For George Johnstone's letter to Robert Morris, see Henry Laurens to Robert Morris, April 27, 1778, note 1.

[3] See Samuel Huntington's Proposed Resolution, April 22–23?; and William Henry Drayton's Proposed Resolution, May 1, 1778.

Henry Laurens to Francis Bailey

Sir,   30th April [1778]

I writ to you the day before yesterday by Messenger Sharp.

Under Cover with this you will receive an Act of Congress for inviting Officers & Soldiers in the Service of the King of Great Britain not subjects of the said King, to settle within these States.[1]

This Act you are desired to translate & print in the German Tongue one Thousand Copies.[2] Let the translation be pure & the work done with the utmost expedition not delayed a single moment. Inform me if you please when the Copies will be out of the press & I will immediately give the necessary directions for sending them to the places intended. Let me strictly enjoin you not to suffer a single

Copy to get abroad, but return the M.S. & all the impressions as you shall be directed.

Please to observe on the first page a pointer, meaning to join the next Paragraph with the preceeding except the seperation by a short hyatus & also the marks directing new Paragraphs.

Let me hear from you immediately & oblige, Sir, your most huml Servt.

LB (DNA: PCC, item 13).
¹ See *JCC,* 10:405–10.
² No German translation of this "Act" has been found.

Henry Laurens to Francis Bailey

Sir,   30th April [1778]
After I had written to you this Morning it was discovered there had been a Small error in Copying the Declaration to foreign Officers &ca.

If this shall reach you in time, please to make the necessary alterations directed in the paper here inclosed. Dispatch alone will render the present effort successful or otherwise, I shall therefore be every hour in expectation of hearing the Impressions are made. You may send 500 Copies immediately to York dry & hold in readiness the other 500, to be delivered to a Messenger who will call for them in his way to Camp.

I am, Sir, your obedt. Servt.

LB (DNA: PCC, item 13).

Henry Laurens to Thomas Burke

Sir,   30th April 1778
Within this Inclosure you will receive the draught of a Letter which you sent last night for my perusal.¹

If I were called upon to give Evidence in the Case, I should deliver my sentiments without Bias or partiality. I might vary in some particulars from your account, nevertheless upon a fair comparison, I think your narrative would not appear to be uncandid, especially if any consideration should be had to its coming from the party most nearly affected.

I have the honour to be &ca.

LB (DNA: PCC, item 13).
¹ Burke had probably sent Laurens the draft of his April 29 letter to North Carolina governor Richard Caswell.

Henry Laurens to Noirmont de La Neuville

Sir,[1]   30th April [1778]
For answer to your Letter of last Night relative to Majr. General
Conway's resignation I beg leave to refer you to the General's Letter
& the consecutive Act of Congress, both which you may see & peruse
at the Secretarys Office.[2]

In me, it would be as unbecoming to arraign the determination
of Congress, as an attempt to reverse their Resolves would be unavail-
ing; but if, as you seem to apprehend Sir, General Conway did not
mean actually to resign his Commission, I am persuaded the Candor
of Congress will not refuse to receive & consider his explanation.

I am, Sir, your most obdt. Servt.

LB (DNA: PCC, item 13). Addressed: "Noirmont de Lanuville, ADC. to General
Conway, York Town."
  [1] René-Hippolyte Penot Lombart de Noirmont de La Neuville (1750–92), a
French infantry officer, entered the Continental Army as a volunteer and became
aide-de-camp to Gen. Thomas Conway in December 1777. Following the appointment of his older brother, the chevalier de La Neuville, as inspector of the
northern army on May 14, Noirmont became deputy inspector of this force, and
on July 29, 1778, was granted a brevet commission as major. After serving in the
southern campaign in 1779 and rising to the rank of lieutenant colonel, he returned
to France and was honorably retired from Continental service in 1781. See JCC,
11:508; and Lasseray, Les Français sous les treize étoiles, 2:356–58. See also Laurens
to Lafayette, May 11, 1778, note 2.
  [2] See Henry Laurens to Washington, April 28, 1778, note 3.

Henry Laurens to George Washington

Sir,   York Town 30th April 1778.
I had the honor of writing to Your Excellency the day before
yesterday by Sharp.

This bearer is dispatched by special order of Congress to return
with the bundle of Papers, sent to Head Quarters some time ago by
the Committee appointed to collect Evidence &c. on the loss of
Tyconderoga & Mount Independence which Your Excellency will be
pleased to deliver to him.[1]

I have the honor to be, With the highest Respect & Esteem, Sir,
Your Excellency's Obedient & most humble servant, Henry Laurens,
President of Congress.

RC (DLC).
  [1] This "special order" is not recorded in the journals, but for the subject at
issue see Committee of Congress to Washington, February 7, 1778; and Washington,
Writings (Fitzpatrick), 11:333.

James Lovell to John Adams

My dear Sir   [April 30–May 2? 1778] [1]
  In aid to your scrutiny after the real robber of the Commissioners
Dispatches,[2] I send what I think a good Confirmation of Folgiers
honesty. By comparing the Governors letter[3] with Folgiers Examination[4] you will find the Govr. led into a mistake about the number of
Seals broken, by Folgiers forgetting that the outside Cover of the
whole had any thing more than "Dispatches" wrote on it. He told us
differently 2 days after we had sent an Express to Nth. Carolina. I am
glad he did forget it at first as it strengthens eventually the nature
of the Evidence.

  You must not wonder that I make so much of this matter. It is of
the highest Importance to you to be guarded against Bosom-Traitors
yourself and to tear them from your Colleagues. I must add that no
one here thinks Folgier's Employment by them a discreet Choice, tho
he does not appear to be the arch Traitor.

  Affectionately your Friend,   James Lovell

May 25th, 1777[5] The Commissrs. refer to Letters of March 14 and
Apr 9th which have never reached us, nor any Letter since May 25th.

RC (MHi). Addressed: "To The Honble John Adams Esqr., Paris." Endorsed by
Adams contemporaneously: "Mr. Lovell 25 May 1777." Endorsed by Adams at a
later date: "This date is a Mistake. It Shd. have been 1778." For an explanation
of these conflicting endorsements, see notes 1 and 5 below.

  [1] This undated letter was probably written during the interval between Lovell's
April 29 letter to Adams and Simeon Deane's arrival in York on May 2 with dispatches from the commissioners at Paris announcing the conclusion of the Franco-
American treaties of alliance and commerce. Writing to Lovell from Paris on
July 9, 1778, Adams reported that he had received Lovell's April 29 letter but
not the "eight or nine scrawls" mentioned in it. Wharton, *Diplomatic Correspondence*, 2:642. And on July 26 Adams wrote to Lovell again acknowledging
that "Your favours of May 16 and 25 by Captain Barnes reached me yesterday."
Ibid. Despite Adams' explicit testimony, however, it seems clear that the "May
25" letter from Lovell is the one printed here, and actually was written several
weeks earlier. No letter to Adams from Lovell or the Committee for Foreign
Affairs dated May 25, 1778, has been found. On the other hand, it is evident from
Adams' July 26 letter that the "May 25" Lovell letter he then acknowledged dealt
with the case of Capt. John Folger, which is the subject of the present letter.
The confusion over the letter's date, which led Adams to endorse it "25 May
1777," derives from the physical appearance of Lovell's postscript. There he
explained that Congress had received no communications from Paris in nearly a
year—"nor any Letter since May 25th"—and as an afterthought wrote at the left
of the postscript "May 25th 1777" to identify a letter from the commissioners
containing a reference to other letters not received ("of March 14 and Apr 9th").
Assuming then that this document is the letter Adams hastily concluded was
written on May 25, but that it was not one of the "eight or nine scrawls" written
before April 29, it must have been penned after Lovell had written Adams on the
29th and before the afternoon of May 2 when Simeon Deane arrived in York

with letters from Paris dated as late as February 1778—a circumstance that would have made it impossible for Lovell to complain subsequently that Congress had not heard from the commissioners since May 1777.

[2] For a discussion of this issue, see Committee Examination of John Folger, January 12, 1778, note.

[3] For Gov. Richard Caswell's January 31, 1778, letter to President Laurens on the subject of Capt. John Folger's role in the theft of dispatches from the commissioners, see N.C. State Records, 10:178–79.

[4] See Committee Examination of John Folger, January 12, 1778. Congress' May 8 resolve exonerating Folger in connection with the theft of the dispatches from the commissioners, which seems to have been passed after this letter was written, is in JCC, 11:482.

[5] This date was added by Lovell to identify the letter from the commissioners referring to "Letters of March 14 and Apr 9th which have never reached us," not, as Adams assumed when he endorsed this document, the date of the postscript.

New York Delegates to George Clinton

Sir,   York Town 30th April 1778

By Major Genl. Gates we take the Opportunity of informg. your Excellency that we hope in a few Days to transmit you some Resolutions of Importance to the State we represent at which Time we shall write fully upon the subject.[1] At present we have to request that you will afford Genl. Gates such Assistance in his important & extensive Command as may be in your Power.

We have the Honor to be with great Respect, your Excellency's most obedient & humble Servants,   Gouvr Morris

Wm. Duer.

RC (NN). Written by Morris and signed by Morris and Duer.

[1] The anticipated "Resolutions of Importance" no doubt concerned Vermont. See Henry Laurens to George Clinton, April 20, 1778, note 2.

William Henry Drayton's Proposed Resolution

[May 1, 1778][1]

Resolved

That the commissioners of Congress at the Courts of France & Spain be instructed to inform those Courts respectively, that Congress are assured the King & Parliament of Great Britain intend very shortly to open a Treaty with these United States to procure a reconciliation with that Kingdom—that Congress believe Great Britain will consent to the Independence of America, only in consequence of the most absolute compulsion—that Great Britain is inclined to

sacrifice much of her claim to bind these States in all cases whatsoever—that as it is the true Interest of America to be an Independent
power, she will be inclined to relinquish her Independency, only
from the most absolute necessity to do so—that the strength & resources of the two Countries are considerably diminished by the
War—that these States wish to be assisted with loans of money ⟨*in
gold & silver*⟩ sufficient to enable them to support the credit of their
paper money—and that an annual supply of ⟨*gold & silver*⟩ money to
the amount of   Millions Livres & an immediate declaration of War by France & Spain against Great Britain would enable
these United States to continue the War & with the blessing of God
to establish their Independence. In addition to these representations,
the said Commissioners shall demand a categorical answer of France
and Spain to this point.

Whether or not they will grant to these United States an annual
loan upon Interest of   millions of Livres during the continuance of the war, & make an immediate declaration of War against
Great Britain.

MS (ScHi). In the hand of William Henry Drayton and endorsed by Henry
Laurens: "Mr. Draytons Mo. 1st May—for Mr. Huntington's."

[1] As Henry Laurens' endorsement on the document indicates, Drayton prepared
this motion this day as a substitute for Samuel Huntington's proposed resolution
on entering into peace negotiations with the British on the basis of American
independence. Although Huntington probably brought his resolution to Congress'
attention as early as April 22 or 23, apparently the delegates did not formally
consider it until April 30 and May 1 when they turned their attention to the
issue of "the state of America with respect to foreign nations." On May 1, according to the journals, "Congress resumed consideration of the motion made
yesterday," but the entries for both dates fail to identify the motion offered or to
mention that a substitute was proposed. Despite this omission, Laurens' endorsement on this document and his comments on the subject in his correspondence
with John Laurens and Rawlins Lowndes strongly suggest that the Huntington
and Drayton motions were the focus of debate on those days.

Although debate on the entire matter appears to have stalled on the first when
Congress ordered "that the farther consideration thereof be postponed," it was
briefly resumed the same afternoon until Congress simply resolved to appoint a
committee of three "to report proper instructions to be transmitted to the commissioners of the United States at foreign courts." In any event, the proposals of
Drayton and Huntington as well as the committee's assignment were quickly over-
taken by events, for the following day Simeon Deane arrived in York with official
texts of the treaties of alliance and commerce that had been signed at Paris in
February, news of which completely altered the assumptions the delegates had
been operating upon since word first reached York on April 20 that the North
ministry was prepared to offer fresh terms for opening peace talks with her
colonies. See *JCC*, 10:374–80, 411, 413–14; Samuel Huntington's Proposed Resolution, April 22-23; and Henry Laurens to John Laurens, April 28, and to Rawlins
Lowndes, May 1, 1778. For the committee appointed "to report proper instruc-
toins" to the commissioners at Paris, see Gouverneur Morris' Draft Report on
Instructions for the American Commissioners, this date.

Henry Laurens to Matthew Clarkson

Sir,   York Town 1st May 1778
  Immediately upon receipt of your favor of the 28th Ulto. which
reached me yesterday afternoon I presented it to Congress, but the
business then before the House excluded every other consideration, I
will endeavor to call their attention this Morning to your representation but as I am doubtful of success I will not detain your Messenger.
In the mean time you may receive as my single opinion Sir that an
augmentation to your Salary will be made, I am of this sentiment because I think it just. You shall hear from me when I am furnished
with subject for writing.[1] I beg Sir you will present my Compliments
to your Coadjutor Majr Clarke & believe me to be, With great regard,
Sir, Your obedient hum st.
                                     Henry Laurens, President of Congress

RC (MHi).
  [1] See Laurens to Clarkson, May 6, 1778.

˙Henry Laurens to George Galphin

My Dear Sir,   1st May 1778.
  I have barely time to tell you I am indebted for several of your
favors, not enough to admit of answering them properly—this I will
endeavor to do in a few days[1]—in the meantime let me present you
with papers which accompany this & which have afforded much satisfaction in this part of the Union. I trust the whole will be as well
pleased. We hourly expect confirmatory accounts of a Treaty between
France & the United States of America by which our Sovereignty &
Independence are acknowledged & guaranteed. This I hope will
operate to good effect upon the Savages of all Colours who are at this
time attempting to ravage & distress us a little more in front & rear.
If War is closed between France & England which is inevitable, the
British Troops may be wanted for defending their Islands—in this
Case their worthy friends the Indians will be left in an unpleasing
Situation. I am glad to find those near our Country are so well dis-
posed; On the frontiers of Virginia, this state & New York they are
very troublesome. God bless you, Sir, I am with great regard

LB (ScHi).
  [1] No further letters from Laurens to Galphin, a Continental Indian commissioner in South Carolina, have been found.

Henry Laurens to Rawlins Lowndes

Sir[1]

1st May 1778.

No less than seventeen days have elapsed since I had the honor of receiving Your Excellency's Letter of the 16th March importing an extract from the Journals of Assembly of the 5th, yet within this time I have not found a proper space of one moment for addressing Congress on the subject of Indian Trade.[2]

Congress have been closely engaged on one branch of a proposed arrangement of the Army, which has been long pending. The first article on the tapis, an half pay establishment for Officers who shall continue in the Army to the end of the War having met such opposition, has engrossed, with very little exception, our time for a Month past. This subject is at present suspended, for reasons which if I judge truly, are not assigned. The supporters of the measure perceive danger of losing the question should it be put at this time when there are only ten States on the floor & therefore wait to avail themselves of the voices of two in three which are daily expected[3]—but this grand business is succeeded by another said to be equally momentous & to which every other consideration must give place, the state of our affairs at foreign Courts. The reading Letters as a prelim[in]ary step employed completely the six hour session of yesterday. I have however introduced my Colleague Mr. Chf. Justice Drayton into the Committee of Indian affairs[4] & will enjoin him to collect the Committee & press for a consideration of the Resolve of Assembly alluded to above, thence a Report will follow & be properly inducted to Congress—& I have no doubt in my own mind of obtaining all that our State expects relative to the expence of supporting an Indian Trade, unless our late acquisition of Land from the Cherokee people should be faintly urged in bar. I know some Gentlemen veiw that circumstance with a jealous eye, be this as it may, I think a demand so well grounded & which may be well supported by applicable precedents with which our Journals abound can suffer but slightly from opposition.[5]

Two days ago Congress completed a Declaratory Invitation to foreign Officers & Soldiers in the service of the King of Great Britain to quit such service & settle in these States a Copy of which I will endeavor to lay before Your Excellency,[6] I like the scheme in general, my objection was to the last Clause.[7] Maryland, Rhode Island & New Jersey peremptorily refuse to bear any part of expence which may arise from the purchase or laying out the intended Grants of Land. New York & Virginia meaning the Delegates from these States, promised on behalf of their constituents to supply large quantities, & it was intimated that the Carolinas & Georgia might well make up the deficiency. Whatever were my sentiments respecting the policy of the measure, I felt a repugnance to binding my Country by any engagements exceeding the powers vested in me & which she might for this & other obvious reasons refuse to confirm, hence I shall be found upon Record, No.

All the States had for many Months been exceedingly remiss in Representation in Congress. Fear I believe had operated upon many minds, partly of the excessive expence attending very bad fare in this Town & partly of a sudden surprize by the Enemy. Certainly had Sir William Howe been a Man of enterprize he might have possessed himself of Congress. This delinquency has cost the Union Millions of Dollars. The days lengthen, the weather mends, the Army is receiving reinforcements & Delegates drop in. We have lately been joined by some very able Men & shew upon the floor about 25—New Hampshire, Delaware & No. Carolina empty—New Jersey & Rhode Island one Delegate—the important Crisis to which we are now verging may possibly rouse the deficient States.[8]

North River which had been left in a defenseless State from the time Sir H. Clinton had rendred it so will in the course of half this Month with permission of the Enemy be secured—but I tremble every arrival of a Messenger from that quarter with apprehensions of hearing of the destruction of our embryo works, of our Stores & Magazines at Albany & that our communication with the Eastern States [is] cut off—all this danger & an hundred other Evils are chargeable to deficiency of Representation. General Gates will proceed to Morrow to Valley forge Camp, there join a grand Council for planning the operations of the rising Campaign, thence proceed to Fish Kill & Albany & take upon him the Command of the whole Northern or middle department—with power to call for the Militia from New York & the Eastern States—if our affairs remain uninterupted when he arrives, all will be well.

The printed papers which I shall send within the present Inclosure will shew your Excellency a late fruitless attempt for settling a Cartel & the sentiments of Congress on Lord North's speech of the 19th Febry & his Draughts of Conciliatory Bills—an Insolent Letter from the Quondam Governor Tryon to General Washington & the General's modest reply will accompany them. Notwithstanding the seperation of the Commissioners who had assembled at New Town an Exchange of prisoners is in motion conducted by the Commissaries on each side. General Lee has been exchanged for General Prescot, & there are many other instances but the work is slow & not satisfactory. Besides from a fatal negligence in our public Officers we have lost an amazing number of prisoners. I have the best authority for saying near two Thousand have escaped or been winked at, a circumstance tending to prove our Riches in that branch, when it is considered that we have still a very large balance of Rank & file.

In addition to the Act of Congress of the 22d April Congress had been moved to confirm a Resolve, Copy of which will also be Inclosed. Upon its first appearance it was a favorite & I felt some anxiety lest it should succeed but after lying a few days & a full discussion this Morning it was postponed generally.[9]

General Washington intimates that he is well informed General Amherst, Admiral Kepple & General Murray are named for Commissioners to treat with America on terms of peace.[10] These or some other great personage, perhaps Lord Howe who it was supposed had been lost between Rhode Island & the Capes of Delaware probably arrived at Philadelphia the 28th April when there was heard at Camp much firing of Cannon in the City. A person of Credit from thence assures us, that Transports were halling to the Wharfs in order to receive Troops & Baggage, the conjecture is, that the foreign Troops are recalled. 'Tis as likely that an embarkation of wounded & other Invalids is intended, the season of the year & the numerous sick among the British Troops favors this opinion.

Major General Conway lately for the second time taunted Congress by an application for leave to resign his Commission, & in notes so extremely rough as secured a Majority of 8 States of 9 in his favor. I say taunted, because I have since received a Letter from his Aid de Camp who knew the contents of the General's & probably the intents of it also, assuring me it was not the General's meaning to resign & praying my Interest to obtain a Repeal of the Resolution. He certainly was not in earnest in his first attempt, but I beleive the door is now shut. His conduct respecting General Washington is criminal & unpardonable, severely censured by all the foreign Officers.[11]

I must now acknowledge & thank your Excellency for your favor of the 30th March[12] & for the Copy of the Constitution of South Carolina, the Title page is all that public business has suffered me to be acquainted with.

The loss of the Randolph & of the many precious lives in the same stroke is affecting. This account came in contact with intelligence of the Capture & loss of the Frigates Virginia, Columbus & Alfred, ancient & venerable characters, but we have Wood enough to Christen with the same Names; our Enemy has suffered great losses & have not Wood & other materials in such abundance, therefore we have least cause for despondency. A New York paper which will go inclosed to Mr. Gervais will shew the Enemy's account of the Ill fated Randolph. Had we had Men on this spot competent to the arrangement of our Treasury & finances, Men of knowledge, virtue & spirit, adequate to the Labour of stemming the torrent of peculation which has overwhelmed us with debt & brown paper Dollars, we should have less cause to regret the loss of four Frigates. These are gone; I trust, & I devoutly pray, the Eyes of these slumbering states may be opened, &

wise measures adopted for averting the loss of their Independences.

We shall probably soon be called upon to meet by a proper Deputation the Commissioners expected from White Hall. For this momentous interview, my private sentiment is, that the Wisdom of the Union should be selected, that we should go beyond the bounds of Congress & of any particular State in our choice of Character. It is probably too late to ask advice or Instruction, & if I do not misunderstand we shall find our Men in York Town. Your Excellency shall receive early intelligence of determinations on this Subject.

The Tax of £5 on Lands &ca is high, but I feel no disposition to repine, excepting only when I reflect upon the gross frauds upon Public Money which overflow this Land & consider the burthens prepared for us, through such Wickedness.

I shall do everything in my power to obtain Captn. Pickerings enlargement but this will be a work of difficulty while he is kept afloat, an object of peculiar resentment, rendered so by his own vanity.[13]

Although I have so long trespassed upon your time, permit me Sir, before I conclude to congratulate with your Excellency on your appointment to the presidency of South Carolina & to express my wishes that your Excellency may enjoy as much satisfaction & pleasure in the discharge of that important trust as I am persuaded your Excellency's Administration will afford to the people. I have the honour to be with great Respect & Regard &ca.

LB (ScHi).

[1] Rawlins Lowndes (1721–1800) was a conservative planter, lawyer, legislator, and judge who served as president of South Carolina from March 6, 1778, to January 9, 1779. *DAB.*

[2] A transcript of President Lowndes' March 16 letter to Laurens is in the Laurens Papers, ScHi. Enclosed with it was a report of a committee of the South Carolina Assembly that has not been found but which, according to Lowndes' description of it, asked Congress to reimburse South Carolina for supplying low cost trade goods to the Indians to preserve peace. There is no evidence in the journals that Congress ever took action on this request.

[3] See Gouverneur Morris to Washington, this date.

[4] Drayton had been appointed to this committee on April 29. *JCC,* 10:402–3.

[5] For a discussion of the acquisition of Cherokee land by South Carolina and other southern states as a result of their victory over this tribe in 1776, see James H. O'Donnell, III, *Southern Indians in the American Revolution* (Knoxville: University of Tennessee, 1973), pp. 54–59.

[6] See *JCC,* 10:405–10.

[7] At this point Laurens inserted an asterisk to key the following note he wrote at the end of the letter: "originally an Agreement & altho amended & made a Recommendatory Clause it is understood those states are to be exempted from all expences." The last clause of this "Invitation" requested states "who have vacant lands" to set some of them aside so that Congress could make good on its promised land grants to foreign officers and soldiers who left British service, adding that "for which lands no charge is to be made against the United States." *JCC,* 10:409.

[8] The delegates who had "lately" arrived in Congress were: Joseph Reed of Pennsylvania (April 6), Richard Hutson of South Carolina (April 13), Charles Carroll of Carrollton of Maryland (April 15), Thomas Adams of Virginia (April 16), George Plater of Maryland (April 18), John Mathews of South Carolina (April 22), Roger Sherman of Connecticut (April 25), and Richard Henry Lee of Virginia (May 1). They were soon joined by the following delegates who arrived in York before Congress adjourned to Philadelphia on June 27: Philip Livingston of New York (May 5), Thomas McKean of Delaware (May 11), John Witherspoon of New Jersey (May 16), Josiah Bartlett of New Hampshire and Samuel Adams of Massachusetts (May 21), Jonathan Elmer of New Jersey (May 26), John Wentworth of New Hampshire (May 30), Thomas Heyward of South Carolina (June 6), John Hancock of Massachusetts and Nathaniel Scudder of New Jersey (June 19), John Collins of Rhode Island (June 22), Samuel Holten of Massachusetts (June 22), and Titus Hosmer of Connecticut (June 23). On the other hand, North Carolina was unrepresented in Congress from May 4 to July 16, 1778, when John Penn attended.

[9] Although Lowndes did not mention the document in his June 17 reply to Laurens, the enclosed "Resolve" was almost certainly a copy of Samuel Huntington's Proposed Resolution, which is printed above under the date April 22–23, 1778.

[10] See Washington, *Writings* (Fitzpatrick), 11:307–8.

[11] For a discussion of Congress' acceptance of Gen. Thomas Conway's most recent resignation offer, see Laurens to Washington, April 28, 1778, note 3. In commenting on this paragraph, Edmund C. Burnett erred in stating that Conway first offered his resignation in an April 6 letter to Laurens, as that letter simply announced Conway's intention of complying with a congressional order that he serve under Gen. Alexander McDougall at Peekskill. Burnett, *Letters*, 3:211n.10; and PCC, item 159, fol. 496. In fact Conway had first offered to resign from the army in November 1777 as a result of Congress' failure to approve his repeated requests for promotion to major general. Conway's earlier letter of resignation has not been found, but he refers to it in a November 14, 1777, letter he wrote to "Charles Carrol esqr. or in his absence to secy of Congress." PCC, item 159, fols. 461–67; and *JCC*, 9:958.

[12] This letter is in the William Gilmore Simms Collection deposit, MHi; a transcript of it is in the Laurens Papers, ScHi.

[13] Lowndes had discussed this issue in his March 30 letter to Laurens, ibid.

Henry Laurens to William Thomson

Dear Sir,   1st May 1778.

The papers[1] which I send inclosed with this have afforded much satisfaction in this Quarter, I trust the whole Union will be as well pleased as we are. I may add that you may almost depend upon it as a fact, France has confirmed a Treaty with our Commissioners & acknowledge the Sovereignty & Independence of America, & that a few days will bring a confirmation of this grand event.

My present circumstances will not allow me to write so fully to my friends as I wish, I work 16 & sometimes 21 Hours in a day which affords short intervals for repose.

My best wishes attend you & Mrs Thomson & all yours.

I am with great regard &ca.

LB (ScHi).

[1] These probably included the same "printed papers" on Congress' response to Lord North's Conciliatory Bill and General Washington's recent dealings with General Howe and Governor Tryon that Laurens described in his letter of this date to Rawlins Lowndes.

Henry Laurens to Andrew Williamson

Dear Colonel, 1st May 1778.

The papers which I send inclosed with this have afforded much satisfaction in this part of America, I trust the whole Union will be as well pleased with them as we are.

You may expect very soon after this reaches you to receive authentic accounts that France has confirmed a Treaty with these States honourable & beneficial to us, & that particularly Spain & Prussia will follow France in the acknowledgement of our Sovereignty & Independence. This will give us a moment of respite. The thousand things I have to do & the Thousand interruptions I am exposed to, allow me only time to add my Compliments to Mrs. Williamson & assurances of continuing with very great Regard.

LB (ScHi).

Gouverneur Morris' Draft Report on Instructions for the American Commissioners

[May 1, 1778][1]

It is proposed to adopt the Motion from Connecticut[2] and then to pass the following Resolution, viz.

Resolved. That a Letter be written to the Commrs.   by the Committee of Correspondence inclosing the foregoing Resolutions & also the Report of the Committee upon the Genls. Letter containing the Draft of two Bills &ca. containing the Reasons for the said Report & Resolution[3] viz.

That the Inhabitants of the united States having suffered greatly by the War become daily more desirous of terminating it.

That the Resources of the States being greatly exhausted by their Exertions as well as by the many Disorders attendant upon Great Revolutions which are scarce conceivable by those who administer established Governments the Difficulty of prosecuting the War increases in Proportion to its Continuance.

That the Derangement of our Finances & the consequent Depreciation of our Currency render a Peace with G Britain not only eligible but necessary.

And That the manifest Advantages which will arise from an Alliance with the Greatest naval Power on Earth over and above those which Peace would in itself produce have prompted us to smoothe the Way to so desirable a Purpose.

That the said Committee do further inform the said Commrs. That Congress conceive it to be the true Interest of America.

To guarantee to the several European Powers their Possessions in the Islands the same being a Pledge in the Hand of this Continent for the Security of their Subjects in every Part of the World & also for the free Trade to those Islands.

To give equal Privileges to all Persons fishing on their Shores Reserving to them the Determination of Disputes arising on that Subject between foreign Powers.

To open the Ports of America to the Ships of all Nations freighted with the Produce & Manufactures of the respective Countries they belong to except such as may shut their Ports to the Subjects of America, &

To be at Peace with all the World & derive Accessions of Wealth & Subjects from the various Commotions of other States.

That the said Committee do further inform the said Commrs.

That Notwithstanding the Situation of this Country and its evident Interests Congress are determined faithfully to adhere to such Treaties as may on their Part have been entered into consistent with the Instructions heretofore given or any of them.

That if no Treaty is yet made by them they are to govern themselves according to Circumstances being assured that the British Force now in America is not adequate to the Purpose of subduing it and that if such Loans or Subsidies can be procured in Europe as to establish the Value of our Paper Emissions of Money there is no Doubt but that we can still continue the Conflict notwithstanding the Disadvantages before enumerated. Wherefore they shall propose & accede to such Terms within the Line of their former Instructions as shall upon the whole appear to them most conducive to the Interests of these united States &

That if War should be declard against Britain by any of the greater Powers of Europe they are immediately to take Advantage of such favorable Circumstance and borrow all the Money in their Power in Holland & keep the same to answer the Drafts or other Orders of Congress.

MS (NNC). In the hand of Gouverneur Morris.

[1] Morris apparently drafted this document as a result of his appointment this this day, with Richard Henry Lee and Roger Sherman, to a committee that was charged "to report proper instructions to be transmitted to the commissioners of the United States at foreign courts." *JCC,* 10:414. For the circumstances leading to the appointment of this committee, which reflected the concerns of some delegates

that Congress should not be seen as intransigently opposed to a new peace initiative believed to have been launched by Lord North, see Samuel Huntington's Proposed Resolution, April 22–23; and William Henry Drayton's Proposed Resolution, this date.

² Undoubtedly the motion of Samuel Huntington mentioned in note 1 above.

³ Although the immediate debate that precipitated the appointment of this committee focused on "the state of America with respect to foreign nations," it had had its origin in a report which reached York on April 20 that the North ministry had proposed two bills in Parliament containing new proposals for opening peace negotiations with the United States. This information had been enclosed in Washington's April 18 letter to Congress, which was referred to a committee consisting of Morris, Francis Dana, and William Henry Drayton, whose report—"the Report of the Committee upon the Genls. Letter containing the Draft of two Bills &ca"— had been adopted on April 22. See *JCC*, 10:367, 374–80; and Henry Laurens to James Duane, April 20, 1778, note 1.

The arrival the following evening, Saturday, May 2, of the texts of treaties of alliance and commerce that had been signed by French officials and the American commissioners at Paris in February, immediately rendered this draft report by Morris moot.

Gouverneur Morris to George Washington

Dr General.　　　　　　　　　　　　　　York Town 1st May 1778

Knox is to attend the Council.[1] Conway hath resigned & his Resignation is accepted. The Affairs of the Army are necessarily delayed by the foreign affairs which have broken in upon us. As to the Half Pay, Matters stand thus. The Questions have been carried but by an Entry on the Minutes there is an Agreemt. that a final Question shall be put whether it be finally determined in Congress or sent to the several States.[2] When a Motion is made for this Purpose the yeas will be Massats., Rhode Island, Connec., Jersey, & South Carolina. The Nays will be N York, Maryland, Virginia & Georgia. Pensilvania is in a mighty flimsy Situation on that Subject having indeed a mighty flimsy Representation. I wish Boudinot were here. Delaware is absent who is with us as is N Carolina also absent. New Hampshire is absent who is against us.[3] This is to go by Gates. I am, respectfully yours,

Gouvr Morris

[*P.S.*] I pay my Respects to Mrs. Washington.

RC (DLC).

¹ See Gouverneur Morris to Washington, April 18, 1778, note 4.

² Congress had entered into this agreement on April 1. *JCC*, 10:300.

³ When on May 13 Congress rejected a motion to refer the issue of half pay to the state legislatures, the state delegations in Congress voted exactly as Morris predicted, with Pennsylvania, reinforced by the timely arrival of Robert Morris, casting its vote with the majority. *JCC*, 10:495–96.

Nathaniel Scudder to Joseph Scudder

My Dear Son,   York Town May 1. 1778
   As I suppose you are now at home with your Honored Daddy &
Mama, I wish you to use every Endeavour to make them and your
Brothers & Sisters comfortable and happy; and at the same Time to
improve your Vacation in such a Way as will prove advantageous to
your own Education, and honorable to you in Point of Behavior
among your Friends & Acquaintances.
   Carefully avoid the Allurements of every Vice, and shun industriously the Temptations of youth. Tread diligently in the Paths of
Virtue, & strive above all to obtain, through the Merits of your
Redeemer, the inestimable Blessings of true Godliness & undefiled
Religion.
   A Scene is opening, my Dear Child, in this Country for the greatest
imaginable Display of Talents and Education, and a Young Man
with your Capacity, Abilities and Learning can't fail under God, if he
sets out right, of making a Figure in public Life on the great Stage
of this new World. Indeed I cannot help contemplating my Sons as
shining in future in some of the most splendid Departments of this
mighty rising American Empire, the Glory of the western World—
and greatly eclipsing their Father in every civil Accomplishment.
This is surely in their Power, since they now may improve themselves
designedly for this Purpose; whereas he from this amazing Change in
human Affairs was unexpectedly & reluctantly, as well as unprepar-
edly and rapidly pushed from Stage to Stage to the most important
Seat he now has the Honor to fill, and to which he finds himself Alas,
but too unequal. But how will it ring my Heart, if by any false Step,
if by any fatal vicious Indulgence these my fond Hopes shall be disappointed? Then indeed will my grey Hairs descend with Sorrow, &
perhaps a speedy Pace, to the Grave.
   O my Son, let it be your daily & nightly prayer to be delivered from
every Evil & every Temptation, and to be prepared for the whole will
& Pleasure of God your Creator, Preserver and constant Benefactor.
   Love & Respects to all, & am my Dear Son, your affectionate &
Indulgent Father,   Nathl Scudder

RC (NjHi).

Roger Sherman to Jonathan Trumbull, Sr.

Sir,   York Town May 1st. 1778
   I arrived here the 24th of last month. I dont know of any thing
very material that has passed in Congress Since Col. Dyer left it. Sev-

eral important Matters are depending unfinished respecting the regulation, & provision for the army, & for fixing the Credit of the Currency. There is a report of a Committee for Sinking 20 Million dollars, of the first Emissions of the Continental Bills by a Loan, to recommend to the serious consideration of the Southern states the Report of the N. Haven convention for stating prizes, and to such of the States as have not sunk their outstanding Bills immediately, to do it & refrain from further Emissions.[1] The Assembly of Pensylvania have passed an Act to sink all their outstanding Bills & that they shall not be receiv'd in the Treasury after the 12th of next month. They also passed an Act regulating prices of Labour & Commodities the first day of April, to be in force the first of June. The regulating Act, in New York State, was in force & the Inholders Conformed to it, when I passed thro', New Jersey practised on their former Law, but it was said it would be altered agreeable to what was agreed to by the Commissioners met at New Haven. The prices of articles here at present are high. Your Excellency will doubtless have received the papers Containing Lord Norths late Speech & the two Bills purposed for Acts of parliament as a foundation for reconciliation with America, with the remarks of Congress thereon before this Comes to hand; it seems pretty evident that the ministry find it difficult to carry on the war & have not much hope of Conquering & therefore they will try every Artifice to divide us; but all ranks of people in this part of the Country that I have heard talk on the Subject are for supporting the Independance of these States at all events. A Committee is appointed to make preparation for the trial of the Genl. Officers, who Commanded in the northern Department, when the Fortresses of Ty & Independance were abandoned. In behalf of the Committee, I request your Excellency to transmit to me any depositions or other Information which you are possessed of that may be of use in that enquiry.[2] The drawing of the Lottery of the united States Commences to Day the numbers & prizes are in the wheels. I am with great Esteem & Regard your Excellency's Obedient humble Servt.

Roger Sherman

P.S. The Articles of Confederation have not been yet taken up.[3] No Returns are made from New Hamshire, N Jersey or Georgia; New York Assembly has Agreed, to them without any alteration, North Carolina Agreed to only a small part & advised to defer the rest till the Conclusion of the war, tis said they will reconsider the matter & probably agree to the whole. New Hampshire, Delaware & North Carolina have no Delegates in Congress at present. All the States except N Hampshire were Represented last week. Col McKean is a Delegate for Deleware, he is now on the Circuit as Chief Justice for Pensylvania.

Tr (Ct).

[1] See Oliver Wolcott to Andrew Adams, April 25, 1778, notes 3 and 4.

[2] On April 29 Sherman had been appointed to a committee "to examine the evidence collected, and state charges against the general officers who were in the northern department when Ticonderoga and Mount Independence were evacuated." *JCC*, 10:403. It is not known whether Governor Trumbull responded to this request for additional information before the committee reported on June 12, but his January 23 response to a previous request from Henry Laurens and Richard Henry Lee is in PCC, item 66, fol. 382.

[3] See James Lovell to Samuel Adams, March 10, 1778, note 1.

Henry Laurens to John Houstoun

Sir,[1]
                                                          2d May 1778.

My last to Georgia went under the 19th March by the hands of the Honble. Mr. Wood.[2]

Hitherto Sir, I have not been honoured by a single acknowledgement of any of the many transmissions which I have made to that State, hence Congress are kept ignorant not only of the measures adopted in consequence of their Recommendations but even of the safety or miscarriage of them. I intreat your Honour will be pleased to give the necessary directions that I may be informed the dates of all my Letters which had reached the Honorable Gentleman lately in the Administration of Government.

I beg leave to congratulate with you Sir, upon your appointment & to add my good wishes that you may experience as much satisfaction in your Administration of Government as I am persuaded you will afford to the good people among whom you preside.

Within the present Inclosure Your Honor will receive

1. An Act of Congress of the 6th August 1777 with a Note subjoined.[3]

2. An Act of the 22d Inst. confirming the Report of a Committee on General Washington's Letter of the 18th[4] & several Copies.

3. An Act Recommending to pardon such American Citizens as may have joined the Enemy & who shall return & surrender themselves before the 10th June ☞ this short limit intended chiefly for the neighboring States.[5]

4. An Act to encourage Officers & Soldiers in the service but not subject of the King of Great Britain to settle in these States.[6]

5. Of the first Instant Recommending the exemption of artificers in the immediate employment of the States from Militia Duty.

To these I shall take the liberty of adding a Newspaper containing many articles of Interesting Intelligence & will keep open my packet 'till I can inclose in it a paper of much more importance the contents of which demand the congratulations of all the faithful Citizens of our Union. The treaties between France & these States have been once solemnly announced in Congress & I have good grounds for presuming to say a Ratification & publication will take place in the course of the present Week. I am now at the 3d May. I have the honor to be

LB (DNA: PCC, item 13).

[1] John Houstoun (1744–96), who had represented Georgia in Congress during the autumn of 1775, served his state as governor in 1778 and 1784. *Bio. Dir. Cong.*

[2] See Laurens to the Massachusetts Council, March 19, 1778, note 2.

[3] On August 6, 1777, Congress had taken two actions relating to Georgia. The first dealt with the appointment of three Continental officials in the state and the second concerned an appeal from a decision of the Georgia Court of Admiralty. *JCC*, 8:616–17. It is not clear which of the two acts Laurens enclosed with this letter.

[4] This was Congress' initial response to Lord North's conciliatory proposals. *JCC*, 10:374–80.

[5] See *JCC*, 10:381–82.

[6] See *JCC*, 10:405–10.

Henry Laurens to Rawlins Lowndes

Sir,   2d May 1778.

I have the honour of inclosing under the present Cover the under-mentioned Acts of Congress, which Your Excellency will be pleased to lay before the Legislative or Executive powers of South Carolina as each Case may require.

1. An Act of 11th March for defraying the expence of carrying into execution an Act of the 9th Febry.[1]

2. of the 12 March for obtaining from each State the constant attendance of at least three Members during the War.

3. Confirming the Report of a Committee the 22d April on General Washington's Letter of the 18th &ca. & spare Copies.

4. of the 23d April, Recommending to the Legislatures of the several States to pass Laws or Issue proclamations for pardoning such American Citizens as may have join'd the Enemy & who shall return & surrender themselves before the 10th June.

5. of the 29th April an Address to Officers & Soldiers in the service of the King of Great Britain, not subjects of said King inviting such Officers & Soldiers to settle within these States, & Recommending to the several States who have vacant Land to lay off a sufficient quantity to answer the purposes intended.

I received with a just sense of the favor, a notification of the leave of absence from Congress granted me by the Honble. the House of Assembly & at the same time an Account that the House had been pleased to re-elect me for this Duty, which implied, at least, a desire that I should continue in it for some time longer. Had our public affairs been in a better Situation than they were when these advices reached me, had there been a full Congress generally, or could I have left Colleagues who had gained an insight into the proceedings of Congress I should have considered the permission to return as a Blessing, circumstanced as we are I hold it my Duty to remain, until I see a large Representation of the States & my Colleagues led into the course of business, which will require some Months even for Men of experience.

I have the honour to be

LB (DNA: PCC, item 13).
[1] The object of this resolve was to reimburse state executives for expenses incurred in implementing a February 9 resolve that authorized them to dismiss supernumerary Continental officials who were not directly appointed by Congress. See *JCC,* 10:139–40, 243.

Richard Henry Lee to Thomas Jefferson

Dear Sir York May 2, 1778.

We are this moment made acquainted by the War Office that an Express was immediately to depart for Virginia, and I take the opportunity of enclosing by him the last papers, which contain all our news, except it be a report that seems not illy founded, that Genl. Amhers[t] and Adml. Keppel are arrived at Philadelphia as commissioners from the King & Parliament of G. B. to carry into execution the very curious plan that one of the inclosed papers contains. Tis happy for America that her enemies have not sufficient ability to give even a specious appearance to their wicked designs. In this case the Peasantry here develope the cheat. We have no news, not a scrip from our Com[mission]ers. The Gold and the Sea power of our enemies have [preva]iled to deprive us of most important dispatches. Adieu my dear Sir, Richard Henry Lee

[*P.S.*] Gen. Lee is fully exchanged and is sent for from Berk[eley] to attend the Army. For Gods sake, for the love of our Country, my dear friend, let more vigorous measures be quickly adopted for reenforcing the Army. The last draft will fall greatly short of the requisite number. Our enemies are sore pressed, wisdom and vigor now will presently compel G.B., proud as she is, to acknowledge our Independency.

RC (DLC). Jefferson, *Papers* (Boyd), 2:175–76.

Robert Morris to James Lovell

Dear Sir   Manheim May 2d. 1778
   Just as I was about to return from Lancaster last Night for this place I heard of Mr. Simeon Deanes arrival there from France & had the pleasure of hearing from him the Good News he brings to Congress. He delivered me the five enclosed Packets directed to me as Chair Man of the Committee & expecting there might be some private letters for me I opened them but was disapointed. I have hardly read them through being desirous they shou'd be with you soon as Mr Deane who leaves Lancaster this Morning and I send these by Mr. Charles Miller by whom I beg you will send my letters if any there be, for me, made up with the Public dispatches.[1] You will add greatly to the favour if you will write me a few lines with a summary of the intelligence & the heads of the Treaty. Mr Miller will wait Your leisure for this. Mr Deane tells me my Brother has paid the last Forfeit of his Follies by his Death on the 1st Feby last. It is the happiest thing that cou'd befall him but has in some degree renewed my Feelings on his Acct. I am Dr sir, Your Obed hble sert.[2]
                                                              Robt Morris.

RC (DNA: PCC, item 137).
   [1] On May 4 Morris wrote to Lovell again in the same vein. "I return you herewith several of the Packets you sent me by Mr. Miller being all that relate to public matters except a Packet or two of English Newspapers so old as August, Septr & Octr last, which I dont think worth sending to You now. Mr. Duer had given us great joy here in relating the News. We most sincerely Rejoice & Congratulate you & every Friend of America on the fair prospect of Peace & Independance & with thanks for your care of my letters I remain, Dear sir, Your obliged & Obed servt." PCC, item 137, Appendix, fol. 241.
   [2] On May 5 Morris wrote a business letter to his associate William Bingham which contains a report of the death of Morris' brother Thomas and the following lines pertaining to public affairs. "I am happy to tell you the Congress have granted an order for your drawing on the Commissioners at Paris for 100,000 Livres, I have often urged the necessity of your being reimbursed, but not Attending Congress for some months past I could not do therein all I wished to do. . . . I must before long return to my Duty in Congress again, altho' I have not half finished the business that caused me to retire. However I must Suspend the Prosecution of it for a few Months and at the end of that time I hope to be in Philadelphia again and that our Public Affairs may then be in such a train that I may retire without being missed, for as I never embarked from Ambitious Motives, I wish to become a Private Man again soon as possible." Bingham Papers, DLC.

Oliver Wolcott to Laura Wolcott

My Dear,   York Town 2 May 1778

I have wrote to you one Letter since that which you recd. by Brown.[1] I then told you that I was well, and by the Blessing of God I continue to injoy good Health. I have not heard from you, nor recd. any Letters from my Freinds since yours of the 6t of April. I expect that Mr. Adams will be here by the latter end of this Month. As soon as he comes I shall Return. Nothing Material has occurred since my last. It is said and it is probably true that Genl. Amherst, Admiral Keppell and Genl. Murray are Appointed to Negotiate upon the Plan proposed by Ld. North—and it is Reported that Ms Amherst and Keppel are Arrived at Philadelphia. There is no doubt but that Genl. Howe has or is going to England. My Opinion is that the Veiws of the British Administration are to delude and endeavour to divide— Altho' I do not perceive that any Attempts of this Kind have any Effect. A false forged Resolution of Congress has lately been published both in Philadelphia and N York, setting forth an order to Genl. Washington to retain in his Army till the end of the War all Soldiers however inlisted or brot. into Service and this forged Resolution they take much Pain to spread in the Country.[2] We are too much uninformed as to European Affairs. But I trust that will not long be the Case. My own Situation here is comfortable—so that you will suffer no Concern on my Account. Take Care of your Health and Banish Care. Every Thing I trust will operate for the best. God who takes Care of and Protects Nations, will take Care of this People and give us still farther and greater Occasions to rejoice in his Goodness. My Love to my Children and Freinds. I am your's, with the greatest Affection   Oliver Wolcott

P.S. Genl. Gates went yesterday to Head Quarters and from thence proceeds to Hudsons River. The Lottery began to draw yesterday in this Town, it will finish in four Weeks. I am not able to congratulate you upon any of the Familys having made their Fortune as yet, but I have or rather perhaps ought to Wish that it might be so, Altho I cannot say that I have much sensation in Regard to this Matter. However I wish that when Brown Returns you will inclose the Tickets. The small Prizes will be paid off in the several States, and perhaps those which are to be paid by Certificates. I beleive it will be so but this Matter is not yet settled.[3]

RC (CtHi).

[1] The last letter from Wolcott to his wife that messenger Jesse Brown carried from York to Connecticut is dated April 14, 1778. Since Brown's departure from York on April 21 Wolcott had also written to Laura on April 25.

[2] See Henry Laurens to George Washington, April 24, 1778, note 7.

[3] For Congress' May 2 resolves regarding the payment of lottery prizes, see *JCC*, 11:415–16.

John Banister to Theodorick Bland, Jr.

Dear Sir.[1]   York 3d May 1778.

By an Express, of yesterday, sent by the board of War, I wrote Mr. Davis all the News preceding that date.[2] Before he got away a Messenger arrived from France charged with the most important Papers from our Commissioners at Paris containing a Treaty of alliance, and a Treaty of alliance and Commerce, between the Court of France and America. By these Treaties our Independence is made a grand Object on the Part of the King of France who has with great liberality that he takes no advantage of the present Situation of the States, but has made the same Treaty with them as if they had been in the most flourishing Prosperity.

The Treaty which was concluded & signed the 6th of Feby. guarantees to America all her Possessions in America, together with Bermudas.

If England declares War against France or occasions a War by attempts to obstruct her Commerce, we are to make common Cause with her & join her forces & Councils.

The States guarantee to France all her Possessions in America. Ext. of D. Franklin's letter.[3]

28 Feby. We have found the greatest cordiality in this Court and that no advantage has been taken of our difficulties to obtain hard Terms of us, but such has been the King's magnanimity and goodness, that he has proposed none we might not have agreed to in a State of full Prosperity and established Power. The Principle laid down in the Plan of the Treaty, being as declared in the Preamble, "The most perfect equality & Reciprocity," the Priviledges in Trade are mutual, and none are given to France but what we are at Liberty to grant to any other Nation. When we mention the good Will of this Nation to our Cause we may add that of all Europe, which having been offended by the Pride and Insolence of Britain wishes to see its Power diminished. The Preparations for war are carried on with immense Activity and it is very soon expected. When this last Event shall take Place, America will be in a Situation to prosecute the War with Ease to herself, but at present the utmost Exertions should be made in opposition to those of G. Britain, which will be thro Rage & disappointment as great as her utmost ability in Men & Resource will admit; and it would be happy if the People at large could be persuaded that one vigorous Effort would restore them to what they so ardently wish, a State of perfect Tranquility, which with established Independence. The present Treaties, Advantageous as they are, have no immediate operation on our military Conflict with G. Britain, but promises eventually assistance, by G. Britain's being

provoked to a declaration of War, or drawing on one by an Interruption of the Commerce of France.

I am your affect. Friend & [. . .]   J Banister.

[P.S.] Let your Father & Mr. Davis have this News as soon as possible. I am in a low State of Health being [. . .] reduced since I saw you, by frequent Retu[rns of a] disorder in my Bowells, greatly a[ggravated] by the Limestone Water of this Place.

RC (ViHi).

[1] Theodorick Bland, the brother of Banister's late wife Elizabeth, was undoubtedly the recipient of this letter, which was found among Bland's papers in the early 19th century and printed in Theodorick Bland, *The Bland Papers*, ed. Charles Campbell, 2 vols. (Petersburg, Va.: Edmund & Julian C. Ruffin, 1840), 1:84–85. At this time Colonel Bland was in Virginia procuring horses and arms and recruiting men for the Continental cavalry. For General Washington's instructions to Bland, see Washington, *Writings* (Fitzpatrick), 11:28–29, 274–75, 339–40.

[2] Not found.

[3] The next four sentences were extracted from the American commissioners' February 8, not 28, letter to the Committee for Foreign Affairs, which is in Wharton, *Diplomatic Correspondence*, 2:490–91.

Charles Carroll of Carrollton to Charles Carroll, Sr.

Dear Papa,   Sunday 3d May 1778

Yesterday evening arrived here Mr. Dean brother to Mr. Silas Dean, with the Treaty of Alliance & commerce Signed the 6th of February by our Deputies at Paris, & Monsr. Gerard commissionated for that purpose. This treaty is bottomed on principles of the most liberal, wise, & generous Policy; the only thing required of us, is the maintainance of our Independance. If France should be involved in the war, & acquired at the treaty of peace any Islands in the West Indies, we are to guarantee the possession of those & their present Islands. It is not even required of us to continue the war (provided we make peace on the footing of independant States) even if France should be obliged to continue the war if She should be engaged in one in consequence of this alliance formed with us.

Our latest letters from our Deputies at Paris are of the 8th March.[1] They promise us immediate & considerable supplies of clothing, arms &c. It is not expected that the military stores already supplied us are to be paid for. The King of Prussia has prevented the German mercenaries from coming over, so that G B will receive few or no soldiers from that quarter; her funds are fallen 10 per Cent. In short, by our Agent's letters it appears that all the great Powers of Europe are favourably disposed towards us. I sincerely rejoice with you on this happy prospect of our affairs.

Mr. Dean was brought over by a French frigate & landed in Canso Bay.

I wrote to you & Molly by Mr. Digges. I shall write to you again by Tuesday post. My love to Molly, Mrs. Darnell & the little ones. God grant you a continuance of health. I am, Yr. affectionate Son,

Ch. Carroll of Carrollton

RC (MdHi).

[1] Actually February 28, a correction Carroll made in his letter to his father the next day.

Samuel Chase to Thomas Johnson

My Dear sir   Yorktown Sunday morning, May 3d. 1778

On Yesterday afternoon arrived here from France, Mr. Simeon Dean (Brother to the Commissioner) with Despatches to Congress from our Commissioners, to the 28 February.

On the 6th of February two Treaties were concluded and sign'd by Monsr. Jerard Plenepotentiary appointed by his most Christian Majesty on the 30th January preceding for that purpose, and by our Commissioners, B Franklin, S Deane, & A Lee Esqrs. The first is a Treaty of *Amity & Commerce* on the plan proposed by Congress and almost in the words of it. The second is a Treaty of Alliance of Amity and Commerce. I cannot better inform you of the substance of these Treaties than in the words of the Commissioners. "If England declares War against France, or occasions a War by attempts to hinder her Commerce, we shall then make a common Cause of it & join our Forces & our Councils. The grand aim of the Treaty is declared to be *"establish the Liberty, Sovereignty and Independency, absolute and unlimited of the United States, as well in matters of Government as Commerce* and *this* is *guarranted* to us by France *together* with all the Countries we possess, or shall possess at the conclusion of the war; in return for which the states Guarrantee to France all its possessions in America. We have found the greatest cordiality in this Court, and that no advantage has been taken of our present difficulties to obtain hard terms from us, but such has been the Kings Magnanimity & Goodness, that he has proposed none which we might not readily have agreed to in a state of *full prosperity and established power*. The Principal laid down as the basis of the Treaty being as declared in the preamble "The most perfect Equality [*and*] Recepro-city; the priviledges in Trade &c. are *mutual* & none are given to France but what we are at liberty to grant to any other Nation." By the Second Treaty France has renounced for ever possession to any part of the Continent lately or now in the possession of Great Britain, or acceded to her by the Treaty of Paris & to the Island of Bermuda.

The account of General Burgoine's defeat was received in Paris the beginning of Decemr. Our Commissioners immediately pressed for the Conclusion of the Treaty, and a Council was called the 12th in which it was decided to acknowledge and support our Independancy.

Our Commissioners are of opinion "That the Treaty with France will certainly be followed by the whole house of Bourbon, and probably by Holland. The Preparations for war Continue daily, & France is determined to protect her Commerce with you." The King of Prussia is well disposed towards you & on application prevented the Hesse & Hanau Troops from passing thro' his Dominions & now waits the Measures of France. Very considerable supplies sailed from France in February under Convoy, and may be hourly expected. Mr. Carmichael is on board.

I do most cordially and sincerely congratulate you on this most important Intelligence. America has now taken her rank among the Nations & has it in her power to secure her Liberty & Independance. Let us be grateful to our God for this singular unmerited Mark of his favour & protection and continue to exert every Means in our power to support the war; this can only be effectually done by speedy and liberal Loans of Money to the Continent and a respectable Army. Congress some time past recommended that subscriptions should be opened in each County.

I am &c.   Saml Chase

Tr (MdAA).

William Ellery to Nicholas Cooke

Sir,   York Town May 3d. 1778.
I take this earliest opportunity to inform your excellency that a Messenger arrived here yesterday P.M. from France, with dispatches, containing among other Things a copy of the Treaties of Alliance and of Amity and Commerce entered into between the Court of France and our Commissioners; which will without doubt be ratified by Congress.

The former hath the protection and support of the Independency of these States for its basis, and the latter is founded in perfect equality and reciprocity.

If War should be commenced by Great Britain agst France it is to be made a common cause. The Independency of these States is to be supported. If any particular enterprize should be undertaken we are to join and act in concert.

No truce to be made without the consent of each, unless our Independency is absolutely acknowledged.

France guarantees our Independency, and all we possess or shall possess at the conclusion of the war and we guarantee to France her Possessions in America.

Admission of other Nations to equal advantages in Commerce.

These are imperfect minutes of some of the principle heads of the treaties as I took them at the Table last evening while they were reading. Hereafter when the treaties shall be ratified copies of them will be transmitted to the several states.

The Letters from the commissioners show a good disposition in the powers of Europe towards us.

Prussia shows a disposition to share in our commerce; but will not open her ports to our privateers until the arrangement of Independency shall be made.

The Ambassador of the Duke of Tuscany hath given our commissioner favorable expectations from his Court.

Portugal will accede to the family compact. The House of Bourbon & all the powers of Europe will soon acknowledge our Independency. We are desired to forget any animosities we may formerly have entertained against France, & to cultivate a friendship for her.

These minutes were made as the other and must of course be very imperfect also.

The Treaties of Alliance &c were signed the 6th of February; and display a spirit of magnanimity and a soundness of policy scarcely to be parallelled. Instead of pursuing that narrow policy which regards only the present moment and present Interest, and nobly disdaining to take an advantage of our situation, France hath, with but a small variation, acceded to our own proposals, thereby doubtless intending to bind us to them by the indissoluble Ties of affection & Gratitude.

It is reported that Genl. Amherst and Admiral Keppel are arrived at Philadelphia; but by an officer whom I saw this morning, and who came directly from Camp it seems to be only a report. Commissioners are daily expected from Britain with proposals for a reconciliation. Congress will abide by their Independency at all events, and I have no doubt but that it will be acknowledged this Campaign even by Britain herself, provided we bring into the field, a respectable Army. She is reduced to the greatest straits. From Germany She cannot collect recruits for their stipulated Troops, From her own Island but few can be drawn. Her credit is sunk in Holland, and her Stocks are fallen. France hath a large body of troops in Normandy and Bretagne, her Navy in good preparation and is determined to protect her commerce to America. She waits only for Britain to strike the first blow. Rather than do this it is my humble opinion that if our people will but step forth this campaign as I have said before She will acknowledge our Independency, and be contented with that part of our commerce which it may suit us to give her.

Mr. Collins will set off in a day or two. He will take with him One hundred and fifty thousand Dollars, and a Warrant on our Loan Office for the same Sum.[1] I am afraid you will be disappointed, but this was not obtained without difficulty. Unless Commissioners should be appointed to settle our accounts before you make another demand, and they are adjusted; or you should send your auditor with the vouchers for every Article, and direct him to tarry until the accounts shall be liquidated I am afraid any Application would be fruitless. Permit me to desire that two of the Delegates, if they should not have come on before this reaches you, may be sent forward immediately; for my health, and the situation of my family oblige me to quit York-Town. I continue to be with great Respect Yr. Excellency's very hble Servant,   Wm Ellery

RC (RHi).
[1] See Ellery to Cooke, April 25, 1778, note 1.

Henry Laurens to Baron de Bonstetten

Sir,[1]   3d May 1778.
Some Twenty days have elapsed since I had the honor of receiving your favor of the 1st March.

I am much concerned that from a want of opportunity it has not been in my power to pay this respect earlier.

It is impossible Sir, for me to determine what might happen if a Gentleman of your Merit & Military abilities were "actually on the spot, where Congress is convened," or where the "Army under General Washington is encamped," but when I assure you that besides those returning French Officers to whom you allude, there are many valuable Characters of different Nations at both places unemployed, & that according to an arrangement now in agitation there will be many American Officers dismissed as supernumerary, you will admit the propriety of forbearing to hold out encouragement to you to encounter so long & expensive a journey, at the end of which there is at present no certainty of promotion, nor even of honorable service. This uncertainty does not arise from a superabundance of Good Officers in our Army, it must therefore be the consequence of our having too many Officers, there would be room enough for some of the first if it were practicable to remove with safety an equal number of the latter class. But Sir, our Army is in its infancy, a State which does not exhibit perfection, & there is a necessity from motives extremely obvious for retaining persons in the list of Officers who are not unexceptionable & we have ground to hope that objections which now are urged against some of our young Men will be removed by time.

Should you think proper to adventure upon a journey this way, although I dare not flatter you with the assurance of a Commission, you may rely on me Sir, for every mark of Civility & respect.

I have the honour to be

LB (ScHi). Addressed: "Baron de Bonstetten, Charles Town."

[1] Baron de Bonstetten, described by one of Laurens' correspondents as "a Gentleman belonging to one of the first families at Bern," was a former Prussian army officer who had recently arrived in South Carolina in quest of a major's commission in the Continental Army. Despite Laurens' attempt in this letter to dissuade him from this quest, Bonstetten remained in America and continued his efforts to obtain a Continental commission until at length Congress decided on November 22, 1779, to inform him that it had no need for his services. See *JCC*, 15:1287, 1298; and John Lewis Gervais to Laurens, March 16, 1778, in Raymond Starr, ed., "Letters from John Lewis Gervais to Henry Laurens, 1777–1778," *South Carolina Historical Magazine* 66 (January 1965): 30. The journals refer to Bonstetten as "Bonstellen."

Henry Laurens to John Lewis Gervais

My Dear friend,   3d May 1778

I can, as I ought in good manner & gratitude, acknowledge the receipt of your very obliging Letters of 17th December, 16th Febry, 16th March[1] & a shorter epistle without date, but circumstanced as I am, continually full handed in public duty; which I say always must be done & to which every other consideration must yield, exposed also to incessant interruptions against which it is impossible to parry, it is equally impossible for me to answer in that respectful manner which I would wish to preserve & particularly when I address Gentlemen who are my friends. I will not therefore even unfold your Letters to look for any thing concerning myself or my own affairs, these I leave to providence & you the Instrument of providence, I know you will do as much for me without, as you would with, my fullest directions & probably in the former case much better. There is one subject, which has constantly dwelt in my mind contained in one of your Letters, this I remember without unfolding, because it has made me very unhappy. The circumstance of Mrs. Gervais's loss of health & the State which you describe, is very extraordinary & indicates much trouble to my friend. Either the Dear Lady is no more & you are left with young Children in your hands, or she is still a melancholy spectacle—You Struggling between wishes of affection & Charity for her Life & her Death. I might be very troublesome with words but tis best on such occasions to say little; the mind will have its course & that of a good Man, as you are, will sum up the whole in God's

Will be done. Wisdom will lead you to this point. This uniform submission is the best & safest pilot through the mazes of a Life of vanity & nothingness. If Mrs. Gervais Lives present me in the most affectionate & respectful terms to her, if she is lost, get another good Wife.

Already in the writing the few lines above I have been taken off near an hour by visits of mere compliment & I must expect every moment, fresh breaks. Let me therefore hasten to say something, for upon my honour I was once very near dismissing this Messenger without a line to you.

Upon the arrival of Mr. Chf. Justice Drayton, our public affairs looked extremely gloomy, every thing was dark & dangerous. By his hand I received a permission from the Assembly of South Carolina to retire from Congress. I told that Gentleman at our first interview the true Situation of America as far as circumstances gave me insight & my resolution, since my Countrymen had been pleased to re-elect me, which I esteemed as a desire, at least, that I would continue here, not to turn my back upon danger, that I would stay & take the worst that should happen or till better times, or till Congress should be more respectable in numbers or till South Carolina, my very delinquent Country, should be more amply Represented. The Chief Justice expressed his pleasure, your friend Colo. John Laurens to whom I had previously written on this head, Strongly encouraged me in my determination—& now our faces are a little brightned, I have a new instance for felicitation, "whatever is is best."

One grand subject had employed Congress in a Committee of the whole & in the House near a Month, an establishment of half pay for Officers who should continue in the Army to the end of the War. I had in the Committee Strongly opposed the measure before Mr. D's arrival, if I have time you will receive within the present inclosure the grounds of my objections & nearly in the words I delivered them.[2] That Gentleman on the same side *in Congress* has offered his sentiments with much energy & perspicuity. There was used a good deal of what in my judgement is *foul play* & you will allow there was some *violence* when I tell you the declaration of a Majority Man. "If the majority, said he, would be guided by me, we would take up the matter & carry it through at all events." When the question was put, if I remember right that Majority was 7 to 4 or 6 to 5—a Member or two dropped off & the business has since been Stagnant, auxiliaries are waited for.[3] The Minority proposed to digest a plan & transmit it to the States for Instruction. It was no convincing argument, that "perhaps, or I should say, probably the people will not agree to it"—convincing I mean, of the rectitude of the intended Act, for how dare we establish a pension List, or attempt *any* measure repugnant to the good Will of the people. My reasonings were

POSTSCRIPT to the PENNSYLVANIA GAZETTE of May 2, 1778.

Y O R K - T O W N, MAY 4.

On Saturday laſt SIMEON DEANE, Eſq; arrived at Congreſs, expreſs from the American Plenipotentiaries at the Court of France, and delivered his Diſpatches to his ———— the Preſident.———The important Contents are, by a Correſpondent, thus communicated.

THE news of the defeat and captivity of General Burgoyne were received in France the beginning of December, with as much joy as if a victory by their own troops had been announced. Our Plenipotentiaries took this opportunity again to attract the attention of the Court of France to the object of their negotiation. On the 16th, Monſieur Girard, Royal Syndic of Straſburgh, and Secretary of his Majeſty's Council of State, waited upon our Plenipotentiaries, and informed them, *by order of the King,* " That after long and full conſideration of our affairs and propoſitions in Council, it was decided, and his Majeſty was determined to acknowledge our Independence, and make a Treaty with us of Amity and Commerce. That in this treaty, no advantage would be taken of our preſent ſituation to obtain terms from us, which otherwiſe would not be convenient for us to agree to, his Majeſty deſiring that the treaty, once made, ſhould be durable, and our amity ſubſiſt for ever, which could not be expected, if each nation did not find its intereſt in the continuance as well as in the commencement of it. It was therefore his intention, that the terms of the treaty ſhould be ſuch, as we might be willing to agree to if our ſtate had been long eſtabliſhed, and in the fulneſs of ſtrength and power, and ſuch as we ſhould approve of when that time ſhould come. That his Majeſty was fixed in his determination, not only to acknowledge, but to ſupport our Independence by every means in his power. That in doing this, he might probably be ſoon engaged in war, with all the expences, riſque and damage uſually attending it; yet he ſhould not expect any compenſation from us on that account, nor pretend that he acted wholly for our ſakes, ſince, beſides his real goodwill to us and our cauſe, it was manifeſtly the intereſt of France, that the power of England ſhould be diminiſhed by our ſeparation from it. He ſhould, moreover, not ſo much as inſiſt, that, if he engaged in the war with England on our account, we ſhould not make a ſeparate peace for ourſelves, whenever good and advantageous terms were offered to us. The only condition he ſhould require and rely on would be this, *that we, in no peace to be made with England, ſhould give up our Independence, and return to the obedience of that government.*"

That upon theſe principles, by virtue of full powers by the King of France to Monſieur Girard, Royal Syndic of the City of Straſburgh, and Secretary of his Majeſty's Council of State, dated the 30th of January, 1778, this Miniſter, with our Plenipotentiaries, ſigned at Paris, on the 6th of February, a Treaty of Alliance and Commerce between the Crown of France and the United States of America, almoſt in the very terms in which the American Plenipotentiaries had been inſtructed by Congreſs. In the Treaty of Alliance, the following articles are conſpicuous.

" ARTICLE I. If war ſhould break out between France and Great-Britain, during the continuance of the preſent war between the United States and England, his Majeſty and the United States ſhall make it a common cauſe, and aid each other mutually with their good offices, their councils, and their forces, according to the exigence of conjunctures, as becomes good and faithful allies."

" ARTICLE II. The eſſential and *direct* end of the preſent defenſive alliance is, to maintain effectually *the Liberty, Sovereignty and Independence, abſolute and unlimited,* of the ſaid United States, as well in matters of government as of commerce."

" ARTICLE VI. The Moſt Chriſtian King renounces for ever the poſſeſſion of the Iſland of Bermuda, as well

as of any part of the continent of North-America, which before the treaty of Paris in 1763, or in virtue of that treaty, were acknowledged to belong to the Crown of Great-Britain, or to the United States, heretofore called Britiſh Colonies, or which *are at this time, or have lately been,* under the power of the King and Crown of Great-Britain."

The Treaty of Commerce ſtands upon the broad baſis of equality; and, conſidering the eſtabliſhed great power of France, and the infancy of the United States, is an act without parallel. In a word, the ſentiments delivered on the 16th of December by Monſ. Girard, by order of the King of France, are ſentiments rarely entertained by Princes, and which, together with theſe equal treaties, muſt rank him, not only among the greateſt Monarchs of France, but in hiſtory.

The Independence of America is a favourite object with all thoſe powers of Europe, who entertain commercial views.---With reſpect to the acknowledgment of our Independence, they have waited the example of France, and will now be determined in our favour by her conduct. The Emperor, Spain and Pruſſia are determined to ſupport us. On the 6th of November laſt the Pruſſian Miniſter wrote in the following terms to one of our Plenipotentiaries, " As to the reinforcements of troops which Great-Britain may receive from other powers of Europe for the next campaign, I can aſſure you, Sir, that your Nation has nothing to fear from Ruſſia or Denmark; and that even Germany will not furniſh but ſome hundred men which the Duke of Brunſwick, the Landgrave of Heſſe, and the Margrave of Anſpach, in conformity to their treaties, cannot but ſend annually, to recruit the troops which thoſe Princes hold in America in the pay of England. It is with ſincere ſatisfaction that I give you this agreeable information."---The King of Pruſſia would not allow the troops of Heſſe and Hanau, in Britiſh pay, to paſs through his dominions,----he has promiſed to be the ſecond Power in Europe to acknowledge the Independence of America.

The American priſoners in England were treated with ſuch inhumanity, as induced our Plenipotentiaries to write to Lord North on the ſubject; and to employ a gentleman of rank in London to relieve their diſtreſſes. The Britiſh government thereupon relaxed their ſeverities. The friends of America in London called a meeting on the 24th of December, 1777, to collect ſubſcriptions for the relief of American priſoners, and on the 5th of January they collected £ 2677 : 8 : 6 ſterling for that purpoſe. Among the ſubſcribers ſtand the names of Marquis of Rockingham, Marquis of Granby, Earl Shelburne, Earl Abingdon, Lord Cholmondely, Viſcount Middleton, Viſcounteſs Middleton, Sir George Saville, Hon. Thomas Townſhend, Hon. Thomas Townſhend, junior, Hon. Thomas Walpole, beſides many Aldermen and Gentlemen of the firſt diſtinction. Our Plenipotentiaries aſſure us that Britain, failing in this campaign, cannot poſſibly make another in America, ſo low are her finances reduced, ſo ruined is her credit abroad, and ſo difficult is it for her to procure men at home. That the greateſt preparations of war were making in all parts of France. That near 50,000 French troops were actually marched into Normandy and Brittany; and that the navy of France and Spain now conſiſted of 270 ſail ready for ſea.

Theſe important advices were brought over in Le Senſible, Monſ. Marignie, Commander, a Royal Frigate of France, of 28 twelve-pounders and 300 men. She left Breſt on the 8th of March, and after a paſſage of 35 days arrived at Caſco-Bay, from whence ſhe ſailed on her return, after two days ſtay to take in water.

Printed by HALL and SELLERS.

Franco-American Treaties of Alliance and Commerce

grounded upon the unconstitutionality, & the danger & the inadequateness of the remedy to the necessity complained of but you will hear more of it by & by.

For the News of the day, I beg leave to refer you to several papers which will accompany this & to my Letter to His Excellency the President,[4] I have referred that Gentleman for an account of the Randolph to a New York paper which I had intended to send you but some freind has kindly Slipped it off my Table.

I must not content myself with referring you to the print for an account of the Treaty between the Court of Versailles & the American Union. I must add my most hearty congratulations upon the promising event. I will not say the Treaty, specious & engaging as it appears, is altogether unexceptionable—but all circumstances considered 'tis very well. I am indebted to Mr. Chief Justice for the compilations in this Room to day—'tis a very good abstract.[5] The whole Treaty, a Secret Article excepted,[6] will be ratified & published very speedily.

Some people who are more Sanguine & more elate than I am talk of moving to Philadelphia. In adversity I am not accustomed to sink, in prosperity it becomes us to pause & be wary.

I intend by this opportunity to pay my respects to Monsr. le Baron de Bonstettin whose Letter lies before me in a pile which I shall never be able to reduce, if I addict myself to being so very prolix as I am in the present Case. Excuse me & beleive me to be with the warmest wishes for the happiness of your self & family.[7]

P.S. I pray you send some of the spare papers of News to Colonel Hammond with my Compliments.

I am very angry with Mr. Chf. Justice for an advantage he has taken of me, in Exelencising the President.

LB (ScHi).

[1] The last two of these letters are in Raymond Starr, ed., "Letters from John Lewis Gervais to Henry Laurens, 1777–78," *South Carolina Historical Magazine* 6 (January 1965): 23–28.

[2] This enclosure has not been found, but see also Laurens' Notes on Half Pay, April 17–21, 1778.

[3] It is not clear to which of the several April roll call votes on half pay Laurens is referring here.

[4] See Laurens to Rawlins Lowndes, May 1, 1778.

[5] Laurens is undoubtedly referring to the May 4 Hall and Sellers broadside announcing the signing of the treaties of alliance and commerce with France (see illustration). This broadside, which bears the heading "Postscript to the Pennsylvania Gazette of May 2, 1778," is a compilation of intelligence from, among other sources, the following letters from Paris: Arthur Lee to the Committee for Foreign Affairs, November 27; William Lee to Charles Thomson, December 18; Commissioners at Paris to the Committee for Foreign Affairs, December 18, 1777, February 16, 1778; and Ralph Izard to Laurens, February 16, 1778. See Wharton, *Diplomatic Correspondence,* 2:429–31, 452–55, 495–501. A number of delegates were offended by the failure of Laurens and Drayton to obtain congressional approval for pub-

lishing this broadside. See Charles Carroll of Carrollton to Charles Carroll, Sr., May 4; and Laurens' letters to William Smith and to Washington, May 5, 1778.

[6] The secret article dealt with the contingency of Spain's accession to the Franco-American alliance. *JCC*, 11:454–55.

[7] Laurens noted in his private letter book that on May 4 he wrote Gervais "A short Letter recommending Mr. Curson." Laurens Papers, ScHi. The letter itself has not been found.

Henry Laurens to Baron de Kalb

Dear General   3d May 1778.

The arrival of Mr. Simeon Deane at York Town & the Intelligence which he imported were circumstances more agreeable than an account of landing even the Manchester Volunteers would have been.

The Act of Congress of the 22d April Subjoined to Lord North's Letter &c shews the firmness of the people on this Side & will mark out a new departure for the British Commissioners arrive when they may.

If France shall succeed in her vision of seperating America from Great Britain without involving herself in a Long War & 'tis possible by the aid of Allies she may do so, the stroke of politics will blaze in history.

Inclosed Sir you will find a compilation of the Intelligence we have received, tis possible I mean probable the treaty will be ratified in a few days. The Inclosed paper will answer your enquiry concerning the frigate.

I have the honour to be[1]

LB (ScHi).

[1] This day Laurens also wrote a brief letter to Joseph Kershaw of Camden, S.C., acknowledging receipt of a letter from Kershaw "concerning the Robberies which the Waggoner is said to have committed on Baron de Kalbs Trunks." Laurens Papers, ScHi.

Henry Laurens to the Marquis de Lafayette

Sir,   3d May 1778

I had the honour of addressing a few apologetic lines to Your Excellency the 27th April & was exceedingly mortified when I learned that Monsieur Your Excellency's Valet had left York without my knowledge. I should certainly have repeated my respects by his hand. Let me at the same time confess I had not intended to have troubled Your Excellency this Morning, if I had not been called upon by the pleasure of forwarding with all possible dispatch four Letters received at 10 oClock last Night from France. The largest of these appears to have been made free with on the Road but whether the fact be so or not is uncertain, all the Letters having been carelessly sent 400 Miles on Horse back in a Canvas Bag were much rubb'd & some of them without Covers, the Letter I allude to was nearly in that condition when I joined the fractured parts by a bit of Wax.

I have before me Your Excellencys favor of the 26th April,[1] to which I must particularly reply & in such manner as I trust will be satisfactory to Your Excellency.

'Tis true I had not quite forgot the Money which I had the honour of advancing & for a reason of some weight, my shattered fortunes will keep me in remembrance of events which in these hard days are important. But no anxiety dwelt in my breast concerning the time or the manner in which a reimbursement was to be made. Let these be as shall be most convenient to your self in Bills of Exchange or simple paper Dollars. I neither take nor attempt advantages of this nature when I advanced the Money we are speaking of, it was done as a convenience to the Marquis delafayette to whom as an American I hold myself indebted for all the conveniences & all the services, & all the respects & devoirs & more than all, in my power. Hence Dear Marquis order the Money to be repaid as you please, but yet I wish to be near Your Excellency for half an hour on this same Money-score, which is not so well understood by every Man at one Age as at another & there are in the World who deem it legal prize to convert a little of the Cash of a Rich Young Nobleman to their own use. Hints of this kind are better to be known than talked of & I know my Dear Sir you will receive this as it is intended.

Your Excellency's Accounts for Money advanced for public service are so exceedingly clever as to convince me they are not the operation of a person who had seen above seven years transaction in a Merchants Counting House, in a word I do not know what to make of them but I will catch half an hour one day this Week & attempt some arrangement.

Our Courier from France left that Kingdom the 8th March, he says every face & every thing from Paris to Brest indicated an immediate War with England.

If your Excellency learns from the dispatches which I have now the honor of transmitting any thing more Interesting than the signing of Treaties of Alliance & Commerce at Versailles between that Court & the United States of America a communication of such intimations as are proper will be extremely acceptable.

There is somewhere afloat between France & this Country a squadron of 4 64, 4 28 Gun ships & several Armed American Vessels convoying divers ships laden with Clothing, Warlike Stores &ca &ca for

American service. I hope we shall soon hear of their arrival at Boston or Portsmouth.

Permit me Noble Marquis to repeat that I continue to be with the highest Esteem & Regard

LB (ScHi).
¹ Lafayette's letter is in Lafayette, *Papers* (Idzerda), 2:39.

Henry Laurens to the Marquis de Lafayette

Sir,   3d May 1778.
An hour after I had dispatched my trouble of this Mornings date by McClosky I was honoured with both your favors of the 1st Inst.¹

Your Excellency will perceive from the former Epistle as well as by the inclosed compilation which I have taken some pains to procure, that I am not quite unfeeling to the good News from the other side the Atlantic.

Let other people fire feu de joy,² I rejoice as heartily as any of them & drudge on, here have I been sitting from sun rise this Morning till now past 11 oClock at Night, except when Miss Kitty came in about half an hour ago, I rose to tell her she was very pretty & to give the best assurance in my power of my sincerity.

Dear Marquis your Trunks & every of your Commands are welcome to me, but I have not seen your Trunks.

Monsieur Francy asked me some questions to day about Bills of Exchange which he is to receive from Marquis delafayette. I could only say "whatever you promised & engaged to do, comply with, there is no danger in this mode of proceeding." He was not very explicit & I could not form opinions without knowing both sides of the question.

Dear Sir I must beg leave to wish your Excellency good Night, Major Brice has promised to call on me very early & to be in Camp tomorrow Night, if he does not appear at 6 oClock I'll send for him. If these papers are good for any thing the sooner they get to the Army & into the Enemy's Army too, the better. I have the honour to be

[*P.S.*] What would your Excellency have me to do respecting Monsr. Capitaine, he intimates that he is going on some surveying & Engineering work on the Susquehana.

LB (ScHi).
¹ Lafayette's May 1 letters to Laurens are in Lafayette, *Papers* (Idzerda), 2:40–43.
² In one of the May 1 letters cited above, Lafayette had expressed the wish that "a grand, noisy *feu de joy* will be ordered" to celebrate the French alliance. Ibid.,

p. 41. For a discussion of the ceremonies celebrating the alliance that were conducted under Washington's auspices and in Lafayette's presence at Valley Forge
on May 6, see Charles Royster, *A Revolutionary People at War: The Continental
Army and American Character, 1775–1783* (Chapel Hill: University of North
Carolina Press, 1979), pp. 250–54.

Henry Laurens to John Laurens

My Dear Son,   York Town 3d May 1778
    You will receive under this Cover a Letter the Contents of which
so far as is proper I long to know, because I have received nothing
from my old friend Mr. Manning nor my Brother nor yours.
    You will learn at Head Quarters the Contents of a Letter which
gives the great lines of our Treaty with France. There is an exceptionable article or two which might not have been, if Doctor F. had been
as extensively knowing in Commerce a very important knowledge to
a Commercial Nation, as he is in some other matters for which he is
universally celebrated.[1] Mr Izard writes to me very long Letters &
marks out unhappy bickerings Franklin & Deane Vs. Lee & Izard[2]—
the Letters long & I have not even time to attempt to read them this
morning. I had a strong inclination as they seem to contain much
matter to have sent them to your General but this would not be so
proper before I have perused the whole Contents.
    I observe in one part he writes the King of Prussia has promised
to be second in declaring our Independence.[3] Poor Old England, she
is said to be in great distress & I beleive it.
    Tell me what effect this intelligence has at Camp. My Dear Son I
pray God preserve you.   Henry Laurens

RC (MHi: William Gilmore Simms Collection deposit, 1973).
    [1] For the objectionable 11th and 12th articles of the treaty of commerce with
France to which Laurens is referring, see Committee for Foreign Affairs to the
Commissioners at Paris, May 14, 1778, note 2.
    [2] See, for example, Izard's February 16 letter to Laurens in Wharton, *Diplomatic
Correspondence*, 2:497–501.
    [3] Although in December 1777 Frederick the Great's foreign minister did indeed
inform the American agent in Berlin, William Lee, that Prussia would recognize
American independence if France took the lead, the Prussian monarch was unable
to keep this promise because the outbreak of the War for the Bavarian Succession
in 1778 made it imperative for him to maintain friendly relations with England,
a nation he otherwise detested. The United States and Prussia did not enter into
diplomatic relations until 1783. See Hans Karl Gunther, "Frederick the Great,
the Bavarian War of Succession and the American War of Independence,"
Duquesne Review 16 (Spring 1971): 59–74.

Henry Laurens to John Laurens

York Town, 3 May 1778 very near the 4th. From 5 A.M. to 12 Mid N. makes 19 hours—deduct ½ at Breakfast. 1 at dinner—1½ or 2 visits—16 hours writing would make some younger people weary.

My Dear sir.

I writ to you this Morning by McKlosky, being of opinion that a general Account tolerably well digested of our recent intelligence from France would be acceptable & might be made useful. I intreated Mr Drayton to compile for me the inclosed. If it be in earnest the French will consent to our making an advantageous Peace with Britain, that Court has no wish to go to War & will not, but in the last necessity, should she succeed in this coup de politique—seperated America from Great Britain, humbled the latter, extended her own commerce at the expence of their folly & keep the King's Peace too, History will say Lewis 16th played his Cards with Judgement—a midnight part of my [dull?] imagination. Adieu My Dear Son,

Henry Laurens

[*P.S.*] Now to Bed.

RC (MHi: William Gilmore Simms Collection deposit, 1973).

Henry Laurens to William Lux

Sir,[1]   3d May 1778.

I thank you for your favor of the 1t Inst. which came to me in Congress late last Night by Mr. Hanson to whom I have ordered Ten pounds to be paid for his services.

You will be soon fully informed of the Treaties of Alliance & Commerce between the Court of Versailles & the United States of America. Copy a Letter which I here inclose will in the mean time give the great outlines.[2] I have the honour to be &ca.

LB (DNA: PCC, item 13). Addressed: "Wm. Lux Esquire, Baltimore."

[1] William Lux, the Continental prize agent in Maryland, died only a week after this letter was written. See *JCC,* 4:301; and *Pennsylvania Packet and General Advertiser,* May 23, 1778.

[2] The enclosure was a copy of the February 8 letter from the commissioners at Paris to Laurens announcing the conclusion of the Franco-American treaties of alliance and commerce. Lux had that letter as well as the last paragraph of Laurens' letter printed as a broadside in Baltimore on May 4. Evans, *Am. Bibliography,* no. 16111.

Henry Laurens to Baron Steuben

Dear sir,   York Town, 3 May 1778
   I take the liberty of Inclosing an Abstract of the recent Intelligence
from France.
   If Louis 16th should succeed in humbling the Power of an haughty
Enemy, extend his own Commerce, establish a New World & spill
none or but little Blood, his Name will pass through posterity to the
end of history—the freind of Mankind.
   I have the honor to be, With very great Regard, Sir, Your Excellency's Obedient humble servt.   Henry Laurens

RC (NHi).

Henry Laurens to George Washington

Sir.   York Town 3d May 1778.
   My last trouble to Your Excellency was dated the 30th Ulto. by
Ross.
   The present will cover an Act of that date for ascertaining the
Rank & Pay annexed to Brevet Commissions. Whether this is, or is
not intended to have a retrospective effect, I think is not clearly ex-
pressed by the Letter, & as I apprehend such operation may in many
Instances give Umbrage I shall embrace the first proper opportunity
for obtaining an explanation of the Act or information to my own
understanding.[1]
   I dispatch this Messenger principally to inform Your Excellency of
an event the knowledge of which may nevertheless very probably have
reached Camp before this can arrive there, as our Messenger from
France Mr. Simeon Dean had spoken every where on his Journey to
York of the Treaties between the Court of Versailles & the United
States of America which were executed on the 6th of February 1778.
These were read in Congress late last Evening & will probably be
ratified & published in the course of the present Week, except a Secret
Article which it is also probable is very well known abroad. Be this
as it may I view the Treaties of Alliance & Commerce, although not
free from exception, as circumstances of advantage to these United
States & which afford a bottom for vast improvements. I beg leave
therefore to congratulate with Your Excellency & with every friend
to the great American Cause. I shall move Congress tomorrow to
order duplicates of the Treaties to be immediately transmitted to
Your Excellency. In the mean time this of a Letter from Doctor
Franklin & Mr. Deane which will go enclosed will communicate the
great outlines.

I have the honor to be, With the highest Esteem & Regard, Sir, Your obliged & obedt. servant,

Henry Laurens, President of Congress

RC (DLC).
[1] See *JCC*, 10:410. Washington expressed no concern about possible ambiguities in this "Act" in his May 12 response to Laurens' letter. Washington, *Writings* (Fitzpatrick), 11:379–81. See also ibid., pp. 477–78.

Henry Laurens to George Washington

Sir,   York Town 3d May 1778

Soon after I had dispatched my Letter of this Morning by Mc-Klosky, the Secretary sent in the Inclosed Act of Congress dated 2d Inst. for raising two Regiments for the protection of the Western frontier & for authorizing your Excellency to appoint a proper Officer to the Command of Fort Pitt. A Copy of the Letter mentioned in this Act will also be inclosed.[1]

I likewise transmit about 100 Copies of an abstract account of intelligence lately received from France which I have by the aid of Mr. Cheif Justice Drayton had printed to day from an opinion that such an account will be acceptable in the Army, & not unuseful in the City.

I have requested Major Brice who is so obliging as to take the charge of these to receive from Mr. Bailey printer at Lancaster 500 Copies of the Address to foreign Officers & Soldiers printed in the German Tongue which he has promised to deliver to Your Excellency.

I have the honor to be, With the highest Esteem and Regard, Sir, Your Excellency's Most obedient & Most humble servant.

Henry Laurens, President of Congress.

RC (DLC).
[1] See *JCC*, 11:416–17; and Laurens to the Commissioners at Fort Pitt, April 9, 1778, note 1. Laurens also sent copies of the May 2 resolves on western frontier defense and a May 1 resolve on exemptions from militia service to President Thomas Wharton of Pennsylvania on May 4 and to Gov. Patrick Henry of Virginia on May 5. See PCC, item 13, fols. 293–94; and *JCC*, 10:412.

Richard Henry Lee to Thomas Jefferson

Dear Sir   York 3d. May 1778

Having detained the Express that he might carry you the news that we heard was on its way from France, I am furnished with an opportunity of congratulating you on the important event of a Treaty of

Commerce, and one of Alliance and Amity, having been signed at Paris on the 6th of February last, between France and these United States. Having been as particular as we could on this subject in the Delegates letter to the Governor, I must beg leave to refer you to that for further information, being compelled to shortness here as the Express waits. Great Britain has now two Cards to play but which she will choose we cannot tell, altho we certainly ought in wisdom to be prepared for the worst. She may either acknowledge the Independency of America and make a Treaty of Commerce with her and thus be at peace with us and with all the World; or she may submit to the uninterrupted progress of French commerce to avoid a war with that Power and yet push her whole force against us this Campaign and thereby injure us extremely if we are not prepared with a strong force to prevent it. She has now at Philadelphia 12,000 Veteran Troops, and may possibly collect and send over 8000 more for a last effort. This consideration points out the necessity of having a strong Army immediately. I do sincerely hope that our Assembly will vigorously and early take up this consideration, because I am sure that their last plan will not procure our quota by a considerable number.

I am dear Sir most affection[ately,]   Richard Henry Lee

RC (DLC). Jefferson, *Papers* (Boyd), 2:176–77.

James Lovell to Arthur Lee

Dear Sir   York Town May 3d. 1778

Your Favour of Novr. 24 was Yesterday delivered to me; and I feel myself greatly obliged by the affectionate and honorary Terms in which you speak of my Sufferings, my regained Liberty and my Engagement in the Service of my Country.

In the month of October 1775 I used the Freedom of writing to you from Boston Prison by a Mr. William Powel who had also in Charge some Papers to enable you to stigmatize the mean Cruelties of Gage who was then quitting his Command. But the Papers which I afterwards sent to you from Halifax Jail by an amiable Lady afforded proofs of scientific Barbarity in Howe which tended to obliterate the Memory of what I had endured under his Predecessor. I had the Imagination, at that Time, of pursuing those Men personally to Europe, but when I heard my Countrymen had wisely declared Independency, I felt myself instantly repaid for all my Losses & bodily Injuries. I will not endeavour to cons[. . .] that I am governed, at this Day, by [. . .] Motives of the most laudible Patriotism. I am not anxious to disavow a Degree of the Spirit of Retaliation which our Enemies seem to have been industrious to excite in us. It would be false affectation of universal Benevolence to say I lament the present Disgrace of Britain. Whether she mends upon it or not, I must rejoice at it, though upon different Principles.

As your worthy Brothers will be particular to you in Addition to public Letters, I will only add my Congratulations upon the present Alliance with France, and close by assuring you of my most sincere Wishes for your personal Felicity, being, Sir, your obliged, humble Servant,   James Lovell

RC (MH–H).
  ¹ Lee's November 24, 1777, letter has not been found, but for his July 28, 1778, response to Lovell, see Richard Henry Lee, *Life of Arthur Lee, LL.D.* 2 vols. (Boston: Wells and Lilly, 1829), 2:143.

James Lovell to the Massachusetts Council

Sir   York Town May 3d. 1778.
After being almost a compleat year without a packet from our Commissioners in France, we had yesterday the pleasure of receiving a most important one, Extracts of which I do myself the honour of inclosing to your Discretion.

The letters of Sepr. Octr & November, contained information which, comparatively, would not now be interesting to the Honble Council; you will be pleased therefore to excuse, to my present great official hurry, my omitting extracts of those dates.

I have the honour to be, Sir, your most obedient Servant,
                                                               James Lovell

P.S. 4th May. Pardon my having mentioned your *Discretion*; the paper No. 4 will prove that I did it with an ill grace from *York Town*.

The Treaties are ratified in whole.¹

RC (M–Ar). Addressed: "Honble President of the Council, Massachusetts Bay."
  ¹ See *JCC*, 11:457.

Gouverneur Morris to John Jay

Dear Jay,   York Town 3d May 1778.
I shall plague you with very few Words. I congratulate you on our Alliance with France; for Particulars I refer you to our Friend Robert. I enclose you a News Paper containing a Report I drew on North's Bills which were sent us by the Genl.¹ I have marked in the Margin two Clauses inserted by the House. You may find perhaps some Difficulty to discover how they shew the Wickedness or Insin-

cerity of the Enemy. The following Clause (the Reason of which you will see) was struck out. "Your Committee &ca that in the present Conjuncture of Affairs when the unalienable Rights of human Nature may probably become the Subject of Negotiation the Wisdom of America should be as far as possible collected and therefore that the States be called upon to send a full and adequate Representation to Congress upon the present *special Occasion*."

Sundry smaller Alterations were made as is the Case in Matrimony for better for worse. We have recommended an Act of Grace with Exceptions.[2] How to make these Exceptions will be a nice Card if Gentlemen have *particular* Friends in the Legislature. A Word to the Wise. I do not chuse to be explicit but I shall set some Sums to our numerical Correspondent when I have time &ca.

Love to Sally. Adieu. Yours,   Gouvr Morris

RC (Windsor Castle: Royal Archives).

[1] The "Report" in question was Congress' April 22 reply to Lord North's conciliatory proposals. *JCC*, 10:374–80. In the absence of the original manuscript report, it is impossible to identify the "two Clauses" added by Congress. But see Jay, *Papers* (Morris), 1:482.

[2] On April 23 Congress urged the states to consider offering pardons to loyalists who repented of aiding or abetting "the British forces in America." *JCC*, 10:381–82.

Gouverneur Morris to Robert R. Livingston

Dear Livingston,   York Town in Pensilvania 3d May 1778

If you have not received Letters from me it is not my Fault for I have written many to you, but from your long very long silence I conclude that something prevents me the very great Pleasure I feel in Hearing from you and yours something which I know not but which I will not for your sake as well as my own suppose to be any Neglect or Forgetfulness for I am determined to beleive that the Friendship which exists between us is built upon that Foundation which the Incidents of Time and Space will neither alter, diminish or take away. What Situation your Politicks are in I will not even pretend to know. For this I know full well that I can hear Nothing so particular as to ground a Judgment on. Generally let me say from what I did hear that things have not gone so well as could be wished. I almost am desirous of being with you. My Heart says yes but in Times and Situations like the present it is not a small Misfortune that the Language of the Heart is not to be attended to. Could I have been of Use in your Legislature? Your Politeness, your Amity will say yes and if you ask whether I am of Use where I am perhaps my Vanity will make the same Answer. I beleive all is right but you know I am quite a *Candid*. Let what will happen the ships Crew must remember not without Gratitude those who threw themselves on Board in the Hour of Distress and saved her from the Storm at the generous Risque of all that this World counts valuable. This is my firm Opinion and being so I cannot but beleive that whatever Men may prevail at a particular Instant in the Flow of Time and however weak, wicked or despicable their Measures my Fellow Citizens will always pay to my Friends that Attention & Respect which are due to their Abilities, their Virtues and the splendid, the essential Services they have rendered to the Republic. Let me intreat you to make my sincere Love & Respects to all your Family and gratulate with the Warmth of Tenderness upon the approaching Prospect of *Post Imbres Sol;* If you see Duane remember me to him. Have his services been properly noticed? Or hath the Council of Appointment neglected him. I suppose they have because if it is lawful and right to judge of Conduct from Character they have done those things which they ought not to have done and have left undone those things which they ought to have done. When you see or write to Schuyler assure him of my Attention to his Interests. I have written to Jay fully upon that Subject lately and therefore will avoid Repetitions. To him, to you and to our worthy Governor I have recommended *Gates*.[1] He has sense enough to see that he hath made some wrong Steps and tho I will not promise his Amendment as a Man I think I can venture to say that as a Politican he will not differ with the State who may afford him such essential Aid or do him so irreparable Mischief as ours in his present Situation. At the same Time my Love of the public leads me to desire that he may fall into good Hands and in such have I put him. If therefore he doth not work well Remember you my Friends are answerable for the Consequences. The little Incursion made on our Northern Country I do not conceive to be of such Importance as to demand a very serious Notice. My Countrymen will I hope agree with me in Opinion that while the Enemy are drawing all the Forces in their Power to Philadelphia it behoves us in the weak divided Situation of Pensilvania and the harrassed & exhausted State of New Jersey to draw thither so respectable a Force that we may meet the Enemy well prepared to answer on the great Theatre of War. It is there and there only that they can make such Propositions as we shall attend to. For the Sentiments of Congress on the Subject of Treaty I enclose you the York Paper of the 24th April. If I can lay my Hands on a Lancaster Gazette you shall have the newer news contained in it. One more Effort my Friend and we are free.

Yesterday Afternoon Mr. Deane Brother of Silas Deane, Esqr. arrived here. He brought with him a Variety of public Dispatches which were the more agreeable as nearly one Year had elapsed since we had received any authentic Intelligence. As you live much to the Eastward of me you doubtless are acquainted with the Manner of his Arrival &ca &ca &ca. I shall therefore mention to you some of those Particulars which I am at Liberty to give to the Curiosity of my Friends and which they cannot learn but from Hence.

Among the Dispatches are two Treaties the one of Alliance the other of Commerce signed at Paris the 6th Feby last between the Count de Vergennes[2] Plenipo. on the Part of his most Christian Majesty and Silas Deane, Doctor Franklin &   Lee Plenipotentiaries on the Part of the United States of America. When these Treaties are formally ratified Copies I take it will be transmitted to the several Governors. At present in Substance:

The first is a Treaty by which France acknowledges and undertakes to maintain our Independence both in Government and Commerce and Guarrantees to us our Possessions together with what we shall hold on the Continent (or Bermudas) at the End of the War Ceding to us all her Titles & Claims to every Part of the Continent of America & its Apendages reserving only her Fishing Islands & such Ports as in Case of War she may take from Britain in Newfoundland. And America guarantees to France her present Possessions in the Islands with such as in Case of War she may take from Great Britain. &ca. &ca. &ca.

The second is a treaty of Commerce upon broad, equal, just Principles. An Enumeration of Particulars would fatigue us both, but both the Treaties are upon Principles of the most perfect Equality and such as the greatest Friend to America would have framed had the important Word *Louis* been put in his Hands at the Bottom of a blank Paper.

The Conduct of the French Court hath been marked by Wisdom and Magnanimity. The Monarch declared that it was his Intention to treat with America as an Equal without Regard to her Weakness or his own Strength but to frame such Treaties as the united States would have entered into when in Possession of that Power which they must arrive at in Consequence of their Independence because he wished that the Alliance might be perpetual.

This will be followed by similar Proceedings throughout Europe where we can count upon Spain, Austria & Prussia as our Friends and Allies. The two latter have rendered us essential Services already and so indeed has the former. You may assure all good Whigs from the best Authority that no Russians, Danes or Swedes will (or shall) come to America. That after the Month of March they will be puzzled to get any more Germans of any Kind. Write the news to our good Domine whom I would write to if I could see a Probability of his getting my Letter.

Should you see poor Smith assure him of my sincere Regret that he hath made the unhappy Choice of being a Subject to the King of

Great Britain instead of to the State of New York.[3] Shake Walter
Livingston by the Hand for me most cordially and tell him to bury
a Bottle of his Falemian with mystic Rites For that I intend when the
Storm abates a little more to come and make a Riot. Go to the old
Gentleman and make him very happy by the Assurance that the
British Ministers equally proud & abject have courted our Ambassa-
dors to save their Nation from the impending Ruin.

I am at the Bottom of my Paper.

Adieu, Adieu. Remember me, yours,   Gouvr Morris

P.S. Without the Knowledge of our alliance with France stocks in
Engld. were down 10 (I think 12 per Cent). At Lancaster upon the
Arrival of Mr. Deane an Article fell from 20/ per lb to 12/6—which
is near 40 per cent. Gold fell from 13 to 5—in the City of Phila. it
fell from 5 to 3.

RC (NHi).
[1] See Morris to John Jay, April 28; and New York Delegates to George Clinton,
April 30, 1778.
[2] In reality, Conrad Alexandre Gérard, not Vergennes, signed the treaties of
alliance and commerce on behalf of the French government. *JCC*, 11:444, 453.
[3] Although William Smith, Jr., the celebrated historian of colonial New York,
had thus far refused to renounce the king or swear allegiance to the state government, it was not until August 1778 that he emerged from retirement in the
country and moved to New York City openly to embrace the British cause. See
L. F. S. Upton, *The Loyal Whig: William Smith of New York & Quebec* (Toronto:
University of Toronto Press, 1969), pp. 103–9.

Jonathan Bayard Smith to Thomas Wharton

York Town May 3d. 1778

I have the pleasure of advising you that yesterday brought us dispatches from our agents in Europe, of a most important and favourable nature to these states. I will not trouble your Excellency with
minute circmstances; But think it my duty to advise you that the
King of France by powers dated January 30th to his secretary of state
did on February the 6th by the said secretary enter into one treaty of
perpetual peace and amity and trade with these United states: And
on the same day into another treaty of commerce with said states.
For the present I beg leave to refer you to the following extract of a
letter from Doctor Franklin and his colleagues as sufficiently indicita-
tive of the spirit of said treaties.[1]

"Mr. Gerrard one of the secretarys came yesterday to inform us by
order of the King that after long and full consideration of our affairs
and propositions in Council, it was decided and his Majesty was determined to acknowledge our independence and make a treaty with us

of amity and commerce. That in this treaty no advantage would be taken of our present situation to obtain terms from us which otherwise would not be convenient for us to agree to, his Majesty desiring that the treaty once made should be durable, and our amity subsist for ever, which could not be expected if each nation did not find its interest in the continuance, as well as in the commencement of it. It was therefore his intention that the terms of the treaty should be such as we might be willing to agree to, if our state had been long since established, and in the fulness of strength and power, and such as we shall approve of when this time shall come. That his majesty was fixed in his determination not only to acknowledge but to support our independence by every means in his power. That in doing this he might probably be soon engaged in war, yet he should not expect any compensation from us on that account, nor pretend that he acted wholly for our sakes, since beside his real good will for us and our cause, it was manifestly the interest of France that the power of England should be diminished by our separation from it. The only condition he should require and rely on would be this. That we in no peace to be made with England should give up our Independance, and return to the obedience of that Government."

Thus our Commissioners. The treaty is such as might be expected from such established principles. And we may be assured of as determined a spirit in other courts. It now only remains with ourselves to act with spirit.

Tr (PHarH). Author and recipient established from transcriber's note and internal evidence. Transcribed under the heading "Copy of a letter from York Town May 3d. 1778" and followed by the note "Indorsed as from Jona B Smith."
[1] This letter from the commissioners at Paris has not been found.

Virginia Delegates to Patrick Henry

Sir,   York, 3d May 1778.
   Having heared that a Messenger from France was on his way to Congress with important dispatches, we detained the Express who otherwise would have set out yesterday that we might furnish your Excellency with the intelligence he brought. It is with singular pleasure we inform you Sir that this Messenger has brought to Congress authenticated copies of a Treaty of Commerce, and a Treaty of Amity and Alliance signed at Paris on the 6th of February last between France and these United States, and we understand there is abundant reason to suppose that the whole Bourbon family will immediately acceed thereto. The Treaty of Commerce is exactly conformable to our own proposals, and it is upon the most generous and

equal principles. The Treaty of Alliance &c is professedly for security of the Sovereignty and absolute Independence of these States both in Government and Trade, and it agrees that if G.B. declares war against France on this account, or causes a war, or attempts to hinder her Commerce, that we shall make a common cause, and join our Arms & Counsels against the common enemy. Each Country guarantees to the other the possessions that they do or may possess at the end of the war. Having heared these Treaties read but once in Congress, we cannot be more particular now. In general we find that his most Christian Majesty has been governed by principles of Magnanimity and true generosity, taking no advantage of our circumstances, but acting as if we were in the plenitude of power and in the greatest security. We are shortly to receive considerable Stores from France that come under a Convoy of a fleet of Men of War. The King of Prussia has actually refused to permit the Hessian and Hannau Troops that England had engaged for America to pass thro his Territories. We congratulate you Sir and our Country on this great and important event, but we beg leave further to observe that it is in our opinion of infinite consequence that the Army should be quickly and powerfully reenforced. Because, if Britain should meanly permit the trade of France to proceed without interruption, and push her whole force against us this Campaign, it might be attended with very pernicious consequences. But with a strong Army, we shall, under God, be perfectly secure, and it will probably compel G.B. to a speedy recognition of our Independence, and thus secure the peace of Europe, with the peace, happiness, and glory of America.

We have the honor to be, with much esteem, Sir your Excellencies most obedient and very humble servants. Richard Henry Lee

P.S. It is very prudently wished by our Commissioners that those of the French nation in our State may be treated with kindness and cordiality.[1]   Francis Lightfoot Lee

John Banister

Thomas Adams

RC (Vi). Written by Richard Henry Lee and signed by Lee, Adams, Banister, and Francis Lightfoot Lee.

[1] The following notes were added below the postscript by Patrick Henry.

"P.S. The postcript not to be printed. P.H."

"N.B. A pen was drawn across the postscript that the printer might not publish in his hand Bill which was deemed improper. P. Henry."

The handbill printed in Williamsburg by Dixon and Hunter containing this delegate letter, without signatures and postscript, is no. B4702 in Roger P. Bristol, *Supplement to Charles Evans' American Bibliography* (Charlottesville: University Press of Virginia, 1970).

Charles Carroll of Carrollton to
Charles Carroll, Sr.

Dear Papa,   Monday P.M. 4th May 1778
I wrote to you yesterday by an Express going to Baltimore Town. In that letter I acquainted you with the arrival of Mr. Simeon Dean from Paris with treaties of Amity, Alliance & Commerce signed by Our Agents the 6th of February & Mr. Gerard Secretary to the King's privy Council. These treaties we this day ratified. They are founded on a generous & true policy.

The articles of information in the printed paper was handed to the press by a member of Congress[1] tho' without the consent of Congress which has given offence; however the information may be relied on in every thing except "that the King of Prussa has promised to be the Second power in Europe to acknowlege the Independance of America." Our Agents write in their official letters that the King of Prussia would open the Port of Embden to us: he is certainly favourably disposed towards us. Mr. Izard, who has been long appointed an Agent at the court of the Grand Duke of Tuscany, writes our President, the information as printed in the handbill. By the inclosed scrap of paper you will see the dates of the Several letters brought by Mr. Dean; the 28 of Febry is the last, on the back of said paper you will find two very material extracts from that letter.[2]

Gen. Heath has recd. from Newport 96 thousand sylver dollars for fuel supplied to Burgoyne's army.

We hourly expect the arrival of a little fleet from France loaded with cloathing & military Stores; they are all armed vessels but one; one of them is stranded at Ocrocock in No. Carolina but the greatest part of the cargo, it is hoped, will be saved. The Capt. writes that this fleet of which he was one left France the 13th of February & was bound for Boston; that in Quiberon Bay they fell in with a French Squadron, who returned our Salute; that this little fleet, consisting of 5 vessels, I think, was convoyed out by 4 French men of war; but I apprehend this convoy will not come all the way with our fleet, so that there is danger of their being intercepted off our coast.

The letters of our General which were published in Pha. & to which you allude in your last, are forged.[3]

I sent you in mine of yesterday a newspaper containing a good deal of interesting intelligence. I hope the Express left my letter with Miss Goddard, as I directed on the back of it.

The words in the printed paper which are underlined are a mistake of the person who sent the intelligence to the Press. If France should not be involved in this war, we may make peace with G B, provided she acknowleges our Independance; for instance, suppose

G B should acknowlege our Independance, & make peace with us, & then a war should break out between France & G B, we are not bound to assist France, & therefore I hope G B will acknowledge our Independance, & on that footing conclude a peace with us, but if France should be engaged in this war in consequence of these treaties we are not to make a separate peace. For notwithstanding Ld North's speech, she finds great difficulty in raising men, & her credit is sinking fast; the legality of raising men by Subscriptions has been questioned in Parliat & in the County of Norfolk (according to the English papers) a remonstrance was preparing against that measure.

The defeat of Burgoyne & the maneuvres of the English Emissaries at Paris who were endeavouring to sound our Agents there to see whether they would listen to accomodation & treaty with England, it is presumed determined the French Ministry to be beforehand with them. I sincerely congratulate you on this important event, which I think puts our Independance beyond a doubt.

It gives me pain to hear that Molly still continues indisposed. God grant her a speedy relief from all her complaints. I flatter myself the approach of Spring will greatly contribute to remove them; my affectionate love to her. Do inform me very circumstantially in yr. letters of her health & of your own, both of which are very dear to me. My love to Mrs. Darnall & the little ones. I am, Yr. affectionate Son,

Ch. Carroll of Carrollton

P.S. I think I have sent you very important news since I came to Congress. Generals Gates & Mifflin are gone to camp to hold with Gen. Washington & the other Major Generals a council of war about the operations of the ensuing campaign.

RC (MdHi).
    [1] Henry Laurens. See Laurens to John Lewis Gervais, May 3, 1778, note 5.
    [2] "The inclosed scrap of paper" contained a list, in the hand of James Lovell, of "Letters recd. May 2d. 1778" from France. These included, from "The Commissioners, BF, SD & AL," letters of September 8, October 7, November 30, December 18, 1777, and February 16, 28, 1778; from Ralph Izard, letters dated October 6 and December 18, 1777; from Arthur Lee, letters of October 6, November 27, and December 8, 1777; and from William Lee, letters of November 24 and December 8, 1777.
    The extract from the commissioners' February 28, 1778, letter written "on the back of said paper" reads: "the preparations of War continue in the Ports with the utmost industry & troops are marching to the Sea coasts, where 3 camps are to be formed. As France is determined to protect her commerce with us, a war is deemed inevitable." To this extract Carroll appended the following note: "N.B. in their letter of the 16th Feby. they Say they had been sounded by emissaries of the British Ministry respecting proposals of a treaty with the Americans."
    [3] Carroll is referring to seven forged letters supposedly written by Washington to members of his family in June and July 1776 that purport to show he secretly opposed American independence. These forgeries, which have been variously attributed to John Randolph or John Vardill, two loyalist refugees living in

London, first appeared in England in 1777 in the form of a pamphlet entitled *Letters from General Washington to several of his Friends in the Year 1776* (London: J. Bew, 1777). In the following year the loyalist printer James Rivington published an edition of this pamphlet under much the same title in New York that was first advertised for sale in Philadelphia in mid-April and is undoubtedly the work Carroll refers to as "published in Pha." See *Pennsylvania Ledger or the Market-Day Philadelphia Advertiser,* April 15, 1778; Washington, *Writings* (Fitzpatrick), 5:126n.56, 35:414–16; Evans, *Am. Bibliography,* no. 15868; and Worthington C. Ford, *The Spurious Letters Attributed to Washington* (Brooklyn: Privately printed, 1889).

Henry Laurens to Francis Bailey

Sir,   4th May 1778
    Yesterday I received your favor of the 1st with the German Copies of addresses &ca. by Ross.[1]
    The Gentleman who bears this, will receive from you the 500 Copies intended for His Excellency General Washington if he can possibly carry them. If he cannot, please to employ a messenger for the purpose & dispatch them without the loss of a moments time. These are badly rubbed, I request you to avoid such damage to the other set by causing better package. Two or four Bundles will be more convenient & safer than one.
    Your specimen of Paper pleases much more than the price—this is beyond any I have yet heard of. I must endeavor to be more frugal in the distribution of public Money. I am &ca.

LB (DNA: PCC, item 13).
    [1] See Laurens' two April 30, 1778, letters to Bailey.

Henry Laurens to Alexander Gillon

Sir,[1]   4th May 1778.
    Your favor of the 4th March reached me, the original about the 14th, Copy on the 21st April. I should have hoped the Commercial Committee had long before that time give you their determination on the proposed plan for importing goods. Why the necessary measures had not been pursued on our part in due time I cannot tell. Probably some delay was occasioned by the lowness of our Treasury, there were calls from every Quarter for Money & every department had suffered exceedingly from want of supplies in due time. But I remember to have heard a Gentleman say who came to Town after you had left us that had he been present the bargain with you should not be concluded. His reason was a failure on your part in a former contract

when you promised to go to Europe in person, & sent an Agent in your place & that the Accounts of that transaction remained unsettled.[2]

This is all I know of the subject. I cannot doubt your having heard fully from the Committee, but my hands are so effectually or perhaps with more propriety, actually, employed in my own duty, that I have not time, nor would it be pleasing to those Gentlemen that I should further interfere than to remind them now & then of the necessity for writing to you. I sincerely wish you success in your maratime engagement; the Noble part which France has taken in our quarrel with Great Britain will smooth your road.

I have the honour to be &ca.

LB (ScHi).
[1] For Gillon's identification, see these *Letters*, 2:254.
[2] In November or December 1777 the Committee of Commerce had concluded a contract with Gillon, stipulating that he was to go to Europe and purchase certain military supplies designated by the committee. Owing to his appointment in February 1778 as commodore of the South Carolina navy, however, Gillon was unable to carry out this contract, and therefore on March 31 Congress resolved that "it would be inexpedient to proceed" with the agreement. See *JCC*, 9:944, 978–80, 1023, 10:294, 298. For Gillon's June 25 response to this letter containing an account of his activities pertaining to the congressional contract, see "Letters from Commodore Alexander Gillon in 1778 and 1779," *South Carolina Historical and Genealogical Magazine* 10 (January 1909): 6–9.

Henry Laurens to Abraham Livingston

Sir,[1]   4th May [1778]

I have supplied the bearer hereof Samuel Cross & taken his Receipts, One Hundred & fifty two Dollars without which he said he could not return to Carolina. Two are for a Cloth to wrap his Letters & preserve them from rubbing which he ought not to be charged with.

This Man has been very long detained yet I am afraid the Board of Commerce have not written by him; I have often urged them, but the Board is crouded with business which I know from circumstances passing through my hands.

I shall dispatch another Messenger in a few days & shall give & repeat timely notice of which the Gentlemen may avail themselves. I have the honor to be

LB (ScHi).
[1] Livingston, a Continental agent at Charleston, S.C., had been appointed in February 1778 one of three attorneys "for claiming the continental share of all prizes libelled in the admiralty court in the State of South Carolina." See *JCC*, 10:114, 311.

Henry Laurens to John Rutledge

Dear Sir,   4th May 1778.

Since my last of the 11th March I have been honoured with your several favors of the 16th Febry & 8 March.

The Account of your resignation gave me inexpressible concern.[1] All your friends, & every Man here, if I may judge from the respectful terms in which you are always spoken of, is your friend, expressed concern, General Lee in particular.

All agree your principle was good—but many say, & among these be pleased to number me & forgive my candor, you ought to have done every thing you did, the last act excepted.

I am exceedingly desirous of transmitting to you much of the minutia of our public affairs but at this time it is impossible, permit me therefore Sir, to refer you to the papers of intelligence which will accompany this. These papers contain subjects of the utmost importance. I have two objections formed in my mind upon the first reading of the Treaty—Bahama unmentioned & a total exemption of duty on French exports from America in return for exemption of Duty on Molasses imported.[2] Possibly at the next reading & upon consideration I may go further—upon the whole however, 'tis very well. In the course of this Week we shall ratify.

If Louis 16th shall have humbled an imperious & dreaded power—established a new World—extended the Commerce of his own people—obtained means for becoming a great Maratime & all without bloodshed or with very little—his name will be transmitted to posterity with Lustre. I am not without feelings for poor old England.

At the arrival of Mr. Chief Justice Drayton all our affairs were not only gloomy but tottering. I had communicated to a friend in Camp[3] my determination not to turn my back upon distress—this I repeated to the Chief Justice. Therefore after thanking you Sir for the permission which you were pleased to obtain from the House of Assembly for my return, it is necessary to intimate, that for such reasons as appeared to me solid I had determined not to avail myself of the benefit. The public aspect is now somewhat brightened, the approaching season not the most inviting to a Southern Journey, Congress not yet so respectable as it probably will be a Month hence. I have resolved to continue here a little longer.

The British Commissioners are hourly expected. My sentiment is to collect the Wisdom of America to meet them, if a meeting is to be had, not to confine our choice to York Town. On this occasion I have taken the liberty to mention your Name. I find it acceptable & we have only to regret that from the distance a timely attendance will be impracticable.

I wish you Sir every degree of happiness & have the honour to be with the highest Esteem & Regard, Sir, your obedt. & obliged Servt.
P.S. I have hinted to Mr. Drayton a fine stroke which may be made on Bahamas, if we have strength for such an important Coup from So Carolina. He will probably extend his Ideas—time will not allow me to add.

LB (ScHi).
[1] See Laurens to John Laurens, March 29, 1778, note 4.
[2] See Committee for Foreign Affairs to the Commissioners at Paris, May 14, 1778, note 2.
[3] John Laurens.

Richard Henry Lee to John Page

My dear Sir,   York the 4th [May] 1778
    I am greatly obliged by your very kind letter of condolance of the 24th last,[1] and I am to thank you for another of your favors that I found here on my arrival. I beg leave to congratulate you on the very important intelligence that we yesterday conveyed to Government by Express. There appears a magnanimity and wisdom in his most Christian Majesty exemplified in these Treaties with France that does him great honor. It was surely magnanimous not to take advantage of our situation so as to obtain unequal advantage, and it was wise to leave open a door for all the Maritime States (England not excepted) to enter and share the Commerce of N. America. Without this last, the intrigues of G.B. might have combined the other Trading powers with her to distress us and our new Ally. As it is, all will be with us against England because our Commerce is open and profitable to all. If England were wise, she would immediately acknowledge our Independence and make, as France has done, a Treaty with us, which, if agreed to on her part without making war on France, might give peace to the world, and guilty Britain alone suffer for her folly by the loss of N. America. But England is proud, and has long been Mad (I mean since the present accession) in her conduct to No. A. Pursuing her plan, if she meanly submits to the French commerce with us, and pushes all her force against us this Campaign, as I think she will, it may injure us much unless we wisely and timely prepare to resist her greatest efforts by quickly and strongly reenforcing our Army. This done, I am clearly of opinion that G.B. will and must acknowledge our Independence before the close of the year.
    General Lee is hourly expected here in his way from his seat in our Berkeley County to the Army, being certainly and fully exchanged for Gen. Prescot.
    I am, dear Sir, most sincerely and affectionately yours,
                                                        Richard Henry Lee

P.S. The inclosed extracts are of most undoubted authority and I beg you will insist on both our Printers publishing them.[2]

In our dispatches by the Express it was mentioned that Gen. Amherst & Admiral Keppell were arrived at Philadelphia as Commissioners.[3] That Account came direct from Philadelphia, but it has since been contradicted, and therefore please have it contradicted in our papers if such news has got into them.   R.H. Lee

RC (PPRF).

[1] For further details about the death of Lee's brother Thomas Ludwell, see Richard Henry Lee to Arthur Lee, May 12, 1778.

[2] The May 4 Hall and Sellers broadside Lee enclosed was reprinted in the May 15 issue of the *Virginia Gazette* (Dixon & Hunter), along with the Virginia delegates' May 3 letter to Governor Henry and the American commissioners December 8, 1777, letter to the Committee for Foreign Affairs. See also Henry Laurens to John Lewis Gervais, May 3, 1778, note 5.

[3] Richard Henry Lee had reported the rumored arrival of these commissioners in his May 2 letter to Thomas Jefferson, but unfounded reports of their appointment had reached Williamsburg even earlier. In the May 8, 1778, issue of the *Virginia Gazette* (Dixon & Hunter) the following extract was printed under the heading "*Postcript of a letter from* York, *in* Pennsylvania, *dated* April 26." "Since writing the above, Congress is informed by the General, that, from good intelligence from the city, he learns that the Commissioners, consisting of Lord Amherst, Admiral Kepple, and Mr. Murray, formerly Governor of Quebec, are appointed, and are to hold a plenitude of civil and military powers for negociation or war, and their arrival may be shortly expected, as the long delay of the former Commissioners was reprobated by the nation. It is probable, if no negociation or pacification, under the propositions, should take place, these new leaders of the British bands will act with great energy and decision in the field. Should we not determine immediately to augment our army?" See also John Mathews to Thomas Bee, April 26, 1778, note 4.

Thomas Burke to Richard Caswell

Dr Sir   York town May 5th 1778

I never addressed you on any public Subject with more pleasure than I do at present. A Treaty is arrived from France Executed by that power and our Commissioners which explicitly Cedes and Guarantees to the United States their Teritories and acknowledges and guarantees their Independence. The only Conditions required of us is that if France must enter into a war for that purpose we unite our Forces with her against our Common Enemy. But the inclosed handbill[1] will more fully inform you, and I shall without ceremony Congratulate you and my Country on this most Auspicious Event. The wisdom of France appears as conspicuously Superior to that of Britain as her Justice and Magnanimity. France wisely foreseeing that a very close union with America and Exclusive advantages must not only be Irksom to the People to whom it might be immediately disadvantageous but make her self the object of the Jealousy of other Powers has forborn every such requisition, and She indeed requires us to do nothing but follow our own true Interests, and what we had unanimously resolved on in Congress some days previous to our knowing any thing of the Treaty.[2] As you will see by the paper I inclosed you by Mr Harnett England who evidently wished to make us every Concession, in my Opinion even Independance, lost the opportunity of gaining our alliance and Political Confidence by a vain Endeavour of shallow puerile Artifice to cheat us out of Resolutions which we had already so liberally sealed with our blood, and which she might see we were determined to support or Perish.[3]

In short Sir I am unable to express the satisfaction I feel on this Occasion. The Prospect of a free, happy, gallant, flourishing People obtrudes every moment on my Imagination and I enjoy by anticipation the future felicity of my Country.

Having yet heared nothing from you relative to the Delegation for our State, and my time being now completely elapsed I shall set off for home in a few Hours.[4] I know not who Succeeds me, but am happy to consider that they will find our affairs in so prosperous a Situation. Soon as I arrive at home I shall trouble you with a Letter, at present I have time only to add that I am, Dr Sir with the most perfect Esteem and regard your Obed Servt,   Thos Burke

RC (PHi).

[1] See Henry Laurens to John Lewis Gervais, May 3, 1778, note 5.

[2] See Congress' April 22 reply to Lord North's conciliatory proposals in *JCC,* 10:374–80.

[3] During Burke's leave of absence in North Carolina he wrote a letter on related matters to Elbridge Gerry in July 1778 that is worth quoting in part here:

"Ever Since the Treaty with France came to my knowledge I am anticipating Peace and all its prospects and I am anxious to improve them to the utmost. I am persuaded England is not in Condition to carry on war against us and our allies, and must make a peace at all Events, and as our Terms will not be extravagant for I suppose they will be no more than that they shall withdraw their forces, and forego all claims to any part of the Continent and the adjacent Isles Including Bermuda, I think the war cannot long Continue. My mind is full of Ideas of future prosperity, and I am constantly Searching out the probable means for improving and securing our Happiness. A Naval Force alone can secure us from abroad, and a wise distribution of political Power from Oppression or Anarchy at home. A Liberal Extensive and emulating Commerce can alone create a naval force for such only can produce Ships and Seamen, and I hope our Chimerical Jealousies of each other will not Nip this in the bud." Burke to Gerry, [July 1778], Preston Davie Papers, NcU.

[4] Shortly after arriving back in North Carolina, Burke wrote to Robert Morris urging him to support a measure Burke favored but had apparently never brought up in Congress. "I had a design," he wrote Morris, "to purchase for General Gates the farm on which he was encamped near Saratoga, this I thought would be a handsom Compliment to him for the Essential Services he has rendered us, and wnat might become the dignity of Congress to present him with. I beg leave to recommend it to your attention. The gallant Arnold ought also to be handsomly remembered." See Burke to Robert Morris, May 25, 1778, Miscellaneous Manuscripts, N.

John Henry to Thomas Johnson

Dear Sir.   York Town Apl. [*i.e.* May] 5th. 1778.
I acquainted you in my former Letter that the Delegates had obtained from Congress the loan of one hundred thousand Dollars. I expected when I wrote you, that I would have been able to have sent you the Money in a day or two,[1] but the great Demands on the Treasury has prevented me. In the course of this Week you may expect the whole or at least some part of it.

Congress yesterday ratified the Treaties of Alliance and Commerce between France and these states. You will soon have a Copy sent to the state. Mr. Chase writes you fully upon this subject.

I am Sir with great respect yrs,   J Henry Junr.

RC (MdAA). Addressed: "His Excellency Thomas Johnson Esquire, Governor of Maryland." Endorsed by Henry: "To be opened by the Council in the absence of the Governor."

[1] See Charles Carroll of Carrollton to Thomas Johnson, April 27, 1778, note.

Henry Laurens to Richard Caswell

Sir,   5th May [1778]
Permit me to refer your Excellency to my last Letter of the 27th Ulto. by Barry.

This will cover an Act of Congress of the 1st Inst. Recommending an exemption from Militia Duty such persons as are employed in manufacturing Military Stores &ca for the use of the United States.[1]

No account yet of the arrival of the expected British Commissioners. Lord Carlisle, Mr. Pultney & Lord Westcote had among others been nominated. The Treaty of the 6th Febry. must have given a new momentum to British Councils & measures.

I have the honour to be

P.S. Congress this day Ratified the Treaties of Paris—of the 6 Febry, & an accot. by authority will speedily be published.[2]

LB (DNA: PCC, item 13).

[1] See *JCC*, 10:412. Laurens also enclosed copies of this act with brief covering letters that he wrote to Govs. William Livingston of New Jersey on May 4 and Thomas Johnson of Maryland on May 5. See PCC, item 13, fol. 293; and Red Books, MdAA.

[2] Congress resolved to ratify the treaties of alliance and commerce with France on May 4 but did not approve the formal instrument of ratification until the fifth. *JCC*, 11:457–58, 462–63.

Henry Laurens to the Marquis de Lafayette

Dear Marquis   5 May 1778

Permit me to refer your Excellency to what I writ the 3d by Major Brice.

Mr. Chief Justice Drayton will do me the honor to deliver this. Will you do me the Honor Sir, to be acquainted with this Gentleman. He is Learned, sensible & strongly attached to the Interests of America, consequently loves all her friends.

This is the Gentleman who from the Bench had the Wisdom & fortitude to Indict the King & Parliament of Great Britain for invading the Rights & Liberties of these States.[1]

Congress this day Ratified the Treaties of Paris of the 6th Febry. & very speedily an account will be published by authority.

I have the honor to be with the highest Esteem & Regard[2]

LB (ScHi).

[1] See William Henry Drayton, *A Charge, on the Rise of the American Empire, delivered by the Hon. William-Henry Drayton, Esq.; Chief-Justice of South-Carolina: to the Grand Jury for the District of Charlestown* (Charleston: David Bruce, 1776). Evans, *Am. Bibliography*, no. 14741.

[2] Laurens also wrote a letter this day to Matthew Troy of Salisbury, N.C., thanking Troy for the help he had given to Michel Capitaine du Chesnoy, a French officer who had fallen ill in North Carolina shortly after arriving in America with Lafayette in the summer of 1777. Laurens Papers, ScHi.

Henry Laurens to John Laurens

My Dear Son,   5 May 1778.

Let me again intreat you to Interest your self in getting my Chariot from Bringhurst, but I do not mean as much as I want it, to urge you to accomplish the end by irregular unlawful means, I know you will not practice such for Elijate's Chariot—all I mean is to keep the subject in your mind.

Mr. Chief Justice Drayton will tell you everything that is going forward here, I request you to wait upon him to the General, introduce him in the Character of Chief Justice of So Carolina, a Delegate in Congress from that State, & my friend & do me the honor to devote all the time you can spare to his service & conversation. Remember he is the Man who upon the Bench had the Wisdom & fortitude to Indict the King & Parliament of Great Britain for attempting to bind America in all Cases whatsoever & Rob her of her Rights & privileges.

God bless you. I am with an affection which by every Act I endeavor to prove your faithful friend.

[*P.S.*] Did Ross deliver you a packet of Striped White Cotton, what quantity? I think it would be no greater Crime—necessity considered, to get a little good Paper from Sir Wm. Howes Stationary—he is truly Stationer—than it was in David to act the shew Bread.

LB (ScHi).

Henry Laurens to Matthew Locke

Dear Sir,   5th May 1778

I wrote to you a few days since by Collo. Harnet who promised to forward my Letter with Safety & dispatch.[1]

This will cover Intelligence the most important & Interesting to the United States, to which I beg leave to refer you.

Congress this day solemnly Ratified the Treaties of the 6th Febry. & very speedily an Account by authority will be published.

The Treaties had thrown the British Administration & Counsels into the deepest confusion & distress & I suppose had operated to delay the Embarkation of their intended Commissioners, who are not yet arrived.

God grant we may make a wise improvement of the advantages & benefits put into our hands. One essential measure which we ought not to neglect, will be to augment our Army & be ready to hear propositions from Great Britain without any fear of consequences from our refusal to accede to such articles as may appear to be unjust or unreasonable. By such means we shall be able to blunt the edge of the Sword & these Infant States may give peace to Europe in securing it to themselves. My best wishes to Mrs Loke & your whole family.

I am with great regard &ca.

LB (ScHi).
[1] This letter has not been found. Laurens' last extant letter to Locke was written on March 31, more than three weeks before Cornelius Harnett left Congress and returned to North Carolina.

Henry Laurens to William Smith

Dear Sir,   5th May 1778.

The kindness of your favor of the 3d Inst. obliges me very much, I wish for opportunity to make a proper acknowledgement.[1] If I have not mentioned Claret in my late Memorandum & there is of a good quality such as I lately received from Baltimore please to add two Boxes, these contained two dozen each.

The inclosed if it has not or a Copy of it already reached you will give a very fair abstract of the recent intelligence from France. Some Gentlemen have questioned the article of the King of Prussia's promise—the authority is contained in a Letter to me from Mr. Izard 16th Febry. & may be depended on—"the King of Prussia has promised in the most explicit & unambiguous terms that he will be the second power in Europe to declare the Independence of America."

I congratulate with you & every friend to our Cause. Congress Ratified the Treaties this Morning & an Account by authority will soon be published.[2] Among the Commissioners nominated from the British Court are Lord Carlisle, Mr. Pultney & Lord Westcote, but no doubt the Treaties of Paris had given a new momentum to British Councils. Lord Mansfield had actually "with Tears in his Eyes" applied to Lord Camden to interpose as a good Man all his endeavors to save the Nation. Lord Camden replied he had predicted long ago what had come to pass but a deaf Ear had been turned to him. He feared now the Door was shut.

I wish time would permit I would with pleasure tell you many other little anecdotes but you know Sir how I am circumstanced. I am with great Esteem

LB (ScHi).
[1] In a letter dated April 28, Laurens had asked Smith to purchase some cheese, lime juice, sugar, and vinegar on Laurens' private account. Laurens Papers, ScHi.
[2] Laurens noted in his private letter book that on May 9 he sent Smith "an Abstract of Intelligence from Philadelphia & 6 Pensylvania Gazettes containing Act of the Congress of the 6th—Articles of the Treaty." Ibid.

Henry Laurens to Baron Steuben

My Dear Sir,   York Town 5th May 1778.
I did my self the honor of shewing my attention by transmitting under your address two or three days ago, a succinct account of the recent intelligence from France, but I believe I had not time to write any more than a direction. This day Congress Ratified the Treaty of Paris of the 6th February. I should have said the Treaties, for there be three. The Public will speedily be informed by authority.

Congress have Resolved to appoint you & you are accordingly appointed Inspector General of the Main Army with the Rank & Pay of Major General; the former to commence from the day of your arrival here.[1]

When the Secretary enables me, by sending in the Act Certified, I will transmit the necessary Commission. I most heartily congratulate you Sir, & as heartily wish it was upon an appointment more adequate to your high Merits & more worthy your acceptance.

Do me the honor Sir, to be acquainted with my friend & Compatriot the Honorable Mr. Chief Justice Drayton from whom you will receive this. This Gentleman's Character is high in So. Carolina & will appear with Lustre in American History—your time will not be mis-spent in conversation with him.

Continue me I intreat you Sir in your Regard & believe me to be with the most respectful attachment, Sir, Your most Obedient & Most humble servant,   Henry Laurens

RC (PHi).

[1] See *JCC*, 11:465. Laurens was perplexed about the starting date for Steuben's pay and wrote the following note on the copy of the resolve appointing Steuben inspector general that was sent to Washington: "I think the Pay is to commence from the Baron's arrival in America, some Gentlemen are of the same opinion—which shall be enquired into & adjusted if the minute above is erroneous." Washington Papers, DLC. Laurens' uncertainty on this point is difficult to understand because the journals clearly state that Steuben was to be paid "from the time he joined the army and entered the service of the United States."

Henry Laurens to George Washington

Dear sir,   York Town 5 May 1778

In a public Letter which I had the honor of writing to Your Excellency the 3d Inst. by Major Brice, I sent a number of hand Bills calculated for giving satisfactory information to the Public who were anxious to learn the recent intelligence from France.[1] One article of this has been questioned, respecting the King of Prussia's promise—the only part of the performance that can be called mine.[2] I believe my authority is good. Mr Izard, under the 16th February, informs me, "The King of Prussia has given the most explicit & unequivocal assurance that he will be the second power in Europe to acknowledge the Independence of America." Tis true our Commissioners in their public advices are not so express, nor are they in my opinion so full & clear in some other respects as they might have been. Human nature pervades every human breast—a residence at Paris will not exempt Men from infirmities of the Mind, nor is even the momentous concern of Guardianship to thirteen united States, an Infant World in danger of being crushed by the hand of violence paramount to those Curses upon Mankind, Pride & Covetousness, sources from whence all the Evils of this Life spring. Our ambassadorial Commissioners of which Your Excellency cannot be ignorant, are unhappily divided in sentiment, Jarrings & Appeals have followed, intelligence intended for the Public loses part of that fulness & perspicuity which would have appeared in candid & united Counsels.

I have seen so much of the World as to be guarded against surprise at any thing, no inconsiderable benefit results from attempts to reconcile & even sweeten the most untoward circumstances which happen in ones journey through it. I apprehend it would break in upon Your Excellency's time, otherwise I would have troubled you with Mr. Izard's Letter not merely for information but from a hope that something might be devised for promoting Concord between our friends yonder, or the Public good, by a Wise seperation, but I will not dwell upon this subject.

Last Night I had the honor of receiving Your Excellency's favor of the last of April & am happy in finding a confirmation of my sentiments respecting persons proper for treating with the expected deputation from our Adversary.[3] I fear the determination, where only this point can be determined, will be contrary. Be it so, thank God we have here some Men of abilities & Integrity, I hope we shall make a judicious choice.

The Act of Congress of the 22d April will blot out Pages of the British Instructions, the Commissioners from that side will perceive a necessity for taking a new departure from the Tower of Independence & what happened in France on the 6th February will oblige them to shape a new course. From the absence of the Commissioners I presume they had not sailed from England at the 10th March. It may have been found expedient at St. James's to vest them with more ample Powers, if they meant to come, than were originally intended, & under new sanctions of Parliament—a work of slow progress. The People would have much to say—that the Nation were more than a little agitated appears from a Letter which I take the liberty of inclosing for Your Excellency's perusal. I have likewise a Letter from the Mercantile line in London which proves to me the people in general had very sensibly felt the weight of the War, were ardently desirous of Peace & anxious lest Congress should reject the intended propositions.

The long & as I humbly think, unnecessary, delay of the Army arrangement is very affecting, I know it must give extreme pain to Your Excellency—it is improper for me to touch upon the causes, especially when it is so well known that Congress have been engaged in very much important business. The Plan introduced for that part of it which is intended to establish an half Pay for Officers during Life, I have been uniformly averse from, & in a Committee of Congress delivered my objections, these appear to me at this moment of more weight because they have not been removed by the reasonings which have been offered against them & I may without vanity think my self not obstinate. I am open to convertion & always without murmuring submit to a Majority.

I view the scheme as altogether unjust & unconstitutional in its nature & full of dangerous consequences. Tis an unhappy dilemma to which we seem to be reduced—provide for your Officers in terms dic-

tated to you or lose all the valuable Soldiers among them—establish
a Pension for Officers, make them a seperate Body to be provided for
by the honest Yeomanry & others of their fellow Citizens many
thousands of whom have equal claims upon every ground of Loss of
Estate, health &c &c & lose your Army & your Cause. That such provision will be against the grain of the People has been unwarily testi-
fied by its Advocates whom I have heard converse upon the subject;
indeed they have furnished strong ground for opposition against an
immediate compliance with the demand.

If we cannot make Justice one of the Pillars, Necessity may be submitted to at present, but Republicans will at a proper time withdraw
a Grant which shall appear to have been extorted.

Were I in private conversation with an Officer on this point I
should not despair of fairly balancing every greivance he might suppose to be peculiar to the Army, by instances of losses & inconveniences in my own property & person—and I count myself very very
happy compared with thousands who have as faithfully adhered to
our original Compact. 'Tis said Gentlemen did not think the War
would have continued so long, forgive me Sir, a ludicrous remark
which I made early in our Contest, indeed in England before the
commencement of Contest.

"I know my Countrymen are good for the Quarter but I have
doubts of their going the Course." There is a certain versatility
habitual if not almost constitutional in Men born south of 38 Degrees
of Latitude in these States—circumstances which have occured in the
process of this War have given strength to my observation, there are
within that division of America not only objects inviting, but temptations almost irresistable, to Change—to say nothing of the general
train of Education; hence tis easy to account for resignation of a
Commission which had been anxiously solicited by scores. The want
of something is made an excuse & even sometimes by worthy Characters who do not Suspect themselves.

Would to God Gentlemen had followed the Noble Patriotic example of their Commander in Chief, a Plan which reflection will shew
them in a shade of disgrace would never have found a place in their
minds. How superior are many of the Gentlemen now in my contemplation, for I know many with whom I don't converse, to the
acceptance of an half pay, contributed to by Widows & Orphans of
Soldiers who had bled & died by their sides, shackled with a condition of being excluded from the Privilege of serving in Offices in common with their fellow Citizens, bated in every House of Assembly as
the Drones & incumbrances of Society, pointed at by Boys & Girls—
there goes a Man who robs me every Year of part of my pittance. I
think Sir I do not overstrain—this will be the Language of Republicans—how pungent when applied to Gentlemen who shall have

stepped from the Army into a good remaining Estate, how much deeper to some who in Idleness & by peculation have amassed Estates in the War.

This Sir is a large field. Virtue & Honor might be summoned to answer, but it is time for me to forbear. I am obliged to write in haste called upon by particular public duties, besides I feel a full assurance, notwithstanding the present seeming contrariety, that my sentiments when fully explained will not differ essentially from Your Excellency's. I must not however conclude without these declarations— that I am not among those to whom may be applied "Our God & Soldiers we adore in a time of danger" &c.

I am most heartily disposed to distinguish the Gallant Officer & Soldier by the most liberal marks of Esteem—desirous of making proper Provision for all who shall stand in need. I would not except even some of the brave whose expences have been Princely, in extravagance, while they complained of insufficiency of pay.

I have ever detested & never practiced Parliamentary Jockeyings for procrastinating an unpalatable business, which as a silent auditor & spectator I have within some time past known to be alternately adopted.

I most sincerely wish this of the Army had been wisely attended to. The high Esteem I, from gratitude, bear for Your Excellency whose sufferings from a contrary conduct I know must have been great as well as my love of dispatch makes me wish it, & I lament that in some degree we are likely to be more indebted to the Policy & deep projects of other Men for our deliverance than to our own Wisdom & fortitude.

I ask Your Excellency's pardon for taking up so much of your precious time, & this the more particularly, because I know Sir your politeness & punctuality in making returns to correspondents. I intreat Your Excellency pay no regard to me in this respect, I am a very plain unceremonious person not ignorant that a multiplicity of affairs are continually crowding upon a Gentleman in your high station & know your mind must be as continually employed in the most important speculation. I only request Your Excellency, if you think me wrong, will believe me Candid & be assured I am with the most sincere attachment & the most respectful affection & Esteem, Dear sir, Your much obliged Servant,   Henry Laurens

[*P.S.*] If it be not improper I request Your Excellency will cause the Inclosed Letter to Thomas Pike to be sent in to Philadelphia.[4]

RC (DLC).
¹ See Laurens to John Lewis Gervais, May 3, 1778, note 5.
² See Laurens' first letter to John Laurens, May 3, 1778, note 3.
³ See Washington, *Writings* (Fitzpatrick), 11:331–33.

⁴ This day Laurens wrote a private letter to Thomas Pike of Philadelphia concerning the care "of the Children of the late Mr. Brewton." Laurens Papers, ScHi. He also enclosed a copy of it with a brief letter he wrote on May 7 to Charles Pinckney of Charleston, S.C., asking Pinckney to inform him "If you think I can be serviceable in the case of the Orphan Children." Ibid.

Marine Committee to Jonathan Trumbull, Sr.

Sir   May 5th 1778
    As a swift sailing Packet is immediately wanted to carry despatches to France, we must request your Excellency should the Armed Vessel belonging to your State, called the Spy be in port, that you will order her to be got ready for that purpose, but if she should not be in Port that you will give directions for some other suitable Vessel being procured and prepared for the sea with all dispatch.¹ The Committee for foreign Affairs will forward in a short time the dispatches, and we beg leave to request your Excellencys attention to what they shall write you on that subject.² We are Sir, with great respect, Yr. most humble servants

LB (DNA: PCC Miscellaneous Papers, Marine Committee Letter Book).
   ¹ This day Congress ordered the Marine Committee to provide vessels for carrying six copies of the ratification of the treaties of alliance and commerce to France. See *JCC*, 11:463–64. The Marine Committee also wrote similar letters to John Langdon and the Eastern Navy Board this day, directing Langdon to prepare one vessel for this special packet service and the board to prepare two. PCC Miscellaneous Papers, Marine Committee Letter Book, fol. 145; and Paullin, *Marine Committee Letters*, 1:234–35. For evidence that Patrick Henry was also asked to prepare two vessels for this purpose, see Marine Committee to John Young, May 6, 1778, note 3.
   ² See Committee for Foreign Affairs to Jonathan Trumbull, Sr., May 19, 1778.

William Ellery to William Vernon

Dr Sir   York Town 6th May 1778
    The marine Comee. of wch. I am a member last Eveng. in conformity to a resolution of Congress, met and determined to send Six Vessels to carry imports & dispatches to France, the said Vessels to be under the direction of the Comee. of Foreign affairs.¹ As the Letters for your Navy board is not yet written² and Capt. Collins is about to set out immediately, I take this oppty. to request you upon receipt hereof forthwith to send off an express to Bedford to Capt. Rathburn of the Sloop Providence, wch. is one of the Vessels Pitched upon for this business, if he shou'd not have sail'd, directing him not to proceed to Sea untill he shall have recd. Orders from the Comee. of

foreign affairs wch. will soon be transmitted to him, and he is most implicitly to obey.[3] I most heartily congratulate you on the Treaties of Alliance, Amity & Commerce wch. were executed the 6th day of Febry. last at Paris, and unanimously ratified by Congress the 4th Instt. I have only Time to say that those Treaties are magnanimous & founded in our Independency, equality & reciprocity. Inclosed is a hand bill published imprudently & without the knowledge of Congress—but wch. contains some truths.

A respectable Army in the Field this Campaign and the War will be our own. Yours in hast,   W E

P.S. Dont let the occation of the Sloop Providence being detained be known to anyone, no not even to the Capt. of her himself. You will let the Navy Board in Boston know that you have stopped the Sloop Providence Otherwise upon the receipt of the Letter of the Commee. Mr Warren may send off an Express to Bedford.

Tr (RNHi).
    [1] See *JCC*, 11:463–64.
    [2] The Marine Committee's letter to the Eastern Navy Board asking it to "procure two swift sailing Vessels for Packets to carry dispatches to France" is dated May 5 in the Marine Committee Letter Book. See Marine Committee to Jonathan Trumbull, Sr., May 5, 1778, note 1.
    [3] No letter from the Committee for Foreign Affairs to John Peck Rathbun has been found.

Henry Laurens to Matthew Clarkson

Sir,   6th May 1778.
    I had the honour of writing to you on the 1st Inst. by return of your Messenger who I saw about Town two days after.

Within the present inclosure you will receive an Act of Congress of yesterday establishing the Salary of the Auditors of the Army accounts at five Dollars per day & forage for a servants Horse whilst in Camp.[1]

I beg Sir you will do me the favour to communicate this to Major Clarks[2] with the addition of my Compliments & believe me to be with great regard, Sir, Your obedt. Servant.

LB (DNA: PCC, item 13).
    [1] See *JCC*, 11:467. Matthew Clarkson had requested an increase in his salary as auditor of army accounts in an April 28 letter to Laurens. It was read in Congress two days later but is not in PCC. See *JCC*, 10:410; and Laurens to Clarkson, May 1, 1778.
    [2] John Clark, who was also an auditor of army accounts.

Henry Laurens to Horatio Gates

Sir,   York Town 6th May 1778.
  You will receive within the present Inclosure the undermentioned
Papers which I am ordered by Congress to transmit.
  1. Copy of a Letter of 24th April from the Honorable James
Duane Esquire.[1]
  2. Extract from the minutes of a Board of Commissioners of Indian
affairs Albany 15th April 1778.[2]
  3. An Act of Congress for affording protection to the Oneida &
Tuscarora Tribes & other Indians.[3]
  4. a Brevet appointing Majr. Stevens to the Rank of Lt. Colonel.[4]
  I sincerely wish you Sir, a good Journey & every degree of happiness
being very truly & with very great Respect & Esteem, Sir, Your obedient & Most humble servant.
                        Henry Laurens, President of Congress

RC (NHi).
  [1] See Duane to Laurens, April 24, 1778. Laurens wrote a brief note to Duane on
May 8, stating that he had sent only "extracts" of Duane's letter to Gates and
Washington. Laurens Papers, ScHi; and Laurens to Washington, this date.
  [2] The minutes of the April 15 meeting of the commissioners for Indian affairs in
the northern department—attended by James Duane, Gen. Philip Schuyler, Volkert
P. Douw, and Timothy Edwards—are in PCC, item 153, 3:298–303. The extract
sent to Gates consisted of a request by the commissioners for military protection
for the Oneidas and Tuscaroras, two members of the Iroquois confederation who
had declared their desire to live in peace with the United States. JCC, 11:456.
  [3] Congress passed this "Act" in response to a report by the committee on Indian
affairs on an April 16 letter from General Schuyler. See JCC, 10:402, 11:456; and
PCC, item 153, 3:294.
  [4] Congress had resolved on April 30 to grant this commission to Ebenezer
Stevens "in consideration of his services and the strict attention with which he
discharged his duty as commanding officer of artillery in the northern department,
during two campaigns." JCC, 10:410.

Henry Laurens to William Livingston

Dear Sir.   6th May [1778]
  Affairs have assumed a different aspect from that which appeared
when your Excellency writ the Letter which I am just now honoured
with of the 27th April.[1]
  I took the earliest opportunity to transmit an Abstract account of
the intelligence which Congress received from France on the 2d Inst.
by putting under Cover 3 or 4 Copies directed to your Excellency the
3d but I had not time to write a decent Syllable. The performance
was Mr. Drayton's, I had given him the article relative to the King
of Prussia. This has been Since questioned because so Interesting a

circumstance had not been intimated in the public Letter from our Commissioners, but I rely on my authority. Mr. Izard writes to me the 16th Febry.—"the King of Prussia has given the most explicit & unequivocal assurance that he will be the second power in Europe to declare the Independence of America."

Congress have Ratified the Treaty or Treaties & a Committee have prepared Somewhat for public information by authority in which many, probably all, of the articles relative to Commerce & for regulating Marine conduct will be included.

I think myself happy in being entirely of opinion with your Excellency respecting Independence & the half pay scheme.[2] This last business lags exceedingly, I beleive we wait for auxiliaries. I have no objection against Liberal acknowledgments of the services of Officers & Soldiers, any thing that will not strike at our Constitution, but if we can't make Justice one of the Pillars necessity will prove a temporary support. We may submit to it at present, Republicans will at a proper time withdraw a Grant which shall appear to have been extorted. This & the natural consequences, I dread.

When the Account of the Treaties of the 6th Febry had reached White Hall Administration were perplexed, they were stunned. I have a Letter which may be trusted, informing me that Lord Mansfield in tears applied to Lord Camden as a *good Man,* to interpose for the salvation of the Kingdom, his Lordship alluded to his repeated predictions which had been treated with Contempt & intimated his fears that the Door was shut.

Another Letter which I have received from the Mercantile Line convinces me the weight of the War lay heavy, that the whole Nation were violently agitated. My influence is even asked to prevail upon America to accept the terms intended to be proposed, meaning the Conciliatory Bills. I do not know that I have a spark of Influence, if I had much, the whole should be thrown into the opposite Scale. From the continued absence of the expected Commissioners 'tis probable new measures were to be projected & parliamentary sanction obtained.

I remember something of Doctor Franklin's having proposed to a certain King a plan for reducing a great Empire to a Small Kingdom,[3] the Inclosed Evening post contrasts to Alfred the Great a certain Emperor of a floating Island.

Having a spare Constitution of the State of South Carolina I send it for your Excellency's amusement.

I wont forget to enquire tomorrow concerning the Money for the light Horse,[4] I am sensible that in numberless Instances we improve our Talents in the same degree of loss. The mismanagement of our finances I often lament, our Children will feel the effects.

&c &c omitted Copying.

LB (ScHi).

¹ There is a transcript of Governor Livingston's April 27 letter to Laurens in the Laurens Papers, ScHi.

² Livingston had praised Congress' April 22 reply to Lord North's conciliatory proposals and criticized the projected half-pay plan for military officers, observing of the latter: "It is a very pernicious Precedent in republican States, will load us with an immense debt and would render the Pensioners themselves in great measure useless to their Country." Ibid.

³ See "Rules by Which a Great Empire May Be Reduced to a Small One," Benjamin Franklin's 1773 satire on British colonial policy, in Benjamin Franklin, *The Papers of Benjamin Franklin,* ed. Leonard W. Labaree et al. (New Haven: Yale University Press, 1959–), 20:389–99.

⁴ See also Laurens to Washington, April 28, 1778, note 1.

Henry Laurens to George Washington

Sir,   York Town 6th May 1778

My last was under the 3d Inst. by Major Brice,¹ since which I have had the honor of presenting to Congress Your Excellency's several favors of the 30th Ulto., 1st, 3d & 4th Inst.²

The present will cover the undermention'd Papers.

1. An Act of Congress of the 2d Inst. for the Protection of the Western frontier—amended.³

2. of the 5th for establishing a Plan of a well organized Inspectorship.⁴

3. A Letter from Lt. Colo. Sutherland of the 47th British of the 11th April accompanied by a State of this Gentleman's health by Doctr. Weir.

4. A Letter of the 15th April from Major Agnew of the 24th & Lieutt. Poe of the 47th—also a State of the health of these Gentlemen respectively by Doctor Weir.

5. Copy of a Letter from the Honorable James Duane Esqr. dated Albany the 24th April.

6. A Commission appointing the Honorable Baron Stüben Inspector General with the Rank of Major General.⁵

The Cases of the British Officers are submitted by Congress to Your Excellency referring to a Resolve of the 3d March.⁶ I received only verbal directions on this head & that not very explicitly, if I understand right Congress mean that an Exchange should be attempted with Sir William Howe being willing to gratify Colo. Sutherland & the other Gentlemen upon equitable terms.

I have the honor to be, With the greatest Respect, Sir, Your Excellency's Most Obedient humble servt.

Henry Laurens, Presidt. of Congress

[*P.S.*] The bearer of this is charged with a Packet containing 500 blank Oaths.

RC (DLC). LB (DNA: PCC, item 13).

[1] Laurens is referring to his last official letter to Washington. He had also written privately to him on May 5.

[2] These letters are in PCC, item 152, 5:535–42, 6:1–9, and Washington, *Writings* (Fitzpatrick), 11:328–33, 343–44, 348.

[3] See *JCC*, 11:416–17; and Laurens to the Commissioners at Fort Pitt, April 9, 1778, note 1.

[4] This act merely confirmed the plan for the inspectorship of the army that Washington had proposed in his April 30 letter to Laurens. *JCC*, 11:465–66.

[5] Immediately preceding this paragraph in the LB Laurens first wrote and then deleted: "The Commission for Baron Stüben shall be transmitted to your Excellency when returned from the Board of War where it is to be entered." See *JCC*, 11:465, for the May 5 resolve appointing Steuben inspector general of the army.

[6] See *JCC*, 10:219.

Richard Henry Lee to George Washington

Dear Sir   York the 6th of May 1778

The unfortunate cause which hath prevented me from attending to your last favor sooner,[1] will, I hope, be my excuse. The long sickness and death of my much loved brother of Belleview, has for some time past confined me in Virginia, and removed every other consideration from my mind. I now embrace the first good opportunity of sending you the pamphlet of forgeries that I formerly mentioned.[2] Tis among the pitiful arts of our enemies to endeavor at sowing dissention among the friends of liberty and their country. With me, such tricks can never prevail. Give me leave dear Sir to congratulate you on the happy event of our Treaty with France being so effectually concluded—Congress has ratified on their part and ordered the ratification to be delivered in due form. This will be announced to the public immediately. The counsels of France have been governed in this affair by true magnanimity and sound policy. It was magnanimous in his most Christian Majesty not to avail himself of our situation to demand unequal and oppressive terms, and it was wise to leave the Commerce of America open to all the Maritime States; which will prevent their jealousy & enmity, and make them foes instead of friends to England. Great Britain has its choice now of madness, or meanness. She will not war with the house of Bourbon and N. America at the same time, so that I incline to think meanness will be her choice as best befitting her present State and the minds of her rulers. It will probably happen that the Trade of France will not now be interrupted; and thus, by affording no pretext for war, the whole force of our enemies may be devoted to one last and vigorous Campaign against us. As wise men we ought to be prepared for such an event by collecting a strong army, and by every other means that can discourage and defeat such intentions of our inveterate enemies. Being disappointed this Campaign, must infallibly compel the acknowledgement of our independence and keep the world for some time longer in peace. England alone will pay for her wickedness and folly by the loss of North America.

Our information is good that very few Troops can come here from Germany, and private letters, as well as public papers say that the plan of getting Regiments by subscription, tho much boasted of at first, has fallen very low. From the Highlands of N. Britain some men will be obtained, and perhaps a few from England and Ireland, but there seems no reason to suppose that their every exertion can add more than four or five thousand to the present force in N. America. But this will require a very considerable strength on our part to make the event certain. An unsettled dispute between the Emperor and the King of Prussia (which England will undoubtedly foment) concerning the division of the estate of the late Elector of Bavaria has threatened a rupture in Europe not for our advantage, because the former of these Princes being with us, the latter might be disposed to favor the views of G.B. to our injury. Alderman Lee writes that there is some hope of this being negotiated happily.[3] An intelligent Correspondent in England writes Alderman Lee that it was uncertain whether Lord Norths bills would be agreed to or not, but that they were industriously sent over here and circulated to prevent our Treaty with France from being concluded. Vain and unwise Men, their means are always destructive of their ends. Norths delusive and indecent propositions have accelerated an adoption of the agreement with France. I am much concerned to find in Virginia such want of method and industry in collecting and bringing forward the Drafts.[4] When I came away there were all the Men (amounting to forty one or two) both of the former and the latter drafts remaining in King George—Merely for want of an Officer to bring them away, and I am misinformed if it is not the case in other Counties. As far as I have been able to learn, it is probable, that if dexterous recruiting Officers were properly furnished for the business, and sent out, almost all these Veterans that have been discharged from our 9 Regiments would reenlist in a short time.

I am, with sincere esteem, dear Sir, your most affectionate and obedient servant,   Richard Henry Lee

P.S. Alderman Lee says they talk of sending Lord Westcote and Hans Stanley here to treat with us, and that they are to bring half a million guineas to bribe the Congress. From their own corruption these men reason to the corruption of all others.

I had almost forgot to mention that four expresses have been sent from St. James's on the subject of Generals Howe and Clinton. The latter had leave to go home, the Court was disgusted with the former and had recalled him, but recollecting that Clinton might be come away, another Messenger was sent to stop Howe if that should be the case. I hope they are both gone.

RC (DLC).

[1] Washington's last extant letter to Lee was dated February 15, 1778. Washington, *Writings* (Fitzpatrick), 10:464–66.

[2] For a discussion of this pamphlet containing seven spurious Washington letters, see Charles Carroll of Carrollton to Charles Carroll, Sr., May 4, 1778, note 3. Lee had mentioned the original English edition of this pamphlet in a January 2, 1778, letter to Washington that was written at Chantilly, Va., and is in Lee, *Letters* (Ballagh), 1:371. For Washington's comments on these forged letters, see his May 25 reply to Lee in Washington, *Writings* (Fitzpatrick), 11:450–52.

[3] The intelligence from William Lee reported here and in the postscript was contained in his February 28 letter to President Laurens, which is in PCC, item 90, 2:410–13, and Wharton, *Diplomatic Correspondence*, 2:510–12.

[4] Lee's concern over Virginia's slowness in meeting her quota was also the subject of a letter John Page wrote to him this day assuring him that the Virginia Board of War was attending to Lee's request to expedite the departure of the "Drafts" from King George County. Lee Family Papers, ViU.

Later in May both Mann Page and Governor Henry informed Lee that the Virginia Assembly had voted to raise 350 cavalry and 2,000 infantry for the Continental Army, but neither offered much hope of expeditious implementation. Mann Page to Richard Henry Lee, May 21, 1778, Lee Family Papers, ViU; and Henry, *Patrick Henry*, 3:175.

Marine Committee to John Young

Sir   May 6th 1778

We have received your Letter of the 26th ultimo from Edenton and are sorry to hear of the loss of the Continental Brig Independence under your Command.[1] We have no doubt but you have done all in your power for Saving as much as possible from the wreck & we desire that you will deliver the same to our Agents Messrs. Hewes & Smith making out an Inventory thereof and taking their receipts for what you deliver, which you must transmit to the Navy Board at Baltimore.[2]

As we have immediate service for yourself, officers & men, we desire that on receipt hereof, you will march them to Portsmouth in Virginia, and advise Governor Henry of your getting there to whom we have wrote respecting your employment[3] and you must follow such Instructions as you shall receive from the Governor.   Messrs. Hewes & Smith will advance you Money to pay the Expence of your Journey in which you will make despatch. We are sir, Your Hble Servants

LB (DNA: PCC Miscellaneous Papers, Marine Committee Letter Book).

[1] On April 15 during a return voyage from France with dispatches from the American commissioners, the *Independence* was wrecked off the North Carolina coast. For further details of this voyage, see William Bell Clark, *The First Saratoga*

Being the Saga of John Young and His Sloop-of-War (Baton Rouge: Louisiana State University Press, 1953), pp. 16–18.

[2] The Marine Committee's letter of this date to Joseph Hewes and Robert Smith of North Carolina, requesting them to receive the cannon, arms, stores, and cargo salvaged by Captain Young and to advance him money for his expenses, is in PCC Miscellaneous Papers, Marine Committee Letter Book, fol. 146, and Paullin, *Marine Committee Letters,* 1:237.

[3] No such letter has been found, but Patrick Henry's letters of May 15 and 28 to Richard Henry Lee suggest that he had been asked by the Marine Committee to secure two packet boats to carry dispatches to France and that Captain Young was to command one of them. Henry's responses were to letters from Lee of May 7 and 18 that have not been found. See Henry, *Patrick Henry,* 3:166, 175.

Dispatches for France were eventually sent to Governor Henry in late June, but before then the Marine Committee ordered Captain Young to Baltimore for a court of inquiry into the loss of the *Independence*. See Marine Committee to John Young, June 18; and Henry Laurens to Patrick Henry, June 27, 1778.

Committee of Commerce to John Langdon

Sir   Committee of Commerce   York May 7th 1778
    We are exceedingly sorry to find that after all the trouble you have had with the Officers and Crew of the Flamand, and after the trouble we have had in sending monies to South Carolina and preparing a Cargo for her,[1] the Captain of that ship should refuse to proceed on her destined Voyage to Charles Town in South Carolina; but we are sorry[2] not on that account only but because we shall loose an Opportunity to make a Remittance. As for any other disadvantages we are unconcerned; for we are sure we shall not be obliged to pay a freight on that Vessel to France, as the Captain of her hath refused to comply with his Orders. We have only to request you to Protest formally against the conduct of the Captain of the Flamand which will effectually secure us against the payment of freight. We have shewn to Mr. Francey your letter, he informed us that he received a Similar one from you, and in consequence thereof had ordered the Captain of the Flamand immediately to France. The Captain and Crew of this Vessel would have behaved better if the latter had not been deceived. Mr Francey when your letter was read to him told us that the Crew were shipped for the West Indies and home to France, and that when they found they were bound to the Continent they mutinied, and it was not without great dificulty that they were subdued to go to Portsmouth, and the same reason with the dread of Capture now induces them to refuse to go to Carolina.

    You will forward to us an Account of the Disbursments on this Ship as soon as possible that we may charge them. In the mean Time, We are with great respect, Yr. Obedt servants,

                                        William Ellery, Chairman

RC (Capt. J. G. M. Stone, Annapolis, Md., 1973). In the hand of John Brown and signed by Ellery.

[1] For the committee's prior instructions to Langdon regarding the *Flamand*, see Committee of Commerce to John Langdon, February 23, 1778.

[2] Preceding four words inserted by Ellery.

Henry Laurens to Thomas Conway

Sir,   7th May 1778

I duly received & presented to Congress your favour of the 22d Ulto. which having been taken under consideration the 28th the House Resolved to accept your resignation as will appear by an Act of that date here inclosed.[1]

I have the honour to be &ca.

LB (DNA: PCC, item 13).

[1] See also Laurens to Washington, April 28, 1778, note 3.

Henry Laurens to Richard Caswell

Sir.   York Town 8th May 1778.

My last to Your Excellency was the 5th Inst by Post.

Within the present Inclosures Your Excellency will receive several Copies of the Pennsylvania Gazette in which is contained an Act of Congress for publishing such parts of the Treaty of Paris, of the 6th February as Congress have judged necessary for public information & for government of Conduct in particular Cases.[1]

The Ratification shall be transmitted when the Secretary enables me, but his Office at present is a scene of hard labour & some articles unavoidably delayed.

I have the honor to be, Sir, Your Excellency's Obedient humble servt,   Henry Laurens, President of Congress

[P.S.] I have sent on to Governor Henry Copy of a Letter from a Man of Character containing News of the day very important if true,[2] & have requested that Gentleman to pass it on to Your Excellency.

RC (MiU–C).

[1] Selected portions of the treaty of commerce with France and related resolves of Congress appeared in the May 9 issue of the *Pennsylvania Gazette*. See also *JCC*, 11:468–71. Congress did not officially release full texts of the treaties of alliance and commerce until November 1778, shortly after the French had agreed to remove from the latter two articles the delegates deemed detrimental to American interests. See *JCC*, 12:1101; and Committee for Foreign Affairs to the Commissioners at Paris, May 14, 1778, note 2. It should be noted, however, that without authorization from Congress Laurens had published parts of the treaty of alliance

in a broadside that appeared in the form of a postscript to the May 2 issue of the *Pennsylvania Gazette*. See Laurens to John Lewis Gervais, May 3, 1778, note 5.

[2] The enclosed letter has not been found, but see also Laurens to Patrick Henry, this date.

Henry Laurens to George Clinton

Sir,
                                                                    8th May 1778.

My last was the 26th Ulto. by Jones since which I have received none of your Excellency's favors admitting the Secretary's return to ¹·e right, but I feel a kind of remembrance that I have; which shall be further examined into.

The present will cover an Act of Congress of the 1st Inst. recommending an exemption from Militia Duty of such persons as shall be employed in manufactoring Military Stores &ca for public service.

An Act of the 6th & several Printed Copies in the Pennsylvania Gazette publishing such parts of the Treaties of Paris of the 6th Febry as are necessary for public information & the government of conduct in particular Cases.[1]

I congratulate with your Excellency on this great event which may by Wisdom on the part of America be improved to the most happy purposes.

A Gentleman just from Philadelphia reports, there were great appearances in that City of a General embarkation of the Enemy—the foreigners were to return to Europe—that he read in an English News paper Lord George Germane's Speech in Parliament advising the House to confirm the Independence of these States & to form an Alliance against France.[2]

Your Excellency will receive this only as Report. Congress have Resolved upon an Address which is now in press which will discover no present disposition in that Body to such confederacy.[3] I have the honour to be

LB (DNA: PCC, item 13).

[1] Laurens also enclosed copies of these May 1 and 6 acts with brief covering letters that he wrote this day to President Meshech Weare of New Hampshire, the Massachusetts Council, and Govs. Nicholas Cooke of Rhode Island and Jonathan Trumbull, Sr., of Connecticut; and on the following day to President Caesar Rodney of Delaware. See *JCC*, 10:412, 11:468–69; PCC, item 13, fols. 303–5, 307; Revolutionary Papers, M–Ar; Meshech Weare Papers, Nh–Ar; and American Manuscripts, MH–H.

[2] There was no truth to this report about Secretary of State Lord George Germain's speech.

[3] See the May 8 "Address of the Congress to the Inhabitants of the United States of America" in *JCC*, 11:474–81.

Henry Laurens to William Heath

Dear sir,   York Town 8 May 1778

By the next opportunity I shall at least acknowledge the Rect of your late Letters now at the Secretary's Office & I have no Command from Congress.[1]

I feel your distress from a want of Money & shall continue urging Congress & the Treasury.

My present purpose amidst throngs of people & business is to convey the Inclosed papers & assure you, I am with great regard & Esteem, Your Obedient & Most humble servt,   Henry Laurens

RC (MHi).

[1] Since Laurens' last letter to General Heath of April 26, Congress had read and referred to the Board of Treasury an extract of Heath's April 13 letter to Washington as well as his April 21 letter to Laurens. See *JCC*, 10:403, 11:419. The RC of Heath's April 13 letter to Washington on "the great and almost insuperable embarrassments under which we labour here on account of the insufficient Supplies of money"—a perennial source of complaint in Heath's correspondence—is in the Washington Papers, DLC; his April 21 letter to Laurens is in the William Gilmore Simms Collection deposit, MHi.

Henry Laurens to Patrick Henry

Sir.   York Town 8th May 1778.

My last was the 5th Inst by Post.[1] Inclosed with this Your Excellency will receive several Copies of the Pennsylvania Gazette in which is contained an Act of Congress for Publishing such parts of the Treaty of Paris of the 6th February as Congress have judged necessary for public information & for government of conduct in particular Cases.

The Clerks at the Secretary's Office are & have been so closely engaged in Copying the Treaties & Ratification for Exchange as to deprive me of Certified Copies of the latter for transmission to the several States, these shall be duly forwarded when I receive them.

I have the honor to be, Sir, Your Excellency's Obedient humble servt,   Henry Laurens, President of Congress.

[P.S.] I have sent Govr Johnson Copy of a Letter containing Reported News from Philadelphia, important if true—which I have requested that Gentleman to forward to Your Excellency. Be so good to pass it on to Govr Caswell, it comes from a Man of Character & is the News of the Day.[2]

RC (PBL).

[1] See Laurens' second letter to Washington, May 3, 1778, note.

Henry Laurens to William Livingston

Sir,   8th May 1778

In Company with this Your Excellency will receive several Copies of the Pennsylvania Gazette containing an Act of Congress of the 6th Inst. announcing such parts of the Treaty of Paris of the 6th Febry. as Congress have judged necessary for public information & for Government of conduct in particular Cases.

An Address to the Inhabitants of these States which as I read it at the Table appeared to promise benefit is now in the press & will be dispersed on Tuesday next.

I have the honour to be

LB (DNA: PCC, item 13).

Henry Laurens to Alexander McDougall

Sir.   York Town 8th May 1778.

On the 28th I had the honor of receiving & presenting to Congress your favor of the 23d Ulto. when it was committed to the Board of War & I have received no Commands respecting the Contents.[1] Major General Gates now on his way to Fish Kill being Ordered to reassume the Command of the Northern department is charged with powers & Instructions from Congress.

Major General Conway in a Letter of the 22d April asked leave to resign his Commission, which was accepted by an Act of the 28th & the inclosed Letter which I take the liberty of requesting you to deliver or forward to that Gentleman contains the necessary notification.[2]

I have the honor to be, With very great Respect & Esteem, Sir, Your Obedt. humble servant,

Henry Laurens, President of Congress.

[P.S.] I likewise inclose an hand Bill containing a succinct & pretty accurate Account of the recent Intelligence from France. The article respecting the King of Prussia is an extract in substance from a Private Letter which I received from Mr Izard who writes the 16th February. "The King of Prussia has in the most explicit & unequivocal terms given assurances that he will be the second power in Europe to declare the Independance of America." Congress have Ratified the Three Treaties of Commerce—Alliance—and Secret—possibly I may transmit by this conveyance an Accot. published by Authority now in the press.   H L private.

RC (NHi).
[1] General McDougall's April 23 letter to Laurens, containing a comprehensive account of the condition of his command in the Highlands, is in PCC, item 161, fols. 87–94. On April 25 Washington ordered McDougall to relinquish this command and rejoin the main army, pointing out that Gen. Horatio Gates' return to active duty as commander of the northern military department made it unnecessary for McDougall to continue in the Highlands. Washington, *Writings* (Fitzpatrick), 11:297–98.
[2] See Laurens to Conway, May 7, 1778.

Henry Laurens to James Mease

Sir   8th May 1778
I presented this Morning your favor of yesterday received by the hand of the bearer of this Mr. Thos. Smith to Congress together with the several papers which came inclosed.[1]

Congress Issued their former Resolution prohibiting the payment of Mr. Demere's draughts because it did not appear that he had accounted either to your Self or to the Treasury for Thirty Thousand or some such number of Dollars advanced him for the Service of the Clothier General's department, at Philadelphia last Summer[2]—upon the same ground the Bills in Mr. Smith's possession are now refused that reception which they would have met if he had transmitted his Accounts.[3] If he has expended the Sum for public Service the difficulty of transmitting an Account could not have been great & the omission of so necessary a part of his duty exposes him to all the inconveniences which may follow.

One of the Delegates from Georgia intimated to the House that it was not necessary for Mr. Demere to expend even the Amount of the first grant because the Georgia Troops had been provided with Clothing by other means. Be this as it may, I am persuaded Sir, you will approve the Conduct of Congress in refusing to pay the draughts of a Gentleman who has rendered no Account.

A Sum of about 54 Thousand Dollars was granted two or three days ago for discharging Bills drawn by Messrs. Otis & Andrews & if do not misunderstand Congress it is the intention to discharge the Bal-

ance of their demand whenever a regular Stated account shall
appear.[4]

I am with great Respect

LB (DNA: PCC, item 13).

[1] Clothier General James Mease's May 7 letter to Laurens is in PCC, item 78,
15:329–30. In it he requested an explanation of an April 6 resolve forbidding him
to pay any bills submitted by his Georgia agent Raymond Demeré and urged
Congress to reimburse his Boston agents Otis & Andrews for the clothing purchases
they had made for the army. Along with this Mease enclosed a letter Demeré had
written to him from Savannah on March 20, describing Demeré's efforts to procure
clothing for the troops in Georgia.

[2] See JCC, 10:312. Congress finally decided on August 29, 1778, to rescind this
April 6 resolve and allow Mease to pay Demeré "for amount of cloathing purchased for the troops in the continental service." See JCC, 11:770, 819, 842, 850–51.

[3] Thomas Smith was the Continental loan officer in Pennsylvania. JCC, 7:14.
There is no mention in the journals of the rejection of his accounts.

[4] See JCC, 11:464. Congress had agreed to pay this money to Otis & Andrews in
response to a request by Mease in his April 30 letter to the Board of Treasury.
PCC, item 78, 15:325–27.

Henry Laurens to the Northern Department Indian Affairs Commissioners

Gentlemen   York Town 8h May 1778

Within the present Inclosure you will receive an Act of Congress of
the 4h Inst. for the protection of the Oneida, Tuscorora and other
Tribes of Indians, for augmenting the Salary of Mr. James Deane and
allowing his extra-Expences, for authorizing you to draw on the pay
Master in the Northern Department 10000 Dollars for opening a
Trade at Fort Schuyler with Indians &c. to which I beg leave to refer.[1]
I have the Honor to be &c.

                              Henry Laurens, President of Congress

Tr (NN).

[1] See JCC, 11:456. Congress adopted these resolves in response to the commissioners' recommendations set forth in an April 16 letter from Gen. Philip Schuyler
to Laurens and an enclosed copy of the minutes of the commissioners' April 15
meeting in Albany. See PCC, item 153, 3:298–303. Laurens also wrote a brief
letter this day to James Deane, the commissioners' Indian interpreter, notifying
him of the resolve "for augmenting your Salary & for reimbursing your extra
expences." PCC, item 13, fol. 300. See also Laurens' letters to Gates and to Washington, May 6, 1778.

Henry Laurens to Philip Schuyler

Sir   York Town 8th May 1778

On the 28th I had the Honor of receiving & presenting to Congress your Favors of the 16th & 16th April.[1] The Commands of the House are contained in the inclosed Letter to the Commissioners for Indian Affairs.

The papers relative to the Loss of Tyconderoga are returned from Camp and committed to a special Committee. I think Mr. Morris is one. I remember Mr. Drayton is and I am persuaded the necessary Report will not be retarded by either of those Gentlemen, both of them diligent & attentive in public Business. If it shall be needful I will take the Liberty to jog them.[2]

Inclosed Sir, you will find a Hand Bill containing a Brief Account of our recent Advices from France. The Article respecting the King of Prussia is taken from a private Letter from R. Izard Esqr. to me, dated Paris 16th February. "The King of Prussia has given the most explicit and unequivocal Assurance that he will be the second power in Europe to declare the Independence of America." Congress have ratified the Treaties of Commerce, Alliance and Secret. An Account by Authority is now in press for the Information of the public. If possible Copies of this shall also be inclosed.

I have the Honor to be with very great Respect, Sir, Your obedient & most humble Servt. Henry Laurens, President Congress

Tr (NN).

[1] General Schuyler's two April 16 letters to Laurens—one dealing with Indian affairs in the northern department and the other with Congress' investigation of Schuyler's role in the 1777 loss of Ticonderoga and Mount Independence—are in PCC, item 153, 3:298, 306–7.

[2] See also Committee of Congress to Washington, February 7, note; and Laurens to Washington, April 4, 1778, note 2.

Henry Laurens to Thomas Wharton

Sir   8th May 1778.

Since my last of the 4th Inst. I have had the honor of presenting your Excellency's favor of that date to Congress which was then Committed part to the Treasury & part to Committee on Indian affairs.[1]

This will be accompanied by several Copies of a Pennsylvania Gazette containing an Act of Congress of the 6th Inst. announcing such parts of the Treaty of Paris of the 6th Febry as Congress judge necessary for public information & government in particular Cases.

On Tuesday I shall have the honour of transmitting an Address to the people now in press.

I am with very great regard

LB (DNA: PCC, item 13).
[1] President Wharton's letter is not mentioned in the journals and is not in PCC.

Marine Committee to the Eastern Navy Board

Gentlemen   May 8th 1778

The many interesting subjects contained in your last Letter shall shortly receive a full answer, for the present we shall confine ourselves to the disagreeable business of the Alfreds loss, and the conduct of Captain Thompson upon that occasion.[1] From various concurring informations as well as from Captain Thompsons letter to this Committee of the 7th of April last, The Committee are of opinion that both the public Interest and the honour of Captain Thompson render it necessary that a Court of Enquiry should be held on his conduct. But this Enquiry the Committee think cannot properly be made until Captain Hinman or some of his Officers can be heard upon the Affair and in the mean time it is not fit that the public should be deprived of the use of the Raleigh. It is therefore the desire of the Committee that you forthwith suspend Captain Thompson from the Command of that Frigate until a full and fair enquiry can be made into his Conduct, on the Occasion of the Alfreds loss, and that the Raleigh be got ready for Sea with all possible expedition. By the time this will happen the Committee will appoint a Captain to take the Command of her.[2] The Committee are intirely of Opinion with you that it will be proper to send out a Collected force to Cruize against our enemies that we recover the injured reputation of our Navy and the losses we have sustained. With this veiw the Committee wish that the Warren and any other of the Continental Vessels that you approve, may be quickly made ready for Sea and you shall shortly hear further and fully from us concerning the destination of these Ships. We have the pleasure to enclose you the late Resolves of Congress concerning Marine misconduct, and the mode of trying it, which we hope may in future remove the dificulty that hitherto subsisted in Affairs of this nature.[3] It seems from your information of the Enemy at Rhode Island hawling three additional Ships into the Channel thro' which you proposed sending the frigate Providence to intercept her, that the chance of her escaping is too great to be unnecessarily run. We would therefore propose you should endeavour to man the Warren with the hands of the Providence and lay aside the attempt to get her out unless through a change of circumstances you should discover a fair

Opportunity of effecting it—in case this should happen we would have her ordered round to Boston there to join the Continental frigates.[4]

We are Gentlemen, Your Hble servants.

LB (DNA: PCC Miscellaneous Papers, Marine Committee Letter Book).

[1] See Marine Committee to John Bradford, April 28, 1778, note 2.

[2] John Barry was subsequently appointed to command the *Raleigh*. See Marine Committee to the Eastern Navy Board, May 30, 1778.

[3] For the May 6 resolves outlining procedures for investigating naval officers involved in the loss of Continental vessels, see *JCC*, 11:469–71.

[4] On April 30 the Continental frigate *Providence* escaped from Narragansett Bay and sailed for France. Morgan, *Captains to the Northward*, p. 129.

Robert Morris to John Brown

Dear sir   Manheim May 8th. 1778

This will be delivered you by an Express Mr. Jona. Hudson of Baltimore sent up to me for Money which it will be most Convenient for me to send from York Town. You will find herein a letter for Mr. De Francy open for Your perusal & enclosed the set of bills drawn by the Marquis de Fayette mentioned therein also my acct against the Marquis. Mr. dc Francy assured me he wou'd repay me this whole acct by the end of this Week & I am sure he will do it. You'l please to wait on him, deliver the letter & receive the Money giving up those bills & a receipt for the rest of the Money in full of my demands against the Marquis. You will then be pleased to send three thousand Pounds of that Money by this Express to Mr. Jona. Hudson Mercht in Baltimore on my Acct. & Credit me for the remainder yourself.

You will also find herein an order of James Walsh on behalf of Goodwin & Russell on Mr. Wm Sellers junr to deliver Me a Sum of money or an order for it, if you get the Money send it down to Mr Hudson by the Express, but if he delivers you the order on Mr Potts, send it to me. Mr. Hudson has remitted Mr Helligass a draft on Colo. Blane for near £3000, let him know of the Express going to Balto. that he may send the Money if he has it & oblige, Dr sir, Your Obedt hble servt,   Robt Morris

P.S. Tell Jemmy Reese his Father is here at Work & will be glad to see him before he returns which may be in 2 or 3 weeks.[1]

RC (PHi).

[1] Morris also wrote to Washington the following day acknowledging the general's April 27 letter concerning delays in the preparation of "our Elaboratories" in Pennsylvania and their correspondence on the subject of Col. Charles Armand-Tuffin. See Washington Papers, DLC; and Washington, *Writings* (Fitzpatrick), 11:315–16, 453.

Henry Laurens to George Washington

Sir.   York Town 9th May 1778.
My last to Your Excellency was dated the 6th by Sharp.

This will be accompanied by a Petition of Lt. Colo. Dircks which
I am directed to transmit & to request Your Excellency will do or
advise therein as Your Excellency shall judge conducive to public
service.[1]

Also by, several printed Acts of Congress of the 6th Inst. contained
in a Pennsylvania Gazette announcing such parts of the Treaty of
Paris of the 6th February as are necessary for Public information &
the Government of conduct in particular Cases.

I have the honor to be, With the highest Esteem & Regard, Sir,
Your Excellency's Most Obedient servt,
                                Henry Laurens, President of Congress.

RC (DLC).
[1] Jacob Gerhard Diriks' petition to Congress—undated but endorsed by Secretary
Thomson: "Petition of J. Gerhard Dercks. read in Congress 8 May 1778. referred
to Genl Washington"—is in the Washington Papers, DLC. In it Diriks, who had
resigned a captain's commission in the Fourth Continental Artillery Regiment in
July 1777, asked Congress for permission "to raise a Body Composed of two or
more Companies which might be Joined to the Corps under the command of
Brigadier General Count Pulaski." But Washington deemed Diriks' request unwise
and refused to approve it. See JCC, 11:509; and Washington, Writings (Fitzpatrick),
11:380.

Marine Committee to the Eastern Navy Board

Gentlemen   May 9th 1778
We have received yours of the 6th, 9th, 15th, 20th & 22d April last
under the signature of Mr. Warren and now sit down to give them an
Answer. The loss of the Columbus altho' considerable yet by the
prudence of your Board in taking out her Cannon & Stores before
she left Providence, is much less than it would have otherwise been.

As it is highly proper that a Strict enquiry should be made into the
causes of the loss of any of the Continental Vessels, you will institute
a Court of Inquiry for the purpose of Inquiring into the loss of that
Ship.[1] We have given directions respecting the frigate Providence in
ours of yesterday which went by Express to which we refer you.

With regard to the Trumbull, the Governor & Council of Connecticut were desired to assist in getting her out of the River because
you were not then assembled at Boston, and not from any the most
distant Idea of your incompetancy to the business.[2] How it hath happened that you have not received notice of their being requested to

aid in that Affair we know not but suppose it to be owing to a multiplicity of business. However we hope that this circumstance will not prevent your exerting yourselves on this occasion. We don't doubt but that you will attend closely to the equiping and manning the Warren and Raleigh, so that they may be ready to go on a Cruize in company as soon as possible agreeably to what we have written to you in the letter already referred to.

The Sloop Providence is to be stopped if she hath not already sailed and to wait the orders of the Committee of foreign affairs.[3] We lament the death of that gallant Sea Officer Captain Chew. Fourteen or fifteen hundred Barrels of Flour and about 15 Tons of Iron are at Senepuxent waiting the arrival of the Vessels you may have ordered to receive them. We should have directed the whole thither had you not expressed a doubt whether you should be able to succeede in procuring Vessels. If you should collect a sufficient number of vessels to carry all the flour and Iron let us know it and we will immediately send the remainder to Senepuxent. The price of 30/ per Ton and insure so far from being thought enormous is so low as to induce a Suspicion that there is some error in your manuscript. No pursers have as yet been appointed for the navy, when there are their pay will be established. Captain Landais is here—hath been before us and his business is submitted to Congress. We have procured a Continental Commission for Captain Burke.[4] Captain Skimmer if he should behave well, which we cannot doubt after reading the good character you have given will be promoted Ceteris Paribus according to his Rank.[5]

To yours of the 9th of April we reply, that we have wrote fully respecting the loss of the Alfred &c by the Express,[6] and that we have transmitted to you the Resolve of Congress respecting the pay & Rations of officers not in actual service.[7] We would observe here with regard to rations that none in fact are allowed to Navy officers by the Regulations of the Navy, all that was intended by the Resolve is the allowance made to Seamen on Ship Board. We should not be sorry to get rid of our bad officers, as for the good ones they may depend upon receiving every encouragement that Congress can reasonably give.

On yours of the 15th we would observe that we approve of your ordering the Raleigh to Boston. That part which relates to an enquiry on the conduct of Captain Thompson is already answered. We shall transmit Instructions for the Frigates in Season. We shall attend to supplying you with Money from time to time as the Treasury will admit of it, so as to enable you to execute the business of your Department with advantage and satisfaction to the public and reputation to yourselves. We are glad to hear that one of the Warrens prizes is arrived, the other we fear is lost. We will attend to the affair of the Peggy. We had received Letters from Captain Jones of the Ranger before we received your Account of him. In the Paragraph in answer to yours of the 9th we answered part of yrs. of the 20th. If it be meant that Tea, Coffee & Sugar should be allowed to officers not in actual service in lieu of the Rations of Meat &c we shall not object to it provided they do not receive of those articles more than to the Amount in value of that Ration. It was thought improper that Captain Skimmer & Tucker or any other Officers appointed by General Washington should be ranked in the Continental Navy at the time the Rank of Continental officers were determined by the Marine Committee. They must take Rank after them and their Ranks as they respect each other ought to be determined by the Senority of their appointments under General Washington. We now enclose you Commissions & Warrants.

In reply to your last of April the 22d we are glad to hear that Captain Manly is exchanged. It is our intention that he should take the Command of the Frigate Salisbury, If upon enquiry into the loss of the Hancock it should turn out it was not owing to any mal conduct in him.[8] The Resolve of Congress, which we have transmitted to you empower the Navy Boards to order Courts of Enquiry & Courts Martial in the cases mentioned in the said Resolve. Captain McNeill should be tried by a Court Martial. When the Resistance shall have arrived it may be time enough for us to appoint a Commander for her. We are somewhat Surprized that the Governor & Council of the state of Rhode Island should make any dificulty about sending in Captain Furneaux, as it would seem improper that he should [be] exchanged for a Captain of a Privateer if any One of that state should be in captivity.

We have nothing more to Add at present, but our wishes that you continue to exert the utmost vigor and Industry in getting the ships and other Vessels of war to sea, that we may avail ourselves of the extensive property which our enemies have upon the Water. We understand our enemies have a practice of detaining all the Boys that they make prisoners from us. We desire that this practice may be retaliated by not exchanging Boys that the Continental Frigates may captivate from them. We are Gentlemen, Your Hble Servants

P.S. Inclosed is an account of Disbursements on the Continental Sloop Providence at Charles Town South Carolina amounting to £5009.2.6 S. Currency, also an account of Slops furnished the Commander of the said Sloop by the Agents at that Port amtg to £3493.12.3 of both which Accounts you will make due note and see that the Slops are properly Accounted for.

LB (DNA: PCC Miscellaneous Papers, Marine Committee Letter Book).
  [1] In June a court of inquiry cleared Hoysted Hacker of negligence in the March loss of the ship *Columbus* while attempting to run the British blockade of Narragansett Bay. See Morgan, *Captains to the Northward*, pp. 128, 148–49.

[2] No letter from the Marine Committee making such a request of Governor Trumbull or the Connecticut Council has been found.

[3] See William Ellery to William Vernon, May 6, 1778.

[4] See Marine Committee to John Bradford, April 28, 1778, note 5.

[5] On John Skimmer's appointment to command the *General Gates,* see Morgan, *Captains to the Northward,* pp. 140–41.

[6] See Marine Committee to the Eastern Navy Board, May 8, 1778.

[7] These resolves were enclosed with the committee's April 6 letter to the Eastern Navy Board.

[8] For the committee's determination on a commander for the Continental frigate *(Alliance)* at Salisbury, see the postscript to its May 30 letter to the Eastern Navy Board.

Oliver Wolcott to Laura Wolcott

My Dear,   Yorke Town 9th May 1778

I Wrote to you the 4t instant.[1] A few Hours after I had sent away my Letters Mr Simeon Dean arrived here, who bro't Congress Two Treatys the one commercial the other Defensive which our Commissioners had entered into with the Court of France—which Treatys have been much Approved of and Ratified by Congress. They are founded upon the broad Basis of Mutual Interest and Security, and Nothing in them which indicates any Design of obtaining any advantage over us. But seem adapted to secure a lasting Friendship which it is certainly the highest Interest of France to Cultivate. I enclose to you a Hand bill published here prematurely and not by any order of Congress, and which contains something in it *"false"*[2] but which as it is published here and abroad you may as well conjecture what is true and what false as others—and shall leave it to your Ingenuity to Make the Discovery. Congress have not tho't proper to Say more at present upon those Treatys than what is contained in a Paper now in the Press and which I hope I shall be able to enclose to you. G Britain now must immediately desist from this cruel War and admit at once our Independency, or else be invovld in a War with France and probably Spain and Prussia. As soon as France announces our Independency which before now she has probably done she will not suffer G Britain to interrupt her Trade to these States. Indeed every Thing forbids G. Britain to be at Peace with her neighbours if she prosecutes the War against America. Our Peace I consider as now dawning upon us. And whenever it shall be established, may these Independent States thankfully Acknowledge that Great Goodness of God who by his kind Providence so evidently affords us his Protection.

Nothing Material has occurred here since my last. The Military Operations I hope will before long begin as most certainly We ought not to Relax for a Moment our most Vigorous Exertions on Accot. of these Events. For a safe and just Peace cannot be established with so inveterate a Foe while the Enemy have it in their Power to carry on the War—which I am Very confident they cannot do but a Very little while unless We become supine and inattentive to our own safety.

By the Blessing of God I injoy good Health. The Disorder which I mentioned in one of my Letters was the same as every one has had, who at first has used these Waters. I then tho't it was a Return of bilious Disorders—but I was intirely Mistaken. I expect that Mr Adams will soon releive me, when he does so I shall Return, and I hope in future I may injoy that domestick Happiness which this Merciless War has for some years so much interrupted. Peace as I said before I think is not farr distant and as I Write this part of my Letter particularly for you, It is my opinion that the War is about over. I think that G. Britain can proceed no farthar. I consider our Independcy as established. And as I Wished not to continue in the bustle of Business Abroad any longer than till the happy Days of Peace returned, I shall hope therefore in future it will please God to grant that for the short Time I may have to live in the World I shall injoy with you the humble unenviable Condition of Rural blissfull Retirement. Take Care of your Health, and may the Almighty Bless you and our Children.   Oliver Wolcott

P.S. I have recd. £35.10.0 L[awful] Money for my Services and Expences as a Commissioner for Indian Affairs, which I mention to you so that if I should not Return you might know that an order of mine of £27 on our Treasurer in part pay for this Service is included in what I have now recd.

RC (CtHi).
  [1] Wolcott is referring to his May 2 letter to Laura, which had been written before Simeon Deane arrived at York later the same day.
  [2] Prussian recognition of American independence was the "false" report alluded to here. See Henry Laurens to John Laurens, May 3, 1778, note 3.

Jonathan Bayard Smith to George Bryan

[May 10? 1778][1]

1. That 20,010,000 Dollars emitted from 22d day of June 1775 till [. . .] be borrowed on Loan Office Certificates of the United States & destroyed.[2]

2. That it be recommended to the respective States forthwith to provide laws for stopping the circulation of all Bills of the emissions abovesaid after the ——— day of ——— next by not considering them as legal tender, but that they be received in exchange for Loan office certificates, or in payment of a continental tax to be raised by the States agreeable to a resolution of Congress of ——— day of ——— last.

3. That the Commissioners of the Contl. L[oan] Offices be directed to cut by a circular punch of an Inch diameter an hole in each bill which they may receive of the said emissions, to cross the same &c. &c. & to transmit such bills to the continental Treasurer to be in presence of a Committee of Congress destroyed.

5. That it be recommended to the several states by laws &c. to levy taxes, cancel their respective emissions, confiscate & sell the estates of persons who have forfeited &c & lending to the United States on Loan office certificates the money arising from such sales & for ceasing to make farther emissions of bills of credit.

8. That the proceedings of the Convention of Committees at N Haven be transmitted to the Southern states; the propriety of adopting similar measures be referred to their serious consideration; & that it be recommended of states Eastward of Delaware to suspend the execution of the plan of the convention for regulating prices, untill Congress shall inform them of the proceedings of the southern States upon the same subject.[3]

Sir   Sunday morng.

I shall be very glad to have your sentiments on the propriety & safety of [calling?] in some part of our bills of Credit in manner as above.[4] The Credit of our money is an [object] now in view here. I confess I fear too great an effect on the public mind from adopting [such a?] measure. I thank you for your several Letters. The accts. from the City are *flattering*. [Is it] a Mr. Ball who several years ago was connected with Stephen Carmicks family? But *timeo donaos & dona firentes*. By Mr. Baily I send you a packet containing several fresh & some old English Papers which you'l please to return when you shall have sufficiently satisfied yourself. I will endeavor for later ones. The acct from Genl. Lacey is clever & does him credit. I have made it accompany the accounts from the City, so that it has been in almost every hand here. By Mr. Delany I shall give you more of the treaty this day.

I am Dr Sir yr affect.

[P.S.] Near 1 week ago we heard that 2 French & 1 Spanish Vessel were taken off the Capes [of Virgin]ia havg. fought 2 hours a 60 Gun Ship. Hearing no more since it is now [doubted]. Be pleased to thank Colo. Matlack for me for his letter.

[Was]hington had a great & genteel well conducted entertainment at Camp.

RC (PHarH). *Pa. Archives*, 1st ser. 6:545–46. RC damaged; missing words supplied from Tr.

[1] This document consists of a single sheet on which Smith copied five paragraphs from a nine-point committee of Congress economic report, which had been read in Congress on April 8, before he penned the brief letter that he dated only

"Sunday morn'g." The conclusion that he wrote these on Sunday, May 10, 1778, rests upon his references to "the treaty," which Congress had ratified on May 4, and to General Washington's "great & genteel well conducted entertainment at Camp" that took place on May 7, as well as upon the fact that Congress had finally begun consideration of the committee report on the seventh.

² For the text of the report Smith extracted here for Bryan, see *JCC*, 10:322–24. For Congress' consideration of the proposal to liquidate Continental bills by borrowing against loan office certificates, see Oliver Wolcott to Andrew Adams, April 25, 1778, note 4.

³ Although this recommendation had been before Congress since April 8, the delegates did not finally adopt it until June 4. See *JCC*, 11:569–70; and James Lovell to Samuel Adams, April 18, 1778, note 11. Pennsylvania had sent a commissioner to the New Haven economic convention who returned to the assembly on February 24 with a report which provided the basis for "An Act for regulating the prices of the several articles herein mentioned for a limited time" passed by the assembly on April 1, 1778. However, this act was "suspended" by the assembly on May 25 during a brief special session. The suspending act was apparently adopted in response to a petition of the citizens of Lancaster as well as in anticipation of congressional adoption of this recommendation. *Minutes of the Second General Assembly of . . . Pennsylvania*, February 1778 session, pp. 46, 73, 78, 85, DLC(ESR).

⁴ Although the Pennsylvania Assembly did not take up the issue of calling in the state's bills "in manner as above," it had already on March 23 adopted a more narrowly focused "Act for calling in the Bills of Credit, issued by the Legislative Authority of Pennsylvania, under the sanction and authority of the Crown." Pennsylvania, Session Laws, 2d Assembly, 2d session, February 1778, pp. 117–19, DLC(ESR). For correspondence on the difficulties the state's treasurer, Michael Hillegas, encountered in complying with this act, including a May 30, 1778, letter of Chief Justice Thomas McKean interpreting the law, see *Pa. Archives*, 1st ser. 6:538, 548–49, 565–67.

Charles Carroll of Carrollton to Charles Carroll, Sr.

Dear Papa,   Monday P.M. 11th May 1778

I have your letter of the 7th & one from Molly. Inclosed you have the last York Paper & an Address of Congress to the People. Mr. Digges pressed me to take the money, but I declined it; I told him I would take the interest; he said he had paid the interest. This was all he could, I thought, in reason expect from me; he did not press the matter farther. I am surprised you have not heared from Mr. Rutherford: his Silence gives room to conjecture he will not take the money. Our taxes, I suppose, will amount to upwards of £1500 for this year. I wish you could obtain the certificates of our different assessments. If peace should soon take place, with proper œconomy in the expenditures of public money, a little skill in finance, heavy taxes, & a prosperous trade we might soon put our paper money on a sure foundation—but if the war should continue, & G B should remain mistress of the Seas we shall find it difficult to Support & prop up the tottering

Fabric of public Credit, unless we manage much better than we have hitherto done.

We have a report this evening, that the Enemy are fortifying Haddonfield & Mountholly in the Jersies; from this I conjecture they are meditating a movement from Pha. to N. York, but we shall hear more of their designs by tomorrow, as it is said, an express is on his way to Congress from Our General. If he should bring any thing new & interesting I will write you another letter tomorrow morning. Wishing you a long continuance of health I remain yr. affectionate Son,

Ch. Carroll of Carrollton

P.S. I made an agreement about 4 years ago with a person, whose name I have forgot for the Sale of Thompson's Lot. It was not Day or Goldsmith, the agreement must be among the papers in one of the chests at Dorhoragen. If you make the agreement, make it with the condition you mention, of its not being engaged by me for Sale. What did they offer for it?

14th May 1778. The Enemy on the 8th instant went up the Delaware with 5 armed vessels & between 20 & 30 flat bottom boats containing about 1000 chiefly light infantry. They burnt our 2 frigates & several other vessels. The frigates were ordered to be sunk but I suppose they were not sunk deep enough so as to [be] covered entirely with water. Inclosed you have the postscript of the Pena. newspaper containing very interesting intelligence.[1] I am, Yr. affectionate Son,

Ch Carroll of Carrollton

RC (MdHi).
[1] See Henry Laurens to George Clinton, May 11, 1778, note 3.

Charles Carroll of Carrollton to Thomas Johnson

Dear Sir,   1778. 11th May.

Mr. Brown of Annapolis has applied to me to intercede with you & some gentlemen of the Council to grant him leave to go to Pha. from which place he may embark for England. I would not endeavour to persuade or influence you or any man to do what I would not do in a similar situation. I think Mr. Brown's request highly reasonable; from indulging it no possible inconvenience can result to the Public. If it should be thought necessary Mr. Brown may be put on oath not to devulge to the Enemy any thing of importance that may come to his knowledge respecting our situation or preparations. It seems to be very hard to detain a man in a place in which he is cut off from all intercourse with his friends & connections & even from the means of subsisting. If this matter should appear to you in the same light it strikes me, neither you or the Council will make the least difficulty in granting Mr. Brown his request.[1]

Yesterday Mr. Henry Sent to Mr. Wm. Lux by one David Poe 36,000 dollars, part of the 100,000 obtained lately from Congress. Mr. Henry wrote by the same opportunity to Mr Lux desiring him to forward the money on to you as soon as possible.[2]

I sincerely rejoice with you on the treaty entered into with France & on the favourable disposition of the most considerable European States. For news I refer you to my letter to Mr. Chase, which I shall write tomorrow morning,[3] as I understand an express from our General is on his way to Congress. I am with great regard & esteem, Dr. Sir, Yr. most hum Sert.   Ch. Carroll of Carrollton

RC (MdAA).
   [1] The journals of the Maryland Council do not indicate that any official response was returned to Mr. Brown's request for permission to enter Philadelphia to embark for England.
   [2] John Henry's letter to William Lux has not been found.
   [3] Not found.

John Henry to Thomas Johnson

Dear Sir   York Town May 11th. 1778.
   I sent you yesterday by Mr. David Poe 36 thousand Dollars part of the Warrant of one hundred thousand lately granted by Congress to the state of Maryland.[1] This Gentleman promised to deliver the 36 thousand Dollars to Mr. Lux at Baltimore, whom I have requested to forward it immediately to you.

I received to Day a Letter from Mr. Brown of Annapolis. He has expressed a strong desire to return home to his native Country. His Intentions are to apply to You and the Council for leave to go to Philadelphia and from thence to England. I cannot discover any reasonable objection against granting his request. Mr. Carrol will also write to you upon this subject; You will easily perceive this Gentleman is very desirous of appearing before you, with the assistance of some of his acquaintances to strengthen his application. I assure you if I could apprehend the least danger from granting him leave to depart in the way he desires, I would be one of the last who would give him permission, but I am persuaded he cannot, if he had an Inclination, communicate any thing to the Enemy which they do not know already. When you consider the particular Situation of this Gentleman I am inclined to think you will be of opinion that he has some claim to your attention and indulgence. If you should join with me in opinion in this and there are no particular state reasons for detaining this Gentleman, I hope he will meet with your assent.

We have nothing new since Mr Chase left us, except a report that the Enemy are preparing to leave Philadelphia.

I am Sir with great respect & Esteem Yrs.   J Henry

RC (MdAA).
[1] See *JCC,* 10:402.

Henry Laurens to Richard Caswell

Sir.   York Town 11th May 1778

My last was dated the 9th Inst[1]—recommended to Govr Henry's protection.

Your Excellency will receive with this twenty Copies of an Address by Congress to the Inhabitants of these United States[2]—& three of a Proclamation for restricting within proper bounds the conduct of Captains, Commanders &c of American Armed Vessels.[3] These papers your Excellency will be pleased to disperse in such manner as shall most effectually answer the purposes intended.

I have the honor to be, With great Esteem & Regard, Sir, Your Excellency's Most obedient humble servt.

Henry Laurens, President of Congress.

12th. General Howe by a Letter the 10 Inst. to General Washington had made new overtures for an Exchange of Prisoners & talks of the prospect of suffering on our part as the hot weather approaches. What Congress will determine may be known to morrow.[4] The Letter this Instant reached me. I recollect General Burgoyne asked of General Gates Parol enlargement for two of his Officers to come into his Camp in order to adjust their Regimental Accounts only for a Month when he had but two days Provision.

RC (NjMoHP).
[1] Laurens is in error here. The RC of his last letter to Governor Caswell is clearly dated "8th May 1778," but he mistakenly noted in his presidential letter book that he wrote it on the ninth. PCC, item 13, fol. 308. Laurens made the same mistake with his last letter to Governor Henry of Virginia.
[2] See *JCC,* 11:474–81.
[3] See Committee for Foreign Affairs to the Commissioners at Paris, May 14, 1778, note 3.
[4] On May 13 Congress referred General Howe's proposals for a prisoner exchange to a committee of three, which reported on the 21st that his recommendations were "ambiguously expressed and so liable to misconstruction" that the committee had been obliged to formulate a more acceptable set of terms, which Congress approved the same day. See *JCC,* 11:492, 520–21. Howe's May 10 letter to Washington and the May 11 letter from Washington to Laurens with which it was enclosed are in PCC, item 152, 6:21–26, and Washington, *Writings* (Fitzpatrick), 11:372–73. Along with these Washington also sent Congress an extract of a May 5 letter from Gen. William Smallwood describing "the painful alternative to which the prisoners in Philadelphia will be reduced, unless they are relieved." PCC, item 152, 6:29.

AN

ADDRESS of the CONGRESS

TO THE

Inhabitants of the *United States* of *AMERICA*.

FRIENDS AND COUNTRYMEN,

THREE Years have now passed away, since the Commencement of the present War. A War without Parallel in the Annals of Mankind. It hath displayed a Spectacle, the most solemn that can possibly be exhibited. On one Side, we behold Fraud and Violence labouring in the Service of Despotism; on the other, Virtue and Fortitude supporting and establishing the Rights of human Nature.

YOU cannot but remember how reluctantly we were dragged into this arduous Contest; and how repeatedly, with the Earnestness of humble Intreaty, we supplicated a Redress of our Grievances from him who ought to have been the Father of his People. In vain did we implore his Protection: In vain appeal to the Justice, the Generosity, of Englishmen—of Men, who had been the Guardians, the Assertors and Vindicators of Liberty thro' a Succession of Ages: Men, who, with their Swords, had established the firm Barrier of Freedom, and cemented it with the Blood of Heroes. Every Effort was vain. For, even whilst we were prostrated at the Foot of the Throne, that fatal Blow was struck, which hath separated us for ever. Thus spurned, contemned and insulted—thus driven by our Enemies into Measures, which our Souls abhorred—we made a solemn Appeal to the Tribunal of unerring Wisdom and Justice. To that Almighty Ruler of Princes, whose Kingdom is over all.

WE were then quite defenceless. Without Arms, without Ammunition, without Cloathing, without Ships, without Money, without Officers skilled in War; with no other Reliance but the Bravery of our People and the Justice of our Cause. We had to contend with a Nation great in Arts and in Arms, whose Fleets covered the Ocean, whose Banners had waved in Triumph thro' every Quarter of the Globe. However unequal this Contest, our Weakness was still farther increased by the Enemies which America had nourished in her Bosom. Thus exposed, on the one Hand, to external Force and internal Divisions; on the other, to be compelled to drink of the bitter Cup of Slavery, and to go sorrowing all our Lives long; in this sad Alternative, we chose the former. To this Alternative we were reduced by Men, who, had they been animated by one Spark of Generosity, would have disdained to take such mean Advantage of our Situation; or, had they paid the least Regard to the Rules of Justice, would have considered with Abhorrence a Proposition to injure those, who had faithfully fought their Battles, and industriously contributed to rear the Edifice of their Glory.

BUT, however great the Injustice of our Foes in commencing this War, it is by no Means equal to the Cruelty with which they have conducted it. The Course of their Armies is marked by Rapine and Devastation. Thousands, without Distinction of Age or Sex, have been driven from their peaceful Abodes, to encounter the Rigours of inclement Seasons; and the Face of Heaven hath been insulted by the wanton Conflagration of defenceless Towns. Their Victories have been followed by the cool Murder of Men, no longer able to resist; and those who escaped from the first Act of Carnage have been exposed, by Cold, Hunger and Nakedness, to wear out a miserable Existence in the tedious Hours of Confinement, or to become the Destroyers of their Countrymen, of their Friends, perhaps, dreadful Idea! of their Parents or Children. Nor was this the outrageous Barbarity of an Individual, but a System of deliberate Malice, stamped with the Concurrence of the British Legislature, and sanctioned with all the Formalities of Law. Nay, determined to dissolve the closest Bonds of Society, they have stimulated Servants to slay their Masters in the peaceful Hour of domestic Security. And, as if all this were insufficient to slake their Thirst of Blood, the Blood of Brothers, of unoffending Brothers, they have excited the Indians against us; and a General, who calls himself a Christian, a Follower of the merciful Jesus, hath dared to proclaim to all the World his Intention of letting loose against us whole Hosts of Savages, whose Rule of Warfare is promiscuous Carnage, who rejoice to murder the Infant smiling in its Mother's Arms, to inflict on their Prisoners the most excruciating Torments, and exhibit Scenes of Horror from which Nature recoils.

WERE it possible, they would have added to this terrible System, for they have offered the Inhabitants of these States to be exported by their Merchants to the sickly, baneful Climes of India, there to perish. An Offer not accepted of, merely from the Impracticability of carrying it into Execution.

NOTWITHSTANDING these great Provocations, we have treated such of them as fell into our Hands with Tenderness, and studiously endeavoured to alleviate the Afflictions of their Captivity. This Conduct we have pursued so far, as to be by them stigmatized with Cowardice, and by our Friends with Folly. But our Dependence was not upon Man. It was upon Him, who hath commanded us to love our Enemies, and to render Good for Evil. And what can be more wonderful than the Manner of our Deliverances? How often have we been reduced to Distress, and yet been raised up? When the Means to prosecute the War have been wanting to us, have not our Foes themselves been rendered instrumental in providing them? This hath been done in such a Variety of Instances, so peculiarly marked almost by the direct Interposition of Providence, that not to feel and acknowledge his Protection, would be the Heighth of impious Ingratitude.

AT length that God of Battles, in whom was our Trust, hath conducted us thro' the Paths of Danger and Distress to the Thresholds of Security. It hath now become morally certain, that, if we have Courage to persevere, we shall establish our Liberties and Independence.——The haughty Prince, who spurned us from his Feet with Contumely and Disdain,—and the Parliament which proscribed us, now descend to offer Terms of Accommodation. Whilst in the full Career of Victory, they pulled off the Mask, and avowed their intended Despotism. But, having lavished in vain the Blood and Treasure of their Subjects in Pursuit of this execrable Purpose, they now endeavour to ensnare us with the insidious Offers of Peace. They would seduce you into a Dependence, which necessarily, inevitably leads to the most humiliating Slavery. And do they believe that you will accept these fatal Terms? Because you have suffered the Distresses of War, do they suppose that you will basely lick the Dust before the Feet of your Destroyers? Can there be an American so lost to the Feelings which adorn human Nature? To the generous Pride, the Elevation, the Dignity of Freedom! Is there a Man who would not abhor a Dependence upon those, who have deluged his Country in the Blood of its Inhabitants? We cannot suppose this; neither is it possible that they themselves can expect to make many Converts. What then is their Intention? Is it not to lull you with the fallacious Hopes of Peace, until they can assemble new Armies to prosecute their nefarious Designs? If this is not the Case, why do they strain every Nerve to levy Men throughout their Islands? Why do they meanly court each little Tyrant of Europe to sell them his unhappy Slaves? Why do they continue to embitter the Minds of the Savages against you? Surely this is not the Way to conciliate the Affections of America. Be not, therefore, deceived. You have still to expect one severe Conflict. Your foreign Alliances, tho' they secure your Independence, cannot secure your Country from Desolation, your Habitations from Plunder, your Wives from Insult or Violation, nor your Children from Butchery. Foiled in their principal Design, you must expect to feel the Rage of disappointed Ambition. Arise then! To your Tents! And gird you for the Battle. It is Time to turn the headlong Current of Vengeance upon the Head of the Destroyer. They have filled up the Measure of their Abominations, and like ripe Fruit must soon drop from the Tree. Altho' much is done, yet much remains to do. Expect not Peace, whilst any Corner of America is in Possession of your Foes. You must drive them away from this Land of Promise, a Land flowing indeed with Milk and Honey. Your Brethren, at the Extremities of the Continent, already implore your Friendship and Protection. It is your Duty to grant their Request. They hunger and thirst after Liberty. Be it yours to dispense to them the heavenly Gift. And what is there now to prevent it?

AFTER the unremitted Efforts of our Enemies, we are stronger than before. Nor can the wicked Emissaries, who so assiduously labour to promote their Cause, point out any one Reason to suppose that we shall not receive daily Accessions of Strength. They tell you, it is true, that your Money is of no Value; and your Debts so enormous they can never be paid. But we tell you, that if Britain prosecutes the War another Campaign, that single Campaign will cost her more than we have hitherto expended. And yet these Men would prevail upon you to take up that immense Load, and for it to sacrifice your dearest Rights. For, surely, there is no Man so absurd as to suppose, that the least Shadow of Liberty can be preserved in a dependent Connexion with Great-Britain. From the Nature of the Thing it is evident, that the only Security you could obtain, would be, the Justice and Moderation of a Parliament, who have sold the Rights of their own Constituents. And this slender Security is still farther weakened, by the Consideration that it was pledged to Rebels (as they unjustly call the good People of these States) with whom they think they are not bound to keep Faith by any Law whatsoever. Thus would you be cast bound among Men, whose Minds (by your virtuous Resistance) have been sharpened to the keenest Edge of Revenge. Thus would your Children, and your Childrens Children, be by you forced to a Participation in all their Debts, their Wars, their Luxuries, and their Crimes. And this mad, this impious System they would lead you to adopt, because of the Derangement of your Finances.

IT becomes you deeply to reflect on this Subject. Is there a Country on Earth, which hath such Resources for the Payment of her Debts as America? Such an extensive Territory? So fertile, so blessed in its Climate and Productions? Surely there is none. Neither is there any, to which the wise Europeans will sooner confide their Property. What then are the Reasons that your Money hath depreciated? Because no Taxes have been imposed to carry on the War. Because your Commerce hath been interrupted by your Enemy's Fleets. Because their Armies have ravaged and desolated a Part of your Country. Because their Agents have villainously counterfeited your Bills. Because Extortioners among you, inflamed with the Lust of Gain, have added to the Price of every Article of Life. And because weak Men have been artfully led to believe that it is of no Value. How is this dangerous Disease to be remedied? Let those among you, who have Leisure and Opportunity, collect the Monies which Individuals in their Neighbourhood are desirous of placing in the Public Funds. Let the several Legislatures sink their respective Emissions, that so, there being but one Kind of Bills, there may be less Danger of Counterfeits. Refrain a little while from purchasing those Things which are not absolutely necessary, that so those who have engrossed Commodities may suffer (as they deservedly will) the Loss of their ill-gotten Hoards, by Reason of the Commerce with foreign Nations, which their Fleets will protect. Above all, bring forward your Armies into the Field. Trust not to Appearances of Peace or Safety. Be assured that, unless you persevere, you will be exposed to every Species of Barbarity. But if you exert the Means of Defence which God and Nature have given you, the Time will soon arrive, when every Man shall sit under his own Vine, and under his own Fig-tree, and there shall be none to make him afraid.

THE Sweets of a free Commerce with every Part of the Earth will soon reimburse you for all the Losses you have sustained. The full Tide of Wealth will flow in upon your Shores, free from the arbitrary Impositions of those, whose Interest, and whose declared Policy it was, to check your Growth. Your Interests will be fostered and nourished by Governments, that derive their Power from your Grant, and will therefore be obliged, by the Influence of cogent Necessity, to exert it in your Favour.

IT is to obtain these Things that we call for your strenuous, unremitted Exertions. Yet do not believe that you have been or can be saved merely by your own Strength. No! It is by the Assistance of Heaven, and this you must assiduously cultivate, by Acts which Heaven approves. Thus shall the Power and the Happiness of these Sovereign, Free and Independent States, founded on the Virtue of their Citizens, increase, extend and endure, until the Almighty shall blot out all the Empires of the Earth.

By Order of Congress,
HENRY LAURENS, President.

In CONGRESS, May 9, 1778.
RESOLVED,

THAT it be recommended to Ministers of the Gospel, of all Denominations, to read, or cause to be read, immediately after divine Service, the above Address to the Inhabitants of the United States of America, in their respective Churches and Chapels, and other Places of religious Worship.

Published by Order of Congress,
CHARLES THOMSON, Secretary.

YORK-TOWN: Printed by HALL and SELLERS.

Address to the Inhabitants of the United States of America

Henry Laurens to George Clinton

Sir, 11th May [1778]

By the common post this Morning I directed a packet to your Excellency containing about ten Copies of an Address by Congress to the Inhabitants of the United States of America & I believe, two or three Copies of a proclamation forbiding certain Malpractices of Captains, Commanders & other Officers & Seamen belonging to American Armed Vessels.[1]

Under the present Cover will be found ten other Copies of the former & two of the latter Acts both dated 9 Inst.[2] Your Excellency will be pleased to take such measures as shall appear most effectual for communicating a general knowledge of these papers to all the Citizens of New York.

I have the honour to be

12th. I have just received a Letter from His Excellency General Washington inclosing one of the 10th from Sir Wm. Howe, renewing proposals for exchange of prisoners. His present ground is danger of peutred fevers from confinement in hot weather. This circumstance gives much scope for conjecture.

14th. I add a P.S. of the Pensylvania Gazette May 9th Containing interesting intelligence.[3]

LB (DNA: PCC, item 13).

[1] Laurens also noted in his presidential letter book that this day he sent "Under blank Covers by the Eastern Post" copies of Congress' May 8 address to the American people and May 9 proclamation on neutral shipping rights to the governors or presidents of all the states north of New Jersey; to Gens. Philip Schuyler, Alexander McDougall, and William Heath; and to absent or former delegates James Duane, Henry Marchant, Nathaniel Folsom, and George Frost. See PCC, item 13, fol. 313; and *JCC,* 11:474–81, 486.

[2] Although Congress approved the address to the American people on May 8, the printed broadsides containing it were dated the ninth. See *JCC,* 11:474–81; and Evans, *Am. Bibliography,* no. 16097. Laurens also enclosed copies of this address and the May 9 proclamation on neutral rights with brief covering letters that he wrote this day to the governors of Rhode Island, Connecticut, New Jersey, Maryland and Virginia; the presidents of New Hampshire, Pennsylvania, and Delaware; and the Massachusetts Council. See PCC, item 13, fols. 308, 310, 314–17; Revolutionary Letters, M–Ar; Americana Collection, DNDAR; and Red Books, MdAA.

[3] The May 13 postscript to the May 9 *Pennsylvania Gazette* contained an account of the marquis de Noailles' rather insulting March 13 announcement to George III of the conclusion of the treaty of amity and commerce between France and the United States. The king was so outraged by the tone of the French ambassador's statement that he immediately ordered the recall of Lord Stormont, the British ambassador in Paris. Laurens added similar postscripts to the May 9 letters to the chief executives of the New England states cited above in note 2. For several documents bearing upon this incident, see *The Annual Register . . . for the year 1778* (London: J. Dodsley, 1779), pp. 290–92.

Henry Laurens to
the Chevalier de Mauduit Du Plessis

Dear Colonel   11th May 1778

I was yesterday honoured with your Lettere Comique by Colonel Gimat.

I will not be "angry" nor will I "chide" you, when you are a good Child, but when you fret for a new Coat or because the Lace upon the old one does not please your fancy, & that when you lose your play things Heaven & Earth & Congress must all stand still as the Sun at Joshua's Command till Papa goes to the Shop & gets a new Toy for you; a little grave reasoning will be necessary, you are now of an Age to bear it, you are grown too big to be wheedled asleep with a pretty Story, & I know you wont take "beating" from any body; but that matter is adjusted; jocularity apart, I receive & return with the highest satisfaction your gratulations on the late happy event of an Alliance between France & these United States.

Your King, throughout Christendom, will be stiled "protector of the Rights of Mankind,"—better founded than "Defender of the Faith," more lustrous than King of Navarre, & an excellent adjunct to "Most Christian." This happy Tribute of America's sensibility will be more mortifying to a certain deluded Prince than any thing that has befallen him in the course of the War.

If His Majesty will now play his other Cards so skilfully as to command peace he shall be further Stiled "Le politique." Then His illustrious Titles in plain English will read.

"His Most Christian Majesty Louis 16th. King of France & Navarre, Protector of the Rights of Mankind, who by the Magic of Policy, humbled, without bloodshed, a powerful, haughty & much dreaded Rival & gave peace to both Shores of the Atlantic. 6th Febry 1778."

But do you think Great Britain will be Jockeyed, out of her Rice, Indigo, Tobacco, Pitch, Tar, Turpentine, Iron, Hemp, Masts, Peltry &c &c &c &c &c &c &ca & an hundred more without a Struggle, at least for revenge. This cannot be, we must expect War & a bloody one too—let us prepare for it as the best means for securing peace.

But tell me if peace comes soon, what will you do, go to France & be Vigneron, or to Carolina & learn to make Rice & Indigo? I know which would be most pleasing to me. By this you will learn that I am disposed Dear Colonel to be very much your friend & humble Servant,

[*P.S.*] Your letters for France shall go in the Same Vessel which is preparing to conduct Our Ratification of the Treaties of 6th Febry.—Commerce, Alliance & Secret.

Common circumstances in my way, people continually coming in have obliged me to write in haste, you will pardon imperfection.

LB (ScHi).

Henry Laurens to Pierre Étienne Du Ponceau

Sir,   11th May 1778

I am sorry to learn by your favor of the 7th Inst. that circumstances have occured which have disturbed your accustomed tranquility.

The Brevet which you have, is to the best of my knowledge exactly such an one as Baron Stüben applied for, I am sure it is such as I was ordered to grant, & you widely mistake, if you believe the disposal of Commissions rests with me.[1] The Resolves of Congress are my Orders—from these I never swerve, be my own inclinations as they may.

Your Brevet intitles you to Rank & pay of Captain, neither one nor the other are depreciated by such assistance as you may give to General Stüben.

Command was not asked for, if it had been, your experience of our Army has shewn you, it could not have been granted.

Major Des Epinier's Commission has been more than once retorted. The importunity of some Gentlemen & their friends at particular times, when Congress were not at leisure for minute enquiries, may have led the House unwarily into error. This perhaps may be produced as an Instance, 'tis impossible to escape without adhering strictly to Rules from which Congress indulgently to their friends from France have sometimes deviated—but when Monsr. Des Espinier shews his Commission & talks of his advantages every circumstance relative to his obtaining that Commission should be disclosed.[2]

'Tis impracticable for me Sir, to be more minute, my Duty to the public will not afford time. I shall only observe further, on two parts of your Letter.

You say, "I certainly mistook the Baron when he applied for a Commission for you" & you tell me what his "meaning" was—the interpretation of the Barons meaning was his expression & I am persuaded you will be tender in an attempt to prove he did not mean what he said.

But Sir, as an Individual what is all this to me? As the President of Congress I repeat, I act faithfully to the orders of Congress. I have no will of my own.

I have heard no complaint from Baron Stüben that his "meaning" had been mistaken or perverted & I beleive there is no ground for complaint.

"You will freely subscribe to my Decision."

I decide then with your permission, that you cultivate the acquaintance you have made among Strangers into friendships, & remain tranquil in your present Sphere until you can fairly & advantageously enlarge it. This is advice I would give to my Son, whether you adopt it or otherwise, you will do me but justice to believe it is well intended, & that I wish to be, Sir, Your most Obedient humble Servt.

LB (ScHi).
    [1] See JCC, 10:180.
    [2] Auguste des Epiniers, a nephew of Caron de Beaumarchais, had been promoted to major on February 2 "in consideration of the services rendered by his uncle, Mons. de Beaumarchais, and of his having served with reputation in the American army." Ibid. See also JCC, 8:663, 9:875–78, 902–5.

Henry Laurens to Udny Hay

Sir.   11th May [1778]
    This Instant Mathuselack Davis has delivered me your favor of yesterdays date & assigned in the same moment several reasons for his immediate return to Camp.
    At the meeting of Congress tomorrow morning your Letter & the papers which accompany it shall be presented to Congress & no time shall be delayed in communicating such Commands as I shall receive.[1]
    I have the honour to be

LB (DNA: PCC, item 13). Addressed: "Colonel Udney Hay Esquire, Camp."
    [1] On January 9, 1777, Congress appointed Udny Hay assistant quartermaster general at Ticonderoga and granted him a commission as brevet lieutenant colonel. After Gen. Nathanael Greene became quartermaster general early in March 1778, however, he insisted that Hay accept a new appointment from him. Hay refused, fearing that this would entail the loss of his lieutenant colonel's commission, and instead wrote to Laurens on May 10 asking Congress to appoint him deputy quartermaster general in the northern department. See JCC, 7:23; and PCC, item 41, 4:273–77. Shortly before this Greene also wrote a letter to Laurens on the same issue, asserting that no deputy quartermaster should hold a colonel's commission and insisting on his own need to appoint his subordinates. See Green to Laurens, May 5, 1778, in PCC, item 155, 1:61–62. After considering both letters, Congress decided the matter in favor of Greene on May 29, resolving not only that Hay could not serve in the quartermaster's department under his own commission or enjoy "any privilege or emolument" of his military rank but also that "no persons, hereafter appointed upon the civil staff of the army, shall hold or be entitled to any rank in the army by virtue of such staff appointments." JCC, 11:554–55. Laurens transmitted copies of the first resolve, and of the first and the second, with brief covering letters he wrote on May 31 to Hay and to Green respectively. PCC, item 13, fols. 343, 346. Hay regarded Congress' action as tantamount to a call for his resignation and therefore in a June 9 letter to Laurens he announced that he was giving up his position in the quartermaster's department. Laurens replied in a brief note on June 17, 1778, that he had submitted Hay's letter of resignation to Congress but that no action had yet been taken on it. See PCC, item 13, fol. 370, item 78, 11:303; and JCC, 11:607. There is no further mention of this issue in the journals, but it is clear from other evidence that despite his offer to resign Hay served as deputy quartermaster general in the northern department until October 1780, though without his former military rank. See Hay's August 15,

1780, letter to Samuel Huntington and his April 31, 1781, memorial to Congress in PCC, item 41, 4:265–66, item 78, 12:77–78.

Henry Laurens to Francis Johnston

Sir, 11th May [1778]

Several Gentlemen your friends in Congress having put you in Nomination a Candidate for the Office of Commissary of Prisoners you were this day unanimously elected & I have transmitted to His Excellency General Washington the Act of Congress Resolving your appointment which I judged to be necessary, being informed that you were in Camp & immediately under his Command.[1] If Colonel Boudinot held the Office by Commission please to inform me & if you desire it I will apply to Congress for permission to transmit a Commission to you.[2]

I have the honor to be

LB (DNA: PCC, item 13).

[1] Upon the recommendation of Thomas McKean, Col. Francis Johnston of Pennsylvania was appointed this day to succeed Elias Boudinot as commissary of prisoners. Johnston informed Congress that he would accept this appointment if he were allowed to retain his "Rank in the Line" and immediately declined to serve after Congress decided on May 21 that he could keep his rank "but no command in the line, nor be entitled to receive the half pay lately granted to the military commissioned officers." Accordingly, on May 28 Congress elected Maj. John Beatty as Boudinot's successor. See JCC, 11:490, 518–19, 525, 546; and Johnston's May 20 and 22 letters to Laurens in PCC, item 78, 11:79–83. Laurens notified Beatty of his selection in a brief letter dated May 29. PCC, item 13, fol. 341. See also Thomas McKean to Sarah McKean, May 16, 1778.

[2] Laurens also wrote a brief note this day to Elias Boudinot, informing him that "Upon a Ballot this day in Congress Colonel Francis Johnson was unanimously elected to succeed you in the Office of Commissary of Prisoners." Elias Boudinot Papers, DLC. Boudinot had been elected a delegate from New Jersey in November 1777 and one reason he wished to resign as commissary was to take his seat in Congress. It is interesting to note that Boudinot informed his wife that Washington and a number of other officers wanted him to serve in Congress so that he could represent the army's interests. Boudinot did not attend Congress, however, until July 7, 1778. See JCC, 11:672; and J. J. Boudinot, The Life, Public Services, Addresses, and Letters of Elias Boudinot, 2 vols. (Boston: Houghton, Mifflin and Co., 1896), 1:109.

Henry Laurens to the Marquis de Lafayette

Sir, 11th May 1778

I have had the honor by Colonel Gimat's hand to receive Your Excellency's favor of the 5th.[1]

Monsr. Lanuville is so well recommended from all quarters & so warmly recommends himself as to Insure him every thing that Congress can with propriety Resolve in his favor. Notwithstanding all this, if I can judge from appearances, that Gentleman will not obtain the Rank he aspires to, until he has given some actual proofs of his abilities as a Military genius. His papers are in the hands of Gentlemen who Seem heartily disposed to serve him—the issue will be known in a few days.[2]

I have not had a proper opportunity for introducing into Congress the business of Chevalier defayolls, but in private chat with a Gentleman most versant in foreign applications, I learn the Chevalier had some time ago adjusted his demands & received Money for conducting him to France, hence I conclude Congress will readily recommend him to a passage in the Warren or in any other Ship of War bound to France in the service of the States.[3]

You will receive by this conveyance several of the publications of the Treaty of Paris so far as Congress have judged necessary to inform the public at this time. The knowledge of the Treaty in general & of those particulars spread among the Indians can have no bad effect but may do good to our cause.

Colo. Gimad has reminded me of an affair relative to Colonel Armand which he says your Excellency had mentioned in a late Letter.[4] I do not at this moment recollect that matter clearly. This Evening I will review & refresh my memory in order to do what shall appear to be needful. I have the honor to be with the utmost esteem & regard &ca.

P.S. Just as I was going to close this paper, Monsr. Lomagne brought me your Excellency's favor of the 10th.[5] You will pardon me Dear Marquis for recommending to write every thing you intend for Congress quite distinct from private intimations & commands to me. I have told this Young Gentleman I can not flatter him with hopes of the Commission he seeks for. If he is inclined to address Congress I shall faithfully deliver his Memorial—but from the nature of things I may venture to predict that his application will be rejected.

Congress determined this Morning to proceed on the arrangement of the Army,[6] the Members are exceedingly anxious to finish that business, wherefore I have no prospect of an opportunity until that is over, of introducing Colo. Armand.

Inclosed with this are a few French papers; these are all I could collect.

LB (ScHi).
[1] This letter is in "Lafayette-Laurens Letters," *SCHGM* 8 (1907): 126–27.
[2] Although the chevalier de La Neuville sought the rank of brigadier general, Congress on May 14 merely appointed him to the post of inspector of the northern army under General Gates and promised that after a three-month probationary period it would "confer on him such rank as his merits may justly entitle him to." Congress no doubt refrained from granting La Neuville the rank he wished

because Laurens had just been informed by his son John that Washington was privately of the opinion that it was not "politic or proper" to make the Frenchman a brigadier. But the chevalier's performance as inspector of the northern army impressed Congress and led it to grant him a commission as brevet brigadier on October 14, 1778. See *JCC*, 11:466, 492, 498–500; Washington, *Writings* (Fitzpatrick), 10:337, 11:357; Simms, *Laurens Army Correspondence*, pp. 170–71; and Laurens to the Chevalier de La Neuville, January 27, 1778, note. The index in volume 12 of the journals frequently confuses the chevalier with his younger brother, Noirmont de La Neuville, and erroneously indicates that Congress appointed the latter inspector of Gates' army.

³ Lafayette had informed Laurens in the letter cited above that the chevalier de Fayolles, whose offer to serve in the Continental Army Congress had rejected the year before but whose travel expenses it had then agreed to defray, was still in America and wanted Congress either to grant him a lieutenant colonel's commission or arrange for his passage back to France on the Continental frigate *Warren*. See *JCC*, 8:743–44; and "Lafayette-Laurens Letters," *SCHGM* 8 (1907): 126.

⁴ Lafayette had written to Laurens on April 21 and informed him that Charles Armand Tuffin, marquis de La Rouerie, who had been commissioned colonel in the Continental Army in May 1777, "is gone on to Boston where he hopes, says he, to raise an independent corps of Americans, Frenchmen, and foreigners desertors (or prisonners) if leave is granted to him." See Lafayette, *Papers* (Idzerda), 2:30. The Board of War prepared a report on May 17 calling for the creation of an independent corps under Armand's command and Congress approved a modified version of it on June 25, 1778. *JCC*, 11:643–45. For a study of Armand's career, see Townsend Ward, "Charles Armand Tufin, Marquis de La Rouerie, Brigadier-General in the Continental Army of the American Revolution," *PMHB* 2 (1878): 1–34.

⁵ Lafayette's letter is in "Lafayette-Laurens Letters," pp. 128–29. In it he tepidly recommended the promotion to major of Jean-Baptiste, vicomte de Laumagne, who had been made a captain in the Continental Army in February 1778 and was now serving under Colonel Armand.

⁶ See Committee at Camp to Laurens, February 5, 1778, note 1.

Henry Laurens to John Laurens

My Dear Son,   11th May 1778.

The great improvements in the discipline of your Army marked in your favor of the 7th must afford a Gentleman of good taste in the Military Science all that Satisfaction which you have expressed & probably a little more than can be described upon paper.¹ I, who love order & etiquette & particularly love your General, participate your pleasure; go on improve till that which was impudently said & sarcastically intended shall be verified, Washington in War shall be equal to Frederic—in many respects he is far superior.²

The public is indebted to Baron Stüben, their minds I hope will in due time be impressed with a Sense of his Merits & that proper effects will be produced.

Your sounds of rejoicing were no doubt heard in the City. What feelings were raised in the minds of Some worthy Characters in the other Army! How deeply will their King be mortified when he reads "protector of the rights of Mankind" & reflects upon his own folly in abdicating the most valuable part of his Dominions!

I am not ignorant of the conduct you complain of respecting your General.[3] In the recent instance I have suffered not a little Chagrin. I think I did not much err in my opinion delivered in Congress that General Washington should be made acquainted with all the Treaties even the Secret Articles; these might have been intrusted to a Commander in Chief of all the Forces of the United States of America, to a friend, a Virtuous patriotic Citizen with equal propriety & safety as they have been to the Member who lay snoring fuddled on one of the Benches while those papers were reading. The conveyance to & from Camp would not have been attended with more risque than the Journies & Voyage between Paris & York but the Treaties could not be spared, they were to be immediately Ratified & transmitted for Exchange—admitted, but in the mean time appoint a Committee or direct your President to write a Letter of congratulation & transmit an Abstract of the Articles intimating that the whole shall be sent for his information at a proper time. *Extract,* from Letters written by the Commissioners at Paris such parts as will shew the complexion of affairs in Europe, somewhat like this in my opinion ought to have been done, & why it was not is not to be answered by me, except that I am persuaded the omission was not the effect of design in a Majority who love & Esteem that valuable Man.

I wished & endeavored even to send the General a few of the latest News papers, these for once came into my possession but under a pretence or promise of sorting them were while I was engaged taken from before me & I have never seen them since save a few of November & December which we had read a Month before, & yet every one affects to wonder what became of the papers.

The foreign Letters are always in possession of a Committee of foreign Correspondence, & for some time heretofore have not as I have reason to beleive always made proper public appearance. This is unpleasant ground to walk on. I must retire from it, much former history should be recited, the State of parties introduced & other circumstances extremely disagreeable to me, in order to give you a tolerable understanding of matters alluded to.

I hope we shall recollect & still though late Act with becomingness towards your friend, his good sense & moderation will lead him to make a true judgement of Causes. If he were disposed to complain he could be at no loss for subjects of a much older date than the one before us.

With respect to Monsr. Lanuville I shall have no peace till he is disposed of, he asks for a yes or no but poor Gentleman he has discovered a mortal aversion to the latter. Congress are not disposed to gratify his demand immediately & I have intimated as much to him & recommended his attending General Gates in a State of probation pointing to the example of the Inspector general.[4] What will be his resolve I can't tell but if I judge rightly he will not immediately succeed in his expectations—or rather demands.

We long to hear from Camp hoping a confirmation of accounts just Reported here as from the City.

You will find inclosed with this two papers with my Name subjoined. The proclamation is the most horrible botchery & verbosity that ever was seen.[5] It was introduced & passed in a moment when Men were impatient for adjourning & I can't persuade the Gentleman whose Cookery it is to reconsider—a word by the bye which in public proceedings I am not a friend to. It encourages rash determinations & impedes business—but Adieu. I am called upon by a variety of business.

LB (ScHi).

   [1] John Laurens' May 7 letter to his father is in Simms, *Laurens Army Correspondence*, pp. 168–71.

   [2] Gen. Thomas Conway had sarcastically compared Washington to Frederick the Great in a December 31, 1777, letter to the commander in chief. See Laurens to John Laurens, January 8, 1778, note 12.

   [3] John Laurens had criticized Congress for not keeping Washington fully informed of recent diplomatic developments in Europe. Simms, *Laurens Army Correspondence*, p. 170.

   [4] See Laurens to Lafayette, this date, note 2.

   [5] See Congress' May 9 proclamation on neutral shipping in *JCC*, 11:486.

Henry Laurens to Baron Steuben

Sir.   York Town 11th May 1778.

I had the honor of writing to you the 5th & since that, of receiving your favor of the 7th.

You seem to have fallen in with the general opinion that immediate Peace is to be the consequence of the Treaty of Paris the 6th February—and as a Man of Modesty & diffident of his own judgement, it would become me to be, at least, silent, but I know who I speak to, a Man of honor & experience in the World, who will always receive a freind's sentiment & judge of it with Candor—tis mine, that we are not to roll down a green Bank & toy away the ensuing Summer. There is blood much blood in our prospect—& in all appearance Sir, I mean all appearance in my view, there will be opportunity & incitement to unsheath your Sword. Britain will not be humored by a stroke of Policy—she will be very angry, & if she is to fall, her fall will be glorious. We, who know Sir, ought to be prepared—a powerful Army in our own field may, I should say, will, be the only means of securing an honorable peace.

If we universally adopt & indulge the Idea of Peace, it would be presumptuous in me to intimate to a Gentleman of Baron Stüben's experience—what probably will be the consequences. I am desirous of banishing from the minds of the people the assurance, even the hope, of a Peace the present Year.

'Tis impracticable for me, from a want of time, to be so Copious upon this subject, as the subject seems to require, but Sir to you—a word is sufficient.

I have a Letter from Capt. Duponceau of the 7th on his Commission which tis impossible for me to answer at this Instant. I think he has all that was asked, the Rank & Pay of Captain, & I am persuaded that a further application at this juncture would be attended with no success, but this being only my private opinion I would not mean to pass it upon him as a Rule. If he is disposed to make an application to Congress I shall faithfully present a proper Memorial. Your patronage in that case will certainly have weight, but I do not venture to encourage it.

No less than five times have I been called off by intruders since I began this Letter, you will therefore Sir, kindly excuse its imperfections & me for its brevity. Colo. Gimat will call upon me in a few minutes if I do not conclude. I must defer to another opportunity to tell you what I wish to repeat every day that I am with very great truth & Regard, Sir, Your Obedient & Most humble servant,

Henry Laurens

[*P.S.*] Having found a minute I have written to Monsr. duPonceau.[1]

RC (NHi).
[1] See Laurens to Du Ponceau, this date.

Henry Laurens to George Washington

Sir,   York Town 11 May 1778.

Since my last of the 6th Inst. by Sharp[1] I have not received any of Your Excellency's favors.

Colonel Gimad takes the trouble of conveying this & also of a Packet containing 50 Copies of an Address by Congress to the Inhabitants of the United States of America. Your Excellency will be pleased to direct a dispersion of those Papers so as most effectually to answer the purposes intended.

Congress by a Ballot this Morning elected Colonel Francis Johnson Commissary of Prisoners to succeed Colo. Boudinot. As I am informed Colonel Johnson is in the Army under the immediate Command of Your Excellency, I inclose the Resolve of Congress of this date for that appointment & I shall by an additional line transmit the proper notifications to the Gentlemen abovementioned.[2]

I have the honor to be, With the highest Esteem & Respect, Sir, Your Obedient & Most humble Servant,

Henry Laurens, President of Congress.

RC (DLC).
[1] In reality Laurens had last written to Washington on May 9.
[2] See also Laurens to Francis Johnston, this date.

Richard Henry Lee to Thomas Jefferson

Dear Sir   York the 11th of May 1778

We have once more ventured into the field of composition as the inclosed Address will shew you.[1] And I have the pleasure to acquaint you that Congress have unanimously ratified the Treaties with France, and directed the ratifications to be presented for exchange in due season. The inclosed pamphlet I t[ake to] be a production of Dr. Franklin. It is well written, and was published first in Holland. When it began to make a noise, the B. Minister procured its suppression, but this, as usual, raised the public curiosity and procured it additional Readers. We have translated it here, and omitting one or two paragraphs that are not now true, it will be published next week in the Gazette of this place.[2] The reasons are good and may be well used in these States to support public credit. Suppose you were to have a translation published by way of supplement to our Virginia Gazettes?

My heart is so bent upon the success of our Country that it grieves me extremely to hear a probability of measures being adopted that I am sure will injure us. I am told that application will be made to this Assembly to revoke Monsr. Loyeautes commission from the last. Is it possible that such an application can be attended to? Thus to treat a Gentleman of unquestioned ability, of reputation in France, and after we have applied to that Court to obtain leave for his longer residence among us than his furlough permitted! His character will not be hurt by it, but how mutable shall we appear. And how totally wrong it will be thus to dismiss an able, zealous, and most industrious Artist, whilst we remain utterly ignorant of the necessary knowledge that he is both able and willing to instruct us in. I think the wise Men of our Assembly will suppress the spirit of vain ambition that prompts to this selfish application.[3]

We are told that the enemies movements at Philadelphia denote their departure, but these perhaps may be designed to amuse us, and prevent the collection of a strong army.

I am dear Sir sincerely yours,   Richard Henry Lee

RC (DLC). Jefferson, *Papers* (Boyd), 2:177–78.

¹ Lee was a member of the committee appointed May 6 to prepare an address to the people "upon the present situation of public affairs" that was approved by Congress two days later. *JCC*, 11:471, 474–81.

² This version of Franklin's pamphlet comparing the basis of credit in the United States and Great Britain was published in the May 16 issue of the *Pennsylvania Gazette*. A 1777 draft is in Franklin, *Writings* (Smyth), 7:1–8.

³ Loyauté resigned on May 20 after the Virginia Assembly ruled that his appointment as inspector general of Virginia artillery did not entitle him to military command. For Lee's previous efforts to secure Loyauté's services for Virginia, see Richard Henry Lee to Patrick Henry, October 8, 1777, note 2.

Thomas McKean to Sarah McKean

Dear Sally,   York-Town. May 11th. 1778.

About sun-down I arrived safe here, tho' I cannot say quite sound. The Treaty between the United States of America & the *most Christian* King proves that his Majesty of France is not only so, but also the most wise, most just & most magnanimous Prince not only in the World at present but to be found in history. The treaty was unanimously approved of by Congress, and the King of France has the signal honor of the thanks of Congress.

Mr. Davison purposes to begin a grammar school at Portor's mill on Octorara about 26 miles from Lancaster on Friday next. I have agreed to send Josey & Robert to him, and have secured lodgings either at Doctor Ewings or some place approved by him. Shall I beg you to get them put in some order as to clothing. You must employ some Taylor & Semstress without delay. As soon as you let me know by Sam that they are ready I shall return home and take them to the school—the sooner the better. Have no news to be relied upon, but expect to celebrate the anniversary of Independance in Philadelphia for it appears to [me?] that the British army will soon quit it.

I am, with love to the children, dear Sally, Your affectionate,

Thos M:Kean

RC (PHi). Addressed: "To Mrs. Mary M:Kean. By Negro Sam." McKean confused the name of his first wife, Mary Borden McKean, who died in 1773, with that of Sarah Armitage McKean, whom he married in 1774.

Gouverneur Morris to Robert Morris

Dear Duer   Monday Evening [May 11, 1778]¹

Livingston is so ill he can't attend Congress. Monsr. La Neuville is kept in dilatory attendance.² The half Pay cannot be postponed (for now we are the Postponers) beyond To Morrow Morning. Tell Morris his Portugueze Affair is settled much against the wishes of his

Eastern Friends.[3] I could not get the Papers till last Night and this Morning I did the needful whereupon the delay was not chargeable on his and your, Friend,   Gouvr. Morris.

The above is a Copy of a Letter written two Hours ago delivered to Duer who unfortunately arrived in Town without you very contrary to my Expectations. James Smith assures him that his *worthy* Colleague Jonathan B Smith hath absolutely declared off upon the Half Pay Business. Clingan is of the true Eastern Stamp and Clay. I need say no more when you know that Massachusetts is against us except that Hall is daily expected from Georgia and some of the *Un* true Blues from New Hampshire. Think one Moment and come here the next. My respectful remembrances wait on Mrs Morris. I send somewhat for your Evenings Amusement.

Adieu, Yours sincerely,   Gouvr. Morris

[*P.S.*] The Question for referring the half pay Establis't to the States cannot be deferr'd longer than to Morrow. Pensilvania being at present against us it will be carried to refer it to the States, which will defeat the Measure.[4] When I have mentioned this I am sure I need not add any thing more to induce you to be here by Eleven o'Clock to Morrow.   W. Duer

MS not found; reprinted from Burnett, *Letters*, 3:230–31. Endorsed by Gouverneur Morris: "Let the Bearer of this Letter pass to and from Manheim—*York Town*." The postscript was written and signed by William Duer.

[1] Although Robert Morris endorsed this letter "Monday Evening Feby 11th 1778 Gouver. Morris," it is clear from internal evidence that it was actually written on May 11.

[2] See Henry Laurens to Lafayette, this date, note 2.

[3] See Committee for Foreign Affairs to the Massachusetts Board of War, May 14, 1778.

[4] Morris was back in Congress on May 13 to help defeat a motion to submit the half-pay plan to the states, but his return to Congress at this time was a brief one. In addition to his vote on the half-pay issue on May 13, the journals also record his votes on two other issues on May 14 and 15, but two private letters he wrote on May 16 and 17 bear a Manheim place line. See *JCC*, 11:495, 500, 503; Morris to John Wendell, May 16, Photostat Collection, MHi; and Morris to William Bingham, May 17, 1778, Gratz Collection, PHi. For the six-month leave of absence from Congress granted to him in November 1777, see Robert Morris to Thomas Wharton, November 11; and Robert Morris to the Committee of Commerce, December 17, 1777.

Henry Laurens to Matthew Locke

Sir,   12th May [1778]

I had the pleasure of writing to you the 5th Inst. by Mr. Brandon & transmitted Copies of Interesting public papers. This is intended for a like purpose.

You will receive within this Enclosure

10 Copies of an Address by Congress to the Inhabitants of the United States.

3 Copies of such parts of the Treaties of the 6th Febry at Paris between the Court of France & these States as Congress judge necessary to make public at present.

These you will extend as far as you can for the information of all our fellow Citizens.

I am not among those who are flattered by a prospect of immediate peace. I think too highly of Great Britain to admit a belief that she will tamely Submit to the political manœuvres of her Neighbor. It is our Duty however to be guarded against her utmost efforts which I have no doubt will be made the ensuing Summer on some part of the Continent. The disappointment, if she should pursue measures more pacific, will be very acceptable to us.

We are told that War is declared & hostilities commenced between England & France.

That Sir William Howe is preparing to embark his foreign Troops for Europe—British Troops to the West Indies. We also hear he has established a Camp on the Jersey Shore perhaps to facilitate his embarkation or to divide our forces, but these I say are Reports.

I am with great respect &ca.

LB (ScHi).

Richard Henry Lee to Arthur Lee

My dear Brother   York in Pennsylva. 12 May 1778

Your favors of Octr. 24, Decr. 6, 8, & 19 by Capt. Young and Mr. Deane came safe to hand and deserve my thanks on many accounts, but on none more than for the care you have taken, and propose to take of my dear Son Ludwell. Under your kind protecting hand I hope he will be reared to much use both public and private. I approve altogether of your designs respecting him. It grieves me extremely to hear of the indolence and extravagence of my son Thom. They are qualities the direct reverse of those that must carry him thro life, if he passes with honor and ease to himself. I hope his Uncle Alderman's attention to him, and your advice, with what I have written him will work a change. It is with infinite pain that I inform you our dear brother of Belleview[1] departed this Life on the 13 of April last after sustaining a severe Rheumatic fever for 6 weeks. Dr. Steptoe attended him the whole time, and I was also with him. Both public and private considerations render the loss most lamentable. He had been just appointed one of our five Judges of the General Court, in which station he was well qualified to do his Country eminent service. He has left behind him a numerous little family (7 children) and a very disconsolate Widow. It is not necessary now to say much about {Deane}.[2] His {recall} which I now rejoice at will prevent all future {machinations} from him, at least in {Europe} and himself as well as all others shall be well attended to here. Our friend Mr. Adams who {succeeds Deane} is a wise and worthy Whig who will not {form cabals} for any private sinister purpose. I advise you to {cultivate} his {friendship}. Congress has now resolved the same for the support of their Commissioners at Madrid, Vienna, Berlin & Tuscany as for those at Paris, and they are authorised to draw bills of exchange on the Commissioner or Commissioners that may be at Paris for the money they want to defray their expences.[3] This makes each {independent} and will, for a time at least, render it unnecessary to send particular remittances to those places in the way of Commodities. You may be assured that Congress are ready and willing to send powerful remittances to Europe in the way of commodities; but the attempt now would be only supplying the enemy, whose Cruisers are so numerous on our Coast and in our Bays, that almost every Vessel is taken. When a war with France and Spain shall take place, the numerous Ships of England will find some other employment than bending their whole force against us. Then it will be in our power to make the remittances we wish to make. Congress has not yet taken up the consideration of appointing another Commissioner. When they do, I think there can be no objection to the Gentleman you recommend or that he should be appointed to Spain.[4] Gen. Burgoyne has leave to return to England upon parole, but his Army is detained until the Court of London shall notify to Congress their ratification of the Convention of Saratoga. The detention of this Army was founded partly on the reasons you assign, and for other powerful ones which Burgoyne himself furnished us with. In the inclosures which our public letter contains you will see the reasons more at large. I am very happy to be able to observe to you, that the unalterable attachment of Congress to Independence is clearly evidenced by their resolutions upon Ld. Norths insidious bills of pacification some days before they had any notice of the Treaty with France. I think you may make a good use of this with those who may doubt our firmness. We have now no danger but what may arise from our {funds}. Necessity has made our {paper emissions} very large, and may render it indispensable that a solid support shd. be derived from {specie}. Therefore {loans} from {Europe} are necessary, and the desires of Congress on this head demand great attention. New Orleans is so removed from us, and so situated, as to make the difficulty of getting anything from thence very great, that the Havannah would answer much better. The English Ships have taken and destroyed so many French & some Spanish Vessels the last winter and spring upon our Coast, that it appears to me upon every principle of policy unwise for these powers to keep their Marine force unemployed, whilst the whole active Naval force of England is warring upon their Commerce. That part of it at least, which approaches our Shores. I should be glad to know the particulars of Mr. Elliot's theft of your papers.[5] If you can contrive me any valuable new publications in England I shall be glad to have them, and I pray you not to forget an annual supply of Jesuits Bark for we have very little here. I have yet received only 8 pounds of what you formerly mentioned, but I thank you greatly for this. God bless and preserve you.

Richard Henry Lee.

[*P.S.*] The British Army have been closely confined in Philadelphia this winter. It is yet there, our Army is daily growing stronger both in numbers and discipline, and we expect soon to begin offensive operations against them. My brother Frank and myself, are both of us eligible to Congress for three years to come; our brother appears inclinable to quit the service, but it shall depend upon my Country whether I do so or not until I see a proper peace upon proper principles.[6]   R.H.L.

RC (ViU).
  [1] Thomas Ludwell Lee.
  [2] Words in braces here and below are written in cipher in the RC. The key was an early edition of John Entick's *New Spelling Dictionary,* with the cipher number indicating the page in Arabic numerals, the column as *a* or *b,* and the place of the word in the column in Roman numerals. For example, the cipher for "Deanè" is 115bXXXVIII." Although the edition used by the Lee brothers has not been found, Edmund C. Burnett used various letters containing interlined deciphered words and a 1782 edition of the dictionary to develop the code list from which the words in braces have been supplied.
  [3] For this May 7 resolve, see Committee for Foreign Affairs to Ralph Izard, May 14, 1778, note 2.
  [4] In his October 4, 1777, letter to Richard Henry, Arthur had recommended that Edmund Jenings be appointed commissioner to Madrid, "his reserve and circumspection being excellently adapted to that court." Richard H. Lee, *Life of Arthur Lee,* 2 vols. (Boston: Wells and Lilly, 1829), 2:114–17.
  [5] Arthur Lee considered British envoy Hugh Elliott responsible for the theft of his papers during his June 1777 mission to Berlin. For Lee's description of the circumstances surrounding the theft, see his letters of June 28 and July 29, 1777, to the Commissioners at Paris and the Committee for Foreign Affairs, respectively, in Wharton, *Diplomatic Correspondence,* 2:351–54, 369–72.
  [6] Francis Lightfoot Lee was granted a leave of absence on May 30, but returned to Congress in early November 1778, soon after Richard Henry returned home on his next leave. See *JCC,* 11:556, 12:1087, 1112.

Henry Laurens to Samuel A. Otis

Sir   13th May [1778]
    I had the honor of writing to you the 21st Ultimo by Messenger Brown.
    I have remarked in Congress some difficulties which have arisen upon applications for Money on Account of the Clothier general said to be intended for discharging the debt contracted by you for the purchase of Clothing on public Account.[1] Possibly no obstacle would have been thrown in as a Bar to payment of a Stated account directly from your self, or as I should say from Messrs. Otis & Andrews. It is not necessary to account for causes of the demurs which have happened. Therefore waving an enquiry give me leave to recommend to you to transmit an Account of all your expenditures & engagements opposed by all the Sums you have received & drawn for, Strike the balance & either draw for such Balance or desire it may be remitted to you & from the Justice of Congress & their readiness to pay every fair account you will meet no farther disappointment.[2] If your Vouchers are not too bulky send them, if they are, Note at the foot of your Account that if required you will transmit the whole or produce them for inspection to any person authorized for that purpose by Congress. It may be proper to give some account of the thin & ordinary Clothing which have been produced in Congress, how the imposition upon you happened & why you had been obliged to submit to it.
    My regard for the Honor of Congress & my Esteem for a Gentleman who, as I judge from the tenor of his whole conduct, has acted the part of a faithful Steward to the public has induced the present interposition. In this light you will be pleased to receive my private Sentiment & be assured I am with great respect, Sir, your most obedient Servant.

LB (ScHi).
    [1] See Laurens to James Mease, May 8, 1778.
    [2] Otis & Andrews was a Boston mercantile house employed by Clothier General James Mease. On May 7 Otis & Andrews had written to Laurens asking Congress to provide them with at least $150,000 to liquidate debts they had incurred in procuring clothing for the Continental Army. Congress read this letter on May 21 and four days later agreed to pay them the $150,000 they requested as well as an additional $500,000 for Mease's department. See *JCC*, 11:517, 524, 531; and PCC, item 78, 17:289–91. See also Laurens to James Mease, May 8, 1778, note 4. For additional payments by Congress to Otis & Andrews, see *JCC*, 11:696, 717, 811, 842.

Richard Henry Lee to John Adams

My Dear Sir,   York, in Pennsylva. 13th May 1778
    Our public letter[1] does not leave me much to add, but friendship will not suffer me to let this opportunity pass, without expressing my wishes to congratulate you on your safe arrival in France. You will find our affairs at your Court in a much more respectable Train than they have been heretofore, and therefore no doubt more agreable to you. Finance seems now the only rock upon which we have any danger of splitting. How far European loans may help us you can judge, but I fear that the slow operation of Taxes, which indeed are pretty considerably pushed in many States, will not be adequate to the large emissions of paper money which the war compels us to make. The number and activity of the British Cruisers on the coast, and in the Bays of the Staple States, render it utterly impossible with any degree of safety, and therefore very unwise, to attempt making remittances to Europe at present. It is in fact furnishing the enemy with what they want extremely, and much to our injury. Surely the Court of France will now give protection to their Commerce to and from America, the clearest policy demands it. Sir you would be greatly surprised at the number and value of the French Vessels taken and destroyed by the English on our Coasts this last winter and spring. Thus the Marine force of G.B. is actively employed in ruining the Commerce of France, while her powerful Navy remains unemployed. Can this be wise? Gen. Howe remains yet in Philadelphia, and our Army where it was, but daily growing stronger in discipline and in numbers. I am inclined to think that the enemy will this Campaign act chiefly on the defensive (carrying on the small war to plunder and distress) holding all they can in order to get the better bargain of us when a Treaty shall take place. I wish, for the sake of future peace, that we could push these people quite off this Northern Continent. Monsr. Beaumarchais by his Agent Monsr. Francy has demanded a prodigious sum from the Continent for the Stores &c furnished the States. His accounts are referred for settlement to the Commissioners at Paris,[2] and I hope they will scrutinize most carefully into this business, that the public may not pay a large sum wrongfully. We have been repeatedly informed that the greater part of these Stores were gratuitously furnished by the Court of France. How then does it come to pass that a private person, a mere Agent of the Ministry, should now demand pay for the whole? It will give me singular pleasure to hear from you by all convenient opportunities, for I am dear Sir, with great sincerity your affectionate humble servant,   Richard Henry Lee

P.S. Be so kind as to take care of the letters for my brothers and get them conveyed.

RC (MHi).
  [1] Perhaps the Committee for Foreign Affairs' May 14 letter to the Commissioners at Paris, which probably had been drafted before the 14th.
  [2] For Beaumarchais' accounts, see Committee of Commerce to the Commissioners at Paris, May 16, 1778.

Gouverneur Morris to Robert R. Livingston

Dear Livingston, York Town 13th May 1778.
  Having nothing to communicate to you worth your Hearing I will enclose you the Prints which lie on my Table. Assure you that our public Affairs are in tolerable good Train. That I am tolerably in Health, excellently in Spirits & at least as happy as I deserve to be. Make my Love to all my Friends Male and Female particularly the latter for whom I feel an Attachment proportioned to the Distance they are from me. It is strange but it is [true?] that we love our Friends more when absent. At least it is so with me.
  Heaven bless you. Adieu. I am affectionately yours,
                                                    Gouvr Morris

RC (NHi). Addressed: "The honle. Robt. R. Livingston Esqr. Chancellor of the State of New York, Manor of Livingston."

Committee for Foreign Affairs to William Bingham

Sir May 14th. 1778.
  At length, on the 2d Instant, we received Dispatches from our Commissioners at Paris with Treaties of Alliance & Commerce concluded on the 6th of February between France and these United States. They were ratified here on the 4th of this Month, and the Prints herewith sent to you will show the Principles upon which they were founded. We are persuaded you will greatly partake of the Satisfaction which we feel on this Occasion.
  We do not find by the Letters we have received that Congress may venture to enlarge the Power which was given to you by the Resolve of Apr. 16th.[1] But it becomes less necessary that you should be furnished in that Way, as Commerce will in all human Probability be more easily carried on between this Continent and your Island.

Great Hurry of Business must be an Excuse of our Brevity at this Time, though it would not warrant an Omission of sending you our Congratulations & the Gazettes.

We are, With much Regard, Your Friends,

Robt Morris

Richard Henry Lee

James Lovell

RC (PHi). Written by Lovell and signed by Lovell, Lee, and Morris.

[1] For Congress' April 16 resolve authorizing Bingham to draw bills of exchange on the commissioners at Paris, see *JCC,* 10:356.

Committee for Foreign Affairs to the Commissioners at Paris

Gentlemen   York Town May 14th 1778

Our Affairs have now a universally good appearance. Every thing at home and abroad seems verging towards a happy and permanent period. We are preparing for either War or Peace; for altho we are fully perswaded that our Enemies are wearied, beaten and in dispair, yet we shall not presume too much on that belief, and the rather, as it is our fixt determination to admit no terms of Peace, but such as are fully in Character with the dignity of Independant States and consistent with the Spirit and intention of our alliances on the Continent of Europe.

We believe, and with great reason too, that the honor and fortitude of America, have been rendered suspicious, by the Arts, intrigues and specious misrepresentations of our Enemies. Every proceeding and Policy of ours has been tortured to give some possible colouring to their assertions of a *doubtful disposition* in America as to her perserverance in maintaining her Independance; and, perhaps, the speeches of several of the Minority in both houses of the English Parliament, who seemed to persist in the possibility of a reconciliation, might contribute towards that Suspicion. We, at this time, feel ourselves particularly happy in being able to shew from the accidental arangement of Circumstances, such as we could neither have policy to foresee or power to alter, that the disposition of America on that head was fixt and final. For a proof of this we desire your attention to the following.

The English Ministry appear to have been very industrious in getting their two conciliatory Bills (even before they had been once read) over to America as soon as possible, the reason of which haste we did not then foresee, but the arrival of your dispatches since with the Treaties have unriddled the Affair. General Howe was equally industrious in Circulating them by his emissaries thro' the Country; Mr Tryon at N York did the same, and both those Gentlemen sent them under sanction of a flag to Genl Washington, who immediately sent the first he received to Congress. Mr. Tryon's Letter which covered them, and General Washington's answer thereto, you will find in Hall's and Seller's Gazette printed at York town May 2d.

Those Bills are truly unworthy the attention of any National Body; but lest the Silence of Congress should be misunderstood, or furnish the Enemy with New Ground for false insinuation, they were instantly referred to a Committee of Congress, whose judicious and spirited report thereon was unanimously approved by the House *April 22d* & published and circulated thro' the several States with all possible expedition.[1]

The dispatches in charge of Mr. Dean did not arrive till the second of May, eight days after the said reports were published; and his expedition in bringing the dispatches to Congress, prevented any Intelligence arriving before him. Inclosed are the reports referred to, to which we recommend your attention in making them as public as possible in Europe, prefacing them with such an explanatory detail of Circumstances as shall have a tendency to place the Politics of America on the firm basis of National honor, Integrity and fortitude.

We admire the true Wisdom and dignity of the Court of France, in her part of the Construction and Ratification of those Treaties; they have a powerful and effectual tendancy to dissolve that narrowness of mind which mankind have been too unhappily bred up in. In those treaties we see the Politician founded on the Philosopher, and harmony of affections made the ground Work of mutual Interest. France by her open Candor has *won* us more powerfully than any reserved treaties could possibly *bind* us, and at a happy Juncture of Times and Circumstances laid the seeds of an eternal freindship.

It is from an anxiety of preserving inviolate this cordial union so happily begun that we desire your particular attention to the 11th and 12th Articles in the Treaty of Amity and Commerce. The unreserved Confidence of Congress in the good disposition of the Court of France will sufficiently appear by their having unanimously ratified those treaties, and then trusted any alterations or amendments to mutual negociation afterwards. We are apprehensive that the general and extensive tenor of the 12th Article may in future be misunderstood, or rendered inconvenient or impracticable, and, in the end, become detrimental to that friendship we wish ever to exist; To prevent which, you will herewith receive instructions and authority for giving up on our Part the whole of the 11th Article proposing it as a Condition to the Court of France, that they, on their part, give up the whole of the 12th Article, those two being intended as reciprocal Ballances to each other.[2]

It is exceedingly distressing to Congress to hear of Misconduct in any of the Commanders of Armed Vessels under the American flag. Every authentic information you can give on this head will be strictly attended to and every Means taken to punish the offenders and make reparation to the Sufferers. The Chief consolation we find in this disagreeable business, is that the most Experienced States have not always been able to restrain the Vices and irregularities of Individuals. Congress has published a Proclamation for the more effectually suppressing and punishing such Practices.[3] But we are rather inclined to hope that as the line of Connection and friendship is now Clearly Marked and the minds of the Seamen relieved thereby from that unexplainable Mystery respecting their *real* prizes which before embarrassed them that such irregularities will be less frequent or totally cease; to which end, the magnificent Generosity of the Court of France to the owners of the Prizes which *"for reasons of State"* had been given up will happily contribute.

We are, Gentlemen, Your Obt. humble Servts,

Richard Henry Lee

James Lovell

RC (PPAmP). In a clerical hand and signed by Lee and Lovell. Endorsed by John Adams: "Comtee. foreign Affairs, May 14. ans. July 29, 1778."

[1] See *JCC*, 10:374–80.

[2] Congress had instructed the commissioners on May 5 to seek a revocation of articles 11 and 12 of the treaty of commerce with France, which provided that in return for charging no duties on molasses imported by Americans from the French West Indies, Frenchmen were to be exempt from duties on United States goods they imported for use in those islands. In addition to conceding too much to the French, this arrangement also seemed to many delegates like an open invitation to illicit trade insofar as there was nothing in it to prevent Frenchmen from buying goods in America, declaring they were destined for the West Indies, and then shipping them to France, thus avoiding payment of any American duties. Consequently, after ratifying the treaty of commerce, Congress resolved on May 5 to instruct the commissioners at Paris to request the French government to agree to the suppression of articles 11 and 12. This task proved to be easy to accomplish, for shortly after this matter was brought to his attention Louis XVI acceded in September 1778 to Congress' wishes. See *JCC*, 11:428–29, 459–62; and Wharton, *Diplomatic Correspondence*, 2:477–82, 485, 497–501.

[3] On May 9 Congress had adopted a proclamation directing American captains to honor neutral shipping rights. Congress had taken this action at the urging of the commissioners, and in drafting this statement followed closely the outline suggested by Arthur Lee. See *JCC*, 11:486; and Wharton, *Diplomatic Correspondence*, 2:429–31, 433–36, 495–97.

Committee for Foreign Affairs to
Charles W. F. Dumas

Sir,   In Committee for Foreign Affairs, York Town, May 14 1778
Your several Favours down to the Letter Y had come to our Hand before the 2d Instant;[1] on which Day we received Dispatches from our Commissioners in France after an Interruption of eleven Months. Judge therefore, Sir, how very agreable your Letters must have been to us, though you wrote but briefly, always supposing we received more full accounts of European Politicks from our Friends in Paris.

We observe with great pleasure that the States of Holland are discovering a proper Spirit in the Conduct of their Commerce by granting Convoys in Consequence of the insolent Behavior of their British Neighbours. The magnanimous Part taken by his most Christian majesty must have great Influence upon all around him. We doubt not of your hearty Congratulations upon the Success of our Cause which you so early & so warmly espoused, and which you have aided with such Judgment and Resolution with your Pen. We shall write particularly to the Gentlemen at Paris respecting the Injuries you have received from our Enemies and shall instruct them to pay the strictest Attention to our Engagements made to you at the Commencement of our Correspondence.

We must refer you to the Prints now sent and to our Commissioners for the general State of our Affairs, only remarking here that we were actuated in our Proceedings on the 22d of April intirely by the uniform Spirit which we have maintained ever since our Declaration of the 4th of July 1776 being not then acquainted with the favourable state of our Cause in France; as an uncommon Fatality had attended the Letters of our Friends for nearly a whole year before the Arrival of their present important packet.

We are with much Esteem, Sir, your humble Servants,

Richard Henry Lee

James Lovell

Robt Morris

RC (DLC). Written by Lovell and signed by Lovell, Lee, and Morris.

[1] In their most recent letter to Dumas that has been found the committee had acknowledged his letters through dispatch "F." See Committee for Foreign Affairs to Dumas, August 8, 1777. The 17 letters he subsequently wrote to the committee "down to the Letter Y," from May 9 to December 16, 1777, are in PCC, item 93, fols. 72–153; and Dumas' letterbook, fols. 73–113, Inventaris I, C.W.F. Dumas Collection, Algemeen Ryksarchief, The Hague (DLC microfilm). Dispatches "H," "J," "P," "S," and "Y" are also in Wharton, *Diplomatic Correspondence,* 2: 320–21, 340–41, 377–78, 407–8, 451.

Committee for Foreign Affairs to Ralph Izard

Sir

York Town 14 May 1778

Your favor of December 18th[1] came to hand the 2nd of this Month with the dispatches of our Commissioners at the Court of Versailles from whom we had received nothing regularly for almost a whole year.

The decided part which his most Christian Majesty has at length taken in our cause must greatly influence other Crowned Heads in Europe not immediately allied to Britain, to desire a portion in our Friendship and Commerce, and must prepare the way for your welcome reception at the Court of Tuscany. We are pleased to find that you have formed a Connection with one who promises to be so friendly to your Commission as your correspondent the favorite minister of the grand Duke; and we think you could not have done better than in following his past advice.

The enclosed resolve of Congress of the 7th Instant will remove any doubts about your support which may have arisen in your mind from an omission on our part, which did not occur to us untill we had received a hint of it from the Gentlemen at Paris in their Letter of Feby 16th.[2]

Other papers herewith sent will convey to you a general Idea of our affairs; and we hope you will be particularly industrious to expose those attempts of our Enemies which are calculated to lead Europe to think we are not thoroughly fixed in our plan of independence. You may observe that we proceeded on the draughts only of two intended Bills which had been sent to America by the British Ministry. We should not have done this but from a conviction of insidious intentions founded upon former attempts to hurt our character abroad. We were so well satisfied of the spirit of these States to persevere in a noble cause that we should have waited for the Bills themselves, if we had not been anxiously attentive to the good opinion of Europe and the rest of the world. We were altogether stranger to the happy state of our affairs in France, accident and knavery having suppressed the Dispatches of our Friends; as our former Letters will prove, if any attempts shall be made to attribute our late determined conduct to a knowledge of our new alliance. Congress unanimously ratified the Treaties on the 4th and the people have showed their satisfaction wherever the knowledge of the proceeding has reached. The army also which is daily increasing in strength has expressed its Joy, and is now prepared either for honorable Peace or the continuance of the just war.

We shall indeavour to procure an enlargement of your powers, and shall immediately forward them to you. There can be no danger of any clashing of future Treaties, with those now made, provided the plain principles of mutual benifit, without any exclusive privileges are made the Basis. We send you the first volume of the journals of Congress; another will be out in a few days and shall be forwarded also. We recommend to you the frequent communication of your proceedings, and we wish you every Felicity, being Sir, your affectionate humble servants,

Signed { Richard H Lee
James Lovell
Robert Morris

P.S. You are to have a plenepotentiary Commission with instructions not limiting the terms of the proposed treaties of amity & Commerce.

FC (DNA: PCC, item 79).
[1] Izard's December 18, 1777, letter to the committee is in Wharton, *Diplomatic Correspondence*, 2:455–56.
[2] On May 7 Congress authorized the commissioners for the courts of Spain, Tuscany, Vienna, and Berlin to "live in such style and manner . . . as they may find suitable and necessary to support the dignity of their public character" at public expense and promised that Congress would provide an additional "handsome allowance" for their services. See *JCC*, 11:473.

Committee for Foreign Affairs to Arthur Lee

Sir   In Committee for foreign Affairs, York Town, May 14th 1778
Your several Favours of Octr. 6th, Novr. 27th & Decr. 8th[1] were delivered to us on the 2d Instant, the Dispatches by Mr. Deane and those by Capt. Young arriving on the same Day. We had before received your short Letter of the 11th of June, but are yet without that of the 29th of July, in which you had informed us "at large of your Proceedings in Prussia." [2] Its Contents would have proved highly agreable to us in those Months when we were quite uninformed of the Proceedings & Prospects of your Colleagues, at Paris. Impressed with a Sense of the Value of the King of Prussia's "warmest Wishes for our Success" we give assurances of equal Wishes in Congress for that Monarch's prosperity. We have little Doubt of open Testimonies of his majesty's Friendship in Consequence of the late Decision of the King of France.
Your Information in Regard to our Connection with the fictitious House of Hortales & Co. is more explicit than any we had before received, but we further expect that all Mystery should be removed: Surely there cannot now be occasion for any, if there ever was for Half of the past.[3]
Our Commercial Transactions will very speedily be put under the Direction of a Board consisting of Persons not Members of Congress, it being impracticable for the same Men to conduct the deliberative

and executive Business of the Continent now in its great Increase.

It has been next to impossible to make Remittances for many months from the Staple Colonies the Coasts of which have been constantly infested by numerous and strong Cruisers of the Enemy. We hope the Alliance of maritime Powers with us will remove our Embarrassments and give us Opportunity to carry into Effect our hearty Wishes to maintain the fairest commercial Reputation.

There will be great Impropriety in our making a different Settlement for the Supplies received from Spain from that which we make in Regard to those received from France. We are greatly obliged to the Friends who have exerted themselves for our Relief, and wish you to signify our Gratitude upon every proper Opportunity. But, having promised to make Remittances to Hortales for the prime Cost, Charges, Interest & usual mercantile Commission upon whatever is justly due to that House, we must keep the same Line with Gardoqui. On the one Hand, we would not willingly give Disgust by slighting princely Generosity, nor on the other submit to unnecessary Obligations.

The Unanimity with which Congress has ratified the Treaties with France and the general glad acceptance of the Alliance by the People of these States must shock Great Britain who seems to have thought no Cruelty from her would destroy our great Partiality in her Favor. What plan she will adopt in Consequence of her Disappointment Time only can discover. But, we shall aim to be in a posture either to negociate honorable Peace or continue this just War.

We stand in Need of the Advice and Assistance of all our Friends in the matter of Finance; as the Quantity of our Paper Currency necessarily emitted has produced a Depreciation which will be ruinous if not very quickly checked. We have encouraging Accounts of the Temper of the Hollanders of late and expect we may find Relief from that Quarter among others.

A few Weeks if not a few Days must produce fruitful Subject for another Letter when we shall in our Line of Duty renew our Assurances of being, with great Regard, Sir, Your affectionate humble Servants,   Richard Henry Lee

James Lovell

Robt Morris

RC (NN). Written by Lovell and signed by Lovell, Lee, and Morris.

[1] These letters are in Wharton, *Diplomatic Correspondence*, 2:401–3, 429–31, 445–47.

[2] For Lee's July 29, 1777, letter, see ibid., pp. 369–72. Congress did not receive a copy of it until at least July 23, 1778, when a copy arrived with Lee's April 8, 1778, letter to the committee. PCC, item 83, fols. 193–98.

[3] In his October 6, 1777, letter to the Committee for Foreign Affairs, Arthur Lee recalled his meetings with Caron de Beaumarchais in London in the spring of

1776 and stated that the military supplies shipped by Roderique Hortalez & Co. had been "gratuitous." However, in this account Lee distorted what had already been reported to Congress, for in letters of December 1776 and January 1777 he had previously conceded that the explicit arrangements with Beaumarchais had been made by Silas Deane, and the commissioners' January 5, 1777, letter to Vergennes, signed by Deane, Franklin, and Lee, refers to transactions made previously by Deane as a "purchase." Notwithstanding the discrepancy in Lee's October 6 explanation that no American returns were expected for Beaumarchais' shipments, the letter struck a responsive chord in Congress and reinforced its increasingly cautious approach to negotiations with Beaumarchais and his agent Théveneau de Francy. See Wharton, *Diplomatic Correspondence*, 2: 242, 244–45, 401–3.

Committee for Foreign Affairs to William Lee

Sir   York Town 14 May 1778

Your favors of Novr. 24 and Decr. 18[1] reached us only the 2d of this month with the letters of our friends at Paris from whom we had not received a regular packet for Eleven months.

You will readily conceive how much We wish to hear from you; and how very agreable your informations would have been at an earlier period. It is evident that You yourself were in a degree of doubt as to the conduct of France even after the Conference of our Commissioners in December; you will therefore be naturally led to give us due credit for the resolute manner in which We proceeded upon the two draughts of bills which the British Ministry had hurried over to America. Be assured we were unacquainted with the spirit of the French Court. The decisive part it has taken was really unexpected upon what accounts we had collected from travellers.

The dates of the papers herewith sent will enable you to put this matter in a clear point of view. The turn of affairs in Europe will make it needless for us to attempt the finesse of recruiting in Germany, which you hint at, and which would have a good effect in Case of necessity.[2] Doctor Lees letters make it quite probable that your Commission will prove successful at Berlin, and there appears the best agreement between the King of Prussia and the Emperor.

The enclosed resolve of Congress of the 7th Inst. will show their intentions with regard to your support, which was not properly attended to when your Commission was made out.[3]

Other papers herewith sent will give you a general idea of our situation. You may be assured that Independence is firmly adopted by the states; and the unanimity of Congress is truly emblamatic of all America. Nova Scotia has long ago expressed its wishes to be adopted by Us, and now afresh Solicits.[4] Canada will be greatly affected by the news of our alliance with its former parent state. In Short, Sir every thing which could be added to our own determination of being free and independent is ensured by this eclairrissment of the Court of Versailles.

Our army is growing daily so that if we are to negotiate with Britain we shall do it in a proper posture. There are some reports of her drawing away her troops, that she may with a proper grace enter into parley. But this must be done without disguise, or no treaty can be held. For surely no one can suppose that we shall now give up a point which we had made a preliminary before we knew what powerful friendship was secured to us in Europe.

The powers which had been given to our Commissioners in France and our great Anxiety to keep perfect faith in Treaties induced a caution with regard to the powers given in after appointments which is now become unnecessary. Perfect equality being the basis of our present treaties without any exclusive privileges to France there can be no chance of discontent from the conclusion of similar treaties with other powers of Europe; therefore we shall doubtless soon forward to you more full powers than what were sent with your commission. As you seem to think it may be advantageous to have a cypher for correspondence we would propose the same which has been mentioned to Doctor Franklin formerly by Mr Lovell,[5] and this is the rather chosen because it may serve between the Doctor and you or any number of your friends taking a different key word for each. The Scheme is inclosed marked L.

Signed { R.H. Lee / James Lovell / Rob Morris

P.S. You are to have a plenipotentiary commission with instructions *not* limiting the term of proposed treaties of amity and Commerce.

FC (DNA: PCC, item 79). FC (DNA: PCC, item 79 appendix).

[1] Lee's November 24 and December 18, 1777, letters to Secretary Charles Thomson and to the committee are in Wharton, *Diplomatic Correspondence*, 2:426–27, 454–55.

[2] In his November 24, 1777, letter to Charles Thomson, Lee had suggested the possibility of raising troops in the German city-states as a means of embarrassing the British. Silas Deane had also proposed the raising of mercenary troops in a November 28, 1776, letter to the Committee of Secret Correspondence. Ibid., pp. 198–99, 426–27.

[3] See Committee for Foreign Affairs to Ralph Izard, this date, note 2.

[4] See Henry Laurens to the Massachusetts Council, May 23, 1778, note 3.

[5] See James Lovell to Benjamin Franklin, [ante July 4, 1777].

Committee for Foreign Affairs to the Massachusetts Board of War

Gentlemen   York Town 14 May 1778

A resolve of Congress respecting a Portuguese Snow and her Cargo is sent to you by the President in which you are requested to transmit an account of Sale to the Committee for foreign Affairs.[1] We ask the favor of you further to procure for us an authentic copy of the proceedings of the Court of Admiralty relative to the said snow as it is our duty to enclose them with the other papers to our Commissioners abroad.

We are Gentn, your humble servants, (Signed) James Lovell, for the Committee

FC (DNA: PCC, item 79).

[1] On May 11 Congress had directed the Massachusetts Board of War to sell the Portuguese snow, *Our Lady of Mount Carmel and St. Anthony,* even though it had not been condemned by the Massachusetts Admiralty Court, because no representatives of the owners were available to reclaim the ship and its perishable cargo. *JCC,* 11:487–89. For further information on this incident, see Robert Morris to John Rowe, October 27, 1777; and Henry Laurens to Samuel Adams, March 7, 1778.

William Ellery to Unknown

Sir,   York Town May 14th 1778

This will be accompanied by half a dozen Postscripts to the last Pennsylvania Gazette,[1] which please to distribute in manner following to wit, one to Govr. Cooke, one to Govr. Hopkins, one to the Secretary, one to the Genl. Treasurer, one to Genl. Sullivan and the other to the Honorable Jabez Bowen Esq.

The old enfeebled *Lion* growls out an *if* at the aggression on his honour, while the *Cock* crows round him determined to pick up his share of commerce. A war seems to be unavoidable. Can Britain, will Britain submit that France should carry on an unmolested Commerce with these States? Her proud Spirit I think cannot brook it, whatever sound Policy may dictate. Will she risk the Loss of her West India Islands, the Loss of Canada, the Loss of rank amidst the Empires of the world rather than acknowledge the Independence we are in *full possession of?* I think she will. Quos deus vult perdere prius demontat. I have not time to ask another Question, nor to add only that I am with great respect, Your very humble Servant,

Wm Ellery

RC (RHi).

[1] See Henry Laurens to George Clinton, May 11, 1778, note 3.

Henry Laurens to William Bedlow

Sir,[1]   14th May 1778

I duly received & presented to Congress your several favors of the 6th March & 23d April, but I have not at this moment any commands from the House, you will be pleased therefore to accept this as it is intended to afford you the satisfaction of knowing that your Letters had reached their destination. When the last came to hand I applied to the Treasury Board where the former had been committed, for information & received in answer "the Board had not yet taken Mr. Bedlow's Memorial under consideration." [2] I have since urged the Gentlemen & shall continue to remind them & when any determination is had, you shall be immediately informed.

I am Sir &ca.[3]

LB (DNA: PCC, item 13).

[1] William Bedlow was deputy paymaster general at Fishkill, N.Y. JCC, 9:901.

[2] On March 26 Congress had referred to the Board of Treasury a "memorial" from Bedlow for which no date is given in the journals but which was doubtless the March 6 document mentioned by Laurens. This memorial is not in PCC, but on August 26, 1778, Congress approved the board's report on it, recommending that Bedlow "be allowed thirty-five dollars per month . . . in addition to his former allowance of fifty dollars per month." See JCC, 10:284, 11:839. Bedlow's April 23 letter to Laurens is also not in PCC.

[3] Laurens also wrote the following brief letter this day to William Denning of New Windsor, Conn. "In answer to your favor of the 9th Inst. this moment come to hand, please to be informed that your attendance as a Commissioner of accounts at the Board of Treasury is expected here, where the Treasurers Office is fixed for the present." PCC, item 13, fol. 319. Laurens had just received a letter from Denning, who had been appointed a commissioner of accounts on March 30, stating that he was unsure of the duties of his office and had recently been informed by letter from Francis Lewis that he need not serve in York. At the foot of Denning's letter, which was read in Congress on the 15th, Secretary Thomson wrote the following note: "The business of a comr. of accounts at the board of treasury is to liquidate and settle all accots that shall be transferred to them by that board under the direction of the Auditor genl. Such comrs must therefore necessar[il]y attend where the board sits." See PCC, item 78, 7:195; and JCC, 11:501. Lewis, who had advised Denning to the contrary, was a member of the committee of claims that had been superseded by the Board of Treasury in July 1776. JCC, 5:620.

Henry Laurens to Rawlins Lowndes

Sir.   14th May 1778

I had the honor of writing to your Excellency the 2d Inst. by Messenger Cross—& yesterday of receiving your Excellency's favors of the 13th & 18th Ulto. together with the Copy of General Howe's Letter referred to, and also the public accts. All these were immediately Committed—the Letters to a Select Committee & the Accounts to the Board of Treasury.[1] Your Excellency shall be duly informed of such Commands as I shall receive on the several Subjects.

Within the present Inclosure will be found

1. An Act of Congress recommending to exempt from Military

Duty such persons as may be employed in manufacturing Military Stores &ca. for the use of the United States, dated 1st May.

2. An Act of 6th May in the Pennsylvania Gazette containing such parts of the Treaty of Paris of the 6th. Febry 1778, as are judged necessary for public information & government of conduct in particular Cases.

3. An Address by Congress of the 9th Inst. to the Inhabitants of the United States of America.

4. A proclamation of the same date for restraining Malpractices of Captains, Commanders & other officers & Seamen of American Armed Vessels.[2]

of No. 2, these will be contained in the packet 6 Copies

of No. 3—20 Copies. No. 4, 3 Copies.

These papers Your Excellency will be pleased to dispose of in such manner as you shall judge will most effectually promote public good.

I have the honor to be &ca.

LB (DNA: PCC, item 13). Addressed: "President Lowndes, So. Carolina, by Sharp 19th May."

[1] President Lowndes' April 13 and 18 letters to Laurens dealt with a variety of issues, including an uprising of South Carolina loyalists and their irruption into Georgia, requests by the Board of War for certain military supplies, South Carolina's accounts with Congress, a dispute over pay between Lowndes and deputy quartermaster general Francis Huger, and Lowndes' need for blank letters of marque and bonds to commission privateers. PCC, item 72, fols. 445–48, 454–59. Along with his second letter Lowndes enclosed an April 14 letter from Gen. Robert Howe, the commander of the southern department, asking Lowndes to dispatch troops and supplies to Georgia as soon as possible to repel an anticipated invasion of the state. Ibid., fols. 449–50. Congress addressed a number of these issues in a series of resolutions passed on May 29. JCC, 11:551–53. See also Laurens to Lowndes, May 17, 1778.

[2] Laurens also transmitted all but the first of the items listed here with a brief letter he wrote this day to Gov. John Houstoun of Georgia. PCC, item 13, fol. 318. To that letter he also added a postscript on May 15, enclosing a copy of Congress' resolution of that date on half pay. See JCC, 11:502-3.

Henry Laurens to the Massachusetts Board of War

Gentlemen.   14th May [1778]

You will find within the present Inclosure an Act of Congress of the 11th Inst. relative to the Portugueze Snow Our Lady of Mount Carmel & St. Antonis, requesting you to make Sale of that Vessel & her Cargo now in the State of Massachusets' Bay & to deposit the Net proceed in the public funds of these United States &ca, to which I beg leave to refer for particulars.[1]

I have the honor to be

LB (DNA: PCC, item 13).
[1] See Committee for Foreign Affairs to the Massachusetts Board of War, this date.

Committee for Foreign Affairs to the Commissioners at Paris

In Committee for foreign Affairs

Gentlemen   No. 8   York Town May 15 1778

Your pressing request for 5000 Hhds of Tobacco is a matter as embarrassing to Congress as to yourselves.[1] Their anxiety to get it to you is as great as yours to receive it. We have already lost considerable Quantities in the attempt and thereby furnished our Enemy, Gratis, with what was designed to discharge your Contracts with, and promote the Interest and Commerce of our Friends. We request your particular attention to this information. It is a matter of the highest moment to our allies as well as to ourselves. In the present State of things it is very probable that England will not interrupt the Trade of France in her *own* Bottoms, and our desire is, as well for her Benefit as ours, that France would open the Trade from her own Ports, so that the Intentional advantages of the Treaties may fully operate to both Countries. We need not enlarge on this head, as your own discernment and judgment will furnish you with all the reasons necessary therefor.

In addition to what is mentioned in our Letter No.   [2] respecting the 11th & 12 Articles we observe that the 12th is capable of an interpretation and misuse which was probably not thought of at the Time of Constructing it, which is that it opens a door for all or a great part of the Trade of America to be carried thro the French Islands to Europe, and puts all future regulations out of our Power, either of Imposts or Prohibition, which tho' we might never find our Interest to use, yet it is the keeping those in our Power, that will hereafter enable us to preserve equality with, and regulate the Imposts of the Countries we trade with. The General Trade of France is not under the like restriction; every article on our part being staked against the single Article of Molasses on theirs. Therefore the Congress thinks it more liberal and consistent that both Articles should be expunged.

We have no material military Transactions to acquaint you with. The Enemy yet remain in Philadelphia, but some late movements make it probable they will not stay long. Our Army is yet at the Valley forge. The Enemy thro' the Course of the winter have carried on a low, pitiful, and disgraceful kind of War agst Individuals whom they picked up by sending out little parties for that purpose and revengefully burning several of their houses. Yet all this Militates against themselves, by keeping up an inflamable Indignation in the Country towards them; and on the whole we know not which most to wonder at, their folly in making us hate them after their inability for Conquest and desires of Peace are confest, or their Scandalous barbarity in expressing their resentments.[3]

You will see, Gentlemen, by the Contract which the commercial Committee has signed with the Agent of Mr. Beaumarchais that Congress was desirous of keeping a middle Course, so as not to appear to slight any determined Generosity of the French Court, and at the same Time to show a Promptness to discharge honourably the Debts which may be justly charged against these States by any Persons.[4] We depend upon you to explain the affair fully, as you seem to make a Distinction between the military Stores & the other Invoices, while no such Distinction appears in the Letters of Mr. Deane & Mr. Beaumarchais. In short, we are rather more undetermined by your late Dispatches than we were by your long Silence.

Congress being at this Time deeply engaged in a Variety of pressing Business and the foreign Committee thin of Members you will be pleased to excuse us from being more particular in our Answer to your several Dispatches as well as in our Information of the State of our Affairs.

We are, Gentlemen, your very humble Servants,

Richard Henry Lee

James Lovell

P.S. You will see what we have written to Mr. Dumas, and will point out to us what will be our Line of Honour to him & Justice to these States.

RC (PPAmP). Begun in a clerical hand and completed by Lovell; signed by Lovell and Lee. Endorsed by John Adams: "Comtee. foreign affairs May 15, ans. July 29, 1778."

[1] In their February 16 letter to the committee, the commissioners at Paris had requested this tobacco in order to pay the expenses of American diplomatic missions to Germany, Italy, and Holland. Wharton, *Diplomatic Correspondence*, 2:496–97.

[2] See Committee for Foreign Affairs to the Commissioners at Paris, May 14, 1778.

[3] Remainder of RC written by Lovell.

[4] See Committee of Commerce to the Commissioners at Paris, May 16, 1778.

Henry Laurens to Ethan Allen

Sir,   15th May [1778]

Yesterday I had the honor of presenting to Congress your favor of the 9th which came to hand the preceeding Evening.[1]

The Contents were heard by the House with much satisfaction &

a Vote immediately passed to grant you a Brevet to Rank as Colonel in the Army.[2] The necessary Certificate to which is annexed the Act of Congress for that purpose, will be delivered to you by His Excellency General Washington.

Permit me Sir to congratulate with your numerous friends on your deliverance from a cruel Captivity, to assure you, I admire your almost unexampled fortitude & respect you highly for your Zeal in the glorious Cause in which we are engaged. And that I shall be happy in any opportunity to testify that I am, With very great Regard

LB (DNA: PCC, item 13). Addressed: "Colonel Ethan Allen, Valley Forge."

[1] Ethan Allen's May 9 letter to Laurens, in which he announced the news of his release from British captivity and thanked Congress for "the Honour done me in passing Several Resolves in order to have long ago expedited my Exchange," is in PCC, item 152, 6:35–36. For the steps Congress had taken to secure Allen's exchange, see *JCC*, 7:12, 10:213, 295.

[2] See *JCC*, 11:496.

Henry Laurens to Benjamin Chew and John Penn

Gentlemen,   15th May [1778]

Your joint Address of the 10th Inst. having been presented by the Board of War to Congress, was this day taken under consideration & an Act which you will receive within the present Inclosure for discharging you severally from your Parole thereupon Resolved.[1]

I shall immediately transmit a Copy of the Act to His Excellency the President of this State & another Copy to Governor Livingston of New Jersey.[2]

I have the honor to be

LB (DNA: PCC, item 13).

[1] In their May 10 letter to Congress, Benjamin Chew and John Penn, writing from "Union Iron Works, New Jersey," had asked to be discharged from their parole so they could return to Pennsylvania and comply with a recent state law "requiring all persons who had enjoy'd Office under the Crown of Great Britain to take the Test prescribed by a former act by the 1st of June next, under pain of Confiscation of their Estates." PCC, item 147, 2:29–30. Chew and Penn, who had been respectively chief justice and governor of Pennsylvania under the proprietary regime, had been arrested and dispatched to New Jersey by order of Congress in August 1777 because of their British sympathies. See Laurens to John Rutledge, August 12 and 15, 1777.

[2] Laurens enclosed copies of the resolve discharging Chew and Penn from their parole with brief covering letters he wrote this day to Gov. William Livingston of New Jersey and President Thomas Wharton of Pennsylvania. See PCC, item 13, fol. 322; Emmet Collection, NN; and *JCC*, 11:497, 503. It should be noted, however, that there was an important difference between the text of the resolve Laurens transmitted this day and the one printed in *JCC*, 11:503. According to

Horatio Gates

the manuscript journals, Congress first resolved somewhat ambiguously "That John Penn and Benjamin Chew, Esqrs., be discharged from their parole," but later amended this to state more specifically "That John Penn and Benjamin Chew, Esqrs., be conveyed, without delay, into the State of Pensylvania, and there discharged from their parole." PCC, item 1, 16:30. According to notations in his presidential letterbook, Laurens did not send texts of the amended resolution to Chew, Penn, Livingston, and Wharton until May 16. PCC, item 13, fols. 321–22.

Henry Laurens to Horatio Gates

Dear sir.   York Town 15 May 1778
    Yesterday I had the honor of presenting to Congress your favor of the 11th which brought on a Vote for a Dep. Ad. General for the Army under your Command. Lieutt. Col. Troup was appointed & you will receive Sir, within this Inclosure the Resolve of Congress & a Commission in terms.[1]
    Your intimation My Dear Sir, of the process & conclusion of the grand Council at Valley forge has raised a peculiar degree of satisfaction in my mind, I feel a happy presage from thence of a glorious Campaign, let us keep our friends in harmony & we shall have nothing to fear from our Enemies.
    Monsr. de la Neuville has obtained a vote extraordinaire "that it is the Interest of the United States to employ Monsr. de la Neuville as Inspector of the Army under the Command of Major General Gates." [2] He will receive a Commission this Morning, intends to proceed immediately to the destined station & after a probation of three Months, according to his Merit he is to expect Rank. In the meantime one hundred & five Dollars per Month & six Rations per day is to be his stipend.
    If you have not seen any thing like the Inclosed Paper the Contents will afford some amusement. Believe me to be with the most respectful attachment & Esteem, Dear sir, Your most Obedient & humble servant,   Henry Laurens, President of Congress.

RC (NHi).
    [1] Robert Troup declined to accept this appointment and was replaced by Col. William Malcom on June 2, 1778. JCC, 11:496, 560.
    [2] See JCC, 11:498–500; and Laurens to Lafayette, May 11, 1778, note 2.

Henry Laurens to George Washington

Sir,   York Town 15 May 1778
    The last I had the honor of writing to Your Excellency was dated the 11th by the hand of Colo. Gimad.

I have since presented to Congress Your Excellency's favors of the 11th & 12th which were immediately Committed & remain unconsidered.[1]

Your Excellency will receive under this Cover an Act of Congress of the present date for allowing Officers in the Army certain half Pay after the end of the present War & a gratuity to each Non Commissioned Officer & Soldier.

The bearer hereof will also deliver a Packet containing 500 forms of an Oath for the Army, more of these shall be sent by next opportunity.

I have the honor to be, With very great Regard & Esteem, Sir, Your Excellency's Obedient & most humble servant

Henry Laurens, President of Congress.

[*P.S.*] Extracts from the Philada. Paper which Your Excellency was so obliging to send I caused to be made & Printed the Evening the Paper came to hand much to the satisfaction of Congress & I believe of everybody. Possibly many Gentlemen in the Army may be uninformed of these Interesting transactions & therefore I shall transmit by the present bearer about 50 Copies.

Congress have Ordered a Brevet to Colo. Ethan Allen to Rank Colonel in the Army, I take the Liberty to inclose a Certificate of the Order & request Your Excellency will be pleased to cause it to be delivered to that Gentleman.   Henry Laurens

RC (DLC).
  [1] These letters are in PCC, item 152, 6:21–22, 31–34, and Washington, *Writings* (Fitzpatrick), 11:372–73, 379–81.
  [2] See Laurens to George Clinton, May 11, 1778, note 3.

James Lovell to John Adams

My dear Sir   15 May 1778.

I find it impossible to write to you at this Time so fully as I wish being greatly overplied with business from the neglect of others. I cannot however consent that Dispatches for France should go off without a line in Testimony of my personal attachment to you and in proof of remembrance of my promises, which kind of proof I have given 9 Times before since you left Boston.

Ever more uneasy when Negociation was talked of than when fresh Troops were destined against us, I am not quite at ease now, though a powerful Alliance is formed in our favour with which the States are much pleased. I cannot be free from concern least the insidious arts of Britain should prevail to induce us to neglect the Oppertunity which is now offered to exterminate the Curses that yet remain on this Continent nested in three Capitals. I fear a temporary Cessation of Hostilities would ruin our best Prospects; when a month of vigorous Exertions wd. free us from the Enemy altogether. The same time spent in Negotiation under a suspension of Hostilities would familiarize the persons of our Foes to us, and give them the advantage of reviving our former feeling Attachments to Britain and to sow Discord and Division in Places where the Government is yet wanting a consistency to render it proof against the Attack of an artful & designing Adversary. We owe Britain neither Love nor Money, but they owe us a vast Reparation. I have spoken here, without seeing, at present, the least opening for a Negociation, but I felt haunted by the simple Idea of such a Thing.

A sort of half pay Establishment is made for the Officers and a grant of 80 Dollars for the Men who shall continue to the end of the War, in Addition to former Encouragement. The Officers Provision will be either Life redeemable at six years Purchase or else for 6 years only absolute. The Soldiers 80 Dollars outright.[1]

Genl. Gates attended a Council in his Way to PeeksKill, and the Plan of Opperations was settled with great Harmony and Unanimity. This is a good Opening, may the Close be answerable![2]

Our little Navy is sadly destroyed but we have every natural Advantage for repairing our Losses. If it was not for the Justice of our Cause, no one could unravel the mystery of the manner in which we have so well supported ourselves against the most formidable naval Power in Europe. We have even made her afraid. As the Dispatch goes from the Eastward you will get News of your lovely family. The Independance was lost on Ocracock bar but we got the dispatches the Same Night that Folgiers came to hand: I send you a few Papers of a different kind from those sent to the other Gentlemen; and am most affectionately, your humb Servt.   J L

RC (MHi).

[1] Lovell was the only Massachusetts delegate to vote against the half-pay plan resolution passed this day in Congress. *JCC*, 11:502–3.

[2] At the May 8–9 council of war Washington and his general officers agreed "to remain on the defensive and wait events," rejecting any attempts to recapture New York or Philadelphia. Washington, *Writings* (Fitzpatrick), 11:363–66.

James Lovell to Benjamin Franklin

Sir,   York May 15th. 1778.

Your Favour of Decr. 21st I read in Congress that it might have the Operation which you benevolently generously and honourably intended.[1] But really Sir, when you say you "perceive he (Mr. D——) has Enemies," I am not inclined to determine that you form your

Opinion upon the Proceedings of Congress alone, to which you refer in the Beginning of your Letter.

You can have no adequate Idea of the bold Claims & even Threats which were made against Congress inducing the Necessity of disavowing Mr. D's Agreements and the consequent more disagreable Necessity of recalling him. You will have seen by past Letters of the Committee how formidable some here thought the Enmity of disappointed foreign Officers would prove both to Mr D—— and to these States. That Gentleman's Embarrassmts. have always been considered as Apologies for his Compliances; and you may rely upon it that imagined, if not real Necessity alone has governed the Decissions of Congress in respect to him; and that he will find he commands general Regard for the Manner in which he has conducted our Affairs abroad. He is exceedingly wanted here to explain some things; especially the Connexion with Mr Beaumarchais; and, in my Opinion, he may return with renewed Honour in Commission to Holland.

Folgier is to be dismissed with his Expences. I wish some Explanation may procure him a Gratuity.

I am, Sir, your most humble Servant, James Lovell

RC (PU).
[1] Franklin's December 21, 1777, letter to Lovell defending Silas Deane's contracts with sundry French officers is in Franklin, *Writings* (Smyth), 7:77–78.

Gouverneur Morris to George Washington

Dear General.   York Town 15th May 1778

Permit me to congratulate you on the passing a Resolution for a Kind of Establishment at this late Hour. It is not what you wished but it may do. You must pardon a little to the Republicanism of our Ideas. What is a little extraordinary there was no dissentient State and only two Individuals.[1] Yet no Measure hath ever been more severely contested. We shall now go thro the Regimental & other Arrangements. Those rapidly. You will perhaps get something like an Army by September. How happy are we that even our Negligence cannot ruin us. Had any Man ventured to say we should have been so exceeding dilatory last March and had he said it with Authority the most gloomy Ideas must have filled every Bosom. Your Council of War by what I can learn ended satisfactorily (nay amicably) to all. Thus Wags the World. I am respectfully & sincerely yours,

Gouvr Morris

RC (ViU).
[1] James Lovell and Oliver Wolcott were the only dissenters to the half-pay plan approved by Congress this day. *JCC*, 11:503.

Virginia Delegates to Patrick Henry

Sir: York May 15th, 1778.

The situation of the affairs of the United States urges (in our opinion) the necessity of a speedy confederation of the states, and as we are doutful whether we can be justifiable in departing a little, even in matters of form, from the strict letter of the instruction we are possessed of on that subject, we are apprehensive it may greatly impede the carrying into execution this salutary work.

We have therefore to entreat that you will lay the same before the General assembly for their consideration, and that they will give such further, or other instructions for our government in this particular, as they may judge expedient.[1]

We are with great respect, Your mo. Ob't. Servts.

Richard Henry Lee.

Francis Lightfoot Lee.

Thos Adams.

MS not found; reprinted from Henry, *Patrick Henry*, 3:166.

[1] The Virginia Assembly was the first to approve the proposed Articles of Confederation and had instructed their delegates on December 15, 1777, to ratify them without qualification. The journals of the Virginia House of Delegates do not indicate that the Virginia delegates received "other instructions" on ratification until a December 3, 1778, resolution directed them to propose to Congress that the confederation become binding on all states that ratified and that provision be made for the remainder to ratify later. *Journal of the House of Delegates of the Commonwealth of Virgina, 1777–81* (Richmond, 1827), October–December 1777, pp. 80–81; October–December 1778, p. 98.

In his June 5, 1778, letter to Richard Henry Lee, Thomas Jefferson explained why the Virginia Assembly did not respond to the delegates' request. "Your letter, about enlarging your powers over the confederation, was not proceeded on, because the nature of the enlargment was not chalked out by you so intelligibly as enabled the house to do any thing, unless they had given a *carte blanche.* Indeed, I believe, that, had the alterations proposed been specified, unless they had been mere form indeed, it might have been difficult to obtain their consent." Jefferson, *Papers* (Boyd), 2:194.

Committee of Commerce to the Commissioners at Paris

                                        Committee of Commerce,
Gentlemen   York in Pennsylvania May 16. 1778.

This will be accompanied with a Contract entered into between John Baptist Lazarus Theveneau De Francy agent of Mr. Peter Augustine Caron de Beaumarchais representative of the House of Roderique Hortalez & Co. and the Committee of Commerce.[1] You will observe that their Accounts are to be fairly stated and what is justly due paid. For as on the one hand Congress would be unwilling to evidence a disregard for, and contemptuous refusal of the Spontaneous freindship of his most Christian Majesty; so on the other they are unwilling to put into private Pockets what was gratuitously designed for Public benefit. You will be pleased to have their Accounts liquidated and direct in the liquidation thereof that particular care be taken to distinguish the property of the Crown of France from the Private property of Hortalez and company, and transmit to us the accounts so stated and distinguished. This will also be accompanied by an Invoice of articles to be imported from France and resolves of Congress relative thereto,[2] You will appoint if you judge proper an Agent or Agents to Inspect the quality of such Goods as you may appy for to the House of Roderique Hortalez & Co before they are shipped to prevent an imposition.

The obstructions of the Bays & Harbours to the Southward by British men of war, hath prevented our shipping Tobacco as we intended. We have ordered several Vessels lately to South Carolina for Rice and have directed the Continental Agent in that state to consign them to your address. So Soon as we can venture to send out Tobacco with any probability of Success we shall certainly do it.

This goes by a dispatch Vessel under the direction of the Committee of foreign Affairs. Five Others are employed in the same business which you will load with such articles as you may have ready to transmit to us.

We congratulate with you on the treaties entered into with his most christian Majesty and are with the greatest respect, Gentn, Your very humble servts,   William Ellery

Richd. Hutson

Thos. Adams

RC (PPAmP). In the hand of John Brown and signed by Adams, Ellery, and Hutson. Endorsed by John Adams: "Comtee of Commerce May 16. 1778 ansd. July 29."

[1] See Robert Morris' Proposed Report on the Claims of Roderique Hortalez & Co., March 12, 1778, note 1.

[2] A 15-page "Invoice of articles to be shipped from France by Roderique Hortalez & Co. for account and risque of the United States of America in whole or in part as the Commissioners of the United States at the Court of France shall direct" that was signed on May 18 by Adams, Ellery, and Hutson, is in the Franklin Papers, PPAmP. This "Invoice" is in a clerical hand, but a part of the heading was written by Ellery and portions of the list are in the hand of Théveneau de Francy. The May 16 resolves authorized the commissioners "to apply to the house of Roderique Hortalez & Co. for such of the said articles as they shall not have previously purchased or contracted for" and requested that the articles shipped by Hortalez & Co. not be insured, but that the commissioners "endeavour to obtain convoy for the protection thereof." JCC, 11:505.

Committee of Congress to Thomas Johnson

Sir,   York-Town, May 16th 1778.
Inclosed we send you Extracts from a Letter found on board a sloop which stranded on Cape-Henlopen the 1st instant.[1] We should have sent your Excellency the original, but that there were other matters in it which concern the State of Virginia. You will perceive, Sir, how necessary the utmost vigilance will be to detect and punish these nefarious practices, which we have reason to apprehend are frequently repeated on the Eastern shore in your State and in Delaware. Congress, having obtained several Letters which were found in the afsd. sloop, referred them to a Committee. As we find nothing in any others of them, that we conceive may be useful to you, we have only to assure you that it will afford us a singular pleasure to render you any service in assisting to secure and bring to trial such wicked Traitors. We have the Honor to be, Your Excellency's Most obedient humble servants,   Wm. Duer

Thos. M:Kean

Richard Henry Lee

RC (MdAA). Written by McKean and signed by McKean, Duer, and Lee.

[1] On this day, according to the journals, Congress referred a "number of intercepted letters" to a committee consisting of Richard Henry Lee, James Lovell, and John Witherspoon and authorized them to "pursue such measures as they judge necessary for the interests of the United States." *JCC*, 11:506. It seems clear, however, that Secretary Thomson erred when he listed the names of the members of this committee in the journals. An examination of the manuscript journals reveals that Thomson entered the names of Lee, Lovell, and Witherspoon sometime after May 16. This fact, considered in conjunction with the variation between their names and those who signed this letter, suggests that the secretary made an erroneous entry and that Duer and McKean, not Lovell and Witherspoon, were actually Lee's colleagues on this committee. See PCC, item 1, 16:32. This conjecture is also supported by the fact that when Gov. Richard Caswell of North Carolina replied on May 28 to another letter of this date from the committee, which has not been found, he addressed his response to Duer and Lee. *N.C. State Records*, 13:140.

The committee sent Governor Johnson an "Extract of a Letter from John Lancaster of New York to Mr. James Parker at Philadelphia, dated April 27. 1778," reporting that the British had recruited 130 men in Somerset County, Md., and that 170 more were ready to join the enemy. *Md. Archives*, 21:89–90. For the Maryland Council's May 22 reply to the committee, see ibid., pp. 106–7.

William Duer to Horatio Gates

My dear General,   York Town May 16th. 1778
This Letter will be deliver'd to you by Monsr. de la Neuville who is appointed Inspector to the Army under your Command agreable

to your Wishes.[1] I could have wished with many others that Congress had conferr'd on him at present the Rank of a Brigadier; but there was no Softening some of your Eastern Freinds, so that we have been obliged to content ourselves with a Promise from Congress to promote him to a Rank agreable to his Merit after an Experience of his Talents and Services for Three Months. At the Expiration of This Time I have no doubt but he will manifest himself Worthy of the Rank his Well wishers were anxious to procure for him in which Case I doubt not he will meet with your Patronage and favorable Recommendations to Congress.

From the Acquaintance I have had with this Gentleman I feel myself interested in his Behalf because I think him a Person of Modesty and Merit, capable of promoting in an Essential Degree the Discipline of our Army. I beg my Respects to Mrs. Gates, and am with much Respect, Your very Obedt. Hble servt.   Wm. Duer

RC (NHi).
[1] See *JCC*, 11:498–500; and Henry Laurens to Lafayette, May 11, 1778, note 2.

Henry Laurens to Ethan Allen

Sir,   16th May [1778]
I beg leave to refer to a Letter under the 15th Sent by Messenger Wilkinson,[1] I am now to add that Congress came this Morning to the following Resolution

"That Colonel Eathan Allen be entitled to all the benefits & privileges of a Lieutt. Colonel in the service of the United States during the time of his late Captivity."

When the Secretary sends me a Certified Extract from the Minutes, that shall be forwarded. In the mean time, this being of equal validity will be properly regarded by the pay Master General. The Resolve is general but I know of nothing it refers to but pay & Rations.

I am with great Regard

LB (DNA: PCC, item 13).
[1] See Laurens to Allen, May 15, 1778.

Henry Laurens to George Clinton

Sir,   16th May [1778]
I had the honor of writing to your Excellency the 11th Inst. by Messenger McClosky.

This will cover an Act of Congress of the 15th for obtaining proofs of infractions said to have been committed on the part of the Conquered in the Convention of Saratoga & for requesting Your Excellency to take the necessary measures for ascertaining Facts, so highly Interesting to the honor & welfare of these States.[1]

Congress have this day ordered the Treasury Board to remit to Your Excellency the Sums specifically, which are provided, by the last Resolve of the Act, for this service.

I have Honor to be &ca.

LB (DNA: PCC, item 13).

[1] Congress wanted Governor Clinton to ascertain the truth of reports that the British were violating the Saratoga Convention by forcing Canadian soldiers, who had been captured at Saratoga and released on condition they take no further part in the war, to fight against the United States again. *JCC,* 11:501–2. Clinton transmitted "several Affidavits respecting the Infraction of the Convention of Saraghtoga on the Part of the Enemy" with a September 1, 1778, letter to President Laurens and promised to send further evidence of British violations as soon as possible. Clinton did gather additional information about British infractions of the convention, but there is no evidence he ever forwarded it to Congress. See Clinton, *Papers* (Hastings), 3:717, 4:420–23.

Henry Laurens to John Ettwein

Reverend sir,   York Town Saturday 16th May 1778

Congress have been so closely engaged in affairs of great importance—requiring immediate attention—as to exclude hitherto the consideration of your Memorial, nor do I beleive there will be an opening for bringing it forward even on Monday next, although, as I judge from private conversation, there are many Gentlemen heartily disposed to grant your requests, the whole House may be so for aught I know.[1] As you have waited so many days without effect, you will probably save time by proceeding in your intended application to the State at Lancaster.[2]

Be assured Sir I will lay your Papers before Congress at the first opportunity for taking them under consideration & as speedily as the case will admit of, you shall be informed at Lancaster or Bethlehem of such determination as shall be had thereon.

From an opinion that the granting your requests will be equally consistent with sound Policy & Christian Charity, I cannot do less than wish very earnestly you may be dismissed from Lancaster with an answer which will give joy & satisfaction to the Brethren & eventually produce much benefit to these United States.

I am Reverend Sir, with great affection & Respect, Your friend & humble servt.   Henry Laurens

RC (PBMCA).

[1] John Ettwein's memorial to Congress, dated May 12 but actually written a few days earlier and signed by Ettwein "In the Name of the Bishops & Elders & on Behalf of all the United Brethren," is in the Laurens Papers, ScHi, and Kenneth G. Hamilton, *John Ettwein and the Moravian Church during the Revolutionary Period* (Bethlehem, Pa.: Times Publishing Co., 1940), pp. 197–99. This memorial, which Moravian church officials asked Ettwein to present to Congress because of his long friendship with Laurens, asked Congress to urge state governments—and particularly that of Pennsylvania—to relieve Moravians of the penalties to which they were liable under various state laws for their refusal to bear arms or abjure the king. Congress appointed a committee on May 14 to consider Ettwein's memorial but decided to take no formal action on the committee's report, which advised the delegates that it would be impolitic to grant the Moravian request. Instead, as the letter printed above suggests, Laurens merely gave Ettwein permission to intimate to the Pennsylvania Assembly that Congress would have no objection if it granted the Moravians the relief they sought.

That this was in fact one object of Laurens' letter emerges even more clearly from an account of Ettwein's dealings with Congress that the Moravian leader wrote in 1781. Therein he noted that he arrived in York on May 11 and went on to observe:

"On that very day, there was published an Address to the People by Congress, which seemed to me like a roaring storm. The treaty with France had just become known and all was at a fever heat. I visited President Laurens without delay, acquainted him with my mission, showed him the memorial, requested him to correct the copy intended for Congress. He replied: it would not be necessary, I should present both of them just as they were; he considered it our duty to make representation, whether fruit should come of it or not. After reading the memorials, he said: 'I like your Spirit!' He promised to speak with some members of Congress, naming some whom I should visit and interview privately about this. I did so early on the 12th of May, visiting 6 members of Congress; only Mr. Mac-Kean, Chief Justice of Pennsylv. proved unfriendly and told me: he would vote against it; if I were pledged to obey someone else, I would be no fit subject of the State. Governor [Gouverneur] Morris of New York introduced the memorial in Congress the same day, taking our part warmly, as did several others. Mr. Duane [Dana], a lawyer, said: 'I believe the Moravians are good Subjects, but they will have nothing to do with pulling down old Governments & setting up new ones!' He inquired of me, whether that were not our position, and I answered: 'Yes!' He volunteered to secure a piece of land of 5 to 6 square m. for the Brethren, 40 m. from Boston, together with an act from the State, similar to the act of Parliament, if we should care to establish a settlement there. I replied: now was not the time to contemplate anything like that. The eastern States require an oath of abjuration only from those who hold public office. The President said: should this people be driven into exile, he would be tempted to drop everything and go with them. A committee was appointed to examine the memorial more closely. Mr. Ellers [Ellery] of Rhode Island was purposely named for this; but afterward, by means of private juggling, MacKean replaced him on it. On the 14th, the President showed me their report in strict confidence. Its purport was as follows: that we still were in possession of our privileges, that even a mere representation to the Assembly would be too strong an action, etc. He was dissatisfied with it, laid the blame on M., and said: it should be recommitted! But after I had waited several days, I received the following document from the President himself, when I visited him on the 16th. [*Here follows Laurens' May 16 letter to Ettwein.*]

"Since he gave me verbal permission to make use of this, I gathered his intent, thanked him for his kind treatment, and journeyed to Lancaster." See "A Short Account of the Disturbances in America and of the Brethren's Conduct and Suffering in the Connection," in Hamilton, *John Ettwein*, pp. 203–5. Despite Laurens' assistance, Ettwein failed to persuade the Pennsylvania Assembly to revise the state's militia and test acts in accordance with Moravian wishes. Ibid., pp. 205–11.

In addition to confusing James Duane—who was in New York at this time—with Francis Dana, Ettwein's "Short Account" contains one other statement that is difficult to square with surviving documents, because according to the journals, William Ellery and Thomas McKean were appointed at the same time to the committee that considered Ettwein's memorial. JCC, 11:498. However, for the hazards involved in relying upon the journals as the absolute source for such information, see Congress to Thomas Johnson, this date, note.

[2] For the May 8 Moravian petition for relief which Ettwein submitted to the Pennsylvania Assembly in Lancaster, see Hamilton, John Ettwein, pp. 199–203.

Henry Laurens to Nathanael Greene

Sir,   16th May 1778

I beg leave to refer to an Act of Congress of this date for paying accounts contracted in New Jersey, for Horses purchased for the use of the Army by Governor Livingston's order & to an Extract of the Governors Letter mentioned in the Act, both papers will be forwarded in this Inclosure.[1]

I have the honor to be &ca.

LB (DNA: PCC, item 13).
[1] See JCC, 11:505; and Laurens to Washington, April 28, 1778, note 1.

Henry Laurens to John Laurens

My Dear Son   16th May 1778.

I thank you for your favor of the 12th.[1] I still entertain a respectable opinion of the fortitude & prowess of our Enemy, nor do I doubt but that long before this day thousands of Monsr. Noailles Countrymen have had their heads broke for his sneer.[2] I need not characterize Englishmen to a Gentleman so well acquainted with the Nation & the history. Were you to retort, that of late they have had no Character, I acquiesce, & add, this is a principal part of it. I am not among those who think Englishmen will be bantered out of their Wits, there is nothing galls them so much as the attempt & particularly when the taunts come from that quarter. I am glad of the alliance of France but it behoves us to look about us with Wisdom & firmness. We ought now to prepare for more serious contest than any we have experienced. If Great Britain has declared War against France the whole Nation will be engaged & the whole Nation is Mighty, their full power when exerted, & well directed, is almost Almighty. I am however more afraid of ourselves than I am of their allmightiness—afraid we shall lull our selves into a fatal security in the mistaken weakness of Britain & Strength of our Ally. This excepted, & all my fears vanish. We shall do very well & not the worse for the alliance. General St. Clair I apprehend had mistaken the New Constitution of So. Carolina—you will have had better information from Mr. Drayton who I beleive was almost Father & Mother of that production; to make you a competent judge I transmit a Copy within the present Inclosure.

Monsr. Lanuville vexed me very seriously the other Evening, he brought your Certified Copy of General Washington's Letter[3] & in much warmth asserted "it was not like the original—this had contained much warmer expressions in his favor." I first mildly answered—he must certainly be mistaken—He persisted & warmly too. Sir! I replied, it is, it must be, a true Copy, I will Stake my honor & my life upon it. He retired in much seeming disgust. I sent for Mr. Nourse Secretary pro. tem at the War Office & between chiding for the repeated losses & miscarriages of public papers in that Office, & intreaties to search diligently for the Generals original relative to Monsr. Lanuville, I prevailed on him at an unseasonable hour, not any such hour in my four & twenty to rummage, horrible Idea to rummage in an Office which ought to be accurate in all things. He succeeded, brought the Letter, I sent it immediately to the Gentleman Monsr. Lanuville who returned a deep apology, which covered with blushes he repeated next Morning.

Congress must from necessity have done something for this Gentleman—because he had been detained here after he had asked only for a Yes, or a No, upwards of three Months. There was however more than a little Struggle. Under a droll resolution he is appointed Inspector of the Northern department, where he is to be on probation three Months & then considered according to merit.[4] As he is said to be a competent Soldier & appears active, no doubt he will obtain his wishes, to the hiegth of a Brigadier.

To Inadvertence & not to want of good will must be imputed a deficiency in Congress toward Colo. Ethan Allen. I shall remind the House this Morning to order him a supply of Money, in the mean time I intreat you in my Name offer him any sum he may require, obtain it of the Pay Master, or from any Body & I will remit immediately a Sum to reimburse.[5] Give me leave my Dear Son to ask if you live without Money or how you live. Tell me if there is any considerable alteration in fashions of Gentlemens' apparel & to take if I stand in need as much of your Scarlet as will make me a Coat.

God bless you &ca.

LB (ScHi).
    [1] John Laurens' May 12 letter is in Simms, *Laurens Army Correspondence*, pp. 171–74.
    [2] See Laurens to George Clinton, May 11, 1778, note 3.
    [3] See Washington's January 23 letter of recommendation to Laurens in behalf

of the chevalier de La Neuville and his younger brother Noirmont in Washington, *Writings* (Fitzpatrick), 10:337.

⁴ See Laurens to Lafayette, May 11, 1778, note 2.

⁵ See Laurens to Ethan Allen, this date.

Henry Laurens to Lachlan McIntosh

My Dear General,   York Town 16th May 1778.

An honest North Britain Capt. Innis was wont to say, "here's health to our friends & damn the rest of our acquaintances." Although I never could implicitly adopt the Idea of this sententious Tar, there are circumstances in which my thin skin cannot resist against the power of his axiom. Now we meet again upon even ground; a ground from which I had neither descended nor clambered in the course of twenty six Years.

I have been honoured by the receipt of your favor of the 11th; an answer is anticipated. You have heard I presume in public Orders the Act of Congress respecting half pay for Officers & gratuity to Non Commissioned Officers & Soldiers after the conclusion of the War. The whole is gratuitous, & does not strike at the Constitution, unless Officers shall veiw in that light the exclusion from holding Offices of profit in common with their fellow Citizens, which may appear to some a little invidious. This short Act is the issue of a Mountain of Resolves & debates which had been in labour nearly two Months. The process will be a fitter subject for conversation, I shall not therefore attempt to trouble you with it at present. The original demand was unjust, its warmest advocates receded & shifted their ground, from time to time, compelled by the power of reasoning opposition. What is now Resolved might have been obtained on the 30th March,[1] but as I hope the pleasure of taking you by the hand in York I will only add that *your* conduct has lost you no ground in the esteem of your fellow Citizens.

Colo. Morgan wishes to see you & to accompany you to Fort Pitt.[2] You may be on the Road & this not meet you at Camp. Why should I say more than repeating that I continue with great Regard, Dear Sir, your obedient humble servt,   Henry Laurens

RC (PHi). Addressed: "Lachlan McIntosh Esquire, Brigadier General in the Army of the United States of America, Valley forge Camp."

[1] That is, four days after two members of the Committee at Camp had submitted a half-pay plan to Congress. *JCC*, 10:285–86.

[2] Washington had just appointed General McIntosh to replace Gen. Edward Hand as commander of Fort Pitt, Hand having been relieved of this command by Congress on May 2 "agreeably to his request." See *JCC*, 11:417; and Washington, *Writings* (Fitzpatrick), 11:379, 388, 429, 460–61.

James Lovell to John Adams

Dear Sir   May 16th. 1778

As I hinted to you in my letter of yesterday, which goes by a different Vessel from what bears this, Half-pay for 7 years, if they live so long, is granted to the Officers who serve the War out. It was also resolved to give 80 Dollars to the Men in addition to their Land.

The Commissioners at the Courts of Tuscany, Vienna & Berlin are to have plenipotentiary Commissions and not to be restricted to 12 years Treaties of *Amity* & *Commerce*. They could only propose & treat but not *conclude*. I hope they will not be allowed to make *Alliances*. Great Caution indeed is to be used on that Point.[1] There is but one Power besides France that could tempt me, unless Minhaer[2] should incline.

I presume our Army will not immediately be reformed, the Battalions consolidated and the useless officers dismissed. He, as yr. namesake says, will soon put Things to rights, having been obliged to coax almost instead of order in times past. Our Soldiers deserve all praise for their perseverance in hunger & nakedness but the *Gemmen*[3] have taken improper times to move their schemes of Pension and, will you believe it, Nobility. Some, in a big House, think that there is no Objection to Titles when not *hereditary*: Does it not look well ——— ——— LORD chief Justice of DELAWARE.

It is reported that Mr. S.A. is coming forward. I assure you we who are here have had consummate drudgery day & night ever since you left us in November. Mr. D[4] is a very good man indeed. I wish he would consent to tarry but his Estate is continually destroyed by his *Friends* who are keeping his Enemies *in order*. I mean the Guards over Burgoynes troops. I hope Mr. Deane will come over. I mean I hope he will not throw himself out of use by resenting an Act of Congress founded on Necessity. I think he is peculiarly calculated for Holland if we have a Commissioner there. Howe is not gone from his command. It is reported that the Enemy are embarking their heavy Baggage. This if fact is no proof of their quitting. It may be a prudent preparative to coming out against us: a few days will make something certain. The Council which Gates attended in his way to Peekskill was finished with great unanimity of Sentiments and much Cordiality between the great men tho the latter was not expected from some foolish bickerings which had been raised out of Conways Indiscretion, whose Resignation has been accepted.

I wish you happiness and I think you have the Fund for it whether you are now in Paris or a Prisoner in England.

Give my love to your Son and tell him it is Matris Ergo, that he may try his talent at the Phrase, which teazed me in my Infancy.

I hope soon to have from you Sic Canibus Catulos similis,[5] by way of Confession, and some Substitute, more adapted to my Experience than the Crepoctis of Tityrus, to mark your Sublimities. Be cautious, however, that you do not hint that you have seen any Thing Superior to Philadelphia; unless you are willing instantaneously to forfeit the great Portion you hold of Mrs. Clymars good Opinion.

Genl. R——[6] has been home several Weeks: he has purchased into an Estate about one hundred miles off near to water Carraige, where is an exceeding rich Lead Mine capable of supplying the army, & of repaying him in half a Year or less.

Your affectionate humb servt.   J L

RC (MHi).

[1] Although on May 28 Congress approved new commissions with "full power and authority to communicate, treat, and conclude" for the commissioners at the courts of Vienna, Berlin, and Tuscany, it could not agree on new instructions for new alliances. See *JCC,* 11:505, 546–47; and Committee of Congress Report, June 1, 1778.

[2] That is, "Mijnheer," the Dutch.

[3] Perhaps Lovell means "gemeen," a Dutch word sometimes used to denote "mob" or "rabble."

[4] Francis Dana.

[5] In such a manner (I thought) puppies similar to (grown) dogs, Virgil *Eclogues* 1.19–22. Lovell was apparently calling attention to Tityrus' foolish comparison of Mantua to imperial Rome—a futile exercise in comparing the lesser with the great, puppies with their sires and dams. Having recently arrived at Paris, Adams would doubtless soon be reporting his experiences in France to correspondents in America who had never ventured upon the larger world stage.

[6] Daniel Roberdeau. See Roberdeau to George Bryan, May 30, 1778, note.

Thomas McKean to Sarah McKean

My dear Sally,   York-Town, May 16th. 1778.

Inclosed herewith you will receive an Address from Congress to the Inhabitants of the United States of America, and the Declaration of the Marquiss de Noailles, with all the news of the last week excepting some which I received from Mr. President Rodney & Captain Parry,[1] such as the capture of a sloop laden with wine, rum, sugar, porter, cheese and a large quantity of dry goods valued at £60,000; she stranded on Cape Henlopen the first of this month and was taken by Captain Parry under a heavy fire from an armed English schooner, but without having a man hurt; all the cargo is effectually secured; another company at Duck-creek has taken an armed schooner in Duck-creek with the Captain viz. Cook, two Lieutenants and the crew. There has been a great firing on Wednesday last at Busseltown, about eleven miles from Philadelphia, between General Maxwell & 1000 men, and a party of the enemy, the result not known.

The treaty with France is so favorable to the United States, & so much beyond what has been ever done on such like occasions in the world before, that in return I shall by virtue of my sovereign power, not only recognize the King of France as the *most Christian,* but also the most wise, most just, most generous and most magnanimous of Princes.

Now for some disagreeable intelligence. The Enemy, about a thousand in number, in row-gallies, flat-bottomed boats &c have been up at Bordentown, destroyed our frigates, row-gallies & all the vessels there, and burned Mr. Borden's house, the tavern he devised to Josey M:Kean, Mr. Hopkinson's and on the opposite shore all Mr Kirkbride's buildings.

I should be glad to hear from you by the way of Lancaster, and to know when you imagine the Boys will be ready to go to school. Goods are falling very fast—Coffee is retailed here, the very best, at 17/6, tho' it was 22/6 two weeks ago.

I am, my dear Sally, with love & kisses to the children, Your affectionate,   Thos M:Kean

P.S. Yesterday the Officers in the army are allowed half-pay for seven years after the end of the present war. Colo. Francis Johnston upon my recommendation, and without his sollicitation or knowledge, is appointed Commissary-General of Prisoners in the stead of Mr. Boudinot, who has resigned in order to take his seat in Congress.[2]

RC (PHi).
[1] The following information was contained in Caesar Rodney's May 8 letter to McKean, which is in Rodney, *Letters* (Ryden), pp. 267–68.
[2] See Henry Laurens to Francis Johnston, May 11, 1778, note 1.

Marine Committee to the Middle Department Navy Board

Gentlemen   May 16th 1778
You are to appoint a Clerk & Treasurer for your Board and a Clerk for the Pay Office.

You are to call upon Mr Lux for and Liquidate any Accounts he may have against the Continent as Continental Agent.

You are to call upon & settle Mr Jonathan Hudsons Account for Superintending the building of the Brig Baltimore.

You are to call upon Mr Stephen Steward whom we have appointed to settle the outstanding accounts and pay off the wages of the seamen of the Virginia and receive of him such Accounts as he hath collected as well paid as unpaid, and also his receipts for Seamens wages, and discharge him from any further trouble in that business which you are to take up & settle.

You are also desired to take care of the Timber and other Materials for ship building belonging to the Continent which we are informed are floating about the River Patapsaco.

You are to converse with Mr Wells Ship Carpenter about the building of Small Vessels for the Continent, and after that require of him whether any Continental Timber or other Materials for ship building have been converted to private use.

You are to be strict in the enquiry into the loss of the Virginia,[1] among other things how Captain Nicholson came to attempt to go out of the Cheseapeake without having a Pilot on board his Ship. Why he did not attempt to run his Ship Ashore. If that could not be effected why he did not throw overboard his Guns, ammunition, warlike and other Stores.

Eight Ton of Continental Hemp hath been lately sent from this place to Baltimore and the other part was to be wrought up for the said Brigantine if she should want the whole. We would have you see that such Cordage is made up as Captain Read may want as soon as possible that Vessel lying at a great expence and waiting only for Rigging, and dispose of the Remainder of the Hemp as you may judge proper. We are Gentlemen, Your hble servants

LB (DNA: PCC Miscellaneous Papers, Marine Committee Letter Book).

[1] See Henry Laurens to the Middle Department Navy Board, April 27, 1778, note 1.

New York Delegates to Horatio Gates

Dear General   York Town May 16th 1778

The Bearer Captain Thos. Smith is an old Mariner, born in the City of New York, from which Place he saild for many Years, and, for some Time in the Employ of Mr. Phil. Livingston. Should the Command of one of the Gallies now building in the North River for the Defense of the Chain be vacant, we beg leave to recommend this Gentleman for the Command of it, to which (having served for a Considerable Time as a Lieut. of a Privateer during the last War with Reputation) we doubt not he will be found very adequate. We congratulate you on the Marquis de Noailles Message to the Court of Great Britain and sincerely wish you much happiness, and success in your Command.

We are, dear General, with Respect Your Obedt. Hble. Servt.

                                               Phil Livingston

                                               Gouvr. Morris

                                               Wm. Duer

RC (PHi). Written by Duer and signed by Duer, Livingston, and Morris. Addressed: "To The Honble Horatio Gates Esqr, Majr. Genl. and Comr. in chief of the Northern Department."

Charles Carroll of Carrollton to Charles Carroll, Sr.

Dear Papa,   York 17th May 1778

I wrote to you the 14th instant a few lines just to inclose you the postscript to the Pena. Gazette of the 9th instant, which I now again send you together with Yesterdays gazette. I forgot to mention in my last that I have engaged Mr. Wilson, an eminent lawyer of Pena. who has lately removed into Maryd., in all my law business. He will attend our present provincial court; I wrote by him to Mr. Stone to put off our cause with Trammell. I have also engaged Stone in my law business, so that I think I have secured the two best lawyers that practice in our courts of law.

I am really concerned for the sudden death of poor Mr. Lux. He was useful public man, & his family will feel his loss. There has lately been a council of war at Camp of the Major Generals for concerting a plan of operations. I am informed a plan was unanimously agreed on: that our army is in good health & spirits, & increasing fast. Last Friday Gen. Lee went to camp to take a command in the army. He has applied to Congress to be made a Lieutenant General; he told me before he wrote his letter, that he should write to Congress for that promotion, & asked my opinion about it; I told him I should oppose his promotion; he seemed chagrined & nettled at my frankness, or with my opinion, which I am determined to abide by for more reasons than one. Congress has unanimously agreed to allow the officers 7 years half pay from the end of the war, as a compensation for their hard services, and the depreciation of our currency. I am told half Joes which before the news of the treaty with France, & Ld. North's speech, sold for £24 paper are now hawked about at £12 & £8. I do not however perceive that the price of commodities at or near this place has fallen.

Pray inform me whether the fruit has suffered by the frost which we had about ten days ago. How goes on the vineyard? Do the vines seem to thrive, & do they promise much fruit?

Monday 18th May P.M. This day's post brought no letters from you; which surprises and gives me no little uneasiness, as I know your punctuality in writing. I hope to God you are all well. This morning arrived at Congress from Boston Capt. Courter, late commander of the Oliver Cromwell privateer. He sailed from Corunna in Spain the 10th of March in a French frigate of 40 guns called the Neptune &

brought duplicates of the treaty, which was brought over by Mr. Dean. I have the pleasure to inform you that the Dean frigate, Capt. Nicholson, & a 20 gun ship part of the fleet expected from France are arrived the one at Por[t]smouth the other at Boston. Docr. Cooper of Boston writes to Mr. Lovel a member of Congress of the 6th instant that *most* of the fleet expected from France were safely arrived, & Capt. Courter told me the day he left Boston several vessels were coming into port, so that in all probability all the expected supplies of cloathing &c &c will get safe to hand. This is great & glorious news. We were very uneasy respecting the fate of our little fleet which consisted of about 10 or 11 sail, and which sailed from France very late in February.

I am at loss to account for you not writing to me by the last post. I form a thousand conjectures; perhaps your letter may have been mislaid. I hope you are all well; if that was not the case, I am sure you would send off an express for me, that is Sam with horses to bring me home. Give my affectionate love to Molly. I hope she is much better than when She wrote to me last. My love to Mrs. Darnall & the little ones.

By late accounts from the Camp our army is encreasing fast. God grant you a long continuance of health. I am, Yr. affectionate Son,
                                   Ch. Carroll of Carrollton

P.S. I forgot to mention that Docr. Franklin was presented to the King of France in form the 20th of March and most graciously recd. The King of France has appointed an Ambassador to these States, and a Committee was this day named for fixing the ceremonial of his reception. I am one of the Committee. Mr. Carmichael is arrived at Boston in the fleet above mentioned from France.

In Congress 19th May. Gen. Mifflin has recd. a letter from Col. Biddle containing the following articles of intelligence—vizt that the Enemy have embarked their heavy cannon, that the stalles for their cavalry are compleated; that the Tories of Pha. have hired houses in N. York, in short from every appearance we may soon expect to see Pha. abandoned by the Enemy. It is said Gen. Howe is returned; he probably met when he got to the capes of Delaware with counter orders. We expect every hour dispatches from our General; but if it be true that that this day he will move towards Pha. he will too busy to write.

A hot press has lately taken place in Pha. Whigs & Tories have been pressed on board without distinction.

RC (MdHi).

Henry Laurens to David Espy and Others

Gentlemen.   Sunday Noon 17th May 1778.

Your Petition to Congress under a Cover directed to me, this moment came to hand. The little Lad who brought it discovers some anxiety to return immediately—for this reason & also because I believe his Stay here is not necessary I shall detain him no longer than while I assure you, your Petition shall be presented at the earliest meeting of Congress tomorrow.[1]

Congress is already apprized of the alarming attempts of our Enemies by means of their Savage Allies & we are adopting proper measures for defeating all their hellish Machinations. Great Britain now convinced of the impossibility of subduing these United States, is endeavouring to distress them by such extravagant Acts in predatory War as will Stain the annals of history with marks of Infamy & disgrace upon that once Magnanimous people. Their Soldiers are, as often as they can Steal abroad, making incursions near the Banks of Delaware, burning Houses, captivating, & too often murdering, such Men as they can lay hold of, leaving helpless Women & Children exposed to suffer all the hardships arising from the loss and absence of heads of families & the total destruction of their Habitations, apparel, furniture & provision. They have even improved upon the lessons learned from their Indian Consorts.

Their measure is nearly filled up, the hand of Vengeance directed by God himself will speedily overtake them.

Let each of us by proper spirit & becoming exertions in our respective spheres strive to be an happy Instrument of Providence.

I send in the Present Packet an Address of Congress to the Inhabitants of these States.

A paper containing such parts of the late Treaties between France & the United States of America as are judged necessary for public information.

And also an hand Bill in which is set forth important intelligence from the Courts of France & England.

General Sir Wm. Howe embarked as I am well informed last Tuesday & left Sir Henry Clinton his successor in Command at Philadelphia. If we will act with Wisdom & fortitude in every quarter, Sir Henry will soon be compelled to follow the other hopeless Knight.

You have my best wishes & may depend upon my best endeavors for public good in which your particular happiness is included.

Gentlemen, I am &ca.

LB (DNA: PCC, item 13). Addressed: "David Espy, Charles Cossna, Andrew Huston, William Parker—& others—Petitioners to Congress, in a Petition dated Bedford 12 May 1778."

¹ Although the journals record that on May 18 Congress read and referred to the Board of War a petition from Bedford County, Pa., the petition itself is not in PCC. Later the same day Congress also referred to the board a letter on "the distressed condition of the frontiers" of Pennsylvania from Thomas Smith of Bedford County and authorized the board "in conjunction with General Washington, to take such measures for affording present relief to the western frontiers as can be adopted." See *JCC*, 11:506–7. Accordingly, on the following day Timothy Pickering wrote to Washington on behalf of the board asking the commander in chief to detach troops from his army to help secure the Pennsylvania frontier and revealed that Congress was considering a more radical solution. "Congress," he informed Washington, "have in contemplation an expedition against Detroit, or at least into the indian country, that they may strike at the root of the mischief. But should it be resolved on immediately the necessary preparations cannot be completed 'till September; and until then such a regular force as we have mentioned on the frontiers appears to us indispensible." *Pa. Archives*, 1st ser. 6:528. Washington replied to Pickering on May 23, withholding comment on the projected expedition but pointing out that he was sending reinforcements to Fort Pitt. Although Congress actually authorized an expedition against Detroit on June 11, the delegates agreed on July 25, 1778, to postpone it after Governor Henry of Virginia informed them that such a campaign was "utterly impracticable at this Season of the Year & under our present circumstances." See *JCC*, 11:588–89, 720–21; Washington, *Writings* (Fitzpatrick), 11:439–41; and Henry, *Patrick Henry*, 3:180–84.

Henry Laurens to the Marquis de Lafayette

Dear Sir,   17th May [1778]

The very Morning Colonel Gimat left York I sent to the Board of War an extract from your Letter respecting Colonel Armand & desired Monsr. Lomagne to attend the Board until a plan shall be digested & a Report made to Congress.¹ This I esteem the most eligible & most expeditious mode for bringing the purpose to effect. Your Excellency may rely on my good will & utmost endeavors but such crowds of important business now lie before Congress, increasing every Morning as almost forbid my hopes of introducing this in a few days.

I have not been able to collect one more French paper in addition to those few sent by Colonel Gimat. Mr. Lovel gave me the strongest assurances those were all he was possessed of or knew where to collect. I will keep my attention very closely to future importations.

Congress having finished after long labour, in a very few Lines, the scheme of gratuity for officers, Non Commissioned Officers & Soldiers of the Army; the general arrangement comes next under consideration, this work will be prepared by Mr. Govr. Morris & Mr. Dana.² To these Gentlemen I will present all your Excellency's intimations respecting French Gentlemen & I could wish you would speak in a few Lines on the Subject directly to Mr. Morris & Mr. Dana. There will be time enough, we shall get through the scheme in the course of a Week.

The minute I read the Duke de Noaille's information to the British King, I sent for a printer & ordered 500 Copies to be immediately struck off.[3] Congress received the Impressions next Morning with great Satisfaction & I believe every body is equally well pleased.

I would willingly fill this sheet with some thing or other, but Monsr. Contair has possitively set his Watch an hour forward & looks very unpleasant when I assure him 'tis but 5 Minutes past seven—& that I have been sitting here already two hours & an half. I must submit; he will wait no longer. Your Commands in all respects Sir shall be faithfully attended to by your Excellency's Much obliged humble Sert.

LB (ScHi).

[1] See Laurens to Lafayette, May 11, 1778, note 4.

[2] For the plan of the "general arrangement" of the army adopted by Congress on May 27, see *JCC*, 11:538–43. The first four sections of this plan, relating to the arrangement of the infantry, artillery, cavalry, and provost corps, are taken from enclosures one through four of Committee at Camp to Laurens, February 5, 1778. The remainder, dealing with the appointment, pay, and ranking of certain officers, seems to be based upon an undated report in the hand of Francis Dana, a member of the Committee at Camp, that is printed in *JCC*, 12:1269–71. In June 1778 Congress had John Dunlap print a broadside containing the May 27 plan for the army as well as related resolves of May 28 and June 2 on civil staff officers and rations. Evans, *Am. Bibliography*, no. 16126. See also *JCC*, 554–55, 560–61, 581–82; and Committee at Camp to Laurens, February 5, 1778, note 1.

[3] Laurens is evidently referring to the May 13 postscript to the *Pennsylvania Gazette*, on which see Laurens to George Clinton, May 11, 1778, note 3.

Henry Laurens to John Laurens

17th May 1778

I beg you will deliver the enclosed Letter to Col. Ethan Allen[1] & tell me, if you can discover, whether he is satisfied or otherwise with the Contents.

There are people in the World who suffer themselves to be cheated & bullied out of Millions & who overlook occasions inviting & demanding liberality.

If the Colonel is not quite pleased as possibly he may not be, we must attempt to obtain awkwardly what might have been performed with a good grace.

Perhaps my own feelings are too quick.

God bless you &ca.

LB (ScHi).

[1] See Laurens to Ethan Allen, May 16, 1778.

Henry Laurens to Rawlins Lowndes

Dear Sir,   17th May [1778]

My last private is dated the 1st Inst. & forwarded by Messenger Cross since which I have been honoured with your Excellencys favors of the 13th & 18th April as acknowledged in a public Address of the 14th Inst.

I presented & read these to Congress as public & received great satisfaction from the attention which was paid to the whole & not less from the applause generally expressed upon particular articles. Men are pleased with instances of watchfulness over the public Stock even when they are not themselves half so attentive to expenditures as they ought to be.

As Your Excellency's Letters are Committed, & the Merits of course are to undergo the consideration of Congress, it would be improper in me to decide on any part. I shall therefore speak to a few points in general terms without pretending higher authority than my own.

The insurrections in our State & the affected Invasion upon Georgia were alarming, but I apprehend the whole appearance of danger has vanished before this day. The policy of St. Augustine, 'tis probable, led them to threaten, in order to avert a stroke which in their own weak state they dreaded at home.[1] 'Tis to be lamented that another Season is lost in which we ought to have removed the Enemy from that Quarter. I do not see at present any ground for apprehensions of a preconcerted Plan for attacking So. Carolina in front; we ought nevertheless to be continually prepared, guarded & watchful, this has been my sentiment from the earliest date of the War, & I have not lost the Idea of our receiving a brush from the tail of that Comet which has spread flames in these northern States. The Scotch are indeed exceedingly zealous in raising Troops but these must supply deficiencies in the Numbers expected from Germany & will be wanted there or in the West Indies. The Enemy cannot be ignorant of the value of So Carolina & Georgia, & will assuredly call upon them at a leisure day; a persuasion of this fact on our part will lead us into such measures for defence & safe retreat as will render the work more arduous on theirs.

One branch we ought to be most especially attentive to, it is absolutely necessary to be jealous of *every* stranger & of every doubtful Character in the State, particularly so, in the Capital & other Sea Ports.

If it were possible to procure a person, or more than one person whose business should be unknown to each other, to discover the errand of every Master of Vessel & of every Stranger coming in to our Country no expence would be too great for the purpose; Where bosoms are found impenetrable much discovery may be made by

incessant watchfulness day & night upon external movements. There
has been & is an universal laxity in Government from this, to the
remotest Sothern State which has afforded the Enemy much of their
powers for distressing us. It would seem as if we had not felt our own
dignity & importance or as if we were not in earnest. New Jersey &
New York driven to extreme distress environed by & almost incorporated with them have been necessitated to watchfulness. The Eastern States preserve a policy of *their own;* in all respects they take good
care of themselves, I am not among those who censure. I am grieved
that we content ourselves with censuring & do not imitate them.
From this State to Georgia there has been much foul play by Men of
fair faces, hence the Enemy has drawn large succors of provision,
Men, & Intelligence. To expatiate upon this head to Your Excellency
would be waste of time, If we believe the fact, my aid will not be
required to point out means for the remedy.

I will barely repeat that it appears necessary to keep a watchful
Eye on every one, & add, particularly so, upon Men from among those
who in bulk are our friends the Bermudians & Bahamians. Some of
the former have sold their friendship for us, for British Gold & injured our Cause exceedingly. Was there ever a deeper scheme than
the project of Arthur yet we are indebted for the discovery to his folly
not to our sagacity, & I have yet some doubts of our holding him a
prize.

When I look back to the precipice on which I have been Standing
& on which my Country, more valuable than ten thousand I's, had
been tottering all the past Winter, I shudder. Had the British General
been a Man of Enterprize, Congress would have been on ship Board
& Sir William Howe in quiet possession of York Town & of Albany.
He could not be ignorant of our circumstances but our safety lay in
Mrs. Lowry's lap.[2]

All the dangers to which we have been exposed were the effects of
that languor in the Quarter which I have described, & so is the waste
& misapplication of Millions of Money & loss of thousands of Men by
death & desertion. If we are eventually delivered & without many
more rude strokes, we shall have to regret that we are more indebted
to the selfish views of deep politicians out of the limits of these States,
than to the Wisdom & fortitude within, but while we continue to be
in danger of such strokes is not it sir, our indispensible duty to be
watchful on all sides, & in every place to guard against them?

I have my suspicions that a narrow inspection would discover the
Board of War's expectations of Stores at Charles Town are not without foundation.[3] But suspicions are not proof. This must be produced
by scrutiny, if anybody will take the necessary trouble.

Had your Excellency known in what manner we had just before
treated your worthy predecessor's Certificates for money advanced in

So. Carolina for public services, you would have been more cautious of draining our private Treasury. I had intimated when the draughts were given to Mr. Rose on the Loan Office that there was no Money there & that consequently the Bills would not be paid. I was really affected by the item of advance made on that account although made with the best intentions & my duty obliges me to add that more than one Member on the floor expressed dissatisfaction with the practice of advancing Money from a particular Treasury On general Account without special order. This was indeed rather applied to the advance made to the Commercial Agent. I was well pleased with the hint, persuaded in my own mind Your Excellency will not insist upon a second.[4]

The taking up loan Office Certificates for raising Money seems to be very displeasing; If Money lenders will not deposit in that fund because of the low Interest, can a Negotiation in Trade be effected without a vast discount? Whatever this discount may be, it is kept out of Sight by laying the loss on the purchase. I refer only to the practice in this part of the Union.

It has been asserted in Congress that a gainful infamous traffic has been carried on by some of our numerous hosts of honest Servants, by means of loan office Certificates, which have been, as they impudently pretended, passed for ready money; but the prices of articles produced by them were enhanced 25 to 50 Per Cent to the emolument of the contracting parties, I say sir, this has been asserted, & in a land abounding with practices of peculation & sacrilegious Robberies of public Money I find no difficulty in beleiving it, hence appears in another veiw the necessity for watchfulness. If the Evil had stopped in the instances alluded to, the loss would have been confined, but a door once opened to advanced prices corruption becomes contagious, pervades every branch of Commerce, calls for extra Millions, depreciates the value of our Money, & threatens bankruptcy. There can be no doubt of the payment of Interest Money in Bills of Exchange in terms of the past resolves of Congress, but this is another Evil to be deprecated for the future. An attempt to renew this mode of Payment will be made, I shall as I did the former, oppose it with all my might. Some gentlemen now see the pernicious effects & acknowledge the justness of my predictions but when Men are Interested, their Sight fails on one side & continues extremely clear in the sinister view.

Some shrewd remarks I learn have been made on the charge of our State account for the expence of the expedition against the Cherokees, it has been said, that Gentlemen were pleased with it, the Land Ceded by the Savages must of course be held as common property. The intimation came to me indirectly, through one of my Colleagues; at a proper time I shall be under no difficulty to find as proper an answer —precedent & Confederation will assist me. My Stated avocation will not spare me time for inspecting minutely, but I am pleased to learn that every charge which had been apparently incurred for the general weal is introduced, I am under no doubt but our utmost intent will be fully countenanced.

With respect to the little explanation between your Excellency & Genl. Moultrie it is sufficient to intimate that under the Resolve of Congress of the 9th Febry Governor Livingston Weeded out a number of useless & pernicious Officers in the State of New Jersey, among others a Dep. Qur. Master general, exactly a Case in point, for which I have once returned His Excellency the thanks of Congress—& shall repeat the same tomorrow.

Your Excellency's refusing to grant Money before an account of the expenditure of former grants had been rendered has been marked with particular approbation, more of this will probably appear in the Report of the Committee, had Congress themselves given the example two years ago millions would have been saved—we are but beginning—& seem rather disposed to put the labouring Oar into other hands but 'tis a momentous concern, in which each state is Interested & in which each executive in my humble opinion is in Duty bound seriously to interpose all their powers. It would take up the remainder of the Night were I to enlarge on this head by adducing Cases to prove the necessity for watchfulness over the public Stewards in every branch of expenditure meaning no imputation upon the Gentleman checked by your Excellency.

The Sale of the General Moultries prize in a Dutch port is an Excellent prognostick of determinations at the Hague respecting these United States.[6] Poor old England, first cheat herself & now she will find she is bamboozled by all her Neighbors.

Within this packet your Excellency will find an hand Bill containing the sarcastical declaration of the Ducke de Noailles to the Court of London of His Master's alliance with the United States of America, which may possibly be new at Charles Town.

Two days ago I transmitted an Act of Congress to the Governor of New Jersey & President of this State for conducting the Honorable John Penn & B. Chew, from the place of their confinement in the former to any place within the latter & there to release them from their parole when they will become amenable to the Law requiring all the Inhabitants to take an Oath of Allegiance & Abjuration & may make their election. 'Tis suggested by some Gentlemen they will take the Oaths & save their Estates.

Your Excellency will read in the Connecticut paper the spirited reply of Govr. Trumbull to Mr. Tryon. This haughty Quondam must have suffered extreme mortification from the retorts upon his Certificates & empty Bills.[7]

The Tories & Indians instigated at Detroit are become very troublesome, the latter have committed many cruel Murders & Struck a panic upon the Inhabitants of the Western frontier, measures are adopted for giving these wretches employment at home but we have really been tardy, & much more mischief will be done before they meet a rebuff. The other Allies of Great Britain had affected Government, established a Mock Congress & Issued Money, nine of these I am told have been hanged at Fort Pitt & I saw pass by my Window this Evening about thirty in Irons. No Stone is left unturned, no cruelty unessayed, by our grand Enemy for distressing us. Predatory War in all its horrors is carried on by British Officers & Soldiers upon the Banks of Delaware, as often as they can steal abroad. They burn Houses, Captivate & too often Murder such Men as they can catch, leave helpless Women & Children to suffer all the miseries arising from the loss of heads of families & the total destruction of their habitations, apparel, furniture & provision, improving even upon the lessons taken from their Savage Consorts.

We are told & beleive that Sir William Howe embarked at Philadelphia on Tuesday last, & left Sir H. Clinton successor in Command. From a new proposition made by Sir William some fourteen days since for Exchange of Prisoners, from the vast quantity of Fire Wood which the British Soldiers have cut for exportation, from the embarkation of many families who had remained in the City when we came out, & several other circumstances, an opinion that all the Troops will speedily evacuate & burn it prevails. I feel all this as conjecture. If General Clinton really means to leave us, he covers his design by a mighty bustle in preparations for the field. It is probable he waits for orders which will follow a declaration of War. The expected Commissioners are not yet arrived, this circumstance gives further scope for conjecture.

Doctor Franklin was presented on the 10th March to his Most Christian Majesty & now protector of the Rights of Mankind in the Character of Ambassador plenipotentiary from the United States of America & was most graciously received. The King at the same time named an Ambassador from his Court to the United States. This circumstance has given a little fillip to Congress.[8] After living eight Months in a State somewhat below my Overseers in Carolina, we Talk of a Table; a Committee is appointed for the purpose & I am ordered upon it.[9]

General Washington's Army, as a friend of mine informs me, is amazingly advanced in discipline by the indefatigable attention & great Military abilities of Baron Stüben now a Major General;[10] by a late return it was 14000 Strong, actual Combatants, & Men are daily increasing that Number, but desertions keep it down.

General Gates is about this day arrived at Fish Kill where he is to take upon him the whole Northern department, I have a Letter from that worthy Man in which he assures me the grand Council lately held at Valley forge had been conducted with perfect harmony & that he entertained the most favorable hopes from the plan concerted; hence I infer with the highest pleasure, he had a Cordial meeting & parting with the General & trust he will hereafter be aware of designing flatterers.[11]

General Burgoyne must now be far advanced toward the place where he may end his progress by a sudden stroke before his departure. With great reluctance & not without great murmuring, he paid the Agents appointed by Major General Heath 94000 Dollars in solid Coin for the fuel supplied the British Troops last Winter, Transports are gone round to Boston to return the provision which those Troops consumed, in quantity & quality.

We are now taking Measures for obtaining strong proofs of prevailing Reports, that the Convention of Saratoga was broken on the part of Great Britain, & I am particularly desired by Congress to request your Excellency will without delay, cause an enquiry to be made of Captain Senf lately arrived in Charles Town respecting the Colours & Military Chest, & to transmit such intelligence by a faithful & expeditious Courier as may be received from that Gentleman.[12]

Since his departure from this place it has been repeatedly intimated to me that he had said the Colours had been concealed in part of the Baggage declared sacred by an Article of the Convention & the Cash in the Military Chest deposited, in parts, in the hands of the Officers.

I need not explain to your Excellency the vast importance of a detection of these frauds nor the absolute necessity for dispatch, nor that Captn. Senff ought to be examined touching other articles besides those abovementioned & the whole upon Oath. Here we have also been somewhat dilatory, I urged the present determination upwards of two Months ago, within a few days of Captn Senf's leaving this place.

The fleet expected from France with Cloathing, ammunition &ca &ca arrived about 14 days ago at Boston & Portsmouth & with them several very valuable prizes, no other particulars are received, except the naming 1 French 40 Gun Ship. Captn. Nicholson in one of the States Frigates & one other States Vessel, authentic & special advices I expect every hour.

Spain reserves herself for the arrival of her plate fleet looked for in April, when if England shall have declared War against France she will enter the lists & Portugal has certainly acceded to the family Compact. Spain affects much munificence towards this Infant World, when I am at Liberty I will explain to Your Excellency that my singular opinion respecting her views prove to be well founded. I communicated my suspicions to my Colleague the Cheif Justice & beleive he has improved upon them in some of his advices to Charles

Town, he said he would. At present that Gentleman is a truant, has been a fortnight on a Visit to Camp for which I shall salute his return with a little scold. A Man of his abilities & diligence I wish to have ever present.

After two Months labor on a scheme for half pay to officers, in which, as a Silent auditor & Spectator, I was Witness to many excellent & some violent Strokes in parliamentary Manœvre, a long Report of a Committee, ridden by amendments & New Resolves, the original project by the Grace of God, was the day before yesterday rid to Death, & from the Ashes, the inclosed Act of Congress of the 15th May, produced. I transmitted it Instantly to the Commander in Cheif; I shall learn in a day or two its reception in Camp. Congress have now Entered heartily upon the general Arrangement of the Army & will get through without difficulty.

Your Excellency will receive in a seperate Packet 13 Sets of Marine Commissions &ca all I have at present & all in my opinion that ought to be used until amendments suitable to our change of Circumstances are made. I have addressed Congress on this subject & hope we shall find time for the purpose immediately after finishing the arrangement—also 20 Military Commissions which may serve in cases of exigency until I transmit more, with the Report on your Excellency's Letters. The impropriety of my predecessors conduct in Signing & spreading in every quarter Commissions in the moment of his retiring was obvious, it has been necessary for me to replace thousands in the several departments.[13] It did not become me to restrain the act, but a remark escaped my Lips "My friend imitates General Vaughan who when he found it expedient to withdraw from Hudson's Banks ravaged the Country." Some officers inadvertently hold Commissions under such premature signature, not worth a rash.

Your Excellency will be pleased to receive this as a performance accomplished in scraps of time after 4 or 5 different efforts. Tis now the 19th. I have the honor to be with very great Respect.
19th 3 oClock P.M. Just as I was about to close this Packet an acct. from Camp arrived.

The Enemy in Philada are in motion but their manœvres & Stratagems keep their real intentions inexplicable. All is conjecture. 'Tis said Sir Wm. Howe is returned, that their heavy Cannon are actually embarked. They have commited cruel Ravage on all the fruit Trees in & about the City. These they have stuck in a Semi-Circle on the Common & hung Lantherns upon each. Their design may be to attack General Washington—to get quietly off & go safely down the River with every moveable worth transporting—to penetrate the Jersey & cross over to New York. &c &c.[14]

LB (SCHi). Laurens wrote part of the body of this letter on May 18. See below, notes 8 and 9.

[1] In his April 13 letter to Laurens, President Lowndes reported that about six hundred South Carolina backcountry loyalists had recently entered Georgia, presumably in order to link up with British forces from East Florida and conquer South Carolina's southern neighbor. PCC, item 72, fols. 445–48. However, Lowndes exaggerated the degree of coordination between the loyalists and the British. See Kenneth Coleman, *The American Revolution in Georgia, 1763–1789* (Athens: University of Georgia Press, 1958), pp. 107–8.

[2] Laurens is evidently referring to General Howe's mistress, Mrs. Joshua Loring.

[3] Lowndes had complained that the Board of War was requesting certain military supplies from South Carolina that the state could not spare.

[4] Lowndes had reported that pursuant to an order of Congress of January 26, 1778, the South Carolina loan officer had paid $25,000 to Alexander Rose to reimburse him for the money he had expended purchasing clothing for the army. See also *JCC*, 10:90.

[5] President Lowndes and Gen. William Moultrie were involved in a conflict concerning the limits of state and Continental authority. Lowndes refused to grant a request from Francis Huger, the deputy quartermaster general in South Carolina, for the payment of $20,000 after Huger declined to account with the government of South Carolina for other money he had received from it, arguing that "a Continental Officer was not Amenable to the State for his expenditures." When Moultrie interceded with Lowndes on Huger's behalf, Lowndes not only reiterated his refusal to pay Huger unless he agreed to a state audit of his accounts but insisted he had the authority to dismiss Huger from office by virtue of a February 9 resolution of Congress on supernumerary officers. Although Moultrie was not averse in principle to Lowndes' demand for an audit, he denied the president's right to dismiss Huger, noting "that Officer had his Commission immediately from Congress." Having reached an impasse, Lowndes and Moultrie both brought their dispute to the attention of Congress, which decided in favor of Lowndes on both issues, resolving on May 29 that the president was right in demanding an audit of Huger's accounts and correct in his interpretation of the February 9 resolve. See *JCC*, 11:552–53; Lowndes to Laurens, April 18, PCC. item 72, fols. 454–59; and Moultrie to Laurens, April 20, 1778, PCC, item 158, fols. 453–57. For the February 9 resolution on supernumerary officers and Gov. William Livingston's response to it, see *JCC*, 10:139–40, 11:504; and Laurens to Livingston, March 10, 15, April 18, and May 25, 1778. Huger is incorrectly identified in the index to the journals as Isaac Huger.

[6] Lowndes had informed Laurens that the *General Moultrie* had captured a British ship carrying 370 slaves and brought her "into a Dutch port."

[7] See Connecticut Delegates to Jonathan Trumbull, Sr., May 18, 1778, note 3.

[8] On Monday, May 18 Congress read a duplicate copy of a March 26 letter from the Massachusetts Board of War with a May 6 postscript and an enclosed extract of a March 30 letter from "Mess. Gardoqui & Sons Merchants in Bilboa," which reported on the basis of "letters from Paris," that the "Honourable Doctor Franklin had . . . been presented on the 20th to His Most Christian Majesty, in quality of Embassador of the Thirteen United American States, & that having been graciously received as such, the King of France had likewise named another for your parts." See *JCC*, 11:507; and PCC, item 65, 1:292–94, 342. In fact, as William Lee wrote to Laurens from Paris on March 23, Louis XVI had received all the American commissioners "as the representatives of sovereign States," not just Franklin. Wharton, *Diplomatic Correspondence*, 2:517.

[9] Laurens is referring to the appointment on May 18 of a committee consisting of Gouverneur Morris, Charles Carroll, and Elbridge Gerry to consider the letters

from the Massachusetts Board of War and Gardoqui & Sons cited in the preceding note. *JCC*, 11:507. Although the journals fail to specify more precisely the purpose of this committee, it is clear that its main function was to make recommendations for the proper reception of the French ambassador to America whose appointment had been announced by the Spanish mercantile firm. Accordingly, Morris drafted a report advising Congress that "it will be necessary to the Reception of Ambassadors and other Foreigners of Importance, that the President of the Congress for the Time being should be allowed a House and Table at the Public Expence, and that a Master of the Ceremonies should be appointed to superintend the same, adjust the Ceremonies and the like." PCC, item 23, fol. 351. Although Worthington C. Ford printed this undated report under the date July 31, 1778, in his edition of the journals, there is no evidence it was ever submitted to Congress, Morris' committee being superseded on that day by the appointment of a new committee "to direct and superintend an entertainment to be given by Congress to the Hon. Sieur Gerard, minister plenipotentiary from his most Christian majesty." *JCC*, 11:733–34. Consequently, Congress did not agree to provide the president with "a convenient furnished dwelling house . . . and a table, carriage, and servants" until December 16, 1778. *JCC*, 12:1213–14, 1222–23. Since President Laurens is not listed in the journals as one of the members of the May 18 committee, it seems likely that he was merely asked to consult with it.

[10] See John Laurens to Laurens, May 7, 1778, in Simms, *Laurens Army Correspondence*, p. 169.

[11] See James Lovell to John Adams, May 15, 1778, note 2.

[12] Capt. John Christian Senf described his knowledge of British infractions of the Saratoga Convention in an August 5, 1778, letter to Laurens that is in PCC, item 78, 20:299. See also *JCC*, 10:29–35; and Laurens to Jacob Christopher Zahn, March 10, 1778, note 3.

[13] "There was at least an Impropriety," Lowndes wrote to Laurens on April 18, "in Commissions being given out in the name of Mr. Hancock, long after that Gentleman had vacated his Seat as President of the Congress, and the same Impropriety occurs daily in Commissions Issued out to the Military in the several Regiments." PCC, item 72, fol. 458.

[14] Laurens' May 19 postscript was printed in the June 4, 1778, issue of the *South Carolina and American General Gazette* under the heading "Extract of a Letter from York-Town, dated May 19." The printed text contains a concluding sentence that Laurens did not copy into his private letter book: "Gen. Washington is moving off his heavy baggage, &c. and preparing to face them, or stick in their skirts."

Henry Laurens to the
Middle Department Navy Board

Gentlemen.   York Town 17th May 1778

Congress on the 13th Inst. Resolved that 600 Dollars be allowed to each of you for extra services at Bordenton & to defray expences going to Baltimore.[1] Shall I receive the Amount & transmit it to you or deliver the Resolve to some other freind here? I beg you will command in either way the services of, Gentlemen, Your obedient humble servant,

Henry La[urens]

[*P.S.*] A Gentleman from the City assures us Sir William Howe embarked for England on Tuesday last & left Sir H Clinton in Command.

RC (PHi). Addressed: "Francis Hopkinson & John Wharton Esquires, Baltimore."

¹ See *JCC*, 11:493. In an April 29 memorial to Congress, Hopkinson and Wharton had requested reimbursement for expenses they had incurred while performing services outside the scope of their duties as commissioners. See PCC, item 41, 4:31–32.

This day Laurens also wrote a brief note to William Smith of Baltimore, informing him that on May 9 Congress had appointed him "a Commissioner of the Navy Board in the Middle district." See PCC, item 13, fol. 325; and *JCC*, 11:484. Smith took the place of John Nixon, who had resigned from the board.

Oliver Wolcott to Andrew Adams

Sir,   York Town 17t May 1778

Your Favour of the 2d instant is recd. Your other Letters except that of the 2d March have failed. The Post now rides regularly, Letters put into that offiece will therefore come safe.

I was sorry to hear of your Want of Health. I Wish it may soon be restored to you.

I hope it will be convenient for some one to relieve me in the Course of a Month. Altho I shall think it my Duty to continue in Congress during the present interesting Period 'till a full Representation is had, yet I have not the least Wish to prolong the Period of my Service.

The Count Noalles Memorial, The Speech of Georgientus and his Wise Parliament you have seen. They Observe that they are much Inclined to be Angry at the Conduct of France, but Wheather they will really be so We shall soon know.

As to the Regulating Act which you Mention No one here thinks any Thing of it. A Recommendation would before now have gone from Congress to suspend it had it not been Apprehended it might have been disagreable to our State. I Am Very well perswaded that there is but a single Member in Congress in favour of it.¹ The States may certainly do what they please either to continue or suspend the Act without giving any offence. There is a Regulating Act in the Jersys and N [York. In] this State they made one and immediately suspended it and for ever will suspend it. I shall say nothing as to the Act—you know my Opinion. And I hope that this political Experiment will be so thoroly made as that there can be no Occasion to repeat it.

I am sir, your Obedient Servant,   Oliver Wolcott

P.S. Duplicates of the Treatys with France have just Now been Brot. to Congress. No other Material Intelligence is recd than what We before had—Exceapt that Dr. Franklin was formally recd. on the 20 March as Ambassador to the French Court from these States. That Court has likewise Nominated an Ambassador to Reside here.

RC (CtY).
   [1] For Wolcott's earlier comments on the act for regulating prices, indicating that Roger Sherman favored such legislation, see Wolcott to Andrew Adams, April 25, 1778.

Oliver Wolcott to Laura Wolcott

My Dear,   York Town 17t May 1778
   I have Wrote you three Letters since the beginning of this Month, one a few Days ago enclosed in a Letter to Mr. Lord.[1] I still injoy Health. May I be thankfull to him who bestows it upon me.
   I was in hopes to have recd. a Letter from you, but Brown says he passed the Town so soon that you had not Time to Write. However I was informed by him and by a Letter from Dr. Smith that you was well. By this Letter I am also informed you had the misfortune to lose a couple of your [Cows?]. Evils We must expect. This I hope will give you no great Pain.
   Yale College Corporation Dr. Smith tells me are much offended by a Letter I wrote to Oliver, and suggests it may possibly have some influence pritty Material upon the Elaction.[2] If so I shall give myself no concern. If my Election can depend upon ⟨so precarious a Tenure⟩ such a frivolous Circumstance I should most willingly ⟨quit⟩ lose it, Altho my Desire of continuing in the Assembly was much greater than I certainly know it now is. What Business the Corporation have with a Copy of my Letter I cannot conceive. Does any one think to prevent me from writing to a Freind any Thing which I apprehend to be true. Certainly I never will be under that Restraint. Oliver perhaps was oblidged to shew the Letter to his Tutor, or might have suffered a Freind to take a Copy of it. At most it must have been but an Inadvertance and I have no Inclination either to blame him or myself at present—and beleive I shall have no Occasion to do it. I feel Very Innocent and consequently totally unconcerned about this affair.
   This Day Duplicates of the Treatys with France were bro't to Congress. But no Material Intelligence was bro't—but what you must have heard of. Dr. Franklin was formerly Admitted at the Court of Versailles as Embasedor for these States on the 20t. March. That Court Will soon send over an Ambassador to Reside here.
   Brown bro't Me a Letter from Mr. Adams wherein he says that he

is not well and thinks that he shall not come to Congress. I hope I shall be releived before long. If Mr. Adams does not come I shall expect the Other Gentlemen will and take the Places of Mr. Huntington, and Mine at farthest by the Time that Brown comes back. In the Mean Time may the Almighty Bless you. My Love to my Children and Freinds. I am yours Affectionately,

Oliver Wolcott[3]

RC (CtHi).

[1] Only Wolcott's May 2 and May 9 letters to Laura have been found. Neither Wolcott's letter to "Mr. Lord" nor his letter to his son Oliver mentioned below has been found.

[2] On May 14, 1778, Wolcott and his colleagues Samuel Huntington and Roger Sherman were elected Assistants on the Connecticut Council. *Public Records of Connecticut,* 2:3.

[3] On May 20 Wolcott wrote another brief letter to Laura in which he reported: "Our latest Accounts from Philadelphia are that the Enemy are about leaving that City, this May be probably true. We shall Very soon know What Part G. Britain Will take. This is an important Moment and We are happy by the favourable Appearance of Things, and flatter ourselves that the Power of the Enemy is upon a fast decline. The Indians are ravaging and Murdering the People on the Western Frontiers. The Conduct of G. Britain in setting on the Savages to Murder indiscriminately as they do every human Being who falls into their Power ought never be forgot." Oliver Wolcott, Sr., Papers, CtHi.

Connecticut Delegates to Jonathan Trumbull, Sr.

Sir   York Town May 18th. 1778.

The Inclosd Resolution of Congress is the result of the most painfull & disagreable question that hath ever been Agitated in Congress.[1]

The question was Steerd before Col. Dyer left Congress & he will be able to give Some account of the matter & Sentiments of many of the States thereon.

A most disagreable & serious debate hath Continued about seven weeks, a bill being brot. in for an half pay Establishment for life for the officers & to their widows during their widowhood; Several Collateral questions were determind on the progress of the debate which Shewed that Eight of the States were in favour of the Establishment for life &c as above, Rhode Island, Connecticutt, New Jersey, & South Carolina strenuously in the negative, New Hampshire being absent.

General Washington wrote repeatedly upon the Subject expressing his great concern; & the necessity of the measure, in one of his Letters he Says that altho he never would take any benefit of such an Establishment himself, yet he did most religiously believe the Salvation of the Army depended upon it,[2] many of the States deemed the measure not only absolutely necessary but Salutary, Just & reasonable.

The Justice as well as necessity of doing some thing for the Army was obvious, to Increase their wages would so directly tend to depreciate the Currency it appeard dangerous as well as futile.

Finally after long debate & delay in hope some favourable Event might turn up, even til delay became dangerous the bill was carried for an Establishment for life, but the four States who were in the negative as before mentioned persevering & urging the dangerous tendency of such a measure as being totally Inconsistent with free States, repugnant to principals upon which this great Controversy was begun & by which it must & ought to be defended with many other arguments & observations too tedious to be enumerated; the majority of the Delegates of Massachusetts, came over to the negative Side of the question.

There appearing a Serious concern in Congress to adopt Some mode in this Important matter, in which they might Unite so as to answer the necessities of the Army & preserve harmony & unanimity in all the States, a Reconsideration of the Bill was proposed & an Amendment moved & finally adopted which is the Inclosd resolution, providing both for Officers & Soldiers Such a reward as should be deemed equal in value to their wages at the Original Stipulation.

It is Allmost Impossible to give a clear & full representation of the difficulties attending this debate, on both sides the question to any gentleman who was not present, however many weighty reasons not here mentioned will readily occur to your Excellency.

If the Inclosd Resolve is not the best measure the nature & Circumstances of the Case would admit, it is certainly the best that could be obtaind.

Your Excellencies late Correspondence with General Tryon meets with universal approbation.[3]

We have Just receivd Intelligence that North Carolina have acceeded to the Articles of Confederation.[4] If the Delegates from New Hampshire should arrive with powers to ratify, which we hope will soon be the Case, there is a prospect the Confederation may soon be Compleated.

Duplicates of the Treaties of Alliance & Commerce, with France, arrived here yesterday & by the same packet we have advice that on the 20th of March Docr Franklin was formally receivd as Embassador from these States at the Court of Versailes & that his most Christian Majesty had named an Embassador, to reside here.

We are with much Esteem, your Excellencies obedient, Humble servants,   Roger Sherman

Saml Huntington

Oliver Wolcott.[5]

RC (Ct). Written by Huntington and signed by Huntington, Sherman, and Wolcott.

[1] For the May 15 resolves granting half pay to commissioned officers for seven years and eighty dollars to soldiers and noncommissioned officers at the end of the war, see *JCC*, 11:502–3.

[2] See Washington's April 10 letter to President Laurens in Washington, *Writings* (Fitzpatrick), 11:235–41.

[3] In his April 23 reply to William Tryon's April 17 request that he publicize Lord North's conciliatory bills, Trumbull had observed that "propositions of peace are usually made from the supreme authority of one contending power, to the similar authority of the other; and the present, is the first instance within my recollection when a vague, half blank, and very indefinite draught of a bill ONCE ONLY READ BEFORE ONE OF THE THREE BODIES of the Legislature of the nation has ever been addressed to the PEOPLE AT LARGE of the opposite power, as an overture of reconciliation." After emphatically stating that British recognition of American independence was a prerequisite to establishing peace, Trumbull pointed out that it was to Congress that all peace proposals should be addressed. The conciliatory bill and letters of Tryon and Trumbull had been published in the May 5, 1778, issue of the *Connecticut Courant* and it was probably a copy of this paper that Trumbull enclosed with his May 5 letter to President Laurens, which was read in Congress on May 15. See *JCC*, 11:501.

For Trumbull's subsequent correspondence with William Tryon, see Henry Laurens to Jonathan Trumbull, Sr., June 5, 1778.

[4] Governor Caswell's April 26 letter reporting that North Carolina had ratified the articles of confederation was read in Congress this day. *JCC*, 11:506–7.

[5] Huntington and Wolcott had also written a brief letter to Trumbull on May 15 acknowledging "Your Excellency's Favour of the 5th inst by Brown who arrived last evening & will be detain'd a day or two—by him we shall write more fully." Peter Force Collection, DLC.

William Ellery to Nicholas Cooke

Sir,[1]   York-Town May 18th. 1778.

I have received the powers and instructions respecting the confederation, and agreeably to a resolution of the house laid the proposed alterations and amendments on the table last Wednesday.

The confederation was to have been taken up last Saturday; but was kept back by some pressing business. I do not expect that any of the amendments proposed by our State will take place, excepting that for taking estimates every five years.[2]

If the confederation should be ratified before two delegates should arrive from our State it will be unrepresented; for, as I have long since informed the assembly, I shall be obliged to return home very soon. It is now about two years since I first attended Congress, and during that time, four months only excepted, the State hath been represented by one delegate. The saving thus occasioned will I hope enable the Assembly in future to keep up three members constantly in Congress; so long at least as it shall sit at such a distance from Rhode-Island. The necessity of this measure of having always three members at Congress hath been recommended and urged by Congress to all the states, and I have desired our State to comply with the recommendation.

I informed the Assembly some time ago that it was proposed in Congress that half pay for life should be allowed to all military commissioned officers, who now are or hereafter may be in the service, and continue therein during the war, and desired instructions thereon.

This matter was first agitated in a committee of the whole, afterwards amended in Congress, and when amended a question was had, according to a previous agreement, whether the propositions should be referred to the States for their consideration or not, and passed in the negative by a majority of one vote only. The main question was then proposed, and a debate ensued, during which it was thrown out by the minority that if the half pay was fixed for the term of six or seven years it might produce a coalition; whereupon the question was put off to the next day when this knotty business was settled according to the inclosed Resolution.[3]

Genl Howe, the President informs me, sailed for Britain last Wednesday, and is succeeded by Genl. Clinton. I have heard nothing of Capt. Coddington. I wish he may arrive safe; but the chance is very much against him. We have nothing remarkable. Inclosed is the last news paper. I heartily congratulate with you on the Alliance enter'd into with France, and am with great Respect, Your very humble Servant,   William Ellery

RC (RPJCB).
[1] Although William Greene had succeeded Nicholas Cooke as governor of Rhode Island earlier in the month, news of this did not reach Congress until May 27. JCC, 11:537. Therefore it is to be presumed that Ellery still thought Cooke was governor when he wrote this letter.
[2] Rhode Island's proposal to require land reassessments every five years—the figures to be used to determine state contributions to the confederation—was defeated in Congress on June 23, 1778. JCC, 11:639.
[3] Since Congress approved the half-pay plan on May 15, Ellery's account here suggests that the delegates had also debated this issue on the 14th, a fact that is not recorded in the journals.

Samuel Huntington to Jabez Huntington

Sir   York Town 18th May 1778
By a Hessian Deserter lately escaped from Philadelphia we are told that the Enemy are shipping their heavy Cannon & baggage, taking in wood &c. He Says they are going off & for that reason he deserted as he did not incline to go with them.

Whether this account be true or only a Manoeuvre of the Enemy time will discover, however it becomes us to exert our Selves to be prepared to drive them off, or Burgoyne them where they be.

I Shall be much Obliged if you will please to Send me by the post or first Opportunity a news paper containing the List of Representatives for the present Session of Assembly, all or any Intelligence that Occurs.

As Mr Brown is Setting off must refer you for farther particulars, & the proceedings of Congress to the Governors letter of this date and am with Esteem your humble Servt,   Saml Huntington

RC (CtHi).

Henry Laurens to John Lewis Gervais

My Dear Sir,   18th May [1778]

I beg leave to refer you to mine of the 3d & 4th Inst. by Cross since which I have been honoured with yours of the 19th Ulto.

I can say nothing in reply to it but my gratulations on the apparent recovery of Mrs. Gervais's health. My best Compliments to the good Lady & assure her tis now my firm opinion & serious advice that you ought not & should not get another Wife.

I have poured forth crowds of News to His Excellency the president which you will learn there & I add some of our printed pieces which you may read at home, having gone through the labor of Copying the Treaties, signing, sealing & transmitting for Exchange a Copy of the Treaty of Commerce will be immediately published. I hope that of Alliance too, but some of my friends appear to be more nice than I hold to be discreet, or respectful toward the people at large & there will be some opposition to printing the whole.

Major General Lee has joined the Army which I hear from J.L. is in fine order.

My Dear friend God bless you.

[*P.S.*] I beg you will write to Mr. Galphin. Tell him a Colonel Brown has paid me on his account fourteen hundred & Sixty Dollars—this Sum I request you to pay to Mr. Galphins Order immediately. I will write to my good old friend in a few days, make an apology for present omission.

LB (ScHi).

Henry Laurens to William Moultrie

Dear General,   18th May [1778]

On the 13th Inst I was honoured with your favor of the 20th April; the next Morning I presented it to Congress & it was ordered with

His Excellency president Lowndes's dispatches to a select Committee.[1] When a Report is made & I receive Commands you shall be immediately informed. In the meantime I may safely assure you the Dep. Qur. Master General is liable to suspension by the President, should he, which I hold to be impossible, give Cause by improper conduct. I shall this day return thanks to Govr. Livingston for his attention to public Interest by suspending many staff Officers, among them a person exactly upon a Line with Colo. F. Huger—a Dep. Qur. Master appointed by General Mifflin.[2] I may as safely add, the Presidents' refusing to grant Money before preceeding Grants had been accounted for, is generally applauded & I presume will be more specially noticed by the Committee.

Mr. Dart will probably be confirmed in the office of Dep. Clothier general.[3] I beleive this article rests pretty much in my own power, arising from a singular circumstance, & that gentleman may depend upon my friendship. Will you do me the honor Sir, to present my Compliments to Mr. Dart, I beg his pardon for not writing. This respect shall not be omitted when I can tell him what he wishes to know.

Within the present Inclosure I send several Interesting public accounts & particularly an Act of Congress of the 15th Inst. for intitling Officers to half pay, for a limitted time after the conclusion of the Present War & for making a gratuitous acknowledgement to Non Commissioned & Soldiers. Of this a duplicate will be found which I request you to send to Major General Howe to whom I shall write in a few days.

When I tell you I am annexed to this Table generally eight hours some times ten or twelve & fixed & bated in a Chair five hours every day, that I have crossed a horse but once the last eight Months you will see the impossibility of writing to all my friends by every opportunity. I have the honor to be with great Regard &ca.

LB (ScHi). Addressed: "Brigadier General Wm. Moultrie Esquire, Charles Town."

[1] General Moultrie's April 20 letter to Laurens, which dealt mainly with his dispute with President Rawlins Lowndes of South Carolina over the issue of the accountability of Continental officials to state authority, is in PCC, item 158, fols. 453–57. For Congress' resolution of this controversy, see *JCC*, 11:552–53; and Laurens to Lowndes, May 17, 1778, note 6.

[2] Col. Francis Huger, the deputy quartermaster general in South Carolina, is incorrectly identified in the index to the journals as Isaac Huger. See also Laurens to William Livingston, May 25, 1778.

[3] Congress did not accept a recommendation by the committee to which General Moultrie's April 20 letter was referred that John Sanford Dart "be appointed Deputy Clothier General for the State of So. Carolina." *JCC*, 11:553. Nevertheless, Dart continued to hold this office under the appointment he had received from Gen. Robert Howe, the commander of the southern military department. In addition to Moultrie's letter cited above see Dart's memorial to Congress of August 1, 1780, in PCC, item 41, 2:456–57.

Oliver Wolcott to Jonathan Trumbull, Jr.

Sir,   York Town 18t May 1778

Your Letter of the 30t April to President Laurens, was referrd to the Board of Treasury. By that Board I am desired to Acquaint you That on the Date of your Letter Congress had ordered 250,000 Dollars & 100,000 ditto in an Order on the Loan office of N York, to furnish your Chest which I hope before Now is recd. by you.[1] As to the Stile in which you ought to be addressed, it should undouptedly conform to the Tenor of your Commission.[2] I shall only observe to you, that I believe it never was intended to address you improperly. I suppose that Committees who have reported upon Subjects relative to your office Thro mere Inadvertence and Ignorance of your proper address, have given your office an improper discription. Such discriptions being found in the Journals of Congress, they served tho' improperly as Precedents for future address. This I apprehend is the Case of the present Error in your Stile. I really beleive that nothing was ever intended in the address, injurious. But perhaps the President will not Write to you upon the Subject, as I think that he will not enter into any Debate upon it. However before long I hope that you will have a Stile perfectly unequivocal, as Congress have in contemplation to put the Board of Treasury into Commission, which they douptless Will soon do, In that Case I think it highly probable that you will be invited to take a Seat at that Board.[3]

Yesterday duplicates of the Treatys with France were bro't to Congress. Dr. Franklin on the 20t March was formally recd. at the Court of Versailles as Ambassador from these States. That Court has nominated a Person to Reside here under a like Character.

Please to Present my Service to my Friend Mr. Pierce, and be assured that I am, sir, your Most Obedient, humble Servant,

                                            Oliver Wolcott

RC (CtHi).

[1] See *JCC,* 10:411.

[2] On Trumbull's complaint that he had been improperly addressed in official correspondence, see Henry Laurens to Jonathan Trumbull, Jr., March 12, 1778, note 1.

[3] Although the Board of Treasury's April 15 report proposing the establishment of a new Board of Treasury was currently under consideration, it was not until September 26 that Congress adopted a substitute plan that reorganized the treasury into the offices of comptroller, auditor, and treasurer, and two chambers of accounts. Jonathan Trumbull, Jr., was elected comptroller of the treasury on November 3, 1778. See *JCC,* 10:349–51, 11:731, 779–86, 12:891–92, 956–61, 1096. The Board of Treasury continued as a standing committee of Congress until 1781.

Committee for Foreign Affairs to Jesse Brown

Mr Brown   [May 19? 1778] [1]
Directions have been sent for one Vessel to be prepared in Connecticut; two in Massachusetts Bay and one in New Hampshire: and you have packets marked A. B. C. of great importance put under your care, which you are to carry with proper Secresy & dispatch, and to deliver according to the following directions.

If his Excellency Governor Trumbull has a Vessel quite ready at your arrival there, you will deliver A to him. If he is but in expectation of having one ready Shortly, leave B with him. If he has no prospect or only a distant one, carry all the packets to Boston where you are to leave A B with the honorable President of the Council, and to proceed with C to Portsmouth, where you are to deliver it to the Continental agent John Langdon Esq., taking receipts for each delivery. Should you convey from Connecticut only two Sets, deliver but one at Boston, unless both Vessells are ready or will be ready in the time that would be required for your proceeding to Portsmouth. Should you proceed to the last mentioned place, and find Col. Langdon not prepared, you will let him know the state of the business at Boston and Connecticut, so that he may use his judgement about the keeping the packet for an opportunity of conveyance, or sending it back to one of the other places.   Signed James Lovell

FC (DNA: PCC, item 79). Addressed: "Instructions for the Express."
   [1] These instructions were apparently written as the committee completed preparations to send three packets of foreign dispatches to France via various New England ports. See Committee for Foreign Affairs to Jonathan Trumbull, Sr., this date.

Committee for Foreign Affairs to Jonathan Trumbull, Sr.

York Town, May 19th 1778
Your Excellency having been requested by the marine Committee to have a Packet Boat in Readiness to carry important Dispatches to France, we have now sent such to your Care, conditionally; which we desire you to give in Charge to a trusty Captain, to deliver with his own Hands to our Commissioners at Paris.[1] Your Wisdom will dictate pointed Orders for conveying the Packets without Injury, with Secresy & with Dispatch; but, for sinking them in Case the Vessel should be unfortunately taken.[2]

We are respectfully, Your Excellency's Humble Servants,
                                                        Richard Henry Lee

                                                        James Lovell

RC (Ct). Written by Lovell and signed by Lovell and Lee.

[1] Capt. Robert Niles of the Connecticut schooner *Spy* delivered a packet containing the ratification of the treaties with France to the American commissioners in Paris on July 8. See Wharton, *Diplomatic Correspondence,* 2:642; and Louis F. Middlebrook, *History of Maritime Connecticut during the American Revolution, 1775–1783,* 2 vols. (Salem, Mass.: Essex Institute, 1925), 1:32, 42. See also Marine Committee to Jonathan Trumbull, Sr., May 5, 1778.

[2] The committee sent similar letters this day to the Massachusetts Council and to John Langdon. Revolutionary Letters, M–Ar; and PCC, item 79, fol. 232.

Samuel Huntington to Joseph Trumbull

Sir   York Town 19th May 1778

I am favourd with yours of 29th ult. Am Sorry to say you are not like to obtain any money, Congress have adopted a rule not to pay out money to any gentleman any considerable time after he is out of Office; until his Accounts are Settled, it was Urged in your Case, you was not Supposd in fault, that the accounts were not Settled, but in vain: they Strictly adhere to the rule in all Cases, hope therefore your accounts may Soon be adjusted.[1]

Since you have removd to Norwich Trust you will be kind to the Ladies who are in a widowd State.

We have just receivd Intelligence that Docr Franklin on the 20th of March was formally receivd as Embassador from these States at the Court of Versailes & his most Christian Majesty had named an Embassador from his Court, to reside here.

Am with due regards, your humble Servt, Sam Huntington

RC (Ct).

[1] For Congress' resolve of this date denying Trumbull's request for an advance, see *JCC,* 11:509. Trumbull's commissary accounts were not settled until long after his death in July 1778, for which see *JCC,* 11:852, 12:1091–92.

Henry Laurens to John Adams

Dear Sir,   York Town, 19th May 1778

Will you permit me to congratulate with you upon the favorable appearances in our American concerns & particularly upon your safe arrival at Paris, and further to request you will forward in the best manner the times will afford, the two inclosed Letters, one to Ralph Izard Esquire & the other to my daughter in Law in London.[1] The latter if War is kindled between France & England must take a circuitous route by Holland or Flanders & under particular protection. Command me at any time to do ten times as much in return & be assured of my chearful obedience.

You are so fully informed of the State of affairs in this quarter by the Committee of Foreign correspondence it would be committing waste upon time to repeat. We have this Instant an account of the Enemy's movements from Philadelphia under clouds of manœvre & stratagem, time will shew whether they mean to attack General Washington or to penetrate Jersey & cross over to New York. Our Commander in Chief is also in motion & if they don't face him he will be on their skirts.

I wish you every degree of happiness & am with great Respect, Dear Sir, Your Obedient humble servt,   Henry Laurens

RC (MHi).
[1] No letter from Laurens to Martha Manning Laurens has been found. However, the letter in question may have been written by her husband, John Laurens.

Henry Laurens to Horatio Gates

Dear sir.   YorkTown 19th May 1778
I had the honor of writing to you the 15th Inst. by McKlosky. This will convey an Act of Congress of the 15th for entitling Officers to half Pay for a limitted time, & Non-Commissioned Officers & Soldiers to a gratutious acknowledgement, after the conclusion of the present War.

If I were to attempt to give you an hearsay story of the Movements of the Enemy from Philadelphia it would be committing waste upon time. You will certainly receive clear & authentic intelligence of every step they take from fountain head. We have not heard from thence since the 12th.

I am with the most perfect Esteem & Regard, Sir, Your obedient & humble servant,   Henry Laurens, President of Congress

[P.S.] This Morning improved our Stile.
The United States of North America, in conformity to the Treaties of Paris the 6th February.[1]

RC (NHi).
[1] Although Congress decided this day to use the designation "United States of North America" on bills of exchange drawn on the commissioners in France, it agreed on July 11, 1778, to omit the word "North" from these bills. JCC, 11:513, 683. Laurens implies elsewhere that on this day Congress officially designated the new nation the "United States of North America," but there is no resolution to this effect in the journals. See Edmund C. Burnett, "The Name of the 'United States of America,' " AHR 31 (October 1925): 79–81; and Laurens to John Rutledge, May 19, and to Washington, May 20, 1778.

Henry Laurens to William Heath

Sir,							York Town 19th May 1778.

On the 11th Inst. I directed a Packet to you containing Addresses by Congress to the Inhabitants of these States.

At present I have no Commands on me from Congress, the bearer Mr Browne is to conduct a Sum of Money which I am told by the Treasury will amply releive you.

Under this Cover I send an Act of Congress of the 15th Inst. for granting an half Pay to Officers after the War for a limitted time & for making a gratuitous acknowledgement to Soldiers. This is an exception to the first part of the preceeding paragraph.

We have just received intelligence from Valley forge convincing of the Enemy's design to leave the City, but their manœvres leave their real intentions inexplicable. 'Tis generally beleived they mean to penetrate New Jersey & enter New York.

I have the honor to be, With much Regard & Respect, Sir, Your most obedient humble servant,			Henry Laurens

RC (MHi).

Henry Laurens to Ralph Izard

My Dear Sir,							19th May [1778]

I have no time by this Courier but to make a bare acknowledgement of your obliging favors by Mr. Deane & Capt. Courter accompanied by the duplicates referred to but I hope to overtake the Vessel by which this is intended with a more respectful reply & shall follow it by every opportunity in order to keep you acquainted with the state of affairs in this quarter, and I beg you will be assured that upon all occasions I will have at heart your honor & Interest, to the best of my ability & as effectually as if I had made a volume of promises.

This Moment we learn the Enemy are moving out of Philadelphia but manœvre & stratagem cover for the present their true intentions, it is suggested they mean to penetrate through New Jersey & pass over to New York.

I beg my best Compliments to Mrs. Izard & that you will be assured I am with perfect attachment & Esteem &ca.

LB (ScHi).

Henry Laurens to Samuel A. Otis

Dear Sir,   19 May [1778]
    The Packet in which this is Inclosed contains a number of Letters
for France which I recommend to your protection to put on board
the Vessel in which our public Dispatches are to go forward, those—
        to The Honl John Adams Esquire
        from the Marquis delafayette
        to Compte Broglie
        to Monsr. St. Paul
to be Committed to the special care of the Captain.
    Be so good as inform me the Name of the Vessel & Commander by
whom they go & if practicable favor me with an Account of the
Names of other Vessels intended for France & when likely to sail.
    Forgive this trouble & lay your Commands freely at all times on
Sir, &ca.

LB (ScHi).

Henry Laurens to John Rutledge

Dear Sir,   19th May [1778]
    I had the honor of writing to you the 4th Inst. by Messenger Cross.
    The Army at Valley forge gathers Strength in recruits & discipline
daily. General Gates arrives about this day at Fish Kill where he is
to take command of the whole northern department & as we have
heard of no attempts by the Enemy to penetrate Hudson's River, I
feel satisfied from an assurance that before this day, the obstructions
are completed & new fortresses in good order. We shall be stronger in
that quarter than ever. From the enterprizing genius of Major General Sullivan we may expect an effectual Stroke by & by upon Rhode
Island, but nothing of that sort is at present in motion.
    The Indians & Tories are exceedingly troublesome on the Western
frontier & all the old Stories which I had heard thirty years ago are
daily repeated & some of the old tricks practiced by the people we
call back Setlers.
    We are now beginning what ought to have been finished two
Months ago to chastise those Red & White miscreants.
    Their Allies upon the Banks of Delaware are playing as much the
Devil there as the Indians do yonder, they steal out in squads, burn
a house & all its appendages, take off or Murder the Master & leave
a helpless Woman & her Infants to struggle through hunger &
nakedness.

We have this Morning in Congress conformed to the Stile adopted in the Treaty of Paris—the United States of North America. I am with very great Respect

LB (ScHi).

Henry Laurens to John Wells

Dear Sir.   19th May [1778]

I can say nothing more in return to your obliging Letter of the 20th April but that the Bill for 200 Dollars lies on my Table—after your own misfortune I had ventured to disclosure to Mr. Hall the name of his friend & I added for his sake & yours & my own a Moiety of your donation.[1]

His Excellency the President will give you Govr. Trumbull's answer to Mr. Tryon's Complimentary Certificate upon empty Bills, & within this Inclosure you will receive bundles of printed Papers. If you write to me often & copiously I will acknowledge a debt & like other very honest planters if I can't be punctual in payment I will allow Interest & make you my factor.

Govr. Livingston in a private Letter which I have just now opened says Huzza for Congress.

I am with great regard

[P.S.] When you read Dalrymple's encomium on his Countrymen for their immense Zeal in raising Troops for subduing America, you will either be ashamed of being or wish you were not a Scotsman—or neither.[2] They are certainly in that Quarter ardently Striving to play the Devil with us—but they may catch a Tartar & the Devil will catch them. The face of affairs is a little altered since the date of Mr. Dalrymple's piece & poor Sanders may be sent to catch Negroes from Barbadoes to Jamaica or to have his patticoats turned up at Portsdown.

LB (ScHi).

[1] John Wells' April 20 letter to Laurens is in the William Gilmore Simms Collection deposit, MHi. This day Laurens also wrote a brief letter to William Brown of Boston, enclosing "Daniel Beaurdeau's [Beaudreau's?] Bill 8th April 1778 on Wm. Erskine Esqr. Boston payable at sight to John Wells & by him & myself endorsed two hundred Dollars" and asking him to use it to "purchase the best Mens large white Silk Hose [and] if you can find room take in 4 or 6 pounds of the very best Coffee you can get." Laurens Papers, ScHi.

[2] In January 1778 John Dalrymple, the lord provost of Edinburgh, had sent an address to the king in behalf of the government of the city offering to raise a regiment of 1,000 men to serve in America. London Chronicle, January 27–29, 1778.

Richard Henry Lee to Arthur Lee

My dear brother,   York in Pen. 19 May 1778

Your several favors by the Vessel from Spain with duplicates of the treaties with France are arrived and shall have my most particular attention. In Virginia we have determined to retain in our practical jurisprudence the Common law of England excepting such parts as relate to royalty and prerogative. Also some of the Statutes that are of a nature the most general. These, with our own Acts of Assembly constitute our Code of Laws. You see therefore that Ludwell may be fully employed with you in reading the Common law and the Statutes, leaving the Municipal law of Virginia until he comes home. But I wish him much to have the groundwork of the law of Nature & Nations with the Civil law and Eloquence. I have not got the Virga. Acts of Assembly here, & it would be difficult to send them if I had. I am astonished at the {impudence}¹ and {jugglery} of {Deane} and his {associates}. You may depend upon their being {carefully attended} to, and as I have found during the progress of this {contest} that the {offenders} have been uniformly {discredited} and {punished}, so I have no doubt will it happen now. Persevere in {honest patriotism} and all will be well. {Patience} you know is one of the Cardinal virtues, and in this case {we} *must* soon give you {relief} since the late {recall} has broken the {faction}.² The Members of Congress are so perpetually changing that it is of little use to give you their Names.³ From Massachusetts now come Messrs. Hancock Sam Adams, Payne, Elbridge Guerry, Mr. Dana & Mr. James Lovell. Connecticut Messrs. Roger Sherman & Huntington, Dyer, Woolcot & Williams. N. York Duane, Governeer Morris, Duer your Acquaintance, Livingston, Francis Lewis. Rhode Island Messrs. Merchant & Ellery. Pennsylva. R. Morris, Read, two Smiths & Roberdeau. Jersey Dr. Witherspoon &c. Maryland Chace, Colo. Plater, Carrol, Henry, Stone. Virga. R.H. Lee, F.L. Lee, Harvey, Bannister, John Adams. So. Carolina Messrs. Laurens, Wm. H. Drayton, Hayward & 2 new ones. Tis not worthwhile to mention others, you know them not & they are new Men. The Express is going so God bless you & farewell,

Richard Henry Lee

[*P.S.*] Campaign not begun. Love to the Alderman &c & to my Son Ludwell.

RC (ViU).

¹ Words in braces, here and below, are in cipher in the RC. For the cipher used by the Lees, see Richard Henry Lee to Arthur Lee, May 12, 1778, note 2.

² For a contrasting view from the Deane camp, see Benjamin Harrison's assessment of Lee's involvement in a "cabal" against Silas Deane in his June 8, 1778, letter to Robert Morris. Wharton, *Diplomatic Correspondence,* 2:607–8.

³ At least fifteen of the delegates Lee listed below were not currently attending

Congress, although they were members of their state delegations. William Williams, on the other hand, was not in the Connecticut delegation at this time; and Thomas Adams, not John, was attending for Virginia.

Henry Laurens' Speech to Congress

Gentn. 20 May [1778]

I beg to be heard on the point of Order, in behalf of your President.[1] The motion was withdrawn by the Gentn. who made it, the Gent. did not whisper & I had declared it to the House. There was no objection—but how shall the Chair preserve Order when Gentn. differ so much and so often in their sentiments upon Order. Were I now, was the Chair upon every occasion to call Gentn. to Order it must of course bring on debate indeed altercation a term which ought not to be heard in this House. Seeing therefore there is such variety of opinion & so often changed, the Chair is always attentive & complaisant to every Gentleman & obedient to the determination of the House. It is not long since a violent infraction was made upon Order, it stands upon your Journal as violent an infractn. as ever appeared upon a Journal.[2] The Chair endeavored to prevent the evil—I am sure I acted with integrity & to the best of my judgement —but the House by a Vote Resolved it to be order, the Chair submitted. After such an Instance & so many disputes upon Order what part can the Chair Act. When the House condescends to direct the Chair I am obedient. I think I know what is Order, but I cannot Govern Gentlemen who upon different occasions differ from themselves—the Chair must therefore in most Cases wait the decision of the House. When the House desire my opinion I give it without hesitation, with Integrity & candor & in this view I trust the Chair will not be censured now nor upon any occasion for being slack in determining Order & in the present I had declared to the House what was, there were three motions before them, that one was withdrawn, in order to apprize no notice was taken this implied Consent & I proceeded.

MS (ScHi). This document is part of the same manuscript containing Laurens' Notes on Half Pay, April 17–21, 1778.

[1] Aside from Laurens' general concern as president for maintaining order on the floor of Congress, his motive for delivering this speech has not been ascertained. Neither the "motion . . . withdrawn by the Gentn. who made it" nor the "violent infraction . . . made upon Order" has been identified. Despite its uncertain provenance, this brief speech remains a valuable source because of the rare glimpse it provides of Laurens' conduct of his presidential office.

[2] The "violent infraction" referred to has not been identified, but for an incident that he may have had in mind at this time, see his Notes on Half Pay, April 17–21, 1778. In noting an incident that occurred on April 21, Laurens had finally concluded: "The Secretary persists in keeping the Journal thus unfairly misrepresenting the proceedings of the House."

Henry Laurens to
Louis Le Bègue de Presle Duportail

Dear General[1]   20th May [1778]

Your favor of the 2d Inst. having been several days more than ordinary on its journey hither must account for so much of the interval of time, for the remainder I must wave your pardon. You know Sir, how I am circumstanced, not the want of good manners, nor of esteem for General duportail, but truly the want of half an hours leisure has occasioned this long delay of my respects. I had once sat down to write but was hindred by such Visits as I am continually exposed to & was forced to content myself with covering a printed paper in order to shew I had not forgot my debt, although I could do no more than write a superscription.

I have the satisfaction Sir of feeling in my own breast your Ideas of the conduct which true policy will dictate for the observance of the United States towards their new Allies & their abandoned Brethren; If I have any objection, it is to the stress which you seem to lay on the sense of *obligation* which ought to be acknowledged by the States to the former, this is touching a delicate String; a speculative point on which the most sagacious writers may hereafter differ without reproach upon the wisdom or candor of either, & 'tis a maxim with me, that attempts to explain Mystery is waste of time. Let us retire from this ground & I beleive every candid American will subscribe to your positions. The late Acts of Congress warrant this sentiment & the Treaties of the 6th February, mark a line for the government of the contracting parties. Notwithstanding the opening left by the Treaty of Alliance, there remains a strong repugnance in my own mind against any agreement with England, unless on her part an indemnification shall be first granted for the damages we shall have sustained by the present unjust War. This is not a growth from late appearances, I had uniformly expressed opinions to this effect long before Lord North's late speech & his Empty Bills had been ushered upon the Stage, but more particularly I wished to have made it an article in the Act of Congress of the 22d April. Nor had we then any knowledge, I candidly declare I had entertained no expectation, of the Treaties abovementioned. I had always determined to maintain this principle even if a convention with our old friends should have had its commencement beyond those Mountains. Every fresh injury added Strength to my Resolution.

There may be yet an arduous work to perform, it is far from being clear that the English will strike the first blow against France, she had delayed a declaration of War so many days subsequent to the explicit & contemptuous specification by the Duke de Noailles as intimates a different policy, probably she will attempt to treat, if we reject her terms vengeance will follow & this Infant World will be exposed to the pressure of her full power; for it does not appear that France & Spain are yet disposed to make the first declaration of hostility. In this view, I perceive a long train of direful consequences to America, but this is likewise speculative & I am not furnished with sufficient premises for a larger discussion.

Your remarks on the temper of the people on this side the Atlantic I conceive Sir, will not apply to the great Majority. Britain by her unexampled Cruelties has rooted out the former affections of America towards her, it will indeed be her aim, because it is her Interest to recover that loss, but before this can be accomplished, the benefits of an universal acquaintance & of an unrestrained Commerce with the World at large will be so generally experienced as to throw an insuperable Bar against any Bias in her favor. In America Great Britain will be regarded as one of the European States & just so far as Interest & Policy shall direct will she be entitled to the friendships of a people whom she had attempted to enslave, whom she had wantonly proscribed & most unmercifully persecuted; the detail will be transfused in American Almanacs from year to year & every Peasant will be taught to rejoice on the anniversary of deliverance; nor will the stile of "Protector of the Rights of Mankind" be read without its proper impressions & effects.

I wait with some anxiety to learn the further movements in Philadelphia, we are just now told that there is an appearance of retiring from New York, if this be true it works another mystery which time must unfold. Our present policy is to assemble a large Army as the best foundation for treaty & the best guard against tricks. I am rejoiced to learn that at Valley forge the Army is greatly improved by the unwearied attention & great skill of Major General Baron Steuben. I have the honor to be &ca.

LB (ScHi).
[1] Louis Le Bègue de Presle Duportail (1743–1802), a French engineering officer, became colonel of engineers in the Continental Army in July 1777 and rose to the rank of brigadier general in November of that year. Elizabeth S. Kite, *Brigadier-General Louis Lebègue Duportail, Commandant of Engineers in the Continental Army* (Baltimore: Johns Hopkins Press, 1933), pp. 11–34.

Henry Laurens to Baron de Kalb

Dear General.   20th May [1778]

With your favor of the 16th[1] came two Packets directed to Monsr. Gerard, which shall be carefully disposed of, the former of this direction, together with one for Compte Broglie & one for Monsr. de St. Paul are on their way to Boston to be embarked there in the same vessel in which the dispatches from Congress to the Ambassador Franklin are to be sent forward.

I do not find that War was declared in England the 23d March. Commissioners for the American business were named & were soon to proceed on their Embassy, a very valuable French Ship called the Henriette just now arrived at Boston had been 43 hours in possession of the Enemy & suffered to proceed. From these circumstances it appears Great Britain was disposed to more deliberation than when she was wont to commence hostilities antecedent to a declaration.

I have sent your Letter to Mr. Thomson. The Chevalier Failly may safely acquit General Gates who has done every thing in his power to obtain that Gentleman's promotion according to promise; Monsr. Failly I believe received General Gates's paper from me, in which he had signified the Merits of that Officer & earnestly requested Congress to order him a Colonel's Commission, the consideration was postponed till the arrangement of the Army should be completed, this will probably be in three or four days.[2] If Monsr. Failly will reposses me of that paper I will endeavor to introduce it again & to gain the assistance of Gentlemen to obtain what appears to me to be no more than due regard to General Gates & justice to the Chevalier.

I am with very great Esteem

LB (ScHi).
[1] Kalb's May 16 letter to Laurens is in the William Gilmore Simms Collection deposit, MHi; a transcript of it is in the Laurens Papers, ScHi.
[2] The chevalier de Failly finally received a commission as brevet colonel on October 27, 1778. *JCC*, 12:1068. For some account of his previous efforts to attain this rank, see Laurens to Lafayette, March 6, 1778, note 3.

Henry Laurens to George Washington

Sir,   York Town 20th May 1778
I had this Morning the honor of receiving & presenting to Congress Your Excellency's favor of the 18th which is Committed to the Committee on the Army.[1]

Inclosed Your Excellency will receive extract of a Letter from General Sullivan of the 3d Inst. & an Order of Congress thereon.[2] Also one branch of the Army arrangement which Congress Resolved this Morning, for establishing a Provost—the transmission of this detached article arises from an opinion in Congress that the measure ought to be immediately carried into Execution.[3]

A proposition having been intimated for allowing subsistence Money to Officers in lieu of part of the customary Rations[4] this article & that of Pay are reserved as the last points for consideration. The present prospect induces me to believe the whole intended arrangement will be finished in the course of this Week, possibly to morrow.[5]

I have the honor to be, With the highest Esteem & Respect, Sir, Your Excellency's Obedient & most humble servant.

Henry Laurens, President of Congress.

[*P.S.*] Congress have adopted the Stile of the Treaties of Paris, "the United States of North America." [6]

RC (DLC).

[1] Washington's May 18 letter to Laurens is in PCC, item 152, 6:39–41, and Washington, *Writings* (Fitzpatrick), 11:415–17.

[2] In May 1 and 3 letters to Washington and to Laurens, Gen. John Sullivan had requested the services of Brig. Gen. John Stark in Rhode Island. Congress responded this day by resolving to inform Washington that Stark was needed in the northern military department instead but that another brigadier might be sent to assist Sullivan. As a result, Washington, who had already ordered Stark to join Sullivan, was obliged to countermand his order and notify Sullivan that no other brigadier was available for service in Rhode Island. See *JCC*, 11:516; Washington, *Writings* (Fitzpatrick), 11:427, 460–61; and Sullivan, *Papers* (Hammond), 2:45–48.

[3] There is no mention of a plan for the establishment of a provost corps in the journals for May 20, and according to this source Congress did not approve one until May 27, when it was passed as part of a general plan for the arrangement of the army. See *JCC*, 11:515–17, 538–43. Among the Washington Papers at DLC, however, there is a manuscript copy of the provost plan that was approved on the 27th with the following endorsement by Secretary Thomson: "Passed in Congress, May 20, 1778." No explanation has been found for Thomson's failure to record this action in the journals, but as Laurens' letter indicates, the delegates believed it was necessary for Washington to establish a provost corps even before they finished work on the general arrangement of the army.

[4] See Congress' June 2 resolves on this issue in *JCC*, 11:560–61.

[5] In fact Congress did not complete the new arrangement for the army until May 27. *JCC*, 11:538–43.

[6] See Laurens to Horatio Gates, May 19, 1778, note.

Josiah Bartlett to Mary Bartlett

My Dear   York Town May the 21st 1778

I arrived here this morning by the favor of Providence in good health, and hope this will find you & the rest of the family so. I wrote you a line the 17th from Bethlehem in this State which was the first oppertunity I had to write to you. I found great Difficulty on the road in procuring hay &c for our horses. Except that, & a great Cold I had for near a week soon after I set out, we have had a pretty agreable jorney. Saturday the 9th I Crossed Connecticut River at Springfield, the 13th I Crossed Hudsons River at fish kills, Sunday 17th I Crossed Deleware River at Eastown, and this morning Crossed the Susquehannah River, about a mile & half wide, at 11 miles Distance from this place.[1] Mr. Wentworth & his waiter were innoculated at fish Kills and rode with us till last Tuesday when begining to have the simptons, I left them at Reading about 46 miles from this place; I am in hopes they will have the small pox favorable & will Come here in a few Days, I find this Town much Crouded, am in hopes I shall procure good Lodgings in a few Days, at present put up at a Tavern. Our Publick affairs wear a very favorable aspect. General Washington thinks the Brittish army is about to quit Philadelphia. If so tis likely the Congress will adjourn there or to some other place nearer the sea. Charles Chace is well.[2] Remember me to my Children & all friends. Hope I shall hear that Rhoda is better & all things go on well with you. The Lottery is Drawing, but can get no account at present of your tickets; the highest prize was drawn to the united States being a ticket unsold & taken to the risk of the Publick. Next week tis probable I can inform you of your luck.

22nd. I am now well, and Sincerely yours &c.   Josiah Bartlett

24th. I send this by the post and least it should fail I shall write in a few Days by a man who is going to Boston.[3]   J.B.

RC (NhHi).

[1] Bartlett's travel diary, which begins with an entry of May 5 1778—"9 am. Set out for Congress rode 2 miles to Haverhill to Dine."—is available in the Josiah Bartlett Papers microfilm, NhHi. According to an account he later filed for his service in Congress during 1778, which he actually attended from May 21 to November 3, Bartlett claimed compensation "to my time from the 4th of May to the 16th of November 1778, 197 days at 42/ per day." Emmet Collection, NN.

[2] Charles Chase (1755–1842) was a New Hampshire hatter who came to York with Bartlett to serve as his personal aide. Bartlett, *Papers* (Mevers), p. 178n.2.

[3] Two days later Bartlett wrote the following brief letter to Mary. "I wrote to you last Thursday by the post, I now Send this by a man going to Boston Just to inform you I am well; have nothing new to inform you. The Lottery which is Drawing in the room under us will finish this Day next week, I Expect to be able to inform you of your luck in it. Mr. Wentworth who I left at Reading about 46 miles from hence to have the small pox is not arrived here yet. I want to hear from you & the family but hope you are all well. In haste I am yours &c." Watt Collection, NhHi.

William Henry Drayton to Baron Steuben

Dr. Sir.   York Town, May 21. 1778

I cannot express to you, the Pleasure in which I travelled from Camp, reflecting upon the rapid advance of our young Soldiers in the art military under your auspices. You are my Dear Baron, intitled to the thanks of every American; & you have mine in the warmest sense.

I have forgot the name of the officer you wish to have a Brevet of Captain of Artillery.[1] Be so good as to mention his name to me; &

I will put the affair in motion. Believe me to be with respect Dr. Sir,
Your most obedient Set.   Wm. Hy. Drayton

RC (PHi).
    [1] Pierre Charles L'Enfant was the officer in question. See Henry Laurens to
Steuben, May 25 and 29, 1778.

Henry Laurens to George Washington

Sir   York Town 21st May 1778.
    I dispatched Barry this Morning with a Letter which I had the
honour of writing to Your Excellency last Night.
    The present is for the sole purpose of transmitting the Inclosed
Act of Congress of this date to enable Your Excellency to answer
General Sir William Howe's late proposition for Exchange of Prison-
ers.[1]
    I have the honor to be, With the greatest Esteem & Regard, Sir,
Your Excellency's Most obedient & most humble servant.
                            Henry Laurens, President of Congress.

RC (DLC).
    [1] See *JCC,* 11:520–21; and Laurens to Richard Caswell, May 11, 1778, note 4.

Gouverneur Morris to George Clinton

Dr. Sir,   Yorktown, 21st May, 1778.
    Yours of the 14th instant by Mr. Barclay I received yesterday morn-
ing.[1] I am much obliged by the returns which I am Sorry to Say came
time enough, as I fervently wish the affairs of the Army, which at this
late hour press upon us much were completed, and indeed that they
had been as they ought to have been completed three months ago.
The plot thickens in Europe every day; what will be the event of the
different movements, God only knows. I am Sorry Jay is under a
necessity of hanging So many,[2] and for that reason almost wish I were
in the State because I flatter myself that I might have been able to
disencumber the hands of government of some few. But as by this
proceeding I might make money instead of Spending it, a thing by no
means too reputable, considering who the rich of the present day are,
I am content. I enclose you a print. Adieu.
    Believe me sincerely yours,   Gouv'r. Morris.

Tr (MH–H).
    [1] Clinton's May 14 letter to Morris, enclosing the returns of two New York regi-
ments and promising to send returns of the rest, is in Clinton, *Papers* (Hastings),

3:308–10. The governor had written in response to April 15 and May 1 letters from Morris that have not been found.

[2] Clinton had merely written that Chief Justice John Jay "fills the Bench with great dignity & pronounces the Sentences of the Court with becoming Grace. It is to be lamented that he has had already so many Opportunities to display his abilities in that Way but it is unavoidable." Ibid., p. 309. But see also Jay's April 29 remarks to Morris on the need to pursue "a harsh System" of justice "repugnant to my Feelings," in Jay, *Papers* (Morris), 1:475.

Gouverneur Morris to George Washington

Dr Genl.   York Town 21st May 1778.

We are going on with the regimental Arrangements as fast as possible and I think the Day begins to appear with Respect to this Business. Had our Saviour addressed a Chapter to the Rulers of Mankind as he did many to the Subjects I am perswaded his Good Sense would have dictated this Text, Be not wise overmuch. Had the several Members which compose our multifarious Body been only wise enough Our Business would long since have been compleated. But our superior Abilities or the Desire of appearing to possess them leads us to such exquisite Tediousness of Debate that the most precious Moments pass unheeded away like vulgar Things.

I am at a loss to determine what the Enemy will do because it is impossible to see what their Interest, Situation and the like require of them or rather because these Circumstances require more of them than they appear to be in Force to perform. It is not so difficult to say what they will not do. They will not go up Hudson's River unless you will insure them a safe Passage down. On the whole it appears to me that they will leave a Garrison at Rhode Island, in Nova Scotia and Canada, possibly a few Men in the Floridas. The Remainder of their Army together with such of the American Rebels as they can force into Service, kid-napp &ca. to the Amount of about fifteen thousand effectives and the large Fleet now in the American Seas and about eight Ships of the Line and a large Convoy of Provisions will serve to carry on an offensive war in the West Indias. This seems to be their only Chance of Safety but of all this the Event will determine much better than we can.

As to what you mention of the extraordinary Demeanor of some Gentlemen I cannot but agree with you that such Conduct is not the most *honorable,* But on the other Hand even you must allow that it is the most *safe* and Certainly you are not to learn that however ignorant of that happy art in your own particular, the bulk of us Bipeds know well how to balance solid Pudding against empty Praise. There are other Things my dear Sir besides Virtue which are their own *Reward.*[1] And the Feelings of others unless I mistake will sooner or later break out into a Retribution of those Act & Neglects which at present pass away unnoticed by the Herd of Observers or rather of Lookers on.

As to your Friend who hath thought proper to *demand* of you a Command, I did beleive from the first that his Resignation was like some former ones from the same Quarter meerly calculated to gain either Promotion or Favor or Revenge.[2] I was therefore led to expect that his Merits and our Misfortune in loosing him would become the Topick of Declamation & took the earliest Opportunity to express in the very strongest Terms my Satisfaction my Joy at the Receipt of the Letter from him and of Consequence to assign the Reasons why this Event gave me so much Pleasure. This gave a very different Turn to Affairs. Panegyrick dwindled to Apology and no Opposition was made to the main Point of accepting his Resignation. The next Day I was informed that he did not intend to resign, that his Letter was quite misunderstood &ca. The Gentleman however had been so unlucky as to use the most pointed terms and therefore his Aid from whom the Information came was told that the observations he made came too late. I am perswaded that he will attempt to get reinstated if the least Probability of Success appears but I am equally perswaded that his Attempts will fail. I beleive his Friends are hitherto of that same Opinion and therefore we have as yet had no attempts made in Congress and possibly we never shall.

I wish you would contrive to get the necessary Returns from Maryland Troops and others who have not made them so as that the arrangement may take Place as soon as possible.

Believe me, Dr General, very sincerely yours,   Gouv Morris

RC (DLC).
  [1] Washington had expressed surprise at the behavior of Thomas Mifflin, "who some time ago . . . was desirous of resigning, now stepping forward in the line of the Army." "That Gentleman's stepping in, and out," Washington went on to observe, "as the Sun happens to beam forth or obscure is not *quite* the thing, nor *quite* just with respect to those Officers who take the bitter with the Sweet." See his May 18 letter to Morris in Washington, *Writings* (Fitzpatrick), 11:414.
  [2] Washington was concerned by reports that his old nemesis Thomas Conway was seeking reinstatement in the army. Ibid.

Gouverneur Morris to Anthony Wayne

Dr Wayne.   York Town 21st May 1778.
    Colo. Johnson delivered me yours of the 16th. I am sorry the business of the Army hath been so long delayed. For your Comfort I have to assure you that it goes on tho not with the Rapidity You and I and every Body else wish. Your good Morals in the Army give me

sincere Pleasure as it hath long been my fixed Opinion that Virtue
and Religion are the great sources of human Happiness. More espe-
cially is it necessary in your Profession firmly to rely upon the God of
Battles, for his Guardianship and Protection in the dreadful Hour of
Trial. But of all these Things you will and I hope in the merciful
Lord you have been made fully acquainted by that pious young Man
Friend Hutchinson. What will be the Success of Colo. Johnson's
Application I know not; hope favorable.[1] Adieu. Pray beleive me
with great Sincerity, yours,   Gouvr Morris

RC (PHi).
   [1] On May 23 Congress rejected Col. Francis Johnston's request to retain his rank
in the line while serving as commissary general of prisoners. See *JCC*, 11:525; and
Henry Laurens to Johnston, May 11, 1778, note 1.

Henry Laurens to Francis Bailey

Sir,   22d May [1778]
   Inclosed you will receive an Act of Congress of this date, for exempting & disqualifying Deserters from the Enemy, from acting as
Militia Men or subsitutes, which you will be pleased to print in
hand Bills in pure German. 500 Copies. I shall direct a person to call
on you to Morrow or on Monday for 250 Copies, send 250 Copies to
me, as the work is short I hope to receive these by the present bearer.
   I am with great respect &ca.

LB (DNA: PCC, item 13).

Henry Laurens to John Bayard

Sir,   22d May [1778]
   Inclosed you will receive an Act of Congress of the 19th Inst. con-
taining a Report from the Board of War on a Memorial from the
General Assembly of this State; and a Resolution founded on that
Report for an enquiry into the building Forts at Ligonier & Hana's
Town & for examining Accounts of the Expence attending the same.[1]
I am with great respect &ca.

LB (DNA: PCC, item 13). Addressed: "John Bayard Esqr. Speaker of the Assembly,
Lancaster."
   [1] On April 14 Congress read and referred to the Board of War an April 2 memorial from the Pennsylvania Assembly asking Congress to pay for the construction of
two forts in Westmoreland County that local officials had recently erected to stave
off British and Indian attacks. After considering this memorial, the board reported
to Congress on May 19 that it had been unable to determine if the two posts

served "only a local, instead of a general purpose," and therefore Congress decided to refer the memorial to the commandant of Fort Pitt, with instructions to ascertain whether or not the building of the two forts should be considered a Continental expense. Eventually the board decided in December 1778 that Congress was not liable for the costs of building the fort at Ligonier, and although it then passed no judgment on this issue in regard to the fort at Hanna's Town there is no evidence Congress ever paid for its construction either. See *JCC*, 10:344, 11:509–11, 12:1182; and PCC, item 41, 8:50.

Henry Laurens to James Mease

Sir,   22d May [1778]

Yesterday I presented to Congress your favor of the day before,[1] this with the several Papers which accompanied it were referred to The Board of Treasury from whom you will now receive a Letter by Mr. Brailsford.[2] I requested the Gentlemen to return the papers which you desired might be sent back.[3] I find that is not complied with by the present Messenger, but it shall be, when the business to which those papers relate is ended.

Inclosed you will receive a packet which came to my hands three days ago.

I am with great respect.

LB (DNA: PCC, item 13).

[1] Clothier General James Mease's May 20 letter to Laurens is in PCC, item 78, 15:343–46. In it Mease announced that the army was well supplied with clothing, asked Congress to pay for the clothes he and his Boston agents Otis & Andrews had purchased, and suggested an end to clothing purchases by Pennsylvania state officials. Congress referred Mease's request for payment to the Board of Treasury, and after reading the board's report on May 25, it agreed to provide Mease with $650,000. On the other hand, Congress failed to follow Mease's advice about state purchasing agents and decided instead on May 29 to suspend all clothing purchases by Mease and Otis & Andrews and to require them to submit their accounts for inspection to the Board of Treasury. See *JCC*, 11:517, 531, 545.

[2] Mease wrote a letter on May 23 to Board of Treasury member Elbridge Gerry in reply to a May 22 letter from Gerry that has not been found. PCC, item 78, 15:339–41. It is clear from Mease's response, however, that Gerry had asked him to send the board detailed accounts of the clothing purchased by Otis & Andrews.

[3] The papers in question were accounts of clothing purchases by Mease and Otis & Andrews. See the May 20 letter from Mease to Laurens cited in note 1.

Henry Laurens to Peter Muhlenberg

Sir,[1]   22d May [1778]

In consequence of a Memorial which I had lately the honor of presenting to Congress to which your name was subscribed the Inclosed Act of the 18th was Resolved for appointing the Reverend Mr.

Henry Miller to be Chaplain to the Germans in the Army under the Command of His Excellency General Washington.[2] I request you Sir, to give the proper notification to Mr. Miller & to beleive me to be, Yours &ca.

LB (DNA: PCC, item 13). Addressed: "Brigr. General Mulenberg, Valley Forge."

[1] Peter Muhlenberg (1746–1807), an Anglican and Lutheran clergyman in New Jersey and Virginia before the War for Independence, was brigadier general in command of the Eighth Virginia Regiment, a largely German unit. *DAB.*

[2] See *JCC,* 11:507. The May 6 "Memorial" to Congress in which Muhlenberg and several other German officers asked for the appointment of Rev. Henry Miller to serve as chaplain to German troops in Washington's army is in PCC, item 42, 5:69–71. This document also contained a May 6 covering note by Steuben endorsing Miller's proposed appointment.

Reverend Miller was only one of a number of military chaplains appointed by Congress around this time. On May 22 Laurens also wrote a brief letter to Gen. Anthony Wayne, informing him of Robert Blackwell's appointment as Wayne's brigade chaplain, and on May 25 he wrote a similar letter to Muhlenberg, notifying him of Alexander Balmain's appointment as Muhlenberg's brigade chaplain. See PCC, item 13, fols. 329, 335; and *JCC,* 11:519, 523. See also Laurens to Francis Johnston, May 25, 1778.

Henry Laurens to George Clinton

Sir.   23d May [1778]

Since my last of the 16th Inst. by Browne I have had the honor of receiving & presenting to Congress your Excellency's favor of the 13th. This & the several papers which had accompanied it were Committed to the Board of War & there remain.[1]

Your Excellency will be pleased to receive with this An Act of Congress of yesterday Recommending to the Legislatures of the several States to exempt from Militia duty, deserters from the British Army & Navy & to disqualify such persons for acting as substitutes during the present War. This Act is contained in the Pennsylvania Gazette of the present date. I likewise transmit 25 Copies of this Act in English & a like Number in the German Tongue, a proper distribution of these will in the opinion of Congress produce good effects. I add barely for your Excellency's information Copy of an Act of the 15th for granting an half pay to Officers of the Army after the War for a limitted time & for making a gratuitous acknowledgement to Non Commissioned & privates. The Retorts which from various quarters have been made to General Tryon's messages & empty Bills must have occasioned a little mortification to a Gentleman of his meekness.

From accounts daily repeated & one in particular this Instant received, there is every appearance of the Enemy's intention to abandon Philadelphia. The Marquis delafayette had been detached with a Command of about 2000 to observe their Motions, intelligence was quickly conveyed to them of his, a Body said to consist of at least 6000, by a forced March had penetrated the Country & nearly surrounded him. We have received no authentic account of his Retreat, but an Officer who had been of the detachment, represents it in a light very honorable to the Marquis, effected without loss. The Enemy came up to the River immediately after he had passed it with Troops & Cannon breast deep. They looked at the Marquis & returned to the City.

Colo. Harrison from Virginia with about 500 of his Regiment of Artillery a Corps of fine appearance is here on his way to Valley forge.

The Enemy's Vessels marked in the Pennsylvania Gazette as taken in Georgia with the Galatia which I hope is also taken or destroyed amount to a Capture of high Value to the United States, they had long infested the Coast & interupted hundreds of Vessels bringing supplies to us & transporting produce from So Carolina & Georgia.

Congress have adapted the Stile introduced in the Treaties of Paris of the 6th Febry. "the United States of North America." I have the honor to be

[*P.S.*] Two French vessels at Wilmington, one at Beaufort, one at Edenton, all in North Carolina are just arrived & said to contain useful & valuable Cargoes.

LB (DNA: PCC, item 13).
    [1] Governor Clinton's May 13 letter to Laurens is in PCC, item 67, 2:114–16. In it Clinton asked Congress to extend the June 10, 1778, deadline for implementing an April 23 resolve that urged state legislatures to pass laws or state executives to issue proclamations offering pardons to loyalists who agreed to submit to American authority. See *JCC*, 10:381–82. This extension was necessary in New York, the governor explained, because he did not have the constitutional authority to issue such a proclamation and the legislature was not due to reconvene until June. Despite this plea, Congress did not extend the June 10 deadline. Along with his letter Clinton also sent Laurens a list of laws passed by the state legislature in response to various recommendations of Congress and a May 4 letter from a New York militia officer dealing with reports of the military situation in northern New York and Canada. PCC, item 67, 2:118–20.

Henry Laurens to William Heath

Sir,   York Town, 23d May 1778.
    My last was the 19th by Brown since which I have not been honoured with any of your favors, as appears by the list sent in by the Secretary, although I think he has omitted one received by Mr. Brailsford, which time will not permit me at this Instant to enquire into. The Gentleman who is so good as to conduct this, waits while I write. I shall address you again by Brailsford in four or five days. At present please to receive an Act of Congress of the 22d Inst. approving your

method of transacting the provision business with Major General Pigot & enjoining you to demand Payment for incidental Charges in unloading, removing & Storing such Provision in solid Coin.[1]

I likewise inclose a Pennsylvania Gazette of this date containing a Resolve of Congress of the 19th & one of the 22d Inst[2] together with scraps of Interesting Intelligence.

I have the honor to be, With great Regard & Esteem, Sir, Your Obedient & Most humble servant,

Henry Laurens, President of Congress.

RC (MHi).
  [1] See *JCC,* 11:523.
  [2] See the following entry.

Henry Laurens to the Massachusetts Council

Honorable sir.   York Town 23d May 1778
My last went by McClosky under the 11th Inst.[1]—since which I have had the honor of receiving & presenting to Congress your several favors of 25th, 27th, & 28th April.[2] These are Committed & remain for consideration.

Please to receive within the present Inclosure an Act of Congress of the 21st Confirming a Report of a Committee on a Memorial from divers Inhabitants of Nova Scotia.[3]

Also a Pennsylvania Gazette containing an Act of Congress of the 19th & one other Act of the 22d—the former for ascertaining Pay & Rations to Captive Land Officers, the latter for exempting Deserters from the Enemy from Militia Duty to which I beg leave to refer for particulars.

I am with great Respect & Esteem, Honorable Sir, Your most obedient & humble Servt.   Henry Laurens, President of Congress

RC (M–Ar). Addressed: "The Honorable Jeremiah Powell Esquire, President, Massachuset Bay."
  [1] See Laurens to George Clinton, May 11, 1778, note 1.
  [2] The Massachusetts Council's April 27 and 28 letters to Laurens, dealing respectively with price regulations and the difficulties of complying with a congressional request to disperse General Burgoyne's captured army throughout Massachusetts, are in PCC, item 65, 1:304–9. For Congress' May 30 resolve on the dispersal of these troops, see *JCC,* 11:556. See also Laurens to the Massachusetts Council, February 20, 1778. The council's April 25 letter has not been found, but according to the journals it dealt with the issue of the expenses Massachusetts had incurred in maintaining Burgoyne's army. *JCC,* 11:518.
  [3] On March 3 twenty-three "late Inhabitants of the Province of Nova Scotia," who were then in Boston, signed a petition to Congress asking for permission to raise men for an expedition against Nova Scotia and requesting that the province be allowed to join the confederation. PCC, item 41, 7:21–23. On May 21 Congress approved the report of the committee to which this memorial was referred stating

that although it would be prudent to delay an attack on Nova Scotia until after war had broken out between Great Britain and France, the Massachusetts Council could launch one sooner if there seemed to be a reasonable hope of success. *JCC*, 11:498, 518.

Henry Laurens to William Nichols

Sir,[1]   23d May [1778]

Your favor of the 21st Inst. this moment reached me. In order to embrace the first conveyance of an answer I delay no time to afford you all the consolation that times & circumstances will admit of.

I will write to my Son & request him to use his utmost endeavors for effecting your Exchange & to Colonel Boudinot for the same purpose.[2] You shall not want Money nor be exposed to the necessity of Exchanging upon unfavorable terms; let me know what sum will be necessary for present occasions. It shall be remitted to you & you may either repay me in a Bill at the highest Exchange or take an opportunity more convenient to your affairs.

If I was Master of such an House here as I have been accustomed to enjoy in Charles Town you Should receive a cordial invitation to take a Bed in it, but at present I live a little below the Stile of one of my Overseers, & tis not even in my power when I please to ask a friend to dine with me.

Your appearance in York Town with permission, may nevertheless be of service to you. Members of Congress have heard of you & tis probable that upon a personal application Some of the Gentlemen may devise means for accomplishing your Exchange, which do not occur to my mind.

You have the best wishes of, Sir, Your obedient huml Servt.

LB (ScHi). Addressed: "Captn. William Nichols, Reading."
[1] For further information on Capt. William Nichols, a captured British naval officer, see Laurens to Nichols, November 21, 1777, note.
[2] See also Laurens to John Laurens, May 29, 1778, note 3.

Henry Laurens to John Sullivan

Sir,   23d May 1778

On the 20th Inst. I had the honor of receiving & presenting to Congress your favor of the 3d Inst.[1]

The House have "directed His Excellency General Washington to order a Brigadier General under your Command if he shall think proper" & have intimated to the General to except "Brigadier Stark who is ordered to the Northern department."[2] The remaining subjects of your Letter are committed to the Board of War & continue unreported.

I have the honor to be &ca.[3]

LB (DNA: PCC, item 13).
  [1] General Sullivan's May 3 letter to Laurens, outlining the needs of his Rhode Island command, is in PCC, item 160, fols. 111–12, and Sullivan, *Papers* (Hammond), 2:46–48. Accordingly, on June 13 Congress asked the delegates of Connecticut, Massachusetts, and New Hampshire to write to their state governments and urge them to send troops to Rhode Island. *JCC*, 11:605.
  [2] See Laurens to Washington, May 20, 1778, note 2.
  [3] Laurens also wrote a brief letter this day to former Commissary General Joseph Trumbull, transmitting a May 19 resolve on the settlement of Trumbull's accounts. See PCC, item 13, fol. 334; and *JCC*, 11:509.

Gouverneur Morris to John Jay

Dr Jay,   York Town 23d May 1778

I send you the Translation of a Letter to which is subjoined the following Note. "The Members of Congress from New York may possibly some of them know the Mr Hartwig above mentioned. A communication of such Intelligence as may be had concerning him will oblige their very humble Servant, B Franklin. Passy near Paris 28 Jany 78."

Mr Johannis Christopher Hartwig or Hartwick a Native of Gotha, having made Theology his study went to London in 1744, was ordained a Minister of the Gospel and sent by Order of the King to America. There he became a Preacher at the Camp and at Rhinebeck for many years. His Reputation & Zeal obtained for him at the Close of the last War the Post of superintendant to the Churches in Virginia and his Circumstances were in other Respects so flourishing that he became possessed of a considerable real Estate in Albany. The last Letter to his Family he dates the 19th Novr 1773 and told them that he is not maried, that his age will no longer permit him to perform the Duties of his office in the manner he formerly had fulfilled them and therefore he had resolved to return and spend the Remainder of his Days in his native Country. Since that time his Family have heard nothing from him and if now living he is sixty five years of Age.

It is requested that Doctor Franklin will have the Goodness to make some Enquiry into the Fate of the said Johann Christoph Hartwick and in Case he should have died to procure the necessary Intelligence as to the Estate he may have been possessed of and the

Steps to be taken by his Representatives to procure the Possession of it.

The Minister Plenipotentiary of Sax Gotha at the Court of his most Christian Majesty will receive the Information which Doctor Franklin shall procure for him upon this Subject with the utmost Thankfulness.

Now Jay what I have to request of you is that you will in the Course of your Peregrinations make Inquiry into this Matter and write me the Result.[1]

I received a Letter from our Friend Robert yesterday dated in Sussex County in which he desires me to write to him without telling me where to direct but as he mentions the having a Wife and two sisters with him I presume he is bound to Lebanon. He adds a wish that I might be in his own words "in this State at the meeting of the Legislature." I presume he means in the state of New York and not New Jersey, if so I say, This is impossible because Frank Lewis is absent. Because Duer hath leave of Absence and will I suppose go as soon as he can. Because Mr. Livingston is sick.[2] On this last head I have to add that I really am very apprehensive on the old Gentleman's account for truly I beleive he will not escape if he does escape without much Pain, Sickness & other of those Circumstances which render Life no such desirable Boon as those who observe the Tenaciousness of Mankind about it would be led to imagaine. What his Disease is no Body pretends to know. I who am no Phisician will however venture to guess that it is an Impostumation in his Stomach or perhaps in some one of the Viscera still more important in a Complaint of that nature. This I gather from a quick Pulse, Languor, continued sickness, some Pain and much Uneasiness about the Part I suppose to be affected, a Decline of strength & Flesh, Hectic appearance. But I will not play the Doctor to you at least who never plays it.

Adieu my Friend. Beleive me in all times, seasons & Circumstances, with sincerity, yours,   Gouvr Morris

RC (NNC).
[1] Jay wrote to Morris on June 3 and informed him that Johannes Christopher Hartwig, a Lutheran missionary, was still alive and had recently been in Albany. Jay, *Papers*, (Morris), 1:484.
[2] Philip Livingston, whose death on June 12 Morris reported is his June 16, 1778, letter to George Clinton. Livingston's son, Henry Philip Livingston, also commented on his father's condition in a letter written at York on May 24 to Governor Clinton. "I take the liberty to inclose three Letters which my father requests you will be kind enough to forward by the first opportunity. He was taken ill two days after his arrival at this place (near a fortnight ago) his disorder is of a complicated nature." Clinton, *Papers* (Hastings), 3:352. The letters mentioned by the younger Livingston have not been found, and the last direct evidence of his father's activities as a delegate consists of his signature on the New York delegates' May 16 letter to Horatio Gates.

Gouverneur Morris to John Jay

Dear Sir   [post May 23, 1778][1]
Casting my eye over a Baltimore paper of the 19th[2] I was struck
with a little publication which relates to the constitution of your
State. The interest I take in all its concerns leads me to enclose you
the paper & to wish that by the return of the Post you will favour me
with your observations on this piece. Pray excuse this liberty & believe me, yours

Tr (MH–H). Endorsed by Jay: "G. Morris recd. 3 June 1778."
   [1] Since Jay received this letter on June 3, the day after he received Morris' May
23 letter, it seems evident that Morris wrote it shortly after completing the former.
Internal evidence indicates only that it was written after Morris had seen a May 19
Baltimore newspaper, which normally would have reached York a few days after
its publication. See Jay's June 3 reply in Jay, *Papers* (Morris), 1:482–84.
   [2] The May 19 issue of the *Maryland Journal*—the only Baltimore paper printed
on that date—has not been found.

Gouverneur Morris to George Washington

Dear General,   York Town Saturday Morning 23d May [1778]
   I wrote you a few days ago by Colo. Johnson; as he is not yet gone,
I will now add two Things I forgot to mention then. The first is that
if you send any General to Rhode Island you will probably find it
most convenient to get rid of Varnom, whose Temper and Manners
are by no Means calculated to teach Patience, Discipline & Subordination.[1] Congress having determined on the Affair of the Prisoners; and
(in my Opinion wisely) dropt for the present all Mention of Citizens;
you will probably be enabled to negotiate a Cartel.[2] If not, severe
Retaliation is the only Mode of compelling the Enemy to Humanity;
and should they as on a former Occasion complain of what they call
Injustice, in punishing innocent Men for the Faults of a few, it will
not be perhaps improper to observe that it is perfectly consonant to
the Law of Nations; which expressly makes this Provision where the
immediate Author of the Evil cannot be brought within the Power
of the Party injured. But at the same time ought to be relaxed whenever Circumstances shall enable us to punish the Delinquents in an
exemplary Manner. The Marquis I hear had like to have been
catched. Pray Sir be pleased to make my Respects to him & Congratulations on his Escape.
   I have the Honor to be, yours,   Gouvr Morris

RC (DLC).
   [1] See also Henry Laurens to Washington, May 20, 1778, note 2.
   [2] See *JCC*, 11:520–21; Washington, *Writings* (Fitzpatrick), 11:372–73; and Henry

Laurens to Richard Caswell, May 11, 1778, note 4. Hitherto Congress had insisted that in his negotiations for a prisoner cartel Washington respect a resolve of December 30, 1777, providing that loyalists captured while in British service be turned over to their respective states for punishment, a policy that hampered Washington's efforts to reach an agreement with General Howe for a general exchange of prisoners. See *JCC*, 9:1069, 10:295; and Washington, *Writings* (Fitzpatrick), 11:216–17.

Robert Morris to John Brown

Dear Sir   Manheim May 23d 1778

As I heard an express passed through Lancaster Yesterday Morning from Boston with Letters from Capt. Green I was in hopes of receiving some letters to day by your means from that quarter but as yet nothing appears. I received a letter from Colo. Griffin by last Post dated at Williamsburg 9th May 1778 wherein is the following Paragraph.

"By last Post I received a letter from Mr Babcock desiring me to receive the Money from the Secret Committee on the terms they proposed and in Consequence thereof, have drawn an order on you for the Amot. The papers were all left in the hands of Mr. Brown with directions to lodge the Money with you whenever you applied.

Mr. Griffins draft on me has not yet appeared but as I wish to be ready to Answer it I beg you will present Mr Ceronios draft to the Committee. It is drawn for hard Dollars, he has been advised that it wou'd be paid & the terms on which it was proposed to be paid was two Dollars for one which Mr Griffin did not choose to accept without orders from his employer Mr. Babcock and as these terms are favourable to the Public I suppose there will be no difficulty. You'l please to receive the Money & advise me when it is ready. I find Cap Brown of the Henrietta arrived in Boston was 43 hours in possession of the Enemy which occasioned his throwing all his dispatches overboard. Mr. Ross had this ship sold in Hamburg and by that means obtained Hamburgee papers & clearances for Hispaniola which has saved her & 600 Bales of Goods she has onboard. My Compts to the Committee. Tell them this Circumstance and they will find good Management prevail in all affairs under that Gentns. care. I am Dr sir, your Obedt hble servt.   Robt Morris

P.S. Advise me the amot of what you receive for Ceronio's bill to Mr Babcock, as I have forgot the Sum & Mr Griffin dont mention it.[1]

RC (NjP).

[1] Morris also wrote brief letters to Brown on May 21 and May 25, both of which are concerned with remittances and the transmittal of letters related to Morris' commercial affairs. DeCoppet Collection, NjP. During this period Morris also wrote

from Manheim on May 19 to commissary of prisoners Elias Boudinot (on the sub-
ject of Lt. Andrew Robinson of the York County, Pa., militia, a prisoner in New
York), Lloyd W. Smith Collection, NjMoHP; and on May 22 to William Lee at
Paris (on the subject of his late brother Thomas Morris), Robert Morris Letters,
ViHi.

Charles Carroll of Carrollton to
Charles Carroll, Sr.

Dear Papa,   24 May 1778
   Your letters by the last post, which I ought to have recd. last Monday, I recd. last Wednesday; they went by mistake to Lancaster &
were returned by the return post.
   A Law has passed in this State, of which you are probably ignorant,
calling in all the money, issued under the Proprietary governt., by
the 1st of next month; after that day it is not to pass:[1] persons having
such monies & residing out of this State have a further time for bringing them in—I believe till sometime in August. Do look over your
cash, and select from it all bills passed by the Legislature of Pennsylvania while under the dominion of G.B. You will find the Law in the
Lancaster newspaper; probably it will be reprinted in Baltimore. I
have written, & sent my letter to Col. Moylan recommending to his
notice the person whom Mr. J. Howard wrote to me about. Please to
inform Mr. Howard of this. It will always give me pleasure to render
him such services. The Marquis de la Fayette crossed the Schuyilkill
last Monday with 2300 men; he was ordered to draw near the city of
Pha. and observe the enemy's motions; it has then imagined they
were about to leave Pha. The Enemy had very early information of
the Marquiss march, & they laid a scheme to intercept him: on Monday night they marched with 7000 men from Pha. in 3 columns taking
different roads: one of these Columns had got in the rear of the
Marquiss unperceived; the other was near his front, the 3d on his
flank: from this perilous situation the Marquiss extricated himself by
a rapid March to the Schuyilkill, which he passed with his whole
detachment & altho the water was middle deep he brought off his men
& cannon safe. As soon as he had gained this side of Schuyilkill he
drew up, the Enemy on the other side looking on; the alarm guns at
Gener. Washington's camp firing gave the alarm to the Enemy's
column which had got in the rear of the Marquiss and they marched
as quick back as they came out. Had this column attacked the
Marquiss detachment, it is probable the whole would have been
killed or taken.
   General Washington in his last letter (I think dated the 18) informed
us he was of opinion, from all the accounts he had recd. from Pha.,

that the Enemy were about to leave that city; his conjecture was that they were going to N. York, & from thence might possibly proceed to the W. Indies. Notwithstanding these appearances & the General's opinion founded on them, I am inclined to think the Enemy will not leave Pha. before the arrival of the Commissioners, who may be daily expected. If they do not acknowlege our Independence, but should have declared war agt. France, I am of opinon they will continue the war in this country and not carry their army to the W. Indies, to perish in that unwholsome climate.

If Joe has finished all the Jobbs at Annapolis, I wish you would set him about preparing stones to line a cold bath; the stones already raised at the soap stone quarry would be sufficient for this purpose, as the bath need not be in the clear more than 10 feet long & 8 broad & 4 feet, 6 inches deep. When I return I will direct where it shall be dug. Joe will be free some time next month, he may be engaged to stay till the bath is finished. I wrote to Skerret by last post to engage the Gardiner at £60 per annum wages. He is a sober & an industrious fellow, & considering the little value of the money, & the dearness of cloaths, I do not think that sum much out of the way.

Inclosed you have yesterday's paper of this place, it contains all the news circulating here except what is above related & what follows.

The only vessels arrived at the Eastward making part of the fleet which sailed from France the latter end of February are the Dean Frigate, and the Queen of France; the Duke de Choiseul one of this fleet is not yet arrived; she parted with the Dean off the western Islands in a gale of wind. Besides the above vessels, the Henrietta, a French Ship with a very valuable cargo, is arrived at Boston. She was in the Enemy's possession 43 hours, all her papers were thrown overboard. The Brigt Resistance is arrived at Boston from Martinico. Mr. Bingham, the Continental agent there, writes that the Govr. has recd. orders to put every thing in a posture of defence, & to be prepared as if war was certain.

Do let me know in your next how the Vineyard thrives. Has the fruit suffered by frost this spring? If it has escaped hitherto, I hope there will be a good deal of it. Remember to answer this part of my letter.

25th P.M. I have yours & Molly's of the 21st instant by this day's post. It will not be in my power to attend the approaching session of our Assembly. There are but 3 Delegates from Maryd. now attending Congress, Plater, Henry, & Self. Mr. Henry will leave this the latter end of this week, or the beginning of next. The death of Mr. Stone's brother will prevent his attendance for some time. Chase won't be here till towards the middle of next month; altho' he is not in our assembly, he will do well to attend it some time. I shall return home about the 20 of next month never to return to Congress, & principally for the reason you suggest. I am sensible business must now be extreamly irksome to you, and I am determined to ease you of it in future by staying at home & minding my own affairs. You know my sentiments of the tender law, I would do all in my power to have it repealed as an unjust, publickly impolitical, & partially oppressive and an ex post facto law; but believe me, my presence in the Senate will not forward the repeal. I much doubt, notwithstanding the major's information, whether a Majority of the Senate would vote for a repeal of it, when it should come to the tryal. You have £11,473. £6000 of it are engaged, remains £5,473—out of this must be paid our assesst., say £1500, remains £3973 for curt. expences; if you are inclined, you may put out at interest to Individuals, this or a much larger sum. If the Senate were to pass a bill to repeal the tender law, it would be rejected by the House of Delegates. I believe every State are too much interested in the law to suffer its repeal. I flatter myself, if we should soon have peace, that our Public debts will be put in a regular course of payt., public credit will revive, and our currentcy settle at par; in that case we shall only lose in the present expenditures of monies paid us. Even this public debt may be of service, and serve as a cement, or bond of Union. It gives me great pleasure to hear that Molly is so much better. I hope she will keep mending, till she recovers a perfect state of health; my affectionate love to her; I would write to her by this opportunity but am tired of writing, and I can say nothing but what she must be convinced on & I have already said. My love to Mrs. Darnall & the little ones. We have not heard lately from Gen. Washington: the report still continues & gains strength of the enemy's approaching departure from Pha. God grant you a long enjoyment of health. I am, yr. affectionate Son,

Ch. Carroll of Carrollton

P.S. 26th May. I write this by Wm. Levy of Baltimore. He has promised me to send it to Mr. Brooke. If there should be any extraordinary intelligence I will write to you again this morning in Congress & send my second letter by the post.

RC (MdHi).
¹ See Jonathan Bayard Smith to George Bryan, May 10? 1778, note 4.

Samuel Adams to James Warren

My dear sir   York Town May 25 1778
    Your favor by Capt Coltor overtook me on the Road; agreeably to your Request I immediately on my Arrival here mentiond to a Gen-

tleman of the Marine Committee the Necessity and Importance of keeping your Board duly supplyd with Cash to enable you effectually to do the duty of your department and was told that 50 thousand of Dollars had been lately remitted to you.[1] I will not fail to do what in me lies to forward that Service, as our Navy has always lain near my Heart.

I am exceedingly pleasd to find that our Army makes a much better Appearance than it has done since the Commencement of this War. It is very respectable in Point of Numbers and Discipline has been happily improvd by the Baron de Stuben who is appointed Inspector General with the Rank of Major General.[2] The invariable Accounts from Philadelphia are that the Enemy are making Preparations for an Embarkation, and it is expected they will soon leave that Place. Where they will proceed next you can as easily conjecture as we. I am not apprehensive of their visiting Boston; I wish however that more effectual Measures might be taken to strengthen & secure that Harbour & Town from Insult to which I think it is too much exposd.

I recollect that your Election of Counsillors will come on the Day after tomorrow. Has Mr ———[3] waited for the Event of that important Day? or is he on his Journey to this Place? It is a matter of so much Uncertainty here, that Nothing, I suppose prevents many wagers being laid upon it, but its being not of so much Moment as some others. Was he present here, he might, if he pleasd, vindicate me against a Report which has given occasion to my Friends to rally me, that I have been called to Account and severely reprehended at a Boston Town Meeting for being in a Conspiracy against a very great Man.[4] You know how little I care for such Rumours. It is easy for me to conjecture by what Means it extended it self from Manheim where I first heard it to York Town; and it may not be difficult to guess how it came from Boston to that Place. Manheim is about 12 miles East of the Susquihanna; there lives Mr R.M. a very intimate Acquaintance of *my* excellent Friend. Mr H *is said* to be on the Road, but no one makes it *certain*. When he arrives Messrs Gerry & Dana propose to set off for N England. I shall be mortified at their leaving us, for I verily think that the Accession even of *that* Gentleman will not make up for the Absence of the other two.

I am happy to find C[ongress] in perfect good humor and attentive to Business though so hard put to it in this place, as hardly to have a Room a piece in which to write a letter to a Friend. It brings to my Mind the Circumstances & Temper of the old Deputies who sat down under a Tree to eat their Bread and Cheese. This is the Kind of Men who are the Terror of Tyrants. I hope I shall shortly be able to write you something of Importance, from the Army at least. In the meantime Vale et me ama.

RC (MHi). In Adams' hand, though not signed.
  [1] Congress had ordered the transmittal of $50,000 for the use of the Eastern Navy Board on May 23, just two days after Adams had returned to Congress. See *JCC*, 11:517, 529; and Marine Committee to the Eastern Navy Board, May 26, 1778.
  [2] See *JCC*, 11:465.
  [3] John Hancock.
  [4] Adams clearly believed that his continuing poltical conflict with Hancock was behind the rumors in York that Adams was an avowed opponent of General Washington. Moreover, it is apparent from this letter that Adams suspected the source of these rumors was Robert Morris' correspondence with Hancock. Adams had not been in Congress during the height of the anti-Washington criticism, having just returned from a six-month leave of absence.

Elbridge Gerry to Robert Treat Paine

My dear sir,   York Town May 25th 1778

I am favoured with yours of March 27th, containing your Sentiments on the Causes of the Failure of the late Expedition against Rhode Island; The papers transmitted by the Commissioners to Congress, I have not been able to examine, from the Multiplicity of Concerns that relate to the Treasury; they were however committed, but no Report has to my knowledge been yet made on them.[1]

Nothing has been done towards regulating Prices in any of the States southward of this, Delaware, Maryland & North Carolina did not choose Members to attend their respective Conventions, & I wish that these States by their independant Conduct may not inadvertantly injure the Cause which they wish to promote, but since there appears to be such a Division amongst the States with respect to the policy & justice of the Measure I think no salutary Effects are to expected from adopting it. Congress are attentive to the affairs of Finance, & as Importations increase, I hope by reducing the quantity of Money that we shall be able to answer the purpose & prevent the Necessity of the other disagreable Measure.

I most heartily congratulate You on the late happy Events in Europe; & hope soon to have the pleasure of seeing You in Massachusetts. If the Oraculum Legis can be spared from the state, I shall recommend your attending Congress this Summer by Way of a [Sacrifice?], which will probably be rendered more agreeable by the Removal of Congress to Philadelphia from whence the Enemy are said to be preparing to remove. I inclose you a Dollar for one recd. & remain sir wth much Esteem your very hum serv   E Gerry

P.S. I have said nothing on the Subject of an Allowance for your services, having before wrote you on that head.[2]

RC (MHi).
  [1] See Rhode Island Expedition Commissioners to Henry Laurens, March 27, 1778.
  [2] See Gerry to Paine, March 27, 1778.

Henry Laurens to Francis Johnston

Sir,   25 May [1778]
    Your favor of the 12th Inst. reached me last Evening. This Morning
I presented it to Congress & agreeable to your Recommendation the
Reverend Doctor David Jones was appointed Chaplain to the Brigade
under your Command, & I beg leave to refer you to the inclosed Act
of this date for that purpose.[1]
    Your refusal of the appointment to succeed Collo. Boudinot as
Commissary of prisoners is Entered on the Journal of Congress, the
duties of that Office must remain on that Gentleman a few days
longer.[2] Accept my best wishes & beleive me to be with great Regard
&ca.

LB (DNA: PCC, item 13).
  [1] See *JCC,* 11:530. Col. Johnston's letter of recommendation is in PCC, item 78,
13:75.
  [2] See Laurens to Johnston, May 11, 1778.

Henry Laurens to William Livingston

Sir,   25th May [1778]
    Since my last of the 15th Inst.[1] by Sharp through the Camp at Val-
ley forge, I received your Excellency's Report of proceedings respecting Dep. Qur. Master Giffor[d] Dally &c which I had the honor of
presenting to Congress. It was Committed & remains in the hands of
the Committee—in the mean time it is my duty in obedience to the
order of Congress to repeat their approbation.[2]
    Your Excellency's application for Money to pay for purchase of
Horses was on the 16th Inst. transferred to the Quarter Master General who was "ordered immediately to pay for such Horses & to settle
the accounts with the persons employed to make the purchases agreeable to the terms upon which your Excellency engaged"—and I
entertain hopes that business is completed.[3]
    Within, your Excellency will be pleased to receive an Act of Con-
gress of the 22d Inst. recommending to the Legislatures of the several
States to disqualify all deserters & prisoners from the Enemy's Army
& Navy from acting as Militia Men or Substitutes during the present
War, & for your Excellency's information I add Copy of an Act of the
15th for establishing for a time limitted an half pay for Officers of the
Army after the conclusion of the present War. I have the honor to be

LB (DNA: PCC, item 13).
  [1] See Laurens to Benjamin Chew and John Penn, May 15, 1778, note 2.
  [2] On May 16 Congress read and referred to a special committee a May 9 letter

from Gov. William Livingston in which he described how he had removed from office certain quartermaster and commissary officers in Morristown, N.J., under the authority of a February 19 resolve of Congress enabling state executives to dismiss supernumerary Continental civil and military officers. No report by this committee has been found. See *JCC*, 11:504; and PCC, item 68, fols. 357–58.

³ See *JCC*, 11:505; and Laurens to Washington, April 28, 1778, note 1.

Henry Laurens to John Stark

Sir   25 May [1778]

Your favor of the 20th April did not reach me till the 12th Inst. when I immediately presented it to the Congress & received directions to inform you that it has not been the practice of Congress to grant Commissions to Brigade Majors, that therefore the further consideration of your application requesting a Commission for your Son Majr. Caleb Stark must be suspended until the arrangement of the Army which is now a subject of deliberation before the House be completed.¹ If it shall be determined to grant such Commissions Mr. Stark will undoubtedly receive one. Hitherto Brigade Major has been appointed by the Commander in Chief or the Commander in a seperate department, I apprehend therefore an appointment or confirmation of appointment by the Honorable Major General Gates will intitle Major Starke to the usual Rank & emoluments.

I beg Sir, you will accept my best wishes & beleive me to be with great Esteem & regard.

LB (DNA: PCC, item 13).

¹ According to the journals, General Stark's April 20 letter to Laurens, which is not in PCC, was read in Congress on May 13. *JCC*, 11:491. Although the Board of War prepared a report recommending the appointment of Caleb Stark as "Brigade Major to Brigadier General John Stark," Congress postponed action on it. See *JCC*, 11:509.

Henry Laurens to Baron Steuben

Dear Sir,   York Town 25th May 1778

I had the honor of writing to you the 11th Inst. by Colo. Gimad which remains unacknowledged although I have since received your favors of the 16th & 21st. The former I presented to Congress, the latter lies before me.¹

There is so great a reluctance in Congress to listen to applications for New Commissions, until the arrangement of the Army is completed, I had judged it best to wait that event before I introduced the name of a Monsieur L Enfant—but seeing you so pressingly desire it,

I will apply to morrow Morning. If we succeed, you will have gained a preference to Marquis delafayette & to Your humble servant. The Marquis has long since applied in favor of Colo. Armand & Officers in his intended Corps,[2] & I, for a Brigadier's Commission which has been due to my own State upward of three Months, both have been postponed.[3] You shall hear from me on this head after to morrow's adjournment. I shall prevail on some of my friends to move for ordering two good Horses to be purchased for Baron Stüben; in this attempt, I flatter myself we shall not fail.[4] Every Gentleman appears possessed of a proper sense Sir, of your Merit, & I am persuaded Congress are disposed to testify their acknowledgements.

Mr. Drayton laid on my Table the Sketch of Encampment you allude to, but I had not been informed before, that I was indebted for it to my good friend Baron Stüben. I beg Sir you will accept my thanks in return. We are anxiously waiting to learn the determinations of the Enemy in the City. Monsieur Wolfen says you Challenge me to meet you there in Six days but I beleive six & twenty will have passed over before I shall see Delaware. I am with perfect Esteem & Respect, Dear sir, Your most obedient & humble servant,

Henry Laurens

RC (NHi).

[1] Steuben's May 16 letter to Laurens, thanking Congress for his appointment as inspector general of the army, is in PCC, item 164, fols. 134–35. A transcript of the baron's May 21 letter, reminding Laurens of his promise to speak to Congress in favor of granting Pierre Charles L'Enfant "the Brevet of Capt of Engineers," is in the Laurens Papers, ScHi. Although Laurens kept his promise, not until April 3, 1779, did Congress appoint L'Enfant a captain in the corps of engineers, "to have rank from the 18th day of February, An. Dom. 1778," the date two other French officers who had also accompanied Steuben to America were commissioned captains in the army. JCC, 10:180, 15:412.

[2] See Laurens to Lafayette, May 11, 1778, note 4.

[3] See Laurens to Isaac Motte, January 26, 1778, note 7.

[4] See Laurens to Steuben, May 29, 1778.

Henry Laurens to George Washington

Sir.   York Town 25 May 1778.

My last to Your Excellency was under the 21st by Wilkinson.

Doctor Scudder on his return to New Jersey is so obliging as to take charge of this, & also of a Packet containing 100 Copies of an Act of Congress, half of these in English & the other half in German— Recommending to the several States to exempt from Militia duty & to disqualify for acting as Substitutes all Prisoners & Deserters from the British Army & Navy during the present War.[1] Congress apprehend that a proper dispersion of these Acts in the Neighborhood of the Camp & even in the Enemy's Garrison if practicable, will produce good effects—more of these shall be sent upon the first intimation from Your Excellency.

I have the honor to be, With the highest Respect & Regard, Sir, Your Excellency's Most obedient & most humble servant,

                    Henry Laurens, President of Congress.

RC (DLC).
[1] This "Act of Congress' had been passed on May 22. *JCC*, 11:522–23.

Richard Henry Lee to John Page

My dear Sir,   York the 25th May 1778
    I am much obliged to you for your kind letter by last Post, by which however I see you had not received any of the several letters I had written to you since my arrival here.[1] The prevailing opinion both here and at Camp is, that the enemy are designed soon to embark their Army and quit Philadelphia, as they have, 'tis said, wooded and watered their Transports, & fixt up Stalls for the horses on board Ship. It is my opinion that this move will depend entirely upon the event of a French war taking place or not. And that this will happen soon seems doubtful at present, for it is very evident that those who direct the Councils of G.B. will submit to every insult rather than venture on a war which must remove for ever all hope of gratifying their revenge upon these States. France may force the war upon them, but they, I think, will not commence the war with France. Marquis Fayette went lately upon the enemies lincs with 2500 men with design to act as occasion should point out; but one of his men deserting and informing the enemy of his force and his situation, they marched almost their whole army quickly in the night to surround the noble Marquis. However, he made good his retreat without any loss save a few Packs. Some Oneida Indians skirmished with the enemy & killed a few of their light Horse. Gen. Gates is gone to command upon the North river where the Eastern Levies are ordered to halt until the designs of the Enemy are more clearly fixed.

    I am yours dear Sir with much affection.

                                         Richard Henry Lee

RC (NN).
[1] Lee's May 4 letter to Page is the only one written since Lee's return to Congress on May 1 that has been found.

James Lovell to William Whipple

Dear Sir   York Town May 25th 1778
    The enclosed letters having been foolishly sent from Cape Ann with a number of others under cover to Mr Geary I take the occasion of writing you a few lines now I am returning them according as they

were originally intended. I am thus formal in telling you why I write, because you seem to have neglected favoring me with a Single line by Mr. Bartlett with the express design of punishing me for a supposed neglect in what was partly the consequence of judgment and partly necessity. I have been expecting you here daily for many weeks and I have been the only one of the Committee for foreign affairs on the Spot for 16 weeks, in which time I have not only performed the regular duty of the absent Secretary, but have endeavored to make up for the neglect of the Committee in some parts of our correspondence during hurry of business last year. At the same time having only 9 States present, and our's requiring 3 for a vote, I was obliged to attendance twice a day in Congress. And now, Sir, think you that, with my duty to the State, my family in the corresponding line, I have had much time to devote to the pleasures of friendship. I will add to what is already written that I have wanted in common with other delegates, a convenient Situation for using a pen in quiet till now that a fire place is not necessary.

So many words look like anxious apology to you, but in truth I am so heartily vexed at your not coming to this forlorn hope of Society, Yorktown, that I care little what you think of me.

The Gazettes have so early & regularly contained our material transactions & intelligence from abroad that I have no occasion to say much on those heads. General Folsom & Commodore Frost are I hope safely arrived. They can tell you a long story about an half pay establishment, it's origin, progress and impediments till they left this place. After being carried, barely, for life, it was by an effort made redeemable at six year's purchase and after a while, made absolute by a sort of common consent, for 7 years. 11 States were unanimous. Only Genl. W[1] of Connecticut and myself were nay, of individuals. I hope as it has passed that the people will be reconciled to it. None out of Congress can sufficiently know the *necessity* though they may judge as well as we about the justice and feel the *unpropriety*.

I am called off by a pretty addition to my other work and plague by the printer's devil who waits for a proof sheet of the Journals. We have finished the 2d Vol and are now going on with '77.

Affectionate regards to the dear partners of my friends not without a little envy towards you and your brother.   J.L.

TR (DLC).
[1] Oliver Wolcott.

Marine Committee to Richard Ellis

Sir   May 25th 1778
We are now to acknowledge the receipt of yours of the 27th of April last. The receipt of yours of the 2d March we have already

acknowledged and fully answered, and refer you to that answer.[1]

We are exceedingly glad to hear of the arrival of the Raleighs Prize loaded with salt at Beaufort. The Continent as we informed you in our last are entitled to One half only of such Prizes as may be Captured by Continental Vessels of War. We would have you purchase the half of the salt belonging to the Captors at the lowest rate you can and remove to and store the same together with the Continental half at Newbern until further Orders as this salt may be much wanted in the fall to pickle meat for the use of the Army. We have delivered your Oath of Allegiance and Oath of office to the Secretary. You will take care not to sell anything belonging to the Continent that may come in your hands without first consulting us, unless the same should be of a perishable nature. We are sir with great respect, Your very hble servts

LB (DNA: PCC Miscellaneous Papers, Marine Committee Letter Book).
[1] For the Marine Committee's April 22 letter to Richard Ellis, Continental agent at Newbern, N.C., see Marine Committee to Thomas Read, April 22, 1778, note.

Elbridge Gerry to James Warren

My dear sir   York Town May 26th 1778
In answer to your agreable Favour of the 7th Inst.[1] I have communicated to the commercial Committee the Invoices of the four Cargoes shipped by the House of Messers Gardoqui's since they dispatched the *Nancy;* And suppose You will receive their Directions for disposing of Capts. Dupree's & Knights Cargoes, or so much of them as belongs to the States. I am apprehensive that the other two have miscarried, & should this be the Case, the Amount of the Invoices will be but a moderate premium for all the Goods shipped by that House on Account of the Continent. I have communicated to the commercial Committee your Demand for Money & desired them to determine the Allowance wch you are to receive for your Services & to settle your former Accounts. 50,000 Dollars are ordered to be sent You for the Use of the naval Department & 650,000 to Messers Otis & Andrews to discharge the Debts wch they have contracted for the publick.[2] Our Friend Mr Adams arrived here last Week & is pleased with the Appearances of Things; Our Army is well officer'd, Generals Washington, Lee & Steuben with the main Army, Gates, McDougal & Starks at the north River, Arnold & Lincoln in Reserve; no Complaint from the Want of provission, Cloathing, Medicine, Arms, Ammunition or Pay, & the officers Minds made easy with Respect to the latter, & a Style of Discipline, introduced by Baron Steuben who is appointed Inspector General wth the Rank of Major General, to

wch the Army have hitherto been Strangers. This great officer has his Inspectors & sub Inspectors with every Corps of the Army; & an Emulation prevails amongst the Officers to merit his Approbation by qualifying themselves for the places which they hold. In speaking of the officers pay, I meant to allude to the half pay Establishment lately made for the officers who shall continue in the Service to the End of the War, which provides that they shall be entitled to their half pay for the space of seven years & has had a happy Effect by making the Commissions of the officers valuable, introducing Subordination, preventing Resignations which of late have been so frequent as to prove very alarming, & promising the most happy Consequences. The Measure was exceedingly disagreable to Congress, as You will suppose when I inform You that it was debated near three Weeks, before it was adopted & the Necessity of it on Account of the State of the Currency was so apparent at length as to make the House unanimous in the Measure. The Soldiers are also provided for, each being entitled to 80 Dollars who shall continue in the service to the End of the War. If Congress should be then of opinion that there is Danger of introducing or fixing a plan of burthening the publick with pensioners & placemen, they may redeem the half pay & put an End to the precedent; for I presume few officers would refuse an offer to discount the Interest if they could be furnished at any Time with the remaining Sum arising on the half pay Establishment. Two Things remain to be accomplished, filling the Batalions & fixing the Value of the Currency, the first is the Business of the several states, the last of Congress who are determined forthwith to attend to it. To accomplish this & Confederate are the only Considerations that detain me here so late in the spring & induce me to consent to ride Home in the warm Month of June. I most heartily congratulate You on late Events in Europe; what a marvellous Change in the System of the political Worlds; the Goverment of England advocates for Despotism, & endeavouring to enslave the evermost loyal Subjects of their King; the Goverment of France Advocates for Liberty, espousing the Cause of Lutherans & Calvinists, & risking a War to establish their Independance; the King of England branded by every Whig in the Nation as a Tyrant; the King of France by every Whig in America applauded as the great protector of the Rights of Mankind. The King of Britain establishing Popery, the King of France endeavouring to free his people from this ecclesiastical Tyranny. Britain at War, & France in alliance with America. The Express is waiting which deprives me of the pleasure of touching on other Matters; I can only add my Compliments to your agreable Lady & Family, & remain wth much Esteem your Friend & hum serv,   E Gerry

RC (ICarbS: Elsie O. and Philip D. Sang deposit, 1975).

¹ Warrens' May 7 letter to Gerry is in C. Harvey Gardiner, ed., *A Study in Dissent. The Warren-Gerry Correspondence, 1776–1792* (Carbondale: Southern Illinois University Press, 1968), pp. 116–17.

² See *JCC,* 11:529, 531.

Henry Laurens to Richard Caswell

Sir,   26th May 1778

Since my last of the 11th Inst. by Post I have had the honor of presenting to Congress your Excellency's several favors of 26th April, 2d & 6th Inst. which remain subjects for Consideration.¹ Capt. Blount is here & will probably be the bearer of the Resolutions of Congress respecting them.

In the mean time this will serve to Cover an Act of the 22d Recommending to the several States to exempt from Militia service & to disqualify for acting as Substitutes all prisoners & Deserters from the British Army & Navy.

Daily Accounts repeat the Enemy's preparations for evacuating Philadelphia—there can be no doubt of the appearance but time will shew the reality.

I have not had a Letter from General Washington later than the 18th, the General never trusts appearances.

The Marquis delafayette lately detached upon a Command of observation with about 2200 Chosen Men & Officers, had nearly been surrounded by 7000 from the City, betrayed undoubtedly by a Tory or a Deserter. The Marquis displayed great Generalship in his retreat which he effected without Loss of Men, Cannon or baggage.

Intelligence of his alarming situation reached the Camp at Valley forge, this was announced by the usual means of firing three Cannon. To the honour of Major General Baron Stüben, the whole Army in fifteen minutes were under Arms, formed & ready to march but the Enemy who had reached one Bank of Schuylkill just as Marquis delafayette had gained the opposite—contented themselves with giving him a look, perhaps a smile, he returned immediately to Philadelphia. The Marquis continues abroad with his detachment of observation.

I have the honor to be &ca.

LB (DNA: PCC, item 13).

¹ On May 18 Congress read an April 26 letter from Governor Caswell to Laurens, announcing that the North Carolina Assembly had "acceded to the articles of Confederation, proposed to the United States by Congress." See *JCC,* 11:506–7; and *N.C. State Records,* 13:102. Four days later Congress read a May 2 letter from Caswell, transmitting three acts passed by the assembly in response to various recommendations of Congress as well as an assembly resolve thanking Capt. Denis Nicolas Cottineau for the services he had performed for the state and forwarding

to Congress the Frenchman's request for a commission in the Continental Navy. See *JCC*, 11:524; PCC, item 72, fols. 47–50; and *N.C. State Records*, 12:734–35, 738, 13:112–13. For further information on Cottineau, see Laurens' letter to him of April 9, 1778. Finally, on May 25 Congress read and referred to the Committee at Camp Caswell's May 6 letter and an enclosed resolve of the assembly authorizing him "to draw on the Continental Treasury for five hundred thousand dollars to be applied in raising and marching men to complete the Continental Battalions belonging to this State." See *JCC*, 11:530; PCC, item 72, fols. 51–52; and *N.C. State Records*, 12:732, 13:122–23. For the steps Congress took on May 29 to reduce Caswell's draft on the treasury to $100,000, see *JCC*, 11:550–51.

Henry Laurens to Samuel Chase

Dear Sir,					26 May [1778]

Under Cover of your favor of the 20th I received yesterday two Packets directed to Mr. M. Ridley, Paris.[1] These come too late to go with the first class of dispatches to our Ambassadors, but tis possible to overtake them. I have sent both packets to Mr. Otis at Boston & presuming one is duplicate of the other have requested his particular care to forward them by the two first good Vessels, those in which the public papers go, if on time.

I am with great esteem &ca.

[*P.S.*] Every day bring similar accounts of the Enemy's preparations for evacuating Philadelphia, but not a word from the General since the 18th. I had a Message yesterday from General Stüben, he hoped to see me in Philadelphia in six days.

The Marquis delafayette had an opportunity of displaying his Generalship last Week in a retreat without loss. To the honor of Baron Stüben when the account of the Marquis's being surrounded had reached the Camp & the Alarm fired, the whole were completely under Arms, formed & ready to March in fifteen Minutes.

LB (ScHi).

[1] Matthew Ridley, a Baltimore merchant residing in France who was appointed by the Maryland legislature in 1781 as an agent to negotiate European loans for the state. Kathryn Sullivan, *Maryland and France, 1774–1789* (Philadelphia: University of Pennsylvania Press, 1936), pp. 52, 121–34.

Henry Laurens to William Heath

Sir,					York Town 26 May 1778

My last was by the hand of Capt. Nevers under the 23d Inst—since which I have been honoured with your favor of the 4th by Mr Adams & presented it yesterday to Congress with the papers accompanying it, the whole of which were Committed to the Treasury, from whence I am assured you will receive ample supplies of Money.[1]

Within the present inclosure I transmit an Act of Congress of yesterday for paying to Brigadier General Glover such Amount as shall appear to be due for supplies by him to the Prisoners of the Convention of Saratoga.[2] And in a seperate Packet 50 Copies of the Act of 22d mentioned in mine of the 23d. Half these are printed in the German Tongue, Congress apprehend that from a proper dispersion among the foreign Troops good effects may be produced.

I have the honor to be, With very great Regard & Respect, Sir, Your obedient & humble servant,

Henry Laurens, President of Congress.

RC (MHi).
[1] General Heath's May 4 letter and enclosures are not in PCC, but see *JCC*, 11:530.
[2] See *JCC*, 11:532.

Marine Committee to the Eastern Navy Board

Gentlemen   May 26th 1778

We now transmit you by the hands of Mr. Norton Brailsford an Express the sum of fifty thousand Dollars agreeably to the enclosed receipt which you will receive and appropriate to the use of the Navy in your Department, crediting this Committee for the same.[1] We hope this sum with the Monies which you will have received for the Warrants on the Loan Offices formerly transmitted will enable you to go on with vigor in your business, and it is our desire that your utmost endeavours be exerted to have all the Continental Vessels of war in your District speedily prepared for the sea & that you send them out to Cruize Against the enemy according to the plan proposed in your Letter of the 9th of March last. We are Gentlemen, your hble servants.

LB (DNA: PCC Miscellaneous Papers, Marine Committee Letter Book).
[1] See Samuel Adams to James Warren, May 25, 1778, note 1.

Josiah Bartlett to Meshech Weare

Hond Sir   York Town May the 27th 1778

I arrived here the 21st Inst. in the Morning.

Mr. Wentworth & his waiter were Innoculated at Fish Kills the 13th, and rode with me to Reading about 46 miles from this place, where by the advice of Genl Gates, they tarried till they should get thro' the disorder. Mr. Wentworth began to have the Symptoms about 20 miles before he arrived there. I have not heard from him since I left there the 19th.

I think it my Duty to inform you that the President of Congress thinks himself neglected in not receiving answers to his letters. He Desired to know of me whether our *Governor* had Receivd any letter from him for Eight months past: that he had Recd no answer to any of his for that time; tho he had taken particular Care to Send Duplicates as often as he trusted them to the Common posts. I Endeavoured to Excuse the matter as well as I could, by telling him that some of his letters were little more than covers to acts & resolves of Congress which were supposed to Require no other answer than a Compliance with their Directions: that I Believed Some answers had been sent since that time, which by reason of the irregularity of the post were not come to hand. He said that Every letter that he wrote by order of Congress, deserved an Answer, at least so far as to let it be Known that it was received; that the way to know whither any letter miscarried, was to keep up a constant Correspondance and note the last letter sent; that it would be but a small matter on the Receipt of Every letter to inform of its being Receivd, if nothing more; and when any thing was done in consequence of any order of Congress to let it be known &c &c &c.[1]

The Confederacy is not yet Ratified, North Carolina being unrepresented & two or three of the other States not having impowered their Delegates to Confirm it; It is the opinion here that it will be Universally agreed to.

I have nothing new to inform you of, more than you will see in the Public papers.

I am with the greatest Respect Sir, your most obedient, Humble Servant,   Josiah Bartlett

RC (MHi).
[1] Bartlett's criticism, which reinforced President Laurens' April 20 request to Weare that he acknowledge official correspondence, struck a responsive chord. In his July 3, 1778, reply to Bartlett, which is in the Josiah Bartlett Papers (NhHi microfilm), Weare promised to correspond regularly with Laurens. Weare's frequent letters to President Laurens after July 4, 1778, are in PCC, item 64.

Henry Laurens to Francis Hopkinson

Dear Sir,   27 May [1778]
The 21st Inst. I received your favor of the 18th & two days ago the twelve hundred Dollars voted to yourself & Mr. Wharton which Sum I now forward by Count de Pulaski, which I believe to be a very

safe opportunity & I trust you will in due time acknowledge it to have proved so.[1]

The paper which came inclosed in that Letter I delivered to Mr. R.H. Lee & Mr. Ellery as they were standing together. Congress this morning added to the Marine Committee, numbers, abilities & diligence in the appointment of four or five auxiliary Members, among these Gentlemen Mr. S. Adams & Mr. Drayton.[2]

News you say Sir in three lines, I will try to come within your Limit.

Three of the Six Nations have signified their desire to be at peace— the other three want a very little Courting. Marquis delafayette—but I refer you to the enclosed paper & save my distance.

My Compliments to Mr. Wharton & believe me, Dear Sir, your obedt. humble Servt.

ENCLOSURE

☞ Caution

The Marquis delafayette having been detached from the Main Army with 2100 picked Men & selected Officers, aided by 45 Indians & about ten French Men in the Indian Corp, proceeded on the 19 May toward Philadelphia to observe the Motions of the Enemy & to make such advantages as circumstances should throw in his way.

On the 20th a proper Chain of Guards & Sentries were Posted to avoid surprize but however vigilant these were, the Enemy having received intelligence of the Marquis's motions by some means unknown to us, probably, from those worse than common Enemies, the Tories, Marched out in large force supposed to be at least 6000, about Midnight, & by a circuitous course passed beyond the Marquis's detachment & then divided by different routs in order to surround the American Troops. It then became necessary for the Marquis to Retreat. The Retreat was executed in most admirable order in presence of the Enemy's advanced parties of Horse. General Clinton who it is said commanded the British was so effectually deceived by the Retreat he judged it was an attempt to draw him into a Snare. This is the only apology to be made for the Commander whoever he was. The loss on our side was three Men Killed & four prisoners. The Enemy lost 2 Horsemen killed & six or eight wounded. When the Indians had discharged their fire upon the light Horse they set up the War Whoop & according to their Custom scampered off. The British light Horse Men terrified by the yelling of the Indians fled precipitantly the other way. The Indians picked up several of their Cloaks & converted them into Boots.

The Marquis's retreat had done him more honor than he would have gained by a drawn battle, or slight Victory.

Citizens are every day Stealing out of the City & deserters from the Enemy come into Camp in great Numbers. Appearances of an intention on the part of the Enemy to evacuate Philadelphia continue & indeed grow stronger, but We know General Washington never trusts appearances—his Army is in fine order & gaining strength every day.

☞ If Mr Hopkinson thinks the above, which is a collection of facts, will afford information & satisfaction to the good people in Maryland he is at liberty to give a Copy to the Printer, but not this writing nor the writer's name.

It may be stiled extract of a Letter from York 27 May—but no more. The Writer loves to please his friends & hates authorship.

LB (ScHi). Enclosure: MS (PHi).

[1] Francis Hopkinson and John Wharton were members of the Middle Department Navy Board, which was originally situated in Philadelphia. In response to their April 29 memorial, which was read on May 1 and referred to the Marine Committee, Congress agreed on the 13th to pay each man $600 to defray the extra costs of transacting navy board business in Bordenton and Baltimore. See JCC, 10:412, 11:493; and PCC, item 41, 4:31–32. Hopkinson's May 18 letter and enclosure are not in PCC.

[2] In addition to Samuel Adams and William Henry Drayton, Josiah Bartlett and Gouverneur Morris were also appointed to the Marine Committee this day. Adams replaced Francis Dana; Morris, Philip Livingston; and Drayton, Laurens himself. See JCC, 11:537.

Henry Laurens to Samuel A. Otis

Dear Sir,   27th May [1778]

I took the liberty of troubling you on the 19th by Brown with many Letters to be sent forward to France; Necessity obliges me to be again troublesome on the same kind of business for my friends at Camp & elsewhere.

In the present Packet will be four bulky Letters

to Monsr. Gerard &ca, Duplicate & triplicate,[1] these to be dispatched by different conveyances but neither of them in the Vessel in which the Original shall have been sent—this went by Brown as abovementioned.

To Mr. Math. Ridley 1 & 2[2]—these to be sent by the first two good vessels & if they reach you in time, one of them to accompany our public dispatches.

An half sheet within contains extracts from Letters which I received last Night from Camp & all the News I know of. I remain with great regard.

LB (ScHi).

[1] Evidently these were letters from French officers in the American army to Conrad-Alexandre Gérard, the French official who signed the Franco-American treaties of alliance and commerce and then served as France's first minister plenipotentiary to the United States, 1778–79.

[2] See also Laurens to Samuel Chase, May 26, 1778.

Henry Laurens to Jonathan Trumbull, Sr.

Sir,   27th May [1778]

Since my last of the 11th Inst.[1] by McClosky I have received & presented to Congress your Excellency's favor of the 5th. Your Excellency's reply to Mr. Tryon is much applauded.[2]

Inclosed herein I transmit an Act of Congress of the 22d recommending to the several Legislatures to exempt from Militia duty & to disqualify for acting as Substitutes all Prisoners & Deserters from the British Army & Navy.[3]

I received a Letter last night from General Washington dated 24th.[4] The Enemy continued in the City, but great appearances of their intention to remove also continued. The General writes "it is certain a great deal of their Baggage is on board & they continue busy packing up, Reports say only a detachment is going for the West Indies." They have been so long about it I begin to suspect the whole is sham. Be this as it may, Citizens & Deserters are daily coming into our Camp, & in great numbers.

I am with very great respect

LB (DNA: PCC, item 13).

[1] See Laurens to George Clinton, May 11, 1778, note 1.

[2] See Connecticut Delegates to Trumbull, May 18, 1778, note 2.

[3] Laurens had transmitted copies of this "Act of Congress" with brief covering letters he wrote on May 26 to Govs. Thomas Johnson of Maryland and Patrick Henry of Virginia. PCC, item 13, fols. 337–38; and Red Books, MdAA. On this day he also sent copies of this act under blank cover by Norton Brailsford to President Meshech Weare of New Hampshire and Gov. Nicholas Cooke of Rhode Island. PCC, item 13, fol. 340.

[4] See Washington, *Writings* (Fitzpatrick), 11:443–44.

Richard Henry Lee to Arthur Lee

My dear Brother,   York the 27th May 1778

Having written you fully and very lately it is not necessary, nor have I time now to be long. All your letters covering missives, certificates &c have safely arrived, and will be maturely attended to. I hope the safe arrival of Mr. Adams and the recall of Deane will benefit

extremely the public business. The latter is in every respect the reverse of Mr. Adams, and so you may form your judgment of the
former. I have found ample cause to love and esteem Mr. Adams in
our joint labors for the public good. My eyes are so extremely injured by their constant application, that without the aid and support
of Spectacles I fear I shall soon loose the use of them. I pray you
then to procure me a pair of the best Temple Spectacles that can be
had. In fitting these perhaps it may be proper to remember that my
age is 46, that my eyes are light colored and have been quick &
strong but now weakened by constant use—My head thin between
the Temples.

The British Army yet remains at Philadelphia and ours at Valley
Forge about 18 miles from the City. The latter growing daily stronger
in numbers & discipline; the former lessening in numbers by various
casualties, but chiefly by desertion. We have the best authority for
believing they are about embarking soon from Philadelphia, so that
my next letter may be from that City.

If the Spectacles are sent to my Son at Nantes he can contrive them
to your ever affectionate brother and faithful friend,

Richard Henry Lee

RC (John F. Reed, King of Prussia, Pa., 1972).

Thomas McKean to George Bryan

Dear Sir,   York-Town May 27th 1778

Your favor of the 21st came safe to hand, together with the extracts of Colo. Piper's & Councillor Urie's Letters.

It may be well to make examples of some of the most wicked of
the prisoners in Bedford as soon as practicable, but when I reflect
on the Savages having scalped eleven women & children within five
miles of the town of Bedford; that the people must be all in arms;
that these criminals might escape for want of testimony or the Attorney General's presence, who cannot well bear the expence of so long
a journey without some salary; that before a Precept could be sent
to the Sheriff of that county, and the legal time for summoning
Jurors &c being allowed, we should be in the beginning of harvest,
with the court; and more especially that in great probability the
Enemy may soon evacuate Philadelphia, which happening will require me immediately to resign my seat in Congress and to repair
thither, as there will be an absolute necessity for a Judge on the
Spot; I say, Sir, when I consider these things I am rather of opinion
it would be adviseable to defer holding a court there yet.[1] As there
will no doubt many more of these wretches be made prisoners, it

would be as well in my judgment, to prevent the expence of two courts within perhaps two months, & try them all at once. If you think differently from me about holding the court in Bedford at this time, be so good to mention it to Mr. Atlee, who can write a Precept & sign it, and afterwards send it to me; he may fix any day for holding the court that he thinks proper, it will be agreeable to me.

I condole with poor Mrs. Wharton on the death of the President.[2] There is nothing new here. Jo. Bone will be executed to day in pursuance of your Warrant.[3] Why did not the General Assembly choose a new President?

I am, dear Sir, with great regard, Your most obedient servant,

Thos M:Kean

RC (NN).
[1] For a second letter Pennsylvania Chief Justice McKean directed to Vice President Bryan this day on the subject of various legal questions that had recently been laid before him, see *Pa. Archives*, 1st ser. 6:555.
[2] For the funeral of Pennsylvania Council President Thomas Wharton, who died on May 23 after a brief illness, see *Pa. Council Minutes*, 11:498–500.
[3] For the Pennsylvania Council's warrant ordering the execution of Joseph Bone, who had been convicted of "Felony & Burglary," see ibid., p. 490.

Thomas McKean to Sarah McKean

Dear Sally,   York-Town. May 27th 1778
Your favor by Mr. Elder I received last night, and am sorry for your situation, but cannot procure a maid here, nor could I on the road, as I came down, hear of one. I think you should not have let that little hussey gone away without a month's notice; however she was weak & lazy besides her being impudent. Miss Nelly Reed will, I hope, stay with you whilst we remain in Paxton, which in all probability will not be longer than the beginning of October, as there are strong circumstances to induce a belief, that the Enemy will shortly depart from this State.

I shall expect Sam and the horses on Saturday week next, which will be the 6th day of June, and am satisfied the boys will be ready to go to school as soon as practicable. A Taylor must be got to mend their clothes, & they ought to have a pair of new shoes each. Until they are sent away, we shall not have it in our power to go to Newcastle county, tho' we must contrive to do as well as possible in this matter when I return. It is so exceeding inconvenient for me to be here that I must resign my Seat in Congress; and yet if you had a good servant or two I should be content to stay a few months longer.

Inclosed you have a printed paper, sent me by Mr. Hopkinson from Baltimore, which contains all I know of the damage done to

Messieurs Borden and Kirkbride by the Enemy, a strange way of tempting the Americans to be reconciled to Great Britain, and conciliating their affections. I have sent you the two last newspapers of Lancaster & York-Town by Mr. Elder, who will forward this. You have no doubt heard of the death of President Wharton on Saturday last. To day Joseph Bone, condemned at the court I held here in April for a Burglary, will be executed. I have nothing more to add, but that I am well, and beg you to kiss Sally for me, and to give my love to the other children. Adieu.

Your most affectionate, Thos M:Kean

RC (PHi).

Gouverneur Morris to George Washington

Dear General In Congress 27th May 1778.

I have a Word to say to you upon the Subject of Promotion which we have just now finished or rather unfinished at least if that Matter was before in an unfinished Situation. That famous incomprehensible Baltimore Resolution (unluckily perhaps) introduced a very tedious Debate which terminated at Length by rejecting the whole of what the Committee reported with Relation to the Promoting of Officers.[1] You may be a little surprized when I tell you that upon the whole Matter I beleive this is best. But how? It is true I confess that much Ground of Heartburning is left under the Baltimore Resolution governing these Matters by the misterious Trinity of *Seniority, Merit & Quota*. Let me however on the other Hand observe that to tie up the Hands of the Republic as to the Officers whom they are to appoint is utterly inconsistent with the republican Principles of Government which ought to prevail among us. No Danger it is true can arise at present but my Dear Sir we are laying Foundations and how Posterity in future Wars may build on the Foundations laid by Ancestors whom they will certainly reverence No Man can be hardy enough to assert. What then you will say is the Effect of the now Rule? In my poor Opinion it is no Rule. What then is the Use of the Resolution? Nothing more than an Apology for Officers whom it may be found necessary to supercede. Congress in Effect seem to have pledged themselves to their Constituents that they will pay a due Attention to the Quota of Troops furnished by the States respectively, to the Seniority of the Several Officers, and to that Degree of military Abilities which Nature or Industry may have conferred upon deserving Individuals. You ask me what is to be the Rule of Promotion below the Degree of a General Officer. I answer that Congress would not with Propriety make any Rule. They have given to the States the

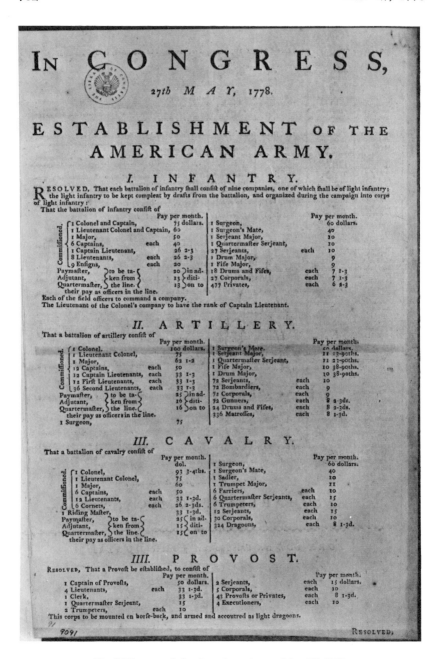

Establishment of the American Army, May 27, 1778

Power of appointing the Officers in their own Regiments;[2] of Consequence therefore it would be idle to restrict them as to the Persons whom they shall appoint. It will therefore be necessary to make Application to the several States on the Occasion. They have already I beleive in most Instances given you the necessary Power and if so then to fix the Order of Promotion will be only a Limitation of such Power. What are my Ideas on the Occasion you will see by the Letter I enclose directed to Governor Clinton[3] which you will do me the Honor to transmit to him.

I am Dr General, most sincerely yours,   Gouv Morris

York Town 28th May

We are going on with the Arrangement of the Army with charming Rapidity after a long stop. A very little Time will I hope compleat it.[4] I hear you expect soon to be in Philadelphia. In my Opinion the Instant the Enemy Evacuate it the best disciplined Troops in the Army should be marched in and the several Inhabitants ordered on Pain of military Execution to confine themselves to their Houses. Proper Persons should then be sent to the several Stores to make out Lists of the Goods contained in them. From these Lists you should mark the Articles which may be necessary for the Army, the Hospital and the like. The next Step should be to levy a Contribution of at least £100,000 Stg. in hard Money which ought to be apportioned upon the Inhabitants according to their Wealth and Disaffection. They may then be permitted to go about their Usual Occupations. But the Quarter Master should take proper Stores and therein lodge under Guard the Articles by you marked and Receipts should be by him given at the Rate such goods sold immediately before the Evacuation and duplicates of such Receipts forthwith transmitted to the Treasury Board. The Propriety of these Steps I will not debate upon. But should they be pursued I think the most beneficial Consequences would accrue to the public.[5] I am once more, yours,

Gouv Morris

RC (DLC).

[1] On May 18 the Committee at Camp submitted to Congress a comprehensive plan for the arrangement of the army, which included a report by Francis Dana on the "Order of promotion," recommending that: "Promotion shall be regimental, to the rank of Captain inclusively. 2d. From that of Captain, to that of Brigadiers inclusively, to be in the Line of the State. 3d. From the rank of Brigadiers, promotion to be in the Line of the Army at large." See *JCC*, 11:507, 12:1269–71; and PCC, item 21, fols. 157–59. This plan to regulate promotions, which Washington had originally suggested to the committee in January 1778, was initially approved by the delegates with certain amendments, but, as Morris goes on to explain, it was then defeated after they realized it would interfere with the right of the states to appoint officers below the rank of general officers. However, on November 24, 1778, Congress did recommend a similar promotion plan to the states. See *JCC*, 12:1157–58; Washington, *Writings* (Fitzpatrick), 10:380–82;

and Committee at Camp Minutes of Proceedings, February 16–20, 1778. The "famous incomprehensible Baltimore Resolution" was the one passed on February 19, 1777, which provided that promotions of general officers were to be governed by "the line of succession, the merit of the persons proposed, and the quota of troops raised, and to be raised, by each State." *JCC,* 7:133. For a discussion of problems of promotion and rank in the Continental Army, see Louis C. Hatch, *The Administration of the American Revolutionary Army* (New York: Longmans, Green and Co., 1904), pp. 35–46.

[2] See Congress' September 16, 1776, resolution on this issue in *JCC,* 5:763.

[3] The letter to Clinton in question, dated May 28, 1778, is printed below. See also Washington, *Writings* (Fitzpatrick), 11:496.

[4] See also Henry Laurens to Lafayette, May 17, 1778, note 2.

[5] In his May 29 response to this letter, Washington criticized Morris' proposed treatment of the citizens of Philadelphia as "inconsistent with sound policy" and "an arbitrary stretch of military power." Washington, *Writings* (Fitzpatrick), 11:482–86.

Committee of Commerce to the Commissioners at Paris

Committee of Commerce,
Gentn.   York in Pennsylvania May 28th 1778.

You will receive this by Thomas Read Esqr who was Captain of the Frigate Washington but is now Commander of the Armed Brigantine Baltimore. This Brigantine was intended for A dispatch Vessel, but now hath A Cargo on board of Forty nine hogsheads of Tobacco which was all she coud take in and accomodate her men. We have addressed her to John Danl. Schweighauser Mercht in Nantes, and have directed him to dispose of the net proceeds of her Cargo, and also a balance which he hath in his hands belonging to these States according to your order. We have order'd Captain Read to wait for and pursue your directions, and have desired Mr. Schweighauser to Ship such Goods on board the Baltimore, belonging to these States, as Captain Read can receive consistantly with your directions.

We have the pleasure to inform you that the Frigate Dean, Captain Nicholson, the Queen of France, Captain Green, and the Henrietta, Captain Brown, are safely arrived at Boston and our Agent there in A Letter of the 13th May advises us that "they had another valuable arrival from France yesterday" which we hope is the Duke de Choiseuil.

We are with the greatest Respect, Your most Obed humble servants,
William Ellery

Richd. Hutson

Thos. Adams

RC (PPAmP). In the hand of John Brown and signed by Adams, Ellery, and Hutson. Addressed: "The Honorable The Ambassadors of the United States of America, at Paris." Endorsed by John Adams: "Comtee. of Commerce, May 28. 1778. Ansd. July 29. Came by the Saratoga, Capt. Read."

Henry Laurens to Philip Schuyler

Sir,   28th May [1778]

The day before yesterday I had the honor of receiving & presenting to Congress your favors of the 9th & 11th Inst. together with Copy of the Message from the Oneida, which were immediately committed to the Board of War.[1] A Report from thence has not yet come up & I remain without commands from the House. You will therefore Sir do me the honor to receive this as private, which I dispatch partly to gratify your Messenger who discovers much anxiety to return, but principally from a feeling of my own, a repugnance to delay, holding coadjutors, in the Service of my Country, in suspense when 'tis in my power by any decent means to releive them.

The Acts of Congress of the 22d April & lately an Address to the people of the 9th May[2] were directed as from my self for your information of these important articles in our public proceedings. In the same manner I communicated those papers to other Gentlemen in your Quarter. Indeed I had entertained an assurance that you Sir, in particular ever active in promoting the public Interest would have made the Canadians as well as the Indians fully acquainted with their contents, but having received no direction from Congress, I could not from any consideration think myself entitled to request or even to hint.[3] I now take the liberty of inclosing an hand Bill & News paper containing other intelligence of the proceedings of Congress, possibly if the knowledge of the former were transfused throughout Canada good effects might be produced.

The public Letter which I had the honor of writing the 8th Inst. by Dodd will have informed you of the Resolves of Congress respecting supplies to the Indians.

Colo. Morgan is at present with his family at or near Lancaster. I expect his return to Morrow, Congress will then learn all that he knows relative to Atskeray[4]—solid peace with our Neighboring Indians is so desirable & so very Interesting, I am persuaded no time will be unnecesarily delayed nor any proper means left untried for obtaining it.

Permit me Sir, to congratulate with you on your Reelection to Congress. Self Interest as well as love of Country prompt my wishes for your appearance.[5]

Every day repeats accounts of the Enemy's preparations for evacuating Philadelphia, but the business seems to have been delayed so long beyond the necessary limit for performing it, that every day Strengthens my jealousies of their sincerity.

You will, no doubt, Sir have heard some crude account of the Marquis delafayette late honorable Retreat, the inclosed paper contains a pretty accurate narrative, & I can rely on the veracity of the writer, but as it comes from a young Man nearly allied to me I request it may not be published.

I must not conclude, however troublesome I may have already been, without intimating, that Mr. Drayton yesterday shewed me some parts of an intended Report on the Ticonderoga affair, hence I expect that business will be speedily brought on the Carpet & finished.[6]

The moment I receive Commands from Congress respecting the Subjects of your Letters abovementioned a Messenger shall be dispatched with them. Mean time I beg leave to repeat that I am, With great Esteem & Respect

LB (ScHi).

[1] General Schuyler's May 9 and 11 letters to Laurens, together with the enclosed message from the Oneidas, are in PCC, item 153, 3:310–11, 322–28. For the Board of War's report on "the frontiers of New York, Pensylvania and Virginia," which was based in part on these documents from Schuyler and which was approved by Congress on June 11, 1778, see JCC, 11:587–91. See also Laurens to Schuyler, April 8, 1778, note 1.

[2] See JCC, 10:374–81, 11:474–81.

[3] In the May 9 letter cited above, Schuyler suggested that Congress translate into French for distribution in Canada its April 22 reply to Lord North's conciliatory proposals and extracts of the treaty of amity and commerce with France.

[4] Atskeray was a Seneca warrior who had been wounded and captured by American forces near Fort Pitt. The Senecas thought Atskeray was in Schuyler's custody and applied to him to effect an exchange, but Schuyler was unaware of Atskeray's whereabouts and therefore asked Congress to solicit information about him from George Morgan, the Indian agent for the middle department stationed at Fort Pitt. See Schuyler to Laurens and an enclosed message from the Oneidas, both dated May 11, in PCC, item 153, 3:322–28.

[5] Although Schuyler had been elected "an additional Delegate" by the New York legislature on March 25, he did not return to Congress until November 1779.

[6] For the status of the investigation of the evacuation of Ticonderoga and Mount Independence, see Committee of Congress to Washington, February 7, note 1; and Laurens to Washington, April 4, 1778, note 2.

Gouverneur Morris to George Clinton

Sir,   York Town 28th May 1778.

I take the Liberty of observing to your Excellency that as the appointment of Officers to a Colo., is in the several States, so after the arrangement of the army which I hope will soon be compleated, some mode Should, by the State, be adopted to keep the Regiments full as to Officers, and some Line of Promotion chalked out for their Satisfaction. What I have to propose is, that the General, or the General who may command in a seperate Department, be invested with the Power of filling up vacancies in the following manner, to wit: that from an Ensign to a Major exclusively the Promotions shall be in the Regimental Line and from a Captain upwards in the Line of the State.[1] That generally Seniority shall be regarded but that a Power be given in extraordinary Cases of merit or Demerit to vary from that Principle. These things, Sir, I take it are within the Province of the Council of Appointment, and they will doubtless see the Propriety of giving to the General under whose Eye our troops may be placed the Power of rewarding their Bravery and Conduct or of punishing by neglect the want of these necessary Qualifications. This will give Zeal and Energy to the Service but I will not dilate upon a Proposition of which you will at the first Glance discern the Propriety. I am with great Respect Your Excellency's most obed't & humble Servant,   Gouv'r Morris.

MS not found; reprinted from Clinton, *Papers* (Hastings), 3:371–72.

[1] Cf. Morris to Washington, May 27, 1778, note 1. No response from Clinton to Morris' proposal has been found.

Henry Laurens to William Atlee

Sir,   29 May [1778]

I received by the hand of Count de Montfort[1] your favor of the 26th. After some conversation with that Gentleman he took leave fully convinced that his attempts to enlist prisoners of War had been contrary to the Resolution of Congress under which he was authorized to Act, your opposition was consequently well founded & your conduct commendable.[2]

I am with great Respect

LB (DNA: PCC, item 13). Addressed: "William Atlee Esquire, D. Comissary of Prisoners, Lancaster."

[1] Count Julius de Montfort was a major in Casimir Pulaski's independent corps, *JCC*, 10:364.

[2] This incident underscores the way in which Congress and the new Board of War made up of nondelegates sometimes worked at cross purposes. On March 28 Congress authorized Casimir Pulaski to raise an independent corps of cavalry and infantry and empowered him to ignore a recent congressional ban on the enlistment of prisoners of war. Two days later, however, Congress, for reasons explained elsewhere, reconsidered the matter and decided not to allow the use of prisoners of war in Pulaski's independent corps. See Laurens to Washington, March 30, 1778, note 1. Nevertheless, the Board of War, which had advised allowing Pulaski to recruit prisoners, subsequently issued instructions authorizing him to enlist them

into his corps. Whether the board acted out of willful disregard of Congress' wishes or in good faith is difficult to determine. In any case, Pulaski proceeded to enlist prisoners, earning a rebuke for this violation of congressional policy from no less an authority than Washington himself. Undeterred, Pulaski continued this practice and thereby prompted William Atlee, the deputy commissary of prisoners in Lancaster, Pa., to write to Congress complaining of Pulaski's efforts to enlist German prisoners in his custody. Unfortunately for Atlee, his letter elicited two contradictory responses from York. Whereas Laurens commended him for refusing to allow Pulaski to enlist prisoners, the Board of War wrote letters on May 27 to Atlee and other deputy commissaries of prisoners assuring them that "Altho 'tis prohibited to inlist prisoners or deserters into the Common battalions; yet tis understood that for the purpose of Completing Genl. Pulaski's independent Corps he should be permitted to inlist both." The board's letter reached Atlee before Laurens' and therefore he allowed Pulaski to recruit German prisoners in Lancaster. Upon receiving Laurens' letter, however, Atlee wrote to him on June 2 and enclosed a copy of his instructions from the board. Two days later Congress referred Atlee's letter to the board, intimating "at the same time, that prisoners of war should not be inlisted into *any* corps in the service of the United States." As a result, the board promptly notified Atlee on June 5 that "The license given Genl. Pulaski to inlist prisoners, is to be considered as recalled." See *JCC*, 11:567; Washington, *Writings* (Fitzpatrick), 11:337; Board of War to William Atlee et al., May 27, PCC, item 78, 1:177; Atlee to Laurens, June 2, ibid., fols. 173–74; Board of War to Atlee, June 5, Peter Force Collection, DLC; and Thomas McKean to Atlee, June 5, 1778.

Henry Laurens to the Marquis de Lafayette

My Dear Marquis   29 May [1778]

You have encouraged me to this freedom of Address. I have the honour to use it from feelings of the highest Respect & the most sincere attachment & affection.

One of your Letters is so very comical, I can't attempt a particular reply, if I did, there would follow such a mixture of Laughter & serious reflexion as would detain a very short Letter an hour.[1]

Your Excellency's Notice of the Young Man, does himself & his Father too much honor.

I congratulate with your Excellency most heartily on the late honorable Retreat which is spoke of by every body here in the highest terms of applause.

The Marquis delafayette has acquired new Glory by this great Act of Generalship.

I have manufactured, from all true materials an account for the Pennsylvania Gazette & have desired a friend to make a proper publication in the Baltimore paper.[2]

I consulted Colo. R.H. Lee on the propriety of presenting your Excellency's other Letter to Congress, he advises, not for the present, for reasons which when we have further conversation on the subject shall be communicated to your Excellency.[3] If General Green is well founded in his opinion we are soon to meet in Philadelphia. I do not flatter my Self on appearances so warmly as I perceive some of my friends do.

I have just received a Packet of French News Papers & without opening any the whole shall accompany this. I shall be happy to know these prove acceptable.

I have the honor to be with the most respectful attachment & the highest Esteem &ca.

LB (ScHi).
[1] See Lafayette's somewhat awkwardly written private letter to Laurens of May 25 in Lafayette, *Papers* (Idzerda), 2:58–59.
[2] See Laurens to Francis Hopkinson, May 27, 1778.
[3] Lafayette's "other letter" was his official letter to Laurens of May 25. Lafayette, *Papers* (Idzerda), 2:55–57. In it the marquis asked Congress to support his plan for a Franco-American "expedition against the english West Indias islands under continental colours," to be commanded by himself and with each nation sharing equally in the conquered territory. He also revealed that he had communicated this plan to his cousin the marquis de Bouillé, the governor of Martinique, and enclosed an extract from a March 8 letter from Bouillé in which the governor revealed that he approved the scheme and had urged the French government to support it but advised Lafayette to delay the attack until war broke out between France and Great Britain. Ibid., pp. 57–58. Laurens conferred on this matter with Richard Henry Lee, a member of the Committee for Foreign Affairs, who initially advised him not to bring it to Congress' attention, but Laurens soon disregarded this advice and on June 9 submitted Lafayette's and Bouillé's letters to Congress, which read and referred them to a committee consisting of Thomas McKean, Roger Sherman, and John Witherspoon. Since France had expressly renounced any claim to the British West Indies in her recent treaty of alliance with the United States, however, Congress took no further action on Lafayette's proposal, contenting itself instead with commending Lafayette through Laurens for his "Zeal and good will for our Cause." See *JCC*, 11:580; Laurens to Lafayette, May 31 and June 19, 1778; and Louis Gottschalk, *Lafayette Joins the American Army* (Chicago: University of Chicago Press, 1937), pp. 194–95. Congress was doubtless also deterred by the size of the contribution to the expedition Lafayette expected from it—3,000 men plus shipping and supplies—and by the fact that there was no guarantee the French government would support the venture.

Henry Laurens to John Laurens

York Town 29th May 1778

I congratulate with you My Dear Son on your safe return to Camp & particularly on the honor which is due to Marquis delafayette for his excellent Generalship in the late Retreat, of which you & every Gentleman under that brave Noble Man's Command participate.

I regret much the want of a perfect account of that affair, & expect your next will supply the deficiency of the last, occasioned you say by necessity.

If you study my inclination which I beleive coincides with your own, you will receive no Pay at present, & delay a determination till we meet, or to some future day, if I understand you. You have hitherto received none.[1] By the first Gentleman going to Camp I intend to remit you a Sum sufficient to discharge arrears & leave a small fund.

If a strong Linen Coat Wastcoat & Breeches will be acceptable to my old friend Shrews ——— Berry, let him consult his Taylor & I will send the quantity of Linen required.

We shall have an excellent opportunity for France from Virginia next Week.

I transmitted Baron Stuben's Commission through the hands of the Commander in Chief because I judged that the proper medium but I have some fears of having erred. Pray inform me.[2]

I have a very pressing Letter from Capt Nichols at Reading, I intreat you Interest yourself as far as you can with the General & with the Commissary on behalf of this honest Man.[3]

Gen Weedon this Moment came in & is so good as to take 600 Dollars for you. God Bless you My Dear son,   Henry Laurens

RC (NN).
[1] John Laurens was serving as a volunteer aide-de-camp to Washington.
[2] "The method of sending Baron de Steuben's Commission was according to rule," John assured his father in a letter written on June 1. "Correspondence between the Hon. Henry Laurens and his Son, John, 1777–1780," *South Carolina Historical and Genealogical Magazine* 6 (July 1905): 106.
[3] John informed his father on June 1 that Washington had permitted Capt. William Nichols to go to Philadelphia in order to negotiate his exchange. Ibid., p. 109. See also Laurens to William Nichols, May 23, 1778.

Henry Laurens to James Mease

Sir,   29th May [1778]
I here inclose for your information & government three Acts of Congress—two dated the 28th Inst. & one this day, vizt.

1. of 28th for the preservation & proper disposal of all Clothing &ca imported on account of the United States into the States of Massachuset's Bay & New Hamshire.[1]

2. 28th for prohibiting further purchases by the Clothier General or his deputies on accot of the united States & for obtaining an immediate settlement of their Accounts.[2]

3. 29th for enabling & requiring the Clothier general & his Agents to make up & issue the Clothing which they have already purchased.

I am with great Respect

LB (DNA: PCC, item 13).
[1] See *JCC*, 11:548; and Washington, *Writings* (Fitzpatrick), 11:416–17.
[2] See also Laurens to Mease, May 22, 1778, note 1.

Henry Laurens to Baron Steuben

Dear sir,   York Town 29th May 1778.

Just as I had predicted when I had the honor of writing to you by Doctor Scudder the 25th, so it happened—the next Morning I presented your Letter to Congress—a Motion was presently made to postpone the consideration of granting a Commission to Monsr L'Enfant until the Army arrangement shall be completed & so it passed.[1] I then informed the House, I had heard the Baron Stüben who went through much Duty in Camp was reduced to the necessity often of walking on foot from a want of a good Horse—an order immediately took place, that the Quarter Master General provide two good Horses for the use of Baron Stuben—& by this conveyance I shall transmit the order.[2]

I conceive Sir, your Certificate hereafter of the usefulness of Monsr. L'Enfant in the Army will entitle him to Pay & Rations but I cannot hazard even a conjecture concerning a Commission until the arrangement is completed—this I hope will be in a few days.

I have not a scrap of News, nor any thing at present to add but the repeated assurance of continuing with the great Esteem & Regard, Dear sir, Your Obedient & Most humble servant,

Henry Laurens

RC (PHi).

[1] There is no mention of this motion in the journals. See also Laurens to Steuben, May 25, 1778, note 1.

[2] See *JCC*, 11:533. Laurens also transmitted a copy of the May 26 "Act of Congress for supplying the Baron Stüben with two good Horses" with a brief covering letter he wrote this day to Quartermaster General Nathanael Greene. PCC, item 13, fol. 340.

Henry Laurens to George Washington

Sir,   York Town 29th May 1778.

I had the honor of writing to Your Excellency the 21st Inst. by the hand of Doctor Scudder, since which I have received & presented to Congress Your Excellency's favor of the 24th. This was Committed & has not yet been returned for consideration.[1]

Your Excellency will be pleased to receive Inclosed two Acts of Congress of yesterdays date.

1. For a new arrangement of Major Lee's Corps of Partizan Light Dragoons.

2. For appointing Major John Beatty Commissary of Prisoners.[2]

I have the honor to be, With the highest Esteem & Respect, Sir, Your Excellency's Obedient humble servant.

Henry Laurens, President of Congress

P.S. Capt. Robt. Smith was yesterday appointed by Congress Secretary to the Board of War. I now transmit him the necessary intelligence.[3]

RC (DLC).

[1] Washington's May 24 letter to Laurens is in the Washington Papers, DLC, and Washington, *Writings* (Fitzpatrick), 11:443. Enclosed with it was a memorial from several North Carolina field officers dealing with the case of Capt. John Vance, a North Carolina artillery commander with a Continental commission who had been dismissed from his command by the North Carolina Assembly because of "misbehaviour in office." Washington and the North Carolina officers feared that allowing a state legislature to deprive a Continental officer of his rank would set a dangerous precedent, but evidently Congress did not share their concern. After referring Washington's letter and the enclosed memorial to a committee on May 27 and after reading the committee's report three days later, Congress simply postponed consideration of the issue and did not take it up again. Unfortunately, the committee's report has not been found. See *JCC*, 11:537, 556; and Hugh F. Rankin, *The North Carolina Continentals* (Chapel Hill: University of North Carolina Press, 1971), pp. 132–33.

[2] See also Laurens to Francis Johnston, May 11, 1778, note 1.

[3] Congress appointed Captain Smith to this office after receiving April 11 and May 26 letters of recommendation in his behalf from the Board of War. PCC, item 147, 2:9, 65. In the former the board stated that it was recommending Smith because "Some Gentlemen of Congress have given it as their private Opinion, that a Person recommended by the Board, would be appointed," and in the latter it noted that it could not fill military commissions unless they were signed by the president of Congress and countersigned by the secretary of the board. Laurens also wrote a brief letter to Smith this day notifying him of his appointment. PCC, item 13, fol. 342.

William Ellery to William Greene

Sir[1]   York Town, May 30th 1778.

From the movements of the enemy and sundry intelligence received there are strong reasons to believe that they intend to quit their present quarters at Philadelphia, and from concurring circumstances it is apprehended they mean to rendezvous at some post or place to the eastward of Hudsons River.

If the Fleet should be bound to the W. Indias they may rendezvous in our commodious bay, in which case, unless our shores should be well guarded, the Troops may make incursions into the country, and lay it waste.

Genl. Sullivan will without doubt collect the forces under his command and post them in such places as he judges will best secure the country and prevent surprize.

Inclosed are the last Lancaster and York papers, which will give you all the news we have.

A Letter to the President of Congress hath announced your election

to the place of Governor of the State of Rhode-Island, and Provi-
dence-Plantations, on which occasion your excellency will permit
me to salute you.[2] It gives me great pleasure to see our late worthy
Governor succeeded by a Gentleman so eminently distinguished for
his patriotick firmness, and steady regard for the rights of mankind.
Heartily wishing that your excellency may enjoy health & spirits to
enable you to discharge the arduous duties of your office agreeably to
your own wishes and the expectations of the publick I am with the
greatest Respect, your Excellency's most obedient and very humble
Servant,   William Ellery

RC (R–Ar).
[1] William Greene (1731–1809), a former assemblyman and superior court justice,
served as governor of Rhode Island from 1778 to 1786. *DAB.*
[2] Greene had informed Congress of his election as governor in a May 15 letter
that was read on the 27th. See PCC, item 64, fol. 402; and *JCC,* 11:537.

Henry Laurens to Cornelius Harnett

Dear Sir,   30th May [1778]
Two days ago, at the end of drawing, I collected the Numbers of
the several Lottery Tickets which you had left in my hands, on the
paper inclosed & sent to the Managers for information of their fate.
The marks opposite to particular Numbers, contains their reply.
I am sorry 'tis not in my power to congratulate with your self &
your friends on better luck. Congress yesterday Ordered the Managers
to publish printed lists of all the Numbers drawn, each to be marked
with its prize, this will afford us an opportunity for further examination, in the mean time, let me receive your Commands respecting the
second Class & in whose hands to leave the Tickets when I return to
South Carolina, an early answer is necessary.
The various accounts repeated every day but all tending to one
point, the preparations of the Enemy for evacuating Philadelphia,
has enlivened the hopes of almost every body of our re-entering that
City in a few days. I am among the few who never trust to appearances in War. General Washington is almost silent on this subject,
while other Officers of the next Class are felicitating themselves upon
the prospect of being in Philadelphia in six days. Tories & other Citizens 'tis true have of late in great numbers abandoned that place &
some of the very worst have taken the Oath of Allegiance & abjuration. The more persons General Clinton can persuade to leave him,
the fewer will remain to consume provision which is become very
scarce in his confines, & there is ground for suspecting stratagem
because it is pretended he has forbid all persons leaving the City.
Were he in earnest it would be impossible that so many hundreds

should elude his vigilance. Tis said all the heavy Cannon & baggage are embarked, the Horses unshod for going on ship board. Admit this, how easy may the debarkation & shoeing be accomplished. My sentiment is, trust them not, reinforce Valley forge with all possible celerity, let the Camp be watchful against surprize. Sir Henry will know every step we take, if he finds we are upon our guard & will not be deceived, he will at least give us Credit for good Generalship, whether he goes or Stays. You have heard, but perhaps crudely, how narrowly Marquis delafayette escaped Burgoyning last Week. The inclosed narrative will inform you circumstantially of almost the whole of his adventure but as it comes from a young man nearly allied to me I request you will not suffer it to be published.[1] The Marquis has gained more applause for his Generalship in the late Retreat than would have been bestowed upon a slight victory.

I shall add to the papers already said to be inclosed a Pennsylvania Gazette & refer you to it for further intelligence. If Mr. Penn is still with you my Compliments & tell him I would have paid my respects to him if I had not reason to beleive he is, as he ought to be, on his journey to Congress.

The New intended 74 at New Hamshire, the building of which had been stopped, is now ordered to be finished with all dispatch, to have only two Decks, to mount 28 24 pounders below, 28 18s above upon a plan of Captn. Landais's, a skilful well recommended French Man & who 'tis probable will supervise the whole work & command the Ship[2]—This undetermined, is therefore only my conjecture.

[*P.S.*] This Instant I received an Accot from Camp strengthening all former of the Enemy's intention to quit Philadelphia.[3] Indeed very little doubt can remain in the most incredulous mind—but still I will not trust them. Generals Howe and Clinton were both out & with the whole Army with hopes of catching the Marquis. They lost many Men by the first Nights severe March 35 Miles. The 24th General Howe left Clinton the sole Command, embarked & dined with his Brother on board the Eagle.

I am with great respect &c.

LB (ScHi). Addressed: "Cornels. Harnett Esquire, near Wilmington, North Carolina."

[1] The "young man" was of course John Laurens. See also Laurens to Francis Hopkinson, May 27, 1778.

[2] See *JCC*, 11:555. For further information about Captain Landais, see Marine Committee to the Eastern Navy Board, April 6, 1778, note 7.

[3] See John Laurens' May 27 letter to his father in Simms, *Laurens Army Correspondence*, pp. 174–78.

Henry Laurens to Matthew Locke

Dear Sir,   30th May [1778]

I had the pleasure of writing to you the 12th Inst & then transmitted all the Current intelligence.

Within the present Inclosure you will receive two News papers which will inform you in general terms of the present situation of affairs.

Every day brings us Reports of the Enemy's preparations for evacuating the City of Philadelphia. I have never put much confidence in these Reports, but after so long a time pretendly spent in preparations, I strongly suspect Stratagem.

General Washing[ton] I am persuaded is upon his guard & will not be amused by appearances. If they go, it will be known in proper time but I will not beleive them gone, until their ships are all fairly at Sea, in the mean time, their *fairest* shew will raise my *strongest* jealousy. Never trust an Enemy, is a maxim which ought to be invariably held in time of War, but how much more applicable is this Rule to such an Enemy as Great Britain, in the present War. That Nation or rather, the King & Ministry of that Nation, have been pleased to call us *Rebels,* & all their acts have demonstrated their opinions, that no faith ought to be kept with us, but when it shall be consistent with their own Interest, therefore my sentiment is—trust them not.

As often as opportunities shall offer, you shall be informed of important events in this quarter by, Your obedient & most humble Sevt.

[*P.S.*] My Compliments & good wishes to Mrs. Locke & your family.

LB (ScHi).

Marine Committee to the Eastern Navy Board

Gentlemen   May 30th 1778

We have to acknowledge the receiving of your favours of the 7th, 9th & 12th instant and to reply to their contents.

In answer to that of the 7th we are glad to hear of the arrivals you mention. We observe that you had offered the command of the Brigantine Resistance to Captain Waters who refused accepting it aledging he was intitled to a better vessel. We have determined that Captain William Burke shall command that Vessel of which you will please to notify him,[1] and inform Captain Waters that should he again refuse such command as shall be offered him, we will consider the propriety of dismissing him from the service.[2] You will have the Resistance fitted & manned for the sea immediately.

It was certainly out of the Line of your Department to have the receiving and storeing of Captain Greens cargo of Clothing & Stores— that was the business of the Continental Agent, who in the delivery thereof should be governed by the Orders of Congress, the Board of War or the Committee of Commerce agreeably to the enclosed Resolve of Congress dated the 28th Current which we send to prevent your taking unnecessary trouble in future.[3]

The schooner Loyalty which you dispatched to bring flour & Iron is safely arrived at Sennepuxent, and we expect by this time is Laden'd and ready to proceed back if not already sailed. We Observe what dificulty you have in procuring other suitable Vessels, and only wish that your exertions in that respect be in proportion to your want of those Articles. Principles of humanity & Œconomy direct the establishment of hospitals & that provision should be made for the sick seamen belonging to the Navy, and we doubt not Congress will consider that matter when time will permit. It gave us much pleasure to hear the Providence Frigate had got out but we are sorry to find that you despair of getting out the Trumbull. The Printers were premature in naming the New ship at Salisbury. The Congress have resolved that she be called the Alliance.

Mr. Vernon of your Board writes to Mr. Ellery of this Committee as follows: "The two ships at Salisbury & Norwich are much larger than any yet built, will bear 18 Pd's. very well, at least 16 of their Guns may be of that Size and wish they were Ordered in time before these Guns are provided." If you consider those ships as competant to carry sixteen 18 Pdrs. each we have no objections to their being put on board & should be glad to know whether guns of that size can be provided.

To yours of the 9th we shall answer that we are sorry Mr. Roach hath been so great a sufferer, and should be glad he would Accept of a Lieutenancy until a command can be given him.[4] As you think it would be proper to resume the Building of the frigate in Connecticut River we have determined so to do, and desire you will give the necessary orders for that purpose, agreeable to the plan you have proposed. We have not seen the Petition of the Hancocks officers we suppose it lies with the Secretary of Congress. We shall make enquiry and will duely consider it. We hope Strict enquiry and impartial judgement will be had on the conduct of Captains Manly, McNeill & Thompson. We desire that it may be a particular charge against Captain Manly how he came to surrender the Continental Frigate under his command without fireing as it is said a Gun, and summon Captain William Burke as an evidence on his and Captain McNeills Trial. We have already wrote you that we wished to have as many of the Continental Vessels within your Department as can be ready in convenient Time fitted for Sea, and sent out to Cruize collectively against the enemy. It is our desire that the Warren should join this force and that our former orders respecting her should not be executed. We transmitted you the 23 instant 50,000 Dollars by Mr. Norton Brailsford an Express for your place which we hope will be adequate to the demands of your Department for some Time.[5] When you are obliged to draw we shall answer your Bills, but wish you to be as spareing as possible, as the heavy demands of the Army Departments keeps the Treasury very low. As you have not been able to procure a Hull for the Hamden's Rigging & Materials, we desire that you will order One to be built accomodated to them and employ Mr. Peck to plan the construction thereof.

In answer to yours of the 12th we approve of your drawing in favour of Mr. Shaw for 80,000 dollars and shall pay the Bill when presented. With respect to the ship Queen of France if she be calculated for a Cruizer we would have her employed as such, and joined with the other ships of war which you are to send out, but should she be a dull sailor and otherwise not well calculated for war, it is thought best to employ her as a merchantman, and in that case you will put her under the care of the Continental Agent to be employed agreeable to the orders of the Committee of Commerce.[6] As to the French officers on board that Vessel, they are become useless since the French Seamen have been taken away, and we apprehend it will be impracticable to man her with American seamen so long as they continue on board. We have [directed] therefore that they shall be discharged. Any Contract that may have been made with them in France we would have strictly fulfilled on our part, and you will either pay them their wages or give them Certificates to receive the same from our Ambassadors in France just as the Nature of their Agreement shall require. We are glad to hear the frigate Deane had arrived at your port, and hope she is again preparing for sea. Enclosed is a Resolve of Congress of yesterdays date respecting the ship on the stocks at Portsmouth heretofore intended for a Seventy four but now to be constructed as a 56 Gun ship. We have determined to resume the building of that ship immediately, and now write to Mr. Langdon for that purpose, and that Captain Landais in conjunction with him is to superintend the building of her. You will afford all necessary assistance in the prosecution of that business.

You will give strict orders to all Commanders of Continental Vessels of war, not to take any private property on board their Vessels unless by Order of Congress or this Committee.

We have directed the Continental Agent John Bradford esqr. to exhibit to you his accounts against the Vessels fitted out by order of General Washington, and all other accounts he may have with this

Committee, which you will please to examine and settle. He is to account with you for the Continental share of all Prizes already received, or that he may hereafter receive. This will be handed you by Captain John Barry whom we have appointed to Command the Frigate Raleigh.[7] He is a brave active officer and we doubt not you will find him very attentive to his duty. You will put him in possession of the Raleigh, and he will be governed by your orders. We have only to add that we hope your strongest exertions will be used in getting out the Vessels of war agreeably to your plan, and that their successes will repair the losses and honor of our navy.

We are Gentlemen, Your Hble servts

P.S. We have directed John Langdon Esq to lay his Accounts before your Board which you will please to adjust & settle with him. As we would not in any respect have the cause of Captain Manly prejudged, so we would not have it understood from what we wrote you of the 6th of March that he was by any means appointed to Command the new frigate Alliance.[8]

LB (DNA: PCC Miscellaneous Papers, Marine Committee Letter Book).

[1] On William Burke, see Marine Committee to John Bradford, April 28, 1778, note 5.

[2] On June 19, 1778, the Marine Committee sent the following curt note to Daniel Waters. "We have received your Letter of the 1st Instant and refer you to what we have wrote to the Navy Board touching your refusal of the Command of the Brigantine Resistance." PCC Miscellaneous Papers, Marine Committee Letter Book, fol. 160; and Paullin, *Marine Committee Letters,* 1:262.

[3] See *JCC,* 11:548–49.

[4] On John Roche, see Marine Committee to the Eastern Navy Board, April 6, 1778, note 9.

[5] See Marine Committee to the Eastern Navy Board, May 26, 1778.

[6] "We have received your favour of the 7th May," the Marine Committee informed the commander of the *Queen of France,* John Green, on June 19, and "we are now to inform you that we have written to the Navy Board fully as to the employment of the Ship under your command. We have directed them to discharge the french officers and now desire you will be governed intirely by the orders of the said Board." PCC Miscellaneous Papers, Marine Committee Letter Book, fol. 161; and Paullin, *Marine Committee Letters,* 1:262–63.

[7] The committee's letters of this date to John Bradford, requesting him to settle his accounts with the Eastern Navy Board, and to John Barry, directing him to go immediately to Boston to take command of the Continental frigate *Raleigh,* are in PCC Miscellaneous Papers, Marine Committee Letter Book, fol. 153; and Paullin, *Marine Committee Letters,* 1:249–50.

[8] For the committee's earlier indications that John Manley was being considered for the command of the *Alliance,* see Marine Committee to the Eastern Navy Board, April 6, and May 9, 1778. Although Manley was cleared of blame in the loss of the *Hancock* by a court-martial on June 13, Pierre Landais was appointed on June 19 to command the new frigate *Alliance.* See *JCC,* 11:625; and "Papers of William Vernon and the Navy Board," *Publications of the Rhode Island Historical Society* 8 (January 1901): 247.

Marine Committee to John Langdon

Sir   May 30th 1778

Enclosed herein is a resolve of Congress of yesterdays date whereby you will find that the Ship on the Stocks at Portsmouth heretofore intended for one of 74 Guns is to be constructed to carry 56 Guns only, upon two Batteries, that is to say Twenty eight 24 pdrs. upon the lower deck, & 28 18 Pdrs. upon the upper deck.[1] We have determined to resume the building of this Ship Agreeable to the Resolve of Congress, and now direct that you employ the necessary workmen for that purpose and let them proceed immediately on that business which we expect will be conducted upon the best and most Œconomical terms for the public, under your direction.

We shall direct Captain Landais of our Navy to repair to your place and assist you in superintending the building of this Vessel,[2] and as we consider him as having great knowledge in constructing and building of ships of war, we doubt not you will find him a useful assistant. You will inform us from time to time what occurs as necessary for us to be acquainted with in this business, and apply to the Navy Board at Boston who will furnish you with Money and every assistance in their power, they will also take proper measures for procuring Guns, Stores, and other Materials for the Ship. You will please to exhibit your accounts with this committee to the said Board who we have directed to adjust and settle them.

We are sir, Your humble servants

LB (DNA: PCC Miscellaneous Papers, Marine Committee Letter Book).

[1] See *JCC*, 11:555. These orders were later countermanded and the *America* was eventually launched as a 74-gun ship in 1782 and immediately presented to France. See Howard I. Chapelle, *History of the American Sailing Navy* (New York: W. W. Norton & Company, 1949), pp. 80–83.

[2] See Marine Committee to the Eastern Navy Board, June 18, 1778.

Daniel Roberdeau to George Bryan

Sir   York May 30th. 1778[1]

Mr. Robert Craig a Commissioner of cloathing, appointed, as he informs, by this State, applied to the Board of War and the Board to Congress on his behalf through the Delligates of this State for a supply of Cash for his Department, on a Representation that he had expended Twenty thousand pounds, and could not perform the duties of his office with a less Sum than Ten thousand pounds. This affair came into Congress in so vague a manner from a representation that our Treasury was exhausted, therefore the Requisition was made to Congress, without Mr. Craig's having it in his power to produce an Inventory or inform where the Goods were deposited, but in general that they were in the hands of a number of reputable people in the County of Lancaster, from these Considerations and plainly seeing that Congress would not comply with any such request, but through the State immediately or the Delligates thereof, I withdrew the application to have an opportunity to inform you, as also that I have not the least doubt but Congress would most readily advance the State for the Clothiers Department on a proper application as above. I am, Sir, Yr. most ob. huml ser,   Danl. Roberdeau

RC (PHi).
¹ Roberdeau had just resumed his seat in Congress on May 26 after an extended leave of absence granted on April 11 to supervise the construction of facilities at a western Pennsylvania lead mine being developed, on property he had recently purchased, to relieve the state's ammunition shortage. See *JCC*, 10:337, 11:534. His activities while on leave can be partially reconstructed from the three letters he wrote on April 17, 23, and 27 from Carlisle, Standing Stone, and Sinking Spring Valley respectively, which are in *Pa. Archives*, 1st ser. 6:422–24, 436–37, 446–47.

Charles Carroll of Carrollton to Charles Carroll, Sr.

Dr. Papa,   31 May 1778
Mr. Henry's departure affords me an opportunity of sending you the Lan. & York newspapers. The letter in the former Signed Humphrey Thompson is a genuine letter, and is I think a most original piece in its way.¹ I think you should preserve it as a curiosity. From concurrent accounts strengthened by circumstances there remains little doubt of the enemy's intended departure from Pha. When they will leave that city is uncertain, but if we may judge from appearances, their stay in it will not exceed a week or ten days from this time. Perhaps they have already left it, or may leave it sooner.

There was a report a day or two ago that Spain had acknowleged our Independance and acceded to the treaty of Alliance, and of Amity & Commerce; how ever we have no confirmation of that report. It was also reported that war was not declared between France & England the 7th of April. A ship is said to be arrived at the Eastward which left Nantes on that day, and brings advice that war was then declared at least by France. We have no intelligence of the sailing of the British Commissioners.

I hope to hear from you by Mondays post that you are all well and that Molly continues to grow better. My love to her, the little ones, & Mrs. Darnall. I hope the fruit has not suffered by the late, or indeed present cold weather; if this rainy weather should terminate in a northwester, I fear we shall lose it all.

I shall write to you again by Tuesday's post, and I flatter myself I may then be able to give you a certain account of the Enemy's having left Pha. Such an event would effectually stop the Spirit of Toryism and discredit the reputation of their arms with the European Nations.

By the latest advices from Europe a war in Germany seems very probable between the house of Austria & Brandenburgh. Wishing you health I remain, yr. affectionate Son,

Ch. Carroll of Carrollton

RC (MdHi).

[1] The May 27 issue of the *Pennsylvania Packet or the General Advertiser* printed a letter written by Sgt. Humphrey Thomson "From my sequestered Museum, near the Lancaster Road, April 23, 1778," in which Thomson offered an absurdly florid apologia for deserting his unit and running off with "one of the daughters of Venus."

William Ellery to William Whipple

My Dear Sir,   York Town May 31st 1778

I rec'd your's of the 10th of May a few days ago and wish I could give you any thing new and entertaining. The most interesting intelligence soon grows old, and we are constantly looking out for something new. I don't wonder that Solomon said all was vanity so soon as he had discovered that there was nothing new under the sun, for if it were not for the expectation of something new life would be but a dull scene, like an old reiterated tale. There would be an end to curiosity which stimulates to the acquisition of knowledge; and the world would be involved in one long night of ignorance and darkness. The most important intelligence that we could expect was, that Providence had disposed some European Power to stand forth in support of injured innocence and the violated rights of mankind. France hath been disposed to enter into an alliance with us and upon terms of equality and reciprocity, herein discovering a magnanimity worthy of the most *Christian* King. We have illuminations and fired our feu-de-jois on this occasion, and it is already become an old story. We are now looking out for further alliances and commissioners from Britain to treat with us. We have not as yet heard that war was declared between France and Britain. It will be inevitable unless Britain can bring down her proud stomach to relish sound policy, to acknowledge our Independency and make peace with us. Whether the haughty insolent Thane can stoop to this or not you are a good judge. I should with you, perhaps, have been willing that France should have continued in her usual way to have supported us, had not I in contemplation the divesting of Britain of every foot of land upon this Continent. I think it absolutely necessary to a future, lasting peace that we should be possessed of Canada, Nova Scotia and the Floridas, which we cannot so well effect without the open assistance of France. We have gained great reputation by our arms and humanity throughout Europe, and I believe even Britain herself begins to think us invincible. It is most certain that if she had not been secretly and openly aided by our own countrymen, she must have long since been compelled to give over her vain attempts. Hereafter when peace and independency shall be established, temptations to disaffection, the preservation of property and office, or the expectation of them will cease, and united truly like a band of brothers, we may bid defiance to the world. Commerce and Agriculture must be our great objects, the latter as the basis of the former and the former must be supported by a proper Marine. I wish we had a respectable Navy, but as matters are circumstanced we must go through the war with a small one. Your plan for a Navy is approved excepting that part of it which proposes the turning of the 74 gun ships into frigates which Mr. Landais, whom the Committee imagine is a very good judge thinks would not do. He hath proposed that they should be constructed to carry only two batteries; the lower battery to consist of twenty eight 24 pounders and the upper one of as many 18 pounders. In this way he says that the 56 gun ship will make as good a battle as a 74, be stronger, sail faster, take less men, be built quicker and be much cheaper. The Committee have laid his scheme before Congress, it was approved and I suppose the Committee will direct Mr Langdon to pursue the building of the intended 74 on Landais plan.[1]

Our future frigates will be such as you describe; with two 56 gun ships and half a dozen such frigates under good Commanders, we should oblige our Enemy's ships to go in squadrons, or capture them wherever we saw them. But without brave skilful Captains it is in vain to equip fleets. I don't know which is the most criminal not to assist a ship overpowered by numbers, or to deliver up a ship without firing a gun. If the Devil were a coward I should think that he possessed some of our sea captains; but the Devil it seems, according to Milton, fought boldly against Michael and he is able and valiant enough, we are told, to maintain a dominion in our world even against the Messiah himself; from whence I infer the Devil wants neither courage nor stratagem. But to be serious, it is indeed melancholy to contemplate our little fleet; two frigates burnt in the North River, two burnt and one taken in the Delaware, one taken without firing a gun, and one lost for want of a pilot, I mean the Virginia. The story is briefly this. After being cooped up in the Chesapeake for more than a twelve month, she made several essays to get out, but to no purpose. Once she had almost reached the Capes, but the Lieutenant, who it is said was well acquainted with the Bay, refusing to act as pilot she put back. Captain Nicholson informed the Committee of this cirucmstance, and that it was impossible for him to get a pilot without he had the assistance of Govt; whereupon the Committee wrote to Govr Johnston and desired him to empower Capt Nicholson to impress a pilot if one could not be otherwise obtained, and at the same time ordered Capt Nicholson to push out if a favourable opportunity should offer.[2] The Governor would not give him the power desired and he could not procure one to take the charge of his ship notwithstanding he made very generous offers. It happened at this time that the Purviances had a brig bound to sea with an old pilot on board. Nicholson agreed to give him £100 to pilot him out which he consented to; accordingly they set sail in the evening with a fine wind, ran down the Bay without any opposition until midnight, when they struck on the middle ground. After thumping some time she got over it, but leaked very much and her rudder was broke to pieces. In this situation they anchored and waited for day. When the day dawned they found two or three of the enemy's ships near them. Capt Nicholson ordered out the barge, and with some of his men, the wind blowing violently attempted to reach Cape Henry which he happily effected.

The enemy took possession of the ship with all her guns and stores, towed her up to Hampton Road, repaired or made a new rudder and have since sent her to New York. This acct as nearly as I can remember was given by Capt Nicholson to the Marine Committee and with this shall end the chapter of losses; for I mean to say nothing about the loss of smaller armed vessels, nor will I censure or acquit any officer. Committees of Inquiry are ordered upon Nicholson, Thompson, Manly, Hacker &c &c.[3] I hope that the inquiries will be strict and impartial. Congress have lately passed a resolution punishing cowardice with death. A little Bynging[4] would be of infinite service. Capt. Thompson is suspended and Barre appointed to the command of the Raleigh,[5] and it is proposed that the Warren and Raleigh should sail on a cruise in company. The Commander of those ships are brave men and I dare say will not loose their ships through cowardice.

New Hampshier is at last represented but the representation came too late. The Resolve, respecting half pay, had passed by a majority of one State only.[6] If N.H. had been present, Congress would have been divided. It first passed for life; but the majority being as small as possible, agreed to a kind of coalition and it was finally resolved that the military commissioned officers who should continue in the service to the end of the war should be entitled to half pay for seven years. The opposition which I think was justly made to the half pay establishment hath retarded the arrangement of the army so long that I am afraid it will not take place until next winter. It is proposed to reduce the battalions to 88 which will of course reduce the number of officers, and lessen the quantum of half pay. The number of Battalions will continue to be reduced as vacancies of officers shall happen by death or resignation.

The argument you draw from the confederation was urged against the establishment and every method taken to get it to the States, but N.H. was not represented and so the minority failed, or rather there was a majority against referring it to the States.[7] Some consideration ought certainly to be made to the brave officers who should continue in the service to the end of the war, on account of depreciation and the hardship they have and may endure, and the risk they have and may run of health and life. Taken up in this light, perhaps three and half year's pay may not be too much.

I am exceedingly glad to hear that Dr Stiles and the greatest part of his family have safely got through the small pox. How the Dr mustered courage enough to encounter that distemper I cant conceive. I hope to have the pleasure of seeing him in New Haven, where I expect to be in my way home the latter end of June.

The interest to be paid in certificates in France ceased the 10th of March, and is not continued. General Lee and Col Allen are exchanged. The Clothier's agents are ordered to send forward such articles as they had purchased, and the shoes, stockings and linen and blankets lately imported from France and of which the Army are in want, are also ordered on, but the other clothing is directed to be stored in Springfield with a view of having a complete suit to put on each soldier in the Fall, to prevent their suffering as they did the last winter for want of clothing.[8]

Thus, Sir, I think I have given you a full answer to your long obliging letter. As I am about to return home soon, I must close my correspondence with you for the present. When I return I shall with pleasure resume it. In the mean time and always I shall continue to be with great esteem and respect, Your most humble servant,

Wm Ellery

[*P.S.*] The Masstts representatives send their respects. Give mine to Mr. Stevens.

Tr (DLC).

[1] See *JCC*, 11:555; and Marine Committee to John Langdon, May 30, 1778.

[2] See the Marine Committee's letters to Thomas Johnson and to James Nicholson, March 4, 1778.

[3] See Henry Laurens to the Middle Department Navy Board, April 27, note 1; and Marine Committee to the Eastern Navy Board, May 30, 1778.

[4] John Byng was the British admiral who was court-martialed and shot for his role in the loss of Minorca to the French during the Seven Years War. *DNB*.

[5] See Marine Committee to the Eastern Navy Board, May 8 and 30, 1778.

[6] See *JCC*, 11:502–3.

[7] See *JCC*, 11:495–96.

[8] See *JCC*, 11:545–46.

Henry Laurens to the Marquis de Lafayette

Dear Sir,   31 May [1778]

I had the honor of writing to you the day before yesterday; & this Morning of receiving your favor of the Same date 29th[1] by the hands of a Gentleman who speaks no English & therefore our conversation was extremely limitted.

From the remarks in your Excellency's present Letter I am not displeased with the late determination to withold that which relates to a West India enterprize & when I catch Colo. R.H. Lee half an hour at leisure we will endeavour to produce from the two, a proper representation, as from your Excellency to Congress.[2] I have now abundant materials for an ample & true account of the Marquis's late honorable retreat, which shall be published in Charles Town & in Boston & in Virginia also. From these places it will soon reach France. I wish much for the Paper containing the lying account published by the Enemy & to know if my old friend Grant is really under arrest & wherefore?[3]

I am with the highest Respect & Esteem

[P.S.] I believe I omitted in my last an account of Money which will go within this Inclosure. A Bill on Charles Town will be very sufficient.

LB (ScHi).
   [1] This letter is in Lafayette, *Papers* (Idzerda), 2:59–60.
   [2] See also Laurens to Lafayette, May 29, 1778, note 3.
   [3] Gen. James Grant was widely criticized in the British army for his failure to entrap Lafayette during a recent skirmish. Louis Gottschalk, *Lafayette Joins the American Army* (Chicago: University of Chicago Press, 1937), pp. 189–93.

Henry Laurens to John Laurens

My Dear Son,   York Town 31st May 1778

Your favor of the 27th by Brigadier Mckintosh obliges me much but it has not been long enough before me to be read with great attention.[1]

If I could possibly adore a human being Your General should be my household deity. 'Tis very lawful however to admire, love & revere him. While every body else is overflowing with joy & noises upon the prospect of reentring the City to morrow & to morrow, he is tranquil & watchful, not trusting to appearances.

My sentiment here is at universal War, every other person's is opposed to it. I maintain that notwithstanding all the shew of intentional departure, the whole may be stratagem. Mr. Clinton may get rid of many hundreds perhaps thousands of Mouths which were destroying his provisions become very scarce within his confines—& of a set of people whom he could not govern altogether by the Articles of War & his general Orders—of some who were daily spies upon his movements & critics upon his conduct, he may have in veiw to obtain elbow Room for his Garrison & he may in a very short space of time complete a debarkation of Horses, Cannon, baggage &c. He may entertain hopes also, to relax our proceedings for filling up this Army.

I will not trust him, I will not (although I beleive it) act as if I beleived he was going, until he shall be fairly gone. I would excite in Camp & guards double vigilance Night & day while he remained on this side or within the Banks of Delaware. Whatever may be his designs, go or stay, he will if we are watchful give us Credit, at least, for good Generalship. He knows every step we take.

I rejoice at the measures which you say are adopted for quieting the minds of those who are now under convictions of their errors & Crimes. Good Citizens may be made of many of them & I don't care how full of useful articles they leave for Sale in the City, there are some which I want & may lawfully purchase. Let me hear all that occurs & as minutely as your time will permit. I pray God protect you.

                                        Henry Laurens, President of Congress

[*P.S.*] In one of the Papers inclosed you will see an account which I wrote & caused to be Inserted of a Capture made at Frederica.[2] Those Vessels were certainly going to disburthen poor Breton Island of all my Rice in Barns &c, & the soil of all the buildings. As General McIntosh says he had not heard of the circumstance in Camp I presume you had not. Tell me how you have disposed of the little Pivot or how he disposes of himself, I have learned that he is now much disposed to adulate where he had betrayed & affected to dispise.[3] I cannot love or flatter that Man.

For once I have got hold of a string of English News Papers for the Month of February. Will these be acceptable to the General or to yourself, I will send them if you desire it.

RC (MHi: William Gilmore Simms Collection deposit, 1973).

[1] John Laurens' May 27 letter to his father is in Simms, *Laurens Army Correspondence*, pp. 174–78.

[2] This is evidently a reference to a compendium of recent news from South Carolina that was printed in the May 23 issue of the *Pennsylvania Gazette* under the heading "Intelligence just received from Charlestown, South-Carolina, April 21, 1778," and reads as follows:

"An express arrived this morning from Georgia, with advice, that Col. Elbert, and Col. White, in the Washington and Lee Gallies of that State, joined by the Bullock Galley, had taken, at the island of Frederica, the following vessels, belonging to the King of England, viz. the Hinchenbrook brigantine, commanded by Captain Ellis; a sloop, commanded by the famous Captain Moubray, and an armed schooner; the British crews belonging to these vessels fled as soon as they were attacked, and got on shore in their boats, with what they could carry off; but it is said Captain Ellis was drowned.

"Our gallies are gone to attack the Galatea man of war, said to be on shore at Jekyl island. This ship, the Galatea, has long infested the coast, and interrupted the trade of Georgia and South-Carolina.

"We are menaced with an expedition from St. Augustine against Georgia, and are sending troops from hence to the assistance of our Sister State. Col. Charles Cotesworth Pinkney, at the head of them, marched this evening.

"Incendiaries continue their diabolical attempts to destroy the remaining part of this town—not content with the mischiefs which they have already committed; last night Mr. Clifford's stables in King-street, and a house in Broad-street, were set on fire, but happily prevented from spreading.

"The Rattlesnake privateer, of Philadelphia, Captain McCullough, has carried two prizes into Georgia, one with dry goods for the army at New-York, the other a retaken vessel with salt. She has likewise taken and sent in here a Jamaica schooner, and a brigantine from the Bay of Honduras."

[3] The "little pivot" was doubtless Gen. Thomas Conway, who was engaged in an effort to curry favor with General Washington in order to overturn his recent resignation and resume his Continental Commission. See Douglas S. Freeman, *George Washington, A Biography,* 7 vols. (New York: Charles Scribner's Sons, 1948–57), 5:4–5. But for Laurens' reference to "pivot" in two other contexts, cf. his letters to John Laurens, January 8, note 6, and June 11, 1778, note 2.

Henry Laurens to George Washington

Sir   York Town 31st May 1778.

The day before yesterday I troubled Your Excellency with a Letter by Messenger Gray; last Night Brigadier McIntosh put into my hands Your Excellency's favor of the 21st Inst. which shall be laid before Congress to morrow.[1]

Inclosed herein Your Excellency will receive an Act of Congress of the 29th for reforming the North Carolina Battalions now in Camp.[2] As it will afford Your Excellency some information, I have subjoined two additional Resolves to complete that Act the whole of which I shall transmit to Govr. Caswell to morrow.[3]

I remain with the highest Regard & Esteem, Sir, Your Excellency's most obedient humble servant,

Henry Laurens, President of Congress.

RC (DLC).

[1] Washington's May 21 letter to Laurens is in PCC, item 152, 6:43, and Washington, *Writings* (Fitzpatrick), 11:429–30.

[2] Congress passed this "Act" in response to a report by the Committee at Camp on a May 6 letter from Gov. Richard Caswell and an accompanying act of the North Carolina Assembly for completing the state's Continental battalions. See *JCC,* 11:503, 550–51; and *N.C. State Records,* 13:122–23.

[3] These were evidently the May 29 resolves on North Carolina officers and money for Governor Caswell. *JCC,* 11:551.

Henry Laurens to John Wells

Dear Sir,   31 May 1778
I did myself the honor to write to you the 19th Inst. by Messenger Sharp.

The News papers & Manuscripts which you will find within the present Inclosure will give you much Intelligence. I must not say this is all the time & place affords, but if you knew how closely my own time is applied to discharging the necessary duties of my present Station, you would rather wonder, at my finding time for collecting any news, than blame me for omitting minutia.

From the Copies of Letters from my son, you may if you please manufacture an Account for public veiw of the Marquis's late honorable Retreat, adding that this brave young Nobleman equally wise & discreet, has gained more glory by this late act than could have been derived from a drawn battle or a slight Victory; he must have been well supported by his officers who all participate of the honor. We are assured Majr. General Grant who had the Command of the 4000 that Marched out of the City near Midnight & who by a circuitous hard March of 35 Miles had compassed the Rear of the Marquis, is put under arrest for neglect of duty or breach of orders; had he trod the Ground assigned to him, he would have occupied Matson's ford, where the Marquis successfully passed & must have embarrassed our brave young Hero, who in that case would have been driven to a necessity of plunging into the River without time for ascertaining depth, must have lost his Cannon, Baggage & many lives. A Gentleman who was with the Marquis & who conducted the Retreat as Inspector, has just now sketched out the Marches of both, or rather of the various parties. General Grant instead of crossing directly to Matsons ford turned down a Road at some distance from the River. The Marquis Marched in view at some 300[1] Toises distance between him & the River, gained & passed the Ford without loss or annoyance. This Gentleman, Monsr. Ternon has likewise given me the following account of the loss on each side which he says may be depended on.

British 3 Dragoons killed

       3 Wounded & carried in a Cart to the City

       1 Grenadier ⎫
                   ⎬ Prisoners
       2 Privates ⎭

    16 Deserters

Union, 3 French Jagers of the Indian Corp killed

       2 Missing. & possitively no more.

He confirms the account in very lively description of the flight of the British Dragoons upon hearing the Indian War Whoop, & adds that one of the French Jagers among the Killed had been most cruelly butchered by the British. They had put him under ground but our people hearing of the circumstance took out the Body & exposed it to the view of the Soldiery. After the Marquis had crossed the River, Mr. Jno. Laurens, Mr. Ternon & a small party were ordered to return & reconnoitre. They followed the enemy & overtook them marching by a hasty step into the City. The Marquis had given early intelligence of his unpleasant situation, the alarm was fired in Camp & in fifteen minutes, to the honor of Baron Stüben be it said, the whole Camp was under Arm formed & ready to March. This alarm which the Enemy caught by sound, penetrated a little deeper & their precipitate retreat marks an indisposition to a general engagement.

I have this Instant (now candle light) a Letter from General Washington.[2]

"The Enemy are still (28th) in Philadelphia but the intelligence from thence is so clear & so strong, it is as certain as any event can be that is contingent, that they mean to abandon it. Against the various measures they are pursuing which point to an evacuation, I can learn but of a single circumstance approved. They are working at their Redoubts with great industry, but this last, tho' certainly true cannot be of sufficient weight to raise a doubt upon the subject & must be considered as merely calculated to deceive us & mask their design. We cannot by the most diligent searches discover whether their movement will be by Land or Sea."

The General has detached General Maxwell with a party to join General Dickinson in New Jersey & to annoy them if they go that way. General Smallwood is called in from Wilmington, no surprize is to be feared in that quarter, our Camp is strong & tis said impregnable. My own is at War with all opinions, except General Washington's, and a very few others. I am not inclined to beleive General Clinton is going, until he is fairly gone. When he has got rid of incumbrances & shall have received reinforcement what is to hinder him from Marching up the York Road & compelling our Army to take the Field. Observe I do not disbeleive, but knowing Mr. Clinton to be a Man of enterprize & deep stratagem, I dread the effects of security on our part or as I should say imaginary security.

A Gentleman just now called on me to read a Letter from New Jersey. "The Enemy are shewing preparations for embarkation in New York. 'Tis conjectured a strong Garrison is to be left there & all the rest to go to the West Indies." All conjecture.

Congress have ordered an intended 74 Gun ship building at Portsmouth New Hamshire to be constructed upon a plan given by Capt Landais a skilful French Sea Officer—to be of two decks only—on the tower to carry 28 24—& on the upper 28 18-pounder. She will cost less money, sail faster, be of equal force & require fewer Men by 150.

General McIntosh is here on his Journey to Fort Pitt where he is to

Command. This Gentleman has brought from Valley forge an high Character penned by the Commander in Chief[3] & an Address from the Officers of the Brigade which he commanded containing the strongest marks of respect, affection & applause.

The tryal of General St. Clair will soon come on, this is a subject too delicate to be treated with brevity, & on which candor forbids wanton prediction. Be the event what it may my original sentiment is confirmed.

The prospect of peace with the Six Nations which will be exhibited in one of the inclosed Manuscript affords me much Satisfaction.

The diligent Cheif Justice who has ten times more time for writing News than I have, will transmit to our Town ten times more than I am able to do. You will catch it all by some means or other.

I say you may manufacture from the materials which I furnish you with, being all to the best of my knowledge perfectly true, but I prohibit the disclosure of authorities. None of us are anxious to appear in print, & I am persuaded you will not willingly make an ill requital to your friends.

⟨*I am Seriously projecting an Enterprize beyond Altamaha; General McIntosh to whom I disclosed my sentiments this afternoon is strongly united in them, but I enjoin you to keep this intimation to your self.*⟩[4]

I rejoice in your good fortune, I know you are sober & vigilant, be steady & beleive me to be with great Regard &ca.

P.S. I have heard that Mr. R.H. Powell went some time ago to St Augustine. Pray tell me the rise, progress & event of that extraordinary circumstance.

I have been told the people about Red Stone have prohibited Tacitus Gaillard's proceeding down the Missisipy.[5]

LB (ScHi).

[1] Laurens inserted an asterisk at this point to key a marginal note explaining the French term "Toise"—a "fathom of $6\frac{1}{4}$ feet."

[2] See Washington's May 28 letter to Laurens in Washington, *Writings* (Fitzpatrick), 11:471–72.

[3] See Washington's May 21 letter to Laurens, ibid., pp. 429–30. With this letter Washington enclosed an account of McIntosh's traveling expenses from Georgia to Pennsylvania, which Congress paid on June 2. *JCC*, 11:561–62.

[4] Laurens wrote in the margin next to this paragraph: "Omitted in my Letter."

[5] See Laurens to Benjamin Farrar, March 7, note, and June 12, 1778.

Richard Henry Lee to John Page

Dear Sir,   York May 31st 1778

Your favor of the 19th has just come to hand and I thank you for it. In proportion to my ardent zeal for the prosperity and security of my country so were my wishes that Monsr. Loyeaute had been able to effect those valuable purposes for our Country that I own I thought him capable of doing.[1] I was the more intent upon this, as I well knew the necessity of what he professed to understand, and our utter ignorance of it. We may spend a great deal of money in this way, but I much fear it will be very late indeed, before we shall receive an equivalent in the protection afforded us. We have fortunately been but little tried yet in Virginia, and God of his infinite Mercy keep our enemies at a distance until we are better prepared to meet them.

The enemy, we are told, still continue embarking their Stores, heavy cannon &c, and the Universal opinion is that they will evacuate Philadelphia in a few days. It may be so, but they are so full of guile, it is no easy matter to penetrate their designs. Should a French war take place, they must go, and quickly too, to guard their W. India Islands, now quite defenceless. We have an account from Philadelphia that there has been an engagement between a French & an English fleet in which the latter has been worsted and lost two frigates sunk. I shall be much obliged dear Sir if you will get Mr. Maddisons answer respecting my Nephew and send it by Post to his Mother.[2] Farewell dear Sir, I wish you healthy & happy.

Richard Henry Lee

RC (ICU).

[1] No doubt John Page had reported Loyeauté's resignation as inspector general of Virginia artillery, as had Page's brother Mann in a May 21 letter to Lee. "I am sorry we have lost him," Mann Page commented, "but the Loss must be attributed to his own Caprice, as he received no Slight from the Assembly. Indeed the Words of the Resolution appointing him Inspector General by no means warrant the Claim which he set up for Command." Lee Family Papers, ViU. For Governor Henry's comments on Loyeauté's resignation, see Henry, *Patrick Henry*, 3:174.

[2] In his May 6 letter to Richard Henry Lee, John Page had promised to attend to Lee's April 20 request respecting his nephew, the son of his recently deceased brother Thomas Ludwell Lee. Lee Family Papers, ViU.

Thomas McKean to Caesar Rodney

Dear Sir,   York-Town May 31st. 1778.

Your favor of the 8th instant came to hand on the 15th,[1] but I had no opportunity of moving upon it until the 20th, when I had a referrence to the Treasury Board, who reported in two days in favor of the State, upon which I obtained the President's Warrant for ten thousand dollars. This money may be had whenever you are pleased to send for it. Mr. Thomas White's affair, and the hundred militia requisition were referred to Mr. Duer of New-York, Mr. Carroll of Maryland and Mr. Bannister of Virginia,[2] a Committee specially appointed early last winter to take the direction of Delaware, as it was understood that the Government was at an End, the President & records being captivated, no Delegates having attended Congress & it being reported that I had given it up as lost and therefore left it. The expectation of a report from these Gentlemen daily has prevented my writing to you sooner, but I find the settled opinion that the Enemy are about quitting Philadelphia, if not the Continent, is the principal cause of the delay, as it is thought should that be the case, White might be bailed, and the hundred men would be unnecessary; should the case prove otherwise, you may depend upon the men, as Congress are determined to support the Whigs in Delaware be the expence what it may.

The treaty of amity & commerce will be sent to each State, but the treaty of alliance with France will be kept for some time in Congress; as there was one Judas among twelve Apostles, there may very probably be a traitor to his country in most of the General Assemblies, or at least among their officers, and therefore it may be prudent to conceal the principal articles until the war commences between France and Britain, or some more suitable time. Believe me, Sir, if the United States of North-America had been recognized as Sovereign & Independent by all the Powers in Europe, and in the plenitude of Strength & Greatness, a more favorable treaty & alliance could not have been expected; this transaction equals in point of justice, generosity, policy & magnanimity any thing to be met with in history; it far exceeds my most sanguine expectations. We have just got an Account, that Spain has acknowledged the United States to be among the Sovereigns of the World, and has entered into a commercial & friendly treaty, but this is not received officially, tho' beleived, therefore we must not pronounce it true 'till further confirmation. The King of Prussia's Prime Minister has wrote to one of our Ambassadors at France, "that after the King of France has recognized our Independance he will not ballance," so that we may also expect soon to hear from that quarter.[3]

I am just now favoured with your letter of the 22d instant,[4] and would have set off for Dover without delay, only General Patterson tells me the General Assembly will not sit above ten days, which will probably make my journey there now useless. In my last I told you that I should attend them in the beginning of May; in answer I understood they were then about adjourning. This is unlucky.

When you send for the 10,000 dollars, you may send the draught in my favour for £90.0.11½, and I shall take it out of this money, and remit the draught & a receipt to you. Have the General Assembly made any & what allowance for their Delegates? My Dinner alone, in a club of ten members of Congress at Widow Moore's tavern, has cost me on an average 26/ per day. No small State, and I am sure no private Gentleman, can well bear this expence; and yet I cannot do better.

Unless I have new powers respecting the Confederation, I shall be obliged to quit Congress next Saturday, as it is determined to go on that business tomorrow, and they expect in a few days to finish it. Be so kind to hint the necessity of these powers or instructions, and of a fuller Representation of the State in Congress.

In a few days I hope to write to you from Philadelphia. There seems to be no doubt but that the Enemy are about to quit Philadia. and the Delaware, if not the Continent. I believe they mean to embark at Blackpoint or at South-Amboy. It is rumoured, there has been a [battle] between the English and French, in which the former lost In[tirely] owing, the British officers in Philadia. say, to the great super[iority of the] latter in numbers & [metal?]. The British Commissioners are exp[ected].

Please to present my compliments to Messrs. Read, Killen, [. . .] meaning all my friends. Adieu, Dear Sir, Your most obedient humble servt,   Tho M:Kean

P.S. Please to present my best compliments to Mr. Dickenson when you see him. I must beg you to forward the letter for Capt. Perry.

RC (PHi). Addressed: "His Excellency Caesar Rodney Esquire, President of Delaware, At Dover."

¹ Rodney's May 8 letter to McKean is in Rodney, *Letters* (Ryden), pp. 267–68.

² See *JCC*, 11:519.

³ This is a reference to the repeated assurances of the baron von Schulenburg, Frederick the Great's Minister of Foreign Affairs, that Prussia would recognize American independence after France formally recognized the United States. Wharton, *Diplomatic Correspondence*, 2:457, 466, 473, 489. For a similar report from Ralph Izard, see Henry Laurens' first letter to John Laurens, May 3, 1778, note 3.

⁴ Rodney's May 22 letter is in Rodney, *Letters* (Ryden), p. 268.

INDEX

In this index descriptive subentries are arranged chronologically and in ascending order of the initial page reference. They may be preceded, however, by the subentry "identified" and by document subentries arranged alphabetically—diary entries, letters, notes, resolutions, and speeches. An ornament (☆) separates the subentry "identified" and document subentries from descriptive subentries. Inclusive page references are supplied for descriptive subentries; for a document, only the page on which it begins is given. Eighteenth-century printed works are indexed both by author and by short title. Other printed works are indexed when they have been cited to document a substantive point discussed in the notes, but not when cited merely as the location of a document mentioned. Delegates who attended Congress during the period covered by this volume appear in **boldface type.**

Congress *(continued)*
recommends militia exemptions, 564, 602, 620, 668–69; on brevet commissions, 585; ratifies French treaties, 602–5, 610; appoints Steuben inspector general, 605; increases auditors' pay, 611; requests protection for Oneidas and Tuscaroras, 612, 624-25; reinforces Fort Pitt, 614; reorganizes inspector general's department, 614; proclamation on neutral shipping rights, 637, 639, 647, 660, 669; grants quartermaster power of appointment, 642; appoints commissary of prisoners, 643; debates army arrangement, 644; requests revision of French treaty of commerce, 660; orders William Denning to attend Treasurer's office, 668; investigates Saratoga Convention violations, 682, 701; enlarges authority of commissioners in Europe, 688; plans expedition against Detroit, 694; postpones providing presidential household, 704; reorganizes treasury department, 713; designates nation "United States of North America," 716, 719, 725, 733; President Laurens condemns delegates' disorderliness, 721; establishes provost corps, 725; recommends exempting deserters from militia, 730, 732, 734, 745, 747, 752, 758; rejects Pennsylvania forts as Continental expense, 731; suspends clothing purchases, 731; appoints chaplain to German battalion, 732; endorses proposal to liberate Nova Scotia, 734; assigns brigadier to Rhode Island, 735; recommends promotion plan, 763; opposes Franco-American West Indies expedition, 769; suspends clothier general's purchasing, 770; reorganizes Lee's dragoons, 771; reorganizes North Carolina battalions, 787; shipbuilding plan, 789; *see also* Accounts; Address to the Inhabitants of America; Board of treasury; Board of war; Committee at camp; Committee for foreign affairs; Committee for Indian affairs; Committee of arrangement; Commitee of commerce; Committee of Congress (by subject); Committee of finance; Committee on appeals; Franco-American alliance; Journals of Congress; Marine committee; Secret committee
Congress, president of; *see* Laurens, Henry
Congress, secretary of; *see* Thomson, Charles
Connecticut: Continental loan office, 65, 374, 488; price regulation opposed, 257, 275–77, 286, 292, 414, 705; instructs delegates on confederation, 263, 275, 305, 393; and Articles of Confederation, 317; militia, 414, 430; shipbuilding, 460; price regulations defended, 490; assistance requested to launch *Trumbull*, 628; council elections, 707; *see also* Trumbull, Jonathan, Sr.
Connecticut Courant, 709
Connecticut delegates: letters from, 541, 707; ☆ on half-pay plan, 707–8; request Rhode Island reinforcement, 736
Connor, Morgan, investigates John Swanwick, 408
Contair, Monsr., 695
Continental agents; *see* Agents, Continental
Continental Army: establishment proposals, xxviii, 6–7, 23-30, 205–8, 299, 354, 393, 694–95; unpreparedness, 4, 13–14, 36–37, 79–82, 97–99; draft proposed, 7, 25; German battalion, 7, 23–24, 732; foreign officers, 10, 47–48, 78, 106, 184, 230, 267, 330, 367, 511, 549, 575, 641, 644–45, 676–77, 681, 685, 694–95, 747, 785; New York troops, 15, 240, 299, 475, 727; additional regiments, 23–24; Canadian regiments, 23–24; state quotas, 23–24; provisions crisis, 37, 80–84, 88, 103, 105–8, 111–13, 117, 131, 137–38, 156–57, 177, 190, 256–57, 285, 316; Virginia troops, 41, 106, 325, 340, 355, 397, 419, 441, 546, 617; reforms discussed, 57–61; unprepared for Canada expedition, 74, 287–88; transport shortage, 80, 98, 107, 131, 240, 355; sickness, 93; regulations, 105–6, 132, 149, 154–55, 188; mutiny threat, 108; New York officers, 117, 303; desertion, 131, 192, 194–95; employment of Indians recommended, 144–46; militia draft, 177, 227, 305; New Hampshire troops, 184; New Jersey officers, 184; arms shortage, 185; establishment adopted, 186, 725, 762–63; manpower requirements, 188; recruitment, 190, 194-95, 209, 226, 228, 258, 353, 358, 397, 411, 477, 617, 753; furlough regulations, 206, 236, 238, 268; Massachusetts troops, 240, 436; Pennsylvania quota, 265; Pennsylvania troops, 285, 358, 397; prisoner

Advisory Committee

Library of Congress American Revolution Bicentennial Program

John R. Alden
James B. Duke Professor of History Emeritus, Duke University

Julian P. Boyd*
Editor of The Papers of Thomas Jefferson, *Princeton University*

Lyman H. Butterfield*
Editor in Chief Emeritus of The Adams Papers, *Massachusetts Historical Society*

Jack P. Greene
Andrew W. Mellon Professor in the Humanities, The Johns Hopkins University

Merrill Jensen*
Editor of The Documentary History of the Ratification of the Constitution, *University of Wisconsin*

Cecelia M. Kenyon
Charles N. Clark Professor of Government, Smith College

Aubrey C. Land
University Research Professor, University of Georgia

Edmund S. Morgan
Sterling Professor of History, Yale University

Richard B. Morris
Gouverneur Morris Professor of History Emeritus, Columbia University

George C. Rogers, Jr.
Yates Snowden Professor of American History, University of South Carolina

*Deceased.

☆ U.S. GOVERNMENT PRINTING OFFICE : 1982 O - 379-467

844